ALL · IN · ONE

# MCSE

# Windows® Server 2003

# EXAM GUIDE

Brian Culp, Mike Harwood,
Jason Berg

with Drew Bird

**McGraw-Hill**/Osborne

New York • Chicago • San Francisco • Lisbon
London • Madrid • Mexico City • Milan • New Delhi
San Juan • Seoul • Singapore • Sydney • Toronto

*The McGraw·Hill Companies*

**McGraw-Hill**/Osborne
2100 Powell Street, 10th Floor
Emeryville, California 94608
U.S.A.

To arrange bulk purchase discounts for sales promotions, premiums, or fund-raisers, please contact **McGraw-Hill**/Osborne at the above address. For information on translations or book distributors outside the U.S.A., please see the International Contact Information page immediately following the index of this book.

### MCSE Windows® Server 2003 All-in-One Exam Guide
### (Exams 70-290, 70-291, 70-293 and 70-294)

1234567890 DOC DOC 019876543

Book p/n 0-07-222407-X and CD p/n 0-07-222408-8
parts of
ISBN 0-07-222406-1

**Publisher**
Brandon A. Nordin

**Vice President & Associate Publisher**
Scott Rogers

**Acquisitions Editor**
Nancy Maragioglio

**Project Editors**
Laurie Stewart, Janet Walden

**Acquisitions Coordinator**
Jessica Wilson

**Developmental Editor**
Drew Bird

**Technical Editor**
Matteo Rustico

**Copy Editors**
Lunaea Weatherstone, Chrisa Hotchkiss,
Sudha Putnam

**Proofreader**
Paul Medoff

**Indexer**
Jack Lewis

**Composition**
Tara A. Davis, George Toma Charbak,
Kelly Stanton-Scott

**Illustrators**
Kathleen Fay Edwards, Melinda Moore Lytle,
Jackie Sieben, Michael Mueller

**Series Design**
Peter F. Hancik

This book was composed with Corel VENTURA™ Publisher.

The logo of the CompTIA Authorized Quality Curriculum Program and the status of this or other training material as "Authorized" under the CompTIA Authorized Curriculum Program signifies that, in CompTIA's opinion, such training material covers the content of the CompTIA's related certification exam. CompTIA has not reviewed or approved the accuracy of the contents of this training material and specifically disclaims any warranties of merchantability or fitness for a particular purpose. CompTIA makes no guarantee concerning the success of persons using any such "Authorized" or other training material in order to prepare for any CompTIA certification exam.

The contents of this training material were created for the CompTIA A+ exams covering CompTIA certification exam objectives that were current as of September 2003.

## How to Become CompTIA Certified

This training material can help you prepare for and pass a related CompTIA certification exam or exams. In order to achieve CompTIA certification, you must register for and pass a CompTIA certification exam or exams.

In order to become CompTIA certified, you must:

1. Select a certification exam provider. For more information please visit http:// www.comptia.org/certification/test_locations.htm.

2. Register for and schedule a time to take the CompTIA certification exam(s) at a convenient location.

3. Read and sign the Candidate Agreement, which will be presented at the time of the exam(s). The text of the Candidate Agreement can be found at www.comptia .org/certification

4. Take and pass the CompTIA certification exam(s).

For more information about CompTIA's certifications, such as their industry acceptance, benefits, or program news, please visit www.comptia.org/certification.

CompTIA is a non-profit information technology (IT) trade association. CompTIA's certifications are designed by subject matter experts from across the IT industry. Each CompTIA certification is vendor-neutral, covers multiple technologies, and requires demonstration of skills and knowledge widely sought after by the IT industry.

To contact CompTIA with any questions or comments:
Please call + 1 630 268 1818
questions@comptia.org

For Lt. Colonel Lloyd W. Smith, United States Air Force: the bravery it took to face what you did at Pearl Harbor, D-Day, and in Korea is quite literally beyond my comprehension. Thank you. I hope my life honors the gift you helped provide. For happy Jen, for the sweet way you get indignant at the thought of others editing my work.

—B.C.

This book is dedicated to family and friends whose patience and understanding make all of the difference.

—M.H.

This book is dedicated to Lloyd. Of all the lessons in life I wish to teach you, the most important one is that you can do anything you set your mind to. If your Dad can write a book, then you can become a marine biologist. Or a baseball player. Or even play football for the Ducks.

—J.B.

# ABOUT THE AUTHORS

**Brian Culp** (MCT, MCSE, A+) worked for a small networking outfit called IBM where he discovered why Dilbert is so popular. He is the author of *Mike Meyers' MCSE Windows 2000 Professional Certification Passport* and *Mike Meyers' MCSE Windows XP Professional Certification Passport*. He has also contributed to several other computer titles, including books on Windows XP and Outlook 2003. He can be reached for questions or speaking engagements at bculp@everestkc.net.

**Mike Harwood** (MCT, MCSE, A+, Server+) is a system manager for a multi-site network and manages projects for a TecMetrix communications, a systems integration consultancy. He performs technical training, writes technical courseware, and is co-author of several computer books.

**Jason Berg** is a full-time technical instructor and part-time writer. This is his first book, but definitely not his last. He teaches hardware, networking, Cisco, and Microsoft certification courses. Jason is the founder of 2weekmcse.com, a technical training company specializing in certification classes. Jason is a graduate of the University of Oregon. He has earned the MCSE, MCT, and MCDBA certifications from Microsoft and CCNA certification from Cisco. He lives in Portland, Oregon, with his wife, Rebecca, son Lloyd, and dog Shari. You can reach Jason at jberg@2WeekMCSE.com or on his web site, www.2WeekMCSE.com.

## About the Development Editor

**Drew Bird** has been working in the IT industry since 1988. In addition to writing technical books and exam study guides, he is an established technical trainer with over 500 days of in-classroom experience teaching Microsoft and Novell networking courses. Drew and his wife, Zoë, live in the hills outside of Kelowna, British Columbia, Canada. In his spare time Drew is an avid adventure racer, scuba diver, skier, and snowboarder. He also enjoys watching the odd film or two.

## About the Technical Reviewer

**Matteo Rustico** (MCSE, MCT, OCP, CNE) has ten years' experience in the IT industry and is currently working as an instructor and consultant for Destech Consulting and Education in Toronto, Canada, as part the Oracle database and Microsoft Networking Implementation Teams.

## About LearnKey

**LearnKey** provides self-paced learning content and multimedia delivery solutions to enhance personal skills and business productivity. LearnKey claims the largest library of rich streaming-media training content that engages learners in dynamic media-rich instruction complete with video clips, audio, full motion graphics, and animated illustrations. LearnKey can be found on the Web at www.LearnKey.com.

# CONTENTS AT A GLANCE

# CONTENTS

# ACKNOWLEDGMENTS

This is my fourth book now with McGraw-Hill/Osborne, and I am very fortunate to work for and with such an excellent team of talented people. The people mentioned here deserve much more credit than can be conveyed in these few paragraphs. They do a hell of a lot of work, not the least is dealing with authors who a) can't follow directions, b) won't follow directions, c) have forgotten directions, or d) have lost directions.

I'm starting to repeat myself, as I've worked with many of the same people in some of my books, but each of these people deserves at least a paragraph of thanks:

Nancy Maragioglio, for her guidance and management.

Jessica Wilson, for her input and stewarding influence.

Matteo Rustico, for an excellent technical edit.

Chrisa Hotchkiss, for copy editing my chapters, and for having one of the coolest last names I've ever seen.

Lunaea Weatherstone, for her copy editing efforts, and for having one of the coolest first names I've ever seen.

Laurie Stewart, for overseeing the production.

Bill Ferguson, who helped generate a good many of the questions herein.

Steve Loethen in the Kansas City Microsoft office, for getting me the necessary software.

David Fugate, for facilitating the working relationship.

If you've ever seen the movie *Harry Potter and the Chamber of Secrets*, you can probably get an idea of the working relationship here: I'm the smarmy author guy (played to smarmy perfection by Kenneth Branagh) and the people listed here are the Hermione Grangers. I kind of just show up, wave some words around, let loose a creature that's just barely under my command, and then get to turn tail and run for the hills. They have to make sure that all the words make sense, that I haven't repeated myself three or four times, that all the references and figures refer to the things they are supposed to, that I haven't committed too flagrant an assault on the King's English, and that I haven't re-peated myself three or four times. Oops, I said that al...see what I mean? They really don't get to fix this stuff, and you can see the unhappy result.

What I guess I'm getting at here is that all these people working together make the book happen, and whatever misuses of ink and paper follow in the 291 and 294 sections are mine alone.

—B.C.

The creation of a book is not a simple process. The final product is the compilation of months of work from authors, project editors, technical reviewers, developmental editors, copy editors, graphic artists, and even more people working behind the scenes. Without the commitment from these people, the book you hold in your hands would not have been possible. Special thanks goes out to all of those involved in this project who toiled evenings and weekends to ensure the development of a quality product.

—M.H.

As with any project of this size, there were many people who helped shape the final outcome. The technical editors, graphics, and support personnel helped round out my work and make it readable. Thank you to Matteo Rustico, technical editor; Jessica Wilson, acquisitions coordinator; Drew Bird, development editor and contributor to the CD-ROM; Laurie Stewart, project editor; Lunaea Weatherstone, Chrisa Hotchkiss, and Sudha Putnam, copy editors; Kathleen Fay Edwards, Melinda Moore Lytle, Jackie Sieben, Michael Mueller, illustrators; and Tara A. Davis, George Toma Charbak, Kelly Stanton-Scott, compositors. A big fat thank you to Nancy Maragioglio for her encouragement and confidence in me, as well as her suggestions and her insights. Nancy, you have helped make me a better writer. Thank you! I would also like to thank Jawahara Saidullah for discovering me. I have wanted to write for years, and you gave me an opportunity. A special thanks to Wesley Rhodes for his help in compiling Chapter 5. Thanks for letting me pick your brain. I would like to thank Mr. Morrison and the Aloha High School English staff of 1986–88. Mr. Morrison, you taught me the rules of writing. And how to break them. A special thanks to all my students. I love teaching, and that's because of the people I have had the pleasure of working with. Thanks for your contribution to my life and work. A thanks also to Mom and Dad for your encouragement and for listening to me.

I would like to express my thanks to the other authors for their work and dedication. It has been an honor to be associated with each of you, and I am proud to place my name on the spine next to yours. It has been a pleasure working with each of you.

I would also like to thank my beautiful wife, Rebecca, for her support and belief in me. Your love and support means everything to me. I am truly blessed in having you as a companion and wife. Thanks for picking up the phone.

—J.B.

Bringing a project of this size and complexity to fruition takes a monumental effort by a great many people. This book is a testament to their efforts and hard work. I would like to extend my heartfelt thanks to everyone involved, but from my personal perspective the following people deserve special acknowledgement and my gratitude:

To my fellow authors—Brian Culp, Mike Harwood, and Jason Berg. It has been a pleasure working with you. Special thanks go to Jessica Wilson—I don't even want to think about the challenges involved in coordinating so many elements and so many people. My hat goes off to you. Thanks also to Matteo Rustico for his keen eye and deep technical insights. This book's accuracy is a testament to your efforts and diligence. In the "back room," thanks go to everyone who worked on the editing and production of the book. This finished product wouldn't be, well, finished, without your hard work.

Finally, very special thanks go to Nancy Maragioglio, our tireless acquisitions editor, mentor, boss, sounding board, and all-around solver of problems. It has been a pleasure.

—D.B.

# INTRODUCTION

## MCSE Certification

The Microsoft Certified Systems Engineer program was developed to provide a professional recognition of the skills and understanding required to effectively create and implement technical solutions. The program has seen changes over the years that have been designed to reflect the changing role of the IT professional and to appropriately reflect the demands of their jobs.

The MCSE on Windows Server 2003 certification requires the candidate pass seven total exams—six core exams and one elective exam. Of the six core exams, four are exams on the networking system, one exam covers the client operating system, and one design exam is required. It is also strongly suggested by Microsoft that the candidate have at least one year of experience in implementing and administering operating and desktop operating systems prior to pursuing the MCSE.

The four networking systems exams that every candidate must take are the following:

- 70-290: Managing and Maintaining a Microsoft Windows Server 2003 Environment
- 70-291: Implementing, Managing, and Maintaining a Microsoft Windows Server 2003 Network Infrastructure
- 70-293: Planning and Maintaining a Microsoft Windows Server 2003 Network Infrastructure
- 70-294: Planning, Implementing, and Maintaining a Microsoft Windows Server 2003 Active Directory Infrastructure

Every candidate must also choose one of the following exams as part of the core operating system requirement:

- 70-270: Installing, Configuring, and Administering Microsoft Windows XP Professional

or

- 70-210: Installing, Configuring, and Administering Microsoft Windows 2000 Professional

To meet the design exam requirement, candidates choose either

- 70-297: Designing a Microsoft Windows Server 2003 Active Directory and Network Infrastructure or

- 70-298: Designing Security for a Microsoft Windows Server 2003 Network

Finally, candidates must select one elective from the following list:

- 70-086: Implementing and Supporting Microsoft Systems Management Server 2.0
- 70-227: Installing, Configuring, and Administering Microsoft Internet Security and Acceleration (ISA) Server 2000 Enterprise Edition
- 70-228: Installing, Configuring, and Administering Microsoft SQL Server 2000 Enterprise Edition
- 70-229: Designing and Implementing Databases with Microsoft SQL Server 2000 Enterprise Edition
- 70-232: Implementing and Maintaining Highly Available Web Solutions with Microsoft Windows 2000 Server Technologies and Microsoft Application Center 2000
- 70-284: Implementing and Managing Microsoft Exchange Server 2003
- 70-297: Designing a Microsoft Windows Server 2003 Active Directory and Network Infrastructure
- 70-298: Designing Security for Microsoft Windows Server 2003 Network
- 70-299: Implementing and Administering Security in a Microsoft Windows Server 2003 Network

You should note that some of these exams can be used as credit toward either the core or elective requirement. For the latest information on the MCSE credential and current exam objectives, see http://www.microsoft.com/traincert/mcp/mcse/windows2003/.

Additionally, any of the following Microsoft certifications may be substituted for an MCSA elective:

- MCSA on Microsoft Windows 2000
- MCSE on Microsoft Windows 2000
- MCSE on Microsoft Windows NT 4.0

Alternatively, you can also use a combination of CompTIA exams to fulfill the elective requirement:

- CompTIA Security+

or

- Unisys UNO-101

In this book, you'll find the information needed to prepare for four of the core exams—70-290, 70-291, 70-293, and 70-294—presented in a format that related to the daily performance of an administrator's job. The material has been organized by exam and is written to act not only as an exam preparation tool, but also as a reference book after you've taken the exams. Every exam objective from each of the four exams is included in this text and is highlighted to help you prepare for the exams.

While this book is designed to help you prepare for the exam, no replacement exists for hands-on experience. We included numerous lab exercises to help guide you through many common tasks, as well as case studies to provide real-world insights into administration.

## Test Structure

If this is your first experience with Microsoft's testing structure, or if you haven't taken a Microsoft exam in some time, the first thing you'll notice is the focus on scenario-based questions. While the actual exam questions remain multiple choice, this structure was developed to help test the candidate's comprehension and skill at evaluating information to determine what's important in developing the solution and what isn't.

These performance or scenario-based questions might include graphic elements as exhibits. These graphics could be screen shots or diagrams, designed to clarify the scenario provided.

Other questions might include graphic elements as "hot spots." In this instance, you're asked to click a portion of the graphic to answer the question. For example, to test your understanding of how to configure TCP/IP properties on a client computer, you might be asked to drag the IP address, the subnet mask, and the default gateway from a series of choices to the appropriate location on a screen that looks like the one you'd find in Windows Server 2003. Microsoft has also developed simulation questions, in which a simulation of the actual product is launched during the test, and you're asked to answer the question by working with the product. This is yet another method developed to ensure there's no replacement for hands-on experience.

Adaptive test formats are also being implemented by Microsoft, but at press time not all Microsoft exams are available in adaptive format. Adaptive testing provides successively more difficult questions based on correct answers. The initial question posed to the candidate is of moderate difficulty. If that question is answered correctly, the next question is slightly more difficult. If answered incorrectly, the next question is slightly less difficult. Through this interactive evaluation of the candidate's responses, the exam tailors itself, as necessary, to achieve the proper psychometric algorithm to determine success or failure on the overall exam. Not only does this adaptive format provide added security to the pool of questions, since the number of questions each candidate is exposed to varies, it can also reduce the amount of time a candidate needs to take the exam.

## Taking the Test

Microsoft exams are provided through Prometric and Vue testing centers worldwide. You can locate the testing centers nearest you by visiting http://www.prometric.com/ or http://www.vue.com/. To register, you need your Social Security number or some other unique ID number when you call. You also need to have the name and number of the test you're registering to take.

On the day of your test, you're required to provide two forms of identification, including one photo ID. Plan to arrive early to do any last minute preparations and to ensure that you're focused on the exam when the time comes. You're not permitted to take any notes or study materials into the testing room with you. Most facilities provide scratch paper and pencils in the room for you to make notes during the exam, but all materials must be left in the room when you depart.

Microsoft certification is a proven career enhancement, so achieving your MCSE certification should prove well worth the time and effort.

# PART I

# Managing and Maintaining a Microsoft Windows Server 2003 Environment (Exam 70-290)

# Managing and Maintaining Physical and Logical Devices

In this chapter, you will learn how to

- Install hardware
- Use Device Manager
- Troubleshoot hardware issues
- Use Windows updates and automatic updates
- Configure driver signing
- Install and manage printers
- Install and configure physical disks
- Configure basic and dynamic disks
- Use disk management
- Implement volume types
- Implement a RAID solution
- Configure compression and encryption

Windows Server 2003 supports a myriad of different devices, from SCSI cards to USB cameras, to wireless mice and keyboards, to plain old PCI devices. With the addition of plug-and-play functionality, installing and managing these devices has gotten significantly easier than it used to be. Remember the days of NT 4.0 when installing a new modem into a server could take the entire afternoon and possibly require reinstalling several service packs along with the manufacturer's driver? (If you missed that experience, you really didn't miss anything.) While that was fun, there are many more demands made on an administrator now, and there just isn't time in the day to take a server offline for two hours every time it needs an upgrade! The good news is most devices now can be installed painlessly and quickly, often without needing a restart. Microsoft has added new tools to install and troubleshoot hardware devices, and improved the functionality of some old tools. The Add Hardware Wizard is improved; so is Device Manager. The Hardware Troubleshooting Wizard is new to Server 2003, and it can be very helpful in troubleshooting hardware issues. As part of this chapter, you will

3

learn how to effectively use these tools to implement and manage a variety of hardware devices.

This chapter also will teach you how to implement and manage physical disks and use the different kinds of volumes effectively. Knowing how to manage and configure physical disks is a critical part of network management. With the release of Windows 2000, Microsoft changed the way physical disks are implemented and managed. These changes have carried over to the new release of Server 2003. It is important that you understand what these changes are and how to effectively use them in a server. You will learn the available volume types and how each type of volume solves a different kind of problem.

You might expect the first chapter of this book to cover installing Windows Server 2003. The installation process could probably fill two to three chapters by itself. However, Microsoft now considers knowledge of the install process to be part of an exam candidate's baseline knowledge. The installation procedures for a Windows Server 2003 have not changed significantly from the procedures for Windows 2000 or Windows XP. Of course, one of the ways Microsoft has increased the difficulty of their exams is to test on subjects they consider to be "baseline knowledge." Let's begin with hardware!

# Installing, Configuring, and Troubleshooting Devices

There are two ways to install hardware: the easy way and the hard way. The easy way to install a device is to simply attach the device or plug it into the computer and voilà, it installs automatically. Plug-and-play technology is definitely the easy way. The hard way? Well, you probably know all about the hard way. The hard way usually involves alternating fits of cursing the machine and supplicating to a higher power to perform a miracle. The good news is that Server 2003 includes plug-and-play support for most hardware devices, and it actually works. The bad news: you won't get that easy of a test question, sorry! There are no questions like, "Phil has inserted the device and it automatically installs itself. What do you do next? A. Start working. B. Start working. C. Start working."

## Installing Devices Using Plug-and-Play

The premise behind plug-and-play is the computer should detect a device after it is physically inserted or installed and should automatically install the appropriate software drivers and configure the device so that it is available and ready to use by the operating system. When plug-and-play works as it was intended, it's a wonderful tool, and it makes the job of installing new devices a snap. When it doesn't work…well, we'll get to that in the next section.

For plug-and-play to work properly, you need three things:

- A plug-and-play compatible BIOS
- An operating system that supports plug-and-play (Windows Server 2003, Windows 2000, XP)
- A plug-and-play compatible device

Most BIOS support plug-and-play functionality, and Windows Server 2003 supports plug-and-play functionality, so usually if the device you are installing is plug-and-play compatible, you're in business. When you install a plug-and-play compatible device, Windows detects the device and installs the appropriate driver. You will see a notification bubble in the lower-right corner of your screen notifying you that new hardware has been added and is now ready to use. You can also verify the status of the new device (as well as all devices on the computer) by using Device Manager. Device Manager has been implemented into the Computer Management Microsoft Management Console (MMC). To access Device Manager in Computer Management:

1. Click Start | Programs | Administrative Tools | Computer Management.

2. Expand the System Tools node and click Device Manager.

**NOTE**   You can also access Device Manager through the Control Panel. Double-click the System applet to open the System Properties. Device Manager is accessible on the Hardware tab. The System Properties are also accessible by right-clicking My Computer and selecting Properties.

The default view of Device Manager shows you connections by type. All devices that are attached to the computer are shown in Device Manager, including CPU, physical disks, network adapters, ports, and system devices. Device Manager can be used to install devices, verify devices are working, update drivers, roll back drivers, enable and disable devices, and change device resource settings.

After Windows installs a device using plug-and-play, you can verify that it is installed and working properly by using Device Manager. If the device is installed properly, you will be able to see the device listed under its appropriate type—for example, a new modem will be listed under modems. By clicking the device and viewing the properties, you will also be able to verify the device is working correctly.

If the device was not installed by plug-and-play or is not working correctly, the device will be displayed with a yellow question mark, as in Figure 1-1. The device also may show as an unknown device. If this occurs, you need to either install the device manually or troubleshoot the device further. We will discuss both these topics in the sections coming up.

## Installing Hardware Detected by Server 2003

When Windows is able to detect the new device, but isn't able to locate the appropriate driver automatically, the Found New Hardware Wizard opens, as shown in Figure 1-2, and enlists your help in locating the driver. The Found New Hardware Wizard offers two options:

- Install the software automatically (Recommended)
- Install from a list or specific location (Advanced)

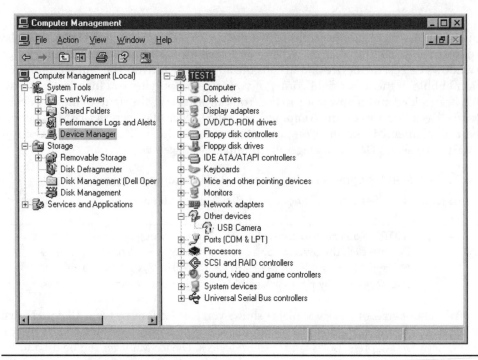

**Figure 1-1**   Device Manager showing a device that has not been installed correctly

**Figure 1-2**
The Found New
Hardware
Wizard

If the first option is selected, Windows will attempt to locate the driver in the Windows install files and on any CDs or floppies that have been inserted in the drives. The second option allows you to specify a particular location, such as a downloaded folder.

For example, you are attempting to install a new digital camera you just bought. It's cool, it's hip, and it's just a tad bit too new to have its driver included on the Windows Server 2003 disk. You plug the camera's USB connector into the USB port of your computer and up pops the Found New Hardware Wizard. If you select the Install The Software Automatically option, Windows will search any CDs or floppy disks that have been inserted, as well as the Windows drivers. If you select the option to install the software from a list or a specific location, you're able to specify a folder on your computer (if you had downloaded the drivers) as the location of the drivers. You can also select a driver from a list. Once the correct driver is selected from the list or provided on the CD, Windows installs the driver and activates the hardware.

The Found New Hardware Wizard is actually part of the Add Hardware Wizard, which can be manually accessed through the Control Panel or the System Properties. The Found New Hardware Wizard appears only when Windows was able to automatically detect the device, but was unable to automatically install the device.

## Installing Devices Using the Add Hardware Wizard

There are many instances where you will need to manually install a hardware device. If Windows fails to detect the device and plug-and-play is unable to complete the driver installation automatically, the Add Hardware Wizard can be used to manually install the device. The Add Hardware Wizard can be found in the Control Panel or on the Hardware tab of the System Properties, as in Figure 1-3.

Let's pretend for a moment that you have installed a USB camera, but Windows was unable to detect the device. You are now going to use the Add Hardware Wizard to install the device.

### Lab Exercise I.I: Installing a New Device Using the Add Hardware Wizard

In this exercise, you will install a device using the Add Hardware Wizard. If you don't have a device just lying around that you can use, you can use Device Manager to uninstall one of your devices, and then use this exercise to reinstall it. For this exercise, a USB camera is the device chosen, but the device could be any type of device.

 **NOTE** Uninstalling a device using Device Manager only removes the driver and uninstalls the device from the operating system, not from the actual machine. If the device is not physically removed from the computer, the next time Windows starts up, the device will be automatically detected and reinstalled. You may also run the Add Hardware Wizard to detect and install the device.

1. Plug in or install your device. If the device is detected by Windows, and the New Hardware Found Wizard appears, click Cancel to cancel the installation.

2. Click Start | Control Panel | Add Hardware to start the Add Hardware Wizard.

3. Click Next. The wizard will scan your system looking for new hardware. The Found New Hardware Wizard appears after a moment and identifies the hardware that Windows found.

4. Select "Install from a list or specific location (Advanced)" and click Next.

5. Select the radio button "Don't search. I will choose the driver to install." (See Figure 1-4.) Click Next.

6. Select the type of device to install from the Hardware Type screen shown in Figure 1-5. If the type of device is not listed (your camera isn't), select Show All Devices and click Next.

7. From the next screen, select your device and driver from the list. If your device is listed, select the correct model and click Next.

8. If the device and driver are not listed, click Have Disk. When the Open dialog box appears, navigate to the location of the drivers and click OK. Your device

**Figure 1-3**
System Properties
dialog box
showing the
Hardware tab

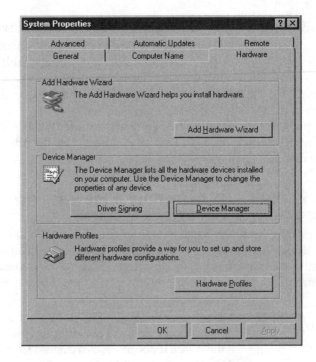

**Figure 1-4**
Choosing your
install options

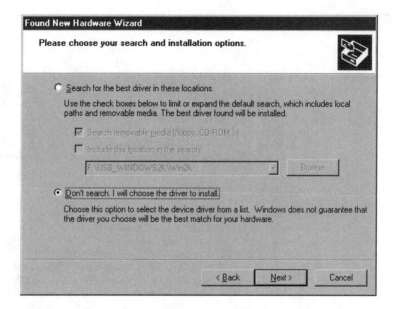

should now be listed, along with the appropriate driver, as in Figure 1-6. Click
the device and click Next.

9. Your device is now being installed. You may see the screen shown in Figure 1-7
appear, warning that the driver has not been tested by Microsoft and is unsigned.
Click Continue Anyway to finish installing the device. (More about unsigned
drivers later in the chapter.)

**Figure 1-5**
Hardware Type
screen in the
Found New
Hardware
Wizard

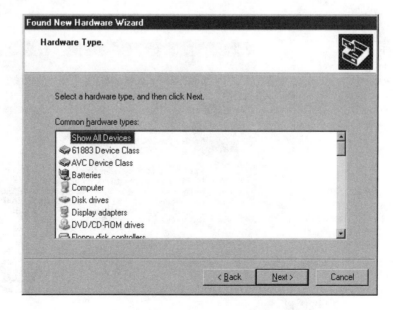

**Figure 1-6**
Select your
device to install.

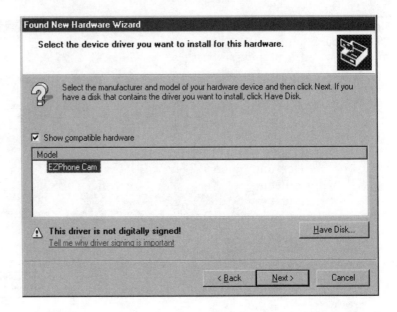

10. The driver is now installed. Click Finish to close the wizard.

11. Open Device Manager and verify the device is installed and working properly.

## Using the Help and Support Center to Install Hardware

If after using the Add Hardware Wizard, the appropriate drivers are not found or not installed, the wizard will display a message informing you that it was unable to install the device.

**Figure 1-7**
Unsigned driver
warning

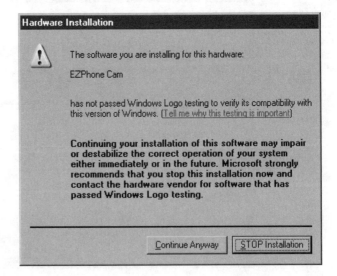

Microsoft has updated the Help feature and renamed it the Help and Support Center. The Help and Support Center interface is easier to use than previous versions of Help and it includes an online assistance feature, which allows you to connect to a Microsoft support professional or newsgroups. If you choose to connect to a Microsoft support professional, you may request e-mail help with valid (non-pirated) products, get incident support for $99 per incident, or log in using a support contract number and password. The newsgroups are free and are usually very helpful. There is also an entire section in the Help and Support Center dedicated to hardware installation, removal, and management.

To open the Help and Support Center, click Start | Help and Support. The home page includes Help Contents, Support Tasks, and Top Issues. The toolbar includes an index, a Favorites option that can be used to mark topics, a History button that keeps track of previous queries, as well as a Support button that takes you online to Microsoft newsgroups. Figure 1-8 shows an example of the Help and Support Center being used to troubleshoot a hardware issue.

The Help and Support Center is very straightforward and self-explanatory. It is a valuable tool and you should definitely devote some time to becoming familiar with how to use the new Help features. Using the Help and Support Center is considered baseline

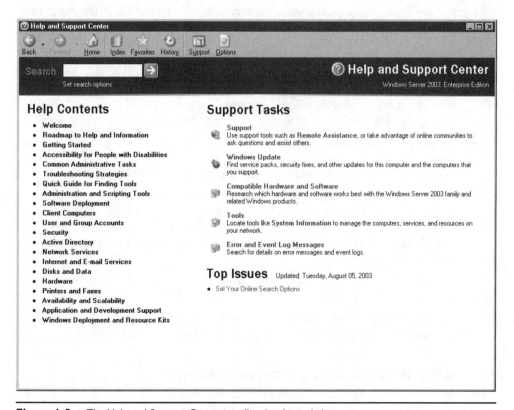

**Figure 1-8**    The Help and Support Center installing hardware help

knowledge, and so is fair game. However, there will probably be very little, if anything, on the 70-290 exam about using the Help and Support Center. Traditionally, Help features have been ignored as an exam topic.

# Using Device Manager

Device Manager is an excellent tool and should become your friend for installing and troubleshooting devices on your Windows server. Device Manager is accessible through the Computer Management MMC or the Hardware tab on the System applet in the Control Panel. You can also add Device Manager as a separate snap-in to a custom MMC.

 **NOTE** The Microsoft Management Console (MMC) is the framework introduced in Windows 2000 for all support tools. All of the Administrative Tools located on the Start menu are preconfigured MMCs. Custom MMCs can also be created by typing **mmc** from a run command and then adding snap-ins to the MMC.

Device Manager can show you devices by type, devices by connection, resources by type, resources by connection, and your hidden devices. Each view enables you to troubleshoot devices in a different manner, as described here:

- **Devices by Type**   Displays a list of all devices on the computer by type of device. All the network adapters present on the machine will be listed under network adapters, all disk drives are listed under disk drives, and so on. Using this view, it is easy to determine if a particular device is working or not. This is the default view and the view that you will use most often.

- **Devices by Connection**   Displays all devices and how they are connected. To see what devices are connected to the motherboard on the PCI slot, for example, you would expand the Standard PC node and expand the PCI bus node.

- **Resources by Type**   Displays the status of allocated resources by type of device. When you view resources by type, you are able to see Direct Memory Access (DMA) devices, input/output (I/O) devices, interrupt request (IRQ) devices, and memory devices. This is the view to use if you need to troubleshoot an IRQ conflict.

- **Resources by Connection**   Displays the status of allocated resources by connection rather than by type.

- **Show Hidden Devices**   Displays all non-plug-and-play devices, and devices that have been removed from the computer but still have drivers installed.

## Updating Drivers Using Device Manager

Probably the most common task you use Device Manager for is to update drivers. If you view resources by type, you are able to see a list of all devices in the computer. When you right-click the device, you will see the following options:

- **Update Driver**   Allows you to quickly update the device driver.

- **Disable**   Disables the current device without uninstalling it from the system. A disabled device is not usable, but is still installed.

- **Uninstall**   Uninstalls the device driver only. If the device is not physically removed, it will be automatically installed at next boot or hardware scan.

- **Scan for Hardware Changes**   Scans the system for any hardware changes and installs any new hardware automatically.

- **Properties**   Opens the Properties dialog box for the device.

 **EXAM TIP**   The easiest way to solve device conflicts between an onboard or embedded device and a PCI device is to disable the onboard or embedded device by using Device Manager. You may see a scenario on the exam where a new sound card is installed that is conflicting with the onboard sound card. You want to use the new sound card exclusively, but unless you are really good with a soldering iron, you won't be able to remove the onboard sound card. Uninstalling the old sound card from Device Manager won't work because the next time the computer is restarted or the hardware is scanned, the device will be found present and will be reinstalled. Simply disable the onboard device to solve your problem.

## Managing Device Properties

It is important, both on the exam and in the real world, that you understand and are familiar with managing devices. When you open a device's properties sheet, you will see tabs for different properties. Figure 1-9 shows the properties for an Intel network card. The properties available will vary according to the device. The most common properties sheets are

- General Properties
- Advanced Settings
- Driver Properties
- Resources
- Power Management

Each of these was designed to provide specific information and to perform administrative tasks. We will look at some of these in the following sections.

## General Properties

The General tab displays general information about the particular device and the manufacturer. The General tab also has a Device Status window that displays whether the device is working properly or not. If the device is not working properly, you can click the Troubleshooting button to access Help topics related to the device and access a wizard that will assist you in identifying the problem. For example, if you are troubleshooting

**Figure 1-9**

Device properties
dialog box for an
Intel network card

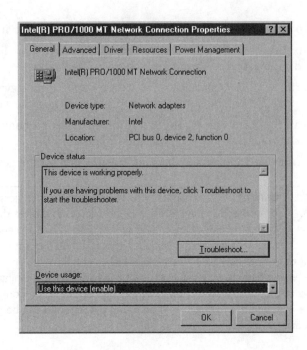

a monitor, clicking the Troubleshooter button opens the Help topics associated with video and monitor problems and asks you a series of questions about the problem. Most of the time if a device is not working properly, it is due to an incorrect or corrupt driver, and reinstalling a working driver fixes the problem. You can reinstall or update the driver on the Driver tab.

**EXAM TIP**  You will probably see a question or two involving devices with incorrect drivers and how to fix them. A video card with an incorrect driver may only display in 800x600, for example. To correct this problem and allow for higher resolutions, update the driver. You may be able to update the driver from the manufacturer's CD or from an updated Windows driver list, or you may have to download a new driver from the manufacturer's web site.

## Advanced Settings

The Advanced tab allows you to set different properties of the device. The Advanced tab allows a great deal of control over the device and includes all of the customizable options of the device. The properties that can be altered will vary depending on the device you have selected. For example, you can alter the link speed and duplex mode of a network card, the SSID of a wireless card, extra initialization commands for a modem, or regional settings on a DVD drive. Not all devices have Advanced settings. On some servers, for example, none of the disk drives have Advanced settings. The same goes for some keyboards and video cards.

## Driver Properties

This is the important one! You must know this dialog box for the exam. On the Driver tab, you are able to view details of the installed driver, update the driver, roll back the driver (new in Server 2003), and uninstall the driver completely.

The Driver Details button shows you the version of the installed driver, whether the driver is digitally signed or not, and the exact location and file name of the driver. You can use this information for troubleshooting.

Updating drivers is simple in Server 2003. By clicking the Update Driver button, Windows launches the Hardware Upgrade Wizard and will locate a new driver for your device.

If the driver you update to doesn't work, you can always roll it back to the previous driver by clicking the Roll Back Driver button. When you click this button, Windows will show you all the drivers that have been previously installed and allow you to choose a driver to roll back to. This functionality first appeared in XP Professional and has been implemented in Server 2003.

Finally, you can uninstall the driver. Uninstalling the driver does not remove the device. You can uninstall the driver if you have been having trouble with the driver and would like to reinstall the device completely. Uninstall the driver, restart the machine, and then reinstall the driver at bootup. Remember, uninstalling the driver does not remove the device. So if you uninstall the driver without removing the device, the driver will be reinstalled the next time you boot the computer or scan for new hardware.

---

 **EXAM TIP**   The ability to roll back to a previous driver is new, and Microsoft tends to test on new features. The simplest way to fix a recently upgraded device that is causing problems is to roll back the driver.

---

## Resources

The Resources tab allows you to troubleshoot interrupt request (IRQ) conflicts. By default, you can't change IRQs if there isn't a conflict. The option will appear grayed out. Also, you can only change IRQs for plug-and-play devices. You can only change the IRQs of non-plug-and-play devices in the CMOS.

## Power Management

The Power Management tab allows you to specify whether the device can be powered off to save battery life or to bring the computer out of standby. Power Management settings are not applicable to servers.

# Hardware Profiles

Hardware profiles are used to support different hardware configuration on the same machine. Hardware profiles are mainly used for laptops. For example, if a user had a docking station at work and a cable modem at home, you could set up a different hardware profile for home and office. Then the user would be able to select the profile that corresponded to where they are and all their devices would work. Sounds tricky, but it's really not.

**Figure 1-10**

Hardware
Profiles
dialog box

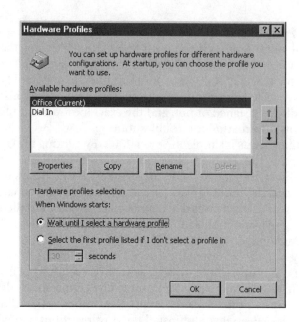

Let's pretend that you support a group of traveling executives. These executives have all been issued laptop computers with both modems and network cards. You want to allow the executives to dial in to your RAS servers when they are traveling, but for security reasons, you want to prevent the executives from using a network connection and a modem connection at the same time.

Here's what you do. Open the System Properties, click the Hardware tab, and select Hardware Profiles. On the Hardware Profiles dialog box, copy the existing profile to create a second profile, as shown in Figure 1-10. Rename the current profile Dial In. On the current hardware profile, enable the modem and disable the network card in Device Manager. Then reboot the machine, choose the second profile, and enable the network card and disable the modem in Device Manager. Call this hardware profile Office. Now instruct your users to boot into the Dial In profile only when they want to dial in to the network. If the user accidentally boots into the Dial In profile when they are at the office, they will not be able to use any network resources or even log onto the network, because their network card will be disabled.

# Driver Signing

Using driver signing can help prevent users from installing harmful drivers that can cause costly downtime. A harmful driver would be any driver that is not compatible with either the device or the operating system. A driver that is signed by Microsoft has been tested and approved by Microsoft and placed on the Hardware Compatibility List

(HCL) as a compatible driver. Attempting to install a driver that has not been thoroughly tested for both the device and the operating system could render your system inoperable.

**NOTE** Microsoft is replacing the HCL on the Web with the Windows Catalog, which can be accessed at http://www.microsoft.com/windows/catalog/. The HCL can be viewed by clicking the Compatible Hardware and Software link under Support Tasks in the Help and Support Center, which connects to the Web. The HCL can still be searched on the Web at http://www.microsoft.com/whdc/hcl/search.mspx.

By default, driver signing is set to warn users before installing the software. Users are able to install driver software after acknowledging the warning. There are three different settings for driver signing, as shown in Figure 1-11:

- Ignore – Install the software anyway and don't ask for my approval
- Warn – Prompt me each time to choose an action
- Block – Never install unsigned driver software

**NOTE** Make sure you check the box under Administrator Option to make the settings applicable to all profiles. Leaving that box unchecked will only configure driver signing for the current profile and users will still be able to install driver software with a warning.

**Figure 1-11**
Driver Signing
dialog box

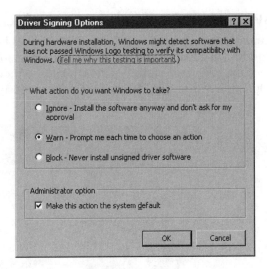

# Signature Verification

You can verify digital signatures of drivers or files by using the Signature Verification Wizard (the File Signature Verification Wizard is shown in Figure 1-12). To open the Signature Verification Wizard:

1. Click Start | Run and type **sigverif.exe**.

2. Click Start to scan for unsigned system files or click Advanced to choose a folder to scan.

You can use the File Signature Verification tool to scan downloaded drivers before installing them.

 **NOTE**   There are many, many unsigned drivers that work just fine. Manufacturers generally test their drivers thoroughly before releasing them and they generally continue to improve the original drivers and post them on their web sites. A driver that has a signature simply means that Microsoft has tested and certified the driver and that they will support the driver. A driver obtained directly from the manufacturer usually works very well, whether it has been signed by Microsoft or not. And if the goal is to prevent users from installing devices, there are better ways to lock users out of their computers. See Chapter 22 for information on using Group Policy and Security Settings to lock down users' computers and prevent users from installing drivers.

# Windows Update and Automatic Update

Windows Update first appeared in Windows 98 and has been implemented in all versions of Windows since. Server 2003 adds scheduling capability to the Windows Update feature, hence the new term of Automatic Updates. Windows Update connects to the Windows Update web site and searches for downloads applicable to your computer.

**Figure 1-12**
File Signature
Verification
Wizard

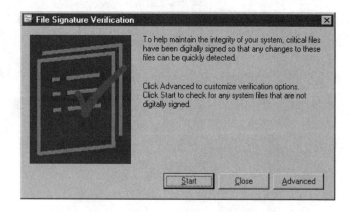

**Figure 1-13**

Automatic
Updates on a
Server 2003
computer

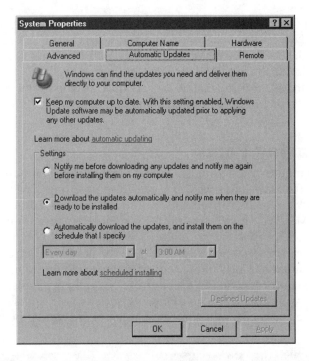

The automatic feature allows Windows Update to run at a specified time and download the applicable updates. Windows Update can be configured to prompt before downloading updates, prompt before installing the updates, or to automatically download and install updates. To access Automatic Updates, open the System Properties and click the Automatic Updates tab, as shown in Figure 1-13.

Windows Update has also now been placed into Group Policy and can be configured as a computer policy and applied to a site, domain, or organizational unit. For more information on Group Policy, see Chapter 23.

# Installing Multiple Processors

Windows 2003 Standard Edition supports up to four processors, and the Enterprise Edition supports up to eight processors. The 64-bit Datacenter Server, the most powerful server Microsoft has ever built, supports up to a maximum of 64 processors with a minimum of eight processors required. With this capability, you will need to know how to upgrade a uniprocessor (UP) to a symmetric multiprocessor (SMP) system. Because Server 2003 supports multiprocessor capability, all that needs to be done is to upgrade the driver of the computer. Failing to upgrade the driver after installing a second processor will render the second processor basically useless. Performance will not improve until the driver has been updated.

To update the driver, open Device Manager and expand the Computer type to view the installed device. Right-click the device and select Update Driver, as shown in Figure 1-14. Follow the Update Driver Wizard prompts, which are nearly identical to the Add Hardware Wizard, and install an SMP driver.

You are able to verify that both processors are working by opening Task Manager and clicking the Performance tab. Task Manager will show all processors installed.

# Managing Ports

Both communication ports (COMs) and parallel printer ports (LPTs) can be accessed and configured using Device Manager. The port settings have settings similar to those of other devices, such as drivers and resources. Parity and transfer rate settings are available for COM ports. An LPT port can be configured to give up its IRQ to another device. Printers are the most common devices attached to an LPT port, and when printers are in an inactive state they don't need an IRQ. The default setting on the LPT port is to never use an interrupt, which allows another device to use the IRQ that would normally be assigned to the device. An LPT port can also be configured for legacy plug-and-play so that the port will detect legacy (old) devices, such as a Zip drives or CD-ROM drives. These settings are located on the Port Settings tab of the Port Properties dialog box.

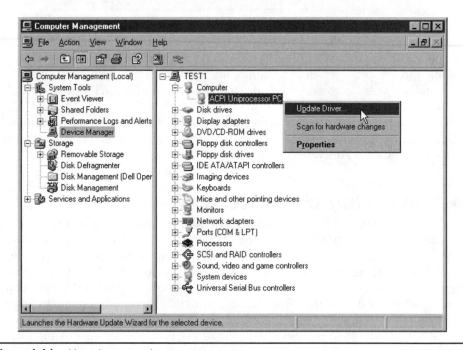

**Figure 1-14**    Upgrading to a multiprocessor server

**EXAM TIP** Some legacy devices plug into the LPT port, such as older CD-ROMs and CD-Ws. If these devices are not detected by Windows, open the Port Properties dialog box and select Enable Legacy Plug and Play on the Port Settings tab.

# Installing and Managing Printers

Before we install and manage printers, we need to get some definitions out of the way. First, quick, look around your office and point to your printer. Did you point to that beige box with the HP logo on the front, the thing that spits out paper every so often? If you did, sorry, you failed Microsoft Printers 101! If you pointed at the printer icon on your computer screen, you are correct.

Now, before you decide that this book must be worthless and use it to line the birdcage, hold on a minute. There is a method to the madness. Microsoft defines that square thing that spits out paper as a *print device*. They define a *printer* as the software interface between the operating system and the print device. The reason for this distinction is that multiple "printers" can be configured to point to the same print device, thus creating some pretty cool features.

The following list summarizes these terms:

- **Printer**   The software interface between a print device and the operating system.
- **Print device**   The physical piece of hardware that actually performs the printing. Most people refer to a print device simply as a printer.
- **Print server**   Any computer on which a local printer is attached. The print server receives documents from clients and sends them to the print device for printing. A print server can be any Windows computer (Server or Professional).

Also, installing a printer is a little different than installing other hardware. Both local printers and network printers can be installed on the computer. Printers are installed by using the Printers and Faxes applet in the Control Panel (see Figure 1-15). The Printers and Faxes applet is also located directly on the Start menu for convenience.

## Installing a Network Printer

It is a common practice to share a single print device with numerous clients. Often, a separate print server is used, such as an HP Jet Direct print server, rather than a Windows Server. Where this is the case, all computers on the network would install network printers and there would be no local printers. A network printer is a print device that has been shared and made available to the network. However, a printer on the network can be managed using Windows Server 2003 by enabling the Print Server role and/or configuring a server as a print server.

To install a network printer, click Add Printer in the Printers and Faxes applet to start the Add Printer Wizard. When asked whether to install a local printer or a network printer, select network printer and click Next. You will have the option of searching

**Figure 1-15**
The Printers and
Faxes applet

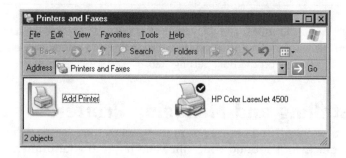

Active Directory for a printer or typing in the share name if known. The wizard will locate the network printer and download and install the appropriate drivers. A network printer can be printed to by users, but can only be managed at the local computer or print server it is attached to.

## Installing a Local Printer

If a local printer is installed, the computer becomes a print server for that printer and will receive print jobs for processing on the attached print device. A local printer can also be managed and additional features such as printer pooling and print priorities can be implemented.

## Lab Exercise 1.2: Installing a Local Printer

In this exercise, you will install a local printer. It is not necessary to have a print device. You can "fake" installing a printer. The printer that you install in this exercise will then be used to demonstrate the additional features of Windows Server 2003 printing.

1. Click Start | Printers and Faxes to open the Printers and Faxes applet.

2. Double-click Add Printer to start the Add Printer Wizard. Click Next.

3. Select "Local printer attached to this computer."

4. Uncheck the box next to "Automatically detect and install my Plug and Play printer," and click Next.

5. Select "Use the following port" and select LPT1, and click Next, as shown in Figure 1-16.

6. Select the manufacturer and model of the printer to install. Select HP as the manufacturer and HP Color LaserJet 4500 for the model (see Figure 1-17). Click Next.

7. Enter **HP Color Laser** for the printer name. Click Next.

8. Select Share Name and type **hpclaser** in the name field. Click Next.

**Figure 1-16**
Select a
printer port.

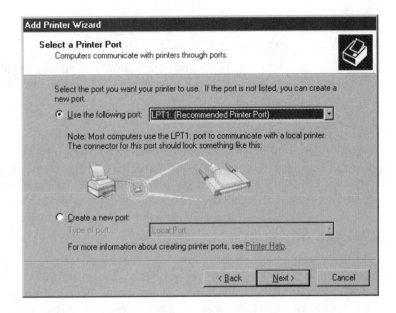

9. Enter a location and comment for the printer. Choose a floor number or building number for the location. Use your imagination for the comment field. Click Next.

10. Select No when asked if you want to print a test page. (You can say Yes, you just won't actually be able to print anything out.)

**Figure 1-17**
Select a printer
manufacturer
and model.

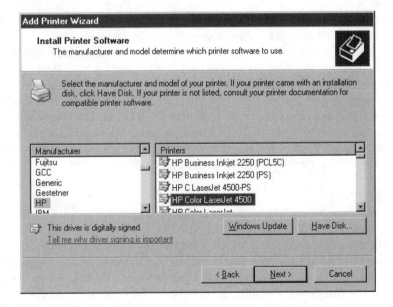

11. Click Finish to complete the Add Printer Wizard.

12. Click Start | All Programs | Accessories and select WordPad.

13. Click File | Print to open the Print dialog box. You should see the printer that you just installed available to print to. Click Cancel and close WordPad.

# Configuring Printers

You must understand how to properly configure a printer for different printing scenarios. The following sections describe how to install additional ports, secure printers using permissions, set up printer pooling, implement print priorities and availability, and set up additional drivers on a printer.

## Installing Ports

We defined a print server as any computer that has a local print device attached to it. You manage printers from the print server. With the widespread use of TCP/IP as a network protocol and most hardware vendors now supporting TCP/IP directly on network printers, it is not necessary to directly attach a print device to a print server. Windows Server 2003 provides the ability to manage a network printer by creating a TCP/IP port on the server and connecting and managing the network printer over IP. Windows Server 2003 also provides a method to create a print server for a printer attached to a Unix system.

### TCP/IP Port

For network printers attached to the network by an Ethernet cable and using TCP/IP, any Windows Server 2003 can be designated as the print server, provided it can communicate with the network printer. Both the print server and the network printer have to have valid IP addresses, subnet masks, and default gateways.

To add a new printer using a TCP/IP port, on the screen in the Add Printer Wizard that asks you to make a port selection, select Create A New Port and select TCP/IP Port from the drop-down list. You will need to enter the IP address of the printer when prompted. The printer must be turned on and accessible over the network or the print server will not be able to make a connection. It is not necessary to know the IP address of the printer as long as you know the share name. When you are prompted to enter the IP address, as shown in Figure 1-18, you may enter the share name of the printer and Server 2003 will locate the printer in Active Directory.

### LPR Port

A Windows Server 2003 can also be used as a print server for a printer attached to a Unix system. Berkeley versions of Unix use the LPR protocol to send print jobs to the line printer spool for printing. In order for a Windows client to be able to forward print jobs to a Unix print spool, an LPR port must be added on the Windows machine. LPR is a protocol and is included with the Print Services for Unix, which are installed through the Control Panel. Installing Print Services for Unix and adding an LPR port allows a

**Figure 1-18**

Adding a TCP/IP port for a network attached printer

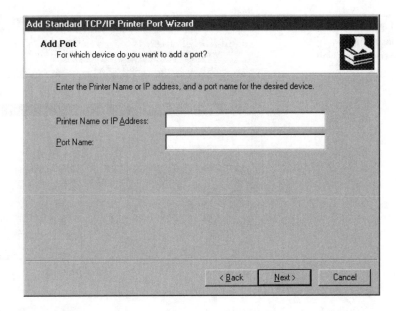

Windows machine to act as a print server to client machines and forward the print jobs to a printer attached to a Unix machine.

## Lab Exercise 1.3: Adding a Unix Printer to a Windows 2003 Print Server

For this exercise, you will add the Print Services for Unix and then add a printer and use the LPR port.

1. Click Start | Control Panel and select the Add/Remove Programs applet.

2. Click Add/Remove Windows Components. You will need to be patient after clicking this button and wait for the Windows Components window to appear.

3. Select Other Network File and Print Services from the components list and click Details.

4. Select Print Services for Unix, as shown in Figure 1-19.

5. Click OK to close the details pane and click Next on the Windows Components window. The wizard will install the drivers for Unix printing. If prompted, insert the disk labeled Windows Server 2003. Click Finish to close the wizard.

6. Click Start | Printers and Faxes to open the Printers and Faxes applet.

7. Double-click Add Printer to start the Add Printer Wizard. Click Next.

8. Select "Local printer attached to this computer."

9. Deselect "Automatically detect and install my Plug and Play printer" and click Next.

**Figure 1-19**
Installing Print
Services for Unix

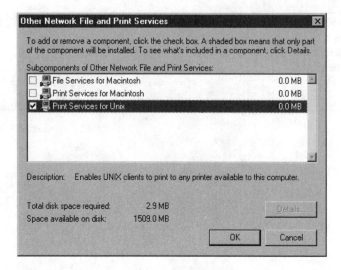

10. Select "Create a new port" and select LPR port.

11. Enter the IP address of the Unix server that the printer is attached to. Also enter the name of the printer or print queue on the server (see Figure 1-20). Click OK.

12. You will receive an error message stating that the port could not be configured because the Unix device could not be contacted. Click OK to close the error message.

13. Select the manufacturer and model of the printer to install. Select HP as the manufacturer and HP LaserJet 5si MX for the model. Click Next.

14. Enter **HPLaser** for the printer name. Click Next.

15. Select Share Name and type **HPLaser** in the name field. Click Next.

16. Enter a location and comment for the printer. Choose a floor number or building number for the location. Use your imagination for the comment field. Click Next.

17. Select No when asked if you want to print a test page.

18. Click Finish to complete the Add Printer Wizard.

**Figure 1-20**
Entering the
name of the Unix
server and print
queue

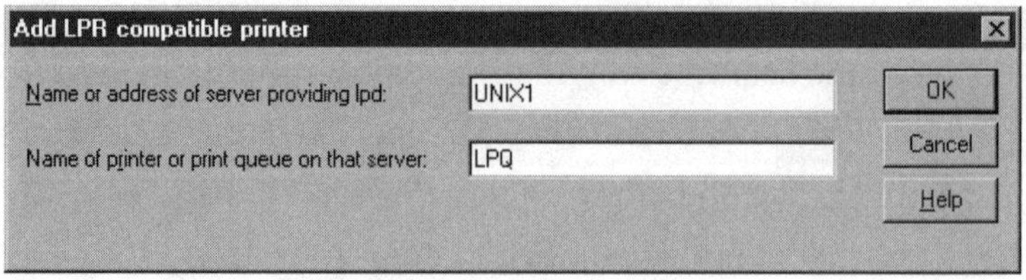

**EXAM TIP**   LPR is a specific Unix protocol used to send print jobs to the print queue. Any time you see LPR, LPD, or LPQ on the exam, think Unix! Or if you see Unix on the exam, think LPR, LPD or LPQ.

## Loading Additional Drivers

Windows Server 2003 has the capability to support printing for multiple client operating systems. A 2003 Server stores print drivers for multiple operating systems (Windows 95, 98, NT 4.0, 2000, and XP) and downloads those drivers to the clients when the client connects to a printer on the print server. Providing print drivers this way is much easier than having to manually install drivers on every client computer in the network. Staying on the Sharing tab on the Printer Properties dialog box, click the Additional Drivers button. You will then see a list of different operating systems that you can select to add drivers for. You must have the Windows disks for each operating system available, as well as the actual print drivers. After performing this operation and loading additional drivers onto the print server, clients will be able to seamlessly connect to a printer, download and install the driver, and print documents without any user intervention.

## Allowing Access to Printers

Printers are resources just like folders and files are, and printers have permissions associated with them as well. (File permissions are covered in Chapter 2.) To print to our HP Color LaserJet that we set up previously, a user must have the Print permission on the printer. Individual users or groups can be granted the Print permission on a printer, although standard practice is to grant Print permissions to groups. Using groups to grant access to resources, such as printers, is discussed in Chapter 2.

To grant access to a printer, open the Printer Properties dialog box and click the Security tab. A sample permissions page is shown in Figure 1-21. Click Add to add a domain local group to the printer and then select the appropriate permissions. Remember, although access has been granted, the users will not be able to see the printer until it is shared.

## Sharing a Printer

Printers were meant to be shared! Sharing a printer allows users throughout the network to access the print device. By default, when a printer is shared at the same time it is added using the Add Printer Wizard, the shared printer is listed in Active Directory and can be located by its name or location attribute.

To share a printer that has already been created, open the Printer Properties dialog box and click the Sharing tab. Select Share This Printer As and enter a name in the share name field. Also, if you would like the printer to be listed in Active Directory, select List In Directory. Conversely, if you have a shared printer that you don't want to be listed in Active Directory, clear the check mark next to List In Directory.

**Figure 1-21**
Configuring the
security of a
printer

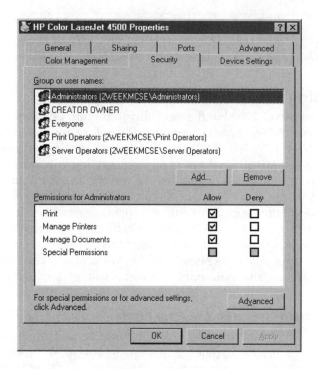

## Print Priorities and Availability

Here's where the ability to create a software printer pointed to a print device gets kind of interesting. Let's suppose that you are the administrator for two groups of users, the executives and the accounting team. Both of these groups have different printing needs, but there was only enough money to buy one print device. Create two software printers and have them both point to the single print device. Then use the priority and availability options to control usage on the printer. To secure the printer so the executives couldn't just use the printer configured for the accountants, add the group that contained the executives to one printer and the group that contained the accounting team to the other printer. Then remove the Everyone group so that each group can only use the printer assigned to them. Now you can modify the properties of the printers and make some changes.

The executives of course want all of their documents printed first! The accountants print huge reports, but they don't necessarily need the reports instantly. You can use the priority and availability settings to control both of these actions. These settings are available on the Advanced tab of the Printer Properties dialog box, as shown in Figure 1-22.

First, assign the executives a priority of 90. When using print priorities, the higher the number, the higher the priority, with 99 being the highest and 1 being the lowest. Then assign the accountants' printer a priority of 50. Now if an accountant and an executive send a print job to the printer at the same time, the executive's print job will print first.

**Figure 1-22**
Setting print
priority and
availability

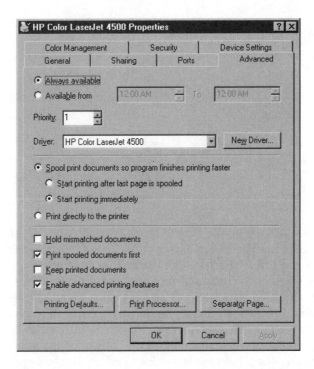

The print server will interrupt the accountant's print job and print the executive's print job as long as the accountant's print job has not finished spooling. If the accountant's print job has spooled, there is nothing that can be done and the executive has to wait.

For the other requirement, you can change the availability of the accountants' printer to something like 5:00 PM to 8:00 AM. Now if an accountant hits the Print button and sends a print job to the printer, the print server will hold the job until 5:00 PM and then send the job to the print device. Using the availability option would essentially queue up all the accountants' jobs until 5:00 PM and then print them all in succession. That's just fine for them and this frees up the printer during the day for the executives. Also, because the priority was set, not just availability, if an executive was working late one evening, his print jobs would still take precedence over the accountants' print jobs.

## Printer Pooling

Printer pooling is used to combine several print devices into one pool, as illustrated in Figure 1-23. The printer (remember, the software interface) will send print jobs to the next available print device. Using printer pooling is useful if a large number of print jobs are performed daily and one print device isn't sufficient. Think of printer pooling as load balancing for printers. Printer pooling is primarily used in large production environments.

**Figure 1-23**
Printer pooling

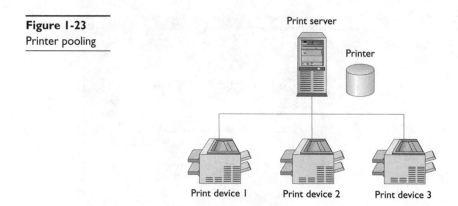

Print server

Printer

Print device 1    Print device 2    Print device 3

The print devices do not have to be identical, but they do have to use the same printer driver. For example, Hewlett Packard builds their printers with backward compatibility, so that a new Color LaserJet 4500 would print just fine using the LaserJet 4 print driver. It is possible then to create a printer pool using a LaserJet 4, LaserJet 5, LaserJet 6L, and LaserJet 4200 DN, as long as the LaserJet 4 print driver was used for all the printers. Each print device must also be directly connected to the print server through a local port or accessible via a TCP/IP port. The print devices need to be in close proximity to one another, for the simple fact that when a user prints a document and the document is sent to the printer, the printer sends the document to whichever print device is available first, and there is no indication of exactly which print device the document went to. Perhaps it would be more fun to place the print devices in the printer pool in opposite corners of the building, or even on different floors, and watch the madness as users go from print device to print device looking for the document they just printed!

## Managing Printers

Of course, it is not enough to simply configure a printer; you must know how to manage and troubleshoot printers when something goes wrong.

### Managing Printers Using Internet Explorer

If a Windows Server 2003 has had web services configured, shared printers on that system can be connected to and managed using Internet Explorer. By default in Server 2003, web services are not installed. This is an important security upgrade. Previously in Windows 2000, IIS was installed automatically and there existed several security holes in IIS that allowed hackers to take control of a system. These holes have been patched with the release of IIS 6.0, and web services are not installed on a server automatically.

To connect to a print server and connect to or manage a printer, type the following into your browser:

```
http://printserver/printers
```

You will connect to the print server and the screen in Figure 1-24 will appear. From this screen, you can click any shared printer located on the print server, and connect to the printer for printing or management.

If you know the share name of the printer you want to connect to and manage, you can type the share name in the address bar directly. For example:

```
http://printserver/hplaser
```

Windows Server 2003 has also placed restrictions on users so that they are unable to connect to a print server or network printer using their browser unless the capability has been explicitly allowed. To manage printers from a browser or to print from a browser, the appropriate Group Policy settings must be turned on. For more information on managing a user environment using Group Policy, see Chapter 23.

**EXAM TIP**   Remember that you can remotely manage printers by using Internet Explorer. Know this path for the exam: http://*printserver*/printers. Substitute *printserver* for the name of the print server, such as http://print1/printers.

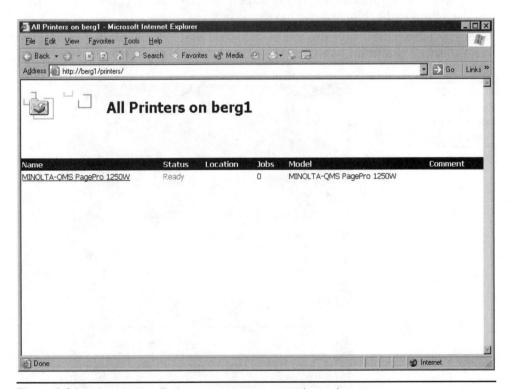

**Figure 1-24**   Using Internet Explorer to manage printers and print documents

## Redirecting Print Jobs

When a user prints a document, that document is first sent to a print queue. If the print device is unavailable for any reason (paper jam, out of toner, powered off), the job will become stuck in the print queue. Print jobs that are stuck in the print queue can be redirected to a different printer. The advantage to redirecting a print job is that users will not have to reprint any of the jobs. If a print job has already started printing, however, and is no longer in the queue when the print device fails, there is nothing that can be done. Only print jobs still in the queue can be redirected.

To redirect print jobs:

1. Click Start | Printers and Faxes to open the Printers and Faxes applet.

2. Right-click the printer that is associated with the failed print device and select Properties from the drop-down menu to open the Printer Properties dialog box.

3. Click the Ports tab.

4. Click Add Port and select the local port from the displayed list. Click New Port.

5. Enter the UNC path of a print device that uses the same printer driver as the failed device, for example, **//poweredge9/hplaserj**. Click OK, then click Close to return to the Printer Properties dialog box.

6. Scroll down the list of ports and click the box next to the local port you just added, as shown in Figure 1-25.

**Figure 1-25**

Redirecting print jobs when a print device has failed

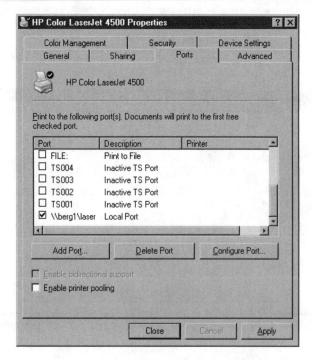

**EXAM TIP**   Knowing the exact steps to redirect a print job is essential for the exam!

## Troubleshooting Printers

Most print problems stem from incorrect printer drivers being loaded. If a user prints a document using an incorrect printer driver, the print job will appear garbled or the print job will print one character on each page. To correct these problems, update the printer driver. The easiest way to update printer drivers on client machines is to first add the appropriate driver on the server, as discussed previously in this section. Then when users connect to the print server, the correct driver will automatically be installed.

For print problems involving the print queue, see Chapter 4.

# Physical Disks

The last type of physical device we are going to talk about is physical disks. Physical disks are critical parts of any network operation, simply because without physical disks, we would have no method of storing large amounts of data and running complex programs, such as Windows Server 2003. A physical disk needs to be installed and formatted before data can be written and stored to the disk. Windows Server 2003 supports both SCSI and IDE hard drives of various sizes. While the differences between SCSI and IDE are not tremendously important for the exam, a brief explanation of both is presented here. What is important to know for the exam is the method used to number physical hard drives, and how to install and manage the physical disks, including tasks such as creating volumes, formatting volumes, and creating fault-tolerant volumes.

## SCSI

SCSI (Small Computer Systems Interface) disks are much more common in enterprise-level computing than the IDE standard. SCSI drives are generally faster and more reliable than IDE drives and for those reasons are much more widely used in mission-critical servers. The second generation of SCSI devices, nicknamed Fast SCSI, can run at 15,000 rpm and support transfer rates of 20 MBps, while IDE only supports up to 7200 rpm and transfer rates of 16.7 MBps. To support SCSI drives, a separate SCSI adapter has to be installed on the motherboard. Almost no personal computers or workstations use SCSI drives, but SCSI drives are very common in enterprise-level servers and storage appliances. SCSI cards also support connecting up to 15 SCSI drives to a single controller, while IDE supports only four. SCSI drives are connected in a daisy chain configuration.

## IDE

AT Attached (ATA), or IDE (Integrated Device Electronics) as they are more commonly referred to, are the standard most commonly used in workstations and personal computers, mainly because it is cheaper than SCSI, and unless multiple drives are required, the SCSI standard isn't needed. ATA or IDE drives were originally used in IBM PC-AT computers, and become the de facto standard for the industry. A parallel IDE cable can hold two drives, and up to four drives can be connected to a single IDE dual channel controller. When connecting two hard drives to an IDE controller using the same cable, it is important to set one of the hard drives as the "master" and the other as the "slave." This is done by setting the jumpers on the hard drive. See the manufacturer's documentation for how to set the appropriate jumpers. Serial ATA has made some improvements over parallel ATA in the area of speed (double that of parallel ATA) and more drives per controller (up to 15).

**NOTE** Many manufacturers use a Cable Select setting, which basically automatically assigns one drive on the cable as the master and the other as the slave. However, there are numerous situations in which the Cable Select setting doesn't work adequately, and it is a best practice to manually set the jumpers.

# ARC Path Designation

All Windows operating systems dating back to NT 3.51 use the Advanced Risk Computing (ARC) numbering scheme to identify the physical disks and the system folder for bootup purposes. Physical disks are numbered ordinally—that is, the numbering starts at 0. This is true both in ARC paths and in Computer Management tasks (such as creating volumes). The boot.ini file on the root directory uses the ARC path to locate the WINNT directory and boot into an operating system. By understanding the numbering scheme, you can troubleshoot boot failures as well as identify specific hard drives in your system.

Every Windows system uses a file to identify where on the hard drive the operating system is located. This file is the boot.ini file. To view the ARC path on your system, open Windows Explorer and navigate to the root drive, usually C. The boot.ini file is located on the root drive, but may be hidden as it is a system file. You will need to change the folder options to view hidden and system files and folders.

Following are two examples of an ARC path:

```
Multi (0) disk (0) rdisk (0) partition (1)\WINDOWS="Microsoft Windows 2003"
SCSI (0) disk (3) rdisk (0) partition (1)\WINNT="Microsoft Windows 2003"
```

Both of these ARC paths identify the exact physical location of an operating system.

**NOTE** Notice the WINDOWS directory in the preceding example. Microsoft has changed the default install folder from WINNT to WINDOWS for Server 2003. This change has caused some problems with applications and scripting. Rather than change all of your scripts and applications, change the default folder to WINNT during the installation process. If you are upgrading an NT 4.0 or Windows 2000 Server, the installation folder will remain WINNT. You should also make sure that you make this change on any images that are being rolled out using RIS or other disk duplication technologies.

If you break the ARC path down into its components, you get

- **Multi (0)**   This identifies which controller the physical disk is located on. Multi is used for IDE drives and for pure SCSI systems in which the OS has been installed on either the first or second SCSI hard drive. If SCSI is being used, Multi refers to a SCSI card with its onboard BIOS disabled. You use ordinal numbers for the value, which means you start counting at 0, then 1, 2, 3, and so on.

- **SCSI (0)**   This identifies which controller the physical disk is located on. You use ordinal numbers. SCSI is only used if the system is using SCSI disks with its own BIOS or if SCSI drives and IDE drives are both present.

- **Disk (0)**   This refers to the actual physical disk attached to the controller. However, this setting is always 0 if Multi is present. Disk (0) is only for SCSI. You use ordinal numbers for the physical disk. A SCSI card can have up to 15 SCSI disks attached, so the value of disk can be anywhere between 0–15. (Yes, that's 16 numbers! Good catch. One of the channels is used by the controller itself.)

- **Rdisk (0)**   This refers to the actual physical disk attached to the controller. However, this setting is always 0 if SCSI is present. Rdisk (0) is only for Multi. You use ordinal numbers for the physical disk.

- **Partition (1)**   This refers to the partition on the hard disk where the WINNT folder is located. Numbering for partitions begins at 1 and is loosely translated to mean 1=C, 2=E, 3=F, and so on. (D is usually reserved for the CD-ROM drive.)

Let's look at an ARC path now and identify exactly which drive and partition the boot partition is located on.

```
Multi (0) disk (0) rdisk (2) partition (2)\WINNT="Microsoft Windows 2003"
```

Multi is being used, so you know that the system is using either IDE or SCSI drives, but probably IDE. You then skip the Disk value, noting that it will always be zero. The Rdisk value is 2, which means the third hard drive. That's because you use ordinal numbers and begin counting at 0. Finally, partition 2 is designated. Partition 2 would be the second partition on the hard drive, probably the E drive.

Here's an easy way to remember what Multi and SCSI refer to:

- There are five letters in the word Multi and five letters in the word Rdisk.

- There are four letters in the word SCSI and four letters in the word Disk.

- Multi goes to Rdisk, and SCSI goes to Disk.

# Using Disk Management

Microsoft has included a Disk Management tool to quickly and easily perform basic disk functions such as installing disks, creating volumes, and formatting. Disk Management is part of the Computer Management MMC. You can access the Computer Management

MMC through the Control Panel, through Start | Programs | Administrative Tools, or by simply right-clicking My Computer and selecting Manage. You can also add the Computer Management snap-in to a custom MMC. To open Disk Management, click Start | Programs | Administrative Tools | Computer Management. Under the Computer Management tree, expand the Storage node and click Disk Management. The Disk Management interface is shown in Figure 1-26.

The Disk Management interface allows you to initialize new disks, create volumes and partitions, and generally manage your hard disks. The default view of Disk Management shows the Volume List in the top pane and a graphical view in the bottom pane. You can alter these settings by clicking View and choosing which view to place on the top and bottom. There is a third view, which shows a list of the hard disks in your computer, including removable storage and CD-ROM and DVD drives. You will also notice that each particular type of volume or partition is represented by a unique color. These colors can be changed by clicking the Settings button on the View menu.

You can also add the Computer Management snap-in to an existing MMC and create a custom console.

## Lab Exercise 1.4: Creating a Custom Console

In this exercise, you will create a custom console and add the Computer Management snap-in to the console. Creating custom consoles will come in handy the more you work with Windows Server 2003. Many administrators sit down and create a custom

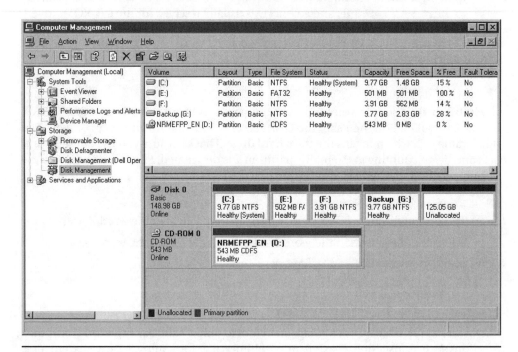

**Figure 1-26** The Disk Management interface

console with all the tools they need before they begin administering the server. It makes the job easier when everything is in one place.

1. Click Start | Run and type **mmc**.

2. After Console1 opens, click File | Add/Remove Snap-in. Click Add and select Computer Management.

3. A dialog box will ask you if you want to manage the local computer or a remote computer. Select the local computer and click Finish.

4. Click Close on the Add Standalone Snap-in box and click OK on the Add/ Remove Snap-in dialog box.

5. Click File | Save As and name the console **Custom1**. Click Save.

6. Close the console.

7. Click Start | Programs | Administrative Tools and select Custom1 to open your saved custom console.

**NOTE** When you save a console, by default it is saved in the user's profile and is available only to the user that created it. Consoles can be saved to alternate locations and then e-mailed to another user. The user must have permissions to perform the tasks in the console, or they will be unable to use the console effectively.

You are now ready to use the Computer Management snap-in!

## Remote Management

The Computer Management snap-in allows you to also manage remote computers. You can connect to any computer in your enterprise and perform the same management functions as if you were physically sitting at the machine. Remember, you must have Administrative rights on the local machine. By default, Domain Admins are part of the local Administrators group, and are able to manage a remote computer that is part of the domain.

To connect to a remote computer:

1. Right-click the Computer Management (local) icon in the tree and click Connect To Another Computer.

2. You can then select any computer in Active Directory. After you select a computer, click OK.

3. Computer Management will now connect to the remote computer.

**NOTE** You will need to use Disk Management to complete the following section. Make sure that you understand how to use the navigation controls. The controls and options in the console are not discussed further in this chapter as they are relatively self-explanatory. Spend a few minutes and push all the buttons and see what happens. Play with the console a little bit.

# Basic vs. Dynamic Disks

With the release of Windows 2000, Microsoft introduced dynamic disks. Dynamic disks use a proprietary format for recording partition information. Whereas a basic disk is divided into partitions, with up to four primary partitions, a dynamic disk is formatted with essentially one primary partition and then individual volumes can be created on the disk. There is no limit, other than how much free space you have on the drive, to how many volumes you can create on a dynamic disk.

## Basic Disks

A basic disk is what we all grew up with. A basic disk uses the normal partition table supported in MS-DOS and most Windows operating systems. It can contain up to four primary partitions or, to allow for more drive letters, three primary partitions and one extended partition. The extended partition could then be divided into smaller units and a separate drive letter assigned to each section, as shown in Figure 1-27.

Basic disks, while simple, suffer from some design flaws that make them less than desirable in mission critical situations. A basic disk's partition table (or file allocation table) is located on the first sector of the hard drive and shares space with the Master Boot Record. With both of these critical components being placed in the same physical sector of the hard drive, should the sector become damaged or corrupted, it would render the entire disk unusable and all data would be lost. The disk would have to be reformatted and data restored from backup. Dynamic disks are an improvement on this design in that they implement a degree of fault tolerance.

Basic disks have been in use for a long time and all Windows operating systems have support for reading and writing to basic disks. This is an important consideration when designing a server with multiple operating systems. Windows 2000, 2003, and XP are the only operating systems that can read a dynamic disk, so if other operating systems need access to the disk, it must remain a basic disk.

**NOTE** NT 4.0 Server introduced volume sets and fault tolerance using more than one basic disk. It is recommended that prior to upgrading from NT 4.0 to Windows 2003, that any volume sets be dismantled and that the volume sets be re-created using the corresponding volume sets in Server 2003. However, if a server running NT 4.0 is upgraded to Windows 2003 without removing the volume sets, Server 2003 will retain the volume sets for backward compatibility.

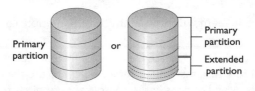

**Figure 1-27** Basic disk configuration using up to four primary partitions or three primary partitions and one extended partition

Using basic disks, you can create the following:

- **Primary partition**   Primary partitions are the only partitions that are bootable, so every system needs to have at least one primary partition. A primary partition is designated by a drive letter or possibly a mount point. A physical disk can be formatted with one primary partition for the entire disk, or can be divided into several sections and each section is a primary partition.

- **Extended partition**   An extended partition is not bootable, but the WINNT directory can be located on an extended partition. An extended partition can create an unlimited number of logical drives.

- **Logical drives**   A logical drive is simply an area of usable space on a physical drive. Logical drives are assigned drive letters. You can't use a logical drive for the system partition, but you can locate the boot partition or the WINNT directory on a logical drive.

In NT 4.0 Server, you were able to use basic disks and create mirrored sets, stripe sets, and stripe sets with parity. Any time you make a configuration change on a basic disk, such as adding a mirror set, the system requires a reboot. With the introduction of Windows 2000, this functionality was discontinued for basic disks and any multi-disk volumes have to be created using dynamic disks.

## Dynamic Disks

Dynamic disks primarily benefit systems with multiple disks, such as network file servers. The main improvements of dynamic disks over basic disks are availability and fault tolerance. Dynamic disks maintain a 1MB database at the end of each physical disk that contains information about all other dynamic disks in the system. By storing this information in multiple places, dynamic disks are less likely to fail, and in the event of failure, are more likely to be brought back online. Dynamic disks can also be reconfigured without having to restart the machine, which is an added plus.

Using dynamic disks to create volumes has become a simpler and less time consuming task and has resulted in less downtime. Previously, creating a mirror set required a reboot of the server. While it may sound harmless, how many times do you really want to reboot your most critical server? Every reboot causes production delays. Dynamic disk configuration changes can be implemented on the fly. A dynamic disk creates one single partition and then allows the creation of volumes within that partition. You can think of a dynamic disk as one great big extended partition. Using dynamic disks, you can create the following volumes (see Figure 1-28):

- Simple volume
- Spanned volume
- Mirrored volume
- Striped volume
- RAID 5 volume

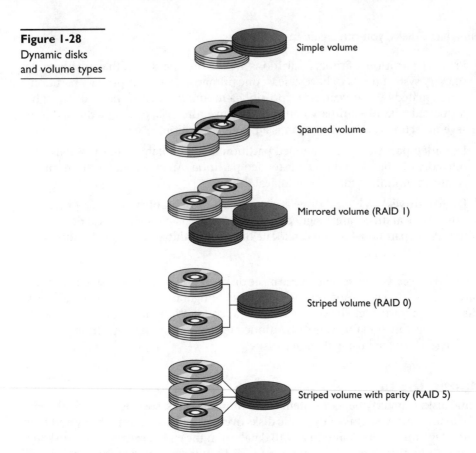

**Figure 1-28**
Dynamic disks
and volume types

Simple volume

Spanned volume

Mirrored volume (RAID 1)

Striped volume (RAID 0)

Striped volume with parity (RAID 5)

A volume is roughly equivalent to a partition in a basic disk. A volume is assigned a driver letter or folder and then formatted for use. These volume types cannot be created on a basic disk. Using basic disks in Windows Server 2003, you are only able to create partitions and logical drives. In fact, if you want to set up any kind of fault-tolerant solution in Windows 2000 or 2003, you must convert your disks to dynamic disks.

If you are using dynamic disks, you can only format volumes using the NTFS format using Disk Management. You will notice when you try to format a dynamic volume, the FAT and FAT32 options are not available, only NTFS. It is possible that a FAT or FAT32 volume is needed for backward compatibility or for certain applications that require that specific format. The workaround for this is to use the command line. You can use the FORMAT command from the command prompt and format the volume using FAT, FAT32, or NTFS. To format a volume from the command line:

1. Click Start | Run. Type **cmd**. Press ENTER.

2. At the command prompt, type **format _x_: /fs:_y_** where _x_ is the volume letter you want to format and _y_ is the file system you want to use, FAT, FAT32, or NTFS. Press ENTER.

3. You will need to verify the current volume name. At the prompt, enter the volume name.

4. You will then be warned all data will be lost if you proceed with the operation. Enter **y** to continue the format or **n** to cancel the format.

5. Enter a new volume label when prompted.

6. Type **exit** to close the command prompt.

7. Open Disk Management and verify the format was completed successfully.

 **EXAM TIP**  If you need to dual-boot a machine with only one physical disk, you must use basic disks, you cannot use dynamic disks. This is the main reason dynamic disks are not supported on laptops! You can dual-boot a machine using dynamic disks as long as the primary disk with the operating systems is basic. You cannot dual-boot a machine when the primary disk is dynamic.

## Simple Volume

Simple volumes are the most common volumes and the type of volume that you will create most often. If you are using a single disk configuration, a simple volume is the only volume type that you can create.

## Spanned Volume

Spanned volumes are created by combining disk space from two or more hard disks. Spanned volumes were called volume sets in NT 4.0. Spanned volumes can be created by using different amounts of space from different hard disks. For example, a 10GB spanned volume can be created from 6GB of unallocated space on hard drive 0, 3GB of unallocated space on hard drive 1, and 1GB of space on hard drive 2. A spanned volume cannot be extended, and there is no fault tolerance in using a spanned volume. If any of the drives fail, the data on the volume is lost and must be restored from backup.

Spanned volumes can be created from two physical disks and can contain up to 32 physical disks. The more disks in a spanned volume, the greater the possibility of a failure. Spanned volumes are generally created when a single volume is required using physical disks with different amounts of storage capacity.

There is no performance gain using a spanned volume. Data written to a spanned volume is written to the first disk in the volume until the disk is full and then the data is written to the second disk and so on.

## Mirrored Volume

Mirrored volumes are created using two physical disks. A mirrored volume requires that the same amount of unallocated space on each physical disk is used. When data is written to a mirrored volume, the data is written to disk and then synchronized on the second disk. An exact copy of the data is available on both physical disks.

A mirrored volume is the only volume available in Server 2003 in which the boot and system partitions can reside besides a simple volume. This is because a mirrored volume can be created from a simple volume or from unallocated space on the physical disk. It is usual practice to mirror the system and boot partition so that in case of a disk failure the server can still be booted.

 **NOTE** You must have a backup of your boot.ini file to ensure that you will be able to reboot the system in case of a disk failure. Remember, the server boots to the OS specified in the boot.ini file and if the boot.ini file is pointing to the failed disk, the server will not boot. It is a common practice and highly recommended that at the time the mirror is created, a copy of the boot.ini file is placed on a floppy disk and the ARC path altered to point to the second physical disk in the mirror. In the case of a failure, the server can be rebooted by supplying the backup boot.ini file.

## Striped Volume

A striped volume is created using a minimum of two and a maximum of 32 physical drives to create a single volume. A striped volume is created by using an equal amount of unallocated space on all the physical disks.

Striped volumes provide the best read and write performance of all the different types of volumes. A striped volume gets its name from how the data is read and accessed on the drive. The data is written across all physical disks in the volume in equal parts, thereby creating a stripe pattern. When data is written to the volume, it is divided into 64KB parts and each part is written to a separate disk. Chopping the data into pieces allows each physical disk to be performing a write operation at almost exactly the same time, thereby increasing speed dramatically. When data is read, it is read in the same way, in 64KB blocks at a time.

Here's an example. Suppose you have a server with four physical disks and you create a 10GB striped volume using all four disks. (That's 2.5GB on each physical disk.) You decide to place a 500MB database on the volume. When you place the database on the volume, Windows immediately begins parsing the 500MB into 64KB chunks and parceling each chunk out one at a time to each of the four physical disks. The first 64KB piece is written to the first disk, the second piece to the second disk, the third piece to the third disk, and the fourth piece to the fourth disk. Because each disk is handling an identically sized piece of data, each disk can begin writing before the other disks are finished. So when the first disk is finished writing the first 64KB block of data, it can immediately begin writing the fifth piece of data before the other disks are finished with their write processes.

A read process works the same way. A file is requested and each physical disk accesses the portion of the file located on the drive.

Striped volumes do not offer fault tolerance. If any of the physical disks in the volume fails, all the data is lost and must be restored from backup. It is recommended that when creating striped volumes, identical physical disks be used—the same size, transfer rate, and manufacturer and model. Using different disks can cause problems in the synchronization of the read and write operations, and can lead to volume failures.

## RAID 5 Volume

RAID 5 volumes provide fault tolerance and performance. RAID 5 write operations are slower than operations using striping. When a write operation is performed, both the disk where the data is being written to and the disk where the corresponding parity information is written to need to be accessed. Parity is a checksum value used to compute data if a drive fails. This leads to multiple operations being required to complete a single write.

The parity information does allow for one disk in the array to fail and the volume to still be operational. When a disk in the array fails, the remaining disks use the data on either side of the failed disk, along with the parity information, to reconstruct the data. When a disk fails, read operations become extremely slow as the data is being rebuilt on the fly.

## Mounted Volumes

Mounted volumes are not really a separate type of volume; they are a method of creating a volume that can be referenced by a name. When you create any type of volume (simple, spanned, and so on), you can choose to "Assign the following drive letter" or "Mount in the following empty NTFS folder" (see Figure 1-29). You have the ability to browse to any folder on your system or to create a new folder. The folder must be empty. If you want to mount a volume to an existing folder containing data, you will need to back up the data, delete the contents of the folder, and then restore from backup after you have mounted the new volume to the folder. The mounted volume is then accessible through a folder.

# Disk Management Tools and Tasks

Knowing how to manage disks properly to configure storage options is essential to effectively managing a serve environment. We have already used the Disk Management

**Figure 1-29**
Mounting a
volume to an
empty folder

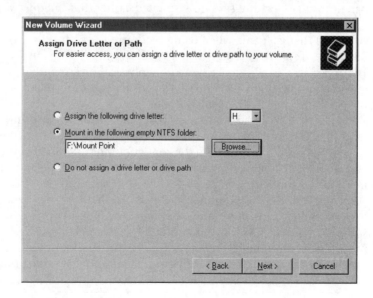

## Hardware RAID

Microsoft has implemented software RAID into all of their server products since NT 4.0, and using software RAID is a low cost alternative to using hardware RAID. Traditionally, the exams have included heavy doses of content about disk management and RAID solutions. Although you should know Microsoft's Disk Management features and tools for the exam, most production environments use special RAID cards with multiple drives as a solution, and Microsoft has begun to place questions that at least reference hardware RAID on their exams.

Hardware RAID offers several advantages over software or OS RAID. First, hardware RAID is much less susceptible to failure. Software RAID has to be written for the kernel level, and it must be perfect or it is susceptible to crashes. Also, software RAID commands have to be executed by the system processor and so are subjected to the normal interrupts and have to share processing time with other applications. By placing the read/write processes on a separate card, the processes are not only speeded up, they are protected as well and are less likely to crash.

Second, hardware RAID is portable. Software RAID is created within the operating system and therefore has OS-specific components that are not transferable between systems, even systems that share the same operating system. In contrast, a mirrored volume using a hardware RAID controller and directly attached to the motherboard can be removed and placed onto a new motherboard and implemented into a new system, regardless of the operating system. The RAID configuration and the data itself would be protected and would remain intact. Hardware RAID can therefore be used in much more elaborate backup and disaster recovery implementations.

Third, hardware RAID of all flavors is supported because it is completely transparent to the operating system. We stated earlier that the only volumes that can have the boot and system partitions on them are mirrored volumes and simple volumes. That isn't true when using hardware RAID. It is very common to use a RAID 0 on a system and then install Windows Server 2003 on the striped volume. That's because, to Windows, two 80GB physical disks configured as a stripe or a mirror appear as one 160GB drive. The OS doesn't know that the two disks are being combined in a RAID configuration.

Hardware RAID is also no longer cost prohibitive. At the printing of this book, hardware RAID cards that supported 0, 1, and 5 were available for as little as $200.

Hardware RAID is usually in the configurations described in this book: RAID 0 (striping) RAID 1 (mirroring), and RAID 5 (striping with parity), but it also comes in a RAID 6 configuration and a RAID 1+0 (commonly referred to as RAID 10) configuration. RAID 6 is similar to RAID 5 in that it stripes data across multiple drives, but the parity information also has its own parity, so two drives can fail and still be recovered. RAID 1+0 or RAID 10 or is a mirrored stripe set. RAID 10 is probably the most interesting of the RAID configurations because it combines optimal performance (striping) with optimal redundancy (mirroring), as shown in

Figure 1-30. Many large corporations and government agencies use RAID 10 for their mission-critical databases and applications. These types of organizations are concerned about being able to recover from any kind of a disaster and have their data back up and running quickly.

An exotic flavor of RAID 10 involves rotating the mirror and keeping a copy off site. Here's how it works. Drive A is striped with Drive B. Drive C is striped with Drive D. Stripe AB is then mirrored to Stripe CD. After the mirror has been synchronized, Stripe CD is removed and replaced with Stripe EF. Stripe CD is kept on site so that if either Stripe AB or EF fails, that redundancy can be quickly restored by simply swapping Stripe CD with the failed stripe set. For ultimate recoverability, a fourth stripe set is configured, Stripe GH. When Stripe EF has been synchronized, it is removed and replaced with Stripe GH. Stripe EF is then taken to an offsite storage facility. The system is then able to be restored completely from Stripe EF should a major disaster strike the corporate location. Each of the four stripe sets is also rotated, as often as daily. At any given time, there are two stripe sets in the mirror on the server, one stripe set on the shelf in the server room, and one stripe set off site. Wow!

snap-in to create different volume types and to format volumes. You also use Disk Management to install and move physical disks from one machine to another. You must also know how to convert volumes to NTFS without losing data and how to manage quotas for users.

## Installing a Physical Disk

Most of the time, physical disks are installed on the system prior to installing the operating system, and they are installed automatically. However, there are situations when a new physical disk is added to the system. A drive may fail or the current drive's capacity has been met and more storage is needed. When a new disk is installed, there are some

**Figure 1-30**
RAID 10
configuration

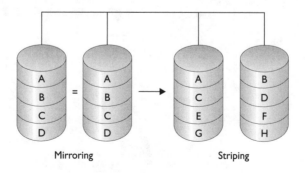

Mirroring          Striping

additional steps that need to be taken before it can be formatted and used to store data. Physical disks are usually plug-and-play compatible and are detected by the operating system. The drivers for the disks are also usually installed; however, the disk will not always appear as a usable disk, as shown in Figure 1-31. All physical disks need to be initialized by Windows. When you initialize the disk, the operating system writes a signature to the disk, an end of sector marker, and a master boot record. After the disk is initialized, it will be ready to be formatted and used.

To initialize a disk, open Disk Management, right-click the disk you want to initialize, and select Initialize Disk. The Initialize and Convert Disk Wizard, shown in Figure 1-32, also allows a disk to be converted to a dynamic disk at the same time.

## Moving a Disk

There are times when you may want to move a disk from one machine to another. After you physically move the drive, you need to rescan the disk to make it accessible from the operating system. Remember that when you initialized the disk, the operating system wrote a signature to the disk. This signature becomes part of the makeup of the disk. When a disk is moved to a different computer, it needs to be rescanned in order for the new computer to properly read the disk. You can rescan the disk either by using Disk Management or by using the command prompt.

Microsoft recommends that you uninstall the disk prior to moving it. To uninstall the disk, open Device Manager, select the disk you want to uninstall, right-click and select Uninstall. You will see a prompt confirming device removal. After clicking OK, the device will be uninstalled. It is now safe to remove the drive. By uninstalling the disk, you

**Figure 1-31**
A recently installed disk that has not been initialized shows as unknown.

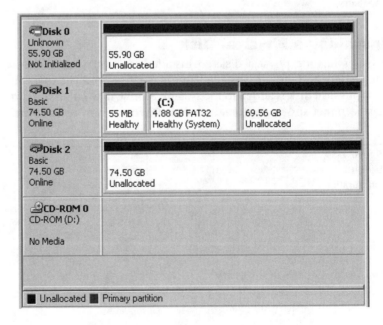

**Figure 1-32**
Initialize and
Convert Disk
Wizard

Initialize and Convert Disk Wizard

**Welcome to the Initialize and Convert Disk Wizard**

This wizard helps you to initialize new disks and to convert empty basic disks to dynamic disks.

You can use dynamic disks to create software-based volumes that can be mirrored, or they can be striped or spanned across multiple disks. You can also expand single-disk and spanned volumes without having to restart the computer.

After you convert a disk to dynamic, you can only use Windows 2000 and later versions of Windows on any volume of that disk.

To continue, click Next.

< Back    Next >    Cancel

have only removed the driver for the disk, not the disk signature. A disk that has been initialized will not need to be initialized a second time if it is placed into a different computer.

**TIP**   Remember our conversation about ARC paths? To identify the appropriate disk to uninstall, right-click the disk and select Properties. On the General tab, you will see a Location heading with a number. This number is the ordinal number assigned to the disk. Match this number with the disk number in Disk Management and you won't go wrong!

After you have moved the disk, restart the computer. Windows will automatically detect the new hardware and you will see the Found New Hardware dialog box. If Windows does not detect the new drive, you will need to add the drive manually by using the Add Hardware applet in the Control Panel.

## Rescanning a Disk

Before you can use the new disk, you must rescan the disk and verify that the disk information is correct. To rescan a disk, open Disk Manager, click the Action menu, and select Rescan.

When you move a dynamic volume, a warning icon will display on the disk and it will display the foreign status. When this occurs, right-click the disk that displays Foreign, and select Import Foreign Disks. Any existing volumes on the dynamic disk will now become accessible.

You can also use the command prompt to rescan a disk. Server 2003 is the most command-line friendly of all the Windows servers, and there are more and more tasks that can be performed from the command line. Purists tend to like command-line administration because they can type faster than they can open windows and navigate to the appropriate box. Also, scripting is very popular with administrators, and having the ability to perform a task in a script is a definite advantage. Some administrators will spend hours perfecting a script to perform a task so they can call up that script whenever they need to perform that particular task again.

## Lab Exercise 1.5: Rescanning a Disk from the Command Prompt

In this exercise, you will rescan a disk using the command prompt. Rescanning disks will not affect any of your data or have any adverse affects on your system. This is a very safe exercise to do.

1. At the command prompt, type **diskpart** and press ENTER.

2. At the DISKPART prompt, type **rescan** and press ENTER.

3. At the DISKPART prompt, type **list disk** and press ENTER.

4. At the DISKPART prompt, type **select disk** *n*, where *n* is the number of the disk you want to import.

5. At the DISKPART prompt, type **import**.

 **NOTE**   To be able to perform any of the Disk Management tasks, you must be a member of the local Administrators group. By default, Domain Admins are part of the local Administrators group.

## Upgrading to Dynamic Disks

To use any of the volumes available in Windows Server 2003, you must be using dynamic disks. You can upgrade your basic disks to dynamic disks. To upgrade a basic disk to dynamic, open Disk Management and right-click the disk you want to upgrade and select the Upgrade To Dynamic Disk option.

## Hot Swappable Drives

A hot swappable drive can be moved in and out of a system without having to shut down or restart the system. Almost all enterprise-level servers use hot swappable drives to avoid costly downtime in the case of a drive failure.

For a drive to be hot swappable, it must be supported on the controller. Most hot swappable drives are SCSI drives and tend to be more expensive. You can't make a drive hot swappable by just yanking it out of the machine.

If you replace or add a hot swappable drive to your system, you simply need to rescan the disk to make it available to the operating system. You can use either method of rescanning the disk mentioned previously.

**NOTE** The storage capacity of hard drives has easily surpassed that of other backup media. As such, it is not uncommon that hot swappable drives are used for backups.

## Converting FAT Volumes to NTFS

You can convert FAT volumes to NTFS to take advantage of the features of NTFS without losing your data or having to reformat. To convert a FAT volume to NTFS, at a command prompt type the following command:

```
convert x: /fs:NTFS
```

where *x* is the volume you want to convert. You can also add the /v switch if you want to run the command in verbose mode. Running any command in verbose mode displays error messages and events. Verbose mode is used for troubleshooting. When running a command in verbose mode, a log is also created in the WINNT directory in the Debug folder. Figure 1-33 shows the convert command syntax and the available switches.

Switches available to the convert utility are shown in Table 1-1.

Converting a volume to NTFS is a one-way change. You cannot convert an NTFS volume back to FAT. To change an NTFS volume back to FAT, you need to back up your data, delete the volume, re-create the volume, and format it as FAT.

# File Systems

There are some important distinctions that must be made in regards to the type of file system to use on your system. Windows Server 2003 supports FAT, FAT32, and NTFS,

```
Command Prompt                                                    _ □ X
Microsoft Windows [Version 5.2.3790]
(C) Copyright 1985-2003 Microsoft Corp.

C:\Documents and Settings\Administrator>convert /?
Converts FAT volumes to NTFS.

CONVERT volume /FS:NTFS [/V] [/CvtArea:filename] [/NoSecurity] [/X]

  volume      Specifies the drive letter (followed by a colon),
              mount point, or volume name.
  /FS:NTFS    Specifies that the volume is to be converted to NTFS.
  /V          Specifies that Convert should be run in verbose mode.
  /CvtArea:filename
              Specifies a contiguous file in the root directory to be
              the place holder for NTFS system files.
  /NoSecurity Specifies the converted files and directories security
              settings to be accessible by everyone.
  /X          Forces the volume to dismount first if necessary.
              All opened handles to the volume would then be invalid.

C:\Documents and Settings\Administrator>
```

**Figure 1-33** The convert utility at the command prompt

| Available Switch | What It Does |
|---|---|
| /v | Enables verbose mode. Verbose mode will show error messages and create a log file for troubleshooting. |
| /x | Forces the volume to dismount before converting to NTFS. This is used only when the volume is a mounted volume. |
| /CvtArea:*filename* | Sets the name of a contiguous file in the root directory to be a placeholder for NTFS system files. |
| /NoSecurity | Removes all security attributes (permissions) and grants the Everyone group Full Control to all files and folders. |

**Table 1-1**　convert Utility Switches

although it is highly recommended to format using NTFS. NTFS is required as the file system when Active Directory is installed. We will cover compression and encryption as features of the NTFS file system. File and folder level security using NTFS will be covered in detail in Chapter 3, and using disk quotas and maintaining hard disks will be covered in detail in Chapter 4.

## FAT

The FAT file system is actually two different flavors: FAT16 and FAT32. FAT16 is generally referred to as simply FAT, and FAT32 is used to differentiate between the versions. FAT16 was widely used in NT 4.0 systems. FAT32 was introduced with Windows 95 SR2 and support for both versions of FAT was built in to all subsequent Windows operating systems, including Server 2003.

FAT gets its name because it uses a file allocation table to keep track of data on the disk. When data is stored on a physical disk, it may be stored in multiple clusters and the cluster may or may not be contiguous. A table is created that maps files to the clusters where they are located and contains information about their sequential order so the file can be located and read. A table entry is 16 bits in length. When FAT32 was introduced, it extended the table length to 32 bits per entry. This increased the amount of disk space supported from 512MB to two terabytes.

FAT needs to be used if you are going to dual-boot a machine with Windows 95, 98, or ME, and any of the 2000, XP, or 2003 products. Previous versions of Windows can only read partitions that have been formatted with FAT.

 **NOTE**　If you are using dynamic disks, you cannot format a volume with FAT or FAT32 using Disk Management. If you need to format a volume on a dynamic disk with FAT or FAT32, you must use the format command from the command prompt. Use the following syntax: format *x*: /fs:fat32 or format *x*: /fs:fat.

## NTFS

NTFS is the file system of choice for Windows Server 2003. NTFS was introduced as a file system with NT 4.0 and has seen some improvements. NTFS version 5.0 was introduced with Windows 2000 Server and is fully supported in Windows Server 2003. NTFS supports compression, encryption, and disk quotas. NTFS is also required for Active Directory. The Active Directory database must be installed on an NTFS volume.

NTFS uses a master file table (MFT) that is similar to the file allocation table used by FAT and FAT32, but much more efficient. Due to the different architecture, NTFS is not readable by Windows 98, 95, or earlier operating systems. If you are creating a dual-boot machine using Windows 98 and Server 2003, you must create a FAT partition for data that must be accessible by either operating system. This does not mean that Windows 98 and 95 computers cannot access network resources placed on NTFS volumes. Any operating system can still access resources across the network.

NTFS supports additional attributes not available on FAT volumes, such as compression, encryption, file and folder level security, and quota management.

### Compression

Windows 2003 supports two kinds of compression: NTFS compression and compressed folders (zipped). Using NTFS compression, you can compress files, folders, and drives. Compression is completely transparent to the user, and users can work with compressed files without having to manually uncompress them. When using compression, it is recommended that you compress folders instead of individual files. By compressing folders, all new files added to that folder will automatically be compressed.

When you compress a folder, you are prompted to choose whether to compress just the folder or files and subfolders, as displayed in Figure 1-34. If you choose to only compress the folder, files currently in the folder are not compressed, however, any new files will be compressed. If you decide to uncompress a folder, again you have the option of uncompressing just the folder or subfolders and files. If you choose to uncompress just the folder, any files in the folder that are compressed will remain compressed, but any new files added to the folder will be uncompressed.

**Figure 1-34**

Compression
dialog box

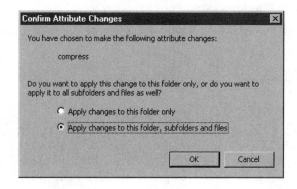

**EXAM TIP** Know this distinction between compressing the folder but not the subfolders and files. You could see some trick questions that combine both uncompressed and compressed files within the same folder.

To compress a folder:

1. Open Windows Explorer and navigate to the folder you want to compress.

2. Right-click the folder and select Properties.

3. On the General tab, click Advanced.

4. In the Advanced Attributes dialog box, select Compress Contents To Save Disk Space.

5. Click OK. Then click Apply.

6. The Confirm Attribute Changes dialog box will appear. Select one of the following:

   • **Apply changes to this folder only**   This will only compress the selected folder. It will not compress any of the files in the folder.

   • **Apply changes to this folder, subfolders and files**   This will compress the selected folder, all files in the folder, and all subfolders and files in the folder.

7. After making your selection, click OK to apply the changes.

8. Click OK to close the folder properties.

## Folder Compression (Zipped)

Folder compression or zipped folders was introduced in Windows XP Professional and is supported in Server 2003. Folder compression uses the compression technology created by WinZip. A folder that has been compressed in this manner is portable; it can be e-mailed to a recipient or copied to a disk or floppy without losing the compression. In fact, you can create compressed or zipped folders on any file system.

To create a compressed (zipped) folder:

1. Open Windows Explorer.

2. Click File | New | Compressed (Zipped) Folder.

3. Type a name for the folder.

You are now ready to move items into the folder. They will be compressed as they are added.

## Displaying Compressed and Encrypted Files in Color

Windows Server 2003 includes the option to display compressed or encrypted files in an alternate color (light blue) so it is easy to identify compressed and encrypted files. By default, this behavior is not set up and needs to be activated. To display encrypted and compressed files in an alternate color:

1. In Windows Explorer, click Tools and select Folder Options.

2. Click the View tab.

3. Select the option "Show encrypted or compressed NTFS files in color."

4. Click OK to close the Folder Options dialog box.

## Moving/Copying Compressed Files

When a compressed folder or file is moved within the same volume, it retains its compression attribute that it received from the parent folder. If the parent folder was compressed, and the option to compress subfolders and files was selected, then any files in the folder hierarchy are compressed and any new files created in the hierarchy also become compressed. When a file is moved within the same volume, the actual physical file isn't moved, only the location in the MFT, so it retains any attributes that it inherited from the parent folder.

## Lab Exercise 1.6: Using Compression

To perform this exercise, you must have a volume or partition available that's been formatted with NTFS. Compression is not supported on volumes and partitions that have been formatted with FAT or FAT32. If you don't have a volume or partition available formatted with NTFS, you will need to create one before continuing with the exercise.

1. Open Windows Explorer.

2. At the root of the drive, create two folders. Name them **Public** and **Private**.

3. Within the Public folder, create a subfolder and name it **Photos**.

4. Right-click the Public folder and select New | WordPad Document. Name the document **photoindex.txt**.

5. Right-click the Photos folder and select New | Bitmap Image. Name the document **babypic**.

6. Right-click the Public folder and select Properties.

7. Click Advanced in the Public folder Properties dialog box.

8. In the Advanced Attributes dialog box, select "Compress contents to save disk space."

9. Click OK. Then click Apply.

10. The Confirm Attribute Changes dialog box will appear. Select "Apply changes to this folder, subfolders and files."

11. When you click OK, the system will now show you the files and folders it is compressing. When it is finished, close all dialog boxes and view Windows Explorer.

12. When you view the root drive with both the Public and Private folders, you will see that the Public folder is blue, indicating that it is compressed. The Private folder is still black, indicating that it is uncompressed.

13. Click the Phone Numbers document and drag it to the Private folder.

14. Open the Private folder. The Private folder is uncompressed, but the Phone Numbers document is showing in blue letters, indicating that it is still compressed.

When a compressed folder or file is moved to a different volume, a new file is created on the destination volume. The new file receives its compression attribute from the new parent folder. A move operation between volumes isn't really a move; it is a copy/delete. Try it sometime; click and drag a file from one volume (C) to a second volume (D). When the dialog box appears to show you status of the move, it doesn't say "moving files," it says "copying." Windows makes a copy of the file and pastes it into the new volume, then deletes the old file from the original location.

Here's the simple rule: If you move a compressed file to a different location on the same volume, it stays compressed. If you move a compressed file to a different location on a different volume, it becomes uncompressed during the move and then inherits the compression attribute from the destination folder. If you copy a compressed file to any location, the file becomes uncompressed during the copy and then inherits the compression attribute from the destination folder.

This rule is applicable to permissions and other NTFS attributes as well. The only exception is encryption using the Encrypting Files System (EFS). If an encrypted file is copied to another NTFS volume, the new file is also encrypted. If an encrypted file is moved or copied to a FAT volume, the encryption is lost. You must have the corresponding public key/private key pair in order to access an encrypted file.

 **EXAM TIP** Convoluted moving/copying compressed files/folders questions are not uncommon on the Microsoft exams. Pay attention to exactly what is being asked. When you move a file from a compressed folder to another folder on the same volume, the file will remain compressed. Always. It retains its compression attribute from the original folder that it was in. If you move the file to another volume, it will inherit the attributes of the target folder. So it is possible that the solution to a problem is opposite what would be normal practice, such as compressing files individually.

## Compressing Files and Folders from the Command Line

Microsoft includes two tools for compressing files and folders from the command line: Compress and Compact. Using command-line tools allows for scripting of processes, which makes life a lot easier!

- **Compress** You can use the Compress.exe tool to compress files to any media, including floppy disks. Compress is a file compression tool that acts like WinZip and allows you to compress files, which can then be e-mailed or copied to floppy disks or other removable media. The Compress.exe file compression tool is included on the Windows 2003 Resource Kit. The Resource Kit tools must be installed before the Compress.exe tool becomes available. The Resource Kit tools can be downloaded from Microsoft's site at http://www.microsoft.com/downloads/ or by searching for Resource Kit tools. For more information on how to use the Compress.exe tool, and for a list of available commands, from a command prompt, type **compress /?**.

- **Compact**  You can use the Compact.exe tool to display and modify the compression attribute on a folder or files within the folder. Compact only works on NTFS formatted partitions or volumes. For more information on how to use the Compact.exe tool, and for a list of available commands, from a command prompt, type **compact /?**.

## Encryption

NTFS supports encryption using the Encrypting File System (EFS). Windows Server 2003 takes advantage of certificate technologies, and EFS uses a public key/private key pair to encrypt contents. Only the user who encrypted the file or folder can view the contents of the file or folder, provided that user's private key certificate is available.

## Public Keys and Private Keys

Windows 2000 included support for public keys and private keys and included a certificate authority as part of the product. Windows 2003 continues this support. A certificate authority is needed to implement secure technologies such as EFS and smart cards for domain logons. If a server is not part of a domain, the appropriate user certificate is created by the operating system if EFS is implemented. The certificate and key pair are then stored on the individual machine. In a domain environment, the certificate and key pair are stored on a domain controller and are accessible wherever the user logs on to the domain.

In general, here's how a public key/private key pair works. The public key is used to encrypt data that only the corresponding private key can decrypt. The public key cannot be used to decrypt something that has been encrypted using that same public key. So if you use a key to encrypt a message, you can't use that same key to decrypt the message in order to read it. You have to use the other key in the pair to decrypt. The public key is freely distributed, and the private key is designated as private and is highly secured.

If anyone uses the public key to encrypt a message, it can only be decrypted by someone using the corresponding private key. In this manner, a public key can be distributed to the general public (hence the name) without compromising the security of data. As long as the private key is protected, any pieces of data that were encrypted using the public key are unreadable to all but the private key user.

On the other hand, if a message or piece of data is encrypted using the private key, anyone who has access to the public key can read the data or message. However, anyone who is able to use the public key and read the message will know that the only user that could have created the message is the private key user. Using a private key to encrypt a message thus ensures authenticity.

**NOTE** A basic understanding of public key/private keys is sufficient for the exams. For a more comprehensive understanding of public key and private key technology, *Cryptography Decrypted* by H.X. Mel and Doris Baker (Addison-Wesley, 2001) is an excellent read and highly recommended.

## How EFS Works

EFS uses an algorithm with random numbers coupled with the user's public key/private key pair to encrypt a particular file or folder. When the user checks the box on the Advanced Properties dialog box of the file to encrypt the data, a file encryption key is generated using a random number. This encryption key is used with the Data Encryption Standard (DES) algorithm to encrypt the contents of the file and write the file to disk. The encryption key is encrypted using the user's public key and is stored with the encrypted file. The file can now only be decrypted with the user's private key.

**NOTE** A file can only be compressed or encrypted, not both. Compression and encryption are exclusive properties. An encrypted file cannot be compressed and a compressed file cannot be encrypted.

The public key/private key pair is created using the user's certificate. On a standalone machine, the user certificate is generated the first time a user attempts to encrypt a file or folder. Once the certificate is created, that certificate is then used to encrypt all files and folders. In a domain environment, a certificate must be issued to the user from a certificate authority. Users are not automatically issued a certificate. Each user has to initiate the process and then have the permission to create the certificate. For more information on certificate authorities and the certificate enrollment process, see Chapter 17.

Since EFS is based on PKI and user certificates, simply moving a file to a different volume doesn't affect whether the file is encrypted or not. If you move an encrypted file to a different location on a different volume, the file is still encrypted. If you copy an encrypted file to a new location on a new volume, the new file will also be encrypted. If an encrypted file is copied or moved to a FAT volume, the encryption attributes are lost and the file is decrypted.

Only the user who created the file can decrypt the file. Users who attempt to access the encrypted file receive an access denied error message and are unable to open the file. Users without access to the file are unable to read, move, or copy the file.

**NOTE** A recovery agent can decrypt an encrypted file, but cannot read the file without decrypting first.

## Assigning Viewing Rights to Additional Users

New functionality in Windows Server 2003 allows for the creator of an encrypted file to allow other users to view the contents of the file. Each user must already have been issued a user certificate for EFS before they can be assigned the right to view an encrypted file by another user. On a standalone computer, a user certificate is automatically generated the first time a user encrypts a file. To allow another user to view the contents of an encrypted file:

1. Right-click the file and select Properties.

2. Click Advanced on the General tab to open the Advanced Properties of the file.

3. Select Encrypt Contents To Secure Data and then click Details.

4. The Encryption Details dialog box will appear and display all users who have been granted rights to view the file and the recover agent for the file (see Figure 1-35).

5. Click Add and select a user certificate from the list of users.

6. Click OK to add the user, click OK again to complete the operation, and then click Apply in the file Properties dialog box.

 **NOTE**  A user who has been granted the Modify NTFS permission for an encrypted file may delete the file, even though they don't have access to view the contents of the file. Also, a user who has been granted access to view the contents of the file may not alter the file or delete the file unless they have also been granted the appropriate NTFS permissions.

**Figure 1-35**
The Encryption
Details dialog box

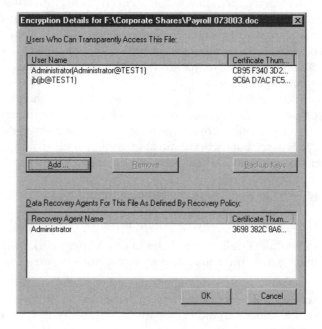

## Cipher

Cipher is the command-line tool to display and alter the encryption attribute on files and folders on NTFS volumes. Using cipher allows for scripting of encryption procedures. Cipher is also used to create the recovery agent certificate on standalone computers. To view a list of all available commands, from a command line, type:

```
cipher /?
```

To view all encrypted files in a specified folder, type **cipher** at the folder root.

Cipher is also used to create the recovery agent certificate. To create the recovery agent certificate for a standalone computer, type:

```
cipher /R:filename
```

The file will be placed in the profile folder of the current user.

Cipher can also be used to overwrite deleted files. When a file is deleted, the file is not immediately deleted from the disk. Instead, the data is still retained on the hard disk until it can be overwritten by other data. Cipher can be used with the /w switch to overwrite deleted data, thus ensuring that deleted encrypted files cannot be recovered.

## Recovery Agents

So what happens if the user loses their key? Or if a user encrypts a file or folder and then leaves the company? You need a method to decrypt files in these situations. Windows provides a recovery agent that is able to decrypt encrypted files. A recovery agent has a master key to all encrypted files on the local computer or in the domain. A recovery agent with a master key is able to decrypt files and folders and make them available to all users again. Simply taking ownership of a file or folder doesn't work. EFS is not dependent on permissions to work. A recovery agent has a public key/private key pair that is able to decrypt the file.

In Windows 2000, the local administrator was by default the recovery agent for the local computer and could decrypt any EFS files on that computer. Windows 2003 does not designate a default recovery agent for a standalone server. By default, there is no data recovery agent set, but users are still able to encrypt files using EFS. To designate a recovery agent for a standalone computer, configure the Public Key Policies node in the local security policy.

To add a recovery agent to the local computer:

1. Click Start | All Programs | Administrative Tools | Local Security Policy.

2. Expand the Public Key Policies node and right-click the Encrypting File System node. Select Add Data Recovery Agent from the menu (see Figure 1-36).

3. The Add Data Recovery Agent Wizard will start and prompt you to add a certificate. The certificate will have the .cer file extension. Browse to the user profile folder that has been issued the recovery agent certificate and add the certificate.

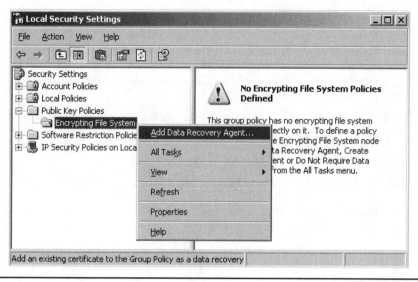

**Figure 1-36**    The local security policy and the EFS recovery agent

4. Click Finish in the wizard to complete the operation. You will be returned to the Local Security Policy snap-in and the user certificate will be displayed as the recovery agent.

5. Close the Local Security Policy MMC.

6. Restart the computer for the policy to take effect.

The EFS policy can also be removed at a later time. Removing the policy does not prevent users from encrypting files. Users will still be able to encrypt file using EFS, even if there is no recovery agent policy.

For computers that are part of a domain, the Administrator account on the first domain controller is by default the recovery agent for the domain. Additional recovery agents can be designated using Group Policy, similar in manner to the procedure for implementing recovery agents on a standalone computer. Before a user can be designated as a recovery agent, a recovery agent certificate has to be issued. It is recommended that once the certificate is issued, the certificate is exported to a floppy disk and kept in a secure location. Certificates can be exported by using the Certificates snap-in. After the export is successful, it is recommended that the original certificate still on the local computer be deleted from the computer, again using the Certificates snap-in. Certificates need to be issued from a valid certificate authority. For more information on certificate authorities and EFS recovery agents in a domain environment, please see Chapter 17.

It is recommended that an encrypted file that needs to be recovered be copied to the recovery agents' computer and the recovery agents' certificate be imported back to the computer to recover the file. Once the file has been recovered, it is recommended to again delete the recovery certificate from the local computer.

To recover a file or folder that has been encrypted:

1. Log on to the computer as the Local Administrator or the Domain Admins if the computer is part of a domain.

2. Right-click the file or folder and select Properties from the drop-down menu.

3. Click Advanced to open the Advanced Properties dialog box.

4. Uncheck the Encrypt Contents To Secure Data check box.

5. Click OK to close the Advanced Properties dialog box.

Click Apply to apply the changes. The file or folder can now be read by users with permissions to the file or folder.

# Chapter Review

In this chapter, we talked about hardware and how to install various devices. Windows Server 2003 uses plug-and-play technology to automatically install the appropriate drivers for hardware. This usually works, but in some cases, the hardware is either not detected or an appropriate driver is not found. To manually install hardware, use the Add Hardware Wizard and supply the appropriate driver from the manufacturer's disk or from the manufacturer's web site. To view all installed devices on the computer, open Device Manager in the Computer Management snap-in. Devices can be viewed by type or by connection, and hidden devices can also be shown. The Device Manager can be used to troubleshoot devices, install drivers, update drivers, roll back drivers, and disable and enable devices. For additional support, the Help and Support Center offers troubleshooting tips and wizards and allows the user to connect to Microsoft newsgroups.

To keep your server functional and up to date with the latest patches and fixes from Microsoft, enable Automatic Updates. Windows Update was introduced in previous versions of windows, but in Server 2003, the ability to schedule updates has been added. Also remember to configure driver signing on your system to prevent users from installing unsigned drivers. Driver signing can be set to warn the user of potential hazards, block the user from installing unsigned drivers, or to ignore any unsigned driver and install it anyway.

We also covered physical disks and the various volume types and configurations that can be created using the Disk Management tool. There are two kinds of disks: basic and dynamic. Dynamic disks allow you to create volumes, which can span multiple physical drives and can be fault tolerant. The volume types that you can create on a dynamic disk are simple volumes, spanned volumes, striped volumes, mirrored volumes, and RAID 5 volumes. Mirrored volumes and RAID 5 volumes are fault tolerant, and the data on the drives can be recovered if one drive in the volume fails. RAID 5 volumes require three physical hard disks; all other volumes require two.

Encryption and compression are features of the NTFS files system, which you must know how to effectively use. Files and folders can be compressed to save disk space; however, the full uncompressed file size is included in any quota calculations. It is recommended that folders be compressed, not files, and that the display color is changed to allow for easier viewing. Compressed files or folders that are moved within the same volume retain their compressions. Files or folders that are copied or moved to any other volume, including FAT volumes, are uncompressed. Compression is not supported on FAT volumes. Folders can also be compressed or zipped and then e-mailed or saved to floppy disks. Files and folders can also be encrypted to protect the contents; however, a file cannot be compressed and encrypted. For a standalone computer, a default recovery agent needs to be created and added to the local security policy. For computers that are part of a domain, the Administrator account on the first domain controller is by default the recovery agent for the domain.

## Questions

1. You have ten Photoshop files totaling 2MB that you want to take with you on a sales call. You have previously compressed these files and they occupy only 750KB of disk space. You attempt to copy the files to a floppy disk, but you receive an error that there is not enough free space on the volume to perform the operation. What could you do to place the ten files on a floppy disk? (Choose all that apply.)

    A. Use the Compress command to compress the files to the floppy disk.

    B. Use the Compact command to compress the files to the floppy disk.

    C. Use the latest version of WinZip to zip the files and place the zipped folder on the floppy disk.

    D. Right-click the parent folder and select Send To Compressed (Zipped) folder. Place the zipped folder on the floppy disk.

    E. From a command prompt, type **cipher /a:photoshop** to create a Photoshop directory on the floppy and compress the files to the directory.

    F. Select the files in Windows Explorer and drag them to the floppy disk.

2. Phil is attempting to install a new web camera on his Windows Server 2003 to be used to monitor the server room. Phil informs you that the device is not detected when he plugs it in. Phil says he also tried to use the Add Hardware Wizard, but the driver was not found. You need to help Phil install the web cam as soon as possible. What should you do?

    A. Open Device Manager and click Scan For Hardware Changes. Insert the driver disk when prompted and install the device.

    B. Start the Add Hardware Wizard and manually install the device. Supply the driver from the manufacturer's disk.

C. Restart the computer.

D. Open Device Manager and select Sound, Video And Game Controllers. Right-click and select Update Driver.

E. Use Windows Update to obtain a signed driver from the Windows Server 2003 update web site.

3. You are setting up a Windows Server 2003 with a four-drive RAID 0 configuration. Each drive in the array is a 36MB SCSI drive. You want to install the OS for optimum performance. What should you do?

A. Install the SCSI driver when prompted during the installation process. When prompted, select to create a RAID 0 configuration. Choose to create a 144MB partition and format the partition as NTFS.

B. Install the operating system onto one of the SCSI disks formatted with NTFS. Create a RAID 5 volume from the remaining SCSI disks and place the paging file on the RAID 5 volume.

C. Install the SCSI driver when prompted during the installation process. When prompted, select to create a RAID 5 configuration. Choose to create a 108MB partition and format the partition as NTFS.

D. Install the SCSI driver when prompted during the installation process. Select the option to remove disk 0 from the RAID array and install the operating system on disk 0. Create a RAID 0 configuration using Disk Management from the remaining three disks.

E. None of the above. You cannot install Windows Server 2003 on a striped volume or a RAID 5 volume.

4. Derek is the night administrator for Garcia Industries. He is responsible for maintaining the file server that users use to save their files to. Currently, the file server has four physical disks configured as a striped volume. Users save their files to a Users folder located on the root of the striped volume. The striped volume is nearly full and Derek has purchased an additional disk to place into the server. He wants to install the additional drive without affecting performance, and users must still be able to save their files to their default folders. What should Derek do?

A. Install the physical drive. Run NTBackup and create a backup of the Users folder on the striped volume and then delete the contents of the folder. Create a single simple volume from the drive and mount the volume to the Users folder. Restore the users' data from the backup.

B. Install the physical drive. Open Disk Management and right-click the striped volume. Select to extend the striped volume onto the new drive.

C. Install the physical drive. Run NTBackup and create a backup of the Users folder on the striped volume and then delete the contents of the folder. Open Disk Management. Delete the current striped volume and then re-create the striped volume using all available disks. Restore the users' data from the backup.

D. Install the physical drive. Open Disk Management. Right-click the unallocated space on the new drive and select New Volume. Create a spanned volume and include the striped volume as part of the spanned volume.

E. None of the above.

5. You want to replace a server's network card with a more up-to-date Ethernet card. You are replacing the integrated 100 MBps onboard NIC with a new PCI Gigabit Ethernet card. After you install the new NIC, you restart the server. After the system boots, you are unable to obtain a network connection, and the system log states that the new adapter is missing or not working.

What should you do to fix the problem?

A. Use the Add/Remove Hardware Wizard to remove the 100 MBps NIC.

B. Use Device Manager to uninstall the 100 MBps NIC.

C. Use Device Manager and to change the IRQ for the 100 MBps NIC to 5 and the Gigabit Ethernet card to 9.

D. Open the Network Connections dialog box. Right-click the 100 MBps network connection and select to disable the network connection.

E. An integrated NIC cannot be uninstalled. Remove the Gigabit NIC and restart the computer.

6. Ian has recently purchased two new drives that he plans on installing on his Windows Server 2003 computer. He wants to implement a RAID 0 solution. After installing the drives, Ian opens the Disk Management snap-in and selects the first disk. When he attempts to create a new RAID 0 volume, the only option he has is to create a new partition or a new logical drive. What should Ian do next?

A. Ian needs to install an additional drive. RAID 0 requires three physical disks to work, as one of the disks is used for the parity information.

B. Ian needs to create a partition before he can create a RAID 0 volume.

C. Ian needs to format the unallocated space on drive 0 with NTFS as RAID 0 only supports NTFS.

D. Ian needs to upgrade the physical disk to dynamic disks before he can create a RAID 0 configuration.

7. You want to implement disk quotas on a file server to deny disk space to users who exceed a 50MB space allocation. All users save files to the Users folder, located on the root drive, and users don't have permission on any other folder on the volume. In addition, David, Scott, Nathan, Roger, and Rob are all web developers who need to be able to save large files to the file server. However,

they should not be able to use more than 5GB of space on the server. David, Scott, Nathan, Roger, and Rob all belong to a global group named webdv.

What should you do to set up quotas for all users? (Choose all that apply.)

A. Enable disk quotas on the volume.

B. Enable disk quotas for the Users folder.

C. Set the disk quota limit to 50MB.

D. Set the disk quota limit to 5GB.

E. Select the "Deny disk space to users exceeding quota limit" check box.

F. In the local security policy, deny the Apply Disk Quotas setting to members of the webdv global group.

G. Add a quota entry for Dan, David, Scott, Nathan, and Roger.

H. Add a quota entry for the webdv global group.

I. Add a quota entry for the Everyone group.

J. On the Security tab of the volume, grant the Full Control permission to the webdv global group.

K. For the Quota entry, select "Do not deny disk usage."

L. For the Quota entry, select "Limit disk space to 5GB."

M. For the Quota entry, select "Limit disk space to 50MB."

8. You are the administrator of a Windows Server 2003. The server has two volumes, C and F. A compressed folder on volume C called Public contains files that now need to be moved to Archive, a folder on volume F. You move the files to the Archive folder, but when you check the files, you discover that none of the files are compressed. You want the files to remain compressed after they are moved. What should you do?

A. Convert the F volume to NTFS. Navigate to the Archive folder and compress the files that have been moved.

B. Convert the F volume to NTFS. Navigate to the Archive folder and compress the folder, selecting the option to compress all subfolders and files.

C. Navigate to the Archive folder and compress the folder.

D. Navigate to the Archive folder and compress the folder and all subfolders and files.

E. Upgrade the disk to dynamic.

9. You are the administrator of a printer pool for your network. You are using HP LaserJet 4300 printers that use the Jet Direct card. You are using PRINTSERV14, a Windows Server 2003, as the print server for the five printers in the printer pool. David comes into your office to tell you that users' documents are stuck in the print queue and won't print. Upon further investigation, you notice that

one of the printers in the pint queue is offline and has a message indicating that it needs service. You need to get the users' documents printed as soon as possible. Another department in your building also has a printer pool set up, but it uses HP LaserJet 2300 printers. Their print server is named PRINTSERV11. You have a spare HP LaserJet 4300 printer attached to ITSERV9 in your IT department. What should you do to get users' documents printed as soon as possible?

A. Replace the offline printer with your spare. Open the print queue and restart the print jobs.

B. Open the HP LaserJet 4300 Printer Properties on the print server. Add a local port named //PRINTSERV9 and select the local port for the printer.

C. Open the HP LaserJet 4300 Printer Properties on the print server. Add a local port named //PRINTSERV11 and select the local port for the printer.

D. Replace the HP Jet Direct card in your print server. Restart the print jobs in the print queue.

E. Open the HP LaserJet 4300 Printer Properties on the print server. Add a TCP/IP port and enter the IP address for PRINTSERV11. Select the new TCP/IP port for the printer.

10. Matt, a user in your department, is responsible for all legal contracts that the company issues. He uses EFS to encrypt all his files. Currently, Matt has 20GB of encrypted data stored on his computer. Matt's computer suffers a hard drive failure and after the hard drive is replaced and his files restored from backup, Matt is unable to access any of his files. You have been designated as the recovery agent for your domain and have previously been issued an encrypted data recovery agent certificate. You need to give access to Matt so that he can access his files again using the least amount of administrative effort. What should you do?

A. Use the runas command on Matt's computer to open Windows Explorer. When prompted for credentials, supply the Local Administrator account and password. Navigate to the folders that hold Matt's encrypted files and decrypt the folders.

B. Log on to Matt's computer as the Local Administrator. Navigate to the folders that hold Matt's encrypted files and decrypt the folders.

C. Retrieve your EFS recovery agent certificate, which is stored on a floppy disk in a locked cabinet in the server room. Log on to Matt's computer using your user account credentials. Import the EFS recovery agent to Matt's computer. Navigate to the folders that hold Matt's encrypted files and decrypt the folders. After Matt's files have been decrypted, delete your certificate from Matt's computer.

D. Run a backup of Matt's files and restore them to your computer. Retrieve your EFS recovery agent certificate, which is stored on a floppy disk in a locked cabinet in the server room and copy the certificate to your computer. Decrypt the files as the recovery agent. Back up the decrypted files and restore them to Matt's computer.

## Answers

1. **A, C, D, and E.** The Compress tool acts like zip and compresses files or folders in such a way that they can be e-mailed or placed on a floppy disk. WinZip is the industry standard for compressing files to floppy disks. Windows 2003 now includes the compressed (zipped) folders feature. You can right-click any folder and select Send To Compressed (Zipped) folder. A compressed folder will be created in the same directory and all the selected files will be placed inside the new compressed folder.

2. **B.** Windows has failed to find the device, so you need to manually install the device. By using the Add Hardware Wizard, you always have the option to use a driver from the disk or from another location. When you supply the correct driver, Windows will install the driver and match it to the hardware connected.

3. **B.** Disk striping or RAID 0 is used for optimal disk performance. However, Windows Server 2003 cannot be installed on a RAID 0 configuration unless it is a hardware supported RAID. You should install the operating system on the first disk, then use Disk Management to configure a RAID 0 volume from the remaining three disks and place the paging file on the RAID 0 volume.

4. **C.** A striped volume provides the best read/write performance of any of the volume types. Once a striped volume is created, it cannot be added to or extended. To add a new drive to the striped volume, you must delete the striped volume and recreate the volume using all available drives.

5. **D.** When an integrated device, such as a NIC or video or sound card, conflicts with an added PCI or AGP device, you need to disable the integrated device. You can disable devices in Device Manager, or in the case of the network cards, you can disable the card from the Network Connections applet.

6. **D.** Only dynamic disks support volumes in Windows 2003. RAID 0 is a striped volume and requires two disks. Before the striped volume can be created, the drives need to be upgraded to dynamic disks. A striped volume can be formatted with any files system.

7. **A, C, E, G, and L.** Disk quotas are applied per volume per user, and quota entries cannot be applied to groups, only users. In this case, you need to first enable quotas on the volume. By default, enabling disk quotas only turns quotas on and allows the amount of disk space used to be tracked. You must select the option to "Deny disk space to users exceeding quota limit" and then specify a limit. Quota entries must be created per user, so you need to create one quota entry each for David, Scott, Nathan, Roger, and Rob. Also, disk quotas are not controlled in the local security policy.

8. **D.** When a compressed file is moved to a different volume, it inherits the target folder's compression attribute. Since the files were compressed and after being moved they are uncompressed, the target folder has to be uncompressed. You know that the volume is an NTFS volume, because permissions are present on the folder and any folder created on a FAT volume can only be shared and does not have permissions associated with it. Therefore, you need to only compress the folder and select the option to compress all subfolders and files.

9. **C.** The problem in this scenario is that the Jet Direct card has quit working, thus rendering all of the printers in the printer pool inoperable. The best way to get users' documents printed quickly is to redirect the print jobs to another printer that uses the same printer driver. HP uses the same base driver in most of their products, so it is easy to redirect a print job on a LaserJet 4300 to a LaserJet 2300. Replacing the Jet Direct card is the proper solution, but it will require more time to replace and reconfigure, and it is advisable to redirect the print jobs until the card can be repaired. The proper procedure to redirect print jobs is to create a local port and then to enter the UNC path to the alternate printer. An IP address can be entered in lieu of a UNC path. You must create a local port, not a TCP/IP port.

10. **C.** This one's a trick question! The preferred method to decrypt files is to copy the files to your computer and then decrypt them using your recovery agent certificate. Except, in this situation, Matt has 20GB of files to recover, and it would be cumbersome and time consuming to back up all of his files to your computer for recovery. It would be much easier to copy your recovery certificate to Matt's computer and then decrypt the files there, deleting your certificate when finished.

# Managing Users, Computers, and Groups

In this chapter, you will learn how to

- Configure local user accounts
- Create and configure domain user accounts
- Implement user profiles
- Configure contacts
- Create and configure computer accounts
- Automate the creation of users, computers, and groups
- Secure user accounts
- Troubleshoot logon problems
- Implement local groups
- Implement domain groups
- Use domain local, global, and universal groups to grant access to resources
- Grant access to resources in other domains
- Use group nesting

With the release of Windows 2000, Microsoft introduced Active Directory, a scalable, robust directory service. However, the fundamental building block of Microsoft's directory service continues to be the domain. A domain is a logical grouping for network resources, including servers, shares, printers, groups, and, of course, user accounts. Every individual who requires access to network or computer resources must have a user account. The user account represents the individual to the domain, and allows for different types of access and different types of tasks. Every user account is unique! It is the uniqueness of the user account that allows administrators to control access for every member of the domain.

There are two types of user accounts that you must be familiar with: local accounts and domain accounts. Local accounts are maintained in the local database of a computer and cannot be used to grant access to network resources. Local accounts are primarily used to administer a computer or to allow several people to share a single computer that is not a member of a domain. Domain user accounts are much more widely used in organizations than local user accounts because they allow for central administration and users can log on to any computer in the domain. Domain user accounts are stored in Active Directory, and a user with a domain account is able to log on to any computer in the domain, except if they have been specifically restricted from the computer. (Users can't log on to domain controllers, for example. A user must be a member of the Domain Admins group, or have been specifically granted rights to log on to a domain controller.) Using local user accounts in a large organization would be extremely cumbersome and impractical, as they would require that each user maintain a different user account for every computer they logged into. The administration of such an environment would be nightmarish.

Although a user account is required to access network resources, granting access to individual users would be a monumental task in larger networks. To make the administration of resources easier, user accounts are collected into groups, and access is granted to a group instead of an individual account. By collecting user accounts into groups, network access can be granted to all members of a group at the same time. When access to a specific network resource, such as a printer, is required, it is simpler to assign access to a group than to assign access to each user account.

Just as there are local accounts and domain accounts, there are also local groups and domain groups. Again, local groups are used to administer the computer or to grant access to local user accounts. Domain groups are much more powerful, and can be used not only to grant access for users in the network, but also to grant access for users in other networks and other domains. Although setting up a group strategy can be complicated, once the groups are implemented, administering access to resources is much simpler than administering access by only using the user account.

Security and troubleshooting will also be covered in this chapter. It is not enough to create accounts for users and then place the accounts into groups to allow access to network resources; you must also concern yourself with ensuring that unauthorized users are not able to gain access to the network. There are many types of network attacks, but some of the most devastating are when an attacker gains access by using a user account and impersonates an authorized user. You will learn some strategies to prevent this type of attack. Also, although logging on to a Windows domain is relatively simple (press CTR-ALT-DEL and enter your name and password), occasionally the logon process fails and users are unable to log on to the network. You will learn how to identify different logon failures and how to troubleshoot them.

# User Accounts

A user account is used to identify an individual to a computer or a network. A user account consists of an account name and password, and a unique identifier. This unique identifier is a binary bit number of variable length that is generated by the computer or the domain where the account is created. This security identifier (SID) identifies the user to the computer or domain, and is used when a user attempts to gain access to a resource. A user account also may have other attributes, such as group membership, remote access permissions, e-mail addresses, and others. Every user who logs on to a Windows computer must have a valid user account, either for that computer or for the domain the computer belongs to. At logon, the user has to select whether they are logging on to a domain or to the local computer. The users' credentials are then either checked against the local database or against Active Directory as appropriate.

There are two types of user accounts: local user accounts and domain user accounts. The two types of accounts share common characteristics, but they vary in scope. A local user account can only be used on a single computer, and a domain user account can be used throughout the entire network.

# Local User Accounts

Local user accounts are stored in the local database of a computer and are only used for accessing resources on the computer. All computers except domain controllers have a local database for storing local user accounts. When a user attempts to access a computer with a local user account, they must enter the correct user name and password and be validated against the local database.

 **NOTE** Domain controllers are different from all other computers in that a local database of user accounts and groups is not kept. The definition of a domain controller is that of a server with Active Directory installed. Since Active Directory is running on a domain controller, the domain controller validates all local logon attempts against Active Directory. In order to log on to a domain controller, a user must be a member of the Domain Admins group, the Enterprise Admins group, or have been explicitly granted the logon locally user right.

The problem with using local user accounts is that they are not portable. If a user needs to use more than one computer, that user needs to have two user accounts, one for each computer they use. Also, if a user attempts to access a resource on another computer, such as a shared folder, they will have to present logon credentials for the remote computer to authenticate and use resources. If a user requires access to resources on several computers, they will require several user accounts, one for each computer. Even if a user only works from a single computer, they may need to have several user accounts for several computers in order to access resources. Also, since each account is unique to the local computer, any account maintenance, such as changing passwords, will have to be done multiple times. As you can see, trying to maintain an environment with local user accounts only would be cumbersome.

Local user accounts are created and administered using the Local Users and Groups snap-in on the Computer Management Console (see Figure 2-1). The Local Users and Groups snap-in can also be added to any custom Microsoft Management Console (MMC). The Local Users and Groups snap-in not only allows you to create and manage user accounts and groups for the local machine, but it also supports connecting to a remote computer and manage user accounts and groups on a remote computer.

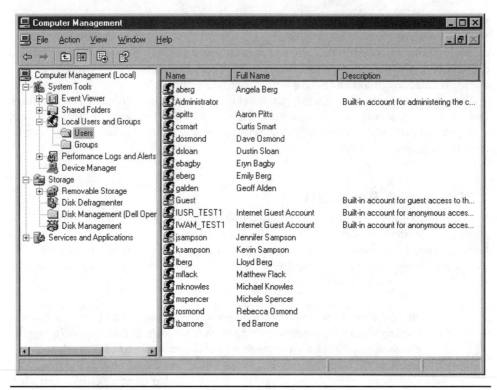

**Figure 2-1**    Local Users and Groups

 **NOTE**    The Local Users and Groups snap-in is not available on domain controllers. When Active Directory is installed on a server, any accounts or groups in the local database are moved to Active Directory and become domain user accounts and domain groups. The Local Users and Groups snap-in is then removed from the system, and is not available as part of the Computer Management snap-in or any other custom MMC. Previously in Windows 2000, the Local Users and Groups snap-in displayed with a red X and a notification screen that local users and groups were not available on a domain controller.

## Built-in Accounts

By default, several accounts are created when Windows Server 2003 is installed. If you have had any experience with NT or Windows 2000, you are probably already familiar with the Administrator and Guest account.

## The Administrator Account

An Administrator account is created when the operating system is installed. The Administrator account has complete control over the local machine and can be used to perform any function. It is used to install software, configure devices, and to perform system tasks. The Administrator account cannot be disabled or deleted, but can and should be renamed. Because it cannot be disabled, hackers will attempt to log on as Administrator because the normal rules of locking out an account after several tries does not apply. Obviously, renaming the Administrator account to Admin really isn't much of a change and isn't a good idea. Rename the Administrator account something that wouldn't be easy to guess, such as Theallpowerfulandgreatmasterofthiscomputer.

Upon installation of Windows 20003 server, you are prompted to enter a password for the Administrator account. If you leave the password blank, Windows prompts you to enter a password and notifies you that for security reasons you really should enter a password. Passwords protect the user accounts from being used by unauthorized users, and leaving passwords blank can compromise the security of the computer. Passwords should be at least seven characters in length, and passwords with number and letter combinations are preferred.

**NOTE** The local Administrator account can be renamed using Group Policy. To do so, open the Local Security Policy MMC, navigate to the Local Policies | Security Options and select "Accounts: Rename the administrator account policy." Enter the new name of the Administrator account and close the Group Policy window. You will need to restart the computer for the change to take effect. For more information about implementing Group Policy, see Chapter 22.

## Guest Account

The Guest account is created to provide access to users who don't have domain accounts. By default, the Guest account is created in a disabled state. If the Guest account is enabled, any user logged on to a local machine can use domain resources to which the guest account has access. Users don't have to log on as Guest with a password because the Guest account includes anyone who doesn't have an account. So if a friend comes to your office and brings his laptop, he can plug his laptop in to your network and access any resources on any computer that the Guest account has been enabled on without ever having to authenticate. All he has to do is log on to his own laptop with a local account. This can be a huge security risk. The Guest account should stay in a disabled state unless there is some compelling reason to enable it.

**NOTE** You may have noticed that the Local Users and Groups contained another user account, the Support_388945a0 account. Support_388945a0 is a vendor account added by Microsoft, and it carries a display name of CN=Microsoft Corporation,L=Redmond,S=Washington,C=US. At the time of this writing, there was very little information available about what this account is for, or under what circumstances this account should be enabled. For additional information about the Support_388945a0 account, please refer to the Windows Server 2003 Resource Kit, http://www.microsoft.com/ or http://www.technet.com/.

### Creating Local User Accounts

To create a local user account, you must have administrative rights for the local machine. User accounts are created and managed in the Users folder of the Local Users and Groups snap-in. To create a new account, right-click the Users folder and select New User. Give the user account a name and select the desired password options. Verify the information and click Finish to create the account.

## Built-in Groups

Groups are built on the assumption that more than one user will access the server or computer and that it is easier to collect user accounts into groups and assign permissions and rights once rather than for each individual. In short, groups are used to ease the administrative burden of granting access to resources.

Windows Server 2003 also installs some default built-in groups, which are not used to grant access to resources but are used to grant rights and privileges to a group of users. User accounts can be added to the built-in groups by right-clicking the group and selecting Add To Group. The default built-in groups on a Windows Server 2003 server are shown in Table 2-1.

| Table 2-1<br>Built-in Groups | Group | Description |
| --- | --- | --- |
| | Administrators | Members have full control of the server and can assign user rights and access permissions to users. The Administrator account by default is a member of the Administrators group and cannot be removed. When a server is joined to a domain, the Domain Admins Global group also is added to the local Administrators group. |
| | Backup Operators | Members of this group can back up and restore files and folders on the server, regardless of the security settings that protect those files. Members of this group can access the server from the network, log on locally, and shut down the system. |
| | Guests | Members of this group will have a temporary profile created at logon. The profile will be deleted at logoff. The Guest account is a member of the Guests group. The Guests group has no default user rights associated with it. |
| | HelpServicesGroup | This group allows administrators to set rights common to all support applications. The only group that is a member of this group is the Support_388945a0 account. This account is associated with the Remote Assistance application. Do not add users to this group. |
| | Network Configuration Operators | Members of this group can make changes to TCP/IP settings and can release and renew IP addresses. |

| Table 2-1 | Group | Description |
|-----------|-------|-------------|
| Built-in Groups *(continued)* | Performance Log Users | Members of this group can manage performance counters, logs, and alerts from the server locally or remotely without being a member of the Administrators group. |
| | Performance Monitor Users | Members of this group can monitor performance counters only from the server locally or remotely without being a member of the Administrators group or the Performance Log Users group. |
| | Power Users | Members of this group can create user accounts and modify and delete those accounts. They can create local groups and modify and delete those groups. Members can add or remove users from the Power Users, Guests, and Users groups. They can create shared resources and manage those resources. Members of the Power Users group cannot modify the Administrators group or add or remove members of the Administrators group. They cannot take ownership of files, back up or restore files and folders, load or unload device drivers, or manage security logs. |
| | Print Operators | Members can manage printers and print queues. |
| | Replicator | The Replicator group supports replication functions. The only member of the Replicator group should be a domain user account used to log on the Replicator service on a DC. Do not add user accounts to this group. |
| | Users | Members of this group can perform common tasks such as running programs and using printers. Users can access the computer from the network and log on locally. All users are members of the Users group by default. |

# Local Groups

In addition to the built-in groups, additional local groups can be created to grant access to resources on the computer. User accounts are added to the group, and the group can be assigned access to a resource. The basic premise is that it is easier to administer users by assigning them to groups and then grant access to a group rather than each user account. On most computers, local groups aren't really necessary and aren't used very much. Local groups are primarily used to secure resources on a computer that is shared by several people.

To create a local group:

1. Select Start | All Programs | Administrative Tools | Computer Management.

2. Expand the System Tools node and select Local Users and Groups.

3. Right-click the Groups folder and click New Group.

4. Enter a Group name and click Create to create the group.

5. Add user accounts to the group by clicking the Add button below the Members section.

To modify the membership of a group after it has been created:

1. Using the Local Users and Groups snap-in, open the Groups folder.

2. Right-click the group and select Add To Group.

3. Click the Add button below the Members section and select users to add to the group. Click OK and close the group.

# Active Directory

It is important to understand some basics of Active Directory before creating and managing domain user accounts and domain groups. Active Directory is the subject of several chapters in this book (see Chapters 18 and 19), but a short explanation follows.

Going back to NT 4.0, user accounts and groups were logically collected into a domain. The domain became a security boundary, and users had to authenticate to the domain before they could use a computer or access a resource. All user accounts and groups in the domain were stored in a database called the Security Accounts Manager (SAM), which was stored on a domain controller. There were severe limitations on the SAM, including what could be stored (user accounts, group accounts, and computers only) and the maximum size that it could grow to (40MB). Windows 2000 introduced a directory service, Active Directory, for storing user accounts, groups, and other objects. Active Directory is now the central repository for all user accounts, groups, workstations, servers, Group Policies, contacts, printers, and even shared folders. Active Directory is much more flexible and powerful than the old SAM.

Active Directory uses domains as containers to hold objects. Each domain is a security boundary. Users must authenticate to the domain in which their user account resides before they can access resources, such as shared folders. Active Directory also links related domains in a hierarchical structure, and users can access resources in any of the domains after they authenticate to the domain in which their user account resides. The hierarchical structure of related domains is called a tree, and all domains in the tree share the same Domain Name System (DNS) namespace. All domains and trees in a single organization are called a forest. All domains in the forest share a common schema.

---

 **NOTE** DNS is the name resolution system of the Internet. Using DNS allows clients to resolve names of hosts to IP addresses so that communication can take place. DNS is the foundation upon which Active Directory is built. For more information about DNS, see Chapters 6 and 8.

**NOTE** A domain controller is a server with Active Directory installed. Domain controllers are used to administer domain objects, such as user accounts and groups. All domain controllers are peers, and so any domain controller can be used to administer objects in Active Directory.

The type of objects that can be stored in Active Directory is defined by the schema. The schema defines the type of objects and the attributes that each object has. The schema is what defines a user account for example. A user account must have a name, a password, and a unique SID. A user account can also have many additional attributes, such as location, address, phone number, e-mail addresses, terminal services profiles, and so on. The schema is also extensible, and additional attributes or objects can be added to Active Directory. Microsoft Exchange 2000 for example, adds a mailbox attribute to all user accounts. The schema is consistent throughout the entire forest.

One of the problems with the old NT 4.0 domain structure was that administration of resources could not be delegated. Any administrator had full control of all objects within the domain. That wasn't always the desired outcome! With larger enterprises, multiple domains were created to separate the administrative realms and to limit administrative powers. With the creation of additional domains, resources and administration became extremely decentralized. Active Directory combines all the resources and domains into one easily accessible structure.

Active Directory also uses a special kind of object called a container object to hold other objects, such as user accounts and computer accounts. While domains are still the primary container and the security boundary, organizational units (OUs) were introduced as sort of a subcontainer. OUs allow objects to be grouped more logically together without having to resort to multiple domains. Though it isn't entirely accurate, if you think of an OU as sort of a miniature domain, you will get the idea. OUs also allow for objects to be grouped together and administered as a unit. For example, all the user accounts of all the accountants in a company can be placed into an OU and then all the accountants can be administered as a unit without affecting the rest of the domain. A user can be assigned the task of resetting passwords for the accountants without having to grant that user administrative rights in the domain.

An OU structure that matches the organization's administrative structure is recommended. Organizational units are used by administrators to group users together for easier administration. By default, there is only one OU created in Active Directory, the Domain Controllers OU, and all domain controllers are subsequently added to the Domain Controllers OU, mainly to add additional security policies to the domain controllers. All other OUs must be created manually and user accounts and groups either added in the OUs or moved into the OUs.

A common practice is to create OUs that match the locations of a business, then create OUs in each location for departments. For example, the administrator of 2WeekMCSE.com would create an OU for Portland, an OU for Honolulu, and an OU for Boston, the locations of the business, as shown in Figure 2-2. OUs could then be created in each location for departments, such as sales, instructors, IT, and so on.

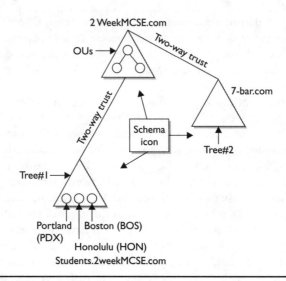

2WeekMCSE.com

OUs →

Two-way trust

7-bar.com

Two-way trust

Schema icon

Tree#2

Tree#1 →

Portland (PDX)    Boston (BOS)
        Honolulu (HON)
    Students.2weekMCSE.com

**Figure 2-2**    2WeekMCSE.com and Students.2WeekMCSE.com make up a two-tree forest

# Domain User Accounts

In contrast to a local user account that can only be used on the local computer, a domain user account can be used to log on to most computers in a domain. A domain user account is created and managed on a domain controller and is centrally stored in Active Directory. Domain user accounts are portable. A user with an account for the domain can log on to any computer in the domain. The only exception is DCs. By default, only Domain Admins can log on to a DC. Users can be given rights to log on locally to a DC by modifying the Default Domain Controllers policy. For information on modifying Group Policy, see Chapter 22.

Active Directory Users and Computers (shown in Figure 2-3) is the tool used to create and manage user accounts, group accounts, organizational units, Group Policies, contacts, printers, and folders. A domain user account can be created and managed on any DC in the domain, provided the user has appropriate rights to the user object.

**EXAM TIP**    Local Users and Groups is not available on a DC. When a DC is created and Active Directory is installed, any users or groups in the local database are moved to Active Directory, the local database is deleted, and the Local Users and Groups snap-in is removed. There are no local accounts for a DC, even local administrator or machine accounts, like there are for other computers. In order to log on to a DC, you must authenticate to Active Directory. Your user account must be a member of the Domain Admins, Enterprise Admins, or Administrators group, or have appropriate rights delegated to your user account.

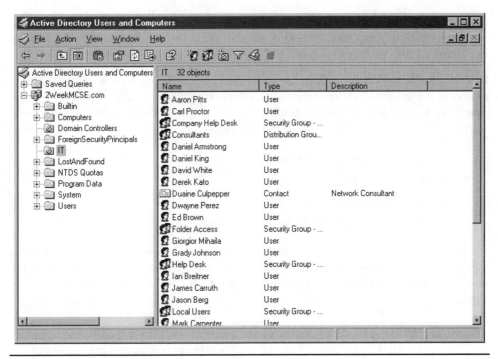

**Figure 2-3** Active Directory Users and Computers

## Built-in Domain User Accounts

Just like the local user account database contained built-in users, Active Directory also contains several built-in accounts. Active Directory Users and Computers also contains an Administrator and Guest. In addition, any user accounts in the local database will be automatically created in Active Directory, and the local database will be removed from the domain controller completely.

### Administrator

Just like there is an Administrator account for a computer, there is an Administrator account for the domain. When a new domain is created and Active Directory installed, the local Administrator account on the server is deleted and a new domain Administrator account is created. The new domain Administrator account has complete control over the entire domain and can be used to perform any function. The domain Administrator account can be used to create domain user accounts, domain groups, implement trusts, configure replication, create and manage Group Policy, and any other domain function. The domain Administrator account is also a member of the local Administrators group on local computers, and so it can also be used to install software, configure devices, and to perform system tasks on individual computers. Like the local Administrator account, the domain Administrator account cannot be disabled or deleted, but can and should be renamed for security reasons. Again, rename the Administrator account something that won't be easy to guess, such as Theallpowerfulandgreatmasterofthisdomain.

**Complex Passwords** When the new Administrator account is created, a new password is required. To increase security, the password requirements of new accounts have been raised, and all new accounts must use complex passwords. Complex passwords consists of three out of four of the following:

- Uppercase and lowercase letters
- Letters and numbers
- A special character, such as a % or !
- No common words, such as orange or sunset

The passwords must also be seven characters or more. Using any part of the server name or the user account name (Administrator) is not allowed. In fact, if you attempt to enter a password that does not meet these criteria, you will see the warning shown in Figure 2-4.

**NOTE** A dictionary attack against a user account is the most common type of attack. A hacker will attempt to guess the password of a user account by entering all words in a dictionary. Dictionary attacks are automated and thousands of passwords can be tried on a user account in a short amount of time. To prevent dictionary attacks, complex passwords should be implemented.

## Guest Account

The domain Guest account is similar to the local Guest account; the only difference is the scope. The domain Guest account can be used by any user who doesn't have a user account in the domain to access resources. Again, by default, the Guest account is created in a disabled state. If the Guest account is enabled, any user can log on to the domain

**Figure 2-4** Password complexity requirements not met

and use resources to which the guest account has access. Because of the security risk of unauthorized users accessing network resources, the Guest account should stay in a disabled state unless there is some compelling reason to enable it. If the Guest account is used, it should be renamed to prevent unauthorized users from simply guessing the Guest account name and logging on.

 **NOTE**  As in the local accounts database, Active Directory Users and Computers contains a Support_388945a0 account. It also contains a krbtgt account. The krbtgt account is the Key Distribution Center Service Account. At the time of this writing, there was very little information available about what these accounts are for, or under what circumstances these accounts should be enabled. For additional information about the Support_388945a0 account and the krbtgt account, please refer to the Windows Server 2003 Resource Kit, http://www.microsoft.com/ or http://www.technet.com/.

## Creating a Domain User Account

Domain user accounts are created using the Active Directory Users and Computers MMC. The Active Directory Users and Computers MMC is located in the Administrative Tools on your Start menu, and is accessible after installing Active Directory. You can also choose to administer user accounts from a workstation and connect to a DC. Active Directory Users and Computers is not installed on workstations; you must install the Admin Pack in order to have access to the Active Directory Users and Computers MMC. Also, you must be a member of the Domain Admins or Enterprise Admins group, or have been delegated the appropriate permissions for the domain.

 **NOTE**  The Admin Pack is available on the Windows Server 2003 CD-ROM in the I386 folder or in the %systemroot%System32 directory.

All preinstalled user accounts—Administrator and Guest—are created in the Users folder in Active Directory Users and Computers. These preinstalled user accounts can be moved to any location in Active Directory. Also, new user accounts can be created in any location in Active Directory. A user account can also be moved to a different OU after being created.

## Lab Exercise 2.1: Creating a Domain User Account

In this exercise, you will create a domain user account. You need to complete the exercise before proceeding with the next section of this chapter so that you can use the user account in further exercises. Also, you must have Active Directory installed before you can complete the exercise. If you have not installed Active Directory, please do so now. For more information on installing and configuring Active Directory, see Chapter 18.

1. Select Start | All Programs | Administrative Tools | Active Directory Users and Computers. Or select Start | Run, type **dsa.msc** and press ENTER to start the Active Directory Users and Computers MMC.

2. Click the plus (+) sign next to your domain to expand the Active Directory hierarchy.

3. Click the Users folder. The contents of the Users folder will be displayed in the right pane.

4. Right-click the Users folder and select New | User from the drop-down menu, or select Action | New | User, or click the New User icon on the toolbar. All of these actions will start the New Object – User dialog box.

5. Enter **Nathan** for the first name, no middle initial, and **Belloli** for the last name of the user account. Use the TAB key to navigate between the fields on the user account. Windows will automatically fill in the Full Name field as you type.

6. Enter a user logon name of **nbelloli**. Also select a UPN from the drop-down menu. If this is the root domain in the forest, there will only be one UPN to select. Click Next to advance to the password screen.

**NOTE** The User Principal Name (UPN) must be unique within the forest. For more information regarding the use of UPNs, see Chapter 20.

7. Leave the password blank and select the Password Never Expires option.

8. Confirm the creation of the user account and click Finish.

9. You will see the warning in Figure 2-5.

**Figure 2-5** Password warning message: You must use complex passwords for Nathan's account.

10. Click OK on the warning and then click Back to return to the password screen. Type in a password of **Unforgettable85**.

11. Right-click your domain and select New | Organizational Unit.

12. Name your OU IT.

13. Right-click the IT OU and select New | User.

14. Enter **Derek** for the first name, no middle initial, and **Kato** for the last name of the user account. Use the TAB key to navigate between the fields on the user account. Windows will automatically fill in the Full Name field as you type.

15. Enter a user logon name of **dkato**. Also select a UPN from the drop-down menu. If this is the root domain in the forest, there will only be one UPN to select. Click Next to advance to the password screen.

16. Type in a password of **Unforgettable85** and select the Password Never Expires option.

17. Confirm the creation of the user account and click Finish.

18. Click the IT OU to verify the creation of the user account.

You should now have two user accounts created in your domain. Nathan's account was created in the default Users container and Derek's account was created within an OU named IT. You will use both of these accounts for further exercises in this chapter and in Chapter 3.

 **NOTE**   By default, the Account Settings in Group Policy are set at a much higher level than they were by default in Windows 2000. All passwords must be seven characters in length or longer and must meet complexity requirements. If you have upgraded from Windows 2000 to Windows Server 2003, these settings will remain whatever they were in your 2000 domain.

# Configuring User Account Properties

There are many properties that can be modified on a user account. Actually, due to the ability of Active Directory to be modified, you may end up with many more user account properties than you started with. Some of the properties that can be modified are obvious, such as user name and password; others are not so obvious, like static IP addresses for dial-in. For each type of modification, there is a separate tab. Depending on what applications are installed on your network, there may be additional user properties available. If Exchange 2000 or above is installed, for example, you will see an E-mail Addresses tab, an Exchange Features tab, and an Exchange General tab, as shown in Figure 2-6. Exchange adds an e-mail attribute to all user accounts in Active Directory. These attributes are then visible as part of the user properties. This is true for any application that extends the schema and adds attributes to the user account.

**Figure 2-6**

A user account with the Exchange attributes added

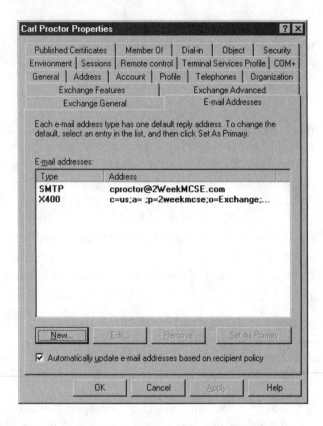

To view the user account properties for Nathan Belloli, for example, right-click Nathan Belloli's account that you created earlier, and select Properties to display his user account properties, as shown in Figure 2-7. Nathan's user account was created with a minimum of account options set. In the following sections, you will learn what options are available and how to configure a user account like Nathan's.

**NOTE** For security purposes, modifying user accounts can and should be audited. For information on auditing account management events, see Chapter 23.

## Configuring User Information

The General tab provides a space for user information, such as first and last name and display name. There are also fields for telephone numbers, e-mail address, and web page address. These fields are simply for contact information only and are not hyperlinked. There is room to store multiple phone numbers and web page addresses. If Exchange 2000 is installed, there will be a separate tab for an e-mail address, which will have the user's active Exchange and SMTP e-mail addresses.

**Figure 2-7**
User account
properties for
Nathan Belloli

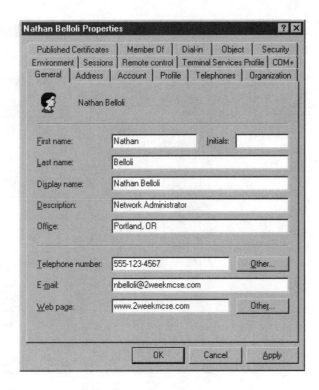

The Address tab provides a space to enter a physical address for the user account. Notice that unlike full-featured address books such as Microsoft Outlook, there is space for only a single address. The Telephones tab provides a space to store numerous telephone numbers for the user. There is also a space to input notes. The address and telephone numbers of a particular user can then be viewed by anyone having access to Active Directory, or can be accessed by applications that access Active Directory. If a telephone number and address are entered on the user account properties, for example, that information will be displayed on the Managed By tab of any computer account managed by the user.

## Configuring Logon Options

The Account tab includes the actual user logon name and logon information, as shown in Figure 2-8. The user logon name is what users enter when they attempt to log on. It is recommended that you implement a consistent naming scheme for all user accounts logon names. A common practice is to use the user's first initial and last name as their logon name, such as nbelloli for Nathan Belloli. Or their first name and the first letter of their last name, such as nathanb for Nathan Belloli. Or their first name, a period, and their last name, such as nathan.belloli. Be consistent. You will make it easier on everyone if you come up with a consistent naming scheme. Users can also use the User Principal Name (UPN) to log on to the network instead of choosing their domain from the drop-down

**Figure 2-8**
Configuring the
account logon
and UPN on
the Account
properties tab

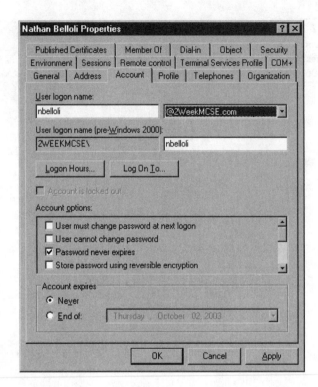

menu on the logon screen. The UPN is the user name and domain reference in e-mail format and is used to simplify user logons. In many situations with multiple domains, users may become confused about which domain to log on to. Using the UPN, a user may log on by typing their user name, the @ symbol, and then a domain reference, such as nbelloli@2WeekMCSE.com, instead of selecting the appropriate domain from the drop-down menu on the logon screen. If more than one UPN is available, the UPN can be changed on the Account tab.

## Configuring Logon Hours

The Account tab also includes Logon Hours and Log On To buttons. The Logon Hours button is used to set the hours during which a user is allowed to log on to the domain. Notice in Figure 2-9 that by default, the user is permitted to log on at any time. To change the user hours, select a block of time and select the Deny option. That will clear the block of time and the user will not be allowed to log on to the domain during those hours. Any user logged onto the domain when the logon hours expire will be allowed to remain logged in, but will not be allowed to log off and then back on. Group Policy can be used to force users to log off when the logon hours expire.

## Limiting Users to Certain Computers

Users can also be limited to certain computers by configuring the Log On To option in the account properties. Figure 2-10 shows that Nathan is only allowed to log on to the

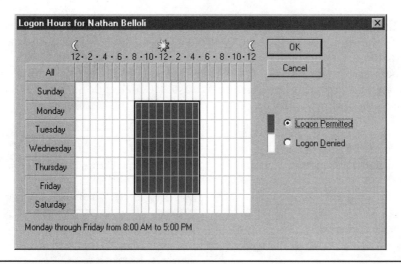

**Figure 2-9**    Logon hours for Nathan

it11, it12 and it13 computers. If Nathan attempts to log on to any other computer in the domain, he will receive a warning and will be blocked from logging on. Using the Log On To feature provides a method to limit users to only certain computers. Users are allowed to either log on to all computers or only specified computers.

**Figure 2-10**

Log on to certain computers

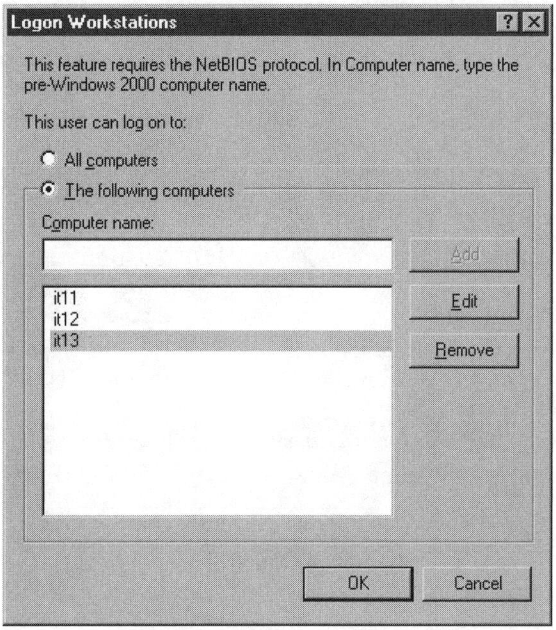

## Configuring Account and Password Options

The account options provide several different administrative functions that can be performed on a user account. Some of these you already know, such as "User must change password at next logon." Others may be less familiar, such as "Store password using reversible encryption" or "Account is trusted for delegation." Table 2-2 describes all the account options available.

| Account Option | Description |
|---|---|
| User must change password at next logon | Forces a user to change their password the next time they log on. |
| User cannot change password | Users are not permitted to change their password. |
| Password never expires | User's password never expires. |
| Store password using reversible encryption | Use this setting when using CHAP as an authentication method. |
| Account is disabled | Account can be disabled or enabled by checking or clearing the box. A user with a disabled account is prevented from logging on. It is common practice to create a user account template and then disable the account. |
| Smart card is required for interactive logon | The user must have a valid smart card and PIN and a smart card reader must be attached to the computer. When this option is set, the "Password never expires" option is also automatically enabled. |
| Account is trusted for delegation | Allows a service running under this user account to perform operations on behalf of other user accounts on the network. This option is only available on Windows Server 2003 DCs with the domain functionality level set to Windows 2000 mixed or Windows 2000 native. On DCs where the domain functionality is set to Windows 2003, the Delegation tab is used. |
| Account is sensitive and cannot be delegated | Allows control over a user account, such as the Guest account. This option is used when the account cannot be assigned for delegation by another account. |
| Use DES encryption types for this account | Provides support for the DES encryption standard. This setting provides all levels of DES encryption up to 3DES 168-bit encryption. |
| Do not require Kerberos for preauthentication | Provides support for alternate implementations of the Kerberos protocol. Preauthentication provides additional security. Use caution when disabling Kerberos preauthentication. |

**Table 2-2**   Account Administration Options

## Configuring User Profiles and Home Folders

The Profile tab provides a place to implement and modify user profiles and home directories. Profiles and Home Directories are used to save user preferences and settings and to provide the user with a default location for saving documents and personal files. Many applications use Home folders as the default Save To location. Profiles can reside on a local computer or a network location. They can also be altered by the user or locked down by the administrator. Both profiles and home folders can be redirected to a network share and accessed by the user from any computer in the network.

### Local Profiles

A user's local profile is located in the Documents and Settings directory on the local machine, as shown in Figure 2-11. When a user logs on to a machine for the first time, a subdirectory matching their user name is created under the Documents and Settings directory. In this subdirectory, the users profile is created and named ntuser.dat. The user profile is copied from the Default User directory. Any changes made to the ntuser.dat file in the Default User directory will only affect new users when they log on. There is also an All Users subdirectory of the Documents and Settings directory. The All Users subdirectory also contains an ntuser.dat file. Changes to this file affect all users logging on to the computer.

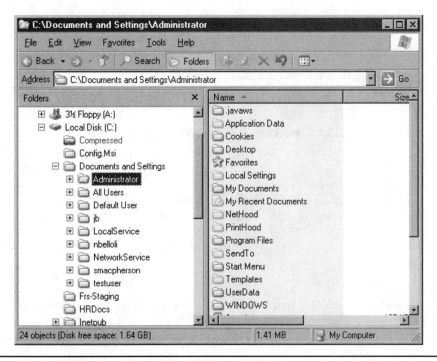

**Figure 2-11** Documents and Settings in Windows Explorer

When a user logs on to the computer, the ntuser.dat file is loaded which contains the users' preferences and settings. Any changes to the user settings or preferences are saved back to the ntuser.dat file when the user logs off the machine.

## Roaming Profiles

If users access more than one machine or move around the network, a roaming profile can be created to ensure that the user will receive his or her user settings and preferences no matter where they log on. When roaming profiles are used, the ntuser.dat file is stored on a network share and loaded to the local machine when the user logs on. Changes made to the user preferences or settings are copied back to the network share when the user logs off. The local profile will remain on the local machine, and should the network share be unavailable the next time the user logs on from that machine, the locally cached profile will be loaded instead. Changes to the local profile will not be saved back to the network share in this case.

**NOTE**   Roaming profiles can cause network problems if users save large files to their desktop or to their My Documents folder. The users' files are pulled from the network every time they log on to a computer, which sometimes causes a great deal of network traffic and creates an extraordinarily long logon. Folder redirection policies in Group Policy allow users' documents to be stored centrally on a server and only accessed when the user wants to open a file. For information about folder redirection, see Chapter 22.

**EXAM TIP**   Using roaming profiles enables users to see their desktop settings anywhere in the network they log on.

## Lab Exercise 2.2: Creating a Roaming Profile

In this exercise, you will create a roaming profile for a user and verify that the profile has been created. To fully test the functionality of the roaming profile, you would need two or more computers. If you have access to two or more computers, after completing the exercise, make a change to the user profile, such as different wallpaper, and then log the user onto the second computer and verify the user gets the same profile.

1. Select Start | All Programs | Administrative Tools | Active Directory Users and Computers.

2. Click the Users folder to display the users in Active Directory.

3. Right-click the user Nathan Belloli and select Properties to open the User Properties dialog box.

4. Click the Profiles tab and enter **C:\Profiles\%username%** in the Profile Path.

5. Click Apply and close the User Properties dialog box.

6. Close all applications and log off the computer.

7. Log on to the computer as Nathan Belloli.

8. Open Windows Explorer and navigate to C:\Profiles\nbelloli to view the contents of the folder. The folder should be empty.

9. Close Windows Explorer, right-click the desktop, and select Properties.

10. Click the Desktop tab and select a new desktop picture. Click OK to close the Desktop Properties dialog box.

11. Log off the computer and log back on.

12. Open Windows Explorer and navigate to C:\Profiles\nbelloli to view the contents of the folder. The folder should now contain all the profile settings for Nathan Belloli.

This exercise is interesting in that the profile isn't copied to the server right away. It is only copied to the server when the user changes the local profile. Changes are saved to the server at logoff. If the server is unavailable the next time the user logs on to the network, the locally cached profile will be used, but changes will not be saved back to the server at logoff. Any changes made while the user is logged on using a cached profile will be lost.

Also, you noticed in the exercise that you typed C:\Profiles\%username% in the profile path, but it reverted to C:\Profiles\nbelloli. Using the %username% wildcard allows for a user account to be copied in order to create new accounts. The %username% is replaced with the current user name.

## Mandatory Profiles

Mandatory profiles can be used when the user should be prevented from saving changes to the user settings or preferences. For example, a profile could be created with many shortcuts to file shares and applications. Users shouldn't be able to delete these shortcuts and then save the changes back to the network share. By creating the profile as a mandatory profile, users are able to make changes to their settings and preferences, but the changes are lost when the user logs off the machine. A mandatory profile can also be used for a group of people, and then every user would get the exact same settings and preferences.

To create a mandatory profile, navigate to the user subdirectory of the Documents and Settings directory. Right-click the ntuser.dat file and rename the file to ntuser.man. This changes the profile to a mandatory profile.

 **NOTE** The ntuser.dat file is a system file and is hidden by default. To see the ntuser.dat file, you need to unhide system files in Windows Explorer. To view system files, click the Tools menu item in Windows Explorer, select Folder Options and click the View tab. Clear the box next to "Hide protected operating system files."

## Home Folders

Users can use home folders to store their personal files. A home folder is a folder on a computer, usually a file server, which can be assigned to users to save documents and files. Home folders are generally used to consolidate user data into one place for easy backup. Also, many applications use the user's home folder as the default location for the Save As and File Open command. A home folder can be located on a single computer or on a network share, where it is available to the user anywhere in the network.

To set up home folders for a user, open the User Properties dialog box and click the Profiles tab. Then select either to place the home folder on the local computer and specify a directory, or select to connect a network drive and then enter the share name, as shown in Figure 2-12.

## Configuring Organizational Relationships

The Organization tab provides a place to enter the user's department and manager. If a manager's user account is entered in the Manager field, that user will list the user in the Direct Reports field. Using this field creates a link between an employee and a manager. By clicking a user's Organization tab, you can see who their manager is and which users directly report to them. Figure 2-13 shows that Derek is Nathan's manager and that Scott reports directly to Nathan, so Nathan is Scott's manager.

**Figure 2-12**

User profiles and
home folders

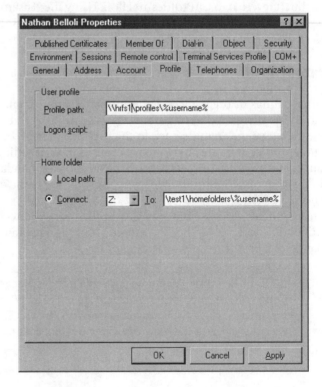

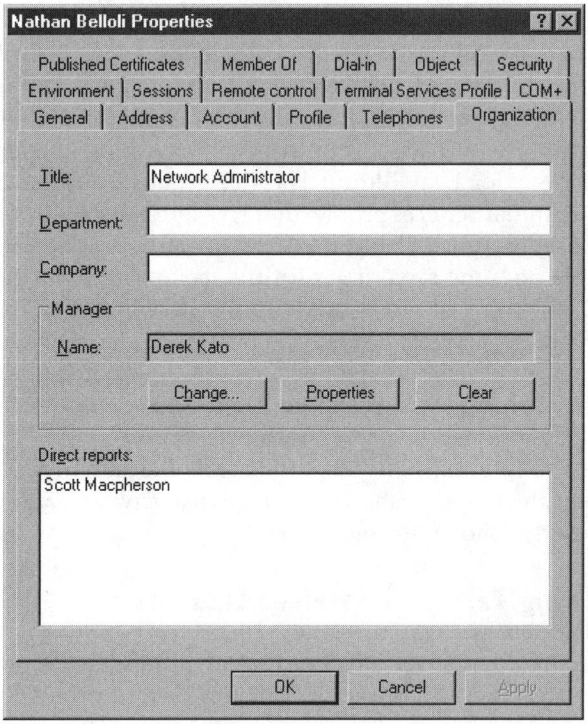

**Figure 2-13**
The Organization
tab showing the
work relationship
between Nathan,
Scott, and Derek

**Nathan Belloli Properties**                                   [?] [X]

| Published Certificates | Member Of | Dial-in | Object | Security |
| Environment | Sessions | Remote control | Terminal Services Profile | COM+ |
| General | Address | Account | Profile | Telephones | Organization |

Title:          Network Administrator

Department:

Company:

Manager
    Name:       Derek Kato

            Change...        Properties        Clear

Direct reports:

Scott Macpherson

                    OK          Cancel          Apply

## Configuring Terminal Services for User Accounts

Terminal Services was introduced as an add-on to Windows NT 4.0 and made a part of the operating system in Windows 2000. The fundamental use of Terminal Services is to provide a server, which can then be used by multiple users to run applications, with each user having their own session on the server. Terminal Services is often used with thin clients rather than desktop computers because thin clients are a cheaper alternative to full-blown workstations and require less administration. Terminal Services will be discussed in much greater detail in Chapter 3. The different user settings are discussed in this section as the settings are part of the user account attributes.

**NOTE**   A thin client is a very low technology computer that runs a Terminal Services client and connects to a server for the operating system and all applications. Thin clients are today's version of the old dumb terminal. Most thin clients have very small amounts of system resources (some don't even have hard drives!) and rely solely on a server for the operating system and all applications, other than the client software (Remote Desktop, for example). Thin clients are much cheaper than desktop computers, and require much less administration and maintenance.

## Configuring Terminal Services Profiles

All users have a profile associated with their user name, as explained in the previous section. The user profile is loaded when a user logs on to a computer. Users can also have a specific Terminal Services profile for use when they log on to a Terminal Services session. When a user initiates a Terminal Services session and logs on, the Terminal Server first attempts to load any Terminal Services–specific profiles. If the user has not been assigned a Terminal Services profile, the server attempts to load a roaming profile, and if a roaming profile is unavailable, the server loads the user's local profile. Only if a profile is unavailable does the server look for the next profile. If a Terminal Services profile is specified, the user will receive that profile and will not load a roaming profile or local profile. Terminal Services profiles can be used to give the users a different look and feel than their normal Windows sessions. This is important because a user profile or a server profile may contain settings and preferences that would have an adverse effect on the bandwidth consumed in a Terminal Services session.

To create a Terminal Services profile, enter the path in the Profile Path field. To specify a home folder, select either a local path or a network path and specify the path for the home folder, as shown in Figure 2-14.

## Configuring Terminal Services Sessions

The Sessions tab, as shown in Figure 2-15, defines how long a user can maintain a connection to the Terminal Server, any timeout and reconnection settings, and what happens to a disconnected session. These settings can, however, be overwritten by the Terminal Server.

**Figure 2-14**
Terminal Services
profile and
home folder

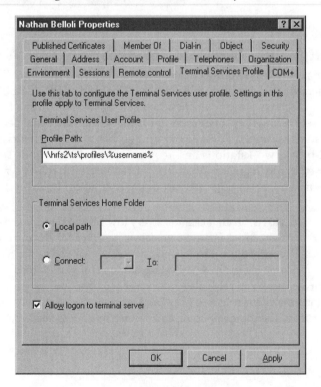

**Figure 2-15**
Terminal Services
Session Limits

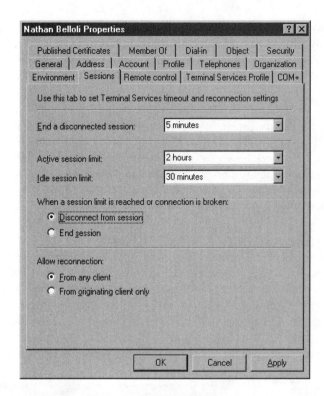

By default, an established Terminal Services session is not ended when the user disconnects from the server. This behavior is to prevent a user session from ending when it is accidentally disconnected due to network or dial-up problems. The session continues to run on the server and can be reconnected to by the user. You can specify that when a disconnection occurs, the session will end after a set time limit. Then if the user does not reconnect, the session would be closed after that period of time. Five minutes is usually ample time for a user who was accidentally disconnected to reconnect again. Leaving the default at Never allows many disconnected sessions to continue to run on the server, not only impacting performance, but also possibly becoming a security risk from someone attempting to access an open session.

The Active Session Limit and Idle Session Limit configurations are both used to control the amount of time a user may use the Terminal Server. A user can be limited to a maximum session time of one hour, for example. Or a user's connection can be ended if they are idle for 20 minutes. You must configure whether a user is disconnected from the server or their session is ended entirely when these limits are met. Disconnected sessions continue to run on the Terminal Server and can be reconnected to without having to reauthenticate. Ended sessions are completely closed on the server, and the user will have to reestablish not only the connection, but will have to reauthenticate to the server as well. If the End A Disconnected Session Limit is set to five minutes, there should be no problem in leaving this setting at the default of Disconnect From The Session. Users can also be allowed to reconnect from any computer or only from the original computer. By allowing a user to reconnect using a different computer, if a user has computer problems, they can reconnect to their session from a different computer without losing any work.

**EXAM TIP** The actual time setting for ending a disconnected setting is irrelevant on the exam. Five minutes, 10 minutes, or 15 minutes are all acceptable intervals. Generally, the question will specify the desired interval. Watch for answers that don't match up with the questions. Also be careful about setting the interval on the user account if the question presents a scenario that would be better served by setting the interval on the Terminal Server. For more information on Terminal Services, see Chapter 3.

## Configuring Remote Control Settings

The remote control feature of Terminal Services is different from the Remote Assistance tool built into Windows XP and Server 2003. Remote control is similar to Remote Assistance, but only works if the user has connected to the Terminal Server and is in application server mode. Remote Assistance can be called up at any time, whether the user is using Terminal Services or not.

The Remote Control tab, Figure 2-16, is where the parameters of remote control are set. In order for the remote control feature to be active, you must select the box next to

**Figure 2-16**
Terminal Services
remote control
settings

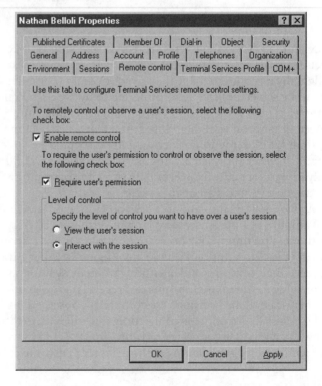

Enable Remote Control. Whether the user's permission is needed to take control of their machine is also a configurable setting. Also, the level of control can be set, whether to view the user's session or to interact with the user's session.

## Configuring the Terminal Services User Environment

The Environment tab, Figure 2-17, is used to specify a program to run when a user logs on to Terminal Services. Enter a name for the application to run and then type in the path to the application in the Start In field. You must type in the path, as there is no browse feature.

There are also three client device settings that can be configured. You can allow users to connect their own local drives, connect their own printers, or to use the main client printer used by the Terminal Server.

## Configuring Group Membership

Use the Member Of tab to add the user account to a global group, as shown in Figure 2-18. (Global groups are discussed later in this chapter.) To add a user account to a group, click Add and select the desired group from the Select Groups properties sheet. Using the Select Groups properties sheet is fairly straightforward. You simply enter the name of the group in the field under Enter The Object Name To Select. If you need to search Active Directory, click Advanced and perform a search. Click OK when finished and click Apply to commit your changes.

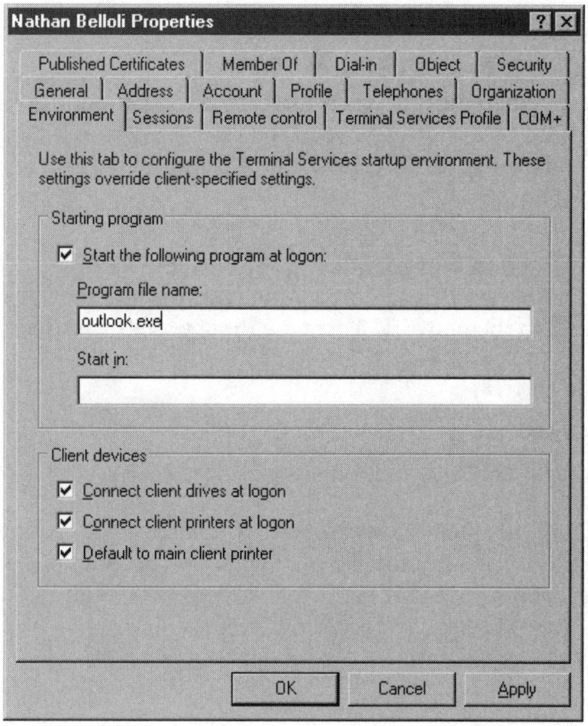

**Figure 2-17**
The Terminal Services Environment tab

**Figure 2-18**

Adding a user
account to
a group

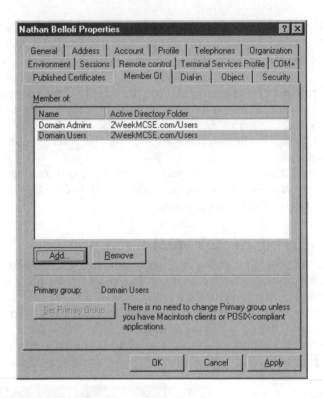

## Configuring Remote Access

There are several remote access settings that you can modify on a user account. To modify the remote access settings, open the User Properties dialog box for Nathan and click the Dial-in tab. Figure 2-19 shows the User Properties dialog box for Nathan; note the Dial-in settings.

### Remote Access Permission (Dial-in or VPN)

The Remote Access Permission setting controls whether or not the user is granted remote access to the network. There are three possible settings:

- Allow access
- Deny access
- Control access through Remote Access Policy

By default, the Deny Access permission is selected. This prevents users from gaining access to the network remotely unless their user account has been specifically granted remote access permission. For example, if you want to allow Nathan to dial in, you must select the radio button next to Allow Access.

**Figure 2-19**

Remote access settings for a user account

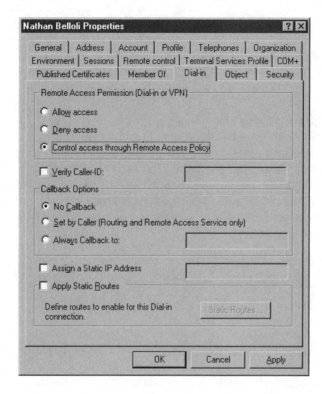

Also by default, the Control Access Through Remote Access Policy option is grayed out and not available. This option is only available when the domain functional level has been raised to that of Windows 2000 or Windows 2003. The domain functional level determines the capabilities and availability of certain features of Active Directory. More detail on the domain functional level is available in Chapter 20.

When the Control Access Through Remote Access Policy option is checked, the remote access policies created on a Routing and Remote Access Service (RRAS) server, or on a RADIUS server if applicable, will control whether the user can gain access to the network remotely. An RRAS server is a Windows 2000 or 2003 server configured to accept incoming connections. A RADIUS server is a Windows 2000 or 2003 server with Internet Authentication Service (IAS) installed. A RADIUS server is used to centralize remote access policies when several RRAS servers are used. Remote access policies are much more powerful and flexible than a simple Allow or Deny. Using remote access policies, you can set certain criteria of when to allow access, such as time of day, days of the week, or group membership. For more information on remote access policies, see Chapter 9.

A user can also be forced to dial in from a particular phone number. To force users to dial in from a pre-set phone number, check the box next to Verify Caller-ID and enter the phone number.

**NOTE** To use the Verify Caller-ID setting, all telecommunications equipment between the user and the remote access server must support caller-ID. If the remote access server is unable to determine the phone number the call originated from, it will deny the connection, even if the call originated from the correct phone number.

## Callback Options

If the remote access server supports callbacks, this option can be used to specify how the remote access server will use callback when a user dials in. When a user dials in to a remote access server, they are authenticated by the server and the server determines if they have authorization to connect remotely. If the user is granted access, the remote access server will disconnect the call and, after a short delay, call the user back. This method can increase security on the network and save users' telephone charges. There are three options for callbacks:

- No callback
- Set by Caller (Routing and Remote Access Service Only)
- Always Callback to

By default, No Callback is selected and the remote access server will not attempt to call a user back after authenticating the user. The Set By Caller option is used to allow users who call in from different locations to be called back. This saves telephone charges for the user. When the user authenticates to the remote access server, the server prompts the user to enter a phone number. The remote access server then disconnects the call and, after a short delay, dials the phone number input by the user.

 **NOTE** The user must have their computer configured to receive incoming calls. Also, this feature doesn't work well at most hotels or places where a switchboard is in use. The user must have a direct phone number that can be called back by the remote access server.

The Always Callback To option is used for security purposes. By selecting this option, you can limit the location that the user is allowed to use to connect to the network remotely. For example, you could enter your user's home number in the Callback field and then your user would only be able to connect remotely from their home. They would not be able to connect remotely from any other location.

 **NOTE** The Link Control Protocol (LCP) must be enabled on the remote access server to support callback. For more information on LCP, see Chapter 14.

 **EXAM TIP** Remote users who frequently travel need to have the callback settings configured to Set By Caller. If the settings are set to call back a frequently called number, the remote user will not be able to connect.

# IP Routing

The Dial-in properties also allow for a specific IP address to be assigned to a user. *This is the only way in Windows Server 2003 that you can assign a specific IP to a user.* To assign a static IP to a user, check the box next to Assign A Static IP Address and enter a valid IP in the space provided. You can also define static routes per user. By defining static routes, you can limit a specific user to only specific parts of your network. If you check the Apply Static Routes box, you must define the static routes. Click the Static Routes button (grayed out by default) and enter the appropriate network IDs.

**EXAM TIP**    Assigning an IP address on the Dial-in tab of the user account is the only way to assign an IP address to a user. This option is only available if the domain functional level has been raised to Windows 2000 Native or Windows 2003.

# Configuring Account Permissions

All objects in Active Directory have a Security tab that displays the Access Control List for that object, as shown in Figure 2-20. Users and groups can be assigned permissions on an object, such as the permission to read the object or to modify the object. You will also notice an Advanced button on the Security tab. The Advanced settings allow for changes to special permissions, changing ownership, auditing, and determining effective permissions. These topics will all be covered in Chapter 3.

**Figure 2-20**

The Security tab for Nathan Belloli

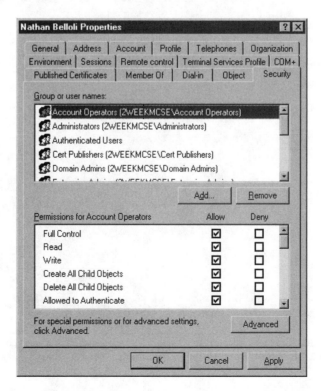

## Viewing the User's Canonical Name

The Object tab, shown in Figure 2-21, displays the canonical name (CN) of the user account object. The CN can be used to extrapolate a computer's distinguished name (DN). For example, Nathan's CN is 2WeekMCSE.com/IT/Nathan Belloli. The DN would then be cn=Nathan Belloli,ou=IT,dc=2WeekMCSE,dc=com. You will see more and more references to distinguished names as you work with Active Directory. Active Directory uses distinguished names to locate objects in the directory service. Some applications also use distinguished names to perform certain operations. For example, if you want to move a user account from one domain to another, you will need to use movetree.exe, a utility available in the Resource Kit, and specify the user's complete distinguished name.

## Implementing Certificates for User Accounts

Previously in Windows 2000, user certificates were managed from the Certificates snap-in. Windows Server 2003 now implements certificates as part of the user account. Certificates issued from a certificate authority can be added to the user account using the Published Certificates tab. Figure 2-22 shows the EFS recovery certificate has been added to Nathan's user account. This enables Nathan to act as a recovery agent.

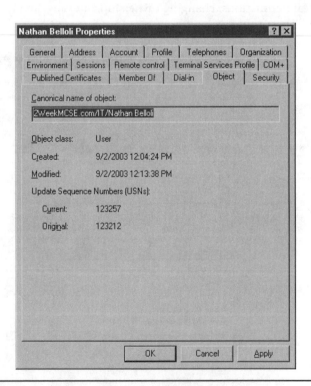

**Figure 2-21**    The Object tab showing Nathan's canonical name

**Figure 2-22**
The published
certificates
associated with
Nathan's user
account

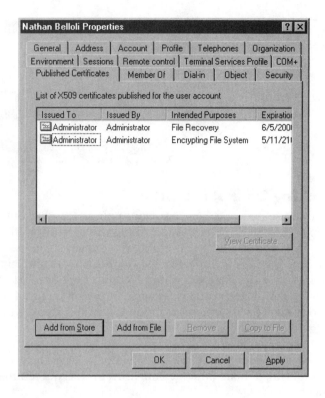

## User Account Administrative Tasks

Besides modifying user account properties, there are a few administrative tasks that you must know how to perform. In any environment, there will undoubtedly be users who fall into the EEOC (Equipment Exceeds Operator Capability) category who constantly forget their passwords, lock themselves out of their account, or both. Also, people change jobs and departments, even domains. This section describes how to perform basic administrative tasks for user accounts.

### Resetting Passwords

Occasionally passwords need to be reset. For example, a password reset is needed when the user has forgotten the password, when a user account has become compromised, a user leaves the company, or occasionally for some other administrative task (such as migrating users to a new domain, which can cause the password to be lost).

The current password is hidden and not visible on the Account tab or on any of the user properties screens. To reset a password, simply right-click the user name and select Reset Password. Figure 2-23 shows how to enter a new password. From this dialog box, enter a new password, confirm the password, and check whether the user should have to change their password at the next logon or not. Usually, when a user's password is reset, they are required to change their password again when they log on, ensuring that their password is known only to them. You don't need to know the user's current password to reset it.

**Figure 2-23**
The Reset
Password
dialog box

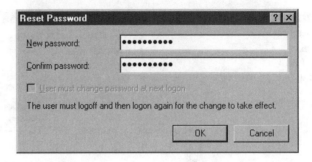

## Unlocking User Accounts

All good secure networks have password policies and lockout policies in place. With these policies in place, users will sometimes mistakenly lock themselves out of the network. A user who has mistyped their password several times will have their account locked out and will not be able to log on to the network until either a set time expires or an administrator unlocks the account. Accounts can be unlocked on the Account tab of the user account. The Account Is Locked Out option is grayed out unless the account is locked out, then it will display the option, with a check box. If the account is locked out, as in Figure 2-24, simply clear the check box to unlock the account. An account cannot be locked out manually. An account is only locked out if a password is mistyped several times. The number of times a user can attempt to log on before being locked out can be set in the default domain policy. Configuring the lockout settings is explained further in this chapter.

**NOTE**   To actually test this, you will need to first set the account lockout policy and then attempt to log on as the user with an incorrect password until the account locks out. Then you can log on as Administrator and unlock the user account. For information on account lockout policy, see the "Configuring a Lockout Policy" section later in this chapter.

As a general rule, most networks implement a policy to lock out user accounts after a certain number of failed logon attempts. The number of attempts allowed can be set to any number, but is usually three or five. If users attempt to log on incorrectly several times, their account is locked out and cannot be used to gain access to the network unless either a period of time passes or an administrator unlocks the account. Lockout settings will be explained in the "Configuring a Lockout Policy" section later in this chapter.

## Disabling and Enabling User Accounts

Accounts can be created in a disabled state and then activated at a later time. This is the recommended practice when creating accounts using a bulk import method and for creating user account templates. A user also may go on vacation for an extended period of time and you want to prevent access from their user account while they are gone.

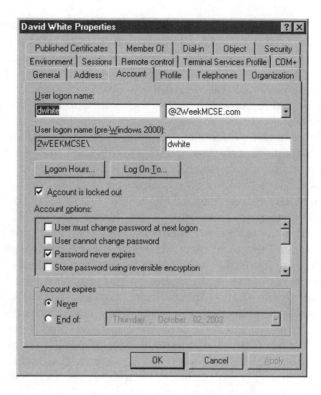

**Figure 2-24**

User account
lockout

To disable an account, right-click the user name and select Disable Account. To enable
the account, right-click the user name and select Enable Account.

**EXAM TIP**   Microsoft recommends that user accounts be disabled, not
deleted entirely, when a user leaves the company.

## Renaming User Accounts

Occasionally, user accounts need to be renamed. It may be that an individual has gotten
married or divorced or just changed their name. Or it may be that a user has left the company and a new user has taken over their job. It is recommended that the user account be
renamed to accommodate a new user taking over an existing position. By renaming the
user account, all the associated permissions and rights of that user are retained for the
new user. The password should be reset at the same time to ensure that the only person
who knows the password is the new user and the old user isn't able to use the account
anymore.

Let's look at an example. Nathan is a junior administrator. He's a good worker. He
studies hard outside of work, and he gets his MCSE. One day Nathan gets an outstanding job offer, and he quits his job with your company. There is a vacancy for a short time

before a new person is hired. To retain Nathan's group membership and user rights for the position, you rename Nathan's account to jradmin to represent the job position. You also disable the account. After a short search, you decide to move Todd Davis into Nathan's old job. All that needs to be done is to rename the jradmin user account to Todd Davis and reset the password. The SID for the account hasn't changed, even though the name has, and Todd has the same rights and permissions that Nathan had previously.

As an alternative, you could make a copy of Nathan's account and name it Todd Davis. Many companies use this method instead of renaming accounts for auditing purposes, and to hold user accounts in case a user returns to the company. However, the new account will have a new SID, so anything that has been directly assigned to the original account will have to be recreated on the new account. For this reason, Microsoft recommends renaming user accounts.

To rename a user account, right-click the user name in Active Directory Users and Computers and select Rename. The user account will be highlighted and you can rename the user account just like you would rename a file or folder in Windows Explorer. After you change the name, a dialog box will appear as in Figure 2-25, and you will be prompted to enter a new first name, last name, display name, and logon name. This window will then alter the appropriate fields within the user account for you.

You can also choose to rename a user account from the user account properties. If you choose this method, you must change the user name, the account name, and the display name. If you just change the user name and account name, but fail to change the display name, you may not be able to find your account in Active Directory again. To rename a user account manually, open the User Properties and change the user name, first name, last name, display name and logon name.

**Figure 2-25**

Renaming a
user account

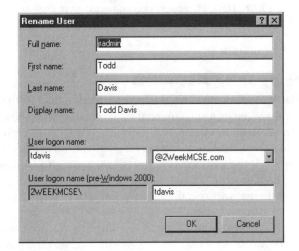

**EXAM TIP** Renaming a user account to accommodate a new employee is classic Microsoft theory. On the exam, look for the phrase, "least administrative effort." Yes, some firms look at renaming a user account as a less desirable option due to the difficulty in tracking user accounts, but renaming a user account is a Microsoft best practice.

## Moving a User Account

Accounts are created and placed into some sort of a container within a domain, whether that be the Users folder or an OU. It is very easy to move a user account to a different container within a domain. When a user account is moved, the policies and settings that apply to the destination container will now affect the user object, and the old policies and settings are completely forgotten.

Moving accounts to different domains is a bit trickier. You cannot use the Active Directory Users and Computers MMC to move users between domains. To move a user account to a different domain in an entirely different forest, you must use some sort of migration tool. Microsoft provides the Active Directory Migration Tool (ADMT) for just such a purpose. The ADMT can be downloaded from Microsoft's site. Go to http://www.microsoft.com/downloads/ and search for ADMT.

If you want to move a user account to a different domain within the same forest, you can use the movetree.exe command from the command line. movetree.exe is part of the Windows support tools included on the CD-ROM. You must install the Windows support tools before the movetree.exe tool can be run from a command prompt. The movetree.exe utility uses an object's distinguished name (DN) to move the object between domains. To move a user object to an OU in a different domain, you must know the destination OU's DN. Here is an example of the context of the movetree.exe tool:

```
movetree /start /s server1.2WeekMCSE.com /d server2.7-bar.com /sdn ou=IT,
 dc=2weekmcse,dc=com /ddn ou=IT,dc=7-bar,dc=com
```

For additional information on using the movetree.exe utility, and for a listing of available commands, type **movetree** from a command prompt.

 **NOTE** The movetree utility is part of the Windows Server 2003 support tools included on the Windows Server 2003 CD. To install the support tools, navigate to the Support | Tools directory on the CD and run the 2003RKST.msi installation file.

## Lab Exercise 2.3: Moving a User Account

In this exercise, you are going to use the accounts that you previously created in Lab Exercise 2.1. If you have not completed Lab Exercise 2.1, please do so now. You are going to move the accounts using two different methods. Microsoft has added the click and drag capability in Windows Server 2003, so moving an account to a different OU is extremely easy. Notice that you cannot move the accounts to any other domain by either method. You must use one of the tools described previously to move user accounts to a different domain.

1. Select Start | Run and type **dsa.msc** to start the Active Directory Users and Computers MCC.

2. Click the Users folder to display all the users in the domain.

3. Right-click Nathan Belloli's account and select Move. Notice that the only containers available are within your own domain. You cannot move Nathan to a different domain.

4. Click the IT OU and click OK.

5. Click the IT OU to verify that Nathan's user account is now in the IT OU.

6. Click and drag Nathan's user account back to the Users container.

7. Click the Users container and verify that Nathan's account now resides in the Users container and not the IT OU.

8. Click and drag Nathan's user account back to the IT OU.

# Implementing Security for User Accounts

When you created the account for Nathan Belloli and Derek Kato, complex passwords were required and you had to implement a password of at least seven characters. Windows Server 2003 has implemented additional security options for user accounts to prevent unauthorized access. You can configure these additional options by configuring the default domain policy in Active Directory Users and Computers, as shown in Figure 2-26. Group Policy is covered in much greater detail in Chapter 23. Account policies and lockout policies are only effective when they are implemented at the domain level.

### Configuring a Password Policy

You have already seen the effects of a complex password. There are several password options that can be set in the default domain policy. They are

- **Enforce Password History**   The initial setting for password history is 24 passwords remembered. That means that a user cannot reuse a password until they have used 24 different passwords. Enabling password history greatly improves the security of a network. It is recommended to keep the initial setting.

- **Maximum Password Age**   Defines how long a user can use a certain password until it needs to be changed. The default maximum age is 42 days. Users are then forced to change their passwords before they can log on to the network.

- **Minimum Password Age**   Defines how long a user must keep their password before changing it again. This setting is to prevent users from changing their passwords back to something familiar after they are required to change their passwords due to the maximum password age setting. Some users will change their passwords several times in order to use a favorite password again.

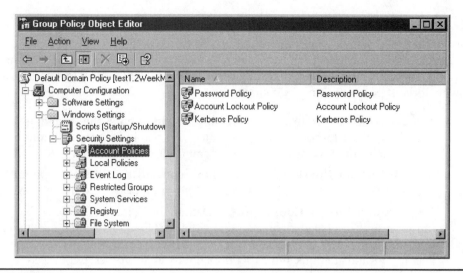

**Figure 2-26** The Account Policies node in the default domain policy

- **Minimum Password Length**   Defines how many characters the password must be. The default setting is seven characters.

- **Passwords Must Meet Complexity Requirements**   Defines that passwords must include letters and numbers, upper- and lowercase letters, special characters, and no common words. Using complex passwords decreases the possibility of someone guessing the password.

- **Store Passwords Using Reversible Encryption**   If Challenge Handshake Authentication Protocol (CHAP) is used for remote access, this setting must be enabled.

To configure password settings:

1. Select Start | All Programs | Administrative Tools | Active Directory Users and Computers.

2. Right-click the domain container and select Properties. Click the Group Policy tab.

3. Select the default domain policy and click Edit.

4. Navigate to Computer Configuration | Windows Settings | Security Settings | Account Policies | Password Policy.

5. Select the desired policy and right-click the policy. Select Properties and then define the policy.

6. Close the Group Policy Object Editor window. Close the Domain Properties window.

7. To immediately apply the password policies, restart the domain controller.

## Configuring a Lockout Policy

One of the best defenses against dictionary attacks is to configure a lockout policy to be applied to all user accounts in the domain. A lockout policy sets the number of times a user can attempt to log on unsuccessfully before their account will be locked. The following lockout policy options are configurable:

- **Account Lockout Duration**   Defines how long in minutes the account is locked out. If the lockout duration is set to 0, an administrator must unlock the user account. A 60-minute lockout duration is recommended.

- **Account Lockout Threshold**   Defines how many unsuccessful attempts are allowed before the account is locked out; 3–5 attempts are recommended.

- **Reset Account Lockout Counter After**   Defines the number of minutes that must elapse after a failed logon attempt before the failed logon attempt counter is reset to 0. If a lockout threshold is set to 5, a user account will be locked out after five invalid attempts. If the user does not try all five times, but instead waits until the lockout counter has been reset, they can again attempt five logons before being locked out. A setting less than the lockout duration is required.

By default, a lockout policy is not configured. It is recommended that a complete password policy be implemented, including a lockout policy, and that users be educated as to what constitutes valid passwords and what the lockout threshold is. When users are locked out, they either need to wait until the lockout duration expires or have their account unlocked by an administrator, which can cause a loss in productivity. To avoid confusion and lost productivity, make sure to communicate to your users what is being implemented.

## Renaming the Administrator and Guest Accounts

Earlier in this chapter, it was recommended that the Administrator and Guest accounts be renamed to increase security. Renaming the Administrator and Guest accounts in Active Directory is relatively simple, because they are domain accounts, and so there are only two accounts to rename. However, every computer in the domain except domain controllers has local built-in Administrator and Guest accounts. Renaming all these accounts would obviously be time consuming if it had to be done at each computer. Luckily, this operation has been placed in Group Policy, and all Administrator and Guest accounts on all computers in the domain can be renamed quickly and easily.

To rename the Administrator or Guest account in Group Policy:

1. Select Start | All Programs | Administrative Tools | Active Directory Users and Computers.

2. Right-click the domain container and select Properties. Click the Group Policy tab.

3. Select the default domain policy and click Edit.

4. Navigate to Computer Configuration | Windows Settings | Security Settings | Local Policies | Security Options.

5. Select the "Accounts: Rename Administrator Account" or "Accounts: Rename Guest Account" policy. Right-click the policy and select Properties.

6. Select to define the policy and then enter a new name for the account.

7. Click OK to close the dialog box. Close the Group Policy Object Editor and apply the changes to the GPO on the domain Properties page.

8. Restart all computers in the domain.

---

 **NOTE** Group Policies that apply to the computer configuration are implemented when a computer boots into Windows. Restarting the computers ensures that the policy changes take effect immediately. Group Policy also has a Refresh setting so that it is not required to restart the computer in order to receive new policies. Each computer in the domain will check with a domain controller at a specified interval to determine if any new settings must be applied. By default, this refresh behavior is not configured. See Chapter 22 for more information about Group Policy.

## Auditing Account Logon Attempts

In order to be aware of network attacks, auditing of logon attempts should be implemented. Auditing can be configured on any container in Active Directory, and so the scope of your auditing policy should be carefully considered. If you want to be aware of all failed logon attempts on your network, you must configure auditing at the domain level. To configure account logon auditing:

1. Select Start | All Programs | Administrative Tools | Active Directory Users and Computers.

2. Right-click the domain container and select Properties. Click the Group Policy tab.

3. Select the default domain policy and click Edit.

4. Navigate to Computer Configuration | Windows Settings | Security Settings | Local Policies | Audit Policy.

5. Select the Audit Account Logon Events. Right-click and select Properties.

6. Select to audit for failed events.

---

 **NOTE** Auditing for successful events will audit all successful logons in your domain. Successful events should be audited when it is suspected that an account has become compromised and you need to determine which computer is being used to log on to the network. Look for odd behavior, such as a logon occurring when most people are out of the office or at odd hours.

7. Click OK and close the Group Policy Object Editor. Apply the changes to the domain Properties and restart all domain controllers.

**NOTE** Auditing for account logons writes events when a user attempts to log on to the network. Since all network logons are directed to domain controllers, you must check the event log on all domain controllers to determine if an unauthorized attempt was made to log on to the network.

**NOTE** Notice that there is also a logon event policy. The logon event policy is for local logons and share logons only, and does not audit for network logons.

# Computer Accounts

It isn't enough to have a user account. Every desktop, workstation, laptop, server, and DC in the network must have a valid computer account in Active Directory. Computer accounts are used to identify a computer to the domain. Computer accounts are accounts for computers, like a user account is an account for a person. Active Directory requires that all logons not only come from a valid user, but that the logon attempt also comes from a valid computer. When a domain controller receives an authentication request, it first checks to make sure the request is coming from a computer that has a valid computer account in the domain. The domain won't accept the user logon, even if it's valid, if it's from a computer that doesn't belong to the domain.

Computer accounts can be manually created in Active Directory Users and Computers, automatically created when the computer is added to the domain, automatically created using Remote Installation Services (RIS), or automatically created using the bulk import methods described in the next section.

**NOTE** Windows 98 clients don't have computer accounts created in Active Directory. If the Windows 98 client has the Active Directory Service client installed, and digital signing for SMB has been disabled, the Windows 98 client will be able to log on. Windows 2000, 2003, and XP machines must have computer accounts to log on.

## Creating Computer Accounts

Computer accounts can be created in Active Directory Users and Computers by anyone having the Create Computer Accounts permission granted to them. The Create Computer Accounts permission can be delegated using the Delegation of Control Wizard (right-click the container and click Delegate) or explicitly granted using the Security tab on the Properties sheet of the container. Administrators, Domain Admins, and Enterprise Admins all have the Create Computer Accounts permission by default. If an administrator joins a computer to the domain, a computer account is automatically created for that computer. By default, computer accounts are created in the Computers folder in Active Directory. Computer accounts can be moved the same way a user account is moved. They can be placed into OUs and specific security policies applied to collections of computer accounts.

To manually create a computer account:

1. Select Start | All Programs | Administrative Tools | and select Active Directory Users and Computers.

2. Right-click the Computers folder and select New Computer.

3. Enter a name for the computer and click Next.

4. If you are going to use RIS to set up this computer, check the box that says this is a managed computer, then add the Globally Unique Identifier (GUID) and click Next.

5. Verify the creation of the computer and click Finish.

## Managed Computers

A managed computer is a computer whose operating system is installed using Remote Installation Services (RIS). RIS can either enter the computer account at the time of installation or it can require that a computer account be present before the operating system is installed. Either way, any computer that uses RIS is a managed computer. If the RIS server has been configured to respond only to known computers, it will not install an operating system on any computer that doesn't have a valid computer account present in Active Directory. Using managed computers reduces administration costs as it relates to the installation of client computer operating systems.

To create a managed computer manually, the managed computer option must be selected and the GUID must be entered, as in Figure 2-27. Most network cards have built-in capability to boot to the network and obtain an operating system from a server, such as a RIS server. The network card must be configured in the system BIOS as a boot device before this functionality will work. When the computer boots using the network card, the GUID will usually display on the screen and can be written down and entered into Active Directory. If this doesn't occur, the manufacturer also usually includes documentation with the computer identifying the GUID. As a last resort, a packet capturing tool, such as Network Monitor, can be used to capture DHCP discover packets and the GUID read from those packets. A DHCP discover packet is what a client computer sends out to obtain an IP address from a DHCP server. The client includes its GUID as part of the packet so the DHCP server will be able to find the client again in order to issue an IP address. DHCP will be covered in much greater detail in Chapter 7.

**NOTE** Remote Installation Services (RIS) is a server configured to automatically install Windows 2000 or XP on client computers. RIS requires that DNS, Active Directory, and a DHCP server be present in order to work. Also, client computers must be PXE (pre-execution environment) enabled. Most network cards manufactured today are PXE-compliant and can boot to a network and look for a RIS server. RIS is the most efficient way to install client machines.

**Figure 2-27**
Setting up
a managed
computer

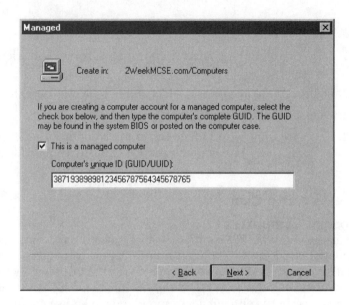

# Configuring Computer Account Properties

A computer account has properties just like a user account. A computer can be a member of a group, be granted dial-in permission, be associated with a RIS server, and more. Following is a brief description of the computer account properties that are available, and how to configure each to achieve an individualized computer setup.

### Viewing Operating System Information

The Operating System tab displays the current operating system and any service packs installed. Any time a new service pack is added on the computer, the Operating System tab will be updated. This properties sheet is a quick way to determine what operating system and service pack are currently installed.

### Configuring Group Membership

The Member Of tab displays the current group membership of the computer account. A computer account can belong to groups, just like user accounts can. To add the computer account to a group, click Add and then select the desired group.

### Configuring Location

The Location tab displays a location for the computer account. The location can be used as a search parameter in Active Directory. The location can be any type of location entered by the administrator. A building and floor can be specified as the location of the computer, or a network location or geographical location can be used.

## Configuring Computer Management

The Managed By tab provides a space to enter the name of the person responsible for managing the computer. The Browse button allows you to search Active Directory and locate the user account of the responsible person. The address and telephone number fields will be automatically populated with that user's information. This information makes it easy to find out who is responsible for maintaining the computer in case of a failure and contact that person quickly. Figure 2-28 shows that workstation2 is currently being managed by Nathan Belloli. Notice that Nathan's phone and fax number are also listed, simplifying the task of contacting him in case something goes wrong.

## Viewing the Computer's Common Name

The Object tab displays the canonical name (CN) of the computer account object. The canonical name of the computer account is the same format as for user accounts. The CN can be used to extrapolate a computer's distinguished name. For example, Workstation2's CN is 2WeekMCSE.com/Computers/Workstation2, as shown on Figure 2-29. The DN would then be cn=workstation2,ou=Computers,dc=2WeekMCSE,dc=com. As in user accounts, the Distinguished Name can then be used to move computer accounts or for other maintenance tasks.

**Figure 2-28**
The Managed
By tab

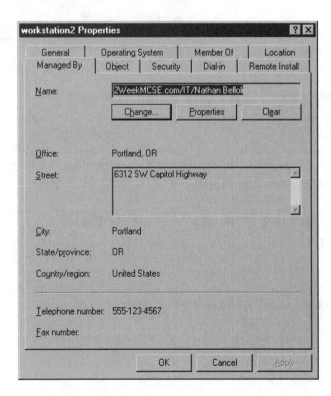

**Figure 2-29**
The object
tab showing
Workstation2's
canonical name

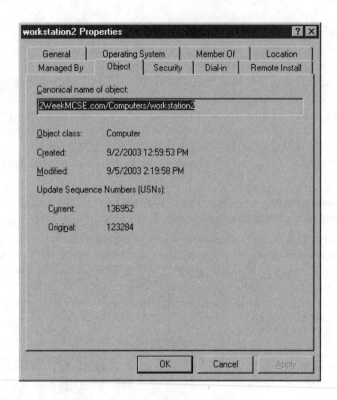

**Configuring Account Permissions**

All objects in Active Directory have a Security tab that displays the Access Control List for that object. Users and groups can be assigned permissions on an object, such as the permission to read the object or to modify the object. The Advanced settings allow for changes to special permissions, changing ownership, auditing, and determining effective permissions. These topics will all be covered in Chapter 3.

**Configuring Remote Install Options**

Using the Remote Install tab, you can configure both client and server options. The Remote Install tab is only available on managed computers and RIS servers. A managed computer is any computer that has used Remote Installation Services (RIS) to obtain its operating system. A RIS server is any Windows 2000 or 2003 server with Remote Installation Services installed and configured. Figure 2-30 shows the GUID for workstation2 and that it is being managed by the TEST1 RIS server. If the Remote Installation Server field is blank, the computer will obtain its operating system from any available RIS server.

**Figure 2-30**
The Remote
Install tab
showing the
GUID and
the RIS server

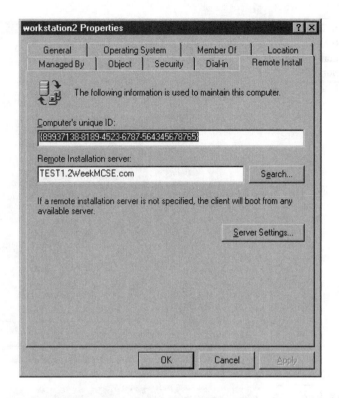

Notice also that there is a Server Settings button on the Remote Install tab. The Server Settings button opens the properties of the RIS server, in this case TEST1, as shown in Figure 2-31. Before a RIS server will respond to client requests, it must be authorized in Active Directory by checking the box next to "Respond to client computers requesting service." If the box is cleared, the RIS server will not respond to clients. Also, to increase security on the network and prevent unauthorized installations, the RIS server should be configured not to respond to unknown client computers. Checking this box forces the RIS server to query Active Directory for a computer account that matches the GUID of the computer requesting service. If a computer account is not found that matches the GUID, the RIS server will not respond to the client. If "Do not respond to unknown client computers" is checked, you must enter the computer accounts into Active Directory before booting the client computers. Entering computer accounts prior to running RIS is known as prestaging the computer accounts.

Just as the client computer contains a reference to the RIS server, the RIS server contains a reference to all client computers that have been assigned to it for installation services. Clicking the Show Clients button displays an Active Directory query with all clients that have been assigned to the RIS server displayed, as shown in Figure 2-32.

**Figure 2-31**
The Remote
Install tab of
a RIS server

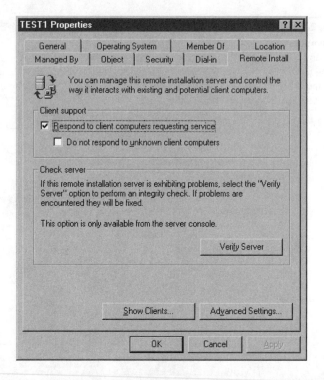

**Figure 2-32**
Active Directory
displaying the RIS
clients of TEST1

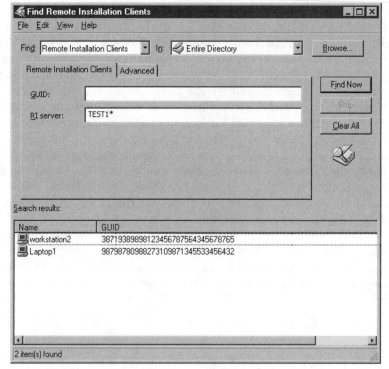

# Contacts

Contacts were introduced in Windows 2000 as objects in Active Directory and look eerily similar to a user account. Contacts aren't user accounts, however, and can't be used to log on to the network. A contact in Active Directory is used similarly to how contacts in Outlook are used. A person's information can be entered into Active Directory and then can be located by querying Active Directory. A contact has some of the same properties sheets that a user has, such as General, Address, Telephones, and Member Of.

If you create a contact, and then right-click the contact, you will see that you have the option to send mail. If you click send mail, your e-mail editor opens up and away you go. It might be a bit cumbersome to query Active Directory for a single person's e-mail address, but you can also group contacts together in a distribution group and then send an e-mail address to the list.

A distribution group is only used for e-mail. A distribution group can have user accounts and contacts as members. Using contacts and distribution groups in this manner, you can enter the Board of Directors members as contacts (they don't need to log on to the network) with all of their telephone and e-mail information, and then add these contacts to a distribution group. When any user in your domain wants to send an e-mail to the Board of Directors, they can address the e-mail to the Board of Directors distribution group and send the message.

Contacts then, in a nutshell, allow you to add contact information for people outside of your domain, and have that information searchable and usable by Active Directory. See Figure 2-33 to view Duaine Culpepper's contact information.

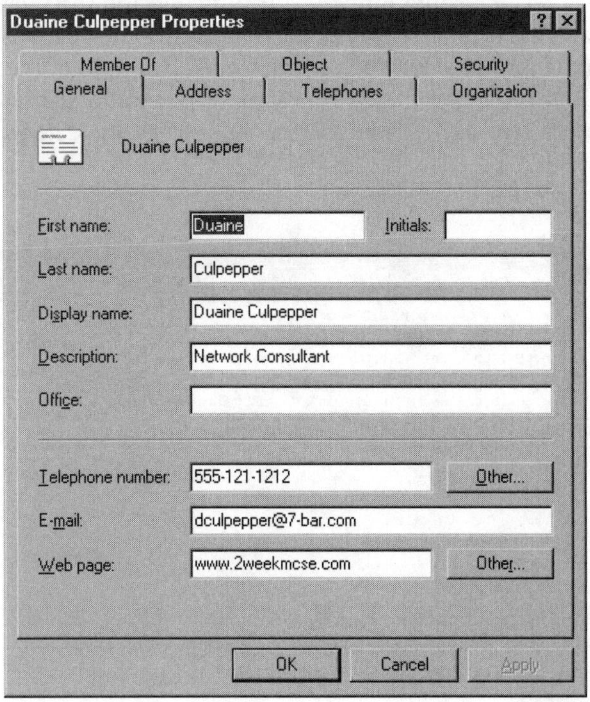

**Figure 2-33**

An Active Directory contact

# Creating and Modifying Objects Using Automation

Windows Server 2003 includes two command-line utilities you can use to automate the addition and modification of user accounts, computer accounts, and other objects in Active Directory. Comma-Separated Value Directory Exchange (csvde) uses comma-separated values (CSV) to bulk import objects into Active Directory. LDAP Data Interchange Format Directory Exchange (ldifde) can be used to modify objects in Active Directory as well as bulk import objects into Active Directory. Both of these utilities can be used for other objects in Active Directory besides user accounts. Both tools require a .txt file with data to work with. csvde is the more commonly used tool to import objects because it uses comma-separated values for data, and almost all databases and spreadsheet programs can export records into CSV format. It is an easy process then to obtain a list of new users from HR and use the same list to perform the bulk import.

## Comma-Separated Value Directory Exchange (csvde)

csvde is a command-line tool that is used to add objects to Active Directory in a bulk import process. csvde cannot be used to modify objects that already exist in Active Directory. It uses text files containing records in the comma-separated value (CSV) format. Most spreadsheets and databases can export records into CSV format. All that is required is a first line defining the fields in each record. This first line is known as the attribute line. The attribute line is followed by the raw data to import. See Figure 2-34 for an example of a text file containing the attribute line and then several raw data records.

The raw data must follow the order of the attribute line. It is okay to leave some values blank in the raw data, but the commas must be in place. There must simply be a blank space in between two commas. For example, when adding user accounts, it's possible that not all users have a middle initial. For those users, the data would read as follows:

```
terry, ,finstad
```

**Figure 2-34**   csvde sample file

Also, if a value includes commas, encompass the entire value in quotation marks. For example, distinguished names include commas, so a distinguished name would read as follows:

```
"cn=Terry Finstad,ou=executives,dc=2WeekMCSE,dc=com"
```

Numerous attributes can be added by using the csvde format. At a bare minimum, a user logon name, account name, and distinguished name are required for user accounts. A UPN can be specified and a control field added. The following line adds Terry's account to Active Directory by using the distinguished name, specifies that the object is a user, specifies the user name is tfinstad, specifies the UPN as tfinstad@2WeekMCSE.com, specifies that the user's display name is Terry Finstad, and adds a control number of 514, which disables the account.

```
"cn=Terry Finstad,ou=executives,dc=2WeekMCSE,dc=com",user,tfinstad,tfinstad@2WeekMCSE.com,Te
rry Finstad, 514
```

## Preparing the Source File

The source file must have two components:

- **Attribute line** Specifies the names of the attributes to be added to active directory and the order in which they will be added. The attribute is the first line in the source file. You must use attribute names as they appear in Active Directory and the attributes must be separated by commas.

- **Raw data (account line)** There will be one line of raw data per object to be added to Active Directory. The raw data contains the value for each attribute in the attribute line.

Here is an example of a source file:

```
dn,department,objectClass,sAMAccountName,telephoneNumber,userPrincipalName,userAcc
ountControl

"CN=Rob Blevins,OU=Production,DC=2WeekMCSE,DC=com",Production,user,rblevins,121-
222-1234,rblevins@2WeekMCSE.com,514

"CN=Scott
Machperson,OU=Production,DC=2WeekMCSE,DC=com",Production,user,smacpherson,121-222-
1369,smacpherson@2WeekMCSE.com,512
```

**NOTE** The control number at the end specifies whether the account is enabled or disabled. The value 512 enables the account and the value 514 disables the account. It is recommended that when you create user accounts using bulk import, you create the accounts in a disabled state and then enable them when they are ready to be used. Accounts created using bulk import have blank passwords and so are a security risk.

## Running csvde

To run the bulk import command using csvde, open a command prompt and type the following:

```
csvde -i -f filename.txt
```

The -i indicates that you are importing, and the -f indicates the file name to use. For more information on using csvde, simply type **csvde** at a command prompt and press ENTER. Figure 2-35 shows csvde from a command line.

## LDAP Data Interchange Format Directory Exchange (ldifde)

ldifde is another tool that can be used to import user accounts and other objects into Active Directory. ldifde can also be used to modify existing objects in Active Directory. Before you can use the ldifde tool, you must first prepare a file that specifies the objects to be added or modified in Active Directory. The file can include an unlimited number of objects, with each object to be added or modified separated by a blank line. The # sign can also be used at the beginning of a line to indicate a comment, which will be ignored by ldifde.

## Preparing the Source File

The source file must contain records consisting of lines that describe an entry. Each line indicates a specific attribute followed by the value of that attribute. For example, a user account would contain a line specifying sAMAccountName followed by the user name value. Each record consists of at least one line, which specifies an attribute, followed by the attribute value. Individual records must be separated by a blank line.

```
Command Prompt                                                    _ □ ×
C:\Documents and Settings\Administrator>csvde

CSV Directory Exchange

General Parameters
==================
-i              Turn on Import Mode (The default is Export)
-f filename     Input or Output filename
-s servername   The server to bind to (Default to DC of computer's domain)
-v              Turn on Verbose Mode
-c FromDN ToDN  Replace occurences of FromDN to ToDN
-j path         Log File Location
-t port         Port Number (default = 389)
-u              Use Unicode format
-?              Help


Export Specific
===============
-d RootDN       The root of the LDAP search (Default to Naming Context)
-r Filter       LDAP search filter (Default to "(objectClass=*)")
-p SearchScope  Search Scope (Base/OneLevel/Subtree)
-l list         List of attributes (comma separated) to look for in an
                LDAP search
-o list         List of attributes (comma separated) to omit from input.
-g              Disable Paged Search.
-m              Enable the SAM logic on export.
-n              Do not export binary values
```

**Figure 2-35**    csvde from the command prompt

The following is an example of the ldifde format:

```
# Create Terry Finstad

DN: CN=Terry Finstad,OU=Production,DC=2WeekMCSE,DC=Com

Ojbectclass: user

sAMAccountName: tfinstad

userPrincipalName: tfinstad@2WeekMCSE.com

displayName: Terry Finstad

userAccountControl: 512
```

You must specify an attribute name as defined in the Active Directory schema, followed by a colon and then the value of the attribute. Only objects and attributes currently in the schema are recognized by Active Directory. If you misspell an attribute, or include an attribute in the file that is not currently in Active Directory, you will receive an error stating that there is no such attribute and the operation will fail.

## Running ldifde

To run the bulk import command using ldifde, open a command prompt and type the following:

```
ldifde -i -f filename.txt
```

The -i indicates that you are importing, and the -f indicates the file name to use. For more information on using ldifde, simply type **ldifde** at a command prompt and press ENTER, as shown in Figure 2-36.

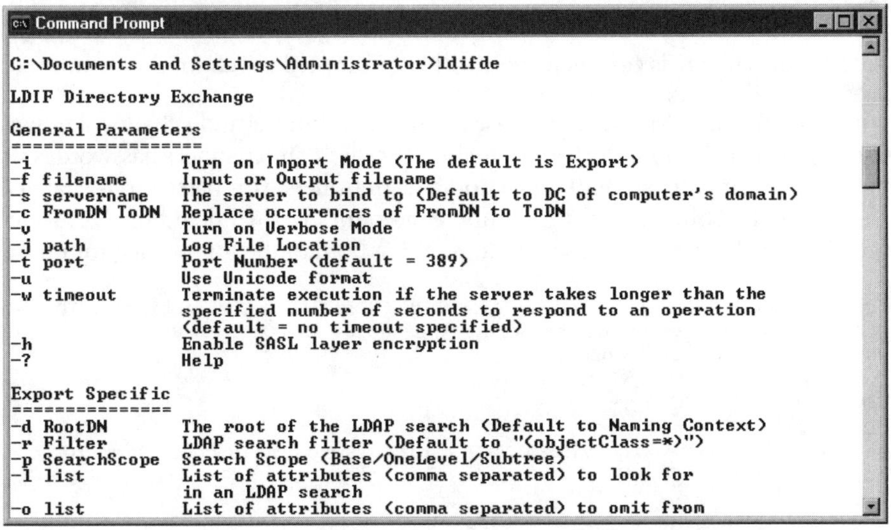

```
C:\Documents and Settings\Administrator>ldifde

LDIF Directory Exchange

General Parameters
==================
-i                 Turn on Import Mode (The default is Export)
-f filename        Input or Output filename
-s servername      The server to bind to (Default to DC of computer's domain)
-c FromDN ToDN     Replace occurences of FromDN to ToDN
-v                 Turn on Verbose Mode
-j path            Log File Location
-t port            Port Number (default = 389)
-u                 Use Unicode format
-w timeout         Terminate execution if the server takes longer than the
                   specified number of seconds to respond to an operation
                   (default = no timeout specified)
-h                 Enable SASL layer encryption
-?                 Help

Export Specific
===============
-d RootDN          The root of the LDAP search (Default to Naming Context)
-r Filter          LDAP search filter (Default to "(objectClass=*)")
-p SearchScope     Search Scope (Base/OneLevel/Subtree)
-l list            List of attributes (comma separated) to look for
                   in an LDAP search
-o list            List of attributes (comma separated) to omit from
```

**Figure 2-36**    The ldifde utility from a command prompt

**EXAM TIP** Ldifde can be used to modify existing objects in Active Directory, but csvde cannot! Know this key difference.

# Troubleshooting Logons

As simple as logging on to a network is, there are situations that arise that prevent users from logging on to their computers and accessing network resources. Often, the user has entered their password incorrectly several times and has locked themselves out. For these situations, simply unlock their account as explained earlier in this chapter. Occasionally though, logon failures have nothing to do with a user entering the correct password. A couple of troubleshooting situations are detailed below.

## Computer Account Is Not valid

As part of the logon process, Windows Server 2003 Active Directory validates not only the user account, but the computer that the logon originated from. If the computer account is not found in Active Directory, or it has been disabled, the logon will not be valid. If the computer that the user is attempting to log on with is not part of the domain, but should be, you must join the computer to the domain before logons will be successful. To join a computer to the domain:

1. Log on to the computer as the local administrator.

2. Right-click My Computer and select Properties. Click the Computer Name tab and click Change.

3. Select the radio button for Domain and enter the domain name to join. You will also be prompted to enter a user name and password with administrative rights in the domain.

4. After the change is complete, you will be prompted to reboot the computer.

Windows 2000 and XP clients also use a discrete communication channel known as a secure channel to communicate with domain controllers. The channel's password is stored along with the computer account on all domain controllers. This password is changed every 30 days. If, for some reason, the computer account's password and the LSA secret are not synchronized, the Netlogon service logs one or both of the following error messages:

```
The session setup from the computer DOMAINMEMBER failed to authenticate. The name
 of the account referenced in the security database is DOMAINMEMBER$. The following
 error occurred: Access is denied.

NETLOGON Event ID 3210:

Failed to authenticate with \\DOMAINDC, a Windows NT domain controller for domain
DOMAIN.
```

To fix this problem and allow logons to resume from the client computer, you need to only reset the computer account. You can reset the computer account in Active Directory Users and Computers by right-clicking the computer account and selecting Reset, or you can use the netdom.exe command from a command prompt. To reset a computer account using netdom:

1. Open a command prompt.

2. Type the following:

```
netdom reset "machinename" /domain:"domainname"
```

### Domain Controller Cannot Be Found

Active Directory is highly dependent on DNS, and the failure to find a domain controller in order to log on is almost always a DNS error, probably on the client. If when the user attempts to log on, they receive an error that a domain controller cannot be located, check the client's TCP/IP settings first and make sure that the correct DNS address is entered. To check a client's TCP/IP settings, type **ipconfig /all** from a command prompt.

If the client has the correct DNS address entered in their TCP/IP configuration, check to make sure the DNS server is responding. To verify connectivity, use the ping command from a command prompt. As a general rule, ping both the IP address of the DNS server and the name of the DNS server if known.

If the client has connectivity and the DNS server is working, it is probable that the domain controller responsible for performing logons is unavailable. Not all domain controllers perform logons; only domain controllers that have been designated as Global Catalog servers perform logons. You may need to check with the domain administrator responsible to verify that an appropriate Global Catalog server is available and operable. For more information about Global Catalog server, please see Chapter 19.

When a successful logon occurs, the local computer from which the logon originated caches the credentials of the user for use in case of a domain controller being unavailable. If a user is logging on to a computer for the first time and is receiving logon failures, you should troubleshoot the failure starting with the DNS settings and working down to a possible domain controller failure.

# Domain Groups

Domain groups allow for user accounts within a domain to be collected into a group that can then be used to grant access to resources or to assign user rights. There are two types of domain groups: security groups and distribution groups. A security group is a security principal and so can be used to assign permissions and rights to a collection of user accounts. A distribution group is not a security principal and cannot be used to assign permissions. A distribution group is used for e-mail. It can be created when a mailbox is desired for a collection of user accounts, but no permissions will be needed. A security group can also be used to distribute e-mail, but it can be assigned permissions as well. The major difference between the two group types is that a distribution group cannot be used to assign permissions or rights and a security group can.

 **EXAM TIP** Watch the language on the exam. It is possible you'll see a question about why a member of a distribution group cannot access a resource. The simple answer is that a distribution group cannot be used to assign permissions or rights. The user attempting to access must be a member of a security group.

## Group Scopes

Within each type of group, there is a group scope. There are three possible group scopes, as shown in Figure 2-37:

- Domain local
- Global
- Universal

The language used to describe the different groups gets confusing. It is very common to refer to group types using the same names as are used for group scopes: domain local, global, and universal. Remember that even though we often talk about groups in this manner, domain local, global, and universal groups are actually the scope of either a security group or a distribution group.

Also, it is common to refer to a domain local group as a local group. Microsoft added the word "domain" to clarify between a local group in Active Directory and a local group on an individual machine. Just remember that when we are talking about a domain environment, a local group refers to a domain local group.

**Figure 2-37**
New Group dialog box showing group type and group scope

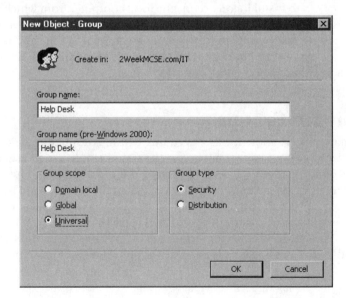

Each group has a different role and Microsoft has defined the groups so that each group plays a distinct part in the overall management of user accounts. Before getting into exactly how they all fit together, it is important to understand what each group does.

## Domain Local Group

A domain local group can contain users and global groups from any trusted domain. However, a domain local group cannot contain domain local groups or local machine groups. Domain local groups are primarily used to assign permissions to resources. (If the domain functional level has been raised, domain local groups can also contain domain local groups from the same domain. You will learn about this later in the chapter.)

## Built-in Domain Local Groups

Just as there are built-in groups on the local computer, there are built-in groups in the domain as well. User accounts and other global groups are added to the built-in local groups to grant specific user rights. The built-in local groups available in Windows Server 2003 are listed in Table 2-3.

| Group | Description |
|---|---|
| Account Operators | Can create and administer domain user accounts and groups. |
| Administrators | Have complete control over the domain. |
| Backup Operators | Can override security restrictions to back up or restore files and folders. |
| Guests | Has the same access as the Domain Users group. The Guests group can be further restricted. |
| Incoming Forest Trust Builders | Can create incoming, one-way trusts to this forest. |
| Network Configuration Operators | Can modify network settings on domain controllers, such as TCP/IP settings. |
| Performance Log Users | Can remotely view performance logs. |
| Performance Monitor Users | Can remotely configure and view Performance Monitor. |
| Pre-Windows 2000 Compatible Access | Has read access to all users and groups in the domain and the right to access domain controllers from the network. This group is included to allow NT 4.0 workstation users to function in a Windows 2000 or 2003 network environment. |
| Print Operators | Can administer printers in the domain. |
| Remote Desktop Users | Can log on to any computer in the domain remotely. Does not grant administrative privileges on the remote computer, only the ability to log on. |
| Replicator | Supports file replication in a domain. |
| Server Operators | Has rights to manage domain controllers. Can shut down the system, create shares, manage disks, and other administrative tasks on the server. |
| Terminal Server License Servers | Local group for Terminal Server license servers. |
| Users | Can run applications on local computers, but cannot install applications. Cannot log on locally to a domain controller |

**Table 2-3**   Windows Server 2003 Built-in Domain Local Groups

## Global Groups

Global groups are used to organize users. A global group can only contain users from its own domain. Use global groups to organize users by job description or function. Organizing users into global groups makes it easy to grant access to resources to a collection of accounts. After users have been added to a global group, the global group is then added to a local group. (If the domain functional level has been raised, global groups can also contain global groups from the same domain. You will learn about this later in the chapter.)

## Built-in Global Groups

There are also some built-in global groups. They are

- **DNS Update Proxy**  Members of this group are able to perform updates in DNS on behalf of other clients. When secure dynamic updates are enabled on DNS, the DHCP servers must be made members of this group to be able to update clients.

- **Domain Admins**  Members of this group have complete administrative rights in the domain. The Domain Admins global group is a member of the Administrators domain local group and all local Administrators groups on all workstations and servers in the domain.

- **Domain Computers**  All computers and workstations that have been joined to the domain are members of this group.

- **Domain Controllers**  All domain controllers are members of this group.

- **Domain Guests**  The Domain Guests group is used to grant access to resources to users who don't have a valid user account in the domain. The Guest account is a member of the Domain Guests group by default.

- **Domain Users**  All users are members of the Domain Users group. Domain Users are granted normal access to workstations in the domain and the domain itself. When a new share is created, the Domain Users group is granted the Read permission.

- **Group Policy Creator Owner**  Members of this group can create and manage Group Policy. The Administrator account is a member of this group by default.

## Universal Groups

A universal group can contain users, global groups, and local groups from any domain in the forest. It cannot contain users or groups from other domains outside of the forest. The purpose of a universal group is to organize users and groups across domains and to grant access to resources across domains. Even though universal groups can contain users, it is recommended to place only global groups into a universal group. The membership of a universal group must remain fairly static because any change to the membership of a universal group triggers replication to every Global Catalog in the forest, regardless of the size of the enterprise.

In order to use universal groups, the domain functional mode must be raised to Windows 2000 native mode or Windows 2003. By default, a Windows 2003 domain is created in mixed mode to allow for NT 4.0 servers to continue functioning alongside the new servers. Only when all servers have been upgraded to Windows 2000 or 2003 can the domain functional mode be upgraded to Windows 2000 or Windows 20003. After the domain functional mode has been raised, universal groups become available.

It may not be completely clear yet what the differences are between the groups and when you should use one or the other, especially universal groups. We will discuss how groups are implemented and how they work together in the next section.

## Built-in Universal Groups

There are two built-in universal groups: the Enterprise Admins universal group and the Schema Administrators universal group.

The Enterprise Admins universal group has administrator privileges for all domains in the forest. By default, the administrator in the root domain is the only member of the Enterprise Admins group and only the Administrator account can manage the membership of the Enterprise Admins group. Because the Enterprise Admins group is extremely powerful, membership should be tightly controlled.

Members of the Schema Administrators universal group are the only users that are able to modify the Active Directory schema. The Administrator account in the root domain is the only default member of the Schema Administrators group. Changing the schema is a complicated procedure and should not be done without careful planning and testing. Because the Schema Administrators group is extremely powerful, membership should be tightly controlled.

## Lab Exercise 2.4: Creating Groups and Adding Members to Groups

In this exercise, you will create a domain local group, a global group, and a universal group and add members to each of the groups. Before completing this exercise, you must have completed Lab Exercise 2.1: Creating a Domain User Account. You will use the account created in that exercise in the following exercise. You will also raise the domain functional level in the following exercise. For additional information on raising the domain functional level, see Chapter 20.

1. Select Start | All Programs | Administrative Tools | Active Directory Users and Computers.

2. Click the plus (+) sign next to the Sports domain to expand the Active Directory hierarchy.

3. Click the Users folder. The contents of the Users folder will be displayed in the right pane.

4. Right-click the Users folder and select New | Group from the drop-down menu, or select Action | New |Group, or click the New Group icon on the toolbar. All of these actions will open the New Object – Group dialog box.

5. Select the radio button next to Domain Local group under Group Scope and the radio button next to Security Group under Group Type. Enter **Folder Access** for the group name of the domain local group. Click OK.

6. Repeat step 4 to open the New Object – Group dialog box again.

7. Select the radio button next to Global under Group Scope and the radio button next to Security Group under Group Type. Enter **Help Desk** for the group name of the global group. Click OK.

8. Repeat step 4 to open the New Object – Group dialog box again.

9. Notice that the universal group is grayed out and not available. Before universal groups are available, the domain functional level must be raised to Windows 2000 native mode or Windows 2003. Cancel the New Object – Group dialog box.

10. Still using Active Directory Users and Computers, right-click your domain and select Properties.

11. On the General tab, click the drop-down list and select either Windows 2000 Native Domain Functional Level or Windows Server 2003 Domain Functional Level. Click OK to accept the change.

12. Close your domain properties.

13. Repeat step 4 to open the New Object – Group dialog box again.

    Select the radio button next to Universal under Group Scope and the radio button next to Security Group under Group Type. Enter **Company Help Desk** for the group name of the universal group. Click OK

14. Right-click the Help Desk global group and select Properties from the drop-down menu, or simply double-click the Help Desk global group to open the Properties dialog box.

15. Click the Members tab.

16. Click Add. The Select Users, Contacts, Computers or Groups dialog box will appear.

17. Enter **nbelloli** in the entry field, or click Advanced to search Active Directory for Nathan's user name

18. Click OK to close the Select Users, Contacts, Computers or Groups dialog box.

19. Verify that Nathan Belloli is present on the Members tab. Click OK to close the Help Desk Properties dialog box.

20. Repeat steps 14–17 on the Folder Access domain local group and add the Help Desk global group.

21. Verify that the Help Desk global group is present on the Members tab. Click OK to close the Folder Access Properties dialog box.

22. Repeat steps 14–17 on the Company Help Desk universal group and add the Help Desk global group.

23. Verify that the Help Desk global group is present on the Members tab. Click OK to close the Company Help Desk Properties dialog box.

24. To verify that Nathan was added as a member of the Help Desk global group, double-click Nathan's user account to open the Properties page, click the Member Of tab, and find the Help Desk group in the list.

25. To verify that the Help Desk global group was added as a member of the Folder Access domain local and Company Help Desk universal group, double-click the Help Desk global group to open the Properties page, click the Member Of tab, and find the Help Desk and Company Help Desk groups in the list.

## Granting Access Between Domains

Groups are created to simplify administration of user accounts as it relates to resources. If an enterprise has multiple domains, in order for a user in one domain to access a resource in another domain, there needs to first be a trust relationship created between the two domains. Once the trust relationship has been created, users from one domain will be able to access resources in the other domain.

When you are adding members to a group, if there has been a trust established, whether it is an automatic parent/child trust or an external trust, you will be able to see and add members from the trusted domain (see Figure 2-38).

## Trust Relationships

Trust relationships have evolved significantly since they were introduced back in the NT days. When trusts were first being implemented, it was a very simple model with one domain trusting another, and administrators in each domain were responsible for

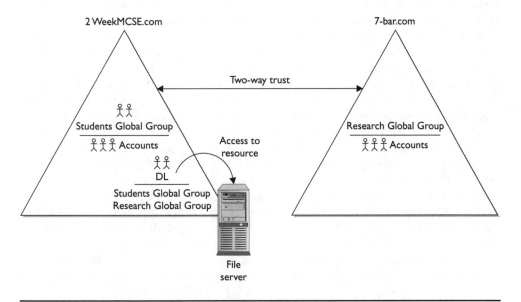

**Figure 2-38**   Granting access to users in different domains

maintaining their part of the trust. Windows 2000 introduced the two-way transitive trust. Windows Server 2003 takes the trust a step further with a forest trust and by enabling a single administrator to configure both sides of the trust.

 **NOTE** A transitive trust is a trust in which the two domains forming the trust not only trust each other, but other trusted domains as well. If domain A trusts domain B, and domain B trusts domain C, then domain A also trusts domain C.

When a user logs on to a domain, the DC validates the account and password and authenticates the user to the domain. Once authenticated, the user is able to access resources for which it has been granted throughout the domain.

If a user attempts to access a resource in another domain, the user is denied access because the user account has not been authenticated to the second domain and the resource does not have an entry that corresponds to the user in its ACL. For the user to be able to access the resource, it would be necessary to create a second account for the user and force the user to log on to the domain using this second account in order to be authenticated. This would be cumbersome and inconvenient to the user, especially if the user needed access to resources spread across several domains. To solve this problem, we use trusts.

A trust is set up between two domains and allows one domain to accept the other domain's authentication. When a user logs on to a domain, they are authenticated to that domain. If a trust has been established to a second domain, when the user attempts to access a resource in the second domain, the second domain accepts the authentication of the first domain and allows the user access to resources. It's almost like the scenario in which the little boy asks his dad for permission to ride his bike and the dad responds with, "If it's all right with your mom, it's all right with me." The dad will accept the mom's decision as to whether to allow the boy to ride his bike. If Mom says no, then Dad will also say no. If Mom says yes, then Dad also says yes.

Back in NT 4.0, there were no default trusts created, and each trust had to be manually set up by an administrator. Also, the trusts were one direction only. A domain could choose to trust a second domain, thereby allowing users from the second domain to access resources within its domain, but not the other way around. For access to be mutual, both domains had to set up a trust for the other domain. Windows 2000 changed all that. Within the same forest, every domain trusts every other domain. There is an inherent trust relationship created between a child domain and a parent domain or a root domain and the forest root domain. This relationship is transitive, which simply means that if domain A trusts domain B, and domain B trusts domain C, then Domain A trusts Domain C. In this way, a user in a domain is able to access a resource in any other domain in the forest, providing they have appropriate permissions. You can see this in action by opening the Active Directory Users and Computers snap-in and adding members to a local group. When you click Add, you will be able to browse any domain where there is a trust present and add user accounts from that domain.

The whole purpose of a trust is to make resources in one domain available in another domain. Trusts are automatically created between all domains in a single forest. Trusts can also be configured between domains outside the forest and, now in Windows 2003, even between two separate forests.

# How Groups Are Used to Grant Access to Resources

Okay, now you have groups and trusts and domain functional levels and users. So how does everything work together? First, you collect user accounts into global groups. By doing this, you are able to grant access to several people at once, rather than having to manually enter every user name on a resource. We said that global groups should be created by job description or job function. That's because users with the same job function have basically the same needs. All the secretaries on the executive floor need to have access to the laser printer at the end of the hall. It is much simpler to add the user accounts of the secretaries to a global group and then grant access to all the secretaries at once.

Now let's put a second laser printer on the floor and let's allow the accountants to also use the two laser printers. It is easier to add both the secretaries' and the accountants' global groups to a single local group and then assign the permissions to the local group.

To make it easy to remember what goes into what and where you assign the permissions, remember AGLP:

- Accounts
- Global groups
- Local groups
- Permissions

  1. Create user Accounts in the domain.

  2. Place user accounts into a Global group.

  3. Place the global group into a Local group.

  4. Assign Permissions on the resource to the local group.

## Windows 2000 and 2003 Group Rules

Now it gets a bit more complicated! If the domain functional level has been raised to Windows 2000 or Window 2003, then:

- Universal groups are available.
- Group nesting is available.

## Using Universal Groups

Let's use our example of the secretaries and accountants again. The secretaries and the accountants both belong to the CORP domain. In the enterprise, there is also a PDX domain. Both the CORP domain and PDX domain have secretaries and accountants. Each domain contains a file server where reports are stored. All the secretaries and the accountants in both domains decide that they want access to the file servers in both domains. You still could use the model of placing the secretaries and accountants into a global group, placing the global group into a local group in each domain, and granting permissions to the local group. But you could save yourself a bit of work by placing the two secretary global groups and two accountant global groups into one Universal group. Now the universal group can be added to the local groups and access granted.

## Using Group Nesting

In domains that have not had the functional level raised, group nesting is not available. Group nesting is the practice of placing a group into another group of the same scope, such as a domain local group into another domain local group or a global group into another global group. After the functional level has been raised, a domain local group can contain other domain local groups from its own domain and a global group can contain global groups from its own domain.

Group nesting allows several smaller groups to be placed into a larger group without having to reenter all the user accounts. For example, if a Headquarters group was desired, then all the departmental global groups at headquarters could be added to the Headquarters global group, saving the administrator from having to manually enter 400 user accounts.

Be careful when using group nesting, however. You should minimize the levels of nesting or it gets complicated. Only nest one or two levels. Also, choose group nesting only where not using group nesting would lead to a duplication of entries.

Universal groups are primarily used in large organizations. To make it easy to remember what goes into what and where you assign the permissions, remember AGULP when using universal groups:

- Accounts
- Global groups
- Universal groups
- Local groups
- Permissions

    1. Create user Accounts in the domain.

    2. Place user accounts into a Global group.

    3. Place the global group into a Universal group.

    4. Place the universal group into a Local group.

    5. Assign Permissions on the resource to the local group.

By using universal groups, you are able to grant access to many users to many resources across many domains. As a rule, it's a good practice to use universal groups when there is a many-to-many relationship. If you have users from many domains who need to access resources in many domains, use universal groups. If you have users from many domains who need to access resources in a single domain, don't use universal groups, stick with global groups and local groups.

# Chapter Review

In summary, there are two kinds of user accounts: local user accounts and domain user accounts. Local user accounts reside in the local database of the computer and are created and managed using the Local Users and Groups snap-in in the Computer Management MMC. User accounts are created to allow multiple users to access a computer. Local user accounts can be granted rights and permissions, which can then be used to access resources and to perform administrative tasks. Local user accounts are only used on a standalone computer or a member server. Local user accounts are not permitted to log on to a domain.

Domain user accounts are created using the Active Directory Users and Computers MMC. The Active Directory Users and Computers MMC can be opened by typing **dsa.msc** from a Run command or by navigating to the Administrative Tools on the Start menu. A domain user account is necessary to log on to the domain. Domain user accounts have numerous attributes that can be modified, and many additional attributes can be added to support applications like Exchange 2000. All attributes are searchable in Active Directory.

Users, computers, groups, and other objects can be added to Active Directory by using one of two bulk import tools. csvde imports comma-separated value text files into Active Directory. csvde cannot be used to modify objects already created. ldifde can be used to import text files into Active Directory and to modify objects already residing in Active Directory. The text files for ldifde are created using object names and attributes, and the file follows the Active Directory naming conventions, using distinguished names.

To grant access to users, you create groups and place the user accounts into the groups. Local groups are created on standalone computers and member servers. Domain groups are created using the Active Directory Users and Computers MMC and are much more powerful than local groups due to their scope. There are two types of domain groups: distribution groups and security groups. Distribution groups are only used for e-mail purposes and cannot be assigned permissions. To grant user access to resources, the user accounts must be placed into a security group. Domain local, global, and universal groups can be created for both types of group. Universal groups are only available if the domain is running in Windows 2000 native or Windows 2003 domain functional level. Universal groups can contain users, domain local groups, and global groups from any domain in the forest. Global groups can contain users from the same domain, and if the domain functional level has been elevated, can contain other global groups from the same domain. Domain local groups can contain users and global groups from any domain with a trust relationship established. Domain local groups are used to grant permissions on resources. Placing a global group inside of another global group is called group nesting and is only available when the domain functional level has been raised to Windows 2000 native or Windows 2003.

The method for creating a group infrastructure is AGLP: accounts are placed into global groups, which are placed into local groups that are assigned permissions. When the domain functional level has been raised and universal groups are available, then

AGULP can be used: accounts are placed into global groups which are placed into universal groups which are placed into local groups which are assigned permissions. Universal groups are primarily used in multiple domain environments, and every domain has to be running in Windows 2000 native mode or Windows 2003 mode for the universal group to work correctly.

## Questions

1. You are the administrator of a Windows 2003 domain. All domain controllers are running Windows Server 2003 and the domain functional level has been raised to Windows 2003. You are in the process of building a new domain controller, which you have named DCSERV. When asked for a password, you enter **dcserv**. You receive an error. What should you do to continue building the server?

   A. Log on to a different domain controller and modify the default domain policy to allow passwords of five characters. Disable the Require Complex Passwords option.

   B. Change the password to Dcserver9.

   C. Change the password to dcse9%rver.

   D. From a command prompt, type **net user dcserver9$**.

2. You are the administrator of a standalone Windows Server 2003 server. Daniel is your new junior administrator. You want Daniel to be able to back up files and folders, run programs, but not shut down the system. What should you do?

   A. Make Daniel a member of the Backup Operators group.

   B. Make Daniel a member of the Backup Operators group. In the local security policy, edit the User Rights node to deny Daniel the right to shut down the system.

   C. Make Daniel a member of the Administrators group.

   D. Make Daniel a member of the Power Users group.

3. You are the administrator of a Windows 2000 and 2003 network. The network is running in mixed mode. You have recently configured a Windows Server 2003 server as an RRAS server. You want to support VPN functionality for your users. You implement a remote access policy to allow access to all users for all days and times. You add the Authenticated Users group to the policy condition. Users are reporting that when they attempt to connect, the connection is denied after a short delay. What is the best solution to allow access to users?

   A. On the Dial-in tab of the User Properties, set the option to Allow Access.

   B. Raise the domain functional level to Windows 2000 native or Windows 2003. On the Dial-in tab of the User Properties, set the option to "Control access through remote access policy."

    C. Open the default domain policy. Click User Configuration | Administrative Templates | Network | Network Connections and disable the "Prohibit connecting and disconnecting a remote access connection" option.

    D. On the Dial-in tab of the User Properties, set the callback option to No Callback.

4. You are the administrator of a Windows Server 2003 network. The domain functional mode has been raised to Windows 2003. You are implementing a remote access configuration. You want the users to receive the same IP address every time they connect via remote access. You have been allotted enough IP addresses from your administrator for every user to have their own IP. How should you configure remote access?

    A. Create a scope on the DHCP server with the IP addresses. Reserve an address for each user who requires remote access. Configure the appropriate options. Also install the DHCP relay agent on the public interface of the RRAS server.

    B. Create a scope on the DHCP server with the IP addresses. Exclude an address for each user who requires remote access. Configure the appropriate options. Also install the DHCP relay agent on the public interface of the RRAS server.

    C. On the Dial-in tab of the User Properties, select to assign an IP address and enter an IP address in the available field.

    D. Create a scope on the DHCP server with the IP addresses. Create a user class with the appropriate options. Set the user class on each user's laptop to identify that user to the DHCP server.

    E. None of the above. You cannot assign IP addresses to users, only to computers using the computer's MAC address.

5. You are the administrator of a Windows 2003 forest. There are five domains in your forest. The root domain is running in Windows 2003 domain functional mode. The child domains are running in mixed mode. There are IT technicians in each domain who require access to a file server in the root domain. The local administrators of each domain have created a global group called ITTech and placed the user accounts of the technicians in the group. You need to grant access to the file server for the IT technicians in each domain. What should you do?

    A. Create a universal group in the root domain. Add the ITTech global group from each domain to the universal group. Create a domain local group in the root domain. Add the universal group to the domain local group. Assign permissions for the file server to the domain local group.

    B. Create a domain local group in the root domain. Add the IT technicians accounts from each domain to the domain local group. Assign permissions for the file server to the domain local group.

    C. Create a global group in the root domain. Use group nesting to add the ITTech global groups to the global group in the root domain. Create a domain local group in the root domain. Assign permissions for the file server to the domain local group.

**D.** Create a domain local group in the root domain. Add the ITTech global groups from each domain to the domain local group. Assign permissions for the file server to the domain local group.

6. You are the administrator of your company's network. The network is running Windows Server 2003, except for a small number of NT 4.0 domain controllers that haven't been upgraded yet. You have created a shared folder on a Windows Server 2003 member server. Giorgio is a member of the ITTech global distribution group. Giorgio attempts to access a folder on a file server, but he is denied access. You open the properties of the folder and review the Security tab. You notice that the ITTech group is not listed and Giorgio's user account is not listed. You also verify that Giorgio is not a member of any other groups. What is the most correct method to allow Giorgio to access the files?

**A.** Add Giorgio's user account to the ACL of the resource and grant the appropriate level of access.

**B.** Add the ITTech group to the ACL and grant the appropriate level of access.

**C.** Create a domain local group called Folder Access. Grant the appropriate level of access on the file server to the Folder Access group. Add Giorgio's account to the Folder Access group.

**D.** Create a universal group. Grant access permissions on the file server to the universal group. Add Giorgio's account to the universal group.

**E.** Change the ITTech distribution group to a security group.

7. You are in the process of prestaging computer accounts. The wizard asks for the GUID, but you can't find the documentation that came with the computer and the GUID isn't anywhere on the case. You attempt to PXE boot the computer, but the computer doesn't display the GUID on the startup screen. How can you proceed?

**A.** Create the computer account without the GUID. You can add the GUID later.

**B.** Capture DHCP discover packets to obtain the GUID.

**C.** Capture DHCP offer packets to obtain the GUID.

**D.** From a command prompt, type **ipconfig /all** and use the MAC address.

8. You have several users in your network who need access to multiple computers in the domain. You want those users to have the same settings no matter which computer they log on to. What should you do?

**A.** Implement mandatory roaming profiles on the User Account Properties in Active Directory Users and Computers.

**B.** Implement roaming profiles for all users in the domain using a Group Policy.

**C.** Create an OU and place the users who need the roaming profiles into that OU. Create a GPO named roam for that OU and assign the roaming profiles policy.

**D.** Implement roaming profiles on the User Account Properties in Active Directory Users and Computers.

9. You are the administrator of your company's network. All servers are running Windows Server 2003 and all client computers are running Windows XP Professional. The domain functional level has been raised to Windows 2003. Rebecca, the company nurse, complains that when she attempts to log on to the domain she receives the following error:

```
The session setup from the computer DOMAINMEMBER failed to authenticate. The name
of the account referenced in the security database is DOMAINMEMBER$. The following
error occurred: Access is denied.
```

You need to allow Rebecca to log on. What should you do?

A. Log on to Rebecca's computer as the local administrator and join the computer to the domain.

B. Log on to a domain controller using the Domain Administrator account and run the following command:

```
netdom reset "machinename" /domain:"domainname"
```

C. Log on to Rebecca's computer as the local administrator and reset the computer account.

D. Using Active Directory Users and Computers, enable the account for Rebecca's workstation.

10. You are the administrator of your company's network. All server are running Windows Server 2003 and all client computers are running Windows XP Professional. Kevin, a user, reports that he is unable to log on to his computer. When he attempts to log on, he receives an error that a domain controller cannot be found. You check the TCP/IP configuration of his workstation by using ipconfig. The results of your investigation are in Figure 2-39. What is probably the problem?

A. Kevin's computer is configured with an incorrect gateway.

B. Kevin's computer is configured with an incorrect WINS server address.

C. Kevin's computer is configured with an incorrect DNS server address.

D. The domain controller that Kevin logs on to has failed.

11. You are the administrator of a network running in Windows 2000 native mode. You need to create and configure several user accounts for new employees. You log on to the Windows Server 2003 domain controller and add a new user with a password of Password. You receive an error that states the computer is unable to create the account because it is unable to update the password. What should you do to be able to create the accounts?

A. Configure the local security policy of the domain controller and require complex passwords.

B. Configure the local security policy of the domain controller and disable the Require Complex Passwords option.

C. Configure the default domain policy and disable the Require Complex Passwords option.

```
Command Prompt                                                    _ □ ×

    Host Name . . . . . . . . . . . : test1
    Primary Dns Suffix  . . . . . . : 2WeekMCSE.com
    Node Type . . . . . . . . . . . : Unknown
    IP Routing Enabled. . . . . . . : Yes
    WINS Proxy Enabled. . . . . . . : Yes
    DNS Suffix Search List. . . . . : 2WeekMCSE.com

Ethernet adapter Local Area Connection:

    Connection-specific DNS Suffix  . :
    Description . . . . . . . . . . : Intel(R) PRO/1000 MT Network Connection
    Physical Address. . . . . . . . : 00-C0-9F-1E-F9-F9
    DHCP Enabled. . . . . . . . . . : Yes
    Autoconfiguration Enabled . . . : Yes
    IP Address. . . . . . . . . . . : 192.168.1.210
    Subnet Mask . . . . . . . . . . : 255.255.255.0
    Default Gateway . . . . . . . . : 192.168.1.1
    DHCP Server . . . . . . . . . . : 192.168.1.200
    DNS Servers . . . . . . . . . . : 192.168.1.210
    Primary WINS Server . . . . . . : 192.168.1.200
    Lease Obtained. . . . . . . . . : Tuesday, September 02, 2003 7:40:41 PM
    Lease Expires . . . . . . . . . : Wednesday, September 03, 2003 7:40:41 PM

C:\Documents and Settings\Administrator>_
```

**Figure 2-39**    ipconfig results of Kevin's computer

    **D.** Re-create the user account and use Basketball2% as the password.

    **E.** Re-create the user account and use a password that is unique in the domain.

12. You are the administrator of a Windows 2003 network. Your network includes four Windows Server 2003 servers that are used by several developers for testing purposes. The developers are all members of the Power Users group and the Developers global group. You want to allow the users to install hardware on the servers without granting them Administrator rights. What should you do?

    **A.** For the Power Users group, grant the right to load and unload device drivers.

    **B.** For the Developers group, grant the right to load and unload device drivers.

    **C.** Configure the driver signing options of the servers to install all files, regardless of signature. Apply the setting as the system default.

    **D.** Configure the driver signing options to prevent the installation of all unsigned files. Apply the setting as the system default.

13. You are the administrator of a Windows network running only Windows Server 2003 servers. Recently you have discovered that some junior administrators are remotely logging on to three file servers and performing incorrect configurations. The three servers are located at the headquarters in a secure location and are also in an OU named HQ Servers. The servers should only be administered by an administrator with access to the secure server room. The junior administrators should not be able to log on remotely to the servers. How can you prevent the junior administrators from being able to remotely administer the servers using the least amount of administrative effort?

A. Create a global group called JRADMIN. Make the junior administrators members of the JRADMIN global group. Create a local group called JRADMINACCESS. Add the JRADMIN global group to the JRADMINACCESS local group. On each of the three servers, deny the logon locally right to the JRADMINACCESS group.

B. On the System Properties of each server, uncheck the "Allow users to connect remotely to your computer" check box.

C. Place the three servers in a separate OU. Deny the logon locally right to all junior admins in a GPO and link the GPO to the domain.

D. Remove the junior administrators from the Administrators group. Make the junior administrators members of the Power Users group.

E. Create a global group called JRADMIN. Make the junior administrators members of the JRADMIN global group. Create a local group called JRADMINACCESS. Add the JRADMIN global group to the JRADMINACCESS local group. Configure the HQ Servers GPO to deny the "Access this computer from the network" right to the JRADMINACCESS group.

14. You are the Enterprise Administrator for the 2WeekMCSE.com domain. You install a Windows Server 2003 server and configure it as a file server. You create a folder and grant access to the folder to a domain local group named Folder Access. Later, you add a new domain named student.2WeekMCSE.com. Grady, a user in the student.2WeekMCSE.com domain, requests access to the folder. Grady is a member of a global group named Students. You want to enable access for Grady and the other members of the Students group with the least amount of administrative effort. What should you do?

A. Add all the user accounts requiring access to the Folder Access group.

B. Add the Students group to the Folder Access group.

C. Add the Folder Access group to the Students group.

D. Create a new global group in the 2WeekMCSE.com domain and add all the user accounts requiring access to the group.

E. Create a universal group in 2WeekMCSE.com and add all the user accounts requiring access to the group.

15. You are the administrator of a Windows 2003 network. James, a help desk technician, leaves the company. Michael, a new hire, will take James's place. You want Michael to have the same level of access that James had. What should you do?

A. Rename James's account to Michael. Reset the password.

B. Copy James's account and create a new account for Michael. Disable James's account.

C. Create a new account for Michael. Recreate the group membership of James's account to Michael's account.

D. Copy James's account and create a new account for Michael. Delete James's account.

## Answers

1. **C.** By default, the complex password policy is enabled for all domain controllers. The complex password requires that a password contain three out of four of the following: both letters and numbers, upper- and lowercase, special characters, no common words in the password. Also the password must be 7 characters or longer.

2. **B.** Daniel needs to back up files and folders, so you make him a member of the Backup Operators group. However, Backup Operators can shut down the system. If you edit the local security policy, you can explicitly deny Daniel the right to shut down the system.

3. **B.** Yes, this requires more administrative effort than simply allowing access, but it is recommended to control remote access through remote access policies.

4. **C.** The only way to assign an IP address to a user is through the Dial-in tab on the User Properties sheet.

5. **D.** Actually, several of these answers will work, but they don't follow AGLP. Global groups have already been created, so adding them to a domain local group and assigning permissions to the domain local group is simple. Because only the root domain has had the domain functional mode raised, you cannot assign permissions using a universal group. The global groups can be placed into the universal group in the root domain, but the permissions aren't effective until the domain functional mode is raised. Adding all the accounts to a domain local group would work, but it requires much more administrative effort.

6. **C.** Adding Giorgio's user account to the Folder Access local group doesn't follow classic Microsoft theory, but it is the most correct answer. Users should be placed into groups and granted access to resources at the group level. Even though our acronym of AGLP states to place accounts into global groups, placing accounts into local groups is possible, and it does meet the criteria of using groups to grant access to resources.

7. **B.** The GUID can be found in DHCP discover packets. The computer sends its GUID as part of the packet so that it can be issued an IP address.

8. **D.** Roaming profiles are enabled on the individual user account properties. To set the profile, navigate to the Profile tab on the User Properties and enter the network UNC where the profiles will be stored.

9. **B.** When the user receives the error that the DOMAINMEMBER failed to authenticate, the machine password and the LSA account are out of synch and the computer account needs to be reset. You can reset the computer account in Active Directory Users and Computers or by using the netdom command.

10. **C.** The DNS address on the ipconfig results screen is the same as the IP address of Kevin's computer. That is probably incorrect and would result in a domain controller not being found.

11. **D.** Windows Server 2003 requires that all domain user accounts be created with a complex password. Complex passwords require that the password use letters, numbers, uppercase/lowercase, special characters, and that common words not be used. Basketball2% works because it uses three out of the four, which is acceptable.

12. **B.** The developers lack the load and unload device driver's user right. Since they are in a Developers group together, grant the right to the Developers group.

13. **E.** The key is to use classic Microsoft theory of granting or denying access to a resource. Place users into a global group, then the global group into a local group, and then grant or deny access to the group. Using this technique ensures that new users added to the global group are able to access resources or denied access to resources without having to reconfigure the user access each time. Place the junior admins into a global group and call it JRADMIN. Create a local group called JRADMINACCESS and add the JRADMIN global group as a member. Then deny the "Access this computer from the network" user right to the local group.

14. **B.** A domain local group can contain users and global groups from any domain. The preferred method to grant access between domains is to place user accounts into global groups and then place the global groups into domain local groups.

15. **A.** Microsoft recommends renaming a user account to a new user when a user leaves the company. Renaming a user account retains all the user rights and permissions for the new user.

# Managing and Maintaining Access to Resources

**3**

In this chapter, you will learn how to
- Configure and troubleshoot NTFS permissions
- Configure and troubleshoot share permissions
- Use special (specific) permissions
- Transfer ownership of files and folders
- Create and manage shared folders
- Implement shadow copies
- Implement the Distributed File System (DFS)
- Solve permissions problems
- Audit access to resources
- Configure and troubleshoot Terminal Services
- Implement Terminal Services licensing
- Configure Terminal Services security

Managing network resources efficiently is one of the greatest challenges an administrator faces. Maintaining appropriate access to resources is an ongoing process, and unless some fundamental rules are followed, this process can become daunting and overwhelming. Also, the ways in which users now access resources have changed and new methods have emerged. Traditionally, users accessed files and folders either locally or as a simple share on a server. In addition to these traditional methods of access, users now more frequently access resources by using tools such as the Distributed File System (DFS), web services, and Terminal Services.

Not only have the methods changed, but the importance of securing resources has too. Bill Gates's famous memo in April 2002 outlined a strategy of increased security for all Microsoft products. Since that time, security has become a focal point in developing Server 2003, and many features have been changed or added to help increase the overall security of a Microsoft network. In this chapter, you will learn how to effectively secure network resources from users who should not have access.

You will also learn the fundamentals of how to provide secure access to files and folders in your network and how to streamline the process so that as needs change, your resource infrastructure will be able to adapt. Emphasis will be placed on managing entire hierarchies and folder trees as a unit and using groups to assign permissions rather than individuals. Also, you will learn how to implement DFS to make the process of locating resources for users easier, and how to implement and administer a Terminal Services environment.

# Implementing File and Folder NTFS Permissions

In Chapter 1, we discussed file systems and some of the various features of the NTFS file system in particular. Although all products still support FAT, NTFS is now the preferred format because of the file and folder level security features. In fact, with the retirement of Windows 95, 98, ME, and NT 4.0, all current Microsoft products now implement the NTFS format natively and it is the only recommended format. Files and folders created on NTFS formatted volumes can be secured using NTFS permissions.

NTFS permissions define what action a user can take on a file or folder. There is a unique permission for every action on a file or folder, and that permission must be explicitly granted to a user before that user can perform the action. There are no "assumed" permissions; either a user has permission to perform an action or they don't. For example, before a user can open a file and view the contents, that user must have the Read permission granted for the file. If the user has not been granted Read access, that user cannot open and read the file. Conversely, access to a file or folder can be explicitly denied. A user who has had the Read permission denied on a file or folder has no access to the file or folder. The specific permissions and how they should be set to allow or deny access is covered in the next section.

## ACLs and ACEs

When you hear the acronym ACL, you may visions of Jerry Rice writhing in pain with a torn ACL. Or possibly you have torn your own ACL, and your knee hurts just thinking about it. Understanding Access Control Lists (ACLs) is a completely different subject and usually a lot less painful! Understanding ACLs and their associated Access Control Entries (ACEs) is fundamental to understanding how access is granted to resources.

Every resource (in fact, every object within Active Directory) has an ACL that is accessed via the Security tab on the resource properties, as shown in Figure 3-1. The ACL is the list of security identifiers (SIDs) that have been granted or denied access to the resource. The ACL is made up of individual ACEs, with each ACE having either an allow or deny action. Users must have an ACE on the resource permitting access in order for them to be able to access the resource.

Every user has a unique SID assigned to them by the domain controller when the user account is created, and the SID is used to identify the user to resources. You don't usually see the actual SID because Windows resolves the SID to a name and presents the name as an ACE. When a user logs on to the network, the user account is authenticated and a ticket is generated that contains the user account's SID and the SIDs of the groups the user belongs to. The user's SID is checked against the ACEs on a resource's ACL (say that three times fast!) and if a match is found, the appropriate action is allowed. If there is no corresponding entry on the resources ACL, the user is denied access to the resource.

**Figure 3-1**

The Security tab of a folder with ACEs

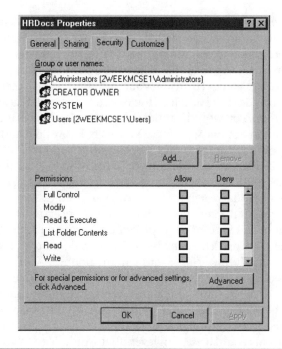

**NOTE** ACEs appear in the Security tab on the resource properties. Although user names and group names appear, the entries are actually security identifiers (SIDs) and are resolved to names to make them readable.

## Permissions

Permissions are assigned to the resource by using the ACL. Permissions either allow an action or deny an action. A deny action takes precedence over an allow action. A user who has been granted the Read permission on a file can open the file and read it. A user who has not been granted the Read permission cannot read the file. If a user has the Read permission set to deny instead of allow, the user doesn't have access to the resource. A deny always overrides any allow permissions, even if the user is part of another group that has been granted access.

Permissions are also usually assigned to groups rather than individual users, to make administration easier to manage. Remember the group discussion back in Chapter 2? User accounts are collected in global groups, which are collected into local groups and assigned permissions on the resource.

Think of the resource as the hottest nightclub in town—the Viper Room in Hollywood, for example—and you want to get in. You approach the bouncer and give the bouncer your ID. He checks your ID against his list that he carries in his jacket pocket to see if you have been granted permission to enter the club. If you aren't on the list, you aren't allowed in, and no amount of patience or bribery will get you in. Brad Pitt and Jennifer Aniston arrive, say hello to the bouncer, and walk right in. They have been granted permission to enter the club. In order for you to get into the club, someone has to place your name on the list and grant you permission to enter. You can ask the owner of the club to let you in (by using your individual user account), or you can be part of a party that includes Brad and Jen (the Brad and Jen global group). If you are part of Brad and Jen's group, you would be allowed in. So let's take the analogy a bit farther. One day you get a part in a movie with Brad. You get to know Brad and he likes you. Brad informs the owner of the club that you will be joining him for drinks that night, your name is placed on the list, and you are granted permission to enter the club. Now you are free to enter the Viper Room as often as you like. You get to hang out with the stars and enjoy life. But then one day you have a few too many and you cause a big scene and get thrown out. The owner of the club now informs the bouncer that you are not to be allowed back into the club, and your name is placed on a second list the bouncer carries in his coat pocket: the deny list. The deny list takes precedence over the allow list, so even if you show up to the club with Brad and Jen, the bouncer won't let you in.

Permissions are the same way. In order to access a resource, a user must have an entry on the ACL of the resource that grants access. The administrator or owner of the resource can grant the allow permission to your user name. Or you can belong to a group that has been granted access. Now life is good. You are able to access the resource as often as necessary. Situations could arise, however, that would lead to your user account or a group account that you belong to being denied access. If you belong to a group with a deny permissions entry, you are unable to access the resource, even if your user name is granted Full Control permission. A deny always takes precedence over an allow permission.

For example, when Scott attempts to access the Public folder on a file server, his credentials are presented to the resource for processing. The resource looks at the ticket containing Scott's SID and all the SIDs of groups that Scott belongs to and searches for a match in its ACL. If no match is found, Scott is not allowed to read the Public folder. If a match is found on the resource, Scott will be granted the appropriate access. In our example, Scott has been granted Read permission on the resource, so he is allowed to open the folder and view its contents. However, if he had been explicitly denied the Read permission on the Public folder, Scott would not be able to open and read the contents of the folder.

**EXAM TIP** When solving permissions problems, remember that deny always wins! No matter what other permissions have been granted, a deny will take precedence and no access is given. This is true even for administrators and the owner of the file or folder.

# NTFS Folder Permissions

NTFS folder permissions apply to a folder and the contents and subfolders within the folder. It is recommended that permissions be granted at the folder level simply because attempting to control access at the file level would become cumbersome. By applying permissions on a folder, all files and subfolders placed in that folder will have the same permissions as the parent unless permission inheritance is altered.

Also, it is recommended that access be controlled using NTFS permissions. Securing resources using NTFS permissions rather than share permissions is more secure. Share permissions do not always apply, but NTFS permissions always do. If a resource is secured using NTFS permissions, there is no back door available to access the files. The general NTFS permissions are

- Read
- Read and Execute
- Write
- Modify
- List Folder Contents
- Full Control

## Read

The Read permission is the most basic of all permissions and is assigned to users and groups when they simply need to view the contents of a folder but do not need to modify the contents in any way. The Read permission also allows users to view attributes of the folder, such as when the folder was created, whether the folder is encrypted or compressed, and the size of the folder.

## Read and Execute

The Read and Execute permission allows users to run programs within the folder as well as view the programs. If an executable file is placed into a folder but only Read access is granted, users will not be able to run the program.

## Write

The Write permission is granted on folders so that users can add files to the folder. The Write permission can be independent of the Read or Read and Execute permission; a user does not need Read permission to have Write permission. Allowing the Write permission by itself would allow users to create files in a folder, but would not allow them to view files created by other users. When a user creates a file, they become the owner of the file, and the owner of the file has Full Control permissions by default.

## Modify

When a user needs to edit files within a folder, the Modify permission must be set to allow. The Modify permission includes the Read, Read and Execute, and Write permissions and adds the ability to delete files. A user who has Read and Execute and Write permissions on a folder will be able to read files and write files, but will not be able to delete files.

## List Folder Contents

The List Folder Contents permission allows a user to view the contents of the folder and to navigate through the hierarchy to other folders, even if they don't have any other access on the subfolders. The List Folder Contents permission allows users to go through a folder to get to a subfolder. This permission only applies to folders, not files.

## Full Control

The Full Control permission includes all the other permissions and adds the ability to change permissions and take ownership of the folder. A user with Full Control permission on a folder will be able to grant access to other users for the folder.

## Applying Permissions

Permissions are cumulative in nature. Users often belong to several groups and it is very likely that a user will be granted access on a resource more than once by virtue of their group membership. In cases where multiple permissions are granted, the user receives the combination of all permissions. For example, Giorgio belongs to the Human Resources global group and the Fourth Floor Users global group. Giorgio is attempting to access a folder for which the Human Resources group has been granted the Modify permission and the Fourth Floor Users group has been granted the Write permission. Giorgio will receive the Read permission plus the Write permission, and will be able to read the contents of the folder and add files to the folder. He will also be able to edit files already in the file. Giorgio will not be able to delete the files because he doesn't have Modify or Full Control permission, which is needed to be able to delete files. If Giorgio had been granted the Read permission and the Modify permission, then he would be able to read files, add files, edit files, and delete files.

# NTFS File Permissions

The permissions for files are nearly the same as that for folders with only a few differences. Obviously, there is no List Folder Contents permission. Also the Read permission is just for reading a file, not subfolders. The most important difference? File permissions take precedence over folder permissions. Because of this difference, it is possible to secure a folder, but still leave some of the individual files easily accessible within the folder. For convenience, a summary of NTFS file permissions is included in Table 3-1.

| Table 3-1 | Permission | Attributes |
|---|---|---|
| NTFS File Permissions | Read | Assigned to users and groups when they simply need to view the contents of a file but do not need to modify the contents in any way. The Read permission also allows users to view attributes of the file, such as when the file was created, whether the file is encrypted or compressed, and the size of the file. |
| | Read and Execute | If the file is a program, the Execute permission is necessary to run the program. |
| | Write | Allows for changes to be made to the file. |
| | Modify | An accumulation of the Read and Write permissions, plus the ability to delete the file. |
| | Full Control | Permits all actions on the file, including taking ownership and changing permissions. |

# Share Permissions

NTFS permissions apply to files and folders, but for access to be granted to users over the network share permissions must also be configured. Share permissions are configured on folders only after they are shared. They only apply to folders and only when the folder is accessed over the network. Creating shared folders is explained later in this chapter, but share permissions are explained here because of the relationship between share permissions and NTFS permissions.

Share permissions are configured on a shared folder and apply only to folders, not files. Share permissions also only apply if a resource is accessed over the network. Most shared folders are created on file servers located in a secure server room, so share permissions must be configured in order for users to have access to the files and folders on the file server, even if NTFS permissions have already been configured. However, if a user is logged on interactively (locally), the share permissions do not apply. For this reason, it is recommended that share permissions are used simply to grant access to folders and the NTFS permissions are used to restrict access to files and folders.

---

 **EXAM TIP**   Be careful with permissions problems involving share permissions. If a problem states that the user is "logged on interactively," the share permissions do not apply and you must simply add up the NTFS permissions.

---

Share permissions are broader than NTFS permissions. For example, there is no Read and Execute permission on a share, only Read. There are three possible share permissions, which are displayed in Figure 3-2:

- Read
- Change
- Full Control

## Read

The Read permission on a share is roughly equivalent to the Read and Execute permission for NTFS. The Read permission also allows users to view attributes of the folder, such as when the folder was created and the size of the folder. Users can also view files and folders within the folder and run programs within the folder.

## Change

The Change permission on a share is also roughly equivalent to the Read and Execute permission for NTFS. The Change permission allows users all the permissions associated with the Read permission, plus the ability to add files and folders to the shared folder, and delete files and folders within the share.

## Full Control

The Full Control permission grants the user the Change and Read permissions on the share, plus allows the user to change share permissions on the share. The Full Control permission does not allow a user to change NTFS permissions.

**Figure 3-2**

Share permissions

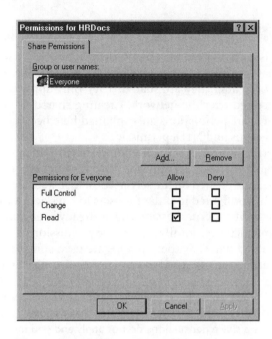

**Combining NTFS and Share Permission**

Most of the time, users are going to access a resource over the network. When resources are accessed across the network, both sets of permissions, NTFS and share, apply. In order for a user to be able to read a file, they must have at least Read NTFS and Read share permissions. A user that has been denied Read NTFS permission, but has been granted the Read share permission still is not able to access the file.

NTFS permissions apply to users whether they are logged on interactively (logged on locally) or over the network. Share permissions apply only to access over the network. It is important, both for the exam and for your real-world network, that you understand what permissions can be assigned, and what the relationship between NTFS and share permissions is.

When a user attempts to access a file or a folder from the network, both NTFS and share permissions are applied, and the most restrictive of the two becomes the user's effective permission. Remember that NTFS and share permissions are both cumulative. Add the NTFS permission together, then add the share permissions together. Then take the set of permissions that is most restrictive and that's what applies to the user. If a user has Read NTFS permissions, but no access from the share permissions, then the user has no access, because the share permission is more restrictive. If a user has Read share permissions, but no access from the NTFS permissions, then the user has no access.

When trying to troubleshoot an access problem, start with the share permissions, simply because they are probably easier to look at. There are fewer possibilities and there are no special (specific) permissions to worry about. Special permissions are explained in the next section. Determine what the share permissions are and then compare them to what effect the user is experiencing.

 **EXAM TIP** Best practice is to grant access at the share level and secure the resources at the NTFS level. NTFS permissions are more restrictive than share permissions and apply to all users, whether they are accessing the resource over the network or locally.

## Lab Exercise 3.1: Solving Permissions Problems

In this exercise, you will solve a permissions problem. In solving the permissions problem, remember the rules: All permissions are cumulative and then the most restrictive of the NTFS and share permissions apply.

Giorgio is attempting to access the HRDocs folder from across the network. Giorgio needs to read, edit, and delete documents in the HRDocs folder. He is a member of the Human Resources and Fourth Floor Users groups. The permissions that have been applied to the HRDocs folder are shown in Table 3-2.

What additional permissions does Giorgio need? How should he be granted the additional permissions? To find Giorgio's effective permissions, do the following:

1. Find the effective permissions for both NTFS and share permissions separately.

2. Select the most restrictive of the two.

3. Determine what additional permissions Giorgio needs.

Look at just the NTFS permissions first and add the permissions together for the groups that Giorgio is a member of. Since Giorgio is a member of both the Human Resources and the Fourth Floor Users groups, you need to combine the permissions for both groups. The Human Resources group has been granted the Modify permission and the Fourth Floor Users group has been granted the Read and Execute permission. Since the Modify permission includes the Read and Execute permission, Giorgio is granted Modify permissions for the NTFS folder.

Giorgio's share permissions are slightly different. The Read share permission has been granted to both the Human Resources and the Fourth Floor Users groups, so Giorgio only has Read access to the share.

| User/Group | NTFS Permission | Share Permission |
| --- | --- | --- |
| Administrators | Full Control | Full Control |
| Human Resources | Modify | Read |
| Fourth Floor Users | Read and Execute | Read |

**Table 3-2**   NTFS and Share Permissions for the HRDocs Folder

Now look at the two sets of permissions and decide which is more restrictive, the NTFS permissions or the share permissions. In this case, the share permissions are more restrictive because they grant only Read access, while the NTFS permissions allow Modify. If Giorgio attempts to access the resource from across the network, he will only be able to read the contents of the folder. Remember though, that share permissions only apply to network access. If Giorgio had physically logged onto the server, only the NTFS permissions would be applicable, and Giorgio would be able to read, write, edit, and delete the contents of the folder.

If the permissions were reversed, that is Giorgio was granted Change permissions on the Share but Read permissions for NTFS, the result would be the same. The most restrictive set of permissions would apply (the NTFS) and Giorgio would only be able to read the contents of the file. Remember, the most restrictive set of permissions always applies.

The easiest way to grant Giorgio the access he needs is to change the share permissions to Change for one of the groups Giorgio belongs to. But be careful: doing so may not be the best method. If Giorgio is the only member of the group who needs Modify permission, it would be better to grant the Modify permission to Giorgio directly. Changing the group's permissions would allow all members of the group to modify the files in the shared folder, which is an undesirable side effect.

# Special (Specific) Permissions

The NTFS permissions explained previously are general permissions. They are actually made up of specific permissions or special permissions. (There's really nothing "special" about them other than they are specific.) You can view the special permissions by accessing the Advanced Security Settings on a file or folder, as shown in Figure 3-3. To access these special permissions, open the properties of a file or folder, click the Security tab and then click the Advanced button.

To illustrate, the Read permission is comprised of the special permissions List Folder/Read Data, Read Attributes, Read Extended Attributes, and Read Permissions. Special permissions can be used when a more specific level of access is desired. For example, if you want to grant a group of users the ability to only read permissions of a folder without granting additional access, the Read Permissions special permission could be allowed. Most of the time, general permissions are adequate; however, special permissions are available and can be used under certain circumstances. The available special permissions are explained in Table 3-3.

 **EXAM TIP**   The most commonly tested special permission is the Take Ownership permission. In Windows 2003, ownership can now be given to another user, not just taken as was the case in Windows 2000.

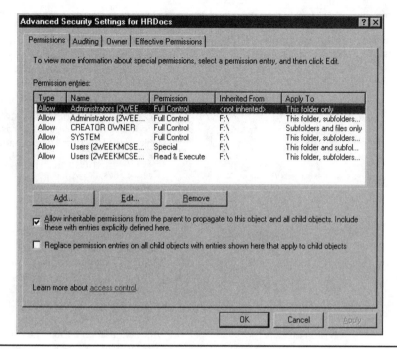

**Figure 3-3**  The Advanced Security Settings dialog box displaying special permissions

| Table 3-3 Special (Specific) Permissions | Special (Specific) Permission | What It Does |
|---|---|---|
| | Traverse Folder/Execute File | Traverse Folder allows a user to move through folders to reach other files or subfolders, even if the user has no permissions on the subfolders. Execute File allows a user to run program files. Setting the Traverse Folder permission on a folder does not automatically set the Execute File permission on all files within that folder. |
| | List Folder/Read Data | List Folder allows a user to view file names and subfolder names within the folder and only affects the contents of that folder. Read Data allows a user to view data in files. |

| Table 3-3 | Special (Specific) Permission | What It Does |
|---|---|---|
| Special (Specific) Permissions *(continued)* | Read Attributes | Allows a user to view the NTFS attributes of a file or folder, such as whether the file or folder is read-only, compressed, encrypted, or hidden. |
| | Read Extended Attributes | Allows a user to view the extended attributes of a file or folder. Extended attributes are defined by the programs in which the file was created, not the NTFS file system, and may vary by program. |
| | Create Files/Write Data | Create Files allows a user to create files within the folder. Write Data allows a user to write changes to a file. |
| | Create Folders/Append Data | Create Folders allows a user to create subfolders within the folder. Append Data allows a user to add data to a file, but not modify or delete any existing data in the file. The original data in the file may not be overwritten, but may be added to. |
| | Write Attributes | Allows a user to change the NTFS attributes of a file or folder, such as read-only, compressed, encrypted, or hidden. |
| | Write Extended Attributes | Allows a user to change the extended attributes of a file or folder. Extended attributes are defined by the programs in which the file was created and may vary by program. |
| | Delete Subfolders and Files | Allows a user to delete subfolders and files, even if the Delete permission has not been granted on the subfolder or file. If this permission has been granted, a user will be able to delete files and folders within the folder, as long as the Delete permission has not been explicitly denied on the folder or file. |
| | Delete | Allows a user to delete the file or folder. |
| | Read Permissions | Allows a user to read the permissions of the file or folder. The user must be granted the Change Permissions permission in order to modify permissions in any way. |
| | Change Permissions | Allows a user to change the permissions of the file or folder. By default, the owner of a file or folder has the Change Permissions permission granted. |

| Table 3-3 | Special (Specific) Permission | What It Does |
|---|---|---|
| Special (Specific) Permissions *(continued)* | Take Ownership | Allows a user to take ownership of the file or folder. The owner of a file or folder has the Change Permissions permission granted and can always modify permissions, regardless of any existing permissions. The owner can change the permissions on a file or folder, even if that user has been denied access to the file or folder. The only exception is encryption. The owner of a file or folder must have the correct public key/private key pair to decrypt the file or folder. |
| | Synchronize | The Synchronize permission only applies to multithreaded, multiprocess programs, not users and groups. |

# Assigning and Modifying Permissions

Microsoft provides a Security tab on all object properties dialog boxes to assign permissions. To assign and modify NTFS permissions on files and folders, use the Security tab on the properties of the file or folder, as shown in Figure 3-4. The Security tab shows the ACL and all ACEs.

**Figure 3-4**

The Security tab of the HRDocs folder

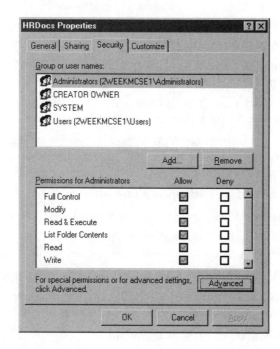

## Lab Exercise 3.2: Assigning NTFS Permissions

In this exercise, you will assign NTFS permissions to a user and then test the user's access to resource. If you have not completed Lab Exercises 2.1 and 2.3, please do so now. You will need to have created a valid user account and appropriate global and local groups in order to complete the exercise. You will use the user's account that was previously created to test NTFS security.

Also, it is required that the folder be created on an NTFS volume. Make sure that an NTFS volume is available. If you don't have a volume formatted with NTFS, use the Disk Management console and create an NTFS volume.

1. Log on to your computer using the administrator user account.

2. Click Start | All Programs | Accessories | Windows Explorer.

3. Click your Local Disk to select the root drive. Click File | New | Folder and name your folder **HRDocs**.

4. Right-click the folder, select Properties from the drop-down list, and select the Security tab from the HRDocs Properties dialog box.

5. Click Add and enter Folder Access as the group name.

6. For the Folder Access local group, check the appropriate boxes in the ACL to grant Read and Execute permissions to the group.

7. Log off and log back on as Nathan Belloli.

8. Double-click My Computer and navigate to the volume where the HRDocs folder is located.

9. Attempt to access the HRDocs folder. You should be able to read the folder.

10. Attempt to create a new folder within the HRDocs folder. You should receive an error that access is denied.

11. Right-click the folder and access the Properties of the folder. Attempt to compress the folder. Again, you should be denied access.

12. Click the Security tab. You will see a message stating that you can only read the permissions. When the ACL appears, the Add and Remove buttons will be grayed out.

13. Log off and log back on as Administrator.

14. Open Windows Explorer and navigate to the HRDocs folder.

15. Right-click the folder and select Properties to open the HRDocs Properties dialog box. Select the Security tab.

16. Click Add, and enter **Nathan Belloli** as the user name.

17. For Nathan's user account, check the appropriate box in the ACL to grant Nathan Full Control of the HRDocs folder.

18. Log off and log back on as Nathan.

19. Again, attempt to access the HRDocs folder. Verify that you have Full Control permissions on the folder by attempting to create and delete new files and folders within the HRDocs folder.

20. Right-click the HRDocs folder and click the Security tab. Verify that you can alter permissions.

In this exercise, you not only learned how to add permissions and modify permissions for files and folders, but you also saw firsthand how permissions are granted to a user with multiple permission entries. Nathan was able to modify all the attributes of the folder when his user name had been added and granted Full Control. He had only been granted Read access through his membership in the Folder Access local group. When a user belongs to more than one group, all the permissions are combined and the user receives the least restrictive of all the permissions.

## Lab Exercise 3.3: Assigning Special Permissions

There are situations when assigning special permissions is preferred over assigning a general permission. In this exercise, you will assign a special permission and then attempt access by using the user account previously created.

1. Log on to your computer using the administrator user account.

2. Click Start | All Programs | Accessories | Windows Explorer.

3. Navigate to the HRDocs folder.

4. Right-click the folder, select Properties from the drop-down list, and click the Security tab from the HRDocs Properties dialog box.

5. Click Advanced to access the Advanced Security Settings of the HRDocs folder, and click the Permissions tab to display all permissions on the folder.

6. Click Add and type **dkato** in the Enter The Object Name To Select box. Click the Check Names button to resolve Derek's user account. If Derek Kato's user name is not found, click the Advanced button and perform a search for Derek Kato in Active Directory. When Derek Kato's name is resolved, click OK.

7. The Permission Entry dialog box will appear. Grant the Allow permission to the Traverse Folder/List Data and the Create Folders/Append Data.

8. Select This Folder Only from the Apply Onto drop-down list, as displayed in Figure 3-5.

9. Navigate to the Public subfolder and open the Properties dialog box.

10. Click the Security tab to access the ACL.

11. Add Derek Kato's name to the ACL and grant Derek Full Control access to the Public folder.

12. Log off and log back on as Derek Kato.

**Figure 3-5**

Assigning special permissions

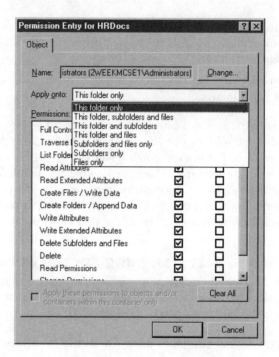

13. Double-click My Computer and navigate to the volume where the HRDocs folder is located.

14. Attempt to navigate through the HRDocs folder to the Public folder and create a new folder within the Public folder. Derek should be able to perform both operations.

## Transferring Ownership

By design, the owner of a file or folder always retains the Change Permissions permission, which ensures that the owner of a file or folder will always be able to access the file or folder, even if they have been denied access. (The owner first needs to change the permissions to allow access.) The creator of a file or folder is the default owner, but ownership can be transferred to other users. Previously in Windows 2000, ownership had to be taken by a user after they had been granted the Take Ownership special permission. New in Windows 2003 is the ability to grant ownership to a user. Ownership is transferred by using the Ownership tab of the Advanced Security Settings screen, as shown in Figure 3-6.

To view the current owner of a file or folder, right-click the folder and select Properties. From the file or folder properties, click the Security tab and then click Advanced

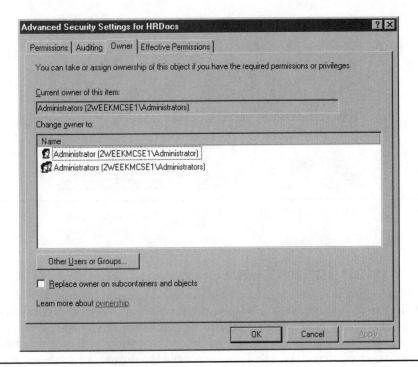

**Figure 3-6**    Transferring ownership

to open the advanced options. Click the Ownership tab to display the current owner and to change ownership. Notice that the user name of the currently logged-on user is displayed in the Change Owner To field. Below the box is a button marked Other Users or Groups. Clicking this button brings up the Select User, Computer, or Group screen that you should be familiar with by now. (See Figure 3-7.) You are able to search and select any user in the forest to be the new owner of the file or folder. Before clicking Apply, decide whether you want the user to be the new owner of all subfolders and files or just the file or folder you have selected.

To take ownership, you must have Full Control permission on the file or folder or have the Take Ownership special permission. To grant ownership to another user, you must have the restore files and directories user right. User rights are different from permissions because user rights generally refer to actions a user performs, not access. An example of a user right is the right to log on locally to a computer. By default, administrators, server operators, and backup operators have this right. Changes to this user right must be performed using Group Policy. For more information on Group Policy, see Chapter 22.

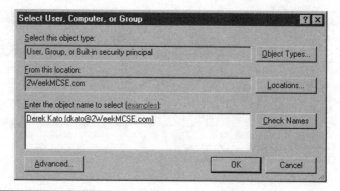

**Figure 3-7**    Select User, Computer, or Group

# Permission Inheritance

It would be impractical and cumbersome to have to manually enter permission entries for all files and folders on a server. To solve this problem and to make administration of resources easier, all files and folders inherit the permissions that have been applied to the parent folder. This is true even of the first folders that are created on a volume. When a volume is created, default permissions are assigned to the root volume, and each subsequent folder created on the volume inherits the default permission attributes from the root. Any change in the permission entries on the root folder impact the entire folder hierarchy within the volume.

You can use permission inheritance to your advantage. When setting up the folder hierarchy, if you create permissions entries on a root folder, you can then automatically have those permissions applied to all subfolders. If you decide at a later date to make a change to the folder hierarchy, you can make the change at the root and have the change propagated throughout the folder hierarchy. When a permission is applied to a specific user for a folder, that permission is also granted to all subfolders as well. The inherited permissions of a folder show up as grayed out, as in Figure 3-8.

When viewing the Security properties of a file or folder, there will generally be two types of permissions present. You will see permissions that have been inherited from the parent folder, and these will be grayed out and not allow you to make any changes to them. You will also see permissions that have been explicitly assigned to the file or folder. These permissions can be altered or removed. Explicitly assigned permissions on a folder become inheritable permissions on any child file or folder, unless the child file or folder has blocked permission inheritance.

It is not only possible, but probable, that folders and files will have a combination of inheritable permissions and explicitly assigned permissions.

**Figure 3-8**
Viewing inherited
permissions

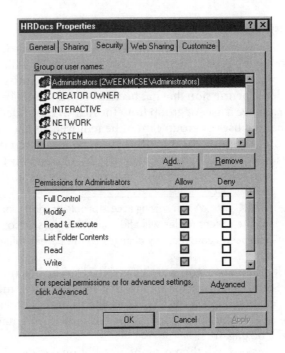

## Default Permissions

In previous versions of Windows, the Everyone group was granted the Full Control – Allow permission on the root of the volume. The Everyone group includes everyone who accesses a resource, whether that user is authenticated to the network, logged on as a guest, or a user from the Internet. By virtue of the Everyone group being granted Full Control access on the root drive and thereby being inherited to all folders on the drive, anyone could then access folders and files on a server by default. The Everyone group was assigned the Full Control – Allow permission for backward compatibility to ensure that programs installed under the old FAT file system would run when converted to NTFS. However, the risk of unwanted access outweighs the gain of backward compatibility, and the Everyone group has now been granted only Read and Execute permissions on the root of the drive. The Domain Users group has been added and granted Read, Read and Execute, and List Folder Contents permissions on the root drive.

**EXAM TIP**   Remember that the Everyone group is no longer assigned Full Control by default. So when solving permissions problems, be careful that you don't remove the Everyone group as you had to in previous versions of Windows. Now all that has to be done is users or groups need to be assigned the appropriate permissions.

## Blocking Inheritance

Inherited permissions appear on the Security tab of the file or folder, but are grayed out and cannot be modified. There are many situations in which the permissions that are needed for a particular folder are in conflict with the permissions already present on the parent folder. A permission that has been inherited cannot be altered or removed. If you attempt to remove a user or group from the ACL of the folder, you will receive a security warning that the user or group cannot be removed, as shown in Figure 3-9. You must then turn off the option for inheriting permissions, or remove the user or group from the parent folder's ACL. It is not always possible or desirable to remove the user or group from the parent folder, so removing inheritance is generally preferable.

**EXAM TIP**   When solving access problems, don't forget that a permission added to the parent folder will affect all subfolders. Also, if permission inheritance has been removed, any changes to the parent folder will not affect subfolders.

To block inheritance, you simply need to clear the box on the Permissions tab of the Advanced Security Settings dialog box that states to allow inheritable permission from the parent, as shown in Figure 3-10. Once inheritance is blocked, the folder will no longer receive any permissions from the parent folder. Inheritance can be added back by checking the box again.

Clearing this box will then prompt an additional response, as shown in Figure 3-11. You will then need to specify whether to remove the inherited entries or copy the inherited entries to the folder.

## Removing Permission Entries

If you choose to remove permission entries, all permissions that were inherited are completely removed and only explicit permissions remain. This completely removes the entries from the ACL and only permissions that have been directly applied to file or folder remain. Removing permissions is preferred when the inheritable permissions are not desired, only explicit permissions.

## Copying Permission Entries

If you choose to copy the permission entries, all permissions that were inherited are copied to the file or folder and become explicit permissions. When you copy permissions, the ACL doesn't look like anything changed, only the grayed-out portion of the entries changes and allows you to then modify permissions.

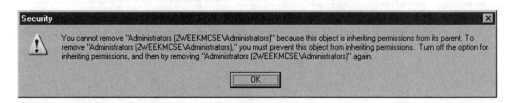

**Figure 3-9**   You cannot change inherited permissions.

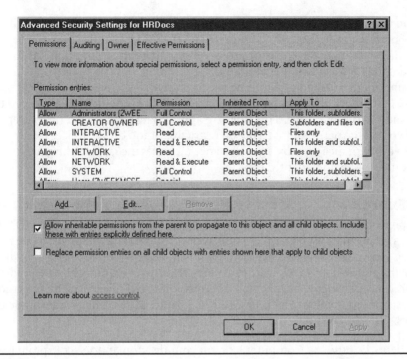

**Figure 3-10**   Blocking inheritance

Removing the inheritable permissions only removes inheritance from that particular folder or file. If you have a folder tree that you are administering, and you remove inheritance from the top-level folder, only the permissions on the root drive will not be inherited. Any folder that is a subfolder of your top-level folder will still inherit permissions from the top-level folder, and any subfolders of the subfolders will inherit their permissions, and so on and so forth. Removing inheritance severs a folder from the folders higher up the hierarchy and creates two points at which the folder hierarchy needs to be administered.

**Figure 3-11**
Copy or Remove
permission
entries

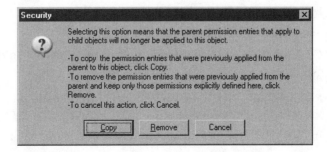

If you want to add a permission entry for the entire folder hierarchy, you will need to add the permission on both the root drive and the folder that has inheritance blocked. Any changes you make to the root drive will not affect the folder that has inheritance blocked or any folders below that folder.

It is important to set permissions on the root drive correctly to avoid access problems later on. Remember, the permissions that are set on the root drive are inherited to every folder and file on that drive. This is where appropriate settings can have a serious impact. If you set the permissions to be too restrictive or too broad, the temptation is there to remove inheritance. Removing inheritance increases the task of administering folders and should not be done lightly.

## Lab Exercise 3.4: Setting Permissions on the Root Drive

In the previous exercise, you created a new folder, HRDocs, and assigned NTFS permissions to a group and a user. In this exercise, you will set NTFS permissions on the root drive and then view permissions as they are inherited to folders located on the root drive. You will test the permissions to make sure that they are inherited throughout the folder hierarchy, and you will remove the inheritable permissions from subfolders. Before proceeding, you must have completed Lab Exercises 2.1, 2.3, and 3.2. If you have not completed these exercises, please do so now.

1. Right-click the My Computer Icon on your desktop and select Explore from the menu.

2. In Windows Explorer, right-click the D drive you created earlier and select Properties.

3. From the D drive Properties dialog box, click the Security tab to show the drive's ACL.

4. Click Add to open the Select Users dialog box.

5. In the Select Users dialog box, type **Help Desk** and click the Check Names button to resolve the Help Desk global group. Click OK.

6. Check the Allow Full Control check box to grant the Full Control permission to the Help Desk group.

7. Click OK to close the Drive D Properties dialog box.

8. In Windows Explorer, click File | New | Folder.

9. Name the folder **Web**.

10. Click the Web folder to select it and click File | New | Folder.

11. Name the folder **Graphics**.

12. Right-click the Web folder in Windows Explorer and select Properties to open the Web Properties dialog box.

13. In the Web Properties dialog box, click the Security tab to show the ACL.

14. Verify that the Help Desk group has Full Control access to the Web folder and that the check boxes are grayed out.

15. Close the Web Properties dialog box and repeat the verification process on the Graphics folder.

# Viewing a User's Effective Permissions

Windows 2003 has implemented an easy method for an administrator to view a user's effective permissions on a file or folder (see Figure 3-12). To view a user's effective permissions:

1. Right-click the file or folder desired. Select Properties.

2. From the file properties dialog box, click the Security tab and click the Advanced button.

3. In the Advanced Security Properties, click Effective Permissions.

4. Click Add to add a user and view the effective permissions.

**EXAM TIP**   It is doubtful that Microsoft would allow you access to this tool on the exam. Know how to solve permissions problems manually!

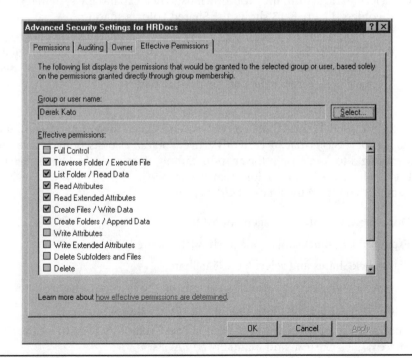

**Figure 3-12**   Viewing a user's effective permissions

# Creating and Managing Shares

Storage has evolved and currently almost all resources have been migrated to file servers and accessed by users over the network. Before a resource can be accessed by network users, it must be shared. Shares can be created from the Shared Folders snap-in, in Windows Explorer, by using the Manage Roles Wizard, or at the command prompt. Microsoft recommends using the Shared Folders snap-in, which is a component of the Computer Management MMC.

To manage share permissions, simply access the Sharing tab from the folder properties on an existing share. Share permissions are managed the same way that NTFS permissions are, only there are no special permissions and inheritance cannot be blocked.

**EXAM TIP**  Although the method you use is entirely up to you, you need to know how to manage shares from the MMC that Microsoft provides for the exam.

## Creating and Managing Shares from the Shared Folders Snap-In

The Shared Folders snap-in is part of the Computer Management MMC and is located under the System Tools node. To access the Shared Folders snap-in, right-click My Computer and select Manage from the drop-down list. Then expand the system tools and select Shared Folders. Figure 3-13 shows the Shared Folders snap-in.

**NOTE**  The Shared Folders snap-in can also be added to a custom MMC by itself without the Computer Management MMC, and can also be used to manage shared folders on remote computers.

Using the Shared Folders snap-in, you can view all shared folders on the computer, and any open files or sessions that are currently active. You can also disconnect users and send console messages to users using the snap-in. Simply right-click the Shares, Sessions, or Open Files node to see a list of actions that can be taken.

To create a share from the Shared Folders snap-in:

1. Open the Computer Management MMC.

2. Expand the System Tools node to show the Shared Folders.

3. Right-click Shares and select New File Share.

4. Browse to the folder you want to share using the Browse button.

5. Name the shared folder and enter a description if desired.

6. Choose the appropriate level of basic access. To modify the ACL of the share directly, click Custom and manually add ACEs.

7. Click Finish.

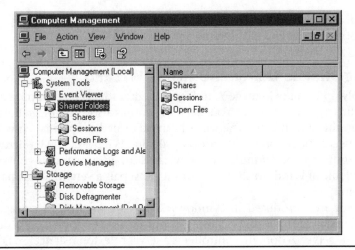

**Figure 3-13**    The Shared Folders snap-in

You can also use the Shared Folders snap-in to modify the permissions of existing shared folders. To modify an existing shared folder:

1. Open the Computer Management MMC.

2. Expand the System Tools node to show the Shared Folders.

3. Right-click a share and click Properties from the drop-down menu.

You will also notice additional options, such as configuring offline caching and adding comments. These additional settings can be configured from either the Shared Folders snap-in or from the Sharing tab of the folder properties. You will learn to configure these additional settings later in the chapter.

## Creating Shares from Windows Explorer

The most common method of creating shared folders is to use Windows Explorer. To create a shared folder from Windows Explorer:

1. Open Windows Explorer.

2. Navigate to the folder you want to share.

3. Right-click the folder and select Sharing And Security.

4. Select Share This Folder and give the share a name.

5. To modify share permissions, click Permissions.

6. To modify the offline caching properties, click Caching.

The properties of the share can be modified in Windows Explorer by opening the properties of the folder and clicking the Sharing tab.

## Creating Shares Using the Roles Wizard

You probably noticed the Manage Your Server Wizard that keeps popping up whenever you start your server. The Manage Your Server Wizard is also available in the Administrative Tools on the Start menu. (The wizard can be turned off permanently by a simple click.) In between the releases of Windows 2000 and Windows 2003, Microsoft had the time and resources to add a multitude of wizards for administrative convenience. The wizards available in Windows 2003 are for the most part a very welcome part of the operating system.

Server roles are introduced in Windows 2003 as a method to configure a server quickly and easily. A server role is simply a common set of applications or tasks combined into one server. A domain controller is a server role, for instance. So is a file server. You can use the wizard with the appropriate server role to configure the server, and in the case of the file server, add shared folders.

### Lab Exercise 3.5: Creating a Shared Folder Using the Manage Your Server Wizard

In this exercise, you will use the Manage Your Server Wizard to configure shared folders on your server. There are many additional tasks you can perform using this wizard. We are going to just stick with the shared folders. Notice that several roles can be placed on one server and the roles can all be administered from the Manage Your Server Wizard. Of course, you can always do things manually, and that's usually the best way to learn how to administer a server, but the wizards give you a head start in configuring a server.

1. Click Start | All Programs | Administrative Tools | Manage Your Server to open the wizard if it's not already open.

2. The Manage Your Server Wizard will show all current roles on the server. Your server should show that it is a domain controller and a file server. If the file server role is not showing, click Add A Role and configure your server as a file server.

3. Click Manage This File Server.

4. The File Server Management MMC, shown in Figure 3-14, will appear, enabling you to manage your shared files, defragment your drive, and perform disk management functions all in one MMC. You will also see tasks listed to add a shared folder, run a backup, send console messages, and configure shadow copies.

5. Close the File Server Management MMC.

6. In the Manage Your Server Wizard, click Add Shared Folders.

7. The Share A Folder Wizard appears. Click Next.

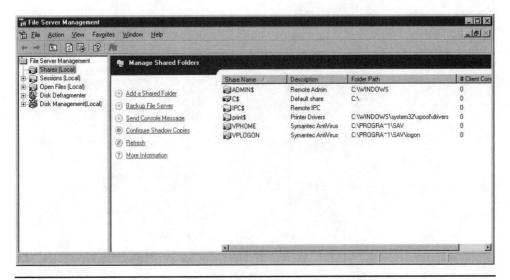

**Figure 3-14**  The File Server Management MMC

8. Browse to the HRDocs folder on your server and select to share it, as shown in Figure 3-15.

9. Give the share a name and a description.

10. Click Change and set the option to "files or programs from the share will not be available." Click OK.

11. Click Next and configure the permissions so that administrators have full access, and other users have Read Only access. Click Finish.

12. You can select to run this wizard again to share another folder or just click Close.

In this exercise, you actually used the Share A Folder Wizard that is also available on the Shared Folders snap-in. You would use the same procedure to share a folder from the Shared Folders snap-in as you did in this wizard.

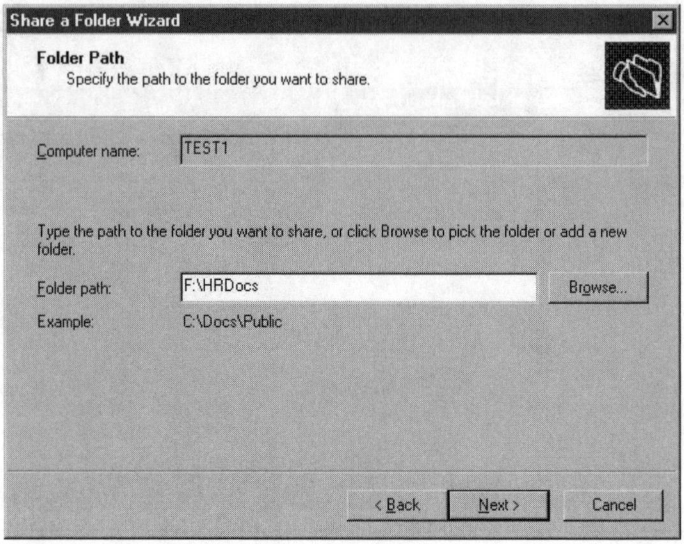

**Figure 3-15**
Share the
HRDocs folder

Share a Folder Wizard

**Folder Path**
Specify the path to the folder you want to share.

Computer name:    TEST1

Type the path to the folder you want to share, or click Browse to pick the folder or add a new
folder.

Folder path:    F:\HRDocs                                    Browse...

Example:    C:\Docs\Public

< Back    Next >    Cancel

## Creating Shares Using the Command Line

Shares can be created by using the command line as well. To create a share using the command line, click Start | Run, type **cmd**, and press ENTER to open the command prompt. From the command prompt, enter the following:

```
NET SHARE Web Graphics=c:\Web\Graphics /remark:"Folder for Web Graphics"
```

To remove the share, enter

```
NET DELETE Web Graphics
```

**NOTE**   The net command is very powerful and there is a wide variety of tasks that can be performed using the command. To see a list of all available net commands, type **net** from a command prompt. To view help on each command, type **net help** *command*.

## Sharing Folders Using Web Sharing

Folders can now be shared as a web folder and accessed through Internet Explorer or another browser such as Opera (http://www.opera.com/) or Netscape (http://www.netscape.com/). Internet Information Server (IIS) must be installed before web sharing is available, however, IIS is not installed on Windows 2003 by default. For more information on installing and configuring IIS, see Chapter 4. For web folders to be displayed correctly, the directory browsing permission has to be enabled on either the folder properties or the virtual folder location on the Internet Information Services.

To enable web sharing, right-click the folder you want to share and select Properties. Click the Web Sharing tab and select the option to Share This Folder. You will be prompted to configure appropriate permissions. Select Directory Browsing and Read for the permissions and click OK. Click OK again to close the Properties dialog box.

 **EXAM TIP**  If Directory Browsing is not enabled, only .htm and .asp files will display correctly. Users will receive an error that they are not authorized to view the web page. This error has nothing to do with anonymous logons or authentication. The Directory Browsing permission allows users to view the contents of the web folder, including all files and subfolders.

Use web sharing with discretion. Yes, it is an easy way to share files and folders, and almost all users are familiar with using a browser, but often the risks outweigh the benefits. IIS is the most heavily attacked service by hackers. Web sharing is a feature of Windows 2003 and so is fair game on the exam, however, very few businesses implement web sharing because of the risks associated with it. If you are looking for a way to make shared folders easier for users to access, try using the Distributed File System (DFS). DFS is discussed later in this chapter.

## Offline Caching

All Windows client operating systems and servers have an offline files feature built in. Enabling offline files allows network resources to be cached locally on the client computer and accessed even if the network resource becomes unavailable or if the client disconnects from the network. Using the offline files feature allows users to access network resources on their computers when they are away from the office or otherwise not on the network.

Before a folder can be configured for offline use by the client, offline caching needs to be configured on the actual network resource, as shown in Figure 3-16. By default, offline caching is enabled when a share is created. If you don't want to allow users to cache the contents of the shared folder on their local hard drives, you must disable offline caching.

There are three configurable options for offline caching, as shown in Table 3-4.

**Figure 3-16**
Configuring offline caching options

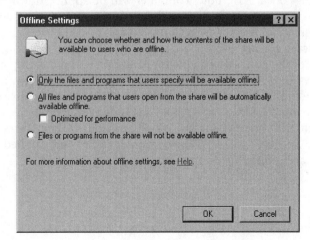

| Table 3-4 Offline Caching Settings | Caching Setting | Explanation |
|---|---|---|
| | Manual Caching of Documents | Users specify which documents to cache and make available offline. Any document opened by the user is automatically made available offline. |
| | Automatic Caching of Documents | All documents in the folder are cached on the user's computer and made available offline. |
| | Automatic Caching of Programs and Documents | Allows applications normally run from the network to be cached on the user's computer and run locally. |

Before configuring caching settings, review your users' needs. Offline files are a nice feature for users, and when used correctly, can help mobile users work more efficiently. However, offline files can be used inappropriately and can lead to confusion. Versioning can be a problem if the files made available are frequently accessed and changed by users. Windows does keep track of file versions and prompts users at synchronization if the file has changed since they downloaded the file, but users can save the file back to the server and overwrite other changes. In these situations, it is recommended to disable offline caching completely.

## Group Policy Settings for Caching

Client settings for offline files can also be controlled in Group Policy. Group Policy will be completely explained in Chapters 22 and 23. A short explanation of the types of settings that can be controlled using Group Policy is included here.

Group Policies either apply to computers or users. Some settings only apply to computers, such as account policies, and some settings only apply to users, such as desktop settings. Caching and offline files can be applied to both computers and users. Any policy settings on the computer container will be applied during bootup, and any policy settings on the user container will be applied at logon. This subtle difference can make the difference between a policy only affecting certain users and a policy affecting every computer in the network.

Most of the policies available for offline files and caching options were available in Windows 2000. Using Group Policy, the size of the cache and synchronization options could be configured in a GPO and then applied to all users in a site, domain, or organizational unit. Windows Server 2003 has added several policy settings to the Offline Files setting in the Computer and User nodes of Group Policy. The new policies are displayed in Table 3-5 and Table 3-6. The computer settings are applied at bootup and the user policies are applied at logon.

| Table 3-5<br>New Offline<br>Settings for the<br>Computer Node<br>of Group Policy | Computer Setting | Explanation |
|---|---|---|
| | Allow or disallow use of the offline files feature (enabled) | This was previously the Enabled setting. Turns offline files on or off as desired. If the setting is disabled, the Make Available Offline setting in Windows Explorer is disabled. |
| | Synchronize all offline files when logging on | Initiates a synchronization when the user logs on to the computer. If this setting is configured, it also disables the "Synchronize all offline files before logging on" setting in the Synchronization Manager so that users cannot override the settings. |
| | Synchronize offline files before suspend | Synchronizes offline files before the computer enters suspend mode. Setting the action to quick ensures only that files in the cache are complete. Setting the action to full forces a full synchronization and all files are brought up to date with the current version on the server. Entering suspend by closing the display on a laptop does not initiate a synchronization. |
| | Encrypt the offline files cache | Encrypts the client-side cache (CSC). The CSC is located on the %systemroot% directory on client computers. The CSC is indexed and the files are saved in binary mode, but can be opened if the appropriate application is used. Encrypting the cache ensures that offline files can only be accessed by the appropriate user. |
| | Prohibit Make Available Offline for these files and folders | Removes the Make Available Offline command from the drop-down menu in Windows Explorer. If the folder has been shared and caching configured as Automatic Caching the files are automatically cached and made available to the user. |
| | Configure slow link speed | Use this setting to configure a threshold below which the connection will be treated as "slow." If a slow connection is detected, the client will not reconnect to the server and attempt a synchronization until the connection exceeds the slow link threshold. |

## Lab Exercise 3.6: Configuring Offline Settings in Group Policy

In this exercise, you will configure several offline settings in Group Policy. Group Policy will be discussed in greater detail in Chapters 22 and 23. You will not test the settings that you configure in this exercise. If you would like to test the configurations, you will need at least one client computer, a domain controller, and a valid user account for the

| Table 3-6 | User Setting | Explanation |
|-----------|--------------|-------------|
| New Offline Settings for the User Node of Group Policy | Synchronize all offline files when logging on | Initiates a synchronization when the user logs on to the computer. If this setting is configured, it also disables the "Synchronize all offline files before logging on" setting in the Synchronization Manager so that users cannot override the settings. |
| | Synchronize offline files before suspend | Synchronizes offline files before the computer enters suspend mode. Setting the action to quick ensures only that files in the cache are complete. Setting the action to full forces a full synchronization and all files are brought up to date with the current version on the server. Entering suspend by closing the display on a laptop does not initiate a synchronization. |
| | Prohibit Make Available Offline for these files and folders | Removes the Make Available Offline command from the drop-down menu in Windows Explorer. If the folder has been shared and caching configured as Automatic Caching the files are automatically cached and made available to the user. |
| | Do not automatically make redirected folders available offline | Redirected folders such as My Documents, Start Menu, Application Data, and Desktop are not automatically available offline. By default, redirected folders and all subfolders are cached and made available offline. If this setting is enabled, users must manually configure those folders that they want to cache for offline use. |

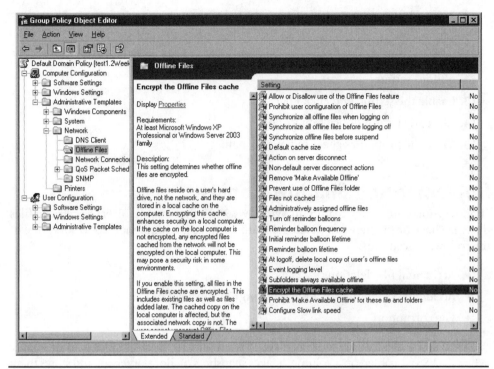

**Figure 3-17**   The Group Policy Object Editor

domain. In order to complete the exercise, you must have already installed Active Directory. You must log on as a Domain Admin or Enterprise Admin.

1. Click Start | All Programs | Administrative Tools | Active Directory Users and Computers.

2. Right-click your domain and select Properties.

3. From the Properties dialog box, click the Group Policy tab.

4. Click Edit from the Group Policy tab to open the Group Policy Object Editor (see Figure 3-17). Click the Computer Configuration node | Administrative Templates | Network | Offline Files.

5. Right-click the Default Cache Size setting and select Properties.

6. Enable the setting and set the size to 10%. Click OK.

7. Right-click the Encrypt The Offline Files Cache setting and select Properties.

8. Enable the setting and click OK.

9. Click the User Configuration node | Administrative Templates | Network | Offline Files.

10. Right-click the Turn Off Reminder Balloons setting and select Properties.

11. Enable the setting and click OK.

12. Right-click the "Do not automatically make redirected folders available offline" setting.

13. Enable the setting and click OK.

14. Close the Group Policy Object Editor.

15. Close the properties sheet of your domain.

# Implementing Shadow Copies

Shadow copies are a new feature in Windows 2003 that enables users to retrieve files that may have been altered or deleted. Shadow copies are implemented to solve one of the following scenarios:

- Accidental file deletions
- Accidental overwrites of a file (clicking Save instead of Save As)
- File corruption

The Volume Shadow Copy Service (VSS) is the driving force behind shadow copies. When the VSS is enabled on a volume, it takes snapshots of files at intervals and stores them for later retrieval. (You can alter the interval as you see fit.) A user can view previous versions of a file and restore a previous version if necessary. When a user accesses a file over the network, they will see a Previous Versions tab on the Properties of the file, as shown in Figure 3-18. Users can then restore a previous version of the file all by themselves.

 **NOTE**  VSS is the service that makes shadow copies possible. VSS also makes itself available to applications that are equipped to take advantage of the service, such as the Backup utility for Windows, which can now back up open files by using VSS.

Shadow copies are primarily intended for situations in which a user has accidentally deleted a file or overwritten the file and need to revert back to a point in time. Shadow copies by themselves are not a backup solution. A separate backup solution should be part of the overall management strategy. Backups are discussed in Chapter 5.

## How the Volume Shadow Copy Service (VSS) Works

When shadow copies are enabled on a volume, an interval is specified. If no interval is configured, VSS uses the default interval of twice per day. At the specified interval, VSS takes a snapshot of the shared folders and the contents. It does not make a backup of the files at that time. When a user opens a file, works on the file, and saves the file back to the original location, VSS uses the snapshot taken earlier to recognize that a file has changed. The VSS then makes a full copy of the file as it was at the interval and saves the file in the System

**Figure 3-18**
Previous versions
of the payroll file

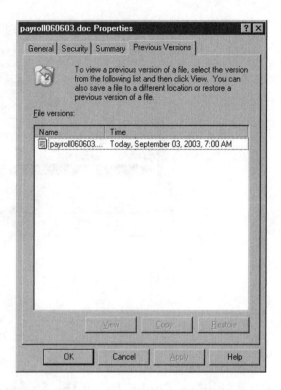

Volume Information folder, a hidden folder on the volume. Now the file on the server is up to date as the user saved it, and a backup of the previous file also resides on the server. If a user accesses the file properties, they can see the previous version of the file as well.

What VSS does not do is make a backup of the file every time a user saves the file. If the default interval is used, a snapshot will be taken at 7:00 A.M. and 12:00 P.M. each weekday. If a file is accessed by a user at 9:37 A.M. and changed and then saved, two copies of the file will be available: the old file as it was at 7:00 A.M. and the new file as it was changed at 9:37 A.M. If another user accesses the file at 11:32 A.M. and changes the file, only the current change and the file version as of 7:00 A.M. will be available.

There are three methods you can use to implement shadow copies: Windows Explorer, the Shared Folders snap-in, and the command prompt.

## Implementing Shadow Copies Using Windows Explorer

Enabling shadow copies on the volume will back up all shared folders on the volume. To implement shadow copies, right-click any volume in Windows Explorer and select Properties. Click the Shadow Copies tab and select the volume to enable, as shown in Figure 3-19. Click Enable and configure the schedule if necessary.

**Figure 3-19**

Implementing shadow copies using Windows Explorer

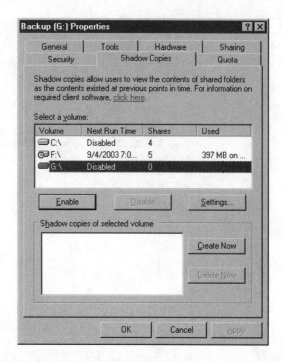

## Implementing Shadow Copies Using the Shared Folders Snap-in

To implement shadow copies, open the Computer Management MMC. Right-click the Shared Folders node, select All Tasks | Configure Shadow Copies, as shown in Figure 3-20. Configure the appropriate volume and schedule.

## Implementing Shadow Copies Using the Command Line

From a command prompt, type

```
vssadmin create shadow /for=forvolumespec
```

For additional help and to see a list of commands, from a command prompt, type

```
vssadmin
```

## Scheduling Shadow Copies

By default, a snapshot is made of the shared folders at 7:00 A.M. and 12:00 P.M. Monday through Friday. Windows 2003 only maintains 64 shadow copy snapshots. Once 64 snapshots have been made, the VSS begins overwriting the oldest snapshot to save the new snapshot. Microsoft does not recommend taking snapshots of the shared folders more than once an hour. Increasing the frequency of the schedule decreases the length of time that files are able to be rolled back.

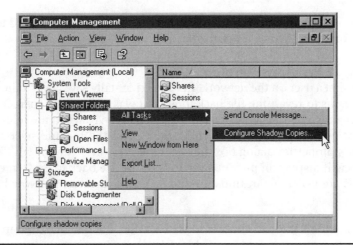

**Figure 3-20** Implementing shadow copies using the Shared Folders snap-in

To configure the schedule:

1. In Windows Explorer, right-click the volume that has VSS enabled and select Properties. Click the Shadow Copies tab.

2. Select the desired volume and click Settings. Click the Schedule button on the Settings window. Notice that, by default, there are two schedules configured, one running every weekday at 7:00 A.M. and the other running every weekday at 12:00 P.M.

3. To create a new schedule, click New.

4. To modify an existing schedule, select the schedule from the drop-down list and then modify the schedule. For additional options, click Advanced.

## Storing Shadow Copies

When shadow copies are enabled, the VSS creates a hidden folder on the volume called System Volume Information and stores previous versions of that folder. It is recommended that the shadow copies are stored on a different volume than where the shared folders reside. You can alter this by clicking the Settings button on the Shadow Copies tab on the volume. Simply store the hidden folder on a different drive.

## Installing the Shadow Copy Client

Windows Server 2003 natively supports shadow copies, however, Windows XP Professional, Windows 2000 Server and Professional, and Windows 98 require a client be installed (twcli32.msi). The client is available on the Windows 2003 server CD, or you can download the client at http://www.microsoft.com/windowsserver2003/downloads/shadowcopyclient.mspx. After the client is installed, Windows Explorer will display the Previous Versions tab in the Properties of the file.

(If you would like to test this out on your own computer, you will need to loopback. From a run command, type //*yourservername*.)

## Recovering a Previous Version

Let's assume that a user on the network, Kevin, accidentally saves over a file on a server. Kevin now wants to revert the file back to what it was previously. There are a few options, all using the Previous Versions tab. First, Kevin navigates to the folder where the file is located and selects the file. Then he right-clicks the file and selects Properties. From the file's properties dialog box, he clicks the Previous Versions tab. The Previous Versions tab will display all previous versions of the file back to 64 (remember, only 64 snapshots are kept). Kevin finds the file he wants to revert to. Now he has some choices:

- **View the file**   If Kevin chooses to view the file, the file is opened in the application it was created in (such as Word). Kevin can then choose to save the file to a different location using the Save As command in the application.

- **Copy the file**   If Kevin chooses to copy the file, he is presented with the dialog box shown in Figure 3-21 and navigates to a new location. Kevin clicks Copy to complete the operation.

- **Restore the file**   If Kevin chooses to restore the file, the previous version will be restored to the current location. When Kevin chooses this option, he sees the dialog box shown in Figure 3-22. Restoring the file overwrites the current file and any changes to the file are lost.

## Restoring a Deleted File

If you delete the file altogether, there isn't a previous version to go back to because you can't access the file. Now what do you do? Not to worry: shadow copy not only takes

**Figure 3-21**

Copying a previous version to a new location

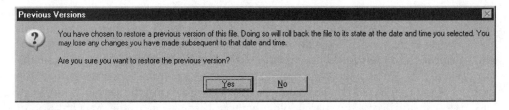

**Figure 3-22**    Restoring a previous version of a file

a snapshot of the files, but of the shared folder as well. So if you delete a file accidentally, you can restore the file by restoring the shared folder. Be careful when you restore the folder because other files may have been changed in the folder and those changes will be lost if you restore the whole folder.

# Implementing and Managing the Distributed File System (DFS)

The Distributed File System (DFS) isn't really a new kind of file system; it's more like an index for all of your shares in your network. Using DFS makes it much easier for users to connect to shares because they only have to remember one share. With DFS, you create a root, and then within the root you create links to your file shares anywhere in the network. Users can map to the DFS root and then find any file share in the network instead of having to remember all the different file shares and which servers they happen to be on.

Let's use an environment with five servers in it as an example. The servers and shares are listed in Table 3-7.

| Table 3-7 Servers and Shares | Server | Shares |
|---|---|---|
| | \\APPSERVER1 | Marketing<br>Photos<br>Docs |
| | \\HRSRV1 | Payroll<br>Payroll Archive<br>Benefits |
| | \\HRSRV2 | Compliance<br>Legal |
| | \\WEBSRV1 | Training<br>Upload |
| | \\FINANCE | Annual Reports<br>Current Year Results |

Using the current infrastructure, if a user wants to access the 2000 Annual Report for the company, they need to navigate to the \\FINANCE server and then access the Annual Reports share. Some users may have mapped the shares to their desktop or Windows Explorer and can quickly access the share. Other users may have to manually browse to the \\FINANCE server each time they need to access the files. Either way, if the location of the \\FINANCE share is changed, users have to learn the new location. With DFS, users can still access the shared folder without being aware of the exact location of the share.

## Lab Exercise 3.7: Creating a DFS Hierarchy

In this exercise, you will create a domain-based DFS, create a root, and add links to the root. You will use the HRDocs share created earlier in Exercise 3.2. If you have not created an HRDocs shared folder, do so now.

1. Click Start | All Programs | Administrative Tools | Distributed File System.

2. Right-click the Distributed File System node and select New Root. The New Root Wizard appears.

3. Select a domain-based root and click Next.

4. Select your domain and click Next.

5. Select your server and click Next.

6. Enter the name of your root. Previously in Windows 2000, it had to be an existing share. In Windows 2003, you can create the share on the fly, as in Figure 3-23. Enter **Corporate Shares** for the root name. Click Next.

7. Since the share Corporate Shares does not exist, you must select a folder to share as Corporate Shares or create a new folder. Click the Browse button

**Figure 3-23**
Creating the
Corporate
Shares root

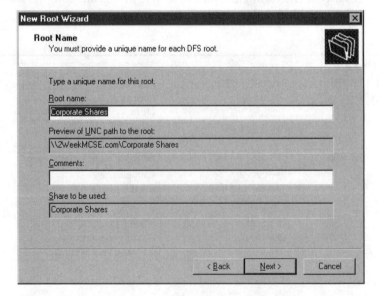

to view all the available folders on your server. Click an NTFS volume and then click Make New Folder to create the Corporate Shares folder. Click OK.

8. Click Next and then click Finish. You will now see that a root has been added to the DFS. Right-click the root and select New Link.

9. Name the link **Human Resources Documents**. Click the Browse button and navigate to the HRDocs share. Add a comment if you wish and then click OK.

10. Click Start | Run and type your server name, such as \\**TEST1**.

11. You will see a list of all the shares on your server, and right there at the top of the list is Corporate Shares.

12. Double-click Corporate Shares to be directed to the HRDocs folder.

As you saw in this exercise, it is very easy to create a link to a different server in your network and to various shares on servers as well. You can create several DFS roots based on your organization's needs and then place all of your shares as links in the roots. One of the benefits to you, the administrator, of using DFS is that when you decide to migrate a file server, all you have to do is go back to the link and repoint it to the new location. No need to retrain users or send out an e-mail!

DFS was introduced in NT 4.0 and greatly improved to the point of real usefulness in Windows 2000. Some additional features and functionality have been added to Windows 2003. For example, DFS now supports more than one root on a server and the ability to browse for shares and create new shared folders within the wizard. It can also be installed one of two ways: as a domain-based root or a standalone root.

## Domain-Based Root

First, the domain-based root is the preferred method because it provides replication and fault tolerance. Replication is achieved by adding a link replica to an existing replica and then setting up replication. To add a link replica, right-click the HRDocs link that you created previously and select New Target from the menu. Browse and select a second shared folder. When you click OK, you are prompted to set up replication, as in Figure 3-24. You must select a master for the replication to ensure that all shares have the same information for the initial replication. The multimaster replication model is used after the initial replication, and a change in any file in any folder triggers replication.

Fault tolerance is provided because the DFS root is stored in Active Directory, and so the root can be accessed from any DC in the enterprise. In this way, if the DC that initially hosted the root fails, the other DCs in the network are able to provide the root and the links to clients by querying the DFS root.

## Standalone Root

A standalone root DFS is not fault tolerant and does not support automatic replication. Standalone DFS is primarily implemented when Active Directory is not present in the network.

**Figure 3-24**
Setting up
replication

## Auditing Access to Resources

Part of maintaining a structured and secure network is auditing the resources once they are created and made available to users. Auditing can be performed on a local server or as part of a Group Policy applied to a site, domain, or organizational unit (OU). Auditing for a local computer only applies if the computer is not part of a domain. Once a computer joins a domain, the default domain policy takes effect and overrides any local policies in effect. Auditing works exactly the same way whether it is configured locally or on a Group Policy Object (GPO).

Auditing can be used to track possible breaches of network security, system events, changes to user accounts, and access to various resources. In the following section, we will concentrate on auditing files and folders and printers, and we will cover auditing as it relates to a local policy only. To audit a computer that is joined to a domain, configure auditing on the appropriate GPO.

**EXAM TIP**   Although we've focused on the most common auditing options here, make sure that you have a basic understanding of what each event covers so you can sort out incorrect answers.

### Enabling Auditing

Auditing files and folders and printers is a two-step process:

1. Enable the auditing for object access policy.

2. Enable auditing on individual files and folders.

The auditing for object access policy can be configured on the local machine by using the local security policy (see Figure 3-25), or on a site, domain, or organizational unit by

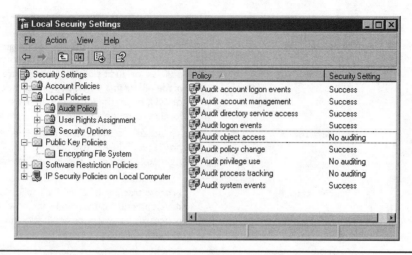

**Figure 3-25**  The local security policy MMC showing auditing options

using the appropriate Active Directory MMC. If the server is a member of a domain, the local security policy cannot be used to enable auditing. When a server is a member of a domain, the server will receive the default domain policy and any other policies applied to the container the server resides in, and the local policy is overridden.

After the audit policy has been configured, auditing must be enabled on the specific file or folder. Auditing is configured for either success or failure of a particular action. When auditing is enabled, an event will be written to the Security log every time a corresponding action is performed.

## Types of Auditing

You can audit for the events shown in Table 3-8.

| Table 3-8 | Type of Auditing | Explanation |
|---|---|---|
| Audit Policies | Account logon events | Audits success and failure of users attempting to log on to the domain. |
| | Account management | Audits account management tasks, such as resetting passwords, modifying user properties, and so on. |
| | Directory services | Audits an event any time a user accesses Active Directory, including searches for objects. |
| | Logon events | Audits success and failure for a local logon or for a logon to a shared folder or file. |
| | Object access | Used to record events related to file and folder access and printer access. |

| Table 3-8 | Type of Auditing | Explanation |
|---|---|---|
| Audit Policies (continued) | Policy change | Tracks changes and attempted changes to security options, user rights, account policies, or audit policies. Changes are made either in a GPO, such as on a domain or OU, or on the local computer using the local security policy settings. |
| | Privilege use | Tracks the use of certain user rights and privileges. Privilege use does not track the right to log on locally, as logons are tracked by enabling auditing for logons. |
| | Process tracking | Process tracking is useful for application development. You can audit the flow of processes between the application and Windows 2003. |
| | System | Tracks system events such as shutting down the system or clearing event logs. |

 **EXAM TIP**  Remember that to audit a folder, you need to turn on auditing for object access. There is no such thing as file or folder access.

# Installing and Configuring Terminal Services

Terminal Services provides a way for users to connect to a Windows Server 2003 server by using a low bandwidth protocol, and run programs or perform administrative tasks on the server. All that is needed is a Terminal Services client installed on the user's machine and network connectivity. The beauty of the Terminal Services client is that it requires very little processing power and memory in order to run. The Terminal Services client can be installed on any Windows-based operating system, including CE devices, and requires only a 386 processor and 8MB of RAM. Using Terminal Services can extend the life of older computers while providing a way to run the latest applications.

To run Terminal Server in remote administration mode, there is no need to install Terminal Services. Remote administration mode is now accessed using the Remote Desktop on the Start menu. Using remote administration mode will be covered in detail in Chapter 4.

First, some terminology. In Windows 2000, Terminal Services was not installed by default. When Terminal Services was installed, it was either installed in remote administration mode or application server mode. Remote administration mode has now evolved to Remote Desktop. There is no longer any such thing as Terminal Services in remote administration mode. Remote Desktop is covered in more detail in Chapter 4. When Terminal Services is installed on Windows Server 2003, it is set up to accept connections from users and to allow them to run programs on the server. Using Terminal Services can be completely transparent to the user, depending on the hardware deployed. Thin clients are computers designed to connect to a Terminal Server for the operating system and all applications and have very little resources. When a thin client is used, the user is not required to even initiate a session; the thin client boots directly to the Terminal Server and the user is prompted to log on and begin working.

A Terminal Server allows users to connect to the server and run applications using Windows XP Professional as the operating system platform. The Terminal Server can also be used with thin clients instead of full workstations. Terminal Services in Windows 2003 now also supports sound and redirected serial and USB ports, which means users can synchronize PDAs and other devices using Terminal Services. This is a huge improvement over Windows 2000 Terminal Services in which these sorts of features were not supported.

When a user initiates a session, the Terminal Server opens a session in its memory space and allows the user to run programs in their own memory space. Generally, 4–8MB of RAM per user is required on a Terminal Server. A Terminal Server running in application server mode should have plenty of processing power and RAM. A dual processor system with 1GB of RAM works very nicely.

## Installing and Configuring Terminal Services

To install Terminal Services, open the Add/Remove Programs applet from the Control Panel and select Windows Components. Select Terminal Services from the list of available components and click Next. You will be prompted to enter the Windows Server 2003 setup CD, so make sure you have it available.

Terminal Services is installed with two management consoles that are used to administer and configure the server, Terminal Services Manager and Terminal Services Configuration. Terminal Services Manager is used to control user sessions and monitor usage. Terminal Services Configuration is used to configure the RDP protocol. Also, after Terminal Services is installed, you will need to install software for users to run. Software must be installed using the Add/Remove Programs applet. If you attempt to install a program from the Setup file, you will see an error notifying you that you must use the Add/Remove Programs applet.

It is recommended that you install Terminal Services on a member server and not a domain controller. Domain controllers have increased security that must be negated to allow users to connect and run programs. By default, domain controllers have tight restrictions on who is allowed to log on locally. Domain Admins and Enterprise Admins are the only user accounts with the logon locally right on domain controllers. In order to allow users to connect to the Terminal Server, they must be granted the logon locally right to the domain controller. Granting this right to users lowers the security on a domain controller severely and is not recommended. Even in small environments, it is recommended that an additional domain controller be purchased and the Terminal Services machine be run on a member server.

## Terminal Services Licensing

All clients that connect to the Terminal Server must have a valid client access license (CAL). Windows 2000 and XP Professional clients have a built-in CAL for Terminal

Services. All other clients must obtain a license prior to establishing a session. To provide licensing, Terminal Services Licensing must be installed on a domain controller with Internet access. The Terminal Services Licensing computer must be able to connect to the Microsoft Clearinghouse to manage licenses. The Microsoft Clearinghouse is a facility that activates Terminal Services Licensing computers and issues individual CALs for use on the clients. Terminal Services Licensing only provides licenses for the Terminal Services client and does not provide licensing for any other software product or operating system.

To install Terminal Services Licensing, use the Add/Remove Programs applet from the Control Panel. When the Licensing component is installed, the type of licensing computer must be selected. To support a multiple domain environment, install an Enterprise Licensing Computer. If the Terminal Services Licensing computer will be used in a single domain model, install a Domain Licensing Computer. The Licensing component must be installed on a domain controller. It is recommended that the Licensing component be installed on a separate computer from the Terminal Server, but it can be co-located for smaller scenarios. The Licensing component requires very little processing power or RAM to function. The licensing database requires only 5MB for every 6,000 licenses.

A Terminal Services Licensing computer must be activated before it can issue and validate CALs.

## Licensing Process

When a client attempts to connect to a Terminal Server, the server attempts to validate the CAL. If the client is running Windows 2000 or XP, or presents a valid CAL, the client is allowed to connect. If the client does not have a CAL, the Terminal Server will connect to the Terminal Services Licensing computer and request a valid license for the client. If there are no licenses available, the Terminal Services Licensing computer will issue a temporary license with an expiration date 120 days from the date of issue. The Terminal Services Licensing computer will monitor the temporary license and will require the purchase of a valid CAL at the end of the 120-day period. If a client with a temporary license attempts to connect to the Terminal Server, the Terminal Server contacts the Terminal Services Licensing computer and checks the validity of the temporary license. If the temporary license is expired, the connection is not allowed until a valid CAL is obtained. Temporary licenses cannot be extended or reissued.

## Terminal Services Licensing Tool

The Terminal Services Licensing tool is provided for the administration of licenses on the licensing computer. Using it, an administrator can activate a license server, install licenses, view both available and installed client licenses, and administer the license server. The licensing tool is pictured in Figure 3-26.

## Remote Desktop Connection (Terminal Services Client)

Windows Server 2003 and Windows XP Professional machines have a built-in Terminal Services client called Remote Desktop Connection, shown in Figure 3-27. The Remote Desktop Connection can be used to connect to a Terminal Server running in either

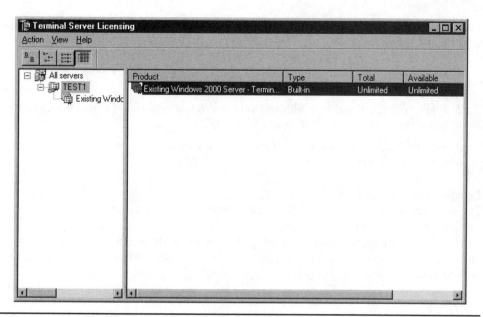

**Figure 3-26**  Licensing tool

remote administration mode or application server mode. The Remote Desktop Connection is found in the Start | All Programs | Accessories | Communications menu. The Remote Desktop Connection replaces the Terminal Services client introduced in Windows 2000.

The Remote Desktop Connection client is made available on the Windows Server 2003 CD for installation on previous versions of Windows. The client, msrdpcli.exe, is located on the Windows 2003 CD-ROM in the Support | Tools folder. The client can be installed on any Windows-based computer and some non-Windows–based computers, such as Unix terminals, MS-DOS, and Macintosh computers. Using Terminal Services with these non-Windows operating systems may require a third-party add-on.

Windows Server 2003 also includes a Remote Desktops MMC to allow an administrator to connect to multiple machines through one interface. The Remote Desktops

**Figure 3-27**

The Remote Desktop Connection in Windows 2003 and XP Professional

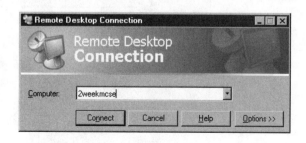

MMC is located in the Administrative Tools applet in the Control Panel. To connect to a server using the Remote Desktops MMC:

1. Click Start | All Programs | Administrative Tools | Remote Desktops to open the MMC.

2. Right-click the Remote Desktops node and select Add New Connection. Enter the server name or IP address and click OK.

3. Expand the Remote Desktops node to see the new connection. Right-click the server and select Connect.

## Configuring Options

The Remote Desktop client has been greatly expanded and now includes the ability to bring sound to the user, and to connect serial and USB devices located on the client machine to the Terminal Server. Connecting USB and serial devices to the Terminal Server allows users to synchronize devices such as a PDA to their Terminal Server profile. To enable these options:

1. Click Start | All Programs | Accessories | Communications | Remote Desktop Connection.

2. Click Options to expand the window and then click the Local Resources tab.

3. From the Remote Computer Sound drop-down menu, select Bring To This Computer, as shown in Figure 3-28.

4. Check the appropriate boxes for disk drives, printers, and serial ports.

**Figure 3-28**
Configuring
sound and
other options

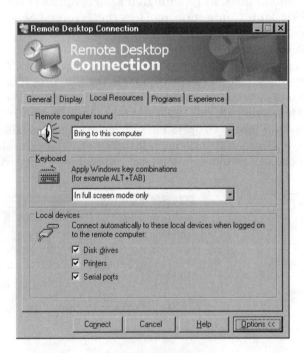

# The Remote Desktop Protocol

Terminal Services uses the Remote Desktop Protocol (RDP), a low bandwidth protocol to send mouse movements, keystrokes, and bitmap images of the screen from the server to the client computer. RDP does not send data over the network, only screen shots and keystrokes. A user is actually performing functions on the Terminal Server and is only viewing the results over RDP.

Before users can connect to a server with Terminal Services installed, you must configure RDP to allow the connections. You can also configure RDP for Remote Control settings, Sessions settings, and Logon settings.

## Configuring RDP Permissions

Users must also be granted the appropriate permissions on RDP before they are allowed to connect and establish sessions on the server. RDP is configured using the Terminal Services Configuration MMC. To configure permissions:

1. Click Start | All Programs | Administrative Tools | Terminal Services Configuration.

2. Select the Connections node. Right-click the RDP-TCP connection and select Properties.

3. Click the Permissions tab and add the appropriate groups to the ACL. Notice that you can grant Administrator, User, or Guest access.

4. Click OK.

RDP can be configured with permissions to allow groups of users to connect to specified servers and not other servers, as shown in Figure 3-29. The RDP protocol also allows an administrator to take control of a session from a user for troubleshooting assistance. This is different than the Remote Assistance feature in Windows XP Professional. For the remote control feature to work, the user has to be connected to the Terminal Server in application server mode.

## Lab Exercise 3.8: Installing the Remote Desktop Client and Connecting to a Terminal Server

In this exercise, you will install Terminal Server, the Remote Desktop Client, and connect to a Terminal Server. By default, the Remote Desktop client is installed on all Windows 2003 and Windows XP Professional servers. If you don't want to reinstall the client, skip steps 3–8, and complete the exercise by connecting to the Terminal Server that you set up.

### Part 1: Installing Terminal Services

1. Click Start | All Programs | Control Panel | Add/Remove Programs.

2. Click the Add Windows Components button. Select Terminal Services from the list of components and click Next.

**Figure 3-29**
RDP permissions

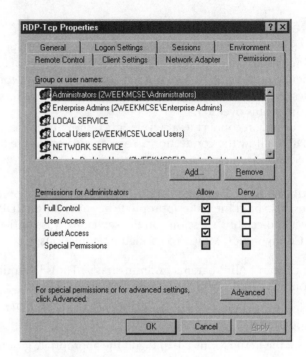

**Part 2: Installing the Remote Desktop Client**

3. Insert the Windows Server 2003 CD into your CD-ROM drive. If Auto Run is disabled, open My Computer and double-click the CD-ROM drive to start the Windows Server 2003 welcome screen.

4. Select the option to Perform Additional Tasks.

5. Select the option to Set Up Remote Desktop Connection. Wait while the Install Shield Wizard starts. Click Next at the welcome screen.

6. Accept the licensing agreement.

7. Enter your user name and organization. Select to install the application for anyone who uses this computer (all users) and click Next.

8. Click Install to begin the installation and Finish when the installation completes.

**Part 3: Connecting to a Terminal Server**

9. To connect to a Terminal Server, click Start | All Programs | Remote Desktop Connection.

10. Enter the host name of your server where Terminal Services is installed and click Connect.

11. When the remote screen appears, enter your user name and password.

# Chapter Review

Managing resources is a challenging task in any network. Doing it well can make the difference between a network that runs smoothly and a network that is constantly requiring the administrator to be a fireman. In this chapter, you learned some new techniques in managing resources effectively.

The first part of the chapter focused on NTFS and share permissions and how to effectively solve permissions problems. It is a best practice to grant access using share permissions and then to secure resources using NTFS permissions. NTFS permissions apply when users are logged on interactively and over the network. Share permissions only apply when a user accesses the resource over the network. Remember that permissions are cumulative. A user with Read and Modify permissions granted to them on a resource effectively has Modify permissions. Effective permissions can be viewed using the Advanced settings on the Security properties sheet.

Creating and managing shared folders is a large part of maintaining appropriate access to resources. You learned several methods of creating and managing shares. Shared folders can be managed from the Shared Folders snap-in on the Computer Management MMC or from the File Server Management MMC. Shared folders can also be managed from Windows Explorer and from a command prompt. Folders can also be shared using IIS and accessible using Internet Explorer or other browser. IIS must be installed and configured before web sharing is accessible.

You also learned how to use the Distributed File System as a pointer for the shares in your network. Using DFS helps users to locate files more easily and with less assistance. Also using DFS, an administrator can migrate files and folders to a new server and users will never know. The pointer to the file share can remain consistent, regardless of the location of the server or share. DFS also supports replication and, when a domain-based root is implemented, fault tolerance.

You learned about using shadow copies to allow users to revert back to previous versions of files. Using shadow copies effectively can save a tremendous amount of time and effort in reclaiming lost or overwritten files.

Finally, you learned about using Terminal Services. Terminal Server has gained a real foothold in today's networks, as it extends the life of older desktops, reduces overall cost of workstations, and severely cuts down on desktop support issues. The Remote Desktop client has been integrated into Windows XP and Windows Server 2003 products and is available to install on any previous version of Windows.

## Questions

1. Rob informs you that he has attempted to access the Marketing folder over the network but is denied access. He tells you that he needs to add and delete several files to the Marketing folder. Your corporate policy states that all share permissions are Everyone Full Control and that access is controlled by using NTFS permissions. You don't remember the path of the Marketing folder. You need to locate the full path name of the Marketing folder and grant Rob the appropriate permissions. What can you do? (Choose all that apply.)

A. From a command prompt, type **net share** to locate the Marketing folder and path. Then at the command prompt, type **set ntfs :prs /(the path) \rblevins=full control**.

B. From a command prompt, type **net use** to locate the Marketing folder and path. Open Windows Explorer and navigate to the appropriate folder and change Rob's permissions to Modify.

C. From a command prompt, type **net share** to locate the Marketing folder and path. Open Windows Explorer and navigate to the Marketing folder and change Rob's permissions to Modify.

D. From the Shared Folders snap-in, click the Shares folder to view all shared folders on the server. Right-click the Marketing share and select Properties. From the shared folder properties dialog box, click the Security tab and change Rob's permissions to Modify.

E. From the Shared Folders snap-in, click the Shares folder to view all shared folders on the server. Open Windows Explorer and navigate to the Marketing folder and change Rob's permissions to Modify.

2. You are the administrator of a Windows Server 2003 network. The network contains two file servers, which contain all the company data. The file servers are in different OUs. Mark, an executive, notifies you that some of the files on the server that should be kept confidential were deleted over the weekend. You need to implement auditing on the servers so that you are aware of any attempted unauthorized access in the future. Which of the following should you do? (Choose all that apply.)

A. Implement a local security policy for each file server.

B. Implement a security policy and apply it to the OU that the file servers belong to.

C. Implement a security policy and apply it to the domain.

D. Create a new OU and move both servers into the OU.

E. Configure Auditing for File and Folder Access.

F. Configure Auditing for Object Access.

G. Enable auditing for success on the folder in which the confidential files are stored on the server.

H. Enable auditing for failure on the folder in which the confidential files are stored on the server.

3. You are the administrator of your company's network. All servers are running Windows Server 2003 and all client computers are running Windows XP Professional. Phil, the director of marketing, informs you that an important presentation that he needs to give tomorrow has been deleted. The presentation was stored on a file server that has shadow copies enabled. You need to help Phil recover the deleted file. What should you do? (Choose all that apply.)

A. Install the twcli32.msi file onto Phil's computer.

B. Install the msrdpcli.exe file onto Phil's computer.

C. Instruct Phil to access the properties of the file and click Previous Versions. Have Phil restore the file.

D. Instruct Phil to access the properties of the folder where the deleted file was located and click Previous Versions. Have Phil restore the folder.

E. Have Phil supply you with the name of the file and when it was last accessed. Restore the file from backup.

4. You are the administrator of a Windows Server 2003 file server. The file server is located in a secured room and only authorized administrators have physical access to it. You are responsible for assigning appropriate permissions for several groups for access to the Departments folder located on the server. The Departments folder contains subfolders named Marketing, Sales, Support, and Call Center.

The sales managers must be able to view the data in the Sales subfolder and create new files, but must not be able to delete any existing files. The marketing managers must be able to view the data in the Marketing subfolder, modify existing files, and create and modify additional files. The support managers must be able to view the data in the Marketing and Sales subfolders, but must not be able to modify any existing data, or create additional files or folders. They must also have access to the Support subfolder, and be able to modify existing data, create additional files, and grant other users access to the Support files. All call center employees must have Read Only access to the Call Center subfolder.

Select the appropriate steps to take. (Choose all that apply.)

A. Use the Shares snap-in and create a share for Marketing, Sales, Support, and Call Center.

B. For the Marketing, Sales, Support, and Call Center shares, grant the marketing managers, sales managers, support managers, and call center users the Change permission.

C. Use the Shares snap-in and create a share for the Departments folder.

D. For the Departments share, grant the Users group Full Control.

E. For the call center employees, grant Read access to the Departments folder.

F. For the call center employees, grant Read access to the Call Center folder.

G. For the marketing managers, grant the Change permission to the Marketing folder.

H. For the marketing managers, grant the Modify permission to the Marketing folder.

I. For the sales managers, grant the Modify permission to the Sales folder.

J. For the sales managers, grant the Read and Write permissions to the Sales folder.

    K. For the support managers, grant the Read permission to the Departments folder.

    L. For the support managers, grant the Read permission to the Sales and Marketing folders.

    M. For the support managers, grant the Change Permissions permission to the Support folder.

    N. For the support managers, grant the Full Control permission to the Support folder.

5. You are the administrator of a Windows Server 2003 network and the manager of the IT department. David, an administrator in your department, leaves the company. Grady, also an administrator in your department, takes over David's work. Each administrator has a personal folder located on a file server formatted with an NTFS volume. Grady needs to have access to all of David's old files. What should you do?

    A. Grant Grady the Take Ownership permission to David's folder.

    B. Move all of David's files in the folder to Grady's folder.

    C. Transfer ownership of David's folder to Grady.

    D. Run a backup of David's folder and restore the backup to a FAT volume. Copy the files to Grady's folder.

6. You are the administrator of a Windows Server 2003 network. You configure a Windows Server 2003 server as a Terminal Server. You install Terminal Services licensing on a different server and activate the licensing server. Half of your clients are running Windows XP Professional and the other half are running Windows NT 4.0. You install the Remote Desktop Client software on the NT 4.0 machines. You instruct users how to use the Remote Desktop Connection to connect to the Terminal Server. Users begin connecting to the server and running their applications. After four months, the NT 4.0 users are unable to connect to the server and run their applications. What should you do to ensure that users are able to connect to their sessions on the Terminal Server?

    A. Install Terminal Services in application server mode.

    B. In Terminal Services Manager, configure the RDP protocol to grant access to the Pre-Windows 2000 Compatibility group.

    C. In Terminal Services Manager, reset all users' connections.

    D. Purchase additional CALs for the NT 4.0 Workstations.

7. You are the administrator of a Windows Server 2003 network with Terminal Services installed. Users have been connecting to the server and working normally. After several weeks, you discover that many users are disconnecting their sessions from their client computers, but the session continues to stay open on the server. You investigate and discover that the users' accounts have the End A Disconnected Session property set to Never. You want to ensure that when a user disconnects from the Terminal Server, the session is ended. What should you do?

A. Using the Terminal Services Manager, disconnect all sessions.

B. On the Sessions tab of the User Properties screen, set the End A Disconnected Session property to 10 minutes.

C. On the Terminal Services Configuration, set the End A Disconnected Session property to 10 minutes.

D. Configure a GPO to end a disconnected session after 5 minutes. Apply the GPO to the domain.

8. You are the administrator of your company's network. All of the servers are Windows 2003 and all of the client computers are Windows XP Professional. You configure a server as a print server for a color laser printer. The marketing department uses the color laser printer for brochures and other projects. The marketing manager reports that other users in the office have used the color laser printer without authorization. You need to find out which users are printing to the color laser printer. What should you do? (Choose all that apply.)

A. Configure a new GPO for the domain. Enable auditing for success and failure of object access.

B. In System Monitor, monitor for jobs in the Print Queue counter.

C. Configure the local security policy of the Windows Server 2003. Enable auditing for success and failure of object access.

D. Audit for success for Print on the color laser printer.

E. Audit for failure for Print on the color laser printer.

9. You are the administrator of your company's network. All of the servers are Windows 2003 and all of the client computers are Windows XP Professional. Mark, a user in your company, shares a folder that stores files on his workstation that are accessed by other users. The other users complain that sometimes they are denied access to the files. You investigate and discover that when the number of users accessing the files reaches 10, other users are denied access. What should you do to enable all users to be able to access the files?

A. On the Sharing tab of the folder, enable the option to allow unlimited connections.

B. Modify the Share permissions to include the Domain Users group and grant Read access.

C. Upgrade Mark's computer to Windows Server 2003.

D. Move the shared folder to Windows Server 2003.

10. You are the administrator of a Windows network. You install Windows Server 2003, FS1, and implement a file server. You create a Users share on the server for users to save documents to, and create user directories under the share. You implement volume shadow copies on the server and configure the schedule to back up files four times a day. All clients are running Windows 2000 Professional or Windows XP. Kevin, a user, informs you that a presentation that he created

and stored on the file server is garbled and unreadable when he opens it. You determine that the file has been corrupted. The last time Kevin accessed the file successfully was two weeks ago. You instruct Kevin to access the Previous Versions tab in Windows Explorer and restore a copy of the file. Kevin informs you that when he accesses the properties of the file, there is no Previous Versions tab. You need to help Kevin restore the file. What should you do?

**A.** Instruct Kevin to access the file by using the UNC name, //FS1/Users/Kevin/filename.

**B.** Restore the file using Backup utility for Windows from a backup tape made two weeks ago.

**C.** Install the twcli32.msi client on Kevin's client computer.

**D.** Use the Volume Shadow Copies Restore Wizard to restore a copy of the file.

11. You are the administrator of a Windows Server 2003 server named 2week9. You have configured a shared folder named CompanyInfo and assigned the appropriate permissions. You also enable web sharing of the folders. Users report that when they access the shares by typing **http://2week9/CompanyInfo**, they receive an error stating that access is denied. You need to enable users to view the files in CompanyInfo from their web browser. What should you do?

**A.** Open Internet Services Manager. On the Directory Security tab of the Default Web Site, allow Anonymous access.

**B.** Open Internet Services Manager. On the General tab of the CompanyInfo properties, check the Directory Browsing permission.

**C.** In Windows Explorer, open the Properties of the CompanyInfo folder and check the Read permission on the Web Sharing tab.

**D.** Instruct users to log off and log back on to the network.

**E.** Upgrade all Internet Explorer programs to version 5.5.

12. You are the administrator of your company's network. All of the servers are Windows 2003 and all of the client computers are Windows XP Professional. Your company has doubled in size in the last year and you have added three new locations. You expect to add three additional locations by the end of the year. Your users frequently travel between the locations and access shared files located in the main office. You want to deploy a flexible file system to allow users to easily connect to the shares regardless of what location they are at. What should you do?

**A.** Install an IIS server in each location. Copy the shared folders to the IIS server and enable web sharing.

**B.** Install an IIS server in each location. Create a web page that points to each shared folder. Configure site settings to point to the local IIS server as the default web page.

C. Implement DFS at the main office. Store the shared folders on two file servers at the main office. Instruct the users to access the shared folders by using the DFS link.

D. Implement DFS at the main office. Store the shared folders on a file server at each location. Configure link replicas on the shared folders and configure replication. Instruct the users to access the shared folders by using the DFS link.

## Answers

1. **D.** The easiest way to locate a share and path according to Microsoft is to use the Shared Folders snap-in. You must modify the NTFS permissions on the folder once you locate it.

2. **C, F, G, and H.** It is best to configure a policy for a single OU rather than the domain. However, in this case, the servers are in different OUs, so you must configure the domain policy. You must configure auditing for object access. You must enable both success and failure on the folder. If you only enable failure, you will only be aware of users attempting to access the folder and being denied, not users who successfully access the folder and delete files.

3. **A and D.** You need to install the shadow copy client onto Phil's computer first, then have Phil restore the entire folder. The file has been deleted and is not accessible.

4. **C, D, F, H, J, L, and N.** The easiest method of granting access to shares is to share the root folder and then secure the resources by using NTFS permissions. Call center employees need Read access to the Call Center folder only. The marketing managers need the Modify permission to read, write, and delete files. The sales managers need Read and Write permission to the Sales folder. The support managers need the Read permission to the Sales Marketing folder. They also need to have the Change Permissions and Modify permissions on the Support folder. Although the support managers do not require the Take Ownership permission, granting them Change Permissions permission would in effect grant them the Take Ownership permission and also require that they alter their own permissions in order to receive the appropriate access.

5. **C.** Transferring ownership is a new feature in Windows 2003, which enables an administrator or the current owner of a file or folder to transfer ownership to another user. This is easier than instructing a user to take ownership, which is still available but not preferred.

6. **D.** By default, a Terminal Server requests a client access license of all clients connecting to the server. Windows 2000 and XP have a built-in Terminal Services CAL. If a CAL is not present, a temporary CAL is issued. The temporary license expires after 120 days. The license cannot be renewed; a valid license

must be purchased and a Terminal Services Licensing computer must be installed and have connectivity to the Microsoft clearinghouse. Since the Licensing computer has already been configured and activated, the only thing remaining is to purchase additional licenses.

7. **C.** User settings can be overridden by configuring sessions in the Terminal Services configuration. To override the user settings, open the Terminal Services Configuration MMC, select RDP, and click Properties. On the Sessions tab, select to override the user setting and configure the server to end a disconnected session after 10 minutes.

8. **A and D.** To enable auditing for printers, you must enable auditing in a policy applied to the computer. On a standalone server, you would enable auditing on the local security policy. Since the server is a member of a domain, you must configure a domain GPO and enable auditing of object access. After configuring the policy, you must enable auditing on the printer for success.

9. **D.** Windows XP only allows 10 users to connect to a shared folder at a time. In order to accommodate all users, you must move the folder to a Windows Server 2003 server.

10. **C.** The Previous Versions tab is only available on Windows Server 2003. In order for other versions of Windows to display the Previous Versions tab, the twcli32.msi file must be run on the client computer to install the shadow copy client.

11. **B.** By default, the directory browsing permission is not set on web sites or virtual directories. In order for users to view files, documents, and other folders, they must have directory browsing permission. You can enable directory browsing either in Windows Explorer or by using the Internet Services Manager. To enable directory browsing in Internet Services Manager, open the properties of the virtual directory and check the Directory Browsing permission on the General tab.

12. **D.** DFS is a highly flexible file system that will also point users to file shares in their own location. You should configure replicas of all shared folders on a file server in each location.

# Managing and Maintaining a Server Environment

In this chapter, you will learn how to

- Monitor system events
- Use the Event Viewer
- Use System Monitor
- Use Performance Monitor
- Manage virtual memory and performance settings
- Use Network Monitor
- Install updates using the software update infrastructure
- Manage servers remotely using Remote Desktop
- Implement disk quotas
- Implement and manage Internet Information Services (IIS)
- Secure Internet Information Services (IIS)

There's a lot that goes into managing a server. The first three chapters of this book have contained information on how to manage a server to install hardware, share files, and manage permissions. But in addition to managing individual resources, you need to also manage the overall condition of the server itself. You need to be aware of out-of-control resources, mismanaged memory, and possible hardware failures. (The hardware does fail. It may take several years, but eventually, everything breaks.) Ignoring these possibilities can create disasters later on. There are few things worse than losing a critical hard drive to a hardware failure that could have been detected. And while having a solid backup strategy in place can certainly help, life is much easier when a proactive approach is taken and possible problems are avoided before they happen. Microsoft has included performance and monitoring tools as part of the Windows Server 2003 operating system to help administrators detect early warning signs and to provide valid information about the overall performance of the server. The first part of this chapter will focus on those tools.

The second half of the chapter will be devoted to configuring and managing a web server. Managing a web server requires much more than simply hosting content. Many times, a single web server is used to host multiple web sites. You will learn several strategies of hosting multiple sites and how to use application pools, a new feature, to improve the stability and scalability of the server. You will also learn how to secure the web server, from securing sites and directories to configuring services in order to reduce the possibility of a successful attack against your server. An administrator who is on top of these issues and can manage an IIS server efficiently is worth his or her weight in gold.

**NOTE**  Most hardware vendors include their own proprietary server monitoring software with the hardware that they build and ship. Dell (http://www.dell.com/), HP (http://www.hp.com/), and IBM (http://www.ibm.com/) all include their own proprietary monitoring and performance tools. Although each is different, knowing the basics of performance and monitoring will enable you to at least look competent with other management software.

# Monitoring Performance and System Events

Microsoft has included several tools to help you manage and troubleshoot performance issues. In this section, you will learn to use

- Task Manager
- Event Viewer
- System Monitor
- Performance logs and alerts
- Network Monitor

Each of these tools monitors a different segment of your server and your network. Using them effectively calls attention to possible bottlenecks and failures before they become serious problems, and thereby helps extend the life of your system.

### Using Task Manager to Monitor and Improve System Performance

Task Manager is the most commonly used of the monitoring tools, and you are probably already very familiar with how Task Manager works. Microsoft does test on Task Manager, and you should review the different features before taking the exam.

Task Manager displays applications and processes currently running on the server, and provides an interface to start new programs or processes and close programs or processes. Task Manager also can monitor memory usage, processor usage, and—new in Windows Server 2003—network usage and user data. Task Manager can be started by pressing CTRL-SHIFT-ESC, by pressing CTRL-ALT-DEL and then clicking Task Manager, or by right-clicking the task bar and selecting Task Manager.

## Starting and Ending Programs

The Applications tab of Task Manager displays all running programs and programs that have stopped responding. Applications that have hung or stopped responding need to be manually stopped. Right-clicking an application and selecting End Task will close a hung application. There is also an End Task button on the bottom of the screen that can be used to end the program.

New applications can also be started from the Applications tab. To start a new program, click the New Task button on the Applications tab. Type the executable file or click Browse and navigate to the executable file you want to run. To start a new program, you can also select File | New Task.

## Viewing Processes

When a program is started, the executable file is added to the list of processes in Task Manager. The Processes tab displays the executable files of all running programs and processes that are part of the operating system, as shown in Figure 4-1. The process listed is known as the image name. Each image name can have multiple processes associated with it, depending on how the code was written.

## Ending Processes

It is a common occurrence that when an application fails it leaves behind processes that are still active. Even ending the application using Task Manager sometimes leaves behind

**Figure 4-1**

Viewing running processes

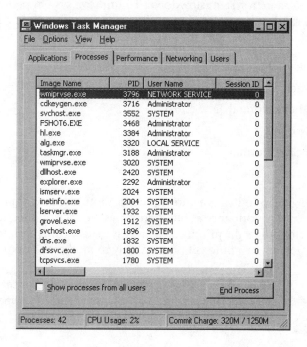

a process or a family of processes. You can use the Processes tab in Task Manager to end these processes.

Processes can be ended either singly or as a group. It can be difficult to ascertain which processes belong together. If you are sure that the listed process is not associated with any other related processes, it can be ended by simply clicking the End Process button at the bottom of the screen. If you are unsure of any related processes and want to end all associated processes, right-click the process and select End Process Tree. Ending the process tree will end the selected process and any child processes. For example, if you end the process tree for Microsoft Outlook, the mapisp32.exe process, the MAPI spooler, will also be ended.

 **NOTE** Windows Server 2003 supports 16-bit applications by running them in their own NT Virtual DOS Machine (NTVDM). If more than one 16-bit application is running, the processes will display NTVDM and NTVDM#2. Each NTVDM is treated as a separate process and can be assigned to a specific processor in the case of multiple processors, or can be monitored and modified separately.

## Changing Priority

When an application is started, the system assigns processor time and system resources to the application. By default, all programs start with the same priority for these resources. It is common to have one particular application interfere with other applications and cause a system slowdown. To improve system performance, the priority of a process can be altered. To change the priority of a process, right-click the process and click Priority, then specify the level desired. The various levels are

- Real Time
- High
- Above Normal
- Normal
- Below Normal
- Low

Setting the priority higher for a process allots more I/O time for that process. This can slow overall performance as other processes are then allotted less I/O time. Only an administrator can set the priority on a process to Real Time. Task Manager cannot be used to start a program in a different priority, only to modify the priority of running processes.

 **NOTE** To start a program with a priority other than Normal, you must use the command prompt. You can use the start command or the cmd command. To start a program using the start command, type

```
start <application> /<priority>
```

```
H1.exe /high
```

To start a program using the cmd shortcut, from a command prompt type

```
cmd /c start /<priority> <application>
```

```
cmd /c start /high hl.exe.
```

**EXAM TIP**   Programs cannot be started with a different priority from the run command, only from the command prompt.

## Monitoring Processor Performance and Memory Usage

The Performance tab, shown in Figure 4-2, displays information about processor performance and memory usage. If more than one processor is present, a separate graph is displayed for each processor. Windows Server 2003 has built-in load balancing for processors; however, if a hard affinity has been set for an application, it is possible for one processor to become overloaded while the other processor does very little work.

- **CPU Usage**   Displays the current CPU usage. It is not uncommon for a CPU to hit 100% while performing intense tasks.

- **CPU Usage History**   Displays the CPU usage over time. If the CPU usage is consistently above 50%, it is possibly time for a new CPU or an additional CPU.

**Figure 4-2**
The Performance tab of Task Manager

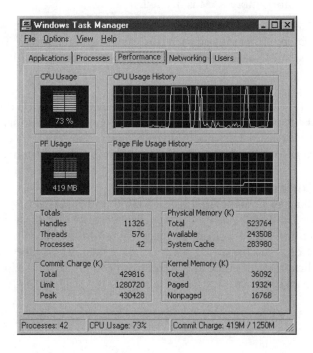

- **PF Usage**   Displays the amount in MB that is being used by the page file. Check this against the total size of the page file (see the "Allocating Virtual Memory" section on page files for information on how to check the file size and make modifications).

- **PF Usage History**   Displays the amount in MB that is being used by the page file over time.

---

 **NOTE**   Double-clicking anywhere on the Performance tab brings up an enlarged graphical view of the CPU usage.

---

Below the graphs, there are other indicators that are used to monitor memory. These indicators are

- **Commit Charge**   Displays the total amount of memory available, including virtual memory, and what is currently being used by the operating system. If the amount being used is within 10 percent of the limit, more RAM is needed.

- **Kernel Memory**   Displays the total amount of memory used by the operating system kernel. Some part of the kernel must be run from physical memory and cannot be placed on the paging file.

- **Physical Memory**   Displays the amount of physical memory or RAM available and being used. If the available memory is less than 5 percent of the total memory, more RAM is needed.

- **Totals**   Displays information about the CPU. Processes are made up of different threads and each thread has several handles. Totals displays how many I/O handles, threads, and processes are currently running on the system.

## Monitoring Networks

Server 2003 includes a tab for monitoring network traffic on the server. The Networking tab only displays traffic coming to or originating from the server; it is not intended to monitor the entire network. It does display the current state of all network adapters on the server, how they are responding, and how much of their network capacity is in use.

## Monitoring Users

Task Manager now includes a Users tab that displays all users logged onto the server, whether locally or by using Terminal Services. The user name, session ID, and computer the user has logged in from are displayed. Administrators can use this feature to take control of a session or log users off of a session. To take control of a user session, right-click the user name and select Connect. You will need to supply the user's password to take control.

## Using the Event Viewer

The Event Viewer is the catchall for myriad error messages and notifications generated by applications, services, and systems running on a Windows Server 2003 server. By default, a basic installation of server includes the following event logs:

- Application
- Security
- System

These logs are fairly straightforward. The Application log contains messages and errors pertaining to operating system functions, applications, and other general operating errors. When a roaming profile fails to load for example, an error is found in the Application log. The Security log contains audit events and other security-related events. The System log basically contains anything that doesn't fit into one of the other two logs.

Additional logs can be viewed in the Event Viewer. In fact, as additional services and applications are added to Server 2003, additional logs become available. Installing Active Directory creates a Directory Service log and a File Replication Service log. If DNS was also installed, a DNS Server log is added. Any log file created with an .evt extension can be viewed using Event Viewer. To open a log file, right-click the Event Viewer and select Open Log File, then navigate to the location of the log file.

## Viewing Events

Each log file can contain hundreds or even thousands of events. These events are sorted with the most recent events listed first. You can also view the events sorted oldest first by right-clicking the log and selecting View | Oldest First. To view a particular event, double-click the event in the log. The date and time of the event, as well as event codes and a short explanation appear. The tricky part is always figuring out what you are really looking at and trying to make sense of it all. Let's look at a typical event. Figure 4-3 displays the source of the problem to be an application hang at 8:58 P.M. If you look at the description, you see that application HL.EXE (Half Life) was the offending application.

The description also displays a link to a Microsoft web site that will be brought up in the Help and Support Center after you click the link, as is displayed in Figure 4-4.

Quite often, you will receive a message stating that there is no additional information available. For those messages, you're on your own! Searching the Internet for the error code using Google sometimes helps.

## Filtering Events

To make searching through hundreds or thousands of records easier, a filter capability is included with the Event Viewer. Filtering is especially helpful when trying to view security events related to auditing. You can filter the log by event type, event source, category, event ID, user, computer, or a date range. Applying a filter to an event log will help narrow the search for a specific event.

**Figure 4-3**
Error message in
the Application
Log showing a
hung application

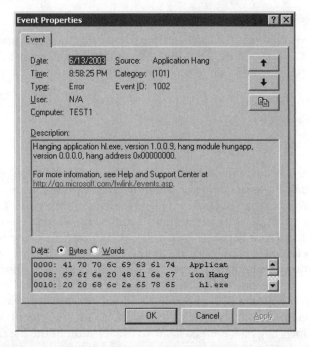

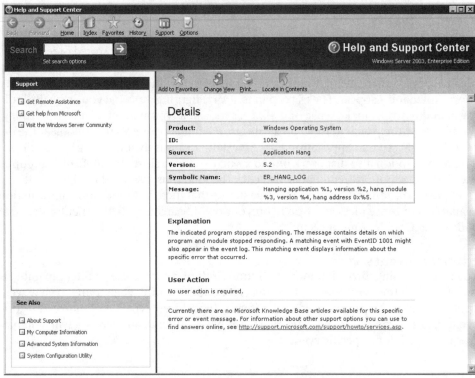

**Figure 4-4**    Viewing the Help and Support Center details of hung application

**EXAM TIP** Filtering event logs is one of those off-the-wall topics that you can expect on a Microsoft exam. Be familiar with the filters that can and cannot be added to an event log. If a user changed another user's account, for example, you cannot filter by the user name to discover the culprit. You must filter for account events and then view all entries to locate the entry.

## Configuring Event Viewer Settings

Each individual log file can be modified as to how large it is allowed to grow and how new events are written to the log. To view the various settings shown in Figure 4-5, right-click the log file and select Properties from the drop-down list.

The following settings can be altered:

- Maximum log size
- Overwrite events as needed
- Overwrite events older than ___ days
- Do not overwrite events (clear log manually)

When a log file reaches its maximum size, events need to be cleared to make room for new events. Setting the log to overwrite events as needed requires the least amount of maintenance. As new events are generated, the oldest events are simply overwritten.

**Figure 4-5**
Modifying log file settings

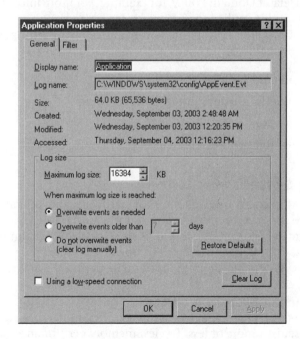

Configuring the log file to overwrite events older than a specified amount of time lends itself very well to a set schedule. Microsoft recommends seven days as an appropriate time period and then recommends that the log file be saved and cleared manually once a week. The problem with overwriting event logs after a certain time period is that if the event log becomes full and there are no events in the log file older than the specified time period, new events are discarded and not written to the file.

The log can also be cleared from the Properties screen. You are prompted to save the log file before clearing it. Also notice the Using A Low-Speed Connection item on the Properties sheet. This is checked if the log being viewed is located on a remote computer that is being accessed by a low-speed connection, such as a modem.

 **EXAM TIP**   Know the various log file settings! You can expect a question about how often events are overwritten, whether the log is cleared manually, and so on.

## Configuring Event Viewer Settings in Group Policy

As you might expect, log file settings can also be controlled in Group Policy, making administration of multiple servers much easier. On a domain controller, the Event Viewer settings are found in the Default Domain Controllers Policy. On other servers, the Group Policy settings will be in the corresponding container that the server belongs to—the Default Domain Policy, for example. For more information on how Group Policy works and is applied to computers, see Chapter 22.

Using Group Policy, you can modify the following settings for the Application, Security, and System logs:

- Maximum log size
- Prevent local guests group from accessing
- Retain log
- Retention method

## Using System Monitor

System Monitor is used to monitor hardware and operating system components. Using System Monitor, you can monitor your hard disks, memory performance, and even print queues. System Monitor is also flexible. For example, you can monitor memory usage with System Monitor. To open System Monitor, click Start | Run and type **perfmon**. System Monitor will open up in graphical display mode.

## Configuring System Monitor

To view performance, you must add a specific counter to System Monitor. A counter is a specific statistic more or less. To view memory performance, you may add the Memory: Pages/sec counter. This specific statistic informs you how frequently data has to be accessed from the paging file on the disk. A large number would indicate that more memory needs to be added to increase performance.

Think of each counter as a specific statistic in a football game. You are the coach (or the administrator). It's not usually enough to know the score (Bob, the system is really slow!) to try to determine where your football team needs to improve (improve system performance). Knowing that your team lost the last game 27–10 doesn't tell you the story of the game. However, if your stat boy informs you that your team only rushed for 61 yards in the game and the other team rushed for 312 yards, you can begin to see a bit more. Then to follow that up, you may want to know what the average yards per carry was. Let's say that your team only rushed the ball one time and the other team rushed the ball 47 times. Your team's average yards per carry is 61 and the other team's average yards per carry is 6.6. You may want to run the ball a few more times. It seemed to work well the first time!

Just like statistics in the football game, if the only statistic you keep track of is Processor: % Processor Time, you can't really tell if the problem with your system performance is due to the processor. You also need to monitor the disk performance and the memory performance to determine if the processor is causing a system bottleneck or if the performance of the processor is being affected by other factors. Monitoring all three counters is kind of like determining the average yards per carry.

Be careful, though, in compiling your statistics. While monitoring the disk, memory, and processor is valuable (average yards per carry), monitoring every statistic in the performance monitor isn't. Kind of like finding out that your team has never won a game on a Thursday, on the road, in Oregon, when it was raining and the temperature was below 45 degrees. There are many, many different counters that can be added to System Monitor. Focus on a few that can really help you.

To add a new counter, right-click in the graph area and select Add Counters from the drop-down list. Select a performance object (such as memory) and then select an individual counter. Notice there is an Explain button available, which helps define each counter. Click Add to commit the change. The results can be displayed in chart mode, histogram mode, or report mode (shown in Figure 4-6).

Table 4-1 contains some of the more common counters, an explanation, and a column that explains what the reading means and what action to take.

 **EXAM TIP**   One of Microsoft's favorite questions over the years has been about memory usage and how to increase performance. Watch for the parameters of the question. The question may indicate that you want to increase performance without spending any money or by using the least amount of effort. Adding memory is always a good idea, but may not be the correct answer to the question. Look for other things, such as increasing the paging file or moving the paging file to a different drive.

## Using Performance Logs and Alerts

It is helpful to know what performance has been like over time in order to analyze trends and predict future performance levels. Good administrators don't just pay attention to what a system is doing right now. They also pay attention to how the server has

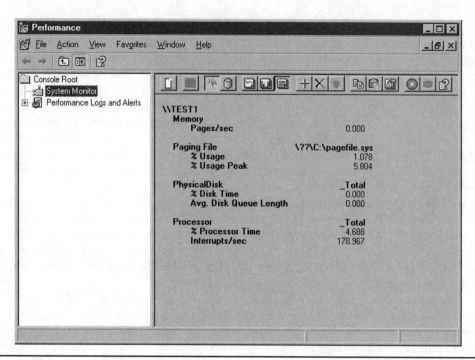

**Figure 4-6**    System Monitor in report mode

| Counter | Explanation | How to Decipher the Info |
|---|---|---|
| Memory: Available bytes | Displays the amount of memory available for use on the server. | If the amount of available bytes is less than 10 percent of the total amount of memory, it is possible your server is low on memory or an application is experiencing a memory leak. |
| Memory: Pages faults/sec | Displays the number of times a set of code or data is not found in the working set of the processor. The data may be found in physical memory (soft page fault) or located on disk (hard page fault). | Most processors can handle large amounts of soft page faults. Compare this reading to Memory: Pages/sec. |
| Memory: Pages/sec | Displays the current rate at which data is written to or retrieved from physical disk to resolve hard page faults. Memory: Pages/sec is the key indicator as to whether more RAM is needed. | A rate of 20 or more indicates a substantial amount of paging is taking place. Add more RAM to the server. |

**Table 4-1**    System Monitor Counters

| Counter | Explanation | How to Decipher the Info |
|---------|-------------|--------------------------|
| Paging File: % Usage | Displays in a percentage what portion of the paging file is currently in use. | If this reading approaches 100 percent, either the paging file is too small and needs to be enlarged or additional RAM needs to be added. |
| Physical Disk: % Disk Time | Displays in a percentage the amount of time the disk spends in read and write operations. | Check this reading with the Memory: Pages/sec and the Paging File: % Usage readings. A percentage of 70 percent or more is too high and indicates that the disk is too busy. In conjunction with high paging file usage it indicates that there is not enough RAM in the system and the physical disk is being used for the paging file. If the paging file readings are low, it could indicate a bottleneck on the disk itself and it's time to upgrade disks or install additional disks. |
| Physical Disk: Avg Disk Queue Length | Displays the number of read/write requests in the queue waiting to be performed by the disk. | This number should generally be under 2. If the number is increasing or consistently above 2, check the paging file and physical memory. If there is adequate physical memory, the disk itself could be the trouble spot. |
| Physical Disk: Current Disk Queue Length | Displays the current number of read/write operations waiting to be performed. | This number should be very small. A value greater than 2 indicates that the disks are impacting users. |
| Processor: % Processor Time | Displays the amount of time in percentage that the processor is busy. | It is not uncommon for a processor to reach 100 percent for short bursts, or during processor intensive operations, such as DVD playback. If the number is at or near 100 percent for extended periods of time, a new or additional processor is needed. |
| Server: Bytes Total/sec | Displays the total number of bytes the server has sent to and received from the network per second. | This indicates how busy a server is. This figure should be compared over time to a baseline figure as there is no general rule for all servers. |
| Server: Files Open | Displays the total number of open files at any given time. Does not display a running counter of the daily total. | This can indicate how busy a server is. |

**Table 4-1**    System Monitor Counters *(continued)*

been performing over time and make judgments as to whether the system is performing as it should. A good strategy to collecting data is to determine different times during the day or week when system performance is high, medium, and low, and then monitor the system at those points. Taking repetitive readings can help determine whether a system is performing adequately. It would be silly to base all your decisions on the data collected from the server at midnight on a Tuesday when there was no activity. It would be equally silly to base decisions on the data collected on Monday morning at 9:15 A.M. when the server is the busiest. Collecting data over time and compiling an average is called creating a baseline. A good baseline takes into account all these variances. To achieve an adequate baseline, it is recommended that data be collected over the course of three to four weeks.

System Monitor is great for monitoring current activity, but to analyze the information over time, log files are necessary. Performance Logs and Alerts is actually a subset of System Monitor and compiles the information into a log that can be displayed in System Monitor. Performance Logs and Alerts supports three types of logs: counter logs, trace logs, and alerts (see Figure 4-7). The counter log uses the counters available in System Monitor, such as the physical disk and memory counters. Trace logs are event driven, such as process creations/deletions, disk input/output, and page faults. Alerts contain counters and events, but only record an entry when a user-defined threshold is met, such as when the Processor: % Processor Time exceeds 80%. Using all three logs in conjunction with each other can help to establish a good baseline for your server and to consistently monitor activity.

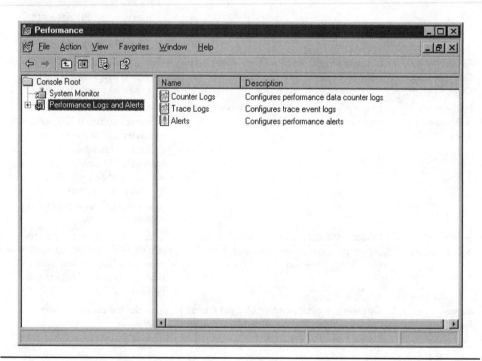

**Figure 4-7**    Performance Logs and Alerts

To create a new log file, right-click the log file and select New Log Settings or New Alert Settings. You must then choose events and counters to monitor, select a location to place the log file (C:/Perflog by default), and specify a schedule. The log can be configured to run manually or to run at a future time. There is not a mechanism to set up recurring sessions. To create a good baseline, you must run the log files at predetermined intervals.

## Lab Exercise 4.1: Using System Monitor and Performance Logs

In this exercise, you will use System Monitor to take several current readings of your server. You will also use Performance Logs and Alerts to create log files that can be analyzed over time.

1. Open System Monitor by clicking Start | Run and typing **perfmon**. System Monitor will open up in chart mode.

2. Right-click in the gray chart area and select Add Counters.

3. Select to use the local computer counters. Select Memory from the Object menu and select Pages/sec from the counters list. Click Add to add the counter.

4. Select Memory from the Object menu and select Available Bytes from the counters list. Click Add to add the counter.

5. Select Processor from the Object menu and select % Processor Time from the counters list. Click Add to add the counter.

6. Select Physical Disk from the Object menu and select Avg. Disk Queue Length from the counters list. Click Add to add the counter. Click Close to return to System Monitor.

7. Click the report icon (looks like a notepad) to display the data in report form.

8. Right-click the gray report area and select Save As. Name the file test1 and save it as an .htm file.

9. Navigate to the location where you saved the file and double-click the test1.htm file to display the report in your browser.

10. Click the chart icon (looks like a notepad with a line graph on it) to display the data in report form.

11. Repeat steps 8 and 9 to display the chart view in your browser.

12. Click the Performance Logs and Alerts node to display the Counter Logs, Trace Logs, and Alerts.

13. Right-click the Counter Logs and select New Log Settings. When prompted, enter **Test123** as the log name.

14. Click Add to add counters. Add the Memory: Pages/sec, Memory: Available Bytes, Processor: % Processor Time, and Physical Disk: Avg. Disk Queue Length counters to the log file.

15. On the Log Files tab, confirm that the log file will be created in C:\Perflog.

16. On the Schedule tab, confirm that the log will start manually. Click OK to close the log file properties.

17. Right-click the Test123 log file and select Start. Wait about five minutes and then right-click and select Stop.

18. To view the log file, click System Monitor, right-click in the chart area, and click Properties. On the Source tab, select Log File and navigate to the C:\Perflog directory and select the Test123 log file.

## Using Network Monitor

Network Monitor is a very basic IP traffic monitoring tool included with Windows Server 2003. It can only be used to monitor traffic to and from the server, and cannot monitor traffic on the local segment or across routers. For a full-featured network monitoring tool, install the Network Monitor included with Microsoft Systems Management Server (SMS). Network Monitor can be used to capture data, filter data, identify other Network Monitor users on the local segment, and view packet data.

Network Monitor, pictured in Figure 4-8, is automatically installed with Windows Server 2003. To start Network Monitor, click Start | All Programs | Administrative Tools | Network Monitor.

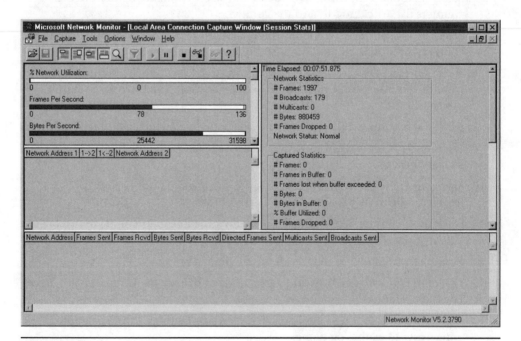

**Figure 4-8**   Network Monitor

# Increasing Performance by Modifying Virtual Memory

Before we proceed with the other tools available, let's talk about some ways to increase memory performance. Although a large amount of RAM is desirable, it is not always possible to add more RAM to a system. Many applications require a large amount of memory to run effectively. To prevent applications from using all available RAM on a system and to keep memory usage efficient, the operating system will move less important data from physical memory (RAM) to a location on a hard disk to create virtual memory. You can modify how much virtual memory is available and how it's used to increase performance.

Processors are designed to guess what set of instructions or commands are going to be run next and to load those commands prior to actually having to execute them. If a processor guesses wrong, a page fault occurs. A page fault is when the processor has to turn to another source to obtain the set of instruction, either RAM (which is very fast) or a paging file on a hard drive (not as fast as RAM). Although a paging file is not as fast as RAM, it is still much better than not having the command available, and so the paging file helps to increase the overall performance of the system.

To modify the virtual memory:

1. Click Start | Control Panel | System to open the System Properties.
2. Click the Advanced tab and then click the Settings button in the Performance section.
3. Click the Advanced tab and then click the Change button in the Virtual Memory section.
4. You will see the virtual memory settings shown in Figure 4-9.

## Allocating Virtual Memory

The amount of disk space allocated to the paging file can be modified to increase performance. Basically, the more space allocated to the paging file, the more improvement in performance. So what size should you set the paging file to? There are a number of answers to how large a paging file should be, and it often depends on the applications installed. The stock Microsoft answer has been to set the paging file to 1.5 times the physical memory installed. So in a system with 1GB of RAM, the paging file should be 1.5GB. Other publications recommend 2.5 times the physical memory installed. If Exchange 2000 is installed, it recommends setting the paging file to two times the physical memory installed.

Try setting the paging file to 0 or No Paging File. Restart your computer and see what happens. If you have a large amount of memory (over 512MB), you probably won't see much of a drop in performance, as there is plenty of RAM available for the applications running. The drawback is you will receive periodic nag screens (I mean, helpful pop-ups) stating that you don't have enough virtual memory and so Windows is creating a paging file for you.

**Figure 4-9**
Virtual Memory
dialog box

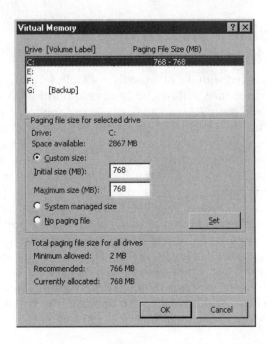

If you make sure you have enough physical RAM to run things properly, the amount of virtual memory becomes secondary. And to answer the question about how large of a paging file to create: go with what you are comfortable with. The paging file should be at least the same size as the amount of physical RAM installed. Whatever size you decide, make sure that you set the initial size and maximum size of the paging file to be the same. If the initial size and maximum size are different (as the default), the paging file will constantly resize itself, which leads to the paging file becoming fragmented and negatively affects performance. Whatever you do, do not allow the system to manage the paging file!

**NOTE**  After making changes to the paging file, you must restart the computer to commit the change.

## Moving the Paging File

One strategy to improve the performance of the paging file is to move it off the system volume and onto another physical disk. If a RAID 0 (disk striping) volume is available, that would be the ultimate. To move the paging file, open the Virtual Memory dialog box that you previously used to change the size of the paging file. The dialog box shows all available volumes on the system. Select a different volume, select the Custom Size radio button, and enter in a minimum and maximum size. Then clear the paging file from the system volume.

The drawback to moving a paging file from the system volume is that memory dumps will not run. When the system suffers a critical failure, a stop error occurs (the Blue Screen of Death) and the system is halted. Whenever a stop error occurs, a memory dump also takes place. A memory dump logs the contents of RAM into a log file, MEMORY.DMP, and places it in the %systemroot% folder. Memory dumps can help diagnose problems, kind of like an autopsy on a computer. Retaining memory dumps may or may not be a big deal. It depends on your environment and any service contracts that you may have in place. Service providers may require that memory dumps be sent to them for troubleshooting and research.

## Modifying Processor and Memory Performance

You probably noticed the screen shown in Figure 4-10 as you clicked through to the Virtual Memory Properties screen. The Performance options enable you to modify how the processor and memory are allocated. For servers, the processor should be allotted to background services. Programs may respond a bit slower on the server, but you really shouldn't be using a server to write reports anyway.

Don't automatically assume, however, that memory should be allotted to the system cache. Windows servers automatically assume that they are going to be used as file servers and allot a large block of memory, 25 percent, to the system cache for serving up files. If you are not using the server as a file server, change the memory allotment to programs. It will reduce the amount of memory allotted to the system cache, and services such as DNS will operate better.

**Figure 4-10**
Processor
and Memory
Performance
options

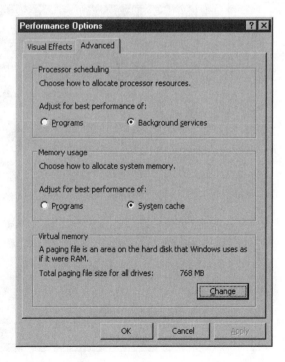

# Windows Update and Automatic Updates

Windows Update first appeared in Windows 98 and has been implemented in all versions of Windows since. Server 2003 adds scheduling capability to the Windows Update feature, hence the new term of Automatic Updates. Windows Update connects to the Windows Update web site and searches for downloads applicable to your computer. The automatic feature allows Windows Update to run at a specified time and download the applicable updates. Windows Update can be configured to prompt before downloading updates, prompt before installing the updates, or to automatically download and install updates, as shown in Figure 4-11. Windows Update settings are accessed in the System Properties page, by clicking the Windows Update tab.

Windows Update has also now been placed into Group Policy and can be configured as a Computer Policy and applied to a site, domain, or organizational unit. For more information on Group Policy, see Chapter 22.

# Maintaining Software by Using Software Update Services

Think of Software Update Services as Windows Update for your intranet. Software Update Services (SUS) is a service that runs on a server with IIS installed and acts as the distribution point for all clients in the enterprise for patches and critical updates obtained

**Figure 4-11**

Automatic
Updates on a
Server 2003
computer

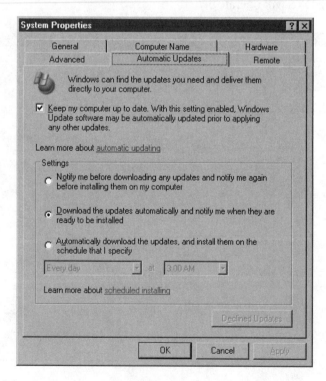

from the Microsoft Windows Update site. SUS obtains the patches and updates from Microsoft's site and distributes them to clients configured to use Windows Update. As noted in the previous section, Windows Update can be configured in Group Policy.

To use SUS, the program first must be downloaded and installed. SUS10SP1.exe can be downloaded from http://www.microsoft.com/windows2000/windowsupdate/sus/. (If the file is not in the preceding location, perform a search of Microsoft's web site for SUS.) Also, IIS 5.0 or higher must be installed. If IIS 5.0 or later has not been installed, the installation program will fail. A virtual directory named SUSadmin is created under the default web site and is accessible in Internet Explorer by typing **http://***yourserver*/ **SUSadmin**. This virtual directory enables an administrator to create a synchronization schedule, approve updates, view logs, set options and monitor the server, as shown in Figure 4-12. A synchronization schedule can be created so that the server will obtain all current patches and critical updates from the Microsoft Windows Update web site at regular intervals. These patches and critical updates will then be distributed to clients as they request them. An administrator must approve the patch or critical update or before

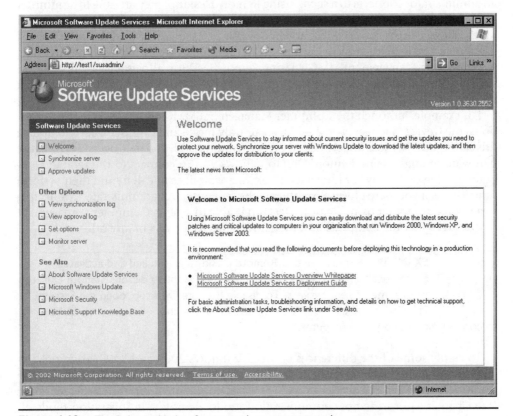

**Figure 4-12**    The Software Update Services web management tool

it can be distributed. The approval process is facilitated on the SUS web page by clicking Approve Updates in the navigation area.

Before clients can use the SUS server, they must be pointed to the server. Using Group Policy, an SUS server can be specified and then all clients affected by the GPO will direct their Windows Update requests to the intranet server. The Group Policy setting is located under Computer Configuration | Administrative Templates | Windows Components | Windows Update. This setting will only work with Windows Server 2003, Windows XP, and Windows 2000 with SP3 installed.

# Managing Servers Remotely Using Terminal Services (Remote Desktop)

All Windows Server 2003 servers have the built-in ability to be managed remotely by using Remote Desktop, the next generation of Terminal Services. Remote Desktop is installed with a default installation and allows up to two concurrent connections. When an administrator connects to a server using Remote Desktop, they are able to administer the server as if they were sitting at the machine. This is very useful, because although MMCs allow remote connections, not all operations are possible using an MMC, and it is often necessary to log directly onto a server. (Try updating a driver remotely by using the Computer Management MMC!) Using Remote Desktop allows an administrator to perform administrative tasks remotely that otherwise would need to be performed at the server.

For example, although the Computer Management MMC allows for remote connections, the Device Manager is opened in a read-only mode and cannot be used to update drivers from. You must log on directly to the computer to update drivers or configure hardware settings. Using Remote Desktop allows you to connect to the remote computer and log on locally (or interactively, as Microsoft likes to call it) and then perform functions as if you were physically sitting at the computer. An administrator connecting to a remote computer using Remote Desktop is able to open a Computer Management MMC directly on the computer and then update device drivers or any other task.

 **EXAM TIP**   Remember that Remote Desktop is installed and activated automatically. For security reasons, you may want to disable Remote Desktop from some of your servers. To disable Remote Desktop, open the System Properties and click the Remote tab. Clear the check box next to "All users to connect directly to your computer."

To clarify some of the differences between Windows 2000 and 2003, Terminal Services was not installed by default in 2000, but had to be manually added by using the Control Panel. Terminal Services was then installed in either application server mode (see Chapter 3) or in remote administration mode. Remote administration mode allowed administrators to connect to a server remotely and perform administrative functions as if they were physically sitting at the server. In Windows Server 2003, remote administration mode has become Remote Desktop and is automatically installed and available out of the box. Terminal Services must still be manually installed to be used as an application server to clients.

Either the Windows 2000 Terminal Services client or the new Remote Desktop client can be used to remotely connect to a server. Windows Server 2003 also ships with a Remote Desktops (notice the S) MMC, shown in Figure 4-13, which can be used to manage multiple servers at once. The Remote Desktops tool is located in the Administrative Tools. The 2003 Remote Desktop clients are much cleaner and simpler to use than the 2000 version. The Remote Desktop client is included with the Server 2003 CD and can be installed on virtually any Windows operating system. To connect to a server remotely, all you need is either the server name or IP address. You must also be a member of the Administrators group or have been granted the logon locally right to the server in order to establish the session.

To connect remotely to a Windows Server 2003 server:

1. Click Start | All Programs | Accessories | Communications | Remote Desktop Connection.

2. Enter either the IP address or the computer name of the server you want to connect to.

**Figure 4-13**   Remote Desktops MMC with multiple connections open

3. You may also configure additional options, such as sound and screen size by clicking the Options button.

4. Click Connect.

# Managing File and Print Servers

The most common use for a Windows server is that of a file and print server. You have already learned how to make files available for use by creating shares and granting appropriate permissions. In this section, you will learn how to manage and troubleshoot a Windows Server 2003 file and print server by using tools such as disk quotas, Disk Defragmenter, and print queues.

## Using Quotas

Quotas are sometimes necessary to keep users from overwhelming a server with massive amounts of useless data. Who needs to save that three-year-old draft of the company picnic memo anyway? Using quotas on a Windows Server 2003 server can limit the amount of space a user has to use and prevent users from saving items above and beyond their allocated space amount.

Quotas are implemented on a per user per volume basis. User quotas are calculated based on the size of files and folders owned or created by that user. Also, if a user has compressed files on the volume, the entire amount of uncompressed space is charged against their quota limit. When a user creates a memo in Word, the size of that document is counted against that user. If a user installs a program, the size of the program is also counted against the user's quota limit. You can use quotas to restrict the amount of disk space a user can use on a particular volume.

## Enabling Quotas

To enable quotas, select the Enable Quota Management box on the Quota tab of the volume properties, as shown in Figure 4-14. However, a specific limit must also be configured. By default, enabling quotas only enables the reporting aspect of quotas and enables an administrator to view how much disk space is being used by each user on the volume. Quotas do not by default deny disk space or set limits for users. When a limit is set, it applies to everyone who accesses the volume, except administrators. We get a free pass! This is simply because the Administrator account is used to install Windows and other programs, and a quota limit would be impractical for an administrator.

To enable quotas:

1. Open Windows Explorer, right-click the drive where you want to implement quotas, and click Properties from the drop-down list.

2. Click the Quota tab.

3. Click in the box next to Enable Quota Management.

4. Click in the box next to Deny Disk Space To Users Exceeding Quota Limit.

**Figure 4-14**
The Quota tab
on the volume
properties
dialog box

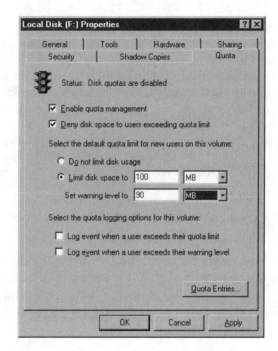

5. Click the radio button to Limit Disk Space To and specify a limit.

6. Set the warning level to the desired setting.

You can also choose to log when a user exceeds their quota limit or exceeds their warning limit. By default, the administrator is not notified when a user reaches their limit or is warned that they are reaching their limit.

If the option to deny disk space to users exceeding their quota limit is checked, users will not be able to save any additional files to the volume until they either move some of the files to a different volume or delete some of their files. Moving a file from one folder on a volume to a different folder on the same volume doesn't work, and neither does compressing current files. Remember that the quota limit counts the entire uncompressed file size.

**NOTE** Be careful when setting low quota limits in an attempt to prevent users from saving documents to a server. If a quota limit of about 1MB or less is set on the system volume, users who have not logged onto the server previously are prevented from logging on. A user's profile must be loaded for the user to log on. If the profile is larger than the quota limit set, the user cannot log on.

## Creating and Modifying Quota Entries

To view how much disk space is being used by individual users, click the Quota Entries button on the Quota properties page. You will see a screen similar to Figure 4-15. The quota entries will show you a report of all users who have saved at least one file to the volume and how much space they are currently using. Every user has a quota entry based on their user account.

By creating or modifying quota entries, exceptions can be made for individual users who need more space than is allotted. By default, the quota setting applies to all users. If a user needs additional space, you can create a new quota entry for them if they haven't saved anything to the volume yet, or you can modify their existing quota entry. To create a new quota entry:

1. On the Quota tab of the volume, click the Quota Entry button.

2. Select File | Quota | New Quota Entry.

3. Enter the name of the user or browse Active Directory. Notice that you can't add a quota entry for a group, only a user. Click OK.

4. Either click to limit the disk space and enter a maximum level and a warning level, or click Do Not Limit Disk Usage. (See Figure 4-16 for an example of a quota entry.)

To modify an existing quota entry:

1. On the Quota tab of the volume, click the Quota Entry button.

2. Select a user and right-click their user name. Select Properties from the menu.

3. Click to either limit the disk space and enter a maximum level and a warning level, or click Do Not Limit Disk Usage.

Quotas can only be set per user. Quota entries cannot be set for groups. The recommended procedure is to implement a quota and specify a limit that will be applied to all users. Then as needed, create quota entries for individual users who require a different limit than has been set globally. By default, administrators have a quota entry created with no limit set.

 **EXAM TIP**   Remember that quota entries cannot be created for groups. Quota entries are per user per volume only. If you need to create an entry for a group of users, you need to specify each individual user.

## Using Disk Defragmenter

It is highly recommended that you defragment your disks on a regular basis. Over time, as files are created, removed, moved, copied, and edited, they can become fragmented. When a file is written to disk, it is written to clusters. Clusters are tiny parts of the drive

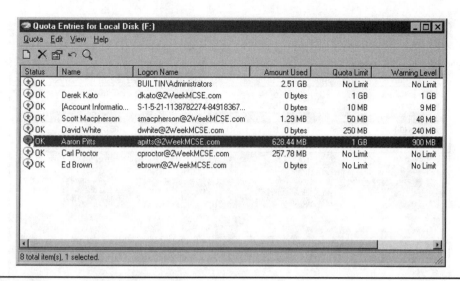

| Status | Name | Logon Name | Amount Used | Quota Limit | Warning Level |
|---|---|---|---|---|---|
| OK | | BUILTIN\Administrators | 2.51 GB | No Limit | No Limit |
| OK | Derek Kato | dkato@2WeekMCSE.com | 0 bytes | 1 GB | 1 GB |
| OK | [Account Informatio... | S-1-5-21-1138782274-84918367... | 0 bytes | 10 MB | 9 MB |
| OK | Scott Macpherson | smacpherson@2WeekMCSE.com | 1.29 MB | 50 MB | 48 MB |
| OK | David White | dwhite@2WeekMCSE.com | 0 bytes | 250 MB | 240 MB |
| OK | Aaron Pitts | apitts@2WeekMCSE.com | 628.44 MB | 1 GB | 900 MB |
| OK | Carl Proctor | cproctor@2WeekMCSE.com | 257.78 MB | No Limit | No Limit |
| OK | Ed Brown | ebrown@2WeekMCSE.com | 0 bytes | No Limit | No Limit |

**Figure 4-15**    The Quota Entries dialog box

where information is stored. A file may take up several clusters and the clusters might not be contiguous. When a file is moved or deleted, often the noncontiguous clusters are not removed as well, thereby creating a fragment. The process of defragmenting removes lost clusters and also reorders clusters in a more efficient order. Defragmenting will improve the performance of your system.

Microsoft includes a disk defragmenter as part of the system tools, as shown in Figure 4-17. You must have approximately 15 percent free space available to defragment a drive. If you don't have adequate free space, you will need to free up some space before defragmenting. You may also have to defragment several times to achieve the desired results.

**Figure 4-16**
Creating a
quota entry

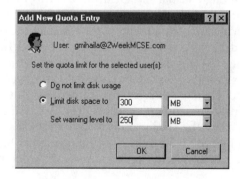

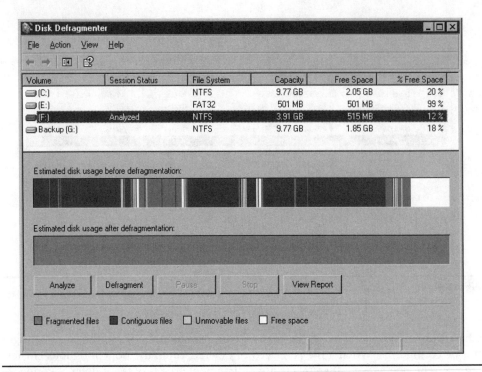

**Figure 4-17**    Disk Defragmenter

 **EXAM TIP**    It is recommended that you defragment disks every 1–2 months. If a server's disk performance is suffering and no new changes have been made for several months, defragmenting the disk is a possible fix.

The two major drawbacks to the disk defragmenter included with Windows Server 2003 are that it is only capable of using a single processor and a defragment cannot be scheduled. Although Visual Basic can be used to make the Windows defragmenter work, it requires additional knowledge of scripting. (For more information on VB scripting for Windows defragmenter, see *Windows & .Net* magazine article #8276, by Zubair Alexander at http://www.winnetmag.com/Articles/Index.cfm?ArticleID=8276). There are some excellent third-party products available with scheduling and multiple processor capabilities. Diskeeper 7.0 by Executive Software (http://www.executive.com/) and Defrag Manager by Winternals (http://www.winternals.com/) are highly acclaimed defragmenting tools. The interesting thing is, when you install Diskeeper, it installs the product directly into the Computer Management snap-in, and you use it just like you would the basic defragmenter that ships with Windows.

You can access Disk Defragmenter in three different ways:

• Click Start | All Programs | Accessories | System Tools | Disk Defragmenter.

- From the Computer Management snap-in, expand the Storage node and click Disk Defragmenter.

- From My Computer, right-click the drive you want to defragment and select Properties from the drop-down list.

Once the Defragmenter is open, click the Tools button and select Defragment Now.

## Using Disk Cleanup

To remove temporary Internet files, compress old files, and empty the recycle bin, Disk Cleanup is provided as a utility. Disk Cleanup provides a user-friendly interface to perform these basic functions. Disk Cleanup can be run from either the properties of the volume or by typing **cleanmgr** from a command prompt and specifying the drive to be cleaned up.

As you can see in Figure 4-18, there isn't a whole lot to the Disk Cleanup utility. It helps organize the deletion process and makes it easy to get rid of temporary files. If you click the More Options tab, you will also have an option of going to the Windows Components applet to remove unwanted operating system components or of opening the Add/Remove Programs applet to remove programs. There are many things the Disk Cleanup does not do, however. Disk Cleanup does not remove all temporary Internet files, cookies, or off-line content. To remove these files, you need to manually browse to the appropriate folders and delete the contents. It does not help you remove old

**Figure 4-18**
Disk Cleanup
utility

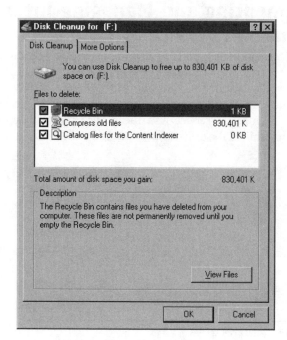

documents or clean up an inbox. You should definitely keep an eye on these types of files and delete them manually on a regular basis.

**NOTE** Two good third-party tools to remove temporary Internet files, spyware, adware, cookies, and other temporary files are AdAware (http:// larasoftusa.com) and Windows Washer (http://www.webroot.com).

### Monitoring and Managing Print Jobs

When a user clicks the Print button and sends the print job to a print server, that job becomes the responsibility of the print server and is monitored and managed from the print server. From the print server, you can start or stop a job, cancel a job, or check the properties of a job. In Chapter 1, you learned how to install a print device and configure a print server. In this section, you will learn how to monitor, manage, and troubleshoot print jobs.

### Using the Print Queue

You can view current print jobs by opening the Printers and Faxes folder and double-clicking the printer. The print queue, shown in Figure 4-19, will display any pending print jobs. It will not display completed print jobs. From the print queue, you can stop a pending job, resume a print job, delete a print job, or pause the printer.

## Implementing and Managing Internet Information Services (IIS) 6.0

Internet Information Services (IIS) 6.0 is a powerful upgrade to IIS 5.0, included with Windows 2000 Server. The first thing you will notice is that IIS is not installed by default. The next thing you will notice after installing IIS 6.0 is that it installs with only a few very basic services. These are dramatic steps in increasing the overall security of a network. IIS is the most heavily attacked service and the service most susceptible to hacking attempts. Microsoft has shifted the thinking in securing a network from one of plugging holes as they

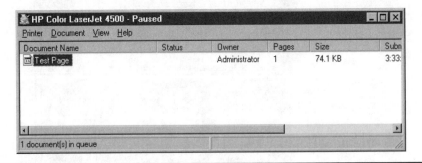

**Figure 4-19** The print queue

are discovered to one of securing servers out of the box, and adding services and programs as needed.

# Installing and Configuring IIS

The architecture of IIS 6.0 is significantly different than previous versions. Application pools are introduced for the first time as a method of keeping processes separate, and compression of HTTP responses is now natively supported within IIS. These changes implemented in Server 2003 have increased the stability and scalability of web services. This section outlines some of these changes and covers material necessary to pass the exam.

**NOTE** There are many additional topics that are not covered in this book. For a more complete reference, please see *IIS 6.0 The Complete Reference*, by Hethe Henrickson and Scott Hoffman, McGraw-Hill/Osborne, 2003.

IIS security is now much improved as well. For starters, IIS is not installed with Server 2003 by default; it must be added manually. This subtle change has been universally applauded by security professionals. In Windows 2000, IIS was installed as part of the default installation, and IIS was also configured to host .asp pages, scripts, and other dynamic content. This became a favorite target of hackers and indeed spawned more than one patch from Microsoft to plug the holes. Having to manually install IIS 6.0 means that there will be very few servers, if any, that have an unintended installation of IIS running.

## Installing Internet Information Services 6.0

You can install IIS manually by using the Control Panel or you can enable the application server role in the Add A Role Configuration Wizard. The Add A Role Configuration Wizard is accessible through the Configure Your Server Wizard in Administrative Tools. Microsoft has created roles for their servers, and a particular type of server can now be configured by using a wizard, shown in Figure 4-20, instead of manually adding all necessary components through the Control Panel. Using the wizard simplifies the setup and configuration of components.

To install IIS from the Configure Your Server Wizard:

1. Click Start | All Programs | Administrative Tools | Configure Your Server.
2. Click Next until you reach the Server Role page.
3. Select the Application Server Role and click Next.
4. If you intend to use FrontPage or Active Server Pages, select the check boxes next to the options and click Next.
5. Click Next to start the installation.
6. If you would like to view additional help, click the link on the Finish screen. Otherwise, click Finish.

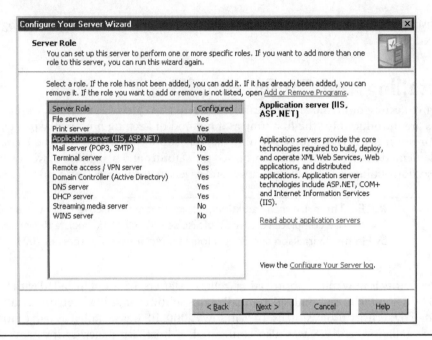

**Figure 4-20**   Adding the application server role

Whichever method you use, IIS is installed in a locked-down state, and services and components must be installed before they can be used. For example, the SMTP service is not installed by default. You must enable SMTP manually by using the Control Panel. To see a list of components installed, open the Add/Remove Programs applet in the Control Panel and bring up the Windows Components dialog box. Click Application Server and click Details. Then click Internet Information Services (IIS) and click Details. Figure 4-21 shows that the only components installed by default are Common Files, the IIS Manager, and the World Wide Web Service. If you click the World Wide Web Service and click Details, you will see that none of the services supporting dynamic content, such as .asp pages, are installed.

## Lab Exercise 4.2: Installing IIS 6.0

In this exercise, you will install Internet Information Services 6.0. IIS is not installed with a default installation of Server 2003, and so it must be added after Server 2003 has been installed. You will notice in the exercise that the naming of IIS and components is slightly different than in previous versions of IIS.

1. Click Start | Control Panel | Add/Remove Programs.

2. Click Add/Remove Windows Components.

**Figure 4-21**

Details of the IIS installation

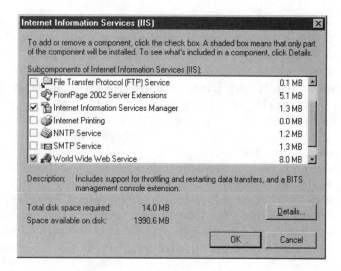

3. Select the Application Server from the list of available components.

4. Click Details to view the underlying components and services installed with the application server. Click OK when finished and click Next.

5. Insert the Windows Server 2003 CD-ROM when prompted.

6. Click Finish when the Completing Windows Components Wizard appears.

7. Click Start | All Programs | Administrative Tools | Internet Information Services (IIS) Manager.

8. Expand the Local Computer if necessary and click Web Service Extensions.

9. In the Details pane, select Active Server Pages and click Allow.

10. Select the Server Side Includes and click Allow.

11. Close the IIS Manager.

12. Open the Add/Remove Programs applet again and navigate to the Windows Components list.

13. Select Application Server and click Details.

14. Select World Wide Web Services and click Details.

15. Notice that Active Server Pages and Server Side Includes are now installed and available for use.

## Configuring Web Sites

A default web site is made available when IIS is installed. The default web site only supports static content, such as .html files. The default web site can be renamed to a more descriptive name, such as 2WeekMCSE.com or Osborne.com. To rename the default web site, right-click it and select Rename. Or right-click it and select Properties, then change the description of the web site. Other configuration changes include performance options, logging options, implementing certificates, and other authentication options. These configuration changes will be discussed in the following sections.

## Changing the Home Directory of the Default Web Site

When IIS is installed on a Windows Server 2003 server, a default web site is created, with the home directory being the %systemroot%\inetpub\wwwroot. If only one web site is going to be hosted on the server, the default web site can be configured to host the content. All that needs to be done is to place the web content into the %systemroot%\ inetpub\wwwroot folder. However, in most cases, developers have already established folders in which they have placed web content, and it is easier to simply change the location of the home directory. IIS can draw files from any folder on the server, or a shared folder located on another server, or a redirection to a URL. To change the home directory, open the web site properties and click the Home Directory tab, as shown in Figure 4-22. If the files are located on the server, select the corresponding radio button and browse to the appropriate folder. If the files are located on a shared folder on another server, select the corresponding radio button and enter the UNC path to the share. The Connect As button also allows an account to be specified to connect to the share. If the files are located on a different URL, select the corresponding radio button and enter the URL.

**Figure 4-22**
Changing the
home directory
of the default
web site

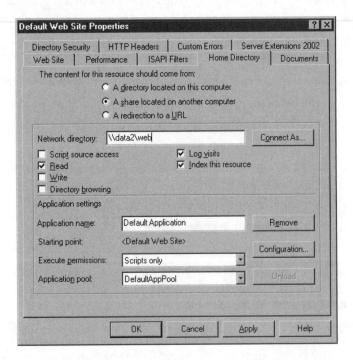

## Creating New Web Sites

A single web server can host multiple web sites. Before multiple sites can be hosted, however, one of three methods has to be implemented. (See the following section entitled "Hosting Multiple Web Sites on a Single Web Server.") By default, any new web site created will be stopped and won't be able to respond to requests for pages.

## Lab Exercise 4.3: Creating a New Web Site

In this exercise, you will create a new web site, provide content, and test the server to verify that content is viewable. Before proceeding with the exercise, you need to complete Lab Exercises 3.4 and 4.2. In Lab Exercise 3.4, you created two folders that you are going to use in this exercise: Web and Graphics. If you have not completed these exercises, do so now. Also, you will need the CD-ROM that came with this book, as the web content is located on the CD-ROM.

1. Click Start | All Programs | Administrative Tools | Internet Information Services Manager to open the IIS Manager MMC.

2. Right-click the Web Sites node and select New | Web Site.

3. Click Next to begin the Web Site Creation Wizard.

4. In the Description field, type **2WeekMCSE.com** and click Next.

5. Accept the default of All Unassigned for the IP address and Port 80 for the port. Do not enter a host header. Click Next.

6. For the Web Site Directory, navigate to the Web folder created in Lab Exercise 3.4. Click Next.

7. Uncheck the permission to run scripts and verify that Read is the only permission present. Click Next.

8. Click Finish to complete the operation.

9. Right-click the Default Web Site and select Stop.

10. Right-click the 2WeekMCSE.com web site and select Start.

11. Insert the CD-ROM that was included in this book.

12. Copy the contents of the Web folder to the Web folder you created in Lab Exercise 3.4.

13. Copy the contents of the Graphics folder to the Graphics folder you created in Lab Exercise 3.4.

14. Open Internet Explorer and type **http://***yourserver* into the navigation bar to view the web site.

## Hosting Multiple Web Sites on a Single Web Server

There are three methods to hosting multiple web sites on a single web server:

- Assign a unique IP address to each site

- Assign a unique port number to each site
- Assign host headers to each site

Each of these methods has some sort of drawback, so it is important that you evaluate what is most important before selecting a method. The settings are on the Web Site tab of the properties page.

Assigning a unique IP address to each site is the easiest of the three methods. However, you need to either configure a single network card with multiple IP addresses or install a new network card for each web site. An IP address has to be specified when a new web site is created, but All Unassigned is the default option. All Unassigned then assigns all IP addresses associated with the server to the web site. If an IP is selected that is in use by another site on the same server, the web site will be created in a stopped state. To start the site, either the other site has to be stopped or a unique IP has to be assigned.

Assigning a unique port number to a site is more a security procedure than a method of supporting multiple sites on a single server. By default, all web sites use port 80. Any traffic coming into the server on port 80 is automatically directed to the web site. If a unique port number is used for a site, only traffic coming into the server on that port number will be directed to the site. The problem with this is that Internet Explorer and other browsers automatically request pages on port 80, and any other port has to be specified in the address bar of the browser by the user. If a second web site was configured to use port 6767, for example, users would need to type **www.2weekmse.com:6767** to access the site. If you want your users to check e-mail on a publicly accessible web site, but you want the site to remain hidden from the public, you could create the web site on a different port number than 80 and then require your users to enter the port number in the address field to access the site. Excellent for keeping a particular site hidden, not so excellent as a method of hosting two sites on the same server.

Host headers require a bit more administration to use, and are not as popular a method because they don't support SSL encryption and are unable to be used by earlier versions of browsers that don't support HTTP 1.1. To use host headers, you must configure DNS and IIS. To configure host headers:

### Part 1 – Configure IIS

1. Click Start | All Programs | Administrative Tools | Internet Information Services.

2. Expand the Web Sites node and select the Default Web Site. Right-click the Default Web Site and select Properties.

3. On the General tab, select the IP address from the drop-down list. Click Advanced.

4. In the Advanced Web Site Configuration Properties page, select the Default IP address and click Edit.

5. Enter a value for the Host Header. Click OK and close the Web Site Properties.

Part 2 – Configure DNS

1. Click Start | All Programs | Administrative Tools | DNS.

2. Navigate to the appropriate zone.

3. Add a CNAME record in the zone. For the Alias name, enter the Host Header value. For the Fully Qualified Name of the target host, enter the FQDN of the web server.

**EXAM TIP**   Remember that host headers do not support SSL or HTTPS and so are not a preferred method of assigning multiple web sites to a single computer. The preferred method is to either install a second network card or configure a second IP on the original network card. Installing additional cards is not usually done, especially if the server is supporting several web sites.

## Changing the Default Document

When a user types in a web site address, such as www.2weekmcse.com, they are directed to the home folder on the web server, and a default file is called up. This default file is set on the web server. IIS 6.0 automatically uses Index.htm, Default.htm, Default.asp, and IISStart.htm as default files. Most sites use Index or Default as the home page, so it is possible that the web site will load properly right out of the gate. However, developers are a bit of a mixed breed, and the home page may be named something different, such as newdesign.htm or opening.htm. In this case, IIS needs to be aware of the different file name and call that file up when a user hits the directory and requests a page. In some cases, the file may be named Index, but have an .html extension (notice the l). In either case, there has to be an exact match or no file will be loaded and the user will receive a File Not Found error.

It is also very common that once a web site is built, additional changes are made to the site using a different naming context, such as index2.htm or altdefault.htm. This practice enables web developers to create several pages that are essentially the same and to test out different designs. After a site is ready, it is easy to add the name of the new default page to the documents tab and then all requests will automatically load the new file.

In any case, the default document needs to be changed on the server to match the appropriate file and therefore load the site. To change the default document, open the web site properties page and click the Documents tab. Verify that the Enable Default Content box is checked and then click Add to add a default document. Type in the name, such as home.htm or index2.htm. Also, move the current default page to the top of the list to make sure that's what people see when they request a page. It's also a good idea to remove the old default page from the list.

## Configuring FrontPage Extensions

First, what are FrontPage extensions and why do you need them? The answer to the second part of that question is you might not. FrontPage server extensions are server-side components that allow a user to update web content by using the FrontPage client. If you are not using FrontPage for your web development tools—many developers live and die by Macromedia products (http://www.macromedia.com/), not FrontPage—then you don't need to enable FrontPage server extensions.

FrontPage extensions first need to be installed from the Windows Components menu before they are able to be configured in IIS. To install the extensions, select Application Server from the Windows Components menu and click Details. Select IIS and click Details to view the IIS components. Select FrontPage 2002 Server Extensions from the list to install the component. After installation is complete, you will notice a Microsoft SharePoint Administration web site listed in the IIS Manager. This web site, shown in Figure 4-23, replaces the wizard and properties pages included in IIS 5.0.

**EXAM TIP** If you see FrontPage on the exam, look for server extensions. Remember, server extensions won't work for any other product! If the scenario uses Macromedia Dreamweaver, for example, you can't use FrontPage extensions.

## Configuring Performance Parameters

By default, every web site is created with the floodgates wide open and will allow as much traffic to and from the site as it receives. The flow of traffic can be limited on a per site or per server basis. You should be careful before configuring bandwidth throttling

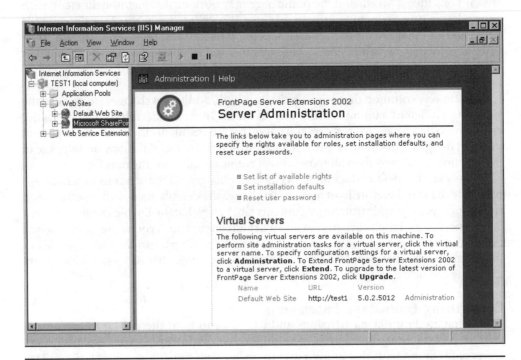

**Figure 4-23** The SharePoint Server Administration web site as viewed in IIS Manager MMC

or web site connections, as any requests over the limited amount will be denied. This may not be the desired result!

To view the performance parameters, open the web site properties and click the Performance tab. Notice that the performance settings are disabled, as in Figure 4-24. To enable bandwidth throttling, click the check box next to "Limit the network bandwidth available to this Web site." Maximum bandwidth can then be limited up to 32,767 KBps (kilobytes per second). The average data transfer is 50 Kbps (kilobits per second). Setting the bandwidth to the maximum would allow over 5,000 simultaneous connections! This is probably more than enough for most operations. The maximum number of connections can also be limited. Notice that the default is set to unlimited connections.

**NOTE**  To help with the calculations: there are 8 bits in a byte. There are 8 kilobits in a kilobyte. A kilo is a thousand, as in kilometer (1,000 meters), but a kilobit is actually 1024 bits, not 1,000 bits. 32,767 kilobytes is 262,136 kilobits.

If you right-click the Web Sites container and select Properties, you can also configure bandwidth throttling and maximum connections per server. If the performance properties are set per server, the maximum amount of bandwidth will be shared by all web sites hosted on the server.

**Figure 4-24**
Configuring
bandwidth
throttling and
maximum
connections

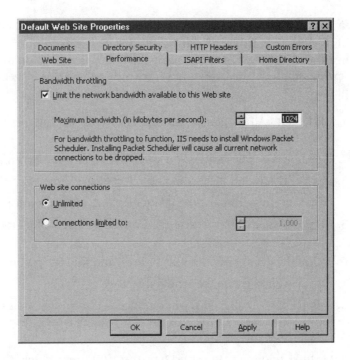

Bandwidth throttling and maximum number of connections can be set to avoid overloading a server that isn't capable of handling excessive traffic, either because of hardware capabilities, network connectivity, or both. Also, if a particular site is expected to receive a small amount of traffic, the performance properties can be set that would then allow more bandwidth and connections to other sites hosted on the server.

## Configuring Virtual Directories

Virtual directories allow IIS to display content not found in the home directory. Virtual directories can be used to pull content from several sources into one web site. Virtual directories are especially valuable in an intranet setting because individual departments can be responsible for their own content without having to have permissions or access to the web server.

Windows Server 2003 provides a wizard to configure a virtual directory. The wizard does not allow browsing to a network location other than the local computer, but a UNC path can be entered and credentials entered as well.

A sneaky way to configure a virtual directory is to enable web sharing on a shared folder and select the appropriate web site to place the directory into. You also will notice a Printers virtual directory already configured. This Printers virtual directory displays the web site used to manage shared printers on the server. The Printers virtual directory by default is located in %systemroot%\web\printers.

## Lab Exercise 4.4: Configuring a Virtual Directory

In this exercise, you will configure two virtual directories, one using the wizard located in the IIS Manager MMC and one using the Web Sharing tab on the folder itself. Notice that permissions can be configured from either the IIS Manager or the Web Sharing properties.

1. Click Start | All Programs | Administrative Tools | Internet Information Services Manager.

2. Click the Web Sites folder and select the 2WeekMCSE.com web site.

3. Right-click 2WeekMCSE.com and select New | Virtual Directory.

4. Click Next to start the wizard. Enter an alias of **CorporateShares** and click Next.

5. Click Browse and navigate to the CorporateShares folder located on your server. Click Next.

6. Accept the default permissions of Read and Run Scripts and click Next.

7. Click Finish to create the virtual directory.

8. Refresh the default web site and notice the CorporateShares virtual directory is located in the root of the web site. CorporateShares is displayed with a gear-like icon, as in Figure 4-25.

9. Open Windows Explorer and type **http://*yourservername*/CorporateShares**.

10. Notice the error you receive: Directory Listing Denied. Verify that you have configured the appropriate NTFS and share permissions previously as instructed

**Figure 4-23**
The
CorporateShares
virtual directory

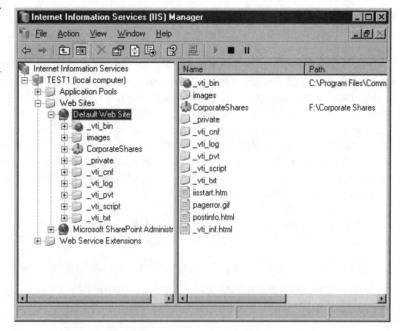

in the exercises in Chapter 3. The domain users should have Read permission configured for both NTFS permissions and for share permissions. If the permissions are not configured correctly, please do so now.

11. Refresh the page. Notice that you still receive the error: Directory Listing Denied. The problem isn't with the underlying permission, the problem is with the permissions on the web site itself. There are no .html or .asp files in the CorporateShares folder, so no content is able to be displayed. To display the contents of the folder itself, you must configure the appropriate permissions.

12. Right-click the CorporateShares virtual directory and select Properties from the drop-down list.

13. On the Virtual Directory tab, enable Directory Browsing permissions.

14. Refresh the page in Internet Explorer. You will now be able to view the Human Resources Documents folder.

15. Open Windows Explorer and navigate to the HRDocs folder.

16. Right-click the folder and select Properties from the drop-down list. Click the Web Sharing tab.

17. Select the Default Web Site from the drop-down list and select the radio button for Share This Folder. Accept the HRDocs alias when prompted and also enable directory browsing.

18. Click OK twice to back all the way out and accept the changes. Open Internet Explorer and type **http://*yourserver*/HRDocs** to view the payroll060603 file.

## Using Application Pools

Application pools are a new feature in IIS 6.0. Using application pools increases a web server's ability to handle more traffic and to manage multiple web sites more effectively. Each web site or application can now be assigned to a separate dedicated process. Separating web sites and resources in this way isolates problems, and a failed process or bug in one site will not affect other sites located on the same server. Think of application pools as separate memory space for web sites, much the same way NT places applications in their own memory space and a problem in one application doesn't affect other applications. By default, all web sites are assigned to the DefaultAppPool, located under the Application Pools node in IIS Manager, as shown in Figure 4-26.

Additional application pools can be created and assigned to individual web sites as desired. To create a new application pool:

1. Right-click the Application Pools node in IIS Manager.

2. Select New | Application Pool.

3. Enter a name for the application pool in the Application Pool ID and click OK.

4. The new application pool will appear under the Application Pools node.

**Figure 4-26**

IIS Manager showing all available application pools and web sites

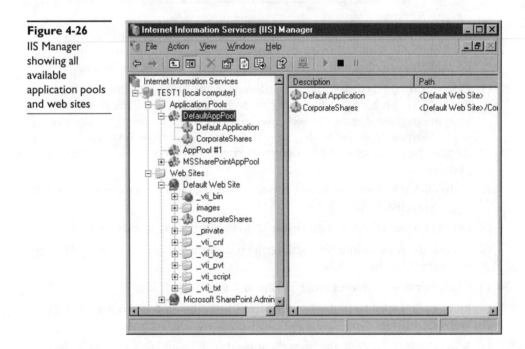

## Configuring Application Pools

By configuring application pools, you can set the parameters for processes and memory usage, protect the server from becoming overloaded, monitor the health of the processes, and specify a security account to be used with the application pool. To view the configuration settings of an application pool, right-click the DefaultAppPool and select Properties. You will see four tabs: Recycling, Performance, Health, and Identity, as shown in Figure 4-27. The application pool parameters can be set for each individual application pool, or globally by right-clicking the Application Pools node in IIS Manager and selecting Properties.

The Recycling tab is used to set the parameters for process and memory recycling. When an application pool is created, a separate worker process is associated with the application pool. A worker process is a separate instance of the w3wp.exe service, the service that runs IIS. Recycling occurs as new worker processes start and old worker processes are shut down. Setting the recycling parameters forces old processes to shut down and new processes to start at certain intervals. Memory recycling can also be configured to prevent memory leaks from occurring.

The Performance tab is used to set parameters for protecting the server from becoming overloaded and to set monitoring options for the server. The Idle Timeout setting shuts down worker processes after being idle for 20 minutes. This is to prevent a multitude of worker processes from starting and then standing idle until the end of time. The Web Garden (following the new tradition of networking words like forest and tree) specifies how many worker processes can be created at any time. If the site is expected to

**Figure 4-27**

Application pool properties sheet

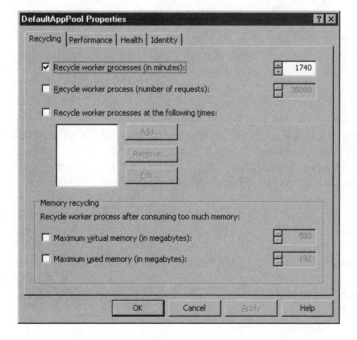

receive a large number of hits, the number of worker processes should be increased to allow the workload to be distributed among several worker processes.

The Health tab contains additional settings that monitor the web server and will perform certain actions to protect the health of the server. If pinging is set, the worker processes will be pinged at set intervals to determine if it is still running. If the worker process does not respond to a ping, the process will be terminated and a new worker process started in its place. The startup and shutdown time limit ensure that worker processes don't hang on startup or shutdown. If a worker process does hang, the server will forcibly terminate the worker process.

The Identity tab allows an account to be specified for the application pool to use when accessing resources on the server. By default, the Network Service account is specified.

## Assigning a Web Site to a Separate Application Pool

By default, all web sites are assigned to the DefaultAppPool. After you create additional pools, web sites can be assigned to a different application pool. To assign a web site to an alternate application pool:

1. Right-click the web site desired and select Properties.

2. Click the Home Directory tab.

3. In the Application Settings section, click the Application Pool drop-down list and select a new application pool to use.

4. Click OK to save and close the properties sheet.

## Monitoring Web Sites

The IIS Manager includes logging and monitoring options. To configure monitoring, open the web site properties and click the Web Site tab. The Enable Logging check box is selected by default, which automatically turns logging on. The default format for logging is W3C Extended Log File Format, but additional formats can also be used, such as Microsoft IIS Log File Format, NCSA Common Log File Format, or ODBC Logging. When logging is enabled, events are written to the application log in Event Viewer. To view additional logging options for the W3C Extended Log File Format, as shown in Figure 4-28, click the Properties button. Notice that logging can be scheduled or based upon a preset file size. Also, there is an option to use local time for all logging. When users request pages from the web site, they transmit their own system time to the web site. If local time is not used, it is possible for events that occur very late in the day would be logged in the following day's log file, based on the time of the remote system.

Also, when IIS is installed, additional counters are automatically added to System Monitor. These counters are used in the same way that other counters are used, and they can either be monitored in real time or stored as a log file. For more information on System Monitor and adding counters, please see the section entitled "Using System Monitor" earlier in this chapter.

**Figure 4-28**
Logging Properties
of the W3C
Extended Log
File Format

## Securing Web Sites

As soon as a connection to the Internet is established, security becomes a concern. Luckily, there are a few things that can be done to drastically improve the security of your web server. To start with, if a server isn't going to be used as a web server, then uninstall IIS. This isn't quite as critical with 2003 as the basic installation no longer installs IIS by default, but every server should still be verified that it isn't running IIS.

Also, a good firewall is an absolute must. Cisco (http://www.cisco.com/) and Watchguard (http://www.watchguard.com/) make excellent firewall appliances. Yes, Windows Server 2003 can be configured as a firewall by using Network Address Translation (NAT) and other services as part of the Routing and Remote Access Server (RRAS), but a dedicated hardware firewall is better.

That said, there are still a couple of areas that need to be addressed on the web server itself.

## Install Patches and Updates

This one seems obvious, but it's still relevant. Microsoft works extremely hard to be responsive to bugs and security holes in their IIS server, and usually manages to release a patch or fix prior to the problem being exploited by hackers. Microsoft had patches in place prior to the Code Red, Code Blue, and Nimda viruses running rampant through the Internet. Any server that had the relevant patch installed was impervious to these viruses and worms. The patches and updates can be installed using the Software Update Server.

Microsoft has also made available a tool to assist in installing hotfixes. Most hotfixes require a reboot of the server, and having to install nine different hotfixes and reboot the server nine times isn't practical. Qchain.exe is a downloadable program from Microsoft that allows multiple hotfixes to be installed with only a single reboot. To obtain Qchaine.exe go to http://www.microsoft.com/downloads and search for qchain. For detailed information on using Qchain, see Microsoft Knowledge Base article 296861.

## Configure Authentication and Restrictions

All users of a web site actually have to authenticate to the domain before being able to access information, even anonymous users. By default, browsers attempt to access resources anonymously. If anonymous users are allowed access to the web site, they are authenticated to the IUSR account. (Go ahead, check your AD Users and Computers, it's there!) The IUSR account is an Internet user account created just for the purpose of allowing anonymous access and has very limited permissions granted.

Anonymous users can be prevented from accessing your entire site or only specific directories. For example, you might run a personal web page where you post a letter to your family with recent pictures and so on. But you might also have a link on your personal web page to Outlook Web Access, which you use when you're on the road. Anyone with nothing better to do can access your personal web page, but they must have a valid user account in your Active Directory to log on to your Outlook Web Access directory. In this case, the anonymous user has been removed from the proper directory, and users must be a member of the appropriate group before they can log on and check e-mail. If you wanted to go one step further, you could remove the anonymous user from your entire site, and users would have to be authenticated to your Active Directory to even view the letter and pictures.

To restrict a site, right-click the web site and select Properties, then click the Directory Security tab. Click Edit in the Authentication section to display the authentication options, as shown in Figure 4-29. Notice that anonymous access is allowed by default, and all requests will be authenticated to the IUSR account.

The following authentication methods can also be used:

- Integrated Windows authentication
- Digest authentication for Windows domain servers
- Basic authentication
- .NET Passport authentication

**Integrated Windows Authentication**    When this type of authentication is selected, a domain user account must be present for the user attempting to access the web site. The user is authenticated against the Active Directory in which the IIS server is a member. The user also must be a member of the appropriate groups to have access to the content and directories located on the web server. When a user attempts to access a web site, they are prompted for their user name and password, as shown in Figure 4-30. If the user is already logged onto the domain in which the web server is located, they are not prompted for a user name and password as their current domain account is used automatically. Integrated Windows authentication uses either Kerberos or NTLM as the

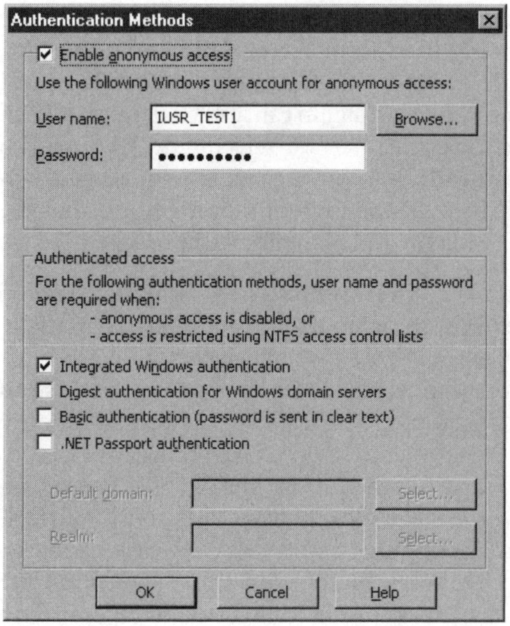

**Figure 4-29**
The
Authentication
Methods
properties page

authentication protocol, depending on the capabilities of the client, ensuring that passwords are not passed over the Internet in clear text. Integrated Windows authentication is most commonly used in intranets.

**Digest Authentication**    Digest authentication is used when Integrated Windows authentication is not supported, and is most commonly used over the Internet. An MD5 algorithm is transmitted instead of the actual password, and the values are compared against the password in Active Directory. Users must still have a valid user account in Active Directory to be authenticated using this method.

**Figure 4-30**
User name and
password prompt
when attempting
to access a
secured site

**Basic Authentication**     Basic authentication is the most widely supported and the most commonly used form of web authentication. Passwords are sent in clear text across the Internet and verified against the domain in which the IIS server is a member. Accounts on a different domain can also be used by entering a domain in the appropriate field or by clicking Browse and selecting the desired domain. Basic authentication is supported by nearly all browsers and all operating systems, which is why it is so commonly used. Using basic authentication ensures that nearly everyone visiting the site will be able to log on and authenticate in order to use web resources.

**.NET Passport Authentication**     .NET Passport is Microsoft's baby and the method they have come up with to authenticate users to multiple web sites by using a single e-mail account. .NET is natively supported in Windows XP and Windows Server 2003, and you've most likely seen the pop-ups to register a .NET Passport with your user account. Microsoft has switched all of their secure directories and sections on their web site to .NET Passport, and so you have probably been forced already to establish a .NET Passport account. On the up side, using .NET Passport really does mean that a single e-mail address will work for multiple sites. .NET Passport was created with e-commerce in mind to make signing on and shopping easier and faster. .NET Passport supports all the good web stuff as well, such as SSL, cookies, and JavaScript, and is compatible with IE 4 and higher, Netscape 4 and higher, and Opera 7.11 and higher.

## Configuring IP and Domain Restrictions

In addition to requiring users to authenticate to the site, certain users can be blocked from accessing the web site by their IP address or their domain name. This technique is especially useful to prevent hackers from gaining access to the web server. Access can be either blocked or allowed based on a source IP or domain name, as shown in Figure 4-31.

Let's say you are configuring a secure site that only your own network and one of your clients is going to be authorized to use. You will first enable Integrated Windows authentication and make sure that each user has a valid user account in your Active Directory. But you can go one step further. You can enter the network ID of the client and the network ID of your own internal network, and allow access to only those specific blocks

**Figure 4-31**
Allowing access to a specific IP address

of IP addresses. Using this in conjunction with user names and passwords makes a very secure web site indeed.

To enter a specific IP address or a network ID, click Edit to bring up the IP Address and Domain Name Restrictions page. Then click Add and enter a single IP or network ID or domain name, as shown in Figure 4-32. Be aware that if a domain name is entered, a reverse DNS lookup will be required for every user attempting to access the site, which can significantly slow performance. (You are even warned about this behavior when you click the option.)

## Use Secure Sockets Layer (SSL) and Certificates

If Secure Sockets Layer (SSL) is configured to be required for a particular site or directory, all users attempting to access the site or directory are required to use HTTPS, and all information transferred between the client and the web server is encrypted. E-commerce sites should use SSL at a bare minimum to protect credit card transactions, viewing of account data, user logons, and other personal services. To enable SSL, click Edit under Secure Communications and select Require Secure Channel (SSL). Windows Server 2003 servers built and used only in the United States also have the option to require 128-bit encryption, also known as strong encryption, rather than the standard 40-bit encryption. It is illegal to export 128-bit encryption outside of the United States.

Certificates can also be used as a method to protect the web site and to authenticate users and allow access. Before certificates can be used, a certificate authority must be installed and configured. See Chapter 17 for more information on certificate authorities.

By configuring the appropriate certificate settings in the Directory Security properties page, and by installing and issuing certificates, an extremely secure web site can be built.

## How Delta Airlines Uses Web Certificates

Using certificates to provide secure web access is actually a very common process. Delta Airlines, one of the largest U.S. airlines, uses a secure web site for their employees to access their schedule, send and receive company e-mail, request vacation time, and related tasks.

Here's how it works. Rebecca is a flight attendant for Delta. Rebecca is required to put in a bid for her upcoming schedule on a monthly basis. She can put in her bids at either a Delta lounge at one of the airports or at home by using a secure web site. Rebecca connects to the Internet at home and then enters the address for the Delta scheduling web site, which is a secure site. She is prompted to log on to the site using her user name and password. However, if that's all it took, any employee could access the site from any computer connected to the Internet, and anyone could attempt to hack into the site. Imagine if Rebecca was able to log on to the site from the coffee shop on the corner and then the next person to use the computer at the coffee shop could try to hack in. Not what Delta had in mind. So Delta uses certificates to secure the web site and ensure that Rebecca is only able to access the site from a designated computer.

When Rebecca attempts to access the web site, she is prompted for a user name and password and asked to provide a valid user certificate. The certificate part is transparent to Rebecca. She was required to obtain the certificate prior to logging onto the secure web site, and Delta provided a procedure that she had to follow. Rebecca had to log onto a different web site and provide personal and employment data to obtain a certificate. Once the information she provided was validated, she was able to download a user certificate and install the certificate onto her computer at home. This certificate is requested when she attempts to log on to the scheduling web site. If the certificate is not present, she is denied access to the site.

Delta has about 15,000 flight attendants who need to request schedules every month. They are providing service to a large number of employees while still maintaining a secure environment to protect themselves against hackers. And although they are using a sophisticated system, it is transparent to the users. Once Rebecca receives her user certificate, she doesn't need to do any additional configuration or perform any additional configuration. She only needs her user name and password to log on to the scheduling site.

## Uninstall SMTP and E-mail Services

IIS 6.0 now ships with Simple Mail Transfer Protocol (SMTP) and Post Office Protocol (POP3) capability; however, IIS really isn't designed as an e-mail server. Microsoft has another product called Exchange, which they would prefer that you use for e-mail. A web server with SMTP and POP3 installed is a target for hackers. It is recommended to remove the e-mail services unless they are explicitly required.

To uninstall the services:

1. Click Start | Settings | Control Panel | Add/Remove Programs.

2. Click the Windows Components button.

**Figure 4-32**

Entering a single IP, network ID, or domain name

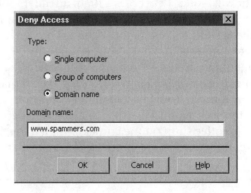

3. Select Application Server and click Details.

4. Select IIS and click Details.

5. Clear the boxes next to the SMTP and POP3 services. Click OK several times to start the process.

# Chapter Review

Managing the guts of a server isn't always the most fun thing an administrator does, but it is certainly a necessary task, and one that should be paid close attention to not just once, but on an ongoing basis. Checking the event logs regularly and taking periodic readings of your server is just the beginning. The event logs can provide valuable information for troubleshooting applications and services. Additional event logs are created as additional services are added, such as DNS or Directory Service. These event logs contain information about the respective services. The Security log contains auditing events and all logon-related events. Event logs can be configured with different size and rollover properties, either locally on the server or in Group Policy.

In this chapter, you learned how to use several management tools to monitor your server and improve the performance. Task Manager is an excellent tool to use to gather information about your processor and memory. Task Manager is also used to manage applications and processes. System Monitor allows you to monitor hardware and operating system components, such as memory, hard disks, and DNS. System Monitor gives real-time output. You can use Performance Logs and Alerts to create log files and to determine a baseline for your server.

You also learned how to use disk quotas to keep users from overburdening a server with too much data. Other disk management tools were also covered, such as Disk Cleanup and Disk Defragmenter. All these tools help you to monitor and manage a file server.

The task of administering a web server is daunting. There are many considerations that must be made when installing and configuring a web server. You must be concerned about security. You must create web sites that are stable and able to handle large amounts of traffic. You must monitor the server constantly to ensure that it is performing well. This chapter covered simply the basics in installing and configuring a web server.

## Questions

1. Your Windows Server 2003 has been operational for approximately six months. The server is used to download streaming video from the Internet and to distribute the content to clients in your organization. You have previously configured a striped volume with three hard drives. The server stores temporary files and content on the striped volume. You schedule the temporary files to be deleted on a weekly basis. Lately, you have noticed a drop in performance. What should you do to improve performance using the least amount of cost?

   A. Add additional RAM and a second processor to your server. Configure the additional processor to load balance the streaming video.

     **B.** Run Disk Cleanup on the striped volume and remove all the temporary files.

     **C.** Convert the striped volume to a spanned volume.

     **D.** Run Disk Defragmenter on the physical disks where the striped volume is located.

     **E.** Run Disk Defragmenter on the striped volume.

2. You are the administrator of a Windows Server 2003 server that has a single 80GB drive. The drive is configured as a single primary partition. The partition contains a shared folder named Users where users save their personal files. You want to prevent users from using more than 100MB of disk space in the shared folder. What actions should you take to accomplish this? (Choose all that apply.)

     **A.** Upgrade the disk to a dynamic disk.

     **B.** Enable disk quotas for the Users shared folder, set the default quota limit to 100MB.

     **C.** Enable disk quotas for the entire volume, set the default quota limit to 100MB.

     **D.** Create a quota entry for the Users global group, set the quota limit to 100MB.

     **E.** Enable shadow copies for the Users shared folder.

     **F.** Select the "Deny disk space to users exceeding quota limit" check box.

3. Todd is the administrator of a Windows Server 2003 server configured as a web server. Todd has enabled logging on several of the web sites hosted on the server. As Todd's supervisor, you require that all logs are directed to you for verification. You notice that all of the logs end at 9:00 P.M. and all of the data between 9:00 P.M. and midnight shows up on the following day's log. What should you tell Todd to do to ensure that each log contains data for that day only?

     **A.** Ensure that the log type is set to W3C Extended Log File Format.

     **B.** Ensure that the log type is set to ODBC.

     **C.** Change the Log Rollover property in the web site logging properties to local time.

     **D.** Change the system time of the server, and adjust the time for the correct time zone.

     **E.** On the Advanced tab of the logging options, enable Time and Date.

4. You enable disk quotas on a Windows Server 2003 file server. You configure a quota limit of 100MB. A user named Mark reports that he can still save large files to the server, even though he is well above his quota limit. What should you do to correct the problem?

     **A.** Check the "Deny disk space to users exceeding quota limit" check box on the Quota tab for the volume.

     **B.** Instruct Mark to take ownership of all of his files.

C. Create a quota entry for Mark and specify 100MB as the limit.

D. Change the quota limit from 100MB to 50MB.

5. 2WeekMCSE.com is a technical training company that employs instructors, salespeople, and office staff. 2WeekMCSE.com also employs seven developers and programmers for consulting work. There are approximately 40 users, including the developers and programmers. The developers and programmers are members of a global group called Consultants. You are the administrator of the network. You build a new Windows Server 2003 server and configure a hardware RAID 5 controller with two partitions. Volume C contains the boot files and system files, and Volume D contains shared folders, which will be used to store user data. 2WeekMCSE.com has decided to implement quotas for all users and limit the amount of disk space per user to 30MB. You are instructed that the developers and programmers are not to be limited as to how much space they are allowed to use. How should you configure disk quotas? (Choose two.)

A. Enable quota management on Volume D. Select the "Deny disk space to users exceeding quota limit" check box and specify a quota limit of 30MB.

B. Create a new quota entry for the Consultants global group. Select "Do not limit disk usage for this entry."

C. Create a new quota entry for each developer and programmer, using their individual user accounts. Select "Do not limit disk usage for this entry."

D. Enable quota management on Volume D. Select "Deny disk space to users exceeding quota limit." Select "Do not limit disk space" as the default quota limit.

E. Create a new quota entry for each user account that will be accessing the volume. Select a quota limit of 30MB for each user.

6. You are the administrator of a Windows network running only Windows Server 2003. Recently you have discovered that some junior administrators are remotely logging onto three file servers and performing incorrect configurations. The three servers are located at the headquarters in a secure location. The servers should be administered only by an administrator with access to the secure server room. The junior administrators should not be able to log on remotely to the servers. How can you prevent the junior administrators from being able to remotely administer the servers using the least amount of administrative effort?

A. Create a global group called JRADMIN. Make the junior administrators members of the JRADMIN global group. Create a local group called JRADMINACCESS. Add the JRADMIN global group to the JRADMINACCESS local group. On each of the three servers, deny the logon locally right to the JRADMINACCESS group.

B. On the System Properties of each server, uncheck the "Allow users to connect remotely to your computer" check box.

    **C.** Place the three servers in a separate OU. Deny the logon locally right to all junior admins in a GPO and link the GPO to the OU.

    **D.** Remove the junior administrators from the Administrators group. Make the junior administrators members of the Power Users group.

7. Every morning you run an Excel spreadsheet locally on the Windows Server 2003 server to analyze data collected the night before. Users report that access to files at this time is significantly slower than at other times. What should you do to resolve the problem?

    **A.** Run the Start /normal csrss.exe command before starting Excel.

    **B.** Run the Start /normal Excel.exe command to start Excel.

    **C.** Use Task Manager to set the Explorer.exe process to high priority.

    **D.** Use Task Manager to set the Excel.exe process to low priority.

8. You are the administrator of a Windows Server 2003 file server, on which all users have their home folders stored. You have implemented a 25MB disk quota on the volume, with the option to deny disk space to users exceeding their limit. On the same volume is a shared directory named Public that all users can save files to. Tim attempts to save a file to his home directory, but receives a message that he is out of space. What can Tim do to save the file?

    **A.** Move some of his files to the Public folder.

    **B.** Compress the contents to his home directory.

    **C.** Delete some files from his home directory.

    **D.** Save the new file to the Public directory.

9. You are the administrator of your company's network. You are running Windows Server 2003 on all servers and Windows XP Professional on all workstations. You have decided to implement Software Update Services to keep all desktops and servers up to date. You install SUS10SP1.EXE. You configure Group Policy to direct all Windows Update requests to the SUS server. You use the SUSadmin tool to synchronize the server with the Windows Update web site. However, none of your clients are receiving updates. What should you do?

    **A.** Nothing. There aren't any updates to install.

    **B.** Package the updates into an .msp file and deploy using Group Policy.

    **C.** Approve the updates.

    **D.** Instruct your users to run Windows Update on their computers.

10. You are the administrator of your company's network. You have three servers which you are responsible for managing, PDX2, PDX4, and PDX6. All three servers are maintained in a secure server room at the company's main location. For security purposes, you don't want to allow administrators to connect remotely to PDX4 to perform administrative tasks. What should you do?

A. Uninstall Terminal Services.

B. Deny the Logon Locally right to administrators.

C. On the System Properties tab, clear the Allow Users To Connect Remotely box.

D. Uninstall the Remote Desktop Connection client from the administrators' computers.

## Answers

1. **E.** A fragmented volume will slow overall system performance. It is recommended to defragment volumes on a monthly basis. Volumes can be defragmented, not disks. Disk Cleanup is a simple utility to assist in removing temporary Internet files and other temporary files, however, in this case you have been keeping up on the deletion of these files. The problem is not that there are too many temporary files, but rather, with the load on the volume, the volume has become defragmented. While adding more RAM and processors to a system is hardly ever a bad idea, neither solution would compensate for the fragmentation of the drive and both would cost additional money. A striped volume is the highest performance in terms of read/write for volumes. Converting a striped volume to a spanned volume would drastically decrease performance.

2. **C and F.** Disk quotas can only be set on a volume or partition, not a folder or shared folder. You must first enable the quota limit for the primary partition and then select the option to "Deny disk space." By default, when quotas are set, the quota only keeps track of use, it does not deny space to users exceeding the quota limit. Quota entries can only be created on a per user basis, not for groups. Also, it is recommended to enable quotas and then use quota entries to account for exceptions (users needing more space than is generally allotted). Shadow copies have nothing to do with quotas.

3. **C.** Enabling the log rollover to be set for local time, all logs will end at midnight and a new log file will be created for the following day. By default, the logging format is set to W3C Extended Log File Format. While verifying that this format is being used is a good idea, it would not solve the issue of the logs ending at 9:00 P.M. Enabling ODBC logging enables an entirely different set of logging properties, none of which have anything to do with the time of the logs rolling over. Changing the system time would actually cause additional problems, such as not being able to log onto the system, and would not fix the problem.

4. **A.** Remember that by default, enabling quotas only allows for reporting of disk space used, it does not prevent users from using additional space. You must check the box to "Deny disk space to users exceeding the quota limit." Instructing Mark to take ownership of the files would not prevent him from saving additional files. If anything, it would increase the amount of space he was currently using. Also, you almost never want to involve the users in any kind of administrative task. Mark already has a quota entry for 100MB. Lowering the quota limit would not prevent Mark from saving additional files.

5. **A and C.** Remember that quotas are set per volume per user. You must first enable quota management on the volume and set a quota limit of 30MB. Then you must create a quota entry for each developer and programmer. You cannot create a quota entry for a group. Also, it makes no sense to create individual quota entries for every user who is going to save data to the volume. Create a default quota limit and then add exceptions to the default limit.

6. **B.** The question states that the servers will only be administered locally by users with physical access to the servers; therefore, you have no need to use Remote Desktop to manage the server. Simply disabling Remote Desktop is the simplest thing to do. Answer A is classic Microsoft group theory. It's also a bit overkill for the scenario. Moving the servers into a separate OU is not called for. In fact, moving the servers into a separate OU may prevent certain policies from taking place that were already configured. Removing the user accounts from the Administrators group would prevent the junior administrators from being able to administer any server.

7. **D.** Change the priority of the Excel process to low, thereby decreasing the amount of I/O time on the processor and allowing other processes to have more I/O time with the processor. The csrss.exe process, the client/server runtime server subsystem, is responsible for graphics and windows functions. Starting this process in normal priority would not affect system performance. Raising the priority of the Explorer.exe process to high would have a further negative impact on the server.

8. **C.** Quotas are per user per volume and once the limit is met, files need to be moved off the volume or deleted to make space for new files.

9. **C.** Before the updates will be available to clients, they must be approved by an administrator. You approve the updates by using the SUSadmin tool. Connect to the SUS server by typing **http://*yourserver*/susadmin** into your browser and select the Approve Updates link.

10. **C.** To disable Remote Desktop, simply clear the "Allow users to connect remotely to your computer" check box under Remote Desktop on the Remote tab of the System Properties.

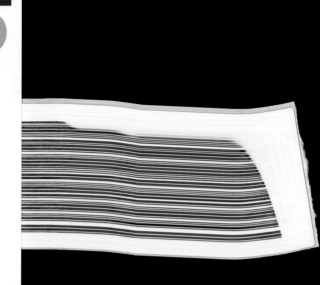

# Managing and Implementing Disaster Recovery

In this chapter, you will learn how to

- Develop a backup and recovery solution
- Use Backup Utility for Windows
- Back up data
- Back up the system state data
- Schedule backups
- Test and verify backups
- Restore data
- Restore the system state data
- Recover from boot failures
- Implement an Automated System Recovery (ASR)

While having a backup and recovery plan is great, it's important to actually put your plan into action. Being prepared to recover from a failure is the most important task an administrator can be concerned with. In fact, if you learn nothing else from this book but how to recover from a failure, you will be a hero someday! Knowing how to share files, create groups, run a web server, and set up networking components are all great things, and certainly part of your job, but to a certain degree they can be learned as you go. There is no such thing as learning backup and recovery when you most need it. You either have it or you don't.

There are two parts to a backup and recovery strategy: implementing a plan and testing that plan on a regular basis. There are many firms that have a plan that is untested and untried. What if something is wrong with the backups? You don't want to find out that the tape drive has been writing blank disks for two months after a virus wipes out your servers. It is vitally important to actually test your backup and recovery strategy regularly to make sure that it works. This chapter will cover the basic principles of creating and implementing a backup and recovery plan, and how to test this backup plan.

Also, there are times when a server crashes, sometimes to the point where the operating system fails to boot properly. Windows Server 2003 includes an Advanced Boot menu to help you get the server back up and running quickly. Also, for occasions when that doesn't help, Microsoft's emergency repair process comes in handy. The emergency repair process, Automated System Recovery, has been improved, gotten a new name, and is better than ever. In this chapter, you will learn how to use the ASR process to repair a failed server.

## Backup and Recovery Solution

be given some steps to take during the planning stage. Make answer the questions posed. Get the opinion of the owner of the IT manager, and anyone else who would be affected by the plan. Then make sure that whatever plan you develop, you implement the plan isn't half as important as actually implementing the backup, so whatever plan you adopt, make sure you implement it.

### Document, Document, Document

Your backup and recovery plan should be written down. You have heard the expression "a goal not written down is a wish"? The same is true of a backup plan. If the backup and recovery plan is not documented, how do you know it will get implemented? Documenting a backup and recovery plan can take a significant amount of time, but is worthwhile. Your disaster recovery document should include not only the steps, but screen shots, passwords, IP addresses, and other information needed to restore your network. Your backup and recovery document should be easy to follow. If a new administrator is hired, he or she should be able to perform a complete backup and recovery by following the document.

After completing the documentation, test the entire solution. Compare the document to what you actually did. If you run into a minor problem, document what you did to fix it. It may be something simple that you are able to intuitively fix, but other people may not know what to do. Create your document as if someone else is going to implement it, not you. Write your document for the mailroom guy. It is unlikely that a mailroom guy would ever have a need to run your recovery solution, but write it for him anyway. If you document well, you won't have to cut short that long overdue vacation if something goes wrong in the office.

### Build a Disaster Recovery Kit

In addition to the document that you create, you should also build a disaster recovery kit. What is a disaster recovery kit? It is a kit that includes additional components that you will need to recover from a disaster, such as critical manuals, copies of software, software keys, serial numbers and passwords. These items all need to be in a single location and easily accessible in case of a disaster. Your kit should also include any specialized hardware that is difficult to obtain. Servers are fairly easy to replace and can be done so quickly, but if you use any specialized cards or components that came from over seas, you should have a spare in your disaster recovery kit.

A must-have for your disaster recovery kit is a phone list of all important parties. You need to have a contact list for your vendors, suppliers, and consultants so they can be reached quickly. You also need to have a contact list of internal people that need to be informed of a disaster. It is critical to notify your own internal people as quickly as possible in case of a disaster for two reasons: 1) decisions have to be made quickly as to how to proceed and 2) coordination needs to be established quickly between your company and the outside vendors and consultants providing services. Often a single person is chosen ahead of time to coordinate all disaster recovery efforts and to oversee the project.

# Developing a Backup Strategy

Before you sit down and whip out a backup and recovery document, there are some planning scenarios that you need to consider and plan for. Should you plan for a complete disaster, like the World Trade Center? How about rolling blackouts? Or should you just plug in a backup tape and run things every few days? To help you develop a sound backup and recovery solution, there are several questions you should answer. What should I back up? What is my recovery point? What is my time frame for recovery? How critical is this particular server to my business? What is my risk tolerance, if any? Answering these questions will help you develop a backup and recovery solution that is right for your company.

## What Should Be Backed Up?

The easy answer is *everything*! However, backing up everything isn't always practical or desireable. Backing up every computer in your enterprise is probably out of the question. Backing up every server completely may still be a bit daunting and require more resources than you have at your disposal. You may only have the resources available to back up the most critical servers in your network.

When designing a backup solution, make sure you back up the following:

- Data, including user files, e-mails, and databases
- Critical system files (including Active Directory)
- Exchange Server or other e-mail server
- SQL Server or other database server
- Critical applications

Your backup plan should start with backing up user data. We live and die by our data. Businesses keep customer information, product information, prospects, sales leads, and just about everything about the business in electronic form. If this information is lost, it is not unrealistic that the company could go out of business. As an example, let's suppose that the server where the contents of this book were stored failed beyond repair and there wasn't a backup of the material. We would lose the entire book. That's a lot of work to re-create! Whether you need to protect sales data, production work, or e-mails, the data that makes your business or organization run is critical and should be protected.

Mission-critical applications, including Exchange or SQL Server, are important to backup. Installations of Office or screen savers or other production applications aren't as critical. Most applications can be reinstalled fairly easily, especially using Group Policy (see Chapter 22 for information on how to install software using Group Policy). Exchange is particularly picky about reinstallation. If you don't do it right, you can lose your entire information store, which really isn't much fun. Make sure the mission-critical applications are backed up and able to be recovered in case of a failure.

You should also try the restores on some preplanned schedule to insure all still work. That little issue has killed many an IT fellow. Also, your DR plan should be retested every 12 to 18 months and parts of your DR should be tested after applying maintenance...such as new microcode, or new drivers, or the obvious new tape software release.

 **NOTE**   Backing up Exchange is different from backing up the data store. If the Exchange Server is not backed up, it may be impossible to recover user data, even if the user data was backed up.

## What Is the Recovery Point?

The recovery point is a determining factor as to how often backups are done and what technologies are used to implement recovery processes. The recovery point is at what point it is acceptable to restore back to. Is every piece of data that comes into the network so critical that the recovery point needs to be up to the minute? Or is it acceptable to lose some data, maybe the stuff everyone was working on today? Also, do critical system files have the same recovery point?

Let's look at the recovery point for data first. Most small and medium-size businesses are satisfied with a 24-hour recovery point for their data. It is acceptable to recover data up to the day before in case of a catastrophe. For their situation, a daily backup of data is acceptable. Very few organizations would accept a recovery point of longer than a day. Larger organizations that perform millions of transactions a day may not be satisfied to lose a day's transactions. The recovery point for them is much, much shorter. Think of a company like eBay. eBay performs millions of transactions per day. What would be the effect if something were to happen to its systems and it lost an entire day's transactions? For eBay, the recovery point is maybe 30 seconds. eBay takes precautions then to protect its critical data up to the minute.

The recovery point for critical system files may differ simply because system files change much less than user data does. A small or medium-size organization may be satisfied with a recovery point of a week or a month. Why? Because once a system is implemented (whether it be a web server, e-mail server, domain controller, or application server) the system itself doesn't change drastically on a daily basis. In fact, it may not change for several months. For most small and medium-size companies, a recovery point of a week for critical system files is acceptable. In some cases, a longer interval is acceptable. On the other hand, a large organization may make changes to its systems more often. A large company with 40,000 employees will probably make at least a few changes to Active Directory each day. For a large company, a recovery point of a single day may be required on its critical servers and domain controllers.

So what should you implement? Do some digging to discover your own company's recovery point, then design your backup and recovery solution to fit. As a general rule, a daily backup of data and a weekly backup of critical servers are adequate for most businesses.

## What Is the Time Frame for Recovery?

The answer to this question determines how long after a disaster occurs you have to get everything back up and running. After the recovery point is determined, the amount of time to recover to that point is determined. The previous day's data may need to be recoverable, but it may be able to be done over a couple of days. Or it may in fact need to be up and running again in two hours. The amount of time required for recovery will directly impact the type of backup technology that will be used. The recovery time begins the moment the disaster happens, not when you finally decide to recover. So if a recovery time of three hours is desired, but it takes two hours to consult with responsible persons to decide on recovery, you only have one hour to actually recover.

Let's look at a couple of examples:

- **Two hours** A very short time frame for recovery such as two hours would necessitate using a server technology, such as clustering servers or mirroring hard drives. Using traditional methods of backup, such as tape, would probably be too slow, depending on the amount of data.

- **Eight hours** Eight hours is the typical workday of an IT administrator. Having an entire day to work with is actually fairly typical. In this case, tape drives might work, depending on the amount of data backed up. If the backup is over several hundred GB of data, a high-speed DLT tape drive or large capacity hard drive is necessary.

- **48 hours** A weekend. Having this amount of time basically allows for any type of backup technology to be used. Tape drives are going to be adequate.

- **One week** A week may be needed in an extreme case such as a disaster. With proper backups, most servers and equipment can be rebuilt and data recovered in a week.

- **Longer than a week** This is a fairy tale! No one ever gives you more than a week to recover from a crash.

## What Is the Risk Tolerance?

Determining risk tolerance will actually help answer some of the other questions. A weekly backup may seem fine until the tolerance for risk is determined, and then how often a backup is run may be altered. Determining risk tolerance is a classic technique used by stockbrokers when interviewing potential new clients. The stockbroker asks, "What are your investment goals?" to which the potential client usually responds something like, "To retire when I'm 50," or "To double my money," or other such lofty expectation. The stockbroker then asks a follow-up question: "Would you be able to survive if your entire investment was wiped out?" The answer to that question helps determine the amount of risk tolerance the investor has and what kind of a portfolio the stockbroker will create.

The same kind of question should be asked about your data center. What kind of loss is acceptable? Realize that the greater the aversion to risk, the more money it's going to cost. The ultimate in backup and recovery systems is to implement a hot site, a secondary site located in a separate location with all the capabilities of the main data center. Hot sites can be switched to if the main building is disabled or unavailable due to a disaster. Implementing a hot site can easily cost upwards of $1 million, and require significant expertise to implement. For some companies, the cost of not being open for business is far greater than the cost of a hot site, and so the cost is easily justified. For most businesses, much less exotic backup and recovery plans are adequate.

## How Critical Is this Server to My Enterprise?

Implementing a backup solution costs money, so priorities should be placed on different servers. It is not possible to back up every computer in the enterprise. It may not even be possible to back up every server in the enterprise. Make a list of all the critical servers in your company, and then prioritize those servers. Domain controllers are considered critical to the enterprise. In many companies, Exchange, SQL, and other database servers are considered critical. And every company has at least one application which they consider mission-critical. Make sure that the servers considered absolutely critical to the enterprise are backed up frequently.

### The Ultimate Backup Strategy

A lot of us work in small offices where a relatively simple backup solution is adequate for our needs. If we are able to recover data from the day before, and bring a server online in a couple of hours, everyone is happy. However, larger enterprises require a different level of preparedness.

There are some companies that do thousands of transactions worth millions of dollars daily. For them, the prospect of being out of business for several hours, let alone several days, is downright scary. When these companies analyze their needs and create their backup and recovery plan, they plan for a complete loss of the main data center, whether it be from fire, weather, terrorism, earthquake, or other disaster. The concern is not only to be able to recover quickly, but to keep from missing transactions. To keep from losing millions of dollars, they implement a hot site.

Here's how a hot site works. A location completely separate from the main headquarters is built, often in a different city. The hot site may be located in a different region of the country to avoid being affected by the same disaster that affects the main headquarters. (Remember rolling blackouts? Or the entire Northeast losing power for two days?) Many companies place their hot site with a disaster recovery solution provider to avoid the costs of completely constructing a new building. Then the company can duplicate the data center in the new building, or implement just a core infrastructure that would enable the company to function. Communication lines are added that are capable of supplying the amount of bandwidth the main site requires on a daily basis. DNS is configured to direct traffic to both sites, with the main site being primary and the hot site being secondary. Transactions are recorded at each location, and all systems operate at both locations as if they are live. In case of a disaster, the hot site is brought on line as the primary location, and all traffic is switched over to the hot site.

The September 11, 2001, attacks were a wake-up call on many fronts, and IT and disaster recovery solutions were no exception. The World Trade Center towers were home to some very large financial institutions. The terrorist attacks were not planned for or predicted by anyone, yet most of the large institutions had prepared for a disaster that would render the building inaccessible for a long period of time, such as a fire. Many of these firms implemented hot sites in other locations that could be switched over to in a very short amount of time. When the first airplane hit the World Trade Center, everyone was stunned and, at first, unaware of what was happening. To IT departments, it was clear there was a problem, although the extent wasn't known. At the first sign that something had gone wrong and service had been interrupted, these firms began to switch their business processes over to their hot site.

Some of these companies had created their own team of disaster recovery specialists and had created their own hot sites in-house. Other companies outsourced their disaster recovery solutions to specialists, such as IBM Global Services (http://www.ibm.com).

For much smaller companies that lack the $1 million budget, web backups can be implemented as a method of protecting the business. A web backup allows data to be backed up over the Internet to a separate location. Web backups are usually facilitated by a third-party solution provider, who takes responsibility for storing the data. The data can then be restored to any location with Internet connectivity. Web backups are an excellent solution for small companies that don't have the resources to manage their own storage facility for backups. The advantage to storing backups offsite is that, in case of a disaster, the backups can be restored to an alternate location. One thing the World Trade Center disaster showed us was that a backup maintained at the office is useless in a situation where the office is destroyed. Firms that had taken steps to store backups at a separate site were able to rebuild their data. Firms that had not planned for such a disaster were not.

Interesting factoid—70 percent of the business who were not adequately prepared for a disaster were not in business one year later. The 30 percent that did survive suffered great economic loss.

# Implementing Your Backup and Recovery Plan

Developing a backup and recovery solution is a two-part process: develop the plan and then implement the plan. The questions posed in the previous section are excellent starting points for creating backup and recovery solutions, however, unless the plan is put into action, the backup and recovery plan is just that: a plan. Make sure that after the plan is developed, you actually put it into place. Whatever your plan is, implement it.

## Test the Solution

There's nothing worse than discovering a failed backup at the moment when you need to recover from a failure. Things do go wrong with backups, and it is critical to make sure that your backup solution is working. Ideally, you should test each backup every time to make sure that it worked. It may not be practical to do this, so at a bare minimum you should check the backup reports and logs each time to verify the backup operation was successful. It is recommended that you perform a full test of your solution on a regular basis as well.

To fully test a backup job, restore the data to an alternate location, then test the server and verify that you can access the files and that everything is there. (How to restore data to an alternate location is discussed later in the chapter.) Don't just test the backup for data integrity, test the entire backup and recovery solution. Granted, it's a little scary to purposely crash a production machine just to make sure that it can be rebuilt and recovered. That's what test labs are for. Build a duplicate machine and test your backup and recovery solution on that. Run a complete backup, as specified in your plan, and then crash the machine and make sure that it can be rebuilt and data recovered. Check the actual test against your backup and recovery plan and make any adjustments necessary. Data backups should be tested at least weekly and the entire backup and recovery system should be fully tested on a monthly basis. The time you invest in testing your backup and recovery solution will be well worth it.

 **NOTE** One way to crash a machine is to delete critical boot files, such as the boot.ini file or the ntldr file. Loading incorrect drivers for devices often works as well. Try using NT 4.0 drivers for an XP device.

# Backup Types

There are five different types of backups and each type handles data in a slightly different way. Many solutions involve a combination of two or more backup types. It is important to understand the archive bit and what it does to understand how each of the types is different. Every file contains an archive bit as one of its hidden attributes. The archive bit is set to 1 to indicate that the file was created or after it has been modified. This setting of the archive bit indicates to backup programs that the file was created or modified and needs to be included in the backup set. The backup program then will set the archive bit to 0, which is known as clearing the archive bit, to indicate that the file has been backed up. If the file doesn't change by the next scheduled backup, that file will be skipped.

**NOTE** This explanation of the archive bit is a little oversimplified for clarity. As you will see in the next section, the archive bit is not always cleared by the backup program. Whether or not the archive bit is cleared (set to 0) is dependent on what type of backup is being run.

## Normal

A normal backup is sometimes referred to as a full backup. A normal backup disregards the archive bit in all files and backs up all files and folders selected, regardless of when they were modified. A normal backup is the most complete type of backup, and the only type of backup that can be used to back up the registry and other critical system files. A normal backup takes the longest amount of time to back up and recover. A normal backup clears the archive bit on all files after backing up.

## Incremental

An incremental backup is the quickest method for performing backups of data. An incremental backup only backs up files that have been created or modified (their archive bit is set to 1) since the last normal or incremental backup. An incremental backup also clears the archive bit (sets the archive bit back to 0) of all files that it backs up.

Since the incremental backup only backs up files that have been changed or modified since the last full or incremental backup, to do a complete restore you must restore the normal backup and then any previous incremental backups as well. For example, if you run a normal backup on Sunday night, and an incremental backup on Monday, Tuesday, Wednesday, then you must restore the normal backup and each incremental backup in order (Monday, Tuesday, Wednesday) to achieve a full restore.

## Differential

A differential backup backs up all files that have changed or been added since the last full backup. When a differential backup is used, it backs up all files with the archive bit set to 1, but it doesn't clear the archive bit. By not clearing the archive bit, a differential backup will back up the same file on two separate days, even if the file didn't change. To do a complete restore, only the last normal backup and the last differential backup are needed.

## Copy

A copy is just that, a copy. A copy backup is generally used for archiving files. A copy only backs up files specified, regardless of whether the archive bit is set to 1 or not, and it does not clear the archive bits. A copy backup probably will not be used to recover from a failure; normal backups are used for recovery. Copy backups may be made when a company is required to keep data for an extended length of time. For example, insurance companies and banks are required to keep records about customers for several years. A copy backup can be used for this situation, and the copy stored offsite.

## Daily

A daily backup only backs up files that were created or modified on the day the backup is run. A daily backup does not clear the archive bit. For a side-by-side comparison of each backup type, see Table 5-1.

 **EXAM TIP**   Know the differences between the backup types and be prepared to answer a question where you have to design a backup strategy using several of the backup types.

# Using Backup Utility for Windows

Backup Utility for Windows was jointly designed for Windows by VERITAS and Microsoft. Backup Utility for Windows is essentially Backup Exec Lite by VERITAS. The new version of Backup Utility for Windows is a very good basic backup program that can back up to hard drives or tape drives and supports a wide variety of hardware, but it does have a few limitations. You cannot use Backup Utility for Windows to back up and restore critical system files on remote machines. If you need additional functionality from your backup solution such as remote backups, Backup Executive by VERITAS (http://www.veritas.com/) is an excellent choice.

| Backup Type | Clears Archive Bit | Best Use |
|---|---|---|
| Normal | Yes | To perform a full backup of all data, system state data, and applications on a regular basis. |
| Incremental | Yes | To perform backups as quickly as possible. Only backs up data that has changed since the last full or incremental backup. To restore data using an incremental backup, first restore the last normal backup and then restore all incremental backups. |
| Differential | No | Backs up data to the last backup and is the quickest method to restore data. Only the last differential backup and the last full backup are needed for a complete restore. |
| Copy | No | Best used for archiving data. |
| Daily | No | Backs up all data on a given day. Best used for performing snapshot type backups. |

**Table 5-1**   Backup Types and Features

Backup Utility for Windows includes some new features and wizards to make backing up and restoring files easier. One new feature of Backup Utility for Windows is the use of shadow copies to run backups of open files. A shadow copy is a snapshot of files that can be taken even when the files are open or being modified. How the Volume Shadow Copy Service (VSS) backs up files was explained in Chapter 3. If the VSS is enabled on the server running the backup, Backup Utility for Windows is able to take advantage of the service and back up files that are open or in use. Previous versions of Backup Utility for Windows did not support shadow copies, and any open files were skipped.

The backup tool also includes a simplified wizard, which can be started from the welcome screen. The wizard, as shown in Figure 5-1, allows for both backup and restore operations. To run the wizard, click the Wizard Mode hyperlink on the welcome screen.

To start Backup Utility for Windows, click Start | All Programs | Accessories | System Tools | Backup. Or simply type **ntbackup** from the Run command. By default, Backup Utility for Windows starts in advanced mode and displays the welcome screen at startup, with the option to run several wizards: a Backup Wizard, a Restore Wizard, or an Automated System Recovery (ASR) Wizard. The wizards are easy to use and provide a section at the end to configure advanced settings, such as the type of backup to use and scheduling options. Figure 5-2 shows the welcome screen. The wizards can also be run from anywhere in the backup utility by clicking the Tools menu and selecting the appropriate wizard.

## Using the Backup Wizard

The first selection screen in the Backup Wizard asks what needs to be backed up and displays three options: back up everything on the computer, only back up selected drives,

**Figure 5-1**

The Backup or Restore Wizard

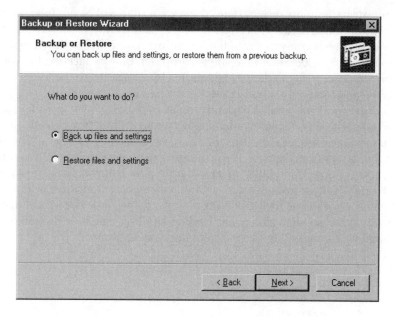

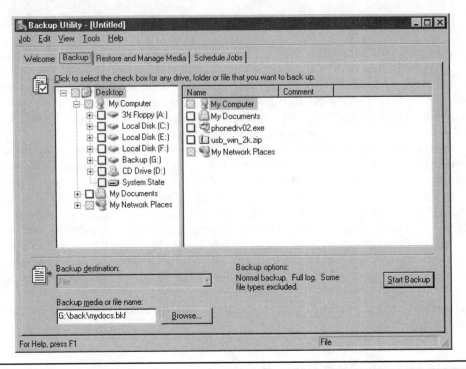

**Figure 5-2**    Backup Utility for Windows in advanced mode

or only back up the system state. The system state will be discussed later in this chapter. If the option to back up selected files and folders is chosen, the screen shown in Figure 5-3 will display, and any folder or file on the local computer or any shared folder on the network can be selected. From a single computer, then, a backup of network resources can be run. Also, a single file may be selected by navigating to the folder where the file is located and then only selecting the file for backup.

After choosing what to back up, you must choose where to back up to. By default, the wizard will only display available options, so if the server you are backing up does not have a tape drive, that option will be grayed out, and you will only be able to back up to a file, as shown in Figure 5-4. The backup can be saved to a local hard drive or to any network location. The ability to save backups to a file was not available under the old Backup Utility for Windows in NT 4.0; only tape backups were available. After choosing where to locate the file, click Next to finish the wizard. The wizard does provide an Advanced tab so that additional backup options can be configured. These advanced backup options will be discussed in the next section.

**Figure 5-3**
Selecting what
to back up

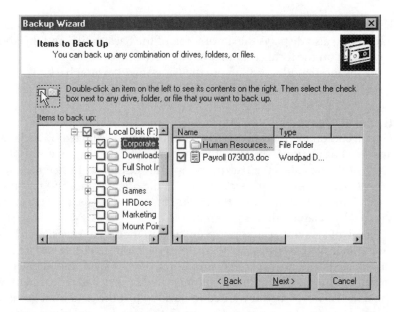

**Performing a Backup Using Advanced Mode**

When Backup Utility for Windows is opened, it displays the welcome screen with the three available wizards. The Backup Wizard can be skipped by clicking the Backup tab and creating a backup job from scratch. The Backup tab displays a screen to select any drive, folder, or file to back up, and includes a separate entry for the system state data.

**Figure 5-4**
Backing up
to a file

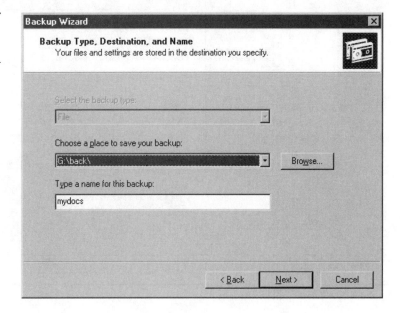

Use the screen to select the files and folders to back up, as shown in Figure 5-5. The Backup tab also displays the destination of the backup file, and the ability to browse to any folder on the local computer or any network location.

In advanced mode, you can use the Tools menu to alter backup options or to save the backup job and schedule it for later. The following options are available.

## General Options

Once a backup job is created, backup options can be selected by clicking the Tools menu and selecting Options. The available options on the General tab are displayed in Figure 5-6. The "Verify data after the backup completes" option will force Backup Utility for Windows to compare the data backed up with the original data and report if there are differences. If there are differences, the backup failed and needs to be rerun. This option is not selected by default, but it is recommended.

You will also notice an option to back up mounted drives, which is checked by default. If it is not checked, only the path to the mounted drive will be backed up, but not the actual data. Remember that a mounted drive is a volume mapped to a folder. Backing up just the path and not the volume could be very bad if the intent was to back up all the data. However, if you wanted to back up just the data on a volume, and not additional data stored on mounted volumes, this would need to be unchecked.

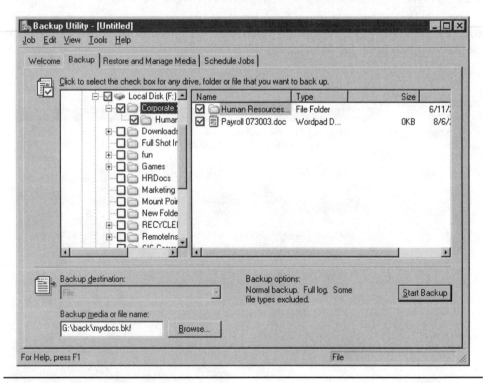

**Figure 5-5**   Selecting files to back up

**Figure 5-6**

General options

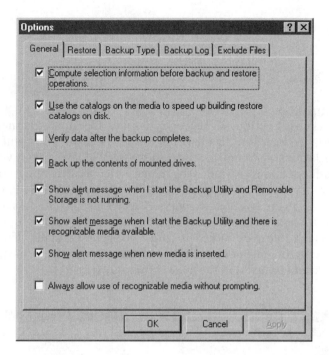

Also, by default, Backup Utility for Windows uses catalogs written to the backup file to restore data. If you are restoring from damaged media, deselect the option to use catalogs. This will force the backup utility to scan the entire backup set.

## Restore Options

There are three possible restore options for dealing with files that are already on the disk:

- Do not replace the file on my computer
- Replace the file on disk only if the file on disk is older
- Always replace the file on my computer

The "Do not replace" option is the default, and Windows recommends this setting. This will speed up the restore process as files that are present are skipped and not overwritten. Skipping files restores only the files that are missing.

## Backup Type

By default, all backups are normal backups unless otherwise specified. To change the backup type, click the drop-down menu and select from the list. The available types are

- Normal
- Copy
- Differential

- Incremental
- Daily

The backup types and their unique characteristics were explained earlier in this chapter.

## Backup Log

The backup log options include options for no log (not recommended), a summary log, or a detailed log. If the detailed option is selected, the report will show every folder and file backed up or attempted. The detailed log will also display whether the backup was successful or not. The detailed log can be a bit overwhelming with the amount of information included. For example, Figure 5-7 shows there were 2,627 critical system files backed up on the 2weekmcse.com test1 server. Keeping records of all 2,627 files is probably unnecessary. The summary log option will only display individual folders and files that weren't able to be backed up, and will display the status of the backup job, whether it succeeded or not. For most situations, the summary log is adequate. The summary log is the default option and the most commonly used.

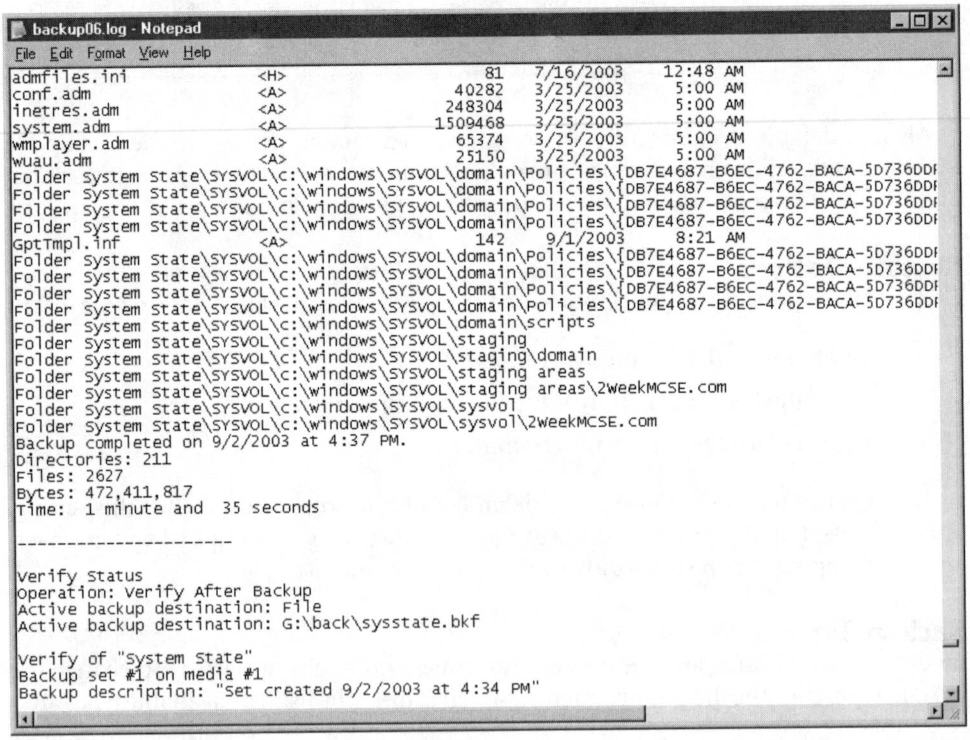

**Figure 5-7**   Detailed log view of a recent backup job

## Excluding Files

Backup Utility for Windows also includes a nifty little feature that will automatically exclude certain files from the backup job. For example, you can exclude the paging file (virtual memory, see Chapter 3) and the hibernate file from any backups. (The hibernate file is equal in size to the amount of RAM in the machine and is used to store the contents of RAM in case of a power failure so that the machine can be brought back on line quickly.) To view the current list of excluded files, click the Exclude Files tab, as shown in Figure 5-8. Notice that pagefile.sys (the paging file) and hiberfil.sys (the hibernate file) are both excluded, along with some other non-critical system files. If you want to exclude additional files, click Add New and choose either a file type to exclude or browse to a file. Notice also that files can be excluded for all users or for only the current user.

# Scheduling Backups

Of course, no backup solution would be complete without the ability to schedule backups to run automatically, and Backup Utility for Windows doesn't disappoint. Backups can be scheduled to run daily, weekly, monthly, or when the system has been idle for a predetermined amount of time. Staying on the backup tab, a job can be scheduled once it has been created. To schedule a job:

1. Click the Start Backup button on the Backup tab.

2. Click the Schedule button.

**Figure 5-8**
Excludable files

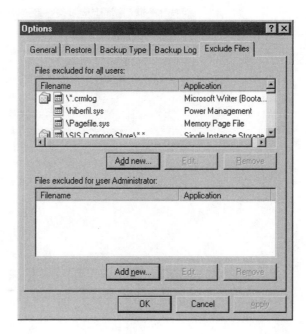

3. Before a schedule can be created, the backup job must be saved. You will be prompted to save the backup job before proceeding.

4. After saving the backup job, you will be prompted for logon credentials to use when running the job. You may use the credentials of any user who is a member of the Backup Operators group.

5. Name your job, as shown in Figure 5-9.

6. Click Properties to access the scheduling component. Backup jobs can be scheduled to run once, daily, weekly, monthly, or when the server is idle. Choose the increment you want to run the backup at. Also notice there is an Advanced tab that can be used to schedule additional increments, such as every other day

7. When finished, click OK to close the scheduling screen and click OK again to close the job screen. Your backup job is now scheduled.

A Scheduled Jobs tab is provided which displays all scheduled jobs and includes a scheduled Backup Wizard to create additional scheduled jobs. To create a scheduled job, click the Add Job button. You will be presented with the Backup Wizard, which will include a scheduling component at the end of the wizard. After following the prompts and creating the job, it will display on the Scheduled Jobs tab. Notice that the job displays with a letter to designate what kind of backup the job is: N for normal, I for Incremental, D for differential.

**Figure 5-9**
Naming a
scheduled
backup job

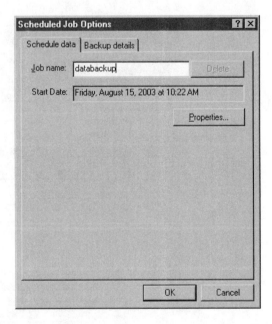

# Backing Up the System State

Microsoft has bundled critical operating system files into a single category and called it the system state data. Backing up the system state data will back up the registry, critical boot files, the COM+ Class Registration database, and will also back up the Active Directory database, certificate services, the SYSVOL folder, and cluster services if present. Selecting the system state data to be backed up automatically selects all of the components, and the individual components cannot be separated or selected individually. Figure 5-10 shows the components of the system state data for a domain controller.

 **EXAM TIP** Any mention of boot files, Active Directory, or the COM+ Class Registration database is an automatic system state data backup. Boot files and other critical system files could be backed up individually if you really knew what you were doing, but Backup Utility for Windows does not support splitting the components up. If you need to back up the boot files, you must back up all the system state data.

Because of this packaging of the critical boot files, backing up the registry and so on is very easy. The system state data can be backed up by using any of the wizards and selecting System State, or by using the Backup tab and selecting the system state data. The system

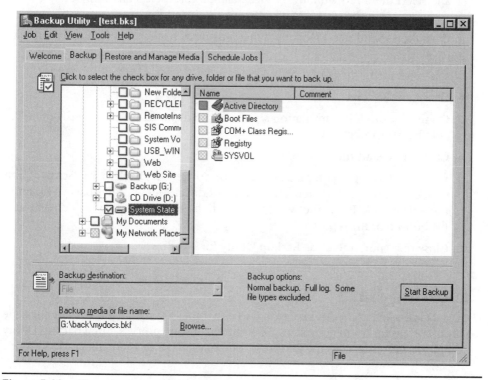

**Figure 5-10** The system state data components

state data can only be backed up and restored on the local machine. It cannot be backed up over the network or restored over the network.

---

 **NOTE** Many third-party backup programs, including VERITAS Backup Exec, include the capability to back up and restore the system state data across the network.

---

### Lab Exercise 5.1: Backing Up and Verifying the System State Data

In this exercise, you will back up and verify the system state data on your server. You must complete this exercise before proceeding to Lab Exercise 5.2: Performing an Authoritative Restore.

1. Click Start | Run, then type **ntbackup** and press ENTER to start Backup Utility for Windows.

2. Click the Backup tab.

3. Select System State Data in the left pane. Attempt to right-click the boot files and select them individually. Notice that you can't select any individual components in the system state data: it's all or nothing.

4. Click Browse and select Desktop. Enter a name of **backup.bkf** for the backup file.

5. Click the Tools menu and select Options. Select the Logging Options tab and select Detailed. Click OK.

6. Click Start Backup.

7. On the Backup Job Information screen, click Advanced. Select to verify data after backup and click OK.

8. Click OK to start the backup.

9. When the backup is complete, click Report to view the backup log. Scroll all the way to the bottom and view the number of directories and files backed up and the time it took. If any files were not able to be backed up, they will display at the bottom of the report.

10. Close the report and close Backup Utility for Windows.

## Restoring Data

Once data is backed up, it can be restored to either the original location or an alternate location, such as for testing purposes. To begin the restore process, open Backup Utility for Windows and either click the Restore Wizard or the Restore and Manage Media tab.

## Restoring Data Using the Restore Wizard

The Restore Wizard first prompts for the backup file to restore, as shown in Figure 5-11. Backup Utility for Windows keeps track of all backups run on the server, and displays each backup file and the corresponding files backed up in each file. This is great when the backups have been meticulously run on the server, and you only need to restore a couple of files. If you are working with a clean install of a server, however, no backup jobs will be displayed. Any backup file can be restored to the server by importing the file into the restore process. To import a backup file, click Browse and navigate to the location where the backup file is stored. Backup files can be located on network shares and then restored to a local server over the network. After selecting the backup file, Backup Utility for Windows will catalog the backup file and display the name of the file, the date it was run, and any drives, folders, or files contained in the backup file.

 **NOTE** All files contained in a backup file (.bkf) retain all of their original attributes and properties. An encrypted file is backed up in an encrypted state, for example, and remains encrypted when it is restored. However, if files originally backed up from an NTFS volume are restored to a FAT volume, these attributes and properties are lost without warning.

After selecting the data to restore, click next to finish the wizard. By default, the wizard will restore all files to their original location and will not replace any existing files. These options can be changed by clicking Advanced, choosing the location to restore to, and choosing whether to replace existing files or not. In a situation where a server is being rebuilt, data would be restored to a location other than where it was backed up.

**Figure 5-11**
Choosing files to restore

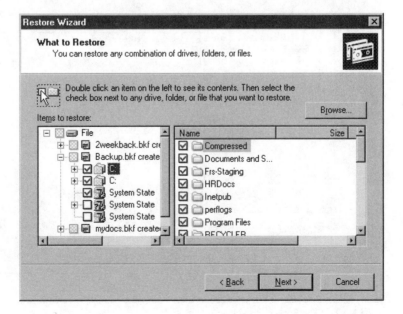

## Restoring Data Manually

If you'd like to skip the wizards, click the Restore and Manage Media tab, as shown in Figure 5-12. You are presented with a screen that allows you to choose your backup to restore, and to choose whether to restore it to the original location or to an alternate location. Again, previous backups are displayed in the left pane, with the individual files displayed in the right pane. A single file can be restored by selecting the appropriate backup, navigating to the parent folder, and then selecting the individual backup for restore.

## Restoring the System State

Earlier in this chapter, you learned what the system state consists of and how to back it up. The system state is unlike regular data, and requires some special handling when restoring, especially if you are restoring a domain controller. If you need to restore the system state data to a computer that has been rebuilt, you must restore it before you boot the machine for the first time. Also, if you are restoring the system state data to a domain controller, you must restore in Directory Services restore mode, which is basically safe mode for DCs. To restore the system state data on a domain controller:

1. Start the server and press F8 to view the Advanced Boot Options menu.

2. Select the option to enter Directory Services restore mode. You will need the Directory Services restore password that was specified when the server was built.

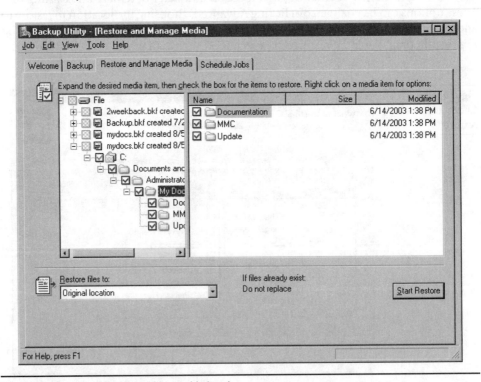

**Figure 5-12**    The Restore and Manage Media tab

3. Open Backup Utility for Windows by typing **ntbackup** from the Run command.

4. Click the Restore and Manage Media tab and select the appropriate file of the backup. Select the system state and click Restore.

Directory Services restore mode allows for the maintenance of Active Directory as well as its restoration. You will learn how to maintain Active Directory in Chapter 21. Before restoring a domain controller, it is important to know that there are two methods of restoring Active Directory: non-authoritative and authoritative.

## Authoritative vs. Non-authoritative

The term "authoritative" is used to describe a restore in which the domain controller being restored has the master, or authoritative, copy of Active Directory. A non-authoritative restore is a domain controller being restored that does not have an authoritative copy of Active Directory. When a domain controller is started, replication occurs during the boot phase, and Active Directory is synchronized. Whether the restore is authoritative or non-authoritative then specifies the direction of replication. An authoritative restore pushes Active Directory out to other domain controllers, and a non-authoritative restore synchronizes changes to the domain controller being booted.

 **NOTE** Domain controllers use Universal Sequence Numbers (USNs) to keep track of Active Directory data and to determine if an update is available. Each domain controller keeps its own USN, and checks its USN with the USN of other domain controllers on a regular basis. If the USN of the other domain controller is higher, that indicates an update is available, and replication is started. If the USN of the other domain controller is the same or lower, replication is not started. Using USNs is a more accurate method than using time stamps.

To explain further, let's suppose that a domain controller fails due to hardware failure. It takes several days to obtain a replacement part for the machine and to repair the domain controller. During this time, other domain controllers have continued to function normally, and various changes in the network and Active Directory have taken place. When the failed domain controller is started for the first time after completing the recovery process, replication occurs and the changes in Active Directory are replicated to the previously failed computer. The domain controller is brought up to date with the rest of the network. This is a non-authoritative restore.

Now let's suppose that the failure you suffered was due to human error, and an administrator deletes significant portions of Active Directory. If you follow the normal procedure of restoring Active Directory from yesterday's backup and rebooting the server, replication will occur, and all the changes and deletions made by the administrator will be replicated back to the domain controller. Performing a normal restore would not bring back the deleted objects. To recover your lost users and OUs, you must perform an authoritative restore and specify the objects that you want to replicate to the rest of the network.

**EXAM TIP** Look for when replication occurred to determine whether an authoritative restore is needed. The only time an authoritative restore is needed is if something was deleted from Active Directory that needs to be brought back and replication has already occurred. Remember that the first thing a domain controller does upon starting up is to check for changes in Active Directory and replicate with other domain controllers.

## Performing a Non-authoritative Restore

A non-authoritative restore is the simpler of the two types to perform. After the restore process is complete, the domain controller will replicate with other domain controllers upon reboot and synchronize Active Directory. When the domain controller finishes booting, it will contain the most up-to-date version of Active Directory.

To perform a non-authoritative restore, follow these steps:

1. Boot the domain controller into Directory Services restore mode.

2. Enter the restore password that was created when the domain controller was created. This password may be different than the administrative password.

3. After logging on, start Backup Utility for Windows by typing **ntbackup** from the Run command.

4. At the welcome screen, choose the Restore Wizard.

5. Follow the prompts, selecting to restore the system state data.

6. When the restore process completes, verify that it was completed without errors and restart the domain controller.

## Performing an Authoritative Restore

There are situations when simply restoring Active Directory from a backup tape is not enough. Remember, when a domain controller boots, it replicates with other domain controllers. If an adverse operation was performed (think user or OU deletion) and replication has occurred, the change will be replicated back to the domain controller on reboot, even though a backup was restored. In this situation, you can use the ntds utility, shown in Figure 5-13, to mark the restore as authoritative and replicate the restored Active Directory to the other domain controllers.

To perform an authoritative restore, perform a system state restore and then perform the following steps:

1. Before rebooting the server, open a command prompt and type **ntdsutil**. Press ENTER.

2. From the ntdsutil prompt, type **authoritative restore** and press ENTER.

3. From the authoritative restore prompt, type **restore database** and press ENTER.

4. After the operation completes, restart the computer.

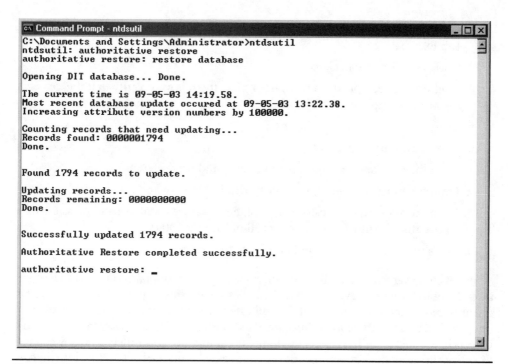

**Figure 5-13**   The ntds utility

   **NOTE**   The ntds utility provides a mechanism to authoritatively restore a single object instead of the entire database. For more information about authoritatively restoring Active Directory, see Chapter 21.

## Lab Exercise 5.2: Performing an Authoritative Restore

In this exercise, you will perform an authoritative restore. You will see the marking process the system performs to mark objects as authoritative. Before doing this exercise, you need to have completed Lab Exercise 5.1. If you have two domain controllers at your disposal, delete an object, such as an OU, before undertaking this exercise.

1. Shut down and restart the server.

2. When the boot menu appears, press F8 to view the advanced options.

3. Select to boot into Directory Services restore mode.

4. Log on to the server using the restore password. (The restore password was selected when Active Directory was installed.)

5. Click Start | Run and type **ntbackup** to start Backup Utility for Windows.

6. Click the Restore and Manage Media tab and select the file that you created in Lab Exercise 5.1.

7. Click to restore the backup.

8. After the restore operation completes, view the report to verify that the operation completed successfully.

9. Close Backup Utility for Windows.

10. Open a command prompt.

11. From the command prompt, type **ntdsutil** and press ENTER.

12. From the ntdsutil prompt, type **authoritative restore** and press ENTER.

13. From the authoritative restore prompt, type **restore database** and press ENTER. Notice that the ntdsutil increments all objects by 100,000.

14. Close the command prompt and reboot the server.

When the server reboots, replication will occur with other domain controllers. However, since the objects on this server have had their USN incremented by 100,000, they appear as the most recent and the changes will be replicated out to the other domain controllers. If only a subtree was marked as authoritative and not the entire database, then only those objects in the subtree will replicate out to the other domain controllers, and any changes to Active Directory that are not part of the subtree will replicate back to the domain controller on which the restore process took place. This allows for a certain object, such as an OU, to be restored while still maintaining any other changes in Active Directory.

 **NOTE** The ntds utility allows for only specific objects to be marked as authoritative. To mark an object as authoritative, you must use the distinguished name of the object. The ntds utility is discussed in greater detail in Chapter 23.

# Troubleshooting Boot Failures

Backing up and restoring data, even Active Directory, is only half of the recovery process. There are going to be times when a server fails and will not boot. For those times, you will need to know how to bring a server back to life or, if the server cannot be brought back to life, how to recover from a server failure as quickly as possible.

Occasionally, a server's hardware fails and the failure to boot isn't due to any change or mistake that was made to the operating system. If the motherboard, disk drives, or CPU has failed, there isn't much you can do other than replace the hardware and reinstall the operating system. Replacing the motherboard, disk drives, or CPU usually requires a full reinstall of the operating system. If your server doesn't make any noise, lights don't come on, or you aren't able to boot farther than the memory test, chances are something major has malfunctioned or reached its life expectancy. If one of these components fails, it will need to be replaced and the operating system will probably need to be reinstalled.

In extreme cases such as this, the Automated System Recovery (ASR) tool comes in handy. You will learn how to use the ASR later in this section.

If, however, the boot failure is due to a misconfiguration, incorrect driver, corrupted file, or other operating system–related failure, there is hope. Microsoft has provided several boot options to enable a server to be booted and fixed. Starting with Windows 2000, a Recovery Console is also available. The Recovery Console must be installed before it will appear on the boot menu, but it can be accessed from the installation CD. The Advanced Options menu includes the following:

- Safe Mode
- Safe Mode with Networking
- Safe Mode with Command Prompt
- Enable Boot Logging
- Enable VGA Mode
- Last Known Good Configuration
- Directory Services Restore Mode (Windows domain controllers only)
- Debugging Mode

## Safe Mode

Entering safe mode boots Windows with a bare minimum of components loaded (just enough to get the system up and running), but still allows for most operations to be performed. Drivers can be loaded and unloaded, video settings can be changed, and the registry can be accessed in safe mode.

To enter safe mode, press F8 when prompted during the boot process. Windows will then boot into safe mode. Safe mode does not load any networking components, such as network cards or protocols. To troubleshoot network issues or protocols, Windows must be started in safe mode with networking.

## Safe Mode with Networking

This mode loads the system the same way as in safe mode, but also includes network interface card drivers and protocols. Booting into safe mode with networking allows for network, connectivity, and protocol issues to be resolved.

## Safe Mode with Command Prompt

This mode loads the system the same way as in safe mode, but also includes the command prompt shell. Use the safe mode with command prompt when you need to run command-line utilities or perform operations that can only be done from a command prompt.

## Enable Boot Logging

Enabling boot logging creates a log file, which is placed in the system root, of all drivers and files loaded during the boot process. The log file also will display any files or drivers that were not loaded. Some of these drivers and files aren't loaded until they are needed and can be ignored. Others are critical to the system and need to be loaded before the system will operate correctly.

As a matter of practice, it's a good idea to use boot logging when you have a perfectly healthy system, to make a record of what is and isn't loaded during the boot process. If you create this log, it can later be compared to the log of a system that isn't working properly, and any differences in the two log files are the possible suspects.

## Enable VGA Mode

The Enable VGA Mode option was created especially for video card problems. Any time you boot a system and the screen is unreadable, you can use the Enable VGA Mode option to boot into a standard 640×480 VGA resolution and begin troubleshooting.

## Last Known Good Configuration

The Last Known Good Configuration can be loaded only if a logon has not been performed since the trouble arose. As part of the boot process, Windows saves a successful logon to the registry, under the HKLM\System\CurrentControlSet registry key. Choosing Last Known Good Configuration loads Windows by using the configuration saved in the registry. If a logon has been performed, the Last Known Good Configuration menu won't do any good.

Here are two examples. Scott logs onto a Windows Server 2003 server and upgrades the drivers for the motherboard to support multiple processors. He is prompted to reboot the machine after the upgrade. During the boot process, Scott receives a stop error (the famous blue screen) and the boot process fails. Because Scott has not logged onto the computer after performing the upgrade, he is able to restart the computer, press F8 to access the Advanced Boot menu, and select Last Known Good Configuration. The system will then boot with the configuration saved to the registry before Scott upgraded the drivers.

For the second example, Scott installs new drivers for the motherboard to support multiple processors, is prompted to reboot, and logs onto the system. After several minutes, Scott receives a stop error and the system fails. Because Scott logged onto the system, the Last Known Good Configuration contains a corrupted configuration, and the system will not boot properly. Scott has to remove the offending driver by using safe mode or the Recovery Console. If Scott is unable to recover using either of these methods, he may resort to the Automated System Recovery.

 **EXAM TIP**  Be careful with questions regarding boot problems. The Last Known Good Configuration is a great tool, but only works if the user hasn't logged on since the problems arose. Remember, if the user hasn't logged on, try the Last Known Good Configuration. If the user has logged on, try something else.

## Debugging Mode

Booting into debugging mode sends debugging information to another Windows Server 2003 server connected via the serial port. You must have a computer attached by the serial port before entering debugging mode. Using debugging mode allows you to monitor the progress of one server from another server. You will only see status information on the debugging (attached) computer. The server will load the operating system as normal, and you won't see any status messages on the original machine.

## Recovery Console

The Recovery Console is a command-line interface that can be used to troubleshoot boot problems. The Recovery Console can be installed at any time by running winnt32.exe /cmdcons from a command prompt. During the installation process, you will be prompted for a password. This password can be different than the Administrator account. Do not forget this password! Without this password, the Recovery Console is useless because it is required to run the Recovery Console. After installation, the Recovery Console will appear on the boot menu and in the boot.ini file (see Chapter 1). You can enter the Recover Console by choosing it at the startup menu.

To install the Recovery Console:

1. Open a command prompt and navigate to the Winnt directory.

2. Type **winnt32.exe /cmdcons**.

If the Recovery Console was not installed previously, and you have encountered a problem that can be fixed by using it, you can enter the Recovery Console by inserting the original Windows Server 2003 installation disk and pressing R when prompted to repair the installation using the Recovery Console.

---

 **EXAM TIP** Because you can always enter the Recovery Console, you can usually fix boot problems using it.

---

The Recovery Console can be used to start and stop services, create directories, format drives, copy files, and repair the boot sector. Using the Recovery Console is an excellent method if the failed system needs a file copied from the setup CD to the hard drive. However, the Recovery Console is difficult to use, especially if the cause of the boot problem is unknown.

One particular problem the Recovery Console can help you fix is the error that states:

```
Windows Server 2003 could not start because the following file is missing or
corrupt:<Windows 2003 root>\System32\ntldr. Please re-install a copy of the
above file.
```

All NT-based systems rely on system files to boot up: ntldr, ntdetect.com, boot.ini, ntfs.sys, ntbootdd.sys, IO.sys, and config.sys are some examples. If one of these files is deleted or corrupted, your system won't boot. The good news is that you can use the Recovery Console to copy these files from another Windows Server 2003 or the Windows Server 2003 CD-ROM back to the failed server. Once the files are restored, the server should boot again.

### Directory Services Restore Mode

Think of Directory Services restore mode as safe mode for domain controllers. You must use Directory Services restore mode to restore Active Directory and to perform maintenance, such as performing an offline defragmentation. Active Directory is a database and cannot be active at the same time as a restore is taking place. Booting into Directory Services restore mode loads the system without loading the Active Directory database.

## Creating an Automated System Recovery

For those situations when the server you are tasked to repair seems as if it has gone to the great circuit board in the sky, using the Automated System Recovery (ASR) can bring the system back to life, assuming of course the hardware is operable. If the server has stopped responding due to a hardware failure, that needs to be resolved before an ASR will help.

The Automated System Recovery replaces the Emergency Repair Disk (ERD) used in NT and Windows 2000. The ERD and now the ASR allow a system that is not responding to be booted. Creating an ASR does two things: it creates a floppy disk that can be used to boot, and it creates a complete system state backup of the server. Creating an ASR does not back up any of the data on the server. In fact, at the end of the ASR creation process, the system prompts you to also back up your data. If the server was created with multiple partitions or volumes, each additional volume must be backed up.

To create an ASR:

1. Click Start | All Programs | Accessories | System Tools | Backup, or click Start | Run and type **ntbackup**, then press ENTER.

2. On the welcome screen, click to open the Automated System Recovery Preparation Wizard (shown in Figure 5-14).

3. Specify the backup path for the system state data and click Next. Click Next again to start the process.

4. Insert a floppy disk when prompted.

5. When the process completes, remove the floppy disk, mark it as an ASR, and store in a safe place for later use.

---

 **EXAM TIP**  The ASR is a new method to recover from boot failures. Look for questions on the exam about when to use it, how to use it, and what to use it for.

**Figure 5-14**
The ASR
Preparation
Wizard

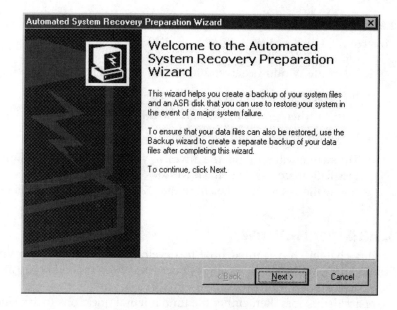

## Lab Exercise 5.3: Creating an Automatic System Recovery

In this exercise, you will use the Backup Utility for Windows to create an Automated System Recovery disk in preparation for a failed system. You will need a newly formatted floppy disk to complete the exercise. You will need to complete this exercise before proceeding to Lab Exercise 5.4.

1. From the Run command, type **ntbackup** to open the Backup Utility for Windows.

2. From the welcome screen, click the ASR Preparation Wizard and click Next to start the wizard.

3. Select the destination for the backup file and click Next.

4. Click Finish to start the ASR process.

5. When prompted, insert the blank floppy disk.

6. When the ASR is complete, mark the disk and keep it in a safe place.

# Restoring from the ASR

Using the Automated System Recovery process is quite painless and can work miracles for failed systems. You need to have the Windows Server 2003 setup CD and the ASR floppy disk on hand for the process to work properly.

## Lab Exercise 5.4: Using ASR to Recover a Failed System

To recover a failed system, follow these steps:

1. Insert the Windows Server 2003 Setup CD and restart the computer.

2. If prompted to boot from the CD, press any key.

3. Press F2 when prompted to start the ASR process.

4. When prompted, insert the floppy disk.

5. The system will reformat the drives, as you would expect from the normal installation process. After the drives are reformatted, the system will automatically restore the system state data from the ASR disk you supplied and reboot the system.

# Chapter Review

In this chapter, you learned how to develop a backup and recovery solution. You learned the importance of having a documented and tested backup and recovery solution. Data has become a firm's most valuable asset, and it is your job to protect this data from accidental loss. Remember the fundamental questions to ask when developing a solution. What should be backed up? What is the recovery point? What is the time frame for recovery? What is the risk tolerance, if any, of the firm? Finding the answers to these questions will help you develop a plan that is appropriate for your firm.

Windows Server 2003 includes a basic but very capable backup solution, Backup Utility for Windows. Backup Utility for Windows now includes the ability to back up data to a file and place the backup on a network share, removable media, or other hardware device, such as a tape drive. An entire drive, volume, folder, or individual file can be backed up. Also, the registry, critical boot files, and Active Directory can be backed up by selecting to back up the system state data.

In case of a failure, the system state data can be restored to recover Active Directory. Under normal circumstances, a domain controller replicates with other domain controllers upon startup, and any changes in Active Directory are replicated to the domain controller. In case of an accidental deletion of an Active Directory object, an authoritative restore can be performed to restore a particular object. By using ntdsutil, a particular object can be authoritatively restored, without disregarding other changes in Active Directory.

You also learned that occasionally servers become sick and have boot failures. Sometimes a boot failure is due to a hardware failure, such as bad memory, a hard drive failure, or motherboard failure. In these situations, the hardware must be replaced before you can troubleshoot the operating system. In some cases, Windows will even have to be reinstalled. However, there are plenty of situations in which the operating system isn't working correctly due to a misconfiguration or other software issue. In these situations, the Advanced Boot options can be used to restore a server to full functionality quickly and easily. In previous versions of Windows, an Emergency Repair Disk was provided to recover from a major failure. Windows 2003 now implements an Automated System Recovery (ASR) process. Using the ASR is an easy way to restore a server to a previous operational state. An ASR disk is created by using Backup Utility for Windows.

# Questions

1. You are the administrator of a Windows 2003 network. Your network consists of three domain controllers, an Exchange 5.5 server running on NT 4.0, and a SQL server running on a Windows 2003 member server. As part of your disaster recovery plan, you back up the system state data on all domain controllers on a weekly basis. You back up domain controller 1 on Mondays, domain controller 2 on Wednesdays, and domain controller 3 on Fridays.

   On Tuesday, you add a new branch office to Active Directory, which includes several additional servers, 37 workstations, and 43 users. On Thursday, a developer in your company adds additional classes to the schema, which cause the SQL database to fail. You need to restore Active Directory to its previous state, without losing the changes you made on Tuesday. Place the steps to restore Active Directory to its previous state in the correct order. (Choose only the steps that apply.)

   A. Shut down DC1 and enter Directory Services restore mode.

   B. Shut down DC2 and enter Directory Services restore mode.

   C. Shut down DC3 and enter Directory Services restore mode.

   D. Start the ntds utility and type **authoritative restore**.

   E. Start ntbackup and restore the system state data from the last backup.

   F. Reboot the domain controller.

   G. Force replication between DC1 and its replication partners.

   H. Force replication between DC2 and its replication partners.

2. Todd installs a new video card, and adds the drivers from the manufacturer's CD. The installation requires a reboot of the server. Todd reboots the machine and receives a stop error. Todd needs to return the server to operational mode using the least amount of administrative effort. What should he do?

   A. Restart the computer and select Last Known Good Configuration from the Advanced Boot Options menu.

   B. Restart the computer and use the Recovery Console to disable the device driver.

   C. Restart the computer and select VGA mode from the Advanced Boot Options menu. Roll back the video driver.

   D. Use the ASR to restore the computer.

3. Rebecca administers a Windows Server 2003 server. The server is configured with a single 36GB volume. She wants to back up her registry and the critical boot files, as well as her My Documents folder. What should Rebecca do?

   A. Use Backup Utility for Windows and back up the system state data and the My Documents folder.

   B. Use Backup Utility for Windows and create an ASR.

 **C.** Use Backup Utility for Windows and back up the registry, critical boot files, and the My Documents folder.

 **D.** Use Backup Utility for Windows and back up the C drive.

4. You are the administrator of a Windows 2003 network. Part of your network is shown as follows:

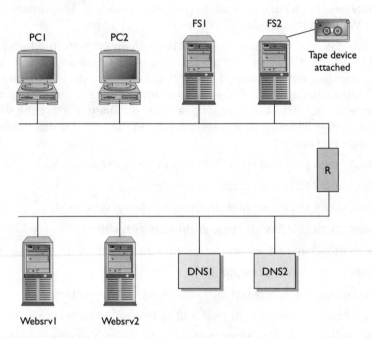

 You back up all of the system state data for each server and place the data on the tape drive attached to FS2. To which server or servers can you restore the system state data?

 **A.** DC1

 **B.** DC2

 **C.** FS1

 **D.** FS2

 **E.** Websrv1

 **F.** Websrv2

 **G.** DNS1

 **H.** DNS2

5. You are the administrator of a Windows 2003 network with six domain controllers in two sites. A backup of each domain controller's system state data

is run each Friday evening. In addition, once a month an Automated System Recovery is created for each server, and the backup file is placed on a tape drive. The tape drive and the floppy disk are then stored in a cabinet onsite. On Thursday, the motherboard of one of the domain controllers fails and has to be replaced. The new motherboard is not received until the following Tuesday, at which time the server is rebuilt. You must return the domain controller to active service as soon as possible while retaining any changes in Active Directory that have occurred since the failure. What should you do?

A. Reinstall Windows Server 2003. After completing the GUI mode of setup, reboot into Directory Services restore mode and restore from the server's last completed backup. Restart the server and boot normally.

B. Reinstall Windows Server 2003 and run dcpromo to install Active Directory. Reboot the server.

C. Use the ASR floppy disk to boot the server and perform a recovery. Boot the server normally.

D. Use the Windows Server 2003 setup CD to boot the server, and repair the installation using the Recovery Console. Reboot the server normally.

6. You are the administrator of a Windows Server 2003 server. The server is configured with three hard drives. The operating system is installed on the first drive and the additional drives are used for storing temporary files and for testing purposes.

To test an application, you install Windows NT 4.0 on a 10GB partition on the second drive. When you restart the server and select the Windows 2003 installation, the server fails to boot and displays the following message: "Windows Server 2003 could not start because the following file is missing or corrupt: <Windows 2003 root>\System32\ntldr. Please re-install a copy of the above file." What should you do to resolve the problem?

A. Start the computer with the installation CD and select to repair the installation using the Recovery Console. Modify the partition parameter in the boot.ini file.

B. Start the computer with the installation CD and select to repair the installation using the Recovery Console. Copy the ntldr file from the installation CD to the root drive.

C. Boot the computer using the installation CD and insert the ASR floppy disk when prompted.

D. Start the computer and press F8 to enter the Advanced Boot Options menu. Select Last Known Good Configuration.

7. 2WeekMCSE.com has two offices, one in Portland and one in New York. Each office contains two domain controllers: ny1, ny2, pdx1, and pdx2. System

backups are run weekly and the tapes are shipped to the Portland office. ny2 fails and you need to restore it as quickly as possible. What should you do?

A. Run Backup Utility for Windows on pdx1 and restore the backup tape across the network to ny2.

B. Ship the backup tapes for ny2 to the New York office. Restart ny2 in Directory Services restore mode and restore the system state data locally.

C. Restart the ny2 domain controller in Directory Services restore mode and start ntbackup. Restore the file across the network and reboot the server.

D. Ship the backup tapes for ny2 to the New York office. Run ntbackup and restore the system state data locally.

8. You are the administrator of a Windows Server 2003 server that is equipped with an IDE RAID card and three physical drives, configured in a RAID 5 hardware array. You use the manufacturer's disk to install the drivers for the RAID 5 array. After booting the server, you are prompted to check the manufacturer's web site for an updated driver. You obtain an updated driver from the web site and install the driver, which prompts a reboot. Upon reboot, you receive a stop error stating that the boot device is inaccessible. What should you do to correct the problem?

A. Use the Recovery Console to copy the old driver to the %system32%drivers folder and overwrite the new driver.

B. Reboot the system and specify Last Known Good Configuration from the Advanced Boot Options menu.

C. Boot into safe mode and roll back the driver using Device Manager.

D. Use the ASR disk to recover the server.

## Answers

1. **B, D, E, and F.** You must perform an authoritative restore to roll back Active Directory to the state it was in prior to the changes. DC2 was backed up on Wednesday, so it has the most recent backup of Active Directory. Shut down DC2, restore the system state data using ntbackup, use the ntds utility to specify an authoritative restore, and reboot the domain controller.

2. **A.** The stop error occurred before Todd logged onto the computer, therefore he can use the Last Known Good Configuration option.

3. **A.** The system state data includes the registry and critical boot files, as well as the COM+ Class Registration database and Active Directory if installed. Rebecca also wants to back up her My Documents folder.

4. **D.** The system state data can only be restored locally using the Backup Utility for Windows. Other third-party applications, such as Backup Exec by VERITAS, do allow for the remote backup and restoration of the system state data.

5. **A.** In case of a major hardware failure, such as the motherboard, Windows Server 2003 must be reinstalled. In addition, the system state data must be restored prior to a full boot of Windows to preserve the original SID.

6. **B.** The ntldr file becomes overwritten when an old installation of Windows is installed. By using the Recovery Console, the ntldr file can be copied back to the root drive.

7. **B.** When the system state data for domain controllers needs to be restored, you must boot the computer into Directory Services restore mode and then run ntbackup and restore the files. You also must restore the system state data locally.

8. **B.** The Last Known Good Configuration can be used to recover from most stop errors if the user has not logged onto the server after receiving the stop error.

# Implementing, Managing, and Maintaining a Microsoft Windows Server 2003 Network Infrastructure (Exam 70-291)

# Administering DNS in a Windows Server 2003 Network

In this chapter, you will learn about
- The NetBIOS namespace
- The DNS namespace
- Fully qualified domain names
- Zones
- Host names

Welcome to the 291 section of this *All-in-One* certification guide. This section will prepare you for the test entitled Implementing, Managing, and Maintaining a Microsoft Windows Server 2003 Network Infrastructure. Just what exactly does that mean? Mostly, it's about getting Windows computers to talk to one another.

For computers in a Windows 2003 network infrastructure to talk to one another, one of the key ingredients is the DNS service. DNS is the name resolution mechanism used by Windows Server 2003 clients to find other computers and services running on those computers. A client consults its configured DNS servers for a list of Active Directory domain controllers where it will then submit its logon credentials.

Before we get too far along, however, you need to understand a few background concepts about the network infrastructure—any network infrastructure. This chapter will explain the concepts at work in DNS. If you are already familiar with the DNS service and terms such as zones, FQDNs, iterative queries, and the PTR records, you can probably move right ahead to Chapter 7 where the exam objectives are met with a discussion of TCP/IP. The topic of how to install, configure, and manage DNS in a Windows Server 2003 implementation is explored in Chapter 8.

## The NetBIOS Namespace

We start our discussion of DNS with the NetBIOS (Network Basic Input Output System) namespace. Namespaces make it easier for humans to work with computers because both the best thing and the worst thing about computers is that they work with numbers. Humans, however, like to work with names.

Computers and network services are therefore given names in these namespaces, and services like the DNS service exist to resolve the names that humans prefer into numbers computers rely on so that the computers can communicate. This is the essence of a namespace.

But no two namespaces are exactly alike. There are important differences between the DNS namespace and the NetBIOS namespace, and identifying some of the advantages and disadvantages of each namespace can help you understand them. It can also help explain why almost all computer networks today use DNS as the namespace of choice.

Prior to Windows 2000, the Windows networking model was built upon the NetBIOS namespace, not the DNS namespace. The NetBIOS namespace uses NetBIOS names. NetBIOS is actually an application-layer protocol (more on that in the next chapter) that can use the transport services of TCP/IP when used in a routed network.

A NetBIOS name is a 16-byte address that identifies a NetBIOS resource on a network. The important thing to keep in mind about the NetBIOS namespace, especially when contrasting it to the DNS namespace, is that it's a *flat* namespace. DNS, conversely, is a hierarchical namespace. Every NetBIOS name must be unique, period. There is no structure of parent and child namespaces that allows computer or service names to be used. For example, if the Internet used the NetBIOS namespace, there could only be one computer with the name of www. Of course, we know that www is used millions of times, because each instance of the www service only needs to be unique in the parent domain. In the NetBIOS world, there is no such thing as a parent domain.

In the NetBIOS environment, computers and services register unique NetBIOS names by using a 15-character computer name appended with a 16th hexadecimal character that identifies the service on the network. If the computer name does not contain 15 characters, the protocol of NetBIOS dictates that the name is padded with as many spaces as necessary to generate a 15-character name.

What's more, there are still some services running on the default Windows Server 2003 installation that register NetBIOS names. An example is File and Print Sharing for Microsoft Networks (also known as the Server service). At startup time, your Windows Server 2003 system registers this unique name, which is generated by using the computer name given to the system during operating system installation.

You can look up the NetBIOS name your computer uses by looking at the System Properties dialog box and choosing the Network Identification tab. Click Properties, then click More to display the NetBIOS name.

Also by default, your system registers this name by broadcasting it to the network and listening to see if any computer has already registered the name. If there is no response, the system registers the name in its NetBIOS name cache. You can look at the NetBIOS name cache by using the nbtstat utility from the command prompt with the -n switch, as shown in Figure 6-1.

If you see that it appears your Windows Server 2003 computer has registered its name more than once, as you should, it hasn't; you are really looking at different NetBIOS names, because the 16th hexadecimal character makes the names unique. However, if there were another computer on the same network trying to use the same computer name, that computer would not be able to successfully register its name at startup time,

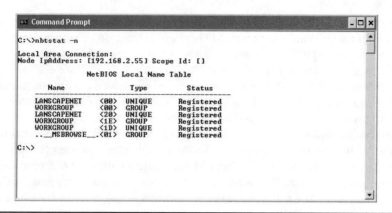

**Figure 6-1**    A list of registered NetBIOS names

because the NetBIOS names would conflict. For example, the Server service will always identify itself with the 16th hexadecimal character of 0x20, so two computers running the Server service with the same computer name would both try to register the same NetBIOS name, and a conflict would result.

There is also an application that can be installed on a Windows Server 2003 computer that provides name registration, renewal, and resolution services for NetBIOS names to IP addresses. In Windows, this NetBIOS name server is called the Windows Internet Naming Service, or WINS (the Internet, in this instance, is a misnomer; WINS is *not* used on the Internet). WINS eliminates the need for broadcast resolution of NetBIOS names to TCP/IP addresses by keeping a centralized database of name-to-IP-address mappings. In other words, WINS does for the NetBIOS namespace precisely what DNS servers do for the DNS namespace.

In Windows 2003, WINS can still be deployed, and it may even be a good idea depending on whether the applications or operating systems in your network still rely heavily on NetBIOS name resolution. However, it should not be needed when the computing environment is entirely Windows 2000 or newer. Furthermore, you should not expect to be tested on your knowledge of WINS.

So why did we start here? Because DNS is also a namespace, a much more flexible and scalable namespace, albeit one that is considerably more complex.

# The DNS Namespace

The Domain Name System (DNS) is a vital component in a Windows 2003 network, as will be made clear throughout this chapter and throughout your pursuit of the MCSE certification. Without DNS, you would have to know the IP address of every computer you are communicating with. DNS exists to resolve the names of computers to IP addresses. It also aids in locating services on a network. In the DNS namespace, the computer names are known as hosts, although the word *host* can refer to about any network interface card (NIC) with an IP address bound to it.

Furthermore, DNS organizes these resources into a hierarchy of domains. The DNS you implement on a Windows Server 2003 system is built on the same standards as the DNS in use on other TCP/IP networks, such as the Internet. It provides a mechanism through which user-friendly names (such as ftp.beanlake.com) are resolved to IP addresses (such as 10.100.9.23) so that computers can establish a communications channel using protocols such as HTTP, FTP, or SMB. The TCP/IP protocols are the transport mechanism that carries data from one system to the other.

And more important, at least in reference to the study of Windows 2003 networks, DNS provides the naming infrastructure for Active Directory. When you build your Active Directory domains, you name them in accordance with the DNS naming conventions in use in the Internet. That way, Active Directory can easily integrate with existing networks that follow the same naming conventions, using the same name resolution technologies—namely, DNS.

In fact, DNS not only provides a *possible* namespace—an alternative to the NetBIOS namespace, say—it's the *required* namespace for Active Directory. You can choose to integrate with the Internet or create a completely private Active Directory network, but you have no choice about the naming standards. As implemented in Active Directory, DNS provides a parent/child architecture for the naming of objects, and using this architecture, the DNS namespace allows for a virtually unlimited number of Active Directory objects.

## DNS Components

There are three main components you'll find in the Domain Name System. Not just Microsoft's implementation, but any DNS solution. These three items are

- Domain name servers
- DNS resolvers
- The logical namespace

The domain name servers are servers running the DNS software component, which store information about a zone file (we'll get to zones in just a bit). These name servers provide address resolution and other information about the computers that you access in both Active Directory domain and in the named domains across the entire Internet.

DNS resolvers are pieces of code that are built into the operating system. These pieces of code, known also as DNS clients, request resolution of FQDNs to IP addresses by querying their configured name servers. FQDNs are defined in the next section.

Finally, the namespace is the logical division of names where DNS objects are stored. The emphasis here is on the word *logical*. There is nothing you can point to, for example, and say, "That's the domain." To illustrate, ask yourself, "Where is the Microsoft domain?" You can't really say. That's because the DNS domain, much like an Active Directory domain, is an organizational entity. The only physical thing you can point to are the name servers, which are the computers that store information and service requests about the resources in the domain.

Keep in mind, too, that in an Active Directory domain, the namespace can often reflect the organizational chart of a particular company, where the company name starts at the root of the namespace, and then from there breaks into domains that provide a hierarchy for your domain enterprise.

## Fully Qualified Domain Names

As just mentioned, the job of a resolver is to request resolution of a fully qualified domain name (FQDN) to an IP address. A fully qualified domain name represents a host name appended to the parent namespaces in a hierarchy. In other words, within the fully qualified domain name you can see the different levels in the namespace hierarchy. Figure 6-2 helps you visualize this hierearchy—the root level namespace, top-level domains, and so on—in use throughout the Internet today.

Note that the leftmost portion of the FQDN is the host portion of the name. A host name is an alias we give to an IP address. Typically, any computer in a network is also considered a host, but other devices, such as routers and network print devices, can have names assigned to them, too.

All other naming information—every name to the right of the first name—contained in the FQDN identifies the logical parent namespace where the host lives.

There are organizations outside of your control that manage the topmost levels of the domain namespace. InterNIC is the organization that manages the top-level namespaces.

---

 **NOTE**  For full information on the InterNIC and what it governs, visit http://www.internic.net/.

---

The InterNIC, in fact, controls the first two levels of the DNS namespace: the root-level and top-level domains. There is only one root domain, which acts as the starting point of all fully qualified domain names. This root domain is designated with a dot (.), and in days of yore, people had to type this dot when using FQDNs. Now, however,

**Figure 6-2**
The logical DNS hierarchy

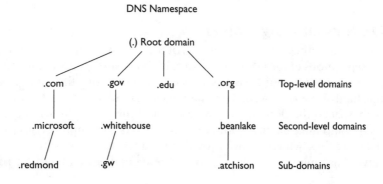
DNS Namespace

applications like Internet Explorer assume the last dot is implied, and you no longer have to enter the root domain when browsing to an Internet address.

The top-level domains, also under the governance of InterNIC, include familiar domains like .com, .edu, .gov, .net, .mil, all of which were intended to be used in the United States. Other top-level domain names include country codes like .ca, .uk, and .au (for Canada, the United Kingdom, and Australia, respectively). New top-level domains like .tv, .law, .info, .biz, and many more are either being proposed or implemented to accommodate new entities entering the Internet fray.

To register a first-level domain, you need to ask the InterNIC whether your domain will be unique in the parent namespace, or at least have a company like register.com do so on your behalf. For example, if you want to register beanlake.com, you're out of luck. However, if you want to register beanlake.org, you may. The domain beanlake can be used multiple times; the only requirement is that it be unique in the parent-level namespace.

Likewise with host names. There are most likely several thousand computers with the host name of COMPUTER1. That's okay, as long as the COMPUTER1 name is not reused within a single domain—for instance, there can only be one COMPUTER1 in the beanlake.com parent domain, just as there can only be one COMPUTER1 in the microsoft.com domain.

Also, when you register a name for use on the Internet, you're responsible for providing the addresses of two name servers (NS records; discussed next) that will resolve the names of hosts and other domains as well as other resources in that second-level domain. The second-level domains are controlled by you if you're the one who registers the domain. From there you're free to add records on your DNS servers representing individual computers in that domain space, subdomains in that domain space, or even provide the addresses of Active Directory domain controllers.

Furthermore, in order to communicate with other computers, both in your own domain and across the Internet, you need to be able to resolve fully qualified domain names to an IP address. How is this done? You ask your configured DNS server for resolution.

But before we examine the process for resolving a name to an IP address, we must understand what information is kept on the name servers. To store the name-to-IP-address mappings so crucial to network communication, name servers use *zone files*.

## Understanding Zones

If domains represent logical division of the DNS namespace, zones represent the physical separations of the DNS namespace. In other words, information about records of the resources within your DNS domains is stored in a zone file, and this zone file exists on the hard drive of one of your name servers. So there are logical parts of the DNS namespace—the domains themselves—and there are physical parts—both the name servers and the zone files. Domain name servers are simply servers that store these zone database files, which in turn provide resolution for records in the zone files. The DNS servers also manage how those zone files are updated and transferred.

Zone files are divided into one of two basic types:

- **Forward lookup zone**   Provides host-name-to-IP-address resolution
- **Reverse lookup zone**   Provides IP-address-to-host-name resolution

Generally speaking, humans are more concerned with the proper configuration of a forward lookup zone, as this is indeed more vital for successful computer communications. For example, a forward lookup zone is consulted when a domain user in a Windows Server 2003 Active Directory domain is looking for a domain controller where logon credentials can be submitted. And let's not forget the web browser, which also relies on forward lookup zoned to resolve FQDNs such as ftp.beanlake.com or www.beanlake.com into IP addresses, either when typed in the address bar or coded within a hyperlink. As administrators everywhere know, users without working Internet access are unhappy users.

Reverse lookup zones, on the other hand, are generally used by utilities like nslookup. In fact, nslookup, which we will discuss in Chapter 8, requires a properly configured reverse lookup zone in order to work like it should.

When a zone file is first created on a DNS server, that server is said to be authoritative for that zone. Then, for each child DNS domain name included in a zone, the zone becomes the authoritative source for the resource records stored in that child domain as well. This means that the DNS server can provide resolution for multiple domains within a zone file, and all changes to the resource records in both domains are made to the authoritative zone it stores.

Additionally, keep in mind that a zone can be authoritative for a single domain or multiple domains. This can be a little confusing because it's possible that one zone file can be authoritative for multiple domains. If you have a DNS hierarchy that, for administrative reasons, you have broken into multiple domains, yet those domains don't have vast number of resources, it may be good planning to store records about both namespaces, or all three or all five namespaces, on a single DNS server. In this example, this single zone would be authoritative for multiple portions of the DNS namespace.

It usually helps if you can remember the distinction between the logical part of DNS (the domains) and the physical part (the zones). In Figure 6-3, name server A stores a zone file that's authoritative for two domains, while name server B is authoritative for only a single domain.

**Figure 6-3**

A zone can be authoritative for one domain or multiple domains.

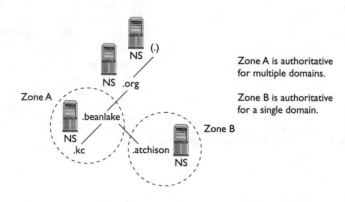

Zone A is authoritative for multiple domains.

Zone B is authoritative for a single domain.

## Zone Categories

The DNS zones kept on Windows Server 2003 computers can be further broken down into one of three categories. For each forward or reverse lookup zone, the file will be one of these types of zones:

- Primary zone
- Secondary zone
- Stub zone

What's more, all of the zones you can create in Windows 2003 can be integrated in Active Directory. Each of these zone categories is discussed in Chapter 8.

## Resource Records Stored in a Zone File

Each record stored in a zone file has a specific purpose. Some of the records set the behavior of the name server, others have the job of resolving a host name or service into an IP address. Table 6-1 explains the most common resource records you will administer, in no particular order.

| Record Symbol | Record Name | Purpose |
|---|---|---|
| A | Host | A host record populates a forward lookup zone and is the workhorse record of a DNS zone. It provides host-name-to-IP-address resolution. |
| PTR | Pointer | This record populates the reverse lookup zone files, if configured, and does just the opposite of an A record: it provides IP-address-to-host-name resolution. |
| SRV | Service | A service record helps identify services running in a domain namespace. When a user submits a domain logon, his DNS server must resolve the domain to the IP address of a domain controller. The SRV records help perform this task. |
| MX | Mail Exchange | This record identifies the IP address of a mail server for a given domain. All mail destined for a domain such as yahoo.com is dropped at the IP address specified by the MX record in the zone files authoritative for the yahoo.com domain. |
| NS | Name Server | These specify the name servers that are authoritative for a given potion of the DNS namespace. These records are essential when DNS servers are performing iterative queries to perform name resolution. |

**Table 6-1**    Resource Records Stored in a Zone File

| Record Symbol | Record Name | Purpose |
|---|---|---|
| SOA | Start Of Authority | This resource record indicates the name of origin for the zone and contains the name of the server that is the primary source for information about the zone. The information in an SOA record affects how often transfers of the zone are done between servers authoritative for the zone. It is also used to store other properties such as version information and timings that affect zone renewal or expiration. |
| CNAME | Canonical Name | Also referred to as an alias record, the CNAME can be used to assign multiple names to a single IP address. For example, the server hosting the site www.microsoft.com is probably not named www, but a CNAME record exists for resolution of www to an IP address all the same. The CNAME record actually points not to an IP address, but to an existing A record in the zone. |

**Table 6-1**    Resource Records Stored in a Zone File *(continued)*

# Updates to Windows Server 2003's DNS

DNS is open standards–based. Modifications and improvements are constantly being developed by the open standards community through a series of Requests for Comment (RFCs). These RFCs help shape DNS into a better name resolution service with each iteration, and help it integrate with the improvements in other areas of network communications.

As such, there have been several enhancements to the DNS features available with the Windows 2003 implementation of DNS, especially when compared to Microsoft's earlier deployments of the DNS service. Some of the improvements include the following:

- **Conditional forwarders**   DNS queries can be sent to specific DNS servers if they meet a defined set of conditions. For example, the 2003 DNS server can be set so that all queries of FQDNs that end in whatisthematrix.com be forwarded to a specific DNS server.

- **Stub zones**   Stub zones keep a DNS server that hosts a parent zone aware of the authoritative DNS servers for its child zone. This improves efficiency of DNS name resolution.

- **Enhanced DNS zone replication in Active Directory**   You now have four replication choices for Active Directory–integrated DNS zone data.

- **Enhanced DNS security features**   Windows Server 2003's DNS now provides greater flexibility when administering security for the DNS server, DNS client, and DNS zone information data.

- **Enhanced debug logging**   The DNS server has been written with enhanced debug logging options to aid in troubleshooting of DNS name resolution.

# Resolving a Host Name

Now that you have an understanding of the components of the DNS infrastructure, you need to understand how a DNS client resolves an FQDN to an IP address. There are actually many ways. A client can sometimes answer a query using information cached from a previously successfully resolved name. In fact, this is the first location the DNS resolver checks.

If the check of the cache is unsuccessful in providing IP address resolution, the resolver gets help from its configured DNS server, as outlined in the next section. This process is known as a recursive query.

The DNS server in turn can use its own cache of resource record information to answer a query. Barring a quick resolution from the DNS servers cache, the server begins a "walk" of the DNS tree through a series of iterative queries. The next section describes the navigation through the DNS namespace.

## Forward Lookup Resolution of FQDNs

Any time you enter a fully qualified domain name into an application, your operating system uses the resolver piece of code to query its configured DNS server (or servers) to get an IP address for the name you have just entered. If your locally configured DNS server has a zone file that contains a record for the resource you're trying to browse to (or if it's contained in the server's cache), that resource's IP address is returned to your resolver. In most cases, the zone file is not going to hold the IP address for the record that you're trying to look up. In that case, the DNS server will resolve that name to an IP address on your behalf. The DNS server does that by walking the DNS hierarchy.

For example, if you type ftp.atchison.beanlake.com into a browser, the browser needs to look up this fully qualified domain name using its resolver. The computer doesn't care what the name of the computer is; in order to communicate, it needs the IP address. The first place it looks for resolution is its configured DNS server. This query to the locally configured DNS server is called a recursive query.

If the local DNS server does not have an A record that maps ftp.atchison.beanlake.com to an IP address, the client's local DNS server—if it's configured to do so—will begin looking through the entire DNS hierarchy on behalf of the DNS client. The DNS server performs the name resolution; the DNS client sits there and waits for a response to its recursive query. The client's local DNS server then talks to other DNS servers throughout the DNS hierarchy using a series of iterative queries.

It begins with a check with one of its configured root-level name servers. Every Windows Server 2003 installation of DNS comes with several root-level name servers already known, and the server will query one of the servers in the list unless it's been configured to be a root-level server of a private network not directly connected to the Internet. You can access this list of root-level name servers by opening your DNS console, right-clicking your server, and choosing Properties. The Root Hints tab, shown in Figure 6-4, contains the entries for the root-level name servers. In Chapter 8, we investigate the DNS console in greater detail.

**Figure 6-4**

The preconfigured list of root-level name servers

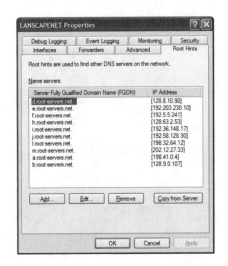

The root-level name servers won't know how to resolve ftp.atchison.beanlake.com to an IP address either, but they'll know to steer the client's local DNS server to a top-level name server. Subsequently, one of the top-level name servers in the .com level namespace will be asked the same question by the local DNS server: "What's the IP address for ftp.atchison.beanlake.com?" They won't have records for that resource in their zone files either, so they'll return their best answers, which in this case will be the NS records of the DNS servers authoritative for the domain .beanlake.

And so it goes. When the client's local DNS server finally locates the IP address for the DNS servers authoritative over the .beanlake subdomain, the local DNS server will then ask those servers for the record for the name ftp.

At long last, the DNS server that's just been queried—the one responsible for the zone file that stores host (A) records for the atchison.beanlake.com zone—will indeed have the IP address for that ftp name, and will return said IP address to the local DNS server. The local DNS server will hand the IP address back to the resolver, and then communication can be established from one IP address to another IP address (the FTP client and the FTP server in this case). This procedure is diagrammed in Figure 6-5.

After the resolution is complete, the DNS server caches the successful resolution in its DNS cache. If the next request for a resource from the same name is requested, the name can be resolved without a query through DNS. Likewise, the entry is usually cached on the DNS server for the same purpose. If another client of the DNS server were to request resolution before the entry's time-to-live (TTL) expires, the name would be resolved without walking the DNS tree.

## Recursive Queries and Iterative Queries

As mentioned, the process takes place with two types of queries. The client asks its local DNS server using a recursive query. A recursive query says, basically, give me the answer or tell me that you can't find it. It's a pass/fail type of proposition. The other type of query, where other DNS servers are talking to each other as the local DNS server is walking the domain tree, is called an iterative query. When your DNS server uses an iterative

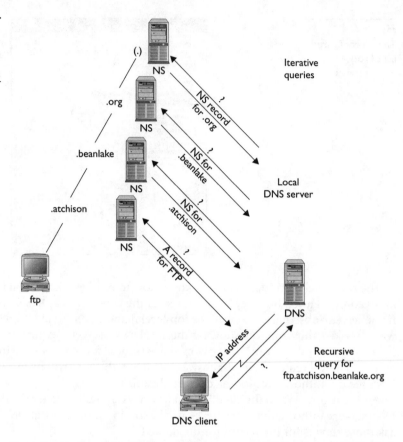

**Figure 6-5**
Iterative queries "walk" the DNS hierarchy.

query, it's asking for a "best guess." So the root-level name servers don't have the IP address for ftp.atchison.beanlake.com, but they will give you their best response, which is, "I don't have it, but I'll send you down to the .com level name servers—you can go ask them." If you're asking for something in the .com level namespace, the root-level name servers aren't going to send you the IP address of .net name servers or .gov name servers. They will give you the NS records for the name servers that govern the .com level namespace.

## Reverse Queries

What was just described was the forward lookup process, where a client is looking for a name-to-IP-address mapping. This is the most common type of lookup, in which an IP address is the expected resource data that is to be provided by the response.

But DNS also provides a mechanism to extract names from IP addresses. This enables clients to use a known IP address during a name query and look up a computer name. Instead of asking, "What's the IP address for ftp.atchison.beanlake.com?" a reverse query asks, "What's the name of the computer with the IP address of 10.169.254.23?"

This is more common with IP diagnostic and troubleshooting utilities like nslookup, which uses the IP address of the client's configured DNS server to query for resource records on that server. It is also used by reporting utilities that might collect information about who is accessing a particular web site. When HTTP "request" packets (they're technically HTTP *gets*) enter a web server, the information in the packet contains the IP address of the requester, but not the requester's computer name. So how do you find out who is hitting your site? With the reverse lookup zones. Utilities use reverse lookup zones to pinpoint either certain users or certain domains that are most frequent guests of the web site.

When DNS was first designed, it wasn't built to support this type of IP-address-to-name query. If you look at Figure 6-6, you see an FQDN, with an arrow representing the flow of the FQDN from general to specific. Below it, you see an IP address with the same arrow. As you can see, the FQDN resolves from the big namespace to the host from right to left, while the IP address identifies the network and then the host from left to right.

So a modification was made to the DNS namespace to get IP addresses to look like FQDNs. To support this reverse lookup query, there's a special domain called the in-addr.arpa domain, which is an abbreviation for "inverse-address. Advanced Research Projects Agency." (ARPA was the Department of Defense agency that was instrumental in the development of the Internet.)

The in-addr.arpa domain is now defined in RFC standards and is reserved in the Internet DNS namespace to provide a practical way to perform reverse queries. To create the reverse namespace, subdomains within the in-addr.arpa domain are formed using the reverse ordering of the numbers in the dotted-decimal notation of IP addresses. In other words, IP addresses are flipped around so that a query for the host name for 200.23.102.9 becomes a query resembling an FQDN, like so:

```
9.102.23.200.in-addr.arpa
```

Notice that the order of host's IP address will be reversed when building your reverse lookup zone files. The IP addresses of the DNS in-addr.arpa tree can be delegated to companies as they are assigned a specific or limited set of IP addresses within the Internet-defined address classes.

**Figure 6-6**
The "flow" of an FQDN and an IP address

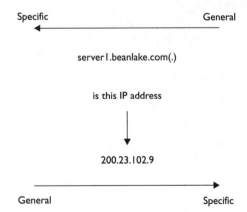

**NOTE** Forward lookup zones are built with A records, but reverse lookup zones are built with PTR records, which, strangely enough, *point* to A records in existing forward lookup zones. It doesn't necessarily matter in what order you create your zones, but you definitely want a forward lookup ready when you're populating the reverse lookup zone. In fact, you can populate the reverse lookup zone with PRT records at the same time you add host (A) records with a single check box.

# Chapter Review

The Domain Name System is the central name resolution component of a Windows Server 2003 network, and is even required for when it's time to implement Active Directory. In this chapter, you were either introduced to or reviewed some of DNS's underlying concepts.

We started with a look at the NetBIOS namespace, which is an alternate, flat namespace that can be used in Windows networking, and in fact was in versions prior to Windows 2000. It is not, however, used to resolve names on the Internet.

We then looked at how the DNS hierarchy is put together. We looked at the purpose of domains, which are the logical divisions of the DNS namespace, and then at the job of the zone files, which hold the resource records that resolve (among other things) host names to IP addresses. We also looked at some of the improvements that have been made recently to DNS, which have been integrated into Windows Server 2003's implementation.

In Chapter 8, we'll build upon this foundation and look at the many management tools and tasks needed to maintain your organization's Windows Server 2003 DNS deployment. Because there aren't that many things you will be directly tested on in this chapter, the review questions are fewer than usual. Don't worry, we'll make it up in chapters to come.

## Questions

1. You are installing the root domain controller for your forest. You have decided that the fully qualified domain name for the computer will be birmingham1.taylortoys.com. The system prompts you with a suggested NetBIOS name for the computer. Which NetBIOS name is prompted?

   **A.** birmingham1.taylor

   **B.** birmingham1

   **C.** taylortoys

   **D.** birmingham1.taylortoys.com

2. You are installing the root domain controller for your forest. You've decided that the fully qualified domain name for the computer will be birmingham1 .taylortoys.com. The system prompts you with a suggested NetBIOS name for the computer. You decide to use a different name. Which names could you use? (Choose all that apply.)

   A. birmingham.1

   B. birminghamserver1

   C. bham

   D. birmingham1

3. You are the Domain Admin of a Windows Server 2003 network for a company named Taylortoys. You currently use the same DNS name, taylortoys.com, on both sides of your firewall. Management is concerned that a breach in the firewall could expose the Active Directory. Which other names could you use on the inside of your firewall? (Choose all that apply.)

   A. taylortoys.com.ad

   B. ttoys.ad

   C. taylortoys.toys.ad

   D. whateveryouwant.com

4. You are the Enterprise Admin of a Windows Server 2003 network. You are currently using only standard primary and standard secondary zones. Another administrator asks you what would be required to upgrade all zones to Active Directory integrated zones. Which statement is true?

   A. All servers in the forest would have to be Windows Server 2003.

   B. All servers in the forest would have to be Windows 2000 or Windows Server 2003.

   C. All DNS servers would have to be domain controllers.

   D. The domain will need to be in at least Windows 2000 native mode.

5. You are the Domain Admin of a Windows Server 2003 network named eaglesinc.com.ad. You have a computer in the domain named computer1. What is the fully qualified domain name of this computer?

   A. eaglesinc.com.ad.computer1

   B. eaglesinc.computer1

   C. computer1.ad.eaglesinc.com

   D. computer1.eaglesinc.com.ad

## Answers

1. **B.** The NetBIOS name is used by Windows Server 2003 computers for backward compatibility with legacy clients and legacy applications. It can be up to 15 characters in length and cannot contain any hierarchical symbols such as "/" or ".". The system will add a 16th character that indicates what service that name provides. Computers that supply multiple services to the network will have multiple NetBIOS names. The system will suggest a NetBIOS name for the computer based on the prefix of the fully qualified domain name.

2. **C and D.** You can choose any NetBIOS name that meets the parameters and that is unique in the forest. In this case, since the computer established a forest root, uniqueness is not an issue.

3. **A, B, C, and D.** Management's concerns in this scenario are valid. Since you are using the same name on both sides of the firewall, a breach in the firewall could expose the Active Directory. You have two other options. You could use an appended name to the current name (such as taylortoys.com.ad) or you could use a completely different name. Each strategy has its own advantages and disadvantages.

4. **C.** Active Directory integrated zones replicate their databases along with Active Directory replication. Therefore, all servers that host Active Directory integrated zones must be domain controllers. There is no functional level requirement and no requirement that all servers be Windows 2000 or Windows Server 2003. However, all of the DNS servers would need to be Windows 2000 or Windows Server 2003 domain controllers.

5. **D.** A fully qualified domain name consists of a prefix and a suffix. The prefix is the name of the computer or other object (user). The suffix is the full name of the domain in which the object is contained. In this case, the prefix is computer1 and the suffix is eaglesinc.com.ad.

# Implementing, Managing, and Maintaining IP Addressing

In this chapter, you will learn how to

- Configure TCP/IP addressing on a server computer
- Implement IP addressing
- Install TCP/IP
- Install and configure DHCP
- Configure a DHCP server
- Integrate DHCP with Active Directory
- Manage DHCP in a routed environment
- Troubleshoot DHCP

The foundation of virtually every modern computing network is the TCP/IP protocol suite. There are entire books devoted to this subject; this chapter serves as an introduction and overview. What you learn in this chapter is by no means a doctoral dissertation on TCP/IP; rather, the information herein will arm you for the 70-291 test and will give you what you need to understand other Windows Server 2003 concepts and technologies that rely on TCP/IP. For example, when you configure an Active Directory site, as you will in Chapter 19, TCP/IP knowledge will be a prerequisite. This chapter will help provide some of that understanding.

All modern operating systems offer TCP/IP support, as you'll find that it's the default networking language these operating systems use. Windows Server 2003 is no different. What's more, an installation of Active Directory, which is what you're spending the majority of time studying on your path to the MSCE, *requires* TCP/IP as the networking protocol.

Most of this chapter, however, deals with just one portion of the TCP/IP suite: the IP address. You will not get far in your certification studies, or in your computer administration career, without a thorough understanding of this computer numbering system that makes sure that information gets from sender to recipient.

# Configure TCP/IP Addressing on a Server Computer

In short, a protocol is the "language" a network interface card (NIC) uses to communicate with other NICs on the network. The principle is much like human-to-human spoken communication. Network cards that want to exchange information must adhere to one of the two following rules:

- They must both "speak" the same language.

- There must be a language translator between the two.

Although TCP/IP is the default, Windows Server 2003 actually supports several network protocols, including NWLink (Microsoft's version of Novell's proprietary network protocol), Internetwork Packet Exchange/Sequenced Packet Exchange (IPX/SPX), and AppleTalk (for communication with older Macintosh clients), to name a few. However, because of the reason stated above, it's likely that you won't need these other network protocols in your administrative career, especially if said administrative career began with the purchase of this book.

## TCP/IP Overview

Because it is the core protocol used to transport packets of information back and forth across the Internet, TCP/IP is the most widely used protocol today by a wide margin. In addition to the advantage of enjoying the support of almost all network operating systems, it also offers the following advantages:

- **It's scalable.**   TCP/IP is scalable, allowing for use in networks large and small.

- **It's routable.**   TCP/IP is routable, which means that the data being sent and delivered may be transported to and from the local physical network and onto a wider network. In other words, what makes a protocol routable is its ability to be transferred from one network to another. The network device that sends information from one network to another is called, appropriately, a router.

- **It supports open standards.**   TCP/IP works with open standards–based companion services like Dynamic Host Configuration Protocol (DHCP) and Domain Name System (DNS) to offer additional functionality and ease of use. These two services automate the assignment of TCP/IP addresses to client computers (DHCP) and automate the resolution of user-friendly host names to IP addresses (DNS). Furthermore, because of the modular architecture of the TCP/IP suite, improvements to these companion services—or even improvements to the protocol itself—can be developed independently of each other. The latter part of this chapter deals with DHCP, and in Chapter 8 we'll look at DNS.

All networking protocols, however, share the following characteristic: they are designed to communicate with other network-accessible devices that are running the same protocol. The protocols accomplish this by first breaking up data to be sent—documents, pictures, executables, and the like—into packets, which, along with the data, contain affixed header and trailer information so the packets can reach their destination. At its very essence, the protocol's job is to define what information is stored in these packets and how that information is processed.

## The Role of the Packet

First, understand that information sent over a network is not placed on the network wire as a single entity. It is broken up into pieces, and then those individual chunks of data are packaged and sent over the network in something called a packet (or frame or datagram; the terms are really interchangeable, but we'll stick with packet for the discussion here). The role of the packet is to make network communication more diplomatic and efficient. If your message is sent as one chunk, the e-mail would tie up the wire for a considerable amount of time, not letting other computers send data until the entire chunk had been transmitted. Furthermore, if the single data message were corrupted, it would need to be resent in its entirety, doubling the amount of time the data transmission would take.

Through the use of packets, however, these problems are addressed. Using packets, a smaller portion of the e-mail transmission can be placed on the wire, tying it up for a much shorter period of time. This allows other computers to send their own packets when your system is not sending, allowing for more diplomatic network communication. The single e-mail is sent as many constituent pieces, and the system at the receiving end knows how to assemble the pieces because of the information contained therein.

Also, suppose a piece of data becomes corrupted as it reaches its destination. With packet transmission, only the packet with the corrupted data need be retransmitted, instead of the entire chapter. Communication is more efficient.

You can think of a packet the same way you think about a piece of mail, where the envelope is analogous to a data packet. When you drop a piece of mail into the old mailbox, it contains a destination address and a sender address, and inside the envelope is the "data" meant to get to the recipient—likewise the packet. It, too, contains a sender and destination address, plus the information meant for the target application.

In certain parts of the mail system, mail sorting components look only at the zip code. They don't care about the street address or about the name on the envelope, and to look at the "data" would constitute a felony. In certain parts of the TCP/IP suite, the only thing looked at is the destination network address. These components don't care what application is going to pick up the data or what that data says.

## The TCP/IP Protocol Suite

As might be inferred from the preceding paragraph, today's networking protocols are implemented as protocol *suites*, or stacks, which represent a combination of several pieces of networking software and services working in tandem to provide network functionality. Protocol suites precisely define the series of steps that are applied to a piece of data—the preparation of a packet—that is to be sent over the network wire.

For example, let's take a look at web site browsing and the protocols involved: the TCP/IP suite contains Hypertext Transfer Protocol (HTTP) services to support TCP/IP file transfer, which can be sent over an Ethernet network. If you were to diagram it schematically, the HTTP protocol lives on top of the transport services of the TCP and IP protocols. As represented in Figure 7-1, below TCP/IP lives the Ethernet protocol, which defines how the network wire is accessed. Each layer of the protocol suite performs specific actions to a packet of information before the data is either sent from a web server or received by a web browser.

Protocols must be configured properly on each computer on the network where the protocol is used. In fact, most troubleshooting of network protocols comes down to fixing improper configuration of a particular protocol. For example, for TCP/IP to work, every network device must be configured with an IP address and a subnet mask.

There are a couple of ways this IP address can be configured: either manually, by typing a number into the TCP/IP Properties dialog box, or dynamically, through the services of either DHCP or Automatic Private IP Addressing (APIPA), as will be discussed later in this chapter.

**Figure 7-1**
Representation of the TCP/IP stack

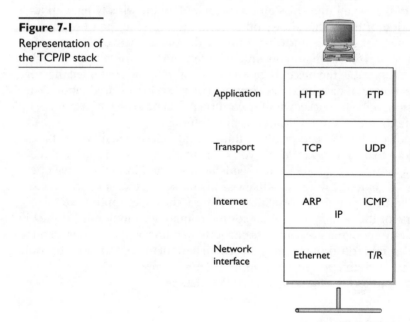

| | | |
|---|---|---|
| Application | HTTP | FTP |
| Transport | TCP | UDP |
| Internet | ARP     IP | ICMP |
| Network interface | Ethernet | T/R |

## The Role of the Redirector

In addition to the networking protocols, there are operating system components necessary that must also support networking. One critical software component that runs on client computers that access file and print services from server computers is called the redirector. The job of the redirector is to play traffic cop: it decides whether a request for a resource is to be serviced locally by one of the disk device drivers or remotely on a network server. Just like transport protocols, the redirectors and server components in a network must also be compatible.

You've seen a redirector at work, even if you aren't aware of its existence. For example, the Microsoft redirector on Windows Server 2003 systems, as well as XP and 200 systems, is called the Client for Microsoft Networks. Right-click My Network Places and choose Properties, select the Local Area Connection and right-click, and choose Properties. As seen in Figure 7-2, you should see the redirector, which goes by the alias of Client for Microsoft Networks. (Just to confuse matters, it's listed as the Workstation Service when you investigate the Services MMC snap-in of your Administrative Tools.)

This Microsoft redirector is used to request file and print resources from the other Microsoft operating systems that are running File and Print Sharing for Microsoft networks. (To further confuse, this service goes by the alias Server service when examined under the Services MMC.) You can look at and modify the startup behavior of both these services when you look in the Services MMC under the Administrative Tools.

Both the Microsoft redirector and the Microsoft Server service "speak" the same file and print sharing protocol: Server Message Blocks (SMB). This allows server and client to exchange file and print resources using a transport protocol like TCP/IP.

**Figure 7-2**

The Microsoft redirector: Client for Microsoft Networks

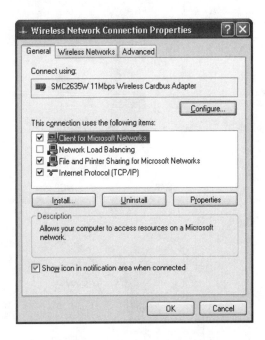

If you want a Microsoft client to access a NetWare server, you must install another redirector that is compatible with NetWare. The redirector for accessing a NetWare server is called Client Services for NetWare (CSNW), which also relies on the installation of the NWLink transport protocol. It is important to know that these two redirectors (client software) can live happily side by side; this is practical, because a lot of organizations are still running both Windows Server 2003 and NetWare servers to provide network resources. The Workstation service will be used to access the Microsoft servers, and the NetWare client will be used to access resources from the Novell servers.

Just as Microsoft clients cannot talk to a NetWare server by default, a NetWare client cannot talk to the Microsoft Server service. Neither can the Macintosh client software. For these clients to interact with a Microsoft Server service, additional software components must be installed on the Windows Server 2003. These components include File and Print Services for NetWare and File and Print Services for Macintosh. They exist to speak the same file and print sharing language as non-Microsoft clients, so that non-Microsoft clients think they are talking to non-Microsoft servers, as illustrated in Figure 7-3.

But your concern as you study Windows Server 2003 is its default networking protocol—TCP/IP—and how to properly configure it for network communication. The next section looks at the basics of this vital protocol.

## Understanding IP Communication

To help you understand TCP/IP, let's start by illustrating a more simplified protocol, one that people already use every day: the telephone system. When you place a long-distance

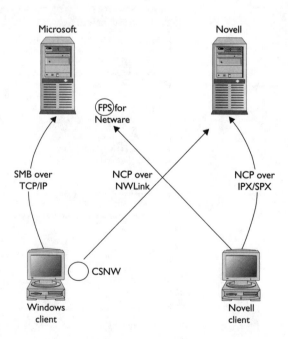

**Figure 7-3**
Clients and servers must speak the same language to exchange data.

phone call, you must dial the area code first. Your call won't connect with the desired recipient if you decide to dial the area code after you dial the seven-digit number. Dialing the area code first, not last, is part of the set of rules—the protocol—of telephone communications. The area code must be dialed first and be three digits in length, and everyone who uses the Public Switched Telephone Network (PSTN) follows this standard. If you were to dial an imaginary four-digit area code, the phone system would get confused about your request, and communication would fail. These same concepts hold true for the protocols used in computer communication.

We also use a protocol when sending data along a computer network, and as mentioned, TCP/IP is the most commonly used network protocol today. It, too, defines the steps that are taken when computers communicate with one another. When you install Windows Server 2003 on a system, it is installed as either a member server or a standalone server. On these clean installations, TCP/IP is the default networking protocol installed.

What follows is the condensed version of a lesson in TCP/IP. Entire books have been devoted to exploring TCP/IP, and with good reason. Microsoft, back when they were certifying folks on NT 4, used to teach it in a five-day class. Microsoft assumes by now that you have already gained much of this understanding of TCP/IP via real-world networking experience or through preparation certifications like Network Plus.

Any understanding of TCP/IP begins with a look at how computers view IP addresses—that is, with an understanding of binary notation.

## Binary Addressing

You're no doubt aware (especially after Chapter 6) of the concept that computers use numbers to talk to each other on a network. The IP address, then, is just the number assigned to your network card that uniquely identifies your computer on a network. Further, in the case of a routable protocol like TCP/IP, the IP address not only designates a unique computer number, but also identifies what unique network your computer is living on.

But computers don't see numbers the same way that humans do. Humans look at numbers in terms of 0 through 9, but computers only deal with 1s and 0s. That's because computers deal with information as states of on or off, yes or no. An IP address is no different. When configuring an IP address, you are giving the computer a 32-bit number that will be part of its identity on the network for as long as it keeps that address. There are 32 1s and 0s in this address, and since a bit is either a state of on or off (1 or 0, respectively), the entire address is 32 bits in length.

Human beings, when configuring IP addresses, deal with these 32 bits of binary 8 bits at a time, by dividing up the IP address into octets. The octets are then given decimal equivalents and separated by periods, and humans use these dotted decimal equivalents when configuring IP addresses. But to a computer, these decimal numbers are meaningless.

Every IP address you encounter when configuring Windows Server 2003 will be denoted in decimal notation and will look something like 192.168.2.200. But to the operating system, the network card, and so forth, that decimal address is just a string of 32 1s and 0s that, in binary notation, looks like this:

11000000.10101000.00000010.11001000

(The periods separating the octets are to make it easier for you to understand; the computer does not use the periods.) We're not used to dealing with numbers in binary notation, but when configuring IP addresses—and when preparing for the exam—it becomes an essential skill. If it helps, think of the bits in an octet as placeholders. A binary numbering system is such because it uses the number 2 as its base. (The decimal numbering system uses a base of 10.) The binary numbers are generated by doubling the value of the "on" bit by increasing the value of the placeholder by a power of 1. (Try this with the base-10 numbering system we use and you'll see that the same concept holds true. For example, the number 327 can be represented as $3 \times 10^2$ (300) plus $2 \times 10^1$ (20) plus $7 \times 10^0$ (7), for a total of 327.) The illustration in Figure 7-4 may make this easier to follow. Now that you've seen it, what would an octet look like to a computer if the decimal equivalent were 12? Like this: 00001100.

To represent a 12, all you need is the $2^4$ placeholder and the $2^3$. The $2^4$ placeholder's decimal equivalent is 8, and the $2^3$ placeholder's value is 4, and 8+4=12. You can also check your skills (or my accuracy) with the scientific calculator, which you'll find as one of your Windows accessories. Type in the number 12 and then click the Bin radio button to see what it looks like. Remember, though, that the calculator doesn't know you're working with an octet, so it won't append the other zeros necessary to make an octet.

As another reference point, Table 7-1 converts the addresses from binary code to their decimal equivalents. You can use in conjunction with or instead of the sketch in Figure 7-4.

**Figure 7-4**
A sketch to help you visualize the concept

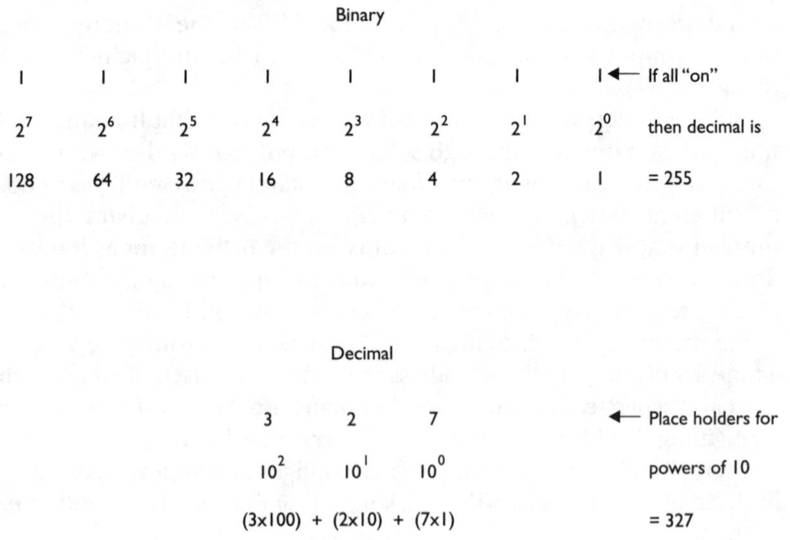

Binary

| | | | | | | | | ← If all "on"
$2^7$ $2^6$ $2^5$ $2^4$ $2^3$ $2^2$ $2^1$ $2^0$ then decimal is
128 64 32 16 8 4 2 1 = 255

Decimal

3 2 7 ← Place holders for
$10^2$ $10^1$ $10^0$ powers of 10
(3×100) + (2×10) + (7×1) = 327

| | Binary Code | "On" Bit Value | Decimal Value |
|---|---|---|---|
| **Table 7-1** Binary Octets and Their Decimal Equivalents | 00000000 | n/a | 0 |
| | 00000001 | 1 | 1 |
| | 00000011 | 2+1 | 3 |
| | 00000111 | 4+2+1 | 7 |
| | 00001111 | 8+4+2+1 | 15 |
| | 00011111 | 16+8+4+2+1 | 31 |
| | 00111111 | 32+16+8+4+2+1 | 63 |
| | 01111111 | 64+32+16+8+4+2+1 | 127 |
| | 11111111 | 128+64+32+16+8+4+2+1 | 255 |

As you can see, if all the bits are set to on, the decimal equivalent is 255. That's as high a number as you'll see in any octet. Conversely, if all the bits are set to off, the decimal equivalent is 0. Therefore, the range of numbers in any given octet in an IP address (or a subnet mask or default gateway; more on that later) is 0–255. But before we do that, let's delve further into the IP address.

## TCP/IP's Big Three

When configuring TCP/IP, the first order of business is to assign an IP address and a subnet mask. There are no exceptions to this rule when setting up TCP/IP parameters, and in a minute you'll learn why. There is also another parameter, the default gateway, that's essential for communicating on larger networks, such as the Internet. You can think of each of these parameters as TCP/IP's Big Three, and they each get special attention in the following sections.

## The IP Address

This is the number associated with your computer, analogous to the address of a house or a number of a telephone line. Every IP address is composed of two parts: the network ID and the host ID.

The network ID represents the network the computer belongs to, while the host ID uniquely identifies the computer on that network. Every network ID on a TCP/IP network (such as the Internet) must be unique, in the same way that every zip code in the United States must be unique. Further, every host ID on each network must also be unique to that network, in the same way that every house on a street must have a different number. If you accept the foregoing as true, then you must also posit that there must be a way to separate the IP address into a network portion and a host portion. But how does IP do this? How does the computer know which part of the IP address is the network identifier and what part is the host identifier? Read on.

## The Subnet Mask

The subnet mask is used to divide the IP address into the network portion and the host portion. It is a required TCP/IP setting. Without the subnet mask, the computer has no idea what network it belongs to. The subnet mask is also a 32-bit binary number broken into four octets for easy human consumption, like this: 255.255.0.0.

The interesting thing to note about the subnet mask is how it looks to the computer, as shown in Figure 7-5.

Notice anything peculiar about the binary number shown in Figure 7-5? That's right; it's a string of *contiguous* 1s followed by another string of *contiguous* 0s. The contiguous nature of the binary notation makes the subnet mask easy to spot.

Note also that the decimal number 255 octet is a string of 8 binary 1s. The decimal 0 octet is a string of 8 binary 0s. The job of the 1s, then, is to mask out the network number—they identify which of the 32 1s and 0s in the IP address are used as the network ID. Everything else—everything that lines up with the 0s in the subnet mask—denotes the host ID.

If you use the IP address with the subnet mask here, you are able to determine which 1s and 0s of the IP address are the network ID, and which 1s and 0s are the host ID. The subnet mask tells you that the first 16 binary numbers are the network number, which when you convert back to decimal is 192.168. The next 16 binary numbers are the host ID, which translate into 2.200.

If any of this is confusing, think back to the example of the telephone protocol. Part of the telephone number you dial represents a big grouping of phone lines (the first three numbers), and part represents an individual line within that larger grouping (the last four numbers). You can think of this as the network ID and the host ID in IP communications.

So why is this determination of network ID and host ID important? Why is a subnet mask required for a valid IP address? It is needed for the successful delivery of information to the proper network, and it helps make TCP/IP a routable protocol.

Each and every packet of TCP/IP communications has a source address and a destination address. And once TCP/IP determines the network ID of the source and destination computers, an important decision is made about how to deliver the packet to its destination. If the network IDs match, the packet is delivered to the local segment of computers. But if the network IDs of source and destination do not match, the packet must be routed to a remote network via a default gateway.

## The Default Gateway

Here's another key ingredient in IP configuration, which is why it's included in the Big Three. Although it is not technically required, your network communication would be very limited without the default gateway parameter.

---

**Figure 7-5**
The subnet mask displayed in decimal and in binary

Decimal ⟶   255.255.0.0

Binary ⟶   11111111111111110000000000000000

A default gateway is the IP address of the router, which is the pathway to any and all remote networks. (Why the default gateway isn't called the default router, especially since there are devices called gateways whose purpose differs from routers, is a matter of late-night conjecture.) To get a packet of information from one network to another, the packet is sent to the IP address of the default gateway, which then helps forward the packet to its destination network. In fact, computers that live on the other side of routers are said to be on remote networks. Without default gateways, Internet communication is not possible, because your computer doesn't have a way to send a packet destined for any other network.

**NOTE**   We tend to think of a router as a big box with the letters C-I-S-C-O etched on the front, but it can be any device that simply passes information from one network to another. Almost any Windows machine with multiple network cards can be configured to act as a router, as you'll learn in Chapter 9.

## Address Classes

You should also know when dealing with IP addresses that they are broken up in to different categories or classes. Each of these categories help define a range of networks in each class, and also help define how many hosts can exist on every network. Also, these address classes have a default subnet mask associated with them, which actually does the dirty work of defining the number of networks and the number of hosts per network.

The different classes are defined by the first few bits in the first octet of the IP address, as you will see. Keep in mind that these IP addresses are seen only as 1s and 0s, and this concept should fall into place.

Let's look at each of these address classes now.

### Class A Addresses

The first bit of the first octet in a Class A IP address is always set to 0. If you refer to the binary-to-decimal chart in Table 7-1, you can see this puts a ceiling on the decimal equivalent of that first octet. If the first bit is set to off (0), the highest number you can make in the first octet is reached by turning all the other seven bits to on (1). When you do, the decimal equivalent is 127, which represents the upper range of a Class A address. Actually, it's 126, because the 127 network is a reserved address, as will be explained next.

A Class A network has a default subnet mask of 255.0.0.0. That means that, by default, the first octet of a Class A address is the network identifier, and the last three octets will be the host identifier. Because of this, there are only 126 Class A networks available for use, with a range in the first octet from 1–126 (the 0 network cannot be used; that, too will be explained below).

To test this, open your TCP/IP Properties page (right-click My Network Places, select Properties | TCP/IP, right-click and choose Properties). Enter a Class A address and then tab down to the subnet mask. The mask that Windows Server 2003 offers you is a Class A mask of 255.0.0.0.

So how many hosts can you create on a Class A network? Well, since the subnet mask tells you the first 8 bits of your 32 total bits will define the network ID, that means you can mix and match the rest of the 24 bits in the remaining three octets to define the hosts in a given Class A network. If you have 24 bits left to define hosts, there are $2^{24}$ such combinations of 1s and 0s. To save you a trip to the calculator, $2^{24}$ comes out to 16,777,214 hosts per network. ($2^{24}$ is actually 16,777,216, but you can't use the first and last host IDs. Again, this will be explained in the following section.)

## Class B Addresses

In a Class B address, the first 2 bits of the first octet are always set to 10. This means that the first octet's decimal value will always be at least 128. And if the second bit will always be set to 0, the highest the first octet will be is 191.

The Class B addresses have a default subnet mask of 255.255.0.0. These addresses are assigned to medium to relatively large companies and organizations, with the network numbers ranging from 128.0.x.y to 191.255.x.y, where x and y are the host values.

There are $2^{14}$ Class B networks (remember that the two bits are locked), or 16,384. Since you have 16 bits to mix and match to define the hosts on each of these networks, you end up with a possibility of $2^{16}$ or 65,534 hosts (when you remember to subtract 2).

## Class C Addresses

In a class C address, the first 3 bits of the first octet are always set to 110. Those three bits are set in stone. That means the smallest decimal number the first octet can be is 192. And since the highest binary you can produce on that octet is 11011111, the upper range for the first octet of a Class C address is 223.

Class C addresses have a default subnet mask of 255.255.255.0, and are assigned to small companies, who sometimes get several Class C addresses at a time. The network numbers range from 192.0.0.x to 223.255.255.x, where x is the host value for the network.

There are $2^{21}$ possible Class C network addresses, or 2,097,152. Each Class C address has one octet's worth of hosts, which is $2^8$ less 2, or 254.

These address class differences are summarized for your review in Table 7-2.

| Address Class | Default Subnet Mask | Range | Number of Networks | Hosts per Network |
|---|---|---|---|---|
| A | 255.0.0.0 | 1.0.0.0–126.0.0.0 | 126 | Approximately 16 million |
| B | 255.255.0.0 | 128.0.0.0–191.255.0.0 | 16 large | 64 large |
| C | 255.255.255.0 | 192.0.0.0–223.255.255.0 | 2 million | 254 |

**Table 7-2**   The Address Class Differences

## The AND Operation

When a computer sends a packet of IP traffic to another computer, there must be a way to evaluate that packet and determine if the packet will be delivered to the local network, or to a remote network, and thus to the default gateway. This evaluation is performed using an AND operation.

It works like this: when a computer builds an IP packet for delivery, that packet will contain both a source IP address and subnet mask, as well as a destination IP address. Just like when you wrap and address a mail package, you include the address of where the package is going and an address of where it's being sent from.

Once the packet is composed, the computer will then AND the subnet mask to both source and destination IP addresses. ANDing combines the IP address and subnet mask, spawning a third number as a result. Where there are 1s and 1s, a 1 is produced once the AND operator does its evaluation. Where there is a 0 and any other number, a 0 results.

It's best to look at an example of the AND operator at work for full understanding. Suppose your system, whose IP address was 192.168.2.200 and subnet mask was 255.255.255.0, composed a TCP/IP packet whose destination IP address was 192.168.8.100. That information would be part of the header information in the packet.

Now, your network card needs to know where that packet will be sent. Will it be delivered locally or remotely? Here's where the AND operator steps in.

When the computer takes the source IP address and ANDs it to the subnet mask, the result is a binary number (see Figure 7-6). Note that this number matches the network identifier, which you have already determined by looking at the subnet mask.

The destination IP address is ANDed to the system's subnet mask (see Figure 7-7). The results of the source ANDing and the destination ANDing are then compared. If the number is a match, the packet is sent only to the local network. In our example, however, the ANDing results do not match, and therefore the computer determines that the packet needs to be routed to another network. It is then sent to the computer's default gateway for routing.

When it's all said and done, ANDing is just the computer's way of determining the source and destination network numbers, and then forwarding the packet as necessary based on that determination. The computer just uses binary when evaluating these numbers.

**Figure 7-6**

The result of the source ANDing process

Source

192.168.2.200
255.255.255.0          ◄——— Decimal

11000000 10101000 00000010 11001000
11111111 11111111 11111111 00000000   ◄——— Binary

11000000 10101000 00000010 00000000   ◄——— ANDing result

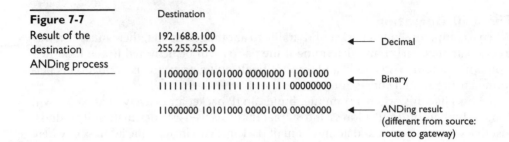

**Figure 7-7**
Result of the destination ANDing process

Now let's talk more about the IP addressing rules referred to in the preceding sections.

## IP Addressing Rules

There are a few rules you should be aware of when assigning IP addresses to computers:

- The network ID cannot be set to 127. This address is reserved for loopback and diagnostic purposes.

- The network ID and host IDs cannot be all 1s. If all bits are set to 1, the address is interpreted as a broadcast address and will not be routed under normal circumstances. A Class B address of 151.255.0.0 is a perfectly good network ID. The network ID is 16 bits long, and only the last 8 bits in the network number are all 1s.

- Neither the network ID nor the host ID can have the bits be all 0s. If all of the host bits are set to 0, for example, that is interpreted as the same as the network number. In the example above, the network number is 151.255.0.0. The first host on that network, then, is 151.255.0.1.

- The host ID must be unique to the local network ID. There cannot be two 0.1 hosts on the 151.255 network.

- A unique network ID is needed for each network connected to a wide area network, which is usually the public Internet. (This network ID is typically provided by your ISP.) On the Internet, for example, there is only one 151.255 network.

- Every TCP/IP host requires a subnet mask. The IP address is useless without one because of the mask's role of separating out the 32 bits of the IP address into distinct network bits and host bits.

**EXAM TIP**  Be able to easily spot bogus IP addresses from a list. It should give you a chance to score a "gimme" question on the 70-291 exam.

## Classless Internet Domain Routing (CIDR) Notation

There is another way of expressing the IP address without having to spell out the subnet mask in octets of 255s and 0s. Instead, you can count out the number of 1s in the subnet mask and then represent the IP address and subnet mask with a slash followed by the number of 1 bits in the subnet mask, like 192.168.2.200/16.

This notation is called classless inter-domain routing (CIDR, pronounced "cedar") notation. The notation here specifies the same IP address as used in the previous example. The IP address part is very straightforward. The /16 tells you that this IP address has a subnet mask with the first 16 bits set to 1. And 16 1s gives you a subnet mask of 255.255.0.0, same as before.

CIDR notation is used to simplify entries on routing tables and is the notation used by a majority of backbone Internet routers. It is also used to cut down on the number of wasted IP addresses in the Class B address space. You should know how to recognize the CIDR notation when you see it and to convert the CIDR subnet mask notation into a decimal equivalent.

## Configuring TCP/IP

After you install and bind TCP/IP to a LAN or a WAN adapter (remember that this will be done automatically by Windows Server 2003 Setup), the core tasks for configuring TCP/IP include the assignment of an IP address, the configuration of name resolution, and the configuration of TCP/IP security.

**NOTE** Binding is the process of associating a network protocol with a network card, or associating a network protocol with a communications service, such as the Client or Server services. In Windows Server 2003, the binding is done with a check box.

A client can get an IP address statically or dynamically. Static addressing is accomplished through the Internet Protocol (TCP/IP) Properties dialog box by an administrator who manually types in the IP address, the subnet mask, and the default gateway, as shown in Figure 7-8.

To open the Internet Protocol (TCP/IP) Properties dialog box:

1. Open the Control Panel and choose the Network Connection applet. (Alternatively, you could right-click My Network Places and choose Properties if the desktop icon has been added by adjusting your default Display properties.)

2. Right-click Local Area Connection and choose Properties.

3. Select Internet Protocol (TCP/IP) and click the Properties button.

But rather than typing all this information on hundreds or thousands of computers in your network, you can let DHCP do it for you by selecting Obtain An IP Address Automatically. As one of the companion services of TCP/IP that can run on a Windows 2000

**Figure 7-8**
Configuring
TCP/IP

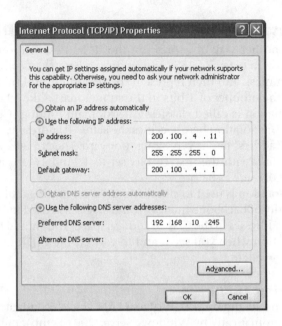

or .NET Server, DHCP's job is to hand out valid IP addresses to computers on the network at bootup time. It must always be configured to assign the two required IP address components—the IP address and the subnet mask. It can be, and usually is, also configured to assign configuration information about the default gateway and any name resolution servers in use on your network. By using this vital component of modern TCP/IP networks, you can automate the IP address allocation to network computers to reduce confusion, administrative overhead, and problems related to human error.

If you accept the Typical network settings at Server 2003 installation time, TCP/IP is installed, and the computer is configured as a DHCP client. After installation, this configuration can be done at any time from the Internet Protocol (TCP/IP) Properties dialog box.

Although it's counterintuitive, a DHCP client does not even need a DHCP server to get an IP address. A DHCP client that cannot locate a DHCP server will assign an IP address to itself through a mechanism called Automatic Private IP Addressing (APIPA). APIPA is not new to Windows, as it was used beginning with Windows 98. It was first introduced to the NT product family with Windows 2000.

## Diagnose and Resolve Issues Related to APIPA

When a DHCP client is unable to locate a DHCP server, the client picks out a random IP address from the private APIPA address range of 169.254.*x.y*, with a subnet mask of 255.255.0.0. The 169.254.*x.y* IP range is private because that network number is not in use on the Internet; it is random because the client generates an arbitrary host number (the *x.y*) for that network. Let's say the client picks the host ID of 100.23. The client will then announce to the network that it wants to use the IP address of 169.254.100.23. If no other computer on the network claims the address, the client registers that IP address and binds it to the network card.

The significance of APIPA is that DHCP client computers that cannot find a DHCP server can still be assigned an IP address and communicate with other computers on the same subnet that also cannot find a DHCP server. It allows communication when the DHCP server is down or just plain not there. Note that APIPA does not assign a default gateway, and therefore it cannot communicate with any computers that live on the other side of a router.

At times you might prefer this behavior, as it can be an effective method for easily administering TCP/IP in a small network. Keep in mind, however, that the addresses assigned will not be able to communicate with Internet hosts or with a host that exists on any other network, because APIPA assigns an IP address and subnet mask but not a default gateway.

---

 **EXAM TIP**   Be prepared to identify the indicators of an APIPA-configured machine (an IP address of 169.254.x.y), what its significance is (the DHCP server is down or nonexistent), and what its symptoms are (computers on the same physical network segment can communicate with one another, but not with remote computers).

---

You can also disable APIPA when using DHCP for IP configuration by using an alternate configuration. This feature is new to Windows Server 2003, so it is a ripe topic for an exam question or two.

## Using an Alternate Configuration

An alternate configuration ensures that your Server 2003 system never uses APIPA for TCP/IP configuration. It does this by using a manually configured IP address configuration, but only in the event that a DHCP server cannot be located. This can be a good solution in instances where a server is moved from one network that uses DHCP to another that uses static addresses. This should not be the case very often when using a system-installed Server 2003 computer, but it's worth knowing.

Alternate configuration is something that's of more value when implemented on laptops that move frequently, so look for it possibly in future XP service packs, and definitely in future Microsoft operating system releases for the desktop.

Here's how you will give your Server 2003 computer an alternate IP configuration, thus disabling APIPA:

1. Open the Network Connections Control Panel applet, right-click the network connection for which you will configure the alternate settings, and choose Properties.

2. From the General tab of the connection's Properties dialog box, choose the Internet Protocol (TCP/IP), and then click Properties.

3. From the General tab of the TCP/IP Properties dialog box, click the Obtain An IP Address Automatically option.

4. On the Alternate Configuration tab, click the User Configured option, and then type values for the following TCP/IP parameters:

- IP address

- Subnet mask

- Default gateway

- Preferred and alternate DNS server

- Preferred and alternate WINS server

## Subnetting and Supernetting

If you stopped after reading about the different classes of IP addresses, you might get the impression that subnet masks will always be a set of 255s followed by a set of 0s. But remember that the rule of subnet masks deals with how these values are expressed in *binary* notation: a string of contiguous 1s followed by contiguous 0s. The 255 and 0 values are just decimal equivalents of an entire octet of 1s or 0s. As long as the 1s and 0s are clearly demarcated, other decimal values may be present in the subnet mask.

But you won't see just any decimal value. For example, you won't see the decimal value of 131 in a subnet mask. Why? Because 131 in binary looks like this: 10000011. That doesn't follow the subnet make rule of all 1s followed by all 0s. Table 7-3 shows you the other values you might see in a subnet mask besides 255, along with their binary equivalent.

So why might you see other subnet masks when configuring IP addresses?

Let's say you were given a Class C network number of 192.168.2.0. Recall from earlier that you therefore have 254 possible hosts you could add to that network. But what if you wanted to split that single network into two networks? Into ten networks? Could you? Yes, if you altered the default subnet mask.

The default subnet mask for a Class C network (255.255.255.0) allows for a single network. To make more subnets from this single network, you need to "borrow" bits from the default host portion of the IP address, and mix and match these bits to define additional networks. By borrowing bits from the host portion of the IP address, you increase the number of potential networks you can create. The more bits you borrow, the more possible networks.

| Table 7-3 | Decimal Value | Binary Equivalent |
|---|---|---|
| Other Possible Subnet Mask Values | 128 | 10000000 |
| | 192 | 11000000 |
| | 224 | 11100000 |
| | 240 | 11110000 |
| | 248 | 11111000 |
| | 252 | 11111100 |
| | 254 | 11111110 |

You can think this subnetting as "sliding" the subnet mask bits to the right. In this example, let's slide the subnet mask 5 bits to the right. In binary, the new make would be

255.255.255.248

or

11111111 11111111 11111111 11111000

if you were to see it as the computer does. You now have masked 5 more bits to define more network numbers. How many networks can you generate? If you recall the shortcut from earlier, that leaves you with $2^5$ possible combinations of 5 bits, or 32 possible subnets.

When you borrow 5 bits from your default Class C host portion, you are left with 3 bits you can mix and match to define the individual hosts on the subnets. How many possible combinations are there of 3 bits? If you remember the shortcut from earlier, you know there are $2^3$ combinations, for a total of 8, as shown in Table 7-4.

Remember our previously iterated IP addressing rules, however: the first value and the last value cannot be used to define the hosts on a network. The all-0s value and the all-1s value are not valid host numbers.

So with that in mind, here's what the first IP address on the second subnet (the first subnet would be the 192.168.2.0 subnet) would look like when expressed in binary:

11000000 10101000 00000010 00001 001

with the subnet mask of

11111111 11111111 11111111 11111 000

This host's IP address, if you were to look it up using ipconfig, would be 192.168.2.9, with a subnet mask of 255.255.255.248. (Again, the periods show the separation of the network portion of the IP address from the host portion; the computer doesn't do it this way.) But the host, because of that administrator-configured subnet mask, would live on the network of 192.168.2.8. When you use custom subnet masks, the network number is not as easily identifiable as when using the default subnet masks. As you can see, the network number is hidden in the IP address and is only visible when you look at the IP address the way a computer does.

| Table 7-4 Potential Combinations of 3 Bits | Binary | Decimal |
|---|---|---|
| | 000 | 0 |
| | 001 | 1 |
| | 010 | 2 |
| | 011 | 3 |
| | 100 | 4 |
| | 101 | 5 |
| | 110 | 6 |
| | 111 | 7 |

Recall that you are just as likely to see this expressed in CIDR notation, which in this case would look like this: 192.168.2.9/29.

Supernetting just reverses the direction of the subnet mask "slide." Instead of moving the subnet mask to the right, thus dividing up a given network, supernetting moves the subnet mask to the left, combining many networks into one. This is significant because it can simplify entries on routing tables. Suppose that a single large company was using several consecutive Class C network numbers. Rather than having a routing table entry for each network, supernetting allows the combination of all these networks into a single supernet, and one routing entry can route traffic to all networks.

If this is the first time you've seen this, you will probably have to repeat the process a few times in order to understand it. But once you see it, you see it. It's very much like riding a bike or doing an algebra equation correctly for the first time.

For exam purposes (and this comes in quite handy in the real world), learn the short-cut tricks that quickly tell you how many subnets can be made with a custom subnet mask, and how many hosts can be created on a given subnet. It would not be surprising if you were asked questions that made sure you know how to define custom subnet masks for a given network situation.

For example, you might have a question that asks you to pretend you have a Class B address, and you need to create 95 subnets. That question might ask what the subnet mask should be, and how many hosts you will be able to create per subnet.

How to proceed? Here's one of the shortcuts: convert 95 to binary. You get 1011111. That's 7 bits needed to represent the decimal of 95. You should slide the default Class B subnet mask of 255.255.0.0 (11111111 11111111 0000000 0000000) 7 bits to the right, giving you a new subnet mask of 255.255.254.0 (11111111 11111111 11111110 0000000). And again, remember your CIDR. You could also express this new subnet mask by changing the default /16 mask to the new value of /21.

How many subnets can you create with this new custom subnet mask? $2^7$, or 128. That's more subnets than are absolutely necessary, but if you use fewer bits—6, for example—you only can create $2^6$, or 64 subnets, which won't meet your requirements.

So, how many hosts per subnet? Add the 1 bit remaining in the third octet with the 8 in the fourth octet, and that gives you a total of 9 bits that the subnet mask leaves unmasked for defining the hosts. $2^9$ is 512. Remember to remove the first and last combinations of 9 bits, and you can define 510 hosts for each of your 128 networks created from a single Class B network ID.

Make sense now? It will, and once you do one all by yourself, you'll be able to do 100 without any problem. Again, it helps when you can see the IP address the same way the computer does.

Because Windows Server 2003 systems, along with all computers on the Internet, use TCP/IP to talk to one another, knowledge of IP is essential to administrating any modern network. You'll need to have a firm grasp of IP configuration especially when installing and configuring a DHCP server, because the job of the DHCP server is to automate IP address assignment. So just how do you set up and manage this vital service? Microsoft expects you to know, and the next section gives you the details.

# Installing and Configuring DHCP

Dynamic Host Configuration Protocol (DHCP) is another complementary service that works in conjunction with TCP/IP. Its function is fairly easy to understand: it automatically configures TCP/IP on client machines. Beyond that, understanding DHCP is a study of how to manage this service on a Windows Server 2003 machine. Let's first examine how to get this service up and running.

## Lab Exercise 7.1: Installing a DHCP Server

You can set up a Windows Server 2003 to run DHCP in a matter of minutes. Here's how to install a DHCP server:

1. Open the Control Panel, and double-click Add/Remove Programs. Then click the Add Windows Components selection.

2. Choose Networking Services from the Components window, and click Details.

3. From the list of Networking Services, select Dynamic Host Configuration Protocol, as shown in Figure 7-9.

4. Click Next, and you may be prompted for the Windows Server 2003 source files. Required files will be copied to your hard disk. Click Finish to close the Windows Components Wizard.

---

 **NOTE** The DHCP server cannot also be a DHCP client. You should configure your DHCP server with a static IP address. This prevents DHCP clients, at renewal time, from having to search all over the network for the DHCP server, which may have moved if it, too, is a DHCP client.

---

**Figure 7-9**
Installing a DHCP server

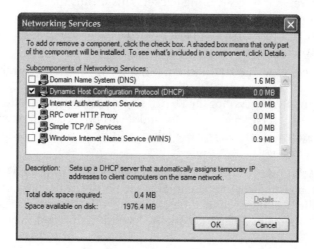

## DHCP Overview

DHCP is an extension of the Boot Protocol (BOOTP), which has been around for quite some time doing the very thing DHCP does: handing out IP addresses. They both do just about the same thing, DHCP just gives you more to deal with. In fact, Microsoft's version of DHCP software that ships with Windows Server 2003 can also serve BOOTP clients as well, but it's important to learn all you can about DHCP for the 70-291 exam.

DHCP centralizes the management of IP address allocation and reduces human error associated with manual IP configuration. (Because humans still must set up and configure this product, it does not completely eliminate human error.)

Using a DHCP server means that users no longer need to keep track of their IP addressing, or receive this information from an administrator, when configuring a system to communicate on the network. The DHCP server supplies all necessary networking parameters. Two things are always handed out as a part of DHCP configuration: the IP address and the subnet mask. Further, DHCP will also frequently configure clients with optional values, such as a default gateway, DNS server address, and the address of a Windows Internet Naming Service (WINS) server, if one is present. Even more configuration options are available, as you will soon see.

## DHCP Lease Process

The DHCP lease process consists of a four-packet conversation between the DHCP client and DHCP server. The conversation can be remembered with an mnemonic called DORA:

- **Discover**   The DHCP client initiates the process by trying to discover any DHCP servers in the network. This discover packet is a broadcast packet (technically, clients are looking for a server running BOOTP, and most computers getting the request ignore it).

- **Offer**   Any server running the BOOTP service responds with an offer of an IP address if it receives the packet. This means that if two DHCP servers are running on your network, two IP addresses will be offered to the DHCP clients. This is also broadcast back to the DHCP client, because as of yet the client has no IP address.

- **Request**   The DHCP client is not picky; it will request the first offer it receives. Also broadcast back to the network, this packet contains the server identifier (the IP address) for the DHCP server who made the offer. That way, if another DHCP server made an offer and it was not accepted, it will know that the IP address it offered was not taken, and it can put it back into its pool of available addresses.

- **Acknowledgement**   The ack packet is sent from the DHCP server to the requesting client and contains the pertinent IP configuration information—the IP address, subnet mask, and any other optional information. Also in the contents of this packet are the lease duration and the server identifier of the DHCP server that offered the lease. That way, at renewal time, the client does not have to broadcast to re-up its IP address lease.

Note that the nature of DHCP lease process traffic is broadcast-based. This can be a problem in a routed network because routers drop broadcasts. They have to; it's the very essence of the Internet that traffic from one computer isn't received by each of the millions of computers connected. For example, if you are administering an office building where each floor represents a different subnet separated by a router, it's entirely possible that one or two DHCP servers can happily meet the needs of this office building. In fact, it's very likely, as the traffic and processing involved in running the DHCP service is relatively light. But how? Didn't we just assert that routers drop broadcasts? How will discover messages, not to mention all of the other DHCP traffic necessary for configuration, get through? There are several ways:

- **Install an RFC 1541 router.** This is also described as a BOOTP forwarder, or a router with built-in DHCP relay. RFC (Request for Comment) 1542 describes the behavior of a router that listens for and then forwards BOOTP broadcasts to other subnets.

- **Configure a DHCP relay agent.** A DHCP relay agent listens for BOOTP requests and passes them on to a DHCP server that it knows about. In Routing and Remote Access, you can configure a Windows Server 2003 computer as a DHCP relay agent. We'll discuss again later in the chapter.

- **Configure a DHCP server on each subnet.** Obviously, this would require the most administrative overhead as you would need multiple installations of Server 2003 and DHCP, and you would furthermore have to set up and maintain multiple DHCP scopes. DHCP scopes are discussed in just a bit.

**NOTE** If you type **rfc** into any search engine, you should find out volumes about RFCs. They define the open-standard protocols in use on the Internet. If you are so inclined, you can suggest improvements to any Internet protocol by submitting your own RFC.

## DHCP Clients and Leases

Configuring a Windows Server 2003 computer—or any Windows computer for that matter—is a matter of selecting a single button. Here's how to make a Windows Server 2003 a DHCP client: (The procedure will work the same from a Windows Server 2003 or 2000 computer as well.)

1. Right-click My Network Places, select Properties | TCP/IP | Properties to access the TCP/IP Properties page.

2. Select Obtain An IP Address Automatically.

That's it! You're now a DHCP client, along with any other computer you instruct to get an address automatically. For purposes of exam preparedness, however, it is more important to know how to manage the DHCP server. The next section examines how.

## DHCP Server Configuration

The nice thing about DHCP is that you don't have to do much administration once you've got it set up and configured. From then on, DHCP pretty much takes care of itself. As a quick reference, take note of the following general steps that are needed to run DHCP on Windows Server 2003:

1. Install the DHCP server (procedure described previously).

2. Create a pool of valid IP addresses from which the DHCP server will select to offer leases.

3. If participating in an Active Directory forest, authorize the server in Active Directory.

4. Reserve IP addresses for certain clients if necessary.

5. Configure Server and Scope options as necessary.

We'll deal with each of these last four items in the sections that follow.

## Scopes

Before a DHCP server has any functionality, you must create a scope. This will serve as the pool of IP addresses the DHCP server will pick from when it receives a discover packet from a DHCP client.

You can set up a scope with a few clicks, as follows:

1. Open the DHCP MMC snap-in.

2. Choose the DHCP server you will create the scope for, then right-click and choose New Scope.

3. The New Scope Wizard launches, leading you through the process of scope creation.

## Manage Reservations and Reserved Clients

There are some clients that you will want to be DHCP clients, but you will also want to make sure they always get an IP address. You also might want to ensure that they get the same address. This gives you the best of both worlds: the ease and automation of DHCP, with the assurance of configuration available with a static IP address.

## Lab Exercise 7.2: Creating a Client Reservation

There are certain clients you will want to always be given the same address. For these clients, you can still receive the automatic configuration benefits of DHCP while effectively configuring a static address. This is useful in instances where application servers need an unwavering IP address, as some client applications are hard-coded to make requests of a specific server. It can also be useful if you have more computers on your network than you have IP addresses in your scope. With a reservation, you can ensure there is always an IP address for that important computer on your network (yours).

You can create a client reservation by right-clicking the Reservations node in your DHCP MMC snap-in, and from the context menu choosing New | Reservation. The New Reservation dialog box opens, as shown in Figure 7-10. Note that you'll need the MAC address of the NIC of the host for which you are creating a reservation. (Unlike IP addresses, which can frequently change, the MAC of a network adapter never changes. It's the thumbprint of the network card that's burned into the chipset of the card, so that when the network card is thrown out, the MAC address goes with it forevermore.) Assign one of the IP addresses from your scope to a MAC address and enter a name for the reservation, and a description if you wish.

 **NOTE** To get a network card's MAC address, use the ipconfig utility with the /all switch. You'll see it listed as the physical address, which it is. The IP address is a logical address.

Furthermore, you can create a reservation for two types of clients: DHCP or BOOTP (or both). DHCP reservations are available to true DHCP clients, such as systems running any of the Windows family of operating systems. A BOOTP reservation is handy for other types of devices that don't necessarily come with the full-fledged DHCP client software, such as might be the case with a network printer.

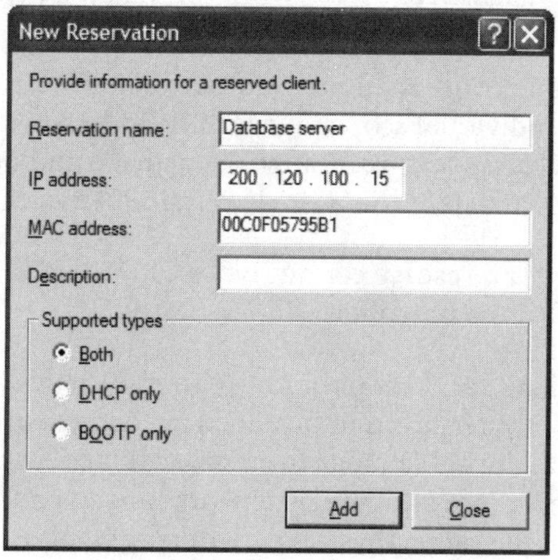

**Figure 7-10**

Adding a client reservation

New Reservation

Provide information for a reserved client.

Reservation name: Database server

IP address: 200 . 120 . 100 . 15

MAC address: 00C0F05795B1

Description:

Supported types
- Both
- DHCP only
- BOOTP only

Add     Close

## Verifying DHCP Reservation Configuration

Once you've created the reservation, the only way to let the IP address back into the IP pool is to delete the reservation. You can change the name of the reservation, or even change the MAC address the IP is reserved for, but the IP address that's reserved cannot be modified.

Because of the broadcast nature of DHCP, and because of a router's typical unwillingness to pass such broadcast traffic, you might think that DHCP would be limited to handing out IP addresses to only one subnet. After all, even if a client from a second subnet on your network were to get a discover packet through the router, the IP address that was given back would not contain the configuration requirements needed for that computer to communicate. The default gateway, for example, of the one subnet wouldn't match the one required for the other. Wouldn't you need another DHCP server configured with another scope that was geared for that other subnet?

Not necessarily. Modern DHCP implementations do allow for configuration of multiple subnets, using a variety of methods. One such method is a superscope.

## Superscopes

A superscope can be used to combine two or more scopes, each serving different subnets, and can make the administration of several scopes on a Windows Server 2003 DHCP server more manageable. Using a superscope, you can group multiple scopes as a single administrative entity that allows clients to lease from either one. With this feature, a DHCP server can

- Support DHCP clients on a single physical network segment (such as a single Ethernet LAN segment) where multiple logical IP networks are used. When more than one logical IP network is used on each physical subnet or network, such configurations are often called multinets.

- Support remote DHCP clients located on the far side of DHCP and BOOTP relay agents (where the network on the far side of the relay agent uses multinets).

- In multinet configurations, you can use DHCP superscopes to group and activate individual scope ranges of IP addresses used on your network. In this way, a DHCP server computer can activate and provide leases from more than one scope to clients on a single physical network.

Superscopes can resolve certain types of DHCP deployment issues for multinets, including situations in which

- The available address pool for a currently active scope is nearly depleted, and more computers need to be added to the network. The original scope includes the full addressable range for a single IP network of a specified address class. You need to use another IP network range of addresses to extend the address space for the same physical network segment.

- Clients must be migrated over time to a new scope—for example, to renumber the current IP network from an address range used in an existing active scope to a new scope that contains another IP network range of addresses.

- To provide fault tolerance, you want to use two DHCP servers on the same physical on a network segment to manage separate logical IP networks.

You can easily create a superscope from your existing scopes. Simply right-click your DHCP server in the DHCP MMC snap-in and choose New Superscope from the context menu. Give the superscope a name, and then add the scopes you want to include. You can add additional scopes to existing superscopes by right-clicking the superscope and choosing New Scope. You'll then create a new scope that's automatically part of the existing superscope.

## Integrating DHCP with Active Directory

The process of authorizing DHCP servers is a necessary step in a network that is running Active Directory. This is a measure taken by Active Directory to prevent "rogue" DHCP servers from being installed and configured with improper IP address pools. DHCP clients are not the most discerning audiences in the world; they will take any IP address offered to them, and servers that hand out wrong IP addresses can wreak havoc on network communication. This was just the case in versions of Windows prior to Windows 2000.

## How DHCP Servers Are Authorized

The authorization process for DHCP server computers depends on the installed role of the server on your network. In the Windows Server 2003 family, there are three roles or server types for which each server computer can be installed:

- **Domain controller**   The computer keeps and maintains a copy of the Active Directory database and provides secure account management for domain member users and computers.

- **Member server**   The computer is not operating as a domain controller, but has joined a domain in which it has a membership account in the Active Directory database.

- **Standalone server**   The computer is not operating as a domain controller or a member server in a domain. Instead, the server computer is made known to the network through a specified workgroup name, which can be shared by other computers, but is used only for browsing purposes and not to provide secured logon access to shared domain resources.

If you deploy Active Directory, all computers operating as DHCP servers must be either Active Directory domain controllers or domain member servers before they can be authorized and provide DHCP service to clients. A standalone DHCP server in a workgroup cannot be authorized in Active Directory and will therefore be unable to lease IP addresses in the domain.

## Lab Exercise 7.3: Authorizing a DHCP Server

You can authorize a DHCP server in just a couple of steps:

1. Open the DHCP MMC snap-in.

2. Right-click the root of the DHCP console and choose Manage Authorized Servers.

3. From the Manage Authorized Servers dialog box, as shown in Figure 7-11, click Authorize, and then type the name or the IP address of the DHCP server you want to authorize.

4. Click OK to complete the procedure.

Although it is not recommended, you can use a standalone server as a DHCP server as long as it is not on a subnet with any authorized DHCP servers. When a standalone DHCP server detects an authorized server on the same subnet, it automatically stops leasing IP addresses to DHCP clients.

## Manage DHCP Options

As we examined earlier in the chapter, the function of DHCP is to get an IP address and subnet mask to a DHCP client. Every other configuration parameter is optional. In this section, we look at how to specify this optional information.

### Server Options

Server options enable you to configure settings that will apply to all DHCP clients, regardless of which scope they pull their IP address from. Options available for configuration include:

- Router (the default gateway) addresses
- DNS server(s) address
- WINS server(s)address
- DNS domain name
- POP3 server names

**Figure 7-11**

Authorize your DHCP server via this dialog box.

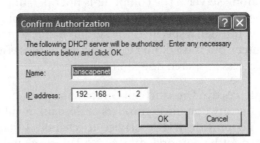

## Scope Options

Scope options, as the name implies, assign values to clients of a particular scope. One common example of a scope option is the address of the default gateway. If DHCP is configured to assign IPs to multiple subnets, each subnet will need a different default gateway in order to successfully communicate with remote computers.

## Client Options

Client options are useful whenever you want to set values for a client reservation. These options are overridden only by parameters you've set at the client machine itself. Everything you can set at the server or scope level you can also configure for a single client. You usually configure client options when you want to set exceptions to the options set on the scope or server level, or to configure parameters over and above those set on the server or scope levels, such as setting a mail, news, or Internet Relay Chat (IRC) server address.

## Option Classes

You will use option classes to further subdivide the options set at the server, scope, or client level. These classes are used to define different computer types and operating systems. There are two kinds of option classes:

- **Vendor classes**   These include options for clients running specific vendor software. Say, for example, you wanted to assign WINS address to Windows 98 clients, but not to Windows Server 2003 clients, or that you wanted the lease duration of the older machines shorter than the newer operating systems. You could accomplish this via a vendor class. Windows Server 2003's vendor classes let you divide your configuration options so that the WINS address, for example, are only handed out to the clients you want.

- **User-defined classes**   These options are custom-defined. You might want computers on a particular floor configured with their own set of options. For this, you will create custom user-defined classes.

In order for a DHCP client to use a class option, it must identify itself as a member of the option class. Some of this behavior happens automatically, as when a Windows 2000 computer automatically identifies itself as a member of the Microsoft RRAS user class when dialing in.

Once you've defined your own classes, you need to configure each client so that it identifies itself as a member of the class. The tool you use to accomplish this is the ipconfig command in conjunction with the /setclassid switch.

 **EXAM TIP**   You may never use this ipconfig switch, but you should know its purpose.

## Lab Exercise 7.4: Creating a DHCP Option

Whether you're creating an option at the server, scope, or client level, the procedure remains consistent. In this exercise, you'll set DNS options for all clients of your Windows Server 2003 DHCP server.

1. Open the DHCP MMC snap-in and right-click your server. Choose Configure Options from the context menu.

2. In the Server Options dialog box, as shown in Figure 7-12, you'll see the available options that all clients will receive (the options won't look much different when configuring for scopes or clients).

3. In the Available Options list, click 006 DNS Servers. Type either the server name or the IP address of the DNS server(s) you will include as part of your optional configuration parameters, and click Add.

4. Click OK to close the Server Options dialog box.

Now that you've set up options, you can verify the options configured in the DHCP console tree by selecting the Server Options node of the tree. Note that the new options will take effect only after the clients renew their current leases or obtain a new address from the DHCP server.

**Figure 7-12**
The Server
Options
dialog box

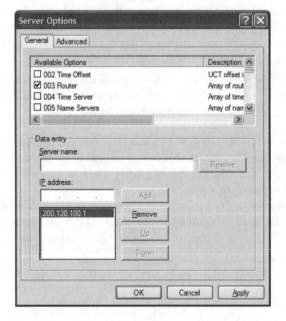

## Manage DHCP Databases

Occasionally, you'll have reason to move the DHCP installation to another server. The information in the DHCP database is not considered crucial under normal circumstances for a couple of reasons. First, it's a dynamic database of information (in other words, who has what IP address and for how long—and that information is constantly being modified). Second, as long as you know the address scope to use, it doesn't take very long to recover from complete DHCP disaster. Just reinstall DHCP or install at another Windows Server 2003 system and create the scope again, and you'll be right as rain.

You might think that backing up a DHCP database or exporting it would be something accomplished from the DHCP MMC console, like all your other administrative tasks. You would be mistaken. The procedure is actually a bit more complex.

The DHCP database is made of several files stored in the \%*systemroot*%\system32\dhcp folder (where %*systemroot*% is the directory where Windows Server 2003 has been installed). The database itself is called DHCP.mdb. but the folder also contains log files and temporary working files.

By default, the database is backed up every 60 minutes, but you can modify this behavior and change the backup directory path to best suit the needs of your network by editing these registry keys:

- HKLM\SYSTEM\CurrentControlSet\Services\DHCPServer\Parameters\ BackupInterval

- HKLM\SYSTEM\CurrentControlSet\Services\DHCPServer\Parameters\ BackupDatabasePath

HKLM, by the way, is the common abbreviation for the registry hive HKEY_LOCAL _MACHINE.

## Lab Exercise 7.5: Backing Up a DHCP Database

Here's how to export the DHCP database to another system. First, you will need to back up the existing database:

1. Stop the DHCP server and disable the DHCP Server service in the list of services (Administrative Tools | Services). This prevents the DHCP server from starting after the database has been transferred.

2. Copy the DHCP server directory tree, %*systemroot*%\system32\Dhcp, to a temporary location on the new (destination) DHCP server. For example, copy the directory tree to C:\Temp\system32\Dhcp.

3. Start the Registry Editor (Regedt32.exe) and go to the following subkey: HKEY_LOCAL_MACHINE\SYSTEM\CurrentControlSet\Services\DHCPServer. Then save the specified key to a text file.

Now that you've ported the contents of the DHCP information to another system, you're able to install DHCP and configure it with the current DHCP scopes, leases, options, and so on. Follow this procedure:

1. Stop the DHCP Server service. Rename the System.mdb file to System.src in the temporary folder, such as the C:\Temp\system32\Dhcp directory.

2. Copy the DHCP server directory tree from the storage location of your copied DHCP files *%systemroot%*\System32\Dhcp to replace the existing DHCP server directory.

3. Start Registry Editor (Regedt32.exe) and go to the following subkey: HKEY_LOCAL_MACHINE\SYSTEM\CurrentControlSet\Services\DHCPServer.

4. Select the DHCPServer key and restore the registry hive information from the file you saved in the previous procedure.

5. In Restore Key, for File Name specify the following: *%systemroot%*\System32\Dhcp\Backup\Dhcpcfg. When prompted, click Yes.

6. After clicking Yes to the prompt to overwrite the existing registry entries, if you have problems completing the restore operation, retry the previous step.

7. Exit Registry Editor. From the Services MMC, start the DHCP Server service.

8. Open the DHCP console and right-click the Server or Scope node and choose Reconcile Scopes from the context menu.

When you reconcile, Windows Server 2003 compares the active leases in the DHCP database to those in the registry. You can reconcile all scopes on the server, which is usually the case, or only selected scopes.

Microsoft expects you to have a grasp of this DHCP database management as you sit down for the 70-291. However, you're not likely to have to manage the DHCP database very often in the real world, if at all.

## DHCP in a Routed Environment

As you've seen, DHCP traffic between client and server is broadcast-based. This is by necessity, as computers can only send directed traffic once they have been configured with a working IP address.

But many routers—in fact, most of them—do not pass broadcast traffic. You won't be able to broadcast traffic to computers on the Internet, for example, because that traffic will almost assuredly be dropped by the first router along the way.

Even within an enclosed LAN like an office building, routers are often employed to reduce the broadcast traffic passed between subnets, thus improving network performance. At the same time, these office buildings will have a single DHCP server assigning IP addresses to all subnets. How is this possible?

Administrators in environments such as these understand how DHCP can be implemented in a routed environment. The next couple of sections discuss the different deployment options for DHCP in routed networks, which is essential knowledge for the 70-291 exam.

## Using BOOTP Forwarding

Earlier in the chapter, we mentioned that you could use a special kind of router that would forward certain types of broadcast messages. These routers are called BOOTP forwarders, or 1542-compliant routers, and actually they aren't all that special. Almost all modern routers, if they do not support this feature out of the box, can be configured this way.

A 1542-compliant router listens for BOOTP Discover messages, and then forwards those specific messages to all other subnets. It does not pass other kinds of broadcast traffic. In this way, a routed network with a 1542 router still gets the bandwidth conservation benefits of a router and is able to implement just a single DHCP server to serve all subnets. Bus as common and simple to implement as this solution is for modern networks, you are much more likely to be asked about your knowledge of a Microsoft's DHCP relay agent.

## Managing and Configuring DHCP Relay Agent

Another option you have for using DHCP in a routed environment is implementing a DHCP relay agent. The relay agent is a software component that listens for DHCP discover packets and then forwards them to a DHCP server it knows about. On Windows Server 2003 systems, the DHCP relay agent can be enabled as a part of Routing and Remote Access (RRAS).

## Lab Exercise 7.6: Configuring a Relay Agent

To configure a relay agent, follow these steps:

1. Open the Routing and Remote Access MMC under Administrative Tools.

2. In the console tree, expand the Server object, then IP Routing, and click General.

3. Right-click, and from the context menu, choose New Routing Protocol.

4. In the Select Routing Protocol dialog box, click DHCP Relay Agent, and then click OK.

**NOTE** The DHCP server knows which scope (or part of a superscope) to offer an IP address from by examining the IP address of the relay agent, or the address of the 1542-compliant router interface that forwards the message. These forwarding agents' IP source addresses are appended to the discover packet, so the contents of the offer packet are generated in kind.

You will know that the relay agent is working correctly when computers from a subnet opposite from that of the DHCP server—the computers on the same subnet as the DHCP relay agent—are able to receive TCP/IP information from the DHCP server.

## Using Multiple DHCP Servers

If the network is routed, and the router is not 1542-compliant (or has had this feature turned off), and if you decide not to implement a DHCP relay agent, then there must be a DHCP server that is local to each subnet. Because DHCP clients won't ever be able to send Discover packets off the local segment, a DHCP server must be present on all subnets where clients are configured to obtain IP addresses automatically. In networks with many segments, this can become an expensive solution, and usually a DHCP Relay Agent would instead be used.

You can also implement multiple DHCP servers even if the network uses a 1542 router. Larger networks might even desire this configuration because of its fault tolerance benefit, as clients who can reach DHCP servers on different subnets can still obtain IP configuration if the local DHCP server goes down.

When configuring DHCP in this manner, make sure to follow the 80/20 rule. The 80/20 rule supposes that there are two subnets in a network, subnets A and B, although the concept works fine when there are more than just two subnets in question. The basic tenet of the 80/20 rule is thus: a DHCP server located on subnet A should be configured with 80 percent of the possible IP addresses for subnet A, and 20 percent of the potential addresses in subnet B. Subnet B's SHCP server, meanwhile, should be configured in the inverse—80 percent of B's IP addresses, 20 percent of A's. Further, the IP address range split between the two subnets should not overlap. This way, if a client of subnet A needs to get an IP address from the DHCP server on subnet B, it won't pull an address that might have already been leased out from the pool of addresses configured on Subnet A's DHCP server.

Another nice benefit of DHCP is its ability to integrate with DNS on a Windows Server 2003 network. This lets clients whose IP addresses are changing from one day to the next always have current IP addresses to name mappings present in the DNS zone files (more about the zone files in the next chapter). The next section looks at the specifics of this feature.

## Integrating DHCP with DDNS

The DHCP server product included with Windows Server 2003 integrates seamlessly with Dynamic DNS (DDNS). Dynamic DNS will be discussed in further detail in the following chapter, but for now know that DDNS automates the updating of host name to IP address mappings on a DNS server. Like DHCP, its job is to make administration of an IP network a whole lot easier.

By default, the DHCP server updates the DNS server with the necessary records of names to IP addresses, so even if you went into a trance during the setup of Windows Server 2003's DHCP and DNS, you would awaken with a network that pretty much does what it should. There is a slight difference between what information is updated for which clients.

If a Windows 2000 or above client (in other words, one that's aware of DNS) grabs an IP address, the client, by default, registers its name and IP address (the A record) with the DNS server while the DHCP server updates DNS with the reverse lookup record (the PTR).

If the client is running an earlier version of Windows, DHCP updates both the A record and the PTR record on behalf of the client (see Chapter 6 for more about the records stored on DNS servers). This behavior is illustrated in Figure 7-13.

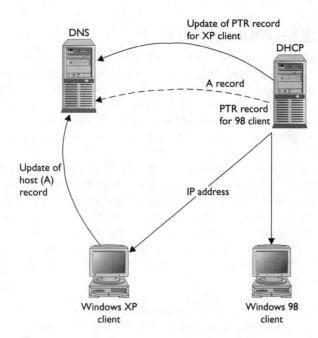

**Figure 7-13**
Different DHCP
Clients interacting
with the DNS and
DHCP servers

Remember, this is the default behavior. To verify this, or to turn off the automatic up-dates of DNS from DHCP, access the DHCP server's Properties page by opening the DHCP MMC snap-in, right-clicking the DHCP server, and choosing Properties. The dia-log box that comes up, as seen in Figure 7-14, will let you specify whether or not the DHCP server updates DNS.

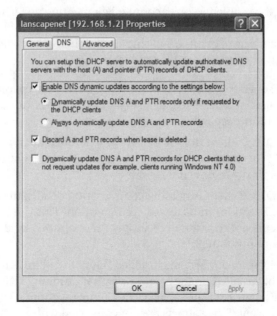

**Figure 7-14**
The DHCP server
updates DNS
with IP address
information for
DHCP clients.

# Troubleshooting DHCP

If you're having problems with DHCP, it usually doesn't take long to find out about it. Users whose machines have incorrect or missing IP address configurations will say they can't check e-mail or surf the Net. In fact, if you're administering a network and more than one user at a time is having problems with connectivity, DHCP status is one of the first things you should check. Subsequently, the root cause of most DHCP problems are that these servers are simply handing out the wrong IP addresses. Your job is to figure out why.

Most computer books are somewhat inadequate in their coverage of troubleshooting. While it'd be great to report that you'll find this book is a sharp departure from such books, alas, that's just not the nature of this title. This book is about communicating computing concepts, not about listing troubleshooting scenarios. The different permutations of networks far and wide make this, for all practical purposes, an impossible task. There are no short cuts to a mastery of troubleshooting. Your ability to troubleshoot is always a function of your understanding of the underlying technology and your personal experience.

 **NOTE** Troubleshooting is done on an ad-hoc basis, and usually one of the first places you start is with the Microsoft Knowledge Base, which can be found at http://www.microsoft.com/support/.

The good news is that most of your exam questions probe your troubleshooting acumen, which is really the best way to demonstrate expertise anyway. So buckle up, configure a DHCP server or two, and fix a few computers that can't connect to the network.

Most of the problems you encounter when setting up DHCP for your network have to do with incorrect or missing configuration details. In other words, human error. What follows is a précis of common problems and their recommended solutions, along with some "best practice" advice for implementing DHCP.

- Use superscopes instead of multiple DHCP servers on each subnet in a LAN. By configuring a superscope, a single DHCP server can provide TCP/IP addresses to multiple separate subnets.

- If a DHCP client does not have an IP address at all (it will read 0.0.0.0 when using ipconfig) or, more likely, has an IP address of 169.254.$x$.$y$, the DHCP server is down or is unreachable.

- If a DHCP client is missing configuration details, the client might be missing DHCP options in its leased configuration. This can have two causes: the DHCP server is not configured to supply these options, or the client does not support the options available.

- The DHCP relay agent is installed but not working. The DHCP relay agent should not be installed on the same server that's running DHCP. They should be installed on separate computers. Also, each subnet without a DHCP server needs a DHCP relay agent if the subnets are not connected with a 1542-compliant router.

- The DHCP console reports lease expirations for reserved clients. If this occurs, it can be caused by a scope set to an infinite lease time, with the reserved client's lease time also shown as infinite, or by a scope lease time that's set to a finite time period with the reserved client using this same lease time. If you want to create reserved clients with unlimited lease durations, create a scope with an unlimited lease duration and add reservations from that scope.

- You create a new scope, but the DHCP server fails to issue leases for this scope. In this case, chances are that the DHCP server has not been authorized in Active Directory. Also, if superscopes are not defined, only one scope can be active on a network at a time. If you have created a scope for a different subnet, remember that the active scope is determined by whether the address in the scope contain the first IP address bound to the DHCP server's network card. You can fix this problem by configuring the DHCP server to use a superscope that includes all the scopes you want to use, or by changing the first IP address (although uncommon, network cards can have multiple IP addresses bound to them) of the network card to a number that's within the range of addresses of the new scope.

# Chapter Review

In this chapter, we've taken a look at the necessary steps to get a network up and running. You need to build your network infrastructure from the ground up, and until you've got TCP/IP configured, you won't be able to do anything else.

We've examined the TCP/IP protocol, and looked at how it can and should be configured on a Windows Server 2003 machine. We've also looked at how you can configure Windows Server 2003 as a DHCP server, and thus let it handle the task of correctly configuring client machines with TCP/IP. In the next chapter, we'll take the TCP/IP foundation and start to learn how we can forget about TCP/IP and just call computers by their names. Using the services of DNS, the names will then resolve to IP addresses so that out computers can communicate.

## Questions

1. You are administering a Windows Server 2003 DHCP server. You have set up a superscope containing five scopes, and you begin to experience issues with one of the scopes assigning bad addresses. You suspect that the database has become corrupted. How do you verify the database is intact?

   A. Select the scope in question, right-click, and choose Reconcile Scope.

   B. Select the superscope, right-click, and choose Reconcile All Scopes.

   C. Select the DHCP server in question, right-click, and choose Reconcile All Scopes.

   D. Select the DHCP server in question, right-click, and choose Reconcile The DHCP Database.

2. You are administering a Windows Server 2003 Active Directory enterprise and are implementing DHCP on a member server of your forest root domain. A user in another domain, thinking they're clever, installs another DHCP server on a Unix system elsewhere in the building. This user is on a separate logical subnet, but is otherwise connected to the network, as other test computers need access to the Internet. How can you ensure your Windows Server 2003 Professional and 2000 Professional DHCP clients do not get IP addresses from the new Unix box?

A. Disable the Unix server computer account in Active Directory.

B. Do nothing. The Windows computers won't know about the existence of the Unix DHCP service.

C. Disable the BOOTP protocol on the router separating the test network from the production network.

D. Manually assign TCP/IP addresses to all the client machines.

3. You have been asked to provide a DHCP installation for a small firm currently using static IP allocation. Which parameters can be assigned by DHCP? (Choose all that apply.)

A. IP address

B. MAC address

C. Default gateway

D. DNS server

4. You are administering a network of four subnets. Each of the subnets has a network interface print device with a static IP address assigned. You add several client systems to one of the subnets and ask a junior administrator to reconfigure the scopes as appropriate. Immediately thereafter, users report they cannot print to one of the print devices. What is the most likely source of the problem?

A. The scope one of the printers received its IP address from has been deleted.

B. One of the existing scopes has been modified so that it overlaps with the addresses reserved for the printers.

C. One of the existing scopes has been modified so that it has a reserved address that's the same as one of the printers.

D. The DHCP service has been stopped by the junior admin for the modifications to the scope, and he forgot to start the service.

5. You have a Windows Server 2003 DHCP server providing IP addressing for your entire network, and you need to be alerted when the number of available addresses drops below 10. How do you set up this alert?

A. Use a third-party product that supports Management Information Base (MIB) objects like HP Open View to monitor the server and send you an alert.

B. Use the Performance console, and set the Available Addresses threshold counter to 10. Performance will then alert you when the threshold is tripped.

C. Install an SNMP third-party product like HP Open View to monitor the server and send you an alert.

D. Use the DHCP console. Right-click the DHCP server, and choose Server Statistics. Click the Alert button and select the Available Addresses parameter. Set the threshold to 10 and select the Send Network Alert check box.

6. Your company has just added a new router that has allowed for the addition of another logical network segment. Now you must set up DHCP to hand out IP addresses to this new segment. You set up the router interface for the new segment with a static address of 200.103.23.1, with the default Class C subnet mask. You need to provide 50 addresses to this segment. What steps must you take to get things working?

A. Add a scope to the DHCP server containing the address with the range of 200.103.23.2–200.103.23.52. Configure a subnet mask of 24 bits. Set the router to forward BOOTP packets, and enable the scope.

B. Install and configure an additional DHCP server on the new subnet to provide the additional IP addresses.

C. Add a scope to the DHCP server containing the address with the range of 200.103.23.2–200.103.23.52. Configure a subnet mask of 24 bits. Set the router to forward BOOTP packets, but do not enable the scope. It will self-enable automatically when a client requests.

D. Add a scope to the DHCP server containing the address with the range of 200.103.23.2–200.103.23.52. Configure a subnet mask of 24 bits. Install a DHCP relay agent on the existing subnet for communication with the DHCP clients on the new subnet. Enable the scope.

7. You are administering a routed network with a single Windows Server 2003 DHCP server. The server is unable to lease IP addresses to clients on the other side of the router, but clients in the same subnet as the DHCP server are being configured with IP addresses as expected. What is the most likely cause of the problem?

A. The BOOTP forwarder feature has not been enabled at the DHCP server.

B. The router is not RFC 1542 compliant.

C. There aren't enough addresses in the scope for the newly added clients.

D. The router interface is a DHCP client as well and has gotten a different address than you originally configured.

8. You are configuring DHCP to integrate with DNS server, and so are going to use the dynamic update feature. Which options are available during the operation? (Choose all that apply.)

A. Update of forward lookups only

B. Update of reverse lookups only

C. Update only if client requests

D. Always update both forward and reverse lookups

9. You are administering a routed office building, and you have installed Active Directory on a Windows Server 2003 domain controller. The domain controller is just one of the domain controllers in your organization's multidomain forest. You decide to implement DHCP on this same machine. What is required before completing this task? (Choose all that apply.)

A. You must have domain administrator rights.

B. You must enable a relay agent on each subnet.

C. You must have enterprise administrator rights.

D. You must configure the machine with a static IP address.

10. You are administering a single subnet network that uses DHCP for allocation of IP addresses. One morning, users report that they are able to get files off of the network file server, but are having problems accessing the Internet to check e-mail. What is the likely problem? (Choose all that apply.)

A. The DHCP server is down.

B. The clients have been assigned IP addresses from the APIPA range.

C. The network hub has lost power.

D. One of the users is using a static address that matches the one the DHCP server is using.

## Answers

1. **C.** Because the scopes are part of a superscope, you need to reconcile all the scopes on the server.

2. **B.** The Unix server cannot be authorized in Active Directory, so the Windows 2000 and Windows Server 2003 computers will not accept any offers from the Unix DHCP server. In an Active Directory domain, the authorization is a mechanism to prevent the allocation of addresses by rogue DHCP servers.

3. **A, C** and **D.** Only the MAC address is not configurable via DHCP. The MAC address is hard-coded into the circuitry of the network card and cannot be changed.

4. **C.** The most likely cause of the trouble is that one of the scopes now overlaps the static address of the print devices, and one of the DHCP clients has grabbed the address. The print devices have static IP address, implying they are not DHCP clients. You can reserve an IP address for them, but since they won't be requesting an address, you are wasting administrative effort.

5. **B.** You need an SNMP management utility like HP Open View to monitor the DHCP server in this way. MIBs are just the management objects collected about network devices, but SNMP is the protocol that makes these pieces of information functional. Answer D sounds like it might work if it weren't a complete fabrication.

6. **A.** These are the steps that must be followed according to the requirements of the question.

7. **B.** The most likely cause is that the router won't forward BOOTP packets to the DHCP server. Answers C and D are plausible, but not likely sources of the problem in this situation.

8. **C and D.** You can update both forward and reverse lookups, and can also elect to update based on client requests. You must enable both the forward and reverse lookups with the options available through DHCP. You cannot individually chooses to update just one or the other.

9. **C and D.** You must be an Enterprise Admin to install Authorize DHCP in Active Directory; Domain Admin permissions are not adequate. A DHCP server cannot also be a DHCP client, so you need to make sure the machine has a static address.

10. **A and B.** The most likely scenario here is that the DHCP server is down, and clients have been assigned APIPA addresses. You should run the ipconfig utility on one of the machines to verify. If users have gotten APIPA addresses, they would be able to communicate with each other, but not with computers on remote networks.

# Implementing, Managing, and Maintaining Name Resolution

In this chapter, you will learn how to

- Install and configure the DNS Server service
- Configure DNS forwarders
- Implement Dynamic DNS
- Integrate DNS and Active Directory
- Set Up Active Directory integration
- Allow updates
- Integrate DNS with DHCP
- Manage and monitor DNS

Now that we've laid the groundwork—you have a better understanding of the DNS namespace after reading Chapter 6 and have learned all about IP addressing in Chapter 7 —we're ready to get down to the business of implementing a DNS on the Windows Server 2003 platform. Without the ability a DNS server provides to resolve computer names to IP addresses, Active Directory function would cease, and network communication in general would be difficult at best.

The DNS server service has been around for some time, however, so as you read through this chapter, be especially mindful of the new features that are available with in Windows Server 2003 network.

## Install and Configure the DNS Server Service

As was mentioned in Chapter 6, DNS provides the hierarchy for Active Directory. If that point hasn't been driven home by now, it will be again in Chapter 19, where we look at the steps to implement an Active Directory domain. If a DNS solution isn't available or installed when you set up a domain controller, you won't be able to create the domain.

Therefore, you need to have a working DNS server *before* you can install Active Directory. If you don't have a working DNS server before you install Active Directory, the Active Directory Installation Wizard will offer to create one for you. So even though it might appear that there's no DNS server present prior to successful Active Directory installation, what's happening under the hood is that the Active Directory installation tool installs DNS for you before it gets around to installing the Active Directory software components.

This section assumes that you know how to install Windows Server 2003 and concentrates on the installation and configuration of the DNS server. One quick note about installation of DNS server: you need to install it on either the Windows Server 2003 server or Windows 2003 Advanced server platforms. Fully functional DNS is not supported on the Windows XP platform. Additionally, you need to have TCP/IP installed and configured before you proceed. If you've chosen the typical options, you should have TCP/IP installed. In fact, there's almost no case in a modern computer environment where you wouldn't have TCP/IP installed on a computer that wants to communicate with any other computers.

It also might be a good idea before you proceed with the installation of DNS to confirm your computer name. To do this, right-click the My Computer icon and choose Properties, then click the Network Identification tab. Make sure the full computer name is correct and, if required, click the Properties button from the Network Identification tab and make the necessary changes to your computer name.

Now it's time to install the DNS server. To do so, follow these steps:

1. From the Start menu, open Control Panel and select Add/Remove Programs.

2. In the Add/Remove Programs applet, click the Add/Remove Components button. This will open the Windows Components Wizard.

3. Select Network Services, and then click Details. The Networking Services dialog box opens, as shown in Figure 8-1.

**Figure 8-1**
Adding the
DNS component
to Windows
Server 2003

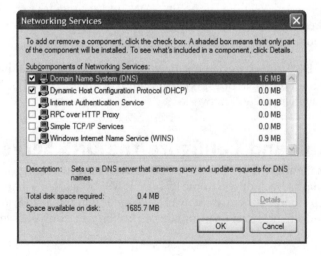

**NOTE**  If you click just the Network Services check box, you're going to install all the Network services, which is probably not a step that you want to take. So, make sure that you just select Network Services and choose Details instead.

4. Select the Domain Name System (DNS), click OK and then click Next. The Configuring Components dialog box appears, showing the progress of the installation. You may also be prompted for the path to Installation Files.

5. Finally, the Completing The Windows Component Wizard screen appears. Click Finish, and then close the Add/Remove Programs dialog box by clicking Close. You can now close the Control Panel. DNS has been installed.

## Managing DNS Server Options

Now that you've installed DNS, you'll next need to make decisions about what role that DNS server will have in your computing environment and subsequently, in your organizational scheme. The role of the DNS server will be dependent on the types of zone file or files it stores. You may also want to note that a single DNS server can provide multiple DNS zone roles. In other words, a single DNS server can be a primary server for one of its configured zones, and a secondary server for another zone.

If your Windows Server 2003 DNS server is a standard primary DNS server, it stores and maintains the original zone file for whatever domain or domains the zone file is authoritative over. The information is kept in a primary zone file is stored in the registry, and also a copy of the zone information is located in the path WINDOWS\system32\dns by default. This can be significant if your Windows 2003 DNS server is set to integrate with other types of DNS servers.

## Lab Exercise 8.1: Creating a Forward Lookup Zone

Here's how you'll create a forward lookup zone on your Windows Server 2003 DNS implementation:

1. Select Start | All Programs | Administrative Tools | DNS. The Microsoft Management Console starts with the DNS snap-in loaded.

2. Expand the server where you are creating the zone, then right-click the Forward Lookup Zones node. From the context menu, choose New Zone. This launches the New Zone Wizard.

3. Click Next to bypass the welcome message, and then on the next screen choose the type of zone. As shown in Figure 8-2, you can choose either a primary zone, secondary zone, or stub zone. If Active Directory is installed, and you're configuring DNS on a domain controller, you will have the option to create an Active Directory–integrated zone with the check box at the bottom of the screen. In this example, choose Primary Zone and click Next.

PART II

**Figure 8-2**

Selecting the type of zone to create

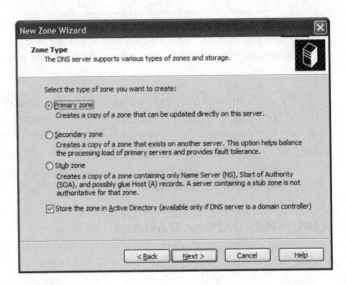

4. Now you'll choose the replication behavior of the zone. You can replicate zone information to

- All DNS servers in the Active Directory forest

- All DNS servers in the Active Directory domain

- All domain controllers in the Active Directory domain

- All domain controllers specified in a scope of an application directory partition

Make your selection, then click Next, and in the following screen, give the zone a name.

5. Click Next, and then select the Dynamic Updates options. You can choose to allow

- Only secure dynamic updates, available only in Active Directory–integrated zones

- Both nonsecure and secure, where dynamic updates are allowed from any DNS client

- Neither, configuring the zone to not accept any dynamic updates

Make your selection and then click Next. Click Finish in the final screen to set up the zone file.

Once you've configured a forward lookup zone, it is often advisable to create a reverse lookup zone to serve as a sort of mirror image of the forward zone. The reverse lookup zone will be populated with pointer (PTR) records, which will allow IP addresses to be resolved into host names.

## Lab Exercise 8.2: Creating a Reverse Lookup Zone

Creating a reverse lookup zone will be very similar, with only a few twists. To do so, follow these steps:

1. From the Administrative Tools menu, open the DNS console.

2. Expand the server you're configuring, and select the Reverse Lookup Zone node, right-click, and choose New Zone.

3. Click Next on the welcome screen of the New Zone Wizard, and again select the type of zone to create. Click Next after you've made the selection.

4. Select the Replication options, and click Next to get to the part that's different.

5. From the Reverse Lookup Zone Name screen, enter the first part of the IP address—the network ID—for which the zone will provide IP-address-to-name resolution. This should be your company's network number. You don't have to worry about flipping it around. The wizard does that for you. For example, if you're using the network number of 123.45.9.0, you would just type the network portion of that IP address. In the bottom section of that window, as seen in Figure 8-3, notice how the wizard takes the network number and reverses it to build the file name that will be used for the reverse lookup zone file. Click Next.

6. Set your Dynamic Updates options as before and click Next.

7. The last page of the wizard confirms your choices. If everything is correct, click Finish. If you see problems, you can click Back to go back and fix the errors.

Once you've got your zone file configured, you still have the flexibility to change your zones as the needs of your network change. Just like most any other software object you'll be dealing with in the Windows Server 2003 environment, a zone includes a set of Properties. These Properties can be managed to change the resolution behavior of the zone.

**Figure 8-3**

Creating and naming a reverse lookup file

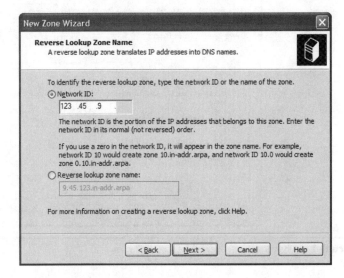

## Lab Exercise 8.3: Changing the Properties of a Zone

Here's how to change the properties of a zone file:

1. Open up DNS Administrative Tools as usual (Start | All Programs | Administrative Tools).

2. Expand the server that contains the server that contains the zone, forward or reverse, that you want to configure.

3. Expand the reverse or forward lookup zone's folder. Right-click the zone that you want to configure and choose Properties.

There are six tabs in the Properties of a zone where you will be able to fine-tune the behavior of the zone files (see Figure 8-4).

**TIP** You should not need extensive knowledge of each and every button and entry on these tabs. For exhaustive information, please see the Microsoft Server 2003 Deployment Kit.

- **General** Sections of the General tab include Status, Type, the Zone File Name, the choice to allow dynamic updates, and Aging Properties.

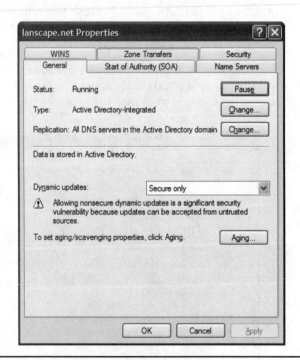

**Figure 8-4** Changing the properties of a zone file

- **Start of Authority**   This tab reflects the information found in the SOA record, and specifies startup behavior of the name server, as well as identification of the server that has authority for a particular domain. The SOA tab really defines the startup behaviors of the DNS server and configures the normal DNS parameters that are part of the zone. These include the Serial Number, the Primary Server, the Responsible Person, the Interval, the Retry Interval, the Expires After, and the Minimum Time To Live, as well as time to live for this record.

- **Name Servers**   This tab is where you'll see a list of name servers for the zone. Again, it is very possible, for fault tolerance or for load balancing purposes, that you implement more than one domain server for a particular domain. If this is the case, you'll want the name servers to talk to each other so they keep a consistent zone file. You don't want one zone file mapping a name to an IP address and then another zone file mapping that same name to a different IP address. So listing a name server or listing a server here will create an NS (name server) record for the zone, which should match the servers that are registered with the domain one level up. The domain one level up then returns these records to any other name server requesting queries of resources in your domain.

- **WINS**   This tab contains information about any WINS servers that might be present in your network. In a pure Windows 2003 environment, as was the case with Windows 2000, you shouldn't need this record because all of your systems will automatically register their host records with the DNS server. But if you need to support older Windows clients, such at 9*x* or NT, you might configure the WINS tab, as shown in Figure 8-5. This tab provides the server with the IP address of one or more WINS servers that your DNS server will use to resolve the query if it doesn't have a record in its own files. The DNS server does this by taking the leftmost portion of a fully qualified domain name resolution request and passing that request on to the WINS server. The options on this tab include Use WINS Forward Lookup, Do Not Replicate This Record, and IP Address. The advanced options include cache timeout and lookup timeout.

- **Security**   This tab is an Access Control List (ACL) that defines who can manage and modify the zone file. Note that the Authenticated Users group has the ability to create child objects, which makes sense when you consider that these users update their A records dynamically—even thought they probably aren't aware of it—when they get an IP address from DHCP.

- **Zone Transfers**   This is one of the most important tabs in terms of managing your zone. This tab allows you to configure how zone transfers occur between the name servers on the Name Servers tab. So here's where you set the server with a primary zone file. You can also do this from the server with a secondary zone file. The options on this tab include whether to allow zone transfers in the first place, and where these zone transfers will go—to any server, only servers listed on the Name Servers tab, or only specific servers that you choose from this tab. The Notify button allows you to choose to automatically notify all other name servers when has been a change to a zone file, just the servers in the name server tab, or, again, name servers that you specify. This tab is where you really configure your security level and replication topology for your DNS server implementation.

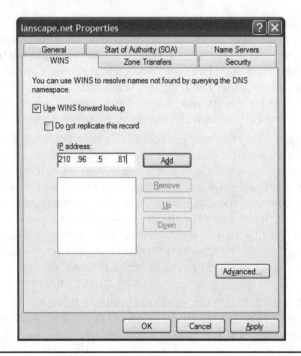

**Figure 8-5**    Integration of WINS and DNS can be configured here.

Besides a forward lookup zone and a reverse lookup zone, DNS administrators using Windows Server 2003 solutions can also create a stub zone. This type of zone was not available under the Windows 2000 environment, and therefore will almost certainly provide fodder for a test question or two on the Network Infrastructure exam.

## Stub Zones

Think of a stub zone as a mini-zone. This mini-zone is kept on a DNS server hosting a parent zone, and its only purpose is to identify the authoritative name servers in child zones. By keeping just this information at the ready, a DNS server is able to more efficiently route name resolution requests to the authoritative servers hosting child zone files.

Records in the stub zone are kept to a bare minimum and contain only these records:

- The start of authority (SOA) record, the name server (NS) resource records, and the host (A) records for the delegated zone
- The IP address of one or more master servers used to update the stub zone's records

 **NOTE**  Master servers for a stub zone can be one or more of the DNS servers authoritative for the child zone. This master server is usually the DNS server hosting the primary zone for the delegated domain name.

So when would it be appropriate to use a stub zone? Consider the following scenario: you have set up a DNS that's authoritative for a parent zone called beanlake.com. Because of the number of resource records, you decide to delegate a subdomain called atchison.beanlake.com to another DNS server in your enterprise. When you first set up the delegation, the parent zone contained only two resource records (the NS records) for the atchison.beanlake.com domain. The records in the zone for the subdomain grow, however, and more than two DNS servers have been added that are authoritative for this subdomain. What's more, you have not been notified of the additional servers.

This results in a DNS server that hosts a parent zone, beanlake.com, that is unaware of the new DNS servers that are authoritative for atchison.beanlake.com, and the parent DNS servers continue to query the name servers for which they are aware, even though more have been added to manage records of the zone.

To fix the above situation, you can configure a stub zone on the DNS server hosting the parent zone of beanlake.com. The stub zone will identify all the servers responsible over the atchison.beanlake.com zone information. After configuration, the stub zone will query the stub zone's master servers to obtain the addresses of all authoritative DNS servers for the subdomain of atchison.beanlake.com. Now that the stub zone has been properly configured, any new authoritative DNS servers added to the child zone will be (almost) immediately learned about if they are added to the growing atchison.beanlake.com resource domain.

## Configuring DNS Forwarding

It's very likely that your network's computers get their IP addresses from an ISP's DHCP server. As a part of that configuration, you are also likely to be handed DNS configuration information from these DHCP servers. But what if, in this case, you implement a DNS server in your network to resolve Active Directory resources? How does that DNS server resolve queries for external resources? Or does it have to? Here's where a DNS forwarder might be a good solution.

A forwarder is a DNS server that takes queries for external resources and passes them on to another DNS server, which in turn will walk the DNS tree resolve the name to an IP address. You can also configure a Server 2003's DNS to use conditional forwarders, described in the next section.

When you use a forwarder, you can designate that names outside your network get resolved by another DNS server rather than the forwarder. In the example mentioned, why have the local DNS server eat up bandwidth sending iterative requests to other DNS servers, especially when the ISP's DNS server is there to do just that? The forwarder will still provide name resolution for local resources, thus improving the efficiency of name resolution for the computers in your network.

## Conditional Forwarders

A conditional forwarder is a DNS forwarder that examines the domain name of the query, and then forwards the query to specified servers based on that name or names. In other words, it's a more precise way of handling forwarding tasks. Continuing the example above, let's say that your network frequently requests external resources from the domain beanlake.com. Using a conditional forwarder, the DNS server can be configured to forward all the queries it receives for FQDNs ending with beanlake.com to the IP address of the DNS server (or multiple DNS servers) that is authoritative for the beanlake.com namespace. This, too, helps improve the efficiency of name resolution requests.

Also new to Windows Server 2003's, the conditional forwarder setting for a DNS server consists of the following:

- The domain names for which the DNS server will forward queries
- One or more DNS server IP addresses for each domain name specified

To configure a conditional forwarder, open the DNS console, access the DNS server's Properties page, and then click the Forwarders tab. You can add conditional forwarders by clicking New and entering a specific domain. Then select the domain you've just added and type the IP address of the DNS server where requests for that domain should be sent, as shown in Figure 8-6.

When a DNS client or server sends a resolution request to a forwarding DNS server, the server looks to see if the query can be resolved with its own zone files or the data stored in its cache. Then, if the DNS server is configured to forward for the domain name designated in the query, the query is passed directly to the IP address of a name server associated with the domain name. This way, the entire DNS tree does not have to be searched.

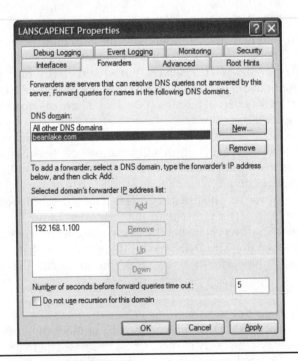

**Figure 8-6**   Adding a conditional forwarder

PART II

# DNS Server Roles

As first touched on earlier in this chapter, a DNS server plays one of several roles depending on what kinds of zones it stores and manages, or, in the case of the caching- only role, the absence of a zone altogether. These next three sections discuss the different roles a DNS server might play in your network. Whether all of these roles are needed will depend on the implementation needs of your network, and it will be your job as test-taker to determine which server roles best address a particular DNS dilemma.

## Primary

The primary DNS server for a zone is the location where all updates to the zone's records are made. All changes to the zone are then replicated to secondary servers. This replication model is called single master replication, where there is a single entity that controls changes to records. Windows NT 4 used this single master model for directory database replication as well.

This also highlights the biggest drawback of the standard primary server model: it includes a single point of failure. Just like when an NT 4 primary domain controller went down, if for any reason the primary server for a zone is unavailable, no updates to the zone can be made. This does not, however, affect resolution of names as long as secondary servers for the zone are available, and name-to-IP-address mappings have not changed.

When you create a new zone, it will be a primary zone, and the server sorting the zone will be a primary DNS server. You can then use primary zones in one of two ways: as standard primary zones or as primary zones integrated with Active Directory.

Using a standard primary zone, only a single DNS server will host and load the master copy of the zone. Further, only that server is allowed to accept dynamic updates, and no additional primary servers for the zone are permitted. You typically implement a standard primary zone when you need to replicate zone information with DNS servers running on other platforms such as Unix.

The good news is that you already know how to set up a primary DNS server. Simply add a primary zone using the procedure described previously in this chapter and you've set up a primary DNS server. There is no button you push to make a server primary or secondary; the designation is made based on the kind of zone(s) it stores. If you want to add more primary servers for a zone, you need to configure an Active Directory–integrated zone, which will then take advantage of Active Directory–integrated storage and replication features of the DNS Server service. To do this, you can either set up an Active Directory–integrated zone when the zone is set up or change the properties of an existing zone.

---

 **NOTE** There really isn't a primary server designation once you've integrated the zone information in Active Directory, as the zone information adheres to the same replication model as Active Directory information: multimaster. Using multimaster replication, there is no single point of failure for zone information, and all DNS servers storing the zone are considered primary.

When you instruct a DNS server to hold an Active Directory–integrated zone, that DNS server needs to also be a computer running Active Directory. Then any other DNS servers operating as part of the Active Directory domain namespace can query the Active Directory database and automatically load all such zones, which will now be stored in the directory database. No other steps are necessary.

Later in the chapter, we'll examine how to change the type of zone a DNS server stores. But first, you need to understand how to set up a secondary server.

## Secondary

So far we've been focusing on configuration of primary name servers where primary zone files will be stored, and configuring some of the options of those zone files. Now we'll look at secondary name servers.

Any time you have a secondary of anything, it is usually for load balancing and fault tolerance. The secondary servers are secondary servers because they store copies of zone files. Changes to the DNS domains are made at the primary zone level and then are copied to secondary zones for secondary zone servers. At the end of the day, they'll both end up storing the same information; it's just that changes to the domain are made at the primary level, not the secondary level.

---

 **TIP** A DNS server can be a primary name server and a secondary name server at the same time. The designation is made by what kind of zone file is stored on the server, and you can store both primary and secondary zones on the same machine. The server would then be a primary server for one zone (or more) and a secondary server for another zone or zones.

---

To set up a secondary name server, all you have to do is configure a secondary zone file that will be stored on that server.

## Lab Exercise 8.4: Configuring a Secondary DNS Server

The following procedure describes how to set up a secondary name server:

1. Open the DNS MMC snap-in from your Administrative Tools.

2. Expand the server that you will configure to be a secondary name server. Right-click the forward or reverse lookup zone that's going to be secondary. Choose New Zone. Click Next to bypass the welcome screen for the New Zone Wizard.

3. Choose Secondary Zone, and make your selection about storing the zone records in Active Directory, and then click Next.

4. Type the name for the zone, and click Next.

5. Here's where the zone truly becomes secondary. Enter the IP address for the master server from which you will copy the zone information. Click Next.

6. On the last screen of the wizard, verify your configuration information. Click Back if you have made any errors.

Another important note about setting your master server is that if you just look at names alone, you might deduce that a secondary server always gets its information from a primary server, but that's not the case. A master server just provides the place where you're going to get your copied zone file from. So a master server can be either a primary server or another secondary server. So don't get confused if you see a reference to a master server and think it's also a primary server. That may not be the case, as the information in a zone might just be a copy of a copy.

## Caching Only

A caching-only server exists only to resolve FQDN queries to an IP address and then cache them for a period of time, usually a bit longer than what is configured on a primary or secondary server. The difference between these servers and caching-only servers is that caching-only servers store exactly zero zone files. They are not authoritative for any part of the DNS namespace, and the information they contain is limited to what has been cached while resolving queries. In fact, when you get your IP configuration from your ISP, you are probably getting the IP addresses of caching-only servers. The ISP's DNS server doesn't need to worry about mapping *your* computer's name to an IP address, it instead needs to resolve your requests for Internet resources as quickly as possible.

To install a caching-only server, simply install DNS on the Windows Server 2003 computer, and then do not configure any forward or reverse lookup zone files. Additionally, you must verify that server root hints are configured or updated correctly.

A caching-only server can help optimize usage of the WAN for resolution requests over time. When first installed, the caching-only server has no cached information. This information is obtained incrementally as client requests are serviced. However, if you are dealing with a slow-speed WAN link between sites, this option might be ideal because, once the cache is built, traffic decreases. In addition, the caching-only server does not perform zone transfers, which can also conserve WAN bandwidth when external resources are located over slower links.

# Integrating DNS with DHCP

Dynamic updates allow a DNS client system to register and update its name resource records and IP address with its configured DNS server. This is especially significant when using a DHCP server to allocate IP addresses, as the name-to-IP-address mappings frequently change. With Dynamic DNS (DDNS) administration, overhead of maintaining zone records is reduced dramatically. DDNS used by Microsoft is standards-based, as described in RFC 2136.

Being able to update DNS dynamically is especially important because the domain controllers are going to create several records for themselves so that users will be able to find them. These include SRV records, A records, and PTR records. It's important that your domain controllers are able to create their records dynamically in DNS, because in order to log on, your client first asks its configured DNS server for a list of all domain controllers for the domain it's trying to log onto. Without these records, your clients will have a very hard time finding a domain controller.

Here's how client machines update their DNS zones with their resource records:

- Computers that have statically assigned IP addresses attempt to dynamically register host (A) and pointer (PTR) resource records for all IP addresses configured by their installed network connections. This means that one computer can resister several IP addresses if multiple network cards are installed. Also by default, DNS clients attempt to register records based on their domain membership settings.

 **TIP** You set the domain membership properties of a computer client through its System Properties dialog box, in either the Computer Name or Network Identification tab, depending on the operating system. You can also set advanced DNS name settings with the Advanced properties of TCP/IP.

- Computers running Windows 2000, XP, or 2003 that are also DHCP clients will only register their host (A) records. The DHCP server then updates the reverse lookup zone (if applicable) with appropriate pointer (PTR) record information for these same clients.

- Clients running operating systems prior to Windows 2000, such as Windows 98 systems, will have both their host (A) and pointer (PTR) resource records updated by the DHCP server on their behalf. This is because, prior to Windows 2000, Microsoft DNS clients were not aware of dynamic DNS. This updating behavior is encapsulated quite nicely in Figure 8-7.

## Implementing Dynamic DNS

The procedure for allowing dynamic updates is very easy. From the General tab of the Zone Properties, as seen in Figure 8-8, the dynamic ability of a zone is set with the drop-down dialog box.

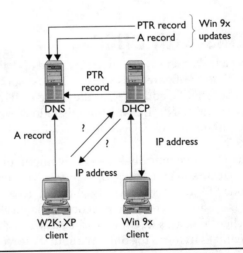

**Figure 8-7**   Dynamic DNS is updated differently depending on the DNS client.

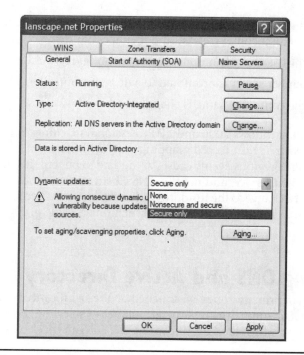

**Figure 8-8**    Configuring a zone for dynamic updates

As you can see, there are three choices here. If your zone type is an Active Directory–Integrated zone, you have the additional choice of allowing only secure updates. When you allow only secure updates, the zone information in an Active Directory zone is stored in Active Directory, and, therefore, you can apply permissions. If you have Secure Only updates selected, only computers with computer accounts in the Active Directory forest will be able to register their resource records with that DNS server.

**NOTE**    When using a standard zone, the default behavior is that the zone will *not* be configured for dynamic updates.

How does your client know that it should update DNS in the first place? This update process is initialized either from the client or from the DHCP server in your enterprise or the client itself, and sometimes both.

By default, 2000 and XP clients will update resource record information on the DNS server, and there are several instances in which this will occur. These include

- A change to one or more of the local IP addresses
- Any time the IP address is leased from the DHCP server, which most often occurs at startup time

- Any time the IP address is refreshed or changed, either as a matter of a normal shutdown or an ipconfig /release and then ipconfg /renew command
- Any time the user forces an update using ipconfig /registerdns
- When a member server is promoted to a domain controller
- Any time the computer name is changed

Also, by default, Windows 2000 and XP Professional machines will contact the DNS server to update with its host record mapping every 24 hours.

When one of the previous events causes an update to be sent, it's interesting to note that the DHCP Client service, and not the DNS Client service, sends the update. This is designed so that if a change to the IP address information occurs because of DHCP, corresponding updates in DNS are performed to synchronize name-to-IP-address mappings for the computer.

# Integrating DNS and Active Directory

In the discussion of primary zones, we touched on the significance of creating an Active Directory–integrated zone. Creating one is a matter of selecting the appropriate check box when specifying which kind of zone to create. (You can check back to Figure 8-2 for a reference.)

But what if you have created a standard primary zone, and now have migrated all DNS servers to Windows 2003, and want to take advantage of the security, fault tolerance, and reduced administration offered by Active Directory–integrated zones? You need to change the zone type.

## Changing the Zone to an Active Directory–Integrated Zone

Changing a standard zone to an Active Directory–integrated zone is a straightforward procedure. To do so, select the zone you want to change, then access its Properties dialog box. From the General tab, click the Change button next to Zone Type: Entry. You get a dialog box as shown in Figure 8-9, which you also saw when setting up the zone for the first time.

So now you can breathe easy knowing that your zones can adapt to serve the current needs of your DNS implementation with a minimum of administrative effort. When possible, implement Active Directory–integrated zones, as explained in the next section.

## Benefits of Active Directory Integration

Converting to an Active Directory–integrated zone makes a couple of significant changes to the way the DNS zones behave or the way DNS updates those zones. One is that the information held in the DNS zones is no longer stored in the files in the DNS

**Figure 8-9**

Converting an existing zone

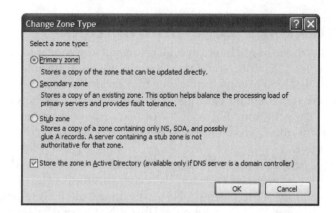

Directory on your hard drive; they are no longer text files. Instead, they become part of the Active Directory database. Another significant change is the way that DNS information is updated or synchronized. Because the DNS information is now part of the Active Directory database, it is synchronized with the Active Directory database. You no longer have to configure a replication topology between your DNS server like you did before by editing the characteristics of the Zone Transfers tab. In fact, if you are using Windows Server 2003 for your DNS solution, it's highly recommended that you go with the Active Directory–integrated zones. It eases the administrative burden of managing DNS. In fact, when you manage Active Directory you're managing DNS, so it takes one more thing out of your administrative mix.

Several important changes are made in your DNS zones when you're working with Active Directory. Some of these changes take place only in Active Directory–integrated zones, but most take place in whatever zone you're configuring. In other words, these changes are made as requirements of installing Windows 2003 Server as a domain controller. For example, in an Active Directory–integrated zone, any domain controller running DNS will be able to accept dynamic updates. So if you've decided to combine DNS service with the Active Directory service on the same machine, you don't even have to worry about configuring dynamic updates. Also, the netlogon service will register with the DNS server so that users can locate the services, because users submit their logon requests to the netlogon service. You can also apply security to DNS updates, and, as mentioned before, zone information becomes part of the Active Directory and is replicated automatically during Active Directory replication. You do not have to configure a separate replication strategy.

 **NOTE** Only primary zones can be integrated in Active Directory. If you are configuring a secondary zone, it will be stored as a standard text file. The multimaster replication model of Active Directory removes the need for secondary zones when zone information is stored in the directory database.

# Transferring Zone Information

If your DNS zone is not integrated, all changes to the zone information will be made at a single server. Therefore, you'll need to replicate the zone among other secondary DNS servers. When you're configuring zone transfers in the standard DNS environment, you do this by selecting and creating secondary servers. You then configure another DNS server to copy the zone file from the primary zone file or another secondary server. In other words, this DNS server that stores the zone file to be copied to other servers is the master server.

One reason why you might do this is to support older, third-party DNS servers that are not part of the Active Directory database. This means Unix DNS servers, which make up the majority of the existing DNS servers in use on the Internet. Here's how you configure Windows 2003 DNS for older Unix BIND secondary servers:

1. Open the DNS MMC snap-in. Right-click the server you want to administer, and choose Properties from the context menu.

2. On the Advanced tab, make sure the BIND Secondaries option is checked, as shown in Figure 8-10, and then close the Properties dialog box.

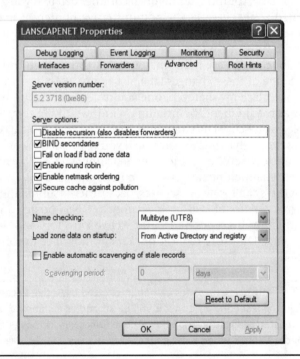

**Figure 8-10**   Enabling Unix BIND

# Monitoring and Management

Once your DNS implementation is in place, it's vital to the operation of your network that it be kept running, and further, that DNS resolution is optimized. Therefore, it is important that you know how to monitor and manage DNS performance.

Fortunately, the knowledge in the preceding section will serve as your best arsenal to help you do this. The next sections will help you leverage that knowledge and give you a few pointers about what kinds of questions to expect on the exam. Many of the questions on DNS, and indeed the entire test, will be based on things that have gone wrong, to see whether you possess the knowledge to put the network right again.

## Managing DNS Record Settings

The DNS records kept by Windows Server 2003's implementation of DNS do not stay in the zone files forever. Computers change IPs, change subnets, and DNS must have a mechanism to deal with all the resource mappings that are no longer valid. To do so, Microsoft's version of DNS supports aging and scavenging features. These features are provided to perform cleanup of the zone files and remove stale resource records, which accumulate over time.

As you now know, when you implement DDNS—and most networks today do—records are automatically added to zones when computers start on the network. However, sometimes they aren't removed when computers leave the network. A common occurrence of this is when a system is improperly disconnected from the network, and its host record is not removed from the zone file because the computer doesn't get a chance to contact its DNS server. If you have a lot of mobile users in the network, this situation can occur frequently.

If resource records are not cleaned from the zone files, problems might occur, including

- If a large number of stale records are kept in the zone file, they can use unnecessary server disk space and cause long zone transfers.

- If DNS servers load stale records, they might answer client queries with improper name-to-IP-address mappings, potentially causing clients to experience communication difficulty when using FQDNs.

- Poor DNS server performance resulting from too many records being searched when trying to resolve resolution requests.

- In certain instances, the presence of a stale resource record could prevent an FQDN from being used by another computer or host device.

Fortunately, Windows Server 2003's DNS implementation combats the existence of stale resource records with the following features:

- Time stamping for any records added dynamically to primary zones. The time stamp is set based on the current date and time at the DNS computer.

- For any manually added records, a time stamp value of zero is used, indicating that they are not affected by the aging process and can remain without limitation. Manually added records must be deleted manually, unless you change this default time stamp.

- It automatically ages resource records, based on a specified refresh time period.

- Only primary type zones loaded by the DNS are eligible to participate in this process. Secondary zones are scavenged by the primary server and then are updated with the appropriate zone information.

- Scavenging continues for all records that persist beyond the specified refresh period.

A DNS server performs a scavenging operation by looking at the time stamp. Using this information, it can determine whether a record has aged to the point of becoming stale. If the record is indeed stale, the record is removed from the zone file. Servers can be configured to perform recurring scavenging operations automatically, or you can initiate an immediate scavenging operation at the server.

## Lab Exercise 8.5: Scavenging Zones

To set the automatic scavenging of zone files, follow these steps:

1. Open the DNS MMC snap-in, right-click the applicable DNS server, and select Properties.

2. Click the Advanced tab. Select the Enable Automatic Scavenging Of Stale Records check box.

3. To adjust the scavenging period, select from the drop-down list an interval in either hours or days, and then type a number in the text box, as shown in Figure 8-11.

To perform a manual scavenge of zones, right-click the applicable DNS server, then click Scavenge Stale Resource Records from the context menu.

## Monitoring DNS

For testing purposes, you will also need to know how DNS can be monitored, especially as part of a troubleshooting routine. There are several tools that can be used to monitor DNS performance, each useful under differing circumstances. It should not be necessary to acquire a working knowledge of each and every one of these tools, but rather identify these DNS tools, and the instances where they would be used.

And while most of these tools we are meeting for the first time, there is at least one we are not. Along with management of the DNS service, one tool useful in the monitoring department is the one we've been working with all chapter long: the DNS snap-in.

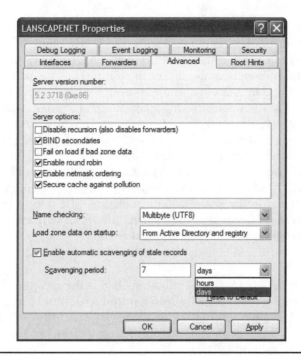

**Figure 8-11**   Configuring automatic scavenging of resource records

**NOTE**   You do not have to be sitting at the DNS server in order to use most of these utilities for monitoring. For example, the DNS MMC snap-in can be installed on any XP Professional computer by installing the Windows Server 2003 Administration Pack (Adminpak.msi).

## The DNS MMC Snap-in

The DNS MMC snap-in not only let's you manage the properties of the server and the zones it stores, it also provides a basic testing tool for the DNS service, as well as the capability to enable logging. You will find these options by opening the Properties pages of the DNS Manager. Two tabs that can be of use when you're trying to troubleshoot problems are Logging and Monitoring. From the Logging tab, you can turn on logging options that will enable you to log activity of the DNS server. The Monitoring tab allows you to test the DNS server to make sure that it is functioning correctly. You can select two different test types, simple or recursive, and you can also choose Test Now to have the test performed on an ongoing basis.

The DNS MMC console can also be used to start, stop, pause, or resume DNS server function, manually update the server data files, or clear the server's resolver cache. As you have seen, the snap-in is the tool used to perform aging and scavenging of stale resource records stored by the server.

## nslookup and dnscmd

Another important troubleshooting tool with DNS is nslookup. It is a command-line utility that looks simple but is actually sophisticated. It has both a command-line interface and what's known as interactive mode. For the purposes of quick testing, you can use just the command-line interface. For more thorough or exhaustive testing, it's recommended that you use the interactive nslookup mode. In order for nslookup to work properly, you must have a properly configured reverse lookup zone. If you get error messages as you are trying to perform queries on your DNS server, it is likely because the reverse lookup zone has not been properly configured.

The dnscmd is also a command-line tool that is used specifically to manage DNS servers. However, it is not available until first installed as past of the Windows Support Tools (Support\Tools on the Server 2003 installation CD). Like most command line utilities, this tool can is often best utilized when called from scripted batch files. You can find help about the dnscmd utility by typing **dnscmd /?**.

## ipconfig

Another important utility for troubleshooting DNS is the ipconfig command. You've probably used ipconfig utility, or have seen it introduced by now, and you will be visiting this crucial IP troubleshooting utility in the chapters to follow. There are several switches that are use with ipconfig to perform different tasks, but some of the ones that are specific to troubleshooting DNS include

- **/all**   This switch provides configuration information for each network adapter, including information about your configured DNS servers.

- **/flushdns**   This switch clears all the cached information you have retrieved from DNS servers. You can use this to force your host to reread information from your configured DNS server. This can be especially effective if an IP address has recently changed and you may be resolving from a cached entry.

- **/registerdns**   This switch renews any DHCP leases you currently have and also will register your host name with your locally configured DNS server.

- **/displaydns**   This switch shows the entries currently in the cache. The /displaydns and /flushdns switches are often used in conjunction with one another.

As a last troubleshooting line of defense, there are many dynamic entries created in your DNS zone files by the netlogon service. You can quickly reregister this information by stopping and restarting the netlogon service to ensure there are no problems with clients trying to locate netlogon servers or the netlogon service for domain authentication.

## Event Viewer

Under Windows 2000, a separate log was kept for DNS information, but was added to the Event Viewer console when DNS was installed. While that's still the case, Microsoft has also included the DNS-specific Event Viewer interface in the Server 2003 DNS console. You don't have to flip back and forth between two applications to view and diagnose the DNS events captured by the DNS service. Figure 8-12 shows the DNS node of Event Viewer and the DNS events node of the DNS MMC snap-in side by side.

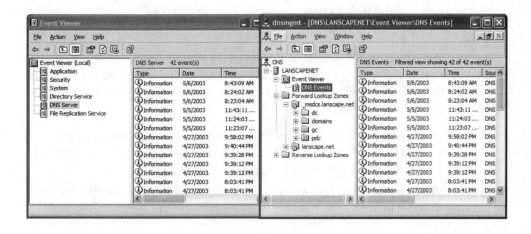

**Figure 8-12**    The DNS console and Event Viewer are now linked.

Just like using Event Viewer, the DNS interface lets you set default properties of the log file. To do so, right-click the DNS Events log file and choose Properties, bringing up the dialog box shown in Figure 8-13.

**Figure 8-13**
The DNS Events
log file properties

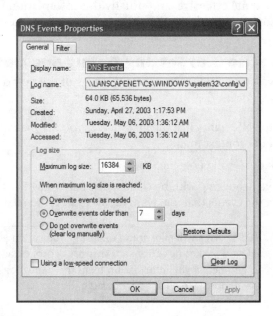

Configuring the log file properties is a fairly straightforward exercise, which most administrators are familiar with by now. Essentially, you're just configuring the properties of a text file: how large it will be, where it will be stored, and what happens when it fills up with collected data.

By default, the logging policy is set so that when the log gets full, the oldest events are deleted to make room for new events, with the stipulation that events are at least seven days old. This is called event log wrapping, and you can customize this policy using options on the General tab:

- **Overwrite events as needed.**  New events will be written even though the log is full. New events will replace the oldest event in the log. If archiving DNS events isn't important (usually it's not), this option is a good choice.

- **Overwrite events older than *x* days.**  The log will be retained for the number of days you specify before overwriting events. The default is seven days. This option is the best choice if you want to archive log files weekly. This strategy minimizes the chance of losing important log entries and at the same time keeps log sizes reasonable.

- **Do not overwrite events.**  This option allows you to clear or archive the log manually rather than automatically. Select this option only if you cannot afford to miss an event (for example, for the security log at a site where security is extremely important).

You can further gather troubleshooting information with DNS's debugging feature. The debugging options can be helpful if you encounter problems that consistently cause your DNS implementation to fail. The information recorded through the debugging options can be quite extensive, and usually this information is used in conjunction with Microsoft support to help resolve these persistent name resolution concerns.

## Lab Exercise 8.6: Setting Debugging Options

Fortunately, setting up DNS to take advantage of the new debugging options is a snap. Here's how:

1. Open DNS, right-click the DNS server you are managing, and choose Properties from the context menu.

2. Click the Debug Logging tab.

3. Enable debugging with by clicking the Select Log Packets For Debugging option. Select the events that you want the DNS server to record.

 **NOTE**  This will take some experimentation on your part, but you need to select a packet direction, a transport protocol, and at least one more option to get meaningful information from the debug logging. Notice that several of the options are enabled by default.

The debug log file will be saved to a location of your choosing, with the default file being dns.log, saved in the *systemroot*\system32\dns directory.

Further, note that in step 2 in the preceding excercise, all DNS debug logging options are disabled until you turn on debugging. Debug logging can be resource-intensive, taxing overall server performance. And, although not really much of a concern on modern hard drives, the log file will take up disk space. Therefore, it should only be used temporarily when more detailed DNS performance behavior is needed to resolve sticker issues.

# Chapter Review

DNS serves as the central name resolution component of a Windows Server 2003 network and is even required for certain components such as Active Directory. In this chapter, we've looked at how the DNS hierarchy is put together and how it has been integrated in the Microsoft software.

We examined important configuration behaviors of DNS, including how to set up and manage a zone, and how zone information could be replicated from server to server. We also spent time looking at the enhancements made in Microsoft's 2003 version of DNS.

Finally, we looked at how the DNS service could be managed and monitored, discussing utilities such as nslookup and Event Viewer. Much of the rest of the book, and indeed the rest of your MCSE studies, rely heavily on your understanding of DNS.

## Questions

1. You are attempting to troubleshoot a DNS problem. You have configured a Windows 2003 server for DNS and intend to use this server as the name server for Active Directory. You set up an Active Directory–integrated zone to store the DNS records. What must you do to ensure successful zone transfers between these different DNS servers?

   A. Configure the existing DNS server as a primary server and configure the rest as secondary servers.

   B. Configure the existing DNS server as a primary, one as master, and the remaining as secondary servers.

   C. Configure the zone files on the other servers as Active Directory–integrated when you create the zones.

   D. You don't need to do anything. Active Directory will handle replication of all DNS records.

2. Your company has five locations around the country. You are currently documenting the DNS structure in place for resolution of internal names. There is a primary DNS server located in Kansas City and a secondary DNS

server located in all other branch offices. The Dallas and Atchison servers transfer from the St. Louis server. Which should be the master server(s)?

A. The master server should be Kansas City only.

B. The master server should be Kansas City, St. Louis, and Atchison.

C. All the servers are master servers.

D. The master server designation does not apply here.

3. You are currently using a Unix BIND DNS solution. There are about 50 internal servers in the BIND servers zone file, and you want to move these records to your Windows Server 2003 server you have just configured with DNS. What is the best way to accomplish your goal?

A. Copy the domain file to the winnt\system32\dns directory on the Windows 2003 DNS server prior to creating the zone.

B. Copy the domain file to the winnt\system32\dns directory on the Windows 2003 DNS server after creating the zone.

C. Copy the file to any location on the Windows 2003 DNS server. Then use the DNS MMC snap-in to import the file.

D. Manually enter the information in the new zone file you create on the Windows 2003 DNS server.

4. You are at a branch office location, setting up a DNS server that will perform local name resolution. You're setting it up as a secondary server to your primary DNS server located in the Kansas City office. You try to transfer the zone, but are unable to do so. What's wrong?

A. You need to configure the secondary server as an IP forwarder.

B. You need to configure the primary server with the address of the new secondary server.

C. You need to install the OSPF routing protocol. The DNS update packets cannot be sent until this protocol is enabled.

D. You cannot create a secondary server on a remote site. The server must be configured with a primary zone file for resolution of local resources.

5. You are trying to troubleshoot a DNS problem and are using the nslookup utility. Every time you use it, however, you experience a timeout error. You are able to get the name resolution you expect, but you want to find out the source of the error. What is the cause?

A. The type of DNS server you are investigating stores an Active Directory–integrated zone. nslookup is useless when querying this kind of zone file.

B. The DNS server has incorrectly configured information, most likely in the SOA record.

C. A reverse lookup zone has not been configured properly, if at all.

D. A secondary server is being queried and had not pulled the latest updates from its master server.

6. You are troubleshooting your DNS server. The server has not been resolving some of the hosts in the network, but is working fine for others. You check the DNS MMC snap-in and everything looks okay. What utility should you use to determine the nature of the problem?

   A. The netstat command

   B. Network Monitor

   C. The nslookup command

   D. The Monitoring tab of the DNS server's Properties page

7. You are configuring DNS for your environment. The servers hosting DNS will be several standalone servers that will be used for server-based applications such as SQL. You want to create a new zone on one of the servers. How should you configure the zones?

   A. Standard primary.

   B. Standard secondary.

   C. Active Directory–integrated.

   D. It makes no difference. Any of the above will work.

8. You are setting up the first domain controller in a new domain. This new domain will be the root domain for an organization's forest. There is a DNS server already in use, but that DNS server is on a Unix system that does not support dynamic updates. It does, however, support SRV records. You do not plan on implementing a new DNS installation. What steps should you take after setting up the new domain controller to make sure that all the correct records have been created on the DNS server?

   A. Use the ipconfig utility with the /registerdns command.

   B. Manually create the records on the DNS server.

   C. Start and stop the netlogon service on the domain controller, causing records to be generated automatically.

   D. You must replace your DNS server solution.

9. You are considering how to configure DNS to best integrate with Windows 2003 Active Directory. You have several options at your disposal. What are they?

   A. Use the same domain name internally and externally.

   B. Use a child domain of the external (public) domain.

   C. Use separate, unrelated domain names for the internal (private) domain and the external (public) domain.

   D. All of the above.

10. You decide to use an older installation of DNS for redundancy and load balancing. The DNS is on a Unix server, and you configure it to act as a secondary server for the zone configured when installing Windows 2003.

When the zone transfers, many of the records don't seem to have survived the journey. What is likely causing this?

A. A Unix BIND server cannot be used as a secondary server.

B. The Windows 2003 DNS server is running in Active Directory–integrated mode.

C. The Unix server does not support Unicode characters.

D. The version of BIND does not support SRV records.

11. You are troubleshooting a Windows XP client machine, and have just changed the name of the computer and the IP address. You now want to make sure the client registers itself with a DNS server. What command should you use to do this?

A. ipconfig /renewdns

B. ipconfig /registerdns

C. nslookup /refreshclient

D. ntdsutil /sendconfig

12. You have just installed and configured five Windows 2003 DNS servers to provide name resolution for your company's domain resources. There are two child-level domains in the enterprise. Which of the following features will help improve the DNS fault-tolerant performance while minimizing network traffic? (Choose all that apply.)

A. Stub domains

B. Zone delegation

C. Primary and secondary zone files

D. Incremental zone transfer

13. You have set up a Windows 2003 server to provide DNS services for a small network that is separate from the Internet. All the resources on the internal network are separated from the rest of the Internet by a router. Users report, however, that the server is able to resolve queries for internal resources, but cannot resolve names for resources outside the LAN. What is causing this problem?

A. The local DNS server is also configured as a root-level name server.

B. The DNS zone is not configured to support dynamic updates.

C. The server's root hints file is improperly configured.

D. The name server needs to be an RRAS server as well. DNS iterative queries cannot be passed through a router.

14. You are configuring a Windows Server 2003 machine to answer queries for hosts on the local network, but you do not want this server performing iterative queries of other DNS servers on the Internet, as you are concerned with bandwidth

use of the WAN. Instead, you want another server to perform the name resolution grunt work. How should you accomplish this?

A. Install the DNS component on the network's RRAS server and let the RAS component do the name resolution.

B. Configure the DNS server as a root-level server and remove all root hints for top-level domains.

C. Make sure that a forwarder is configured for the DNS server.

D. Disable recursive lookups.

## Answers

1. **D.** Because the zone created is an Active Directory–integrated zone, there is no primary or secondary server designation. Configuration information will be replicated automatically to each domain controller in the Active Directory domain.

2. **B.** The master server is the server that provides the source copy of the DNS zone file information to secondary servers. These master servers can be either primary or secondary servers.

3. **C.** The easiest thing here is to copy the files to the directory winnt\system32\ dns. Then create the zone file using the DNS MMC snap-in. During the creation process, you will have the chance to name the file. If you select the imported file, the proper DNS entries should appear.

4. **B.** The most likely problem here is that the primary server is configured to only transfer its DNS zone information to known servers, and it is not aware of the new secondary server. To address this, you will need to add the secondary server to the list of known servers from the DNS server's Properties page.

5. **A.** This error happens when a reverse lookup record cannot be found for the DNS server itself. All your system knows about the DNS server is the IP address, and this IP address must be resolved to a host name for nslookup to work without error messages. The job of the reverse lookup zone is to provide IP-address-to-host-name resolution.

6. **B.** Network Monitor is the only tool that will let you see the request that is sent to and from the DNS server, so that you might be able to find the cause of the problem.

7. **A.** You won't necessarily need Active Directory in a test environment, and you will need to create the standard primary before you create the standard secondary.

8. **B.** If you are using a DNS server that does not support dynamic updates, you need to create the appropriate Active Directory domains and service (SRV) records manually. You need to create records for the Global Catalog server, LDAP directory services, Kerberos services, and so on.

9. **D.** All of these are valid choices when integrating your DNS namespace with Active Directory.

10. **C.** The transfer didn't fail altogether, just some of the records do not make sense. Therefore, the most likely reason this is occurring is that the Unix box does not support Unicode.

11. **A.** A client registers its IP configuration with a DNS server that supports dynamic updates with the command ipconfig /registerdns. The other switches used in these answers are invalid.

12. **A, C,** and **D.** The incremental zone transfers help reduce the amount of network traffic generated when DNS servers replicate zone information. When you set up primary and secondary zone files, you have multiple copies of the zone information stored on many servers.

13. **B.** The likely cause here is that the DNS server has no way of contacting the DNS root name servers to begin walking the DNS hierarchy. Each implementation of DNS includes a file that provides root hints for the root-level servers on the Internet.

14. **C.** If you want to pass along the job of name resolution to other DNS servers, you need to make sure to configure a forwarder. The server doing the forwarding then will not perform any iterative queries in the DNS namespace.

# Implementing, Managing, and Maintaining Routing and Remote Access

In this chapter, you will learn how to

- Install the Remote Access Service
- Configure the remote access server
- Configure routing and remote access user authentication
- Work with remote access permissions and authentication
- Configure routing and remote access policies to permit or deny access
- Manage TCP/IP routing
- Set up a virtual private network
- Manage and monitor remote access

What is remote access? Different wires, different protocols. That's essentially all there is to remote access. The network is still available, and it's still used exactly the same way as it is when users are physically sitting at it. Remote access just uses different lines—the Publicly Switched Telephone Network (PSTN), for example, instead of the CAT 5 cabling in use on the LAN. It also employs different communication protocols—PPTP, for example, which is responsible for carrying a TCP/IP payload, instead of the "naked" TCP/IP packet that might be passed between computers in a LAN.

When you put remote access in to action, you are enabling the extension of your LAN outside the boundaries of your office building's walls. When properly implemented, there isn't any difference between a user operating at a desktop computer hooked to the LAN at your office and a user hooked to their phone jack in their home or hotel room.

But while it's easy to explain in a few words, actually setting up the clients and the servers for remote access is a bit more of a chore. And understanding all of the various details surrounding the securing and managing of that access is even more so. This is material you are likely to be tested on, so it's important to give it your full attention.

# Remote Access Overview

Prior to Windows 2000, the Remote Access Service was installed as an add-on component to the Windows NT 4 Server platform. This add-on provided the capability for the server to receive incoming phone calls and thus grant remote access to the network. Further, you also needed the RAS software client installed on the other end, whether you were connecting to an NT 4 RAS server or dialing into a generic (read: Unix) dial-in server.

Now, however, these components are installed automatically when you set up Windows 2003 (and indeed any other operating system subsequent to Windows 2000). The new software also bundles several features that used to be installed as separate services through NT 4. For example, the capability to set up a virtual private network (VPN) is now included with the Routing and Remote Access Service (RRAS) software.

But notice that the components are only installed. They're not configured. Configuration of routing and remote access is what this chapter is all about.

## Remote Access Clients

Almost any kind of modern operating system today contains the software necessary to establish an RAS connection to a Windows Server 2003 system. This would include any of the Windows family of operating systems. Additionally, Windows Server 2003 computers can still connect to older Unix-based dial-up servers using the Serial Line Interface Protocol (SLIP) protocol, which is discussed later in the chapter.

Usually, the biggest drawback to a RAS connection is the speed. A LAN connection, running today at speeds of 100 Mbps and higher, is many times faster than any dial-up connection.

## Lab Exercise 9.1: Configuring a Remote Access Client

To create a new RAS connection for communicating with a RAS server, perform the following steps:

1. Open the Network Connections window, using any available method. You can always go through the Control Panel.

2. In the Network Connections window, double-click the New Connection Wizard icon to launch the New Connection Wizard.

3. Click Next, and then in the Network Connection Type screen, choose the middle option, Connect To The Network At My Workplace, as shown in Figure 9-1. Click Next.

4. Now you'll choose whether to create a dial-up or virtual private network connection. For this example, choose the dial-up connection and click Next.

5. Give the connection a name, click Next, and then configure the phone number the connection uses. Click Next.

6. Now configure connection availability, click Next, and then click Finish from the summary page.

**Figure 9-1**

Creating a RAS connection

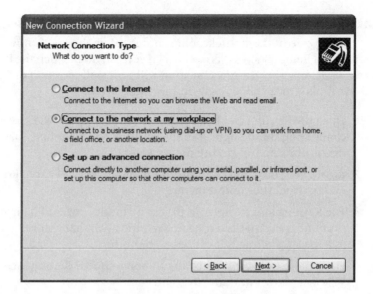

Now you've configured your 2003 machine as a RAS client. But while it may be very practical to configure a RAS client connection from this machine, it's more common that this system will be used as your company's RAS server, and Microsoft, on their 70-291 exam, expects the same.

# Configuring the Routing and Remote Access Service

Before you can learn more about the Routing and Remote Access Service, you'd better know how to get it up and running. As mentioned earlier, the necessary software is installed, but is not functional until configured. The next step, then, is to configure the service and start accepting inbound connections.

## Routing and Remote Access Requirements

Before you begin, a few things must be in place:

- Installation of the hardware needed to support your WAN connections. If you are accepting dial-up connections, for example, you need to make sure a modem is properly installed and configured.

- Installation of the LAN protocols needed for the clients to reach computers on your network. In most cases, TCP/IP will be all you need, and this will be installed by default.

## Lab Exercise 9.2: Configuring the Remote Access Server

After taking care of the housekeeping chores listed above, it's now time to enable the Routing and Remote Access Service, which you can do through the Routing and Remote Access MMC snap-in. The MMC snap-in will be installed as part of your default Administrative tools. Once you're ready, follow these steps:

1. Open the Routing and Remote Access MMC snap-in. The server you are currently configuring should appear in the console tree. Note here that you are given instructions on how to use the console.

2. Right-click your server and choose "Configure and Enable Routing and Remote Access" from the context menu.

3. The Routing and Remote Access Configuration Wizard launches. Click Next from the welcome screen, which reminds you that you can enable the server as a router, a remote access server, or both.

4. From the list of common configurations, choose Remote Access (Dial-up or VPN), as shown in Figure 9-2, and click Next.

5. Now you should see the Remote Client Protocols screen. This screen is used as a verification tool to make sure you have all the necessary LAN protocols installed for the clients the RAS server will serve.

6. Click Next after you have confirmed the necessary protocols (you could add protocols here if you wish).

**Figure 9-2**

Choosing the RRAS server type

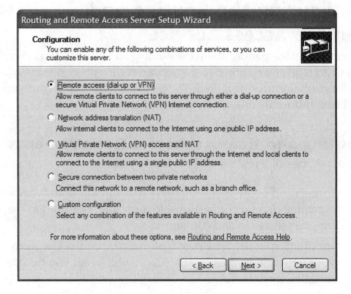

7. You will see the IP Address Assignment screen, where you will select how your RAS clients will receive IP addresses. You can use the services of a DHCP server on your network, or you can configure a DHCP component on the Routing and Remote Access Services server by clicking the choice to assign IP addresses from a specified range of IP addresses. For this example, choose the Automatic option and click Next.

**NOTE**   Later in the chapter, we'll look at the implications of choosing the DHCP option. For now, just know that the RRAS server will go out and grab a block of 10 IP addresses from the DHCP server to allocate to RAS clients.

8. On the Managing Multiple Remote Access Servers screen, you have the option to configure the RRAS server to authenticate clients using the services of a RADIUS server. For now, click Next to accept default selection of No to the RADIUS option. (We'll discuss the RADIUS option later on as well.)

9. Click Finish, and then click OK in the Routing and Remote Access message box. The message tells you that you need to configure your RRAS server as a DHCP relay agent so that clients can obtain IP addresses from the DHCP server.

## Configuring the DHCP Relay Agent

The role of the DHCP Relay Agent was first examined in Chapter 7. If you have a subnet without a DHCP server and the router that divides this subnet will not forward BOOTP protocol packets, then you need to use a DHCP Relay Agent if you want the computers on that subnet to take advantage of the automation of DHCP.

The steps to set up the DHCP Relay are covered here once again, to save you having to flip back to Chapter 7. All it takes is a few steps, as follows:

1. Open the Routing and Remote Access MMC snap-in and expand your server.

2. Expand the IP Routing node and select the DHCP Relay Agent.

3. Right-click the DHCP Relay Agent and choose New Interface. You'll more often than not use the Local Area Connection, and that's what we'll do here. Click OK after making the selection. You've just instructed your DHCP relay agent to contact the DHCP server over the LAN connection.

4. In the Routing and Remote Access console tree, right-click the DHCP Relay Agent and choose Properties.

5. In the Server Address box, as shown in Figure 9-3, enter the IP address of the DHCP server and click Add. Click OK when you're done to close the DHCP Relay Agent Properties dialog box and commit your changes.

**Figure 9-3**
Configuring the
DHCP relay
agent by
specifying the
DHCP server
address

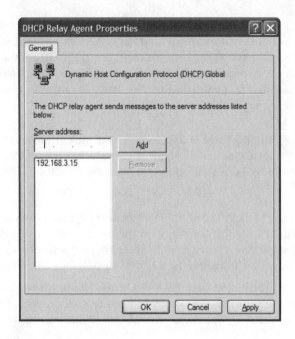

## Managing the WAN Protocols

On a local area network (LAN), transport protocols like TCP/IP are used to get information from one system to another. That's still the case when transmitting data over a wide area network (WAN), but when using a remote access connection over a WAN, other protocols help the TCP/IP packets reach their destinations.

Remember the mantra: different protocols. There are two protocols supported by Microsoft's Routing and Remote Access Service for serial, asynchronous connections. They are

- **Serial Line Interface Protocol (SLIP)**   This is one of the oldest serial line protocols and is only included for support of legacy applications. There are significant drawbacks to the SLIP protocol, which will be discussed, and it is rarely used today.

- **Point to Point Protocol (PPP)**   This is the protocol to use when establishing a connection via modem. The PPP can automatically make connections and even reestablish them when needed. It uses error correction and supports the combining of multiple connections for increased bandwidth. PPP is an open-standard protocol, defined in RFC 1661, and the Windows 2003 implementation is fully 1661-compliant.

**NOTE** Most of the data passed back and forth between the components of your computer is done in *parallel*, multiple bits traveling along a series of wires. However, when data needs to be passed outside the computer, the data is passes one bit at a time—that is, in *serial*. This ensures much more reliable communication than would otherwise be possible using the existing communication technologies for passing data over long distances. The exceptions include the parallel port, which is used mainly for printers, and the SCSI bus, which can be used to connect lots of devices, although not very often anymore.

Windows Server 2003 can also behave as a RAS client of any RFC 1661 dial-up server, and can accept connections from any 1661-compliant computers. The real advantage of this protocol, especially when compared to SLIP, is that it includes support for all commonly used LAN protocols such as IPX/SPX, AppleTalk, and, of course, TCP/IP. SLIP is restricted to passing TCP/IP packets only.

Furthermore, PPP can be used with a variety of authentication protocols, which define how a user is authenticated when they are remotely accessing the network—how their user names and passwords are passed from client to the remote access server.

These authentication protocols will be fleshed out as we move through the chapter. For now, as we start this discussion, let's examine the most basic use of the Routing and Remote Access Service server.

## Managing Ports

When remote connections are made, they are made through a *port*. A port is an entry point into the RRAS server (or any server, for that matter). Ports can be both physical and logical. For example, the computer you work with now most likely has a parallel port, which is a communication pathway for data—in the case of a parallel port, almost always data sent to the printer—to enter and leave the system. But in the case of a Routing and Remote Access Server, you are dealing with *logical* ports. All of the many ports open for RAS traffic come "listen" for inbound connections, usually, on just a single physical interface of the network device; the ports open for RAS traffic serve to help identify the type connection attempt. Without available ports, remote access connections cannot be made.

## Lab Exercise 9.3: Examining Remote Access Ports

Here's how to make sure the remote access clients are able to connect to an available port:

1. Open the Routing and Remote Access console, and select the Ports node in the left pane.

2. A list of available ports appears. Choose the port you want to manage, right-click, and choose Status from the context menu. The Port Status dialog box opens, as shown in Figure 9-4.

**Figure 9-4**

The port status is accessible in this dialog box.

3. In the dialog box, you can see the port condition, the line speed, the call duration, network statistics, and networks protocols being used. You can reset or refresh the statistics by clicking on the aptly named buttons at the bottom, or disconnect a connection by clicking Disconnect.

If you have a network card installed, you should have noticed multiple ports created for each of these two protocols: the Point to Point Tunneling Protocol (PPTP) and the Layer Two Tunneling Protocol (L2TP). These two protocols are used when establishing remote access connections not over phone lines using the phone number of a modem, but rather to IP address assigned to the network card. These two protocols encapsulate, or "tunnel," the TCP/IP traffic sent to the RRAS server, and are thus the protocols that make virtual private networking possible.

# Virtual Private Networking

Ask a computer vendor technician what a virtual private network (VPN) is, and you're likely to get definitions that can vary widely depending on who's doing the explaining. There are VPN solutions built into firewall platforms, and there are dedicated hardware solutions that provide VPN solutions. At the end of the day, however, they all share a common cause: to transmit data privately over a public transit system.

For purposes of discussion here, we will focus on the VPN capability built into the Windows Server 2003 platform. More specifically, we deal with this piece of software as it's implemented through Routing and Remote Access.

# VPN Components

There are several pieces of the VPN puzzle. They include

- **VPN servers**   These serve as one of the endpoints of a VPN connection. When configuring a VPN server, you can allow access to just that server, or pass traffic through the VPN server so that remote users gain access the resources of the entire network.

- **VPN clients**   VPN clients establish connections to VPN servers. They can also be routers that obtain router-to-router secure connections. VPN client software is included in all of the modern Windows operating systems, including Windows Server 2003. Router-to-router VPN connections can be made from computers running Server 2003 and Windows 2000 running Routing and Remote Access. Additionally, any client that supports PPTP or L2TP connections (discussed later) can be VPN clients of a Windows Server 2003 system.

- **LAN and remote access protocols**   LAN protocols like TCP/IP are used by applications to ferry information back and forth. Web browsers, for example, use TCP/IP to carry HTTP get requests to HTTP servers. Remote access protocols, on the other hand, are used to negotiate connections and provide framing for LAN protocol data that is sent over WAN links. More about the WAN protocols will be discussed later.

- **Tunneling protocols**   As discussed in the following section, VPN clients use tunneling protocols like L2TP or PPTP to create the secured VPN connections.

- **WAN options**   These provide the physical mechanism for passing data back and forth. These connections typically include such familiar network technologies such as T1 or frame relay. In order for a VPN connection to be successful, the VPN client and VPN server must be connected to each other using either permanent WAN connections or by dialing in to an Internet service provider (ISP).

- **Security options**   Since a VPN uses a network that is generally open to the public, it is important that the data passed over the connection remain secure. To aid with secure communication, Routing and Remote Access supports such security measures as logon and domain security, data encryption, smart cards, IP packet filtering, and caller ID. The security options will also be discussed in more detail later on.

# VPN Tunneling Protocols

The protocols involved in setting up a VPN encapsulate a TCP/IP datagram or *payload*. The nature of the transmission is public, using public networks such as the Internet. But because of the encapsulation protocols involved, the data itself is kept private; it's as if the network exists only to get your data to its destination. In other words, if TCP/IP transmission delivers envelopes of information from point A to point B, then the VPN protocols add a seal and lock to these envelopes.

There are two protocols implemented in Windows Server 2003 that make this private connection using a public network a reality: PPTP and L2TP.

**Point to Point Tunneling Protocol (PPTP)**   PPTP is Microsoft's legacy protocol for supporting VPNs. It was developed in conjunction with other communications companies such as US Robotics as an extension of the PPP protocol. PPTP encapsulates IP or IPX packets inside of PPP datagrams. This means that you can remotely run programs that are dependent upon particular network protocols. One of the keys to remember about PPTP is that the protocol provides encryption capabilities, making it much safer to send information over nonsecure (read: Internet) networks.

**NOTE**   If you wanted to secure communications between computers within your office—say, to prevent internal business espionage—you certainly have that option. There's nothing that says you can't use the encryption services of PPTP in LAN-to-LAN networking.

**Layer Two Tunneling Protocol (L2TP)**   L2TP is a standards-based encapsulation protocol with roughly the same functionality as the Point-to-Point Tunneling Protocol (PPTP). One of the key differences between Windows Server 2003 implementation of L2TP and its cousin PPTP is that L2TP is designed to run natively over IP networks only. This implementation of L2TP does not support native tunneling over X.25, frame relay, or ATM networks. Like PPTP, L2TP encapsulates Point-to-Point Protocol (PPP) frames, which then encapsulate IP or IPX protocols, allowing users to remotely run programs that are dependent on specific network protocols. But unlike the PPTP protocol, L2TP does not provide encryption of the data. For data security, L2TP relies on the services of another standards-based protocol, IPSec.

Sometimes, it's hard to visualize what these VPN protocols do by description alone. Figure 9-5 represents the role the tunneling protocol plays in data communication.

Table 9-1 provides a handy summary of the differences between the two VPN protocols available with Server 2003. It would be a good idea to have this knowledge handy when preparing for the 70-291 exam.

## Installing and Setting Up a VPN Server

You should now have a pretty good picture of what a VPN server does and what role it plays in the network. You should also have a good understanding if why one would be set up. All that's left now is a few clicks of the mouse and some button pushing.

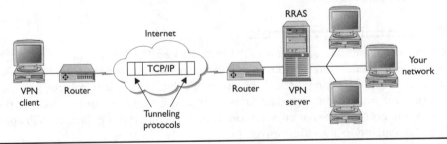

**Figure 9-5**   Role of tunneling protocol in data communication

| PPTP | L2TP |
|---|---|
| Microsoft proprietary | Standards based |
| Only Windows and Linux platforms | Not platform specific |
| Microsoft encryption | IPSec encryption |
| Requires that the transmission network provide point-to-point connectivity | Requires an IP-based transmission network |
| No header compression | Supports header compression |

**Table 9-1**   Comparing the Two VPN Protocols

# Lab Exercise 9.4: Configuring a Virtual Private Network

To configure a VPN, follow these steps:

1. Open the Routing and Remote Access MMC snap-in. Expand the target server, and click the Ports node. There should be several PPTP ports and several L2TP ports, as shown in Figure 9-6. The RRAS server installed with hundreds of user licenses when the Routing and Remote Access Service was enabled.

2. To configure the ports, right-click the Ports node and select Properties. You'll see the Ports Properties dialog box, as shown in Figure 9-7.

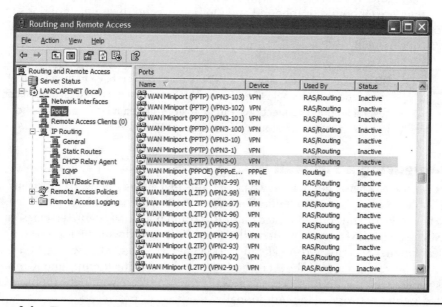

**Figure 9-6**   The configured VPN ports are displayed in the details pane.

**Figure 9-7**
The Ports
Properties

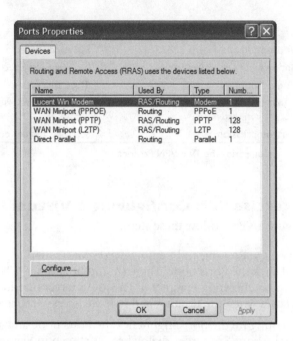

3. From the dialog box, select the protocol you want to modify and click Configure. The dialog box displayed then will let you set the direction of the interface (Inbound or Inbound and Outbound) and the number of ports to enable. You can set the phone number of a device here, although that is of little use with a VPN.

**NOTE** Part of the charm of a VPN is that you can have multiple virtual connections to a single IP address. This way, one network card can host several inbound connections, rather than require a modem and telephone line for each simultaneous remote user.

## Configuring a Firewall with a VPN

This isn't exactly news, but not every type of traffic that enters a network, especially from the public Internet, is wanted traffic. Firewalls serve as a barrier between public and private networks, filtering out unwanted traffic that could potentially harm server resources.

Microsoft's full version of its firewall software is installed with a BackOffice product called Internet Security and Acceleration (ISA) Server. A scaled-down version of this firewall, however, can easily be set up and configured with the Routing and Remote Access Service server. With RRAS's basic firewall, you can secure your network from unsolicited public network traffic. Additionally, the firewall provides a Network Address Translation (NAT) service that hides a private network from public view. When using NAT, your entire private network appears as a single IP address—the IP address of your external interface on the RRAS server.

The basic firewall examines all packets sent from and to the public interface for which the basic firewall is enabled. It then uses dynamic packet filtering, along with a set of static filters, to make decisions on which traffic will pass and which will not. Packet filtering works using a set of rules and exceptions. Packet filters can be configured to either pass all traffic except for those meeting the conditions of the rule, or discard all traffic except for those matching the criteria of the filters. Static filters are configured to accept or discard only a very specific traffic, such as traffic from a particular IP address or destined for a specific port, while dynamic filters can be used to allow or deny access on a per session basis. Dynamic filters can apply to individual users, groups, or IP subnets.

One possible use for the basic firewall is to allow only those communications from VPN clients. If so configured, the firewall will route traffic between the private network and VPN clients that are accessing it through the RRAS server. Keep in mind when you do this that you have just cut off traffic to the Internet for private computers, as the firewall will allow instead only traffic destined for the VPN clients.

**NOTE** You won't need to use the basic firewall if your network has other firewall software installed. For example, if your network is using ISA Server for proxy and firewall purposes, the basic firewall is redundant, and will likely cause more problems than it prevents. You should also configure exceptions for certain types of traffic if the firewall component blocks traffic that your network should receive.

Dynamic packet filters cannot be configured on private interfaces. If you want a greater degree of protection for your network, you can configure a static packet filter on a private interface.

## Lab Exercise 9.5: Setting Up the Basic Firewall

To configure a firewall as a part of the Routing and Remote Access Service server component, you will perform two procedures. First, you'll set up Network Address Translation by following these steps:

1. Open the Routing and Remote Access MMC snap-in, expand your server, and right-click General from the console tree.

2. From the context menu, choose New Routing Protocol.

3. In the Select Routing Protocol dialog box, click NAT/Basic Firewall, and then click OK.

Now you're ready for the second step, which is to configure the firewall component. Here's how:

1. Open the Routing and Remote Access console, expand your server, and choose NAT/Basic Firewall.

2. In the details pane, right-click the interface you want to configure (it will usually be an interface connected to a public network), right-click, and choose Properties.

3. On the NAT/Basic Firewall tab, as shown in Figure 9-8, choose one of the following radio buttons to set behavior for the firewall:

- Private interface connected to private network
- Public interface connected to the Internet, and then select "Enable a basic firewall on this interface"
- Basic firewall only

## Managing Packet Filters

Firewall is another one of those computing terms that seemingly has many different definitions, depending on whom you ask. But a firewall is essentially a packet filter, a piece of software that lives on a router. This software examines the contents of all traffic either leaving the network, entering the network, or both, and makes decisions on whether or not to pass that traffic based on the configuration settings you've set up.

**Figure 9-8**

Selecting the behavior of the firewall

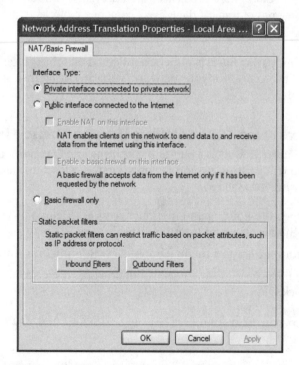

You can easily set up your Routing and Remote Access Service server to act as a firewall by configuring packet filtering. Furthermore, you have the ability to set different packet filters on different network interfaces. This allows for a great degree of flexibility when deciding how traffic flows between outside networks and the RRAS server. Generally speaking, you can configure packet filters for one of these two behaviors:

- Pass through all traffic except packets prohibited by filters
- Discard all traffic except packets allowed by filters

 **NOTE**  This discussion covers just the basics of packet filtering. For a more detailed discussion, see the Resource Kit web site at http://www.microsoft.com/. Be sure to look up Part One: Routing, where you will get further information on filtering configurations and fragmentation filtering.

The packet filtering behavior is based on *exceptions*. That is, you configure filtering rules that are based on a set of one or more conditions, and if the traffic matches the rule, a decision is made to allow or deny packets. You can set a rule to allow all traffic *except* for those packets that meet the conditions of the rule, or configure the RRAS server to deny all traffic *except* for packets that meet the conditions.

If this sounds confusing, it's usually less so once you see it in practice. Probably the best way to get familiar with a packet filter's capabilities is by configuring one. In this example, we'll be configuring a packet filter so that outside computers cannot ping the Routing and Remote Access Service server from the outside. To do so, we'll configure a filter to prevent inbound Internet Control Message Protocol (ICMP) traffic. ICMP is a protocol that reports information on behalf of IP connections. Many utilities, including the ubiquitous ping utility, use the ICMP protocol to verify connectivity.

## Lab Exercise 9.6: Creating a Packet Filter

Here's how to configure a packet filter:

1. Under the Administrative Tools, open the Routing and Remote Access MMC snap-in.

2. Expand the RRAS server where you will be configuring the packet filter, then expand IP Routing, and choose General.

3. In the details pane of the General node, choose the interface where the filter will be added, right-click, and choose Properties.

4. From the Properties dialog box, click the General tab, and select Inbound Filters.

5. From the Inbound Filters dialog box, as shown in Figure 9-9, click New.

6. Now you see the Add IP Filter dialog box where you configure the behavior of the filter. Let's say you want to prevent someone from outside the corporate

**Figure 9-9**

Configuring an inbound filter

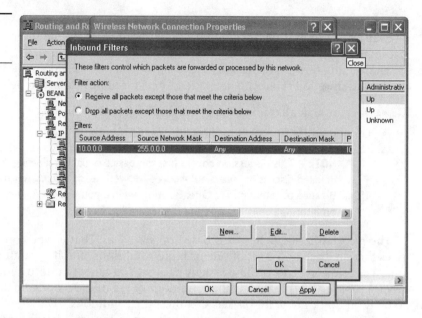

LAN from pinging your RRAS server. Choose the destination network choice, type the IP address and subnet mask, and in the Protocol drop-down box, choose the ICMP protocol. Click OK when you're done.

7. In the Inbound Filters dialog box, select the appropriate filter action. Here's where you set the exception behavior. In this instance, you will configure the action to discard packets that meet the criteria. Click OK twice when you're done.

**NOTE** This is a very common configuration of a packet filter. In fact, the firewalls guarding such Internet servers as microsoft.com and ebay.com do not allow you to ping them. How can you tell? Try opening a web site in your browser, and then open a command prompt and ping the same web site. If it's a popular web site like the ones just mentioned, you can bet the site has a firewall configured to deny inbound ICMP traffic.

Now that you've configured a firewall and added packet filters, you've just made your Windows Server 2003 system a powerful sentry for your network, guarding against undesired traffic from the public Internet.

There are other ways to secure the RRAS server, and therefore your network, besides turning on the firewall software. Users accessing the RRAS server will need to be authenticated, and you should understand the different authentication protocols available.

# Configuring Remote Access Authentication Protocols

Essentially, the authentication protocols define how user names and passwords are submitted to the RRAS server. Why is this important? Because very often the most vital piece of information transmitted over the public network during RRAS server/client communications is the user name and password, which are quite literally the keys that open the private network. Therefore, it's very important to ensure that information isn't being stolen when being sent over the public network.

Here, then is an overview of the authentication protocols available with a Microsoft Server 2003 remote connection:

- **Challenge Handshake Authentication Protocol (CHAP)**   The Challenge Handshake Authentication Protocol (CHAP) is a widely supported authentication method in which the remote access server sends the remote access client a challenge string. The remote access client uses this challenge string in conjunction with the user's password to create a Message Digest 5 (MD5) hash. (Hash algorithms are known as one-way encryption because it is easy to calculate the hash result for a block of data, but it is mathematically infeasible to determine the original data block from the hash.) The MD5 hash is sent to the remote access server. Now the remote access server, who has access to the user's password, performs the same hash calculation and compares the result with the hash sent by the client. If they match, the remote access client's credentials are considered authentic. In other words, CHAP allows for authentication without actually having the user send his password over the network. Further, because it's an industry standard, it allows Windows Server 2003 to behave as a remote client of almost any third-party PPP server.

- **Microsoft Challenge Handshake Authentication Protocol (MS-CHAP)**   MS-CHAP is used to authenticate remote Windows workstations, providing the functionality to which LAN-based users are accustomed while integrating the hashing algorithms used on Windows networks. Like CHAP, MS-CHAP uses a challenge-response mechanism to keep the password from being sent during the authentication process. MS-CHAP uses the Message Digest 4 (MD4) hashing algorithm and the Data Encryption Standard (DES) encryption algorithm to generate the challenge and response and provides mechanisms for reporting connection errors and for changing the user's password. The response packet is in a format specifically designed to work with networking products in Windows 95, Windows 98, Windows Millennium Edition, Windows NT, Windows 2000, and Windows XP. The Microsoft version(s) of CHAP provide stronger data encryption keys, and produce results specifically targeted for Windows-to-Windows remote networking. RRAS clients other than Windows clients will not be able to use MS-CHAP authentication.

- **Microsoft Challenge Handshake Authentication Protocol Version 2 (MS-CHAP v2)**   MS-CHAP version 2 is an enhancement of MS-CHAP and extends the security features offered by MS-CHAP. For example, when using MS-CHAP, a single cryptography key is used for data sent in both directions between RRAS server and RRAS client. With MS-CHAP v2, separate keys are used for the sent and the received data.

**EXAM TIP** If the user is changing passwords during the authentication process to an RRAS server running Windows Server 2003, the client must be using one of the two Microsoft-CHAP authentication methods.

- **Shiva Password Authentication Protocol (SPAP)** SPAP is supported for the sole purpose of allowing Shiva remote access clients to connect to Windows Server 2003 RAS computers and to also allow the reverse. SPAP uses a simple encrypted password authentication protocol where the remote access client sends an encrypted password to the remote access server. Using a two-way encryption algorithm, the remote access server decrypts the password and uses the plaintext form to authenticate the remote access client.

- **Password Authentication Protocol (PAP)** Use only if necessary. Password Authentication Protocol (PAP) is a simple authentication protocol in which the user name and password are sent to the remote access server in unencrypted text, making it possible for anyone listening to network traffic to steal both. PAP is typically only used when connecting to older Unix-based remote access servers that do not support any additional authentication protocols.

**NOTE** If you set up the properties of a remote connection to use a secure password, and you connect to a server that only supports PAP (Unix), Windows Server 2003's remote access client will terminate the connection.

- **Extensible Authentication Protocol (EAP)** EAP is an extension of the Point-to-Point Protocol (PPP) that supports authentication methods that go beyond the simple submission of a user name and password. EAP was developed in response to an increasing demand for authentication methods that use other types of security devices such as token cards, smart cards, and digital certificates. EAP provides an industry-standard architecture for support of additional authentication methods within PPP. Further, it provides better protection against brute-force or dictionary attacks and password guessing than the password-based authentication protocols. EAP, in conjunction with strong EAP types, is a critical technology component for highly secure VPN connections.

## Configuring Routing and Remote Access User Authentication

Once you understand the importance of RRAS authentication protocols, the next task is to enable the protocols for inbound connections. Here are the steps necessary to enable the protocols just discussed:

1. Open the Routing and Remote Access MMC snap-in, and right-click the RAS server and choose Properties.

2. From the server Properties dialog box, select the Security tab and click the Authentication Methods button. This opens the Authentication Methods dialog box, as shown in Figure 9-10.

**Figure 9-10**
Here's where you set the remote access authentication method.

**3.** Select the appropriate protocol, and click OK to return to the server Properties, and then OK to commit the changes.

## Secure Callback and Caller ID

The security features you can set for a remote access session are almost endless. One of the measures you can take is to ensure that remote clients are always calling from a particular phone number. You can also take advantage of Routing and Remote Access Service's caller ID features. Either way, you have the additional security that a user is calling from a trusted location such as a telecommuter's home or a company conference room. Further, the secure callback feature can also save on telephone charges for the user, since the call will be originated at the Routing and Remote Access Service server, and not from the RAS client. We'll take a look at each of these in the following sections.

## Caller ID

The caller ID feature is just what it sounds like. When a dial-up client establishes a remote connection, you have specified the number the user must call in from. If the number does not match, the connection attempt is rejected. Caller ID is designed to provide a greater degree of security for users who telecommute by implementing a level of physical security. Of course, this is also the caller ID's main drawback: users are limited to a specific phone line. It is therefore not a very viable option for mobile users.

To make this work, you must have a phone system that supports caller ID. It must be supported by the caller, the RRAS server, and the phone system between. Fortunately, most phone systems today, for a little extra money, do support caller ID.

Caller ID is available on VPN connections as well. When connecting via a VPN, the caller ID is the IP address of the client. But unless the client has a fixed address (and most ISPs charge extra for a fixed address), this can be very hard to implement. Usually, a dial-up Internet client gets an IP address from a DHCP server.

## Callback

When you take advantage of the callback feature, you are also ensuring the phone number is at a physically secure location. That way, even if someone were to steal a user's logon credentials, the stealing party would still need physical access to the phone line the user calls in from.

But understand that even when using callback, the remote access client still initiates the session. The user calls in and connects with the remote access server, and only after authentication and authorization does the remote access server call back. The remote access server drops the initial call and then calls back to a number set by the caller or a preconfigured callback number.

One advantage of callback is that it's not dependent on the caller ID service from the phone companies providing the phone service. But probably the biggest reason it's used is to reduce the cost of a remote access client making the call, or to make sure that the charge is on the company bill, not the telecommuter's.

Users' callback options are configured from the Properties pages of their user account. As shown in Figure 9-11, there are three callback options to choose from:

- No Callback (the default)
- Set by Caller
- Always Callback to

**Figure 9-11**

Setting callback options

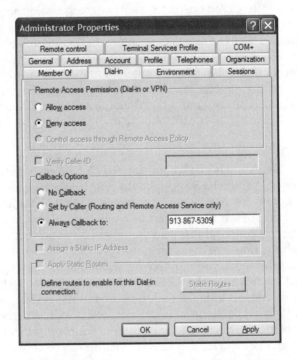

**TIP** With the exception of authentication credentials, no data from remote access client to remote access server is transferred until after the user has been authenticated, authorized, and called back.

## Remote Access Account Lockout

Imagine that someone has figured out the phone number to your remote access server. Imagine further that this person knows someone at your office and has figured out their user account name. With these two pieces of information in hand, they could begin dialing up and trying password after password in an attempt to hack into your network. Or could they?

With the remote access account lockout feature, you have the ability to specify how many times a remote access authentication fails against a valid user account before the user is denied access. This is especially important when configuring remote access over a VPN connection, as no dialing in is necessary, and it is less likely that you will implement any physical security over the connection. Just like you don't want users trying to log on to your domain over and over again on the LAN, you don't want the same when accessing resources via the RRAS server.

Once you've enabled remote access account lockout, any random password hacks are thwarted after a number of failed attempts you specify. When configuring the remote access lockout behavior, there are two variables you must keep in mind:

- **How many failed attempts are allowed before future attempts are denied** After each unsuccessful attempt, a counter for the user account is incremented. If the user account's failed attempts counter reaches the configured maximum, the user won't be able to attempt another connection. If a user mistypes his password, but then successfully authenticates, the failed attempts counter is reset. That is, the failed attempts counter does not accumulate beyond a successful authentication.

- **How often the failed attempts counter is reset** The failed attempts counter is reset after a specific period of time. If an account has been locked out after tripping the failed attempts threshold, it is automatically reset to 0 after the configured reset time.

To configure the remote access lockout feature, you must open the registry and modify settings as follows.

**NOTE** These settings are modified on the computer that's providing the remote session authentication. For example, if the remote access server is configured for Windows Authentication, you will configure the registry on the RRAS server computer. However, if the RRAS server passes authentication along to another authentication server, such as a RADIUS server, you need to modify the registry on that server instead. The role of the RADIUS server is discussed in just a bit.

The first parameter that must be set is turning remote access lockout on. To enable remote access account lockout, you must set the MaxDenials entry in the registry to 1 or greater. To find the MaxDenials entry, look in this registry subkey:

```
HKEY_LOCAL_MACHINE\SYSTEM\CurrentControlSet\Services\RemoteAccess\Parameters\
AccountLockout
```

By default, MaxDenials is set to 0, which means that remote access account lockout is disabled.

You might want to change the default time before the failed attempts counter is reset, which is 48 hours. To do so, you modify the ResetTime (mins) entry in the registry to the required number of minutes. The ResetTime (mins) entry can be found in this registry subkey:

```
HKEY_LOCAL_MACHINE\SYSTEM\CurrentControlSet\Services\RemoteAccess\Parameters\
AccountLockout
```

The default time here is set to the hex value of 0xb40, or 2,880 minutes. Divide by 60, and you get a lockout duration of 48 hours.

### Resetting an Account that Is Locked Out

If you're dealing with a legitimate account whose user has simply forgotten their password, you might not want to wait until the failed attempts counter resets. In this case, you need to manually reset the user account after it's been locked out. To do so, simply delete the following registry subkey that corresponds to the user's account name:

```
HKEY_LOCAL_MACHINE\SYSTEM\CurrentControlSet\Services\RemoteAccess\Parameters\
AccountLockout\domain name:user name
```

And if you've heard all the admonishments about deleting stuff in the registry, and are worried about the implications thereof, don't be. When the lockout count for a user account is reset to 0 due to either a successful authentication or an automatic reset, the registry subkey for the user account is deleted anyway.

# Configure Routing and Remote Access Policies to Permit or Deny Access

A remote access policy is a set of actions that are applied to users as they try to establish a connection to the Routing and Remote Access Services server. You won't get far into the 70-291 exam without seeing a question about Remote Access Policies. They are to the 70-291 what Group Policies are to the 70-294 (to be discussed in Part IV): without a pretty thorough understanding, you're probably throwing money away if you sit for the test. Remote Access Policies work by evaluating each remote connection attempt. A connection attempt either meets or does not meet a set of specific *conditions*. These conditions can include the time, what user or group is trying to connect, and from what IP address they are connecting.

Moreover, each condition has one or more *attributes* that help define the condition, and these attributes can vary from condition to condition. For example, one of the attributes of the Windows Groups condition is the name of the group.

If you've ever taken a logic class, or maybe even written software code, you might already be familiar with some of the underpinnings of remote access policies. At their heart, they are a series of If Then/And Then statements. These remote access policies act as a sort of bureaucratic mechanism over remote access to the LAN. It's as if they question any connections made, asking, in effect (if you've got your remote access policy set this way), "*If* your connection is made between the hours of 8:00 A.M. and 5:00 P.M., forget it. *If*, on the other hand, you are connecting between 5:00 P.M. and 8:00 A.M., *and* you are a member of the Windows 2003 global group Sales and your account has permission to do so, *then* you're granted remote access to the network."

Even if you know what you're doing, it can get quite complex toot-sweet. That's why Remote Access Policy guidelines recommend keeping it as simple as possible, as we'll soon see. Let's first talk more about the logic behind the Remote Access Policy evaluations.

## Evaluating a Connection Attempt

Any time a remote access connection attempt is made, that connection is compared to the policies in place. But not just any policy. A match is tried against the *first* policy in the list of remote access policies. The policies then evaluate and authorize the attempt using a general logic flow as follows:

- If the connection attempt *matches* all policy conditions, RRAS checks the remote access permission setting of the account:
  - If the remote access permission of the user account is set to grant access, the connection settings of the policy profile and user account are applied.
  - If the remote access permission is set to deny access, reject the connection attempt.
- If the connection attempt *does not match* all policy conditions, the next remote access policy in the list is processed.
- If the connection attempt does not match *all* conditions of *any* remote access policy, the connections attempt is rejected.

The behavior of RRAS connection evaluation is summarized in Figure 9-12.

## The Default Remote Access Policies

Once you've activated the Routing and Remote Access Service, two default policies are created in the Remote Access Policies container, as shown in Figure 9-13. These two policies work to deny all remote access attempts unless dial-in permission is specifically enabled for a user's account.

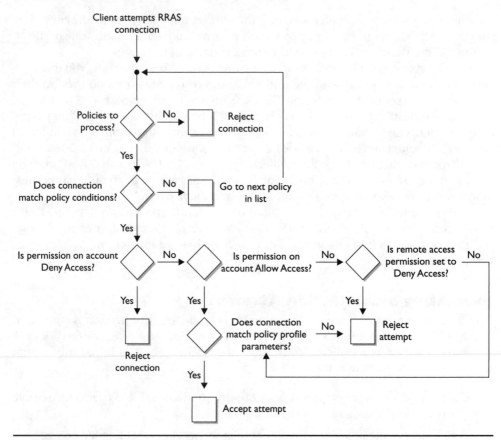

**Figure 9-12**  Evaluating a Remote Access connection attempt

What's more, in an Active Directory domain, all user accounts are set by default to control remote access through remote access policy, so the net result of the default policies and the default settings of a user account is to deny all connection attempts.

This first policy defines connections made from Microsoft RAS software. The second is for pretty much every connection attempt, no matter what the RAS vendor or the time of day the connection is attempted. Notice that both of these policies are set to deny access. To investigate the properties of these two remote access policies, right-click the policy and choose Properties.

If you want to enforce certain restrictions globally of the RRAS server, you might consider editing the conditions or profile properties of one or both of the default policies. For example, you could edit the default Connections to Microsoft Routing and Remote Access Server policy to require encryption.

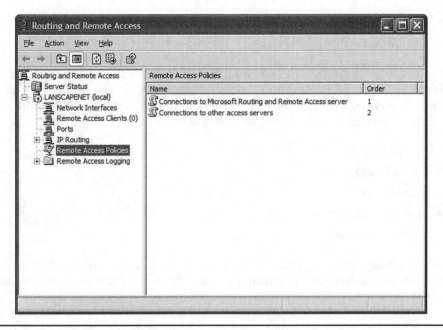

**Figure 9-13**    There are two default remote access policies created.

# Creating a Remote Access Policy

The remote access policies you configure will be made up of a number of connection parameters before determining a match. These parameters include connections that meet the following conditions:

- Group membership
- Type of connection
- Time of day
- Authentication methods
- Remote access permission
- Whether user account dial-in properties are ignored

The policies can be further configured to manage behavior of connections once they've been allowed. These restrictions on connection behavior, known as the profile of the connection, include

- Maximum session time
- Encryption strength
- IP packet filters

- Idle timeout time
- IP address for PPP connections

And you're not done there. Say you want to further specify that members of a particular Windows group have access only during certain periods of the day, or only using a dial-up connection, and then only from a certain phone number You can further set connection restrictions based on the following settings:

- Group membership
- Type of connection
- Time of day
- Authentication methods
- Identity of the access server

So your ability to manage your remote connections is almost limitless. Using the settings in a remote access policy, you can configure whatever restrictions on remote access you choose.

When you create a remote access policy, it will be configured to either allow or deny access. When a connection attempt meets the criteria set in a policy, that's only half of the puzzle. The other half is that policy's decision about whether to grant access to the server.

## Lab Exercise 9.7: Creating a Remote Access Policy

Here's how to create a remote access policy:

1. Open the Routing and Remote Access MMC snap-in from the Administrative Tools.

2. Expand the Routing and Remote Access server where you'll create the policy, right-click the Remote Access Policies, and choose New Remote Access Policy.

3. The New Remote Access Policy Wizard opens. Click Next, and then enter a name for the policy, as shown in Figure 9-14. The radio buttons let you choose whether to set up a custom policy or one that is based on Microsoft suggestions. For this exercise, create a custom policy and click Next.

4. The Policy Conditions screen lets you add conditions for the policy. As we discussed, different conditions will have different attributes. If your condition is Day-and-Time Restrictions, the attributes of that condition would be what day and what time connections can be made.

**Figure 9-14**
The Policy
Configuration
Method screen

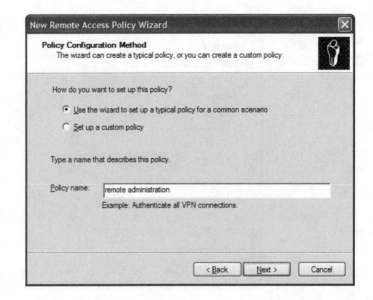

5. For this example, we'll work with the Windows-Groups attribute. Select the attribute and then click Add to open the Select Groups dialog box, as shown in Figure 9-15.

6. After making your selections. Note that you can add multiple conditions to a policy, so that connections would have to meet both criteria in order to have the policy apply.

7. Click Next. The Permissions screen of the wizard appears, as shown in Figure 9-16. Here's where you set the behavior of the policy. You have two choices. If the conditions of the policy are met, you can either grant access or deny access. So if you want to implement the inverse of the example described above (users in the Sales group *cannot* access the network remotely) you would click Deny. To allow access, click the Grant option.

**Figure 9-15**
Add attributes of
a condition.

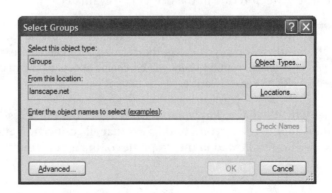

**Figure 9-16**
Remote access
permissions

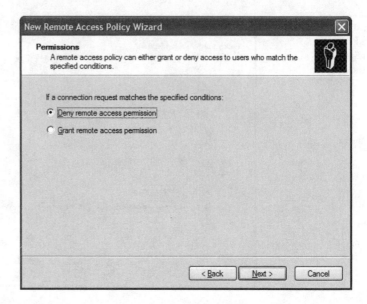

8. Click Next, and the Edit Dial-In Profile screen appears. You can restrict a number of connection parameters here, which we will discuss in detail later on in the chapter.

9. Click OK to return to the User Profile screen, and then Finish to complete the creation of the policy.

**TIP**   Remote access policies are a separate beast than Group Policies, and as such you should know where the remote access policies are stored. They are on the Routing and Remote Access servers, not on the domain controllers, where other domain policies (such as Group Policies) live.

What if you're connecting and you don't meet the conditions of the remote access policy? As you might expect, the policy won't apply then. If there's a list of remote access policies, the next one in the list will be evaluated.

**NOTE**   If all of the Routing and Remote Access policies have been deleted (in other words, you delete the default policy before creating any other effective policies), remote users will be denied access to the network through the RRAS server. Period.

That's why it's vital to know about that default remote access policy and who it applies to. It applies to everyone, and it says that all connection attempts will be rejected unless specifically allowed in the Properties of the user account.

**NOTE**  For this reason, many Routing and Remote Access servers' policies are not trifled with. Usually, you can just enable a few specific accounts for remote access for the ones that really need it and leave the others alone. This is pretty effective in accomplishing most companies' remote access objectives.

# Configuring Internet Authentication Service (IAS)

Remote access servers are nothing new to computer communications, and neither is the requirement that a user be authenticated before being granted access to the network. If you are dialing up to an ISP, that service provider is going to want you to have paid for a valid account before granting access to their network (the Internet). And, if they are charging you for time, they are definitely going to want to know how long you've been using the connection. Even if they are not charging, it is vital to know how long you are using the connection so that capacity needs can be anticipated. How is this authentication done and how is the usage information collected? With a RADIUS server.

In fact, whenever you're being charged in any way for network access (including accessing the Internet from your home connection), chances are that you're being authenticated by a server running the Remote Authentication Dial-In User Service (RADIUS). RADIUS is a standards-based protocol that provides authentication and accounting services.

## The Role of RADIUS

If a RADIUS server provides authentication, a RADIUS client sends user credentials and connection information in the form of a RADIUS message. What is the RADIUS client? In the case of Windows Server 2003, the RRAS server.

The RAS server takes the user logon request and forwards it on to the RADIUS server. The RADIUS server then authenticates the RADIUS client request against whatever database of user accounts that's being used, and subsequently generates a RADIUS message response. This RADIUS client (the RAS server), during the session, also sends RADIUS accounting messages to RADIUS servers so that information can be tracked about network usage.

Additionally, the RADIUS standards support the use of RADIUS proxies. A RADIUS proxy is a computer that forwards RADIUS messages between RADIUS-enabled computers.

If you want to implement a RADIUS server on your network for any of the reasons above, you can use Microsoft's version of the RADIUS server, called the Internet Authentication Service (IAS). IAS is RADIUS that can be installed alongside an existing RRAS solution.

## Lab Exercise 9.8: Installing the Internet Authentication Service

Here's how to install the Internet Authentication Service:

1. Open the Control Panel, and double-click Add/Remove Programs. Then choose Add/Remove Windows Components.

2. In the Windows Components Wizard, click Networking Services, and then Details. In the Networking Services dialog box, choose Internet Authentication Service, and click Next (you might be prompted for the installation files).

3. After IAS is installed, click Finish, and then click Close.

Now you've provided another authentication mechanism for dial-up or virtual private network clients.

 **NOTE**   You aren't required to use Microsoft's IAS if you need to implement RADIUS. Because of its open-standards nature, you are welcome to use an existing RADIUS solution and have the RRAS server send authentication requests to it instead of IAS.

# Managing TCP/IP Routing

Although most computer users are unaware, *every* TCP/IP host on a network also routes packets, not just the devices with multiple network cards. In the case of a simple computer with a single network card, the system decides if the packet's destination network address is the local network or the remote network. (It does this using the logical AND operation on the source and destination IP addresses, which was discussed in Chapter 7.) If the packet needs to be delivered to a remote network, the computer forwards, or routes, the packet to the default gateway.

It makes this decision about where to route packets—which have been determined through the ANDing process (see Chapter 7) to belong on remote networks—based on the entries in its routing table. You can view your system's routing table by opening a command prompt and using the route print command, as shown in Figure 9-17.

The routing table entries allow your system to determine the route to other network computers, including itself.

Upon receiving a packet, a router performs a calculation to determine the packet's destination network address. One this information is in hand, the router makes a decision on where to best forward the packet after it consults its routing table. The router then takes the following considerations:

- If the routing table contains an entry for the destination network address, and the router is directly connected to that network, it will forward the packet to that destination network using the destination host address.

- If the routing table contains an entry for the destination network, but the router is not directly connected to that network, the router will forward the packet to the router specified in the routing table entry.

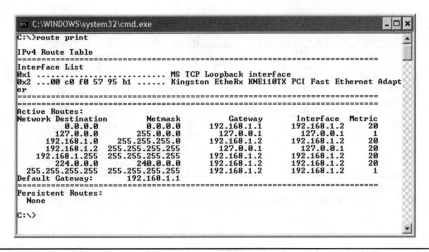

**Figure 9-17** Every TCP/IP computer has a routing table.

- If the routing table does not contain an entry for the destination network, the router forwards the packet along to *its* configured default gateway.

## Managing Routing Tables

Before a packet is forwarded, a chart is consulted to make sure the packet is sent along the best possible path. This chart is the computer's routing table, and on routers, managing the contents of the routing table is paramount to the router's trouble-free operation.

What's more, every computer with TCP/IP installed has a routing table. Figure 9-18 displays what you will see in a typical routing table.

Let's take a closer look at the information in the routing table to see what instructions it gives to the router itself. The entries in a routing table consist of the following information:

- **Destination** The network ID for a route. This number is used in conjunction with the subnet mask to determine the destination network path using the destination IP address information of a packet.

- **Network mask** The subnet mask that helps determine a destination network ID.

- **Gateway** The IP address where the packet is sent. For networks where the host or router is directly attached, the gateway address field may be the address of that interface which is attached to the network.

- **Interface** The interface that's used to send the packet to the destination network ID.

- **Metric** A measurement of the directness of a route. Most often, the lowest metric is the preferred, and fastest, route. If multiple routes exist for a given network destination, the route with the lowest metric is used.

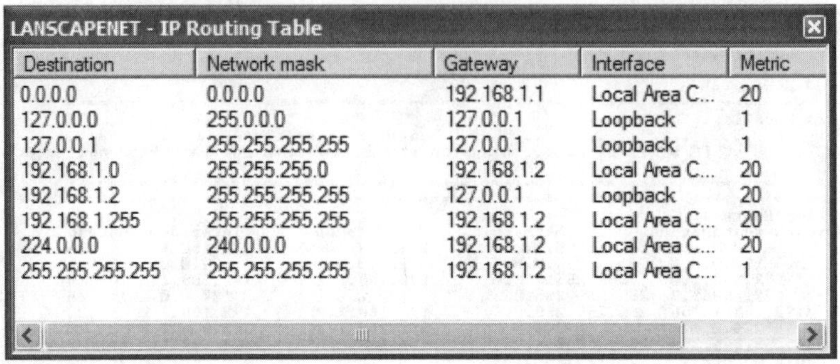
LANSCAPENET - IP Routing Table

| Destination | Network mask | Gateway | Interface | Metric |
|---|---|---|---|---|
| 0.0.0.0 | 0.0.0.0 | 192.168.1.1 | Local Area C... | 20 |
| 127.0.0.0 | 255.0.0.0 | 127.0.0.1 | Loopback | 1 |
| 127.0.0.1 | 255.255.255.255 | 127.0.0.1 | Loopback | 1 |
| 192.168.1.0 | 255.255.255.0 | 192.168.1.2 | Local Area C... | 20 |
| 192.168.1.2 | 255.255.255.255 | 127.0.0.1 | Loopback | 20 |
| 192.168.1.255 | 255.255.255.255 | 192.168.1.2 | Local Area C... | 20 |
| 224.0.0.0 | 240.0.0.0 | 192.168.1.2 | Local Area C... | 20 |
| 255.255.255.255 | 255.255.255.255 | 192.168.1.2 | Local Area C... | 1 |

**Figure 9-18** A routing table as viewed with the graphical RRAS interface

## Working with a Static Route

If you recall our simple definition of a router, it's a computer with two network cards. These two network cards, then, are attached to two different logical IP networks. The routing table helps direct traffic that is passed through the router.

Now that you've got a router, you have a routing table you need to be able to configure in order for that router to pass along traffic to the proper network. There are two ways the routing table can be built and modified: either manually or automatically.

## Adding a Static Route

You can add routes to the routing table with the route add command, or the Routing and Remote Access graphical interface. As part of the route add command, you'll specify the route, the network mask, and the destination IP address of the network card your router will use to get the packet to its destination network.

Here's the syntax to use with the route add command:

```
Route add network_address mask subnet_mask gateway_address
```

In the syntax, *network_address* is the network ID you are configuring a route for, *subnet_mask* is the subnet mask that is used to obtain the network ID, and *gateway_address* is the path the packet will take to get to the network.

Further, you can use the -p parameter when using the route add command to configure the route as persistent. A persistent route will be kept in the registry, and will be recreated each time you restart your server. In other words, you're setting up a permanent routing table record.

When using the graphical interface, you can right-click the Static Routes node below IP routing, and choose New Static Route. You'll get a dialog box like the one you see in Figure 9-19, and you will be prompted for the destination network ID, network mask, and gateway address. It's just like using the route add command with a little less typing.

**Figure 9-19**
Adding a static
route

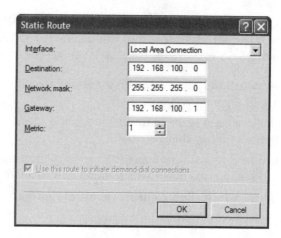

**NOTE** The routes you add using the Routing and Remote Access MMC snap-in are persistent. They remain configured until you delete them manually.

## Managing Routing Protocols

The other way to manage a router's routing tables is to let the computer do it for you. Just like letting DHCP allocate IP addresses, configuring a dynamic routing protocol usually means less errors due to human error, and less administrative overhead.

The routing protocols used by Windows Server 2003 use one of two kinds of algorithms to determine the best possible path for a packet to get to its destination, either distance vector or link state.

## Routing Information Protocol (RIP)

The distance vector protocol in use on Windows 2003 is called Routing Information Protocol (RIP) for IP. This protocol was designed for the exchange of routing information within a small to medium-size IP network. It is not, however, ideal for larger networks, as will be discussed later. It also can be used as a dynamic routing protocol for NWLink networks (Microsoft's version of IPX/SPX), in which case it's called RIP for IPX/SPX.

When you first enable a router on a Windows Server 2003 machine, the routing table includes entries only for the networks that are physically connected. When RIP is enabled for an interface, the router will periodically send an announcement of its routing table to inform other RIP routers of the networks it can reach. RIP version 1 uses broadcast packets for its announcements. RIP version 2 offers an improvement and can be configured to use either multicast or broadcast packets when communicating with other routers. Also, RIP version 2 offers more flexibility in subnetted and classless interdomain routing (CIDR) environments.

The biggest advantage of RIP is its simplicity. With a few clicks in the Routing and Re-mote Access Server MMC console, you can deploy RIP. With the RIP dynamic routing protocol installed on Windows Server 2003, you get the following features:

- RIP version 1 and version 2, with the ability to configure individual network cards with separate versions.
- Calculations used to avoid routing loops and speed recovery of the network whenever topology changes occur.
- Route filters; you can configure RIP to accept information from only certain networks, and also choose which routes will be shared with other RIP routers.
- Peer filters, which allow control over which router announcements are accepted.
- Simple password authentication support.

But there are significant drawbacks, which makes RIP a poor, if not unusable solution for large networks. For example, the maximum hop count used for RIP routers is 15, making networks 16 hops away (or more) unreachable where RIP is concerned. Another disadvantage of RIP is that it's a chatty protocol, broadcasting the entire routing table to its RIP partners. And RIP routers can suffer from slow latency time. When changes are made to the network topology, it can take several minutes before the RIP routers recon-figure themselves to reflect the changes, resulting in lost or undeliverable data until the routing tables are properly updated.

 **NOTE** A hop is an intermediate network device (usually a multihomed device like a router), which a packet must pass through before it gets to its destination.

## Open Shortest Path First (OSPF)

Where RIP is built to work easily in smaller networks, the Open Shortest Path First (OSPF) routing protocol is designed large or very large networks. The goal is the same: information about connections to other networks is shared from one router to another. It offers several advantages over RIP, especially significant in large networks:

- Routes calculated with OSPF are always loop-free.
- OSPF can scale much more easily than RIP.
- Reconfiguration for network topology changes is faster.

The biggest reason OSPF is the choice in larger networks is its efficiency; instead of ex-changing routing tables via broadcast the way RIP does, OSPF-configured routers main-tain a map of the network. This mapping is called the link state database (hence, it's a link state protocol). Much like domain controllers synchronize the Active Directory da-tabase, OSPF routers keep the link state database up to date. As a further contrast to the behavior of RIP, only changes to the link state database are replicated to partner routers.

Once changes have been made to the link state database, an OSPF router's link state database is recalculated.

As networks start to multiply, the size of the link state database increases, and a corresponding hit on router performance results. To combat this, OSPF subdivides the network into smaller sections, called areas. Areas are connected to each other through a *backbone area*, with each router only responsible for the link state database for those areas connected to the router. Area border routers (ABRs) then connect one backbone area to another.

The biggest drawback of OSPF is its complexity; OSPF requires proper planning and is more difficult to configure and administer. If you are implementing a dynamic routing protocol for a smaller network (if you are administering 10 or more routers in your network), RIP is all you should really need.

**NOTE**   The OSPF protocol is not available on the 64-bit versions of the Windows Server 2003 family.

# Configuring Routing and Remote Access for DHCP Integration

If you have users connecting to your Routing and Remote Access Service server, they will still need an IP address before they can pass information to the LAN. Again, this is not really different from using the LAN.

But how will these users obtain their IP addresses? Just like with the LAN, the best way is through the services of DHCP. All you need to do is tell the Routing and Remote Access Service server how and where.

When the Routing and Remote Access Service server is configured to use DHCP, it grabs ten IP addresses from the DHCP server. This DHCP server can be another computer on the network, or the service can live on the RRAS server itself. The Routing and Remote Access Service server uses the first IP address obtained for the network card that serves as the RAS interface, and then allocates the other IP addresses to client computers as they establish their connections.

When all ten IP addresses have been handed out by the RRAS server, another ten IP addresses are requested, and if available, appropriated by the RRAS component.

### Lab Exercise 9.9: Integrating RRAS and DHCP

Here's how to configure Routing and Remote Access for DHCP integration:

1. Open the Routing and Remote Access snap-in, and then right-click the server you want to manage. Select Properties.

2. From the IP tab, click the Dynamic Host Configuration Protocol radio button, as shown in Figure 9-20.

**Figure 9-20**
One click and all remote access clients get their IP addresses the same way they do when at the office.

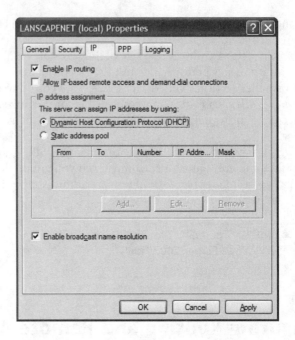

Once configured, the Routing and Remote Access Service server will allocate IP addresses gotten from DHCP to both dial-in and VPN clients.

# Implementing Secure Access Between Private Networks

Because RRAS transmits data over a public network (the Internet), care must sometimes be taken to encrypt not only the user names and passwords, but also the data itself. Fortunately, there are several encryption technologies available with Windows Server 2003's version of RRAS that makes this possible.

Although these topics are discussed in greater detail Part III in this book, it is important to note some of the encryption protocols here, as they will often be implemented in conjunction with an RRAS solution.

## Data Encryption

The available encryption methods for IPSec include the following:

- **Data Encryption Standard (DES)**   Through your IPSec policies, you can implement DES as the encryption method. The DES algorithm is a 56-bit encryption key. This algorithm was published in 1977 by the U.S. National Bureau of Standards, and allows for the ability to frequently regenerate keys during a communication. This prevents the entire data set from being compromised if one DES key is broken. However, its use is considered outdated for business use, and should only be used for legacy application support. Specialized hardware has been able to crack the standard 56-bit key.

- **Triple DES (3DES)**   IPSec policies also allow the choice of a strong encryption algorithm, 3DES, which provides stronger encryption than DES for higher security. 3DES uses a 56-bit encryption key as well, but, as the name implies, uses three of them. As a result, 3DES is considered 168-bit encryption, and is used in high security environments like the U.S. government. All computers to which the policy is assigned will receive this policy.

 **NOTE**   As of this writing, the export of 3DES applications required government approval.

# Chapter Review

We covered quite a bit of material that you should expect to see on the 70-291 exam, and should also expect to encounter in real working networks. We covered the behavior and purpose of remote access, and its two basic versions: dial-up and VPN. Furthermore, we looked extensively at how to secure remote access through such mechanisms as encryption of data and secure callback.

Since the function of a Routing and Remote Access Service server is to route packets between public and private networks, we also spent time covering the essence of IP routing as implemented on RRAS, and how we could further manage routing behavior with the use of packet filters. A thorough knowledge of the RRAS material is essential to ensure the best chance at test success. Now let's look at some questions.

## Questions

1. You are administering the company's RRAS server. The company has many salespeople, many of whom work out of their homes, and therefore there is a heavy reliance on VPNs. You find that you have run out of VPN ports, and need to configure the RRAS server to allow for additional VPN connections. How do you do this?

   A. Run the VPN Wizard and configure the additional ports.

   B. Open the Networking and Dial-Up Connections window and launch the New Connection Wizard. From the wizard interface, select the New Inbound VPN selection, and then follow the prompts.

   C. In the Routing and Remote Access console, edit the properties of the L2TP ports and add the additional required connections.

   D. In the Routing and Remote Access console, edit the properties of the IPSec ports and add the additional required connections.

2. You are administering a small network and need to configure the Routing and Remote Access Service server to implement smart card authentication. What protocol do you need to do this?

   A. EAP

   B. MS-CHAP v2

   C. PPTP

   D. IPSec

3. You are configuring an RRAS server, and have set up multilink so that multiple dial-in connections can be combined into one logical connection. Yet you know that the connections will be heavily accessed. To prevent users from tying up resources, you want to configure the server so that connections that are idle will automatically be dropped. What protocol is required to accomplish your goal?

   A. PPP

   B. BAP

   C. PPTP

   D. EAP

4. You are the RRAS administrator for a company, 80 percent of whose users telecommute. You have just installed and configured a new Windows 2003 Routing and Remote Access Service server. Your clients, though, still use an older third-party PPP dialer used for the old system, and upgrading these remote systems would be an arduous task. What is the most secure protocol that can be used for these connections?

   A. PAP

   B. EAP

   C. CHAP

   D. IPSec

5. You are administering a Windows 2003 RRAS server and have a user who is trying to connect to the LAN through a dial-up connection. He reports that he is given a logon screen, but when he enters his user name and password, he gets a message saying he is not an authorized user. He is able to log in at the office, however. What is the nature of the problem?

   A. He is using a password that is not supported by the RRAS policies.

   B. He is using an account that is not authorized to use the RRAS server.

   C. He is using the wrong account; he needs to log in with his roaming account.

   D. The modem on the RRAS server is likely down.

6. You are administering a company where several researchers are sending in large updates to databases from the field. They always use the same numbers for

their dial-in connections, but are racking up large toll charges on calling cards when they do. How can you configure RRAS to minimize these toll charges and take advantage of cheaper long distance rates?

**A.** Configure a remote access policy to deny connection attempts that are using a calling card.

**B.** Use IPSec to create a VPN tunnel to the RRAS server using the PSTN.

**C.** Secure a personal toll-free number for each dial-in connection.

**D.** Configure Routing and Remote Access to use callback security.

7. You are administering a large global organization with hundreds of field researchers who need to connect and submit data to the organization's database almost daily. The field researchers' computers all have smart cards they use with a RADIUS server for authentication. You have just installed a Windows Server 2003 computer and want to incorporate the RADIUS authentication for the RRAS server. Which authentication protocol should you set the RRAS server to use for the RADIUS server?

**A.** MS-CHAP

**B.** Shiva PAP

**C.** EAP

**D.** PAP

8. You have configured a Windows Server 2003 system with Routing and Remote Access and have created a policy that restricts what time of day users in your Active Directory domain are able to access the dial-in server. The time of day policy does not appear to be working, however, as users are still being granted access to the RRAS server when they should not. What's the problem?

**A.** The time of day policy has not been replicated to all of your Active Directory domain controllers yet.

**B.** The time of day policy is last in the list of policies.

**C.** The time of day policy is listed first in the list of policies.

**D.** The time of day policy is not linked to any remote access profiles.

9. You have configured a Windows Server 2003 system as a VPN server, and you are under instructions from the company's CIO to use only the L2TP protocol for VPN connections. The CIO further instructs that the VPN use data encryption to protect potentially sensitive information. What should you do?

**A.** Use L2TP with a dedicated VPN hardware solution.

**B.** Use L2TP in a Windows Active Directory domain that's been converted to native mode.

**C.** Use PPTP instead of L2TP.

**D.** Use L2TP with the IPSec for encryption.

10. A user in your network is tying to access the networks RRAS server through a VPN connection, but is unable to do so. You check the server to verify that there are free ports for the connection. What else should you check to make sure the VPN connection can be made?

   A. The user must be using compatible VPN protocols.

   B. The user must have dial-in permission.

   C. The connection attempt must match all conditions in at least one remote access policy.

   D. All of the above.

11. A user in your Active Directory domain has been using the RRAS server for several days for access to private resources. Today, however, the connection has been refused. You go to the RRAS server and discover that all of the VPN ports are being used. Which of the following is true about the user's connection?

   A. The user's connection will be held in the RRAS queue until new VPN ports are created.

   B. The connection has been refused.

   C. The connection is being held pending a free port opening up.

   D. The connection has been accepted, but network resources will not be available until a VPN port becomes free.

12. A user in your network is trying to dial in to the company's RRAS server on a Sunday, but is denied access. On Monday, you check the remote access policies you've configured and notice that the conditions for a group she belongs to has day and time restrictions of Monday through Saturday, 5:00 P.M. to 1:00 A.M. What should you explain to her about why the problem occurred?

   A. You forgot to activate the policy.

   B. The policy was not listed first in the list of remote access policies.

   C. The policy was working as designed.

   D. The user met a previous set of conditions as well, and that policy denied access.

13. You are configuring a Routing and Remote Access Service server that will provide access to the Internet for your corporate LAN. Your company has a written policy that the Internet connection should not be used for personal surfing. The Internet connection exists for VPN traffic to branch offices and for delivery of e-mail. Management occasionally uses the Internet access to download new tax forms into their accounting product, and has approved use of the Internet for updates to the Windows operating system. And for fantasy football. How can you best implement this written company policy of restricting Internet access for specific purposes?

    **A.** Configure a Group Policy that removes Internet Explorer from the users' list of available programs.

    **B.** Configure IP packet filters to regulate Internet access.

    **C.** Modify the properties of all client computers' Internet Explorer settings to control which web sites are viewable and which are not.

    **D.** Create static routing entries on the RRAS server to control access to web sites based on which network the web server lives on.

14. You have just set up a new RRAS server with three network cards to route traffic between several subnets in an office building. There are other routers in the building, ten in total. This RRAS server, however, does not seem to be routing traffic, though it is otherwise functioning normally. You check the server settings and everything seems to be configured properly. What is the likely problem? (Choose all that apply.)

    **A.** The router's authentication credentials are wrong.

    **B.** There aren't any RIP routers elsewhere in the network.

    **C.** There is no static default route.

    **D.** No routes are being learned by other peers.

## Answers

1. **C.** You need to open the RRAS console and add more L2TP ports. Five are automatically configured when you install Routing and Remote Access. IPSec is the security protocol used to secure the L2TP connections, not the protocol that establishes the VPN connection.

2. **A.** EAP is needed for support of smart card authentication, and you should expect to get a question requiring you to know this on the exam.

3. **B.** The Bandwidth Allocation Protocol can be configured in conjunction with multilink protocol to drop connections when bandwidth needs to be freed up for additional connections.

4. **C.** The highest level of security you can achieve with this configuration is the CHAP protocol authentication. CHAP is supported by almost all third-party dialers. PAP could be used, but it does not secure the password in any way. IPSec secures the data over an L2TP connection, but is not an authentication protocol.

5. **B.** The user has an account that is not authorized to access the network remotely. You must be authorized in a remote access policy before you can connect to Routing and Remote Access via dial-in. The default remote access policy denies all logon attempts unless the accounts have been specifically enabled in Active Directory Users and Computers.

6. **D.** When you configure the Routing and Remote Access server to use callback, all charges will appear on the company's ling distance plan, and not on a calling card.

7. **C.** You can use multiple authentication methods, but if you are forwarding requests to a RADIUS server, you need to configure the RRAS server to use the Extensible Authentication Protocol (EAP), which allows for proper formatting of the authentication request.

8. **B.** Remote access policies are evaluated in the order in which they appear in the Remote Access Policies node. In this case, the default policy whose time and day parameters match all connection attempts is being applied to the connection attempts. It's assumed that the accounts have the permission to obtain remote access, as they would need to anyway for the time and day policy you have configured to be in effect.

9. **D.** L2TP and IPSec use separate negotiation methods for making a connection. L2TP negotiates the VPN tunnel, while IPSec handles the security handshake. Using L2TP alone would leave an unsecured tunnel.

10. **E.** All of these conditions must be met before successfully running the gauntlet of remote access.

11. **B.** No new connections will be accepted when there are no available ports. There is no such thing as an RRAS queue, and there is no pending status of VPN connection attempts. Either the connection is accepted or it is rejected.

12. **C.** The policy was working. The policy conditions are set to reject connection attempts made on Sundays (as well as weekday mornings), and the connection made by the user on Sunday did not meet that condition.

13. **B.** IP packet filters examine the contents of either inbound or outbound (or both) IP packets and can control which source and destination address can be accessed. In this scenario, you could build a packet filter that drops all IP traffic except for packets bound for specified IP addresses. Modifying the properties of all browsers is not a workable solution and could be modified by knowledgeable users.

14. **C and D.** If no routes from other routers are being sent to a router with a dynamic routing protocol, it won't know about the other networks it can reach. Also, if there is no default route configured, the router is unable to send packets for which it does not have an entry in its routing table.

# Managing Network Security

In this chapter, you will learn how to
- Implement security baseline settings and audit security settings using security templates
- Implement the principle of least privilege
- Monitor and troubleshoot network protocol security
- Use IP Security Monitor
- Use Kerberos support tools

Secure network administration practices are used ostensibly to keep your data safe. In reality, they keep your job safe. Nothing can demonstrate the need for alternate network administration procedures, usually implemented by alternate network personnel, than a loss or compromise of critical data.

In other words, when hackers attack your data, they also attack your livelihood.

Bear in mind that the term "hackers" gets overused. Typically, you'll need to protect the network's data from the actual users of the network, both those who are merely curious and those who have no ill intent, but can't resist clicking around.

To make your network more secure, you should be familiar with implementing a baseline of security settings, and also with some of the governing principles behind computing security.

## Security Baseline Settings and Security Templates

One of the best tools at your disposal for configuring security settings on a Windows Server 2003 system is a security template. A security template is a single file that stores a series of security-related settings. It's a physical representation of a security configuration. By storing several security-related settings in one file, you can use this file to quickly apply tens, if not hundreds, of security settings all at once.

The tool used to view and alter these template files is called the Security Templates MMC snap-in. With this tool, you can painlessly alter existing security templates or create new ones. You do not use the utility to create new security settings, but rather, take existing settings and create new configurations of these settings. These configurations are then stored in text-based .inf files. This organization of security settings can go a long way toward streamlining administration.

 **EXAM TIP** There are a couple of exceptions to what can be contained in a security template. IP Security and public key policies cannot be set with a security template.

To use the Security Templates MMC snap-in, you must first add it to an existing MMC console or create a new one. To do so:

1. Click Start | Run, type **mmc**, then click OK.

2. From the File menu, choose Add/Remove Snap-in.

3. In Add/Remove Snap-in dialog box, click Add.

4. In the Available Standalone Snap-ins window, click Security Templates, choose Add, click Close, and then click OK. As shown in Figure 10-1, you will now have the ability to access the predefined template files, which are stored in the path identified in the Security Templates root node: *systemroot*\security\templates.

5. In the File menu, click Save, and give the new MMC console a name. It will then be added to your list of Administrative Tools.

Once you define and/or modify security templates, they can then be imported into a Group Policy Object to ease domain and OU security administration. Once imported, any computer accounts or user accounts in the site, domain, or OU where the template has been applied will then receive the security settings defined in the template.

Windows Server 2003 includes a collection of preconfigured security templates you can use to rapidly establish a baseline of security settings. The predefined security templates are based on the roles computers play in a computing environment. The roles that these templates configure can be divided into three common security levels:

- **Compatible (compat.inf)**  The compatible template is used to enable development of new applications to a standard security level in the Windows Server 2003 environment, while still allowing existing legacy applications to run under a less secure configuration. Because of its inherent security limitations that allow for maximum compatibility, it should not be applied to domain controllers, and also should not be imported into either the default domain policy or the default domain controller policy.

- **Secure (secure*.inf)**  The secure templates configure recommended security settings for all areas except file, folder, and registry key settings. They are commonly used to apply a range of password, audit, and account lockout policies that are much more secure than the default settings used after operating system installation.

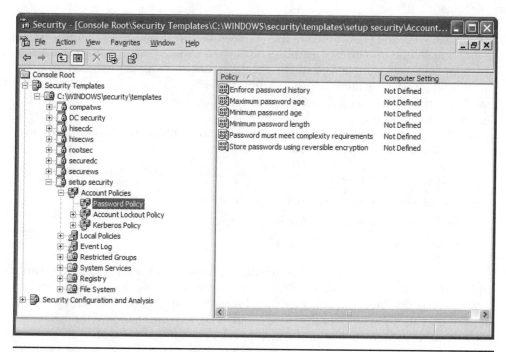

**Figure 10-1**    The predefined security templates

- **Highly secure (hisec\*.inf)**    The highly secure templates enforce all of the security settings the secure templates do and add even tighter security standards. They impose restriction on data that travels between clients and servers, including use of encryption as part of the communication equation. Further, they employ restricted groups to remove all members of the Power Users group, and to ensure that only Domain Admins and the local Administrator account are members of the local Administrators group.

**EXAM TIP**    Computers configured with highly secure templates may make communication impossible with down-level Windows clients, such as Windows 95 and 98 computers because they require secure domain-to-member communication channels, and Windows 95 and 98 clients cannot be members of a Windows Server 2003 domain.

You'll note also that there are certain templates, such as the Setup Security (setup security.inf) template, that act as the "reset button" on security for a given system. The effective settings in the Setup Security template can vary from computer to computer, and represent the default security settings applied during operating system installation. Other templates such as the System Root Security (rootsec.inf) are used to apply security to just a very specific area of the computer, in this case the permissions for the root of the system drive. It would be used if you were concerned that permissions on the root drive had been altered, and you wanted to hit the "reset button" for the root permissions.

Additionally, these predefined templates can serve as a good starting point when creating new templates. For example, you might like the security settings of the Secure Domain Controller template (securedc.inf), only with a few modifications of the password policies. You can make the needed changes to just the password policies, and then save the changes to a new template file.

You will use the predefined security templates to complete the following security tasks based on the needs of your system:

- Reapplying default settings
- Implementing a highly secure environment
- Implementing a less secure but more compatible environment
- Securing the systemroot directory

For example, the setup security.inf template allows you to reapply default security settings. This template is created during setup for each computer and must be applied locally. You should not apply the predefined security templates without testing first, as some of the security settings in the more secure templates can make a Windows Server 2003 machine incompatible with other Windows operating systems that do not support the same security features. For example, the highly secure security template causes servers configured with these settings to refuse LAN Manager and NTLM connections. Also, any client connecting to a Windows Server 2003 machine with the hisec.inf template must use client-side SMB packet signing. All computers running Windows 2000 and Windows XP operating systems enable client-side SMB packet signing by default, but other versions of Windows do not.

## Creating and Modifying Templates

You can create a new security template to best suit the needs of your organization, or, to save time and effort configuring many of the hundreds of security settings, use one of the predefined security templates. Before making any changes to your security settings, though, you should understand what the default settings of your system are and how they influence behavior.

## Lab Exercise 10.1: Creating a Security Template

Here's what to do to start creating your own security templates:

1. Open the Security Templates MMC snap-in.

2. In the console tree, right-click the default path folder (*systemroot*\security\templates), and choose New Template. Give the template a name and optional description, and then click OK.

3. You now have an unconfigured security template you can start modifying. In the console tree of your new template, expand the template to display the security policies, and navigate to the security setting attribute you want to modify.

4. In the Details pane, right-click the security setting and choose Properties from the context menu, or simply double-click the setting.

5. From the setting Properties dialog box, select the "Define these policy settings " check box, and make any desired changes to the setting. In Figure 10-2, you see how to make an audit policy a part of the new template. Click OK when you're finished.

Yet another way this tool can be used is to change existing templates. To do so, just expand one of the preconfigured templates and make changes according to the steps outlined above. When you've made the necessary tweaks, right-click the name of the policy and choose Save As from the context menu. You will then be given the Save As dialog box, which will by default open to the same location where the predefined templates are stored, as shown in Figure 10-3. Give the modified template a name, and it should now show in the Security Templates MMC utility.

## Importing a Template into a GPO

Now that you know how to create and modify security templates, it's time to actually put them to use. You can use these collections of settings by applying the template file to a Group Policy Object. This is the feature that allows the templates to do their magic.

## Lab Exercise 10.2: Applying a Template

Here's how to import a template into a Group Policy Object. In the example, you'll apply a template to a domain-linked GPO, but the method will be the same no matter what GPO the template is imported to:

1. Open Active Directory Users and Computers, and right-click the domain node. From the Properties dialog box, click the Group Policy tab, and then select the Group Policy to which you want the template applied. Click Edit.

2. Expand the Computer Configuration settings, then select the Security Settings. Right-click, then choose Import Policy.

**Figure 10-2**
Modifying a
setting in a
template

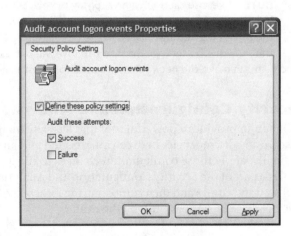

**Figure 10-3**

Saving a modified template

3. In the Import Policy dialog box, select the template you want to import. By default, the dialog box will open to the default template location of *systemroot*\security\templates.

4. You can force an immediate refresh of the new Group Policy security settings using the Gpupdate utility, or you can wait for the default refresh interval. A reboot will also do the trick.

Now the time spent fine-tuning the security templates has paid off. But there is still another important tool that will let you try out the security templates before putting them into play in the production environment. It's called the Security Configuration and Analysis tool.

**NOTE** Exercise caution when applying templates in a production environment. When you apply a policy, it will remove all existing security settings, replacing them with the settings stored in the template file. This can cause problems in the network, as settings that are too low will put data at risk, and settings that are too high can make the network impractical for most users.

## The Security Configuration and Analysis Tool

This MMC snap-in provides a powerful tool that lets you analyze security settings, view results, resolve any discrepancies between an expected and an actual security configuration, and finally, apply those configuration changes to the local machine.

The analysis part of the Security Configuration and Analysis tool works by building a database of security settings and then comparing the local security settings of the computer against the database of settings built by the utility.

The configuration part of Security Configuration and Analysis uses the database of security settings to rapidly apply the settings to the system.

How are the databases of security settings built? With the template files—both the ones already on the machine in the *systemroot*\security\templates folder and the custom templates you configure with the Security Templates utility. Remember that the templates are merely text files full of security settings, and just like almost any other database tool, Security Configuration and Analysis can use these kinds of files to populate the entries of a database table.

As you can see, the Security Templates and the Security Configuration and Analysis tools work hand in hand. Therefore, it's not uncommon to have both MMC snap-ins loaded into the same console.

To add the Security Configuration and Analysis MMC snap-in to a console, follow the same procedure as you did when adding the Security Templates utility, only choose the Security Configuration and Analysis tool, of course.

## Configuring System Security

The Security Configuration and Analysis utility performs a series of complex analysis and configuration to your machine, but the tool itself is not that difficult to learn. What's more, you don't really need to, as there are instructions in the Details pane that will help you use this tool for the first time.

## Lab Exercise 10.3: Creating a Settings Database

Your first order of business when using this tool, however, is to set a working database of security settings. Until this step is completed, the Security Configuration and Analysis utility really isn't capable of much. Here are the steps you'll follow:

1. In the Security Configuration and Analysis snap-in, right-click Security Configuration and Analysis and choose Open Database. This will be your working database of settings that will be either analyzed or applied.

2. Name the database, and then select the security template you want to apply to the database. You can use any of the preconfigured templates or one you have created. Click Open.

3. You won't see anything change except the instructions in the Details pane of Security Configuration and Analysis. However, something important has occurred, at least as far as the utility is concerned. You now have a database of settings you will use for comparison or application (that is, analysis or configuration).

4. To analyze the system with the template's database of settings, right-click the Security Configuration and Analysis root node and then select Analyze Computer Now. Verify the error log location and click OK, and analysis begins, as shown in Figure 10-4.

When the processing is complete, any discrepancies between the local computer settings and the database settings will show up marked with a red X, while settings that

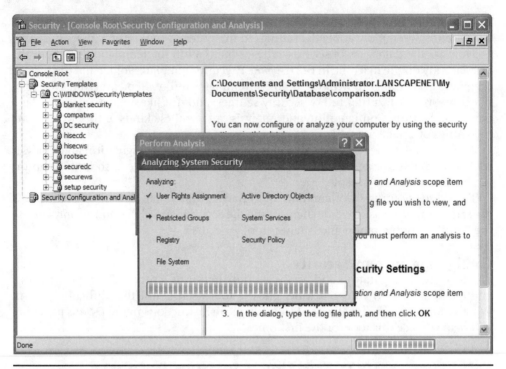

**Figure 10-4**   The Security Configuration and Analysis tool performing its analysis

match will show as a green check mark. Figure 10-5 shows you what to expect when performing the analysis. Settings that do not have either the red X or the green check mark are not configured in the database you just created with the template.

You can then resolve discrepancies between the database settings and the computer settings if you want. You do this by double-clicking on the settings and selecting whether or not to define the setting in the database, as shown in Figure 10-6, and furthermore adjusting the setting to best suit your needs.

You can also repeat the process and import multiple templates. The database will merge the many different templates to create one composite template. Any conflicts encountered will be resolved by having the last setting imported become the effective database setting.

When you are satisfied with the settings in the database, you can apply the settings by right-clicking the Security Configuration and Analysis root node as before, and then choosing Configure Computer Now from the context menu. Set the error log path and click OK.

Using the Security Configuration and Analysis tool, you've just made potentially hundreds of security setting changes to the local machine with a few clicks of the mouse.

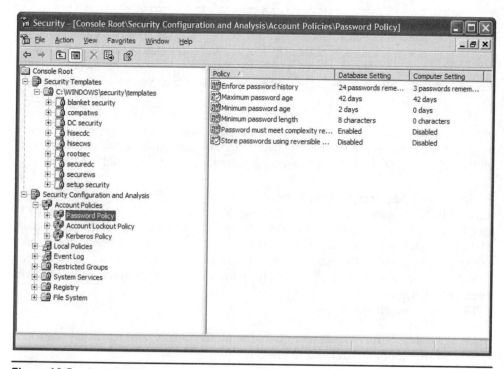

**Figure 10-5**    Results of a security analysis

**Figure 10-6**
Defining a
security setting
in the database

**EXAM TIP** When you apply the secure or highly secure templates, communication attempts that do not conform to the rules of the template are rejected, and some of these connection and encryption technologies are not even available on Windows 9x or NT 4 systems. To ensure compatibility with these operating systems, you should use either the Compatible or Setup Security template.

Also note that when using the Security Configuration and Analysis tool, you are applying local security settings. If this does not produce the results you expect, it could be because the security settings are being overwritten by site, domain, and organizational unit policies. These Group Policy processing order statutes are discussed in Chapter 22.

## Exporting a Security Template

Another handy feature of the Security Configuration and Analysis tool is the ability to save a database of security settings to a new template file. This way, you can take a database of carefully adjusted settings and save them for later use when configuring the security settings of Group Policy Objects. Further, you can later redefine these settings using the Security Templates tool, using the two utilities to take security settings back and forth as often as you please.

To export a security template:

1. Open the Security Configuration and Analysis console, and right-click the root Security Configuration and Analysis node.

2. If you have created a security database by importing multiple templates, you can save the database settings into a separate template file. To perform this task, choose Export Template from the context menu.

3. The Export Template To dialog box appears, by default set to the same location as the other security templates. Give the file a descriptive name and click OK.

Now you should see that template added to your list of manageable templates in the Security Templates console. If you don't, right-click the templates folder and choose Refresh from the context menu.

If you don't quite understand what a Group Policy is yet, this discussion of security templates gets repeated in Chapter 23 as you take a look at the use of Group Policy Objects to manage your enterprise. As you just saw, you can implement a baseline of security quickly for computers in your network by importing a security in to a GPO.

**NOTE** The repeated information is provided in case you are not sitting down to read this book cover to cover, as most of you will read it one section at a time as you progress towards your MSCE certification. As you have no doubt experienced by now, there are several areas of study that overlap in the different testable objectives. For example, you'll need to understand Group Policies to help you establish a baseline of security in the network, and you also need to understand them to properly implement Active Directory.

With that said, here are a few more Microsoft recommendations for using security templates to help secure your organization:

- Do not deploy either predefined or newly created security templates to your production network without first thoroughly testing them in a test environment. This trial period will help ensure that mission-critical applications continue to work after template application.

- Do not ever edit the setup security.inf template. This setup template gives you the option to reapply the Windows Server 2003 default settings. Further, should you ever remove a security template from a Group Policy Object, best practice is to reapply the setup security.inf to restore all default settings.

- Do not apply the setup security.inf template through Group Policy. Because of its relatively low security configuration levels, the setup security.inf template should only be applied one computer at a time with either the secedit or Security Configuration and Analysis utility.

- Do not apply the Compatible template to domain controllers. This sets a level of security on these vital systems that compromises almost all security standards. For example, you should never import the Compatible template to either the Default Domain or Default Domain Controller GPO.

- Do not modify the predefined templates. These predefined templates serve as good benchmarks for security, and having them around means that they can always be deployed. Instead, customize one of the predefined template using procedures previously discussed, and then save the changes under a different template name.

So just what would make a good security template? As with many things, it depends on what your security goals are. Also keep in mind that a good security plan must always be balanced against a good usability plan. A wonderful IPSec policy does you no good if the computer with the policy is unable to exchange information with the other computers on the network, or if the password policies are such that users resort to Post-It notes.

## Recommended Security Practices

Your comprehensive security plan is implemented with more than just security templates. The templates are just a device that makes many of these settings easier to implement.

Table 10-1 lists some general recommendations from Microsoft about how best to secure your Windows Server 2003 environment, along with some of the reasoning behind the recommendations. These security guidelines go beyond configuring settings with a template, and should be practiced whether templates are used in your network or not.

Also remember that implementation of these recommendations requires a thorough understanding of the technologies discussed. You won't be able to deploy a Group Policy Object, for example, without knowing what it is.

| Security Guideline | Why It's Recommended |
|---|---|
| Restrict physical access to computers, especially domain controllers. | The best-laid software security policies can be defeated by a person who has access to the computer, who can then unplug or steal the system itself. Physical access to a server by an intruder could result in unauthorized data access or modification as well as installation of hardware or software designed to circumvent security. This is especially true for your domain controllers. To maintain a secure environment, you must restrict physical access to all servers and network hardware. You might also consider not connecting a keyboard and mouse to the domain controller under normal circumstances to further prevent physical access to that server. |
| For administrative tasks, use the principle of least privilege. | Using the principle of least privilege, administrators should only use an administrative account to perform administrative tasks. For routine, non-administrative, day-to-day work, a different account should be used. To accomplish this without logging off and back on, log on with a regular user account and use the Run As feature to run the tools that require the broader permissions. Later in the chapter, we'll discuss both the principle of least privilege and the Run As feature. |
| Define groups and their membership. | When deciding on the default level of computer access that end users will have, the determining factor is the installed base of applications. That is, users should only be in the groups necessary to do their work. Some older applications require that the user be a member of the Power Users local group to run the application. This gives most users more administrative privileges than are usually necessary. For this reason, Microsoft recommends that your organization only use applications that belong to the Windows Logo for Software Program. If your applications conform to the Windows Logo program, you can make all your end users members of the Users (or Authenticated Users) group.<br>Domain administrators and enterprise administrators should be the only users allowed to link a Group Policy Object to an organizational unit. This is the default setting. To have a GPO apply, the authenticated users need only the Read and Apply Group Policy Object permissions. |
| Secure data on computers. | Ensure that the system files and the registry are protected using strong Access Control Lists (ACLs). For more information on controlling the Access Control List for objects on the computer, please refer to Chapters 3 and 21. |

**Table 10-1**   Recommended Security Guidelines

PART II

| Security Guideline | Why It's Recommended |
|---|---|
| Use strong passwords throughout your organization. | Most Windows Server 2003 Active Directory domain users will use a user name and password to prove their identity. These passwords are normally chosen by the user, who may want a simple password that is easily remembered. In most cases, these passwords are weak and may be easily guessed or determined by an intruder. Also, the default domain security settings, in a nod to increased usability, allow for these weak passwords to be used. Passwords are of no use if they can easily be guessed or stolen (it's why secure networks may opt for smart cards). Weak passwords can negate the use of passwords at all, and can thus become the point of entry for an otherwise strong security environment. A strong password policy will force users to create passwords that are more difficult for a hacker to discern and, as a result, help provide an barrier around your enterprise's resources. |
| Do not download or run programs that come from untrusted sources. | The threat: Viruses. Trojan horses. Spyware. Programs can sometimes contain instructions to violate security in a number of ways including data theft, denial of service, and data destruction. These malicious programs often masquerade as legitimate software and can be difficult to identify. To avoid these programs, you should only download and run software that is guaranteed authentic and obtained from a trusted source. |
| Keep virus scanners up to date. | Virus scanners frequently identify infected files by scanning for a signature, which is a known component of a previously identified virus. The scanners keep these virus signatures in a signature file, which is usually stored on the local hard disk. Because new viruses are discovered frequently, this file should also be updated frequently for the virus scanner to easily identify all current viruses. |
| Keep all software patches up to date. | As Microsoft readily admits, software patches, hotfixes, and service packs (which frequently incorporate the latest patches and hotfixes) are frequently issued to address known security vulnerabilities. Check software provider web sites periodically to see if there are new patches available for software used in your organization. Microsoft can automate this process for the operating system when you configure Automatic Updates. |

**Table 10-1**  Recommended Security Guidelines *(continued)*

# Configuring an Audit Policy

Another important security mechanism is the ability to audit what's happening to and on the computers of the network. This can be especially important on file servers such as DFS or web servers, database servers, DNS servers, and, of course, domain controllers.

By implementing auditing, you gain a "Big Brother"–like ability to monitor what users are doing on the computer. Auditing will show you what activities are happening on a system, who is doing the activities, and what time they were doing it.

There are three main steps to implementing security-related auditing for your system. First, you need to decide which events you want to audit. You can audit events such as user logon and logoff, as well as access to resources on a computer. The categories of events you select will define your overall audit policy for a particular computer. When you first install Windows Server 2003, there are a few audit settings selected in the local security policy. These audit settings are configurable with the Local Security Settings utility, as shown in Figure 10-7. You can access this preconfigured MMC from the Administrative Tools menu.

Once the member sever has been upgraded to a domain controller, there will be another preconfigured MMC created, called Domain Controller Security Policy, and there will be a few more audit settings that are configured by default.

But you don't necessarily have to set the audit settings with either of these two MMC snap-ins. The audit settings can be configured from any Group Policy Object, and they can also be configured and saved as a part of any security template. The template file, as we have seen, can then be imported into a GPO.

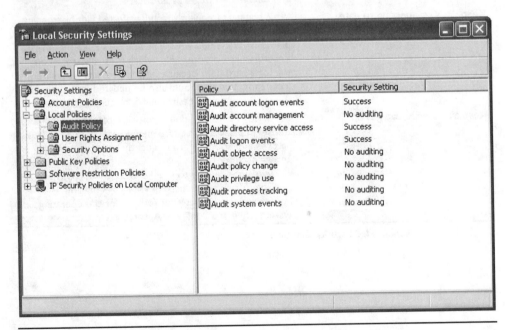

**Figure 10-7**   The default audit settings on a member server

You can audit the following types of events, as shown in Table 10-2. Note also the default auditing setting.

| Audit Policy | Description | Default Setting |
|---|---|---|
| Audit account logon events | Audits logon events which are generated when a domain user account is authenticated on a domain controller. | Success |
| Audit account management | Audits each instance of account management. | Success on domain controllers, No Auditing on member servers |
| Audit directory service access | Determines whether to audit the event of a user accessing an Active Directory object that has its own access control list specified. | Success on domain controllers, Undefined on member servers |
| Audit logon events | Audits each instance of a user logging on or off of their computer; generated on local computers during local account use. | Success |
| Audit object access | Determines whether to audit the event of a user accessing an object that has its own access control list specified. Objects can include files, folders, registry keys, and printers. | No Auditing |
| Audit policy change | Determines whether to audit every incident of a change to user rights assignment policies, audit policies, or trust policies. | Success on domain controllers, No Auditing on member servers |
| Audit privilege use | Determines whether to audit the instance of a user exercising a user right. | No Auditing |
| Audit process tracking | Determines whether to audit detailed tracking information for events such as program activation, process exit, handle duplication, and indirect object access. | No Auditing |
| Audit system events | Audits events that affect either system security or the security log, such as when a user restarts or shuts down a computer. | Success on domain controllers, No Auditing on member servers |

**Table 10-2**   Audit Settings in Windows Server 2003

PART II

After you've decided what to audit, the next task is to set the properties of the security log, including the size of the log file. These topics will be discussed in the next section.

Finally, depending on the audit events selected, you then need to determine what objects are audited. Auditing object access, for example, can be more accurately described as the *ability* to audit object access. Once object access is enabled, you then need to select the objects for which you want to monitor access, and set the audit settings from that object's Properties dialog box accordingly. You can furthermore set up auditing of either success, failure, or both when users try to access that particular file.

## Deciding What to Audit

When you define an audit policy, you get to choose what events to track and whether to track the success or failure of those events. Whether you should track success or failure events depends on the activities you are trying to capture. For example, do you really want to audit each and every successful logon? Probably not. Do you want to audit failed logon attempts? In a secure environment, you probably do. Keep in mind that auditing does generate overhead on the computer, so you want to audit the events that are most likely to indicate a security issue. Unnecessary auditing can be a drag on performance, so you want to focus your audits appropriately.

By default, nothing is audited, so you must configure auditing manually, and it is done on a per-computer basis. It can also be a two-step process, as in the case where you would want to audit who is accessing a confidential file. You would first audit the success of object access, and you'd then set the auditing on an individual resource by accessing the Properties dialog box of that resource and configuring auditing on a per-group or per-user basis through the Advanced button, as shown in Figure 10-8.

**Figure 10-8**
Auditing a resource

**NOTE** Remember, you need to ensure that Simple File Sharing is turned off before you can see the Security tab on an NTFS resource. (This applies to XP machines; Server 2003 doesn't use SFS.) Verify that SFS is unchecked by looking at the View tab in Folder Options.

**TIP** You can only audit access to resources on NTFS partitions.

## Reviewing Results of Your Audit Policy

Finally, the audit policy settings dictate which security settings the Event Log service should log in the Security log. The Security log will identify either the failure or success of audit events. To get detailed information on the events, such as who did what and when, simply double-click the particular event to see the Event Properties window, as shown in Figure 10-9.

This is a tool that may seem overwhelming at first because of the number of settings that can be configured. Finding exactly what you want to configure will be a matter that requires patience, repeated use, and trial and error.

That being said, you will hardly ever configure local security settings in the real world. That's because most security settings that are important enough to set at the local level should also apply to the network as a whole. So that's what you do: set most, if not all, of your security settings at the domain level in Active Directory rather than at the local computer level. A perfect example of this would be password policies. Does it make sense to require an eight-character password on one computer and not on another? Usually not. So you would set this password policy at the domain level, so that all users

**Figure 10-9**
Examining the results of your audit

of your network would need an eight-character password to log on. Moreover, domain policies will by default override local policies, so that even if you set a ten-character password requirement at the local computer using the above scenario, the effective setting would still be for an eight-character password.

While all this is not crucial information for the Windows 70-291 exam, it is required understanding as you progress through the MCSE exam series. It can only help if you enter this test with a basic understanding of Group Policies and how they might apply to an Active Directory environment.

 **TIP** Local security settings are the only GPOs that can be applied to a standalone or workgroup Windows XP computer. All other GPOs are domain-based.

So, when might you want to change any of the local Group Policy settings? Well, it is your only Group Policy lever that is available in a workgroup setting. In this configuration, the Local Group Policies can be quite effective on securing a machine, especially one that is shared by many people.

The greater the number of GPOs that are configured for a computer, and the greater the number of settings within each GPO that is are configured, the longer it takes for a computer to start and complete the logon process. Therefore, best practice is to minimize the number of GPOs applied to a computer in a domain, and minimize the number of settings applied to a computer in a workgroup or a domain.

But configure only what you need. Just because you can audit almost every computing activity doesn't mean that you should. Here is what's recommended when you set an auditing policy in your network:

- **Look before you leap.** Because auditing does carry with it a performance price tag, you should develop an auditing plan before implementing audit policy. Therefore, you should carefully consider exactly what information you want to collect in your auditing practices. Deciding exactly *what* data you're after beforehand can go a long way in defining how the audit policies will be configured.

    For example, your file server may contain sensitive financial information. In such a case, you would likely be interested in intrusion detection; you would want to find out if anyone were trying to access that information. Therefore, you should consider collecting failure audits, thus allowing you to see who was attempting to gain access to the folders for which they were not authorized.

    But be careful. If this data is stored on a publicly available server, such as a web server, enabling failure audits can create so many failure audits that the Security log becomes full, causing a server with degraded performance, and an audit policy that may not be able to collect any more audits (it will depend on how your Security log is configured).

    Furthermore, if in addition to the above setting you also have the "Audit: Shut down system immediately if unable to log security audits" policy setting enabled, users can easily start a denial-of-service attack by exploiting this vulnerability in your audit policy.

- **Consider available resources for collecting and reviewing an audit log.** Just like any log file (or any file, period), an audit log will take up space on your computer. They also don't review themselves; someone will have to spend time and resources configuring the audit policy and reviewing the results of that policy. Therefore, you should only audit those events that have an impact on your organization.

- **Collect and archive security logs across your organization.** If it's important enough to audit, it's important enough to archive. You should get into the habit of saving old audit logs for later review if necessary. If an intrusion occurs, you might not be aware of it until days or weeks later, and isolation of the problem will depend on whether you can refer back to the saved audit logs. Also, archived audit logs can be a valuable resource in the tracking of trends.

 **NOTE** Knowledgeable hackers will commonly clear the Security log, effectively erasing their footprints. You can stay a step ahead of this cloak-and-dagger game by using a tool like the Microsoft Operations Manager, which can automate the gathering and archiving of Security logs. More information about MOM is available at the Microsoft web site: http://www.microsoft.com/mom/.

- **Audit both success and failure events in the system event category.** Any time a hacker attempts to access the computer or the network, signs of telltale activity can usually be found in the System event category. Also, the number of audits generated by these two System Event audit settings are enabled tends to be relatively low, and the quality of information gained from such audited events tends to be relatively high.

- **Audit success events in the Policy Change event category for all domain controllers.** Any time an event is captured by the Policy Change event category, there has been a change to the security policy configuration. If there are only one or two users who are supposed to be making changes to the security policies, and the changes have not been made by those users, you have a situation on your hands.

  If you audit failure events in the Policy Change event category, you can see if unauthorized users are trying to change security policy settings. However, Microsoft cautions you that collecting failure events is resource-intensive, and will open you to the possibility of a denial-of-service attacks from users who could just try to change security settings.

- **Audit success events in the Account Management event category.** In a secure environment, you want to know when changes are made to the accounts of the domain, especially when users are placed into certain groups that may have access to certain resources. Auditing success of account management events ensures that you have this information.

  Auditing failure events can also be useful for the same reason that it could be useful in auditing policy change events, but also leaves open the same vulnerabilities.

- **Audit success events in the Logon event category.**   Auditing the successful logon events gives you a record of when each user logs on or off a computer. In the instance where a user name and password are compromised, you have the ability to track the user of an account to a specific computer and a specific time. Failure event logging can show you attempts to break into the computer using unauthorized accounts, but can also leave open the possibility of a denial-of-service attacks due to repeated login attempts.

- **Audit success events in the Account Logon event category on domain controllers.**   This tells you who has logged on to the domain. While auditing success of logon events is important on domain controllers, it is not necessary on member servers. Auditing success events lets you track who is authenticated to the domain and when.

   Audit of failure events lets you see who has attempted to log on but has not been successful. This can help you catch hackers trying multiple passwords, but it also will log every legitimate user who simple mistypes his or her password. If you have delegated the task of resetting passwords to a junior administrator in your domain, you might *not* want to capture failure events here. The auditing of failure events also exposes the network to a denial-of-service attack form outside users who can repeatedly attempt to log on, thereby shutting down your network.

- **Be specific when setting up auditing on an object.**   To audit access to *any* object on your network, you first need to enable the Audit Object Access policy setting. Only then do you edit the Access Control List (ACL) for specific objects for which you want to audit access, and furthermore define what kind of access is audited.

   For optimum file server performance (this is where you most often implement an object access policy), minimize the number of entries in the ACL for an object. One entry in a ACL that will audit access for a group that contains 100 users does not degrade system performance as much as 100 separate auditing entries on the ACL.

   To reduce the number of audit events generated, you should only audit the actions that will provide meaningful information. For example, are you interested in the auditing the instances where a file is simply read or changed? Remember that when you audit Full Control, you are auditing every permission for the file object.

## Implement the Principle of Least Privilege

The principle of least privilege is not a utility, an application, or a setting you configure in a Group Policy. Rather, it is a security guideline that states the following: a user should have only the minimum privileges necessary to perform a specific task. For example, if a user's job is to edit a specific file on your system, such as a chapter of a computer book, that user should not be placed in the Domain Admins global group just so that you're sure the user can open Word. This would be the antithesis of the least privilege principle at work. Instead, you should create a normal user account, or even let them use the Guest account, and then grant permission only over that one file.

**NOTE** The term "privilege" here is used to encompass both rights, which allow a user to accomplish a task, and permissions, which define a level of access to a resource.

Using least privilege helps to ensure that, if a user account is compromised, the impact is minimized by the limited privileges held by that user. But occasionally, even normal users will need to open administrative utilities to perform a specific task—such as change a static IP address setting or disable a hardware device—or else an administrator will have to make a visit to that computer to do so.

When such is the case, security can be compromised by either a) placing the user account in an administrative account for purposes of accomplishing the task, and then not removing the account when the task is complete, or b) logging on as a user with administrative privileges and then forgetting to log off once the task is done. In each of these scenarios, security is compromised because privileges for the regular user are now higher than they need be. In scenario A, the user is now an administrator, with subsequent access to all administrative tools, and in scenario B, the user is using the wrong account, an account with administrative privileges, and will be until he or she logs off.

These are two common occurrences where guidelines of least privilege are broken. One of your main lines of defense against this, however, is the Run As feature. When a task requires additional privileges, the normal user can use Run As to start a specific process in the context of another account with those additional privileges needed for the process.

In addition, scenario B presents yet another problem: in order to log on with the administrative account, the regular user must first log off. This can be very disruptive of ongoing work. Using the Run As feature will be considerably less disruptive to the regular user, and considerably more secure than either of the other two solutions.

## Using the Run As Feature

To run a program in the context of another user account without logging off and back on, log on with a regular user account and use the Run As feature to run the tools that require the broader permissions.

## Lab Exercise 10.4: Using Run As

Here's how you can use the Run As feature from the Windows Server 2003 graphical interface:

1. In Windows Explorer or on the Start menu, right-click the program executable file (or icon) that you want to open, and then click Run As.

2. Click The Following User radio button.

3. In User Name And Password, type the administrator account name and password.

If you right-click and do not see the Run As option, hold down the SHIFT key while right-clicking. This is a sure-fire way to access the Run As option (if it can be used with the particular program you're right-clicking). Holding the SHIFT key is specifically needed to launch Control Panel items in the context of another user account.

You can also use the Run As feature from the command line. To run a program, type

```
runas /user:UserName program PathToFilename
```

In the above example, you'll replace the *UserName* variable with the user account to use when running the specified program. You can enter the *UserName* information in one of two formats: either enter the user principal name *(user@domain)* for the account or use the syntax *domain\user*. The UPN looks like the e-mail address for the account, and indeed it may be. In Chapter 20, we look further at the significance of the UPN.

The *PathToFilename* specifies the path to the file name that you want to open. This is the program you will run as a different user. For example, to open Active Directory Sites and Services in the context of the Brian account—Brian is the Domain Admin for the lanscape.net domain—use the following syntax after opening the command prompt:

```
runas /brian@lanscape.net "mmc %windir%\system32\dssite.msc"
```

You would then be able to perform all site management tasks without interrupting the work of the currently logged-on user. If you forgot to close the Active Directory Sites and Services, only that utility would be open with administrative privileges. If you were to log on using the Brian account, all domain management utilities would be subject to perusal.

 **NOTE** Not all programs support the Run As feature, but most of the management utilities you'll encounter will, especially those provided by Microsoft. Also, you can use the Run As feature to launch a program in the context of any user account, not just user accounts with administrative privileges. Of course, such regular accounts may not have the permissions to access the program you're trying to run in the first place, but that doesn't mean you can't try.

Furthermore, note that the Run As feature depends on the Secondary Logon service. If you use the Run As feature, and the logon fails, it could be because this Secondary Logon service is not running.

To troubleshoot such a scenario, make sure the Secondary Logon service is running by checking the Services console. If you discover that it is not, you can start it from using this MMC snap-in. Here's what you'll do:

1. From the Administrative Tools, open the Services console.

2. Find the Secondary Logon service in the list of services, and then from the details pane, do one of the following:

   - Right-click the service, and choose Start, Stop, Pause, Resume, or Restart from the context menu as is required.

   - Double-click the service to open the service's Properties dialog box, as shown in Figure 10-10. From the Properties dialog box, you can Start, Stop, Pause, Restart, and configure startup behavior of the service with the drop-down menu. In the case of the Secondary Logon service, note that the default configuration for the service is to start automatically.

**Figure 10-10**
Modifying
properties
of a service

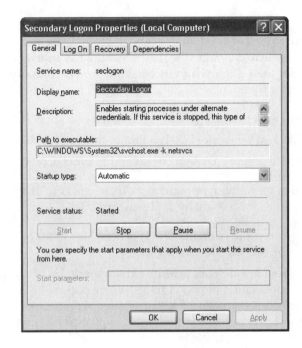

PART II

# Monitor and Troubleshoot Network Protocol Security

Central to your strategy for securing network traffic on you network will be the implementation of IPSec policies. These policies can be applied to examine traffic sent to and from local computers, domains, sites, and organizational units, and will either allow or deny that traffic based on the rules in the policy. There are two tools you can use to create, modify, and assign IPSec policies: the IP Security Policy Management console or the netsh commands for IPSec from the command line.

In this book's next section covering the 293 exam, much more attention will be given to setting up the IPSec policies for your network. However, to effectively discuss this topic, you first need a bit of foundation about IP Security.

## IP Security Background

IPSec, through the encryption of data, can serve as a critical line of defense against attacks on network computers, from both private networks and public networks alike. It is especially designed to secure IP traffic over nonsecure networks such as the Internet.

IPSec is based on an end-to-end security model, establishing trust and security from a source IP to a destination IP address. The IP address itself does not necessarily need to be the identifying factor for the network communication. The system behind the IP address can alternatively have an identity that is validated through an authentication process such as a digital certificate. The only computers that participate in the sending and receiving of secure network traffic are the sending and receiving computers. Each computer handles security at its own end. In this way, the computers using IPSec assume that the network over which the data is to be transmitted is inherently nonsecure. This model allows IPSec to be deployed to successfully protect computer transmission for the following network scenarios:

- **Local area network (LAN)**   Client/server and peer-to-peer
- **Wide area network (WAN)**   Router-to-router and gateway-to-gateway
- **Remote access**   Dial-up clients and Internet access from private networks

And no matter what type of network IPSec works to protect, there will always be are two main objectives sought by deployment of IP Security:

- **To protect the contents of IP packets**   Information in packets should only be seen by the intended recipients.
- **To provide a defense against network attacks**   This can be achieved through implementation of packet filters, where packets both leaving and entering the machine (or network) must meet a set of predetermined conditions. Defense against network attacks is also accomplished by ensuring that communication only occur with trusted entities.

Both of these design mandates are met through the use of cryptography-based protection services, security protocols, and dynamic key management. These underlying technologies provide the strength and flexibility to protect computer communications. Furthermore, the IPSec technologies are only dependent on the IP protocol, and can be used to secure communication between any devices that support it. Settings can be configured to restrict access to and from private network computers, domains, sites, remote sites, extranets, and even dial-up clients. Its flexibility allows for communication to be blocked for either receipt or transmission of specific traffic types. For example, IPSec filters can be configured so that HTTP traffic is allowed to be received, but only HTTP traffic that is bound for port 80.

Once an IPSec policy has been configured, it is vital that you be able to manage and troubleshoot ongoing operation. There are several tools at the disposal of a Windows Server 2003 administrator to do just this. You may use all of these, several of these, or none in your particular environment. As an exam candidate, however, you should be familiar with them all. We begin with what is possibly the most robust of these tools, the IP Security Monitor.

## IP Security Monitor

While the IP Security Monitor is not new to Windows Server 2003—there was a version included in Windows 2000—there have been some significant enhancements. If you've used both, the first thing you'll probably notice is that the Server 2003 version is now implemented as an MMC snap-in, whereas in Windows 2000 it was an executable called ipsecmon.exe.

Quite simply, the IP Security Monitor allows you to view a variety of information about all the IPSec policies that have been applied for a given system or even a domain. The information gathered can include the following:

- Details about active IPSec policies, including the name, description, date last modified, store, path, organizational unit, and Group Policy Object name
- Generic filters and specific filters
- Statistics and security associations

Furthermore, you can use the IP Security Monitor to customize IPSec policy refresh rates, and search for filters that match a specific source or destination IP address.

The IP Security Monitor includes two modes, each displaying different information about the IPSec policies applied and how they influence network traffic behavior. Both modes are accessible as different nodes under the IP Security root, as shown in Figure 10-11. They are

- **Quick mode**   Displays information such as Packets Not Received, Packets Not Authenticated (both because of the security restrictions of the configured policies), as well as Authenticated and Confidential Bytes Received and Sent.
- **Main mode**   Displays more exhaustive information, such as Send and Receive Failures, Authentication and Negotiation Failures, and Invalid Packets Received.

**Figure 10-11**
You can use either main mode or quick mode to view information.

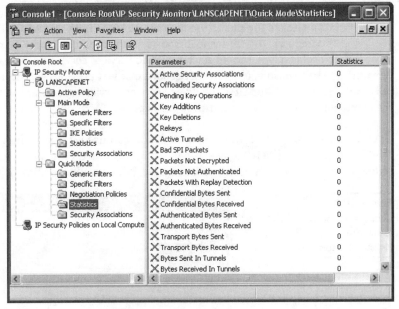

**TIP** These are just a few examples of the collectible data with the IP Security Monitor. As with many management tools presented throughout this book, it is not vital that you memorize all of the information that can be gathered, or even how to use the tool. What remains important is that you have an understanding of *when* and *why* the tool might be used. The *how* is not so important.

First, you'll need to add the IP Security Monitor to a custom MMC snap-in. Here's how:

1. From the Start | Run menu, type **mmc**, and then click OK.
2. From the File menu, choose Add/Remove Snap-in, and then click Add.
3. Choose the IP Security Monitor from the list of snap-ins, and then click Add. Click Close to exit the Add/Remove Snap-in dialog box, and then click OK.

Next, you'll add the computer on which the IP Security Monitor will gather information about the IP protocol:

1. From the console tree, right-click the IP Security Monitor, and then choose Add Computer from the context menu.
2. The Add Computer dialog box will open, as shown in Figure 10-12. You have two choices:
   - For the local computer, click This Computer.
   - For a remote computer, click The Following Computer, and then type the name of the remote computer, or click Browse to find it on the network.

 **NOTE** The IPSec Services service must be started on the computer to be monitored for this to work. If the service is not started on the target computer, the server icon shows as a stopped service. To correct this problem, you should start the IPSec Services service on the target computer using the Services console, using the procedure that was previously discussed. Then, to refresh IP Security Monitor after the IPSec Services service has been restarted, right-click the computer to be monitored and choose Reconnect.

Once the IP Security Monitor is loaded, you can use it to perform a variety of tasks. The first one you're likely to tackle is viewing the active policies on a particular computer. To do so, you'll investigate the Active Policy node, as shown in Figure 10-13.

**Figure 10-12**

Adding a computer to the IP Security Monitor console

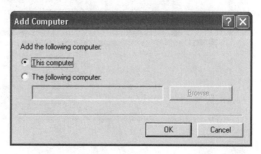

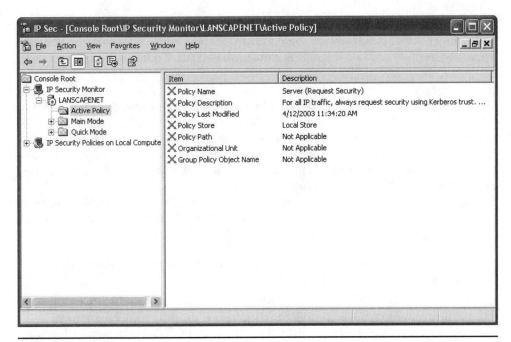

**Figure 10-13**   The Active Policy node

Here, you'll find many pieces of information about the active IPSec policies that have been applied, as summarized in Table 10-3.

| Table 10-3 | Active IPSec Policy Item | Description |
|---|---|---|
| Information Gathered in Active IP Security Policies | Policy Name | Specifies the name of the active IPSec policy. |
| | Description | Optional text that describes the purpose of the active IPSec policy. |
| | Policy Last Modified | Not applicable (this information is displayed only for active IPSec policies that are applied to a computer). |
| | Policy Store | Specifies the storage location for the active IPSec policy. For active IPSec policies that are applied by the domain, this location appears as Domain Store. |
| | Policy Path | Specifies the LDAP path to the active IPSec policy. |
| | Organizational Unit | Specifies the organizational unit to which the Group Policy Object is applied. |
| | Group Policy Object Name | Specifies the Group Policy Object to which the active IPSec policy is applied. |

When using the IP Security Monitor to look at policies that are specific to a local computer, the Policy Path, Organizational Unit, and Group Policy Object Name items do not apply, as these only are relevant to domain-based IPSec policies.

## Using netsh

You can also use the netsh utility from the command prompt instead of the graphical-based interface provided by the IP Security Policy Management console. These commands will let you do everything you can do with the MMC snap-in, including the configuration and viewing of static or dynamic IPSec main mode settings, quick mode settings, rules, and configuration parameters. Further, the etsh commands also give you all the monitoring capabilities of the IP Security Monitor tool.

There are even some features of IPSec management that are not available unless you use the netsh commands. The utility can be especially useful when you want to perform the following IPSec tasks:

- Script IPSec configuration. You can write a script that calls the netsh utility to script IP Security parameters.

- Configure the following features, which are not available in the IP Security Policy Management snap-in: IPSec diagnostics, default traffic exemptions, strong certificate revocation list (CRL) checking, IKE (Oakley) logging, logging intervals, computer startup security, and computer startup traffic exemptions. With these features, you can further extend the security of an IPSec policy.

The netsh utility is one of the most extensive command-line utilities you will encounter. The above-referenced features can be run with the netsh ipsec command, which is just one of the many ways to use netsh (others include -ras, to configure remote access, and -dhcp to configure DHCP). You should also remember the help switch (/?) for assistance with individual syntax.

Once you have specified the netsh ipsec parameter, you will then choose from one of several sub-parameters that will actually configure the IPSec behavior you want. For example, to create a new IPSec policy, you could use the following syntax:

```
netsh ipsec static add policy name= secureclient [parameters]
```

This would create a new policy called secureclient. Behavior of the policy, such as the default polling interval, could then be configured with the additional [*parameters*], but actual setting of the rules and filtering behavior of the policy would be set through entirely different ipsec commands. Again, remember the /? switch for help with individual syntax, which you will not need for the exam.

## Using the Event Viewer

Another monitoring and troubleshooting tool that can be used to help manage IP Security is the Event Viewer. Because of its versatility, the procedure for using the Event Viewer is covered several times throughout the book, including a discussion in Chapter 21 in Part IV of this book.

The Event Viewer in this instance will be used to view the results of Internet Key Exchange (IKE) events. These IPSec events will be written to the Security log, where you will be able to view information regarding both success and failure of IKE negotiations.

Before these events are written to the Security log, however, you'll need to enable success or failure auditing for the Audit Logon Events policy setting for the system's audit policy. This can be configured at either the domain or local computer level using the auditing procedures outlined earlier in this chapter.

Once you have configured success or failure auditing (or both) for the Audit Logon Events policy settings, the IPSec driver records the success or failure of each main mode and quick mode negotiation and the establishment and termination of each negotiation as separate events. However, enabling this type of auditing, especially at the domain level, can cause the Security log to quickly fill with IKE events. For example, if you have a IPSec policy for a file server that requires secure traffic for all connecting clients, IKE events will soon fill the Security log as these clients negotiate their secure sessions. This can be a problem if you have constraints on the Security log's file size.

Therefore, you might want to consider disabling the auditing of IKE events in the Security log. To do so, follow these steps:

1. Open the registry editor by typing **regedit** from the Start | Run menu.

2. Expand the HKEY_LOCAL_MACHINE\System\CurrentControlSet\Control\ Lsa\Audit\DisableIKEAudits registry key.

3. Set the registry setting to a value of 1. Notice that the DisableIKEAudits key does not exist by default and must be created.

4. Once you've made the necessary registry change, either restart the computer or stop and restart the IPSec service by running the following from the command line:

```
net stop policyagent
net start policyagent
```

Also, changes to the IP Security policies can also be written to the Security log when you have the Audit Policy Change setting enabled in your audit policies. This can be a valuable troubleshooting tool when network communications fails, and the explanation can be traced back to a change in IPSec policy that has rendered two computers incompatible in terms of network communication.

## Using Network Monitor

Like many of the tools discussed in this chapter, you should know the function of Network Monitor. This section gives you an overview of that function, but a full discussion of everything you could do with Network Monitor is beyond the scope of this book.

Network Monitor is a packet capturing tool. It records packets that are sent to and from the computer on which it's running. Normally, it captures all traffic sent and received, but you can configure Network Monitor filters to capture only certain kinds of packets, such as DNS queries or traffic from only certain IP addresses.

**NOTE** Network Monitor included with System Management Server (SMS) 2.0 is more robust, allowing for packet capture to and from *any* node in the network.

Network Monitor is a fascinating tool. Many times in your computer education, you're told about the "layered" nature of the network protocols. This tool lets you peel open the packets and look at the information stored in these layers. For example, the IP header information contains information about the source and destination address of the packet. It does not include the destination port number. That information is stored in the TCP or UPD layers. Each of these layers can be examined in complete detail using Network Monitor.

Network Monitor is not installed by default. To add Network Monitor, you must first install it by selecting Control Panel | Add/Remove Programs | Adding A Windows Component. You'll find Network Monitor as a component of the Management and Monitoring Tools.

Once installed, a menu shortcut is placed in your Administrative Tools, and you choose this shortcut to launch Network Monitor. You could also add Network Monitor to a custom MMC console.

To start capturing network packets with Network Monitor, first select a network interface you want to monitor. Then use the toolbar buttons (you could use the Capture menu as well) in the Station Stats window to start the capture, as seen in Figure 10-14. The Station Stats window gives you general information about the capture, including the duration, how many packets are captured, and what nodes are captured from. You can also use this window to get a feel for overall bandwidth usage on your network.

When the capture is finished, either choose Stop or Stop And View to view the packets captured. If the capture is stopped, click the View button (looks like a pair of glasses) in the Station Stats window to go to the Capture Summary window.

When you're viewing the capture, the Capture Summary displays all packets captures, along with general information about the packet, such as where the packet originated and what its destination was. Double-clicking one of the packets brings up the Capture Detail window, where you can look at the component parts of the packet. As seen in Figure 10-15, this Capture Detail window lets you see exactly what the packet was for. The packet shown here was a query for DNS resolution for the name www.yahoo.com.

## Kerberos Support Tools

Kerberos is an authentication system whose design objectives are similar to those of IPSec. Namely, it is designed to enable two parties to exchange private information across an otherwise open network. Just as IPSec does this for data being sent over that open network, Kerberos secures authentication requests, ensuring that user access to network services occurs over a secure communications channel.

The Kerberos version 5 (v5) authentication mechanism works by assigning a unique key, called a ticket, to each user who successfully authenticates to a Windows Server 2003 domain controller. These tickets contain encrypted data, including an encrypted password, which confirms the user's identity to the requested service. The ticket is then used to

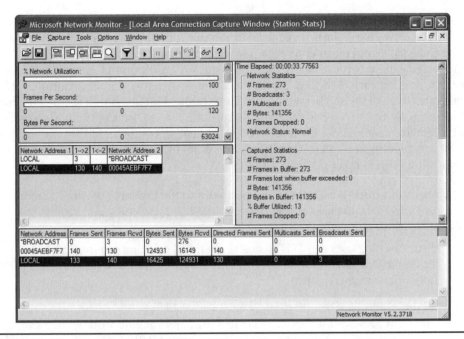

**Figure 10-14** Capturing network traffic with Network Monitor

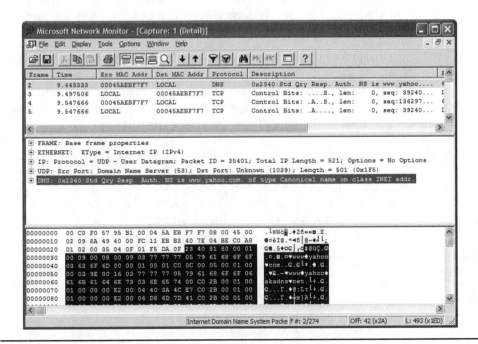

**Figure 10-15** Viewing the packet contents of a capture

secure messages and identify the sender of the message when accessing other network services. Moreover, the entire ticket generation and authentication process is entirely invisible to the end user, except when entering a password or smart card credentials.

The engine of Kerberos v5 authentication is the Key Distribution Center (KDC), a service that runs on each Windows Server 2003 Active Directory domain controller. This KDC stores user names and passwords for clients of the domain, as well as other account information. Kerberos v5 services are installed on each Active Directory domain controller, and a Kerberos client service is installed on each member computer in the domain.

When a user logs on to an Active Directory domain, the following Kerberos v5 authentication process takes place:

1. After submitting a user name and password to the domain (or using a smart card and PIN), the user authenticates to the KDC.

2. The KDC then issues a special ticket-granting ticket (TGT) to the client. The client machine uses this TGT to access the ticket-granting service (TGS) on the Active Directory domain controller. This TGS is part of the Kerberos v5 authentication mechanism.

3. The ticket-granting-service then issues a service ticket to the client.

4. The client presents the service ticket to each requesting network service. For example, if you have configured your DNS server to allow only secure dynamic updates, the DNS server uses the Kerberos-generated ticket for authentication (in other words, you don't have to enter your user name and password again to update the DNS zone file). It's the service ticket that confirms both the user's identity to the service and the service's identity to the user.

As mentioned, every Windows Server 2003 domain controller also serves as a KDC. Additionally, a client uses its configured (DNS) server to locate the nearest available domain controller. That domain controller will then become the client's preferred KDC during the user's logon session. If the preferred KDC becomes unavailable, the client, again using DNS, locates an alternate KDC to provide authentication.

Because a client system also uses the same domain controller where it submits logon credentials for Kerberos authentication, under normal circumstances you should not have to do any configuration of the client's choice of KDC. However, Kerberos v5 is an open-standards protocol, and other servers can provide this same functionality. To configure a client machine to use a server other than a Windows Server 2003 domain controller for Kerberos authentication, you will use a utility called ksetup.

## Using ksetup

ksetup is a command-line tool that can be used to configure a client that authenticates to an Active Directory domain controller running Windows Server 2003 to use an alternate server for Kerberos v5 service ticket generation. When the client uses this alternate Kerberos server instead of its Server 2003 domain, it is said to be using a Kerberos v5 realm. ksetup is used to configure Windows clients for interoperability with other network servers (read, Unix) using Kerberos authentication.

Windows administrators can use the ksetup utility to perform the following tasks:

- Set up a realm entry on the Windows client for a Kerberos v5 realm.
- Set up a list of KDC servers for that realm.
- Set up a Kerberos password (kpasswd) server for that realm.
- Set up a local account to Kerberos v5 account mappings. This is necessary to inform the non-Windows operating system how to authorize a specific security principal.
- Set the computer's password in the Kerberos realm.
- Change a user's password in a Kerberos v5 realm.

**NOTE** Only members of the Administrators or Servers Operations group on the target computer may use ksetup. It only available on Windows Server 2003 machines.

If ksetup is used to let Windows computers use the Kerberos authentication features of a non-Windows system, what about the reverse? Can non-Windows computers be configured to authenticate to Windows network services using Kerberos? They can with the aid of a utility called ktpass.

## Using ktpass

Network services running on Unix systems can be configured for secure integration with services in Active Directory that rely on Kerberos authentication. This allows for full, secure interoperability between the two operating systems. Networks can then mix and match both the services and the operating systems that best meet their needs. To set this up, the ktpass utility is needed.

This command-line tool allows Unix-based services that support Kerberos authentication to use the network service features provided by the Windows Server 2003 Kerberos KDC service. It does this by permitting a Windows administrator to configure a non-Windows Kerberos service as a security principal in the Windows Server 2003 Active Directory domain. To use ktpass, you must specify the server name for the non-Windows host or service in Active Directory. It will then generate an MIT-style Kerberos "keytab" file, which contains the shared secret Kerberos key for the service.

But in order to make this work, you need to generate the aforementioned Unix host keytab file, map a security principal to the account, and set the host principal password. You can't just create a Unix-style account in the Active Directory database. Instead, these Kerberos accounts are generated by using service principal name mappings.

Here is the procedure you'll use:

1. Open the Active Directory User and Computers MMC snap-in (Start | All Programs | Administrative Tools), and create a user account for the Unix service. For instance, you might create a user account called UnixAccess.

2. Set up an mapping for the user account using ktpass. Using the UnixAccess account, the syntax would look like this:

```
ktpass /princ ServiceInstance@REALM /mapuser UnixAccess
/pass Password /out Unixmachine.Keytab
```

3. Merge or replace the new keytab file with the /Etc/Krb5.keytab file on the Unix host.

Now integration of Windows-based Kerberos and Unix, or MIT Kerberos is possible. The Unix Kerberos services use the keytab file to log on and use Windows Kerberos services.

# Chapter Review

In this chapter, we've looked at how to best secure the resources in a Windows Server 2003 network using a variety of administrative procedures. We looked at how we might configure baseline security settings using the Security Templates tool.

We looked at IP Security and its role in securing network communications over a non-secure network, and then used tools such as the IP Security Monitor to manage the implementation of IP Security policies.

Also, we defined the principle of least privilege. Using the principle of least privilege, you ensure that users get only the permissions they need to get work done.

Finally, we looked at the Kerberos v5 authentication process, and how it is used to secure access to network services once domain authentication has been submitted. In Windows-only environments, configuration of Kerberos settings is not necessary. However, when configuring interoperability with non-Windows systems, two tools may be used: ksetup and ktpass. We looked at instances where both might be used.

## Questions

1. You are the administrator for a Windows Server 2003 Active Directory domain called bigcarp.com. You are concerned about protecting data on the company's file server. You implement IPSec policies as part of a GPO that applies to an organizational unit that contains all the domain's member servers. You want to verify that IPSec is working properly on the network. What steps can you take? (Choose all that apply.)

A. Run System Monitor to analyze all IP traffic, and watch counters that specify encrypted IP traffic.

B. Check the Security log of the Event Viewer regularly to watch for events that enable audit policy.

C. Run the IP Security Monitor to check for IP Security Statistics in main mode.

D. Install and run the Windows Security Monitor from the Windows Support Tools, and configure this utility to write all security events to the Event Viewer.

2. You are the administrator of a Windows Server 2003 domain. Although IPSec policies are in effect throughout the network, these policies will not change very often. Further, the infrastructure is spread over a large geographic area, and you do not want computers using much bandwidth checking for changes to the IPSec policies. How can you configure the policy so that you can lengthen the default refresh interval?

   **A.** Right-click the IPSec policy node and change the Refresh Interval setting from the context menu.

   **B.** Configure the IPSec agent not to start automatically from the Services MMC console.

   **C.** Select the active policy in the IPSec node of the Group Policy Object and change the Check For Policy Changes setting on the General tab in the policy's Properties dialog box.

   **D.** Select the active policy in the IPSec node of the Group Policy Object and change the Check For Policy Changes setting on the Schedule tab in the policy's Properties dialog box.

3. You are the administrator for a Windows Server 2003 Active Directory domain called bigcarp.com. You have signed a licensing agreement to license your company's technology to another company. This other company uses Unix servers, but also uses Kerberos v5 authentication. You want to allow these Unix computers access to Windows network services using the Kerberos v5 authentication. What tool should you use to accomplish your goal?

   **A.** ksetup

   **B.** ktpass

   **C.** IPSec Group Policies

   **D.** A Certificate Services server

4. You are the administrator for a Windows Server 2003 Active Directory domain called bigcarp.com. There are several servers in the network, and one of these has been recently been upgraded to Windows Server 2003. You have deployed IPSec policies to secure the flow of traffic to and from these member servers, and want to document the policies that are effective. Which of the following tools can be used to collect information about monitoring IPSec policies from the Windows Server 2003 machine? (Choose all that apply.)

   **A.** Use the IP Security Monitor to view the active policies for the local machine.

   **B.** Use the Computer Management MMC snap-in to verify the IPSec policies that are active for the local computer.

   **C.** Use Network Monitor to capture and analyze network traffic on the local segment.

   **D.** Use the IP Security Monitor to view the active policies for remote machines.

5. You are the administrator of a Windows Server 2003 domain and are troubleshooting the domain's IPSec policies. You want a single policy to apply to all domain users, and another, more secure policy to affect members of the Research organizational unit. The Research OU is a child OU of the Kansas City OU. Upon investigation with the IP Security Monitor, you discover that an entirely different IPSec policy is being applied to the Research OU. What is the most likely cause of the problem?

A. The policy that is last applied becomes the effective policy; here a KC policy is applied after the domain policy, and its settings become the effective setting for the Research OU.

B. The No Override setting configured for the GPO linked to the KC organizational unit.

C. There is a local policy effective for computers in the Research OU, and local policies are always the effective policy when configured.

D. Domain policies are effective only when settings are more restrictive than policies processed later in the processing order.

6. You are the administrator for a Windows Server 2003 Active Directory domain called bigcarp.com. You want to have your domain clients use a different server for Kerberos v5 ticket generation other than the Windows Server 2003 domain controller because they need access to network services running Unix. These Unix machines also use Kerberos v5 authentication before granting services access. What tool should you use?

A. ksetup

B. ktpass

C. IPSec Group Policies

D. A Certificate Services server

7. Which of the following are true about IPSec implementation in a Windows Server 2003 enterprise? (Choose all that apply.)

A. IPSec policies use filters to evaluate traffic leaving and entering a particular computer.

B. IPSec policies can be implemented only at the domain level; this ensures that computers then participate in the secured communication.

C. IPSec policies can be used to allow HTTP traffic only that is destined for a specific port.

D. IPSec policies can be used to block e-mail traffic that contains certain attachments.

8. You are the administrator of a Windows Server 2003 domain and want to implement the Kerberos v5 authentication protocol in your network. The network consists of 15 Windows Server 2003 machines, and 200 client computers that are running either Windows 2000 or Windows XP Professional. What steps

should you take to ensure that Kerberos v5 tickets are generated when users submit their logon credentials?

A. Make sure that smart cards are used for domain authentication.

B. Add the Kerberos v5 protocol to all domain controllers using the Network applet in Control Panel. All client machines will then download the protocol the first time they log on to the domain.

C. Configure the Kerberos authentication password using the ktpass utility for the Windows Server 2003 computers.

D. Do nothing. The Kerberos v5 protocol is automatically installed when a Windows Server 2003 domain is created, and all client computers in this scenario support Kerberos authentication.

9. You are the administrator for a Windows Server 2003 Active Directory domain called bigcarp.com. The network uses TCP/IP exclusively, and confidential data needs to be sent to and from geographically dispersed offices using the Internet as the networking medium. You have been asked to recommend a plan that will secure this data sent over a public network, but have been told to do so without the purchase of additional hardware. What should you recommend to most effectively achieve your goal? (Choose all that apply.)

A. Implement a Kerberos v5 authentication scheme for access to network services.

B. Implement IPSec for all computers in the network, including clients who rely on dial-in access to network servers.

C. Use smart cards to secure the logon process for all users.

D. All of the above.

10. Which of the following are true about the capabilities of the netsh command-line utility?

A. netsh can be used to implement IPSec policies in a scripted file.

B. There are IPSec configuration features available through netsh that are not available with the IP Security Policy Management MMC snap-in.

C. netsh can be used to configure DHCP as well as IPSec policies.

D. All of the above.

## Answers

1. **B and C.** The Event Viewer is used to track events that might indicate a security breach, and is the receptacle for events that are captured by any active audit policies. The IP Security Monitor can collect IPSec statistics for encrypted communication, including authenticated packets sent and received, and packets not encrypted or authenticated.

2. **C.** The Check For Policy Changes value specifies how often the IPSec agent running on the client system will check for changes to policy settings and download them if there have been any. Configuring a longer interval can conserve bandwidth in slower networks.

3. **B.** The ktpass command-line tool allows Unix-based services that support Kerberos authentication to use the network services provided by the Windows Server 2003 Kerberos KDC service. Administrators set this up by configuring a non-Windows Kerberos service as a security principal in the Windows Server 2003 Active Directory domain using the ktpass utility.

4. **A and D.** The Windows Server 2003 IP Security Monitor can be used to view active policies on both the local machine and on remote computers. There are only two tools that can monitor IPSec traffic: the IP Security Monitor and the Security log of the Event Viewer.

5. **A.** The order of GPO processing is local, site, domain, and OU. Although not explicitly discussed in the confines of this chapter, you should be familiar with the processing order for GPOs, as it's liable to appear anywhere in the four core Windows Server 2003 exams.

6. **A.** The ksetup command-line tool is used to configure a client that authenticates to an Active Directory domain controller to use an alternate server for Kerberos v5 service ticket generation. When the client uses this alternate Kerberos v5 server, it can then interoperate with other non-Windows servers that use Kerberos authentication.

7. **A, C, and D.** All of these are true about IPSec implementation. You can implement an IPSec policy to secure traffic for all domain computers or just a single computer, depending on the Group Policy Object where the IPSec policy is configured.

8. **D.** Kerberos v5 is automatically installed and used by Windows Server 2003 computers and by operating systems using Windows 2000 or later.

9. **A and B.** Implement IPSec for all computers if you are concerned with securing traffic sent over public networks such as the Internet. You can configure the IPSec policies in the domain so that data is encrypted and is only sent and received from trusted sources. The Kerberos v5 authentication will ensure that only users who have authenticated to the domain will have access to network services. Smart cards can better secure the logon process, but require additional hardware.

10. **D.** The netsh command-line tool is a powerful utility that can be used to configure IPSec behaviors as well as parameters of other network services such as DHCP and RRAS. One of its primary advantages over the IP Security Policy Management tool is its ability to be called by a script.

# Maintaining a Network Infrastructure

In this chapter, you will learn how to
- Monitor network traffic with System Monitor and Network Monitor
- Troubleshoot connectivity to the Internet
- Troubleshoot server dependency and recovery

Once the network infrastructure is in place, an administrator's job is to keep it functioning at optimal levels and to take corrective action when it is not. This chapter will equip you with some of the knowledge needed for this vital administrative duty. Most of the time, when the network is down, an organization's productivity is down as well.

Part II's last chapter examines how to monitor a Windows 2003 network infrastructure. While there are several software tools available for this task (some manufactured by other software vendors), the 291 exam will expect you to know about the ones provided by Microsoft. This chapter includes an overview of tools such as the Network and System Monitor that are specifically mentioned in the test objectives. Additionally, this chapter includes a look at many of the diagnostic and troubleshooting tools used when computers cannot communicate on the Internet. Normally when computers cannot connect to the Internet, they cannot communicate with each other as well. The tools discussed can help you find the solutions to these problems should they occur.

Finally, the chapter looks at the services running on your Windows Server 2003 machine. These server services provide the functionality that clients of the server rely on, and therefore it's essential that you be able to diagnose the cause of a particular service failure.

## Monitor Network Traffic

After the network infrastructure is in place, after its traffic has been secured and remote access has been granted, administrators must be able to measure and monitor that traffic going back and forth. There are two essential objectives when monitoring traffic. One objective is to measure the performance of a network, to be able to say quantitatively whether performance is good or poor, and why. The other objective of troubleshooting is for root cause analysis—finding out why network communication is not performing as expected.

There are two tools that can help you monitor network traffic: System Monitor and Network Monitor. You can use the information gathered by these two tools to help measure baselines of normal performance and diagnose network problems, both of which will, in turn, help you devise a capacity planning scheme that will prevent future problems from occurring.

## System Monitor

System Monitor is a very robust tool that will let you collect data about not just network performance, but also about almost any usage of hardware and software resources for a Windows Server 2003 computer. It provides for centralized performance monitoring, as it can be used to collect information on both the local system or on any other system in the network. When you use System Monitor, you will make the following decisions about the data you want to collect:

- **Type of data**   The first decision concerns what kind of data to collect. When determining data to be collected, you specify performance objects, performance counters, and performance object instances. Each of these terms will be defined later in this section. For now, just know that certain System Monitor objects are useful for describing performance of system resources (memory, processor, network) and others provide information about the operation of applications (in this case, think system services).

- **Source of data**   After deciding what to collect, you'll then decide what system to collect from. System Monitor has the ability to collect data from either the local machine or from other computers on the network. Note that to gather performance data, you need administrative credentials on the machine where System Monitor will be gathering performance counters.

- **Sampling parameter**   Once you determined what and where the data will be collected, you then decide how the data is collected. You can launch System Monitor manually or automatically by scheduling it to run at certain times or after certain events, as previously mentioned. Further, you will set a sampling interval, which specifies how often data will be sampled. When viewing data captured in a log file, you can also choose starting and stopping times so that you can view data only that falls within a specific time range.

Additionally, System Monitor lets you collect information using counter logs. These log files can be very useful in setting a baseline of performance, and can also be triggered to begin logging data when certain problems occur or when certain performance thresholds are tripped.

In addition to options for defining what kind of data is collected by System Monitor, and from where, the System Monitor administrator is faced with decisions about the method of data display. You have considerable flexibility at your disposal and can vary the data presentation based on your choice of

- **Type of display**   There are three System Monitor views for data captured: graph, histogram, and report views. System Monitor defaults to the graph view, as it makes a meaningful picture of performance data and offers the widest variety of optional settings.

- **Display characteristics**   For any of the three System Monitor views, you can define the colors and fonts for the display. In graph and histogram views, you can select from many different options when you view performance data:

  - **Labels**   You will name the vertical axis in a graph or histogram.

  - **Range of values**   You are not confined to displaying the entirety of the information gathered, but can select just the most relevant data for display.

  - **Format of lines or bars**   Like formatting words (making certain words bold to draw special attention, for example), you have the ability to draw the eye to certain measurements in the System Monitor display using color, width, style, and other graphical elements.

Before you can accurately measure abnormal use on your system, you have to go about defining normal use. This process of appraising normal use is also known as establishing a baseline.

**NOTE**   Sometimes establishing a baseline is described as *benchmarking* a system. No matter what you call it, the question answered by the process is the same: what is normal for this machine?

In real-world use, there is probably no great need to establish baselines for each and every one of your enterprise's computers. You should certainly do this, however, on any servers that will form the backbone of your network, because if these machines perform poorly, so will your entire network. You should especially measure baselines at the following times:

- When the computer is first brought online and begins operation
- When any changes are made to the hardware or software configuration

The reason that baselines are useful for the above-mentioned situations is self-evident: when any changes are made to the system, you will have something to which you can compare the changes. Like a weight-loss advertisement, you will create a "before" snapshot that you can compare to the "after." Good administrative practice is to make sure baselines have been created before making any changes to your Windows Server 2003 computer.

Another use for System Monitor is to identify a bottleneck. A bottleneck is any system resource that causes slowdowns to the computer system as a whole. Bottlenecks cause slowdowns by causing other resources to sit around while the source of the bottleneck completes its task. The thing you need to keep in mind about bottlenecks is that there's *always* a bottleneck. The computer won't operate at the speed of light. So upgrading a component to resolve a bottleneck in one area can shift the focus of a bottleneck to another area. It's just a matter of finding and resolving the ones that are causing a noticeable degradation of performance.

The other monitoring duty you have is to proactively find trends that are occurring on a system. This job goes hand in hand with the creation of baselines and is really nothing more than comparing multiple baselines against one another to determine what kinds of usage patterns emerge. For example, suppose you are taking snapshots of normal usage for one day a month, and the log files show that CPU usage is increasing by about 5 percent each time you measure. You can then assume that within eight months' time, your CPU usage will increase by 40 percent, and you're going to have problems. By tracking trends, you can proactively take steps to ensure that certain performance problems never occur. A bottleneck is caused when one resource is slowing down overall performance.

 **NOTE**   Although you won't need knowledge of Windows 2003 groups for this test, you should be aware that there are two new groups built into the Windows Server 2003 operating system that can help secure access to performance data. These two groups are the Performance Log Users group and the Performance Monitor Users group.

You can use System Monitor to make sense of the information collected in a counter log. Without System Monitor, the data in the log files is just that—data. System Monitor, with its ability to make pictures, can help extract meaning from that data. Also, in Windows Server 2003, you can now simultaneously view data from multiple log files.

You can use the System Monitor functionality in other applications that support ActiveX controls. If you don't speak ActiveX, don't worry, lots of applications do. ActiveX means that the System Monitor views are supported in web pages, and in Microsoft Office applications such as Microsoft Word.

Similar to creating custom MMC consoles that can then be used on multiple computers, you can create multiple computer performance monitoring configurations that can be installed on other computers, allowing you to quickly set up System Monitor measurements on many systems.

## Viewing System Monitor Data

A picture is worth a thousand words, and System Monitor helps you create pictures from the data that is collected during monitoring. System Monitor is part of the Performance console that lets you easily display data generated from either real-time activity or from log files. When you first open System Monitor, you'll notice that nothing is tracked by default. To start making use of the tool, you must tell System Monitor exactly what to track. You do this by adding instances of counters of certain objects to the current graph in the Add Counters dialog box, as shown in Figure 11-1.

**Figure 11-1**

Adding
Performance
Monitor counters

There are three terms you must be familiar with to effectively use System Monitor. They are

- **Object**   The individual system resource that can be monitored.
- **Counter**   A unit of performance of that object that can be quantified numerically.
- **Instance**   A further subdivision of a counter. For example, on a system with two processors, there can be three instances of the %Processor Time counter: one for processor 1, one for processor 2, and a third instance for total processor time.

When you start using System Monitor, the options available can be a little overwhelming. Don't worry; nobody outside of Microsoft has a thorough understanding of every single counter that can be tracked with System Monitor. You won't be able to memorize every aspect of System Monitor, so don't try. The important thing to remember, both for exam purposes and for real-world use, is which counters are most effective for measuring everyday usage of a system. You will have to experiment with System Monitor, of course, to get comfortable with this tool, but one nice feature is a detailed description of what each counter does that pops up when you click the Explain button as you go to add a counter. You can see what happens when you click this button in Figure 11-2.

**Figure 11-2**

The contents
of the Explain
button

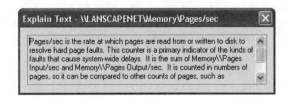

The resources that have the greatest impact on performance on the vast majority of systems, in general order of importance, are memory, processor, network, and disk (depending on how a system is used, that ranking is subject to change). With these four counters, you'll do roughly 80 percent of your performance monitoring, and you've just considerably whittled down your list of objects to which you need to give your day-to-day attention. Of the possible counters for these objects, some are going to be more helpful than others when taking performance snapshots. In the following sections, the most common counters that are measured on the most important objects will be noted.

## Memory Performance

Consider the metaphor of the desktop as it applies to the computer. Windows has been using this metaphor for years because it is an anchor, a link to something that we are already familiar with, and something we've had an understanding of for years—a desk—that helps us relate to this entirely new tool, a computer operating system.

You can also extend this metaphor to help you understand most computer hardware. If you think of your brain as the CPU, all the stuff on your office desk is the area of memory. It is the place you first look when you want to "process" more information. If the information you are looking for is on your desk, that's great, and you can access it quickly. If not, you have to go to the filing cabinet (the hard drive) to retrieve the information you want. The bigger the desk space you have, the more things will quickly be at your fingertips when you want to work with them.

Memory is the most common cause of system bottlenecks. There is virtually no way for a system to have too much memory, and it is a great starting point as you begin to look for bottlenecks. To find out how much memory your system is using, you need to examine two main areas: physical memory and the pagefile.

A system's physical memory are the physical sticks of RAM that hold all the 1s and 0s that make up the instructions for an application, an operating system, or a hardware device. Each location in memory is given a memory address, which is how the CPU keeps track of what application is placing instructions where. So to applications, RAM is simply a long list of numbers that it sees as available. Again, you can't have too much and it's next to free.

The pagefile is logical memory that exists in a file called pagefile.sys located on the root of the drive Windows has been installed on. Like physical RAM, the pagefile is a list of addressable locations where 1s and 0s can be stored. In fact, applications have no idea whether the instructions it is sending to memory are kept on the pagefile or in physical RAM. That's a process usually governed by the Windows operating system. The one who can tell the difference is you, the user, who will notice a considerable slowdown in performance when the pagefile is accessed frequently, as the speed performance of RAM is greater than the performance of a hard disk by a factor of about 100.

Following are the most important counters for monitoring memory:

- **Memory > Available MBytes**  Measures the amount of available memory that is available to run a process. If this number is less than 4MB, you should add more memory.

- **Memory > Pages/Sec**  Shows the number of times that the processor requested information that was not in physical memory and had to be retrieved from disk. For optimal performance, this counter should be set at around 4 or 5.

- **Paging file > %Usage**  Indicates how much of the allocated pagefile is currently in use. If this number is consistently larger than 99 percent, you may need to add memory.

**TIP**  Because of the pagefile, systems that are short on memory will often report high disk usage. This is because the disk is being asked all the time for data that should be living in physical memory. Fix the memory problem and the high disk usage problem disappears.

## Processor Utilization

It's a rare case that a processor is the source of a bottleneck. Most people buy much more processor than they really need. After all, how fast do you need that e-mail to open anyway? However, if you suspect that your processor is cause for concern, you should monitor the following counters:

- **Processor > %Processor Time**  Measures the time that the processor is busy responding to system requests. If this value is consistently above 80 percent, you may indeed have a processor bottleneck.

- **Processor > Interrupts/Sec**  Shows the average number of times each second the processor is interrupted by hardware requests for attention. This number should generally be below 3500. However, problems in this area indicate a problem with hardware that may be malfunctioning and sending unnecessary interrupts.

## Disk Performance

Disk access is the amount of time it takes your disk subsystem to retrieve data that is requested by the operating system. You can monitor two objects when measuring disk performance. The PhysicalDisk object is a sum of all logical drives on a single hard disk, and the LogicalDisk object represents a single logical disk. The following counters can be tracked for both the PhysicalDisk and LogicalDisk object; the PhysicalDisk is used in this example:

- **PhysicalDisk > %Disk Time**  Shows the amount of time a disk is busy responding to read and write requests. If the disk is busy more than 90 percent of the time, you can improve performance by adding another disk channel and splitting the I/O requests between the channels.

- **PhysicalDisk > %Current Disk Queue Length**  Indicates the number of outstanding disk requests that are waiting to be processed. This value should be less than 2.

## Network Performance

The measurement of network performance is usually done by looking at the network as a whole, not the performance of an individual computer. Windows Server 2003 does not include a tool for monitoring the entire network, but you can monitor the traffic that is being sent and received on the local network card, as well as the performance of any protocols bound to that card. Here are the network counters that you will find most useful:

- **Network Interface > Bytes Total/Sec**   Measures the total number of bytes sent and received from the network interface card (NIC). It does not specify which protocol, but looks at total traffic instead. You can compare this number against the total bandwidth capacity of your card. You should not exceed 30 percent of your card's total megabits per second (Mbps) rating for extended periods.

- **TCP > Segments/Sec**   Filters and measures the number of bytes that are sent or received from the network interface that are TCP-specific.

By the way, how does one go about fixing these problems when bottlenecks are detected? In a word, upgrade. Add more memory, swap out to a better processor if the motherboard allows, use faster drives or a striping array, and get a faster NIC of at least 100 Mbps.

---

 **NOTE**   The advice to upgrade makes the assumption that you have first made sure all other network-specific performance variables have been accounted for. For example, is there a driver update and/or firmware revision that could improve performance? What about the settings of the card? Are the protocols bound in the order they are most frequently used? Sometimes, the only way to improve performance is to upgrade, but you should first make sure that the configuration of the network is optimized in the first place.

## Application Performance

If you are consistently running multiple applications concurrently on your Windows Server 2003 system, there are a couple of ways to optimize performance.

To configure application performance, from the Control Panel, double-click the System icon and select the Advanced tab. (You can also right-click My Computer and choose Properties.) From there, click the Settings button in the Performance section to display the Performance Options dialog box, as shown in Figure 11-3.

The Performance Options dialog box allows you to configure application response so that foreground applications are always given a higher performance priority, which is the default, or so that foreground applications and background services are given the same priority. You might want to consider changing the application response option to Background Services if your Windows Server 2003 system is frequently accessed as a file or print server.

**Figure 11-3**
The Performance
Options dialog
box

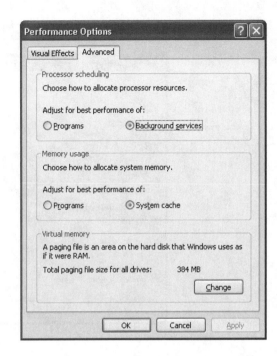

You can also set the paging file (virtual memory) size and location from here. To re-view, the pagefile is the physical location of logical memory—memory that exists on the hard drive. Windows manages virtual memory, and it would be rare for an administrator to change any of the virtual memory settings on a Windows Server 2003 computer. It is possible to improve virtual memory slightly by moving the paging file, pagefile.sys, to a faster hard drive. You can configure this by clicking the Change button on the Perfor-mance Options dialog box. Then, from the Virtual Memory dialog box, as seen in Figure 11-4, you can change the location of the pagefile by selecting the desired drive, choosing the Initial Size and the Maximum Size settings, and clicking Set.

Of course, the best way to optimize the use of virtual memory is not to use it—install more physical memory instead, which is approximately 1,000 times faster than virtual memory.

## System Security

System Monitor can also be used to help you monitor server security. There some useful counters to help you with this task, including

- **Server > Errors Access Permissions** The number of times clients have attempted to open a file and have received a STATUS_ACCESS_DENIED. This counter can indicate whether somebody is randomly attempting to access files in hopes of getting at something that was not properly protected.

**Figure 11-4**
Altering the
default virtual
memory settings

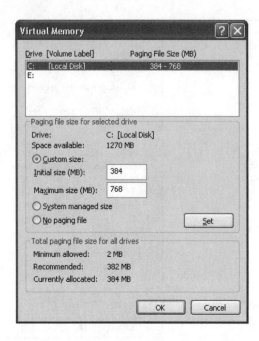

- **Server > Errors Granted Access** The number of times accesses to files opened successfully were denied. Can indicate attempts to access files without proper access authorization.

- **Server > Errors Logon** The number of failed logon attempts to the server. A high reading of this counter is a good indication of whether password guessing programs are being used to crack the security on the server.

## Network Monitor

In Chapter 10, you were introduced to Network Monitor. There is also a command-line version of Network Monitor that can be used to gather packets off the network wire. This command-line tool is called netmon.

The advantage of the netmon utility is the ability to start a Network Monitor user interface from the command line. And, because it can be called from the command line, it can also be called from a scripted file. netmon offers all the functionality of Network Monitor, including the ability to implement filters on captured traffic, both incoming to and outgoing from the computer where Network Monitor is being run. Once you understand that netmon is Network Monitor from the command line, you have pretty much all you need to know other than the exact syntax.

So here is the syntax used when monitoring with netmon:

```
start netmon [/net Number] [/capturefilter Path] [/displayfilter Path]
[/buffersize Number] [/quickfilter {ATM | ETHERNET | IP | IPX | VINES |
 TOKENRING | FDDI}, Address] [/quickfiltername FilterName] [/autostart]
[/autostop]
```

Also, notice that Network Monitor is installed by default on a Windows Server 2003 machine. But that doesn't mean that your Windows Server 2003 came with the default installation. You might have to install Network Monitor before you can use netmon. To install it, follow these steps:

1. Select Control Panel | Add/Remove Programs.

2. In the Add/Remove Programs window, open the Windows Components Wizard by clicking Add/Remove Windows Components.

3. In the Windows Components Wizard, select the Management and Monitoring Tools (don't click the check box; it installs all Management and Monitoring tools), and then click Details.

4. In Subcomponents of Management and Monitoring Tools, select the Network Monitor Tools check box, and then click OK.

5. Here you may be prompted for the Windows Server 2003 installation files, which you can retrieve from the installation CD, or by browsing for a location to the files on a network server.

Once Network Monitor is installed, you can use the netmon tool from the command prompt.

# Troubleshoot Connectivity to the Internet

There are many things that can go wrong when networking computers, and as an administrator, you will become familiar with a good many of them. With the thought in mind that network problems are a fact of life in modern computing environments, it can help stem the tide of trouble calls if you keep some of the following Microsoft recommendations in mind when designing and configuring your network:

- **If you use multiple network adapters, rename each local area connection.** The Windows Server 2003 installation will automatically detect any supported network adapters and then create a local area connection in the Network Connections folder for each adapter. If you have more than one network adapter (which you would commonly have if the machine were to serve as an RRAS server or a proxy server, for example), you can eliminate confusion by renaming each local area connection. In most cases, you will give the adapters descriptive names like Internal and External. This makes it easier to troubleshoot IP address configuration.

- **Add or enable the network clients, services, and protocols that are required for each connection.** Each connection must have the appropriate client services and protocols for each type of server it will be requesting data from, and each connection that will be sharing out services must likewise have the services required by its clients. If you are setting up a Windows-only network, all required services—the File and Print Sharing for Microsoft Networks, the

Client for Microsoft Networks, and the TCP/IP protocol—will all be installed by default. If clients will not be sharing out any resources, you can close possible security holes by disabling the File and Print Sharing for Microsoft Networks on these machines

- **Verify required connection settings for your network adapter.** If you are configuring a static IP address for a computer (sometimes your ISP will require this; other times it is wise to have certain servers have a static IP address) you will want to ensure that these statically configured machines have the following:

  - Specific IP address

  - DNS addresses

  - DNS domain name

  - Default gateway address

  - WINS addresses (if applicable)

---

 **NOTE** By default, even Windows Server 2003 machines are DHCP clients. This means that you will likely get all of the above configuration information automatically from a DHCP server, even if that "server" is just a router interface that can hand out addresses. Automated IP settings are used for all connections by default, eliminate the need to configure settings listed above.

---

- **Create your dial-up, VPN, or direct connections by using the New Connection Wizard.** After configuring a connection, you can then treat the connection objects much like you can treat other software objects on your computer. That is, you can copy the connection, rename it, and easily modify the connection settings via a Properties dialog box. Using such techniques, you can efficiently create different connections to accommodate multiple modems, ISPs, dialing profiles, and so on.

- **Ensure efficient network communications by specifying the order in which network protocols are used.** If your connection uses multiple network protocols, you can set the binding order of those protocols, which establishes a hierarchy of preference when accessing network servers. You should set the most often-used protocol at the top of this list.

  For example, if your LAN connection will be accessing both NetWare and Microsoft Windows networks, two protocols are needed: IPX and TCP/IP. However, the most often accessed servers are the Windows servers using TCP/IP. Therefore, you should ensure the Microsoft Windows Network is at the top of the Network Providers list on the Provider Order tab, and also ensure that Internet Protocol (TCP/IP) is at the top of the File and Printer Sharing for Microsoft Networks binding list.

  You will access network bindings settings from the Network Connections dialog box by choosing Advanced Options under the Advanced menu. As shown in Figure 11-5, you configure the binding order with the two tabs here: Adapters and Bindings, and Provider Order.

**Figure 11-5**

Setting the binding order for network protocols

• **If you don't need it, don't install it.** Just because you can install other protocols doesn't mean you should. In fact, each additional protocol installed for a network or network adapter increases the network traffic generated, and thus is a drag on performance. Limiting the number of protocols on your computer optimizes network speed. If your computer encounters a problem with a network or dial-up connection, it attempts to establish connectivity by using every network protocol enabled. If you only have the protocols installed that your system needs to communicate, the operating system does not attempt connections using protocols it cannot use and will return status information to you more quickly.

## TCP/IP Problems

In your administrative career, you'll discover that anything that can go wrong will go wrong. You'll also discover that a single problem can have a multitude of causes. For example, if you cannot connect to the Internet, the usual cause is with the client's TCP/IP configuration. But what? There are many factors that make up a correct TCP/IP configuration.

Is it the IP address itself? Is it using an IP address that is on the same network as its companions? If not, it could be trying to route traffic that is does not need to, and probably has no way to get to the default gateway.

Is it the subnet mask? If you have incorrectly configured the subnet mask, the host may be on a different logical network than its peers. It will think it has to route local traffic, and it will see its default gateway as living on a different subnet, which cannot be the case for a default gateway. Conversely, the system may conclude, after the ANDing process, that a remote host is on the same local network and therefore not direct the request to the router.

Is it the default gateway? Because the default gateway represents the pathway off the local segment, an incorrectly configured default gateway will not allow any Internet traffic to commence.

Is it the DNS server? As you now know, the DNS server provides resolution of FQDNs to IP addresses. If your computer cannot resolve the name www.ebay.com to an IP address, you can't shop. One way to test for DNS configuration problems is to try to use an IP address (so the DNS server is not involved in the communication attempt) to navigate to a web site or other resource rather than using the fully qualified domain name.

**NOTE** Many of the above-referenced problems are reduced to the point of nonexistence when you have configured the client to receive its IP address via a DHCP server. That's why even the Windows Server 2003 operating systems defaults to DHCP configuration.

As mentioned in Chapter 7 in this 70-291 exam section, every IP address on a network must be unique. If a computer tries to use an IP address that is already in use on the network, the IP address will not bind to the network adapter. This avoids disruption of network communications. Fortunately, Windows Server 2003 is kind enough to inform you when a duplicate address is detected. You will see a dialog box explaining that an IP address conflict has been detected, usually before you are able to log on. If you run the ipconfig utility, the subnet mask will be 0.0.0.0. The ipconfig utility and its brethren are discussed in the section that follows.

There are several TCP/IP tools that can help you troubleshoot connectivity, and if you have to administer a production network for very long, use of these command-line utilities will become second nature. Some of these tools have been mentioned throughout this section and will make cameos throughout the book, but it will serve you well to have them all discussed in one place.

In the discussion that follows, we'll identify some of the most commonly used switches for each utility and explain why they're used. It is not an exhaustive look at each and every one of these utilities, a discussion which could easily fill scores of pages.

## ipconfig

In your troubleshooting lineup, this one will always bat leadoff. ipconfig displays current TCP/IP network configuration value, especially when used with the /all switch. The /all switch displays information such as the configured DNS and WINS servers (if present) and whether or not the host is a DHCP client. When used without parameters, ipconfig displays the IP address, subnet mask, and default gateway, as shown in Figure 11-6.

It is also be used with the switches presented in Table 11-1.

**NOTE** As with all of these command-line utilities, you can get help on exact syntax without thumbing through a computer book by using the /? switch.

**Figure 11-6**

Results of the ipconfig utility

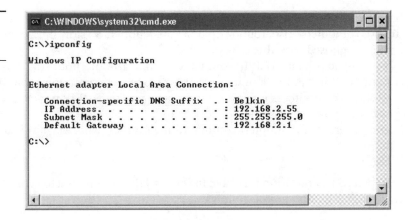

```
C:\WINDOWS\system32\cmd.exe                          _ □ ×

C:\>ipconfig

Windows IP Configuration

Ethernet adapter Local Area Connection:

        Connection-specific DNS Suffix  . : Belkin
        IP Address. . . . . . . . . . . : 192.168.2.55
        Subnet Mask . . . . . . . . . . : 255.255.255.0
        Default Gateway . . . . . . . . : 192.168.2.1

C:\>
```

## ping

The ping utility verifies connectivity from one IP network adapter to another. It does this by sending a small packet of information (it can be used to send a large packet as well) to the computer name or IP address specified in the syntax. When the ping sender receives

**Table 11-1**

Switches Used with the ipconfig Utility

| Switch | Purpose |
|---|---|
| /release | Sends a message to the currently configured DHCP server to release the IP address in use, and is only effective when clients have been configured to obtain their IP addresses automatically. |
| /renew | Causes the client to try to get an IP address from any available Dynamic Host Configuration Protocol server, and is likewise available only for computers that have been configured as DHCP clients. |
| /flushdns | During DNS troubleshooting, you can use this switch to discard negative cache entries from the cache, as well as any other entries that have been added dynamically. A negative cache entry specifies that a given host name could not be resolved. It is kept in the cache to prevent your DNS server from having to walk the DNS hierarchy for names that cannot be resolved. |
| /displaydns | Shows the contents of the DNS resolver cache. This can be checked to see if any incorrect cached DNS entries are the source of a name resolution problem. |
| /registerdns | Forces a manual name registration for all host names for a given computer to its configured DNS server. You use this switch to troubleshoot a failed DNS name registration or resolve a dynamic update problem with the DNS server without rebooting the client computer. |

back a corresponding Echo Reply message, communication has been verified between the two computers. Also, round-trip times are reported, so slow links between computers can be diagnosed with this utility as well.

ping is the primary TCP/IP command used to troubleshoot connectivity and name resolution. You can think of it as sonar for computer communication. If a ping is successful, the computer is on and can send and receive TCP/IP packets. Therefore, other types of communication should work as well.

ping is one of the simplest command-line utilities, whose syntax is thus:

```
ping IP Address or computername
```

When communication is failing, the general flow of pinging to verify TCP/IP connectivity from a computer is as follows:

- Ping the loopback address of 127.0.0.1.
- Ping the local computer's IP address.
- Ping the default gateway.
- Ping the remote computer you are trying to reach.

This is generally done in reverse order to try to isolate the cause of broken network communication.

Furthermore, you can ping other computers using IP addresses or by using host names. This is a good way to troubleshoot name resolution problems. If a ping is successful using the IP address of a computer but not its host name, you should check your name resolution methods for problems. (This might be a good time to run ipconfig /flushdns.)

If ping is unable to resolve an IP address on the network, but pinging the local loopback adapter address of 127.0.0.1 works, use ipconfig to verify that an address has been assigned to the network adapter. Configuration and protocol testing varies from one protocol to the next.

The ping command can be used the following set of modifiers:

- **-t**  Specifies that the ping send a continuous string of Echo Request messages to the destination host until interrupted. To interrupt and display statistics, press CRTL-BREAK. To interrupt and quit ping, press CTRL-C.

- **-a**  Specifies that reverse name resolution is performed on the destination IP address. If this is successful, ping displays the corresponding host name.

- **-l**  Specifies the length, in bytes, of the ping. The default is 32. The maximum size is 65,527. Ping Echo Requests bigger than the default are commonly referred to as fat packet pings. This switch can be used in conjunction with the -t switch to quickly flood a server with traffic, making for a very simple and effective denial-of-service attack. And no, you can't ping Microsoft's servers.

**NOTE** It is very possible that you will be able to browse a web site even though you cannot ping the web server. That is because many firewalls on the Internet filter out the type of packets used for pinging (Internet Control Message Protocol [ICMP] traffic). This is a security measure, because an easy, effective hack is to flood a web server with continuous fat packet pings from one or more computers, which try to overwhelm a server with repeated, large ping packets. One way to combat this is to have a firewall block all ICMP traffic. You can experience this firsthand by surfing to a commonly surfed to web site like http://www.microsoft.com/ and then opening a command prompt and trying a ping.

- **-r** Specifies that the Record Route option in the IP header be used to record the path taken by the Echo Request message and corresponding Echo Reply message. If possible, specify a count that is equal to or greater than the number of hops between the source and destination. The count must be a minimum of 1 and a maximum of 9.

## tracert

The tracert utility is used to follow the path a packet takes as it tries to reach its final destination. This utility uses ping packets with progressive time-to-live (TTL) values, starting with a TTL of 1. Each time a packet hits a router, the TTL value is decremented by at least 1. When the TTL value reaches 0, the packet is dropped. This prevents all undelivered traffic on the Internet from still being out there, passing from one router to another in a never-ending attempt to reach its destination.

In the case of tracert, the TTL of 1 means that the packet will die at its first stop. When it dies, another companion protocol will report back that the packet has, indeed, expired, and also report the IP address of the device that dropped the packet. The next ping packet is sent to the destination has a TTL value of 2. It dies two hops away from its source. The TTL keeps incrementing until the ping reaches its destination, at which time the route from sender to receiver has been reconstructed.

Because it steps through the path a packet takes, the tracert utility is useful for identifying slow or broken links in the chain to get information from point A to point B. The syntax of the command is very similar to ping:

```
tracert IP Address or computername
```

The tracert should begin reporting the route taken by the packet, along with performance indicators for each stop along the way. You will be able to see where the slow links are in the network.

It is also be used with the following switches:

- **-d** Prevents tracert from attempting to resolve the names of the hops along the path to the destination computer. This can improve performance in the display of tracert results.

- **-h** Specifies the maximum number of hops in the path to search for the destination computer. The default number of hops is 30.

## pathping

The pathping utility generates information about network performance and problems that result in packet loss. It also is able to pinpoint exactly where the network slowness or packet loss is occurring, making it an ideal tool for the crucial task of assessing fault.

pathping, like tracert, is also essentially a ping with some modifiers. It sends multiple Echo Request messages to each router between a source and destination over a period of time, and then computes results based on the Echo Reply messages returned from each router. In so doing, pathping performs the equivalent of the tracert command by identifying which routers are on the path. It then sends pings to all of the routers over a specified time period and computes statistics based on the number returned from each.

It is also be used with the following switches:

- **-p**  Specifies the number of milliseconds to wait between consecutive pings. The default is 250 milliseconds (1/4 second).

- **-n**  Prevents pathping from trying to resolve the IP addresses of routers to their names as the path is being generated. This might speed up display of pathping results.

- **-h**  Specifies the maximum number of hops in the path to search for the destination host. The default is 30 hops.

## netdiag

netdiag is not installed by default, but instead comes packaged with the Windows Support Tools. Once installed, you use the Network Diagnostic utility to help isolate networking and connectivity problems.

netdiag does this by performing a series of tests to determine the state of your client connectivity to the network. These tests and the key network status information they expose give network administrators and support personnel a more direct means of identifying and isolating network problems.

Further, because this tool does not require parameters or switches to be specified, support personnel and network administrators can focus on analyzing the output rather than on training users how to use the tool.

Although netdiag does not require parameters, it can still use a few, including these switches:

- **/l**  Sends output to netdiag.log. This log file is created in the same directory where netdiag.exe was run.

- **/d**  Finds a domain controller in the specified domain.

- **/fix**  Attempts to fix minor problems; will cause unresponsive DHCP clients to release and renew their IP addresses, for example.

## netstat

The Network Statistics utility displays information about all active TCP connections, as seen in Figure 11-7. This includes statistics about the ports on which the computer is listening, Ethernet statistics, the IP routing table, and stats for the IP, ICMP, TCP, and UDP

**Figure 11-7**

Information available with the netstat command

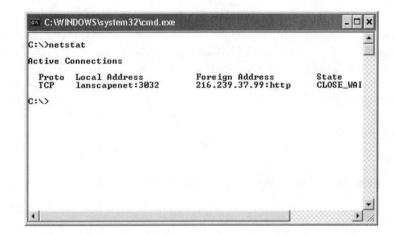

```
C:\>netstat

Active Connections

  Proto  Local Address           Foreign Address         State
  TCP    lanscapenet:3032        216.239.37.99:http      CLOSE_WAI

C:\>
```

protocols. It can be vital to help identify potential security holes on a particular system. Any port on which a TCP/IP host is listening represents a possible way into that system from the network.

It is also be used with the following modifiers:

- **-a**  Displays all active TCP connections and the TCP and UDP ports on which the computer is listening.

- **-n**  Displays active TCP connections without determining the names of the addresses and port numbers. Instead, ports are displayed only as numbers.

- **-p**  Shows connections only for the protocol specified by the protocol switch. Possible protocols displayed include TCP, UDP, TCP version 6, or UDP version 6.

- **-s**  Displays statistics by protocol. By default, statistics are shown for the TCP, UDP, ICMP, and IP protocols. If the IPv6 protocol is installed, statistics are shown for the TCP over IPv6, UDP over IPv6, ICMPv6, and IPv6 protocols. This switch is most often used along with the -p parameter, which is used to specify the protocol for which statistics are generated.

## netsh

As you saw in the previous chapter, the netsh utility can be used to perform a wide range of network configuration procedures from the command line. One advantage this provides is the ability to use the netsh utility in a scripted operation.

To run a netsh command, you first start netsh from the command line and then change to the context that contains the command you want to use. The contexts available depend on which networking components have been installed. Therefore, its syntax is unlike any of the other utilities mentioned here, and it is really not used with switches like the others. It is mentioned here again because the context in which it was discussed in the previous chapter was only for configuration of IPSec policies.

It is also used to monitor and manage. For example, if the Windows Server 2003 computer was acting as the network's DHCP server, you could type **dhcp** at the netsh command line to change to the DHCP context. From within the DHCP context, you could issue a series of commands that would manage the DHCP server, such as adding scopes and options, deleting scopes and options, and even adding and removing a DHCP server to/from the network.

However, if you do not have DHCP installed and try to change to the DHCP context from netsh, the following message appears:

```
The following command was not found: dhcp.
```

netsh can be used to manage not only DHCP and IPSec, as previously mentioned, but also the following network services:

- **Internet Authentication Service (IAS)**   Through configuration of the authorization, authentication, accounting, and auditing (AAAA) database.

- **TCP/IP**   By configuring IP addresses, subnet masks, default gateways, and DNS servers.

- **Routing and Remote Access Service (RRAS)**   By automating commands that manage both routing and remote access behavior, including the addition and deletion of registered RRAS servers and the configuration of routing interfaces.

- **Windows Internet Name Service (WINS)**   Via the addition of WINS servers and the display and verification of the WINS resolution database.

As you can see, netsh is clearly the 800-pound gorilla of your available command-line utilities used to manage and troubleshoot network connectivity. On a day-to-day basis, however, most administrators find the ipconfig and ping utilities to be indispensable. These two utilities are quick, simple, efficient, and able to pinpoint most network problems with ease.

## Other Internet Issues

You'll run into problems that aren't easily solved even with the most sophisticated of troubleshooting utilities. Sometimes, you just have to find out if the thing works. Table 11-2 provides additional reference for common problems when accessing the Internet.

| Problem | Possible Causes | Solution |
|---|---|---|
| When using a local area connection, there is no response. | 1. The network card may not be functioning.<br>2. The network cable is unplugged. | Check the appearance of the local area connection icon. Depending on the status of the local area connection, the icon appears in different ways in the Network Connections folder. Also, if the local area connection media is disconnected (for example, the cable is unplugged), a status icon is displayed in the taskbar. |

**Table 11-2**   Possible Connectivity Issues

| Problem | Possible Causes | Solution |
|---|---|---|
| Modem does not work. | 1. The modem is incompatible with Windows Server 2003. 2. The modem is not installed correctly or is turned off. | Check the Windows Hardware Compatibility List at  http://www .microsoft.com/whdc/hcl/search .mspx Verify that the modem is connected properly to the correct port on your computer. If the modem is external, verify that the power is on. |
| Dial-in sessions with a remote access server are getting dropped. | 1. Call waiting is disrupting your connection or someone is picking up the line. 2. Modem software needs to be updated. | Check to see whether the phone has call waiting. If so, disable call waiting and try calling again. Check with the modem manufacturer for the latest software updates. |
| Unable to connect with a remote access server. | 1. The remote access server is not running. 2. You do not have a valid user account, or the account does not have permission to access the server over a RAS connection. | If the server is down, the administrator needs to check the error and audit logs to see why the service stopped. After the problem is fixed, restart the service. Also, if possible, check to see if other clients are having the same problem. If others are able to connect, the problem is not with the RRAS server. Verify with your system administrator that your user account has been created, and that you have remote access permission. |

**Table 11-2**  Possible Connectivity Issues *(continued)*

# Troubleshoot Server Services

At the heart of the Windows Server 2003 operating system are the services that it provides. If you have a Unix background, the services are akin to Unix daemons and provide the same functionality. The Windows Server 2003 services provide core operating system features, such as the serving of web sites, event logging, help and support, cryptography, and error reporting, to name but a few. Technically speaking, a service is an application that launches and runs in the background, so even though you may not have opened any programs, applications are indeed running through the act of booting up the system.

For example, without the Server service, Windows Server 2003 (or any NT-based computer for that matter) wouldn't be able to provide file and print sharing using the SMB protocol. If the Netlogon service were not running, domain controllers would not be able to accept and process domain logon requests, and thus domain would effectively halt. And in the last chapter, we discussed the importance of the Secondary Logon service.

Therefore, maintaining service operation is crucial to a functioning and secure Windows Server 2003 network. You have to know how to start and stop services, and have an understanding of how many of the services are interrelated.

Toward this end, the first order of business is to understand how to configure the general properties of a service. You can manage these services on both local and remote computers with the Services MMC snap-in. Here is the procedure you'll follow:

1. Open the Services MMC snap-in from your Administrative Tools menu.

2. In the details pane, select the service you want to configure, right-click, and choose Properties from the context menu.

3. On the General tab, in the Startup Type drop-down list, choose Automatic, Manual, or Disabled, as shown in Figure 11-8.

4. If you need to modify the account that the service uses to log on, click the Log On tab, and then do one of the following:

   • To specify that the service uses the Local System account, click Local System account.

   • To specify that the service uses the Local Service account, click This Account, and then type **nt authority\localservice**.

 **NOTE** The Local System account is a special account that has full access to the system. On domain controllers, this access includes the directory service. Therefore, if a service logs on using the Local System account on a domain controller, that service has access to the entire domain. The Local Service account, on the other hand, has the same level of access to resources as members of the Users group. This limited access can help safeguard your system if individual services or processes are compromised. Neither of these pieces of information, however, are meant to convince you to change default account credentials, which use the respective accounts for a reason.

**Figure 11-8**
Configuring
startup behavior
of a service

- To specify that the service uses the Network Service account, click This Account, and then type **nt authority\networkservice**.

- To specify another account, click This Account, then Browse for the user account to use with the Select User dialog box. When you are finished, click OK.

5. Now type the password for the account in Password and Confirm Password, and click OK.

**NOTE**  If either the Local Service account or the Network Service account is specified as the context for the service to use, the password must be blank.

## Service Dependency

There is a very easy way to gather basic information about the service dependencies for the services running on Windows Server 2003. Here's what to do:

1. Open the Services MMC console.

2. Access the Properties dialog box of any service, and then click on the Dependencies tab, as shown in Figure 11-9.

3. To view services that are associated dependencies of the selected service, in the list on the Dependencies tab, click the plus sign next to the service.

**Figure 11-9**
The Dependencies tab of a service provides a quick overview.

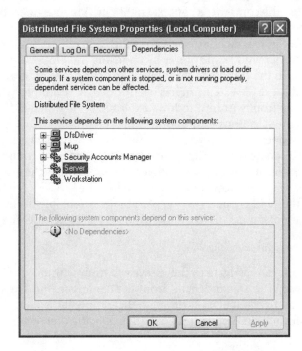

The information provided with this tab can help you determine if a problem with one service will have a cascading effect on other services. For example, as you can see Figure 11-9, logical shared volumes in a distributed network won't be managed DFS service if the Server service is not started as well.

But what if the Dependencies tab doesn't provide you with enough information? Is there a tool that will help you gather more exhaustive information about service dependencies? Well, you've heard us say this before, but it *depends*.

## The Dependency Walker

There is a tool in Windows Server 2003 called depends.exe whose purpose is to walk a dependency hierarchy for a given program or service. In fact, it can be used on any Windows module (.exe, .dll, .ocx, and .sys, files all included) to build a tree diagram of all dependent modules. What's more, the Dependency Walker is not a command-line utility, but rather, a graphical tool. There is quite a lot of information that can be gathered with the Dependency Walker. For any Windows module or program, you can obtain information about that program's minimum set of required files, along with detailed information about each required file, including a full path to the file, the base memory address where the file is loaded, file version numbers, the computer type, and debug information, to name a few.

It is most useful when used to diagnose and resolve problems with services and applications such as missing modules, invalid modules, import/export mismatches, and mismatched computer types for modules.

To open the Dependency Walker, select Start | Run, and type **depends** in the Run dialog box. The Dependency Walker opens, and also causes a View Dependencies item to be added to the computer's context (right-click) menus once the Dependency Walker is configured to handle certain file extensions.

You configure which file extensions the Dependency Walker will handle in the context menus of Windows Explorer by choosing the Options menu and then adding file extensions in the Handled File Extensions dialog box, as shown in Figure 11-10.

Once the .exe file extension has been added, for example, when you right-click an executable file from within Windows Explorer, a View Dependencies choice is displayed as one of the selections in the context menu.

So how does this help you diagnose service dependencies? Remember that all Windows 2003 services are applications that load in the background. These applications have .exe file extensions, just like any other program. To view the executable file that is the service, refer to the Services console and look at the service's Properties dialog box. As you saw previously in Figure 11-8, the path to the executable is noted on the General tab.

For example, the path to the Distributed File System service executable is this:

```
Systemroot\system32\Dfssvc.exe
```

Now you can navigate to the dfssve.exe from within Windows Explorer, right-click, and choose View Dependencies from the context menu. The Dependency Walker will launch, and dependencies for that application will display, along with all of the additional information. You will see a display like the one seen in Figure 11-11.

**Figure 11-10**
Adding file
extensions for
the Dependency
Walker to handle

## Service Recovery Options

Because of the vital nature of the services on a system, it's also crucial that administrators
be able to quickly recover in the event of a service failure. One way you can usually restore a service is to stop and restart it using the available buttons in the service's Properties dialog box. (You can also use the hyperlinks on the left side of the details pane
when using the Extended MMC console view.)

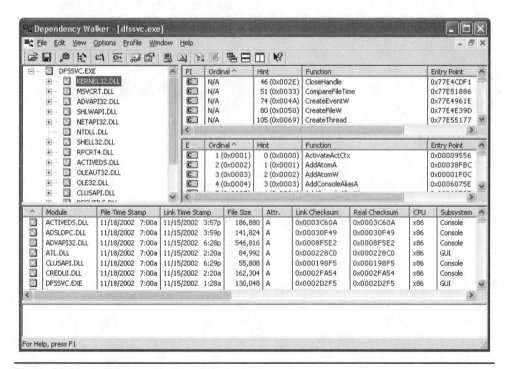

**Figure 11-11**    The Dependency Walker

But what if you're not at the server to open the Services console, and there is no way to connect remotely to open it from another system? Because a Windows Server 2003 machine without services running is little more than an expensive paperweight, Microsoft has an automated process available for recovering from service failures.

To set up the automated procedures, follow these steps:

1. Open the Services MMC console, and access the Properties dialog box for the service for which you want to set up the automated recovery actions.

2. On the Recovery tab, as shown in Figure 11-12, select the action that you want the service to take for the instance of the First Failure, Second Failure, and Subsequent Failures. There are a few additional steps that may need to be taken:

   • If you select Run A Program, type the path to the program for the specified computer under Run Program. Note that UNC names are not supported. You must use the absolute path, which looks like this: C:\recovery\servicecrash.bat. Note also that it does not have to be a program, but can instead be a script, which might in turn start a program, such as a counter log.

   • If you choose to Restart The Computer after a service failure, click Restart Computer Options to specify how long the computer waits before restarting. You can also create a message to send using the netsend mechanism to remote users before the computer restarts.

**Figure 11-12**
Configuring automated service recovery options

**NOTE** When the computer restarts, all services are stopped and restarted, which usually fixes service-related problems. This is why a reboot is often a first line of defense for troubleshooters, albeit one that doesn't address *why* the service stopped working in the first place.

## Using Service Configuration

There's one more thing worth knowing come exam time: how to configure and troubleshoot server services from the command line. The tool you use is called Service Configuration.

sc.exe exchanges management instructions with and gathers information from the Service Controller and installed services on your system. You can use sc.exe for testing and debugging the services programs necessary for a functional Windows Server 2003. sc.exe parameters can configure a specific service, retrieve the current status of a service, and be used to stop and start a service, making it a potentially life-saving utility when a service is stopped and an administrator has to connect remotely to start a service. Like netsh, one of the big advantages of the sc utility is the ability to call its commands in a batch file which then automate startup or shutdown sequences.

Also, like netsh, the sc utility is used not so much with switches, but in one of several contexts, which is then in turn used with a variety of context-specific switches. Each context lets you configure the particulars for a single server service. Contexts include, for example, config, which can be used to modify the service's entries in the Registry, failure, which specifies what action to take upon the failure of the service, start, and stop, which are used to do just that for a specific service. In all, there are 24 different contexts for the sc utility.

You could use the sc tool to start a specific service from the command line in this way:

```
sc [ServerName] start ServiceName [ServiceArguments]
```

where *ServerName* and *ServiceName* are variables for the server where the service will start, and what service that will be, respectively. Like most command-line utilities that have graphical counterparts that save greatly on typing, the sc utility is usually only used when generating a batch file.

# Chapter Review

In this 70-291 section's final chapter, we've looked at ways to keep running at optimal performance levels. We've examined the use of System Monitor in gathering performance information, and furthered our exploration of Network Monitor. Specifically, we looked at how you could use Network Monitor from the command line.

But our look at command-line utilities didn't stop there. We looked at the use of these tools: ipconfig, ping, tracert, pathping, netdiag, and netsh. You will find these tools essential in troubleshooting network connectivity and performance, and you can expect several questions on the exam that will require you to be familiar with the purpose of these tools.

Finally, we concluded with a look at the server services on a Windows Server 2003 machine, their role in a functional server operating system, and how their startup behavior could be managed. Furthermore, you learned how to diagnose service dependencies and how you might recover server services in the event of service failure.

You now have all the essential information you need to tackle Microsoft's 70-291 test. Best of luck, and happy reading as you continue toward the 70-293 section.

## Questions

1. Which of the following are advantages of using the netmon command instead of Network Monitor? (Choose all that apply.)

   A. It can be used in a scripted operation.

   B. It is better suited to make use of a slow network connection.

   C. It can be used in the main mode or the quick mode.

   D. It does not require the Network Monitor software to be installed.

2. Which of the following are symptoms you will see when a client is configured with an IP address that is a duplicate of an address already in use on a Windows Server 2003 network? (Choose all that apply.)

   A. Upon running ipconfig, the client will reveal an IP address of 255.255.255.0.

   B. Upon running ipconfig, the client will reveal an IP address of 0.0.0.0.

   C. The client will only be able to communicate with hosts that live on remote networks.

   D. The client will not be able to communicate with any hosts using TCP/IP.

3. Which of the following are true about the tracert utility? (Choose all that apply.)

   A. It can be run as an MMC snap-in to graphically display network topology.

   B. It works using a ping packet with incrementing TTL values.

   C. It always reveals the complete path to the target host computer.

   D. It is used to verify IP configuration parameters on Windows Server 2003 hosts, but cannot do so on a Windows 2000 or Windows XP host system.

4. You are the administrator of a Windows Server 2003 domain. You are trying to verify the proper configuration of the DNS server on your network. Which of the following would be likely indicators that a DNS server is not providing the correct name resolution? (Choose all that apply.)

   A. The client is able to ping a web site using an IP address, but is unsuccessful when trying to ping a web site using the FQDN.

   B. The client is able to ping local computers using host names, but is unable to ping remote computers using host names.

C. Upon running ipconfig, the client is configured with an IP address of a DNS server that is on a remote network.

D. The client is unable to ping a web site using an IP address, and is unable to ping when using a FQDN.

5. You are monitoring the performance of a file server running Windows Server 2003. You are gathering data using System Monitor, and want to configure it so that it collects data about the frequency of potential security break-ins. Which of the following counters should you enable? (Choose all that apply.)

A. Server > Attempted Logons

B. Network Interface > Submitted Passwords

C. Server > Errors Access Permissions

D. Server > Errors Logon

6. Which of the following are true about a Windows Server 2003 computer with an incorrectly configured subnet mask?

A. It will be able to communicate with remote hosts only.

B. It will be able to communicate with local hosts only.

C. It will not be able to communicate with either local or remote hosts.

D. When diagnosing with ipconfig, the subnet mask will read 0.0.0.0.

E. All of the above.

7. You are the administrator of a Windows Server 2003 domain. You want to ensure that services such as the Server service run continuously, and you want to reboot the system as a last resort. You are setting the Recovery options in the Services MMS console. Which of the following can you configure using the Automatic Recovery tab?

A. You can configure System Monitor to begin a capture of performance data.

B. You can configure to leave the service stopped.

C. You can configure the service to stop and restart.

D. All of the above.

8. The netsh utility allows you to configure which of the following network services from the command line? (Choose all that apply.)

A. IP Security policies

B. DHCP scopes

C. Active Directory user accounts

D. RRAS servers

E. All of the above

9. It is Monday evening, and you are using a Windows Server 2003 machine to remotely connect to a branch office for the download of the day's sales totals. The machine was upgraded from Windows 2000 on Friday evening. You are unable to establish a connection with the remote server. Which of the following are possible explanations for the problem? (Choose all that apply.)

A. The network card on the Windows Server 2003 machine is not functioning and cannot bridge the connection to the modem.

B. The modem is incompatible with Windows Server 2003.

C. The modem of the receiving computer has been turned off.

D. All of the above.

10. You are the administrator for a Windows Server 2003 Active Directory domain called bigcarp.com. On one of your Windows Server 2003 machines, the DNS server service is failing with regularity, but you suspect the cause is a dependent service and not the DNS service itself. Which of the following tools can you use to determine the services upon which DNS relies to successfully run? (Choose all that apply.)

A. The Computer Management MMC snap-in

B. The netsh command-line utility

C. The Dependency Walker

D. The Services MMC snap-in

## Answers

1. **A and B.** The netmon utility is Network Monitor from the command line. Like other command-line tools, one of its main benefits is that it can be called from a script file, which can make it ideal for automated troubleshooting situations. And, because it is not a graphical utility, it is ideally suited for environments where available bandwidth is low. It does require that Network Monitor be installed, however.

2. **B and C.** When a client tries to use an IP address already in use, the client will be informed of this through a dialog box. Upon further investigation with ipconfig, you should find that the client will have an IP address of 0.0.0.0. Because it does not have an IP address bound, the client will not be able to communicate with any other TCP/IP hosts.

3. **B and C.** The tracert utility works by sending ping Echo Request packets to the destination host, only with incrementing TTL values starting at 1. Packets will then expire at each subsequent hop along the path, therefore recreating the route to the destination. However, certain firewalls block ICMP packets, and therefore will drop ping packets, preventing you from discovering the complete path to the destination.

4. **A and B.** If the client is unable to communicate with another computer using a FQDN, there is likely a problem with name resolution. A computer can resolve names to IP addresses by broadcast if the other computer is on the same subnet, but would be unsuccessful trying to do the same for remote hosts. If a client is not able to ping using IP addresses, there is a problem with IP configuration or the physical network. A DNS server does not have to be on the same network as the client system, because name resolution is directed traffic.

5. **C and D.** There are several counters provided by System Monitor that will help you ferret out possible security threats to your network. Of the possible answers here, Server > Errors Access Permissions and Server > Errors Logon will help you the most when trying to evaluate hacking. In fact, they're the only counters that exist to measure attempted hacks through password guessing.

6. **C.** A Windows Server 2003 system with an incorrectly configured subnet mask will believe it is on a different network than it really is, and will try to route network traffic to a default gateway that it cannot reach. Unlike when trying to use a duplicate IP address, there are no telltale signs of a bad subnet mask configuration. This has to be determined by making behavioral observations with utilities such as ping.

7. **D.** With the Recovery tab of the Services MMC, you can configure one of three actions on the first, second, and subsequent failures of the specified service: No Action, Restart The Service, or Run A Program. The program specified can be a script file, which in turn can initiate an almost unlimited set of possibilities, such as starting a diagnostic program.

8. **A, B, and D.** With the netsh utility, you can manage almost any network service from the command line. You cannot, however, use it to manage Active Directory users and computers. To manage a network service, you first need to change to the context of the service you want to manage.

9. **B and C.** The only one of the possibilities that could not cause a dial-up connection to fail is a failed network card. The connection to the remote RAS server is a direct dial-up connection which was working fine last week, so the modem may not be on the Windows HCL for Windows Server 2003.

10. **A, C, and D.** You can view service dependencies with the Dependencies tab of the Services MMC snap-in, and can also get a very detailed look at service dependencies, down to the files the services depend on, with the Dependency Walker (depends.exe). Remember that the Computer Management console gives you access to the services as well.

# PART III

# Planning and Maintaining a Network Infrastructure (Exam 70-293)

# Implementing
# Server Security

In this chapter, you will learn how to
- Plan a secure baseline installation
- Configure default security settings
- Work with server-related default security settings
- Configure security for servers assigned specific roles
- Deploy security configurations
- Create custom security templates
- Choose client operating systems to use in an enterprise

As you can well imagine, servers are a vital part of the network infrastructure. Servers can have a variety of roles, from a DNS server to mail server and database server and so on. We rely on the services these systems provide to keep the network running and to ensure access to data. Recognizing their importance in the day-to-day operations of the network, it becomes essential that they be secured from tampering from outside of the network as well as from network users.

In this chapter, we look at some of the measures you can take to secure servers that are assigned specific roles. But first we will look at some of the general security procedures that are used to secure servers regardless of the role they play on the network.

## Configuring and Planning Security for Servers

There are many elements required to establish a secure server. This can range from everything from creating remote access policies to configuring default security settings, designing security templates and managing file system permissions. With so many areas to be aware of when designing server security, it is essential that administrators take the time to ensure that servers are sufficiently protected from both outside and internal threats.

When designing server security, one of the primary areas that must be addressed is ensuring that the level of access you grant to network users is tightly controlled. To do this, you need to have a clear understanding of users and groups.

## Securing Local Group Access

In an ideal world, you could make all members of your network part of the Administrators group and trust them not to get up to any mischief. This is not an ideal world and assigning regular users to the Administrators group would certainly be a recipe for disaster. As such, you not only have to carefully guard access permissions to the Administrators group, but also control who is added to any of the various default Windows Server 2003 groups.

If you have some system support experience, you have no doubt worked with groups. Groups provide a means to organize users and reduce the amount of time administrators spend managing user accounts. By assigning users to the appropriate group, administrators need not assign individual permissions and rights to each and every account. Rather, they place users in groups that already have the desired permissions and rights assigned. Windows Server 2003 includes several built-in groups from which you can choose, each with a different level of user rights and permissions. Of the built-in groups, there are five key groups: Administrators, Power Users, Users, Backup Operators, and Print Operators.

## The Administrators Group

Placing users in the Administrators group should always be done with caution, as anyone in this group has complete access to the system. Typically, there will be a single user who will be placed in the Administrators group. Each user added threatens the security of the overall system. By default, the administrator account and the first account made during the Windows Server 2003 installation will be a member of the Administrators group, but all other accounts must be added manually.

When deciding whether to assign a user to the Administrators group, you must be clear as to why they need to have administrative rights. By default, members of the Administrators group will be able to perform the following functions:

- Install the operating system and additional system components, including such things as system services, hardware drivers, and updates and service packs.
- Perform upgrades to the operating system.
- Use features within Windows Server 2003 to repair the operating system.
- Establish systemwide policies and parameters such as audit and password policies.
- Take ownership of files.
- View the auditing logs.
- Back up and restore the system.

With the ability to perform such tasks, it becomes easy to see why allowing this level of control to too many users may be a very bad idea. A much better idea is to have groups designed to accommodate specific purposes.

**EXAM TIP** It is considered a best practice to only log on to a system using an administrative account when you need to perform the functions of the administrator. Working on the system as the administrator can make a system vulnerable to Trojan horse attacks and other security risks. If you are logged on with administrator privileges, a Trojan horse could reformat your hard drive, delete all your files, or even create a user account with administrative access.

## The Power Users Group

Next to the Administrators group, the Power Users group offers the most system access. Users in the Power Users group can perform systemwide administrative tasks, but do not have the carte blanche of the Administrators group. Users who are responsible for a certain level of system administration are candidates for the Power Users group, but as with the Administrators group, users should be assigned to it sparingly. The rights and permissions assigned to the Power Users group include

- Install programs that do not modify operating system files or install system services.
- Configure and manage system resources and settings, including printers, date, time, power options, and other Control Panel resources.
- Create and manage local user and group accounts.
- Stop and start system services.

As you can see from the list, even the rights assigned to users in the Power Users group could provide users with the ability to do a lot of damage to a system. For regular users, the best solution is to assign them to the Users group.

## The Users Group

The Users group offers far more security than the Power Users or the Administrators group as the rights and permissions assigned to it are very limited. Most of the users on the system will likely be assigned to the Users group to restrict what they are able to do with the system, including modifying the operating system or tampering with other users' data.

Members of the local Users group are able to create local groups, but are restricted to managing only those groups that they created. Users have full control over their own data files. Recognizing the security of the Users group, administrators should do their best to ensure that most end users are members of the Users group only and that programs that are installed are accessible to the members of the Users group.

## The Backup Operators Group

Another of the built-in groups that is particularly useful is the Backup Operators group. To provide a user with the ability to back up and restore system files, all that needs to be done is to add the user's account to the Backup Operators group. Members of the Backup Operators group can back up and restore files on the computer, regardless of any

NTFS permissions that protect those files. However, they cannot access files outside of a backup program that preserves the integrity of the files. Users assigned to the Backup Operators group can also log on to the computer and shut it down, but they cannot change security settings.

## The Print Operators Group

One of the ways to delegate responsibility on the network is to designate certain trusted users as print operators. Members of the Print Operators group are able to manage all aspects of the printing process, including creating, sharing, and deleting printers connected to domain controllers in the domain. Members of this group can log on locally to domain controllers in the domain and shut them down. This group has no default members.

## Other Local Groups

Besides those local groups mentioned above, Windows Server 2003 does provide a few additional default groups that are designed for very specific purposes. Table 12-1 summarizes the rest of the local groups in Windows Server 2003.

| Table 12-1 | Group | Summary |
|---|---|---|
| Windows Server 2003 Default Local Groups for Specific Tasks | Guests | The Guests group is used to quickly give system access to users who are not regular users. Guest privileges allow the user to logon to a system and shut it down but cannot make permanent changes to the desktop or profile. |
| | Network Configuration Operators | Users in this group have special rights to manage and configure network settings and features. |
| | Remote Desktop Users | Users in this group have the ability to log on through Terminal Services. |
| | Replicator | Members of this group are used to support directory replication, a feature used by domain services. |
| | Help Services | Provides special permissions enabling the support of the computer through Microsoft Help Services. |
| | Terminal Services Users | This group contains any users who are currently logged on to the system using Terminal Services. |
| | DHCP Administrators | Members of this group have administrative access to the DHCP Server service. |
| | DHCP Users | Members of this group have read-only access to the DHCP Server service. |

**EXAM TIP** For the Windows Server 2003 exam, be prepared to identify which groups you can assign users to perform specific system tasks. Do not be fooled into placing a user into the Administrators group unless they really need to be.

## Securing Global Groups

In addition to the local groups for a server, there are several global groups to which users can belong. These groups are created automatically when you install an Active Directory domain. You can use these predefined groups to help you manage shared resources and delegate specific domain-wide administrative roles.

Many default groups are automatically assigned a set of user rights that determine what each group member can do within the scope of a domain. Table 12-2 shows the various global groups available and what group members have permission to do on the domain.

| Group | Summary |
|---|---|
| Account Operators | Members of this group create, modify, and delete accounts for users, groups, and computers in all containers and organizational units in the domain, except within the Builtin folder and the Domain Controllers organizational unit. |
| Administrators | As with the local groups, members of this group have full control of all domain controllers in the domain. |
| Backup Operators | Members of this group can back up and restore all files on domain controllers in the domain. |
| Guests | The Guests group is used to quickly give system access to users who are not regular users. |
| Incoming Forest Trust Builders | Members of this group can create incoming, one-way trusts to the forest of the domain. |
| Network Configuration Operators | Members of this group have the ability to modify TCP/IP settings. |
| Pre-Windows 2000 Compatible Access | Used for backward compatibility, members of this group have read access on all users and groups in the domain. |
| Print Operators | Members of this group can manage, create, share, and delete printers connected to domain controllers in the domain. |
| Remote Desktop Users | Members of this group have access to remotely log on to domain controllers in the network. |
| Replicator | This group can manage directory replication functions. |
| Server Operators | On domain controllers in the domain, members of this group can log on interactively, create and delete network shares, start and stop services, back up and restore files, format the hard disk, and shut down the computer. |
| Users | Default group used for ordinary users. |

**Table 12-2** Windows Server 2003 Default Global Groups

PART III

## Securing User Permissions

Effectively managing files and folders on a Windows Server 2003 system will certainly involve assigning and managing the permissions required to access them. Permissions allow administrators to decide who can and cannot access particular files and folders and what they can do with them when they are accessed. If your system is configured with NTFS partitions, you have the option of controlling file and folder access on a per-user or a per-group basis. If you are using a system with FAT partitions, you are out of luck. FAT partitions do not offer any local security functionality.

To view or modify the assigned NTFS permissions, select the file or folder you want to view from Windows Explorer, right-click the file or folder, and choose the Properties option from the menu. NTFS permissions for a file or folder are configured from the Security tab in the Properties dialog box for that file. When configuring permissions, you can choose either to allow or deny a specific permission for a user or group. Figure 12-1 shows the Security tab and NTFS permissions.

There are six basic NTFS permissions available: Full Control, Modify, Read and Execute, Read, Write, and List Folder Contents. A description of each of these is given in Table 12-3.

## Advanced NTFS Settings

The six basic NTFS permissions discussed above are actually comprised of several more specific NTFS permissions. Knowing the individual NTFS permissions allows the administrator to fine-tune permission settings and give more control over what users can and cannot access. By clicking the Advanced button from the Security tab in a file's Properties dialog box, you

**Figure 12-1**
The Security tab is used to configure NTFS permissions for a file or folder.

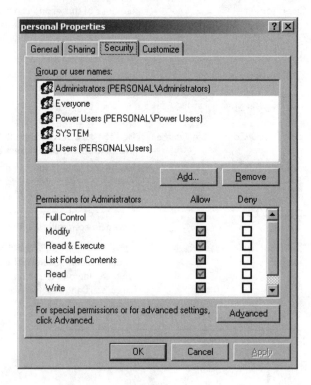

| NTFS Permission | Description |
|---|---|
| Full Control | Gives the user or group complete control, including changing permissions, taking ownership, and all other access given by the other NTFS permissions. |
| Modify | Allows the user or group to create new files and folders, view and change a file's attributes, list and view the contents of a folder, and delete files. Does not allow the user or group to take ownership of a file or to change the permissions for files and folders. |
| Read and Execute | Allows the user or group to traverse folders and execute files within those folders, view the attributes of a file or folder, list the contents of a folder, and read the data in a folder's files. |
| Read | Allows the user or group to list the contents of a folder, read the data in a folder's file, and see the attributes of a file or folder. |
| Write | Allows the user or group to change the attributes of a file or folder, create new files and write data to these files, and to create new folders and append data to the files. |
| List Folder Contents (for folders only) | Allows the user or group to traverse folders, list the contents of a folder, and see the attributes of a file or folder. |

**Table 12-3**    Options Offered by NTFS When Configuring Permissions

can view each of the individual NTFS permissions that form the building blocks for the six basic NTFS permissions. Clicking Advanced will open the Advanced Security Settings dialog box as shown in Figure 12-2.

**Figure 12-2**
The Advanced Security Settings dialog box is used to fine-tune NTFS file permissions.

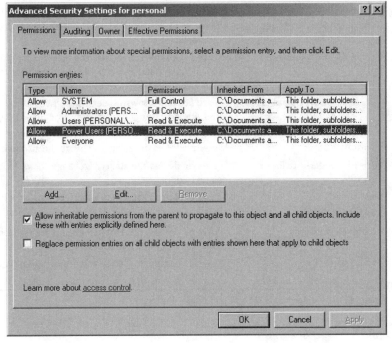

The Advanced Security Settings dialog box has four tabs: Permissions, Auditing, Owner, and Effective Permissions. From the Permissions tab, you can see each of the individual NTFS permissions. Table 12-4 provides a summary of the individual NTFS file and folder permissions.

As mentioned, the permissions listed in Table 12-4 are used to form the six basic NTFS permissions. Table 12-5 shows how these independent NTFS permissions map to the six NTFS permissions.

 **EXAM TIP**   For the exam, you will be expected to know the NTFS permissions, and what they will and won't allow you to do.

## Inherited Permissions

Folders and files on a Windows-based system are often stored in a hierarchical fashion, meaning that folders are quite likely to contain additional folders and subfolders.

| Permission | Description |
| --- | --- |
| Traverse Folder/Execute File | Traverse Folder allows or denies permissions to move through folders. Traverse Folder takes effect only when the group or user is not granted the Bypass Traverse Checking user right in the Group Policy snap-in. Execute File allows or denies running program files. |
| List Folder/Read Data | List Folder allows or denies viewing file names and subfolder names within the folder. Read Data applies to the files only and allows or denies viewing the data in the files. |
| Read Attributes | Allows or denies the ability to view the attributes of files or folders. |
| Read Extended Attributes | Allows or denies the ability to view the extended attributes of files or folders. |
| Create Files/Write Data | Create Files allows or denies the ability to create files within a folder. Write Data allows or denies the ability to make changes to a file and overwrites existing content. |
| Create Folders/Append Data | Create Folders allows or denies the permission to create folders within folders. Append Data allows or denies the ability to make changes to the end of files. |
| Write Attributes | Allows or denies the ability to change the attributes of files or folders. |
| Write Extended Attributes | Allows or denies the ability to change the extended attributes of files or folders. |
| Delete | Allows or denies the ability to delete files or folders. |
| Read Permissions | Allows or denies the ability to read files or folders. |
| Change Permissions | Allows or denies the ability to change permissions of the file or folder, such as Full Control, Read, and Write. |
| Take Ownership | Allows or denies the ability to take ownership of files or folders. |
| Delete Subfolders and Files | Allows or denies the ability to delete subfolders and files. |

**Table 12-4**   Individual NTFS File and Folder Permissions

| NTFS Permission | Full Control | Modify | Read and Execute | Read | Write |
|---|---|---|---|---|---|
| Traverse Folder/ Execute File | X | X | X | X | |
| List Folder/Read Data | X | X | X | X | |
| Read Attributes | X | X | X | X | |
| Read Extended Attributes | X | X | X | X | |
| Create Files/Write Data | X | X | | | X |
| Create Folders/Append Data | X | X | | | X |
| Write Attributes | X | X | | | X |
| Write Extended Attributes | X | X | | | X |
| Delete | X | X | | | |
| Read Permissions | X | X | X | X | X |
| Change Permissions | X | | | | |
| Take Ownership | X | | | | |
| Delete Subfolders and Files | X | | | | |

**Table 12-5**    Mapping Individual NTFS Permissions to the Six Core NTFS Permissions

Normally, when permissions are assigned to a parent folder, each of the folders within inherit the permissions of that parent folder. Inherited permissions can make the job of administrator easier as it is only necessary to assign permissions to one folder instead of numerous subfolders.

There are situations, however, where you will not want to have inherited permissions filtering down to subfolders. In such a case, you can establish explicit permissions that will override any inherited permissions.

Changing the inheritance setting for a file or folder is done through the Security tab of a folder's Properties dialog box. From the Security tab, click Advanced to open the Advanced Security Settings dialog box. At the bottom of the box, deselect the option that says "Inherit from parent the permission entries that apply to child objects. Include these with entries explicitly defined here." Once deselected, the file or folder permissions can be explicitly set independent of any inherited permissions.

 **EXAM TIP**    Explicitly defined permissions override any inherited permissions.

## Determining Permissions

Discussions of permissions can get more involved when a user is a member of different groups and each of the groups has different permissions. In addition, permissions can be assigned to the individual user as well as a group. When a user is a member of multiple groups, there is likely going to be a number of different permissions involved with conflicting levels of access.

In such cases, there are a few things to remember. NTFS security permissions are cumulative. This means that if you are a member of one group with Read permission and a member of another with Modify permission, you will have the permissions assigned to both groups. Any rights you are assigned personally also combine with rights that you receive from a group. However, any Deny entries assigned to a user or group will override any Allow settings.

So, for example, if you were a member of one group from which you were assigned the Read permission and another from which you were assigned the Modify permission, your effective permissions would be both Read and Modify.

 **EXAM TIP**   Remember that Deny permissions take precedence over Allow permissions and that NTFS permissions are cumulative.

## Moving or Copying Files and Folders with NTFS Permissions

One thing that can cause a hiccup for file and folder access is when data is moved or copied from its original location. Before moving or copying files between locations and file systems, there are a few things that administrators need to be aware of. First, and perhaps the most obvious, if files and folders are moved from an NTFS partition to a FAT partition, all NTFS permissions will be lost on the object being moved or copied. Moving or copying files or folders between NTFS partitions becomes a bit trickier. Table 12-6 summarizes the basic rules for moving or copying files and folders around NTFS partitions.

| Data Transfer | Permissions After Move or Copy |
| --- | --- |
| Copying files within the same NTFS volume | Files and folders copied within the same NTFS volume will inherit the permissions of the folder to which they are copied. |
| Copying files between different NTFS volumes | Files and folders copied between different NTFS volumes will inherit the permissions of the destination folder. |
| Moving files or folders within the same NTFS volume | Files and folders moved within the same NTFS volume will retain the permissions from the source folder. |
| Moving files and folders between different NTFS volumes | Files and folders moved between different NTFS volumes will inherit the permissions from the destination folder. |

**Table 12-6**   Moving Files and Folders

## Taking Ownership of Files

Every object on a Windows Server 2003 NTFS volume, from files and folders to printers, has an owner. The owner of the object essentially has control over that object in terms of assigning permissions to the object and thereby accessing that object. In most environments, administrators will create and own most objects, such as printers and directories. Users, on the other hand, will have ownership of the files and folders that they create.

At some point it may be necessary to take ownership of a file or folder. An example of this might be if the original owner of a file or folder leaves a company and new permissions must be set. To ensure that you can access these files, you may need to take ownership of them and then modify the permissions. To take ownership of a file or folder, perform the following steps:

1. Log onto the system using the Administrators account or as a member of the Administrators group.

2. From Windows Explorer, right-click the file or folder you want to take ownership of.

3. From the Security tab, click Advanced to display the Advanced Security Settings dialog box.

4. Select the Owner tab, from which you can view the current owner of the file and replace the current owner with one on the list. Figure 12-3 shows the Owner tab.

**Figure 12-3**
The Owner tab in the Advanced Security Settings dialog box is used to take ownership of a file or folder.

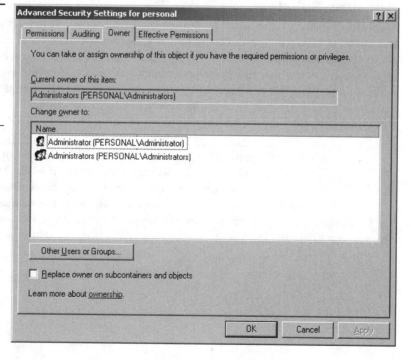

Once an administrator has successfully taken control of a file or folder, the permissions and access to that data can be modified.

# Creating Security Templates

Security templates allow users to create baseline security options for computers that share similar security requirements. For instance, you can create a security template that is to be used for all file servers or domain controllers on the network. Templates allow consistent security settings to be deployed to multiple computer systems. Several elements are needed to create a security template that can be used by systems on the network. Two of the categories that are used to create security templates are establishing account policies and local policies.

**NOTE** All of the security protocols and procedures you employ do not help that much if the server is in the trunk of somebody's car. With this in mind, one of the primary considerations for securing any server is taking care of the physical security. Physical security is basically a combination of common sense and procedure. The purpose of physical security is to restrict access to server equipment to only those people who need it. Depending on the environment, this may involve simple procedures such as a lock and key or complex procedures such as biometrics.

## Account Policies

Account policies are established to define how a user account interacts with the system and are used to help increase account security. Account policies are systemwide and apply to all user accounts on the local system. There are three areas to configure when setting an account policy: the password policy, the account lockout policy, and the Kerberos policy. To access the account policies, choose Start | All Programs | Administrative Tools and the Domain Controller Security Policy icon. This will open the Default Domain Controller Security Settings window, as shown in Figure 12-4.

**NOTE** If the system is not a domain controller, you will not find the Domain Controller Security Settings icon. Instead it will be the Local Security Settings Policy. The Account Policies can be set from both of these areas. Password policies are normally set at the domain level with the domain group policy, unless you are working in a workgroup environment, in which case you would use the local policy.

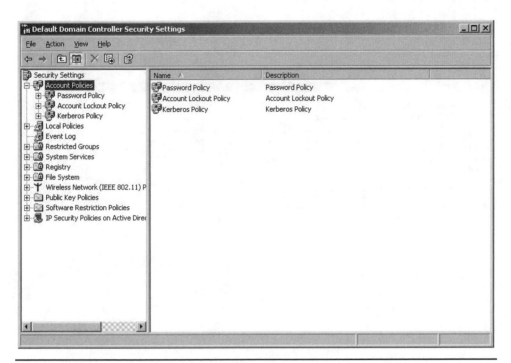

**Figure 12-4**   The Default Domain Controller Security Settings window is used to configure and secure account policies.

## Password Policies

Passwords represent one of the biggest security concerns on a computer system; once a password is compromised, access to the system is an easy logon process. To help make system passwords more secure, you can enforce password policies. Password policies are set from the Default Domain Controller Security Settings window, as shown in Figure 12-5.

As shown in Figure 12-5, there are six settings you can use to increase password security. Table 12-7 summarizes the available security options for passwords.

For many environments, the default password policy settings will be sufficient. However, for those systems that require additional security, configuring the password policies is one of the first steps in securing the system.

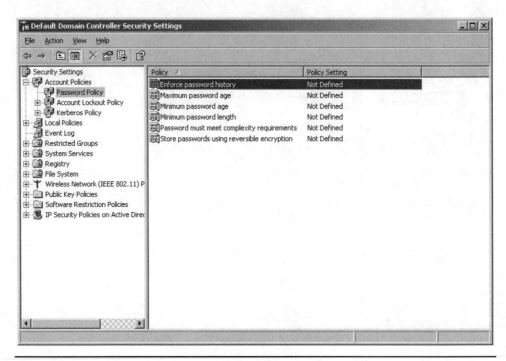

**Figure 12-5**  Password policies are used to increase the password security.

## Account Lockout Policy

Account lockout policies are used to configure how the system will respond to invalid logon attempts. The danger here is that if there is no account lockout policy in place, it is possible to keep guessing user names and passwords in an attempt to gain access to the system. An example of this is programs that run through a dictionary of words and

| Password Policy | Description | Default Setting for a Domain Controller |
|---|---|---|
| Enforce password history | The password history policy sets the number of unique new passwords that have to be associated with a user account before an old password can be reused. This prevents the same password from being reused over and over, increasing the difficulty in obtaining the password. The value must be between 0 and 24 passwords. | Not Defined |

**Table 12-7**  Available Security Options for Passwords

| Password Policy | Description | Default Setting for a Domain Controller |
|---|---|---|
| Maximum password age | The maximum password age sets the number of days that a password can be used before the system requires the user to change it. You can set passwords to expire after a number of days between 1 and 999, or you can specify that passwords never expire by setting the number of days to 0. When enabled, the default setting is 42 days. | Not Defined |
| Minimum password age | The minimum password age sets the number of days that a password must be used before the user can change it. You can set a value between 1 and 999 days, or you can allow changes immediately by setting the number of days to 0. | Not Defined |
| Minimum password length | Passwords using more characters are typically more secure than those using fewer characters. The minimum password length allows you to set the least number of characters that a password for a user account may contain. You can set a value of between 1 and 14 characters, or you can establish that no password is required by setting the number of characters to 0. | Not Defined |
| Passwords must meet complexity requirements | Many users choose a password based on the ease of remembering the password. This policy ensures that the passwords chosen must meet a certain complexity requirement making them harder to guess. | Not Defined |
| Store passwords using reversible encryption | This password policy provides support for applications that use protocols that require knowledge of the user's password for authentication purposes. Storing passwords using reversible encryption is essentially the same as storing plaintext versions of the passwords. For this reason, this policy should never be enabled unless application requirements outweigh the need to protect password information. | Not Defined |

**Table 12-7**   Available Security Options for Passwords *(continued)*

characters trying to access an account. To prevent these brute force attacks, you can use account lockout policies that allow you to shut the account down after a preset failed number of logon attempts are exceeded. Setting account lockout policies is done from the Security Settings window, as shown in Figure 12-6.

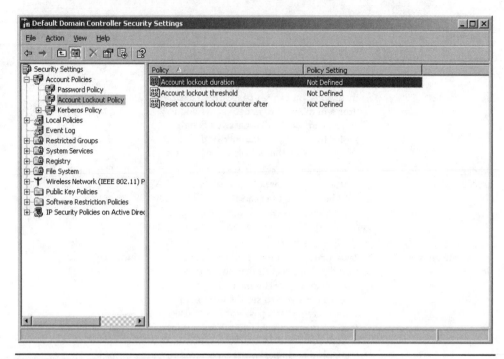

**Figure 12-6**   An account lockout policy is used to help prevent unwanted account access.

As shown in Figure 12-6, there are three options for configuring account lockout options. Table 12-8 summarizes the account lockout options for Windows Server 2003.

| Account Lockout Policy | Description | Default Setting for a Domain Controller |
|---|---|---|
| Account lockout duration | The lockout duration defines the number of minutes that an account remains locked out. Once the time has been exceeded, the account will automatically be enabled. The available range is 1 to 99,999 minutes. You can also specify that a locked-out account will remain locked out until an administrator explicitly unlocks it, by setting the value to 0. | Not Defined |
| Account lockout threshold | The threshold policy sets the number of failed logon attempts that must be exceeded before a users account is locked out. The value can be between 1 and 999 failed logon attempts. | Not Defined |
| Reset account lockout counter after | This policy specifies how long the counter will remember unsuccessful logon attempts. The available range is 1 minute to 99,999 minutes. | Not Defined |

**Table 12-8**   Options for the Account Lockout Policy

## Kerberos Policy

Kerberos policies are used for domain user accounts. As you might have guessed, Kerberos policies set security baselines for Kerberos settings, including such things as ticket lifetimes and enforcement. Kerberos policies do not exist in local computer policy. There are five Kerberos settings as shown in Table 12-9.

## Creating Local Policies

Local policy settings apply to the computer on which the security policy is specified. They are composed of three categories: audit policies, user right assignments, and security options. Like the account policies, these are accessed through either the Local Security Settings window or the Default Domain Controller Security Settings window.

## Creating Audit Policies

Network administrators are often a little paranoid, always wanting to keep an eye on who is doing what on the system. Auditing is one of the methods you can use to monitor your system. Auditing is simply a means of tracking the occurrence of certain system events, including such things as the creating or deletion of user accounts and successful or unsuccessful logon attempts.

| Kerberos Policy | Description | Default Setting for a Domain Controller |
|---|---|---|
| Enforce user logon restrictions | This setting is used to identify if the Kerberos V5 Key Distribution Center (KDC) will validate all requests for a session for a session ticket against the user rights policy of the user account. | Not Defined |
| Maximum lifetime for service ticket | This setting is used to specify (in minutes) the maximum amount of time that an issued session ticket can be used to access a local service. | Not Defined |
| Maximum lifetime for user ticket | This user ticket setting configures the maximum amount of hours that a user's ticket-granting ticket may be used. When the ticket expires, a new one must be requested or the existing one must be renewed. | Not Defined |
| Maximum lifetime for user ticket renewal | This setting identifies the number of days during which the user's ticket may be renewed. | Not Defined |
| Maximum tolerance for computer clock synchronization | This computer clock synchronization setting specifies the maximum time difference that Kerberos V5 tolerates between the time on the client clock and the time on the domain controller running Windows .NET that provides Kerberos authentication. | Not Defined |

**Table 12-9**   Kerberos Settings

PART III

**EXAM TIP** Auditing is considered a security measure as it is used to track system security violations.

The first thing to decide when implementing auditing is what system events you want to monitor. Windows Server 2003 allows you to monitor the success or failure of those system events. For instance, if you were auditing logons, you could choose to log all unsuccessful logon attempts, which may indicate that someone is trying to gain access to your system. On the other hand, you may want to audit successful attempts to see who is logging on and when. Hyper-diligent administrators can log both failed and successful attempts. However, over-ambitious audit policies and excessive logging can be cumbersome, take up a lot of space, and reduce the overall system performance.

Auditing is not enabled by default and has to be enabled manually. To access the audit feature, go into the Control Panel, select Administrator Tools, and finally the Domain Security Policy icon. Figure 12-7 shows available options for creating an audit policy. Table 12-10 provides a brief description of the event categories that you can choose to audit.

 **NOTE** The results from the auditing policy you set up are viewed from the Event Viewer.

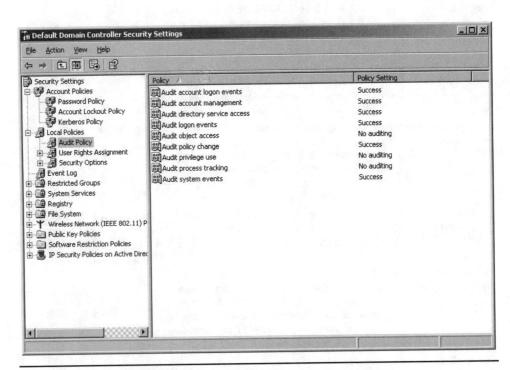

**Figure 12-7** Audit policies are designed to track events on a computer system.

| Audit Policy | Description | Default Setting for a Domain Controller |
|---|---|---|
| Audit account logon events | Allows you to audit a user logging on to or logging off from another computer in which this computer is used to validate the account. | Success |
| Audit account management | Audits account management such as the creation or deletion of groups or users. | Success |
| Audit directory service access | Tracks a user accessing an Active Directory object that has its own system access control list (SACL) specified. | Success |
| Audit logon events | Tracks each instance of a user logging on to, logging off from, or making a network connection to this computer. | Success |
| Audit object access | Tracks a user accessing an object—such as a file, folder, registry key, printer, and so forth—that has its own system access control list (SACL) specified. | No Auditing |
| Audit policy change | Enabling the audit policy change will track changes to the audit policy. | Success |
| Audit privilege use | Auditing privilege use will record each instance of a user exercising a user right. | No Auditing |
| Audit process tracking | Process tracking involves auditing such things as program activation, accessing an object, or exiting a process. | No Auditing |
| Audit system events | When auditing system events, you can track such events such as shutting down or restarting the system as well as monitoring changes to system security or the security log in the Event Viewer. | Success |

**Table 12-10**    Available Event Categories to Audit

**NOTE**    To enable auditing of local objects, you must be logged on as a member of the Administrators group.

# User Rights Assignment

It is a common mistake to confuse user and group rights with standard permissions, but they actually refer to different security methods. User and group rights refer to the actions a user can perform to the system, such as backing up and restoring system files. Permissions refer to controlling resource and file access. Setting user and group rights can be done from the Default Domain Controller Security Settings window. Figure 12-8 shows the Default Domain Controller Security Settings window and the available user and group assignments.

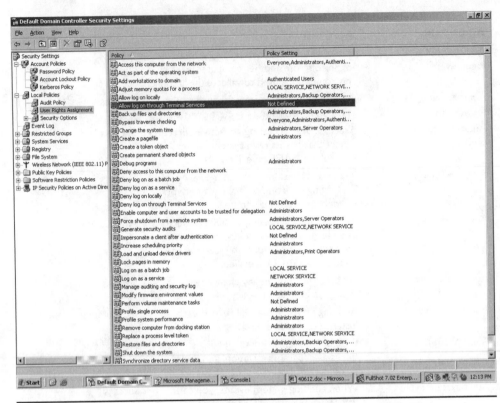

**Figure 12-8**   The Default Domain Controller Security Settings window is used to assign user and group rights.

As shown in Figure 12-8, there are a number of different rights that can be assigned. To allow a user or group a particular right, or to view who is assigned a right, double-click any of the system rights on the right side of the Security Settings window. For instance, if you want to assign users or groups the right to shut down the system, click that right to open the Shut Down The System Properties screen shown in Figure 12-9. From this screen, you can view which users and groups have the rights to shut down the system. You can also add or remove users or groups from the list.

## Privileges and Logon Rights

When working with the User Rights Assignments in the Security Settings window, the configurable rights can be broken down into two categories, privileges and logon rights. Privileges typically affect the entire computer system and are essentially used to perform a specific task. Logon rights define the way in which a user can log on to the system. Both

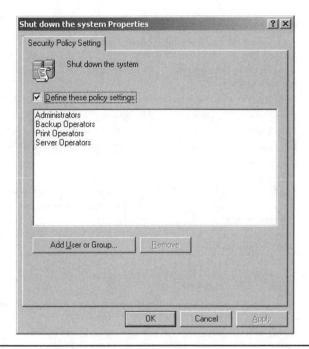

**Figure 12-9**    Using the User Rights Assignment configuration menu, you can view, add, or remove
users and groups to a system right.

are used to help define the security of the overall system. Table 12-11 summarizes the
configurable logon rights, and Table 12-12 summarizes the configurable privileges.

Privileges are generally assigned to groups rather than individual user accounts, with
the rights of the group being applied to the users once they are added to the respective
group. Table 12-12 lists the available privileges in Windows Server 2003.

## Configuring Security Options

Like user and group rights assignment, setting security options is performed from the
Default Domain Controller Security Settings window. Unlike user and group rights
that apply to the user or group, security settings apply to the entire computer. Most of
the security settings require you to enable or disable a number of security-related settings, such as renaming the Administrator or Guest accounts, restricting CD-ROM or

| Table 12-11 | Logon Right | Function |
| --- | --- | --- |
| Configuring User Rights Assignments for Logon Security | Access this computer from the network | Allows a user to access the local computer over the network. |
| | Deny access to this computer from the network | Denies access to the local computer over the network. |
| | Deny logon as a batch job | Prevents user logon using a batch file. |
| | Log on as a batch job | Allows a user to log on using a batch file. |
| | Deny logon as a service | Denies option to log on as a service. |
| | Log on as a service | Allows option to log on as a service. |
| | Deny logon locally | Prevents the specified user from being able to log on locally. |
| | Log on locally | Allows the user to log on from the local system. |
| | Deny logon through Terminal Services | Prevents a user from logging on through Terminal Services. |
| | Allow logon through Terminal Services | Allows a user to log on through Terminal Services. |

| Privilege | Function |
| --- | --- |
| Act as part of the operating system | Allows a process to authenticate as if it were a user and gain access to the same system resources as a user. |
| Add workstations to domain | Allows a user to add a computer to the domain. |
| Back up files and directories | Allows a user to back up the files and folders on the system without needing permissions to access the files and folders. By default, the members of the Administrators and Backup Operators groups have this privilege. |
| Bypass traverse checking | Allows users to move through folders for which they do not have permissions to access. This allows them to look through the contents of a folder, but not to change or view the files within the folder. |
| Change the system time | Allows the user to change the internal clock for the computer. By default, the Administrators and Power Users groups have this privilege. |
| Create permanent shared objects | This advanced privilege allows a process to create a directory object in the Windows Object Manager. It is unlikely that you will have reason to modify this one. No groups have the privilege by default. |
| Create a pagefile | With this privilege, users can resize the current pagefile or create a new one. Only the Administrators group has this by default. |
| Debug programs | Provides the user with the right to attach a debugger to a process. |
| Enable computer and user accounts to be trusted for | Users with this privilege have the ability to change the Trusted For delegation setting on a user or computer object in Active Directory. |
| Force shutdown from a remote system | Allows a user to shut down the system from a remote system on the network. Only the Administrators group has this by default. |
| Generate security audits | Assigning this privilege allows a process to generate entries in the security log. |
| Increase scheduling priority | Allows the user to increase the execution priority of a process using Task Manager. Only the Administrators group has this by default. |
| Load and unload device drivers | As you might expect, this privilege allows a user to install and uninstall device drivers, but only plug-and-play device drivers. Drivers for non–plug-and-play devices can be installed only by administrators. |

**Table 12-12**    Privileges in Windows Server 2003

| Privilege | Function |
|---|---|
| Lock pages in memory | With this privilege, it is possible to allow a process to lock data into physical memory, preventing it from going to the pagefile. This is not assigned to any groups by default. |
| Manage auditing and security log | Allows the user to configure the system's auditing and to specify object access auditing. This privilege also allows viewing the security log in Event Viewer. Only the Administrators group has this by default. |
| Modify firmware environment values | Allows the user to modify the system environment variables. Only the Administrators group has this by default. |
| Perform volume maintenance tasks | Allows the user to use volume-specific tools such as the Disk Defragmenter tool or the Disk Cleanup utility. By default, only the members of the Administrators group have this privilege assigned. |
| Profile a single process | Assigned to allow a user to use monitoring tools used to monitor non-system processes. The Administrators and Power Users groups have this privilege by default. |
| Profile system performance | Allows the user to use system performance monitoring tools that monitor system processes. Only the members of the Administrators group have this privilege by default. |
| Remove computer from docking station | Assigns the privilege to remove a system from the docking station. By default, members of the Administrators, Power Users, and Users groups have these privileges. |
| Replace a process level token | Specifies user accounts that can replace the default token associated with another process. |
| Restore files and directories | Allows the user to restore files and directories regardless of file or folder permissions. Members of the Administrators and Backup Operators groups have this privilege. |
| Shut down the system | Allows the ability to shut down the local system. By default, members of the Administrators, Backup Operators, Power Users, and Users groups have this privilege. |
| Synchronize directory service data | This privilege involves synchronization services and is relevant only to domain controllers. |
| Take ownership of files or other objects | Allows a user to take ownership of any objects in the system. These objects include files and folders. By default, only members of the Administrators group have this right. |

**Table 12-12**    Privileges in Windows Server 2003 *(continued)*

floppy access, driver installation, and logon prompts. Figure 12-10 shows the Default Domain Controller Security Settings window and some of the available configurable security settings.

There are more than 60 configurable security options in Windows Server 2003 that allow you to completely customize the security of the entire system. Some of these settings are more commonly implemented than others, but when defining a security policy they may all come into play. Some of the settings you are more likely to configure are described in Table 12-13.

 **EXAM TIP**    Before taking the 70-293 exam, familiarize yourself with the security options available for configuration.

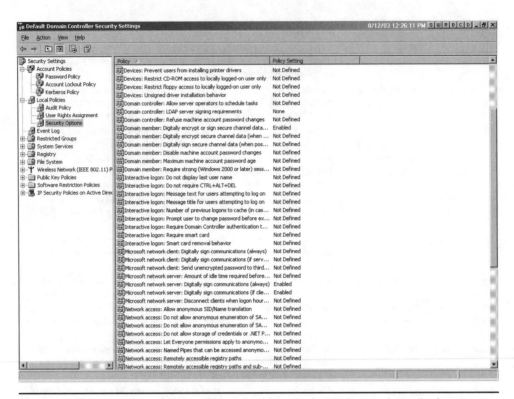

**Figure 12-10** Setting a local security policy is done from the Default Domain Controller Security Settings window.

| Security Option | Description |
|---|---|
| Accounts: Rename administrator account | It is not possible to delete the Administrator account, but it is recommended for security purposes to rename the account. Renaming the account increases the difficulty of gaining access to the Administrator account as both the user name and password need to be obtained. |
| Interactive logon: Number of previous logons to cache (in case domain controller is not available) | This setting identifies the number of times a user can log onto a Windows domain using cached account information. Cached account information is stored in case the Windows domain server is unavailable, allowing the user to still be able to log on. The default is set for 10 logons. |
| Network access: Do not allow Stored User Names and Passwords to save passwords or credentials for domain authentication | This option prevents the storing of user names and passwords. |
| Accounts: Rename Guest account | As with the Administrators account, it is often a good idea to rename the Guest account. |

**Table 12-13**  Commonly Implemented Security Policy Settings

| Security Option | Description |
|---|---|
| Network security: Force logoff when logon hours expire | Determines whether to disconnect users who are connected to the local computer outside their user account's valid logon hours. Users will be forcibly disconnected if they exceed their predefined logon hours. |
| Interactive logon: Do not display last user name | Determines whether the name of the last user to log onto the computer is displayed in the Windows logon screen. For security, the previous user name should not be displayed in the Windows logon screen. |
| Devices: Prevent users from installing printer drivers | This security setting determines who is allowed to install a printer driver as part of adding a network printer. |

**Table 12-13**    Commonly Implemented Security Policy Settings *(continued)*

These are just a few of the available settings, but they provide a good idea of what the security options are able to do. A word of caution: when first implementing a security policy, it is tempting to "nail down" the system. Unfortunately, too much security can make things more complicated for the administrator and less useful for the end user. The security policy is really a practice of finding the middle ground.

 **EXAM TIP**    Because a computer can have more than one policy applied to it, there can be conflicts in security policy settings. The order of precedence from highest to lowest is organizational unit, domain, and local computer settings.

## Additional Security Settings

In addition to the account policies and local policies, the Default Domain Controller Security Settings window identifies nine other areas used to secure the system and create baseline templates. A brief description of these other configurable security features is provided here:

- **Event Log**    There are twelve configurable options for the Event Log. They are used to define the properties of the Application, Security, and System Log files. Configurable options include who can and cannot access the logs, the size of the log files, log retention times, and actions to take when log files exceed maximum size.

- **Restricted Groups**    This setting is used to define members of security groups. When adding members to these security groups, there are two configurable options: Members Of This Group, and This Group Is A Member Of. The Members list defines who belongs and who does not belong to the restricted group. The Member Of list specifies which other groups the restricted group belongs to.

- **System Services** This setting is used to specify the startup mode (manual, automatic, or disabled) as well as the access permissions (Start, Stop, or Pause) for all system services.

- **Registry** This setting is used to configure security for registry keys and their subtrees. From here, administrators can configure who has access to specific registry keys.

- **File System** The file system is used to configure access permissions on discretionary access control lists (DACLs) and audit settings on system access control lists (SACLs) for file system objects using Security Configuration Manager. To use this policy, NTFS needs to be used.

- **Wireless Network** This setting is used to specify the type of wireless security to use on the network. This includes using IEEE 802.1x and the EAP type to use. Wireless security methods are discussed in Chapter 16.

- **Public Key Policies** Public key policies are used to manage the key policies. Using these policies, it is possible to automatically issue certificates to computers, manage encrypted data recovery agents, create certificate trust lists, or automatically establish trust of certificate authorities.

- **Software Restriction Policies** A software restriction policy is used to control software on the system and its ability to run the local computer, organizational unit, domain, or site.

- **IP Security Policies on Active Directory** The IP Security (IPSec) policy is used to configure IPSec settings for the system. Configuring IPSec is covered in Chapter 16.

Now that you have seen how baselines and security templates are made, you can look at the default templates used with Windows Server 2003.

## Default Security Templates

Windows Server 2003 includes several security templates that are designed to create a starting point for creating security policies for the system. A security file is a text file that defines a security configuration. Once this file is configured, you can use these same security templates on all systems that you manage. The type of template used on a system will depend on what the system is used for, whether a server or a workstation. If none of the default security templates meet your needs, custom ones can be created as shown in the previous section. The security templates available in Windows Server 2003 are listed next.

---

 **EXAM TIP** Security templates are located on the local computer in the c:\windows\security\templates directory.

- **Default security (setup security.inf)**  The setup security.inf template holds the default security settings applied to the system when the operating system was first installed and is sometimes used for disaster recovery purposes. While the setup security.inf file is created on systems during setup, it can vary during the installation on different computers. The setup security.inf file can be used for servers and workstation computers, but it cannot be applied to domain controllers.

**NOTE**  .inf files can be viewed in Notepad or another word processor. To view the settings in each of the .inf files discussed in this section, locate them in the systemroot/security folder and double-click them.

- **Domain controller (DC security.inf)**  The DC security.inf file is created when a server is promoted to a domain controller. It provides increased default security over that of the setup security.inf because of its role as a domain controller.

**NOTE**  Security templates are applied using the Security Configuration and Analysis snap-in, the secedit command-line tool, or they can be imported through the Group Policy editor.

- **Compatible (compatws.inf)**  The compatws.inf or compatible template is designed to relax the default file and registry permissions granted to the Users group, allowing them to run legacy applications more easily and without having to add them to another group such as Power Users. Microsoft recommends that the compatws.inf template not be applied to domain controllers.

- **Secure (securews.inf or securedc.inf)**  Secure templates define enhanced security settings, including stronger password, lockout, and audit settings. These .inf files are designed to increase security without affecting application compatibility.

- **Highly secure (hisecws.inf or hisecdc.inf)**  These default templates offer increased security over the securews.inf and securedc.inf files. They configure further restrictions on the levels of encryption and signing that are required for authentication and for the data that flows over secure channels and between clients and servers.

- **System root security (rootsec.inf)**  The rootsec.inf template specifies the root permissions. This template can be used to reapply the root directory permissions if they are inadvertently changed.

**NOTE**  It is important to point out that nottssid.inf, compatws.inf, secure*.inf, and hisec*.inf files are incremental files. This means that they can only be applied on top of the default security templates. They are designed to augment the security provided by the default configurations.

## Viewing and Configuring Security Templates

With a basic knowledge of the default security templates available with Windows Server 2003, you can now look at how you can modify these default templates to better suit your needs and even create new templates.

To view the existing templates, open the Microsoft Management Console by selecting Start and typing **mmc** in the Run dialog box. With the console open, add the Security Templates snap-in by selecting File | Add/Remove Snap-in. In the Add/Remove dialog box, click Add. From the Available Standalone Snap-ins, select the Security Templates option as shown in Figure 12-11.

To modify the settings on one of the default .inf files, expand the tree of the desired .inf file in the left pane of the window. With the tree expanded, select the policy category you want to view or change and click it. As an example, Figure 12-12 shows the default password policy for the setup security.inf file.

Modifying and viewing the existing default .inf file is one thing, but it may be necessary to create one from scratch. To create a new security template, right-click the main file folder and select New Template from the menu as shown in Figure 12-13.

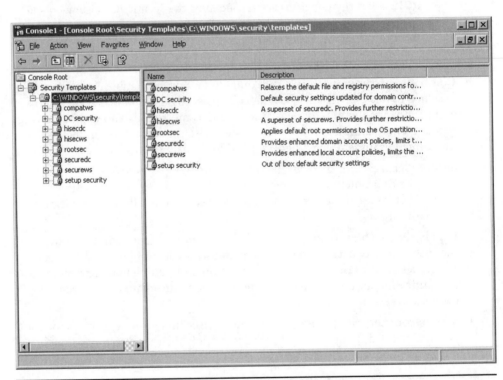

**Figure 12-11**   The Security Templates snap-in is used to view and configure the default security .inf files.

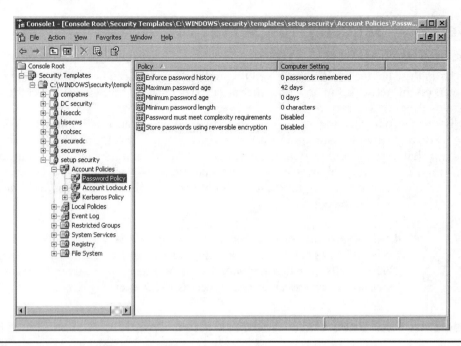

**Figure 12-12**   The default setup security.inf file can be viewed and modified.

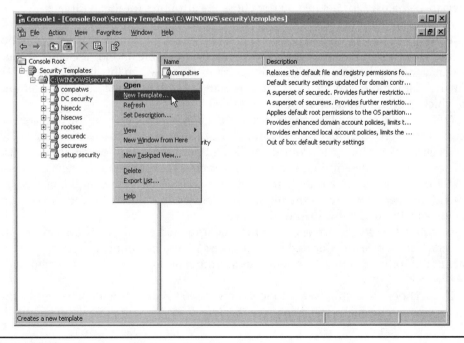

**Figure 12-13**   Creating a new security template

# Defining Security for Servers Assigned Specific Roles

So far in this chapter, we have reviewed the mechanisms that can be used to secure the servers on the network. But how does the role a server plays on the network affect the security settings of that server?

The first step in deciding on the security to be used on servers is to identify the computers on the network that require similar security settings. This is done by identifying the role that a system will play on the network. For instance, file servers, workstations, and domain controllers all have very specific security needs. Each of these roles will be associated with a security template that will identify the baseline security for the various classes of systems on the network.

---

 **NOTE** One of the complaints about older Windows Server operating systems such as Windows NT 4 was that it wasn't secure after the installation. Windows 2000 and 2003 were designed with these default templates to ensure that after installation, there was a measure of security to the operating system.

---

## Securing Servers that Are Assigned Specific Roles

To design an effective security template for a specific server, it is important to know the intended function of that server. For example, if you were creating a security template for a mail server or a web server, you need to know how these servers function and what they are being used for before you can chose the attributes for that template.

As an example, if a database server is being used on network, you need to know whether both local clients and remote clients will access the database. If both, you modify the security template to secure access both from remote and local clients. As such, you may want to define a template to include force logoff when logon hours expire. This can increase remote security. As a generic precaution, you may create a security template in which the Administrator account is disabled.

Once you are aware of the role a system is to play on the network, the next step is to scroll through the template options and create security measures specific to that role.

To take a closer look, let's consider a file and print server. Almost all networks use a file server of some description. The role of file servers is to provide and manage access to files and folders and to ensure that this data is accessible to users on the network. Of course, you need security on the file server to ensure that the data on the server is not tampered with or seen by unauthorized eyes.

Closely tied into file servers and often incorporated on the same system are print servers. Print servers provide and manage access to printers. In many network environments, the ability to print is as essential as any other network service and therefore must be secured.

If you choose to configure a Windows Server 2003 system as a file server and a print server, the system will be installed using the default security template setup security.inf.

This will provide a measure of security for the file server, but you may need to increase the security as you develop a single security template for multiple file servers on the network. As an example of securing the file server, Table 12-14 highlights some of the default settings of setup security.inf and how they may be changed to increase server security.

**NOTE** As mentioned above, making changes to the existing template and creating new ones are done in the MMC using the Security Template snap-in.

Table 12-14 provides a quick overview of a few of the changes that can be made to increase security on a security template. Once the security is assigned as needed, the template can be deployed to all similar servers on the network.

| Security Setting | security.inf Default Setting | Changed Setting | Description |
|---|---|---|---|
| Accounts Policies/ Password Policy: Password must meet complexity requirements | Disabled | Enabled | Enabling this policy ensures that the passwords chosen must meet a certain complexity requirement, making them harder to guess. |
| Accounts Policies/ Password Policy: Minimum password length | 0 Characters | 8 Characters | This policy ensures that passwords chosen must be at least eight characters in length. |
| Accounts Policies/ Account lockout policy: Account lockout threshold | 0 invalid logon attempts (account will not lockout) | 3 invalid logon attempts | This policy specifies that the account will be locked out after three unsuccessful logon attempts. |
| Local Policies/User Rights Assignment: Take ownership of files or other objects | Administrators | Print Operators | Adding the Print Operators group will allow members of that group to take ownership of printers and manage them. |
| Local Policies/Security Options: Unsigned driver installation | Not defined | Do not allow installation of unsigned drivers. | Prevent using unsigned drivers, for example, as printer drivers may cause system malfunction. |

**Table 12-14**  Modifying the Default Security Template to Increase Security for File Servers

Securing file and print servers using security templates is just the first part of the security puzzle. Security also involves assigning users to the correct user groups with predefined levels of access to the server and the files it maintains. Further, restricting access to data using NTFS permissions is also part of a secure server strategy.

### Domain Controller (Active Directory) Role Overview

Domain controllers store directory data and manage communication between users and domains, including user logon processes, authentication, and directory searches. Domain controllers do a lot of the work on the network and as such will often require a higher level of security than other servers on the network. When a security template is created for the domain controller, you can increase specific security settings.

When a system is converted to a domain controller, the setup security.inf is replaced with the DC security.inf file. Securing the domain controller and creating a security template will involve updating the DC security.inf template or replacing it with a newly designed one.

 **EXAM TIP** Before taking the exam, take the time to carefully review the security options available when creating a security template. Try creating one for a specific server role and applying it to the server to see how it affects its overall security.

## Deploying Security Templates

Once a security template is created for a group of similar servers or an individual system, the next step is to deploy that security template. How this is done will depend on whether the network is a workgroup or a domain.

### Deploying Security Templates in a Workgroup

In a workgroup environment, it is not possible to deploy security templates using Group Policy, therefore the only way to apply security templates is to import them into the local computer policy. There are two methods to import the security policy: from the Windows interface using the Security Configuration and Analysis tool, and from the command line using the secedit utility.

The Security Configuration and Analysis tool is an MMC snap-in utility and needs to be added to the console. Once added, the following steps outline the procedures for adding security templates using the Security Configuration and Analysis tool.

1. Within the MMC, right-click Security Configuration and Analysis, and then click Open Database. This will open the Open Database dialog box.

2. You can create a new database by simply typing a file name in the File Name text box and then clicking Open. You will be prompted to locate the security template you want to use for the database. Click any of the listed security .inf templates and select Open.

3. In the console tree, right-click Security Configuration and Analysis, and then click the Configure Computer Now option.

4. You will be prompted to specify the location of the error log file. Identify the location and select OK. Once the error log location is identified, the security template will be applied to the local computer system as shown in Figure 12-14.

**NOTE**   To perform this procedure, you will need to be a member of the Administrators group or have been delegated the permissions necessary to perform the procedure.

If you do not want to use the Windows utility, the security template can be applied using the command line and the secedit utility with the /configure option. An example syntax for the command follows:

```
secedit /configure /db hisecws.sdb /cfg hisecws.inf /overwrite /log hisecws.log
```

In this example, the /db option identifies the path to the database file that contains the stored configuration. The /cfg option specifies the name of the security template to use in the database. The /overwrite option is used to ensure that previous security templates are overwritten with the new information, and finally, the /log option identifies the name of the log file.

secedit allows you to analyze security settings using a security database, configure settings based on a template or database, validate a security template file, refresh Group Policy of a local computer, and export the current security settings to a template file. The commands used to perform these actions are as follows:

- secedit /analyze
- secedit /configure
- secedit /export
- secedit /validate

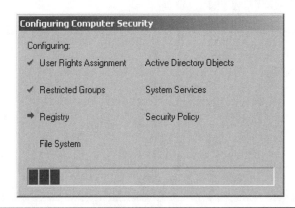

**Figure 12-14**   The Security Configuration and Analysis tool can be used to apply a security template.

**EXAM TIP** It is important to remember that the security settings on a system can be analyzed and configured using both the Security Configuration and Analysis tool and the secedit command-line utility. Using secedit, it is possible to regularly analyze security information by configuring a scheduled task that would execute the secedit utility with the appropriate parameters at specific intervals.

## Deploying Security Templates in a Domain

Security templates deployed on a domain level are imported directly into Group Policy objects. The steps for importing a security template for a Group Policy object are as follows:

1. Choose Start | Run, type **mmc** and click OK. This will open the MMC.

2. Select File | Add/Remove Snap-in to open the Add/Remove Snap-in dialog box.

3. Click Add, and from the Add Standalone Snap-in menu, add the Group Policy Object Editor. This will open the Select Group Policy Object dialog box.

4. Click Browse, select the policy object you would like to modify, click OK, and then click Finish. Click Close and then click OK.

5. In the console, expand Domain Policy | Computer Configuration | Window Settings. Right-click the Security Settings icon and choose Import Policy from the menu. Figure 12-15 shows this process.

6. Select the security template you want to import and select Open. The policy will be applied.

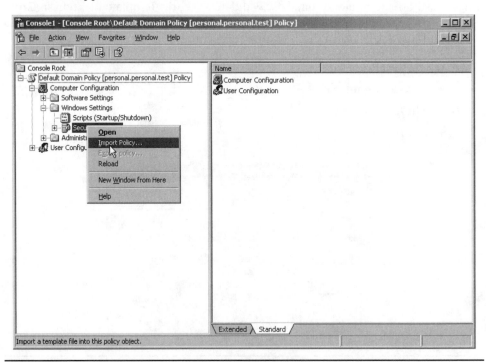

**Figure 12-15** Importing a security template using the Group Policy Object Editor snap-in

# Selecting Operating Systems to Install on the Network

When a security strategy is designed for an organization, it is important to consider the operating systems that will be used on client systems and whether they support the proposed or current security infrastructure. With that in mind, it's a good idea to review some of the security measures discussed in this chapter and which operating systems may be inappropriate to use.

## NTFS Security

NTFS is one of the primary mechanisms used to secure files and folders on an operating system. This means that, without question, NTFS is the file system of choice to be used with server systems and many client systems where local computer security is a concern. In such environments you can choose from several operating systems, including Windows XP, Windows Server 2003, Window 2000 Server, Windows 2000 Professional, Windows NT 4 Workstation, and Windows NT 4.0 Server. Each of these operating systems will allow you to configure NTFS partitions on your system.

 **NOTE** Windows NT uses a different version of NTFS, the new version supported in more recent Windows operating systems offers many new features, but is incompatible with the older version.

Client operating systems such as Windows 9x and Windows Me do not support NTFS partitions and therefore offer no local security for files and folders.

## Security Templates and Client Operating Systems

The security templates used in a security strategy can also impact what client operating systems can be used on the network. As mentioned previously, the secure*.inf and hisec*.inf files are used to incrementally augment the default security of a current security template. However, these templates do not work with all client operating systems.

- **secure*.inf files** The secure*.inf security templates are often used in a mixed environment of Windows 200/XP systems and down-level clients. This security template is applied when the strongest level of security is needed that will not exclude down-level Windows clients.

- **hisec*.inf files** High security templates are designed for use in environments where no down-level Windows clients exist on the network. This template provides very high security, but excludes many of the lower-level operating systems, leaving you with Windows 2000/XP client systems on the network. If a server is configured with hisecws.inf, a user with a local account on that server will not be able to connect to it from a client that does not support NTLMv2. Windows clients that do not natively support NTLMv2 include Windows for Workgroups, Windows NT clients prior to service pack 4, and Windows 95 and Windows 98 platforms that do not have the Active Directory Client Extensions Pack installed.

In addition to these considerations, legacy Windows client systems do not offer a means to locally apply a security template. Windows 2000/XP systems use default security templates and therefore offer a measure of security as soon as the operating systems is installed. Taking all of these considerations into account, discussions of client operating systems in terms of security at least weigh heavily in favor of Microsoft's high-end professional client operating systems such as Windows 2000 Professional and Windows XP Professional.

# Chapter Review

In this chapter, we have explored some of the mechanisms that are employed to form a security strategy in an enterprise. We began by exploring the group memberships and looking at assigning members to the groups to provide the correct level of access to a computer system. In addition, we reviewed how NTFS permissions can be used to secure access to files and folders on a computer system.

Security templates are used to provide a security baseline for Windows Professional and Server operating systems. Each system has a security template installed by default. This is designed to provide a measure of security for a system directly after installation.

There are many default security templates that may be used, and these can also be modified or new ones created to increase the level of security. When creating or modifying a security template, you can design them to meet the security needs of servers functioning in a variety of roles. The key is to create a security template for a specific server role and then apply that security template to all systems on the network with a similar role.

Many of the security features discussed in this chapter are better suited for implementation on modern Windows operating systems such as Windows 2000/XP. Older legacy Windows operating systems do not offer the same level of versatility in terms of security.

## Questions

1. You are the administrator of a network that uses several different versions of Windows, including 100 Windows 9x systems, 40 Windows NT 4.0 systems all with service pack 4, 200 Windows 2000 Professional systems, and 100 Windows XP systems. You decide to apply an incremental security template to the existing default security. Which of the following will you apply as the new security template?

    A. hisecws.inf

    B. secure.inf

    C. DC security.inf

    D. setup security.inf

2. PeopleChoice, a company that makes potato chips, has asked you to help secure their network. Several users have been logging onto the network and attempting to access a new and secret chip recipe and print it out. They ask

you to design a method of tracking those who are attempting to access one of the network's printers. Which of the following methods would accomplish this?

A. Configure audit policies to track account logon events.

B. Configure audit policies to track account management.

C. Configure audit policies to track directory service access.

D. Configure audit policies to track object access.

3. You need to design a policy that includes the ability to prevent the use of unsigned drivers that may cause system malfunction. Which of the following would you choose?

A. Navigate to Local Policies/Security Options: Unsigned driver installation option, select the option not to accept unsigned drivers.

B. Navigate to Account Policies/Security Options: Unsigned driver installation option, select the option not to accept unsigned drivers.

C. Navigate to the Group Policy editor/Security Options: Unsigned driver installation option, select the option not to accept unsigned drivers.

D. Navigate to Account Policies/Audit Options: Unsigned driver installation option, select the option not to accept unsigned drivers.

4. Your network has recently grown to more than 300 Windows XP systems. You are no longer able to manage the system alone and need to delegate some of your administrative tasks. You want to give a user named Homer rights to configure, create, and manage local user and group accounts. You want to give a user named Alfredo the ability only to restore system files and directories. What is the best way to accomplish this without assigning too many privileges?

A. Add Homer to the Administrators group and add Alfredo to the Backup Operators group only.

B. Add Homer to the Power Users group and add Alfredo to the Backup Operators group only.

C. Add Homer to the Power Users group and modify the local security policy to allow Alfredo to restore files and directories.

D. Add Homer to the Backup Users group and modify the local security policy to allow Alfredo the right to restore files and directories.

5. Your boss has decided that he wants to review the security logs in the Event Viewer. She is currently a member of the Power Users group. What is the best way to allow her to view the logs?

A. Add your boss's account to the Administrators group.

B. Modify your boss's account to include the "Manage auditing and security log" privilege.

    **C.** Have your boss log on to the system using an Administrator account when she wants to view the logs.

    **D.** Do nothing; Power Users can view system security logs.

6. You suspect that a user is attempting to gain unauthorized access into your system. Which of the following can you do to determine a potential security breach and prevent unauthorized access? (Choose all that apply.)

    **A.** Implement an audit policy to track successful logons.

    **B.** Implement an audit policy to track failed logon attempts.

    **C.** Implement an account lockout policy to lock out an account after three failed logon attempts.

    **D.** Implement an account lockout policy to reset the password after three failed logon attempts.

7. Which of the following groups offers the most security?

    **A.** Users

    **B.** Administrators

    **C.** Power Users

    **D.** Backup Operators

8. You are the administrator for a medium-size network that uses several legacy applications. All members of the Users group need to run these legacy applications, but they are experiencing some compatibility problems. Which of the following templates is designed to relax overall security and allow users to run legacy applications more easily, without having to add them to another group such as Power Users?

    **A.** hisecws.inf

    **B.** compatws.inf

    **C.** DC security.inf

    **D.** setup security.inf

9. You have set up a password policy that requires users to change their passwords every 30 days. After some time you discover that the users are not changing passwords, but simply reusing old ones to make them easier to remember. Which of the following could you do to ensure that network users use unique passwords when a change is required?

    **A.** Configure the Enforce Password History setting to 12.

    **B.** Configure the maximum password age to 15.

    **C.** Configure the minimum password age to 15.

    **D.** Configure the minimum password length to 15.

PART III

10. Which of the following settings is used to specify the maximum amount of time that an issued session ticket can be used to access a local service?

    **A.** Maximum Lifetime for Service Ticket

    **B.** Enforce User Logon Restrictions

    **C.** Maximum Lifetime for User Ticket

    **D.** Refresh Time for Service Ticket

## Answers

1. **B.** Secure (securews.inf or securedc.inf) provides enhanced security, including stronger password, lockout, and audit settings. This security template is applied when the strongest level of security is needed that will not exclude down-level Windows clients, including Windows 9x systems and higher.

2. **D.** Auditing object access tracks a user accessing an object—such as a file, folder, registry key, printer, and so forth—that has its own system access control list (SACL) specified.

3. **A.** To set a policy to prevent the use of unsigned drivers, navigate to Local Policies/Security Options: Unsigned driver installation option, and select the option not to accept unsigned drivers.

4. **C.** Adding Homer to the Power Users group will allow him to create and manage user accounts. Modifying Alfredo's account to include the right to restore files and directories would allow him to restore files. It is not necessary to add Homer to the Administrators group as being a member of the Power Users group provides enough permissions. Adding Alfredo to the Backup Operators group is not necessary as he needs permission to restore files only, not back up and restore.

5. **B.** If you modify the boss's user account to include the "Manage auditing and security log" privilege, she will be able to review security logs without accessing an administrative account or being added to the Administrators group. Power Users cannot view security logs by default.

6. **B and C.** To determine if someone is attempting to gain unauthorized access to your system, you can enable auditing to track the occurrence of unsuccessful logon attempts. To help reduce the chances that someone can gain access using that account, you can implement an account lockout policy to lock out the account after a certain number of failed logons is exceeded.

7. **A.** The Users group has by default the least rights and therefore can change less on the system. All users for the system should be members of the Users group only, unless they need to perform other system tasks.

8. **B.** Compatible (compatws.inf) is designed to relax the default file and registry permissions granted to the Users group, allowing them to run legacy applications more easily, without having to add them to another group such as Power Users. Microsoft recommends that the compatws.inf template not be applied to domain controllers.

9. **A.** The password history policy sets the number of unique new passwords that have to be associated with a user account before an old password can be reused. This prevents the same password from being reused over and over, increasing the difficulty in obtaining the password. The value must be between 0 and 24 passwords.

10. **A.** The Maximum Lifetime for Service Ticket setting defines the number of minutes that an issued session ticket can be used to access a local service.

# Planning, Implementing, and Maintaining a Network Infrastructure

In this chapter, you will learn how to
- Analyze IP addressing requirements
- Plan network routing
- Subnet IP addresses
- Troubleshoot client TCP/IP configuration
- Work with DNS
- Plan DNS security
- Troubleshoot DNS
- Manage WINS replication
- Use the LMHOSTS file
- Plan an Internet connectivity strategy
- Troubleshoot Internet connectivity
- Monitor network traffic

A well-designed network does not happen by accident; instead, creating a network infrastructure involves paying close attention to many elements. These elements include everything from choosing and configuring protocols, to implementing network services such as DNS and WINS, hardware placement and network monitoring. In this chapter you'll work through some of the technologies and strategies that must be considered when designing or managing a network infrastructure. Perhaps the best place to start is with today's protocol of choice, TCP/IP.

## Introduction to TCP/IP

In the IT world, technologies have a way of coming and then disappearing almost overnight, replaced by something faster and cheaper. In such an environment, it is tough to find technologies with any staying power, but TCP/IP is one such technology. TCP/IP has been with us since the early 1980s and today is the default protocol used in most modern networks and for the Internet.

All of the various operating systems available today not only support TCP/IP, but also have it as their default protocol. Windows Server 2003 uses TCP/IP as its primary protocol, and it forms the foundation for Active Directory. There are many reasons why TCP/IP has become the protocol of choice, including

- **Scalability**   TCP/IP can be used on networks of all sizes and can grow with networks. This is accomplished through IP addressing and subnetting, which are discussed later in this chapter.

- **Routability**   TCP/IP is routable because it uses network and device addresses. This allows data to be routed from one network to another. Today's networks often have data leaving the local physical network making routable protocols such as TCP/IP necessary.

Both the scalability and routability of TCP/IP will be discussed in the following sections.

## Inside TCP/IP

TCP/IP is actually a protocol suite, meaning it is not a single protocol, but rather, is made up of several individual protocols. Each of these protocols provides a different function and as a whole, provides TCP/IP functionality. The protocol gets its name from two of the main protocols in the suite, TCP and IP. TCP provides the reliable transmission between systems, and IP is responsible for addressing and route selection. A few of the other common protocols are included in Table 13-1.

| Protocol | Description |
|---|---|
| User Datagram Protocol (UDP) | Provides connectionless transportation between devices Connectionless transport means that UDP does not verify that the data was received by the intended recipient, data transmissions are not guaranteed. |
| File Transfer Protocol (FTP) | Protocol used for uploading and downloading files to and from a remote host. |
| Trivial File Transfer Protocol (TFTP) | Connectionless protocol that does not have the security or error-checking capabilities of FTP. |
| Simple Mail Transfer Protocol (SMTP) | Protocol used for e-mail transfer. |
| Hypertext Transfer Protocol (HTTP) | Protocol designed to retrieve web pages from a web server. |
| Hypertext Transfer Protocol Secure (HTTPS) | Secure protocol designed to retrieve web pages from a web server |
| Post Office Protocol (POP) | Protocol used to retrieve e-mail messages from an e-mail server. |
| Telnet | Opens a session on a remote host. |
| Address Resolution Protocol (ARP) | Protocol used to resolve IP addresses to MAC addresses. |

**Table 13-1**   Protocols Included in the TCP/IP Protocol Suite

# Introduction to IP Addressing

There can be no argument that TCP/IP is a flexible and scalable protocol. On the other hand, it can be very complex, specifically when it comes to IP addressing. We are sure that discussions of IP addressing have left more than one administrator scratching his head. There really is no easier way to learn about IP addressing than to start from the beginning.

In an IPv4 network, the IP address consists of four numbers called octets (8 bits), each separated by dots. If you do the math, this means that each IP address is 32 bits in length (4 bits × 8 bits). An example of an IP address is 192.168.2.1.

Each of the octets can range from 0–255, as shown in the above example. An IP address can also be displayed in binary values. In this case, each bit in an octet can either be a 1 or a 0. When calculating the binary value of an IP address, the leftmost bit starts with a value of 128 and counts down from there according to the values of a binary-to-decimal conversion: 128, then 64, 32, 16, 8, 4, 2, and 1 for the far right bit. Figure 13-1 demonstrates the conversion of 192 to decimal format.

Binary calculations for IP addresses are an important consideration and as such have a way of appearing in one form or another on exams. With that in mind, Table 13-2 provides some examples of binary conversions.

## Subnet Mask

Unlike other protocols, an IPv4 address uses the single address to identify both the node on the network and the network segment. Every IP address is composed of two parts: the network ID and the host ID. You need to know which portion of the address represents the node address and which of the octets represent the network segment. The leftmost portion of the address identifies the network ID, and the remaining numbers identify the host ID. This sounds simple, but the complexity comes when you have to draw the line between left and right numbers in the IP address. To determine which numbers in an IP address represent the network ID and the host ID, you use the subnet mask. The subnet mask is a 32-bit address expressed in the same way as that of the IP address.

IP addresses are assigned to specific address classes with each class having an associated default subnet mask. There are three main classes of IP addresses. Table 13-3 displays the default IP address classes.

 **NOTE** Notice in Table 13-3, number 127 is not listed. The first octet of an IP address cannot be 127; this is saved for local loopback procedures.

| 128 | 64 | 32 | 16 | 8 | 4 | 2 | 1 | =255 |
|-----|-----|-----|-----|-----|-----|-----|-----|------|
| 1 | 1 | 0 | 0 | 0 | 0 | 0 | 0 | =192 |

**Figure 13-1** Binary-to-decimal conversion for an octet of 192

| Binary Value | Decimal Calculation | Numeric Value |
|---|---|---|
| 00000000 | n/a | 0 |
| 00000001 | 1 | 1 |
| 00000011 | 2+1 | 3 |
| 00000111 | 4+2+1 | 7 |
| 00001111 | 8+4+2+1 | 15 |
| 00011111 | 16+8+4+2+1 | 31 |
| 00111111 | 32+16+8+4+2+1 | 63 |
| 01111111 | 64+32+16+8+4+2+1 | 127 |
| 11000011 | 128+64+2+1 | 195 |
| 11111111 | 128+64+32+16+8+4+2+1 | 255 |

**Table 13-2**   Converting Numeric Values to Decimal Values

## IP Addressing Rules

There are a few rules you should be aware of when assigning IP addresses to computers:

- A network ID cannot be set to 127. This address is reserved for loopback and diagnostic purposes.

- The network ID and host IDs cannot be all 1's. If all bits are set to 1, the address is interpreted as a broadcast address and will not be routed under normal circumstances. A Class B address of 151.255.0.0 is a perfectly good network ID. The network ID is 16 bits long, and only the last eight in the network number are all 1s.

- The network ID and host IDs cannot be all 0s. Of all bits are set to 0, that is interpreted as the same as the network number. In the example above, the network number is 151.255.0.0. The first host on that network, then, is 151.255.0.1.

- The host ID must be unique to the local network ID. There cannot be two 0.1 hosts on the 151.255 network.

- A unique network ID is needed for each network connected to a wide area network, which is usually the public Internet. (This network ID is typically provided by your ISP.) On the Internet, for example, there is only one 151.255 network.

| Address Class | IP Range | Default Subnet Mask |
|---|---|---|
| Class A | 1.0.0.0 to 126.0.0.0 | 255.0.0.0 |
| Class B | 128.0.0.0 to 191.255.0.0 | 255.255.0.0 |
| Class C | 192.0.0.0 to 223.255.255.0 | 255.255.255.0 |

**Table 13-3**   Default Subnet Masks Matched to IP Address Classes

- Every TCP/IP host requires a subnet mask. The IP address is useless without one because of the mask's role of separating out the 32 bits of the IP address into distinct network bits and host bits.

**Determining the Network ID and Host ID**   The calculations used to determine the host ID and network ID can look somewhat ominous, but once you get the process, it is straightforward. To determine the portions of an IP address, you use something called a bitwise logical AND operation. Essentially what this involves is comparing two IP addresses on the binary level. The result of this comparison will reveal which portion of an IP address is the network and which is the host ID. To demonstrate, let's take the IP address of 192.168.20.5, which converted to binary is

    1100000.1010100.00010100.00000101

    (128+64.128+32+8.16+4.4+1)

With the binary for the IP address calculated, look at the default subnet mask for the IP address. Using Table 13-3, you can see that in this case, the 192.168.20.5 address falls into the Class C range of subnet masks. This gives you the default subnet mask of 255.255.255.0. The next step is to convert this subnet mask into binary as follows:

    11111111.11111111.11111111.00000000

The next step is to compare the two binary values to determine the host and network ID. There are two rules to remember when performing the bitwise logical AND operation:

- If both numbers being compared are 1s, the result of the calculation is a 1.
- If any of the numbers in the calculation are a 0, the result is 0.

Okay, let's perform the operation:

    11000000.10101000.00010100.00000101 =192.168.20.5

    11111111.11111111.11111111.00000000 = 255.255.255.0

    11000000.10101000.00010100.00000000 = 192.168.20

Using the calculation, you have determined that the network ID of the IP address is the final three octets, 192.168.20. This leaves the final 8-bit octet for the host IDs.

**EXAM TIP**   Determining host and network portions of an IP address is an important consideration for determining how big a network can grow. Be sure you are comfortable with identifying host and network IDs for the exam.

## Determining IP Class Range for a Network

If you were ever to set out to design a network, you would need to choose one of the classes of IP address to use with the network. It is far from an arbitrary decision, and determining the correct IP address range to use requires considerable consideration.

Each of the IP classes yields a different amount of total network and host IDs. To determine which IP class will be needed, you will need to know how many of each are available and if this is sufficient for the network. Table 13-4 shows the available network and host IDs for the various IP classes.

Table 13-4 identifies the default numbers for host and network IDs. The next step is to determine the number of hosts and network IDs available for a specific IP range.

**Calculating Network IDs**    There are several steps involved in identifying the number of network IDs assigned to a particular IP range. The following provides the procedures for calculating network IDs:

1. The first step is to convert the lowest IP address in the range to binary and then do the same to the highest IP address in the range. In this example, let's assume the lowest ID is 192.168.0.0 and the highest address is 192.168.15.0. In binary, these numbers are as follows:

   192.168.0.0: 11000000.10101000.00000000.00000000

   192.168.15.0: 11000000.10101000.00001111.00000000

2. In this calculation you are only concerned with the portion of the IP address that falls within the subnet mask. Recall that for the 192 range, the subnet mask is 255.255.255.0. This means you only use the three leftmost octets. Using the binary numbers, you must identify the highest bit position used in the network ID portion of the IP addresses, in this case, the fourth bit position of the third octet. Therefore, the number of bits available for the networks is 4.

3. In the final step, you need to identify the difference between the network IDs of the two IP addresses. The first IP address has a binary value of 0, and the second has a binary value of 15 (8+4+2+1). When calculating network IDs, you always increment the value by 1. Therefore in this case, you have 16 network IDs available.

| IP Address Class | IP Range | Number of Default Networks | Default Hosts |
|---|---|---|---|
| Class A | 1.0.0.0 to 126.0.0.0 | 126 | 16,777,214 |
| Class B | 128.0.0.0 to 191.255.0.0 | 16,384 | 65,534 |
| Class C | 192.0.0.0 to 223.255.255.0 | 2,097,152 | 254 |

**Table 13-4**    Identifying Default Host and Network IDs for IP Classes

**Calculating Host IDs**  Host IDs represent the total number of network devices you can add to the network. The total is restricted by the number of unique IP addresses you have to assign to devices on the network.

Using the above example, you know that the first three octets were reserved for the network ID, which leaves the last 8-bit octet for the host IDs. This means there are 256 total IDs available. However, you cannot use all 1s or all 0s, which means you have 256 minus 2 available hosts. Class C networks therefore have 254 available hosts.

As you can imagine, 254 may not be enough, and the large number of hosts for the other IP classes may be too many. This is where subnetting comes into play.

---

**EXAM TIP**  When configuring the available hosts, all 1s and all 0s cannot be used. Therefore, in the final calculation, the total number of hosts is calculated minus 2.

## Subnetting Default IP Address Classes

The default network and host IDs were shown in Table 13-4, but what happens when more hosts or networks are needed than the default allows? This is when you need to configure IP subnets.

For example, suppose you have a Class B address of 132.132.0.0. Using the default subnet mask would assign the first two octets as the network ID and the rest of the address to be used as host addresses. This leaves a large number of host addresses. With subnetting, you can take some of these host addresses and use them as network addresses. All you need to do is change the subnet mask. For example, if you change the Class B default of 255.255.0.0 to 255.255.255.0, it would give you an extra octet and an additional 254 network addresses (132.132.1.0 to 132.132.1.254). In this scenario, you restrict your host IP addresses to 254, which may or may not be enough for the network. Table 13-5 provides some subnetting examples for a Class B network.

| Subnet Mask | Total Network IDs | Total Host IDs |
|---|---|---|
| 255.255.0.0 | 1 | 65,534 |
| 255.255.128.0 | 2 | 32,766 |
| 255.255.192.0 | 4 | 16,382 |
| 255.255.224.0 | 8 | 8,190 |
| 255.255.240.0 | 16 | 4,094 |
| 255.255.248.0 | 32 | 2,046 |
| 255.255.252.0 | 64 | 1,022 |
| 255.255.254.0 | 128 | 510 |
| 255.255.255.0 | 256 | 254 |

**Table 13-5**  Subnetting Examples for a Class B Network

The Class B address range provides a large number of IP addresses to work with, too many for most organizations. Class C networks, on the other hand, are well suited to be subnetted for smaller companies. When working with Class C IP addresses, the same subnetting principles apply. Table 13-6 provides a summary of subnetting a Class C network.

## Private IP Address Ranges

While IPv4 addresses are scalable, the limits of that scalability are being tested. After years of loyal service, IPv4 addresses are running out. In the future, IPv6 is destined to overtake version 4 and bring with it enough IP addresses to last a lifetime. Until it is here and widely adopted, you need a method to stretch the IP addresses you currently have available.

The solution has come in the form of classes of nonroutable IP addresses. These nonroutable addresses are designed to be used within an organization, and because they are nonroutable, they can be used over and over and be unique to that organization. The three ranges of nonroutable IP addresses include

- 10.0.0.0 to 10.255.255.255

- 172.16.0.0 to 172.31.255.255

- 192.168.0.0 to 192.168.255.255

Many organizations will use two sets of IP addresses: the private ones used on the internal network, and external IP addresses obtained from an ISP that will allow traffic out to the Internet.

 **EXAM TIP**  Look for TCP/IP questions on the exam expressed in the CIDR method.

| Subnet Mask | Total Network IDs | Total Host IDs |
|---|---|---|
| 255.255.255.0 | 1 | 254 |
| 255.255.128.0 | 2 | 126 |
| 255.255.192.0 | 4 | 62 |
| 255.255.224.0 | 8 | 30 |
| 255.255.240.0 | 16 | 14 |
| 255.255.255.252 | 32 | 6 |
| 255.255.255.254 | 64 | 2 |

**Table 13-6**  Subnetting a Class C Network

## Classless Inter-Domain Routing (CIDR) Notation

There is another way of expressing the IP address without having to spell out the subnet mask in octets of 255s and 0s. Instead, you can count out the number of 1s in the subnet mask and then represent the IP address and subnet mask with a slash followed by the number of 1 bits in the subnet mask, like this:

192.168.2.200/16

This notation is called classless inter-domain routing (CIDR, pronounced "cedar") notation. The notation here specifies the same IP address as used in the previous example. The IP address part is very straightforward. The /16 tells you that this IP address has a subnet mask with the first 16 bits set to 1. And 16 1s gives you a subnet mask of: 255.255.0.0, same as before.

CIDR notation is used to simplify entries on routing tables and is the notation used by a majority of backbone Internet routers. It is also used to cut down on the number of wasted IP addresses in the Class B address space. You should know how to recognize the CIDR notation when you see it and to convert the CIDR subnet mask notation into an octeted decimal equivalent.

# Troubleshooting TCP/IP Addressing

IP addressing can get somewhat confusing, and as a result there may be times to troubleshoot the addressing scheme used for a network. First, let's review the basic requirements necessary for a system to function on a network.

To gain network access, a client system needs only two key pieces of information: a unique IP address and the corresponding subnet mask. While a system can gain access to the network with just an IP and subnet mask, there are other key information pieces needed for further functionality. These configuration settings include the default gateway, DNS server, and WINS server. A brief description of each of these is provided here:

- **IP address**   Each client system must have a unique IP address to log onto a network.

- **Subnet mask**   As mentioned earlier, the subnet mask identifies which portion of the IP address represents the network and which identifies the node. All systems require a subnet mask.

- **Default gateway**   The default gateway allows the client system to communicate with systems on a remote network without the need to manually add routes to the client system.

- **DNS server**  The DNS server resolves fully qualified domain names (FQDN) to IP addresses. DNS configuration is covered later in this chapter.

- **WINS**  WINS converts NetBIOS names to IP addresses. WINS is also covered in detail later in this chapter.

The way in which this data is entered into a system depends on the operating system used. Figure 13-2 shows the TCP/IP configuration screen from a Windows Server 2003 system.

## Resolving Client Configuration Issues

TCP/IP information is entered into a computer system either manually or automatically using the Dynamic Host Configuration Protocol (DHCP). In smaller networks, statically assigned IP addresses are quite common. In this configuration, the administrator must manually enter all of the TCP/IP settings into each computer on the network. This can lead to all sorts of problems as the network grows. For instance, one common problem when IP information is manually entered is duplicate IP addresses used on two different machines. When this occurs, the second machine that boots up will display an error message notifying the administrator that it cannot log onto the network because there is a duplicate IP address.

Most of the client configuration issues can be traced to the wrong settings being entered. When faced with a client connectivity problem, consider the following:

- **Unique IP address**  Verify that the IP address is in the correct class of IP addresses used for the rest of the network. When manually entering addresses, be sure that the number is unique from others on the network.

**Figure 13-2**
The TCP/IP
configuration
screen is used
to configure the
IP, DNS, default
gateway, and
subnet mask.

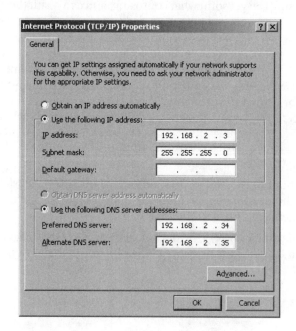

- **Subnet mask** The subnet mask has to match the subnet mask being used on the network. Verify that the correct subnet mask is being used.

- **DNS configuration** If the system is unable to resolve domain names to IP addresses, the wrong DNS information may be entered.

- **Default gateway** One common error is that client systems are able to log on to the local network, but are unable to communicate with systems on a remote network. The first thing to verify is that the correct default gateway information is entered.

To review the current TCP/IP settings on a client system, the ipconfig /all command can be issued from the command prompt. The output from the command is shown in Figure 13-3.

## Resolving DHCP IP Assignment Errors

When a DHCP server is configured correctly, it rarely causes problems, but like any other technology, sometimes things don't work as planned. In this section, we review a few of the errors that may occur with a network's DHCP server.

## Managing DHCP Scopes

A DHCP scope is a grouping of IP addresses that can be assigned to client computers on a network. A defined scope has the following elements:

- A client system will be assigned an address from a range of private IP addresses.

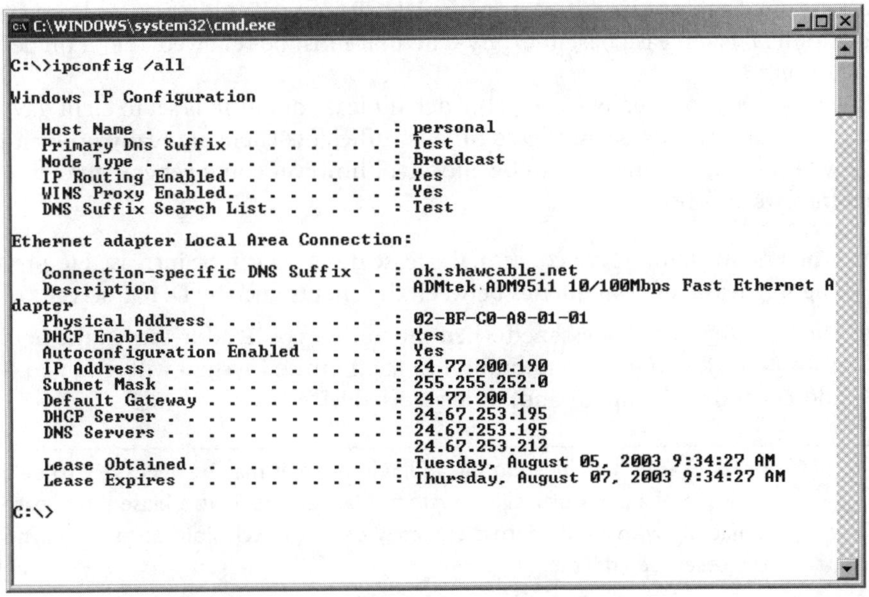

```
C:\WINDOWS\system32\cmd.exe

C:\>ipconfig /all

Windows IP Configuration

        Host Name . . . . . . . . . . . . : personal
        Primary Dns Suffix  . . . . . . . : Test
        Node Type . . . . . . . . . . . . : Broadcast
        IP Routing Enabled. . . . . . . . : Yes
        WINS Proxy Enabled. . . . . . . . : Yes
        DNS Suffix Search List. . . . . . : Test

Ethernet adapter Local Area Connection:

        Connection-specific DNS Suffix  . : ok.shawcable.net
        Description . . . . . . . . . . . : ADMtek ADM9511 10/100Mbps Fast Ethernet A
dapter
        Physical Address. . . . . . . . . : 02-BF-C0-A8-01-01
        DHCP Enabled. . . . . . . . . . . : Yes
        Autoconfiguration Enabled . . . . : Yes
        IP Address. . . . . . . . . . . . : 24.77.200.190
        Subnet Mask . . . . . . . . . . . : 255.255.252.0
        Default Gateway . . . . . . . . . : 24.77.200.1
        DHCP Server . . . . . . . . . . . : 24.67.253.195
        DNS Servers . . . . . . . . . . . : 24.67.253.195
                                            24.67.253.212
        Lease Obtained. . . . . . . . . . : Tuesday, August 05, 2003 9:34:27 AM
        Lease Expires . . . . . . . . . . : Thursday, August 07, 2003 9:34:27 AM

C:\>
```

**Figure 13-3** The ipconfig command is used to review the TCP/IP settings on a Windows Server 2003 system.

- A scope can also consist of addresses that are excluded from the range that can be assigned to clients. These addresses are able to be reserved and are assigned to devices such as servers or network printers.

- The DHCP server can automatically assign the subnet mask, which determines the subnet for a given IP address.

- Each address assigned to clients is given a certain lease period. The lease period determines how long a client system will use an IP address before it needs to be renewed with the DHCP server. Lease time is determined by the administrator and can be set from hours to days.

- Any DHCP scope may include configuration options for DHCP clients, such as DNS server, router IP address, and WINS server address.

- Within a DHCP scope, IP address reservations can be configured and used to ensure that a DHCP client always receives the same IP address.

**Troubleshooting Scopes**    DHCP scopes can sometimes cause problems. When troubleshooting a scope, ensure that

- There are enough IP addresses within a scope to assign to client systems.

- The lease time for IP addresses is correctly set.

- The scope is active, meaning it can assign IP addresses.

- The exclusion range for IP addresses is correctly set.

## Managing Leases

Unless assigned a reserved address from the DHCP scope, IP addresses are leased to client computers. Each lease has an expiry date that must be renewed after a predefined period of time.

When a scope is originally created, the default lease duration is set to eight days. For most organizations, this default lease time is sufficient. There are really no firm rules that govern how lease times are to be allocated, however some general guidelines for lease times are as follows:

- When network traffic is a concern, the lease duration can be increased to prevent ongoing lease renewal queries between the clients and the DHCP server.

- The lease time can be lessened when the number of IP addresses in the pool is limited. This limits the amount of time an unused system will retain an IP address and free it up for another network device.

 **NOTE**   When troubleshooting a DHCP lease, it may be necessary to delete the lease of a particular client system. Manually remove a lease if the lease is conflicting with an IP address that may be in an exclusion range or assigned to a reserved address.

## Spotting a DHCP Error

When a DHCP client is unable to locate a DHCP server, the client picks out a random IP address from the Automatic Private IP Addressing (APIPA) address range of 169.254.*x.y*, with a subnet mask of 255.255.0.0. The 169.254.*x.y* IP range is private because that network number is not in use on the Internet and because routers on the Internet are configured not to forward packets with this address. If you operate a DHCP server and clients cannot get the IP address from the server, the client system will register with a 169 address.

The significance of APIPA is that DHCP client computers that cannot find a DHCP server can still be assigned an IP address and communicate with other computers on the same subnet that also cannot find a DHCP server. It allows communication when the DHCP server is down or just plain not there. Note that APIPA does not assign a default gateway, and therefore it cannot communicate with any computers that live on the other side of a router.

At times you might prefer this behavior, as it can be an effective method for easily administering TCP/IP in a small network. Keep in mind, however, that the addresses assigned will not be able to communicate with Internet hosts or with a host that exists on any other network, because APIPA assigns an IP address and subnet mask but not a default gateway.

---

 **EXAM TIP** When a client system cannot obtain an IP address, it will be assigned a private address In the 169.254 range.

# Developing IP Routing Strategy

The days of a network being held in the confines of a single location are long gone. Today's networks branch out between interconnected offices all over the world. What we have today is any number of separate physical network segments connected together using routers. Routers are devices that route data between networks. Essentially, when a router receives data, it must determine the destination for the data and send it there. To accomplish this, the network router uses two key pieces of information, the default gateway address and the routing tables, as follows:

- **Default gateway**  A default gateway is the IP address of the router, which is the pathway to any and all remote networks. To get a packet of information from one network to another, the packet is sent to the default gateway, which helps forward the packet to its destination network. In fact, computers that live on the other side of routers are said to be on remote networks. Without default gateways, Internet communication is not possible, because your computer doesn't have a way to send a packet destined for any other network. On the workstation, it is common for the default gateway option to be configured automatically through DHCP configuration

PART III

- **Routing tables** There is nothing magical about routing tables, they are simply a list of the network routes and destinations. This list includes the destination IP addresses and subnet masks needed to find the destination host. The route print command can be used to view the routing table on a client system. Figure 13-4 shows the routing table from a client system.

## Developing an IP Routing Solution

When designing the network, it is important to give careful consideration to the routing strategy you plan to use. Some of the decisions you will need to make include the physical placement of the routers, whether to use dynamic or static routing, and the IP configuration of the router.

As far as router placement is concerned, there are some common placement practices, including

- **Between network segments** One of the standard placement strategies for routers is to place them between network segments to localize network traffic and keep it inside the private network.

- **Between a private network and the Internet** A router is often placed between a private network segment and the Internet. This allows an organization to securely change data over a public network using technologies such as VPN.

- **Between dissimilar network architecture** Routers allow one type of network such as Ethernet and Token Ring to communicate with each other.

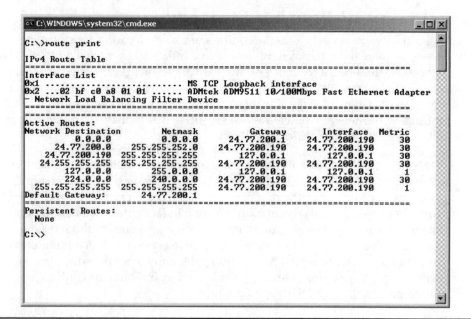

**Figure 13-4** The route print command shows the routing table on a client system.

## Static and Dynamic Routing

The way in which routers communicate is an important factor to consider when planning a routed network. Routers maintain a routing table, which allows them to determine the destination for a data packet. Some routers are configured to share routing table information to keep up to date with network routes. This type of route sharing is known as dynamic routing. Dynamic routing requires the use of routing protocols to perform the router-to-router communication. Two of the more common dynamic routing protocols are the Routing Information Protocol (RIP) and Open Shortest Path First (OSPF).

**NOTE**   Discussions of RIP and OSPF are covered in Chapter 14.

If dynamic routing protocols are not being used, routing tables must be updated statically to manually to allow routers to know where to forward data packets. As you can imagine, having to manually update routing tables can be a time-consuming task, and if the information is entered incorrectly, the router may not find the destination for a packet.

There are some situations where statically updated routing information may be used, including

- On smaller networks where changes to routing information is infrequent
- To reduce the network overhead caused by using routing protocols such as RIP and OSPF
- When a default router for a demand-dial interface is required

**NOTE**   A detailed discussion of static and dynamic protocols is covered in Chapter 14.

# Domain Name System

The Domain Name System (DNS) is the standard name resolution strategy used on Windows Server 2003 systems. The function of DNS is to resolve host names such as www .earlybird.com to an IP address. Resolved host names are easier for people to remember than IP addresses.

DNS operates in what is known as the DNS namespace. The DNS namespace is an organized, hierarchical division of DNS names. At the top level of the DNS hierarchy is an unnamed DNS node known as the root. All other nodes in the DNS hierarchy are known as labels. Together they form the DNS tree.

Perhaps the best example of a DNS tree can be seen on the Internet. At the top level are domains such as .com, .org, or .edu as well as domains for countries such as .ca (Canada)

| Table 13-7 | Domain Name | Description |
|---|---|---|
| Top-Level DNS Domain Names | .com | Commercial organizations |
| | .gov | Government organizations |
| | .net | Network providers |
| | .org | Not-for-profit organizations |
| | .edu | Educational organizations |
| | .mil | Military |
| | .ca (for example) | Country-specific domains |

or .de (Germany). Table 13-7 shows some of the more common top-level domain names and their intended purpose.

Below these top-level domains are the subdomains associated with organizations, such as Microsoft.com. Figure 13-5 shows a sample of the DNS namespace of the Internet.

## Planning a Namespace Design

When it comes to designing the DNS namespace for a business, there are a few things to keep in mind. First, it is unlikely that you will be able to get a top-level domain name.

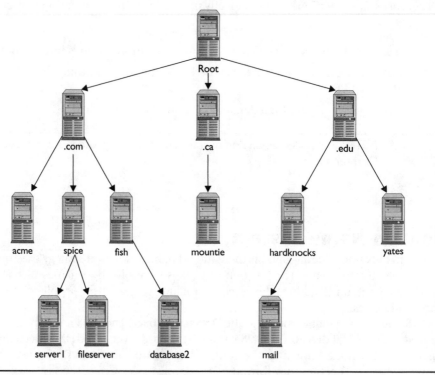

**Figure 13-5**   The DNS namespace for the Internet

## Understanding the DNS Name

A DNS name can at first seem quite cryptic, but there is a method to the madness. Consider the DNS name library.div1.acme.com.

When reviewing a DNS name, start from the leftmost part, which identifies the machine name. In this case, the machine name is library. Moving to the right, you see div1, which is actually a child domain to acme.com. In this case, whoever created the div1.acme.com domain would have needed permission from acme.com to create the domain.

Continuing to the right, you see acme.com, which is effectively a child domain of the top-level domain .com. In this case, whoever wanted to create the domain acme.com had to contact the owners of the .com domain to get permission to create the subdomain acme.com.

From reading the DNS name, we can see the hierarchical structure of the DNS namespace.

Top-level domain names are tightly controlled; the lower domain names are the ones you need to be concerned with. Top-level domains include those mentioned in Table 13-7.

Most of the Windows Server 2003 networks you'll use will certainly be using DNS. This means that someone will need to create the DNS namespace that will be used. There are several things to consider when creating a namespace for an organization. It is important to take the time to create the right one, as changing a namespace can be a cumbersome and costly endeavor.

The first thing to do is choose the top-level domain name that will be used for hosting the organization's name on the Internet, such as .com. The next step is to choose the second-level domain name, which will give you a two-tired domain name, such as acme.com. This is often referred to as the parent domain name or simple as the domain name used on the Internet.

The next step in the namespace design is combining the parent domain name with organizational names used internally to form subdomain names. For example, acme.com may have an accounting division, accounts.acme.com, and a test division, test.acme.com. To take it one step further, the test division has both a support and development team. Their namespace may be support.test.acme.com and dev.test.acme.com.

Many organizations map out the namespace to get a look at how it will work within the organization. The namespace mapping will create a namespace tree similar to the one shown previously in Figure 13-5.

## Planning DNS Zones and Zone Transfer

You could read a thousand definitions for a DNS zone and still be as confused as when you started. The trick for understanding DNS zones is to keep it simple. Essentially, the DNS namespace can encompass many computers and as many individual domains. A DNS zone gives you the ability to carve up the namespace into manageable chunks—or in more technical terms, DNS zones are delegations of authority for a downstream namespace. Figure 13-6 shows how the DNS namespace from Figure 13-5 may be segmented into zones.

Each zone contains DNS information, known as resource records, for a section of the DNS namespace domain. For each DNS domain name included in a zone, the zone becomes the authoritative source for information about that domain and responsible for maintaining information for that portion of the DNS namespace.

Many zones start out containing only a part of a subdomain, but as the network grows they may encompass an entire subdomain and even multiple subdomains. If other domains are added underneath a current zone, that domain can either have its own zone or be added to the previously created zone.

## Zone Transfers

In most cases, a DNS zone will have more than a single DNS server for both load balancing and server redundancy reasons. As you might expect, multiple servers means that both of these databases must have a way to be consistent. The information must be

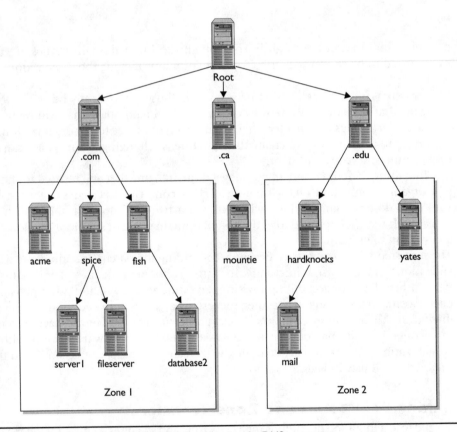

**Figure 13-6**    Zones provide a method of partitioning the DNS namespace.

synchronized between DNS servers in a process known as zone transfers or replication. There are two types of zones used in the transfer process, primary and secondary.

 **NOTE** Just to clear up a little potential confusion, the physical databases are also called zones.

The primary zone is king, a read/write database, and there can only be a single primary zone for any portion of a DNS namespace. Secondary zones allow for updated databases by the primary zone. Secondary servers can be accessed by clients in the same way a primary system can. Their job is to provide database redundancy and DNS load balancing. DNS servers that become the source for the zone transfers are known as the master servers. Master servers can take the role of either a primary or secondary system. As mentioned, you can only have one primary, but you can have many masters. The number of masters is generally determined by load balancing requirements and/or line speeds between remote sites, assuming there is a secondary in the remote sites. The primary will always be a master to at least one secondary.

 **NOTE** The master is defined as the source of zone database files for the purpose of replication. In a DNS environment, you are not limited to one master.

When a new DNS server is added to the network, it will need to replicate its database with the primary zone to obtain an up-to-date copy of the zone information. If it does not, clients cannot get accurate DNS information from the master or secondary server.

Just as there are two types of zones for DNS servers, there are also two types of zone transfers, full transfers and incremental.

A full zone transfer, known as an AXFR, replicates the entire zone database. The incremental, or IXFR, zone transfer updates only the information that has changed in the primary database. This is the method of choice to reduce the network traffic a full zone transfer can create. AXFR transfers are often performed when a new DNS server is added to a zone or when there are inconsistencies in a database and a complete update of the zone database is required.

 **EXAM TIP** Zone transfers use both the AXFR and IXFR transfer methods. IXFR is preferred as less data is passed between servers.

## Securing DNS

For something as important as DNS, there is no doubt that DNS security is a concern. There are many strategies you can use to secure DNS servers, many of which involve verifying that the DNS server is correctly installed. Before looking at some of the ways to protect the DNS service, let's take a quick look at the types of attacks that are sometimes used against DNS systems.

- **Denial of service (DoS)**   Denial-of-service attacks attempt to overflow the DNS server with recursive queries. The intended result is to tax the resources of the server, leaving it unable to handle name resolution requests.

- **Footprinting**   In this type of attack, the attacker is attempting to obtain DNS zone data, which may provide the domain names, computer names, and even IP addresses of network systems.

- **Address spoofing**   IP address spoofing is designed to allow the attacker to reroute or access and change data. Essentially, IP spoofing involves convincing a sending computer that the spoofing system is the intended recipient when it isn't. Network devices often use the IP address to determine the sender and receiver for a data transmission. In a spoofing scenario, the hacker, assumes the identity of an IP node.

- **Redirection**   In a redirection attack, the attacker attempts to redirect DNS queries to servers operated by the attacker.

Having reviewed some of the potential attack areas, we can now examine some of the security measures that can be used to protect the DNS service.

## Securing the DNS Namespace

Often overlooked is the ability to secure the DNS namespace. As mentioned above, the DNS namespace is the hierarchical organizational structure of DNS. When implementing a DNS namespace, consider the following namespace security strategies:

- If public network names will not need to be resolved for the private network, do not allow DNS communication with that network. Basically, this means that a private DNS namespace will be used solely within the private network. Internet name resolution will not be possible.

- Split the DNS namespace. In this configuration, the namespace is split between either side of the firewall. Internal DNS servers function within the firewall and external servers function outside of the firewall. This means that the company's parent domain—for example, orion.com—is outside of the firewall, while the subdomains, support.orion.com, are kept within the firewall.

- Split the DNS servers. In this configuration, there are separate DNS servers for the internal and for the external networks. The internal DNS server will handle queries made by internal hosts and will forward queries for external names to the external DNS server. Such a design protects the privacy of the internal DNS names.

## Securing the DNS Service

Many of the default settings used for Server 2003 were made with at least some level of security in mind. Some of the settings for securing the DNS service are likely already configured securely by default. However, if you are called in to secure a DNS system, these settings will need to be checked:

- **Access permissions** Verify who has access to change or modify the DNS service. By default, the following groups have varying levels of access to the DNS service: Administrators, Authenticated Users, Creator /Owner, DNSAdmins, Domain Admins, Enterprise Admins, Enterprise Domain Controllers, and System groups. As part of security procedures, it will be necessary to review which accounts are members of these groups and what level of access to DNS they should have.

- **Network interfaces** In its default configuration, if a Windows Server 2003 DNS server is using multiple network cards, it is configured to listen for DNS queries using all of its IP addresses. To secure this, it may be necessary to isolate only the IP addresses the DNS server listens to from DNS clients.

- **Cache pollution** Windows Server 2003 has a Secure Cache Against Pollution option, which is on by default. Cache pollution is caused when DNS query responses contain non-authoritative or malicious data.

## Securing DNS Zones

When securing DNS zones, there are two primary sources to be aware of: dynamic zone updates and access permissions.

Dynamic updates enable DNS client computers to register and dynamically update their resource records with a DNS server whenever changes occur. This may in fact cause some security issues. By default, the Windows Server 2003 system is not configured to allow dynamic updates, which is the greatest level of update security. On the other hand, it prevents the use of a beneficial DNS feature. To securely use the dynamic update feature, it is recommended to store DNS zones in Active Directory and use the secure dynamic update feature. This feature restricts DNS zone updates to only those servers that are authenticated and joined to the Active Directory domain where the DNS sever is located.

The second strategy for securing DNS zones is to be aware of access permissions. As mentioned in the previous section, several groups are allowed DNS configuration access by default. Ensure that only those accounts that need to have access to DNS configurations are in fact allowed to do so.

## Securing DNS Records

The last area of DNS we should discuss is securing the DNS records. DNS records are stored on the DNS system, and security measures involve controlling access to the server and these records. Assigning appropriate users and groups with the correct levels of permissions is the key to DNS record security.

## DNS Forwarding

DNS forwarding is used to forward DNS queries for external DNS name resolution to DNS servers outside of the local network. To accomplish this, one of the DNS servers on the internal network is designated as the DNS forwarder. Once the DNS forwarder is established, other DNS servers on the network will forward name resolution queries that they are unable to resolve locally to the DNS forwarder.

---

**NOTE**   It is possible to configure all DNS servers on the network to send queries outside of the network. This could potentially allow sensitive DNS information to be exposed to the Internet.

---

When configuring a DNS forwarder, some administrators like to create a large cache of external DNS information. This strategy reduces the number of queries the forwarder needs to send to the Internet, as DNS queries can be resolved using the cached data information. This will reduce DNS query response time and also decrease Internet traffic.

Another type of DNS forwarder is known as a conditional forwarder. Conditional forwarders are DNS servers designed to forward queries based on domain names. In this configuration, the DNS server will not forward all requests it cannot resolve locally. Instead, Windows Server 2003 DNS servers can be set to only forward queries according to the domain names contained within the query. This is known as name-based forwarding.

In application, here is how name-based queries work. When a client queries the DNS server, the DNS forwarder checks to see if it can be resolved using the information in the cache of the local zone database. If it cannot be resolved locally, the DNS server

### Answering the Query

In the DNS query process, there are many different ways that a client query can be resolved. In fact, the DNS query may be resolved on the local system before it even reaches the DNS server. This can happen by the local system using cached information from a previous query.

Next, a client query can be resolved for the DNS server's cache. Name resolution information received from the local cache or from the DNS server's cache provides a quicker means of name resolution as the DNS forwarder does not need to query external DNS servers to obtain the information. This also reduces the amount of network traffic required to resolve names externally.

If information is not in cache, external name resolution is performed in a process known as recursion. Recursion refers to the process whereby a DNS server queries other DNS servers on behalf of the requesting client to fully resolve the name and send an answer back to the client.

will forward to the domain name specified in the client query. From there, the client query is sent to the IP address of the server associated with the domain name. Figure 13-7 shows an example of name-based DNS forwarding.

## DNS Hosts File

In the early days of host name resolution, a text file called a Hosts file was used to perform host name resolution. The Hosts file contains a mapping for the host names to IP addresses. Using the Hosts file, clients can resolve host names without needing to use a DNS server. The Hosts file is a standard text file that can be modified in Notepad or any other word processor.

The format of the file is straightforward: IP address <TAB> Hostname. An example of an Hosts file entry is shown here:

```
17.54.94.97 app.tester.com
```

Entries in the Hosts file are checked sequentially. DNS lookup time can be increased by placing the most often used host name entries near the top of the Hosts file.

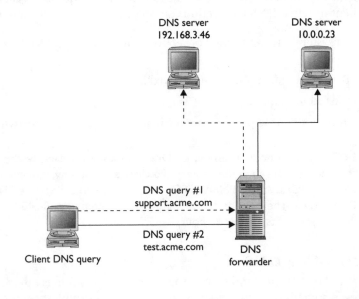

**Figure 13-7**   With name-based forwarding, each of the queries for the domain names is forwarded to a DNS server associated with the domain name.

**NOTE** Be aware, entries in the Hosts file are case sensitive. It is important to get those host names in the Hosts file exactly right. Further, the Hosts file is checked before DNS and could lead to errors if it has invalid entries, even if the DNS server has the correct data.

## Dynamic DNS

One of the drawbacks of DNS has been that it wasn't dynamic. It did not automatically collect information about the names and addresses of computers on the network. WINS, for all of its drawbacks, had one up on DNS in this respect. WINS registration was done automatically when a machine booted up or when a DHCP lease was renewed. WINS had the ability to automatically keep a current database of the machines on the network. DNS required more manual intervention.

Windows Server 2003 supports a feature known as dynamic DNS (DDNS), which reduces the effort required on the administrator's part by allowing clients to register with a DNS server automatically.

DDNS registrations are client initiated, which means that the DNS server does not request that clients on the network register—rather, the client requests registration from the server. Client-initiated DNS registration can occur in a number of ways, including

- The client system has just booted or rebooted and the request to the DNS server is initiated.
- A DHCP-assigned address has just renewed a lease.
- The command ipconfig \registerdns is issued.
- Twenty-four hours have passed since a client system has registered with DDNS.

**NOTE** The 24-hour threshold for DNS renewal is a default setting that can be changed in the registry. To change the setting, navigate to HKEY_LOCAL_MACHINE\SYSTEM\CurrentControlSet\Services\Tcpip\ Parameters:. The current default setting is represented as 86,400 seconds, which represents exactly 24 hours.

## Troubleshooting DNS

DNS is a tried and true service, and when properly configured, things rarely seem to go wrong. However, sometimes things do go wrong and when troubleshooting DNS, you need to do so from both the server level and the client level.

### Troubleshooting DNS Clients

When a client system is unable to use name resolution services, there are three key areas where you can focus your troubleshooting efforts: the physical connection to the network, the local system's network settings, and database consistency.

Common causes of not being able to access DNS services can be directly traced to a client's physical network connectivity. Such things as a hardware failure or cabling issue could cause this. To test if this is the case, you need to verify that the client system is connected to the local network. This can be done by browsing the network or trying to ping the DNS server. Once you know that the client system is physically connected to the network, you can move to the next troubleshooting area.

The next thing to check is that the DNS client computer has a valid IP configuration for the network. This includes the subnet mask, IP address, and the IP address of the DNS server. The ipconfig /all command can be used to verify these settings on a Server 2003 system. It may be a good idea to ping the DNS server to ensure that the client system can see it on the network. If confirmed, it begins to look like the DNS problem may lie with the server itself.

One last problem we should mention on the client end is when client computers receive incorrect or stale information from a DNS server. There are a few things that can cause this problem, but most likely it is related to the DNS database in some way. For instance, if the client computer is getting its zone information from a secondary server, that server may not have up-to-date information. The trick for testing this is to manually update the zone information to the secondary servers.

**NOTE** When troubleshooting DNS clients, you can also start by flushing the local client cache (ipconfig /flushdns) just in case you have an invalid mapping in there. Also you can check the contents of the cache (ipconfig /displaydns) to see if you need to flush it.

## Troubleshooting DNS Servers

If more than a single DNS client is having problems with name resolution, the problem likely lies with the DNS server/servers. If a single DNS server is not responding to client requests, the problem may be found with the physical network connectivity. The first thing to verify is that that server is connected to the network.

If the DNS server has physical connectivity to the network and clients can ping the server, verify that the DNS service is running on the server. The nslookup command can be used to test whether the server can respond to DNS clients.

If the DNS service is enabled and running, the problem may lie with some of the configuration settings of the DNS server. For instance, verify that the DNS server is not configured to use a nonstandard port instead of the default port of 53. This may be done to increase firewall security, but it can also adversely affect DNS functionality. It may also be that the DNS server is configured to limit service to a specific list of its configured IP addresses. This is not often the case, but if you're brought in to troubleshoot a server, all DNS settings need to be verified.

Finally, if the DNS server is unable to respond correctly to queries it receives, it is a sign of incorrect data on the server. If this occurs on a secondary server, it may be necessary to force a full zone transfer to ensure that all of the most recent DNS zone information is received from the primary. It may also be necessary to manually clear the DNS cache to ensure that stale name resolution information is not being accessed.

# Managing WINS

The Windows Internet Naming Service (WINS) is responsible for providing name resolution for a network by resolving NetBIOS names to an IP address. On a Microsoft network, each computer uses a unique NetBIOS name to identify itself on the network. The NetBIOS name can be up to 15 characters long and is the name you see when you browse a network. Often, the NetBIOS name reflects the computer's user, such as johnscomp, or the function of the computer, such as librarylab.

When a WINS server is being used, all of these NetBIOS names are kept in a database located on the WINS server. Using this database, the WINS server can perform NetBIOS name to IP address translation. For instance, the WINS server will identify that johnscomp is using the IP address of 192.168.3.45.

There are two primary ways for NetBIOS names to be resolved to IP addresses: using a WINS server that is dynamically updated with computer NetBIOS name to IP mapping or by using an LMHOSTS file which has static NetBIOS name to IP mappings and is maintained manually.

---

 **NOTE** It is possible for a network node to broadcast to the network when name resolution is required. This broadcast message is sent to the entire local network and each device must determine if it is the intended target. The intended target system will respond to the request. The problem with broadcast resolutions is that they can use value bandwidth in the resolution process. This leaves broadcast NetBIOS resolutions suitable only for smaller networks where the generated traffic would not adversely affect the network. Broadcast resolutions cannot be performed on a routed network. In the real world, most broadcast traffic is blocked at the routers to avoid broadcast storms. But some routers can be configured to allow NetBIOS broadcasts through (not smart, but not impossible).

---

## Using the LMHOSTS File

In its day, WINS was the primary way for name resolution on the network. In those early days, the function WINS provides was configured using a text file called the LMHOSTS file. This file is stored locally on each of the client systems and provides NetBIOS to IP address resolution for that system. In smaller networks, this LMHOSTS file can be used to provide WINS resolution; however, because it is a static file, if the name of a computer changes, each individual LMHOSTS file will need to be updated. The LMHOSTS file could also be stored centrally if you used the #INCLUDE option.

The LMHOSTS file is a text file and not overly complex to configure. The basic structure is an IP address of the server the client will connect to, then the server's NetBIOS name, such as 24.54.94.97 AppServer.

Table 13-8 contains a few keywords used to customize the LMHOSTS file.

As mentioned, the file is easy to set up, but can require a lot of administrative overhead in terms of maintenance. Individual LMHOSTS files maintained on each client system can

| Table 13-8 | Keyword | Function |
|---|---|---|
| Using Options to Customize the LMHOSTS File | #PRE | Used to load the LMHOST entry into memory. This allows for dynamic cache allocation. |
| | #DOM | The symbol used to designate the system as a domain controller. |
| | #include | This option is used to identify a LMHOSTS file located on a remote host. |

be too much work, especially where changes to the file are commonly required. If an LMHOSTS file is used, it can be done by using the #include switch, which references the location of a central LMHOSTS file on a remote server. In this configuration, only the file on the remote server needs to be changed to accommodate the changes to the NetBIOS names.

The LMHOSTS file can be opened using Notepad, and the directions for doing do will be displayed. The name of the file is LMHOSTS.sam: once it is edited, you will need to save it as LMHOSTS with no extension.

**NOTE** For extra name resolution protection, LMHOSTS files can be created for client systems in the event that the WINS servers should go offline.

## Designing a WINS Strategy

Like any other service on a network, when implementing WINS on a network, there are many design considerations to keep in mind. These include

- WINS convergence
- WINS replication
- WINS redundancy

## WINS Convergence

When we talk about WINS convergence, we are referring to the time it takes the WINS database to be replicated to the other WINS servers on the network. Convergence is an important consideration; on networks with slow WINS convergence, it is possible that some hosts on the network may have the wrong NetBIOS information for the period of the convergence. In such a case, some hosts may be unable to resolve NetBIOS names to IP addresses and may be unable to access certain network resources.

**EXAM TIP** The convergence time for a WINS server is controlled by the frequency of the replication process.

## WINS Replication

On a network, it is common practice to use more than one WINS server. This is both to provide redundancy and to share the workload of WINS resolutions. When multiple WINS servers are used, each server maintains a copy of the WINS database. To keep the WINS database current among all servers, WINS servers synchronize the database in a process known as WINS replication.

To create WINS replication, each of the WINS servers on the network must be configured as a push partner, pull partner, or both. A pull partner is a WINS server that requests database updates from another partner. This occurs at preconfigured time intervals or in response to a database update notification from a push partner. Both of these update criteria are configured by the administrator. A push partner, on the other hand, is a WINS server that responds to the requests of the pull partner for database updates. It can also be configured to send out update notifications to the pull partner informing it of a change in the database.

**EXAM TIP**   When designing a WINS replication strategy, it is recommended that each of the WINS servers be designed as both a push partner and a pull partner.

**NOTE**   As you might imagine, WINS servers have to be configured in pairs. This means that there have to be both push and pull partners.

**Replication Considerations**   As an administrator, the day may come when you need to decide which servers will be the push partners and which will be the pull partners. This decision is often based on the performance of the server. Pull partners are often used on the far side of WAN links, as they can be configured to replicate at predefined time intervals. This allows the administrator to configure replication when it will have the least impact on the network.

On faster links, push WINS servers are often used. WINS servers configured as push servers can be configured to force WINS updates based on the number of changes made to the WINS database. Microsoft recommends that each of the WINS servers be configured as both a push and pull partner. This allows all WINS servers to update the WINS database based on either time intervals or the number of changes made to the database. To summarize, the following are the WINS replication options:

- Administrator can update the WINS database manually from the WINS Manager utility.

- System startup replication can be configured.

- Replication can occur at a predefined time interval. For example, the replication can occur every eight hours. This is the configuration used with pull partners.

- Replication can occur after a predefined number of updates or changes to the database are surpassed. This is the configuration setting for push partners.

## WINS Fault Tolerance

Multiple servers are often used for redundancy. In such a configuration, if one server should fail, there is another ready to take over and prevent a disruption to network users. This is also true of WINS servers.

In practical network application, multiple WINS servers are used not only to provide redundancy but also for load balancing. As mentioned earlier, when multiple WINS servers are used, they must be configured as a push partner, pull partner, or both.

When implementing WINS, there are a few other fault-tolerant strategies to be aware of:

- **Configure client systems with a primary and secondary WINS server** The reason for this configuration is straightforward: if the client cannot locate the primary WINS server, it will check for the secondary one. Though it is rarely done, Windows operating systems from Windows 98 can be assigned 12 WINS servers. That may be a bit more than most organizations need.

- **WINS server placement** It is strongly advised that each local network segment have a local WINS server. If the WINS server is not local, should the WAN link fail, the local clients could not receive WINS services. Such a configuration may work if the local network segment is small and LMHOSTS files could provide NetBIOS name resolution.

- **Replication paths** Not only is it advisable to have redundant WINS servers on the network, but wherever possible, it is advised to have redundant replication paths. As in networking, sometimes links fail, and if they do, WINS servers may be unable to replicate with each other. They will just sit and push and pull into midair.

# Plan an Internet Connectivity Strategy

It would be hard to find an organization in this day and age that does not have and require a connection to the Internet. The way in which this connection is established can vary among organizations. In this section, we provide an overview of the different methods used to access the Internet.

## Network Address Translation

It wasn't too long ago that configuring Internet access for small companies was a bit of a problem. Any office with 5–10 computers would need to set up a modem on each system and create an individual dial-up account for each user. This method was not only expensive but also created large administrative overhead. Later versions of Microsoft Windows introduced something called Network Address Translation (NAT) that changed the way the Internet can be accessed by organizations. By enabling NAT on a Server 2003 system, you allow connected users on a private system to share a single connection to access a public network such as the Internet. Figure 13-8 shows an example of NAT in action.

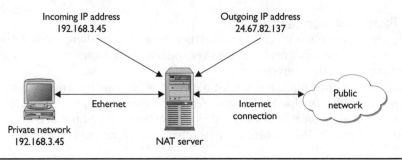

Figure 13-8   A NAT server translates private IP addresses to public addresses.

 **EXAM TIP**   NAT eliminates the need for a large number of IP addresses by mapping externally assigned IP addresses to privately assigned addresses.

NAT does have its detractors, specifically when it comes to some protocol restrictions. These include

- NAT blocks the Simple Network Management Protocol (SNMP) and the Lightweight Directory Access Protocol (LDAP).
- NAT does not offer support for Kerberos v5.
- NAT does not support Remote Procedure Call (RPC), therefore applications such as the MMC, which use RPC for client/server communication, are incompatible with NAT.
- When enabled, NAT is a mini-DHCP server. No other DHCP servers can be used on the network segment other than NAT.
- In most configurations, the network must be a single nonrouted network segment.

As you can see from this list, these limitations of NAT preclude it from the infrastructure of many network environments. However, smaller organizations may not use all of these features and as such are well suited for NAT implementation.

 **EXAM TIP**   There are three main components to NAT. First is the network translation, which translates the IP addresses and TCP/UDP port numbers of packets that are forwarded between the private network and the Internet. The second component is the IP addressing assignments. NAT automatically assigns IP addresses in the 192.168.0.0 private address range. The third element is the name resolution. The NAT computer becomes the DNS server for the other computers on the network.

**Deploying NAT**   When deploying NAT, you need to configure settings on both the NAT server and the client. To begin, let's take a look at what is needed to configure the NAT server.

On the client side of NAT, you need to configure client systems to obtain IP addressing information automatically and then restart the client systems. Assuming NAT is used for address assignment, the client systems will receive TCP/IP information from the NAT server. The client information includes

- IP address from the 192.168.0.0 private address range
- Subnet mask (255.255.255.0)
- The default gateway, which would be the IP address of a directly reachable IP router
- DNS server address, which would be the address of the NAT interface on the server

With the client side configured, there are a few things to do on the NAT server:

1. The first step to configure NAT is to actually install the Routing and Remote Access service. To do this, you need to start the Routing and Remote Access Server Setup Wizard. Choose Start | All Programs | Administrative Tools | Routing and Remote Access. This will open the Routing and Remote Access dialog box.

2. Choose Action from the task bar and then the Add Server option. This will allow you to add your local server to the Routing and Remote Access dialog box.

3. Right-click the server you added and select the option to Configure And Enable Routing And Remote Access. This will start the Routing and Remote Access Server Setup Wizard.

4. Select Next when the wizard first appears to select the type of routing and remote access you want to install. For this exercise, select the NAT option, as shown in Figure 13-9.

5. The next screen in the wizard allows you to select an existing interface or create a new demand-dial interface for client computers to connect to the Internet. It also allows you to enable a basic firewall for that connection. If a new demand-dial interface is required, the Demand-Dial Interface Wizard will start.

6. With Routing and Remote Access installed, you can configure NAT on the server. First we need to configure the IP information for the internal network card. For example:

IP address: 192.168.0.1

Subnet mask: 255.255.255.0

No default gateway

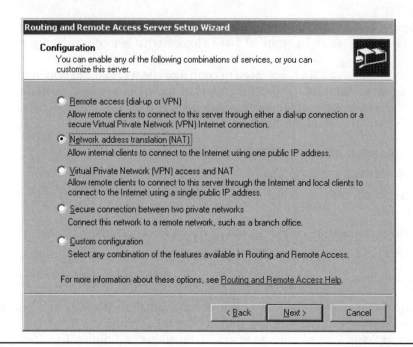

**Figure 13-9**   The Routing and Remote Access Server Setup Wizard is used to configure NAT
on a server.

7. To enable routing on your dial-up port, from the Routing and Remote Access
   dialog box, expand the tree for the installed server, right-click Ports, and select
   Properties from the menu. From the Ports Properties dialog box, click the
   Configure button.

8. To add your Internet and home network interface to the NAT routing protocol,
   from the Routing and Remote Access dialog box, expand the IP Routing tree,
   right-click NAT/Basic Firewall, and select the New Interface option. Figure 13-10
   shows the dialog box used to attach network interfaces to NAT.

9. To enable NAT addressing and name resolution, from the Routing and Remote
   Access dialog box, right-click NAT/Basic Firewall and select Properties to open
   the NAT/Basic Firewall Properties dialog box.

10. Select the Address Assignment tab to enable automatic assignment of IP
    address. Choose the Name Resolution tab to enable NAT name resolution.
    Figure 13-11 shows both tabs.

**EXAM TIP**   Before taking the exam, familiarize yourself with NAT server
configurations.

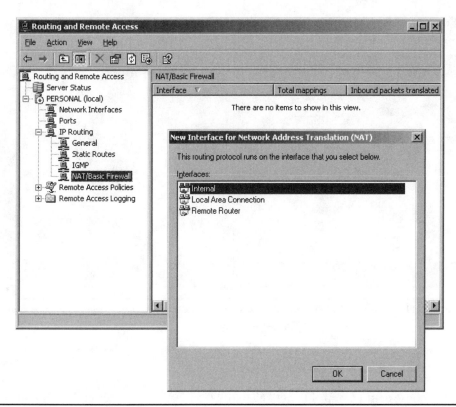

**Figure 13-10**   Network interfaces have to be added to the NAT routing protocol.

 **NOTE**   As shown in Figure 13-11, the Address Assignment tab includes an Exclude button. This is used to exclude IP addresses that are not to be handed out, such as addresses to network printers or other network servers.

## Internet Connection Sharing

Internet Connection Sharing (ICS) provides an alternative to NAT as a method to achieve Internet connectivity. ICS is designed to be as simple as possible and, in fact, enabling it is as simple as checking a single box. While it may be a little easier to enable than NAT, it is not as versatile. Once enabled, there isn't much that can be configured.

Like NAT, ICS provides three key services to the network: network address translation, automatic IP addressing, and name resolution. When ICS is enabled, it will appear in the Network Connections dialog box as a shared connection.

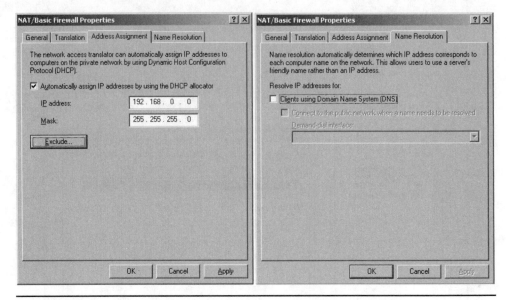

**Figure 13-11**   The NAT/Basic Firewall Properties dialog box is used to enable name resolution and automatic address assignments.

The following steps are used to enable ICS:

1. Choose Start | Control Panel | Network Connections and select the network adapter on which ICS is to be enabled.

2. In the Properties dialog box for that adapter, select the Advanced tab.

3. Select the check box to "Allow other network users to connect through this computer's Internet connection" to enable ICS.

Once the check box has been selected, ICS will be enabled. Other systems networked to this system will be able to access the Internet through the ICS system.

 **EXAM TIP**   ICS requires a server with two network interfaces, one for the private internal network configured with 192.168.0.0 address and an adapter for a public connection.

ICS requires two connections in order to work: one public and one private. The private connection, typically a LAN adapter, connects the ICS host computer to the computers on your home or small office network. The public connection, typically a DSL, cable, or dial-up modem, connects your network to the Internet.

**NOTE**   ICS, while being easy to use, is not configurable. Using ICS, you will not be able to modify the default configuration. This includes disabling the DHCP allocator or modifying the range of private IP addresses that are distributed, disabling the DNS proxy, or configuring a range of public IP addresses.

**EXAM TIP**   You can enable ICS only when two or more network adapters are installed.

# Troubleshooting Internet Connectivity

Troubleshooting Internet connectivity is just one of those necessary evils for the network administrator. In this section, we review some of the areas to keep an eye on when troubleshooting Internet connectivity.

## Troubleshooting Basics

When a connection to the Internet fails, the first response is often to check through all of your system settings. While this may need to be done, it is likely not the first troubleshooting step to take. There really are no rules on how to approach a computer-related problem, just apply a little common sense and practice. The first step may be to determine if an Internet connectivity problem is isolated to a single system, single network segment, or single server. Determining the scope of the problem will certainly assist you in isolating where the cause lies. For example, if no client computers are able to access the Internet, but they are able to access the network, it is likely the problem is not with the clients. It may be a server, the firewall, or even the ISP. If you assume the problem lies with a server, for instance, you could perform the following troubleshooting procedures:

- **Verification of physical connections**   When searching for physical connectivity problems, you are looking for wiring and cabling issues. This may be the cabling going to the hub or out to the Internet.

- **Verification of recent changes**   Have there been any recent changes to the system? If there has, it may be that one of the changes has had an unexpected result.

- **Network interface card**   When checking the cabling, verify that the LED on the NIC is still lit or flashing. It may be that there is something wrong with the NIC itself.

- **Protocol configuration**   Using the ipconfig command, you can determine if you have the appropriate IP addresses for both the internal and external network interfaces. You can also determine if the default gateway is correctly configured.

## The Right Tool for the Job

One of the tools an administrator uses over and over and therefore should know how to use well, is the ipconfig utility. The ipconfig command provides the ability to see the IP configuration for all installed network adapters. The information provided includes the IP address, default gateway, DNS servers, MAC address, whether the system is DHCP enabled, and the DHCP lease expiry date.

ipconfig is more than just a utility to show the current IP configuration; it can also be used in the troubleshooting process using a variety of switches. For example, if you think the system may have incorrect IP configuration, you can use the ipconfig /renew command to get new IP information for that adapter. Table 13-9 shows the available options for the ipconfig command.

 **EXAM TIP** For the exam, review the available options for the ipconfig command and when they may be used.

These simple suggestions show the troubleshooting process can begin. Effective and systematic troubleshooting can make a seemingly difficult issue into a quick fix.

## Troubleshooting NAT

NAT is really not that complicated, and therefore, there are few places to look if there are problems with gaining Internet access through a NAT server. When troubleshooting NAT, consider the following:

- **Connectivity** Before checking settings, verify that the client system or server is physically connected to the network.

| Table 13-9 | Option | Description |
| --- | --- | --- |
| ipconfig Command Options | /? | Displays help message |
| | /all | Displays complete IP configuration information for all installed adapters |
| | /release | Releases the IP address for the specified adapter |
| | /renew | Renews the IP address for the specified adapter |
| | /flushdns | Purges the DNS resolver cache |
| | /registerdns | Refreshes all DHCP leases and reregisters DNS names |
| | /displaydns | Displays the contents of the DNS resolver cache |
| | /showclassid | Displays all the DHCP class IDs allowed for the adapter |
| | /setclassid | Modifies the DHCP class ID |

- **IP configuration**   NAT will assign IP addressing to client computer systems. To verify that the client system is obtaining the IP address, the ipconfig command can be issued. On Windows 9*x*/Me systems, the winipcfg command will provide IP information. If clients are not receiving IP information, verify that network address translation addressing is enabled on the interface that corresponds to your small office or home office network segment.

- **Inoperative name resolution is not working**   Verify that network address translation name resolution is enabled on the interface that corresponds to your small office or home office network segment. Ensure that in the IP configuration, the DNS server address is assigned. This would be the address of the NAT interface on the server.

- **Default gateway**   Ensure that the default gateway points to the correct location. In this case, it would be the IP address of a directly reachable IP router.

There isn't much more to troubleshooting NAT connections than this. Most NAT connectivity problems can be traced to a simple configuration change.

## Troubleshooting ICS

When it comes to troubleshooting ICS, there are even fewer places to look than with NAT. As previously mentioned, ICS really doesn't have any configurable settings; rather, it uses default settings when ICS is enabled. This helps isolate ICS-related problems.

First, check the physical connectivity to the network. To use ICS, client systems must belong to the same workgroup or network. Verify that they are connected to the network and can browse to the ICS server.

Verify the IP configuration information. We have found, however, that sometimes the information is stale, so make sure the system can be rebooted to get new IP information from the ICS server. Alternatively, the ipconfig /renew command will provide the same results.

One final thing to try is to reboot both the ICS server and the client.

## Name Cache Troubleshooting

From time to time, you may notice that the DNS server is not correctly resolving names. This can have a few causes, such as a corrupt or outdated database. One more option that can cause this is stale information maintained in the cache.

When troubleshooting name cache problems, you can use the ipconfig command to flush out and reset the contents of the cache. In this case, you would use the /flushdns option with the ipconfig command. During DNS troubleshooting, if necessary, you can use this procedure to discard negative cache entries from the cache, as well as any other dynamically added entries.

Keep in mind that flushing the DNS cache does not affect any of the entries in the DNS hosts file. To eliminate those entries from the cache, remove them from this file.

**NOTE**   The /flushdns option is only available for computers running Windows 2000, Windows XP, or Windows 2003.

# Plan and Modify a Network Topology

Most organizations today have established networks, and the chance of an MCSE being called upon to create a network from scratch is uncommon. However, networks are dynamic and are constantly being changed and updated to increase efficiency, security, and functionality. MSCEs will need to know how to effectively design a network, including knowing how to configure the network topology. This requires deciding on the physical placement of network resources.

## Placing DNS Servers

When it comes to the physical placement of network resources, there are really no absolute rules. It often boils down to common sense and some general guidelines. For DNS servers, common-sense placement would be in a location on the network that is centrally available to DNS clients. To reduce network traffic, wherever possible, it is recommended to separate DNS servers on different subnets. This way, a local DNS server can maintain name resolution for the local segment.

There are a few questions you need to ask when deciding where to place a DNS server on a network:

- If there are separate network segments used, will clients have name resolution if a DNS server fails?

- If network segments are separated over a WAN, how will name resolution occur if the WAN link fails?

- If multiple DNS servers are to be used on a network segment, will one of the DNS servers be required to be configured as a forwarder?

- How important is DNS redundancy?

The answers to these questions will help decide where on the network DNS servers should be placed. For example, let's assume you are deciding on DNS placement for a routed network separated by a high-speed link. In such a scenario, you could implement a single DNS server solution on one side of the high-speed link to resolve DNS queries for both sides. In this case, name resolution queries must cross over the link. This may be fine if there are few queries and bandwidth is not an option. However, if that link should fail, DNS is not possible for one of the network segments. Further, if the DNS server itself goes down, both sides are unable to resolve host names.

Knowing this, when you design the network you may decide to place a DNS server on either side of the high-speed link to provide redundancy and failover capability. How would this same scenario look if the networks were separated by a slow WAN link?

Over a slow link, you would certainly consider placing a DNS server on either side of the slow WAN link to reduce the queries that must go over the link. Database synchronization would still need to occur and most likely incremental replication would be used.

At the end of the day, in most organizations multiple DNS servers are going to be used for fault-tolerant reasons. The question becomes where these servers can best be placed on the network, and which ones to configure as the primary and secondary servers.

## Placing DHCP Servers

The placement of DHCP servers follows the same general placement guidelines as those for a DNS server. Within a local segment, place DHCP servers in a location on the network that is centrally available to DHCP clients. There are a few additional considerations when using DHCP on a routed network.

On a routed network that uses DHCP server and divided network subnets, there must be at least one DHCP server to supply addresses for the network segments. It is typically placed on the subnet that has the most client systems. In addition, in order for a DHCP server to provide IP address information to clients on remote segments separated by routers, a DHCP and BOOTP relay agent must be used to forward traffic between subnets.

**NOTE** The DHCP/BOOTP relay agent is the program or component responsible for relaying DHCP and BOOTP broadcast messages between a DHCP server and a client across an IP router. A DHCP relay agent supports DHCP/BOOTP message relay as defined in RFCs 1541 and 2131. The DHCP relay agent service is managed using the Routing and Remote Access service.

**EXAM TIP** One very broad rule when determining placement for WINS, DNS, and DHCP servers is to place them where they can maximize response time while at the same time minimizing network traffic.

Like DNS servers, if multiple network segments are to be used, it may be a good idea to have a DHCP server resident on each segment instead of relying on a single DHCP server. This reduces overall network traffic and at the same time provides a potential redundant DHCP solution.

## Placing WINS Servers

As mentioned earlier, WINS provides another option for name resolution on a network. While DNS may be the preferred solution, there are many legacy networks still using a WINS naming solution.

On a routed network, it is necessary to consider the potential effect that WINS replication and WINS name resolution traffic will have on the network. Client name requests and responses that occur as a system powers on pass through the traffic queues on the routers and can cause delays at peak times. Such considerations can greatly affect where you place the WINS servers.

PART III

In common application, more than a single WINS server is used. In such a configuration, it is common to provide each network segment with its own WINS server and configure a push/pull partnership between the WINS servers to keep the databases consistent. If WINS servers are separated over a slow WAN link, replication can be configured to occur at non-peak periods.

---

 **NOTE** How many WINS servers are needed to provide name resolution for a network? On smaller networks, two WINS servers can provide efficient name resolution and fault tolerance. As the network grows, Microsoft recommends one WINS server and a backup server for every 10,000 computers on the network.

---

When WINS servers are used on multiple network segments, such as a series of remote offices, Microsoft suggests implementing WINS in something called the hub-and-spoke configuration. This model is designed to maximize convergence speeds and at the same time reduce administrative overhead. As the name suggest, one WINS server forms the hub of the model, perhaps at a central office, and is configured as both a push and pull partner. The other WINS servers are located at remote branch offices and are also configured as push and pull partners.

The model provides for both efficiency and redundancy. Figure 13-12 shows the WINS hub-and-spoke model.

### Network Firewalls

While there are a few choices when placing DHCP, WINS, and DNS servers, the placement of firewalls is pretty straightforward. Firewalls sit at the edge of the network separating the public and private networks. In most cases, they are the entry and exit points for the network, but under some situations it may be necessary to place a server outside of the firewall. In most cases, however, everything is tucked in behind the firewall server.

## Monitoring Network Traffic

With the network set up the way you want, the next step is to monitor the network to ensure there are no bottlenecks or performance lags in the system. One of the more common tools used to monitor network traffic is Network Monitor.

One of the main functions of Network Monitor is to capture and analyze network data to determine a potential problem before it affects network users. Network Monitor is an advanced tool that allows the administrator to capture very specific types of network information sent to or from the computer on which Network Monitor is installed.

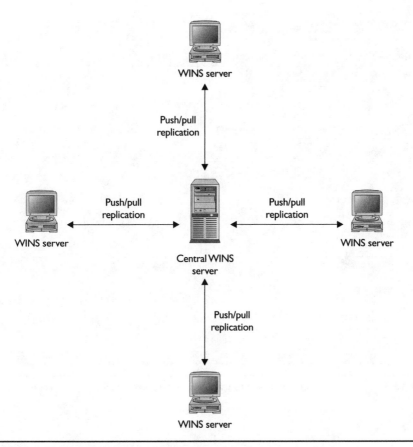

**Figure 13-12**   The WINS hub-and-spoke model provides efficiency and redundancy.

 **NOTE**   To capture remote packets sent to other systems in the network, you need the network component that ships with Microsoft Systems Management Server.

## Using Network Monitor

Using Network Monitor allows the administrator to gather detailed network statistics. In this section, we review some of the ways to capture and analyze network traffic. To start Network Monitor, select Start | All Programs | Administrative Tools | Network Monitor. Figure 13-13 shows Network Monitor.

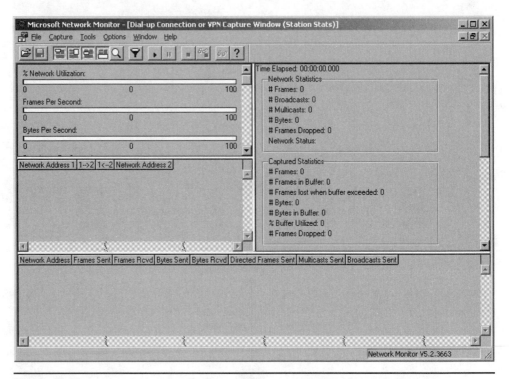

**Figure 13-13**   Network Monitor is used to track data coming into and leaving the server.

**NOTE**   Network Monitor may not be installed by default on a Windows Server 2003 system. To install network-monitoring tools, use the Add/ Remove Programs applet in the Control Panel.

## Capturing Network Frames

To capture to and from a local computer, you need to set a capture filter for a set of frames. After the data is captured, it can be viewed and interpreted by the administrator. To begin to capture network frames, select Capture | Start.

On the right side of the Network Monitor window is the Total Statistics pane. This is used to provide a summary of all network traffic sent to and from the system during the capture process. There are five areas that are summarized:

- **Network Statistics**   The Network Statistics section displays the total amount of traffic that has been sent to or from the local computer since the current capture began. The information gathered includes the total number of frames sent and received, total number of broadcasts, total number of multicasts, and the total number of frames dropped.

- **Captured Statistics**   This section summarizes the current network capture. This includes such statistics as total number of captured frames, number of frames in the temporary capture file, total number of captured bytes, and the number of frames dropped by Network Monitor.

- **Per Second Statistics**   The per second statistics give a summary of averages on the network capture. For example, elements included would be the average number of frames per second detected since the capture began, average bytes per second, average number of multicast and broadcast messages, and the percentage of network utilization.

- **Network Card Statistics**   The NIC statistics provide a summary of the activity detected by the network card since the capture was started. Included in these statistics are elements such as the total frames detected by the network adapter, broadcast and multicast frames detected, and the total bytes detected by the network adapter.

- **Network Card Error Statistics**   Provides a summary of the errors detected in the current capture. Elements in this summary include the cyclical redundancy check (CRC) errors and number of frames dropped.

## Trigger Actions

One of the features of Network Monitor allows administrators to set triggers that respond to events on the network. For example, you can configure an event trigger depending on how full the capture buffer is or even if a specific pattern is detected in a captured frame. There are three possible actions that can occur when an event is triggered:

- An audible alarm will sound, using a series of computer beeps.

- Network Monitor will automatically stop recording frames.

- The operating system can start an executable file.

**Configuring Triggers**   The following steps outline the procedures for configuring event triggers:

1. Select Capture | Triggers to open the Capture Triggers dialog box.

2. To configure an event trigger to occur when a specific ASCII or hexadecimal string appears in a frame, select the Pattern Match option. In the Pattern text box, identify the string that Network Monitor should detect.

3. If you want to configure a trigger action when a percentage of the capture buffer is full, select the Buffer Space option and specify the percentage desired. Figure 13-14 shows the settings for trigger events when a percentage of the capture buffer is full.

4. If you want to configure the event trigger to occur when a specific pattern in a frame is detected after a specific percentage of the capture buffer becomes full, click Buffer Space Then Pattern Match, followed by the desired percentage.

PART III

**Figure 13-14**

An event trigger can be configured to occur when a specific percentage of the capture buffer is full.

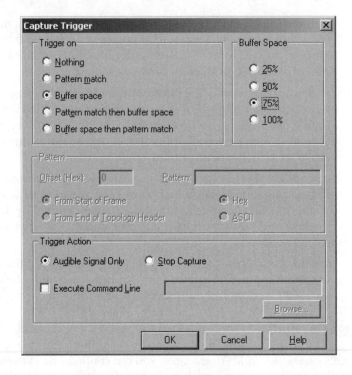

5. If you want to configure the event trigger to occur when a specific percentage of the capture buffer becomes full after a specific pattern in a frame is detected, select Pattern Match Then Buffer Space, followed by the desired percentage. Figure 13-15 shows this configuration option.

 **EXAM TIP**  You are almost certain to have questions on the exam pertaining to Network Monitor. Before taking the exam, familiarize yourself with Network Monitor, including capturing and analyzing frames.

# Chapter Review

In this chapter, we have reviewed the basics of TCP/IP addressing and how this addressing is used to increase scalability of IP-based networks. We discussed how the IP address and the subnet mask are used together to define the network and host IDs. In addition, we highlighted the procedures used to subnet an IP-based network to extend the number of networks or the number of hosts allowed on a segment.

We reviewed name resolution strategies used on today's networks, including DNS and WINS. We identified some of the considerations when planning a host name resolution strategy, including the namespace design, zone replication, forwarding, and DNS security. For WINs, we looked at replication strategies and resolving NetBIOS names using the LMHOSTS file.

**Figure 13-15**
A trigger can
be set to occur
when a specific
percentage of
the capture buffer
becomes full after
a specific pattern
in a frame is
detected.

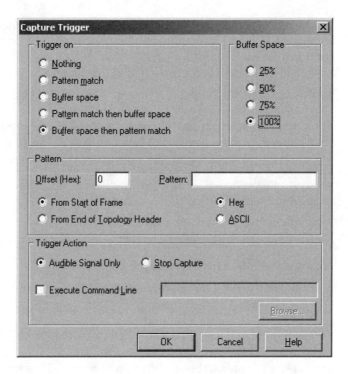

NAT and ICS provide a method for small to medium-size companies to gain Internet access. Both technologies provide IP translation, name resolution, and automatic IP address assignment. While both technologies provide a single point for Internet access, NAT is more configurable and more versatile than its counterpart.

Network Monitor is an invaluable tool to monitor events on the network. It can be configured to perform actions when specified criteria are exceeded.

## Questions

1. Your network consists of a single Windows Server 2003 domain named acme.local.support. You have been asked to ensure that all internal name resolution traffic never passes outside the network. External name requests must be handled by an external DNS server. What should you do?

   **A.** Configure all internal DNS servers to forward name resolution requests to the external DNS server.

   **B.** Configure all internal DNS client systems to forward name resolution requests to the external DNS server.

   **C.** Configure all internal DNS clients to forward name resolution requests to the NAT firewall.

   **D.** Configure all internal DNS servers to forward recursive name resolution requests to the internal client systems.

2. You are the administrator of the acme.com domain. The network is currently comprised of a main office and two branch offices. The branch offices are connected to the main office by 256 Kbps leased lines. You have a single DNS zone, and all DNS servers are located at the main office. The network is not currently connected to the Internet.

Users are reporting that response times are extremely slow when they attempt to access intranet resources. When you monitor the network, you discover that DNS name resolution queries are generating heavy traffic across the WAN links.

You take the following actions:

- Create a new secondary DNS zone at each branch office. Use the primary zone at the main office as the master zone.

- Configure the client computers to query their local DNS servers.

Which result or results do these actions produce? (Choose all that apply.)

A. Name resolution traffic across the WAN links is reduced.

B. Response times for name resolution queries are reduced.

C. Response times for name resolution queries are increased.

D. Because a new secondary DNS zone is created at each branch office, name resolution traffic across the WAN links is increased.

3. You are the administrator of a Windows Server 2003 network. The network has four segments connected by a router. Each segment contains its own WINS server and two other DHCP servers. The network uses 300 client systems, a mixture of Windows NT Workstation 4.0, Windows 2000 Professional, and XP Professional systems. Users in each network segment inform you that they cannot browse any network resources on the other network segments. They do not have problems browsing their own segment. How should you configure the network to enable users to browse for network resources on all three network segments?

A. Configure a central WINS server and configure it as a pull server for the other three WINS servers.

B. Upgrade the Windows NT 4.0 client systems to allow for WINS database registration.

C. Configure an uphill proxy for the WINS servers and direct them to replicate as push/pull partners.

D. Configure the four WINS servers as replication partners of one another.

4. You are creating a home network that uses a Windows Server 2003 system, two Windows 98 Second Edition systems, and Windows 2000 Professional system. You want to have Internet access on all of the computers in your home office, but isolated to a single entry point.

You perform the following tasks:

- You enable Internet Connection Sharing.

- You create a connection between the network and the Internet.

- You install and configure LAN adapters connecting the client computers to the network.

Which of the following is true of your configuration? (Choose all that apply.)

A. It provides network address translation for the private IP addresses.

B. It provides name resolution.

C. It provides IP address configurations for the entire network.

D. It enables a direct-dial Internet connection for client systems.

5. Your network consists of a Windows Server 2003 system and a mixture of Windows XP and 2000 client systems. The Windows Server 2003 system maintains a dial-up connection to the Internet. All client computers are configured to use APIPA. There is no DHCP server on the network. You want to implement ICS to allow client computers to access the Internet. How should you configure the server? (Choose all that apply.)

A. Enable Internet Connection Sharing on the dial-up connection of the server.

B. Enable Internet Connection Sharing on the dial-up connection of the client systems.

C. Configure the server to use APIPA for the LAN interface.

D. Configure each client to use APIPA for the LAN interface.

6. Your network consists of a single Windows Server 2003 domain and uses TCP/IP. DHCP is used to assign addresses to your Windows XP client computers. Due to a large company expansion, numerous client computers are added to your network. Users report that occasionally they cannot access network resources or log onto the network. The TCP/IP configuration of a computer that is experiencing this problem shows that it is using the address 169.254.0.16—an invalid address in your network. What should you do?

A. Configure the DHCP server in a push/pull configuration and designate IXFR replication.

B. Add new addresses to the existing DHCP scope to include the new client computers.

C. Reduce the lease times assigned to client systems.

D. Configure a superscope to include the 169.0.0.0 address range.

## Answers

1. **A.** By configuring the internal DNS servers to forward name resolution requests to the external DNS server, internal DNS names will not be published to the Internet. Any DNS entry that internal DNS servers cannot recognize will be forwarded to the external DNS server. The external DNS server sends the client query to other external DNS servers on the Internet.

2. **A and B.** Creating a new secondary DNS zone at each branch office and configuring the client computers to query their local DNS servers will reduce the name resolution traffic across the slower WAN links. Also, response times for name resolution queries are reduced as client computers will query local DNS servers.

3. **D.** If the WINS servers were configured as replication partners, they would have a synchronized database and local client systems would be able browse systems on the other three segments.

4. **A, B, and C.** When Internet Connection Sharing is enabled, network address translation for the private IP addresses, name resolution, and automatic IP address configuration information are provided.

5. **A and C.** To allow the client computers to access the Internet through ICS, it has to be enabled on the dial-up connection of the server and the server must be configured to use APIPA for the LAN interface.

6. **B.** It is likely that after the additional systems were added to the network, there weren't enough addresses in the current DHCP scope to accommodate the new systems. Therefore the solution is to add more addresses to the DHCP scope. The problem may also be lessened by decreasing DHCP lease times, but this would not solve the long-term problem.

# Planning, Implementing, and Maintaining Routing and Remote Access

In this chapter, you will learn how to
- Identify routing protocols
- Work with multicast traffic
- Plan security for remote users
- Manage remote access policies
- Identify protocol security requirements
- Plan remote access authentication methods
- Create an IPSec policy
- Troubleshoot TCP/IP routing

It really wasn't that long ago when the concept of remotely accessing a network was relatively unheard of. Remote access methods and access security were in their infancy, and remote access technologies were too complex and expensive to implement for most organizations. Remote access was the domain of skilled technicians who had the time and motivation to configure it.

Today all that has changed, and remote access and telecommunication have become integral parts of an organization's IT strategy. Organizations have come to rely on anywhere, anytime expectations for their networks. This has made the job of network administrator that much more difficult. Not only do remote users have to have access to a network, but that access has to be restricted and secured.

Microsoft's response to remote access is the Routing and Remote Access Service (RRAS). In one form or another, RRAS has been with us since Windows NT 4, but there have been significant improvements along the way. The version of RRAS offered with Windows Server 2003 products is the cumulative effort of years of development. What we are left with is a complete and comprehensive RRAS implementation with an easy-to-manage graphical interface and enough features to address the remote access needs of modern organizations.

In this chapter, we provide an overview of RRAS and take a look at what it takes to plan, configure, and securely deploy it.

# Planning and Deploying a Routing Strategy

In today's network environments, the question has shifted away from whether remote access is required to what type of remote access is going to be used. For system administrators, when the decision to allow remote access into the network is made, their job begins. When designing a routing strategy, many key decisions have to be considered, from layout to network protocols, security considerations, and remote access protocols.

## Remote Access Protocols

Before we get too far in discussions of maintaining routing and remote access, it is important to have an understanding of some of the primary remote access protocols. While you may not have questions specific to these remote access protocols on the exam, you are sure to see references to them.

### Point-to-Point Protocol

The Point-to-Point Protocol (PPP) is a commonly implemented remote access protocol and the most popular method for transporting IP packets over a network. PPP offers full interoperability between software vendors and various remote access implementations. PPP provides encryption of user names and passwords during the authentication process and requires that remote clients and servers negotiate data encryption methods and authentication methods. This authentication process is performed using specific PPP authentication protocols. These protocols include the Challenge Handshake Authentication Protocol (CHAP), Microsoft Challenge Handshake Authentication Protocol (MS-CHAP), Password Authentication Protocol (PAP), and Extensible Authentication Protocol (EAP).

**NOTE** PPP authentication methods are described later in this chapter in the section entitled "Planning Security for Remote Access Users."

**PPP Dial-up Sequence** The following provides a quick look at the steps required when a PPP remote connection is established.

1. To allow communication between the connecting devices, framing rules are established between the client and the server. The Link Control Protocol (LCP) is used to establish and configure link and framing settings such as maximum frame size.

2. Authentication protocols are used to determine what level of security validation the remote access server can perform and what the server requires. The level of security that can be negotiated ranges from unencrypted (plaintext) password authentication to encrypted, highly secure smart card authentication.

3. Network Control Protocols (NCPs) configure the remote client for the correct LAN protocols, TCP/IP, IPX, and so on.

Once these steps have been negotiated between the client and the server, data can be exchanged.

## Point-to-Point Tunneling Protocol

You are sure to see references to the Point-to-Point Tunneling Protocol (PPTP) in the Microsoft exam. PPTP is used to create a tunnel between two points on a network over which connectivity protocols such as PPP can be used. This tunneling functionality provides the basis for creating virtual private network (VPN) connections. A VPN is a form of remote access and essentially provides an extension to the local LAN. A VPN uses a public network such as the Internet to create a point-to-point dedicated link between the remote client and the network. The function of the VPN link is to give anyone with a connection to the Internet the ability to log on to and access a remote network as if they were connected to that network locally.

To establish a PPTP session between a client and a server, a TCP connection known as a PPTP control connection is required to create and maintain the communication tunnel. This PPTP connection exists between the IP address of the client system and the IP address of the PPTP server and uses TCP/IP port 1723.

## Layer Two Tunneling Protocol

Like PPTP, the Layer Two Tunneling Protocol (L2TP) is used to create a VPN connection. L2TP is actually a combination of two technologies, PPTP and Layer 2 Forwarding (L2F) technology from Cisco. L2TP uses tunneling to provide secure data transmissions in a two-phase process. L2TP first authenticates the computer and then the user. By authenticating the computer, it prevents data from being intercepted, changed, and then forwarded to the user. This is known as a man-in-the-middle attack. L2TP uses the IPSec protocol to provide security.

 **NOTE**   Securing data communications using IPSec is covered later in this chapter.

Both of these protocols use PPP to move data between systems, however, PPTP requires that the connection be made over TCP/IP whereas L2TP supports other technologies such as x.25 networks. PPTP and L2TP can be used to encrypt data passed between two systems, but the method of encryption is different. PPTP is a Microsoft technology and uses PPP encryption. L2TP uses IPSec for encryption and for tunnel authentication.

 **EXAM TIP**   L2TP uses IPSec for encryption and is available for systems other than Microsoft. PPTP is a technology specific to Microsoft.

## General Security Considerations

As you might expect, you cannot use something like routing and remote access without there being some security implications. This chapter does not address security concerns in detail, but when planning a remote access strategy, it is a good idea to have a general idea of some of the security concerns that may arise.

 **NOTE**   A detailed discussion of network security is provided in Chapter 16.

- **Be a member of the Administrators group.**   In a Windows Server 2003 environment, you need to be a member of the Administrators group to administer RRAS. As you might expect, you also need to be a member of the Administrators group to access command-line configuration utilities such as the netsh command. With this in mind, careful consideration must be given to who is in the Administrators group.

- **Streamline the configuration.**   When it comes to installing and configuring RRAS, install only what you need. When configuring the connection, ensure that you clearly understand the configuration options. Do not enable options you are unsure of and that may inadvertently allow unwanted access to network and server.

- **Simplify the network.**   As networks grow, devices and services are often added as a stopgap solution to keep things running. Before long, the network is more complex than it needs to be. Before enabling RRAS, clean up the network and reduce the number of attack points. Strategies for streamlining the network may include

  - **Cleaning up routing**   Clean up the number of routes currently used. For example, use as few demand-dial and static routes as possible.

  - **Streamline protocols**   Use as few routing protocols as necessary. For example, if AppleTalk or IPX/SPX is not needed, ensure that it is not installed.

- **Know your protocols.**   Part of creating a secure routing and remote access strategy is understanding what the various protocols are designed to do and which ones offer the greatest level of security. For instance, if using a virtual private network (VPN) and configuring a router-to-router VPN, consider using L2TP instead of PPTP.

- **Identify network protection strategies.** One of the key strategies of securing network traffic is to simply restrict routing network traffic to the minimum level required by your network. Other strategies include using the IP filter option to identify whether a remote access client is authorized, using packet filters, and enabling firewalls on external network interfaces. Such strategies are well documented and are part of the security design of the majority of RRAS implementations.

## Working with Routing Protocols

It really does seem that the word "protocol" is overused and can make things somewhat confusing. When we are talking about routing protocols, we mean the protocols that allow routers to communicate with each other. This communication is necessary to ensure that routers keep aware of the network topology and any changes that may happen to it. There are two types of routing protocols commonly used: distance vector protocols and link state protocols.

## Distance Vector Protocols

Distance vector protocols are popular in today's network environments and have a straightforward approach to router-to-router communication. With distance vector communication, each router communicates all the routes it knows about to all of the other routers to which it is directly attached. This means that routers only communicate routing information to their router neighbors.

Because routers in a distance vector network only know about the routers to which they are directly attached, they can only actually make the connection to those routers. The communication from router to router for distance vector protocols is known as *hops*. On the network, each router constitutes one hop. For example, if there are five routers in the network, there are four hops between the first router and the last.

To keep the routing information between routers current, distance vector protocols send each other route updates. The update interval is configurable in Microsoft RRAS as well as the routers. The default in Windows Server 2003 is 30 seconds, but can be set as high as 24 hours. If any changes are detected in the routing information, the routing tables are altered to reflect the change. However, network topology changes are not that frequent, and while it is a good thing to have up-to-date routing table information, this constant update cycle increases network traffic. If a change in the routing is detected, it takes time for all of the routers to detect and accommodate the change. This process of learning routing information and changing the routing information is known as convergence.

Convergence is typically not a problem on smaller networks, but on larger networks that may use several routers, convergence can have a significant impact on the functioning of the entire network. In such a case, there are two strategies commonly used to reduce the effects of convergence:

- **Hold-down timers** Used to limit the number of changes to a given route within a period of time.

- **Triggered updates**   Triggered updates are a more proactive approach to topology updates. If a change is made to a node's routing table, an update containing the new information for the changed route is sent to all the neighboring nodes so they can be informed of the change. Triggered updates cause a flood of initial update packets that eventually calm down to correct routes much more quickly than the other methods—sort of a short-term pain for long-term gain approach.

Networks with slow convergence may suffer from routing loops. Routing loops occur when routing tables on routers are slow to update and a communication cycle is created between routers. For example, a packet arrives at Router A. Router A has an updated routing table and therefore assumes that the best route for a destination calls for Router B to be the next stop (hop). Router A sends the packet to Router B, but if this router has not been updated, it may still decide that the optimal next hop is Router A. Router B sends the packet back to Router A, and the packet continues to bounce back and forth between the two routers until Router B receives its routing update or until the packet has timed out.

When using distance vector protocols, you have two strategies you can use to prevent routing loops:

- **Split horizon**   In a split horizon configuration, routes are not advertised back to the router from which they are learned. Thus two nodes would not create loops that involve packets bouncing back and forth.

- **Split horizon with poison reverse**   With poison reverse, routes are advertised back to the router from which they are learned; however, they are done so with a hop count of infinity, which tells the node that the route is unreachable.

The most popular distance vector protocols used today are both called the Routing Information Protocol (RIP). One version of RIP is used with the IPX/SPX protocol, while another version is used with TCP/IP.

### Routing Information Protocol (RIP)

Because RIP is a distance vector protocol, routers using RIP keep their routing tables updated by communicating routing information to neighboring routers. The neighboring routers update their information and broadcast those changes to the routers nearest them. As a distance vector protocol, RIP uses hops to isolate the best route to a destination. RIP is an easily implemented routing protocol and well designed for smaller networks.

While RIP is easy to configure, it does have some drawbacks. First among them may be the fact that RIP routing announcements consume considerable bandwidth. While this may be less apparent on local LANs, the impact can be felt when the updates are occurring over slower WAN links. A second drawback of RIP lies in its scalability. RIP routing is limited to 15 hops; if the network has more than this, RIP cannot be used.

When RIP is configured, it determines the best route for data packets based on the shortest number of hops to a destination. This strategy can sometimes lead to an unexpected routing decision. For example, one destination may only be two hops away, but the link between the source and destination may be particularly slow. In such cases, the route with a larger hop count may even be faster. To prevent this, you can assign a higher hop count to the slower link and then it will be ignored in preference for the faster link. Naturally, if the faster link should ever fail, the slower one will still be chosen as a backup route.

There are two versions of IP RIP available, appropriately named version 1 and version 2. When implementing RIP, it is advised to use RIP 2 wherever possible as it offers some significant improvements such as multicast and password authentication. RIP v1 and RIP v2 can be combined in the same network, and network routers that support RIP v2 can communicate using both RIP v1 and v2 broadcasts and accept announcements from both versions.

---

 **EXAM TIP** IP RIP is commonly used in environments where there are frequent changes to the routing table, where there are no more than 14 hops between routers, and when using a demand-dial interface.

---

## Link State Protocols

Link state protocols take a different approach than their RIP counterparts. The link state protocol builds a map of the entire network and holds this map into memory. When a link state protocol is used, routers send out link state advertisements (LSAs) that contain network information. These LSAs are sent to every other router on the network and this information is used to create their network maps.

In a link state network, route information updates are completed like that of the distance vector networks, but they are performed less frequently. Infrequent updates and the fact that routers maintain a map of the entire network make convergence less a problem than that of distance vector. This advantage comes with a price. Link state protocols place a higher demand on resources and require additional RAM and more powerful hardware.

The most common link state protocol in use today is the Open Shortest Path First (OSPF) protocol.

**Open Shortest Path First (OSPF)**   Where RIP is built to work easily in smaller networks, the OSPF routing protocol is designed large or very large networks. Unlike IP RIP, OSPF requires that routers maintain a map of the entire network using a link state database. Network changes are reflected in the database, and when updates are made, only changes are synchronized between routers. When changes are made, the information of the change is flooded across the network to ensure that each router on the network is synchronized and has the most recent updated information. Although it is an efficient routing protocol, OSPF is more difficult to configure and manage than RIP.

To determine the path a data packet should take, OSPF uses a shortest path first algorithm; this algorithm is responsible for finding the shortest path between the source and the destination. Because routers maintain a map of the entire network, routing loops are not a problem.

As networks grow, the size of the link state database increases and router performance declines. To combat this, OSPF subdivides the network into smaller sections, called areas (collections of contiguous networks). Areas are then connected to each other through a backbone, with each router only responsible for the link state database for those areas connected to the router. Area border routers (ABRs) connect one area to another.

At the end of the day, whether a network will use RIP or OSPF is dependant upon the network environment and the size of that network. The following provides a summary of the two routing protocols:

- **Hop count limitation**   RIP has a limit of 15 hops; beyond 15, the host is considered unreachable. With OSPF, there is no limitation on the hop count.

- **Convergence**   RIP converges more slowly than OSPF. This is because routing changes with OSPF are propagated through routers instantaneously and not periodically.

- **Path determination**   RIP has no concept of network delays and link costs. Routing decisions are based on hop counts. Even if the destination is on a lower hop count but a slower link, it will be chosen.

- **Network design**   OSPF allows for a logical definition of networks where routers can be divided into areas. This is designed to limit the link state updates over the whole network. RIP has no concept of network areas or boundaries.

- **Routing loops**   Because RIP only sees the direct router neighbor, routing loops can occur. OSPF maintains a complete map of the network eliminating routing loops.

## Planning Routing for IP Multicast Traffic

In traditional IP communication, there were two choices, unicast and broadcast transmissions. Unicast transmissions are designed to transmit a packet to a single destination, whereas broadcast transmissions are used to send a datagram to an entire subnetwork. What we need is a communication method that falls between these two, and that is where multicast transmissions come into play. Multicast transmissions are designed to enable the delivery of datagrams to a set of hosts that have been configured as members of a multicast group in various scattered subnetworks. Basically, this increases the scope of unicast transmissions while at the same time compensating for the randomness of broadcast transmissions.

 **NOTE**   Packets delivered to group members are identified by a single multicast group address. Multicast packets are delivered to a group using best-effort reliability, just like IP unicast packets.

While multicasting can be a great addition to any network, if you are planning on using multicast traffic on the network, the network must support it. This means that computer systems and routers must be multicast-capable.

All of the Windows Server 2003 products are multicast-capable, allowing them to both send and receive multicast packets. If specific applications want to use multicast communication, they must construct IP packets with the appropriate IP multicast address as the destination IP address. Applications wanting to receive multicast traffic must make TCP/IP aware that they are listening for all traffic to a specified IP multicast address.

> **NOTE** The Internet Group Management Protocol (IGMP) is used by IP systems to announce their interest in receiving IP multicast traffic from IP routers.

As far as routers are concerned, they must be able to receive multicast traffic from nodes and forward multicast traffic to nodes listening for multicast communication. Before deciding on whether or not to use multicast communication on the network, ensure that both the nodes and the routers can support it.

# Planning Security for Remote Access Users

Opening up your network to remote users can be an uncertain endeavor. While most users are harmless, you never know if there is a malicious user who wants to gain access to your server through the remote access door you have opened. To combat this, part of planning for allowing remote access is to establish a security strategy to help ensure that only those whom you want to access your system are indeed doing so.

## Remote Access Policies

One of the tasks assigned to the system administrator is to establish remote access policies that help enforce when remote users can access the network and what they can do once they are in. The remote access policies you configure will be made up of a number of connection parameters that a remote user must meet before access to the network is granted. According to Microsoft, there are three distinct elements to creating a remote access policy: defining conditions, setting remote access permissions, and configuring the profile. We will look at each of these components individually followed by a step-by-step procedure for creating a remote access policy.

## Defining Conditions

Conditions for remote access policies refer to certain attributes that must be met before the remote user can log on. If there are multiple conditions, all of these must match the settings of the connection attempt in order for it to match the policy. There are numerous attributes that can be used to create remote access conditions. Table 14-1 highlights these conditions.

> **NOTE** In this section, we will create a remote policy and select attributes from this table to include in the policy.

| Condition | Description |
|---|---|
| Authentication Type | The type of authentication that will be used. The specific authentication types will be discussed later in this chapter. |
| Called Station Identification | The phone number of the network access server. |
| Calling Station Identification | The phone number used by the caller. |
| Client Friendly Name | The name of the RADIUS client that is requesting authentication. |
| Client IP Address | The IP address of the RADIUS client. |
| Day and Time Restrictions | The time of day or the day of the week of the connection attempt. |
| Framed Protocol | Protocols operate differently; this attribute specifies the type of framing for incoming packets. |
| Network Access Server Identifier/ IP Address | The name or the IP address of the network access server. |
| Network Access Server Port Type | The media that will be used by the client to access the server, such as ISDN or Ethernet. |
| Tunnel Type | The type of tunnel that will be used by the client, such as L2TP or PPTP. |
| Windows Groups | The groups to which the user attempting the connection belongs. |

**Table 14-1**   Creating Remote Access Conditions

## Setting Remote Access Permissions

As mentioned previously, remote users have to meet certain conditions as determined by the remote policy. When these conditions are met, you have two choices, grant remote access permission or deny remote access permissions. As we work our way through the creation of a remote access policy in the next section, this will become clear. For example, if you added an attribute of MC-CHAP v2 to your remote access conditions, you can choose to deny or grant access to those remote users using MS-CHAP v2. In the world of wizards and advanced options, it is nice sometimes to just have two choices.

## Configuring the Profile

The term "profile" in this context can be a bit misleading, but it refers to a group of settings that can be applied to a connection upon authorization. As shown in the next section on creating a remote access policy, the profile is created as you work your way through the New Remote Access Policy Wizard. From the Edit Dial-in Profile dialog box, you have six configurable tabs to modify the profile:

- Dial-in Constraints
- IP
- Multilink

## RADIUS

When reading about routing and remote access, you are sure to read references to something called RADIUS. The Remote Authentication Dial-In User Service (RADIUS) is a standard protocol used to centralize the authentication of dial-in users. When configuring remote access policies for a network, it is possible to have numerous policies each located on different RRAS servers throughout the network. As administrator, you may find yourself having to configure the same remote access policy on each RRAS server, a task that can quickly become cumbersome.

RADIUS functions in a client/server system. The remote access user connects to the RRAS server as usual. However, this server acts as a RADIUS client and instead of checking for local policy files, the system will pass the request to a RAIDUS server. The RADIUS server provides all authentication, authorization, and auditing functions. The RADIUS server then passes the information to the RADIUS client, which is a remote access server running the RADIUS client software. The connection request is either accepted or rejected depending on the information received. Several RRAS servers acting as RADIUS clients all use the same RADIUS server, which enables centralized management of remote access.

- Authentication
- Encryption
- Advanced

**Dial-in Constraints**   While dial-in constraints are not new in Windows Server 2003, they are an important consideration for a remote access policy and therefore likely to appear on the exam. If you have had experience configuring remote policies for Windows Server 2000, you will no doubt recognize the familiar options.

Shown in Figure 14-1, the Dial-in Constraints tab provides many options for configuring dial in procedures. These include

- **Minutes server can remain idle before it is disconnected**   The parameter configures how long the connection will remain active when there is no activity.

- **Minutes client can be connected**   This field specifies the maximum amount of time that the user can stay connected.

- **Allow access only on these days and at these times**   This field specifies the days of the week and hours of each day that a connection is allowed.

- **Allow access only to this number**   This parameter specifies a specific phone number that the user must call to gain access to the network. Any other numbers than those specified will be rejected.

**Figure 14-1**
The Dial-in Constraints tab is used to configure dial-in procedures.

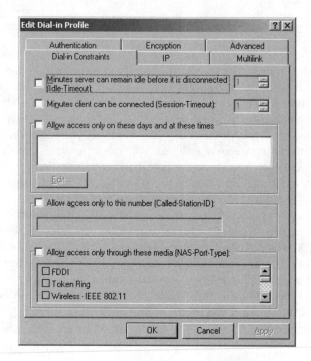

- **Allow access only through these media** This parameter allows the system administrator to choose the media that will be accepted to make the connection.

**IP** The IP tab is used to establish the IP address assignment behavior. The IP tab is also used to configure IP packet filters, a feature used with the Routing and Remote Access Service. Figure 14-2 shows the IP tab of the Edit Dial-in Profile dialog box, which includes these options:

- **Server must supply an IP address** IP assignment is managed by the server.
- **Client may request an IP address** This allows client systems to request and IP address.
- **Server settings determine IP address assignment** IP address assignment is determined by the access server (this is the default setting).
- **Assign a static IP address** A static IP address assigned to the user account overrides this setting. The IP address assigned is typically used to accommodate vendor-specific attributes for IP addresses.

**Multilink** Multilink allows you to aggregate multiple physical links. An example of a multilink connection is when B channels of a Basic Rate Interface (BRI) connection are combined. You can use a multilink connection for any ISDN adapter, but the multilink connection must be supported on both sides of the connection. While the multilink feature allows you to combine physical links, it does not dynamically maintain those links.

**Figure 14-2**
The IP tab is used to set the IP configuration for remote access.

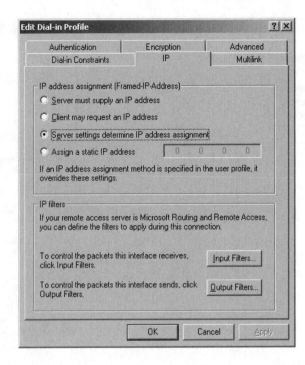

In other words, it does not allow for changes in the physical bandwidth conditions such as adding or removing links. The Bandwidth Allocation Protocol (BAP) makes up for this shortcoming by allowing the dynamic management of links.

The Multilink tab is used to set multilink properties that both enable multilink and determine the maximum number of ports that a multilink connection can use. The options include

- **Server settings determine multilink usage**  This option ensures that the multilink settings will be determined by the server.

- **Do not allow multilink connections**  This option prevents the use of multilink connections.

- **Allow multilink connections**  This option allows the use of multilink connections.

- **Maximum number of ports allowed**  This option specifies the number of ports that can be used.

The bottom of the Multilink tab allows you to configure the BAP policies that both determine BAP usage and specify when extra BAP lines are dropped.

**Authentication**   As you might expect, the Authentication tab is used to set the type of authentication that will be allowed to make the connection. As shown in Figure 14-3, there are many configurable options for authentication. By default, the Microsoft

**Figure 14-3**
The Authentication tab is used to set the remote authentication configuration.

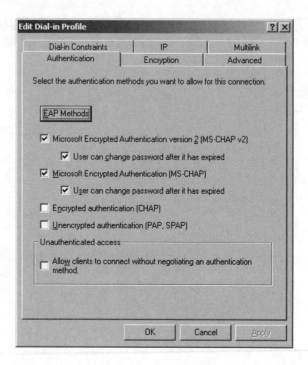

Challenge Handshake Authentication Protocol (MS-CHAP) and Microsoft Challenge Handshake Authentication Protocol version 2 (MS-CHAP v2) are enabled. Also, the setting to allow users to change their password after it has expired is set. Changing from these default options is as simple as selecting a different check box. For most environments, these default settings should be fine.

**Encryption**    Continuing in the tradition of well-named tabs, the Encryption tab is used to configure the encryption used with remote access. There are four options from which you can choose, Basic, Strong, Strongest, and No Encryption. In most environments, some level of encryption is required. A detailed discussion in provided later in this chapter.

**Advanced**    The Advanced tab is used to configure RADIUS attributes that are sent back by the IAS server to be evaluated by the RADIUS client.

 **EXAM TIP**    For the exam, make sure you are comfortable with the process of planning and implementing a remote access policy.

## Creating a Remote Access Policy

It is likely that the default remote policies will not be sufficient and as system administrator you will be tasked with creating and modifying remote access policies. With

Windows Server 2003, this is straightforward, just a matter of finding the right wizard. The following is the procedure to add remote access policies:

1. Open the Routing and Remote Access MMC snap-in from the Administrative Tools.

2. Expand the routing and remote access server where you'll create the policy, right-click Remote Access Policies, and choose New Remote Access Policy.

3. The New Remote Access Policy Wizard window opens. Click Next, and you will be asked to enter a name for the policy. Your other option on this screen is to decide whether to set up a custom policy or one that is based on Microsoft suggestions. In this example, we'll create a custom policy. Click Next.

4. The Policy Conditions screen lets you add conditions for remote users to successfully make the connection. Click Add to add an attribute. Figure 14-4 shows the Select Attribute screen.

5. Select the attribute you want to add to the policy and click Add. In this exercise, we added Authentication Types, as shown in Figure 14-5.

6. Click Next. The Permissions screen of the wizard is displayed. Here's where you set the behavior of the policy. You have two choices. If the conditions of the policy are met, you can either grant access or deny access.

7. Click Next, and the Edit Dial-in Profile screen appears. You can restrict a number of connection parameters.

8. Click OK to return to the User Profile screen, and then click Finish to complete the creation of the policy.

To view the remote policies currently established for a server, click Start | All Programs | Administrative Tools | Routing and Remote Access Server. With the Routing and

**Figure 14-4**

To create a custom remote policy, attributes are added to the policy.

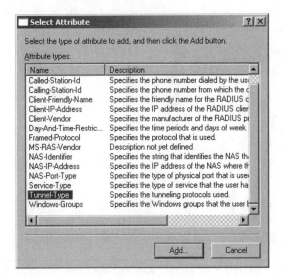

**Figure 14-5**
Once the
attribute is added
it is shown in the
Policy Conditions
screen.

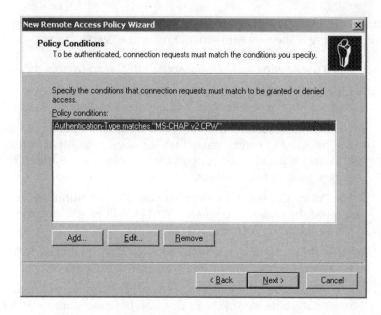

Remote Access window open, double-click the Remote Access Policy icon in the left hand pane to display the policies currently in place. Figure 14-6 shows the Routing and Remote Access window and the default policies.

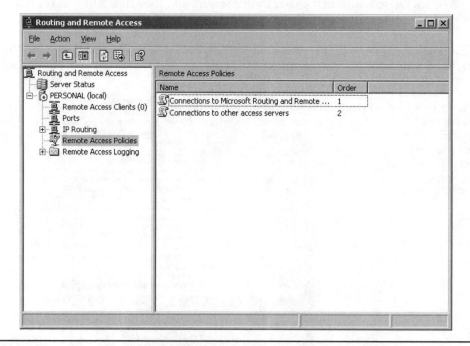

**Figure 14-6**    Remote policies are configured to control access to the network.

# Analyzing Protocol Security Requirements

Talking about all of the security features available in Windows Server 2003 is one thing; deciding which ones are needed for a particular organization is quite another. When it comes to implementing protocol security, the obvious assumption is that it is always going to be part of a security strategy. Most of the time it is, but not always.

When we are talking about protocol security in Windows Server 2003, we are talking about IP Layer Security (IPSec). IPSec is well suited for network traffic transmissions, right down to the IP layer, in fact. Its ability to provide secure transfer is not in question. The trick is finding the middle ground between making information available to users and protecting an organization's sensitive data.

In the Microsoft world, finding the balance for protocol security involves many factors, including

- **Analyzing the risk**   This is the first step in determining the security level used. Some environments are at greater risk than others for intrusion. For example, a childcare agency is less likely to be a target than a government agency. That is not to say that someone wouldn't want to access the childcare agency, just that it is less likely. The security measures can be adjusted accordingly.

- **Assessing information value**   The data transferred over the network in some organizations is extremely valuable, both in monetary and privacy terms. If the information used in an organization has an external value, the risk is higher and communication security must be higher as well. Security measures have to be implemented to protect the information.

- **Security compatibility**   As a network grows, additional services are added along the way. When a network is first built, it is unlikely that the same level of security measures were needed or even available with earlier operating system versions. When deciding on a security strategy, ensure that it fits within the organization's current framework.

- **System use**   One other factor that can greatly influence how protocol security will be implemented is the way in which the system will be used. A domain controller, for example, may require a higher level of security than a web server or a print server.

As you can see from the above points, the rules for security deployment are not set in stone. There is a vagueness to them that can be difficult to work with. They can vary widely, depending on an organization's policies and infrastructures.

While there are no set rules, Microsoft provides some very general guidelines to consider for IPSec deployment:

- **Minimal (basic) security**   Use a minimal approach to security if the organization does not exchange any sensitive data. Determining what is and is not sensitive data can be tricky—what isn't valuable to one person may be to another. When configuring a system with a minimal security, IPSec is not active.

- **Standard security** When computers may contain valuable data, they need to be secured. Herein lies the balance: they must provide enough security to prevent unwanted access, but not so much that they become a hindrance to users trying to perform their tasks.

**NOTE** Windows Server 2003 provides default IPSec policies that secure data, but do not necessarily require the highest level of security: Client (Respond Only) and Server (Request Security).

- **High security** Those organizations that maintain very sensitive data, such as banks or government agencies, will typically implement very secure IPSec policies. Protection overrides all other considerations, such as the impact on network users.

## Authentication for Remote Access Clients

One of the most important decisions you need to make when designing a remote access strategy is the method by which remote users will be authenticated. Authentication simply refers to the way in which the client and server will negotiate on a user's credentials when the user is trying to gain access to the network. Windows Server 2003 supports a number of different authentication methods, each offering a different level of security. Which one is used by an organization will depend on security policies. The authentication methods for Windows Server 2003 are the following:

- **Microsoft Challenge Handshake Authentication Protocol (MS-CHAP v2)** The second version of MS-CHAP brings with it enhancements over its predecessor, MS-CHAP. These enhancements include support for two-way authentication and introduced a few changes in which the cryptographic key is analyzed. As far as authentication methods are concerned, MS-CHAP v2 is the most secure. MS-CHAP v2 works with PPP, PPTP, and L2TP network connections.

- **Microsoft Challenge Handshake Protocol (MS-CHAP)** MS-CHAP is used to authenticate remote Windows workstations, providing the functionality to which LAN-based users are accustomed while integrating the hashing algorithms used on Windows networks. MS-CHAP works with PPP, PPTP, and L2TP network Connections. Ms-Chap Uses A Challenge/Response Mechanism To Keep The Password from being sent during the authentication process. MS-CHAP uses the Message Digest 4 (MD4) hashing algorithm and the Data Encryption Standard (DES) encryption algorithm to generate the challenge and response, and provides mechanisms for reporting connection errors and for changing the user's password.

- **Extensible Authentication Protocol (EAP)** EAP is an extension of the Point-to-Point Protocol (PPP), which supports authentication methods that go beyond the simple submission of a user name and password. EAP was developed in response to an increasing demand for authentication methods that use other types of security devices such as token cards, smart cards, and digital certificates.

- **Challenge Handshake Authentication Protocol (CHAP)**   CHAP is a widely supported authentication method and works much the same way as MS-CHAP. A key difference between the two is that CHAP supports non-Microsoft remote access clients. CHAP allows for authentication without actually having the user send his password over the network, and because it's an industry standard, it allows Windows Server 2003 to behave as a remote client of almost any third-party PPP server.

- **Shiva Password Authentication Protocol (SPAP)**   SPAP is supported for the sole purpose of allowing Shiva remote access clients to connect to Windows Server 2003 RAS computers and to also allow the reverse. SPAP uses a simple encrypted password authentication protocol where the remote access client sends an encrypted password to the remote access server. Using a two-way encryption algorithm, the remote access server decrypts the password and uses the plaintext form to authenticate the remote access client.

- **Password Authentication Protocol (PAP)**   Use only if necessary. Password Authentication Protocol (PAP) is a simple authentication protocol in which the user name and password are sent to the remote access server in unencrypted text, making it possible for anyone listening to network traffic to steal both. PAP is typically only used when connecting to older Unix-based remote access servers that do not support any additional authentication protocols.

- **Unauthenticated Access**   Users are allowed to log on without authentication.

Choosing the correct authentication protocol for remote clients is an important part of designing a remote access strategy. Remember, once authenticated, those users have access to the network and servers, so choose wisely. In most instances, you would start with the most secure, MS-CHAP v2, and work your way down the list.

**NOTE**   Windows NT 4 does not support MS-CHAP v2.

**EXAM TIP**   Before taking the exam, make sure you are aware of the different remote access authentication methods and where and when they may be used.

**NOTE**   If you set up the properties of a remote connection to use a secure password, and you connect to a server that only supports PAP (Unix), Windows Server 2003's remote access client will terminate the connection.

## Configure Routing and Remote Access User Authentication

Once you have decided on the authentication method to use for clients, implementing client authentication is actually a straightforward process. Here are the steps necessary to enable the protocols just discussed:

1. Select Start | All Programs | Administrative Tools, and select the Routing and Remote Access MMC icon to open the Routing and Remote Access window.

2. With the Routing and Remote Access window open, ensure that the Routing and Remote Access Service is started. To do this, right-click the computer you want to start the service and select the Configure And Enable Remote Access option from the menu.

3. Once the Routing and Remote Access Service is started, a green arrow icon will appear on the system on which the service is running. Right-click this system and select Properties to open the Personal (Local) Properties dialog box, as shown in Figure 14-7.

4. From the Personal (Local) Properties dialog box, select the Authentication Methods button to open the Authentication Methods dialog box as shown in Figure 14-8. Click the type of authentication method desired for remote client access.

**Figure 14-7**
The Personal (Local) Properties box is used to establish the remote client connection options.

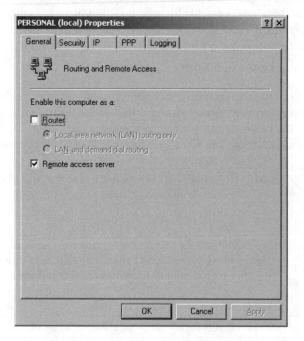

**Figure 14-8**
Choosing the remote access authentication method to be used for allowing remote access

# Securing Access Between Private Networks Using IPSec

Securing access between private networks is a significant concern for system administrators. One of the tools you can use to provide this security is configuring IPSec.

## Creating an IPSec Policy

Earlier in this chapter, we took a look at IPSec and under what circumstances it is used. The following steps outline the procedure for creating an IPSec policy:

1. To install the IP Security Policy Management snap-in, choose Start | Run and type **mmc** in the Run box to open the console.

2. With the console open, select File | Add/Remove Snap-in to open the Add/Remove dialog box. Click Add to open the Add Standalone dialog box.

3. Click the IP Security Policy Management icon and click Add.

4. Select the computer for which you want to manage IPSec policies. Click Finish to have IP Security Policy Management added to your console.

Now that the IP Management tool is installed, you can create an IPSec policy using the following procedures:

1. Right-click the IP Securities Policy icon on the left side of the console screen and choose Create IP Security Policy from the menu. This will start the IP Security Policy Wizard.

2. On the first screen of the wizard, you will be required to enter a name for the IPSec policy. Once done, click Next to open the Requests For Secure Communications screen. This screen is simply used to select or deselect the option to Activate The Default Response Rule. A default rule is simply used to respond to security requests when no other rule is assigned.

3. Clicking Next will take you to the Default Response Rule Authentication Method screen. This screen is straightforward; it allows you to set the initial authentication method that will be used. By default, Kerberos v5 is used.

4. Click Next to complete the creation of the IPSec policy. The new policy will be added to the console's main window.

 **NOTE** This chapter deals exclusively with the creation of the IPSec policy. Refer to Chapter 16 for information on editing and configuring an existing IPSec policy.

## IPSec Data Encryption

You are no doubt curious about the specific data encryption methods that are supported by IPSec. For those of you who cannot wait to see them in Chapter 16, here is a brief overview of IPSec data encryption.

- **Data Encryption Standard (DES) (40-bit)**   This encryption method provides the best performance, but at a cost, as the encryption security is lower. Can be used in environments where data security is a little lower.

- **Data Encryption Standard (56-bit)**   Through your IPSec policies, you can implement DES as the encryption method. The DES algorithm is a 56-bit encryption key. This algorithm was published in 1977 by the U.S. National Bureau of Standards, and allows for the ability to frequently regenerate keys during a communication. This prevents the entire data set from being compromised if one DES key is broken. However, it is considered outdated for business use, and should only be used for legacy application support. Specialized hardware has been able to crack the standard 56-bit key.

- **Triple DES (3DES)**   IPSec policies also allow the choice of a strong encryption algorithm, 3DES, which provides stronger encryption than DES for higher security. 3DES uses a 56-bit encryption key as well, but, as the name implies, uses three of them. As a result, 3DES is considered 168-bit encryption and is used in high security environments like the U.S. government. All computers to which the policy is assigned will receive this policy.

**NOTE** If you choose not to create a custom IPSec policy, you need to be aware of the default one used by the system. Microsoft stresses that this default policy is just a guideline and should be modified to suit the individual needs of an organization.

# Troubleshooting TCP/IP Routing

You can't really have a chapter on routing without a section on troubleshooting remote connections. After all, system administrators working with remote access will certainly find themselves troubleshooting the connections at some point.

When troubleshooting TCP/IP, it is often necessary to view, test, and configure the TCP/IP configuration of the system. For that reason, a complete suite of tools is supplied with Windows Server 2003. Table 14-2 lists some of the tools commonly used in TCP/IP troubleshooting on Server 2003 and their purpose.

**EXAM TIP** While reviewing for the exam, we strongly recommend that you take the time to try each of the commands discussed in this section. Pay close attention to how the output from each command is displayed and the command's available options.

The commands in Table 14-2 give you an idea of what tools are available. Now let's look at how some of these are used in the troubleshooting process.

## ping

Of all the tools discussed here, ping is perhaps the most used and the most useful. ping allows you to test the connectivity between two devices on the network. When the

| Table 14-2 | Utility | Purpose |
|---|---|---|
| Troubleshooting Utilities | arp | Shows the Address Resolution Protocol table for the local system |
| | hostname | Displays the host name for the local system |
| | ipconfig | Displays the local TCP/IP configuration |
| | nbtstat | Provides information about NetBIOS over TCP/IP connections |
| | netstat | Provides statistical information and connection status for TCP/IP protocols |
| | pathping | A route tracing tool that combines features of the ping and tracert commands with additional statistical information that neither of those commands provides |
| | ping | Used to test connectivity between two devices on the network |
| | route | Displays a copy of the local routing table for the system and provides the ability to modify the local routing table |
| | tracert | Tracks and displays the entire route between two systems |
| | netsh | Allows you to configure a computer's network configuration remotely or locally |

command is issued, special packets called "echo" packets are generated and sent to the remote host. If the remote host is able to respond to the packets, it returns each of them and the ping utility on the system that generated the query displays the amount of time, in milliseconds, that it took to complete the round trip. You can see an example of the output from a successful ping command in Figure 14-9.

As you would expect, the ping command is not always successful, in which case you can use the utility to locate the problem. It should be pointed out that if you are having a problem, ping does not help you determine *what* the problem is, though it does help you determine *where* the problem lies.

## Troubleshooting with ping

When using ping to locate a communication problem, there is a specific order in which to proceed. The following numbered steps define the process normally taken, but it is possible to skip straight to the last step and then, if that doesn't work, work your way back to determine the location of the problem.

1. Ping the address of the local loopback. The local loopback is a special function built into the TCP/IP protocol stack, which allows it to be tested. You can use any valid address in IP address range of 127.0.0.1–127.254.254.254 in your test, though 127.0.0.1 is most commonly used. If the ping of the local loopback is successful, it indicates that the TCP/IP protocol is loaded correctly and bound to the network interface properly. What it does not test is the physical connectivity of the system, as the loopback is a software function.

2. Ping the IP address of the computer you are testing.

3. Ping the IP address of the default gateway. As well as testing that the TCP/IP configuration of your system is valid, this also tests the physical connectivity.

4. The last step is to ping a host on a remote network.

**Figure 14-9**

The output from a successful ping command

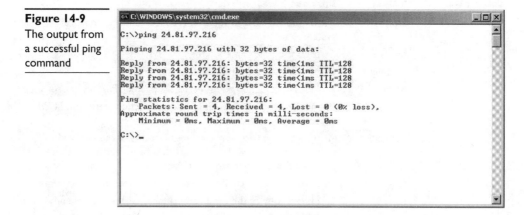

```
C:\>ping 24.81.97.216

Pinging 24.81.97.216 with 32 bytes of data:

Reply from 24.81.97.216: bytes=32 time<1ms TTL=128
Reply from 24.81.97.216: bytes=32 time<1ms TTL=128
Reply from 24.81.97.216: bytes=32 time<1ms TTL=128
Reply from 24.81.97.216: bytes=32 time<1ms TTL=128

Ping statistics for 24.81.97.216:
    Packets: Sent = 4, Received = 4, Lost = 0 (0% loss),
Approximate round trip times in milli-seconds:
    Minimum = 0ms, Maximum = 0ms, Average = 0ms

C:\>_
```

## tracert

When you are unable to access a remote host, one tool that can assist in determining where the problem is the tracert command. The function of tracert is to trace the path to the destination IP address and record the results. The tracert display shows the succession of IP routers used in the delivery of packets and how long the process took. Figure 14-10 shows the output of a tracert command.

As far as troubleshooting with tracert is concerned, as the path to the destination IP address is traced, the command will display the last router that successfully forwarded the data packets. Such information is helpful in pinpointing where the communication failure is.

Some of the common options used with tracert are displayed in Table 14-3.

## pathping

The pathping utility provides the middle ground between the ping utility and tracert. Like tracert, pathping is used to trace the route an IP packet along its destination. Unlike tracert however, pathping sends packets to each router over a period of time, and then computes results based on the packets returned from each hop. pathping makes it possible to determine where a routing problem lies as it shows the degree of packet loss at any given router or link. Figure 14-11 shows the results of a pathping command.

As with many of the other commands, the pathping utility has numerous options available. Table 14-4 shows some of the pathping options and their descriptions.

## route

The route command is a commonly used utility designed to display and modify the entries in the local IP routing table. As shown in Figure 14-12, issuing the command route print will provide a snapshot of the routing table of the local system.

| Figure 14-10 | |
|---|---|
| The tracert command is used to trace the path to the destination IP address. | |

```
C:\>tracert microsoft.com

Tracing route to microsoft.com [207.46.134.155]
over a maximum of 30 hops:

  1    23 ms    24 ms    23 ms  24.81.97.1
  2    24 ms    23 ms    25 ms  rd1ht-ge3-0.ok.shawcable.net [64.59.170.2]
  3    55 ms   215 ms    35 ms  rc1wh-atm0-2-2.vc.shawcable.net [66.163.76.233]

  4    35 ms    35 ms    35 ms  rc1wt-pos2-0.wa.shawcable.net [66.163.76.110]
  5    39 ms    35 ms    35 ms  rx0wt-microsoft.wa.shawcable.net [66.163.68.18]

  6    34 ms    35 ms    35 ms  pos0-0.core1.sea1.us.msn.net [207.46.33.13]
  7    39 ms    35 ms    35 ms  207.46.36.210
  8    49 ms    47 ms    48 ms  207.46.155.17
  9     *         *         *    Request timed out.
 10     *         *         *    Request timed out.
 11     *         *         *    Request timed out.
 12     *         *         *    Request timed out.
 13     *         *         *    Request timed out.
 14     *         *         *    Request timed out.
 15     *         *         *    Request timed out.
 16     *         *         *    Request timed out.
 17     *         *         *    Request timed out.
```

| | Option | Description |
|---|---|---|
| **Table 14-3**<br>Options Used<br>to Customize<br>tracert Packets | -h | Determines the maximum number of hops used by tracert packets to reach the destination. |
| | -w | Specifies a time-out interval for the tracert packets. The default is 4000 milliseconds. |
| | -4 | Identifies trace as an IPv4 trace. |
| | -6 | Identifies trace as an IPv6 trace. |
| | -d | tracert does not try to resolve the names of the routers in the path. |

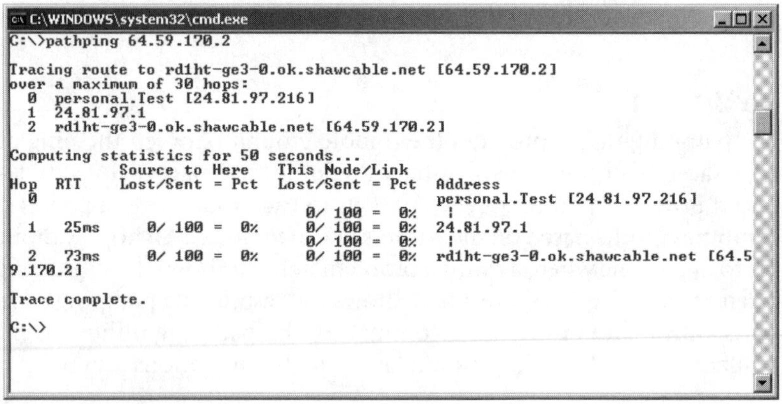

**Figure 14-11**
The pathping utility is used to trace an IP packet toward its final destination.

| | Option | Description |
|---|---|---|
| **Table 14-4**<br>Options Used<br>to Customize<br>the pathping<br>Command | -h | Similar to the tracert option, identifies the maximum number of hops to search for target. |
| | -p | Specifies the time to wait between pings |
| | -n | Informs the pathping to not resolve addresses to host names. |
| | -w | Specifies the time to wait for each reply (measured in milliseconds). |

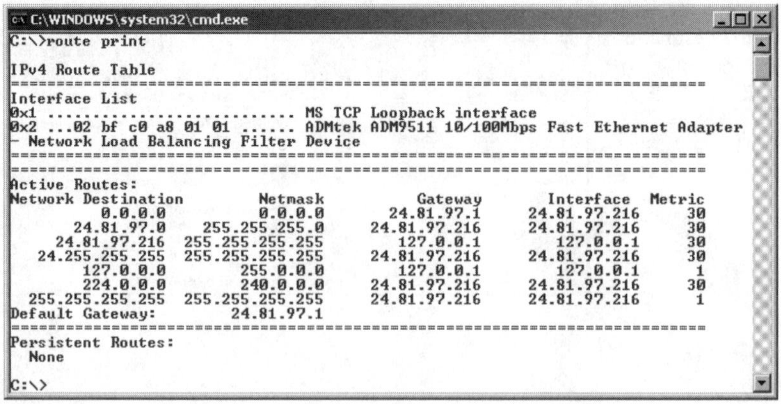

**Figure 14-12**
The route command is used to both display and modify the local routing table.

| Table 14-5 | Option | Description |
|---|---|---|
| The route Command Options | add | Adds a route to the local routing table. Added routes are temporary unless used in conjunction with the -p option to make the route persistent. |
| | change | Modifies an existing route. |
| | delete | Deletes a single route or multiple routing entries. |
| | print | Shows a display of the current routing information. |

In addition to providing a look at the current routing table, the route command can be used during troubleshooting to add routes to the system or remove routes that may be causing problems. The options to view and modify the local routing table using the route command are shown in Table 14-5.

# Chapter Review

In this chapter, we have taken a whirlwind journey through the world of Windows Server 2003 Routing and Remote Access Service. Along the way, we have reviewed routing protocols and outlined the advantages and disadvantages of distance vector routing protocols such as RIP and link state protocols such as OSPF.

We identified some of the considerations for implementing a routing and remote access strategy, such as highlighting some general security concerns, planning multicast traffic support, developing remote access policies, analyzing protocol security requirements, and understanding remote access authentication methods.

Finally, we concluded by reviewing some of the common utilities used to troubleshoot TCP/IP routing. These tools include ping, tracert, pathping, and route.

## Questions

1. You are designing a PPTP connection between an office in Vancouver and one in Chicago. You have been asked to implement the strongest possible level of encryption for the connection. Which of the following would you select?

   A. PAP

   B. ESP

   C. MS-CHAP

   D. MS-CHAP v2

2. You are the administrator for a company that has a central corporate office and a remote sales office. You have been asked to provide a tunneling technology to connect the offices and the connection should be secured using IPSec. Which of the following strategies could you employ?

   A. Use L2TP to create dial-in remote access between the two office sites.

   B. Use PPTP to create dial-in remote access between the two office sites.

    C. Use L2TP to create a VPN connection between the two office sites.

    D. Use PPTP to create a VPN connection between the two office sites.

3. Which of the following commands can be issued to show the current routing table information?

    A. route display

    B. route print

    C. pathping -route

    D. pathping -display

4. You are configuring a server that will become the network's access server. The server will be used to enable clients to dial into the corporate network. The remote clients use a variety of operating systems, including Mac OS X, Windows XP/ 2000, and Unix variants. You are configuring the security for the remote connection and want to use the most secure protocol. Which of the following should you choose?

    A. MS-CHAP v2

    B. MS-CHAP

    C. PAP

    D. CHAP

5. You are troubleshooting remote access connections to a network. Several users report that sometimes they have no trouble gaining access to the network while other times access is denied. After some research, you determine that the problem likely lies with the servers and that remote access policies are different on some of the RRAS servers and some policies are out of date. Which of the following can you do to ensure that policies remain current and users are consistently allowed, or denied, remote access?

    A. Configure a single RADIUS server and place the remote policies on it.

    B. Configure the Automatic Remote Policy Wizard to replicate remote policy changes to all RRAS servers.

    C. Configure the modem properties to forward incoming remote requests to a single server that stores all remote access policies.

    D. Use the remote policy replication utility (RPU) to schedule policy updates.

6. Which of the following technologies uses a link state database?

    A. RIP v2

    B. OSFP

    C. PPTP

    D. L2TP

7. Routers using RIP keep their routing tables updated by communicating routing information to neighboring routers. How many hops is RIP routing limited to?

   A. 255

   B. 15

   C. 6

   D. 1

8. You are the network administrator for a large network and are involved in designing a routing solution for the network. You want to implement a solution in which routing loops are unlikely to occur. Which of the following routing protocols would you implement to accomplish this?

   A. OSPF

   B. RIP

   C. PPTP

   D. L2TP

9. You have been asked to assist in configuring access from remote laptop users who use smart card readers. Part of the process requires that you select the correct authentication protocol to support the smart card readers. Which of the following would you choose?

   A. CHAP

   B. SPAP

   C. EAP

   D. MS-CHAP v2

10. You are the administrator of a small network and have been assigned the task of designing the network's routing strategy. Which of the following routing protocols would be best suited for the network routers and would require the least amount of administrative effort?

    A. OSPF v2

    B. RIP v2

    C. OSPF

    D. NTP

## Answers

1. **D.** MS-CHAP v2 is the most secure encryption method to use for the PPTP connection.

2. **C.** L2TP is used to create a VPN between two points. L2TP provides security for the data transmissions using IPSec.

3. **B.** Issuing the route print command will show a display of the current routing information. This is often used in the troubleshooting process to verify the routing information for a system.

4. **D.** Because you have to support clients that are using other protocols, CHAP is the best answer.

5. **A.** The Remote Authentication Dial-In User Service (RADIUS) is a standard protocol used to centralize the authentication of dial-in users. All remote requests will be authenticated from the central RADIUS server.

6. **B.** OSPF requires that routers maintain a map of the entire network using a link state database. Network changes are reflected in the database and when updates are made, only changes are synchronized between routers.

7. **B.** RIP routing is limited to 15 hops. If the network has more than this, RIP cannot be used.

8. **A.** Because RIP only sees the direct router neighbor, routing loops can occur. OSPF maintains a complete map of the network, eliminating routing loops.

9. **C.** Whenever you need to work with smart cards, or see a reference to smart card authentication on the exam, remember that smart card authentication is not a standard form of authentication. The authentication required is incorporated into extensions to PPP and requires the extensible authentication protocol.

10. **B.** The best choice in this case would be to use the Routing Information Protocol version 2. RIP v2 is a dynamic routing protocol that is easy to configure and administer, making it well suited for smaller networks.

# Maintaining Server Availability

In this chapter, you will learn how to

- Work with cluster services
- Manage cluster services
- Work with server load balancing
- Manage Network Load Balancing using wlbs/nlb and NLB Manager
- Identify system bottlenecks using System Monitor
- Identify solutions for correcting system bottlenecks
- Plan a backup and recovery strategy
- Use volume shadow copy
- Create ASR recovery disks

Ever since the first server was wheeled into a business, the need to provide uninterrupted access to mission-critical applications and data has been a priority for server administrators. The reasons for this are straightforward—when the server goes down, the business may lose money. In the past, maintaining high availability has not always been easy, often requiring specialized hardware and software and complex management tools. Windows Server 2003 builds on the technologies of past Windows versions and includes many enhanced tools and procedures for designing and implementing affordable high-availability server solutions.

In this chapter, we look at some of these tools and procedures and how they are used to ensure continued access to applications and data.

 **NOTE** Server uptime is typically measured in a percentage as a number of nines. Today, the term "six nines" represents the Holy Grail of high availability. For example, 99.9999% server uptime translates to 32 seconds of downtime per year; 99.9% represents about 8.75 hours of downtime per year.

# Working with Clusters

One of the features used to increase server availability is known as clustering. Clustering is a strategy in which a group of computers works together providing access to common applications and data. In a cluster configuration, a group of servers that are physically separate are viewed and accessed as if they were a single entity. Each server in a cluster is referred to as a cluster node. The entire node cluster is typically accessed through a single unique identifier such as a NetBIOS name, TCP/IP address, or MAC address. Each node in the cluster is not individually accessed by client systems. Rather, incoming requests to the servers are handled by the clustering software, which redirects the client's request to a particular server within the cluster. In the case of a hardware failure, the cluster can function as long as there remains one operational node left. This means that a functioning server cluster can accommodate failure of multiple cluster nodes. This strategy goes a long way in ensuring server availability. The advantages of clustering technology include

- **System redundancy**   Using multiple server nodes in a cluster avoids a single point of failure and provides increased availability to applications and data.

- **Centralized management**   Cluster nodes provide a central point from which network administrators can remotely or locally manage the cluster.

- **Scalability**   As the network grows, more servers can be added to a cluster to increase processing power and provide a greater degree of redundancy.

Windows 2003 offers two clustering services, known as the Microsoft Cluster Service (MSCS) and Network Load Balancing (NLB).

## Microsoft Cluster Service

MSCS is specifically designed to provide high availability to mission-critical databases and file and print services. To provide this high availability, the nodes within the cluster are in constant communication, exchanging periodic messages called heartbeats. If one of the server nodes does not respond, another one of the nodes automatically takes over and provides the appropriate network service. This is known as a *failover* configuration. The switch from servers is transparent to the end users, and service to applications is uninterrupted. MSCS is only available with the Windows Server 2003 Enterprise and Datacenter Editions and supports a maximum of eight cluster nodes.

**NOTE**   When designing a cluster configuration, remember that a cluster cannot be implemented if using systems running both Windows Server 2003 Enterprise and Windows Server 2003 Datacenter Editions. The different operating systems may be running incompatible versions of the cluster service.

**EXAM TIP**   Remember that MSCS is only available with the Windows Server 2003 Enterprise and Datacenter Editions and supports a maximum of eight cluster nodes.

## The Quorum Query

When you read about server clustering, you will no doubt run into the concept of quorums. Quorums are an important consideration when working with MSCS clusters. In each and every cluster, there is a dedicated resource that holds important configuration data that is used in the restoration of a failed cluster. This dedicated resource is known as the *quorum resource*. Quorums are actually recovery log files that contain cluster configuration information and must always be available for the cluster to run. For a device to qualify as a quorum resource, that resource has to be able to provide physical storage that can be accessed by any node in the cluster and it must use NTFS.

When designing a clustering configuration, it is important to keep in mind the type of quorum resource you will use. In Windows Server 2003 there are three ways to three ways to set up the quorum resource:

- **Single node server cluster**   A single node server cluster is a unique configuration often used for system configuration testing. A single node server cluster can be configured with external cluster storage devices or without it. For single node clusters without an external cluster storage device, the local disk is configured as the cluster quorum device.

- **Single shared quorum**   As the name suggest, in this configuration the quorum is placed on a shared storage device in the cluster which all cluster nodes can access.

- **Majority nodes quorum**   New to Windows Server 2003, the majority nodes quorum requires that cluster configuration information be stored on the local disks of each node. The majority node set resource ensures that the cluster configuration data is kept consistent across the different disks. Majority nodes quorum is often used for geographically dispersed server clusters.

Of these three models, the single shared quorum is the most popular design for maintaining the quorum resource. This design is well suited for environments where all of your cluster nodes are in the same location. The single shared quorum also allows a cluster to continue supporting users even if only one node is running.

 **EXAM TIP**   Although we didn't get any questions on our exam specifically on quorums, they may be on there somewhere. However, a general knowledge of what they are designed for may be required to answer clustering-related questions.

## Pre-Implementation Considerations

In Windows Server 2003, the process of designing and implementing a server cluster is fairly straightforward. As with other implementations, there is a bit of planning that should occur to make things run smoothly. In this section, we review some of the general pre-implementation considerations to be aware of before attempting to install a server cluster.

**Hardware Verification**    Hardware verification is certainly nothing new and is as relevant for clustering hardware as any other hardware component you install in a server system. The hardware for the cluster should be verified with Microsoft's Hardware Compatibility List (HCL). The list can be accessed at http://www.microsoft.com/hcl/. To simplify the installation and reduce potential errors, Microsoft recommends using identical hardware for all nodes. While this certainly isn't always possible, it can greatly reduce administrative headaches.

**IP Addressing**    When planning the configuration of a server cluster, keep in mind that every network adapter on each cluster node requires an IP address. Microsoft recommends assigning static IP addresses to the nodes. It is possible to use DHCP, but there is a very logical reason why this is not often done.

If you were to use DHCP to assign IP addresses to cluster nodes, you could inadvertently create a single point of failure. If the DHCP server becomes unavailable, the cluster nodes depending on it may be unavailable as they will be unable to get a valid DHCP address. If DHCP is used, it is recommended to ensure measures are in place to keep DHCP services available. Such measures may include having redundant DHCP servers.

---

**TIP**    If using DHCP, it is a good idea to use long leases for cluster node clients, which will help ensure that they maintain a valid IP address.

---

**EXAM TIP**    When working with IP addresses and server clusters, remember that a static IP address is used for the entire cluster entity and DHCP cannot be used. DHCP can be used for assigning IP addresses to the individual cluster nodes, however.

**Cluster Name**    When implementing the cluster, you will need to assign the cluster a name through which administrators can access it. The cluster name follows the rules of other network naming conventions: it must be unique in the network and not the same as any other domain or system in the network. As with other system names, the name length is limited by the rules of NetBIOS.

---

**NOTE**    As you might expect to work with and configure the cluster, you will need to have access to a user account that is part of the local Administrators group on each node. All nodes must have joined a domain (instead of a workgroup) and be members of the same domain.

**Deployment Considerations**  As discussed in the preceding sidebar, "The Quorum Query," there are three cluster models: the single node cluster, single shared quorum device, and majority node set cluster models. If you use the single shared quorum device or majority node set cluster models, you have a variety of different cluster deployment options. The deployment option chosen will depend on the needs and budget of an organization. These cluster deployment methods include

- **N-node failover pairs**  The failover pair refers to the fact that each application is configured to failover only between two specified nodes. The drawback of this approach is that the failure of two servers in the same pair results in complete failure of all resources they own. To deploy N-node failover pairs, all cluster nodes have to be divided into pairs and assigned groups to each pair.

- **Hot-standby server/N+I**  Unlike the N-node failover pairs, a single node is designated as the failover for all remaining nodes in the cluster. The hot-standby server is capable of running the applications from each node pair in the event of a failure.

- **Failover ring**  In a failover ring configuration, an instance of all applications is run on each node in the cluster. In the event of failure, the responsibility to manage the failed server's applications falls to the next node in sequence. The failover ring cluster requires that a circular list of nodes is created that form the failover sequence.

- **Random cluster**  In a random cluster, the failover sequence is random, left to the server cluster to choose. This works well in environments where clusters contain a large number of nodes and groups and other models are too complex to implement.

## Setting Up a Server Cluster

After the system prerequisites are satisfied and you have an idea of how you would like to implement the cluster, you are ready to build the cluster. There are two tools you can use to create the server cluster, the Cluster Administrator graphical tool and the cluster.exe command-line utility. We will start with creating a cluster using the Cluster Administrator.

Select Run | All Programs | Administrative Tools and then the Cluster Administrator icon to start the Cluster Administrator. Alternatively, the cluadmin.exe command can be typed into the Run dialog box. Figure 15-1 shows the Cluster Administrator.

As shown in Figure 15-1, as soon as the Cluster Administrator is started, the Open Connection To Cluster dialog box is displayed. The Action drop-down menu on this screen provides you with three options, Open Connection To Cluster, Add Nodes To Cluster, or Create A New Cluster. To create a new cluster, select this option from the menu to start the New Server Cluster Wizard. The following steps will guide you through the process of creating the server cluster.

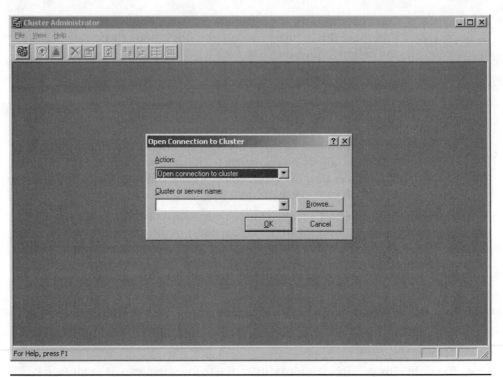

**Figure 15-1** The Cluster Administrator is used to configure server clusters.

**NOTE** If after selecting the option to create a new cluster, things do not work, make sure you are a member of a domain and not a workgroup and that you are using NTFS partitions.

1. With the New Server Cluster Wizard displayed, take the time to read the requirements to complete the procedure on the first screen. When satisfied, click Next.

2. On the second screen of the wizard you will be required to specify the name of the new server cluster and the domain in which it will be created.

3. Next, you will be required to select the computer that will be the first node in the cluster. Click Next once you have identified the system.

4. The wizard will then analyze the system to make sure it meets all the requirements to complete the cluster creation. Successful components will be marked with a check mark, warnings with a yellow exclamation point, and failures with a red X. If there are problems, you can view the log or click Details to gather information on the process. To retest the configuration, click Re-Analyze. Figure 15-2 shows the five steps performed by the New Server Cluster Wizard.

**Figure 15-2**

Verifying system requirements for creating a cluster

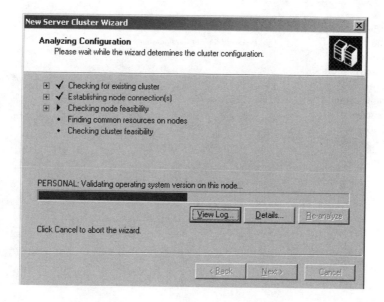

5. In the next screen of the wizard, you will be required to enter a unique IP address that will be used to connect to the cluster. Enter the IP address and click Next.

6. The next screen of the wizard allows you enter the logon information for the domain account under which the cluster service will be run.

7. The final screen of the wizard provides an overview of the cluster information you have entered. From this screen you also have the ability to select the quorum resource; click Quorum to choose. Figure 15-3 shows the Proposed Cluster Configuration screen, which displays a summary of the cluster configuration, and the Cluster Configuration Quorum dialog box, which displays the options for quorum resources.

**EXAM TIP** Before taking the exam, take the time to run through the process of creating a server cluster. Questions on the exam will be easier if you have had some hands-on experience working through the process.

Once the final Next button is clicked, the creation of the cluster will begin. In the process, the system completes four steps: it reanalyzes the system to ensure cluster information is correct, configures cluster services and starts the cluster service, configures resource types, and finally configures the resource. Figure 15-4 shows the creation of the cluster.

With the cluster created, you can view and manage it from the Cluster Administrator. Figure 15-5 shows the newly created cluster in the Cluster Administrator.

**Figure 15-3**
The Proposed
Cluster
Configuration
screen and
the Cluster
Configuration
Quorum
dialog box

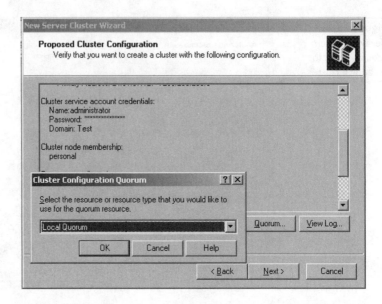

So far we have covered creating a cluster using the graphical utility. All that is left is to do the same using the command-line utility cluster.exe. Creating clusters with the command line requires more effort, but those with experience working at the command line should feel right at home.

**Figure 15-4**
Four final steps
are completed
to create and
configuring
the cluster

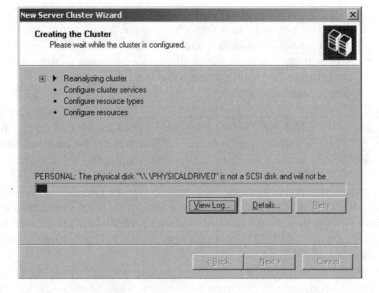

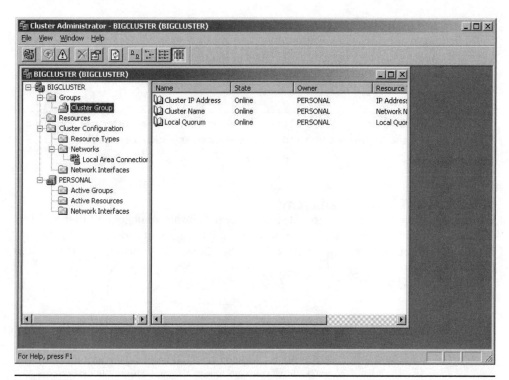

**Figure 15-5** The Cluster Administrator is used to view and manage clustering services.

To create a cluster using the cluster.exe command, the /create switch is used along with a variety of other information. To be specific, the following syntax is used:

```
/create /node:node-name /user:domain\username | username@domain /
pass:password
```

```
/ipaddr:xxx.xxx.xxx.xxx,xxx.xxx.xxx.xxx,network-connection-name
```

where *xxx.xxx.xxx.xxx,xxx.xxx.xxx.xxx* is the IP address followed by the subnet, and *network-connection-name* is the network adapter, and so on.

Confusing? Well, here is an example for creating a cluster named cluster1:

```
cluster.exe /cluster:cluster1 /create /
ipaddr:192.168.1.1,255.255.255.0,"internal" /password:free /
user:test\administrator /node:personal
```

In this example, we are creating the cluster1 cluster with an IP address of 192.168.1.1 and a subnet of 255.255.255.0. We assigned the cluster to the network adapter named "internal" on the node server named personal. Finally, we are using the cluster service account named administrator in the test domain. Once this command is correctly issued, the cluster will be created. Adding clusters to an existing cluster is done with the / add option, removing clients is performed with the /evict option, and stopping the cluster is done with the /stop option.

 **NOTE** For a full listing of the options available for the cluster.exe command, run the following command at the command line: **cluster.exe /?**.

## Basic Server Cluster Management

While the Microsoft objectives do not specifically list cluster management in this objective, it is a good idea to at least have an overview of management procedures. Table 15-1 describes basic cluster procedures from both the Cluster Administrator and the cluster.exe utility.

| Desired Command | Procedure Using Cluster Administrator | Procedure Using cluster.exe |
|---|---|---|
| Starting the cluster service | Right-click the node on which you want to start the service and select the Start Cluster Service option from the menu. | From the command prompt, type **cluster /cluster name node node name /start** |
| Stopping the cluster service | Right-click the node on which you want to stop the service and select the Stop Cluster Service option from the menu. | From the command prompt, type **cluster /cluster name node node name /stop** |
| Pausing a node (while paused, prevents resources on other nodes failing over to the node) | Right-click the node on which you want to stop the service and select the Pause Node option from the menu. | From the command prompt, type **cluster /cluster name node node name /pause** |
| Resuming a node | Right-click the node on which you want to stop the service and select the Resume Node option from the menu. | From the command prompt, type **cluster /cluster name node node name /resume** |
| Verifying node status | Icons, such as a blue and white exclamation mark, visually display the status of the cluster node. | From the command prompt, type **cluster /cluster name node node name /status** |

**Table 15-1**   Basic Commands for Managing the Cluster

## Recovering from a Cluster Node Failure

To ensure high availability and the ability to quickly and effectively recover from a cluster node failure, regular backups of the nodes within a cluster are essential. When performing cluster backups, there are four key pieces of information you need to have to complete a total restoration:

- **Cluster disk signatures and partitions**   Using the Automated System Recovery (ASR) in the Backup Wizard, you can make a backup of the disk signatures and partitions. The process of creating an ASR recovery disk is covered later in this chapter.

- **Cluster quorum data**   The quorum data contains the cluster information and the cluster recovery log. The Backup Wizard can be used to back up the cluster quorum when you perform a system state backup from any node. After you back up the cluster quorum disk on one node, it is not necessary to back up the quorum on the remaining cluster nodes.

- **Data on the cluster disks**   To back up all cluster disks used by a node, perform a full backup from that node.

 **NOTE**   If a cluster disk owned by the node being backed up fails over to another node during the backup process, the backup set will not contain a full backup of that disk.

- **Data on the individual cluster nodes**   To make things run smoothly, it is a good idea to back up the clustering software, cluster administrative software, system state, and application data on the individual server nodes. This can be done using the Windows Server 2003 Backup Utility.

**Restoring an Individual Cluster Node Using ASR**   When a system completely fails, the ASR process can be used to restore the system to a functional state. For the ASR process you will need to have your most recently created ASR recover disk that contains the backed-up cluster disk signatures, partition layouts, and cluster quorum. You will also need a boot disk, preferably the original operating Windows Server 2003 installation CD, and you will need to be a member of the Administrators group on the local computer system.

To begin the recovery process, insert and boot from the original Windows Server 2003 installation CD. When prompted, press the F2 key to initiate the ASR recovery process. Insert the ASR disk when asked and follow the onscreen directions. Once the system recovers using the ASR disk, the node should be able to rejoin the cluster.

PART III

**No ASR Disk!**   Even the most diligent system administrator may forget to create an ASR disk. For such times, there is another option that can be tried to recover from a corrupted quorum log or quorum disk. The procedure is as follows:

1. Stop the cluster service by selecting Start | All Programs | Administrative Tools and the Services icon. Find the cluster service, right-click it and select Stop from the menu.

2. With the cluster service stopped, right-click the cluster service icon again and choose the Properties option from the menu to open the Cluster Service Properties dialog box.

3. At the bottom of the General tab of the Cluster Service Properties dialog box, you have the option to specify start parameters for the cluster service. In the Start Parameters text box, enter the following switch: **/fixquorum**.

4. Restart the service to repair the quorum disk. Figure 15-6 shows the Cluster Service Properties dialog box with the /fixquorum option.

**NOTE**   If you are restoring a disk signature to a damaged cluster disk, power down all other cluster nodes except the one on which you are performing the ASR restore. This cluster node must have exclusive rights to the damaged cluster disk.

**Figure 15-6**
The /fixquorum option is used to attempt to repair a corrupted quorum disk.

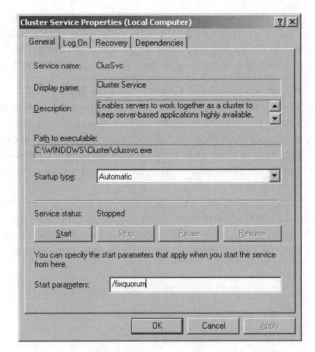

The /fixquorum option can also be used from the command line using the clussv.exe command. The clussvc.exe command should not be used under normal conditions, but only as a temporary diagnostic tool if the cluster service fails to start. Listed in Table 15-2 are some of the available diagnostic options available with the clussv.exe command.

**Recovering System State**   Using the Windows Server 2003 Backup Utility, you can back up the system state, which includes such things as the COM+ Class Registration database, Certificate Services database, Active Directory service, and the cluster service information. In the event of a cluster failure or the failure of an individual node, you may need to restore the system state, for example, if you need to restore the cluster quorum for all nodes in the cluster.

To use the Backup Utility to restore the system state, select Start | All Programs | Accessories | System Tools and finally the Backup icon. Alternatively, you can simply type **ntbackup** in the Run dialog box to start the Backup Wizard. When prompted by the wizard, select the option to Restore Files And Settings and navigate to the location of the backed-up system state data. Once selected, the system state will be restored and you should be able to rejoin the cluster.

## Network Load Balancing Clusters Overview

Although the term Network Load Balancing (NLB) clusters can seem a bit intimidating, the function and implementation of NLB are fairly straightforward. Essentially, NLB is used to disperse incoming client requests across several different servers. Instead of client requests accessing the applications and resources of a single server, the request can be spread across as many as 32 servers. As you can appreciate, this increases not only the availability of those applications but also the response time. Windows Server 2003 NLB software can detect when a server in the cluster stops working and assign new client requests to that server. The design of NLB is to provide continual and uninterrupted access to applications. This makes NLB clusters well suited for web and FTP servers, proxy servers, VPN servers, Telnet servers, and Terminal Services servers.

**NOTE**   Network Load Balancing is included with all Windows Server 2003 products.

| Table 15-2 | Option | Description |
|---|---|---|
| Using the clussv.exe Command | /fixquorum | Allows the system to start the cluster service even if there are problems with the quorum device. |
| | /resetquorumlog | If the quorum log file is not found or is corrupted, creates a new quorum log file based on information in the local node's cluster database file. |
| | /forcequorum | Restores quorum for a majority node set server cluster that has lost quorum. |
| | /debugresmon | Enables the debugging mode. |

PART III

In application, each NLB cluster node runs separate copies of applications or services such as that for a web, FTP, and Telnet server. This is in contrast to the previously mentioned server clusters where only a single instance of a particular application is allowed to run at a time. Windows Server 2003 NLB software has the ability to detect a failed cluster node—typically within ten seconds—and the failed server is removed from the cluster. Client requests are directed away from the failed server and to the remaining functional servers within the cluster. NLB allows all of the computers in the cluster to be addressed by the same set of cluster IP addresses, but also maintains their existing unique, dedicated IP addresses. Table 15-3 summarizes some of the key characteristics of NLB clusters.

 **EXAM TIP** NLB does not use clustered storage devices. Each server runs a copy of the IP-based application or service that is being load balanced, and the data necessary for the application or service to run is stored on local drives.

| Feature | Description |
| --- | --- |
| Increased scalability | Requests for individual TCP/IP services can be spread across the entire cluster.<br>Windows Server 2003 supports up to 32 computers in a single cluster. |
| High availability | NLB nodes can detect system failures and automatically recover failed node.<br>The workloads among nodes are monitored and redistributed when nodes fail or are removed.<br>Recovers and redistributes the workload within ten seconds. |
| Versatile management | Using the Network Load Balancing Manager, it is possible to manage and configure multiple Network Load Balancing clusters from a single computer.<br>Configuration options allow the administrator to direct client requests to a single host. This allows Network Load Balancing to send client requests to a specific node running a particular application.<br>NLB provides the ability to block undesired network access to certain IP ports. |
| Compatibility | NLB does not require specialized hardware or systemwide hardware changes in order to run.<br>NLB requires only standard Windows networking driver components.<br>Clients access the NLB cluster using a single logical Internet name and virtual IP address. Each individual node cluster retains an individual name.<br>Network Load Balancing can be bound to multiple network adapters, allowing you to configure multiple independent clusters on each host. |

**Table 15-3**   Windows Server 2003 NLB Clusters Features and Enhancements

## Pre-Implementation Considerations

NLB was designed to be as compatible as possible. As such, it doesn't take much to get the cluster up and running. With that in mind, in this section we highlight some of the things to consider before implementing your NLB.

**Network Adapters**   Microsoft recommends that when designing the NLB cluster, plan to use two network cards in each cluster node. This isn't for redundancy, but rather, to effectively create two distinct networks. For example:

- **Adapter 1 (cluster adapter)**   Provides for network traffic for the cluster.

- **Adapter 2 (dedicated adapter)**   Provides client-to-cluster network traffic and other traffic originating outside the cluster network.

While it is recommended to use two adapters wherever possible, two network cards are not required. However, if only a single network adapter is used, there are some limitations to be aware of. When using a single adapter in unicast mode, node-to-node communication is not possible and nodes within a cluster cannot communicate with each other. In multicast mode with a single adapter, node-to-node and intercluster communication is possible. However, the single adapter configuration is not recommended for handling moderate to heavy traffic from outside the cluster. Microsoft recommends that for node-to-node communication and to accommodate moderate to heavy traffic, two network cards should be installed.

 **EXAM TIP**   Remember that when a cluster is set to run in unicast mode, NLB cannot distinguish between single adapters on each node. This means that node-to-node communication is not possible unless each cluster host has at least two network adapters.

**IP Addressing**   Configuring the NLB cluster requires a little forethought as far as IP addresses are concerned. It is recommended that TCP/IP be the only protocol bound to the cluster's network adapters. Wherever possible, the IP addresses for the cluster should be statically assigned during the NLB configuration. All dedicated cluster IP addresses must belong to the same subnet and have the same subnet mask.

To provide high availability to clients, NLB uses a virtual IP address for the cluster, and all client requests are directed to this virtual IP address instead of individual node IP addresses. If one of the servers in the NLB cluster should fail, the rest of the servers in the cluster can transparently take over. When the failed server is brought back online, it can rejoin the cluster group without disruption to clients.

To configure the NLB cluster, you will need to have a number of available IP addresses. If you are using a single network adapter approach, you will require an IP address for each adapter in each node and one for the virtual cluster address. These too should all be on the same subnet with the same subnet mask. When using multiple network cards in each node, you will again need an IP address for the virtual cluster and one for each adapter in every node. Cluster and dedicated IP addresses must belong to the same subnet.

## Installing Network Load Balancing

With all of the configuration and hardware prerequisites met, you can begin to install the NLB cluster. There are two primary methods of installing the NLB cluster: using the Network Load Balancing Manager, and using the properties of a network connections dialog box. We'll begin with the Network Load Balancing Manager.

### Installing NLB Clusters Using the Network Load Balancing Manager

The NLB manager is part of, and can be executed from, the Windows Server 2003 Administrative Tools. It can also be executed in the Run dialog box using the nlbmgr.exe command. As shown in Figure 15-7, the NLB Manager is divided into three window sections. The top left window displays a list of clusters and nodes, the top-right window displays the known cluster configurations, and the bottom window is used to display status messages.

To create an NLB cluster, select Cluster | New to open the Cluster Parameters dialog box (shown in Figure 15-8). In this dialog box, you need to enter your cluster TCP/IP configuration, cluster operation mode (unicast/multicast), and whether to allow remote control (and if so, set the remote control password).

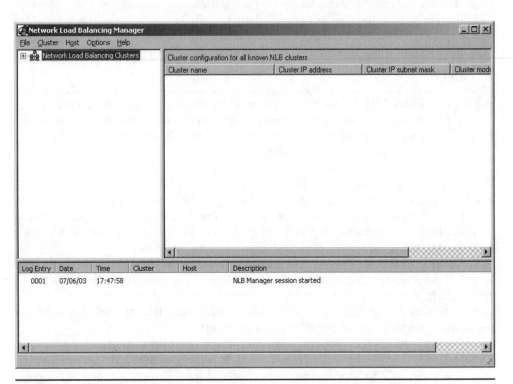

**Figure 15-7**    The Network Load Balancing Manager is used to create NLB clusters.

**Figure 15-8**
The Clusters
Parameters
dialog box

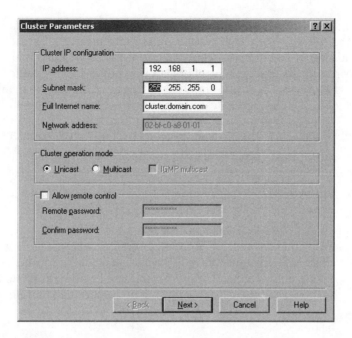

**NOTE** The terms *unicast* and *multicast* are used to describe how a message is communicated in a network. Unicast transmissions send a message to one receiver, typically from a server to a workstation. Multicast transmissions transmit a message to multiple recipients at the same time. Multicast is a one-to-many transmission similar to broadcast network communications, except that multicasting means sending to specific groups, whereas broadcast communication sends to everybody.

**EXAM TIP** Network Load Balancing does not support a mixed environment of unicast/multicast.

As far as the TCP/IP configuration is concerned in the Cluster Parameters dialog box, there are a few things to keep in mind. The IP address you enter on this screen is the virtual IP address and must be set identically for all hosts in the cluster. As mentioned earlier, this virtual IP address is used to address the entire cluster. This should be the primary IP address and subnet mask for the cluster.

One final consideration, the dedicated IP address and the cluster IP address, entered during setup in the Network Load Balancing Properties dialog box, must also be entered in the Internet Protocol (TCP/IP) Properties dialog box. Make sure that the addresses are the same in both places.

**EXAM TIP** Both the dedicated IP address and the cluster's primary IP address must be static IP addresses. They cannot be DHCP-assigned IP addresses.

PART III

Once the information is entered correctly in the Clusters Parameters dialog box, the next screen allows you to enter any additional cluster IP addresses. If there are no additional cluster IP addresses, click Next to open the Port Rules dialog box.

Port rules are used to control of various types of TCP/IP traffic. To add or edit a port rule, click Add or Edit in the Port Rules dialog box. This will open the Add/Edit Port Rule dialog box. The configurable options in this window include

- **Cluster IP Address**   The cluster IP address that the port rule should cover.

- **Port Range**   The TCP/UDP port range that a port rule should cover. Ports numbers ranging from 0 to 65,535 are currently supported.

- **Protocols**   The TCP/IP protocol that a port rule should cover: TCP, UDP, or both.

- **Filtering Mode**   There are three possible filter modes: multiple hosts, single host, and disabled. The multiple hosts filter specifies that multiple hosts in the cluster handle network traffic for the associated port rule. The single host filter option allows network traffic for the associated port rule to be handled by a single host in the cluster according to the specified handling priority. Finally, the disable port range forces all network traffic for the associated port rule to be blocked.

Once you have established and configured the port rules, click Next to display the Connect dialog box where you can specify the host that will be created as the first member of the new cluster. Once the host name is entered, click Next to open the Host Parameters dialog box (see Figure 15-9), which contains the following options:

- **Priority**   Used to set a unique ID for each host. It is important to note that the host set with the lowest number value is chosen to control the network traffic of the entire cluster. This priority setting can be overridden using port rules.

- **Dedicated IP Configuration**   Used to identify a unique IP address for the host to be used for network traffic not associated with the cluster.

- **Default State**   Used to specify whether Network Load Balancing will start, and if it does, to determine if the host automatically connects to the cluster when the operating system is started.

Once the host parameters are entered, click Next to finish creating the new NLB cluster. The cluster will now appear in the NLB Manager. If there are problems with the newly created cluster, it will appear as a red and white X in the bottom information window of the NLB Manager.

**Installing NLB Clusters Using the Network Properties**   The preferred way to create an NLB cluster is using the NLB Manager, but it is not the only way. The following is a quick overview of creating NLB clusters using the Network Properties.

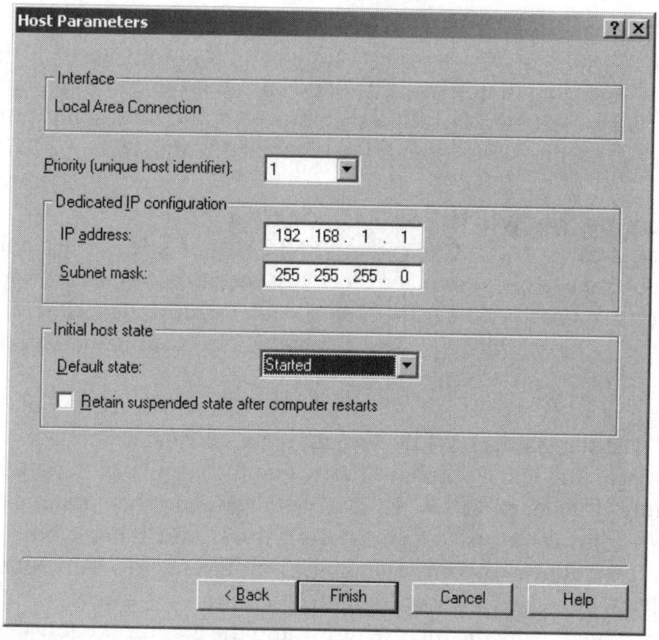

**Figure 15-9**
The Host
Parameters
dialog box

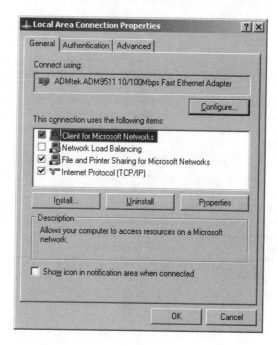

To begin creating the NLB cluster, select Start | Control Panel | Network Connections and finally the Local Area Connections icon to open the Local Area Connection Status Dialog box. Click Properties to open the Local Area Connection Properties dialog box as shown in Figure 15-10.

**Figure 15-10**
Creating NLB
clusters through
the Local Area
Connection
Properties
dialog box

Notice in Figure 15-10 that the check box beside the Network Load Balancing option is unchecked. Check this option and click Properties to open the Network Load Balancing Properties dialog box. The dialog box has three familiar tabs, Cluster Parameters, Host Parameters, and Port Rules. Completing the information on these three tabs will create the cluster just as you did using the NLB Manager.

## Managing Network Load Balancing

Now that you know how to create an NLB cluster, you are also going to need a basic understanding of how to manage those clusters once they are created. There are a few utilities you can use to manage the NLB cluster, including the NLB Manager, command-line utilities (wlbs.exe/nlb.exe), and the Network Load Balancing Properties dialog box in the Network Connection properties.

nlb.exe is the Windows Server 2003 replacement for the older wlbs.exe (Windows Load Balancing Suite). While it might seem unusual to manage an NLB cluster from the command line when you have flashy graphical tools, command-line management can be more efficient and allow for faster changes than their graphical counterparts. nlb.exe allows administrators to manage both local and remote NLB clusters. As far as the graphical utilities are concerned, there is not much to report with them. The procedures involve menus and a lot of right-clicks. Table 15-4 shows some basic commands that can be issued using the nlb.exe utility and the graphical equivalent using the NLB Manager. For a full list of available options, type **nlb /?** at the command prompt.

 **EXAM TIP** Before taking the exam, familiarize yourself with command-line cluster management and available options.

| Command | Procedure Using NLB Manager | Procedure Using nlb.exe |
|---------|------------------------------|--------------------------|
| Provide summary information on the NLB cluster, including IP configuration, event messages, and cluster state | Right-click the cluster and then point to Control Hosts and select Display from the menu. | nlb.exe display |
| Suspend all cluster operations | Right-click the cluster and then point to Control Hosts and select Suspend from the menu. | nlb.exe suspend |
| Prevent new traffic handling for specific ports and stop Network Load Balancing | Right-click a host or a cluster, point to Control Host or Control Hosts and select the Drainstop option. | nlb.exe drainstop |

**Table 15-4**   Basic NLB Commands

| Command | Procedure Using NLB Manager | Procedure Using nlb.exe |
|---------|------------------------------|--------------------------|
| Stop handling Network Load Balancing cluster traffic | Right-click the cluster or host, point to Control Hosts and select the Stop option. | nlb.exe stop |
| Start handling Network Load Balancing cluster traffic | Right-click the cluster or host, point to Control Hosts and select the Start option. | nlb.exe start |
| Disable and block all Network Load Balancing traffic handling for specific ports | Right-click a host or a cluster, and then click Control Ports. Select the port you want to disable or block and then click Disable. | nlb.exe disable |

**Table 15-4**    Basic NLB Commands *(continued)*

# Identifying System Bottlenecks

When a server isn't performing as well as it should, whether applications are slow and unresponsive or error messages start to appear, it is time for administrators to begin the process of performance troubleshooting. Tracking down the cause of a server performance issue is not always an easy endeavor, and as a result, the first response to performance troubleshooting is often to upgrade the server, starting with the memory. While this hit and miss approach to correcting performance issues with a server is often the way business is done, Windows Server 2003 provides some tools that allow you to take a more scientific approach. In this section, we'll take a look at the Windows Server 2003 System Monitor and how it is used to help identify potential performance bottlenecks.

## Bottleneck Basics

When it comes to tracking and correcting server bottlenecks, the first assumption is often that the hardware resources are insufficient to handle the load. Such assumptions have led to situations where components are unnecessarily upgraded to address a performance issue. There is no doubt that insufficient hardware resources can create bottleneck issues, but they cannot always take the blame. The only accurate way to determine where a bottleneck is and what is causing it is to monitor the performance of the system, component by component and program by program.

What makes isolating system bottlenecks particularly tricky is that there are many different factors, or a combination of factors, that can be creating the problem. Here are a few factors that might cause a system bottleneck:

- **Insufficient hardware resources**   Components may need to be enhanced or upgraded to handle the load.

- **Load balancing**   System hardware may be adequate, but the workload is not evenly distributed among hardware.

- **Hardware failure**   Hardware that is not working correctly can cause a bottleneck. Performance counters should be able to isolate this as a cause.

- **Software demands**   Programs that are written poorly or not functioning correctly can monopolize resources and create system bottlenecks.

At the end of the day, deciding whether the performance of a system is acceptable is often a judgment call, as performance concerns vary greatly depending on the environment in which the system is used. For example, a server may function fine as an authentication server, but if the same system is now responsible for file and print services, it may not be able to handle the load. The only way to really know what a system can do is by gauging how hard the components are working and determining at what point a component may need to be replaced. To determine this in Windows Server 2003, you can use System Monitor.

## Using System Monitor

Those who have experience working with the Management Console in Windows 2000 will feel right at home working with the Windows Server 2003 equivalent. When the Performance Monitor is opened, it has the same two components as with Windows 2000, the Performance Logs and Alerts and the System Monitor. The Performance Logs and Alerts maintain the system's logging functions and System Monitor is responsible to display real-time performance statistics. Figure 15-11 shows the Windows Server 2003 System Monitor.

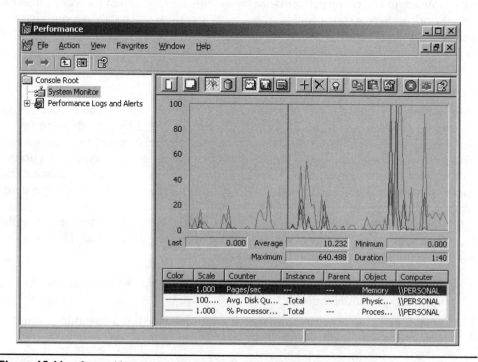

**Figure 15-11**   System Monitor is used to display real-time performance statistics.

**EXAM TIP**  System Monitor can be opened by typing **perfmon** into Run or it can be started by selecting Start | All Programs | Administrative Tools and finally the Performance icon.

As you can see from Figure 15-11, the graphic interface of System Monitor is straightforward. However, before you get into using System Monitor, you need to know the difference between objects, instances, and counters.

## Objects, Instances, and Counters

In the System Monitor world, an *object* refers to a physical component of the server, such as memory or a hard disk. An object may also refer to a logical component such as a disk volume and even a software component such as a system process. When working with System Monitor and looking for a bottleneck, you track the performance of these individual objects using *counters*.

A *counter* is a measurable aspect of an object. For example, memory has many measurable characteristics, such as pages/sec or available bytes. Each of these memory characteristics is considered a counter and provides you with very specific information on that object. When hunting for those performance bottlenecks, you need to choose the correct counter for the job. Choosing the correct counter for troubleshooting the performance of a specific object is discussed later in this chapter.

*Instances* refer to the number of occurrences of an object in the server. For example, if you have two hard disks in a server, two instances of that object are present in System Monitor. When measuring the performance of a particular object, you have the option to monitor all instances, both hard disks, or a single instance.

With a better idea of these concepts, we can now look a bit closer at System Monitor and the process of adding counters to monitor the objects in a server.

## Adding Object Counters to Monitor

As shown in Figure 15-11, System Monitor is first opened, there are three default counters running, one to monitor memory (Pages/sec), one to track hard disk performance (Average Disk Queue Length), and one for the processor (% Processor Time). These three default counters give a good overview of the performance of these objects; however, they are often not enough to track down all performance bottlenecks. In such cases, you need to add a few counters to the mix.

There are two easy ways to add a counter to an object in System Monitor. The first is to click the + button in the menu bar, and the second is to simply right-click in the System Monitor window and choose the Add Counters option from the menu. Whichever method you choose, the result will be to open the Add Counters dialog box, which is where the real fun begins. Figure 15-12 shows the Add Counters dialog box.

**EXAM TIP**  Monitoring system performance is a major consideration for system administrators. As such, you can expect to see questions on the exam highlighting System Monitor. We suggest taking the time to gain some hands-on experience with System Monitor before taking the exam.

**Figure 15-12**
Adding counters
to System
Monitor is
done from the
Add Counters
dialog box.

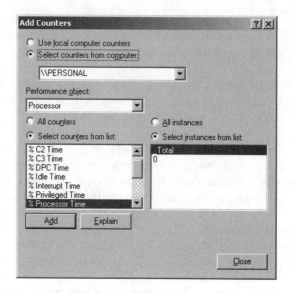

Once the Add Counters dialog box is open, things can get confusing. There are a number of different objects you can choose to monitor, and each object has various counters available to track performance. To add a counter, first select the Performance Object you want to monitor from the drop-down menu, such as the processor or physical disk. Once selected, choose the counter you need and click Add to begin monitoring the object. The monitoring of the object will be viewable in System Monitor's main screen and will be displayed in a different color from the other objects. Add as many counters as you want, but be selective and add only those counters you really need. Too many counters make it hard to get an accurate picture of what is going on in the system.

**NOTE** If you are wondering what a certain counter is designed to monitor, Windows Server 2003 includes an Explain button you can click to describe the function of the counter. While some of these explanations are useful, others seem to confuse more than they clarify. Still, they are worth checking out.

Now that you know how to add counters to measure characteristics of system objects, you can see how adding counters translates to actually troubleshooting a server and identifying bottlenecks.

## Identifying Processor Bottlenecks

There is an array of counters available to monitor processor activity. The names of these counters are somewhat cryptic, and the explanations provided with Windows Server 2003 often serve to muddy the waters. Fortunately, when it comes to monitoring processors and looking for bottlenecks, you only need to use a few of these counters. These include the % Processor Time, Interrupts/sec, and % Interrupt Time.

The % Processor Time counter is the primary indicator of processor activity and displays the average percentage of busy time observed during a sample interval. If the % Processor Time counter consistently displays an average usage above 85%, the processor may need to be upgraded or it may be necessary to track down applications that are too demanding on the processor. Either way, 85% on the processor usage indicates that the processor may be a bottleneck.

The Interrupt counters are used to monitor how often the processor needs to handle requests from hardware such as video cards, networks cards, disk drives, and peripheral devices. If the processor is spending too much time handling requests from hardware—for instance, if the Interrupts/sec counter exceeds an average of 3500/4000—the processor may be having trouble handling the load. A high number of interrupts can also be caused by software problems such as faulty device drivers that can send out a stream of constant interrupt requests per second. Updating old or beta device drivers may help bring the interrupt counters within normal range. Table 15-5 summarizes the important counters for identifying processor bottlenecks.

**EXAM TIP**   A dramatic increase in the Interrupts/sec counter value often indicates a hardware problem. Identify the hardware causing the interrupts.

**Correcting a Processor Bottleneck**   Though processors are not often at the root of your bottleneck troubles, it does happen. When it does, you typically have two choices of what you can do to alleviate the bottleneck:

- Add a processor (if using a dual-processor motherboard)
- Upgrade to a faster processor

Before running out and replacing that processor, it is a good idea to track other objects in the system to see if they may be adding to the problem. You could upgrade the processor only to find that the problem lay elsewhere.

## Identifying Hard Disk Bottlenecks

Like the processor, the hard disk has a number of different counters that can be used to monitor disk activity and overall performance. Of all of the counters available for monitoring the physical disk, the average system administrator will only need two primary

| Table 15-5 Counters Used to Identify Processor Bottlenecks | Counter | Function | Warning Signs |
|---|---|---|---|
| | % Processor Time | Primary indicator of processor activity. | Average usage consistently exceeds 85%. |
| | Interrupt/sec | Displays how much time the processor is interrupted to handle hardware requests. | A counter consistently exceeding 3500/4000 is too high. |

PART III

counters in the search for bottlenecks. The first is the % Disk Time counter, which represents the percentage of elapsed time that the selected disk drive was busy servicing read or write requests. The second, Current Disk Queue Length, displays the number of requests outstanding on the disk at the time the performance data is collected.

When reviewing the % Disk Time counter you will want to see a low number. If you see that the hard disk is busy servicing requests 90% of the time or higher, there is a bottleneck. It could be that the hard disk needs to be replaced for a faster one, but the hard disk may in fact not be the culprit. You may find that adding memory to the system will bring the % Disk Time counter to normal parameters.

The Current Disk Queue Length counter should be low, typically below 2. A high value indicates there is a wait period that is likely impacting users. Unlike many of the other counters, the Current Disk Queue Length counter provides a snapshot picture of performance, not an average over a time interval. Table 15-6 summarizes the key characteristics of the counters used to track potential hard disk bottlenecks.

**Correcting Hard Disk Bottlenecks**   When the hard disk is causing a system-wide bottleneck, the most obvious solution would be to purchase a new and faster hard disk. There are other things that can be tried to eliminate that hard disk bottleneck, however, including

- Upgrade to a higher speed disk, although this may not be enough to completely remove the bottleneck.
- Adding multiple hard disks to the system can reduce the workload on a single disk.
- Create striped volumes across multiple physical disks to increase throughput.
- If multiple servers are used, distribute programs among servers to spread the workload out.
- Isolate tasks that heavily utilize disk I/O; if possible, place these tasks on separate physical disks.
- Basic disk maintenance, such as using Disk Defragmenter to consolidate files, can optimize hard disk performance.
- Update motherboard/host bus adapter drivers.

| Table 15-6 Counters Used to Monitor Disk Activity | Counter | Function | Warning Signs |
|---|---|---|---|
| | % Disk Time | Elapsed time that a disk drive was busy servicing read or write requests. | A hard disk busy servicing requests an average of 90%. |
| | Current Disk Queue Length | Shows the number of requests outstanding on the disk at the time the performance data is collected. | Outstanding requests should be low, on average below 2. |

## Identifying Memory Bottlenecks

When it comes to tracking down bottlenecks, memory counters perhaps get more work than any other counter. It may be a bit of a cliché, but memory is most often at the root of server performance problems. Both the operating system and those programs you put on it are memory hungry. Still, it is a best practice to use System Monitor to confirm your suspicions before running out and buying more memory.

The thing to remember when monitoring memory is that you are using System Monitor to track the performance of the physical memory and hard disk access. This is because of the way Windows operating systems use virtual memory to augment a system's physical memory. In a nutshell, virtual memory is a method of simulating more memory than actually exists in the system by allowing information in physical memory to be swapped out to the hard disk. This allows the computer to run larger programs or more programs concurrently. The hard disk may show high usage, but this is because it is so busy compensating for memory shortages in the system.

 **NOTE** One of the performance issues you are looking for in System Monitor is a memory leak. In application, a program should use the memory it needs and then free up that memory when the program is terminated. Some programs keep taking memory resources even though they are not being used or they do not return memory resources when not terminated. These programs are said to have a memory leak.

When it comes to tracking memory bottlenecks, there are many counters you need to be aware of. Complicating the issue is the fact that some of the counters are not listed under the memory object, as there are counters under the PhysicalDisk object that will assist in tracing potential virtual memory problems. For the exam, you will need to have knowledge of many of the memory counters. Table 15-7 summarizes the counters used with memory to track memory performance bottlenecks.

 **EXAM TIP** Pay close attention to all of the tables provided in this section and familiarize yourself with the values of those counters and what values constitute a bottleneck.

**Correcting Memory Bottlenecks** The most obvious solution to correct performance bottlenecks that are memory-related is to crack open the case and install more memory. There are a few more things to try, including these:

- If using multiple hard disks, use multiple paging files.
- Ensure that the page file is the correct size. Typically, Windows manages the size of the file, but it may need to be manually changed. As a rough calculation, Microsoft recommends the paging file be between 1 and 1.5 times the amount of physical memory available.

- Double-check that the memory settings are all correct.
- If possible, place the network's memory-hungry programs on your highest performing computers.

## Identifying Network Bottlenecks

One of the more frustrating performance bottlenecks to try and isolate are the network bottlenecks. When you are trying to track down network bottlenecks, you are determining how much traffic there is on the network and how efficiently your server is managing that traffic. There are a number of counters you can use to monitor the network and hunt for those network bottlenecks. Two of the more often accessed network-related counters are described in Table 15-8.

| Counter | Function | Warning Signs |
|---|---|---|
| Memory: Available Bytes | Displays the amount of physical memory immediately available for allocation to a process or for system use. | If the counter runs too low it is an indication that the system is low on memory. A low amount of available physical memory can also indicate a memory leak in a program. Should be on average over 4MB available. |
| Memory: Commit Limit | Shows the amount of virtual memory that can be committed without having to extend the paging file(s). | Paging file should be 2.5 times the size of RAM installed in the system. |
| Memory: Pages/sec | Identifies paging activity. | If the counter consistently exceeds a threshold of 20, this could indicate that too much paging is occurring and more memory is needed. |
| Paging File: % Usage | Lists the percentage of the paging file currently being used. | A counter that consistently exceeds 70% indicates that there is too much pressure on the paging file. Add more memory or increase the size of the paging file. |
| Physical Disk: % Disk Time | Elapsed time that a disk drive was busy servicing read or write requests. | Monitor the physical disk on which the paging file is located. A counter exceeding 90% averages may be a memory bottleneck. |

**Table 15-7**    Isolating Network-Related Bottlenecks

| Counter | Function | Warning Signs |
|---------|----------|---------------|
| Network Interface: Bytes Total/sec | Displays the rate at which bytes are sent and received over each network adapter. | If the counter is either too high or too low from what you would expect from the card, it may be faulty. If the speed is too slow given the adapter and network speed, it may be faulty. If the rate displayed is consistently high, it may not be effectively handling the load. |
| Server: Bytes Total/sec | Measures the rate at which the server is sending and receiving network data. | The traffic going in and out of the server indicates how busy the network is. A load too high indicates that the server is struggling to keep up with the load. |

**Table 15-8**    Isolating Network-Related Bottlenecks

**Correcting Network Bottlenecks**    There are many things you can do to alleviate network related bottlenecks. These strategies include

- If a group of systems are shared by common network users, place the users on the same subnet.
- Unbind infrequently used network adapters.
- If possible, switch to a multiple adapter configuration to reduce the load on a single network adapter.
- If you are using more than one protocol, you can set the order in which the workstation and NetBIOS software bind to each protocol.
- Update network adapter drivers.

# Planning a Backup and Recovery Solution

Part of maintaining a high availability solution is preparing for the worst. In the case of servers, the worst is a complete crash of the system and the need to reinstall data from backups. Good server administrators will always have a solid backup strategy, including knowledge of the different types of backup strategies and the best one to choose for a given environment. In this section, we'll look at some of the tools and procedures used to back up server data and how that data is restored.

**EXAM TIP**    Since the dawn of Microsoft certification exams there have been questions on the various backup types and the best one to use in a given situation. Be sure to have a solid understanding of them before taking the exam.

## Working with the Backup Utility

The first and most obvious place to start a discussion of backups is with the Windows Server 2003 Backup utility. As with many of the other Windows utilities, Backup is a wizard that allows you to easily select what to back up and the type of backup to make. There are two methods to access the Backup utility. You can select Start | All Programs | Accessories | System Tools. Alternatively, you can also type **ntbackup** in the Run dialog box to start the Backup utility. Once the utility begins, you can work your way through the wizard's screens. Figure 15-13 shows the Windows Server 2003 Backup Utility.

The second screen in the wizard allows you to select to back up all files and data and create a system recovery disk or choose the data that is to be backed up. Figure 15-14 shows the screen to choose to quickly back up the entire system or select individual files.

If you select to manually choose the files and folders to backup, the Items To Back Up dialog box will be displayed. From here you can select files on the local computer or from the network or trusted domains to be backed up. You can also select to back up the system state.

**NOTE** More information on the system state is covered in Chapter 5.

Once you have selected the data that is to be backed up, you will have to choose the type of backup to perform and specify the destination of the backup file. By default, the backup file is named Backup.bkf and is destined for the My Documents folder for whomever is logged in at the time of the backup. Figure 15-15 shows the screen to select the backup destination, type, and name of the file.

The final screen in the Backup or Restore Wizard provides a brief summary of the backup created and an Advanced button to further customize the backup. As they are likely to appear on the exam, let's review the advanced backup options.

**Figure 15-13**
The first screen in the Backup Utility allows you to restore or back up data files.

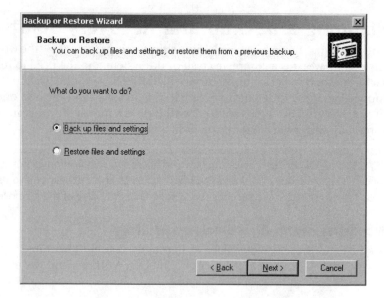

**Figure 15-14**
Choosing to back up selected files or the entire contents of the hard disk

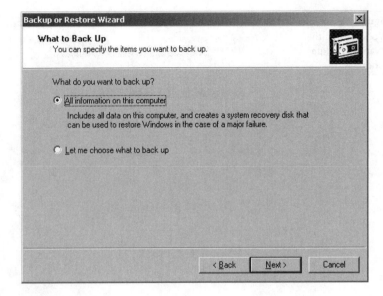

**Advanced Backup Options**

A basic backup using the default options is sufficient for many environments. However, they may be times when it is necessary to customize the backup to tailor it to an organization's specific needs. This is where the advanced options come in. By clicking the Advanced button on the final screen of the Backup or Restore Wizard, you open an Options dialog box (see Figure 15-16).

**Figure 15-15**
The Backup or Restore Wizard allows you to specify the location and type of backup to perform.

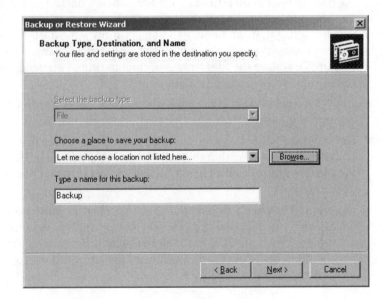

**Figure 15-16**
Working with the
advanced backup
options

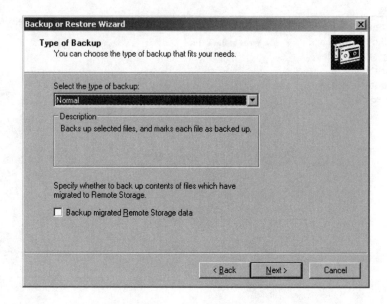

**Backup Type**    When you back up files on a Windows Server 2003 system, you have
five different backup types to choose from. Each of these has a very specific use and offer
specific advantages and disadvantages. You can pretty much count on getting a question
regarding backup types on the exam and in what situations they are best suited.

- **Normal**    This is the default backup option and is most often referred to as a
  full backup. With a normal backup, each of the selected files are backed up and
  the backup system then marks each file as being backed up. Marking files that
  have been backed up is referred to as clearing the archive bit. The archive bit,
  which is a flag that can be set in a file, is simply a means by which the system
  can keep track of the files that have been created or changed since the last
  backup. To restore the files from a normal backup, you need only the most
  recent copy of the backed-up data.

- **Copy**    A copy backup is similar to the normal backup with one notable
  exception: the copy backup does not clear the archive bit.

- **Daily**    The daily backup is used to copy only those files that have been created
  or changed on the day that the daily backup is performed. Like a copy backup,
  the files are not marked as being backed up—in other words, the archive bit is
  not cleared.

- **Differential**    When a differential backup is chosen, only those files that
  have been created or changed since the last normal or incremental backup
  are copied. The archive bit is not cleared with differential backups. To restore
  from a differential backup, you will need the latest full backup as well as the
  most recent differential backup.

- **Incremental** The incremental backup copies only those files that have been created or changed since the last normal or incremental backup. Because the incremental backups are only copying the files that have changed, they are quicker, as less needs to be backed up. The archive bit is cleared with incremental backups. To restore when using incremental backups, you will need the latest normal backup and each incremental you have done since that normal backup.

**Backup Log** Keeping track and reviewing system-generated backup logs is important to ensure that the backups are working correctly. Finding out that backups have failed when you are trying to restore the system is not a good thing.

On the Backup Log tab, you need to decide exactly how much information you need to log. By default, the Backup utility logs only errors and significant system events. From the Backup Log dialog box, you have three options to change what is being logged. The first radio button allows you to select detailed logging. This option logs all information, which may sound good, but it can make the log files too big and any errors listed in the file are harder to find.

The second choice is summary logging. This feature records only key system operations. Because less is logged, errors in the file are easier to find. The final logging option is to not log any system events. This is certainly not recommended and used only in special circumstances.

**Exclude Files** One common strategy when backing up a server is to exclude data that does not need to be backed up. Often, even if you are doing a normal or full backup, there are certain files you don't want to back up. The Exclude Files tab is used to isolate files that are to be excluded from the backup.

## Developing a Backup Strategy

To create a successful backup strategy, you will often have to combine different backup methods. For example, in most organizations losing even one days' worth of data is crippling. As such, a backup would need to be performed daily. Running a full backup once per day is often not practical considering the time it takes and the space required. Therefore, normal backups are often reserved for regular intervals—perhaps once per week. That leaves the rest of the week. To fill in these days you can use either the differential or incremental backup but not a combination of the two.

If you use an differential backup, you may take a normal backup on Sunday, for example, and then daily differentials that provide a daily backup of all the files that have changed since the last normal backup. An incremental backup backs up only those files since the last normal backup or since the last incremental. This makes incremental backups the fastest and the one you should use when there is a very small backup window.

When you restore from these backups, a normal backup is easiest as only a single set of tapes is needed to restore. When restoring from a strategy using differentials and normal backups, you need the latest differential backup and the latest normal backup. Finally, when you restore from a strategy using incrementals, you need all of the incremental backups and the latest normal backup. Because of this, incremental backups are the most difficult and time consuming to restore.

# Using Volume Shadow Copy

It used to be that administrators would run a backup and upon completion of the backup be greeted by a list of files that could not be backed up because they were in use by an application or locked. To get around this, many backups were conducted after hours to ensure that most of the files needing to be backed up were not in use and therefore could be backed up. This created what is known as the backup window, the time in which a backup may be performed when applications and data are not in use. Part a system administrator's role was to develop a solution that allowed a backup to take place within this window.

Windows 2003 helps get around this problem by using Volume Shadow Copy Technology (VSCT). The basic function of VSCT is threefold:

- Applications can continue to write data to the volume during a backup.
- Files that are open are no longer omitted during a backup.
- Backups can be performed at any time, without locking out users.

To enable shadow copies, you use the advanced options in the Backup utility. To access the advanced options, work your way through the steps in creating a backup as described earlier. On the final screen of the Backup or Restore Wizard is an Advanced button used to access the advanced backup options. Clicking this button will guide you through the advanced backup options, including the option to use volume shadow copies.

## Grandfather, Father, Son

One of the more well-known and popular backup strategies is known as the Grandfather, Father, Son (GFS) backup rotation. In this configuration, separate backup tapes are used for monthly, weekly, and daily backups. For example, you could employ the GFS strategy using 12 tapes: 4 for the daily tapes Monday through Thursday (Son), 5 for the weekly tapes (Father), and 3 for the monthly tapes (Grandfather).

When restoring from backup from this strategy, it is possible to recover from a single day to several months back. However, the data from several months back may not be that useful given how fast data changes in modern organizations. Still, the option is there.

# Automated System Recovery

In days gone by (namely, with Windows NT 4 and 2000), you had something called an Emergency Repair Disk (ERD), which could be used to attempt to repair a damaged system. With Windows Server 2003, the ERD has been replaced with the Automated System Recovery (ASR). Not only is the name different, but the contents as well. For security reasons, the ASR disks no longer contain registry data.

ASR is an advanced tool designed to repair a damaged system and is often the last resort when other methods such as Safe Mode, Last Known Good Configuration, and Recovery Console have been unable to restore a system. There are two components needed to create an ASR backup. The first is the actual backup of the data and files, and the second is the creation of a floppy disk required to restore the system to its original state. The following is the procedure to create an ASR disk:

1. Start the Backup or Restore Wizard by typing **ntbackup** in the Run dialog box or by selecting All Programs | Accessories | System Tools and then the Backup icon.

2. The first screen of the Backup or Restore Wizard displays three buttons to access the Backup, Restore, and Automated System Restore (ASR) Wizards. Click the button to start the ASR Wizard.

3. The ASR Wizard will prompt you for a location to save the backup. Choose the location and click Next.

When the disk is created, there are three files created, asr.sif, asrpnp.sif, and setup.log. The asr.sif file contains the server name, master boot record and partition information, and the location of the recovery information. The asrpnp.sif file holds a list of the plug-and-play devices in the system, and the setup.log file contains information on the files that were backed up during the ASR process.

## System Recovery and Restore Using ASR

Once the Windows Server 2003 Backup Utility has been used to create the ASR, if the system were to fail in the future it can be recovered from the time when the ASR backup was created. To restore the system state using the ASR, perform the following steps:

1. Boot from the Windows Server 2003 CD-ROM.

2. When prompted, press F2 to begin the ASR recovery process.

3. Insert your most recent ASR floppy disk in the drive when prompted.

4. Insert the backup data when prompted.

5. Follow the onscreen instructions to complete the installation.

PART III

**EXAM TIP**  ASR is not a utility designed to be used for backing up or restoring data.

 **NOTE**  More information on ASR can be found in Chapter 5.

# Chapter Review

This chapter has presented a whirlwind tour through some of the mechanisms and procedures designed to provide high availability. Server clusters use multiple server nodes to provide failover capabilities in case of system failure. Up to eight nodes can be used in a server cluster. NLB can use up to 32 nodes in a cluster and provides load balancing by dispersing client requests among several nodes.

System Monitor is used to systematically find components or programs that may be causing performance bottlenecks. System Monitor uses counters to measure the physical and logical components in a system. Several of the object counters are specifically designed to track down performance bottlenecks.

There are many considerations when backing up a system. ASR disks are used to back up key system information but not data. The Backup utility is used to back up all data as well as the system state. Volume shadow copy allows backups to record open files that traditionally would have been skipped over with previous backup strategies.

## Questions

1. If a full backup is done Friday night and a differential is done in the evening of every other weekday, what tapes would be required to complete a restore on Tuesday?

    A. The normal backup from Friday only

    B. The normal backup from Friday and three differential tape sets

    C. The normal backup from Friday and every differential backup since Friday

    D. The normal backup from Friday and the latest differential backup

2. As system administrator, you have been reviewing backup logs and discover that many of the files are open and are not being backed up during regular backups. Which of the following strategies can you use to ensure that the open files are being saved?

    A. Using the Advanced options in the Backup Utility, ensure that the system state is being backed up.

    **B.** Using the Advanced options in the Backup Utility, ensure that the option to use volume shadow copy is selected.

    **C.** Using the Advanced options in the Backup Utility, ensure that the option to use volume shadow copy is not selected.

    **D.** Using the Advanced options in the Backup Utility, create an ASR disk and select the Backup Open Files option.

3. You have been tasked with trying to isolate a performance bottleneck in a server system and note the following results:

| Counter | Average Result |
| --- | --- |
| % Disk Time | 94 |
| Pages/sec | 83 |
| % Processor Time | 8 |
| Bytes Total/sec | 10 |

Which system component might you replace to increase performance?

    **A.** Memory

    **B.** Processor

    **C.** Network card

    **D.** Hard disk

4. You are troubleshooting system performance on a server and suspect that there is a processor bottleneck. Which of the following counters would you choose to monitor processor activity? (Choose two.)

    **A.** % Disk Time

    **B.** % Processor Time

    **C.** Current Processor Queue Length

    **D.** Interrupt/sec

5. As system administrator, you decide to implement NLB clusters using a single network adapter in the host nodes. In this configuration, which of the following statements is true?

    **A.** When using a single adapter in unicast mode, node-to-node communication is not possible and nodes within a cluster cannot communicate with each other.

    **B.** When using a single adapter in multicast mode, node-to-node communication is not possible and nodes within a cluster cannot communicate with each other.

    **C.** When using a single adapter, node-to-node communication is not possible.

    **D.** When using a single adapter, NLB cluster protocol must be bound to the network adapter.

6. You are managing an NLB cluster and want to suspend the cluster for maintenance. Which of the following commands will suspend the cluster?

   A. nlb *subnet mask* halt

   B. nlb *ip address* halt

   C. nlb suspend

   D. nlb halt

7. Which of the following commands creates a new quorum log file based on information in the local node's cluster database file?

   A. clussvc /resetquorumlog

   B. clussvc /rebuildlog

   C. nlb /resetquorumlog

   D. clussvc /rebuildlog

8. Which of the following best describes a single shared quorum?

   A. The local disk is configured as the cluster quorum device.

   B. The quorum is placed on a shared storage device in the cluster which all cluster nodes can access.

   C. The quorum requires that cluster configuration information be stored on the local disks of each node.

   D. The quorum requires that cluster configuration information be stored on external storage devices.

9. Which of the following commands is used to verify the status of a server cluster?

   A. clussvc /verify

   B. cluster /*cluster name* node *node name* /status

   C. clussvc /*cluster name* node *node name* /status

   D. cluster /*cluster name* node *node name* /verify

10. Which of the following methods are used to back up the quorum data?

    A. The Backup or Restore Wizard is used to back up the cluster quorum when you perform a system state backup from any node.

    B. The Backup or Restore Wizard is used to back up the cluster quorum when you perform a system state backup from all nodes.

C. The ASR process is used to back up the cluster quorum when you perform a system state backup from any node.

D. The ASR process is used to back up the cluster quorum when you perform a system state backup from all nodes.

## Answers

1. **D.** To restore from a differential backup, you will need the latest full backup as well as the most recent differential backup.

2. **B.** If the volume shadow copy feature is enabled, files that are open are no longer omitted during a backup.

3. **A.** The results of the System Monitor show high average for both the % Disk Time and Pages/sec. This is an indication that there is a lot of paging going on and the hard disk is having trouble keeping up. Adding more memory will reduce the amount of paging necessary. The % Processor time and Bytes Total/sec are within acceptable parameters.

4. **B** and **D.** The % Processor Time is the primary indicator of processor activity, and the Interrupt/sec counter monitors how often the processor is interrupted to handle hardware requests. Answer A is incorrect as % Disk Time is a PhysicalDisk counter, and answer D is not a valid counter.

5. **A.** When using a single adapter in unicast mode, node-to-node communication is not possible and nodes within a cluster cannot communicate with each other. All of the other answers are invalid.

6. **C.** The command nlb suspend will suspend the NLB cluster until it is started again.

7. **A.** The clussvc /resetquorumlog command is used to create a new quorum log file based on information in the local node's cluster database file. All of the other answers are invalid.

8. **B.** The single shared quorum model places quorum resources on a shared storage device in the cluster which all cluster nodes can access.

9. **B.** The cluster.exe command is used to manage server clusters from the command line. The /status option is used to verify the status of the cluster. All other answers are invalid.

10. **A.** When backing up the quorum data, the Backup or Restore Wizard is used to back up the cluster quorum when you perform a system state backup from any node. After you back up the cluster quorum disk on one node, it is not necessary to back up the quorum on the remaining cluster nodes.

# Planning and Maintaining Network Security

In this chapter, you will learn how to
- Identify protocol security using IPSec
- Configure IPSec policy settings
- Plan for secure network communications
- Understand protocol security in heterogeneous computer environments
- Plan remote administration procedures
- Implement wireless security
- Troubleshoot security for data transmissions

In today's network world, data is moving all over the place—through firewalls, over the Internet, across the LAN, and over the WAN. In all of this movement, someone out there wants to access that data and intercept it. Network administrators need to assess the level of risk an organization faces and implement appropriate security measures to respond to the threat.

In this chapter, we look at how to create policies to ensure secure data transmissions over an IP-based network using IP Security (IPSec). We also discuss the unique security needs of wireless networks as well as designing secure remote administration strategies.

## Planning and Implementing Security for Data Transmissions

When data is sent over the network, we assume it will reach its intended destination without being accessed and viewed by anyone for whom it is not intended. The problem is, basic IP transmissions lack security, and anyone with the motivation and know-how can access and modify that data. For many of the data transactions that occur on a day-to-day basis, lack of security is not necessarily a problem because much of what is sent is valueless information. But many communications do require security, and when IP-based communications require security, IPSec is often the answer. Other methods help secure data transmissions, such as Secure Sockets Layer (SSL); however, SSL provides application-layer security, whereas IPSec operates at the IP layer. Working at the IP layer allows IPSec to transparently encrypt pretty much any communication.

## Establishing Secure Connections Between Systems

Understanding how secure communication between systems occurs can at first be a little confusing. With that in mind, this section explores the basics of securing communications and the terms and concepts you need to know.

Before two systems can exchange secure data, they have to mutually agree on a security agreement before communication is to take place. In technical terms, this security agreement is called a security association (SA). For communication to happen, both systems must agree on the same SA.

The Internet Key Exchange (IKE) manages the SA negotiation process for IPSec connections. IKE is an Internet Engineering Task Force (IETF)–established standard method of security association and key exchange resolution. IKE performs a two-phase operation: the first ensures a secure communications channel, and the second phase negotiates the use of SAs.

---

 **NOTE**   Remember that the SA is a compilation of many items. It includes a negotiated key, security protocol, and security parameters index (SPI). When all these elements are added, they define the security to be used from the sender and receiver.

---

## Phase I SA Negotiation

In Phase I negotiation, also known as main mode, the two computers establish a secure and authenticated connection between them. IKE provides the initial protection during this phase. Several items are negotiated during the main mode phase, including the following:

- **Encryption method used**   The encryption methods include Data Encryption Standard (DES) and triple DES (3DES).

- **Integrity algorithm**   Phase I negotiation uses one of two integrity verification methods: Message Digest 5 (MD5), and Secure Hash Algorithm 1 (SHA1).

- **Authentication method**   Authentication methods include Kerberos v5, certificate, or preshared key authentication.

- **Diffie-Hellman**   The Diffie-Hellman represents a base keying strategy. There are three Diffie-Hellman groups: Group 1 (768 bits of keying material), Group 2 (1024 bits), and Group 2048 (2048 bits).

Once these various factors have been negotiated between systems, IKE generates a master key that protects authentication. Without this authentication, the communication fails.

## Phase II SA Negotiation

In this phase, also known as quick mode, a negotiation of which SAs will be used is performed. Three steps must occur to complete phase II:

- **Step 1** Systems exchange requirements for securing data communications. This includes the IPSec protocols, Authentication Headers (AH) and Encapsulating Security Payloads (ESP), integrity and authentication methods (MD5 or SHA1), and encryption methods (3DES or DES). Once an agreement with these elements is achieved, the SA is established. Actually, two SAs are established: one for the inbound traffic, and one for the outbound traffic.

- **Step 2** The security key information between the two systems is updated. In this process, IKE is responsible for refreshing keying material and for creating new or secret keys for the authentication and encryption of packets.

- **Step 3** In the final step, the SAs and keys, along with the Security Parameters Index (SPI), are passed to the IPSec driver.

## Understanding IPSec

IPSec is an IP-layer security protocol designed to provide security against internal and external attacks. This consideration is important because the reasons and methods for securing against attacks from outside the network are well documented. IPSec provides a way to protect sensitive data as it travels within the LAN. As we know, firewalls do not provide such security for internal networks, so a complete security solution requires both a firewall solution and internal protection provided by such security mechanisms as IPSec.

To create secure data transmissions, IPSec uses two separate protocols: Authentication Headers (AH), and Encapsulating Security Payloads (ESP). In a nutshell, AH is primarily responsible for the authentication and integrity verification of packets, whereas ESP provides encryption services. Because they are independent protocols, when implementing an IPSec policy, they can be used together or they can be used individually. Whether one or both are used depends on the security needs of the network.

## Authentication Headers

Before using AH, it is important to understand what its function is and what it can and cannot do. AH provides source authentication and integrity for data communication but does not provide any form of encryption. AH is capable of ensuring that network communications cannot be modified during transmission; however, AH cannot protect transmitted data from being read.

AH is often implemented when network communications are restricted to certain computers. In such an instance, AH ensures that mutual authentication must take place between participating computers, which, in turn, prohibits network communications to occur between nonauthenticated computers.

## Encapsulating Security Payloads

Encapsulating Security Payloads (ESP) is used to provide encryption services to network data; however, it can also be used for authentication and integrity services. The difference between AH authentication and ESP authentication is that ESP includes only the ESP header, trailer, and payload portions of a data packet. The IP header is not protected as with AH, which protects the entire data packet. Relative to encryption services, ESP provides encryption with the DES or 3DES encryption algorithms.

 **EXAM TIP**  Although both AH and ESP provide authentication and integrity services, the difference lies in the exact portion of a data packet that is protected against modification. ESP does not protect the IP header, used to route the packet through the network. AH protects the entire packet.

 **EXAM TIP**  Only network devices and operating systems that support IPSec can take advantage of ESP encryption. If they do not support IPSec, an alternative encryption method, such as SSL, must be employed.

 **NOTE**  As you might imagine, you will rarely need IPSec traffic to pass through a firewall. In previous Windows versions, this was not possible. New features in Windows Server 2003 support IPSec through NAT.

## Using AH and ESP

Given that AH and ESP are indeed separate protocols within IPSec, you need to understand in which instances each may be used. Although no rules are defined, there are some general guidelines. For instance, consider using ESP to do the following:

- Ensure that the contents of a packet are not visible during transport.
- Protect the packet from modification during transport. Recall, ESP does not protect the entire packet from modification, only the TCP/UDP header.

Consider using AH to do the following:

- Ensure mutual client-to-server authentication is required between computers.
- Verify that only authenticated hosts receive transmissions.
- Protect an entire data packet from modification during transport.

 **EXAM TIP**  Although in many circumstances, AH and ESP are combined, be aware of the individual aspects of each protocol for the exam.

## Identifying the Attacks

You know that the purpose of implementing all of this data transmission security is to guard against attacks, but what attacks are you guarding against? You need to be aware of several different types of attacks when configuring a security plan. Knowing the potential threats can help pinpoint the holes that need to be plugged. Some of the types of attacks you need to be concerned with include the following:

- **Eavesdropping** When network communications occur in clear-text format, there is the danger that someone can intercept transmissions and read the data. Of course, once the data is accessed, it can be modified and forwarded. Imagine the impact if this were to occur in a bank. When sensitive data is being transmitted throughout the network, it must be encrypted to protect against eavesdropping.

- **Address spoofing** IP address spoofing is designed to allow the attacker to reroute or access and change data. Essentially, IP spoofing involves convincing a sending computer that it is the intended recipient when it isn't. Network devices often use the IP address to determine the sender and receiver for a data transmission. In a spoofing scenario, the hacker assumes the identity of an IP node.

- **Man-in-the-middle** This attack involves the attacker placing him or herself in between the sending and receiving devices. Once there, the attacker may have the ability to monitor and intercept transmissions between computers and can do so without detection.

- **Denial-of-service attacks** The denial-of-service attack involves flooding a system with unnecessary traffic, which may tax system resources, causing the system to overload. The intent of this attack is not so much to obtain data as it is to block traffic.

- **Sniffer attacks** Sniffer attacks are designed to monitor the network and attempt to access and then view data within a packet. Encryption can be used to encode the data within a packet, reducing the harm of the sniffer attacks.

This list represents only a few of the possible types of attacks you may encounter, but they provide enough motivation to secure those networks and understand how data can be accessed.

PART III

## Choosing IPSec Transmission Modes

IPSec can operate in one of two separate modes: transport mode and tunnel mode. These modes refer to how data is sent throughout the network. In transport mode, IPSec protection is provided all the way from the issuing client to the destination server. In this way, transport mode is said to provide end-to-end transmission security. Figure 16-1 shows an example of IPSec transport mode security.

 **EXAM TIP** When implementing IPSec transport mode, security is maintained for the entire path.

Tunnel mode, shown in Figure 16-2, secures data only between tunnel points or gateways. In this way, tunnel mode provides gateway-to-gateway transmission security. When data is in transmission between the client and the server, it remains unprotected until it reaches the gateway. Once at the gateway, it is secured with IPSec until it reaches the destination gateway. At this point, data packets are decrypted and verified. The data is then sent to the receiving host unprotected.

Tunnel mode is often employed when data must leave the secure confines of a local LAN or WAN and travel between hosts over a public network such as the Internet.

 **EXAM TIP** Tunnel mode provides security only at gateway points; it is not adequate if data needs to be protected on the local network.

For the exam, you will be expected to know not only what tunnel mode and transport mode do, but in what circumstances each may be used. Table 16-1 provides a quick look at some deployment considerations.

## Configuring IPSec

IPSec is used to secure data as it travels between two computers or gateways. Once implemented, network transmissions are free from modification and cannot be read by unwanted eyes. To get to this point, however, many elements are involved in establishing an IPSec policy. These include determining policy rules, defining filter lists and filter

**Figure 16-1**    IPSec transport mode, used for end-to-end transmission security

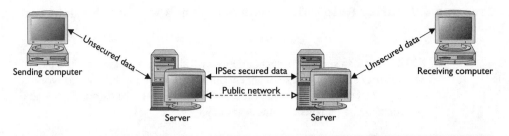

**Figure 16-2**    Tunnel mode, providing gateway-to-gateway transmission security

actions, and identifying the authentication mode used. This section explores each of these individually and what it takes to configure a complete policy.

## IPSec Security Rules

*Security rules* are the element of the IPSec policy that set the behavior of IPSec, and they are used to identify how data communications are to be secured. Security rules are assigned to either network or host IP addresses that are listed in the filter list. Each security rule must contain several configurations, including the following:

- Filter list
- Filter action
- Authentication methods
- Tunnel endpoint
- Connection type

Each policy can have more than a single rule, with rules combined to create versatile IPSec policies.

| Deployment Consideration | IPSec Mode |
| --- | --- |
| An organization's data is being transmitted over a public network. Local network security is not a concern. | Tunnel mode |
| Data is being passed over a WAN that uses a firewall and network address translation. IPSec services must be implemented on perimeter servers to prevent encrypted data from going through NAT. | Tunnel mode between perimeter servers |
| Data is being passed over a WAN that uses a firewall but does not use network address translation. End-to-end IPSec security is required. | Transport mode |
| Secure connection is required between a client and server system only. | Transport mode |
| Highly sensitive data is being transmitted within the local network. | Transport mode |

**Table 16-1**    Deciding to Employ IPSec Tunnel Mode or Transport Mode

**Creating a Security Rule**   The process of creating a security rule can be quite involved.

**NOTE**   Because security is such a concern and IPSec is an important part of a security strategy, we strongly encourage you to take the time to work through the creation and modification of IPsec polices. Hands-on experience will certainly be beneficial come exam day.

The following procedure describes the steps required to establish a security rule.

1. Launch the Microsoft Management Console (MMC) by typing **mmc** in the Run dialog box.

2. In the MMC, select File | Add/Remove Snap-In.

3. In the Add/Remove Snap-In dialog box, click the Add button to open the Add Standalone Snap-In dialog box.

4. In the Add Standalone Snap-In dialog box, select IP Security Policy Management and click the Add button, as shown in Figure 16-3.

5. The Select Computer Or Domain dialog box opens. Here, you have the option to manage the local computer, the domain to which the local computer is attached, or another computer or domain entirely. Figure 16-4 shows the Select Computer Or Domain dialog box. Click Finish to add the policy.

**Figure 16-3**
The Standalone
Snap-In dialog
box, used to add
snap-in features
to the MMC

**Figure 16-4**
The Select
Computer Or
Domain dialog
box, used to
manage local
or remote
computers

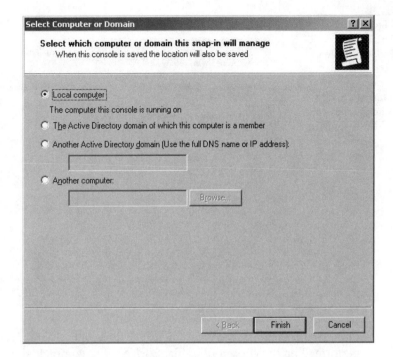

6. Using the recently created snap-in, right-click the desired policy in the right pane, and select Properties from the menu. The Properties dialog box opens for that policy.

7. The Properties dialog box has two tabs: Rules and General. From the Rules tab, click the Add button to start the Security Rule Wizard. Click Next to begin the creation of the security rule.

8. The first wizard screen requires you to specify a tunnel endpoint. The tunnel endpoint determines whether the traffic is tunneled and, if it is, the IP address of the tunnel endpoint. If not establishing a rule for VPN connections, select the This Rule Does Not Specify A Tunnel Point option and select Next. Figure 16-5 shows the Tunnel Endpoint screen.

9. On the Connection Type screen, you determine whether a rule applies to the LAN connection, dial-up connections, or both. Click Next to open the IP Filter List.

10. On the IP Filter List screen, you select a filter to apply to the IP traffic. The filter list contains predefined packet filters that describe the types of traffic to which the configured filter action for this rule is applied. Select the filter type and select Next. Figure 16-6 shows the IP Filter List screen.

**Figure 16-5**
The Tunnel
Endpoint screen,
used to identify
the endpoint of
a tunnel if a VPN
is being used

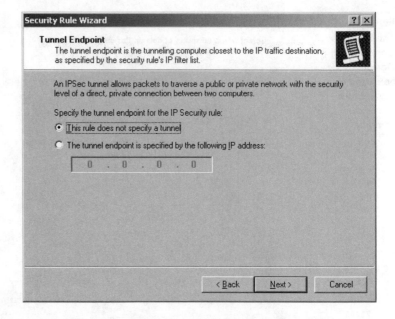

11. On the Filter Action screen, you identify which type of action is to be
performed on the chosen IP traffic. Click Next to complete the creation of
the security rule, which will be added to the Properties dialog box, as shown
in Figure 16-7.

**Figure 16-6**
The IP Filter List
screen, used to
select the filters
to apply to
IP traffic

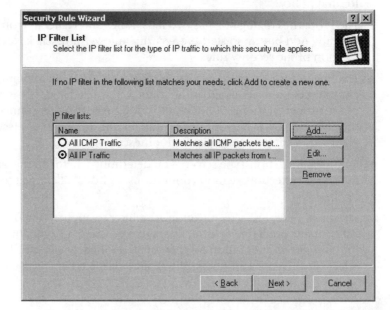

**Figure 16-7**
Added security
rules applied
to current
IPSec policies

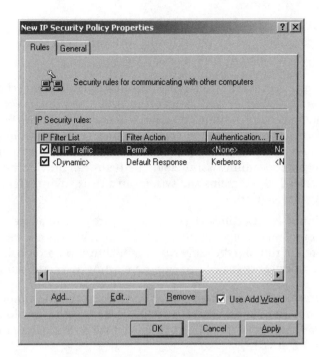

## Choosing the Security Method Used by an IPSec Policy

Another element of managing IPSec policies is to configure the encryption, integrity, and authentication method to be used. Before looking at how these security methods are actually implemented, you should know a little about the security choices supported by IPSec and their respective level of security.

**IPSec Integrity Protocols**   When we talk about integrity verification, we are talking about hash algorithms that are used to verify that the information received is exactly the same as the information sent. A *hash algorithm* is essentially a cryptographic checksum used by both the sender and receiver to verify that the message has not been changed. If the message has changed in transit, the hash values are different and the packet is rejected.

When configuring IPSec integrity security, there are two options: Message Digest 5 (MD5) and Secure Hash Algorithm 1 (SHA1). Of the two, SHA1 is more secure than MD5, but it requires more CPU resources. MD5 offers a 128-bit hashing algorithm. SHA1 uses an algorithm that generates a 160-bit authentication. Although it provides more security than MD5, it can affect overall performance, because it demands more system resources.

PART III

**IPsec Authentication Protocols**   To establish IPSec communications, two hosts must authenticate with each other before SA negotiations can take place. Systems can be authenticated in three different ways:

- **Kerberos**   Kerberos v5 is the default authentication technology used with Windows Server 2003. Kerberos provides the primary security protocol for authentication within a domain; when used, it verifies both the identity of the user and network services. Advantages of Kerberos include the fact that it can provide mutual authentication between the user and the server. Secondly, its interoperability is a strength. Kerberos can provide authentication between Server 2003 domains and systems in a Unix environment that is using Kerberos for authentication.

- **Public Key Certificates (PKIs)**   PKIs are used to authenticate clients that are not members of a trusted domain, non-Windows clients, or computers that are not running the Kerberos v5 authentication protocol. The authentication certificates are issued from a system acting as a certification authority (CA).

- **Preshared keys**   In preshared key authentication, computer systems must agree on a shared, secret key to be used for authentication in an IPSec policy. Preshared keys are to be used only where certificates and Kerberos cannot be deployed.

**IPSec Encryption Protocols**   IPSec offers three primary encryption methods. The one you chose depends on the security needs of your organization. The encryption methods include these:

- **Data Encryption Standard (DES) (40 bit)**   This encryption methods provides the best performance but at a cost: the encryption security is lower. It can be used in environments where data security is a little lower.

- **Data Encryption Standard (56 bit)**   Through your IPSec policies, you can implement DES as the encryption method. The DES algorithm is a 56-bit encryption key. This algorithm was published in 1977 by the US National Bureau of Standards, and it allows for the ability to frequently regenerate keys during a communication. This ability prevents the entire data set from being compromised if one DES key is broken. However, its use is considered outdated for businesses; it should be used only for legacy application support. Specialized hardware has been able to crack the standard 56-bit key.

- **Triple DES (3DES)**   IPSec policies also allow the choice of a strong encryption algorithm, 3DES, which provides stronger encryption than DES for higher security. 3DES uses a 56-bit encryption key as well, but, as the name implies, it uses three of them. As a result, 3DES is considered 168-bit encryption, and it is used in high-security environments like the U.S. government. All computers to which the policy is assigned will receive this policy.

**EXAM TIP**   For the exam, be sure you are aware of the different IPSec encryption methods and under what circumstances they are best used.

**Diffie-Hellman Technique**   The Diffie-Hellman is a cryptographic technique, named after its developers Whitfield Diffie and Martin Hellman. Diffie-Hellman establishes the exchange of public keys, which are used to create secure communication between hosts using IPSec. The Diffie-Hellman requires that two computer systems each have their own private key, which they use together with a public key to devise a common key. The function of this protocol is to allow two systems with no prior knowledge of each other to generate a shared key and securely communicate. (For more information on keys, refer to Chapter 17.)

The keying material exchanged by the two computer systems can be based on three different levels: 768, 1024, and 2048 bits. As you can imagine, the higher the number of bits, the harder it is to crack; but as a tradeoff, it is more demanding on the system's CPU.

## Assigning IPSec Security

Knowing what the various security options are, we can now define the security for an IPSec policy. The following steps outline the procedure for establishing policy authentication and encryption:

1. Using the IPSec snap-in created earlier, right-click the policy in the right pane and select Properties.

2. In the Properties dialog box, select the Rules tab followed by your desired security rule, and finally, click the Edit button.

3. Edit Rules Properties dialog box opens. From here, select the Security Methods tab, as shown in Figure 16-8.

4. Select any one of the security methods, and click Edit to open the Edit Security Method dialog box, as shown in Figure 16-9. This dialog box offers three options: Integrity And Encryption, Integrity Only, and Custom. Each of these options is discussed in the following sections.

**Predefined Security Options**   As mentioned previously, you have three choices when configuring IPSec security. Two of these options are predefined; the third option, Custom, allows customization of the security options. We will look at each of these security options a little more closely:

- **Encryption And Integrity**   This predefined option uses the ESP protocol to establish encryption using the 3DES algorithm, and it uses the SHA1 algorithm to establish authentication and integrity.

- **Integrity Only**   The Integrity Only option uses the ESP protocol to provide data integrity and SHA1 verification; however, ESP does not provide encryption services.

**Figure 16-8**

The Security Methods tab, used to assign security methods to an IPSec policy

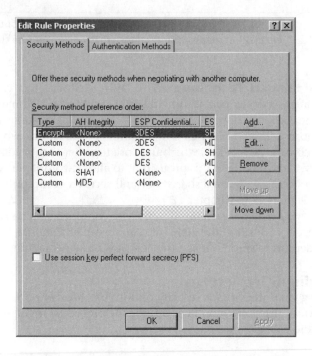

**Figure 16-9**

The Edit Security Method dialog box, used to configure the security methods you will use

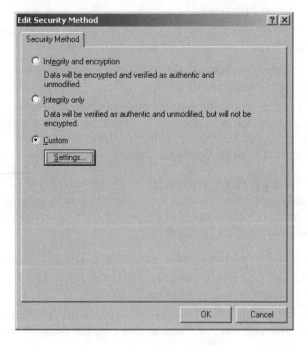

- **Custom** In many cases, the predefined parameters of Encryption And Integrity do not meet the security needs. This is where the Custom option comes in. With the custom security settings, many options are configurable, including assigning ESP and AH protocols, 3DES/DES encryption, and integrity algorithms.

**EXAM TIP** Review the custom options for IPSec security before taking the exam.

## Filter Lists

The IPSec security rule identifies how data communications are to be secured. This task is accomplished by using an IP filter list. The filter list determines which IP traffic is to be affected by the security rule. To better understand filter lists, we can create new ones and modify existing filter lists, as described in the following procedure:

1. Using the IPSec snap-in, right-click the security policy and select Properties.

2. In the Properties dialog box, select the Rules tab, select the desired security rule, and click the Edit button to open the Edit Rule Properties dialog box.

3. Select the IP Filter List tab in the Edit Rule Properties dialog box. Figure 16-10 shows the IP Filter List tab.

**Figure 16-10**
The IP Filter List tab, used to modify the IP addresses and types of traffic affected by the filter

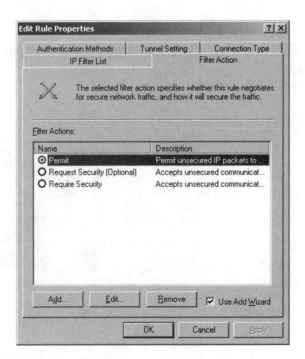

**PART III**

4. From the IP Filter List tab, click the Add button or the Edit button to add a filter list or to edit a current list.

## Choosing IPSec Filter Actions

You use the filter actions to determine how security will be handled for the IP addresses identified in the filter list. You configure filter actions from the Filter Action tab in the Edit Rule Properties dialog box mentioned earlier. Figure 16-11 shows the Filter Action tab.

As shown, three actions can be taken when configuring IPSec filter actions:

- **Permit** The Permit IPSec security option is the absence of security. Packets are allowed to travel around the network without IPSec protection.

- **Block** On the other side of the security spectrum is the Block option. When the Block filter option is used, a protocol that matches an associated IP filter will not be accepted on the network.

- **Negotiate Security** If an IPSec filter is matched, the Negotiate Security option enables the administrator to set the encryption and algorithms that must be used to secure data transmissions.

 **EXAM TIP** Be sure you are familiar with the various TCP/IP port assignments for the exam.

**Figure 16-11**
The New Filter Action Properties dialog box, used to set filter actions

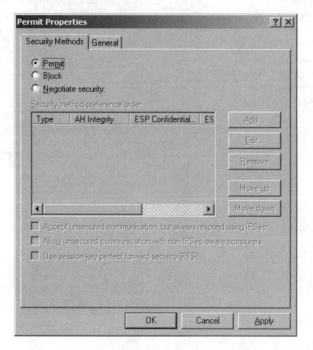

## Working with Ports

When you configure IPSec, you need to know which ports are assigned to the various protocols. Essentially, each protocol within the TCP/IP suite has a port association. During communication, the target port is checked to see which protocol or service is destined for. The request is then forwarded to that protocol or service. As an example, HTTP uses port 80. When a web browser requests a web page, the request is sent through port 80 on the target system.

65,535 ports are available. These are broken down into three distinct designations: well-known ports (1–1023), registered ports (1024–49151), and dynamic ports (49152–65535). Fortunately on the exam, you will not need to know how all these ports are assigned, but you will need to know commonly used TCP/IP port assignments and the service, TCP or UDP, they use. These are included in Table 16-2.

**NOTE**   You can obtain a complete list of port designations from the Internet Assigned Numbers Authority (IANA) at http://www.iana.org/assignments/port-numbers.

**EXAM TIP**   Although not listed previously, IPSec uses ports 50 and 51, and UDP uses port 500. To tunnel through a firewall, these ports need to be opened.

| Protocol | Port Assignment | TCP/UDP Service |
|----------|-----------------|-----------------|
| FTP | 21 | TCP |
| SSH | 22 | TCP |
| Telnet | 23 | TCP |
| SMTP | 25 | TCP |
| DNS | 53 | UDP |
| TFTP | 69 | UDP |
| HTTP | 80 | TCP/UDP |
| POP3 | 110 | TCP |
| NNTP | 119 | TCP |
| IMAP4 | 143 | TCP |
| SNMP | 161 | UDP |
| HTTPS | 443 | TCP |

**Table 16-2**   TCP/IP Ports

## Predefined IPSec Policies

Windows Server 2003 includes three predefined IPSec polices that may meet the security needs of an organization. These security polices may work in their default state, or you can modify them to accommodate the unique needs of an organization. By examining the default options available and reviewing their settings, you get a better idea of what you need to be do when creating a policy from scratch.

### Client (Respond Only)

In this configuration, the client tells Server 2003 not to use the IPSec option by default. Instead, IPSec is engaged only when it is requested by another system or network device. In this configuration, the client system never initiates IPSec security; however, it communicates using IPSec when requested to do so.

This default policy is built from what is known as the *default response rule*. This default rule applies to both inbound and outbound connections. The default configuration settings include the following:

- IP Filter List: <Dynamic>
- Filter Action: Default Response
- Authentication: Kerberos
- Tunnel Setting: None
- Connection Type: All

If any of these default settings does not meet your needs, you can modify them or create a new policy. For example, if necessary, you can change the authentication type from Kerberos to PKI, or you could change the connection type from All to LAN or Remote Access only.

### Server (Request Security)

The Server (Request Security) policy offers more security than the Client policy. In this configuration, the system initially requests IPSec-secured traffic, but then it compromises and allows unsecured communications if the other system does not support IPSec. In this way, the entire communication can be unprotected if systems are not IPSec-enabled.

To see how this policy is made, take a look at the three rules used to create it.

Rule 1

- IP Filter List: All IP Traffic
- Filter Action: Request Security (Optional)
- Authentication: Kerberos
- Tunnel Setting: None
- Connection Type: All

Rule 2

- IP Filter List: All ICMP Traffic
- Filter Action: Permit
- Authentication: N/A
- Tunnel Setting: None
- Connection Type: All

Rule 3 (Same default rule as the Client option)

- IP Filter List: <Dynamic>
- Filter Action: Default Response
- Authentication: Kerberos
- Tunnel Setting: None
- Connection Type: All

## Secure Server (Require Security)

This policy offers the greatest level of security. The Secure Server policy secures all network traffic to or from the computer on which the IPSec policy is applied. This policy rejects all packets from nonaware IPSec clients.

This policy has a rule to require security for all IP traffic, but notice that it allows ICMP traffic, and the default response rule is similar to the other predefined policies:

Rule 1

- IP Filter List: All IP Traffic
- Filter Action: Require Security
- Authentication: N/A
- Tunnel Setting: None
- Connection Type: All

Rule 2

- IP Filter List: All ICMP Traffic
- Filter Action: Permit
- Authentication: Kerberos
- Tunnel Setting: None
- Connection Type: All

Rule 3 (Same default rule as the Client policy)

- IP Filter List: <Dynamic>
- Filter Action: Default Response
- Authentication: Kerberos
- Tunnel Setting: None
- Connection Type: All

By examining the various rules in these predefined policies, you get a better idea of what you need to design policies to meet an organization's standards.

## Application-Layer Security

So far, we have discussed using IPSec to protect data transmissions at the IP layer. It is possible, however, to secure data communications at the application layer. Several protocols are used to provide authentication and integrity at the data transmissions and at the application layer. Let's review a few of them.

Server Message Block (SMB) and the Common Internet File System (CIFS) sign each packet as it is sent, while the receiving computer verifies the authenticity and integrity of each packet it receives. As a result, SMB can protect data transmissions between a client and the server computer. The advantage of SMB over IPSec is that it works with previous Windows versions. IPSec is an option for Windows 2000/2003–based clients; SMB is available to Windows 98 and later Windows versions.

Secure Multipurpose Internet Mail Extensions (S/MIME) and Pretty Good Privacy (PGP) are used to digitally sign e-mails so they cannot be modified in transit. Both protocols also provide the means to encrypt e-mail messages so they cannot be read in transit. If S/MIME is used to encrypt a message, it has to be used on the other end to decrypt that message.

Two other protocols that can secure data at the application layer include Secure Sockets Layer (SSL) and Transport Layer Security (TLS). SSL is most often associated with web pages and is used to encrypt data sent between the server and the client. In addition to securing web pages, SSL is also used to encrypt Lightweight Directory Access Protocol (LDAP) queries, Post Office Protocol v3 (POP3) authentication, Network News Transfer Protocol (NNTP) authentication and Internet Message Access Protocol (IMAP) authentication. However, an application must support the use of SSL encryption to use it. Because IPSec works at the IP level, applications are unaware of it being used, making it more versatile that its SSL counterpart.

TLS is much like SSL in that it can provide authentication and message integrity. A key difference between them is that TLS uses different encryption algorithms. Windows Server 2003 can use TLS to encrypt smart card authentication.

# Configuring Protocol Security in a Heterogeneous Client Computer Environment

You typically use a firewall to protect against attacks from the outside, but something else is required when protecting the data that travels around the LAN and over public networks. In a Windows Server 2003 environment, IPSec and the application-layer security protocols function. But what do you use in heterogeneous computer environments that maintain a multitude of OS's, including Unix, Linux, and even Macintosh systems? The answer is easier than you might think.

Many of the programs and utilities used in a heterogeneous computer environment send data in clear text across the network. Some of these applications include FTP, Telnet, POP3, and IMAP. As with a pure Windows environment, your security choices occur at the application and IP layer.

In a heterogeneous environment, similar methods, SSL and TSL, can be used to protect data over an internal or potentially insecure network and achieve data integrity and privacy. As in a Windows world, TLS and SSL are commonly used to provide solutions to protect users' data from unwanted intruders. They basically provide applications with enhanced sockets that automatically encrypt any data flowing through them. SSL is not platform-dependent and is used by web browsers when they are using the HTTPS protocol.

On the IP level, you can still use IPSec to encrypt clear text that must travel over the network. On non-Windows platforms, IPSec still uses the two independent protocols, AH and ESP, to ensure authentication, integrity, and encryption services.

## Configuring IPSec Policy for Non-Windows Systems

To implement IPSec security polices for data transmissions, you can take a look at the default polices to provide some. If, for example, you have a Unix system that uses Telnet on the network and you wish to secure its clear-text transmissions, you need to define both the filter and the filter actions. When designing the filter, you must configure the inbound and outbound transmissions from a Telnet client to the Telnet server from the MMC console. The creation of an IPSec filter is shown in Figure 16-12.

The figure shows that the filter is designed to verify data transmissions from any IP address to the Telnet's servers address (the My IP Address option). The protocol type is TCP, the source port is any port, and the destination port is 23. With the filter for Telnet created, you can configure the actions that will be taken when someone tries to access the server using Telnet and port 23.

As shown in Figure 16-13, you have the option to permit access, block access, or negotiate security.

In short, you can configure your Windows Server 2003 systems to enforce IPSec-secure communications, or you can customize those filters to allow some secured access while at the same time, allow certain insecure transmissions to pass.

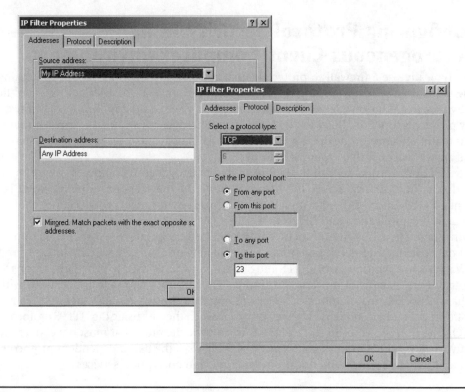

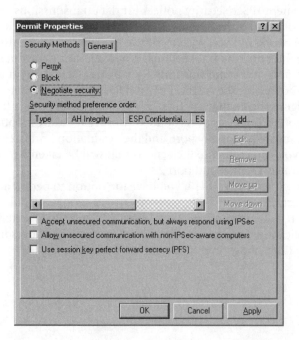

**Figure 16-12**    Configuring an IPSec filter for Telnet access

**Figure 16-13**
Determining filter
actions for a filter

**NOTE**   while working with filters, you may notice an option to enable mirrored filters. This option is used to create two filters based on the filter of your settings: one for traffic to the destination, and one for traffic from the destination.

# Planning Secure Network Administration

Gone are the days when a system administrator needed to walk around from system to system to manage the network. Today's networks are often managed from a single location using remote management tools. Although there are certainly benefits to this scenario, there are some implementation considerations. However, the ability to avoid fixing computer problems over the phone is indeed a step in the right direction.

## Creating a Plan to Offer Remote Assistance to Client Computers

For anyone who has spent time supporting end users, the idea of remote assistance is more than welcome. Remote Assistance enables an expert to remotely assist an end user with a computer problem. The expert has different options for remote assistance: either viewing the computer system or making recommendations to correct the error or remote assistance can be configured to completely take control of the remote system and repair the computer from a remote location.

An end user can request remote assistance through the Windows Messenger Service, through an invitation saved as a file, or through an e-mail. Remote Assistance is a feature of Windows XP and Server 2003 products.

An expert can connect to a remote system through the Internet or over the LAN or WAN. It is even possible to use Remote Assistance behind a firewall. To do this, TCP port 3389 must be open.

**EXAM TIP**   To offer remote assistance through a firewall, the firewall must have port 3389 open.

## Securing Remote Assistance

If someone has complete access to a system using Remote Assistance, that person has total control over that system and its files. This opens up a few very important security issues that must be addressed before you implement a policy to allow Remote Assistance. There are three areas to secure if Remote Assistance is a concern, as described in the following sections.

**Local Computer Security**   Every now and then, the user of an individual system may require Remote Assistance from an expert. Most of the time however, the Remote Assistance feature is not needed and can therefore be disabled on the local system. The following procedure outlines the steps to turn off both incoming Remote Assistance opportunities and to prevent the local computer from requesting Remote Assistance.

1. Choose Start | Control Panel, and select System. The System Properties dialog box opens.

2. In the System Properties dialog box, select the Remote tab, as shown in Figure 16-14.

3. The first check box is Allows You To Turn On Remote Assistance And Allow Invitations To Be Sent Form This Computer. This option is off by default and should remain off until needed. Select the check box to allow Remote Assistance.

4. The bottom check box is used to allow remote computers to access the computer using Remote Assistance. It too is set to off by default. To enable Remote Assistance, select the check box.

5. With Remote Assistance enabled, you can click the Select Remote Users button to identify user accounts, from this or other domains, which can access your local computer.

**Figure 16-14**
The Remote tab, used to enable and disable Remote Assistance for a local Windows Server 2003 system

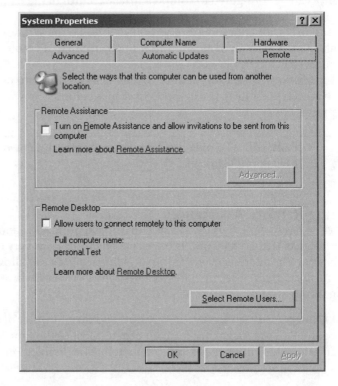

**Securing Remote Assistance at the Firewall**   Much of the Remote Assistance use will come from within the same LAN. However, it is possible to provide remote assistance to computers within a private network from a public network. This is a particularly intimidating thought for network administrators in charge of security. If systems within a LAN are configured to accept Remote Assistance queries, access can be controlled at the firewall to prevent a potential threat. To prevent Remote Assistance at the firewall, port 3389 must be blocked.

**Securing Remote Assistance Using Group Policy**   One final option for controlling Remote Assistance access is to create a Group Policy designed to prevent users from requesting a Remote Assistance session. The same group Policy can be configured to restrict the option to allow someone to remotely access the system.

## Planning for Remote Administration by Using Terminal Services and Remote Desktop for Administration

In Windows 2000, if you wanted to remotely manage a system using Terminal Services, you used something called Terminal Services in remote administration mode. Although the functionality remains practically the same, the name has changed in Windows Server 2003 to Remote Desktop for Administration.

Remote Desktop for Administration is built on Terminal Services technology, and, like other remote administration methods, is designed to reduce support overhead by remotely managing end-user systems. Remote Desktop for Administration establishes the remote connection using the Terminal Services Remote Desktop Protocol (RDP) on port 3389.

**NOTE**   It is not necessary to purchase Terminal Services licensing when using Remote Desktop for Administration.

## Securing Terminal Services Administration

Users who are authenticated over a Remote Desktop for Administration session have remote access to the system and complete control over that system. Therefore, security concerns arise when this type of remote administration is used.  When implementing Remote Desktop for Administration, consider the following:

- **Passwords**   All users who have remote access should use strong passwords. General guidelines for passwords include one that has at least seven characters, does not contain your user name, real name, or company name, and doesn't use a complete dictionary word.

- **Firewall**   Remote Desktop for Administration is built on Terminal Services technology and therefore uses port 3389. To prevent this type of remote access into the network, this port should be blocked at the firewall.

- **Group Policy Restrictions**   Using the Group Policy Editor, it is possible to set restrictions on Terminal Services access, including session length, number of connections, and various encryption and security settings.

# Planning Security for Wireless Networks

In this chapter, we have discussed the methods used to secure data transmissions over the LAN and the WAN, but what about those data transmissions that travel over the air-waves? There is no doubt that wireless communication has changed the way we do business. It has given us unparalleled mobility but has brought with it some security concerns.

Wireless LANs (WLANs) present a unique challenge to administrators. A wired network, for instance, requires a physical connection for tampering; WLANs, on the other hand, present an opportunity for anyone within range of a wireless access point (AP) to eavesdrop on the network. This makes wireless communications a significant security concern for administrators.

## 802.11-Based Basic Security

The 802.11b and 802.11a are the most widely deployed WLAN technologies today. While being widely deployed, they do have their share of security concerns. Out of the box, the 802.11 standards offer some basic security measures, including the use of open and shared-key authentication and wired equivalent privacy (WEP) keys. This combination offers a measured level of security, but over time, it's been shown that each of these elements can be compromised. The following list looks at each of these 802.11 security measures.

- **Open System Authentication**   As strange as it sounds, the Open System Authentication doesn't actually provide authentication services. Instead, it provides identity verification by exchanging data messages between a wireless client and the wireless access point. With open authentication, the use of WEP prevents the client from sending data to and receiving data from the access point, unless the client has the correct WEP key.

- **Shared Key Authentication**   Shared Key Authentication does provide authentication. In the Shared Key Authentication process, the wireless access point sends a client system a challenge text packet that the client must then encrypt with the correct WEP key and return to the access point. If the client is unable to provide the correct key, authentication will not succeed and the client will not be allowed to associate with the access point.

- **WEP**   WEP is defined by the IEEE 802.11 standard and is intended to provide a level of data confidentiality that is equivalent to a wired network by encrypting the data sent between wireless clients and wireless access points. In application, WEP requires that all communicating parties share the same secret key.

> **NOTE** WEP can function in both a 40- and 128-bit versions, but both are easily cracked using easily accessible online tools.

## 802.1x Authentication

802.1x is an IEEE standard designed for authenticating not only wireless 802.11 networks, but also to wired Ethernet networks. The 802.1x standard provides a method for authenticating access to a network and managing keys used to protect traffic. 802.1x uses the Remote Authentication Dial-In User Service (RADIUS) to provide network authentication services to verify a potential client's credentials. In addition, 802.1x uses Extensible Authentication Protocol (EAP) for message exchange during the authentication process.

## EAP and 802.1x

EAP is an extension of the Point-to-Point Protocol (PPP) that supports authentication methods that go beyond the simple submission of a user name and password. EAP was developed in response to an increasing demand for authentication methods that use other types of security devices such as token cards, smart cards, and digital certificates. The support that 802.1x provides for EAP types allows you to use any of the following authentication methods:

- **EAP-Transport Level Security (EAP-TLS)**   EAP-TLS is an authentication method that uses certificates for server authentication and can also use certificates and smart cards for client authentication.

- **Protected EAP with EAP-TLS (PEAP-EAP-TLS)**   PEAP-EAP-TLS provides authentication using certificates and not credentials, user names, or passwords. Smart cards can also be used for authentication. Using PEAP-EAP-TLS, client certificate information is encrypted, providing additional security over EAP-TLS.

- **Protected EAP with EAP-Microsoft Challenge Handshake Authentication Protocol version 2 (PEAP with EAP-MS-CHAPv2)**   Despite the long name, this authentication method is straightforward. Certificates are used to define server authentication and a user name and password for user authentication. Of these methods, this one is easiest to implement because by using MS-CHAP, all client authentication is password-based. This means that certificates or smart cards do not need to be installed on clients.

> **NOTE** More information on MS-CHAP and other authentication protocols is provided in Chapter 14.

PART III

# Troubleshooting Security for Data Transmission

As with everything else in the world of technology, sometimes the tools we use to secure data transmissions don't work like they should. This is where troubleshooting begins. This section looks at two different utilities that can be used to trace transmission problems: the IP Security Monitor and the Resultant Set of Policy (RSOP) snap-in.

## IP Security Monitor

The IP security Monitor snap-in is a utility used to determine if IPSec communications are successfully secured. The tool provides a wealth of information on the status of IPSec, including filters, security associations, IKE policies, negotiation policies, and security statistics. In addition, it can be used to show the number of packets that have been sent over the AH or ESP security protocols and how many keys have been generated since the computer was last started. In short, it is the place to go when you want statistics on the functioning of IPSec on a local or remote system. Some of the detailed information provided includes the following:

Monitor IPSEc traffic on both local systems as well as remote computers.

- View the details of all IPSEc polices.
- View both main and quick mode filters.
- View SA information.

Figure 16-15 shows the IPSec Security monitor.

### Adding the IP Security Monitor Snap-In

As mentioned, the IP Security Monitor is a snap-in tool. The following procedure outlines the steps required to add it:

1. Type **mmc** in the Run dialog box to open the console.

2. With the console open, select File |Add/Remove Snap-In, and then click Add.

3. From the available options, locate and select the IP Security Monitor option, and then click Add.

4. Click Close, and then click OK.

---

 **NOTE** The IP Security Monitor snap-in is designed to monitor IPSec on computers running Windows Server 2003. The IPSecmon command is used to monitor IPSec in a Windows 2000 environment.

---

## Using the Resultant Set of Policy

Resultant Set of Policy (RSoP) is a snap-in used to view existing IPSec policy assignments. It can also be used to test a planned IPSec policy before deployment to work out

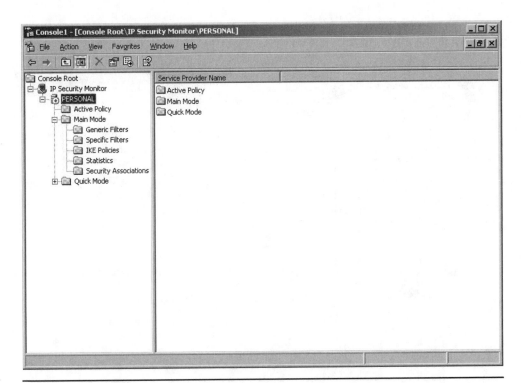

**Figure 16-15**   The IPSec Security snap-in, used to monitor IPSec traffic on a local or remote computer system

the bugs before implementation. To view IPSec policies, you need to add the snap-in to the MMC and then run a query. Two types of queries can be performed: logging mode queries and planning mode queries.

## Logging Mode Queries

A *logging mode query* provides information on current IPSec policies that are assigned to an IPSec client. The query results quickly display which IPSec policies are currently assigned and which are not. It can also display information on specific policy information such as filter rules, filter actions, authentication methods, tunnel endpoints, and connection type. Figure 16-16 shows a logging mode query.

## Planning Mode

Planning mode provides you with a way to test a security implementation without actually putting it into play. In this way, you can troubleshoot IPSec configurations before they do any harm to the network. In planning mode, a wizard guides you through the steps of creating a simulated policy and then allows you to view the results as if that policy were actually implemented.

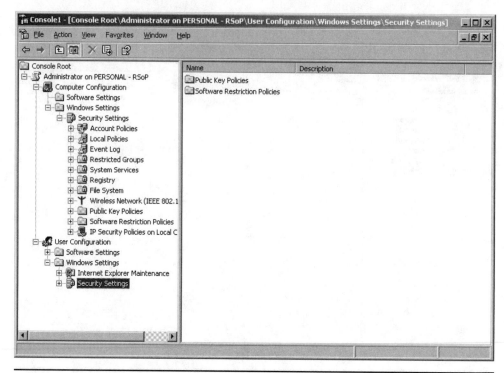

**Figure 16-16**   The logging mode query, showing current IPSec policy assignments

## Configuring IPSec with NETSH

The netsh IPSec commands provide a command-line alternative for the console-based utilities. Using netsh, you can access all the capabilities of the IP Security Policy Management and IP Security Monitor MMC snap-ins. It is also possible to view static and dynamic mode settings and all IPSec configuration parameters.

### Static netsh IPSec Mode Commands

Static commands are used to create, modify, and assign IPSec policies without immediately affecting the configuration of the active IPSec policy. Several static commands can be administered, as summarized in Table 16-3.

**NOTE**   To use static commands, you need to access the command prompt and switch to the IPSec static command prompt. To do this, type **netsh ipsec static**.

| Command | Description |
|---|---|
| Add filter | Adds a filter to the specified filter list |
| AddFilterAction | Establishes a filter action using quick mode security methods |
| Add filterlist | Creates a new filter list |
| Add policy | Creates a new IPSec policy |
| Add rule | Creates a new IPSec rule |
| Delete all | Deletes all current IPSec policies |
| Delete filter | Deletes a specified filter |
| Delete filteraction | Deletes a specified filter action |
| Delete filterlist | Deletes a specified filter list |
| Delete Policy | Deletes a specified IPSec policy and associated rules |
| Delete rule | Deletes specified rules from an IPSec policy |
| Exportpolicy | Exports IPSec policies to a specified file |
| Importpolicy | Imports IPSec policies from a specified file. |
| Restorepolicyexamples | Restores IPSec defaults |
| Set defaultrule | Modifies a default response rule |
| Set filteraction | Makes changes to an existing filter action |
| Set filterlist | Modifies an existing filter list |
| Set policy | Modifies an existing IPSec policy |
| Set rule | Modifies an existing IPSec rule |
| Set store | Identifies the IPSec storage location |
| Show all | Displays the configuration information for all IPSec policies |
| Show filteraction | Identifies the configuration for various filter actions |
| Show filterlist | Identifies the configuration for various filter lists |
| Show gpoassignedpolicy | Identifies the configuration information for active IPSec polices assigned to a specified group policy object |
| Show policy | Identifies the configuration for various IPSec policies |
| Show rule | Identifies the configuration information for a rule for a specified policy |

**Table 16-3**   Identifying Static netsh IPSec Commands

## Dynamic netsh IPSec Commands

Dynamic netsh commands are used to make immediate changes to the IPSec configuration. In some cases, for the changes to take effect, the IPSec service needs to be stopped and restarted. Dynamic IPSec commands take effect only when the IPSec service is running. Table 16-4 summarizes the netsh IPSec dynamic commands.

**NOTE**   To switch to a dynamic IPSec command mode, type the following: **netsh ipsec dynamic**.

| Command | Description |
| --- | --- |
| Add mmpolicy | Creates a new IPSec main mode policy and adds it to the security policy database (SPD) |
| Add qmpolicy | Creates a new quick mode IPSec policy and adds it to the SPD |
| Add rule | Creates a new rule for the main mode or quick mode polices and adds it to the SPD |
| Delete all | Deletes all IPSec policies and filters from the SPD |
| Delete mmpolicy | Deletes a single or multiple main mode polices from the SPD |
| Delete qmpolicy | Deletes a single or multiple quick mode polices from the SPD |
| Delete rule | Deletes a rule from the SPD |
| Set config | Modifies a variety of IPSec settings |
| Set mmpolicy | Changes the configuration of an IPSec main mode policy and updates the SPD |
| Set qmpolicy | Changes the configuration of an IPSec quick mode policy and updates the SPD |
| Set rule | Changes the configuration of an IPSec rule and updates the SPD |
| Show all | Summarizes configuration information for all polices, filters, and security associations in the SPD |
| Show config | Displays the values for various IPSec settings |
| Show mmfilter | Summarizes information for a specified main mode filter or multiple main mode filters in the SPD |
| Show mmpolicy | Summarizes the configuration information for a specified main mode policy in the SPD |
| Show mmsas | Summarizes the main mode security associations in the SPD |
| Show qmfilter | Summarizes information for a specified quick mode filter or multiple main mode filters in the SPD |
| Show qmpolicy | Summarizes the configuration information for a specified quick mode policy in the SPD |

**Table 16-4**    Identifying the Dynamic netsh IPSec Commands

# Chapter Review

In this chapter, we have taken a quick tour through the processes involved in securing data transmissions. On a network, data can be secured on the application layer using such protocols as SSL and TLS. Data can also be protected on the IP layer using IPSec. Because IPSec works on the IP layer, it is transparent to applications.

Many settings and configurations are involved in establishing an IPSec policy. This includes the creation of rules, filters, and filter actions. Additionally, the type of communication, tunnel mode or transport mode, needs to be assigned.

IPSec, SSL, and TLS are not proprietary security measures and can be used in heterogeneous computing environments. When IPSec is used, the server can be configured to accept or reject data based on whether or not the communications are secured with IPSec.

Wireless networks provide unique security challenges to the administrator. 802.11 is the most widely used wireless standard but suffers from some security flaws. It does have built-in security measures, WEP open key authentication, and shared key Authentication. All three are easily cracked using available tools. The EAP and 802.1x is a wireless security strategy designed to compensate for the security weaknesses of 802.11.

## Questions

1. The Accounting department in an organization currently sends unencrypted sensitive data on the network. You have been asked to implement a solution that will both encrypt the data and prevent manipulation of that data. As a solution, you implement IPSec using AH. Which of the following best describes the outcome?

   A. Data will be protected from modification but will not be encrypted.

   B. Data will be encrypted but may still be captured and modified.

   C. Data is both encrypted and protected from modification.

   D. Only the IP header is encrypted while the data is protected from modification.

2. The Accounting department of an organization has decided to transfer payroll requirements to a remote office. Both offices are protected by a firewall, but neither one is using NAT. You have been asked to provide end-to-end security for the payroll data. As a solution, you propose to open UDP port 500 on the destination firewall, configure both AH and ESP, and configure IPSec in tunnel mode. What is the likely outcome of the solution?

   A. Data will be protected from the sending computer all the way to the receiving computer.

   B. Data will be protected from the sending computer to a tunnel endpoint. Data will travel unsecured to the final destination.

   C. Data will not pass through the firewall and packets will be rejected.

   D. Data will pass unsecured to the tunnel entry point, pass secured to the destination tunnel point, and pass unsecured to the final destination computer.

3. Several attempts have been made make Remote Assistance calls into a LAN. You have been asked to ensure that Remote Assistance is not allowed from systems outside of the LAN. You still wish to offer Remote Assistance within the LAN. Which of the following is the easiest way to accomplish this task?

   A. Disable the option to allow remote assistance on each of the individual systems.

   B. Create a Group Policy limiting the acceptance of remote assistance sessions.

**C.** From the Remote Assistance server, block port 500.

**D.** From the firewall, block port 3389.

4. As system administrator, you have been asked to ensure that the highest level of encryption is being employed in the network. The current configuration is shown in Figure 16-17.

Considering the information in Figure 16-17, what, if anything, can you do to increase encryption security?

**A.** Enable AH and configure it to use SHA1 encryption strength.

**B.** Enable AH and configure it to use 3DES encryption strength.

**C.** Configure ESP to use 3DES encryption strength.

**D.** Configure ESP to use MD5 encryption strength.

5. XYZ, a hat manufacturer, has recently had its network security compromised from within. As a result, you have been asked to implement an IPSec policy that secures all network traffic to or from the computer on which the IPSec policy is applied. This policy should reject all packets from nonaware IPSec clients. The company's current IPSec policy is as follows:

- IP Filter List: All IP Traffic

- Filter Action: Request Security (Optional)

- Authentication: Kerberos

- Tunnel Setting: None

- Connection Type: All

**Figure 16-17**
Current
encryption
settings

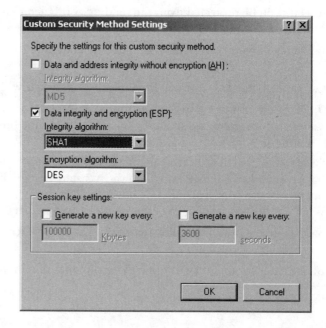

What must you change to meet XYZ's security needs?

A. Change the IP Filter List setting to Block.

B. Change the Authentication setting to Preshared Keys.

C. Change the Filter Action setting to Require Security.

D. Change the Filter Action setting to Request Security (Required), and change the IP Filter List setting to Block.

6. You have been asked to implement an IPSec policy that offers the greatest level of authentication. Which of the following best suits your needs?

A. Preshared keys

B. Kerberos

C. Certificates

D. SHA1

7. Smith and Jones Inc. is an accounting firm with two separate offices across town. Traditionally, they have been unconcerned with sending sensitive data between offices over a public network. However, they have become increasingly concerned with possible eavesdropping both over the public network and inside the local LAN. Which of the following IPSec methods could you employ?

A. IPSec operating in transport mode

B. IPSec operating in tunnel mode

C. IPSec using Advanced Public Encryption (APE)

D. IPSec using SSL secure communication

8. Which of the following netsh commands is used to display all of the IPSec configuration information?

A. netsh ipsec static show all

B. netsh ipsec dynamic show more

C. netsh ipsec static IPSec config

D. netsh ipsec dynamic IPsec config

9. You have recently made a series of changes to the IPSec configuration but have now decided that the security measures you have employed are too restrictive. You need to reduce security measures and implement an IPSec policy that does not explicitly require security for all network traffic to or from the computer on which the IPSec policy is applied. The current configuration is as follows:

- IP Filter List: All IP Traffic
- Filter Action: Require Security
- Authentication: Kerberos
- Tunnel Setting: None
- Connection Type: All

Which of the following changes will accomplish this goal?

A. Modify the IP Filter List setting to Allow Unrestricted IP Traffic

B. Modify the Filter Action setting to Request Security (Optional)

C. Modify the IP Filter List setting to Request Security (Optional)

D. Modify the Filter Action List setting to Allow Unrestricted IP Traffic

10. Which of the following IPSec encryption protocols offers 168-bit encryption?

A. DES

B. Triple DES (3DES)

C. Kerberos v5

D. SHA1

## Answers

1. **A.** AH is designed to prevent the manipulation of data during transit, but it does not have a mechanism for encryption. To achieve the desired results, both AH and ESP need to be used.

2. **D.** IPSec tunnel mode is known as a point-to-point or gateway-to-gateway technology. In this light, if configured, data will be secured only when passing between these two points. It will not be secured on either side of the tunnel. To provide for end-to-end security, IPSec would have to be configured for transport mode.

3. **D.** Remote Assistance can work through a firewall into a local LAN, but only if port 3389 is open. To limit Remote Assistance capability to the internal network, block the port.

4. **C.** To increase encryption security, you can configure ESP to use 3DES encryption, which provides a higher level of security than the currently configured DES encryption method.

5. **C.** Changing the Filter Option setting to Require Security forces the use of IPSec for data communications. This policy rejects all packets from nonaware IPSec clients.

6. **B.** SHA1 will best suite your needs.

7. **A.** IPSec transport mode provides end-to-end security for data communications.

8. **A.** Issuing the command netsh ipsec static show all reveals the configuration for all IPSec policies, including rules, filter lists, and filter actions.

9. **B.** Changing the Filter Action setting to Request Security (Optional) reduces security and allows packets from non-IPSec aware clients.

10. **B.** 3DES offers up to 168-bit encryption and is used to secure communication for organizations with highly sensitive data.

# Planning and Maintaining a Security Infrastructure

In this chapter, you will learn how to

- Understand public key infrastructure terms and concepts
- Publish Active Directory and certificates
- Design a public key infrastructure
- Enroll and distribute certificates
- Authenticate smart cards
- Monitor security
- Update a security infrastructure

In the days of old, user logon security was provided using a combination of user names and passwords. Each time a user logged on, the users credentials had to be compared against a server's database for authentication. The problem with this arrangement is that while the user name and password identified the user, there was no way to validate the server. This opens up the potential for man-in-the-middle attacks where a hacker can impersonate the validating server and the user unknowingly passes data to the wrong location. What was needed was a way to validate both the user and the server and ensure that the information is going to the right place.

Windows Server 2003 provides the tools to do just that. In this chapter, we look at the mechanisms designed to secure communication between server and client systems, namely, designing a public key infrastructure (PKI).

## Planning a Public Key Infrastructure Using Certificate Services

A *public key infrastructure* is a collection of software, standards, and polices that are combined to control certificates and public and private keys. A PKI is comprised of several services and components working together to develop the PKI. Some of the key components of a PKI include the following:

- **Certificates**   A form of electronic credentials that validates users, computers, or devices on the network. A certificate is a digitally signed statement that associates the credentials of a public key to the identity of the person, device, or service that holds the corresponding private key.

- **Certificate authorities (CAs)**   Entities that validate the identity of a network device or user requesting data. CAs issue and manage certificates. CAs can be either independent third parties, known as a *public CA*, or they can be organizations running their own certificate-issuing server software, known as *private CAs*.

- **Certificate templates**   Templates used to customize certificates issued by Windows Server 2003 Certificate Services. This customization includes a set of rules and settings created on the CA and used for incoming certificate requests.

- **Certification Revocation List (CRL)**   A list of certificates that have been revoked before they have reached the certificate expiration date. Certificates are often revoked due to security concerns such as a compromised certificate.

 **NOTE**   Each of the PKI elements mentioned here is discussed in more detail throughout this chapter.

Before we get into actually planning and designing a PKI, we thought it best to first review some of the terms and concepts that you will encounter when working with a PKI.

## PKI in Action

The following sections discuss areas in which a PKI is normally used. Knowing what a PKI is used for gives you a better idea of whether it is needed in a particular network.

## Web Security

In many environments, the Internet has obviously become critical to the daily operation of organizations of all sizes. Despite its benefit to business and the opportunity to expand business, the Internet also brings with it a vast array of security concerns. To increase security and confidence using the Web as a business tool, PKI offers the following benefits:

- **Server authentication**   With PKI, client systems have a way of validating that the server they are communicating with is indeed the intended sever. Without this information, it is possible for people to place themselves between the client and the server and intercept client data by pretending to be the server.

- **Client authentication**   On the other side of the equation, server systems need to have a method of verifying a client's identity. PKI provides the mechanisms necessary to validate the client's identity.

- **Confidentiality** PKI provides secure data transmissions using encryption strategies between the client and the server.

In application, PKI works with the Secure Sockets Layer (SSL) protocol and the Transport Layer Security (TLS) protocol to provide secure HTTP transfers, referred to as HyperText Transport Protocol Secure (HTTPS) protocol. To take advantage of the SSL and TLS protocols, both the client system and the server require certificates issued by a mutually trusted certificate authority (CA).

If the server and client have validated each other's certificate, they can authenticate each other. Then secure communication can occur between the two parties over the Internet.

## Digital Signatures

*Digital signatures* are the electronic equivalent of a sealed envelope and are intended to ensure that a file has not been altered in transit. Any file with a digital signature is used to verify not only the publishers of the content or file, but also to verify the content integrity at the time of download. On the network, PKI allows you to issue certificates to internal developers/contractors and allows any employee to verify the origin and integrity of downloaded applications.

## Secure E-Mail

Today's organizations rely heavily on e-mail to provide external and internal communications. Some of the information sent via e-mail is not sensitive and does not need security, but for those communications that contain sensitive data, a method is needed to secure e-mail content. PKI is a widely deployed method for securing e-mail transactions.

In application, a private key is used to digitally sign outgoing e-mails and the sender's certificate is sent with the e-mail so the recipient of the e-mail can verify the sender's signature. In addition to message verification, PKI can encrypt e-mail messages using a public key to encrypt the message and a private key to decrypt it.

## Encrypted File System

The Encrypted File System (EFS) is a file encryption technology used to store encrypted files on an NTFS volume. Data encryption is certainly not a new concept, and it plays an integral role in a system's overall security strategy. EFS encryption, however, works only on the NTFS 5 file system used with Windows 2000/XP and Server 2003.

The function of EFS is to scramble or encrypt the data on the hard disk, preventing unauthorized users from viewing the protected files. If an unauthorized user attempts to open or copy an encrypted file, he or she will receive an Access Denied error. To authorized users, however, working with encrypted files is no different that working with any other file. For instance, it is not necessary to "decrypt" a file before using it. By default on a Windows Server 2003 system, only the creator of the file and the system's designated recovery agent can access the encrypted files.

In addition to encrypting files, in Windows Server 2003, it is also possible to mark folders for encryption. This means that files created in or copied to an encrypted folder will automatically become encrypted. The folder itself, however, is not actually encrypted: anyone who has the file access permissions to the folder can open it and look at the names of the files within it. They cannot, however, open and access the files within it.

EFS uses PKI technology to provide the mechanisms needed to encrypt files and for EFS file recovery. Each file that is to be encrypted using EFS creates a random key that is used to create the file. A copy of the secret key is associated with the file. When retrieving the file, EFS transparently unwraps the copy of the secret key encrypted with the user's public key using the user's private key. This is then used to decrypt the file in real time during file read and write operations. Similarly, a recovery agent may decrypt the file by using the private key to access the secret key.

## Public and Private Keys

Discussions of PKI will certainly include mention of public and private keys. In fact, it is hard to get started without a good understanding of these and how they are associated with PKI. The term *key* is used for very good reason—public and private keys are used to lock (encrypt) and unlock (decrypt) data. These keys are actually long numbers, making it next to impossible for someone to access a particular key.

When keys are used to secure data transmissions, the computer generates two different types of keys, a public key and a private key. The distinction between the two is as follows:

- **Public key**   A nonsecret key that forms half of a cryptographic key pair that is used with a public key algorithm. The public key is freely given out to all potential receivers.

- **Private key**   The secret half of a cryptographic key pair that is used with a public key algorithm. The private part of the public key cryptography system is never transmitted over a network.

Keys can be used in two different ways to secure data communications: public key encryption and symmetric key encryption.

- Public (asymmetric) key encryption uses both a private and public key to encrypt and decrypt messages. The public key is used to encrypt a message or verify a signature, and the private key is used to decrypt the message or to sign a document. Figure 17-1 provides a simplified look at the process of public key encryption.

- Private (symmetric) key encryption uses a single key for both encryption and decryption. If a person possesses the key, he or she can both encrypt and decrypt messages. Unlike public keys, this single secret key cannot be shared with anyone except people who should be permitted to decrypt as well and encrypt messages. Figure 17-2 shows an example of the private key encryption method.

As you might have guessed, public key encryption has a major advantage over symmetric key encryption. Because symmetric key encryption uses only a single key, it should not be used for communications over an insecure channel unless a secure channel also exists for the key to be distributed to the valid users. It only makes sense that if a secure channel exists, there is no need to encrypt communications and send them via an

**Figure 17-1**    Public key encryption, using both a public and private key

insecure channel. Public-key technology makes it possible through the use of multiple keys to securely transmit sensitive data via an insecure channel.

 **EXAM TIP**    Public key encryption allows two parties to exchange secure communications over an insecure communications network.

## Certificates

Certificates are the cornerstones of the PKI. A *certificate* is essentially a form of electronic credentials that validates users, computers, or devices on the network. A certificate is a digitally signed statement that associates the credentials of a public key to the identity of the person, device, or service that holds the corresponding private key. Certificates can provide a number of security services, including authentication, encryption, and digital signatures.

- **Authentication**    An important part of a security strategy. For authentication to happen, users are required to prove their identity to the network device or server to which they are trying to communicate. Certificates provide the means to ensure that this communication is secure and that the parties involved in the communication are who they say they are.

- **Encryption**    The process of converting something that is in a plaintext form into an unreadable form. This prevents unwanted eyes from viewing potentially sensitive data. *Decryption* is the process of taking the unreadable data and converting it to something that can be read. This can be thought of as locking something valuable into a strong box with a key. Using certificates, we have the ability to protect e-mail messages, files on a disk, and files being transmitted across the network.

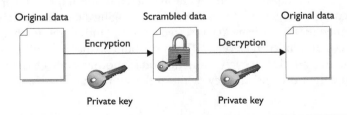

**Figure 17-2**    Private key encryption, using a single key for both encryption and decryption

- **Digital signature**   A way to ensure the integrity and origin of data. Integrity involves ensuring that the data being received has not been altered since it was signed. Digital signatures also provide a method of verifying the identity of the person or entity who signed the data. This enables the important security features of *integrity* and *nonrepudiation*, which are essential for secure electronic commerce transactions.

Certificates are issued for a variety roles, including securing e-mail (S/MIME), ensuring web user and web server authentication, Internet Protocol Security (IPSec), and for Transport Layer Security (TLS). To do this, each certificate must include specific information, such as the following:

- A subject's key value
- Specific requester information such as an e-mail address
- A specified validity period that determines the expiration date of the certificate
- Certificate issuer information and the digital signature of the issuer

## Certificate Stores

*Certificate stores* are essentially a container for certificates and their associated properties. The PKI uses five different types of certificates stores:

- **Personal**   Stores a user's or computer's certificates for which the related private key is available.
- **CA**   Stores the issuing and intermediate certificate authority certificates to use in the CA hierarchy.
- **Enterprise Trust**   Contains Certificate Trust Lists. These are an alternate mechanism that allows an administrator to specify a collection of trusted CAs that must verify to a self-signed CA certificate in the trusted root store.
- **Trusted Root**   Contains only self-signed CA certificates that are trust points in the PKI.
- **UserDS**   Stores a logical view of the certificate container that is located in the Active Directory and is used to simplify access to certificate stores.

## Trusts

The issue of *trust* is an important consideration when looking at the PKI. For instance, in a private key encryption method, the two parties exchanging data trust their shared private key. It is assumed that the private key is stored securely, and therefore, there is message integrity between the sender and receiver. The trust is built on the security of the private key.

A trust built in a public key encryption method is another story altogether. Both parties each secure their own private key, while at the same time, they have to share each other's public key. This means that when we receive a digitally signed message, we need to be able to trust that the digital signature is from whoever claimed to make it. Trusting this public key is a critical consideration for the public key infrastructure to work. The problem is, how can a public key be implicitly trusted?

There are two steps in forming this trust. The first is confirming the validity of the signature using the known public key. Using this key, it is possible to determine the integrity of the signature and ensure that the signature is mathematically valid. The problem is, even if you know the signature is mathematically valid, how do you know you used the right public key? That is, is it the public key from the other end of the communication that made the signature in the first place? It may not be.

To complete the trust in a public key encryption, it is necessary to locate a certificate for the public key that can verify the key belongs to the right entity. To do this, the certificate must be issued by a certificate authority (CA) that is implicitly trusted by the receiver. If the receiver trusts a particular CA, then all certificates issued by that CA are, in turn, trusted.

Once a certificate has verified the public key by a trusted CA, then the signature is trusted.

# Certificate Authorities

Certificate authorities (CAs) are entities that validate user identities and that issue and manage certificates. As outlined previously, the CA provides security certificates that ensure that people are who they say they are. CAs can be either independent third parties, known as a public CA, or they can be organizations running their own certificate-issuing server software, known as private CAs.

## Public CAs

Public CAs are organizations such as Verisign or Entrust, which issue publicly accessible certificates. On the Internet, many of the e-commerce sites use these types of third-party CAs for their secured web sites. Such a strategy is designed to increase consumer confidence in ensuring that the communication is secure. Public CAs are often used in the following circumstances:

- If you are buying or selling products over the Internet, you can use third-party certificates to verify the transaction.

- If the resources or trained personnel are not available to deploy a PKI strategy into an internal network, a public CA can be used.

- If certification use is limited, public CAs have the infrastructure in place to accommodate limited use.

- Third-party CAs can be used for interorganization communication as the certificates are acquired from a common third-party root authority.

PART III

## Private CAs

Public CAs have found considerable success when conducting transactions over the Internet; however, some organizations choose to create and manage an internal CA. While it may take more effort to create an internal CA, it also provides an organization with control over all client-issued certificates and as a side benefit, decreases cost of obtaining certificates from third-party CAs. Private CAs are often deployed under the following conditions:

- An organization requires increased control over client-issued certificates.
- Current infrastructure and expertise are in place to support the PKI.
- An organization wishes to reduce the costs associated with obtaining third-party certificates.

## Certificate Hierarchies

Windows Server 2003 uses a hierarchal CA model. This approach gives PKI a scalable and manageable architecture. In some network environments, a single server CA may be used, but often, multiple CAs are used with established parent/child relationships. This model is sometimes referred to as a *rooted hierarchy* because the initial server is known as the root CA.

The *root CA* is designed to become the most trusted CA in the network's PKI. Because of the role root CAs play on the network, they are typically protected more than their subordinate counterparts. If the root CA on a network is somehow compromised, the certificate security on the network is vulnerable.

Directly below the root CA are any number of subordinate, or intermediate, CAs, which in turn can issue certificates. There is no requirement that all CAs share the same root CA parent. Figure 17-3 shows the rooted CA hierarchy.

**NOTE**  In CA lingo, a *subject* refers to the entity that requests a certificate or holds a certificate.

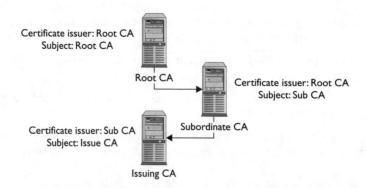

**Figure 17-3**    A rooted CA hierarchy, most often implemented in a Windows 2003 environment

As shown in Figure 17-3, there may be other CAs below the subordinate CA, known as *issuing CAs.* Having these multiple levels of CAs allows increased security for the root CA as the root can be isolated from the network. This allows the subordinate CAs to issue specific certificates to clients.

**EXAM TIP** A rooted CA allows the root CA server to be removed from the network and secured. If the root CA is compromised, all certificates issued will need to be revoked.

Many networks use a single server to act as the CA and issue certificates. However, it may be smart to use a hierarchal CA structure for many reasons, such as fault tolerance, load balancing, security, and organizational reasons.

## Planning the Hierarchy and Certificate Distribution

Deciding to implement the CA hierarchy is the first step; the next is to identify the type of organization to use for the hierarchy. As with any other network design, there are a few options, as described in the following sections.

**Certificate Authority Hierarchy by Location** When designing the organization for the CA, a common design is to use geographical location. Many networks span over many locations, and a location-based hierarchy is well suited for such environments. Consider Figure 17-4, which has a head office in San Diego connected to networks in Vancouver and one in New York.

Figure 17-4 shows a single subordinate CA in Vancouver and New York, but in application, it may be necessary to have additional CAs at both locations.

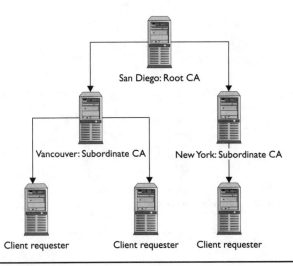

**Figure 17-4** Hierarchal distribution of CAs

PART III

**Certificate Authority Hierarchy by Network Organization**    Many of the networks you work with will have some form of administrative structure. For example, network segments may be broken up according to function, such as accounting, customers, staff, marketing, and so on. In such a case, you can design your CA hierarchy according the overall network administrative layout. Figure 17-5 provides an example of such a strategy.

As seen in Figure 17-5, the third layer of CAs allow a dedicated CA for junior accountants and senior accountants and similarly, full- and part-time staff. This strategy is beneficial in creating different templates for the different users. For example, the different CAs allow an administrator to easily set up different validity dates for certificates for full- and part-time staff.

**Certificate Authority Hierarchy by Usage**    Certificates can be issued for a number of reasons, including securing e-mail, deploying IPSec, performing smart card logon, and securing web transfer. This provides a structure by which you can design the CA hierarchy. In such a configuration, CAs will be assigned to each of these different areas. Figure 17-6 shows an example of the CA hierarchy by usage.

As shown in Figure 17-6, the Server1 subordinate CA issues certificates only for e-mail and SSL requests; Server2 issues certificates for IPSec and smart card requests. Such a strategy adds an extra level of the issuance of certificates.

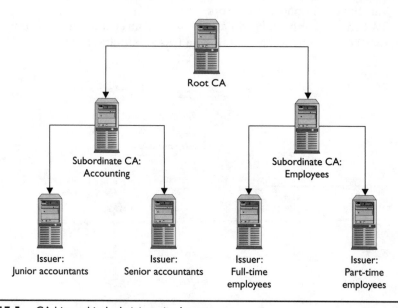

Root CA

Subordinate CA:
Accounting

Subordinate CA:
Employees

Issuer:
Junior accountants

Issuer:
Senior accountants

Issuer:
Full-time
employees

Issuer:
Part-time
employees

**Figure 17-5**    CA hierarchical administrative layout

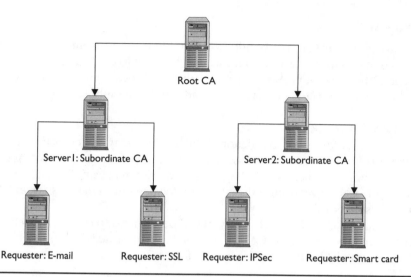

Server1: Subordinate CA

Server2: Subordinate CA

Requester: E-mail    Requester: SSL    Requester: IPSec    Requester: Smart card

**Figure 17-6**    CA hierarchy divided by usage

**NOTE**    The configuration for the offline root CA is contained in a text file known as the capolicy.inf. The capolicy file must be in the system root folder before Certificate Services is installed. The configurations in the file are read during the installation of Certificate Services.

## Offline CAs

One of the strategies to ensure the security of the root CA is to remove it from the network or take it offline. Doing this will ensure that the root CA cannot be compromised because if it is, all certificates issued underneath it will be compromised as well. In fact, in some organizations, the root and second-level subordinate CA are taken offline.

When the decision is made to take the root, and possibly several subordinate CAs, offline, keep in mind a few important considerations. One such consideration is the physical storage of the offline CAs. The best scenario here is lock them away where only administrators have access. Another consideration is the expiration of the root certificate. Like any other certificate, it has a validity date, and this date should be the longest-issued certificate date of any certificate on the network. Finally, even when the root CA is offline, any issued certificates must still be verified against the revoked certificate entries listed in the CRL. If the root CA is offline, the CRL has to be moved to an accessible location on the network.

## CA Types

Before you can deploy CAs in a Windows Server 2003 environment, you need to know which types of CAs there are and what each are designed to do. When installing Certificate Services, there are four CA options from which to choose: enterprise root CA, enterprise subordinate CA, standalone root CA, and standalone subordinate CA.

### Enterprise Root CAs

The enterprise root forms the foundation of the CA hierarchy. An enterprise root CA requires the use of Active Directory and assigns itself a CA certificate. Enterprise CAs can issue certificates for purposes such as digital signatures, secure e-mail using S/MIME, authentication to a secure web server using SSL or TLS, and logging onto Windows Server 2003 domain using a smart card.

When installing Certificate Services, you will be required to choose between the enterprise CAs and the standalone CAs. To help make an informed decision, here are a few points to remember about enterprise root CAs.

- To install an enterprise CA, Active Directory must be used.

- You must be a domain administrator or be an administrator with Write access to Active Directory to install an enterprise root CA.

- The enterprise CA publishes user certificates and the Certificate Revocation List (CRL) to Active Directory. To publish certificates to Active Directory, the server on which the CA is installed must be a member of the Certificate Publishers group.

- Enterprise CAs use certificate templates, and each of these templates has security permissions set in Active Directory. These permissions verify whether the certificate requester is authorized to obtain the certificate type he or she has requested.

 **NOTE**   Like an enterprise root CA, the enterprise subordinate CA requires Active Directory. You use enterprise subordinate CAs when you want to take advantage of Active Directory, certificate templates, and smart card logon.

### Standalone Root CAs

One of the fundamental differences between the enterprise root CAs and the standalone CAs is that the standalone root CA may or may not be a member of a domain. This means it is not necessary to use Active Directory when using a standalone root CA. If Active Directory is used, the standalone CA will use it to publish certificates and to develop the CRL lists.

Standalone CAs issue certificates for purposes such as digital signatures, secure e-mail using S/MIME, and authentication to a secure web server using SSL or TLS.

 **EXAM TIP**   When not connected to a domain, standalone CAs are easily taken offline and securely stored.

Consider the following before installing a standalone CA:

- Standalone CAs do not require the use of Active Directory.

- Certificate templates are not used. This means the certificate requester must provide identifying information in the certificate request. This information would normally be supplied in the certificate template.

- No certificates can be issued for logging on to Server 2003 domain using smart cards.

 **NOTE** The standalone subordinate CA is similar to the standalone root; however, the subordinate must receive its certificate from another CA. Standalone subordinates may or may not be a member of a domain and, therefore, do not require Active Directory.

 **EXAM TIP** Standalone CAs do not support smart card logon.

# Deploying Server 2003 Certificate Services

Deploying Certificate Services in a Windows 2003 environment is a straightforward process. First, thing you need to install the Certificate Services.

1. Select Start, Control Panel, and choose Add/Remove Programs. The Add Or Remove Programs dialog box opens.

2. From the Add Or Remove Programs dialog box, select the Add/Remove Windows Components option. The Windows Components Wizard opens.

3. From the Windows Components Wizard, select the box to install the Certificate Services, as shown in Figure 17-7.

4. The CA Type screen opens, as shown in Figure 17-8. Select the desired type of CA and click Next. To complete this exercise, we will use the Enterprise Root CA option.

5. In the CA Identifying Information screen, you identify the name of the CA and enter the *validity period*: the period of time when the certificate can be accepted as an authoritative credential. Click Next to open the Certificate Database Settings dialog box.

6. The Certificate Database Settings screen is used to identify the location of the certificate database and the associated log files. The default location is systemroot\system32\CertLog. Select a location, click Next, and the configuration of the CA will begin. At this point, you may be prompted to supply the Windows Server 2003 CD for installation files.

7. After several minutes, the Certificate Services will be installed on the local computer system.

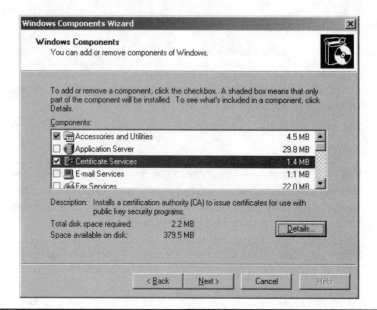

**Figure 17-7**   Certificate Services, installed from the Windows Components Wizard

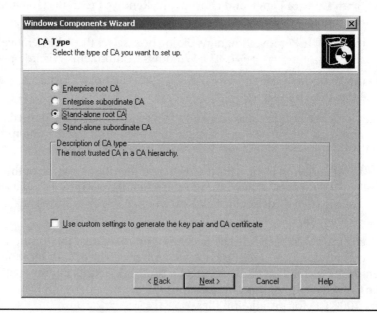

**Figure 17-8**   The CA Type screen, used to determine the type of CA to install

## Managing Certificate Authority

Once Certificate Services has been installed on the computer, you can manage certificates from the MMC console. To do this, the CA must be added to the MMC console. Figure 17-9 shows the MMC console with the Certification Authority snap-in.

As shown in Figure 17-9, there are five areas to administer under the CA server tree: revoked certificates, issued certificates, pending requests, failed requests, and certificate templates.

## Revoked Certificates

When a certificate is revoked, it is invalidated by the system before its natural expiration date and stored in the Revoked Certificates folder. To revoke a certificate, open the Issued Certificates folder, right-click the certificate you wish to revoke, and choose Revoke from the menu. You will be prompted to provide a reason why the issued certificate will be revoked. Figure 17-10 shows the Certificate Revocation dialog box.

A certificate may need to be revoked for a number of reasons; most often, it is related to a security concern. Some of the reasons for revoking a certificate include these:

- A subject's private key has been compromised.
- A CA's private key has been compromised.
- A certificate should not have been issued.
- A change has occurred in the status of the subject holding the certificate.

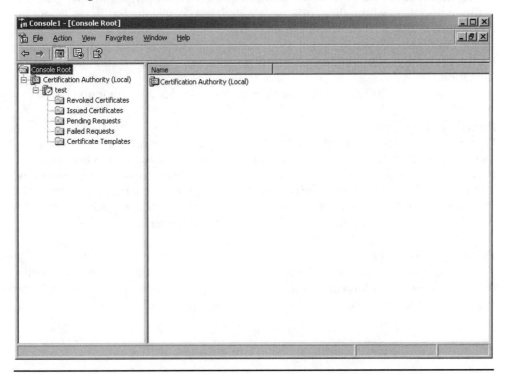

**Figure 17-9**    Management of certification distribution using the MMC console

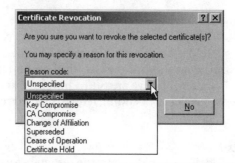

**Figure 17-10**   Supplying a reason to revoke a certificate

   **EXAM TIP**   If you suspect that a certificate has been compromised, you can revoke it using the MMC console and the CA snap-in.

## Issued Certificates

The Issued Certificates folder lists just that—the certificates that have been issued. When you double-click any of the issued certificates, an information dialog box opens, providing details on the issued certificate. The information dialog box contains three tabs that display information. The General tab provides quick reference on the intended purpose of the certificate, to whom the certificate is issued, who issued the certificate, when the certificate was issued, and when it expires.

The Details tab, shown in Figure 17-11 shows all the details of the issued certificate, including security information, signature algorithm, serial number, and public key information.

The final tab is Certification Path, which simply identifies the path to the CA.

## Pending Requests

When the CA receives a request for a certificate, that certificate can either be issued immediately, or it can be held as a pending request. Requests are sometimes held as pending to give the administrator a chance to review the certificate request before issuing it. This is particularity important if the issuing CA has been configured as a standalone CA. Standalone CAs do not verify the certificate requester using Active Directory; as such, there is no way to confirm the identify of the certificate requester.

## Failed Certificates

The Failed Requests folder maintains a list of the certificates that have requested a certificate but were unsuccessful. This is often a result of an administrator rejecting a certificate request from the requester.

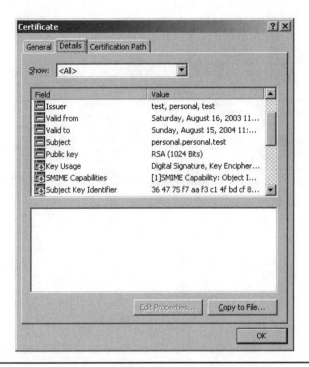

**Figure 17-11** The Details tab, used to highlight specific information of an issued certificate

## Certificate Templates

Certificate templates are an important part of an enterprise CA. They are used to customize certificates issued by Certificate Services. This customization includes a set of rules and settings created on the CA and used for incoming certificate requests. The templates are stored in Active Directory for use by every CA in the forest. Figure 17-12 shows the current certificate templates and those installed by default when the system is set up.

 **EXAM TIP** Certificate templates can be issued by an enterprise CA running only on Windows Server 2003, Enterprise Edition, or Server 2003, Datacenter Edition.

When you double-click any of the templates, the Properties dialog box for that template opens, summarizing the details of that certificate template.

**Managing Certificate Templates** The Certificate Templates folder provides the means to view the current templates, but it may be necessary to add or modify templates. To add a certificate template to be issued, right-click the Certificate Templates

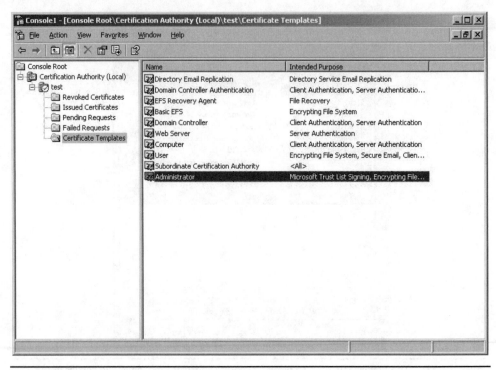

**Figure 17-12**    Installed templates, stored in the Certificate Templates folder in the MMC

folder, select New, and select the Certificate Template To Issue option. The Enable Certificate Templates dialog box opens, as shown in Figure 17-13.

## Certificate Enrollment and Issuance

The process of certificate enrollment involves the entire procedure of requesting, receiving, and installing a certificate. A key part of this process, as you might imagine, is *certificate issuance*. Certificates can be issued in two ways: manually or automatically. The method you use depends on many factors, including the type of CA installed.

In any case, when designing a certificate strategy, you need to configure the default action to take when the CA receives a certificate request. To establish these default settings, follow these steps:

1. Open the MMC console by typing **mmc** in the Run text box.

2. With the MMC open, add the Certificate Authority snap-in to the console.

3. In the console tree, click the name of the CA.

4. From the Action menu, select the Properties option to open the Properties dialog box for that CA. Choose the Policy Module tab, as shown in Figure 17-14.

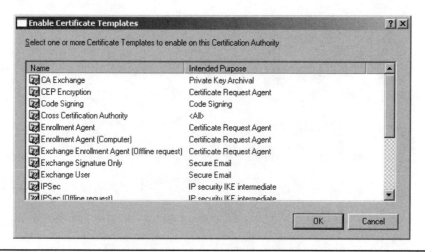

**Figure 17-13**    The Enable Certificate Templates dialog box, used to add a template to the CA

5. On the Policy Module tab, click the Properties button to open the dialog box used to configure how certificate requests will be handled by default. Figure 17-15 shows this dialog box.

**Figure 17-14**
The Policy
Module tab,
providing access
to configuring
certificate
issuance

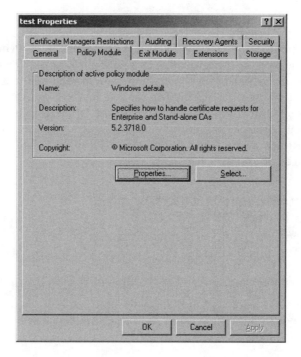

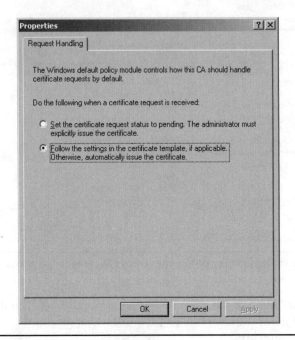

**Figure 17-15**    Configuring the default parameters for certificate requests

As shown in Figure 17-15, two configurable options exist for the default certificate response. The first is Set The Certificate Request Status To Pending. The administrator must explicitly issue the certificate. This setting is high on overhead because the administrator would have to review every certificate request before it is issued.

The second option is Follow The Settings In The Certificate Template, If Applicable. Otherwise, Automatically Issue The Certificate. In this configuration, the certificate template is read first to see if there are issues regarding issuance. If the certification template has no instructions for issuance, the certificate will be issued automatically. The administrator need not review each certificate request.

## Automatic Issuance Using the Group Policy Object Editor

It is also possible to set how certificate requests will be handled using the Group Policy. The configuration for this and the options available are straightforward:

1. Open the MMC and add the Group Policy Object Editor snap-in to the console.

2. Expand the tree as follows: Local Computer Policy/Computer Configuration/ Windows Settings/Security Settings/Public Key Policies. Click the Public Key Policies folder.

3. An icon entitled Autoenrollment Settings displays in the right pane. Double-click it to open the Autoenrollment Settings Properties dialog box, as shown in Figure 17-16.

There are a few options when configuring the autoenrollment behavior. The ability to autoenroll at all can be blocked by selecting the option, Do Not Enroll Certificates Automatically. You also have the choice, Enroll Certificates Automatically. In addition, you can configure more actions such as automatically renewing expired certificates, removing revoked certificates, and updating certificates that use templates.

# Configuring Certificate Renewal

Certificates are issued with a defined lifetime in which they remain active. As such, a strategy must be in place to renew certificates as they near their expiration. User and Computer certificates can be manually renewed from the MMC console. To do this, you must add yet another snap-in to the console, Certificates, as shown in Figure 17-17.

When the certificate is renewed, you have a few choices about how that renewal will affect the currently issued public and private keys. In the renewal process, you can either reuse the same public and private key, or generate a new set of keys. When renewing the certificate, best practice is to obtain a new public and private key for security reasons. Reusing the same keys over and over increases the likelihood of a compromised key. Figure 17-18 shows the renewal options for user and computers.

---

 **NOTE** When renewing keys for a CA, it is sometimes best to keep the same keys because issuing new ones would mean all issued certificates under that CA would be invalid.

---

**Figure 17-16**
The Autoenrollment Settings Properties dialog box is used to configure certificate enrollment.

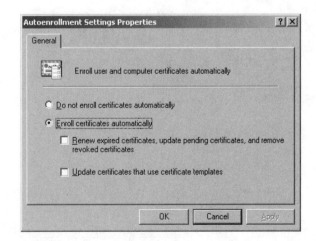

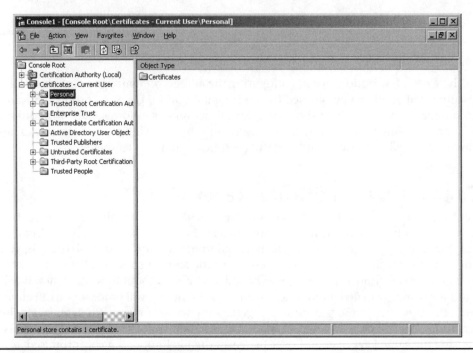

**Figure 17-17**    The Certificate snap-in

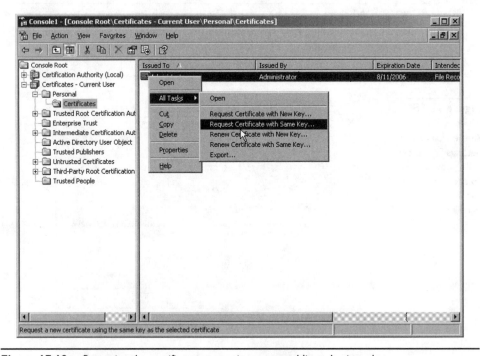

**Figure 17-18**    Renewing the certificate, generating a new public and private key

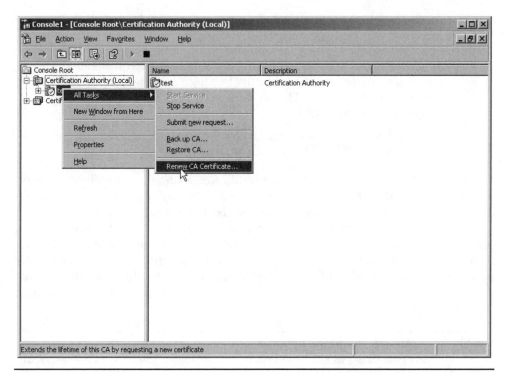

**Figure 17-19** Renewing a certificate for a CA using the Certification Authority snap-in

The process for renewing the certificates on a CA is slightly different. To renew the certificate, use the Certification Authority snap-in. Right-click the CA server, select All Tasks, and select the Renew CA Certificate option, as shown in Figure 17-19.

# Smart Card Authentication

There is no doubt that certificates are a versatile tool—but they can't be used to log on to a system. After all, they can be thousands of bytes long. Instead, most of us still use the traditional logon procedure using a user name and password. This has long been a security concern for administrators.

Perhaps we can't log on to the system using a certificate, but smart cards provide us with a workaround solution. A *smart card* is a credit card–size device that can store a certificate. The smart card can be used for storing signin passwords, public and private keys, and other personal information. Smart cards provide tamper-resistant and portable security solutions for tasks such as securing e-mail and logging on to a domain. To use a smart card, you will need a special smart card reader and you will need a certificate.

## Smart Card Enrollment Station

To issue smart cards from a central location, a smart card enrollment station is used. The smart card enrollment station is part of the enterprise CA service and uses certificate templates to determine which information to include in a certificate. Relative to smart cards, there are two user certificate templates of interest:

- **Smart Card Logon**   This template gives the smart card user the ability to authenticate to the network but cannot be used for other purposes such as securing e-mail. Smart card logon is installed by default when the CA is added to the MMC console.

- **Smart Card User**   This template provides the user with network authentication and other services such as encrypting e-mail.

To issue either one of these smart card certificates, a smart card enrollment station has to be located somewhere within the organization. In addition, to operate the enroll-ment station, someone in the organization must be designated as the enrollment agent. Individuals can be designated enrollment agents by issuing them the Enrollment Agent certificate, which allows them to enroll on behalf of others. You should carefully con-sider who is designated as enrollment agents because this certificate gives them the abil-ity to enroll for smart card certificates for any domain user, including Administrator. By default, the access permissions for the Enrollment Agent certificate are set to Domain Administrators.

 **EXAM TIP**   Only the enterprise CAs can issue templates; therefore, they are the only CAs that can issue smart cards for logon. Standalone CAs cannot be used for smart card logon.

## Web-Based Certificate Enrollment

Three steps are needed to get a certificate: requesting the certificate from the CA, the CA determining if you should be given the certificate, and finally, the issuing of the certifi-cate. While the determination of the certificate is handled either manually or automati-cally from the server, the other two elements can be done via a web interface.

To request a certificate from a CA, make sure the Certificate Services and Certificate Services Web Enrollment support are installed on the server. The process for doing this was discussed earlier in this chapter. (In short, you open the control panel, choose Add/ Remove Programs, and from within the Windows Components, select the Certificate Services to add to the system.)

 **NOTE**   If you intend to create Web Enrollment support to allow clients to obtain certificates via the Web, you should install Internet Information Services (IIS) before installing Certificate Services, and Application Service Provider (ASP) pages need to be enabled. If Certificate Services is installed before IIS is installed, you will need to manually create a virtual root directory by typing **certutil –vroot** at the command prompt.

Once Certificate Services has been installed, client systems can request a certificate from the CA by pointing their web browser to a specific location on the server. Using Internet Explorer, type **http://servername/certsrv**. A default Microsoft web site will open, which allows you to request a certificate, view the status of a pending certificate, or download a pending certificate. When requesting a certificate via the web interface, you can choose between a web browser certificate, an e-mail protection certificate, or submit and advanced certificate request. The advanced option allows you to choose other types of certificates, such as a server authentication certificate, and configure the options for that certificate.

**NOTE** If you get a 404 error when directing the client to the server's CA, ensure that Certificate Services was installed after IIS. If not, the virtual folder for certificates needs to be created.

After the certificate has been requested, you can log back on to the server and view the status of a pending certificate request. All pending certificates will be listed, and if the certificate that was requested is listed as issued, you can install that certificate right from the web site.

# Planning Security Updates

Things change fast in the world of IT: one day your systems are secure, the next someone has found another chink in the armor. In such an environment, it is important that all systems be up to date in terms of security. A Windows Server 2003 system has two key utilities to help ensure that security is kept current: the Microsoft Baseline Security Analyzer (MBSA) and the Microsoft Software Update Services (SUS).

## Microsoft Baseline Security Analyzer

Wouldn't it be nice if there were a utility that scanned your systems looking for common security misconfigurations? It would be, and fortunately, there is. The Microsoft Baseline Security Analyzer was designed to be an easy-to-use utility with the ability to reveal any potential security issues. The Microsoft Baseline Security Analyzer includes a graphical and command-line interface that can perform local or remote scans of Windows systems. MBSA runs on Windows Server 2003, Windows 2000, and Windows XP systems and scans for common security misconfigurations in the following products: Windows NT 4.0, Windows 2000, Windows XP, Windows Server 2003, Internet Information Server (IIS) 4.0 and 5.0, SQL Server 7.0 and 2000, Internet Explorer (IE) 5.01 and later, and Office 2000 and 2002. MBSA also scans for missing security updates for Windows NT 4.0, Windows 2000, Windows XP, Windows Server 2003, IIS, SQL, Exchange, IE, and Windows Media Player. Figure 17-20 shows the MBSA.

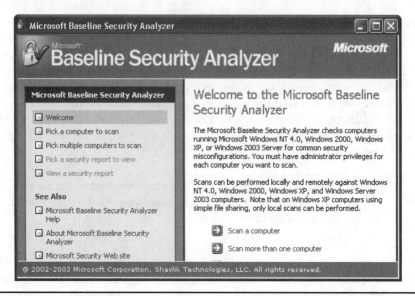

**Figure 17-20**   MBSA, used to scan a local or remote computer looking for potential security holes

**NOTE**   MBSA can be downloaded directly from the Microsoft web site.

To inspect a computer system, simply select the option Pick A Computer To Scan. Once selected, you will have the option to scan for Windows vulnerabilities, weak passwords, IIS vulnerabilities, SQL vulnerabilities, and security updates. Once you have selected the options you want, start the scan.

The scan will provide a security assessment of the system and highlight any security concerns. Each security concern found will be identified with a potential solution. Figure 17-21 shows the results from a test system.

## Microsoft Software Update Services

Microsoft Software Update Services (SUS) is a well-designed utility created to keep systems up to date with the latest critical updates. You can use SUS to deploy updates on single systems or to deploy updates to systems throughout the network running Windows 2000 and

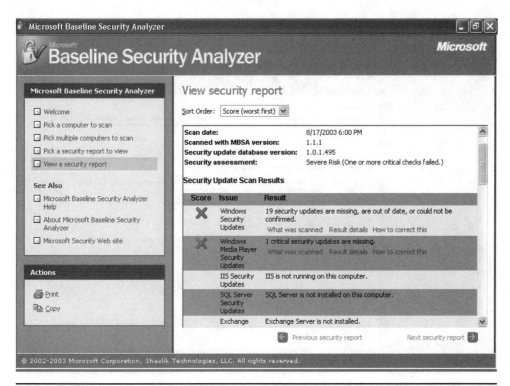

**Figure 17-21** MBSA, displaying the results from the security analysis

later operating systems. You can download the SUS utility from the Microsoft web site. Once installed, it will be accessible through the Administrative Tools program group. Figure 17-22 shows the SUS utility main screen.

**NOTE** You will need to have IIS installed and an NTFS volume installed to install SUS.

To start the update process on a system, select the option, Synchronize Server. You will have the choice to synchronize the server now or schedule the synchronization. This is sometimes done to perform the security updates after hours to preserve bandwidth.

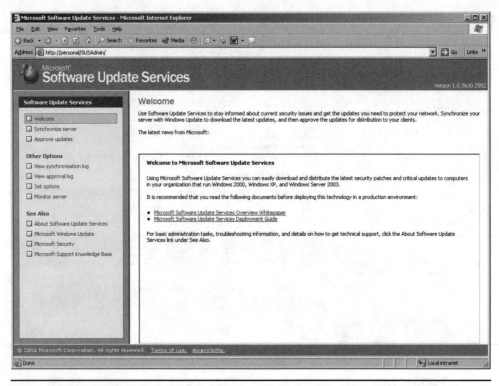

**Figure 17-22**   The SUS utility, used to deploy security updates throughout the network

Once the process has started, updates will be downloaded from the Microsoft Windows Update Services and installed on the local machine. Figure 17-23 shows the downloading process.

**NOTE**   Clients will have to be modified on the internal network so that the Automatic Update service points to the SUS server for updating their systems. This can be done via the registry or through Group Policies. Also, downloads must be accepted by the administrator before they can be deployed. This will give the administrator a chance to test the downloads before they are deployed to the desktops.

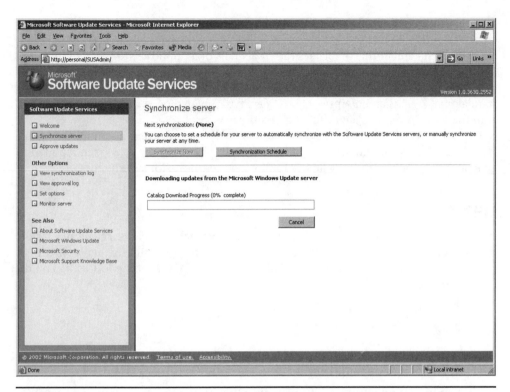

**Figure 17-23** SUS, downloading critical updates from the Microsoft Windows Update Services

# Chapter Review

In this chapter, we looked at managing a PKI. The PKI is comprised of several services and components working together, including certificates, certificate authorities, certificate templates, and Certificate Revocation Lists. PKI also uses both public and private keys. The public key is a nonsecret key that forms half of a cryptographic key pair that is used with a public key algorithm. The public key is freely given out to all potential receivers. The private key is the secret half of a cryptographic key pair that is used with a public key algorithm. The private part of the public key cryptography system is never transmitted over a network. Keys can be used in two different ways to secure data communications: public key encryption and symmetric key encryption.

Certificates are the cornerstones of the PKI. A certificate is essentially a form of electronic credentials that validates users, computers, or devices on the network. A certificate is a digitally signed statement that associates the credentials of a public key to the identity of the person, device, or service that holds the corresponding private key. Certificate issuance is managed by certificate authorities. Certificate authorities can either be installed as a standalone CA or as an enterprise CA. CAs are typically deployed in a hierarchal fashion, with the root CA often taken offline for security reasons.

CAs can be configured to issue certificates to certificate requesters automatically. Once issued, certificates sometimes need to be renewed. When they are, it is often required to generate a new public and private key for the new certificate for security reasons.

## Questions

1. Your company has decide to implement an internal CA to issue certificates inside the network. You wish to use several certificate templates in the deployment of the certificates and secure e-mail transactions. Which of the following could you first install?

   A. Enterprise subordinate CA

   B. Enterprise CA

   C. Standalone CA

   D. Standalone subordinate CA

2. You have been employed by a law firm that requires secure e-mail between clients. This e-mail needs to be trusted and verified; however, all communications must pass over the Internet. Which of the following strategies would you use?

   A. Private Key Encryption

   B. Private Key Encryption with MD-5

   C. Public Key Encryption

   D. Public Key Encryption with MD-5

3. Under which of the following conditions might a certificate be revoked? (Choose two.)

   A. When the validity date is exceeded

   B. When the subject's private key has been compromised

   C. When the CA's private key has been compromised

   D. When the public key has been compromised

4. You are assigning smart cards to ten users within the internal network. Five of the users from the Accounting department will require logon access and e-mail encryption capability. The other five users, from the Marketing division, do not need to send secure e-mail. How should the enrollment agent assign the certificate templates?

    A. Assign the users from the Accounting department the Smartcarduser certificate and issue the Marketing users the Smartcardlogon certificate.

    B. Assign the users from the Accounting department the Smartcardlogon certificate and issue the Marketing users the Smartcarduser certificate.

    C. Assign the users from the Accounting department and the Marketing department the Smartcardlogon certificate.

    D. Assign the users from the Accounting department and the Marketing department the Smartcarduser certificate.

5. You are the administrator of a network that uses 15 Windows XP Professional systems and a single server. Because the network is so small, you have not installed Active Directory and the server is used mainly to provide central storage for data. Your boss has asked that you install a method to issue certificates to the internal network with the least amount of administration. Which of the following best suits your needs?

    A. Enterprise subordinate CA

    B. Enterprise CA

    C. Standalone CA

    D. Configuring static Certificate Services for each of the individual Windows XP systems

6. You have deployed Certificate Services on your network and all users will request certificates via the web interface. The name of the CA server is Server1. Which of the following is the correct URL to access the CA server?

    A. http://www.server1/certsrv

    B. http://server1/certsrv

    C. http://www.server1/certrequest

    D. http://www.server1/certsrvrequest

7. Which of the following files maintains the primary configuration of an offline root CA?

    A. system.log

    B. root.log

    C. c.root.inf

    D. capolicy.inf.

8. You have been contracted to manage a network for a small company. After reviewing the network, you discover that both the server and most of the client systems are out of date and do not have the latest security patches applied to them. All of the network computers use Windows 2000 or later and use NTFS

partitions. Which of the following could you employ to keep the updates current to the client systems on the network?

A. Install Microsoft Software Update Services from the Server 2003 CD and configure clients so that the Automatic Update service points to the SUS server for updating their systems.

B. Download Microsoft Software Update Services from the Microsoft web site and configure clients so that the Automatic Update service points to the SUS server for updating their systems.

C. Install Microsoft Software Update Services from the Server 2003 CD and create a policy to force the system to retrieve updates each time the system is booted.

D. Download Microsoft Software Update Services from the Microsoft web site and create a policy to force the system to retrieve updates each time the system is booted.

9. You have recently finished installing a network using 3 Windows Server 2003 systems and 100 Windows XP Professional computers. As part of the installation, you wish to install a self-authenticating CA that can authenticate other CAs on the network. The issuing CA should be able to use Active Directory to authenticate certificate requestors and provide certificates for smart card logon. Which of the following CAs should be installed on the network?

A. Enterprise root CA

B. Standalone root CA

C. Enterprise issuing CA

D. Standalone issuing CA

10. You are a new administrator working with an unfamiliar network. You suspect that the network server may have been compromised and want to see if all security patches have been applied or if there are any configurations to the server that may be allowing someone access to the system. Which of the following could you do to discover potential security issues on the server?

A. Download and run the Microsoft Baseline Security Analyzer (MBSA) from the Microsoft web site.

B. Download and run the Microsoft Security Assessment Analyzer (MSAA) from the Microsoft web site.

C. Install and run the Microsoft Baseline Security Analyzer (MBSA) from the Server 2003 CD.

D. Install and run the Microsoft Security Assessment Analyzer (MSAA) from the Server 2003 CD.

# Answers

1. **B.** Enterprise CAs use certificate templates, whereas standalone CAs do not.

2. **C.** Public key encryption uses both a private and public key to encrypt and decrypt messages. The public key is used to encrypt a message or verify a signature, and the private key is used to decrypt the message or to sign a document. Only the public key is sent over the insecure network and not each of the private keys. Public-key technology makes it possible through the use of multiple keys to securely transmit sensitive data via an insecure channel.

3. **B and C.** If it is assumed that the subject's private key or the CA's private key has been compromised, the certificate should be revoked.

4. **A.** Assigning the users from the Accounting department the Smartcarduser certificate for their smart cards will allow them to send encrypted e-mail. Assigning the members of the marketing department with the Smartcardlogon certificate will not enable them to use secure e-mail transactions.

5. **C.** Because the network does not use Active Directory, only a standalone CA can be installed.

6. **B.** When requesting or installing certificates via a web interface, you need to direct the client systems to the certsrv location on the CA server. The correct syntax for this is http://servername/certsrv.

7. **D.** The configuration for the offline root CA is contained in a text file known as the capolicy.inf. The capolicy file must be in the systemroot folder before Certificate Services is installed. The configurations in the file are read during the installation of Certificate Services.

8. **B.** The SUS utility is free for download from the Microsoft web site and the Automatic Update service and client systems can be configured to point to the SUS server for updating their systems.

9. **A.** The creation of a CA hierarchy requires a root CA, and in this case, the enterprise root CA is required because it uses Active Directory to identify network entities that request a certificate. Root CAs are able to self-assign digital certificates.

10. **A.** The Microsoft Baseline Security Analyzer (MBSA) can be downloaded from the Microsoft web site and performs security analysis of a local or remote system. Once completed, the scan provides a security assessment of the system and highlights any security concerns. Each security concern found is identified with a potential solution.

# PART IV

# Planning, Implementing, and Maintaining an Active Directory Infrastructure (Exam 70-294)

# About Directory Services

In this chapter, you will learn how to
- Work with a directory service
- Understand Microsoft's Active Directory
- Store objects in Active Directory
- Set up Active Directory

Before we start our discussion of Windows Server 2003's Active Directory, we must take note of a few underlying concepts. While this introductory chapter will not provide vast volumes of information that you'll be tested on when sitting for the 70-294 exam, it provides an essential overview of the concepts presented throughout the rest of this part. You'll find the information presented in this chapter especially helpful if you are new to Windows Active Directory, either because you are new to the computer administration field or because you have recently migrated from a Windows NT 4.0 domain environment.

Although the bulleted items listed are the objectives of the chapter, they are not Microsoft exam objectives. In the chapters that follow, however, the chapter objectives listed will more directly map to testable material. That's not to say that this material isn't important; with a thorough understanding of the concepts involved, you stand a much better chance of assimilating the information in this book's final part.

And, as Active Directory is a directory service, you need to thoroughly comprehend what a directory service is. So we'll start by answering this most fundamental of questions.

## What's a Directory Service?

At the most basic level of computer networking, no matter what operating system is in play, you have a server service that accepts connections from a client service for the purpose of making the resources of one system available to other systems. In Windows Server 2003, these two software components are called Server and Workstation services, respectively, and confirmation that these two services are running can be viewed by opening the Services management tool (select Start | All Programs | Administrative Tools | Services). You can also use this tool to gather general information about the behavior of these services, as well as configure certain aspects, such as startup behavior. Typically, though, you do not perform much management of these services with this utility.

Now once a resource has been shared out—that is, made available to client services via the server service—you often don't want just anyone accessing these shared resources. So as networking software was evolving (some of the earliest network operating systems included Novell's NetWare and Microsoft's Windows for Workgroups), developers also included a way for these systems to provide authentication, so that the only users who could access network resources were the ones who were supposed to.

**TIP** Keep in mind that a *server* is what a computer is *doing* in the network. Windows Server 2003 is just a name of the latest Microsoft operating system; it can be both a server and a client, depending on what it's doing. For example, a system running the Windows 98 operating system could be the company's print server, and that another computer running Windows Server 2003 could be a print client of the 98 machine. At the same time, the Windows Server 2003 system could be providing DNS name resolution services to the Windows 98 client machine.

To perform authentication, a computer that's making resources available (for example, files or printers) will need a list of all the users who are allowed to interact with the resource. In the case of Windows for Workgroups, users were required to know a password in order to connect to resources on remote computers. These remote computers would have a list against which the user name and password were checked to determine whether or not to permit access.

In its simplest iteration, the directory is the list. It's a database of users who have the ability to connect to a given system. The service is the software that makes the list available to the operating system. This service works in harmony with the server service (the software that makes resources available) so it can be checked when connection attempts are established.

## Directory Services in Ancient Times

In older networks, like NetWare 3.12 or Windows for Workgroups, the directory was kept separate on each individual machine. This is still true in Windows peer-to-peer networks (or workgroups) where each machine keeps a unique database of the users who can use that machine. As networks grew, this became a prohibitively large administrative task as user accounts would need to be created at each individual server to which the user needed access. In other words, for one user, you often had many accounts.

In later versions of their respective networking software products, both Microsoft and Novell worked toward a centralized directory of users that could be checked for access to a network's resources. With a centralized database of users who were able to use network components, administrators no longer had to create multiple accounts for a single user, and administration could be centralized. Both of these companies' earlier versions, however, had varying degrees of difficulty accomplishing what some customers most wanted.

What you are working with right now, and are studying to master, is the result of years of Microsoft coders trying their best to build the ultimate piece of networking software. Lots of people trying to write a better mousetrap. For Microsoft, that mousetrap is called Active Directory.

# Microsoft's Active Directory

Now that you know a little more about directory services and directory databases, you may be asking, what is significant about the current Microsoft version of a directory service—namely, Active Directory?

First of all, understand that Active Directory is built upon the networking technologies that preceded it. Active Directory, as a piece of Microsoft software, is certainly not unique in that regard. Microsoft and other software companies have always taken existing technologies and/or the ideas of existing software, including those pieces of software that are openly available (such as the TCP/IP protocol suite), and built upon them. (Microsoft's detractors love to point this out, but there's nothing wrong with this; you can't copyright an idea.) They've taken what's out there and made it theirs by taking the next evolutionary step.

In the case of Active Directory, Microsoft already had a working domain model built into their Server products. When Microsoft moved to the NT operating system, they added the capability to link domains together with *trust relationships*. Using one or more trust relationships between domains, the NT domain model became scalable because multiple domains could be made aware of each other's presence in an enterprise. This linking of domains was done for administrative reasons. Carefully implemented, the enterprise could still be managed centrally or, conversely, could be distributed among multiple administrative groups. This linking also provided for easy access to resources, and it accommodated business mergers and subsidies as organizations redefined themselves.

 **TIP**  Scalable is a tech term that refers to a system's capability to grow and accommodate more users. Exactly what's scalable and what's not is rather nebulous and frequently a matter of conjecture, and the term should be avoided in polite conversation. Software can be described as scalable, but hardware can be too. If it can grow relatively easily, it's said to be scalable. If there are limitations to adding more (users, computers, processors, and so on), it may be termed not scalable.

But scalability, like beauty, is a relative term. In other words, NT's domain model, though scalable, was not *very* scalable. As you started to add multiple domains to the NT mix, several problems occurred, and these problems usually compounded themselves as the organization began to grow.

For example, every time a user accessed a resource in a another domain besides the one where their account lived, it increased network traffic. It also caused extra traffic as the domain controllers in these multiple domains maintained the trust relationships.

A trust is the logical linking of two domains. In Active Directory, trust relationships are created automatically between the domains in a tree or forest. And in the case of Windows Server 2003, two separate forests can be linked with a trust relationship. Trust relationships facilitate two things: cross-domain logon, in which a user in one domain can submit his account credentials across the trust to the domain where his account lives, and universal resource access, in which a user has the ability to access resources in domains that trust the one where his account resides. We'll discuss the different types of trust relationships in Chapter 19.

Remember, as we discuss the significance of trusts here, that *ability* to access resources does not necessarily imply *permission*. It's entirely possible to be able to access something in another domain—to establish a connection—yet have read-only permission or have permission denied altogether.

The NT domain model became somewhat burdensome for growing enterprises. In its next iteration of its Server family of operating systems, Windows 2000, Microsoft set out to address two main areas of concern to help alleviate many of the problems encountered when working with the NT 4 domain model. The two things determined to be most needed in the next version of the directory service software were

- A global list of each domain's directory would need to be available at every domain.

- A system should exist to automatically manage trust relationships, lessening the administrative overhead involved in ensuring the benefits of multiple domains.

There's a corollary to these two driving characteristics. It was as if the folks at Microsoft, during a brainstorming session, thought, "Well, if we're going to change our directory services model to this one central great authentication database, why don't we just go ahead and fill this database up with handy data that would answer queries like, 'Which one of the printers on the fourth floor prints color?' or 'Is that computer located in the North building or the South building?' Let's design our directory database like that."

So they did. These were the driving motivations for the design of the next domain model, the one that would carry Microsoft into the next millennium. The result was Active Directory, which made its debut in Windows 2000. Now Microsoft has carried forward this domain model and built upon it in its release of Server 2003.

Windows Server 2003 includes many improvements to Windows 2000's version of Active Directory, making it even more versatile, dependable, and economical to use. We won't go into too much detail here, but Active Directory improvements in Windows Server 2003 provide the following benefits:

- **Easier deployment and management**   Improved migration and management tools, along with the ability to rename Active Directory domains, make deploying Active Directory significantly easier than when the directory service was first introduced in Windows 2000 Server. Better tools bring drag-and-drop capabilities, multi-object selection, and the ability to save and reuse queries. Plus, improvements in Group Policy make it easier and more efficient to manage groups of users and computers in an Active Directory environment.

- **Greater security**   Cross-forest trust provides a new type of Windows trust for managing the security relationship between two forests—greatly simplifying cross-forest security administration and authentication. Users can securely access resources in other forests without sacrificing the single sign-on and administrative benefits of having only one user ID and password maintained in the user's home forest. This provides the flexibility to account for the need for some divisions or areas to have their own forest, yet maintain benefits of Active Directory.

- **Improved performance and dependability**  Windows Server 2003 more efficiently manages the replication and synchronization of Active Directory information. Administrators can better control the types of information that are replicated and synchronized between domain controllers both within a domain as well as across domains. In addition, Active Directory provides more features to intelligently select only changed information for replication—no longer requiring updating entire portions of the directory.

Throughout the rest of Part IV, we will be dealing with the technologies that make these improvements possible. In fact, most of the terms and tools you will be learning about will impact one of these three areas in some way, and you can be sure that Microsoft will heavily emphasize these areas in the 70-294 exam.

## The Directory Database

Active Directory's job is to store and make available a directory database. While the term "database" can make cold shivers run down the spine of many a computer user, the concept can be simplified quite dramatically. At its core, a database is a list. If you've ever made a shopping list, you have worked—at least in concept—with a database. The biggest difference between a shopping list and a database (besides the fact that when we talk about databases, we are talking about things stored on a computer) is the way the information is organized.

In a database, one of the items in the list has a unique value. This unique value sets the item apart as a distinct entity and is known as a *key* value. In other words, a database stores a single distinct object and then a series of attributes of that object.

Take the example of one of the most common and most easily understood objects stored in Active Directory: the user account. To the Active Directory database, the unique part of the account is a number assigned to the account, called a security identifier (SID). (We'll talk more about the SID in Chapter 20.) Everything else stored in the database about that user account are attributes. The logon name is an attribute of the SID. Likewise the first name, last name, and logon domain are all attributes. Lots of users can have the same domain attribute, and lots of users can even have the object attributes of Brian, as a first name attribute, and Culp, as a last name attribute.

## The Schema

What's especially significant about Active Directory's list of objects that can be added to its directory database is that every Active Directory domain in an enterprise of domains contains the exact same list of potential objects and attributes. This list of what's possible to add to an Active Directory directory database is called the schema, and the schema is consistent throughout the Active Directory enterprise. In Chapter 21, we'll discuss all of these elements of the enterprise in further detail.

Active Directory groups a fixed set of attributes in the schema and defines them as a class. Names, addresses, e-mails, phone numbers, locations, and so forth, all describe the user class object, for example. A class, therefore, is used to describe a type of object. The class—and hence, the schema—can be added to, making Active Directory an extensible database. Active Directory is flexible enough to accommodate any kind of organization and can store just about any type of information. Say, for example, that you wanted to track a user's favorite charity as part of the information used to describe a user account. The Active Directory schema can be modified to include this information.

## The Global Catalog

For each domain, we have a directory of information, and certain attributes from each domain will be copied to a Global Catalog. This "index" domain information is then shared among the multiple domains.

Active Directory uses a Global Catalog to provide a repository of the most commonly searched for objects and their attributes. Certain objects and attributes from each domain will be copied to the Global Catalog and made available to all connected domains.

You can think of the Global Catalog as an index for the domains in the enterprise. Each domain controller stores a copy of all the objects stored in its directory database. But users access the Global Catalog when they want to find information that's stored in domains other than their own.

The Global Catalog's main function is to make the following activities much easier:

- **Logging on at a domain other than the one you're in**   In an Active Directory enterprise, it's possible to use the computers on one domain to log on to another. The Global Catalog is consulted for a list of possible logon domains.

- **Finding objects in other domains**   If you are looking for color laser print resources throughout the enterprise, the Global Catalog will likely store information about these printers.

## The Active Directory Namespace

When you implement multiple domains in an enterprise, it will be easier to locate objects and to replicate information between domains if you impose some sort of consistent structure on them. The Active Directory software writers have done just this by borrowing from an existing domain structuring technology. This technology is used to provide the composition of the Internet domains, and thus provides a way of linking domains together. It's called the Domain Naming System (DNS), and now it's used to provide the backbone of your Active Directory domains.

The DNS namespace is one huge, hierarchical, distributed database of resource record mappings to IP addresses. It works by linking each and every domain into one contiguous namespace. You will need to have a pretty good understanding of DNS in order to successfully prepare for the 70-294 exam. Microsoft assumes that you bring this knowledge to the table before you study this material, but we haven't made the same assumption. Please refer to Chapters 6 and 8 for a full discussion of DNS.

What's significant as far as Active Directory goes is that, by using an existing hierarchical namespace in which the Active Directory domains will be named, you have created a system where trust relationships can be managed automatically. Why? Because the trust relationships can be inferred from the domain names. For example, if you had an Active Directory domain called mcgraw-hill.com, and then created a child domain in the mcgraw-hill.com namespace, and named the child domain brianfanmail.mcgraw-hill.com, the trust relationship could be deduced from the names. If these were Windows Server 2003 Active Directory domains, the two domains would trust each other automatically.

By using the DNS namespace, it's ensured that all your Active Directory domains will have names that are consistent. Additionally, there's a system that makes sure all this happens. The Domain Naming Master (explained in Chapter 21) is the server that handles these duties for an Active Directory enterprise. This system ensures that all domains have names that fit cohesively in the namespace.

So to summarize, then, these are the three keys to the engine that runs Microsoft's Active Directory. All domains in a Windows Server 2003 Active Directory enterprise share the following:

- A common schema
- A common Global Catalog
- A common configuration

And once the engine is ready, it's time to add the fuel. In Windows Server 2003, Active Directory is fueled by the objects it stores.

## Objects Stored in Active Directory

This may not exactly be news, especially of you've ever paid taxes or gotten a driver's license, but *you* are an object. At least you are to Windows Server 2003 running Active Directory. In fact, everything is. Computers, groups, resources, Group Policies, and yes, even you, the user. It may come as some solace, then, to know why you are viewed the way you are by Active Directory: it's primarily to simplify security. All objects stored in Windows Server 2003's Active Directory database will have the following attributes attached:

- **Methods**  Every object will have methods in common, such as creating the object, opening the object, and deleting the object.

- **Properties**  All Active Directory objects have a set of properties or attributes, which you usually see by right-clicking the object and choosing Properties from the context menu. At a minimum, an object will have a name property and a type property.

- **Collections** If an attribute can contain more than a single value (such as the members of a group object), these values are stored as collections or an array of values.

By treating everything as an object, Windows Server 2003 maintains security over the object no matter how a user accesses the object—whether locally, sitting at the domain controller, or remotely from another system. In fact, a significant collection attached to the objects in Active Directory is the Discretionary Access Control List (DACL), as seen in Figure 18-1. This list provides the one and only security model for access to objects in Windows Server 2003. Every time a connection to the object is attempted the DACL is checked before access is granted.

Now that you understand the concept that objects are stored in Active Directory, the question that remains is: What exactly are the objects that can be stored in the Active Directory directory database?

## Computers

A computer object is a software representation of a physical entity, namely, the computer. It represents an important level of participation in the Active Directory domain. This level of participation usually has to do with security. You should also understand, when thinking of computer accounts, that only certain operating systems have the ability to participate in the domain through addition of a computer account.

Any of the Windows Server 2003 or Windows 2000 (both Professional and the varieties of Server) operating systems can participate with a computer account. XP Professional, likewise, can create an account in a 2003 domain. However, the XP Home

**Figure 18-1**

The Discretionary Access Control List

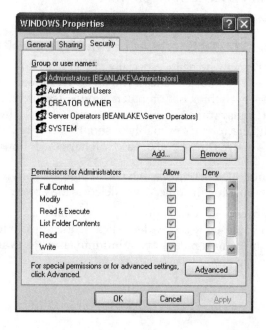

version, along with the 9x family of operating systems, cannot. This can be significant if you want to implement security options such as restricting a user's logon to a single computer or group of computers in an enterprise, or if you want to take the administrative steps of deploying software to computers using a Group Policy Object (Group Policies will be discussed at great length in later chapters, starting with Chapter 22). As will be reiterated throughout these two chapters, you can only deploy Group Policy to those operating systems that support it.

 **TIP** Windows NT 4 systems also have the ability to participate as a computer account in a Windows Server 2003 domain, but since Microsoft is dropping support of NT 4, it's usually assumed for the purposes of computer account discussion that only the latest of Microsoft's operating systems will be used.

## Users

User accounts comprise the meat and potatoes of Windows Server 2003 domain administration. All computing activities, whether it be access to a resource or backing up a file, occur in the context of a user account. An account is needed to interact with the network and is issued an *access token* at logon time. This access token is presented against a resource's Access Control List to determine what level of access a user has. Without a valid user account, a user has no access to a Windows Server 2003 domain.

## Groups

A group object is just another type of account, much like a user account. However, this account's purpose is to store a list. In this list is an inventory of all the user accounts that belong to the group account. It is also used at logon time, in conjunction with the user account, to help generate an access token. The access token is a register of the user account and all the groups to which it belongs. It is proffered to resources in the domain for the purpose of determining access.

The advantage of a group is straightforward: it makes administration of permissions and rights simpler. When you grant a level of access permission to a group, the permission applies to all members of that group. This is especially advantageous as domain accounts grow to hundreds and thousands of accounts.

In Chapter 20, we'll take a more detailed tour of what kinds of groups are possible in Windows Server 2003 domains and the significance of each.

## Printers

In a Windows Server 2003 domain, you have the option of creating a software object in Active Directory for each shared printer in your enterprise. The advantage of creating an Active Directory object for each shared printer (rather than just creating the shared printer on a print server) is that it enables users to find an enterprise's printers more easily by conducting a search through Active Directory. That way, users don't have to know the physical location of the resource they're looking for. Just like when you use the phonebook, you don't have to know what street the business is on when you're looking for it, you just have to know what the business does.

Additionally, more attributes can be listed about the printer than can be with the shared object alone. When you share a printer, you just configure a share name. When you publish a printer in Active Directory, you can include information about the printer's functionality or what floor it's on, which can be a big advantage to users who want to send a job to it.

Note that even though a printer object is created in Active Directory, the printer still exists as an object on a local machine, and that computer handles the security for that printer. The printer object that's stored in Active Directory is really just information about the printer.

### Shared Folders

Much like printers, these resources are shared out from file servers in your enterprise. But also like printers, information about the shares can be published in Active Directory, facilitating easier searches when users are looking for resources. The computer hosting the share will still be responsible for managing the security permissions on that shared folder when it is accessed from the network.

If you're reading this book in sequence, you have already seen shares created and managed. If not, please refer to the first section in Chapter 3.

Also keep in mind that the above are just some of the more common objects you create in a Active Directory directory database. You can also create these:

- **InetOrgPerson**   This kind of object makes it easier to migrate users from non-Microsoft directory databases to Active Directory. The InetOrgPerson object is used in several non-Microsoft LDAP directory database services to represent users of an organization. This is a new feature of Windows Server 2003, so be especially vigilant for an exam question on this.

- **MSMQ Queue Alias**   This object is a logical representation of a message queuing and routing system. An MSMQ server enables distributed applications running at different times to communicate using heterogeneous networks, even though some of the computers may be offline. Message queuing stores the message until the network/computer is available, thus ensuring message delivery, routing, security, and priority-based messaging.

And there are even more that can be added as your needs require.

Now that you've learned about the background of Active Directory, and about what objects it can and commonly does contain, it's time to actually implement Active Directory in a Windows Server 2003 enterprise. The next section looks at how to do this.

# Setting Up Active Directory

Before you can take advantage of benefits afforded by Microsoft's Active Directory, you must know how to implement it. The process for installing Active Directory on a Windows Server 2003 server computer begins by launching the Active Directory Installation Wizard, often referred to by its executable file, DCPROMO.

There are other ways to launch the Active Directory Installation Wizard, just as there are lots of ways to open the Control Panel. As an alternative to the method described in the following, for example, you could choose Configure Your Server Wizard from the list of Administrative Tools. The Configure Your Server Wizard is also the first thing that launches after you've got Windows Server 2003 installed. But for purposes of testing, you should know how to launch the Active Directory Installation Wizard from the Run dialog box, and the utility that launches it, DCPROMO.

Using dcpromo.exe, you can install and remove Active Directory from a Windows Server 2003 computer at will. It provides a wizard-based interface that is as easy to use as any other wizard in the Windows environment. In fact, if you can set up a printer on a Windows 98 machine using the Add Printer Wizard, you have all the requisite button-clicking skill to install Active Directory. The hard part, as with all things Windows Server 2003, is not the button-clicking, but possession of a full understanding of what will happen when the buttons are clicked.

## Running the Active Directory Setup Wizard

As we go through this wizard, it is assumed that you are setting up a test environment, and therefore we will demonstrate the most straightforward way possible. As in most wizards, there are many different paths the Active Directory installation can follow, depending on your goals. Later chapters look at what some of these other goals might be as you configure your Active Directory enterprise.

Before you start the Active Directory Installation Wizard, there are a few important requirements that must be met for successful installation:

- An NTFS partition for the SYSVOL folder

- Free space on your hard disk, about 1GB

- The Installation Wizard must be run in the context of an account with administrative permissions in the domain or administrative permissions in the enterprise. (If you are establishing the forest root domain, which is the first Active Directory domain in the enterprise—that is, the one that establishes the Active Directory network—the local Administrator account will be sufficient, as none of these other accounts will exist yet.)

- DNS, which will be installed if an installation is not present.

## Lab Exercise 18.1: Installing Active Directory

It's also important to realize here that as we go further along in Part IV, we will be taking different paths through the Active Directory Installation Wizard than the one outlined here. These other paths will result in different roles for your Active Directory domain controllers, and will be examined in the detail necessary to fully understand them in later chapters. For now, our goal is just to build an Active Directory domain that we can work with later as necessary.

To launch the Active Directory Installation Wizard:

1. Click Start | Run, and then type **dcpromo** to start the Active Directory Installation Wizard.

2. Click Next to bypass the introductory screen of the Active Directory Installation Wizard.

3. On the Operating System Compatibility page, read the information and then click Next. Note here that the improved security characteristics of Windows Server 2003 set communications requirements of its clients that cannot be met with older operating systems such as Windows 9*x* and NT 4 using a service pack prior to SP4.

4. Here's where the real forks in the road first appear. Since we are assuming that in this first 70-294 chapter you may be setting up a test environment for learning purposes, we will create a new domain in a new enterprise of computers (your enterprise of computers, to be precise). On the Domain Controller Type screen, select Domain Controller For A New Domain, as shown in Figure 18-2, and click Next.

5. Since we're starting a brand new enterprise, and not joining an existing one, from the Create New Domain screen, select Domain In A New Forest, as shown in Figure 18-3, and then click Next.

6. Enter the full DNS name for the new domain and click Next. We'll talk extensively about the naming of your domains in the next chapter.

**Figure 18-2**
Creating a
new domain

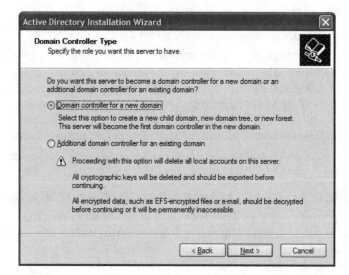

**Figure 18-3**
Creating a new
domain tree in
a new forest of
domains

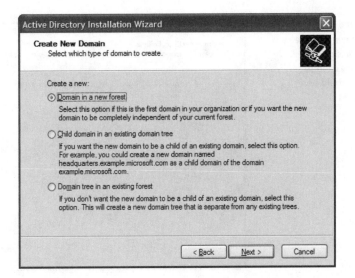

TIP   If you've ever surfed the Internet, you have used DNS domains like
ebay.com or microsoft.com. You can use a similar namespace in the creation
of your Active Directory domain. If you are creating a private namespace (it
won't ever be searched for from a computer connected to the Internet), you
can use any namespace you want, like mydoghas.fleas. For this example, we'll use the fictional
namespace of lanscape.net. (At least as of the time of the writing, the name had not been
registered.) But while the namespace will be fictional, the Active Directory installation will
not. It just won't have resources available publicly.

7. From the ensuing wizard screen, confirm the NetBIOS domain name. This will
   be important if you plan on having non–Active Directory clients, such as NT 4
   clients, access your domain.

8. Confirm the location of the Active Directory database and log files. It is
   recommended practice that you locate these folders on different drives than the
   operating system for recoverability, although, as shown in Figure 18-4, the default
   locations are on the same partition as the operating system. It is recommended
   practice, however, that you store the log files on a separate physical drive (if
   possible) to improve performance.

9. Confirm the location of the SYSVOL, or shared system volume, folder. This
   folder replaces the NETLOGON share functionality of NT 4 domain controllers
   and is the conduit through which logon attempts are submitted. Remember,
   the SYSVOL folder must be placed on an NTFS-formatted drive. In other words,
   NTFS must be present for installation of Active Directory.

**Figure 18-4**
Specifying where the directory services and log files should be located

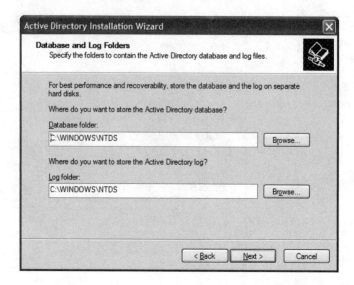

10. The wizard now confirms your DNS server installation on the DNS Registration Diagnostics screen. You should receive a warning if a DNS server is not found. If a DNS server is not found, the wizard will offer to install DNS for you, as shown in Figure 18-5.

**Figure 18-5**
The offer of DNS installation

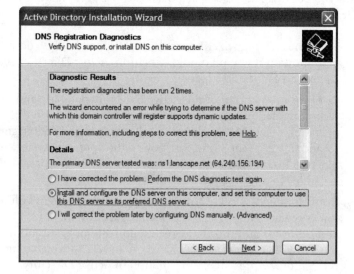

**TIP** DNS installation by the Active Directory Installation Wizard is almost always a good idea when DNS cannot be located. If you choose not to install DNS from this wizard screen, Active Directory will still install, but you will receive numerous startup errors, and indeed Active Directory will not be functional until you address this problem. You must either find or create a DNS server that supports the necessary records that Active Directory creates. Windows Server 2003's DNS server supports these records, and the Active Directory Installation Wizard creates them automatically (you'll likely have to create them manually if using a Unix DNS server solution, for example), so why not take advantage of the automation the Wizard provides?

11. Choose the option that begins "Install and configure the DNS server," and then click Next to let Windows Server 2003 set up DNS on its own.

12. On the next screen, you'll receive a security warning. In NT 4 and prior, the Remote Access Server (RAS) had to allow clients to read domain information before authentication. If your RAS servers are down-level (NT 4.0), you will need to allow this weaker level of permissions. Click Next after you've made your decision, which should be permissions compatible with Windows 2000 or Windows Server 2003 server operating systems unless absolutely necessary.

13. Next, you're prompted for the Directory Services Restore Mode password, as shown in Figure 18-6. This password does not have to be the same as your administrative password, but you should make sure it is safely stored—written down somewhere secure—so that it won't be forgotten.

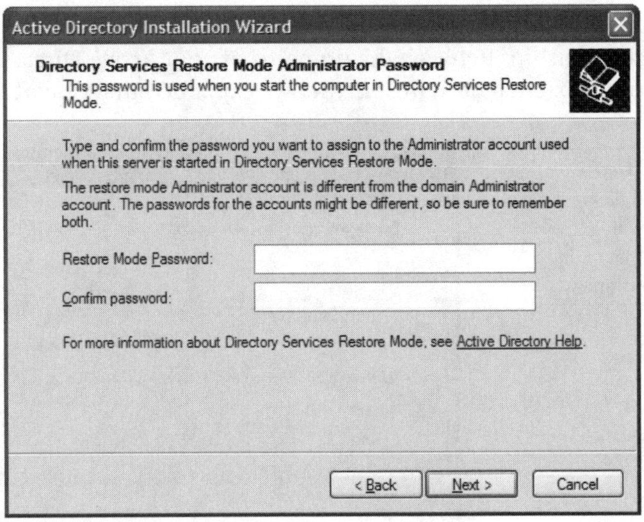

**PART IV**

**Figure 18-6**
The Directory
Services Restore
Mode password

Active Directory Installation Wizard

**Directory Services Restore Mode Administrator Password**
This password is used when you start the computer in Directory Services Restore Mode.

Type and confirm the password you want to assign to the Administrator account used when this server is started in Directory Services Restore Mode.

The restore mode Administrator account is different from the domain Administrator account. The passwords for the accounts might be different, so be sure to remember both.

Restore Mode Password: 

Confirm password: 

For more information about Directory Services Restore Mode, see Active Directory Help.

< Back    Next >    Cancel

14. The next screen will summarize your choices before starting the Active Directory installation. You can click Back to review and/or change any of your settings before clicking Next. Clicking Next starts the installation process. (If you've selected that DNS be configured, you might be prompted for the location of your Windows Server 2003 installation files.)

15. If all has gone according to plan, you'll get a final screen, as in Figure 18-7, confirming the successful installation of Active Directory on the system. Once you've closed this screen, you'll be prompted to reboot the server.

Congratulations! You've just turned an ordinary Windows Server 2003 system into an all-powerful forest root domain controller. Now you've got a system that has all the directory services software necessary to run a computing empire such as mighty Microsoft itself, or, more modestly, to simply study the features of Active Directory from the comforts of your home. Either way, the concepts will remain the same.

After the installation of Active Directory is complete, you will have three new Microsoft Management Console snap-ins added to your Administrative Tools so that you can, appropriately enough, manage what's in your Active Directory directory database. These three tools, which you will find by clicking Start | All Programs | Administrative Tools, are the following:

- **Active Directory Users and Computers**   This is the tool used to manage most of your Active Directory objects, such as User accounts, Computer accounts, Group accounts, published printers, and shares, to name a few. You will also be coming here often to do your Group Policy management.

- **Active Directory Domains and Trusts**   This tool is used to manage trust relationships between the domains of your Active Directory enterprise and other external domains. Earlier we explained that one of the benefits of

**Figure 18-7**
The final dialog screen will sum up your accomplishment.

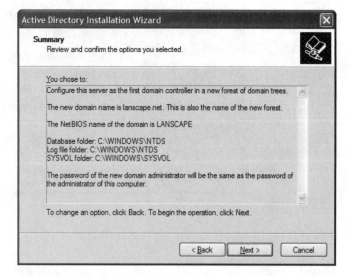

*Active Directory Installation Wizard*

**Summary**
Review and confirm the options you selected.

You chose to:

Configure this server as the first domain controller in a new forest of domain trees.

The new domain name is lanscape.net. This is also the name of the new forest.

The NetBIOS name of the domain is LANSCAPE

Database folder: C:\WINDOWS\NTDS
Log file folder: C:\WINDOWS\NTDS
SYSVOL folder: C:\WINDOWS\SYSVOL

The password of the new domain administrator will be the same as the password of the administrator of this computer.

To change an option, click Back. To begin the operation, click Next.

< Back    Next >    Cancel

Windows Server 2003's Active Directory domain model, especially when compared to NT 4's model, was that administration of trusts in your enterprise is virtually nonexistent. That's still true. What you will use this tool for is to specify and manage trusts between either older NT 4 domains or between domains of external organizations and yours.

- **Active Directory Sites and Services** This is used to create and manage the directory services sites, and to further manage the replication of Active Directory information between these sites.

 **TIP** Throughout this section, you'll see instructions like "Open the Control Panel," or "Open Active Directory Users and Computers." You should see the exact steps used the first time or two, but there are lots of different ways to accomplish these tasks. It's assumed that by this point in your certification studies, you know most of them, or at least the ones that work best for you. Most of my instructions and screenshots throughout Part IV use the XP Theme interface, but with the older "Classic" Windows 9x–style Start menu and icons like My Computer and My Network Places added to the desktop. Just realize that this is *not* how Windows Server 2003 installs out of the box.

There are other tools installed as well, such as Domain Controller Security Policy and Domain Security Policy, but the tools most important to managing Active Directory objects are listed above. We will be using all of these tools, especially Active Directory Users and Computers and Active Directory Sites and Services, extensively throughout this section, so stay tuned if you're aching to find out more about the uses of these MMC consoles.

## Ideal Domain Design

Additionally, keep in the back of your mind throughout all this that Microsoft recommends that, whenever possible, you design your Active Directory infrastructure to include only a single domain. This is because a single Windows Server 2003 domain is scalable (there's that word again) to millions of objects. In other words, a single domain has the potential to accommodate organizations of almost any conceivable size, including Microsoft itself. By the time you are done with this section of the book, you will have a much better understanding about why a single domain probably can—and should—best suit your organization's needs.

When you implement a single domain, all of the Active Directory concepts discussed throughout the section still apply, but you can be blissfully unaware of almost every one of them and still have a good working network. You don't really have to know that much about trusts, forests functional levels, universal group caching, and so on, and you'll still have a network that performs just fine. If you don't have testing in mind, Microsoft makes it awfully easy to administer a small to medium-sized company with its newest version of Server.

But that's not our goal here, is it? You picked up this book to quickly obtain the information that Microsoft expects you to know for the each of its core certification exams. In the next chapter, we start focusing on precisely the information necessary to pass the 70-294 exam.

# Chapter Review

In this chapter, we've examined the foundational information needed to understand Windows Server 2003's Active Directory. With an understanding of these concepts, we will go forward to explore how to best implement Active Directory.

If at any time you get confused about what is being discussed in the upcoming chapters, you can come back to Chapter 18 to regroup and jog your memory. Most of the Active Directory concepts deal with the abstract—things you cannot see, even with your computer.

We started this chapter with a look at the history of a directory service, and the role a directory database plays in a modern computing network. We also examined how a directory service serves to authenticate users on a network, and how it enables access to resources in multiple domains.

We walked through the steps to set up Active Directory on a computer running Windows Server 2003. You need to install Active Directory so that you can follow along with some of the steps later in Part IV. Also, it's generally a good idea install the software you're going to spend a considerable time studying.

In the final part of the chapter, we also looked at the Microsoft recommendation for ideal domain design.

## Questions

1. You are the administrator of a Windows Server 2003 domain. Right now, there is a single domain with the name of beanlake.com. As the company expands, it will be adding several domains to the forest. All child domains will be named after the cities in which a new location is opened, and all will have the existing domain as a parent. Which common Active Directory features exist between these domains? (Choose all that apply.)

   A. Schema

   B. Global Catalog

   C. DNS namespace

   D. Replication schedules

   E. External trusts

2. Which of the following components of Active Directory are shared by all domains in an Active Directory enterprise? (Choose all that apply.)

   A. Schema

   B. Global Catalog

   C. Parent domain

   D. Configuration

3. What are the two items that make up the Active Directory schema? (Choose two.)

   A. Classes

   B. Names

   C. Attributes

   D. Objects

4. What is the utility used to install Active Directory on a Windows Server 2003 computer?

   A. promotedc.bat

   B. dcupgrade.exe

   C. adinstall.exe

   D. dcpromo.exe

5. Which of the following components of Active Directory need to be installed on an NTFS partition? (Choose all that apply.)

   A. The SYSVOL folder

   B. The Active Directory log files

   C. The Active Directory database

   D. The 2003 operating system

## Answers

1. **A, B, and C.** All domains in a Windows Server 2003 Active Directory forest share a common schema and Global Catalog. If the domains are all in the same tree, they will also share a common DNS namespace. The domain controllers in the domains will not necessarily have the same replication schedules, and any external trusts will be configured independently.

2. **A, B, and D.** There are three elements that are common to all domains in a linked Active Directory enterprise. They are the schema (a list of what's possible to add to Active Directory), the Global Catalog (an index of commonly used objects and their attributes), and the configuration.

3. **A and C.** Classes are really preset templates of attributes. There are preset classes for computer, user, printer, and organizational unit Active Directory objects. Attributes store specific information about a class.

4. **D.** dcpromo.exe launches the Active Directory Installation Wizard, which is used to install Active Directory on a given Windows Server 2003 system.

5. **A.** In order for Active Directory to install, the SYSVOL folder must be placed on an NTFS drive. The scripts folder contained within the SYSVOL folder will be shared out as NETLOGON, and will be the location where logon authentication requests to the domain are submitted.

# Planning and Implementing an Active Directory Infrastructure

In this chapter, you will learn how to

- Understand the logical elements of Active Directory
- Implement an Active Directory forest and domain structure
- Understand the physical elements of Active Directory
- Implement an Active Directory directory service forest and domain structure
- Replicate Active Directory information between components
- Plan a strategy for placing Global Catalog servers

We've already looked at some of the building blocks of the Active Directory enterprise. In this chapter, we'll design and implement the logical components of Active Directory. A full understanding of these logical components is critical to exam success and to real-world administration because they define how a computer network is administered.

The discussion of logical computing concepts can sometimes be confusing because we're dealing with mechanisms that, for the most part, you can't see. For example, where is the Microsoft domain? It is everywhere and nowhere at the same time. To understand the logical components of Active Directory, we must answer some of the many questions that naturally arise when considering computing mechanisms that we can neither see nor touch, but rather are best visualized with pen and paper.

And once we have the logical elements of Active Directory mastered, we then turn to the physical elements—the Active Directory infrastructure that you can actually see and touch. The physical components are important because they help determine how the information stored in Active Directory is shared between computers.

Also, the physical Active Directory components house the logical information that is so crucial to a Windows Server 2003 network. Especially significant are the domain controllers, which house components like the Active Directory database and the Global Catalog. Towards the end of this chapter, we'll look at the significance of the Global Catalog and how it should ideally be implemented for a given Microsoft Active Directory enterprise.

# Logical Elements of Active Directory

The logical components of Active Directory are important because they define how the computing enterprise will be administered. By designing and determining the logical elements of Active Directory, we become the architects of the network. Just like building architects, we want to start with the ideal in mind; the structural architect begins with a "perfect" building, and then makes accommodations for the functionality of the building, the landscape on which it must be built, city ordinances, and so on. We, too, as Active Directory engineers, begin with what's ideal for administering, and then we make changes to the Active Directory hierarchy based on the computing goals of the organization. We want to start with an ideal design in mind, and then adjust from that ideal where necessary. But the interesting thing about Active Directory is that usually there is a much greater synergy between the goals of Active Directory administration and the final design. We will do with logical space what Frank Lloyd Wright did with living space.

There are four logical components of Active Directory. They are

- Domains
- Trees
- Forests
- Organizational units

## Domains

A Windows 2003 Active Directory *domain* is a logical collection of users and computers. In other words, it's an organizational entity that groups together the objects in your enterprise. With a domain in place, you have several benefits, including the following:

- They enable you to organize objects within a single department or single location, and all information about the object is available.
- They act as security boundaries. Domain admins exercise complete control over all domain objects. Further, in Windows 2003 Active Directory, Group Policies, another kind of domain object, can be applied to determine how resources can be managed and accessed.
- Domain objects can be made available to other domains.
- Domain names follow established DNS naming conventions, permitting the creation of child domains to best suit your administrative needs.
- Domains allow control over replication. That is, domain objects are fully replicated to other domain controllers within a domain, but not to other domains in an Active Directory enterprise.

Just what kinds of objects are stored in a domain? In a Windows 2003 domain, an *object* refers to those items in our computing enterprise which are stored as a piece of software code—usually the security identifiers (SIDs)—in the Active Directory database. Such objects can include these:

- User accounts
- Computer accounts
- Shared folders
- Shared printers
- Group Policies

The other question to consider when setting up your logical structure is, why should you create domains in the first place? This one is a multiple-part answer. When computing objects are stored and managed in a domain's directory database, three clear advantages over the workgroup model emerge:

- One user, one account
- Universal access to resources
- Centralized administration of resources

In a Windows 2003 domain, as was the case in a Windows 2000 domain, information about the objects in a domain is stored in a central location—the Active Directory database. A copy of this database is stored and replicated between all domain controllers for the domain. So if a domain is the cornerstone entity in an Active Directory enterprise, how does the domain fit into the larger picture of Active Directory?

As first described in Chapter 18, Active Directory is essentially an organizational and administrative collection of all the resources in your network. Notice further, as you open the main tool for Active Directory resource management—Active Directory Users and Computers—that the icon you see representing Active Directory in Windows Server 2003 is that of a phone book. A phone book lists all the numbers of residences or businesses in a city or municipality enterprise; likewise, in a Windows Server 2003 computer domain, Active Directory lists all the objects in a computing enterprise, and also stores all the attributes about them.

In a city or municipality, a phone book provides different ways for you to access information. You can look up an organization by its business name, by the type of service it provides, and so on. Similarly, a Windows 2003 Active Directory domain provides lots of way to reference the objects that are collected therein.

Also significant is that a domain represents a security boundary. For example, the domain administrator of one domain cannot administer other domains in the hierarchy. Even the domain admins in a parent domain cannot administer a child domain within the same tree. Only one group has the power to administer every domain in a Windows 2003 forest: the enterprise Admins group. This group is created on the forest root's domain controller. Chapter 20 discusses some of these built-in security groups.

The same rule applies for the application of Group Policy settings. By default, Group Policy settings do not cross domain boundaries. Therefore, any Group Policy settings that you apply to a parent domain do not apply to any of the parent's child domains. These separate security boundaries allow domains—even the ones within a tree that are tied together with these parent/child naming relationships—to act as distinct administrative and/or security units within an Active Directory forest hierarchy.

And when multiple Windows Server 2003 domains exist in a parent/child relationship, you are building an Active Directory tree.

## Trees

Once you've decided to create domains in your enterprise, you may find that you need more than one domain to best reflect the administrative structure of your company. As you can tell, domains have many benefits; thus, you may find compelling reasons to apply these benefits separately to various groups of users and computers in your organization.

Remember, though, that users and computers actually live in a domain. The domains exist in a tree, and trees subsequently live in a forest. If you want to link your Windows 2003 domains together for purposes of administration and/or sharing of resources, you'll need to start building Active Directory trees and forests.

The hallmark of an Active Directory *tree* is that it is a contiguous linking of one or more Active Directory domains that share a common namespace. In other words, the domains are linked together in parent-child relationships as far as the naming conventions go. Figure 19-1 shows what an Active Directory tree might look like.

**NOTE**  The geometric shape of a domain in every Windows Active Directory schematic you will *ever* see will be a triangle. So you know what you're looking at in this illustration and all the ones to follow: triangle = Active Directory domain.

All domains in an Active Directory tree share a common schema, Global Catalog, and are linked with two-way, transitive trust relationships. The transitive nature of the trusts ensures that the resources in one domain are available to users of other domains in the tree. In the section on trust relationships in this chapter, and again In Chapter 21, we discuss these trust relationships in more detail.

Sometimes, however, even a tree full of domains will not work for your enterprise. Say, for example, you run a company like Microsoft, and you decide to purchase the assets of another company. Let's pretend that said company is hotmail.com. The users, computers, and resources of hotmail.com, then, need to be merged with microsoft.com.

**Figure 19-1**
An Active
Directory tree

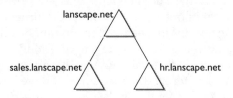

Obviously, these two domains do not share a common DNS namespace, yet you still want to link these two entities in a single administrative structure. You want all constituent domains of these two trees to share the same Active Directory information: a common schema, Global Catalog, and configuration, just like when setting up a tree.

## Forests

A *forest* lets you link together multiple domain trees in a hierarchical arrangement. The goal in designing a forest is the same as when designing a tree: to define and maintain an administrative relationship between the domains.

By creating a forest, you build into your computing environment the flexibility to reflect the real-world business environment of acquisitions, mergers, and spinoffs from your main company—all this while retaining the administrative benefits of domains linked together with trust relationships. All domains in the tree are linked by two-way, transitive trust relationships, and all tree roots in the forest are likewise linked by two-way, transitive trusts. Notice in Figure 19-1, however, that only the top domains in each respective tree are linked with trust relationships. Is the design goal of universal resource access still maintained? Yes. Because of the two-way transitivity of the trusts, users in one domain in the forest can still be allowed access to resources in any of the forest's member domains. Figure 19-2 shows a Windows Server 2003 forest schematic.

What's important to note is that a forest is a group of Active Directory trees that share the following components: a schema, a site configuration, and a Global Catalog.

Also important to note when designing your Active Directory forest is that it is built from the top down. That is, the forest root is the first domain in the enterprise, and it will be the most important domain to your forest structure. You cannot build child domains and then reverse-engineer your Active Directory forest. Child domains, as well as additional trees, must join existing domains or the forest root tree.

In most diagrams of an Active Directory forest, the forest root domain is clearly identified, as it is in Figure 19-2. In fact, when upgrading Windows NT 4.0 domains to Windows Server 2003 domains (or Windows 2000 domains, for that matter), the first domain you decide to upgrade will establish the root of your Active Directory forest.

PART IV

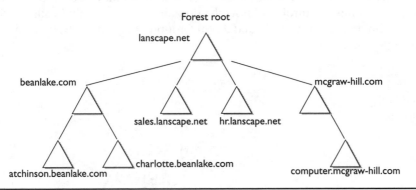

**Figure 19-2**   An Active Directory forest

**NOTE** Choose your forest root domain with caution. Once established, the forest root cannot be changed without decommissioning the entire logical Active Directory infrastructure. In Windows Server 2003, it is now possible to *rename* the forest root domain, but the domain designated as the forest root cannot be changed once established.

## Organizational Units

When properly implemented, an organizational unit (OU) is the administrative lynchpin of a Windows 2003 Active Directory hierarchy. It is a container object within a domain that represents subadministrative entities within an Active Directory. Organizational units are used to group together domain computers, users, and other domain objects into an administrative collection. These collections are kept as separate logical units. Windows 2003 domains are designed to be self-contained, and through the use of organizational units, you have a lot of flexibility about how that domain is administered.

Don't be misled by the word "group" in the preceding paragraph; OUs are not groups; they are administrative containers. Anything you can put into the domain, anything you can put into an Active Directory database, you can put into an organizational unit. That's not true with groups. The only entities groups can contain are users, computers, or other groups. Organizational units, on the other hand, can contain computers, shared resources, printers, as well as groups and users—just about anything you can store in an Active Directory database can live in an organizational unit.

Another big difference between groups and organizational units is that you can apply Group Policy to an organizational unit or an organizational grouping of computers and users; you cannot apply Group Policy to a group. The name might imply otherwise, but that's not what Group Policies are used for.

An organizational unit's structure may be based on cities, like Kansas City, St. Louis, Omaha, Dallas, and so on., or on departments, like I.T., H.R., Payroll, Sales, Accounting, and so on. You can also nest organizational units in parent/child relationships, much like you can create parent/child domain affiliations when you set up a tree. Figure 19-3 shows an example of how a company might build a parent/child OU hierarchy.

As the Active Directory architect, these organizational unit characteristics also gives you almost unlimited control over how the domain objects are administered within a single domain. In the Chapters 22 and 23 on Group Policy especially, you will see this administration in action.

**Figure 19-3**
A parent/child
OU hierarchy

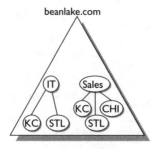

An organizational unit provides two significant benefits: It allows you to delegate control, or even certain kinds of control, over some portions of the domain. Furthermore, applying a Group Policy allows for a set of users in one organizational unit to have a very different end-user experience from the users in another organizational unit.

Within a domain, it is very common that you will have business units or offices that are completely separate from one another. The benefit of organizational units is that they let you administer these separate cities or business units as autonomous units that are administered by completely different administrators. However, you, as a domain administrator, still have control over the entire domain.

For example, you can specify with a Group Policy deployment that a certain collection of users and computers get a certain software package, while another set—another OU—gets a different software package. In fact, instead of creating extra domains to distribute administration, Microsoft encourages system administrators to create a single domain, and then use organizational units within that domain to delegate their administrative tasks.

Furthermore, as you build your Active Directory forest, you will also be building and maintaining trust relationships.

## Trust Relationships

If you followed along with the steps to create the forest root domain outlined in Chapter 18, you are now sitting near a Windows Server 2003 domain controller, which is the only computer in the Active Directory hierarchy. (All Active Directory networks, big and small, share this unassuming origin.) How many domains have you created? One. How many trees? One. How many forests? One! You are now lord over your very own Active Directory forest.

In other words, a forest can contain only one tree, and a tree can contain only one domain. That's how it works. In such an environment as the one you just created, no trust relationships are necessary. And even once you start adding other domains to your Active Directory forest, no configuration of trusts is necessary.

*Trust relationships* serve two important functions worth noting as we expand the Active Directory enterprise:

- **Trust relationships facilitate cross-domain logon.** A user can submit from any domain in the forest logon credentials to a domain controller in the domain where his or her account lives. The logon follows the path of the trust relationships from one domain controller to another. Note, however, that all the domains in the trust path must be "up" for this to occur. Figure 19-4 examines the path of the logon through the trust associations.

- **Trust relationships facilitate access to resources in all other domains in the forest.** Also shown in Figure 19-4, the links between domains in a forest mean that users in one domain can be granted permission to access resources in other domains throughout the forest. Within a forest, the accounts in one Active Directory domain are trusted by the other domains.

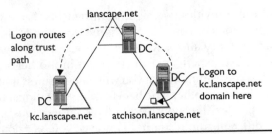

**Figure 19-4**   Logon follows trust link paths and allows for universal access to resources.


These built-in trust relationships are both two way and transitive. In other words, if domain A trusts domain B, and domain B trusts domain C, then domain A will trust domain C. While this was also true of the previous iteration of Microsoft's domain model, this setup was not the case with Windows NT 4.0 domains, and many organizations will make the leap to Windows Server 2003 directly from Windows NT 4.0, rather than from Windows 2000.

# Implementing an Active Directory Directory Service Forest and Domain Structure

Now that you understand a little bit about the logical components of Active Directory, it's time to start building these entities. To start the forest creation process, just as you did in Chapter 18, you run dcpromo.exe from the Run dialog box. Doing so invokes the Active Directory Installation Wizard, as show in Figure 19-5.

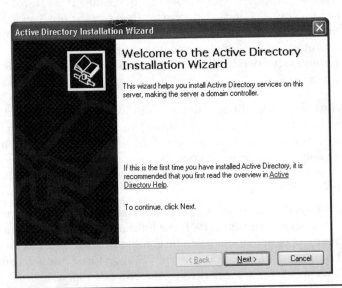

**Figure 19-5**   The Active Directory Installation Wizard

Like many other wizards, the choices you make on the screens determine the subsequent choices on other screens; it's a road with many forks. Probably the most significant fork is the first one, where you decide whether to build a domain controller for a new domain or to create an additional domain controller for an existing domain. If you choose the former, you then have the ability to build the domain controller that establishes a new forest root domain.

## Creating the Forest Root Domain

The *root* of an Active Directory forest is always the first domain created in the logical hierarchy. In many ways, it's the most important decision you make in the building of Active Directory, because the choice you make now is the hardest one to reverse.

When you create the forest root, you're doing far more than just setting up a domain controller. When the forest root is established, you also generate the base schema for all other domains that may be added to the Active Directory forest, and you also designate the server that manages this schema information. The schema will be managed by this first domain controller until it's changed by an enterprise administrator.

Why is this point significant? Because the schema is a list of all the potential components that can be added to an Active Directory database, and a list of all the ways those components can be described. In other words, if a component isn't first defined in the schema, you can't put it in the Active Directory database.

Before you build the forest root, keep these prerequisites in mind for establishing the Active Directory forest root:

- The Windows Server 2003 platform must be installed and running on the intended domain controller.

- A DNS server must be installed and configured with a forward lookup zone for the domain you intend to create. If one is not present, the Active Directory Setup Wizard will offer to install one for you.

- The intended domain controller must have TCP/IP installed and correctly configured. It should be installed by default.

- You need an NTFS partition for the installation of the SYSVOL directory on the domain controller, and you need enough space for that directory. Microsoft recommends about a gigabyte of free space.

- You should ensure that the system time information is correct. During Active Directory installation, the system will also become the domain's time server for the other machines on the domain.

But you probably noticed this if you followed the steps in Chapter 18. As you also probably noticed, the button clicking doesn't present that great of a challenge. More important, you should understand what impact the buttons clicked will have on your organizational and administrative model.

After you have created the first domain controller in the first domain of your enterprise, you can then add additional domain controllers to the existing domain, or create domain controllers that will establish other domains in the forest. (Most of the time, adding more domains or domain trees is unnecessary, as you will see.) The tool you use to build this hierarchy is the same as the one to establish it: the Active Directory Installation Wizard. This time, however, by choosing different paths through the wizard, you have the ability to create other domain controllers in the domain, other child domains of the forest root, or even other domain trees in the forest.

## Creating a Child Domain

Because the button-clicking is so elementary, the test probably won't ask about specific procedures in the wizard. Your job is more to know why a tree might be warranted for a given company. That said, let's identify the screen where the important forks in the road appear.

If, through your selections, you instruct the Active Directory Installation Wizard to create a domain controller for a new domain, you must next decide whether to create a new domain tree, or to create a new child domain in an existing tree. If you create a new domain tree, you must then decide whether that new tree will become the root of a new forest, as shown in Figure 19-6.

Domains in a forest are linked through a two-way transitive trust. These trust relationships are automatically created as you start to build your Windows 2003 Active Directory forest. In other words, parent domains are linked transitively with child domains, and a tree and tree roots in a forest are likewise linked in a two-way transitive trust relationship.

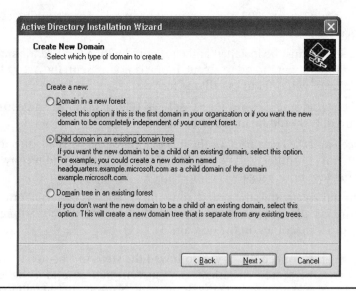

**Figure 19-6** Creation of a child domain

**TIP** Microsoft recommends that, where possible, you design your network for the creation of a single domain.

By combining trees and forests, you have absolute flexibility over the design of your Active Directory enterprise, and, thus, over the administration of the objects in your computing enterprise.

## Installing an Additional Domain Controller for an Existing Domain

Your Active Directory enterprise might not call for additional domains, however. If this describes your organization, you still typically want to install at least one other domain controller for the domain for fault tolerance and load balancing. The Active Directory Installation Wizard makes it almost effortless.

## Lab Exercise 19.1: Adding Another Domain Controller

Follow these steps to create an additional domain controller:

1. Launch the Active Directory Installation Wizard. Click Start | Run, and then type **dcpromo** in the Run dialog box.

2. The Operating System Compatibility screen will be the same as when establishing the forest root; click Next when you've thoroughly read the information.

3. On the Domain Controller Type screen, choose Additional Domain Controller For An Existing Domain. Click Next.

   You now have two choices about where to get a copy of an existing Active Directory database, as shown in Figure 19-7. The additional domain controller can get its information either from the network or from restored backup files. If choosing the latter, you must type the location of the restored backup files, or choose Browse to locate the restored files. Click Next after you've made your selection, and then click Next again.

4. The rest of the wizard screens (Network Credentials, Database And Log Folders, System Volume, and Directory Service Restore Mode) will look identical to those you saw in Chapter 18. Enter the appropriate information and click Next on each screen.

5. Review the Summary screen, and then click Next to begin the installation. Restart the computer to complete the installation procedure.

 **EXAM TIP** You could run the Active Directory Installation Wizard with the option to create an additional domain controller from restored backup files more directly by running dcpromo with the /adv switch. This switch bypasses the first few screens of the wizard. This new feature of the dcpromo utility was not available with Windows 2000.

**PART IV**

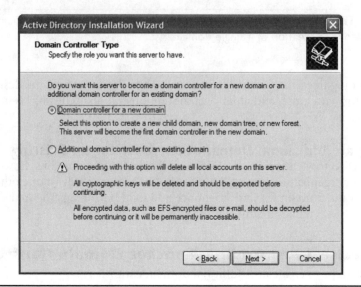

**Figure 19-7**   Adding an additional domain controller

## Uninstalling Active Directory and Removing a Domain

Finally, you should know the procedure to remove Active Directory from a Windows Server 2003 computer. Removing Active Directory turns the server into a member server in the domain where it was previously a domain controller. Follow these steps:

1. Launch the Active Directory Installation Wizard.

2. After the welcome screen, the Remove Active Directory screen appears. Note that if the domain controller is the last domain controller for the domain, you specify this with the check box here, as shown in Figure 19-8. Doing so will decommission the domain.

**NOTE**   If Active Directory is already installed on a server, removing Active Directory is the only option available. Other than using the renaming tools available when your domain is running in Windows Server 2003 functional level, you cannot change the nature of the domain controller without first removing and then reinstalling Active Directory.

When you are decommissioning a domain, you must select the This Server Is The Last Domain Controller In The Domain check box. Otherwise, the domain naming master will still have a record for the domain's existence, and it could present a problem when domains are added later. Chapter 21 discusses the full significance of the domain naming master, but for now, remember that like the schema, only one server manages this information throughout the Active Directory forest.

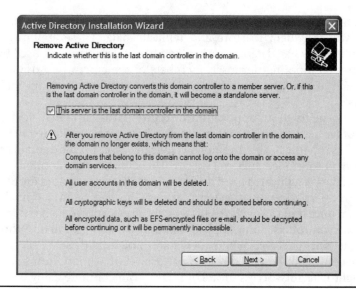

**Figure 19-8**    Uninstalling Active Directory from the last domain controller

When the last domain controller has been removed from the domain, the domain ceases to exist. Removing a domain results in the permanent loss of any Active Directory data contained in that domain, including all user, group, and computer accounts. If you want those accounts retained, you must move them into other domains first.

If you want to decommission a forest, you must first decommission all attached domain trees and child domains before removing the forest root domain. This is part of the reason why the naming of the Active Directory forest root domain is such a critical decision. Any changes to the forest root domain result in considerable administrative time and effort.

## Creating and Configuring Application Data Partitions

A new feature available with Windows Server 2003 Active Directory is an application directory partition. A directory partition is replicated between domain controllers, but only to the domain controllers you choose. A domain controller that participates in the replication of a particular application directory partition hosts a replica of that partition. Only domain controllers running Windows Server 2003 can host a replica of an application directory partition. Furthermore, these partitions can store any kind of file, folder, shared folder, printer, and any other object, except security principals.

 **NOTE**    Any kind of object used to manage control access to resources is a *security principal*. A user account is the poster child for a security principal because permissions will be assigned on this kind of object.

Application directory partitions are usually created by, and sometimes for, the applications that will use them to store and replicate data. These applications include back-end applications like database servers and naming information used by DNS. For testing and troubleshooting purposes, members of the enterprise Admins group can manually create or manage application directory partitions using the ntdsutil command-line tool.

One of the benefits of an application directory partition is that, for redundancy, availability, or fault tolerance purposes, the data in it can be replicated to different domain controllers in a forest. The data can be replicated to a specific domain controller or any set of domain controllers that you specify. This differs from a domain directory partition in which data is replicated to all domain controllers in that domain. Storing application data in an application directory partition instead of in a domain directory partition may reduce replication traffic because the application data is replicated only to specific domain controllers. Some applications may use application directory partitions to replicate data only to servers where the data will be locally useful.

Another benefit of application directory partitions is that applications or services that use Lightweight Directory Access Protocol (LDAP) can continue using it to access and store their application data in Active Directory.

Yet another benefit of creating an application partition is that you don't need to worry about configuring a replication topology; Active Directory takes care of it for you through the services of the Knowledge Consistency Checker (KCC). The KCC automatically generates and maintains the replication topology for all application directory partitions in the enterprise. When an application directory partition has replicas in more than one site, those replicas follow the same intersite replication schedule as the domain directory partition. We'll touch on the KCC and intersite replication again later in the chapter.

 **EXAM TIP** When you are uninstalling Active Directory from a domain controller, make sure no application partitions still reside on the domain controller. They should be deleted and/or moved before performing the uninstall.

## Lab Exercise 19.2: Creating an Application Data Partition

Use the following procedure to set up an application directory partition:

1. Open the command prompt (type **cmd** in the Run dialog box), and type **ntdsutil**.

2. At the ntdsutil command prompt, type **domain management**.

3. At the domain management command prompt, type **connection**.

4. At the connection command prompt, type **connect to server** *servername*, where *servername* is the name of the server on which you are creating the application directory. A message will appear telling you whether you are successfully connected.

5. At the connection command prompt, type **quit**.

6. You will be returned to the domain management command prompt. Once there, do one of the following to set up the directory:

- To create an application directory partition, type **create nc** *applicationdirectorypartition domaincontroller*.

- To delete an application directory partition, type **delete nc** *applicationdirectorypartition*.

The *domaincontroller* variable is the full DNS name of the domain controller where you are creating the application partition (or a replica thereof). The *applicationdirectorypartition* is the distinguished name for the partition. For instance, the distinguished name for finance.beanlake.com is dc=finance, dc=beanlake, dc=com.

 **CAUTION**   If you delete the last replica of an application data partition, you will permanently lose all of the data contained in that partition and will have to recover data from backup.

# Understanding the Physical Elements of Active Directory

Up to this point, we've been dealing mostly with computing concepts that are best managed with pencil and paper. These logical structures are, however, physically created as software objects. But these objects don't live in a vacuum; they have to be created somewhere, and they have to be stored somewhere. Furthermore, the information has to be shared with other computers. Enter the physical components of Active Directory. This section explores how to best plan and manage the physical parts of your Active Directory enterprise.

## Installing and Configuring an Active Directory Domain Controller

An Active Directory structure contains two physical components: *sites* and *domain controllers*. Unlike a domain, these are components you can actually point to and lay your hands on. You can implement a domain controller easily enough by following any of the procedures listed previously when discussing Active Directory implementation. Simply put, you just run dcpromo to create a domain controller.

Once set up, the job of a domain controller is to store a writable copy of the Active Directory database for the domain of which it is a member. Sometimes, these domain controllers will store additional information like the Global Catalog. Sometimes, the domain controllers play important roles in the functioning of the network. And sometimes, they perform many of these tasks at once.

All of the objects in the domain's Active Directory database—the user accounts, the groups, the computer accounts, the organizational units, and so forth—are stored within a domain controller, and all domain controllers within a single domain act as peers. When domain controllers act as peers, they engage in *multimaster* replication. The multimaster replication model is a carryover from the Windows 2000 Active Directory environment, but it represents a significant departure from the single-master replication model used by Windows NT 4.0 domain controllers. All changes to the Windows NT 4.0 directory database were made at a Primary Domain Controller (PDC) and then replicated out to Backup Domain Controllers (BDCs). This is no longer the case.

When Windows Server 2003 domain controllers engage in multimaster replication, a change to the Active Directory database can be made at any of the domain controllers, and these changes will be then reflected on other domain controllers after replication. There isn't a single server that receives preferential notification of changes, as was the case in Windows NT 4.0. It's worth noting, however, that *some* information needed for a working Active Directory environment is still updated using the single-master replication model, as will be discussed in Chapter 21.

A domain controller, one of the physical components of Active Directory, is stored in another physical component of Active Directory, the site.

## Implementing an Active Directory Site Topology

The simple definition of a *site* is a collection of one or more "well-connected" IP subnets. More importantly, though, a site is a unit of Active Directory replication. If the domain controller's job is to store and replicate the Active Directory database, then the site's job is to govern how that replication occurs.

But the site's capabilities don't end here. A site is also used by Active Directory to manage the following:

- Logon traffic, ensuring that a client located and submits credentials to local domain controllers when possible

- Requests to the Global Catalog, by keeping all such requests local (if there is at least one Global Catalog server per site, as is recommended)

- Optimization of traffic for Active Directory–aware applications, such as the Distributed File System (DFS).

Once you understand that a site is a way of controlling Active Directory traffic, you can make more informed choices about how many sites your organization needs. If a company is using Windows Server 2003, and it is located in a single office building or office complex, sticking with the default single-site configuration that's created when Active Directory is set up makes sense. This way, you can let automated processes handle replication with a minimum of administrative interference.

In general, however, you should probably implement a site for each geographic location, because you can better manage how Active Directory replication traffic uses the WAN links that connect the different locations. For example, if your company has major office facilities located in five separate cities, and those offices are connected by WAN links slower than a T3, you should consider a different Active Directory site for each of those cities. You might even want to implement separate sites for office buildings within the same city if office buildings are connected by slower links.

On the other hand, you might not always need to implement a separate site just because domain users are separated geographically. In certain cases, especially where branch offices are small or are connected by fast links, implementing multiple sites can actually cause a decrease in LAN performance. Because a site contains at least one domain controller, creating a site may sometimes cause unnecessary expense. It all depends on the links between physical locations and how many users are at each site. There are no right or wrong answers, of course, but Microsoft does expect you to recognize what works best given a specific set of parameters.

## The Role of the Knowledge Consistency Checker

If the sites exist to control replication traffic, how does Active Directory build the replication topology between a site's domain controllers? Automatically, using the Knowledge Consistency Checker.

During the Active Directory installation process, each domain controller is made aware of other domain controllers within the same domain. The Knowledge Consistency Checker works to ensure that every one of these domain controllers has at least one replication partner, or peer. The end result of the KCC's hard work is that all domain controllers are able to get updated Active Directory information from all others using a fault-tolerant ring topology.

The other job of the Knowledge Consistency Checker is to allow Active Directory to take care of the replication of directory database information without administrators having to worry about it too much, or configure it manually. Manual creation of replication links, or *connection objects*, between domain controllers can still be done, but Microsoft doesn't recommend it. The Knowledge Consistency Checker automates the replication process, ensures the replication topology, minimizes replication latency, and checks all replication links every 15 minutes to ensure that the main controllers are functioning properly. Further, if one of the domain controllers should be taken offline, the KCC automatically regenerates a new replication topology between domain controllers for the domain. So again, you don't have to do much. You can kind of fall backwards into a good working network with Windows Server 2003.

## Replication: How and Why

Replication between the domain controllers in an Active Directory domain, no matter in which sites those domain controllers live, works by keeping track of a version number assigned to the Active Directory database. This version number is called an Update Sequence Number (USN), and it is used to track the changes made to each copy of Active Directory. Every time a change is made to the database, the domain controller updates the database USN where the change was made.

Every domain controller keeps track of its USN and, more important, the USNs of its replication partners. Then, every five minutes (this is the default interval), the domain controller checks for changes from its replication partners in the same site. If a domain controller finds that its replication partner has an update to its USN, it then requests that all changes since the last known USN be sent. Even if a domain controller has been offline for an extended time, it can quickly be sent all updates to the Active Directory database when it comes back online.

When it's time for the test, be sure you understand the differences between how Active Directory information is exchanged among domain controllers within the same site and among domain controllers between separate sites.

## Replication Within Sites (Intrasite)

Replication within a site is handled by the Knowledge Consistency Checker. The job of the KCC is to evaluate the domain controllers within a site and automatically establish and maintain a *ring-based* replication topology. It does this by automatically creating *connection objects* between two domain controllers within a site. Each domain controller will have at least one two replication partners, if applicable (if there are only two domain controllers in a site, those domain controllers will only have one partner, for example). You can manually create these connection objects between domain controllers, or force replication between two domain controllers, but normally you would never need to do so. To force replication over a connection object, right-click the connection object and choose Replicate Now from the context menu.

The ring-based topology is logical in nature; it does not mean that you need, nor will the KCC create, a Token Ring network. Rather, the ring topology is logical and merely ensures that more than one method exists to get Active Directory information from one domain controller to another.

Another reason you would not manually create connection objects is that the KCC is a dynamic process. That is, it automatically adjusts the replication topology as network conditions change. As domain controllers or subnets are added or removed from a site, the KCC constantly checks to make sure each domain controller is able to exchange information with at least two others within the site, thus keeping the ring topology intact. So even though you need to do virtually nothing to tweak the performance of the KCC in a production network, your job as a test candidate is to make sure you understand the purpose of the KCC.

Moreover, here's what else you need to know about intrasite replication:

- **Replication does not use compression.** This behavior reduces the processing load on domain controllers. (Processing cycles are needed to compress and uncompress information.)

- **Replication occurs based on a notification process.** When a domain controller has an update to its Active Directory database, it notifies the other domain controllers in the same site. These domain controllers then contact the notifying domain controller and request that the changes to the database be sent.

Although replication *within* sites is really no big deal, Microsoft expects you to know plenty about replication *between* sites.

## Replication Between Sites (Intersite)

The replication between Active Directory sites is a much more complex process. It needs to be: the replication traffic can have a much more dramatic impact on available bandwidth, and, as such, must include the ability to be governed more carefully.

You should be familiar with the following key information about intersite replication:

- **Replication between sites uses compression.**   The compression of Active Directory increases the processing load on domain controllers. It also cuts back on bandwidth use, which is the more precious resource in Windows Server 2003.

- **It uses scheduling.**   Replication between sites occurs only during scheduled hours.

- **It uses a replication interval.**   The replication is available only during a set schedule; even then, it happens only periodically during those set hours.

These last two behaviors of intersite replication are critical to managing the impact replication traffic has on your WAN. But before you can manage these parameters, you must create a second site and then move at least one domain controller to this other site. After you've moved a domain controller to the other site, you'll need to create a connection object between the domain controllers.

By default, one is created for you called DEFAULTIPSITELINK, but you can use Active Directory Sites and Services to create other sites as needed. Once you've created the links between sites, you can manage the properties of the connection object much like managing the properties of other objects in the Active Directory database.

In short, there's a lot to consider when configuring and managing Active Directory traffic once your organization starts to encompass multiple geographic locales. But to manage this replication traffic, you first need to know the procedure for creating a new site.

## Managing an Active Directory Site

So a site is somewhat easy to define: a collection of one or more well-connected IP subnets. When you first establish an Active Directory domain, you also set up Active Directory's first site. All IP subnets will be included in that first site—which is called, somewhat aptly, Default-First-Site-Name. As a result, all domain controllers in that domain will be placed in this first site, and these domain controllers will exchange Active Directory information using intrasite replication techniques.

In other words, before you start creating additional sites, all domain controllers are considered well connected. If you have one domain controller in Kansas City and one in Reykjavík, Active Directory assumes they are in the same location and replicates database changes accordingly.

To investigate the properties of this initial Active Directory site, you can use the Active Directory Sites and Services MMC snap-in, as shown in Figure 19-9, which you will find in the Administrative Tools.

If your network is relatively contained, or the locations are connected by very fast links (you have a T3 line, say, connecting one office to the other), you might need only

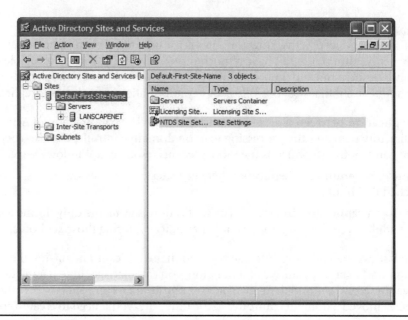

**Figure 19-9**    The Active Directory Sites and Services snap-in

the Default-First-Site for your network. If, however, you find that your enterprise is expanding to multiple geographic locations, and the links between these locations are slow, you should probably implement multiple sites.

> **NOTE**   For a network with thousands of users, a T1 might be slow, but a smaller company might need additional sites only if there is less than 128 KBps of available bandwidth.

## Lab Exercise 19.3: Creating a Site

It won't take you long to create a second site (or third, or fourth...) in your Active Directory enterprise. The button-clicking is easy. Here's the procedure you follow:

1. From Administrative Tools, open Active Directory Sites and Services.

2. Right-click the Sites folder, and choose New Site.

3. Name your new site and choose one of the site links this site will use for replication, as shown in Figure 19-10. We will discuss site links later in the chapter.

4. After clicking OK, a dialog box informs you of the next steps, as shown in Figure 19-11.

**Figure 19-10**    Setting up a new site to control replication

Good! You've just configured a second Active Directory site and are on your way to regulating replication traffic exactly as Microsoft recommends. Note that there's nothing in the site yet; it's just an empty container object, but that will soon change.

Also, bear in mind that office locales, like the businesses themselves, are fluid, often changing over time. Businesses expand, acquire other businesses, are acquired themselves, or go out of business altogether. Fortunately, adapting to these changes in organizational structure and/or business mission, at least for Active Directory, is a breeze.

## Renaming and Deleting a Site

Sometimes, the network will be reorganized or moved, and sites need to be either renamed or deleted as appropriate. The renaming procedure is straightforward: right-click the site and choose Rename. Just like the renaming of a user account, all you're really

**Figure 19-11**    Steps needed to complete the configuration of the site

PART IV

doing is changing one of the attributes of the Active Directory object, and nothing about the object changes except that single attribute.

Deleting is a little more precarious. When you delete an object, you are deleting that number that makes the object unique. The name associated with that number, as far as Active Directory is concerned, is rather irrelevant. If you were to then create an object and give it the same name as the object you just deleted, you would need to reconfigure all of that object's properties if you wanted it to behave just like the deleted item. For example, a site containing several domain controllers that was deleted and then recreated with the same name would be void of any domain controllers. If you were to rename the same site rather than delete it, however, the site would keep its domain controller membership intact.

Of course when you delete a site, the subnets and domain controllers within that site do not vanish into the ether. But their references in Active Directory are deleted, and that can certainly affect replication traffic. Therefore, be cautious when removing sites if you don't want to delete the objects they contain.

To delete a site, right-click the site and choose Delete. A confirmation dialog box appears, as shown in Figure 19-12, warning you that you will be deleting additional items.

## Site Properties

Once you've configured a site, you'll likely begin its management by changing some of its basic properties. The site has properties because, when created in Active Directory, it's a piece of code; an Active Directory object and all objects in Active Directory have properties. To access the site's Properties dialog box, right-click the site node in the left pane of Active Directory Sites and Services and choose Properties. You will see these five tabs:

- **Site**  Describes the site.
- **Location**  Lets you enter a location.
- **Object**  Lets you see the full name of the object and when it was created. There is nothing you can change on this tab.
- **Security**  Allows you to set the Access Control List for the Active Directory object, and also allows you to delegate control of the object to other users in the organization.
- **Group Policy**  Lets you create and attach Group Policies that will manage the objects in the site.

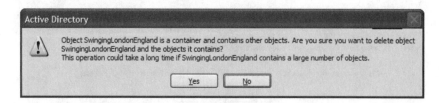

**Figure 19-12**    A warning that additional objects could be deleted as well

You can delegate control of many Active Directory objects, and sites are just one example. You can also delegate administrative responsibility over domains, organizational units, and domain controllers.

## Moving a Domain Controller

Let's tackle the procedure of moving a domain controller to another site. Like moving other objects, the process is just a matter of a few clicks. Here's how:

1. From Active Directory Sites and Services, expand the Sites folder and expand the site where the domain controller you will move is currently located.

2. Expand the Servers node, right-click the domain controller you'll move, and choose Move.

3. In the Move Server dialog box, select the destination site, and click OK to complete the procedure.

**NOTE** Unless you've installed more than one domain controller in your domain using the steps introduced in Chapter 18, you will have only a single domain controller. You can create sites without any domain controllers at all, however.

**PART IV**

## Configuring Site Boundaries

The creation of your Active Directory site topology follows a recommended procedure. It's OK to get this procedure out of order, but when first creating the Active Directory infrastructure presented here, the procedure outlined in this chapter might help you keep these concepts straight: create the container, set the boundaries for that container, and populate the container with objects. So, then, after you create a site, you will set the boundaries for the site using subnets.

You know the simple definition by heart now: sites are one or more well-connected IP subnets. A site will be populated with your network's domain controllers, but they are made up of subnets. In other words, the subnets really give shape to the sites. The site by itself is just an empty shell. Computers, including domain controllers, get associated with sites based on the IP subnets to which they belong.

**NOTE** Because computers are associated with sites based on their IP subnets, Microsoft recommends that you create your subnets and assign them to sites before installing your domain controllers. That way, the domain controller will assign itself to the appropriate site automatically during installation based on the IP address with which it's configured.

Keep the following rules about subnets in mind:

- **All subnets will be assigned to a site.** You won't create a subnet without assigning it to an existing site, so you want to set up your intended sites before creating subnets.

- **A subnet cannot exist in multiple sites.** A site may be defined by several subnets, but a subnet can be assigned to only a single site.

- **A client computer logging on to the domain will try to find a domain controller in the same site as the client computer.** This additional benefit of site behavior keeps logon traffic local whenever possible.

**TIP** Make sure you have a pretty good grasp of TCP/IP for the 70-294 exam. If you need help, you can reread Chapter 7. Microsoft expects you to recognize networking notation like Classless Inter-Domain Routing (CIDR) notation and what a subnet is because these are the building blocks of your Active Directory sites.

## Lab Exercise 19.4: Adding Subnets to Sites

To configure the boundaries of your sites, you need to create subnets and then assign these subnets to them as appropriate. Here's how:

1. Open Active Directory Sites and Services, right-click the Subnets folder, and choose New Subnet.

2. In the New Object – Subnet dialog box, as shown in Figure 19-13, enter the IP address and subnet mask of a computer that will live on the subnet. Alternatively, you can specify a network ID, which will be more inclusive of the computers in the subnet.

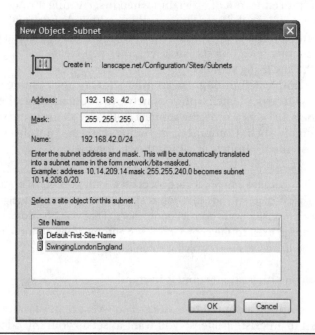

**Figure 19-13** Creating a new subnet for a site

3. Note that Windows Server 2003 automatically extracts the network portion of the IP address and lists the network ID in CIDR notation. It uses this CIDR notation to name the subnet.

4. Now assign the subnet to a site. (This is why you create the container object, the site, before you give shape to the site by creating subnets.) Click OK.

These subnets are created as objects in Active Directory, and just like any other object in Active Directory, the subnets will have a set of properties you can manage. One of these properties is the site to which it belongs.

## Moving a Subnet

But what if you change your mind about which site your subnet belongs to? What if a network ID changes? Or what if the network undergoes a minor reorganization, and you need to move a subnet from one site to another? As you might suspect, this is a very painless process. Here's what you do:

1. From Active Directory Sites and Services, click the Subnets folder, and then in the Details pane, select the subnet you want to move.

2. Right-click and choose Properties. From the General tab of the Properties dialog box, as shown in Figure 19-14, use the Site drop-down menu to select a site where the subnet will now reside.

3. Click OK to complete the move procedure.

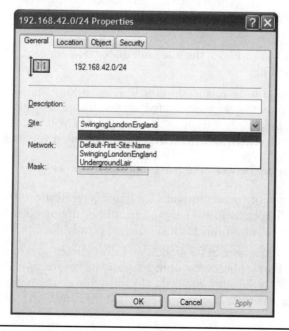

**Figure 19-14**    Moving a subnet from one site to another

So if a site is one or more well-connected IP subnets, what exactly does "well-connected" mean? Is a T1 link between sites well connected? Not if there are thousands of users at each site. Is 128 KBps well connected? In your organization, where you might have offices with only a computer or two at remote locations, it may be. In other words, it depends.

If the sites are not well connected, though, it's up to you to control replication traffic so that WAN bandwidth is optimized. The next section deals with just this topic, and you can be assured that Microsoft will deal with this topic as well on the 70-294 exam.

## Creating Site Links

Now that you've created a new site, defined the boundaries of that site, and populated that site with a domain controller, you're ready to manage the exchange of Active Directory information between the domain controllers in different sites.

Before you do, however, you need to set up a site link that will link the sites. This provides the thoroughfare over which replication can take place.

## Lab Exercise 19.5: Creating a Site Link

Here's how to create a site link:

1. From Active Directory Sites and Services, expand the Sites folder and expand the Inter-Site Transports node.

2. Right-click either the IP or the SMTP folder. Usually it will be IP, but slower links may use SMTP. The following section examines the differences between these two intersite replication protocols. For now, let's use the IP folder. Choose New Site Link.

3. As shown in Figure 19-15, the Site Link dialog box appears, where you will name the site link.

4. Choose the sites to be included in the link by clicking them and choosing Add. Note that if only two sites are created, they will automatically be selected for the new site link. Only if more than two sites exist will you have the choice of selecting which sites will be included. Click OK when you're done.

Here's the difference between the two replication protocols:

- **IP**  IP uses remote procedure calls for sending replication. This protocol is also used for replication within a site, and should be the protocol used if you have a persistent IP connection, as most offices typically do.

- **SMTP**  SMTP can be used for replication only between sites in different domains. It is not used for replication within a site. By its nature, SMTP is asynchronous. Further, SMTP replication can only send schema, configuration, and Global Catalog data. Domain data is not replicated this way.

**Figure 19-15**   Creating a new site link

   **TIP**   When you create an SMTP site link, you must also install a certification authority (CA). The certification authority issues certificates that are used to sign the SMTP Active Directory replication messages, thus assuring the authenticity of Active Directory updates.

## Configuring Replication Schedules

Now that you've created the site link, understand that you've just created another Active Directory object, and this Active Directory object can be managed via the tabs in its Properties dialog box, as shown in Figure 19-16. In fact, through the use of these properties, you'll manage how replication behaves between your Active Directory sites.

You can configure the following properties:

- **Description**   This property is for human consumption—a comment about the link.

- **Sites In This Site Link**   Here's where you can add and remove the sites that will use this site link for replicating Active Directory information between domain controllers.

- **Cost**   This value is relative, and it is used by Active Directory to determine the best route available when replicating information. The least expensive route is always used. More about site link cost in the section that follows.

**Figure 19-16**    The site link properties

- **Replicate Every**    This property is where you set the interval of replication. When the site link is available, replication will take place however often you specify here.

- **Change Schedule**    This property lets you alter the availability of the link. If you want replication between sites to occur only at night, you can set this by clicking the Change Schedule button and altering the dialog box you see in Figure 19-17.

**TIP**    The default replication availability is 24 hours a day, 7 days a week, and the default replication interval is every 180 minutes (3 hours). You can configure the interval anywhere from 15 minutes to 10,080 minutes (1 week). For replication to occur at the scheduled interval, the site link must be available.

## Configuring Site Link Costs

If you refer back to Figure 19-16, you see that the cost of a site link is 100. But just what does this cost indicate? Dollar amount? Bandwidth? The answer is neither. The default site link cost is 100. Anything that is higher has a higher cost; lower has a lower cost. For example, if you assign a link with a cost of 200, Active Directory calculates this link as

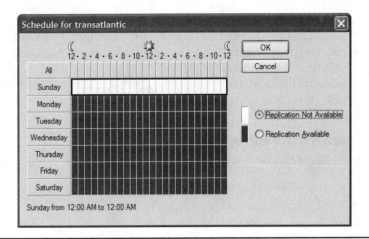

**Figure 19-17**  Specifying the replication interval

being twice as "expensive" as the default value. When replicating between two sites, deciding which link to use is easy—the lowest cost will be used if available. When replicating information between sites that aren't directly connected, the total costs of the links through all sites can be a complex calculation.

To set the site link cost, simply enter a value in the Cost section of the site's Properties dialog box.

## Site Link Bridges

By default, all site links are bridged together. They are transitive in nature, just like the trust relationships between domains in a forest. Thus, all sites can talk to each other and exchange Active Directory updates. If this is not physically possible because of the topology of your network, you will need to create a site link bridge. As shown in Figure 19-18, site 4 has no way to get replication information to site 1; it can only communicate with site 3.

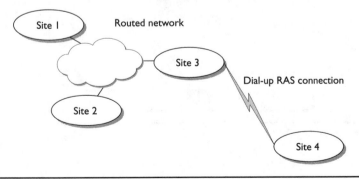

**Figure 19-18**  When to use a site link bridge

In today's networking environment, a site link bridge will rarely be necessary. And just because the link is a dial-up connection does not mean that it's a nonroutable network. A connection made through a Routing and Remote Access Service (RRAS) server or a dial-up connection to the Internet is routed like almost any other connection. One example of a dial-up connection that necessities a site link bridge is a direct-dial connection over the Public Switched Telephone Network.

## Lab Exercise 19.6: Bridging Site Links

To create a site link bridge, you first need to turn off the automatic bridging of the sites, as follows:

1. Open Active Directory Sites and Services, expand the Sites folder, and then expand the Inter-Site Transports node.

2. Right-click the transport for which you want to disable the automatic bridging of site links, and choose Properties.

3. On the General tab, as shown in Figure 19-19, clear the Bridge All Site Links check box, and click OK.

**Figure 19-19**   Disabling the bridging of site links

On the General tab, note there's also a selection to ignore schedules. When you select this option, replication changes are forced to occur regardless of the current availability of the schedule.

After you've turned off the automatic bridging of links, you need to create the site link bridge for your network. To do so, follow these steps:

1. From Active Directory Sites and Services snap-in, expand the Sites folder, and then expand Inter-Site Transports.

2. Right-click the transport for which you'll create the site link bridge, and choose New Site Link Bridge.

3. Name the bridge. From the list of site links not in this bridge, select the site links you want to add.

4. Remove any links you do not want in the bridge, and click OK when you're finished.

 **TIP**   Remember that in a fully routed IP network, a site link bridge is not necessary. Because few companies use networks that aren't IP or fully routed, you'll probably never have to set up a working site link bridge. Of course, you still need to know about it for the exam.

## Configuring Preferred Bridgehead Servers

An easy way to think of the *bridgehead server* is that it's the "spokesperson" for a site. It is the main server used to send and receive replication information between sites. As shown in Figure 19-20, the bridgehead sends replication on behalf of the site, and visa versa.

By default, one bridgehead server is selected by the Inter-Site Topology Generator (ISTG) for each site that contains a domain controller, but you can change this selection using the method outlined next. Normally, you let this background process select the bridgehead server, so this is yet another area of expertise that you will rarely need to perform in a production environment.

**Figure 19-20**
Role of a
bridgehead server

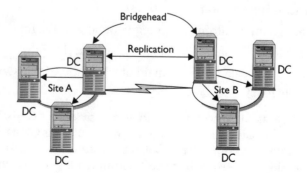

## Lab Exercise 19.7: Designating a Bridgehead Server

Here's how to create a preferred bridgehead server:

1. From Active Directory Sites and Services, expand the site where you are creating the bridgehead server.

2. Expand the Servers folder, right-click the server you will make the bridgehead, and choose Properties.

3. In the Transports Available For Inter-Site Transfer area, select the protocol for which you want to make this server a bridgehead server, and click Add.

4. Click OK to commit your changes, and then close Active Directory Sites and Services.

## The Inter-Site Topology Generator

As mentioned, you won't have to specify a bridgehead server under most circumstances. That's because yet another Active Directory replication process handles this for you behind the scenes. In every Active Directory site, there will be one domain controller (if there is a domain controller in the site) called the Inter-Site Topology Generator (ISTG).

This domain controller's job is to build the replication topology both between sites and within sites. It checks the cost of connections between sites, including whether domain controllers have been added or removed. The KCC process then uses this polling information to update the inter-site replication topology as needed.

When you're designing and implementing your Active Directory sites, you're mostly concerned with the placement of your domain's domain controllers, the other physical component of the Active Directory infrastructure. You will need to know several specifics about these vital computers when you take the 70-294 exam.

## Global Catalog Servers

It's essential that you understand the Global Catalog server's place in the Active Directory enterprise. The Global Catalog stores the following Active Directory information:

- Schema information for the forest
- Configuration information for all domains in the forest
- A subset of domain data for all domains in the forest
- All domain data for the domain of which the Global Catalog server is a member

A Global Catalog server, then, stores a copy of the Global Catalog and replicates changes to other Global Catalog servers. By default, this Global Catalog server is created on the first domain controller installed at the forest root. Other Global Catalog servers should be added as needed. Microsoft recommends you implement one Global Catalog server per site to keep queries of the Global Catalog local. As will be evident in just a few more paragraphs, the Global Catalog is often consulted by clients when retrieving Active Directory information, including a list of available domains at logon time.

It's vital to the day-to-day operation of a Windows Server 2003 forest that a Global Catalog server be available. In every Active Directory forest, at least one Global Catalog server exists. That's because these servers provide three main areas of functionality:

- **They facilitate cross-domain logon.**  The Global Catalog helps find the domain controller where a user's account is stored by resolving *user principal names*—the user's logon name appended to the domain where the account lives, such as matt@nwtraders.msft and brian@beanlase.com—to their respective domains.

- **They facilitate the finding of Active Directory objects in other domains.** A Global Catalog lets users search for directory information throughout the forest, regardless of in which domain the data is actually stored. Therefore, having a Global Catalog server nearby can significantly speed up searches within a forest.

- **They handle universal group membership.**  Information about universal group memberships is stored only in the Global Catalog. When a user logs on to the domain, the Global Catalog is also consulted to provide a list of universal groups to which the account belongs, if any. Chapter 20 discusses the impact this has on network traffic.

With Windows Server 2003, this replication is handled by treating all configured Global Catalog servers throughout the forest as if they were in one site. Therefore, the KCC handles Global Catalog replication automatically.

Your job as administrator, then, is to know where and when to implement Global Catalog servers and to manage how often changes are made to the Global Catalog. You perform this task by either configuring or not configuring a domain controller to hold a copy of the Global Catalog.

## Implementing a Global Catalog Server

In addition to the domain information for the domains in which they live, a Global Catalog server also holds a copy of the Global Catalog for the Active Directory forest. As a result, you create a Global Catalog server on a machine that's already a domain controller. Here's how:

1. Open Active Directory Sites and Services, and expand the Sites folder in which you wish to create the Global Catalog server.

2. Expand the Servers folder, and select the server to hold a copy of the Global Catalog.

3. Right-click the NTDS Settings object, and choose Properties. In the dialog box, as seen in Figure 19-21, select the Global Catalog check box to make the server a Global Catalog server.

4. Click OK, and you're finished.

**Figure 19-21**
Enabling a Global
Catalog server

NTDS Settings Properties

General | Connections | Object | Security

NTDS Settings

Description: [This server will store a copy of the global catalog]

Query Policy: [                                            ▾]

DNS Alias: [A2B456C4-9A4C-404F-9C3A-BB2C843793D5._msdcs.]

☑ Global Catalog

The amount of time it will take to publish the Global Catalog varies
depending on your replication topology.

[ OK ]   [ Cancel ]   [ Apply ]

So every forest will contain at least one Global Catalog server. In fact, if the Global Catalog server is not available and the user has not logged on to the domain previously, the user will be able to log on to only the local machine. If the user has logged on previously, and the domain is set to Windows 2000 native mode or higher, the user will log on using cached domain credentials from the previous logon. We'll discuss the implications of Windows 2000 native mode, along with all the other domain functional modes, in Chapter 20.

Fortunately, every forest has one Global Catalog server by default. A Global Catalog server is an automatically enabled domain controller that establishes the Active Directory forest. You don't have to keep the Global Catalog on this server: you can move it around to best meet your needs. When evaluating the needs of a Global Catalog server for a site, you must consider the replication traffic generated versus the benefits of keeping Global Catalog searches local.

## Adding Attributes to the Global Catalog

Active Directory provides a preconfigured set of attributes that are to be included for Global Catalog replication. Generally, the most commonly searched-for objects, like user objects, are stored in the Global Catalog, along with the most commonly searched-for attributes, such as the user name.

To increase search efficiency, however, sometimes you may want to customize the Global Catalog to include additional Active Directory attributes. But before you do, a word of caution: changing the attributes stored by the Global Catalog will affect network traffic.

**EXAM TIP** The contents of the Global Catalog are replicated to all Global Catalog servers. When you change the contents of the Global Catalog, that information will be replicated among all Global Catalog servers in the Active Directory forest.

Adding an attribute to the Global Catalog requires you to use the Active Directory Schema MMC snap-in. Because changes to the schema are so rare, it is not one of the tools found in your set of Administrative Tools. To use this tool, you must build a custom MMC.

But wait! Because management of the schema is so rare, the schema management is not even available until it's registered on your system. To have it show up as an MMC snap-in option, follow these steps:

1. Open a command prompt. (You can choose Start | Run | and type **cmd**, but there are many ways to do this.)

2. From the command prompt, type **regsvr32 schmmgmt.dll**.

3. A dialog box should confirm the successful registration of the schmmgmt file you just registered. Click OK.

Now the Schema Management MMC snap-in has been registered to your computer.

## Lab Exercise 19.8: Adding an Attribute to the Global Catalog

Now you're ready to add an attribute for inclusion in the Global Catalog. Here's what you do:

1. Click Start, then Run, and then type **mmc**. A blank MMC opens.

2. Select File | Add/Remove Snap-In. The Add/Remove Snap-In dialog box opens.

3. Click Add, and then choose Active Directory Schema. Click OK, and then close the Add/Remove Snap-In dialog box.

4. In the Schema Management MMC, expand Active Directory Schema, and choose the Attributes node.

5. In the details pane, right-click the attribute you want to add to the Global Catalog, and choose Properties from the context menu.

6. In the Properties dialog box, select the Replicate This Attribute To The Global Catalog check box, as shown in Figure 19-22. The example adds the mobile phone attribute to the Global Catalog, so it's easier find when searching through other domains.

Because Global Catalog servers store a copy of and replicate changes to the Global Catalog, it follows that any changes to the Global Catalog will affect network communication.

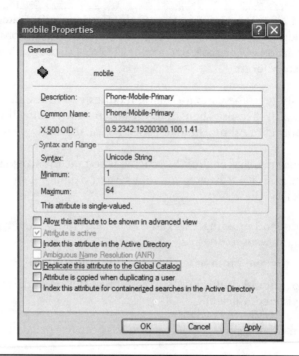

**Figure 19-22**    Adding an attribute to the Global Catalog

Again, Microsoft recommends that you implement at least one Global Catalog server in every site. This keeps queries for forest resources—including ones newly added to the Global Catalog—from crossing slow WAN links in most instances.

And remember, it's entirely possible for a single site to have domain controllers from multiple domains in the forest. For example, Microsoft might have a Sales domain and a Research domain, yet the domain controllers for these two domains reside in the same server closet right next to each other. That's why it's very difficult to represent both the logical Active Directory components and the physical components in the same diagram. Clients in a site consult the Global Catalog for a list of available domains where they can submit logon credentials. A Global Catalog at each site keeps the retrieval of this list local, and also keeps the logon local where possible.

# Chapter Review

In this chapter, we've examined the logical components in our Active Directory enterprise, with an eye toward some of the new features available with a Windows Server 2003–based network. We've examined the function of a domain, a tree, a forest, and an organizational unit. The logical elements in Active Directory define in large part how your network will be administered.

Also in this chapter, we looked at the function of Active Directory's physical components, the sites and domain controllers. We created new subnets and assigned these subnets to sites, learning along the way that any given subnet can be a part of only one Active Directory site. Further, we examined such administrative tasks as renaming sites and moving subnets from one site to another.

In the back of our minds during these procedures was a site's underlying objective: to manage Active Directory replication, especially replication over slow WAN links.

Because this chapter was largely about defining Active Directory concepts, we defined the Global Catalog. For each Active Directory forest, the Global Catalog stores information about the most commonly accessed objects and attributes throughout. Recall that the general rule is that you enable storage of the Global Catalog on one domain controller in every site.

Finally, keep in mind that you probably won't encounter a test question that asks you what an Active Directory tree is, nor will you encounter one that asks you to pick out a domain from a list of geometric shapes. The main function of this material is to set the stage for the other concepts to follow. You'll need to understand these concepts thoroughly; the questions will demand that you synthesize them into a plan that best suits a given computing environment.

## Questions

1. Which of the following groups can administer any and all domains in a forest enterprise?

   A. Domain Admins

   B. Universal Admins

   C. Enterprise Admins

   D. Enterprise Server Operators

2. You have several branch offices connected by slow WAN links. What should you do to reduce Active Directory replication traffic between sites?

   A. Place one domain controller in every site.

   B. Configure a separate child domain for every branch office.

   C. Place only one domain controller at the main office so there will be no replication of traffic.

   D. Place two domain controllers in each site so that replication traffic is always local.

3. You want to implement a Group Policy Object that will distribute the latest Office Service Pack. You are thinking about distributing this GPO to an Active Directory object. What are your choices? (Choose all that apply.)

   A. A tree

   B. A site

C. An organizational unit

D. A domain

4. You have two distinct business units that collect and store information in very different ways. You decide that in your Windows 2003 solution for your enterprise, you will require multiple schemas to best store this information. What kind of enterprise will you create?

A. One forest; one schema.

B. Multiple forests; one for each schema.

C. One tree, two domains; one schema for each domain.

D. It does not matter; the schema is extensible.

5. To combat random password hacking, you decide to implement a Group Policy that will be used to set an Account Lockout Policy to lock out accounts after five unsuccessful attempts. On which Active Directory object will you link this policy?

A. The site; it holds the domain controllers.

B. The OU; it holds all the user accounts.

C. The domain; logons are submitted to the domain.

D. The forest; no matter how many domains, every logon to Active Directory occurs in the context of a forest.

6. You are the network admin for a Windows 2003 Active Directory domain. The domain has 25 domain controllers spread amongst various sites around the country. At one of the locations, you have a 10 Mbps network, and five floors. You want to create a separate site for each floor to keep replication from using a good portion of the available bandwidth. You create five sites and create the site links between them, but you do not notice an immediate difference in replication traffic. What step should you now take?

A. Reboot domain controllers for all the new sites.

B. Wait for the KCC to calculate the new connections.

C. Move the domain controllers to the subnets created for the Sites in Active Directory Sites and Services.

D. Upgrade the network. You have optimized as much as you can, given the limitations of your network.

7. You are documenting the procedure for site creation as your company expands to other cities. Like the Dell server guy, you will be delegating the creation of new sites to junior administrators while you talk about really good coffee with the CEO. What will you recommend as the best method for creating the new sites?

A. Create the site, select the site link, add the subnets, and move the domain controllers.

B. Move the domain controllers to the Default-First-Site, create the site, add the subnets, and add the site links.

C. Create a temporary site link bridge for existing sites, add domain controllers to the Default-First-Site, add subnets, create test sites, add domain controllers, and rename the sites to move them into production.

D. Create the subnets, create a site, create site links, and move domain controllers to the new sites.

8. You are the architect for a Windows 2003 Active Directory domain, and you have decided on a single domain for your company's 1500 users. You have just implemented a branch office in Benchpress, Kansas that is connected by a 56 KBps link. You configure a separate site for this office and configure the site link to use SMTP. Now you find that the replication between the sites doesn't seem to be working. What should you do?

A. Create an enterprise certification authority.

B. Install Microsoft Exchange.

C. Install an SMTP mail system.

D. One word: broadband.

9. You have two sites in your Active Directory domain, one in Kansas City and one in Columbus, Ohio. Users at these two sites report that the links have been slow, and upon investigation, you find that they are running near 100 percent capacity. You run Network Monitor and find that the bulk of the traffic is being caused by Active Directory replication. You investigate the behavior of the site links. What behavior should you check? (Choose all that apply.)

A. Check on the schedule of the site links.

B. Check the Ignore Schedule option.

C. Check how many users have been added in the last 24 hours.

D. Check that the links are checking for changes only every four hours during the day and every two hours at night.

10. You have two sites in your Active Directory forest structure connected by a high speed fractional T1. You are now trying to optimize the replication of Active Directory traffic between sites. You have placed a Global Catalog server at each of the sites, and you want to ensure successful replication between these two systems. What can you do to assure that this will happen?

A. Create a separate site for each Global Catalog server and create a site link for these two sites. Configure a site link bridge between these servers and the other domain controllers in your forest.

B. Ensure the site link specifies these servers as the preferred bridgehead servers.

C. Create a site link bridge that includes the links between the two servers.

D. Create a connection object that specifically links the two Global Catalog servers.

PART IV

## Answers

1. **C.** The Enterprise Admins universal group can be used to administer any domain in the forest, and it is the only group whose members have this ability.

2. **B.** Placing a domain controller for each domain at every site connected with a slow WAN link is the best way to reduce replication traffic because then only Global Catalog information is replicated between domains.

3. **B, C, and D.** These three container objects in Active Directory can have GPOs linked to them. Trees, and forests, for that matter, are not Active Directory containers, but rather describe logical linkings of domains.

4. **B.** Forests share a common schema. Therefore, if you are implementing multiple schemas, you must create multiple forests.

5. **C.** Because logons are submitted to the domain, all account lockout policies should be set at the domain level. In fact, this is where all Account Policies (Password, Lockout, Kerberos) are set.

6. **C.** The domain controllers do not know they are at a new site until you move them using Active Directory Sites and Services.

7. **A.** This is the best answer for this question. There are many ways to create sites and add domain controllers, but none of them are listed in the answers provided. In addition, the method recommended in answer A is the most straightforward.

8. **A.** If you're using SMTP-based replication between sites, you will need an enterprise certification authority. The authority appends a digital signature to all replication packets being sent. Note that the SMTP packets are sent between domain controllers using SMTP; they do not rely on a mail server.

9. **A and B.** You should check the Ignore Schedule option, which can be used to force replication, but it needs to be turned off so that site link schedules are respected. You should also verify the frequency of how often the site links check for replication updates. If this value is too frequent, full synchronization may not occur.

10. **D.** When you create a connection object, you specify the path that replication should take. You should also configure the preferred bridgehead servers for the replication protocol, but creating a site link does not include the option for specifying a bridgehead server.

# Planning and Implementing User, Computer, and Group Strategies

In this chapter, you will learn how to

- Add accounts
- Add groups
- Plan a security group strategy
- Plan a user authentication strategy
- Plan an organizational unit (OU) structure
- Implement an OU structure
- Plan an administrative delegation strategy

Once you've learned about the components of Active Directory—the physical components that participate in directory replication, and the logical components that define how the organization defines its administrative structure—it's time to start populating the Active Directory database with user accounts so users can start using the domain.

In this chapter, you'll learn to add and manage accounts. You'll organize your user and even computer accounts to simplify the administration when assigning permissions or delegating administration.

Every user participating in a Windows 2003 Active Directory domain needs a user account and password. Further, user accounts are sometimes used as service accounts when accessing Back Office applications such as Exchange Server and SQL Server. And even if you are not using an Active Directory domain for access to network resources, you still need an account to use the local Windows Server 2003 machine. In this case, you will be using a local account.

Users will be created, and then they will log on to begin accessing domain resources. But just how the users present their logon credentials is yet another area where administrators can exert discretion. Most networks use user names and passwords to access the domain, although other credential presentation methods, such as smart cards, are also configurable.

After adding accounts and creating security groups, you'll learn more about the organizational unit creation process and how you can use OUs to divide up administrative responsibilities throughout the domain.

# Adding Accounts

Once you've decided how best to implement the Windows Server 2003 operating system, including if and how to deploy the Active Directory environment, the next essential task is creating accounts. Only once an account has been presented and authenticated will a user be able to access a Windows Server 2003 domain's resources.

As first explored in Chapter 18, a user account allows a user to log on to the local computer, or, in the case of a Windows 2003 Active Directory environment, one of the domains in your forest. The user account's credentials are validated against the directory database to which they are submitted, and if authenticated, the user account is granted an *access token* at logon time. Included in this access token is the user account security identifier (SID), along with the SIDs for any group account of which the user is a member. This access token is presented against access control lists (ACLs) to determine a level of access to a resource.

Most of the accounts you'll create in a Windows Server 2003 environment will be domain accounts—they will be created in the Active Directory database. But before we discuss the creation of Active Directory accounts, to set the foundation, we'll examine a local account in some detail.

## Local Accounts

When you create a *local* account, you create a new security identifier in a directory database. That directory database is local to that particular machine; that is, it's stored in a folder on the machine's local hard disk. You can create a local account on any computer that's a part of a workgroup, or on any member computers of an Active Directory domain, as long as the computer is not also a domain controller.

 **NOTE** Potential member computers in a domain include systems running Windows NT 4.0, Windows 2000 Professional, Windows XP Professional, and Windows Server 2003. Other operating systems, such as Windows 98 and XP Home, do not create computer accounts in the domain; therefore, they are not considered members. You can still log on to a domain from one of these "lesser" operating systems, but the computer itself won't be a member of the domain.

With a local account, a user has the ability to log on locally to the machine where the account resides. However, when using a local account, he or she is restricted to using only the resources on that computer. If the user wants to access a resource on a computer elsewhere in the network, the user will have to do so in the context of a user account valid on the target machine.

This caveat becomes a disadvantage as the network starts to grow, because users need multiple accounts defined to access resources that are stored on multiple computers. Figure 20-1 shows the principles of local accounts in a workgroup environment.

How do you know you're using a local account when logging on? You specify where the account will be submitted in the Log On To section of the Log On To Windows dialog box. If the selection in the drop-down menu says *computername* (This Computer), then you are trying to submit a local account for logon.

## Domain Accounts

A *domain* user account, conversely, is created on a domain controller, and is stored in the Active Directory database. The domain controller stores a replica of this database, keeps it up to date with the latest changes by synchronizing with other domain controllers, and checks the database when validating the user logon attempt.

Because the account credentials are submitted to a central location, they can be submitted from any computer in the domain. (Unless, that is, you've restricted which computers the user can log on from, which is your prerogative as the Windows Server 2003 Active Directory administrator. There are exceptions to just about everything, depending on the instructions you've given the computer.)

And because account credentials are stored and authenticated against a single entity—the Active Directory database—it's not wise to create two Brian accounts for logon, one for the domain and one for the local computer. All the user needs is the single domain account. The domain account still gives Brian the right to use every computer in the domain (except the domain controllers themselves, which by default restrict who is able to log on at those machines). As shown in Figure 20-2, a domain account needs to be defined only once per user.

**TIP**    Remember, you don't need to use the *local* Administrator account to perform administrative tasks. The domain account will do just fine, unless the default group memberships have been tempered with. We'll discuss some of the default group memberships, especially the Administrators groups memberships, in the next section.

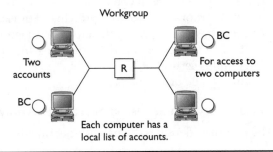

**Figure 20-1**    Using a local account

PART IV

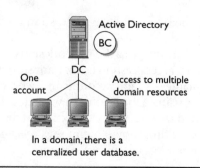

In a domain, there is a
centralized user database.

**Figure 20-2**    A domain, simplifying administration as the network grows

## Creating a Domain User Account

By now, you should know how to create a local user account. Unless you're using the command prompt, you use the Computer Management MMC snap-in (right-clicking My Computer and choosing Manage is one way to launch this tool) and then the Users folder under Local Users and Groups. With the Users node selected, right-click and choose New User, and then fill in the blanks of the ensuing dialog boxes.

But this title, and the test you're preparing for, is not concerned with the creation or use of local accounts. And if you try to attempt this on a Windows Server 2003 machine and succeed, there's one point you should remember about the computer: it is *not* a domain controller. If it were, the creation of a local account would be impossible unless you started up in safe mode or directory services mode.

Because the directory database on Windows Server 2003 domain controllers is the Active Directory database, creation of any user account will be a domain account. In other words, there aren't any local accounts on domain controllers. In fact, when you upgrade a member server to a domain controller, all local accounts present are transformed into domain accounts.

## Creating a Security Principal

Also understand that when you create a user account in Active Directory, you are creating a *security principal*—a software object over which security settings are applied—in the Active Directory database. In other words, if you want to restrict access to a resource, you do so by modifying the permissions of a security principal. For example, you edit the ACL so that the user account, or security principal, named Brian is allowed read-only access to the resource. Other examples of security principals include group accounts, which are discussed later in this section.

A domain user account is made of two parts:

- **The prefix**   The user logon name, also known as the security principal name
- **The suffix**   The part that identifies the parent domain where the user account is housed

When you combine the two parts of the user name using the at (@) symbol, you get the user's user principal name (UPN). You're probably already familiar with this syntax: the UPN will look something like this: brian@beanlake.com. Furthermore, a user in an Active Directory forest can use the UPN to submit account credentials without selecting from the drop-down list of domains. This can come in handy if the user is logging in remotely, or if several domains are linked in the forest and the user is using a computer that's in a domain other than the one where his or her account resides. Chapter 21 looks again at the significance of a UPN, because domains and user accounts in Windows 2003 can use multiple UPN suffixes.

 **NOTE** You can give several users the same name in an Active Directory forest, as long as the full name is unique to the parent OU (container) where the account is created. However, each UPN in a forest must be unique.

If you have mastered the procedure of creating a local account, you won't have any problems creating a domain-based account either. About the only significant difference, besides where the account will live, is the tool used.

## Lab Exercise 20.1: Creating a Domain User

To create a domain user, follow these steps:

1. In Active Directory Users and Computers, select the container where you want to add the user account. You normally put your user accounts in the Users folder, or, better, in one of your organizational units, but you can create a user account in any container in Active Directory Users and Computers. You add a user to the domain container or even to the Computers container if you want. After you've made the selection, right-click and choose New | User.

2. The New Object – User dialog box appears. You first saw this dialog box in the Chapter 19 in the discussion on UPN suffixes. Give the user a first name, last name, full name, and logon name. Remember also that the logon name must be unique to the forest. Click Next.

3. The Password options dialog box opens, as shown in Figure 20-3, in which you set the initial password and password options. The following password options are available:

   - **User Must Change Password At Next Logon**   Forces the user to change the password the first time he or she logs on. It is checked by default to ensure ownership of passwords.

   - **User Cannot Change Password**   Prevents the user from changing the password, and leaves password ownership in the hands of the administrator

**Figure 20-3**
The password
options
at account
creation time

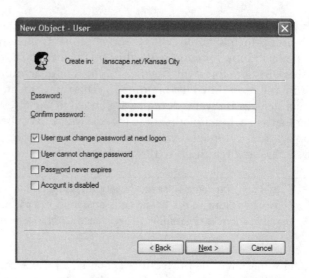

• **Password Never Expires**   Overrides any password expiration settings you've configured through a Group Policy. We will discuss Group Policies in Chapter 21.

• **Account Is Disabled**   Used by the administrator to disable the account. If this box is checked, the account is active but cannot be used to log on. This option can sometimes be useful when creating a template for copying user accounts.

4. Click Next and the Finish dialog box appears, where you can review the settings of the new account.

**NOTE**   Often, you administer the domain from a computer other than the domain controller. If you want to have the Active Directory Users and Computers snap-in available on a computer running Windows XP professional, for example, you need to install the Windows 2003 Administration Tool by running the adminpak.msi installer. This file is placed in the WINDOWS\system32 directory on all domain controllers, and is also available on the Windows 2003 installation CD-ROM in the \I386 directory.

## Creating Accounts Using the Command Line

Microsoft usually slips in a question or two about the command-line utilities, even though you will likely opt to use the graphical tool instead to avoid having to type. Adding and changing a user account can be performed at the command line as well as by using the Active Directory Users and Computers snap-in. The utilities used are discussed in the following sections.

**The dsadd Utility**   The Directory Services add utility lets you add an account to Active Directory. Its syntax is the following:

```
dsadd user UserDN [-samid SAMName] -pwd {Password|*}
```

where *UserDN* is the user distinguished name, and *SAMName* is the user Security Accounts Manager (SAM) name. If it's not specified, the SAM name will be generated using the first 20 characters of the User DN. The –pwd sets the initial password, but if you enter the asterisk as its value, you will be prompted for the password.

For example, to add a user named Brian Culp to your organization, you could type this at the command line:

```
dsadd user "cn=brian culp, ou=gurus, dc=beanlake, dc=com" -samid brianculp
-pwd password
```

You can also use the dsadd utility to create new computer and group accounts, as well as new organizational units.

---

**NOTE**  You can use the dsadd user /? to display the exact syntax for use of the command, in case you haven't committed that to your otherwise photographic memory.

---

**The dsmod Utility**  The Directory Services Modify command-line utility is used to alter a wide range of account properties. An example of its syntax is as follows:

```
dsmod user UserDN -disabled {yes|no}
```

In this syntax example, you specify the user account with its DN, and then use the –disabled switch to disable the account. You can use dsmod to reset user passwords, add users or computer accounts to groups, and convert a distribution group to a security group, to name a few.

**The dsmove Utility**  The Directory Services move utility will let you move a single Active Directory object from its current location in another location in the directory, as long as the move operation occurs within a single domain. You can also use it to rename a single object without moving elsewhere in the directory tree. The syntax is as follows:

```
dsmove ObjectDN [-newname NewName] [-newparent ParentDN] [{-s Server | -d
Domain}] [-u UserName] [-p {Password | *}] [-q] [{-uc | -uco | -uci}]
```

The dsmove utility is a new utility in Windows Server 2003, so you might expect to see it mentioned on the 70-294 exam.

**The dsrm Utility**  The Directory Services remove utility can delete Active Directory objects from the command line. In the following example, the dsrm tool is used to delete a group:

```
dsrm GroupDN
```

where the group's distinguished name is used to specify which group will be deleted.

Group accounts can be safely deleted without affecting the user accounts the group contains. However, note that you can use the dsrm utility to delete organizational units as well. When you do, you must take care not to delete all objects the OU contains, unless that is your aim. The dsrm utility should prompt you to confirm the deletion of individual objects within an OU, but it can also be configured *not* to do so with the –noprompt switch.

 **NOTE** For detailed information about each of the command-line Directory Service utilities, please see the Windows Server 2003 help files, and look up "Command-Line Reference."

Again, why bother learning these tools when the Active Directory Users and Computers graphical tool lets you perform these tasks with a lot less typing? Because you might see these referenced somewhere in the exam, and you need to be able to recognize the significance of the acronyms. In addition, sometimes, the use of the command line is preferable, like when you are performing remote administration over a slower connection.

As you just saw, the command line can be used not only to create accounts, but also to move them around. Accounts can be moved within a single domain or between domains in a forest, but the procedure for each operation differs, as explained in the next section.

## Creating Many Users at Once

If you need to create multiple users in a short period of time, you might want to consider using one of the directory services import utilities. These utilities take the contents of a file and use the entries to quickly generate tens, if not hundreds of user accounts all in one fell swoop. Many of these utilities are also covered in Chapter 2 of this book.

**The csvde Utility**    The Comma-Separated Value Directory Exchange utility works with information stored in a comma-separated value (.csv) file. You can use the values in this file to make bulk imports of user information into the Active Directory database. You can also use this utility to export user account values to a .csv file.

You use the csvde utility in this way:

```
csvde [-i] [-f FileName] [-s ServerName] [-c String1 String2] [-v] [-j Path]
[-t PortNumber] [-d BaseDN] [-r LDAPFilter] [-p Scope] [-l LDAPAttributeList]
[-o LDAPAttributeList] [-g] [-m] [-n] [-k] [-a UserDistinguishedName
Password] [-b UserName Domain Password]
```

Almost any application that deals with storing directory records can work with a .csv file. For example, you can export Microsoft Exchange user information to a .csv file (Exchange can import this data as well), and then you can use the file with the csvde to quickly create Active Directory users. Further, almost any database can be populated with records that come from a .csv file. Because Active Directory is a database, it is no different.

You can also use the csvde utility to export user accounts and all attributes of the user accounts to a comma-separated file. In fact, the default mode of the csvde is export mode. (You use the –i switch to import information into Active Directory.) Using this method, you could export user information in a particular OU or domain and then use that data to populate the Contacts folder in Outlook.

You can also use Active Directory Users and Computers and quickly export Active Directory user information to a .csv file. To export Active Directory user information to a .csv file, choose the container object from which you want to export data using Active Directory Users and Computers, right-click, and choose Export List from the context menu. The Export List dialog box opens, where you can specify a .csv file, as shown in Figure 20-4. The drawback of using this technique is that only the information you see, such as name and description, is exported.

An example of the csvde utility in action might look like

```
csvde -I -f input.csv
```

to import a comma-separated file, and

```
csvde -f output.csv
```

to export to a comma-separated value file.

**The ldifde Utility**  The Lightweight Directory access protocol Interchange Format Directory Exchange utility is a close cousin to csvde. ldifde, however, is a more flexible tool, allowing you to create, modify, and delete almost any directory object from the command line.

**Figure 20-4**
Exporting
Active Directory
information into
a .csv file

Additionally, the ldifde tool can also be used to extend the schema, and to export Active Directory user and group information to other applications or services. As with its cousin the csvde tool, it can also be used to populate Active Directory with records stored in other LDAP-compliant directory services, like Exchange.

Its syntax is as follows:

```
ldifde [-i] [-f FileName] [-s ServerName] [-c String1 String2] [-v] [-j Path]
[-t PortNumber] [-d BaseDN] [-r LDAPFilter] [-p Scope] [-l LDAPAttributeList]
[-o LDAPAttributeList] [-g] [-m] [-n] [-k] [-a UserDistinguishedName
Password] [-b UserName Domain Password] [-?]
```

The main advantage of the ldifde utility when creating large numbers of user accounts at once is that it is not limited to use only .csv files.

On the MCSE exams, it's pretty much assumed that you have the skills necessary to create a user account. Although an important part of any network administrator's daily life, it is not considered a core skill for purposes of testing. Therefore, you will learn the procedure for creating user accounts so that you can have some accounts to manage with security groups, which is the focus of this objective.

## Moving User Accounts

Once a user account is created, you're free to move the account to other Active Directory containers as your organizational needs require. Moving user accounts between containers within a single Active Directory domain is a simple process. It's most often performed to move accounts from one OU to another. To do so, follow these steps:

1. Launch the Active Directory Users and Computers snap-in, and navigate through the tree structure to the user you wish to move.

2. Right-click the account, and choose Move from the context menu.

3. From the Move dialog box, shown in Figure 20-5, choose the folder or OU that will be the new residence for the account. Click OK when you're done.

**Figure 20-5**
Moving an account within a domain

That's it! Remember, you can also use the command line to perform the same task using the dsmove utility. Either way, moving objects between organizational units is a fairly straightforward procedure. Using the Active Directory Users and Computers snap-in in Windows Server 2003, you can even drag and drop accounts between organizational units. This is new in Windows Server 2003, and lets you move users around your hierarchy as easily as you can mange files with Windows Explorer, but don't expect that feature to be the subject of a test question. Too easy.

Moving user accounts between domains, however, is a bit more involved.

## Moving Objects Between Domains

If you are administering a big enterprise with several domains, sometimes a user account needs to be moved between domains. This procedure is a bit more complex to the domain controllers because the user account contains the SID for the domain as well as the relative identifier of the account in the domain. (And as you may recall from Chapter 19, the RID Masters for each domain must be running for the movement to complete successfully.) Consequently, a different utility is used.

The utility is called movetree. movetree is installed when you install the Windows Server 2003 support tools from the \Support\Tools folder on the distribution CD-ROM.

Once installed, you can run movetree from the command prompt, whose syntax will be as follows:

```
movetree /operation /s source server /d destination server /sdn source name /
ddn destination name /u domain\username /p password
```

Remember, the /? switch will help you use the proper syntax when it's actually time to use the tool. It's important to know the function of movetree as you prepare for the exam. Active Directory Users and Computers cannot be used to move users (or computers, or organizational units) *between* domains.

---

**NOTE** Although most often used to move user accounts, you can also use the movetree utility to move organizational units and computer accounts. Keep this in mind as we turn our attention to OUs later on.

---

## Adding Groups in Windows Server 2003

Administrators create groups to make tasks easier, such as managing permissions and user rights. That's because any permission you grant to a group applies equally to all members of a group. So rather than have an access control list populated by tens, hundreds, even thousands of entries, you can secure resources with just an entry or two.

It's also worth delineating here the difference between a user right and a user permission. A *permission* gives a user a level of access to a resource. These resources can include a file or printer, or an Active Directory object, as we've seen. A user *right* is the ability to perform a task. An example is the right to back something up. For example, you don't necessarily need the *permission* to read something to have the *right* to back it up. Or, you might have the right to access a computer from the network, but you don't have the permission to access all the files on that computer.

> **NOTE** In Active Directory, a group is treated like a user account. In other words, a group is a single account, with a SID, just like a user account. The group account just has many other SIDs associated with it.

Before you begin using groups to specify permissions and rights, however, you must first learn how to set them up, and more importantly, learn about all the different kinds of groups that can be set up. The next section examines these issues.

## Global, Domain Local, and Universal Groups

Because the creation of users and groups is, as far as the directory database is concerned, essentially the same operation (in other words, creating a new SID), you use the same tool to create both users and groups. This is true when you create local groups; the utility used is Computer Management (unless you want to use the command line). The tool you use to create domain users is Active Directory Users and Computers, and it's also where you will make your groups.

Therefore, you begin the creation of a group just like you do the creation of a user account: start by selecting the container where the group will live.

> **NOTE** Microsoft recommends creating groups in the same place they recommend creating other user accounts—in an organizational unit.

Once you decide on the container where you will create the group, right-click, choose New, and then choose Group.

The New Object - Group dialog box opens, as shown in Figure 20-6. In this dialog box, you choose to create one of two group *types*:

- **Distribution** If you've ever created an e-mail list, you understand the purpose of a distribution group. It can be used only for distribution purposes (of messages, e-mail, and so on) and is not used to manage permissions or rights. In other words, you will never see distribution groups used in an access control list.

- **Security** This group is used for assigning either permissions to resources or rights to perform certain tasks. It is therefore used to manage security, and it is this group that is the focus of the Microsoft exams. You can furthermore use a security group for distribution purposes. The rest of the objective concentrates on security groups.

So as an administrator, you'll be concerned mostly with creating security groups, which, like user accounts, are security principals. The security group accounts can be used to define levels of permission or rights to objects in the Active Directory environment.

**Figure 20-6**
Creating a new
Active Directory
group account

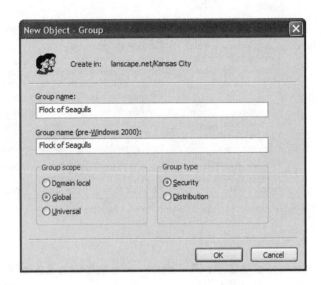

Once you've settled on the type of group, the next consideration is about which group scope best suits your needs. To make an informed decision, you need to understand the differences between the three group scopes. Each type has very specific definitions of who can be a member of the group, and where the group can be used as a security principal. The three group scopes are as follows:

- **Global**   A global group is used to gather accounts from a single domain. No accounts from other domains can be added to a global group. It can be used throughout the forest when configuring ACLs for resources.

- **Domain local**   A domain local group can contain user accounts and global groups from any domain in the forest. It can be used to assign security permissions only in the domain where it was created.

- **Universal**   A universal group can contain user accounts and global groups, as well as other universal groups. It can be used to assign rights and permissions to any resource throughout the entire Active Directory forest. However, universal groups can be created only when the domain functionality mode is set to Windows 2000 native mode or higher.

As you've just seen, you must factor in additional considerations when creating the groups. One of the places where you'll be most aware of the domain functionality level of your domain is when creating groups. Specifically, notice that the universal group scope is not available when operating in Windows 2000 mixed mode. Other differences exist between modes when dealing with groups, and we'll touch on them as needed throughout the discussion.

Table 20-1 encapsulates what is possible with your Active Directory group scopes when using the different domain functionality modes.

| Scope | Windows 2000 Mixed | Windows 2000 Native | Windows Server 2003 |
|---|---|---|---|
| Domain Local | Can contain users and global groups from any domain in the forest | Can contain users and global groups from any domain in the forest, as well as other domain local groups from the same domain | Can contain users and global groups from any domain in the forest, as well as other domain local groups from the same domain |
| Global | Can contain only users from within a single domain where the group is created | Can contain users within the domain where the group resides, and other global groups from within that single domain | Can contain users within the domain where the group resides, and other global groups from within that single domain |
| Universal | Not available in Windows 2000 mixed mode | Can contain users, global groups, and universal groups from any domain in the forest | Can contain users, global groups, and universal groups from any domain in the forest |

**Table 20-1**    Group Behavior at Different Domain Functional Levels

## Lab Exercise 20.2: Adding Members to a Group

Once the group is created, you can begin to define its membership. Group members can include user accounts, computer accounts, contacts, and other groups (with a few restrictions, as you'll see). Why might you include a computer as a member of a security group? To grant access to one computer for a shared resource on another computer, as might be necessary for a remote backup.

The steps for adding group members are very easy:

1. Open Active Directory Users and Computers and navigate to the group whose membership you wish to manage.

2. Right-click the group, and choose Properties from the context menu. From the Members tab, click Add.

3. The Select Users, Contacts, Computers, Or Groups dialog box opens, as shown in Figure 20-7.

You can type the first letter or letters, and Active Directory finds accounts that match when you choose Check Names, or just click OK. Click the Advanced button to help you

**Figure 20-7**
Selecting
members
of the group

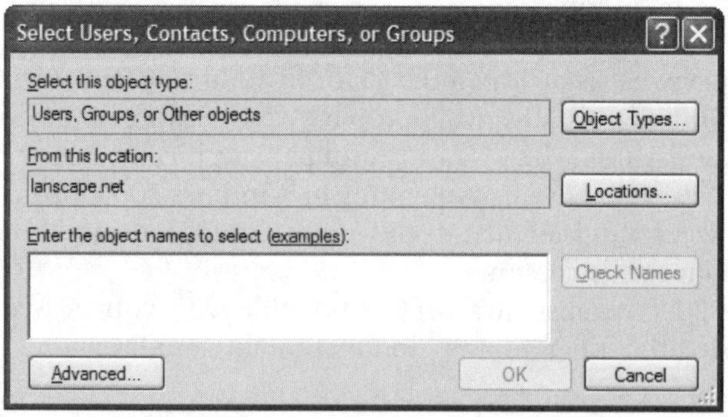

search for specific accounts. Click OK when you're done, and the list of new members appears.

If you have many users in a group already and need to create a new group that includes those same members, you have just presented an ideal case for use of group nesting.

## Built-in and Predefined Groups

Several groups are created by the installation process of the Windows Server 2003 operating system, and still more are created by the installation of Active Directory. In Active Directory Users and Computers, these built-in group accounts are created in two places: the Users container and another container called BuiltIn.

Generally speaking, the significance of these groups is that their members have certain predefined user rights, most of which are suggested by the names of the groups. Members of the backup operators group, for example, have the right to back up and restore. Domain Admins and Enterprise Admins have the most far-ranging rights, and the membership in these groups should be carefully guarded.

Table 20-2 lists the default groups created by the installation of Windows Server 2003 and Active Directory. You shouldn't spend time memorizing all of these built-in groups, but it won't hurt to be familiar with them.

| Group Name | Description | Default Rights |
|---|---|---|
| Account Operators | Members of this group can create, modify, and delete accounts for users, groups, and computers located in the users or computers containers and organizational units in the domain, except the domain controllers organizational unit. Members of this group do not have permission to modify the Administrators or the Domain Admins groups, nor do they have permission to modify the accounts for members of those groups. Members of this group can log on locally to domain controllers in the domain and shut them down. | Allow log on locally; shut down the system. |
| Administrators | Members of this group have full control of all domain controllers in the domain. By default, the Domain Admins and Enterprise Admins groups are members of the Administrators group. The Administrator account is also a default member. | Access this computer from the network; adjust memory quotas for a process; back up files and directories; bypass traverse checking; change the system time; create a pagefile; debug programs; enable computer and user accounts to be trusted for delegation; force a shutdown from a remote system; Increase scheduling priority; load and unload device drivers; allow log on locally; Manage auditing and security log; modify firmware environment values; profile single process; profile system performance; remove computer from docking station; restore files and directories; shut down the system; take ownership of files or other objects. |

**Table 20-2**   The Groups in the BuiltIn Container

| Group Name | Description | Default Rights |
|---|---|---|
| Backup Operators | Members of this group can back up and restore all files on domain controllers in the domain, regardless of their own individual permissions on those files. Backup Operators can also log on to domain controllers and shut them down. This group has no default members. | Back up files and directories; allow log on locally; restore files and directories; shut down the system. |
| Guests | By default, the domain guests group is a member of this group. The Guest account (which is disabled by default) is also a default member of this group. | No default user rights. |
| Incoming Forest Trust Builders (appears only in the forest root domain) | Members of this group can create one-way, incoming forest trusts to the forest root domain. For example, members of this group residing in Forest A can create a one-way, incoming forest trust from Forest B. This one-way, incoming forest trust allows users in Forest A to access resources located in Forest B. Members of this group are granted the permission Create Inbound Forest Trust on the forest root domain. This group has no default members. | No default user rights. |
| Network Configuration Operators | Members of this group can make changes to TCP/IP settings and renew and release TCP/IP addresses on domain controllers in the domain. This group has no default members. | No default user rights. |
| Performance Monitor Users | Members of this group can monitor performance counters on domain controllers in the domain, locally and from remote clients without being a member of the Administrators or Performance Log Users groups. | No default user rights. |
| Performance Log Users | Members of this group can manage performance counters, logs, and alerts on domain controllers in the domain, locally and from remote clients, without being a member of the Administrators group. | No default user rights. |
| Pre-Windows 2000 Compatible Access | Members of this group have read access on all users and groups in the domain. This group is provided for backward compatibility for computers running Windows NT 4.0 and earlier. By default, the special identity Everyone is a member of this group. Add users to this group only if they are running Windows NT 4.0 or earlier. | Access this computer from the network; bypass traverse checking. |
| Print Operators | Members of this group can manage, create, share, and delete printers connected to domain controllers in the domain. They can also manage Active Directory printer objects in the domain. Members of this group can log on locally to domain controllers in the domain and shut them down. This group has no default members. | Allow log on locally; shut down the system. |

**Table 20-2**　The Groups in the BuiltIn Container *(continued)*

| Group Name | Description | Default Rights |
|---|---|---|
| Remote Desktop Users | Members of this group can remotely log on to domain controllers in the domain. This group has no default members. | No default user rights. |
| Replicator | This group supports directory replication functions and is used by the File Replication service on domain controllers in the domain. This group has no default members. You should not add users to this group. | No default user rights. |
| Server Operators | On domain controllers, members of this group can log on interactively, create and delete shared resources, start and stop some services, back up and restore files, format the hard disk, and shut down the computer. This group has no default members. | Back up files and directories; change the system time; force shutdown from a remote system; allow log on locally; restore files and directories; shut down the system. |
| Users | Members of this group can perform most common tasks, such as running applications, using local and network printers, and locking the server. By default, the domain users group, authenticated users, and interactive are members of this group. Therefore, any user account created in the domain becomes a member of this group. | No default user rights. |

**Table 20-2**    The Groups in the BuiltIn Container *(continued)*

You might also want to take note of the default membership of each group. As you can see, most groups either have no default members, or have membership that you cannot/should not modify. You add users to these groups to confer to the user the pre-defined rights of the group.

Along with built-in user accounts including the Administrator and Guest accounts, several groups are also created in the Users folder, as shown in Table 20-3.

Again, no need to memorize this table of group accounts. They are provided mostly for reference purposes, so you don't have to scramble off for the Microsoft help files where you'll find the exact same information, every time one of these groups is mentioned.

| Group Name | Group Description | Default User Rights |
|---|---|---|
| Cert Publishers | Members of this group are permitted to publish certificates for users and computers. This group has no default members. | No default user rights. |
| Dnsadmins (installed with DNS) | Members of this group have administrative access to the DNS Server service. This group has no default members. | No default user rights. |
| Dnsupdateproxy (installed with DNS) | Members of this group are DNS clients that can perform dynamic updates on behalf of other clients, such as DHCP servers. This group has no default members. | No default user rights. |

**Table 20-3**    Default Groups in the Users Folder

| Group Name | Group Description | Default User Rights |
|---|---|---|
| Domain Admins | Members of this group have full control of the domain. By default, this group is a member of the Administrators group on all domain controllers, all domain workstations, and all domain member servers at the time they are joined to the domain. By default, the Administrator account is a member of this group. | Access this computer from the network; adjust memory quotas for a process; back up files and directories; bypass traverse checking; change the system time; create a pagefile; debug programs; enable computer and user accounts to be trusted for delegation; force a shutdown from a remote system; increase scheduling priority; load and unload device drivers; allow log on locally; manage auditing and security log; modify firmware environment values; profile single process; profile system performance; remove computer from docking station; restore files and directories; shut down the system; take ownership of files or other objects. |
| Domain Computers | This group contains all workstations and servers joined to the domain. By default, any computer account created becomes a member of this group automatically. | No default user rights. |
| Domain Controllers | This group contains all domain controllers in the domain. | No default user rights. |
| Domain Guests | This group contains all domain guests. | No default user rights. |
| Domain Users | This group contains all domain users. By default, any user account created in the domain becomes a member of this group automatically. This group represents all users in the domain. | No default user rights. |
| Enterprise Admins (appears only in the forest root domain) | Members of this group have full control of all domains in the forest. By default, this group is a member of the Administrators group on all domain controllers in the forest. By default, the Administrator account is a member of this group. | Access this computer from the network; adjust memory quotas for a process; back up files and directories; bypass traverse checking; change the system time; create a pagefile; debug programs; enable computer and user accounts to be trusted for delegation; force shutdown from a remote system; increase scheduling priority; load and unload device drivers; allow log on locally; manage auditing and security log; modify firmware environment values; profile single process; profile system performance; remove computer from docking station; restore files and directories; shut down the system; take ownership of files or other objects. |
| Group Policy Creator Owners | Members of this group can modify group policy in the domain. By default, the Administrator account is a member of this group. Because this group has significant power in the domain, add users with caution. | No default user rights. |

**Table 20-3**    Default Groups in the Users Folder *(continued)*

| Group Name | Group Description | Default User Rights |
|---|---|---|
| IIS_WPG (installed with IIS) | The IIS_WPG group is the Internet Information Services (IIS) 6.0 worker process group. Within the functioning of IIS 6.0 are worker processes that serve specific namespaces. For example, www.beanlake.com is a namespace served by one worker process, which can run under an identity added to the IIS_WPG group, such as MicrosoftAccount. This group has no default members. | No default user rights. |
| RAS and IAS servers | Servers in this group are permitted access to the remote access properties of users. | No default user rights. |
| Schema Admins (appears only in the forest root domain) | Members of this group can modify the Active Directory schema. By default, the Administrator account is a member of this group. Because this group has significant power in the forest, add users with caution. | No default user rights. |

**Table 20-3**   Default Groups in the Users Folder *(continued)*

Specifically, we'll be dealing with, or have already dealt with, groups such as Schema Admins, Enterprise Admins, and Domain Admins. Membership of these groups needs to be closely guarded because of their power throughout the enterprise.

The characteristics of groups in Windows Server 2003 sometimes depend on the functional modes of the domain or forest. In Windows 2000, a domain was either running in mixed or native mode. Now, however, a few more options are available for domain modes, as well as a set of forest functional modes. Each offers its own set of advantages and disadvantages, as examined more closely in the next section.

## Domain and Forest Functional Modes

Prior to Windows 2003, two levels of domain functionality existed: native mode or mixed mode. With the domain in mixed mode, you still had the option to add a Windows NT 4.0 backup domain controller to the domain. Native mode forbade the addition of NT 4.0 domain controllers, but it gave administrators the ability to implement access to features available only in native mode, such as universal groups.

The same design philosophies have been carried forward to the functionality of Windows 2003 domains. Now, instead of two levels of functionality, however, there are three. Each level offers certain benefits and certain liabilities.

Additionally, two different levels of functionality now apply to the forest. We'll start with a look at domain functionality.

## Domain Functionality

Configuring the domain functional level enables features that affect the administrative features available for the entire domain. Further, the domain functional level setting affects only that domain. Therefore, it's possible for a Windows 2003 forest to have some domains using one type of domain functionality, and other domains using another. Four domain functional levels are available:

- **Windows 2000 mixed**   This is the default domain functional level, and it is the most flexible in terms of adding domain controllers. You can add Windows NT 4.0, Windows 2000, and Windows Server 2003 domain controllers to Windows 2000 mixed level domains.

- **Windows 2000 native**   This level allows the addition of Windows 2000 and Windows Server 2003 domain controllers.

- **Windows Server 2003 interim**   This level lets supports only Windows NT 4.0 and Windows Server 2003 domain controllers, and it is specifically designed for organizations making the transition from Windows NT 4.0 domains to Windows 2003 domains. It will be an option only when upgrading the first Windows NT domain to a new forest and can be manually configured after the upgrade. If this describes your company, know that Microsoft is dropping support of Windows NT 4.0 at the end of the year, so you'd best get cracking.

- **Windows Server 2003**   As you might surmise, this domain functional level supports only Windows Server 2003 domain controllers.

**NOTE**   You can't install Active Directory on servers running Windows 2000 if you've set the functional level to Windows Server 2003 interim. (Well, you can, but they won't be able to participate in domains running in the Windows Server 2003 functional level.)

And although this point is implied in the preceding discussion, I want to make sure it gets across with no ambiguity when discussing domain functionality levels: *they take into consideration only domain controllers*. It does not matter which client operating systems are in use when the domain functional levels are set.

You can have Windows 98, Windows XP, Windows 2000, and Windows NT 4.0 clients all participating in a domain, yet the domain is set to Windows 2003 functionally. This scenario could be the case if all your domain controllers were running Windows Server 2003, and the domain functional level has been upgraded from the default.

Briefly stated, when the domain is running at the Windows Server 2003 functional level, all Active Directory features are available. If set to a level that allows the addition of down-level domain controllers, some of these Active Directory features are either limited or not available at all. Table 20-4 describes exactly which features are available in what mode.

A couple highlights you should note about Table 20-4:

- Notice that universal groups are not available in a Windows 2000 mixed mode domain.

| Domain Feature | Windows 2000 Mixed | Windows 2000 Native | Windows Server 2003 |
|---|---|---|---|
| Domain Controller Rename tool | Disabled | Disabled | Enabled |
| Update logon timestamp | Disabled | Disabled | Enabled |
| User password on InetOrgPerson object | Disabled | Disabled | Enabled |
| Universal groups | Enabled for distribution groups, but disabled for security groups | Enabled for both security and distribution groups | Enabled for both security and distribution groups |
| Group nesting | Enabled for distribution groups, but disabled for security groups, except for domain local that can have global groups as members | Enabled for all groups | Enabled for all groups |
| Converting groups | Disabled | Enabled | Enabled |
| SID history | Disabled | Enabled | Enabled |

**Table 20-4**   Features Available in Different Domain Functional Levels

- You cannot rename a domain controller unless you're running in the Windows 2003 functional mode.

- You can convert groups only in the Windows 2000 native or Windows Server 2003 modes.

 **NOTE**   The reason we don't discuss the Windows 2003 interim level is that you shouldn't be operating in this mode for long, and its features shouldn't make up any testable information. For more assistance on the Windows 2003 interim functionality level, please see the information presented at http://www .microsoft.com/windowsserver2003/upgrading/nt4/default.mspx.

Left-brain stuff, to be sure, but like the rules that govern NTFS and Share level permission interaction, for example, these are rules you should have fresh in your mind come exam time.

## Lab Exercise 20.3: Changing the Domain Functional Level

To raise the level of the domain functional level, follow these steps:

1. Open the Active Directory Domains and Trusts MMC snap-in from your Administrative Tools menu.

2. Select the domain in your forest for which you want to raise functionality, right-click, and then choose Raise Domain Functional Level.

3. In the Raise Domain Functional Level dialog box, as shown in Figure 20-8, choose one of the following from the Select An Available Domain Functional Level drop-down menu:

- To raise the functional level to Windows 2000 native, choose Windows 2000 Native, and then click Raise.

- To raise the functional level to Windows Server 2003, choose Windows Server 2003, and then click Raise.

 **TIP**  Changing the functional level is a one-way process. If you might want to introduce Windows 2000 servers as domain controllers in the future, leave the functional level set to Windows 2000 native. There is now way back to the Windows 2000 native functional mode other than decommissioning the domain and reinstalling.

## Forest Functionality

In addition to setting domain-wide functionality, there are also forest-wide functional levels that apply to a Windows Server 2003 enterprise. Forest functionality enables features across *all* the domains within your forest. The three forest functional levels are as follows:

- **Windows 2000**  This level is the default, and it supports the addition of domains running Windows NT 4.0, Windows 2000, and Windows Server 2003 domain controllers.

- **Windows Server 2003 interim**  This level is meant only for transitions from Windows NT 4.0 domains to Windows 2003 forests. It supports servers running only Windows NT 4.0 and Windows 2003.

**Figure 20-8**
Changing
the domain
functional level

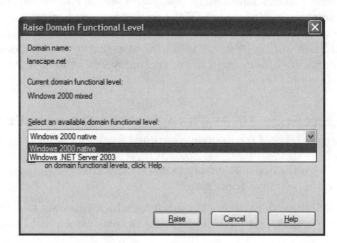

Raise Domain Functional Level

Domain name:

lanscape.net

Current domain functional level:

Windows 2000 mixed

Select an available domain functional level:

Windows 2000 native

Windows 2000 native
Windows .NET Server 2003
on domain functional levels, click Help.

Raise     Cancel     Help

- **Windows Server 2003**   This level supports only Windows Server 2003 domain controllers across the entire forest, to the exclusion of all other domain controllers. It also enables all Active Directory features, as outlined in Table 20-5.

When you create a new Active Directory forest using Windows Server 2003, the forest will be set to the Windows 2000 functional level by default. This enables the addition of other forests running Windows 2000 domain controllers. You can raise the forest functional level to Windows Server 2003.

**TIP**   Here again, we won't spend time on the features of the interim functionality level. If you need to learn more about this level, fine, but don't spend much on your test preparation energy on the 2003 interim levels.

Table 20-5 describes the features available from the different forest functionality levels.

Note in Table 20-5 that many of the new improvements gained from switching from Windows 2000 to Windows Server 2003, Active Directory–wise, are realized when using the Windows Server 2003 forest functionality level. For example, changing the name of a domain was impossible in Windows 2000 without decommissioning the domain and reinstalling Active Directory. Now, if all domain controllers in the forest are running Windows Server 2003, you can rename a domain to better accommodate organization restructuring.

Also note that while you can rename a domain using the Windows Server 2003 forest functional level, including the forest root domain, you still cannot *change* the domain that serves as the forest root. This point should reinforce what was first discussed in the previous chapter: deciding what domain will be the forest root is probably the most significant choice you make in your Active Directory design because it is the one that is most difficult to reverse.

| Forest Feature | Windows 2000 | Windows Server 2003 |
| --- | --- | --- |
| Global catalog replication improvements | Enabled if both replication partners are running Windows Server 2003; otherwise, improvements are disabled | Enabled |
| Defunct schema objects | Disabled | Enabled |
| Forest trusts | Disabled | Enabled |
| Linked value replication | Disabled | Enabled |
| Domain rename | Disabled | Enabled |
| Improved Active Directory replication algorithms | Disabled | Enabled |
| Dynamic auxiliary classes | Disabled | Enabled |

**Table 20-5**   Comparing the Forest Functional Levels

PART IV

Now that you understand a bit more about the forest functional levels, let's look at implementation. The next lab exercise walks you through upgrading the forest.

## Lab Exercise 20.4: Changing the Forest Functional Level

Here's what you do to change the forest functional level:

1. Open Active Directory Domains and Trusts.

2. Because you're not managing any particular domain, but, rather, the forest as a whole, right-click the root-level Active Directory Domains and Trusts node, and then choose Raise Forest Functional Level from the context menu.

3. The Raise Forest Functional Level dialog box opens, as shown in Figure 20-9. From the drop-down menu, select an available forest functional level, click Windows Server 2003, and then click Raise. Note that you will not be able to raise the forest functional level to Windows Server 2003 until *all* domain functional levels in the constituent forest domains have first been raised to Windows Server 2003 (which, in turn, will mean that all domain controllers are running Windows Server 2003).

 **NOTE** Similar to raising the domain functional level, the upgrade of the forest functional level is a one-way process. Once forest functionality has been raised, domain controllers running previous versions of Windows cannot be introduced into the forest. In other words, raising the forest functionality for Windows Server 2003 prevents you from adding domain controllers running Windows 2000 Server *anywhere* in the forest.

A forest functional level will affect the kinds of trust relationships available. The trusts between domains will serve as the administrative link, and it's important that you thoroughly understand the different types of trusts available.

**Figure 20-9**
Changing
the forest
functional level

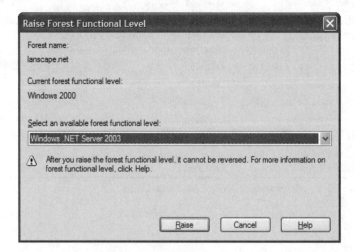

Some of the benefits of forests operating in the Windows Server 2003 forest functional level include that you can create cross-forest trusts. This new kind of trust relationship is available when the forest is upgraded. In Chapter 21, we'll explore what this cross-forest trust means—along with other kinds of trust relationships—in terms of access to resources in domains other than the one you're in.

# Planning a Security Group Strategy

One of the benefits of upgrading the domain functionality mode is that you have the ability to *nest* groups: placing groups of one type inside groups of the same type. In Windows 2000 mixed mode, you can still nest groups by placing a global group inside a domain local group, which is actually Microsoft-recommended practice (discussed in the following section). But in mixed mode, you cannot place a global group inside an existing global group, or a domain local group in an existing domain local group.

Once your domain functional level has been upgraded to Windows 2000 native or higher, however, these limitations are no longer apply. Global groups can be nested in other global groups, and domain local groups can be nested in other domain locals.

## Group Nesting

Microsoft recommends that you follow a specific administration procedure when dealing with group accounts. The procedure can be summarized with the following acronym: A G D L P.

You create user accounts in Active Directory domains, and then gather the user accounts within a domain into global groups. Next, create domain local groups, populate them with the global groups in your enterprise, and finally, assign permissions to the domain local groups.

Following this recommendation, ACLs for resources will be populated with only groups and not individual user accounts. This setup will help you keep groups organized, which, in turn, both saves administrative overhead and reduces the chance for security breaches caused by users getting inappropriate access to resources.

## Changing Group Scope

No matter what the domain functional level, the first group you create will be a security group with a global scope unless you change these defaults. Once you create the group, though, you have the option to change its scope—as long as the domain functional level is Windows 2000 native or Windows Server 2003. If your domain meets this condition, you can then make the following changes to your group scope:

- **Domain local to universal** You can make this scope change as long as the group you want to change does not already contain another domain local group as a member.

- **Global to universal** You can also convert global groups to universal, but only if the group you want to change is not a member of another global group.

- **Universal to domain local**  You can make this change with no limitations.

- **Universal to global**  You can make this scope change if the target group does not have another universal group as a member.

**TIP**  To summarize: notice that you can change any group to a universal scope, and change a universal back if you want to. Remember, however, that the domain must first be in Windows 2000 native mode or greater. This information will almost certainly generate a question or two on the exam.

## The Impact of Universal Groups on Replication

Given the flexibility of universal group membership and use as a security principal, a natural question arises: Why not just make all groups universal and be done with it? The reason is that universal groups—in both their creation and their ongoing use—have an impact on replication traffic. And if you don't carefully manage your universal group membership, this replication traffic can be quite crippling to network performance.

Universal groups affect network performance because group membership is published to all global catalog servers. And, as you've seen, Global Catalog servers participate in replication to keep the contents of the Global Catalog in sync. Therefore, Microsoft strongly recommends two rules when managing your universal groups: keep your universal group membership small, and keep it static.

**TIP**  Domain local groups and global groups are listed in the Global Catalog too, but their memberships are not.

You can accomplish both of these objectives by leveraging the power of group nesting, and also by remembering that a group is just a single account to the Active Directory database.

For example, say you had 500 users from a single domain that you wanted to place into a universal group called Graphics. You could put all 500 user accounts into the Graphics group, but that would populate the universal group with 500 accounts, and all 500 accounts would be replicated among Global Catalog servers. No group administration secret decoder ring for you.

Alternatively, you could place all 500 accounts into a single global group, and then nest that group in the universal group. What's the account membership total of the universal group now? One. Figure 20-10 demonstrates the procedure you should use when implementing universal groups.

What's more, you could later decide to add another 100 users to the Graphics universal group. If you added the user accounts to the global group, these 100 new users would also benefit from membership in the universal group, yet the universal group's membership would still be just the single (global) group account. See? Small and static. A universal group that includes 600 users, but whose membership is a single account.

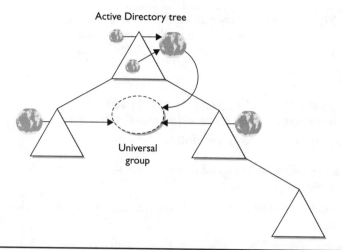

**Figure 20-10**    Universal groups leveraging nesting

## Evaluating the Need to Enable Universal Group Caching

If you have a small site, a link between sites that is very slow, or both, it may not be wise to implement an additional Global Catalog server. A small site might not merit the expense of another domain controller running Windows Server 2003, and precious bandwidth can be conserved by not having Global Catalog servers exchanging updates over a WAN link. In these situations, you can still conserve bandwidth and improve Global Catalog efficiency by caching universal group membership information.

When you use universal group caching, universal group membership is stored locally on the domain where it has been enabled. When a user logs on for the first time, the domain controller will go out and discover what, if any, universal groups the user belongs to. It then caches this membership information for the user indefinitely, with a periodic refresh.

Now that the domain controller has this information locally, the user gets universal group membership from the domain controller rather than having to query the Global Catalog server. This situation can dramatically improve logon times for sites without a Global Catalog server, as well as providing these additional benefits:

- Eliminates potential upgrade of domain controller hardware to handle the extra system requirements needed when storing and replicating a copy of the Global Catalog

- Makes WAN usage more efficient because Global Catalog information, other than universal group membership, will not be sent to the domain controller providing the caching service

**NOTE** Universal group membership caching is configured at the site level on a specific domain controller. It further requires that all domain controllers in the site are running Windows Server 2003.

## Lab Exercise 20.5: Caching Universal Group Information in the Global Catalog

To cache universal group information, follow these steps:

1. Open Active Directory Sites and Services, and select the site where you will enable universal group caching.

2. In the details pane, select the NTDS Site Settings object, right-click, and choose Properties.

3. As shown in Figure 20-11, select the Enable Universal Group Membership Caching check box. In the Refresh Cache From drop-down box, select a site from which the site will obtain its cache information. You should select the nearest (or fastest-linked) site that contains a Global Catalog because universal group membership updates will be published there.

**NOTE** If you leave the refresh location set to <default>, the cache will be refreshed from the nearest site that has a Global Catalog. Otherwise, you can specify a site like you have just seen.

**Figure 20-11**
Enabling
universal group
membership
caching

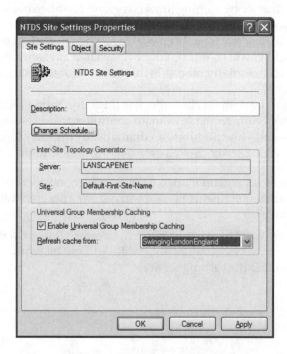

Now you're on the path to optimizing Active Directory replication traffic. The skills you develop here will help you when working within a single domain, and they will also transfer nicely when planning for larger, multidomain organizations.

# Planning a User Authentication Strategy

Now that we've defined a user accounts so that users can access Active Directory forest resources, we want to specify an authentication strategy. Typically, this involves decisions about the passwords: who will control the passwords, how long must they be, when will they expire? But a user name and password, as you'll see, aren't the only way a user can be authenticated on the network. The next few topics will examine some alternative strategies, and also look at ways to make your password authentication strategy as secure as possible for your environment.

## Planning a Smart Card Authentication Strategy

Smart cards are becoming more and more a part of the logon process, because smart cards generally offer an improved security mechanism over traditional user name and passwords. The user name and password mechanism is a relatively weak security measure for a host of reasons, especially when compared to smart card authentication. This is because the smart card logon implements a double-layered security measure. There must be a physical device present, and a user must enter a PIN or password when performing a smart card authentication.

In other words, just because your user name and password are used to access a network, that doesn't necessarily prove you're the one actually using the account. It could be someone else who has either guessed or stolen your logon credentials. (It can be done easier than you think.)

The smart card's security is almost exactly like the safeguard present when you get cash from an ATM. You feel pretty safe that only you can get your money because someone needs your card to access your account, and even if you left your card at a coffee shop table, the person who found it would still need to know your PIN to swipe your money. In other words, successful logon when using a smart card *is* proof that you posses the smart card.

Another big potential security hazard of the user name and password model is if your password were compromised, you'd have no way of knowing about it until it's too late. You could go on using your network resources normally. If, on the other hand, someone were to steal your smart card, you'd know pretty quickly because you couldn't use the network without it.

## Configuring a User for Smart Card Authentication

Once you understand the concepts behind smart card use, you might decide that smart card authentication is the right choice for your network. Before you set up smart card authentication, several technologies need to be in place:

- Ensure that a certification authority (CA) hierarchy is available. This CA can be set up internally or be an external authority.

- Configure the certification authority to issue smart card certificates.

- Enable the security permissions of the Smart Card User, Smart Card Logon, and Enrollment Agent certificate templates to allow smart card users to enroll certificates.

- Install a smart card *enrollment station*: a computer with a smart card reader. An Enrollment Agent Certificate will also be needed for users who will be setting up the smart cards at that system.

- A smart card reader will also be needed at each computer where smart card authentication will be used.

---

 **NOTE** For those who are not reading this book is sequence, the certification authority stuff is all explained in Part III of this book.

---

The step-by-step procedure for setting up smart card authentication, however, is a relatively lengthy process, requiring that a user first acquire a digital certificate. Generally speaking, here's how it all breaks down:

- Log on as an *enrollment agent* (an account—because its been mapped to an Enrollment Agent certificate—that can then generate smart cards on behalf of anyone in the domain) for the domain where the user account lives, which will be using smart card authentication. Then navigate to the web site of the certification authority (CA) that issues smart card certificates using Internet Explorer.

- From the CA's web page, request a certificate using the designated hyperlink. Then, if you're enrolling on behalf of another user, look for a choice that lets you request a certificate for a smart card on behalf of another user.

- You will have two choices about enrolling the Certificate Template: either enrolling for logon only, or enrolling for secure e-mail as well as Windows logon.

- Next, you choose the name of the CA who will be issuing the smart card certificate, as well as the Cryptographic Service Provider (CSP) of the smart card's manufacturer. (A *CSP* is the software that performs the dirty work of encryption and encoding data, including, in this instance, logon credentials.)

- Next, the Enrollment Agent is asked to sign the enrollment request, and then chooses the account that will be the recipient of the smart card certificate.

- Finally, you'll be prompted to insert your smart card into the smart card reader so that the digital certificate can be copied. A PIN will also be selected at this time.

Now that the digital certificate is installed on the smart card, the certification authority web page should give you the option of either viewing the certificate you just installed or beginning a new certificate request.

**NOTE** Most of these steps will be spelled out for you again by any vendor who has just sold your company a smart card solution.

**Requiring Smart Card Use**   Once the smart card apparatus is in place and certificates have been issued, you can require that the user account use the smart cards for access to domain resources. To do so, access the users' Properties pages by right-clicking and choosing Properties, and then access the Account tab. From the Account Options section, select the Smart Card Is Required For Interactive Logon check box. The users will now have to have the smart card ready when they want to access the domain.

**EXAM TIP**   The Smart Card User certificate template requires that the computer where the smart card reader is installed be a part of the domain.

But securing your domain resources goes beyond obtaining and implementing a smart card solution. In fact, before you choose smart cards, you will probably invest a lot more time trying to make sure the passwords your enterprise uses give you the best security possible.

## Creating a Password Policy for Domain Users

Smart cards aren't a feasible choice for every network. And you can still implement a high level of security for your network when you understand some of the recommended practices for using strong password policies.

One point to know about password policies is that they affect the entire domain. We'll get into Group Policies in much more detail starting in Chapter 21, but for now, this is the information you need. The other point you need to know is how to configure a password policy.

## Lab Exercise 20.6: Setting a Password Policy

To configure a password policy affecting all domain users, follow these steps:

1. From Administrative Tools, open the Domain Security Policy MMC snap-in. (Alternatively, you could open Active Directory Users and Computers, select the domain container, and edit its Group Policy, but again, more on that in the chapters to follow.)

2. Expand the Account Policies node. You will see three groups of account settings: Password, Account Lockout, and Kerberos.

To increase the strength of the password settings, double-click one of the settings and make the appropriate changes. Six password policy settings exist, as shown in Figure 20-12 and described on the following page.

PART IV

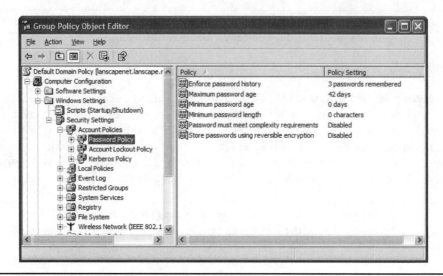

**Figure 20-12**   Configuring password policies

- **Enforce Password History**   This setting determines how many unique new passwords must be created for a user account before an old password can be reused.

- **Maximum Password Age**   This setting determines the number of days a password can be used before it must be changed. Passwords can be set to expire between 1 and 999 days, or you can configure passwords that never expire by setting the number of days to 0. When the password age is set to something over 0, the minimum password age must also have a setting less than the maximum password age. If the maximum password age is 0, the minimum password age can be any number of days between 0 and 998.

- **Minimum Password Age**   This setting determines the number of days a password must be used before it can be reset. This setting prevents users from cycling through a series of passwords quickly until the original password is used.

- **Minimum Password Length**   This setting is self-explanatory. You can set the value of a minimum password length between 1 and 14 characters. Note that the minimum password length is set to 0, which lets users use blank passwords.

- **Password Must Meet Complexity Requirements**   This is an on/off setting, and knowledge of its impact is necessary before deciding to enable this policy.

- **Store Passwords Using Reversible Encryption**   Although this description sounds like it might help tighten password security, it actually does the opposite. Storing passwords using reversible encryption means just that: the encryption can be reversed, which is equivalent to storing plaintext versions of the passwords. The policy provides support for applications that require knowledge of the user's password for authentication purposes. For this reason, you should never enable it unless application requirements usurp your desire to protect password information.

## Recommendations for Strong Passwords

Microsoft also recommends that you implement a stronger password policy model than the defaults configured if your network requires tighter security. You'll find that most of the default password policies favor usability over security, which may not be desirable for you situation. In no particular order, here are some of those recommendations for designing strong passwords:

- Use the Enforce Password History policy so that multiple passwords are remembered, preventing users from using the same password when their password expires.

- Make the Maximum Password Age policy a setting that causes users to change passwords frequently, typically every 30 to 90 days. This prevents hackers who have acquired a password from using that password indefinitely.

- Use the Minimum Password Age policy in conjunction with Enforce Password History so that users cannot simply change their password for a few minutes and then change it back to their original password, thus circumventing the policy that forces password changes.

- Define the Minimum Password Length setting so that passwords must be at least a specified number of characters. Longer passwords are generally stronger than shorter ones, if for no other reason than they are harder to pick off by looking over someone's shoulder. The recommendation is for at least seven characters.

- Enable the Password Must Meet Complexity Requirements setting. This policy setting ensures that all newly created or changed passwords meet strong password requirements. Understanding what these complexity requirements are merits its own topic.

**Complexity Requirements**  When the Password Must Meet Complexity Requirements policy setting is enabled, new passwords must meet these conditions:

- Passwords must not contain all or part of the user's account name.

- They must be at least six characters long.

- They must contain characters from three of the following four categories:
  - English uppercase characters (A through Z)
  - English lowercase characters (a through z)
  - Base 10 digits (0 through 9)
  - Non-alphabetic characters (for example, !, $, #, %)

**NOTE** The Password Must Meet Complexity Requirements setting can be changed, but to do so takes knowledge of the Microsoft Platform Software Development Kit to do so. It's less of a hassle to understand and use the default complexity requirements by either turning it on or off.

No matter how the user authenticates, the account itself will usually be stored in an organizational unit. We've mentioned a couple of times how OUs can be used to help define the administrative hierarchy in your enterprise. Microsoft expects you to have some grasp of how an OU structure can best be planned for a given situation. Let's define that planning more carefully here.

# Planning an OU Structure

Organizational units are really the workhorse of a Windows 2003 Active Directory hierarchy, at least from an administrative point of view. They are container objects within a domain that represent subadministrative entities within an Active Directory. Organizational units are used to group domain computers, users, and other domain objects into separate logical units.

However, organizational units are actually not *groups*, they are *administrative containers*. Anything you can put into the domain, anything you can put into an Active Directory database, you can put into an organizational unit. That's not true with groups. The only Active Directory objects that groups can contain are user accounts or other group accounts. Organizational units, on the other hand, can contain computers, shared resources, printers, as well as groups and users.

Another big difference between groups and organizational units is that you can apply Group Policy to an organizational unit; you cannot apply Group Policy to a group. The name might imply otherwise, but that's not what Group Policies are used for.

An organizational unit's structure may be based on cities, like Kansas City, St. Louis, Omaha, Dallas, and so on, or on departments, like I.T., H.R., Payroll, Sales, Accounting, and so on. You can also nest organizational units in parent/child relationships, much like you can create parent/child domain affiliations when you set up a tree. Figure 20-13 shows an example of how a company might build a parent/child OU hierarchy.

As the Active Directory architect, this organizational unit flexibility also gives you almost unlimited control over how the domain objects are administered within a single domain. In Chapters 22 and 23 on Group Policy especially, you will see this administration in action.

An organizational unit provides two very significant benefits: it allows you to delegate control, or even specific types of control, over certain portions of the domain. In addition, applying a Group Policy allows a set of users in one organizational unit to have a very different end-user experience from the users in another organizational unit.

## Creating OUs

The most important point to remember about an organizational unit is that it's a unit of administration. If you begin with that in mind, your OU design starts to suggest itself.

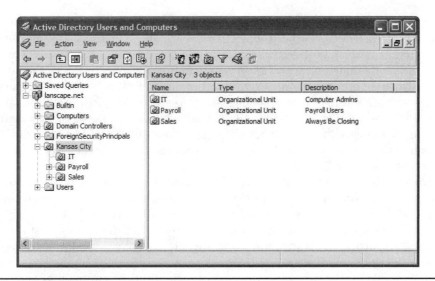

**Figure 20-13** Parent/child OU hierarchy

And once you have the ideal design in mind, implementing an OU structure, like most of the button-clicking you do, is a snap. Here's what you do:

1. Open Active Directory Users and Computers and select the Active Directory container where you intend to create the new OU. You will choose either the domain container or an existing OU.

 **TIP** Notice that you won't be able to create an OU in the Users folder. This can further help differentiate between groups and OUs.

2. Right-click and from the context menu, choose New | Organizational Unit. The New Object – Organizational Unit dialog box appears.

3. In the Organizational Unit dialog box, name the OU and click OK.

That's all there is to it. Now you can populate the resources you'll be administering in the OU by adding user, computer, and group accounts as described earlier.

# Implementing an OU Structure

A small company becomes a big company, and soon the number of users in the company becomes too large for one person to manage. If this is the case, you will find it useful to separate your users into other units of administration.

Organizational units serve just this purpose. With and OU, you can logically arrange all of your Active Directory objects that will need management: users, groups, computers, printers, and so on. With an organizational unit, you can manage one of these units much differently than another unit, yet still retain centralized control of the domain objects. Furthermore, you can delegate to other domain users certain administrative abilities over these units. A branch manager in Kansas City (KC), for example, could administer the users in the KC organizational unit, while a Manhattan branch manager could do the same for the users in her office. You could still set folder redirection policies for users in both offices, and these policies could not be overridden by the administrators of the branch offices if you so desired.

Also, keep in mind that this degree of administrative flexibility was not possible when designing Windows NT 4.0 domains. The domain was the only organizational entity, and if you wanted to split up administration in the manner just described, you had to create entirely separate domains. The ensuing management of trust relationships and resources in two (or more) domains greatly increased administrative cost and complexity.

In a Windows 2003 Active Directory environment, think of a domain as a container for Active Directory objects that also serves as a security boundary. How is it a security boundary? To illustrate, take the example of domain administration. Domain Admins of one domain do not get to set the administrative directives for another domain—hence, the security boundary.

Most administrative needs, however, can be met with an organizational unit. Let's first look at how one is generated.

## Planning an Administrative Delegation Strategy

As you know, one of an OU's main benefits is that is lets administrators delegate control over certain sections of the domains' objects. (This topic was also explored in Chapter 19, when we delegated control over Active Directory sites.)

Conceptually, delegating administrative control over organizational units is no different. As shown in Figure 20-14, just like our site container objects, an organizational unit has an access control list that controls who does what. If you don't see the Security tab when looking at the properties of an Active Directory object, make sure the advanced features are turned on. (Select View menu | Advanced Features.)

---

 **TIP** Some of the default containers like the Users and the Built-In folder are not organizational units; therefore, you cannot delegate control over these containers. Look for the Active Directory icon—the phonebook—when you want to delegate control.

---

By changing the contents of this access control list, you can delegate control over the users. By clicking the Advanced button, you get access to the individual Access Control Entries (ACEs). With these ACEs, you can be very specific about what kind of control is

**Figure 20-14**

The access control list of an Active Directory container

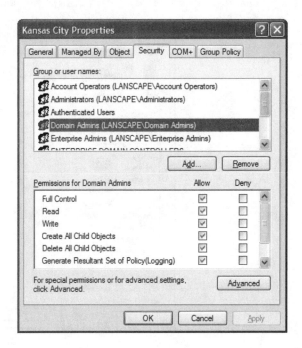

granted. You can give a single user the ability to change passwords for user accounts and no other administrative ability. To perform this task, click Edit for the users Access Control Entry, which opens another dialog box, as shown in Figure 20-15. (You might need to add them to the ACE list first.)

This area is also where I think the difference between security groups and organizational units becomes more clear. An organizational unit is an administrative entity, and we delegate administrative control *over* our OUs; but we delegate control *to* the users in our security groups. Furthermore, the control is granted over the users, computers, and groups, printers, and so forth, *contained* in the OU.

## Using the Delegation of Control Wizard

You can also use the Delegation of Control Wizard to delegate administrative tasks to users. The wizard interface simplifies the process of manually editing the ACL, but the end result is the same. You've already seen this as well in Chapter 19, so we won't cover all the steps again.

What is worth pointing out, however, is that the delegation of control over organizational units can include a few more steps and some different tasks. For example, you don't create user accounts in a site, but that responsibility can be easily delegated over an OU using the wizard. Figure 20-16 shows the screen where you can select common tasks or configure a custom task to delegate.

**Figure 20-15**
Granting only the
ability to reset
passwords

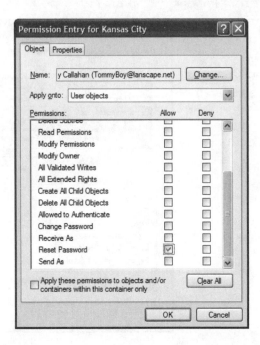

**Analyzing the Administrative Requirements for an OU**

With either of the two methods just demonstrated, you can assign basic administrative functions to everyday users while still maintaining control over the more complex administrative tasks. In other words, delegating administrative responsibility no longer confers the ability to cause a lot of problems the way it did in NT 4.0. Delegating control lets regional users take responsibility over their local network resources. This ability actually helps you implement a higher degree of security because you can restrict the

**Figure 20-16**
Delegating
administrative
control over an
OU using the
wizard interface

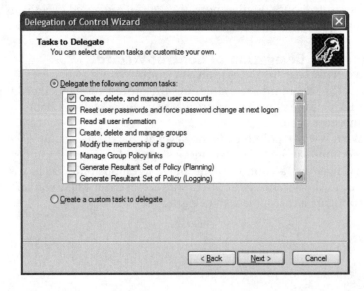

membership of powerful groups such as the Domain Admins and the Enterprise Admins groups.

Windows 2003 domains are designed to be self-contained, and through the use of organizational units, you have a lot of flexibility about how that domain is administered. In making the decision about how best to design your organizational units, you need to consider the structure of your organizations. Are geographic locations self-contained? Can each have its own user who does day-to-day administration? Is your company organized more by department, with department heads in charge of computing decisions?

There are no right or wrong answers, of course, but there are two general methods of designing an organizational unit strategy. The first design strategy is to design by location, as shown in Figure 20-17.

Alternatively, you can implement the delegation of administration over domain objects by factoring in department considerations, as seen in Figure 20-18.

Remember, these are not inflexible rules. Most larger companies especially will end up with a hybrid design resembling something like that shown in Figure 20-19.

Because of the administrative flexibility afforded by organizational units, Microsoft recommends that instead of creating extra domains, system designers create a single domain, then use organizational units within that single domain to delegate their administrative tasks. Because a single Windows 2003 domain can contain millions of objects, scalability and performance are rarely a concern, even in the largest of organizations.

## Authorization Manager

Another tool used to delegate administrative control, new to Windows 2003, is the Authorization Manager. Although you'll probably do most of your delegation with the Delegation of Control Wizard, especially as you are delegating the first few administrative tasks, it is not the best tool for every circumstance.

Both the Delegation of Control Wizard and the Authorization Manager—along with the old-fashioned method of simply editing the access control list—let you assign rights or permissions to individual users or groups. The biggest difference between the Delegation of Control Wizard and the Authorization Manger is that the Authorization Manger lets you delegate control over certain applications. The Authorization Manager can provide greater flexibility, but it is a more complex tool to use. For delegating everyday tasks like adding accounts, it is not the best choice.

**Figure 20-17**
Designing OUs
by location

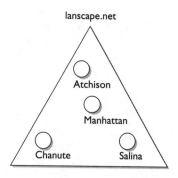

**Figure 20-18**
Designing by
department

When you use the Authorization Manager, you will have the option of choosing between two modes of use:

- **Developer mode**  This mode allows you to create, deploy, and maintain specific applications. In developer mode, you have unrestricted access to all Authorization Manager capabilities.

- **Administrator mode**  This mode is less flexible than developer mode. In administrator mode, you can deploy and maintain applications. You have access to all Authorization Manager features except those that let you create new applications or define new operations. Administrator mode is the default mode of Authorization Manager.

So what does this mean? Well, the Authorization Manager does for applications what the Delegation of Control Wizard does for Active Directory objects. You would use the Delegation of Control Wizard to delegate a specific administration role, like the changing of a password, to a certain user. You would use the Authorization Manager to let a user have a specific role within an application. For example, you might define a role for an Auditors group that would let them audit the debit and credit transactions from a certain accounting application. They might not otherwise be able to use the application in any other capacity other than the role you have defined.

You can also configure roles based on a computer's function. With computer role-based administration, you might allow certain users to install and enable services on a web or file server, for example.

As mentioned, developer mode is used to define roles. However, applications that support administrative roles usually either create an authorization store, or use an existing authorization store, with predefined operations and tasks. In such an event, the developer mode will not be necessary. Applications that can be used with the

**Figure 20-19**
A hybrid of OU
design, which
nests OUs in
parent/child
relationships

lanscape.net

Authorization Manager store an *authorization policy* in the form of an *authorization store*, which, in turn, are stored in Active Directory or XML files. The authorization store is the database that holds Authorization Manager policy files. These authorization files apply the configured authorization policy to the selected users or when the application is run.

> **NOTE** To use the Authorization Manager, your domain must first be running in Windows Server 2003 functional mode.

Before you can use the Authorization Manager to delegate a task, you must create an Authorization store. Here's what you do:

1. Open the Authorization Manager by either creating a custom MMC and adding the snap-in, or by typing **azman.msc** from the Run dialog box.

2. Right-click the Authorization Manager root, and then choose Options from the context menu.

3. Choose the Developer Mode option in the Options dialog box, and click OK

4. In the Authorization Manager, right-click Authorization Manager again, and choose New Authorization Store.

5. From the New Authorization Store dialog box, choose whether to create an Active Directory or XML file.

6. Type the authorization store name in the Store Name dialog box, or click Locations to find the authorization store, and add a description if you wish.

Now that you've configured an authorization store, you can use the Authorization Manager to begin delegating tasks. To begin the process, choose either the application level role or the scope level role to which you want to assign a user or group, right-click, and choose Assign Windows Users and Groups. The wizard should lead you the rest of the way.

A *scope* is used by an application to keep certain resources separate from other resources within that application. Examples of scopes include a specific folder, an Active Directory container, a collection of files like all .xls files, or even a URL that can be accessed by the application and its underlying authorization store. You can use scopes to divide the areas of an application over which you want to delegate control, and also use them to prevent unintended access.

> **NOTE** Because it can be a very complex tool, a full discussion of the Authorization Manager is beyond the scope of this book. Typically, application developers define the roles and the authorization store. Like many testable topics, what's important is an understanding of what the tool does. For further information about the Authorization Manager, please see the following MSDN web site that discusses application authorization: http://msdn.microsoft.com/library/default.asp?url=/library/en-us/security/security/authorization_portal.asp.

PART IV

After deciding how best to organize your domains and organizational units, it's time to implement the design. The next objective looks at how to realize your blueprint for Active Directory greatness by implementing the forest and domain structures.

## Moving Users Within an OU Hierarchy

Moving organizational unit objects within a single domain is also very easy. From Active Directory Users and Computers, right-click the objects and choose Move. The Move dialog box opens, as shown in Figure 20-20, and you make the destination OU selection.

Not only can you move the objects in the OUs, but you can even use the same procedure to move the entire OU.

And although this topic might seem minor, it is significant in real-world Active Directory environments. In the NT 4.0 domain model, once the administrative duties have been divvied up, they are relatively locked in place because of the difficulty in redesigning a domain structure.

One of the big advantages of organizational units, though, is the flexibility they provide. As you've seen, you can easily move OUs within a domain as the administrative needs of the environment evolve.

# Chapter Review

Now that we've added user accounts, Active Directory is officially open for business for the users of your enterprise. In this chapter, we've examined the differences between local and domain user accounts, and after creating domain accounts, looked at how to organize those accounts using the different groups available.

You learned that the domain functional level significantly affects the behaviors of your groups in Windows Server 2003. You also learned which features are available when you upgrade a forest. The forest functional level also determines what is possible in the domains in the forest, and when the forest is in the Windows Server 2003 functional level, a domain can be renamed.

**Figure 20-20**
Moving an
object from one
organizational
unit to another

We investigated many of the command-line utilities that are used to manage user accounts and other Active Directory objects. We also looked at the significance of the organizational unit and its use in designing a delegation strategy within a 2003 domain. The available delegation tools include the access control list for an Active Directory object, the Delegation of Control Wizard, and the Authorization Manager, which is new to Windows Server 2003.

## Questions

1. You are the administrator of a Windows Server 2003 enterprise. There are six domains in the network. Several sites have been implemented, many of which contain only a few users and computers. Some connections between sites are good; others are quite slow. Furthermore, the network uses several universal groups for granting users from many domains access to resources. You are monitoring traffic use and notice that the retrieval of universal group membership is significantly affecting bandwidth use. Which of the following are ways to improve the network impact of universal groups? (Choose all that apply.)

   A. Use universal group caching.

   B. Install a Global Catalog server at each one of your sites.

   C. Leverage the use of group nesting to keep universal group membership small.

   D. Break the single domains into several domains in a single Active Directory tree.

2. You have implemented a universal group in your Windows Server 2003 Active Directory enterprise. There are 10 domains in the forest, and the universal group contains global groups from all 10 domains. Five new users have been added to the global groups in each of the 10 domains. How many new accounts will be added to the universal group?

   A. 5

   B. 10

   C. 50

   D. 0

3. You are a domain admin for a Windows Server 2003 domain. You would like to create an account for a user that allows him to log on to a print server and administer the server. The account should give access to the printers only on the print server itself, and to no other domain resources. Which type of account should you create?

   A. You should create a Domain User account, which will be stored in the SAM on the print server.

   B. You should create a Local User account, which will be stored in Active Directory and be given permissions only for the print server.

    **C.** You should create a Domain User account, which will give access to all printers in the domain.

    **D.** You should create a Local User account, which will be stored in the SAM on the print server.

4. You are the accounts manager for a Windows Server 2003 domain. The domain admin has asked you to create 50 new accounts. Which tools could you use? (Choose all that apply.)

    **A.** Active Directory Users and Computers

    **B.** dsadd on command prompt

    **C.** Active Directory Domains and Trusts

    **D.** csvde

5. You are the accounts manager of a Windows Server 2003 domain. Your manager has asked you to make hundreds of modifications to existing user accounts and to add additional user accounts as well. You would like to use a tool to automate this process. Which tool should you use?

    **A.** csvde

    **B.** Active Directory Users and Computers

    **C.** DNS

    **D.** ldifde

6. You are the enterprise administrator of a Windows Server 2003 network. A domain admin asks you to clarify some rules about universal group creation and membership. Which of the following answer(s) should you give? (Choose all that apply.)

    **A.** The members of a universal group must all reside in the domain where the universal group exists.

    **B.** Neither the members of the universal group nor the resources to which it gives access have to reside in any particular domain.

    **C.** The resources where access is defined for the universal groups must reside in the domain where the universal group exists.

    **D.** A universal group does not exist in any particular domain; rather, it exists in all domains.

7. You are the enterprise administrator for a Windows Server 2003 network. You have decided to enforce a password policy, but you are not sure how to implement it. You have made changes to account policies affecting the site, domain, and OUs in your network. The policy that you now have set for the site requires at least eight characters in the password. The policy for your domain now requires at least six characters in the password. The policy for an OU named Sales, which is contained within your domain, is now set to require at least four characters. If you were to create a new user in the Sales OU, how many characters would be required for a password?

A. 8

B. 6

C. 4

D. 0

8. You are the domain admin for a Windows Server 2003 domain. You want to create a password policy that is very strong. You have implemented a policy that requires at least eight characters in the password and ensures that the password must meet complexity requirements. Which passwords could be used by a user named bobjones? (Choose all that apply.)

A. xyzBoB123

B. 320Xyz123

C. !1zpaSSWord

D. 5joNes!234

E. !@#$%^&*

9. You are the enterprise administrator of your Windows Server 2003 network. You decide to implement a smart card authentication strategy for your network. Which components will this require? (Choose two.)

A. A certification authority

B. All new user names and passwords

C. User training

D. Additional DNS servers

10. You are the domain administrator of a Windows Server 2003 domain. You want to build a hierarchy of OUs that will contain users from various departments within your domain. You decide the logical place to start would be the default Users container. You right-click the Users container, but you do not see the option Create An OU. Why is this option not visible to you?

A. You are not the enterprise admin.

B. You are not right-clicking an OU.

C. You cannot create an OU within an OU.

D. You have to set your own Group Policy first.

## Answers

1. **A and C.** Through universal group caching, domain controllers can store universal group membership only, reducing the need for Global Catalog servers in every site. Also, universal group membership is stored on all Global Catalog servers, and the fewer accounts in a universal group, the less the impact on traffic.

Groups within a universal group will help keep the number of accounts in a universal group small. If you have a Global Catalog server at every site, these Global Catalog servers will participate in Global Catalog replication, and that is not necessary for sites with few resources.

2. **D.** There will be no new accounts in the universal group. Because you have implemented group nesting, the membership of the universal group will remain unaffected, and only the global groups in each domain will see membership increase by five.

3. **D.** Local user accounts exist in the SAM on only one computer. They can be used for access to resources only on that one computer. In this case, a local user account is what you need to make sure that the user can administer the printers only on the print server.

4. **A, B,** and **D.** You could manually add the accounts to the Active Directory using the Active Directory Users and Computers tool. Another alternative would be to use the command-line interface and dsadd. Here, you could create a script that would aid in adding all the accounts to the correct location. Finally, you could use a comma-separated value list to align the account names and their properties and input the information into Active Directory. Active Directory Domains and Trusts is not a tool used to add user accounts.

5. **D.** Because you need to automate changes as well as additions, you will have to use ldifde. csvde can be used to add accounts but cannot be used to make changes or deletions to the Active Directory. Active Directory Users and Computers will not help you automate the process. DNS is a service and not a tool used to add accounts.

6. **B** and **D.** Universal groups exist in the Active Directory and are replicated to all domains in a forest by the Global Catalog servers. They can contain members from any domain, and they can be used to give access to a resource in any domain. When universal group membership is changed, the change must be replicated to the entire forest. For this reason, universal groups should contain only global groups or other universal groups. They should generally not contain users because the frequency of membership changes is much greater with users than with groups.

7. **B.** Account policies (password, account lockout, and Kerberos) that are set at domain level will always override any settings at OU and/or site level. This is one exception to the rules in regard to Group Policy.

8. **B** and **C.** When password complexity is enabled, passwords must meet the following criteria:

   • They cannot contain all or part of the users account name.

   • They must be at least six characters long.

   • They must contain three of the four items listed on the following page.

- English uppercase letters (A–Z)
- English lowercase letters (a–z)
- Base 10 digits (0–9)
- Nonalphabetic characters (e.g., !@#$%^)

In this scenario, only options B and C are valid.

9. **A and C.** Smart card authentication is an available Extensible Authentication Protocol for Windows Server 2003. It requires a certification authority, which is either supplied by you or from a third-party CA. Because it is extensible (added on), it does not require that all user names and password be changed. It will also have no direct effect on the number of DNS servers that you require.

10. **B.** You do not have to be the enterprise admin or set any Group Policies to create a hierarchy of OUs. You do, however, have to start with an OU. The default containers are not OUs and therefore cannot be used as a starting point. You should create a new OU to start your hierarchy of OUs.

# Managing and Maintaining an Active Directory Infrastructure

In this chapter, you will learn how to
- Implement server roles
- Restore Active Directory
- Manage an Active Directory forest and domain structure
- Manage Active Directory database replication
- Troubleshoot Active Directory using Microsoft utilities

Throughout this book, you've learned about the components of the Active Directory infrastructure. We've examined the objects Active Directory stores and manages, and we've built our enterprise using the various physical and logical Active Directory components.

In this chapter, we'll expand on some of these concepts as we manage, monitor, and optimize Active Directory performance. For example, in Chapter 18, we defined the Active Directory schema and its role in the forest. Now we'll look at the instances where that schema might be extended beyond its default settings and learn about the procedures involved.

We'll also cover how to back up and restore your Active Directory database, one of the most critical tasks you will ever face. Hopefully, you won't need to perform a restore operation very often. But if Active Directory information is lost, it can cost your business lots of money, and it could cost you your job. You can be certain that Microsoft expects you to know how to get Active Directory up and running again in the event of a failure.

## Implementing Server Roles

As mentioned earlier, all Active Directory domain controllers are peers, and each of those peers send Active Directory updates using the *multi-master* replication model. With multi-master replication, changes can be made to any domain controller, and eventually those changes—using the replication topology discussed in Chapter 19—are known by all other domain controllers in the domain.

But certain changes to Active Directory information are impractical to replicate using the multi-master replication model. Therefore, some domain controllers in the network perform *single-master* roles, where certain types of changes are made at only one server using the Windows NT 4.0–style single-master model of replication. That is, a change of information is made in only one location, and these changes are then pushed to other servers participating in replication. All domain controllers are made aware of the changes made at these single master servers, but only one server manages the changes. These vital domain controllers are known as the Flexible Single Masters Operations (FSMO; pronounced "fizz-mo") servers.

You can think of the single-master operations roles as the workers in most small companies (and several big ones as well). At times, employees at small companies have to wear different hats, one minute working in sales, the next in marketing, the next in customer service or repair. Similarly, a Windows Server 2003 machine can wear several of these Active Directory hats at once when providing these single-master roles in the Active Directory enterprise. It's like a server being both a DNS and a DHCP server at the same time.

## Planning Flexible Operations Master Role Placement

In every forest, five FSMO roles are assigned to one or more domain controllers. Two of these operations masters are forest-wide: there is only one such server in the forest. Three are domain-wide roles: in every forest, certain single-master roles will be held on only one server per domain. Let's take a look at these roles.

### Forest-Wide Operations Master Roles

Every Active Directory forest must have the following single operations master roles in place: the schema master and the domain naming master.

These two roles must be unique throughout the forest. For every forest, there will be only one domain controller that's the schema master and one that's the domain naming master, even though both of these roles can be located at the same machine.

 **TIP** These two roles are created on the first domain controller installed at the forest root domain. In other words, the first computer in the forest holds these two forest-wide roles by default.

The responsibilities of each role are as follows:

- **Schema master** The schema master controls all updates and alterations to the schema. Whenever you are extending the schema or are installing an application that does so, such as Exchange Server, the schema master must be available.

- **Domain naming master** The domain controller acting as domain naming master is contacted when you are adding or removing domains in the Active Directory enterprise.

**TIP** A domain naming master in a forest set to the Windows 2000 functional level must also be enabled as a Global Catalog server. This is not the case when the domain is set to the Windows Server 2003 functionality level.

## Domain-Wide Operations Master Roles

For a domain to function as it should, every domain must have servers providing these single-master roles:

- Relative ID (RID) master
- Primary Domain Controller (PDC) emulator master
- Infrastructure master

Like the forest-wide operations masters are to the forest, these roles must be unique for each domain. Let's take a look at the importance of each of these roles now.

**RID Master**  The RID master distributes relative IDs (RIDs) to each of the domain controllers installed for a particular domain. Whenever a domain controller creates an Active Directory user, group, or computer, it assigns a security identifier (SID). This user SID is made up of a domain SID number, which will be the same for all objects within a domain, and a RID, which is unique within that domain. The domain controllers get their RID numbers from the RID master. This ensures that the objects created in a domain all have unique SIDs throughout the forest.

Further, when you want to move Active Directory objects from one domain to another, you do so at the computer currently acting as the source domain's RID master. The object then gets a new SID assigned to reflect the membership in the new domain. There is only one RID master per domain.

**PDC Emulator Master**  In the Windows NT 4.0 domain model, directory information was replicated using a single-master model. All changes to the directory database—such as a change of password—were made at the PDC and then replicated to Backup Domain Controllers (BDCs). In a Windows Server 2003 domain, it's still possible to have Windows NT 4.0 domain controllers, but they must be BDCs. (A PDC would indicate the presence of an Windows NT 4.0 domain, not a Windows Server 2003 domain.)

The PDC emulator exists to "fool" Windows NT 4.0 backup domain controllers into thinking they're communicating with a PDC. The PDC emulator is also the first domain controller notified whenever password changes are performed by other domain controllers in the domain. If a password is recently changed, it can take some time for all domain controllers to be notified of the change. If a user submits a logon to a domain controller that does not have the updated password, the logon request is forwarded to the PDC emulator before rejecting the logon attempt.

The PDC emulator also provides other services not readily apparent from its name. By default, this FSMO server is responsible for synchronizing the time on all domain controllers throughout the domain. It's often advisable for the server with the PDC emulator role to be configured to synchronize with an external time server. You can perform this synchronization of the PDC emulator with an external server using the net time command. The syntax to specify the PDC emulator's Simple Network Time Protocol server looks like this:

```
net time \\servername /setsntp: timesource
```

 **TIP** The PDC emulator is also the computer where Group Policy objects are changed, even if the change is being made from another domain controller. Group Policies are discussed in Chapters 22 and 23. The physical file of the Group Policy is changed at the PDC so that multiple changes are not made to the same Group Policy objects.

**Infrastructure Master** The infrastructure master's job is to update objects in its Active Directory database with the objects stored in other domains. The infrastructure master performs this task by comparing its data with that of a Global Catalog. If the infrastructure master finds data that is out of date, it requests the latest Active Directory information from the Global Catalog. The infrastructure master then sends the updated data to other domain controllers in the domain.

Additionally, the infrastructure master is in charge of updating group-to-user references whenever members of groups are modified. This prevents the loss of group memberships that a user account is a part of when the user account is renamed or moved from one container to another within a domain.

Unless your domain consists of only one domain controller, the infrastructure master should not be assigned to a domain controller that's also a Global Catalog server. If the infrastructure master and Global Catalog are stored on the same domain controller, the infrastructure master will not function because it will never find data that is out of date. It therefore won't ever replicate changes to the other domain controllers in the domain. There are two exceptions:

- If all your domain controllers are Global Catalog servers, it won't matter because all servers will have the latest changes to the Global Catalog.

- If you are implementing a single Active Directory domain, no other domains exist in the forest to keep track of, so in effect, the infrastructure master is out of a job.

To demonstrate the roles the domain controllers play in holding these FSMO roles, consider a simple forest of one tree and three domains. In this forest, as shown in Figure 21-1, there will be one schema master and one domain naming master, and three each of the RID master, PDC emulator, and infrastructure master.

## Planning for Business Continuity of Operations Master Roles

As you have just learned, the operations masters roles are vital to the operation of an Active Directory forest. That said, you may not immediately notice when a server holding one or more of these roles is down. As long as the condition is temporary, you need to do little other than bring the domain controller back up again.

**Figure 21-1**
FSMO roles

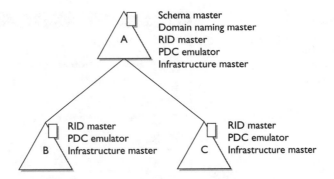

It is possible to move these operations master roles to other computers should the need arise. When moving the location of the FSMOs, you will be performing either a *transfer* or a *seize* of the role in question, as explained in the next sections. Transferring a FSMO role is done when there is a planned change. Computers remain operational during this time. Seizing a FSMO role is a more drastic action, performed when the server holding the role has failed and will likely not recover.

## Transferring the Operations Master

Transferring an operations master role means moving it from one domain controller to another with the cooperation of the original role holder. It is an orderly transfer of power. Depending on the operations master role to be transferred, you perform the role transfer using one of the three Active Directory consoles in Microsoft Management Console (MMC).

You transfer a FSMO role with one of a couple of tools, depending on which role you wish to transfer, as follows:

- To transfer the role of the RID master, the PDC emulator, or the infrastructure master, use Active Directory Users and Computers.

- To transfer the role of domain naming master, use Active Directory Domains and Trusts.

- To transfer the role of schema master, use the Active Directory Schema snap-in.

## Lab Exercise 21.1: Transferring a FSMO Role

Once you know which tools to use, the button-clicking is easy. For example, to transfer the role of PDC emulator, follow these steps:

1. Open the Active Directory Users and Computers MMC, right-click Active Directory Users And Computers, and choose Connect To Domain Controller from the context menu.

2. Type the name of the domain controller you want to hold the PDC emulator role, or select the domain controller from the available list, and click OK.

3. After selecting the target domain controller, right-click Active Directory Users And Computers again, point to All Tasks, and choose Operations Masters.

4. From the Operations Masters dialog box, as shown in Figure 21-2, click the PDC tab, and then click Change.

**Figure 21-2**
Transferring the
PDC emulator
operations
master role

For transfer of the RID master or infrastructure master, you follow the same procedure except for the selection of the tab demonstrated in step 4.

When you transfer roles, there is cooperation from the existing FSMO master. But sometimes those servers are down and cooperation is not possible. In that case, you will need to seize the role.

**TIP**  To transfer an operations master role, you must be a member of either the Enterprise Admins group or the Domain Admins group in the domain where the current FSMO role lives. To transfer the role of the schema master, you must be in the Schema Admins group.

## Seizing the Operations Master

Seizing a FSMO server is done when one of the FSMO servers fails. However, failure of a FSMO, other than the fact that the domain controller is down, can sometimes be hard to detect. In other words, you might not know right away that the server experiencing the problem is also a FSMO server.

Failure of an operations master role can be generally summarized this way: you probably will never notice the failure of one of these servers, provided that you intend to bring the computer back up in the near future. Why? Because most of the information held by the FSMOs is rarely updated. For example, you won't notice the failure of the schema master unless you're trying to update the schema. You won't know that the domain naming master is gone unless you add or remove a domain. These are not functions that occur daily.

The only server role whose absence you might notice immediately is the PDC emulator. Because this server receives preferential updates of passwords, logons might fail if the PDC is not available and a password has been changed.

Therefore, you will almost never *need* to seize these roles from the other domain controllers. In other words, if you plan to bring the domain controller back to life, you won't have to have another domain controller seize the role.

In fact, if you have a domain controller whose schema, domain naming master, or relative identifier roles has been seized by another domain controller, it should *never* be brought back online. A machine that once served one of those roles must be reformatted and reinstalled. If two schema masters attempt to operate in the same Active Directory forest, the forest becomes inoperable.

The utility used to seize an operations master role is called ntdsutil. The NT directory services utility is a very powerful and flexible command-line tool, and its use will be detailed throughout this chapter. In the following example, we'll use it to seize a domain naming master role.

### Lab Exercise 21.2: Seizing a FSMO Role

To seize a FSMO role, follow these steps:

1. Open the command prompt at the domain controller that will be the new holder of the domain naming master role.

2. From the command prompt, type **ntdsutil**.

3. At the ntdsutil command prompt, type **roles**.

4. At the fsmo maintenance command prompt, type **connections**.

5. At the server connections command prompt, type **connect to server** *domaincontroller*, where *domaincontoller* is the target server that will now hold the domain naming master role.

6. At the server connections prompt, type **quit**.

7. At the fsmo maintenance command prompt, type **seize domain naming master**.

Seizing other master roles will look very similar except for the last step.

 **TIP** You should consider transferring FSMO roles when domain controller performance can be better optimized, but seizure of FSMOs is a drastic step that you should almost never take. You should not seize the operations master roles if you can transfer them instead.

Besides knowing how to manage the Active Directory FSMO roles and what to do if they fail, Microsoft also expects you to know how to get the entire Active Directory database back again should a domain controller fail. The next objective examines how, it and specifically points out information that you should expect to see on the 70-294 exam about restoring Active Directory.

# Restoring Active Directory

By the time you reach this point in your MSCE certification path, you should already know how to perform a backup of data using the Windows Server 2003 Backup Utility. You should have also been introduced to the concept of backing up system state data.

To review, *system state data* includes special information critical to the operating state of the computer. Also, the system state takes on different guises from computer to computer, depending on the functions performed. In other words, what makes up the system state will be different on a Windows XP Professional machine than on a Windows 2003 domain controller. In the example of a Windows Server 2003 domain controller, the system state includes the Active Directory service database and the SYSVOL directory. The system state also includes other information, but it's these two that are critical for a restore of Active Directory.

In other words, when you back up the system state on a domain controller, you have the information necessary to restore the domain controller, and thus, the domain, back to its original condition at the time of the last backup.

## Understanding the Significance of the SYSVOL Folder

The SYSVOL folder is critical because it contains the domain's public files. This directory is shared out (as SYSVOL), and any files kept in the SYSVOL folder are replicated to all other domain controllers in the domain using the File Replication Service (FRS)—and yes, that's important to know on the exam.

The SYSVOL folder also contains the following items:

- The NETLOGON share, which is the location where domain logon requests are submitted for processing, and where logon scripts can be stored for client processing at logon time.
- Windows Group Policies, as will be discussed in Chapter 22.
- FRS folders and files that must be available and synchronized between domain controllers if the FRS is in use. Distributed File System (DFS), for example, uses the FRS to keep shared data consistent between replicas.

Microsoft also recommends not to make any changes to the folder structure of the SYSVOL directory. When domain controllers replicate SYSVOL information, the directory structure must be consistent among all domain controllers. This advice also extends to backup and restore operations of the SYSVOL structure. Leave things as they are.

Because this folder is the initial point of contact between a domain client and a domain controller, and because it stores the domain's Group Policies, it is a very important folder to back up. Fortunately, all this is automated when you use the Windows Server 2003 Backup Utility, also known by its executable file, ntbackup, and perform a backup of the system state.

Once backed up, you now have an insurance policy against domain controller failure. Here's hoping you'll never need that insurance policy. But as with other insurance policies, if you're around long enough, eventually you will.

## Examining Restore Types

Over the course of your administrative career, it's bound to happen: a domain controller will fail, and you'll have to perform a restore operation. Once a restore of Active Directory becomes necessary, three restore types are available for you to choose from:

- Primary restore
- Normal restore (also known as nonauthoritative restore)
- Authoritative restore

Each of these restore types gets full attention in the sections that follow.

Before you perform any of these Active Directory restore operations, however, it's crucial to understand that you must first start the domain controller in Directory Services restore mode. To get to Directory Services restore mode, you need to access the Windows Server 2003 Advanced Startup options, which you can do by pressing F8 key the computer is starting up. You can also access the Advanced Startup options from the Boot Loader menu if your system is configured for dual boot.

The next several sections assume you know how to access this Directory Services restore mode, and further assume you are booted into this mode to perform the restore.

## Performing a Primary Restore Operation

Normally, you should need to perform this type of restore operation only when you've lost the entire domain or are restoring a domain with only a single domain controller. You would specify a primary restore on the single domain controller or the first of several domain controllers for the domain. In either case, you are rebuilding the domain from backed-up Active Directory information.

To configure restore as primary, you need to set the advanced options when performing the restore operation. To do so, follow these steps:

1. Open the Backup Utility by choosing Start | All Programs | Accessories | System Tools | Backup. The Backup Or Restore Wizard starts.

2. Click the Advanced mode link on the Backup Or Restore Wizard's welcome screen.

3. Click the Restore And Manage Media tab, select the system state backup file to restore, and then click the Start Restore button.

4. In the Confirm Restore dialog box, click Advanced.

5. Set the advanced restore options you want, and then click OK.

## Performing a Nonauthoritative Restore Operation

If you open the Windows Server 2003 Backup Utility, restore the system state data, and reboot the server, you have just performed a nonauthoritative restore. This is the default mode used when using the Backup Utility. When you perform a nonauthoritative restore, you are telling your domain controller to get the latest changes to the Active Directory database from the other domain controllers once the restore operation is complete. In most cases, this is exactly the restore type you want to perform. Active Directory objects restored during a nonauthoritative restore will have their original Update Sequence Numbers (USNs), which are tags that help Active Directory determine which is the most recent change to Active Directory. A higher USN indicates a more recent change.

If a domain controller goes down, most of the time you will want to perform a nonauthoritative restore. For example, a domain controller goes down and a user changes her password. You would want the domain controller, upon restore, to have that changed password in its Active Directory database, or the user would be rejected when trying to validate at that restored domain controller. If you do not want changes in Active Directory to be reflected in the restored Active Directory information, you should perform an authoritative restore.

### Performing an Authoritative Restore Operation

In certain instances, you will want to restore Active Directory and then have the restored replica become the "master of the domain." When a restore is marked as authoritative, all other domain controllers will synchronize their Active Directory databases with the one marked as authoritative, or, alternatively, selected objects that have been marked as authoritative, instead of the reverse.

Will you do this often? Probably not. In most cases, a domain controller goes down, you restore it from backup, and then you let it grab any changes made to the Active Directory database while the server was incapacitated.

If, however, unwelcome changes have occurred to Active Directory information while the failed domain controller is out of commission, you must perform an authoritative restore. For example, if an OU gets deleted accidentally while the domain controller is down, restoring the domain controller and performing a nonauthoritative restore would not restore the missing OU.

To authoritatively restore Active Directory data, you must still perform a restore as before. However, before you restart the domain controller, you then boot to the Directory Services restore mode, as described previously, and run the ntdsutil utility. The ntdsutil utility lets you mark some or all Active Directory objects as "masters of the domain." This is done by setting an update sequence number on the object to be authoritatively restored that's higher than any other update sequence number in the Active Directory replication system. When the other domain controllers look at the higher USN, they assume the higher USN represents the most recent changes to the object, and therefore will ask for these "new" changes to be sent. Thus, all authoritative restores will eventually be replicated throughout your entire enterprise.

ntdsutil is installed in the systemroot\system32 directory. It is a command-line utility, which means there is syntax to learn. For full instructions on how to use the ntdsutil, remember the /? switch.

**NOTE** As a final thought, you do not necessarily have to perform any of these Active Directory restore procedures. If you have other domain controllers in the domain, you could also just install Windows Server 2003, install Active Directory, and then let the Active Directory database be repopulated through the process of normal replication with other domain controllers, as happens when you add any other domain controllers. But as you no doubt have figured out by now, the real world doesn't always reflect the test world.

# Managing an Active Directory Forest and Domain Structure

If your enterprise consists of a single domain, it also consists of a single tree and a single forest. In other words, a forest can be one tree, and a tree can be a single domain. If this describes your enterprise, no automatic trust relationships will be established. Once you create child domains and add additional domain trees, however, trust relationships are created automatically. These trusts between the domains in a forest are both two-way and transitive.

The *transitive* nature of the trust relationships in Windows Server 2003 simply means that if domain A trusts domain B, and domain B trusts domain C, then domain A will trust domain C. This was not the case with Windows NT 4.0 domains. It was the case, however, with Windows 2000 domains. The *two-way* nature means that the domains trust each other. In NT 4.0 domains, all trusts were one way. One-way trusts are still used to establish trusts to domains outside the Active Directory forest, as you will see.

Trust relationships perform two functions to make the forest a usable logical structure:

- **The trust relationships facilitate cross-domain logon.** Users can submit from any domain in the forest logon credentials to a domain controller in the domain where their account lives. The logon follows the path of the trust relationships from one domain controller to another. Note, however, that all the domains in the trust path must be up for this to occur. Figure 21-3 examines the path of the logon through the trust associations.

- **The trust relationships facilitate access to resources in other domains throughout a forest.** Also shown in Figure 21-3, the links between domains in a forest mean that users in one domain can be granted permission to access resources in other domains throughout the forest. Within a forest, the accounts in one Active Directory domain are trusted by the other domains.

You can create *shortcut trusts* to facilitate more direct communication between domains in a forest. This strategy can be especially helpful if your domain structure has been determined by geographic considerations, and the logon must pass over several slow WAN links to be authenticated by a user's home domain. The shortcut, as shown in Figure 21-4, is a more direct trust link between domains in a relatively deep forest hierarchy.

Note from the figure that a shortcut trust is both one way and nontransitive in nature. One of the significant aspects about creating a Windows Server 2003 domain is that it forms a security boundary between itself and other domains. These security boundaries do not cross over into other domains. In other words, the domain administrator of a parent domain cannot administer child domains in the hierarchy. Only one group has

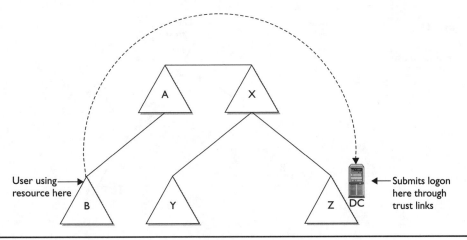

**Figure 21-3**   Logon follows trust links and allows universal access to resources.

**Figure 21-4**
A shortcut trust

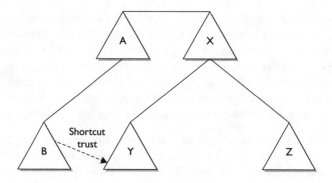

the power to administer every domain in a Windows 2000 enterprise or in a Windows 2003 forest, the Enterprise Admins group, which is created on the forest root's domain controller. Furthermore, any Group Policy settings that you apply to a parent domain do not apply to any of the parent's child domains. These separate security boundaries allow domains—even the ones within a tree that are tied together with these parent/child naming relationships—to act as distinct administrative units and distinct security units within an Active Directory forest hierarchy.

## External Trusts

An *external trust* is used to establish a trust relationship between two domains in different forests, or between a Windows Server 2003 domain and an external Windows 2000 or NT 4.0 domain. They are created to grant access to resources to user accounts that exist in domains that are not part of the Active Directory forest.

External trusts are nontransitive and can be set up as either one-way or two-way trusts, as seen in Figure 21-5.

**Figure 21-5**
The purpose of
an external trust

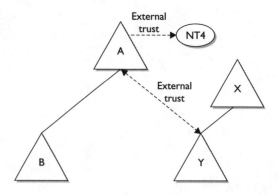

## Lab Exercise 21.3: Configuring an External Trust

To set up an external trust, follow these steps:

1. Open the Active Directory Domains And Trusts MMC snap-in from Administrative Tools.

2. In the console tree, right-click the domain with which you want to establish a trust, and choose Properties.

3. On the Trusts tab, click the New Trust button, and then click Next.

4. On the Trust Name screen, as shown in Figure 21-6, type the DNS name (or NetBIOS name) of the domain, and click Next.

5. In the Trust Type dialog box, choose the External Trust option, and then click Next.

6. Now configure the direction of the trust. The Direction Of Trust screen provides three choices:

   - **Two-Way For An External Two-Way Trust**   Users in the current domain and users in the target domain can access resources in both domains now.

   - **One-Way Incoming For An External Trust**   Users in the target domain will not be able to access any resources in this domain, but users in the current domain will be able to access resources in the target domain.

   - **One-Way Outgoing To Trust Users From Other Domains**   The inverse of the previous selection. Users in the current domain will not be able to access any resources in the specified domain, but the target domain will be able to access resources in the current domain.

7. Complete the wizard to finish the final steps for establishing the trust.

PART IV

**Figure 21-6**

Entering the name of the external domain you will trust

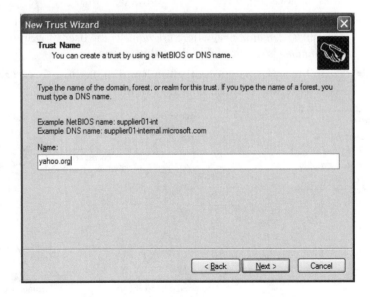

## Forest Trusts

New to Windows Server 2003 is a *forest trust*: it lets you create a trust relationship between two separate Active Directory forests. Although you could create trusts between *domains* in two different Windows 2000 forests, you could not create trusts between different *forests*. If you wanted trusts to exist between all the domains in two separate forests, you had to create individual trust relationships for each trusting and trusted domain.

When you create a forest trust between forests, this is no longer the case. That's because a trust created between Windows Server 2003 forests can be configured as a two-way, transitive trust link. In other words, it's just like the trust created between the domains and trees within a forest. It's also possible to create one-way trusts to other forests. With a one-way forest trust, all the domains in one forest would trust all the domains in another forest, but not visa versa.

The forests will still maintain Active Directory information separately; the schema and Global Catalogs in each forest will be different.

**TIP**   Before creating a forest trust, set the forest functional level in both forests to Windows Server 2003. Also, ensure that DNS has been properly configured so that the domain controllers establishing the trust between forests will be able to resolve domains to IP addresses.

As illustrated in the hypothetical example in Figure 21-7, a forest trust provides several benefits for organizations that need access to resources in other forests.

The benefits include the following:

- Simplified management of resources. Less administrative overhead is associated with maintaining only a single trust between forests.

- Complete two-way trust relationships with every domain in each forest, which eases the locating of resources in other domains.

- Cross-forest logon using the user principal name (UPN), whose syntax is *username@domainname*, where *username* is the user's logon name, and *domainname* is the domain where the account resides.

- Flexibility and separation of administration. Because forests are still separate Active Directory entities, they are administered as such.

**Figure 21-7**
Two-way trust link created when you employ a forest trust

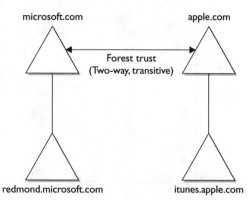

> **NOTE**  Forest trusts are created between only two Windows Server 2003 forests and are not implicitly transitive to a third (or fourth, or fifth...) forest. In other words, if Forest A trusts Forest B, and Forest B trusts Forest C, Forest A does not trust Forest C unless that trust is explicitly created.

## Realm Trusts

*Realm trusts* are useful when a Windows Server 2003 domain needs to trust the accounts and resources in a non-Windows domain, such as a Unix domain. These realm trusts can be configured as either one-way or two-way trusts, and they have the built-in flexibility of being able to switch from transitive to nontransitive and back again.

To create a realm trust, you follow the same procedure as outlined earlier when discussing external trusts, only when you type the DNS name of the domain to trust, you a message will inform you that the domain is not a valid Windows domain. You will then be able to select Realm Trust or Trust With A Windows Domain in the Trust Type dialog box. Once you select the realm trust, you have the option to select whether the trust is transitive or nontransitive.

> **NOTE**  The non-Windows domain that you are trusting must support Kerberos v5 authentication for the realm trust to be configured.

PART IV

## The ntdsutil Utility

We've used the ntdsutil command-line utility several times before in the course of our look at Active Directory. However, it's such a significant management utility, capable of such a wide variety of activities, that it merits its own section here.

The ntdsutil.exe utility, which is located by default in the *systemroot*\System32 folder, provides a host of management services for Active Directory. Some of these have been discussed earlier; some are being introduced for the first time. You can use ntdsutil to perform the following tasks:

- Management and control of the FSMO servers

- Creation and management of application directory partitions

- Perform an authoritative restore of Active Directory information

- Removal of metadata left behind by domain controllers that were removed from the enterprise without being properly uninstalled with the dcpromo utility

- Database maintenance of Active Directory, including compacting and defragmentation

Much like the nslookup utility, you can use ntdsutil one command at a time, or run it in interactive mode, using a series of menus that allow you to move between different Active Directory administration activities. Like most other command-line tools, it is not meant for the inexperienced: you can harm the performance of the network if you use it to make improper configuration changes.

Because you've already seen the uses of ntdsutil mentioned in the first two bullet points, let's take a look at how this tool is used to manage the Active Directory data store.

# Managing Active Directory Database Replication

As mentioned in Chapter 18, the Active Directory is, at its heart, a database. It's stored and managed on the hard disk of a domain controller, within a certain folder structure (to be discussed), and if your domain has multiple domain controllers, then all these domain controllers participate in a replication topology to ensure that the database of Active Directory information is consistent.

The following information lives in this database:

- **Domain data** This is the data most visible to users and even administrators. It includes information about nearly every object within a domain. For example, when a new user is added to your network, an instance of the user account object and any attribute data that describes the object (as long are the attributes exist in the schema) are added to the domain data. Whenever a change to this user account object occurs—a change to the e-mail address, say—this change is reflected in the domain data. Same goes for any other object creation, deletion, or attribute modification.

- **Configuration data** The configuration data is how your Active Directory network is put together, both logically and physically. The configuration data includes a list of all domains, trees, and forests, as well as the locations of the domain controllers and Global Catalogs in the Active Directory topology.

- **Schema data** The schema is a listing of all possible objects and object attributes that can be stored in the directory database. It's vital that all domain controllers share this schema data because if it's not defined in the schema, it doesn't exist in Active Directory. Furthermore, the schema can be extended to allow for the addition of objects unforeseen by the default schema.

- **Application data** This data will be a part of the Active Directory data store only if you have configured application directory partitions. Data stored in the application directory partition addressed the occasional need to replicate information automatically between domain controllers, but not necessarily to all domain controllers. ntdsutil is used to create, configure, and manage the information contained therein.

This directory data is stored in the ntds.dit file on the domain controller, and Microsoft recommends that you store this database file on an NTFS partition for obvious security reasons. And, like any other database file, this one will need occasional management as objects are added and removed from the directory database. The file will sometimes need compacting, and it will also become fragmented over time.

Which utility is used to perform this file management? You guessed it: ntdsutil, using the files commands. For example, to compact the ntds.dit file, use the steps after you have booted Windows Server 2003 using the Advanced Startup Options Menu (F8), and have chosen the Directory Services restore mode:

1. From the command prompt, type **ntdsutil**.

2. Type **files**.

3. Use the following syntax to compact the database

   ```
   compact to target directory
   ```

   where the *target directory* must be an empty directory.

You can then use a variety of switches with the compact to command to write header information to the screen, analyze disk free space and report data file size, and perform an integrity check on the ntds.dit file.

## Monitoring the File Replication Service

The File Replication Service (FRS) replicates specific files using the same multi-master model that Active Directory uses. It is used by the Distributed File System for replication of DFS trees that are designated as domain root replicas. It is also used by Active Directory to synchronize content of the SYSVOL volume automatically across domain controllers.

The reason the FRS service replicates contents of the SYSVOL folder is so clients will always get a consistent logon environment when logging on to the domain, no matter which domain controller actually handles the request.

When a client submits a logon request, he or she submits that request for authentication to the SYSVOL directory. A subfolder of this directory, called \scripts, is shared on the network as the netlogon share. Any logon scripts contained in the netlogon share are processed at logon time. Therefore, the FRS is responsible for all domain controllers providing the same logon directory structure to clients throughout the domain.

## Managing Schema Modifications

Let's say you want to add something to Active Directory (a user object, for example). Before you create this new object in Active Directory, the object is validated against the appropriate object definition in the schema. Only then can it be added to the Active Directory directory database. If there is no definition for the object or the attribute, the object can't be written. Because the user object exists in the schema, an *instance* of it can be added.

But you probably gathered that from reading Chapter 18. Beyond that somewhat elementary concept lies the really exciting feature about the schema, and the reason we're spending some time with it in this chapter as well: the schema is *extensible*. If an object is missing in the default schema that your organization would like to add to Active Directory, or if an existing object would work better if only you could add a different attribute or two, you can change the list of what's possible in your Active Directory network by modifying the schema.

Before you do, you should consider several factors. Because only one schema exists per forest (managed by the schema master, as discussed previously), extending the base schema can have wide-ranging implications for your entire enterprise. For this reason, you should carefully consider each change you make. First, though, let's look more closely at some of the properties of the schema.

## Directory Object Definitions

When you create a new user in Active Directory, you are creating a new instance of an object class. An *object class* contains a list of attributes that are used to define the instances of the class. As you might guess, the User class includes attributes such as givenName and streetAddress. These two attributes *may* be used to help define the instance of the User object, but they don't necessarily have to. An attribute that is required to create an instance of an object class is called a *mandatory* attribute, and any other attribute that can describe the object class is an *optional* attribute. For example, the user object has mandatory attributes that include the objectSID and the SAMAccountName. This means the Active Directory user object must have these attributes defined at the time the object is created. If you don't define one for the user at the time the object is created, you won't be successful in creating the object.

The default schema contains about 250 objects and about 900 attributes. That means you can add 250 types of class objects, like users, computers, and so forth, to the Active Directory database, and you can describe these objects using one of one or more of 900 different attributes. The point? You may never have to extend your schema. What's more, the schema can be modified in two ways: automatically and manually.

Several applications are written to be Lightweight Directory Access Protocol (LDAP) compliant, which is also an open standard to which Active Directory adheres. These applications are said to be Active Directory–aware, and some will make changes to the schema. So you may have to extend the schema after all. You may, but only through the installation of an application like Exchange Server 2000 or 2003, which will be making the changes without your direct intervention.

The other way to modify the schema is manually, using the Active Directory Schema MMC snap-in. Although it won't be at the top of your list of Windows Server 2003 administrative chores, you should know what's involved to manually extend the schema for purposes of exam preparation. After that, it may be a long time indeed until you are called upon to perform such an extension on a production network.

## Schema Storage and Schema Cache

If the schema is a set of software objects and attributes, then that software code needs to be stored somewhere. The schema is stored in the schema directory partition, which, in turn, is a part of the Active Directory information stored on all domain controllers in a forest. This domain controller is called the *schema master,* and the computer providing this role must be available for any changes to the schema to be made. Any changes are then replicated from the schema master to all other domain controllers in the forest.

Moreover, each Windows Server 2003 domain controller caches a copy of the schema in memory to improve performance of schema operations. Each time the schema is modified, the cached version is also automatically updated. This update takes place after a short interval, but you can force a refresh of the schema cache by right-clicking the Active Directory schema root from the MMC snap-in of the same name, and from the context menu, choosing Reload The Schema.

## Schema Security

Not just any user can administer the schema. In fact, this privilege is not even extended to most domain administrators in a forest, save for one. Only one group has the permission to write changes to the schema: the Schema Admins group. Also by default, the group has only one member, the Administrator account in the root domain of the forest. As you saw in the Chapter 20, Schema Admins is one of the built-in groups created during an installation of Server 2003. The membership of the Schema Admins group is shown in Figure 21-8.

Every object and every attribute stored in the schema also has an access control list (ACL) with it, just like every other Active Directory object. However, management of the ACLs for schema objects is rare indeed. You don't want many users having access to the schema, if any. You also might want to employ a Group Policy to make Schema Admins a restricted group, and thus further control exactly who is in this powerful group. We'll talk more about using restricted groups in Chapter 23.

## Managing Schema Modifications

In general, you view schema changes in the same light that you (should) view registry changes: proceed with caution. Just like making the wrong changes to the registry can make the computer unusable, if you make the wrong changes to the schema, your forest can become unusable. For example, you can make it impossible to add objects such as user accounts, or make other objects such as computer objects invalid if you make an incorrect change. It is therefore imperative that you keep the permissions over the schema as tight as possible.

**Figure 21-8**
Default
membership
in the Schema
Admins group

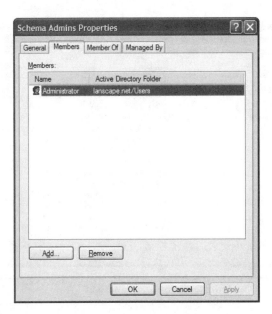

Because modifying the schema has such sweeping implications, you should begin with a cursory knowledge of the base schema at the very least. If existing schema class objects and/or attributes meet your needs, then naturally there is no reason to go and monkey with the schema.

To keep the schema away from prying eyes, the tool needed to change the schema isn't even available from the list of MMC snap-ins until you first register the necessary snap-in to the operating system. You perform this task by either opening the command prompt, or by choosing Start | Run, and typing **regsvr32 schmmgmt.dll**.

Now you're ready to add the Active Directory Schema MMC snap-in to a custom-built Microsoft Management Console. Open a blank MMC and from the File menu choose Add/Remove Snap-In. Then add the Active Directory Schema snap-in to the console, as shown in Figure 21-9.

**TIP**  Microsoft recommends you create a test forest environment to try out schema changes before applying them to a production environment. Any problems with the schema changes can then be identified without affecting the network users—or your employment status.

Now that the Active Directory schema snap-in is open, you can extend the schema by adding or changing either the object classes or the object attributes, as indicated by the two nodes you see in the console. Administrators or developers who know what they're doing can then modify the following:

- A class definition, by expanding the Classes node, right-clicking a class designated for modification, and then choosing Properties
- An attribute definition, by expanding the Attributes node, right-clicking the attribute to modify, and then choosing Properties

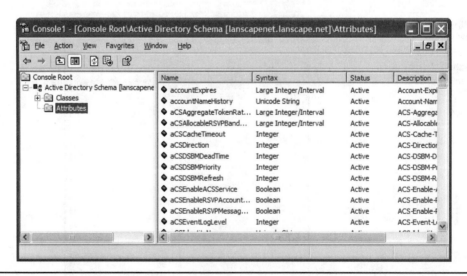

**Figure 21-9**    The Active Directory Schema snap-in

**TIP** Microsoft won't ask you volumes about how to make specific changes to the schema. It will normally be performed by someone with a programming background. You need to understand the general procedure and the tools involved.

In addition, you can add to the schema a class definition or attribute definition by choosing the Create Class or Create Attribute selection after right-clicking the Class or Attribute node. Before you can perform this procedure, however, you need to obtain a valid object identifier (OID) from the relevant International Standards Organization (ISO) issuing authority, or from the American National Standards Institute (ANSI). For more information about obtaining an OID, please visit the web sites of either of these two organizations at http://www.iso.ch or http://www.ansi.org.

**NOTE** If the forest functional level is not set to Windows Server 2003, adding a new attribute to the Global Catalog will cause a full synchronization of the Global Catalog. This can significantly affect network performance, especially as Global Catalog servers synchronize their Global Catalogs between sites.

## Deactivating a Schema Class or Attribute

Once you define a new class or attribute for the schema, it cannot be deleted. (In fact, a dialog box will warn you of just that when you attempt to add something new to the schema.) You cannot delete what's in the schema.

If you have an attribute or class that is no longer needed, though, or if an error occurred when creating the definition, what can you do? You can deactivate the class or attribute. A deactivated class or attribute is considered defunct. A defunct class or attribute is unavailable for use; instances of that object, or descriptions using a defunct attribute, will no longer be possible. However, defunct objects and attributes can easily be reactivated.

You can deactivate an attribute or class with a single check box in the object's Properties dialog box, as shown in Figure 21-10. To activate or deactivate an attribute, select the Attribute Is Active check box. Also note that certain objects, such as the Computer Class object, and certain attributes, such as the AccountExpires attribute, cannot be deactivated.

**TIP** Remember that when you create a new class or attribute, you must obtain an object identifier. When your forest functionality has been raised to Windows Server 2003, you can redefine a class or attribute that's been deactivated.

When you redefine an attribute, you are reusing an existing object identifier and LDAP display name for an attribute that has been deactivated. However, you can now specify a new attribute syntax that better suits your needs. You also need to rename the attribute before you can redefine it.

## Including an Attribute in the Global Catalog

Another useful feature of the Active Directory schema snap-in is the ability to index schema attributes and/or replicate attributes of the schema to the Global Catalog.

PART IV

**Figure 21-10**

Deactivating an Active Directory schema attribute

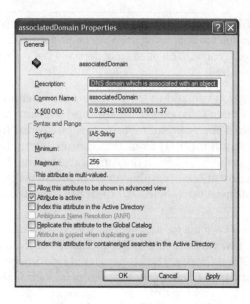

Windows Server 2003, through Active Directory, decides which of the attributes are most commonly used and replicates these attributes to the Global Catalog. But if your network users are constantly performing searches for other attributes, you should include these attributes in the Global Catalog. Doing so can improve performance of queries run against the attribute in Active Directory.

To index a schema attribute, or to include the attribute for replication to the Global Catalog, right-click the attribute from the Active Directory schema snap-in and choose Properties. In the Properties dialog box, as shown in Figure 21-11, include the attribute in the index or replicate it to the Global Catalog by selecting the appropriate box.

**Figure 21-11**

Including an attribute for indexing

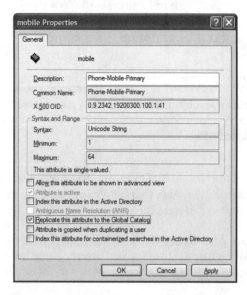

## Adding or Removing a UPN Suffix

When you create a user account in Active Directory, you give that user a logon name, a pre–Windows 2000 user logon name, and a UPN suffix. This *UPN suffix* identifies the domain in which the user account is located. The UPN suffix can (and usually is) the domain name of the domain where the account is created, an alternate domain in the Active Directory forest, or an alternative name used just for logon purposes. If an alternate UPN suffix is created, this suffix does not even have to follow valid DNS naming conventions.

Figure 21-12 shows the UPN of a new user account created in the lanscape.net domain. The user creating the account configures the user logon name, and Active Directory Users and Computers suggests a pre-Windows 2000 logon name using the first 20 characters of the Windows 2003 logon name. The UPN suffix is appended to the user logon name to create the entire user principal name.

By default, this UPN suffix will be the same as the DNS domain name where the account is being created. In most instances, this default UPN suffix will be the only one the user account will ever need. However, you can use alternative UPN suffixes to simplify logon when logging on to other domains throughout the forest, or to provide additional logon security. These alternative UPN suffixes are "aliases" created for the domains in the forest, and they let a user log on using a UPN different from the one he or she is assigned by default.

You might consider using an alternate UPN suffix for a domain when the domain is very deep in a tree hierarchy. For example, you might have a domain called hr.kansascity.lanscapenet.net. This long domain name would be laborious to enter when using a user principal name to log on. (A user principal name uses the user name with the at (@) symbol, and then the UPN suffix.) In this case, a user would log on with a user logon name like jennifer@hr.kansascity.lanscapenet.net. You could create an alternate UPN suffix for the domain to reduce the amount of typing needed when using the UPN. If you created an alternate UPN suffix like lanscape, the same user could log on using the UPN of Jennifer@lanscape.

**Figure 21-12**
The UPN suffix when the user account is created

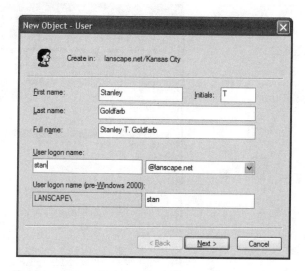

## Lab Exercise 21.4: Adding a UPN Suffix

Follow these steps to add or change the UPN suffix for a user account:

1. Open the Active Directory Domains and Trusts MMC snap-in from the Administrative Tools menu.

2. Select the console root, Active Directory Domains and Trusts, right-click, and choose Properties.

3. From the UPN Suffixes tab as shown in Figure 21-13, type an alternative UPN suffix for the forest, and then click Add. Click OK to complete the procedure.

If you need to add more alternative suffixes for the Active Directory domain, simply repeat the procedure as necessary.

## Routing Name Suffixes Across Forests

When a forest is first put together, all name suffixes are routed across all domains in the forest by default. That is, if a user logs on using the UPN of brian@kc.lanscape.net while in the atchison.lanscape.net domain, the UPN suffix routing mechanism will make sure the logon attempt is routed to the kc.lanscape.net domain. It will do so following the trust path, routing the logon to the parent domain of lanscape.net before sending it along to the kc child domain.

Additionally, forests have a built-in mechanism that routes name suffixes to the appropriate tree roots. As you have learned, forests can employ multiple name suffixes, such as lanscape.net and beanlake.net. In Active Directory Domains and Trusts, both of these name suffixes appear with a wildcard character (the asterisk) at the beginning of the UPN suffix. Therefore, requests for logon authentication for all child domains of beanlake.net from other domain trees will be routed to the beanlake.net tree root domain. That's because all child domains of beanlake.net will include beanlake.net in their unique UPN suffixes (that is, *.beanlake.net).

**Figure 21-13**

Add an additional
UPN suffix

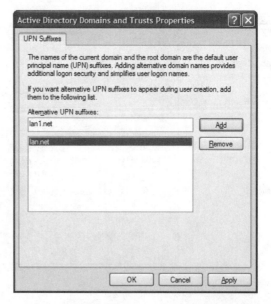

You can further manage how these suffixes are routed between two separate Windows 2003 forests by configuring suffix routing. Using the netdom utility, you can specify if and how UPN names are routed. The next section looks at use of the netdom utility.

**NOTE** Don't include the at symbol in either the user name or the UPN suffix. When authentication attempts are routed to trusted forests, all characters before the first at symbol are interpreted as the user name and everything after the at symbol is interpreted as the UPN suffix.

## Handling UPN Collisions

Sometimes, when two (or more) forests are joined by forest trust relationships, UPN suffixes used in one forest might be the same as UPN suffixes used in another. Thus, when a user sends an authentication request, there is confusion among the routing domain controllers about where to forward the request. This event is called a *UPN collision*. However, with collision detection, you can ensure that each name suffix gets routed to only a single Active Directory forest.

Active Directory Domains And Trusts will detect a UPN suffix conflict under these circumstances:

- The Domain Name System (DNS) name is already in use in another trusted or trusting forest.
- The NetBIOS name is already in use among the forests.
- One domain name suffix SID conflicts with an existing name suffix SID.

If a second instance of a name suffix is detected, the routing for the most recently added name suffix will be disabled by default. Consequently, the UPN routing will be disabled for the newly added trust partner, but only for the domain with the conflict. For example, if you configure a forest trust from a forest with a domain called kc.beanlake.net to a forest with a domain called kc.lanscape.net, a domain name conflict will occur. In this instance, there will be two domains in the trusting forest enterprise with domains whose NetBIOS names are called kc.

When this conflict happens, the kc domain name will be disabled in the newly trusted domain. Despite the naming conflict, however, routing will still work for any other unique name suffixes in the newly trusted forest.

Any UPN suffix conflicts will be listed in Active Directory Domains and Trusts. To view such conflicts, open the forest trust Properties dialog box, and select the Name Suffix Routing tab.

If Active Directory Domains and Trusts detects a name suffix conflict during the creation of the forest trust, the New Trust Wizard will prompt you to save a log file of the conflicts.

## The netdom Utility

The netdom utility is used to manage Active Directory trusts from the command prompt. Using this tool, you can administer trusts both between domains and between forests. It's installed from the Windows Server 2003 CD-ROM as a part of the Support Tools in the \Support\Tools folder.

PART IV

The netdom utility is a powerful tool that lets you perform a wide variety of administrative tasks. Most of the tasks are related to managing computer accounts. They include the following:

- Join a Windows 2000 or XP Professional system computer to a Windows Server 2003 or Windows 2000 domain.
- Specify the organizational unit for a computer account.
- Generate a random computer password when initially joining the domain.
- Manage computer accounts for domain member workstations and member servers.
- Move a computer account from one domain to another within a forest. The move operation also retains the original security descriptor for the computer account.
- Establish one-way or two-way trust relationships between domains.
- View and change the behavior of a trust relationship.

Additionally, with regard to the routing of UPN suffixes as discussed in the previous section, you also use the netdom utility to list all routed names, and to enable and disable routing for certain UPN suffixes should your enterprise require this step. Let's say you had a forest whose root domain was called lanscape.net, and then you create a trust to another forest with a root called beanlake.net. Let's also say both of these forests had child domains called sales. Even though the DNS names of these two domains would be different (sales.lanscape.net and sales.beanlake.net), each of these child domains would have NetBIOS domain names of sales.

Once you create the forest trust from the lanscape.net forest to the beanlake.net forest, routing to the sales domain in beanlake.net would be disabled. If, however, you needed to route the NetBIOS name sales to the beanlake.net domain instead, and you don't use the sales name when referencing the domain in the lanscape.net forest, then you could use netdom to disable the sales domain name in lanscape.net and subsequently enable it in the beanlake.net forest.

**NOTE** Because the netdom utility has several uses, you should refer to the help files for correct syntax for a given situation. The important point is to recognize when netdom might com in handy.

# Troubleshooting Active Directory Using Microsoft Utilities

Microsoft, on the 70-294 exam, will also expect you to troubleshoot Active Directory when problems arise. Not that this *ever* actually occurs, but just in case, let's go over a few items here that will help optimize consistent, reliable performance of an Active Directory enterprise.

A few tools are available to help you monitor replication. You can be certain that a question or two will require familiarity with these tools:

- repadmin
- dcdiag
- replmon

**TIP**  Microsoft expects you to know which tools can help diagnose and resolve problems when they occur.

All of these utilities except replmon are command line–based tools. None of them are installed by default.

These tools, along with several others, are stored in the \Support\Tools directory on the Windows Server 2003 CD-ROM. You must install them first before you can use them. The easiest way to install the support tools is to double-click the suptools.msi setup file in the \Support\Tools folder. This option will install several support tools besides the tools mentioned in the previous list.

If you wish, you can also extract just the tools you want to work with by opening the Support.cab file and then extracting the desired files out of the cabinet.

## The repadmin Utility

The replication diagnostic tool, more commonly known by its short name repadmin, can help you diagnose Active Directory replication problems between domain controllers. Using this tool, administrators can look at the replication topology as seen from the point of view of each domain controller.

You can also use repadmin to force replication between domain controllers or to manually create a replication topology. However, this is not normally required—or even recommended—because of the behind-the-scenes work of the Knowledge Consistency Checker (KCC).

**CAUTION**  If you don't know how to use this tool, don't use it. Incorrect configuration of the replication topology can result in degraded replication performance. This tool is used primarily for monitoring purposes, or for occasionally forcing replication, not for configuring replication topology.

Repadmin uses the following syntax:

```
repadmin Operation Parameters [/rpc] [/ldap]
[/u:Domain\User][/pw:{Password | *}]
```

The repadmin tool then uses a variety of switches to tell it what kind of replication to monitor. For example, if you wanted to know the bridgehead servers for a specific site, you would use the /bridgeheads command. It would look something like this:

```
repadmin /bridgeheads [DC_LIST],
```

where DC_LIST specifies the host name of a domain controller, or a list of domain controllers that you wish to be designated as bridgeheads. The domain controllers in the list need to be separated by spaces.

To force a replication event, you use the /replicate command. Use replicate with further arguments that fine-tune replication behavior. For example, to command a full synchronization between domain controllers, the syntax is as follows:

```
repadmin /replicate Destination_DC Source_DC [/full]
```

The /full switch ensures a full synchronization between the source and destination computer.

## The dcdiag Utility

The domain controller diagnostics tool is yet another monitoring tool that you can use to analyze the state of the domain controllers in either your domain or forest enterprise. dcdiag works by letting you select specific domain controllers to run diagnostic tests. These tests use a given set of scope parameters that you enter at the command prompt. The scope reporting boundaries can include a forest, a site, or even a single domain controller. The syntax is as follows:

```
dcdiag /s:DomainController [/n:NamingContext]
[/u:Domain\UserName /p:{* | Password | ""}]
```

Several switches will allow you to further modify the utility's behavior. For example, if you notice there's an unresponsive server, and you want to perform a simple test to find out why, you could use the dcdiag tool as follows:

```
dcdiag /s:lanscape1 /u: Domain\administrator p:/ password /e
```

The /e switch will test the entire enterprise's domain controllers. You will see a report generated as domain controllers throughout are tested for connectivity, and any domain controllers that do not pass will be identified in this report.

 **NOTE** It is impractical to try to memorize command prompt syntax other than for a few of the most commonly used tools, and Microsoft doesn't expect you to know on its exams. It's much more important to learn when a tool might be used and then to remember the /? switch to get online help about proper syntax when it's actually time to use the utility.

## The replmon Utility

The active directory replication monitor saves you from having to type. The replmon tool provides you with a GUI to many varied replication-monitoring features, allowing you to see what's being transferred between domain controllers with a point-and-click interface.

This tool lets you force replication between domain controllers, and it allows you to quickly generate a visual map of the network's replication topology, as well as generate reports on the performance and history of Active Directory replication.

To run the replmon utility, follow these steps:

1. Type **replmon** in the Run dialog box. The Active Directory Replication Monitor MMC snap-in opens.

2. To select which servers to monitor, right-click the Monitored Servers node, and then click Add Monitored Server.

3. The Add Monitored Server Wizard appears, helping you make a selection. You can type the name of a specific server or browse the directory for a server.

4. If you select the Search The Directory option, you'll choose a domain from the drop-down list, and then click Next.

5. Browse the site containers for servers to monitor. Expand the appropriate site and select your server, as shown in Figure 21-14.

Now that you know how to open the utility and add a server, you should be aware of its monitoring capabilities. Here's a partial list, along with instructions for a few selections:

- See when a replication partner fails.

- View the history of successful and failed replication changes for troubleshooting purposes: right-click the server, and choose Generate Status Report.

- View the properties of directory replication partners: right-click the server object, and choose Show Domain Controllers In Domain. A report similar to the one shown in Figure 21-15 will appear.

- View a snapshot of the performance counters on the computer, and the registry configuration of the server: right-click the server, and then choose Show Current Performance Data.

**Figure 21-14**

Adding a server to Active Directory Replication Monitor

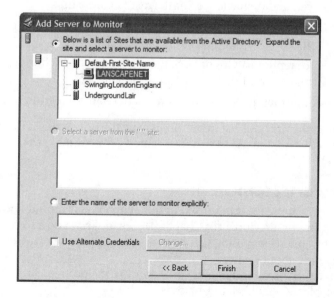

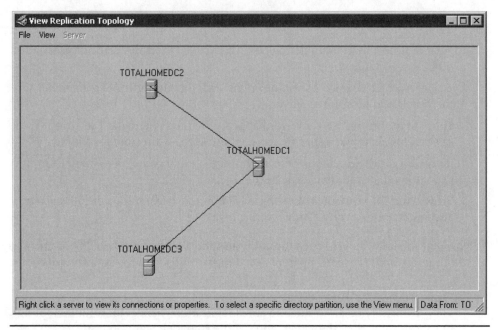

**Figure 21-15**    replmon showing all domain controllers in the domain

- Generate status reports that include direct and transitive replication partners, and detail a record of changes: right-click the server, and then choose Generate Status Report.

- Find all direct and transitive replication partners on the network: right-click the server, and then choose Show Trust Relationships.

- Display replication topology: right-click the server, and then choose Show Replication Topologies.

- Force replication: right-click the server, and then choose Synchronize Each Directory Partition With Replication Partners.

- Monitor replication status of domain controllers from multiple forests.

Given the previous list, replmon may be the only replication-monitoring tool you'll ever need. Also, the use of this tool is pretty straightforward—everything begins with a right-click.

## Network Monitor

Like many of the tools discussed in this chapter, you should know the function of Network Monitor. Previously in Chapter 10, we looked at how to configure Network Monitor. Now just keep in mind that Network Monitor is one of the tools with which you can gather data about replication traffic.

For a full discussion of Network Monitor, including instructions on how to capture traffic, please refer back to Chapters 10 and 11.

# Directory Service Log in Event Viewer

Another diagnostic tool that helps troubleshoot and diagnose Active Directory problems is the Directory Service log in Event Viewer. This log file is added to when the Windows 2003 Server machine is acting as a domain controller.

To view the Event Viewer logs, open the Event Viewer from the Administrative Tools or through the Computer Management MMC snap-in.

Some of the log events captured by the Event Viewer can be very helpful; others are a little esoteric. In the Directory Service log file, three types of log events are captured:

- **Informational**   The icons for informational events are white balloons with blue *is* inside. They provide information only and do not indicate a problem.

- **Warnings**   These icons are yellow triangles with exclamation points that look somewhat like road signs. They indicate potential trouble spots, but they are not necessarily indicators of impending doom.

- **Errors**   Error event icons are red *xs*. Errors should be immediately investigated and resolved if possible.

To display the information captured by an event in the Directory Service log file, select the Directory Service node from the Event Viewer console, and double-click an event to investigate.

The results shown in the Properties dialog box of the event will inform you of the time and date of the capture, the user, and the computer involved, among other information. The other information that is displayed depends on which kind of event has been logged. The example in Figure 21-16 shows a general informational message, informing you that a Global Catalog server has been found.

**PART IV**

**Figure 21-16**
The Event Viewer providing a graphical interface for viewing log files

**NOTE** Remember, you won't see the Directory Service log file in the Event Viewer unless your server is configured as a domain controller. All Windows systems with the Event Viewer should have at least three logs, however: the System, Security, and Application log files.

Configuring the log file properties is a fairly straightforward exercise, one with which most administrators are familiar with by now. Essentially, you're just configuring the properties of a text file: how large it will be, where it will be stored, and what happens when it fills up with collected data.

By default, the logging policy is set so that when the log gets full, the oldest events are deleted to make room for new events, with the stipulation that events are at least seven days old.

You can further customize this policy, referred to as the event log wrapping options, with the options on the General tab of the log file's Properties dialog box. With these options, you set the log file wrapping behavior as follows:

- **Overwrite Events As Needed**   New events will be written even though the log is full. New events will replace the oldest event in the log. If archiving DNS events isn't important (usually it's not), this option is a good choice.

- **Overwrite Events Older Than X Days**   Retain the log for the number of days you specify before overwriting events. The default is seven days. This option is the best choice if you want to archive log files weekly. This strategy minimizes the chance of losing important log entries and at the same time, keeps log sizes reasonable.

- **Do Not Overwrite Events**   Clear or archive the log manually rather than automatically. Select this option only if you cannot afford to miss an event (for example, for the security log at a site where security is extremely important).

You can also set the maximum log file size on the General tab as well using the Maximum Log File Size entry. By configuring a larger maximum log file size than the default of 16384KB, you can put off some of the wrapping behavior just mentioned when the max log file size is breached.

## Chapter Review

In this chapter, we've built on our foundation of Active Directory understanding, and we now know a little bit more about what to do when our Active Directory infrastructure behaves other than as planned. Many test questions on any MSCE test, not just this one, will survey your ability to recognize and fix Windows Server 2003 problems.

Flexible Single Masters Operations (FSMO) servers play critical roles in the functioning of both an Active Directory domain and forest. There are five FSMO roles. Three occur once in each Windows Server 2003 domain: RID master, PDC emulator, and infrastructure master. Two are found only once in each forest: the domain naming master and the schema master.

On those rare occasions where it is warranted, administrators sometimes need to extend the schema. This chapter looked at the tasks involved when this task needs to be performed. We also discussed the impact that schema modification has on the entire Active Directory forest.

Also significant here, especially for real-world purposes, was the discussion of how to back up and restore Active Directory information. We examined the difference between a nonauthoritative and an authoritative restore. We also looked at the restore procedure and the tools necessary to perform one.

Finally, we looked at several tools used to monitor and troubleshoot Active Directory replication. These tools include Network Monitor and the Event Viewer, as well as replmon, dcdiag, and repadmin.

## Questions

1. The following syntax is an example of what?

   ```
   CN= Russell Simkins, OU=Legal, OU=Atchison, DC=bookstore, DC=com
   ```

   A. Fully qualified domain name

   B. User principal name

   C. Distinguished name

   D. Full user LDAP name

2. The following syntax is an example of what?

   ```
   Rsimkins@bookstore.com
   ```

   A. Fully qualified domain name

   B. User principal name

   C. Distinguished name

   D. Full user LDAP name

3. You are the administrator of an Active Directory environment consisting of a single Windows Server 2003 domain. There are four domain controllers, SVR1, SVR2, SVR3, and SVR4. SVR4 does not hold any of the domain or forests' FSMO roles. The system state of SVR4 was last backed up a week ago, and the motherboard fails. You purchase a new server and want that server to play the same part in the Active Directory environment as SVR4. What should you do?

   A. Add the new server to the domain, and then use the Windows Backup Utility to create a copy of the system state of another domain controller. Start the new server in Directory Services restore mode and restore using this backup.

   B. Use the Active Directory Installation Wizard to make the new system a domain controller for the domain.

   C. Use the ntdsutil utility to perform an authoritative restore using the last backup of SVR4's system state.

   D. Use the ntdsutil utility to perform a nonauthoritative restore using the last backup of SVR4's system state.

4. You have just extended the schema using the Active Directory Schema MMC snap-in so that users can track a resource ID for each computer object. After running a Network Monitor capture, you find that queries for this attribute are being run often against domain controllers. What is the best way to improve the performance of the queries?

   A. Install additional domain controllers to distribute the processing of these queries at other servers.

   B. Index the attribute using the Active Directory schema tool.

   C. Configure a site for each subnet in your network and place a Global Catalog server in each site.

   D. Reload the schema cache on the domain controllers.

5. You are administering a Windows 2003 forest for a legal firm, and you need access to several thousands of pages of deposition and saved audit reports that are stored on another company's Unix server. The Unix domain supports Kerberos v5 authentication for its users. You do not want the Unix domain's users to have any access to resources in the Windows Active Directory domain. What kind of trust relationship should you configure?

   A. A one-way: outgoing realm trust

   B. An external Kerberos trust

   C. A two-way realm trust

   D. A one-way: incoming realm trust

6. You are the administrator of a medium-sized company that includes a single Windows Server 2003 domain. There are six Windows Server 2003 domain controllers. On a Wednesday, you back up the system state data on one of your domain controllers. You then add ten new user accounts on Thursday and back up the system state again. On Friday, however, another administrator misreads an e-mail and deletes those ten accounts. Which of the following utilities should you use to recover the ten user accounts?

   A. The repadmin /rollback command

   B. The dcpromo utility

   C. The ntdsutil utility

   D. There is no way to recover the user accounts

7. You are the domain administrator of a small Windows Server 2003 Active Directory environment, with only a single domain and two domain controllers. After heavy rains, water damage forces you to replace both domain controllers and restore from backup. How do you enter Directory Services restore mode to quickly recover the Active Directory database?

   A. Press F12 as soon as the BIOS loads.

   B. Press F8 during the boot sequence and select Directory Services restore mode.

**C.** Select Directory Services restore mode from the Boot menu.

**D.** Boot from the Windows 2000 Server CD-ROM.

8. You are the domain administrator of an Active Directory domain. There are 12 domain controllers in the domain, spread across several sites. You have just written a logon script and want to ensure it runs for every user, no matter which domain controller is authenticating the logon attempt. In which directory should you place the logon script to ensure the desired behavior?

   **A.** The SYSVOL share of one of the domain controllers

   **B.** The root directory of the C drive on every domain controller

   **C.** The WINNT directory on one of the domain controllers

   **D.** The WINNT/System32 directory

9. Which of the following tools can best help you diagnose problems with Active Directory replication from one Windows Server 2003 domain controller to another? (Choose all that apply.)

   **A.** repadmin

   **B.** dcdiag

   **C.** Task Manager

   **D.** replmon

10. You are the network administrator in a Windows Server 2003 Active Directory forest. The enterprise consists of two trees, each with three domains. The root of the forest is called beanlake.com and has two child domains called us and canada. The root domain of the second tree is called griffin.com and also has two child domains named us and canada. As the administrator of us.griffin.com, you would like to make changes to the forest schema. Which domain administrator do you need to contact to add your account to the Schema Admins group?

   **A.** griffin.com.

   **B.** beanlake.com.

   **C.** The Schema Admins group, because it is a universal group, is static, and cannot be modified.

   **D.** None of the above; as domain admin, you will have this ability automatically.

## Answers

1. **C.** This is an example of a distinguished name. The distinguished name identifies the object and also the parent Active Directory containers where that object is located. Every object in Active Directory must have a unique distinguished name. The object names themselves may be used several times, but they must be unique in the parent container where they reside.

2. **B.** A UPN is the user logon name and the UPN suffix joined with the at symbol. When you create a user account in Active Directory, you give that user a logon name, a pre–Windows 2000 user logon name, and a user principal name (UPN) suffix. This UPN suffix identifies the domain in which the user account is located. The UPN suffix is usually the domain name of the domain where the account is created, an alternate domain in the Active Directory forest, or an alternative name used just for logon purposes. If an alternate UPN suffix is created, this suffix does not even have to follow valid DNS naming conventions.

3. **B.** The only step necessary is to install Active Directory on the new server computer. The server will then request the latest version of the Active Directory database. Neither an authoritative nor a nonauthoritative restore is necessary here because the other domain controllers have been providing fault tolerance for Active Directory information.

4. **B.** To improve performance of queries, you should index the newly added attribute by right-clicking the attribute in Active Directory schema, and then selecting Index This Attribute in the Properties dialog box.

5. **D.** A one-way: incoming realm trust would configure the Unix domain to trust the users of the Windows 2003 domain. The Unix admins, if they could get past the insult of your distrust, could then add the Windows domain users to the access control lists of the folder that holds the data needed.

6. **C.** In this scenario, you should use the ntdsutil utility after performing a restore to authoritatively restore the deleted user accounts using the Thursday backup file. With ntdsutil, you can mark just the ten user accounts as authoritative. Before restoring the information, you must take the domain controller offline by restarting the computer in Directory Services restore mode.

7. **B.** Pressing F8 during the boot sequence displays the Advanced Startup menu, allowing you to enter Directory Services Restore mode.

8. **A.** By default, domain controllers running Windows Server 2003 replicate the contents of the SYSVOL to all the domain controllers within a domain using the File Replication Service (FRS). Therefore, you need to add the logon script to the SYSVOL directory on just a single domain controller, and then replication to all other domain controllers in the domain occurs automatically.

9. **A, B,** and **D.** The repadmin tool is an advanced command-line troubleshooting utility used to diagnose problems in Active Directory replication. dcdiag can be used to analyze the state of domain controllers. The replmon tool is used to monitor replication and force synchronization between domain controllers.

10. **B.** The Schema Admins group exists only in the root domain of the forest, which in this case is beanlake.com. Therefore, you will have to contact the domain admins in the beanlake.com domain to be added to the Schema Admins group.

# Planning and Implementing Group Policy

In this chapter, you will learn how to

- Plan Group Policy strategy
- Identify the Components of Group Policy
- Plan a Group Policy strategy by using Resultant Set of Policy (RSoP) planning mode
- Plan a strategy for configuring the user environment by using Group Policy
- Plan a strategy for configuring the computer environment by using Group Policy
- Configure the user environment by using Group Policy

Group Policy is a beast. This chapter introduces you to this versatile, mammoth administrative technology, explains what it is, and describes how it works. (How it works is the important point for you.) It then starts to demonstrate the capabilities of Group Policy, starting with management of the end-user experience. But the discussion is simply too broad to end here.

 **NOTE** Chapter 23 picks up where this one leaves off, highlighting some of the security and software installation capacity that's possible through a Group Policy Object.

You can figure that about 30–50 percent of the 70-294 exam will in some way test your ability to understand and implement a Group Policy Object. Therefore it's imperative that you have a good grasp on the concepts and skills in this chapter before even thinking about registering for the test. Additional experimentation with Group Policies in a test environment is also highly recommended for you to get a better feel how Group Policy behaves when the settings introduced here are configured.

We'll start this chapter with a look at Group Policies in the most general terms, and then start funneling towards specifics later in the chapter. We want to begin painting the

Group policy picture using the broadest of strokes possible, by considering what they are and what they can do.

## What's a Group Policy?

Like files and folder, like users and groups, like domains and organizational units, a Group Policy Object (GPO) is just another software object, typically stored in the Active Directory database. (I say typically because there is one stored in the local machines' directory database as well, but mostly Group Policies are used to manage Active Directory–based computing environments.) This software object is made up of a collection of settings that can potentially affect almost any aspect of user and computer configuration. So far, so good?

Group Policies can then be linked to the container objects in Active Directory: sites, domains, and organizational units. The Group Policies linked will then configure settings that, by default, affect all objects in the container. They can be used to determine what Start Menu options are available, what the background of the desktop will be, what programs will be available. And these are just of few of the configurable settings, as you will soon see. This chapter focuses just on some of the settings that affect the end user experience.

## Planning a Group Policy Strategy

But before we jump into the Group Policies created and linked to the Active Directory containers, let's start with the aforementioned local policy. There are several reasons to start with an examination of the local policy even though you won't see questions that directly test your understanding of it. First, all Windows XP Professional, Windows 2000, and Windows Server 2003 computers have a local policy, so even if you don't have an installation of Active Directory handy on Windows Server 2003, you can still study and understand Group Policies by looking at the local policy. Second, they give you a good starting point for Group Policy comprehension.

One of the challenges of any domain administrator is enforcing a corporate policy about how users' desktops should look. For example, a picture of your favorite NASCAR driver might be appropriate for a home computer, but a manager of a bank might want something a little more stately when making a first impression to a potential bank customer.

Using a Group Policy to manage users also means controlling what content is provided via the desktop. The Control Panel, for example, can be kept from prying, unknowledgeable eyes. The Run or Shutdown options can be removed from the Start menu, and Internet Explorer can be removed from the desktop.

But these are just a few examples. Looking at individual examples is the best way to get comfortable with the capabilities of Group Policy, partly because the scope of manageable settings is so overwhelming. In this chapter and the next, we'll first examine what Group Policy does, how Group Policy Objects (GPOs) are processed, and how they are secured. Once we lay the groundwork, learning about Group Policy becomes an examination of the instances of Group Policy settings. Managing the end-user environment, as discussed at the close of this chapter, is just one example of what a Group Policy can do.

A Group Policy Object is capable of executing many administrative tasks, including the following general possibilities:

- Enforce centralized control of user and computer settings at the site, domain, or organizational unit (OU) level.

- Provide a desktop environment that enables users to accomplish job functions while also ensuring that applications cannot be changed or removed.

- Control the end-user experience by managing the appearance of the desktop, including which software is or can be installed.

- Ensure that a company's written policies regarding computer use and security settings have a computing mechanism for application.

Furthermore, every computer running Windows Server 2003 is governed by at least one Group Policy Object. This is the local GPO, and it serves as a good starting point as we investigate Group Policy.

## The Local Group Policy Object

Every computer running Windows 2000, Windows XP Professional, or Windows Server 2003 has a local Group Policy Object linked to it. With a local GPO, it's possible to configure the settings of just a single computer without affecting any others. In an Active Directory environment, these local settings are low on the totem pole, because the settings dictated by a local policy can be overwritten by settings configured at the site, domain, or OU level. However, in a non-Active Directory environment, the local GPO is the only measure of applying a Group Policy setting.

By now, you've probably used some of the Control Panel tools to make changes to the look and feel of the desktop. You've changed screen resolution, desktop wallpaper, mapped network drives, and so on. However, these changes are not a permanent part of the end-user experience. The desktop can be changed; the network drives can be unmapped.

But what if the administrator wants to take more control of the user environment, dictating the look and feel of the desktop experience? What if, for example, the administrator of a computer—or even an entire domain—wants to remove access to Internet Explorer altogether for all users of a particular computer? What if he or she wanted all users, for purposes of professionalism, to use a uniform desktop theme? Group Policy can be configured to address each of these concerns.

PART IV

## Configuring the Local Policy

To illustrate, perhaps it's best to start with a "blank," or unconfigured GPO. We can configure this unconfigured GPO one setting at a time to become familiar with Group Policy settings.

## Lab Exercise 22.1: Getting Familiar with Group Policy

To open a blank GPO that will apply to the local computer, follow these steps:

1. Open an empty MMC by selecting Start | Run, and then typing **mmc**.

2. An empty console opens. Select File | Add/Remove Snap-In.

3. In the Add/Remove Snap-In dialog box, click the Add button. The Add Standalone Snap-In dialog box opens, where you will navigate to the Group Policy Object Editor.

4. Select the GPOE, click Add, and the screen shown in Figure 22-1 is displayed, where you accept the default choice that the Group Policy will govern the local computer. Click Finish to accept the choice.

5. Close the Add/Remove Snap-In dialog box, and then click OK from the Add/Remove Snap-In dialog box to get back to the MMC, which should now have the Local Computer Policy snap-in loaded.

Now that you have a blank GPO awaiting configuration changes, you need to understand the different components of Group Policy, and also how these components behave as Group Policy Objects are processed to determine the user environment.

**Figure 22-1**
Adding a GPO
for the local
computer

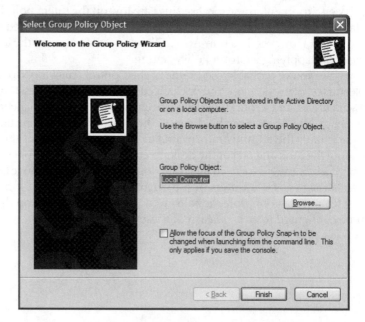

## Components of Group Policy

After you've followed the previous procedure, you will have the MMC loaded with the GPOE, which, in turn, is configured to edit a local policy. As you can see from Figure 22-2, two main categories of Group Policy settings exist:

- **Computer Configuration** This setting is used to set policies that affect the computer regardless of who logs on. It is applied as the operating system initializes, before the user is presented with the logon screen.

- **User Configuration** This setting is used to set policies that apply to users regardless of the computer they are using. User settings are applied after a user identifies himself or herself, usually through a user name a password, and before the desktop is presented.

If you expand each of these main groupings, several subheadings of policy settings appear. Each grouping of configuration settings includes collections for Software settings, Windows settings, and Administrative Templates settings. The individual configuration settings for Users and Computers, however, are not necessarily the same. The setting groupings are briefly described next.

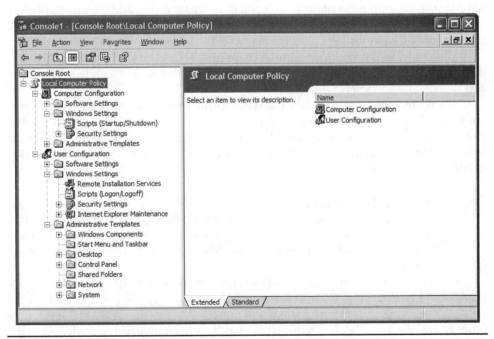

**Figure 22-2**  Settings in a Group Policy Object

## Software Settings

For both User and Computer configurations, the software settings specify software installation options. As you will see in Chapter 23, these settings will help you deploy and maintain installed software for the computers and/or users in your organization.

For example, you could use the software settings to ensure that all computers in a site get a service pack update to an application. The software settings can also ensure that a particular user has an accounting program available no matter which computer he or she logs on from.

## Windows Settings

The Windows settings contain scripts and security settings. The Scripts node is one place where you can most clearly see the difference between which settings affect the user and which ones affect the computer. Notice here that the scripts assigned to computers are Startup/Shutdown scripts, as computers engage in starting up and shutting down. Users, however, are assigned Logon and Logoff scripts, because that's what they do: log on and log off.

In the Scripts node, administrators can attach a script to a Group Policy, with virtually no limitations to the scripting languages used. The script can be written in any ActiveX language, including VBScript, JScript, Perl, and DOS-based scripts such as .bat and .cmd.

The Security settings node allows for manual configuration of security levels. These settings include collections of Audit policies, Password policies, and User Rights assignments, to name a few. Hundreds of security settings are available, and some of these settings are discussed in further detail in Chapter 23.

Additionally, in the Windows settings node under only the User Configuration settings, you'll find policies used for Internet Explorer Maintenance, Public Key Policies, and Remote Installation Services.

If you're creating a Group Policy Object that will apply to an Active Directory container, you'll see a Folder Redirection node. Later in this chapter, as we explore Active Directory–based Group Policies, you'll become familiar with folder redirection: some significant improvements have been implemented in the Windows Server 2003 version as compared to Windows 2000.

## Administrative Templates

The settings configurable with the administrative templates are all registry based. That is, configurations made with the administrative templates are written to the registry at either startup or logon time, depending on whether the setting applies to a computer (startup) or user (logon).

The Administrative Templates include several collections of settings: Windows Components, System, Desktop, Control Panel, and Network. All can be manipulated in a variety of ways. Configuring these settings will noticeably affect the end users' desktop. In other words, if you configure a setting that mandates a certain desktop wallpaper, users are bound to notice.

You can use the System node in part to control behavior of the Group Policy Object it-self, and it will be examined when we discuss Group Policy processing exceptions and the refresh rate, which defines how often clients check for updates to the settings of a GPO.

When you make changes to an Administrative Template setting, you double-click (or right-click and choose Properties) the setting to open the dialog box shown in Figure 22-3. On the Setting tab, three options can be set regarding the configuration of each template setting:

- **Enabled**   This setting enforces the configuration setting for the GPO being configured. A setting that is enabled will edit the registry of the computer where the GPO is effective.

- **Disabled**   This setting will not be enforced for this GPO. The Disabled setting can be used to override a setting configured at a parent container further up in the GPO processing hierarchy. The Disabled setting will also write a change to the registry.

- **Not Configured**   This is the default setting. It means the setting will not be set, but instead, may be inherited from a parent container. Most settings will not be configured as you build your GPOs.

Under the Administrative Templates setting, more than 450 settings exist that affect either user or computer behavior. Which ones you might need to configure for your en-vironment will be a matter of exploration, trial, and error.

**PART IV**

**Figure 22-3**
Configuring an
Administrative
Template setting

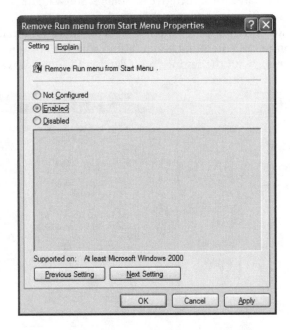

When you configure an Administrative Template setting, the change is written to the registry, thus increasing processing time for the Group Policy Object. Note that this includes configuring the policy setting in the negative, or Not Configured. Therefore, you want to configure as few of these settings as possible while still meeting your administrative objectives.

 **NOTE** If you don't want to scroll through all 450+ Administrative Template settings, you can display only those settings that have been configured. To do so, choose the Administrative Templates node, and then select View | Filtering. The dialog box shown in Figure 22-4 opens, and you can select the option Only Show Configured Policy Settings. Of course, this won't be effective when you are configuring the settings in the first place.

Believe it or not, even more Administrative Template settings are available than you'll see when configuring your first Group Policy Object. To gain access to these settings, you first need to make the Group Policy Object Editor aware of them.

## Making Changes to the Administrative Templates

Also be aware that there are over 220 new administrative settings that are configurable with Group Policy settings.

The administrative settings provided with Windows Server 2003 are themselves stored in an .adm file. Many more .adm files are available than you first see when working with the default administrative templates. Software manufacturers create these .adm files for integration with Group Policies. For example, included with the Microsoft Office 2003 Resource Kit is an .adm file that contains additional settings specific to Office application management. Included in the .adm file are a host of settings not available when tinkering with the settings provided by Windows Server 2003 alone.

**Figure 22-4**

Filtering the display of Administrative Templates settings

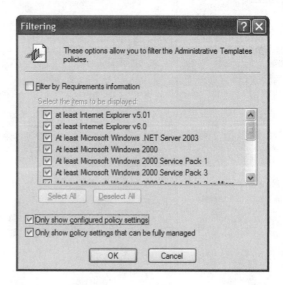

But before you can use any alternate .adm files, you must first make sure Group Policy knows about them. Here's what you do:

1. Open the Group Policy Object Editor and expand either the User node or the Computer Configuration node.

2. Right-click Administrative Templates and choose Add/Remove Templates.

3. In the Add/Remove Templates dialog box, click Add.

4. Select the .adm file to add, as shown in Figure 22-5. If you have copied an .adm file to your hard disk, you browse for it here.

There are also .adm files that help you manage Windows Media Player, Internet Explorer, and NetMeeting settings, to name a few.

---

**NOTE**  For additional information about the many .adm files and how they can be used, please see the Windows 2003 Deployment Kit at http://www.microsoft.com/windowsserver2003/techinfo/reskit/deploykit.mspx.

---

## Group Policy Behaviors

Once you've gotten a foothold on the types of settings that are configurable through a Group Policy, it's time to understand how these policies work when applied to a user or a computer. As you'll see, multiple GPOs often apply to a single user logon, especially in an Active Directory environment. These settings sometimes complement one another, and sometimes they will conflict. You must understand what will happen in each of these situations.

**PART IV**

**Figure 22-5**
Adding an additional administrative template

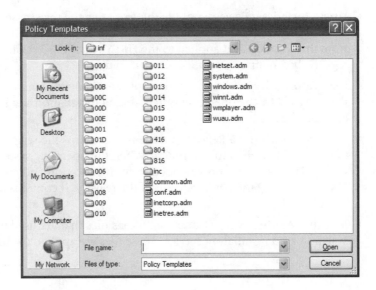

But first, let's take note of where a GPO, once created, is actually stored both on the local computer and then in an Active Directory domain.

## Group Policy Storage Location

As mentioned earlier, every GPO is a software object that stores a collection of configuration settings. And just like every other piece of software, is has to be stored somewhere. Also, every system running Windows Server 2003 will have a single local GPO. This local Group Policy is stored in the following location: systemroot\System32\GroupPolicy.

Domain-based Group Policy Objects, on the other hand, are actually stored in two locations. The *Group Policy container* is a directory service object, and it stores all properties for the GPO, including the latest version of the object, as well as the list of all settings that have been configured.

The other storage location is the *Group Policy template*, which is a folder structure located under the SYSVOL directory. If you recall from the previous chapter, clients connect to the SYSVOL folder when establishing contact with the domain, so it follows that Group Policy information will be stored here. Residing in the Group Policy template are settings that have been configured with Administrative Template settings, security settings, script files, and any information about applications that will be deployed or managed via software installation settings.

The Group Policy template is located in the \Policies subfolder for its domain. The template directories are automatically given names, and there is no need (nor should you) to change these directory names. Each template directory can have several subfolders that store Group Policy settings. These subfolders, examples of which are shown in Figure 22-6, may include the following:

- **Adm**   Contains the .adm files for the Group Policy template.
- **Scripts**   Contains the scripts and related files for the Group Policy template.
- **User**   Includes a Registry.pol file that contains the registry settings that are to be applied to users. When a user logs on, this Registry.pol file is downloaded from this location and applied to the HKEY_CURRENT_USER portion of the registry. It contains an Applications subfolder.
- **User\Applications**   Contains the application advertisement script files (.aas) that are used by the operating system–based installation service. These files are applied to users.
- **Machine**   Includes a Registry.pol file that contains the registry settings that are to be applied to computers. When the operating system initializes, this Registry.pol file is downloaded from this location and applied to the HKEY_LOCAL_MACHINE portion of the registry. It contains an Applications subfolder.
- **Machine\Applications**   Contains the .aas files that are used by the operating system–based installation service. These files are applied to computers.

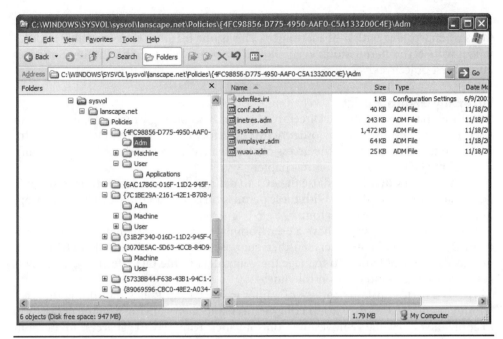

**Figure 22-6**   Directories in the Group Policy template

When a user logs on in an Active Directory domain, several Group Policy settings may apply to the user's environment. Upon further investigation, however, it's apparent that no GPOs apply directly to the organizational unit where the user account resides. Yet Group Policy settings apply anyway. This is because, by default, Group Policy settings are passed down from parent container to child container in the Active Directory administrative hierarchy. In other words, settings are inherited, in much the same way that NTFS permissions are passed down from parent folder to child folder in the directory hierarchy. If you fully comprehend the NTFS inheritance behaviors discussed in Part I of this book, you have a head start on understanding the topic that follows.

## Group Policy Inheritance

Unless some of the exceptions to the processing order have been configured (as discussed in the following sections), Group Policy settings are passed down from parent container to child container. For example, a GPO setting you have configured for a top-level OU also applies to all child OUs within. This inheritance extends to any user and computer objects stored in the parent and child containers.

However, if a GPO has been set for the child container, and that setting conflicts with the parent-level GPO, the child setting will be the effective setting. If a setting is configured for a parent OU, and the setting is not configured for the child OU, the child inherits the setting from the parent.

In this way, Group Policy inheritance works just like the inheritance of NTFS permissions when working with files and folders. This is one reason it's very valuable to be familiar with NTFS permissions even though they are not specifically mentioned as 70-294 test objectives.

## Filtering Group Policy

Because each GPO is an Active Directory object, it is accordingly managed, in part, with a set of properties just like any other Active Directory object, like an OU or a user. Included in these properties is the access control list (ACL). We'll delve into the significance of the GPO's ACL later in the chapter.

For now, know that you can use the ACL to define which users have Read and Apply permissions to Group Policy. With these permissions, you can filter a Group Policy application to a specific user or group.

For example, suppose you have a user, Tommy, who is the designated administrator of an OU's users and computers. Further, suppose a GPO is linked to that OU that removed the Control Panel. To manage the computers in the OU effectively, Tommy is going to need access to the Control Panel.

This is a perfect instance for use of a filter to the Group Policy. By adding the user, Tommy, to the ACL of the Group Policy Object, and then denying him the permission to apply the policy that removes the Control Panel, Tommy will get access to the Control Panel.

This filtering behavior, along with the other exceptions to processing order, give administrators almost unlimited flexibility when deploying Group Policies to manage Active Directory Users and Computers. Another level of filtering lets administrators filter certain settings within a single GPO. This is possible through the use of Windows Management Instrumentation (WMI) filters.

## Windows Management Instrumentation Filtering

Administrators also have the option to further manage Group Policy behavior by configuring WMI filters. These filters allow for additional filtering of Group Policy processing, and they are used much the same way as you use security groups to filter GPO application for a certain group. WMI filters are used to implement exceptions to given policy processing. The WMI filters are written in a language called the WMI Query Language (WQL).

---

 **NOTE** You should use WMI filters sparingly. The more WMI filters apply to a policy, the longer it will take to process the Group Policy Object.

---

To use a WMI filter, you must create one first. WMI filers are written using the WMI Query Language, and can be done right from the WMI Filter tab of the GPO's Properties dialog box. The Filter tab extension to the Properties page of a Group Policy Object allows you to specify a WMI filter for a given Group Policy Object. Furthermore, the

Resultant Set of Policy (RSoP) tool is sometimes used in conjunction with application of WMI filters, because it can display existing WMI filters, and it can also be used to specify alternate filters.

## Lab Exercise 22.2: Adding a WMI Filter

Here's how you add a WMI filter:

1. Open Active Directory Users and Computers.

2. In the console tree, right-click the domain or organizational unit for which you want to set Group Policy, and choose Properties from the context menu.

3. On the Group Policy tab, select the GPO for which you're configuring the filter, right-click, and choose Properties.

4. Select the WMI Filter tab, click This Filter, and then click Browse/Manage.

5. Click Advanced.

6. Click New to clear the Filter Name, Description, and Queries fields.

7. Type in information about the new filters you create. Then save the changes and click OK to finish the procedure.

---

 **TIP** You need not know how to write these WQL filters to pass the test. This skill is usually performed by those with a software development background. For more information, visit http://www.microsoft.com and search for the WMI Software Development Kit (SDK).

Now that you've learned about some of the background issues regarding Group Policies, it's time to create a GPO for use in an Active Directory environment. The concepts you learn here will serve you well in the chapters to follow, because GPOs always follow the same behavior rules, no matter what's being configured with the policy.

## Group Policy Processing Behavior

Here's how the Computer Configuration and User settings are applied at startup and logon time:

1. Upon computer startup, a computer obtains a list of GPOs that will be applied to the computer. This list depends on the following:

   • Whether the computer is a member in a Windows Active Directory domain

   • In which site the computer resides in Active Directory

   • Whether the list of GPOs has changed

2. After the list has been obtained, the Computer Configuration settings are processed synchronously in the order dictated by the processing hierarchy.

3. Any startup scripts assigned to the computer are run synchronously: each script must complete before the next one is run. All this occurs before the user gets his or her user interface, including the Windows logon dialog box.

4. The user presses CTRL-ALT-DELETE and submits user credentials.

5. After the user is authenticated, a list of GPOs for the user is obtained. This list depends on several factors, including the following:

   • Whether Loopback is enabled.

   • Where the user account resides in the Active Directory tree structure (assuming a domain account is used; a logon using a local account to a local machine would not have any domain-based policies take effect).

   • Whether the list of GPOs has changed.

6. The User settings are then processed using the processing hierarchy.

7. Any logon scripts assigned run asynchronously. That is, all scripts are run at the same time by default.

## Group Policy Scope

GPOs adhere to a specific set of rules when applied to users and computers. It is crucial that you learn and fully understand these rules and how they sometimes overlap in their application. One set of these rules defines what happens at each Active Directory container where Group Policy is linked, and how Group Policy settings are inherited from the parent container objects above. Another set defines how settings from multiple GPOs are applied when the individual settings conflict. And a third set of rules deals with how GPOs are processed when several are linked to a single container.

## Group Policy Processing Sequence

Here's how GPO are processed, by default:

1. **Local**   Each Windows Server 2003 computer has exactly one GPO stored locally, which gets processed first.

2. **Site**   Any GPOs associated with a site to which the computer belongs, or from which a user is logging on, is processed next.

3. **Domain**   GPOs linked to the domain container are processed next according to the order listed on the Group Policy tab, as discussed in the next section.

4. **Organizational unit (OU)**   GPOs linked to parent OUs are processed next, followed by GPOs linked to child OUs if applicable. In this way, the immediate parent object of the user or computer account will be processed last, which significantly affects effective settings.

Note that this list spells out the processing order for GPOs from first to last. But the default order of settings precedence is just the opposite. In examining this list, it's important to understand that the local policy is lowest on the GPO processing totem pole. In other words, the last setting processed becomes the effective setting, but only when there is a conflict between settings.

If no configuration conflicts occur, all GPO settings apply. For example, if a local setting specifies auditing of printer access, the domain-level setting redirects the My Documents folder, and an OU setting removes the Control Panel, the user environment will reflect all of these settings. If, however, the OU setting redirects the My Documents folder but uses different settings than the domain policy, the OU's setting will override the domain level settings. Why? It's the last setting applied.

If we could highlight one section from this chapter, that would be it. Until you commit that default processing order to memory, don't bother sitting for the 70-294 exam.

## Multiple GPOs Linked to One Site

For each Active Directory container object, several Group Policy Objects may be linked. Remember that the GPO is the actual software object, which you change and modify according to your requirements, and the link simply allows you to reference the GPO from an Active Directory container object. This lets administrators apply the settings of a single GPO to different levels in their hierarchy without having to re-create another similar GPO for each container. It lets them do more with less.

For each object, the Group Policy tab displays the list of GPOs attached to the object, as shown in Figure 22-7.

**PART IV**

**Figure 22-7**
One GPO linked
to a single Active
Directory object

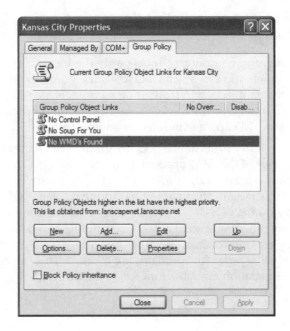

When more than one GPO is linked, the list is processed from the bottom to the top. This means that GPOs at the bottom are processed last, and the top policy is processed last. As with the container processing order, the last setting applied becomes the effective setting where there is a conflict.

Once you learn the default processing order, including what happens when multiple policies apply to a single logon, you can begin to learn all of the multiple exceptions to this rule. A set of rules are applied when processing GPOs, and you must absolutely know these rules when readying for the exam:

- All GPO settings apply unless a conflict is detected. The effective settings are a combination of all settings of all site, domain, and OU Group Policies that might apply to a user login.

- If there is a conflict, the rules of policy inheritance are followed: local, site, domain, OU. The last setting applied where there is a conflict becomes the effective setting.

- If more than one GPO is linked to an Active Directory container object, GPOs are processed from the bottom to the top as they are listed on the Group Policy tab in the Properties dialog box. Again, where there is a conflict in settings, the last setting applied becomes the effective setting.

- Computer settings take precedence over user settings. If a setting is specified from a user and a computer at the same level of GPO processing, the computer settings override the user settings where there is a conflict in settings.

## Exceptions to Group Policy Processing

There are several exceptions to the default GPO processing order:

- **Workgroup computers process only the local GPO**   Because the other containers you can link a GPO to—sites, domains, and OUs—are all Active Directory objects, and workgroup computers are not part of an Active Directory environment, the only way to use GPOs with these computers is by configuring the local GPO on a computer-by-computer basis.

- **Block policy inheritance**   At any domain or OU level, the inheritance behavior of the GPO processing can be blocked. (The Block Policy Inheritance option is grayed out at the site level.) For example, if you are the junior administrator of the finance OU, and that finance OU lives in a domain that has a domain GPO that prevents access to the Control Panel, you can block policy inheritance so that users in your OU have access to the Control Panel. They see Control Panel because the settings configured higher in the default processing order (the domain) are blocked. This can add to the flexibility of administration available for OUs in the domain.

**TIP** Notice that when you block policy inheritance, you block it at the container level, not on an individual GPO. That is, the setting is effective for all GPOs linked to the site, domain, or OU. It doesn't matter where these GPOs were originally created.

- **No override** This is the antidote for the Block Policy Inheritance option. Any GPO linked to the site, domain, or OU can be configured so that its settings cannot be overridden by other GPOs lower down in the processing chain. If more than one GPOs has the No Override setting, the one highest up in the GPO processing chain will be the effective setting. This behavior enables a domain administrator (or an OU admin, and so on) to enforce a container-wide setting that cannot be usurped by a junior administrative.

- **Loopback** This setting is probably the most confusing, and it is definitely the least often used. It is designed for computers that are part of a closely controlled environment such as laboratories or kiosks. Unfortunately, it merits the most discussion, but it is a setting you will configure only rarely, if at all. You may need to know it for the exam, so it's worthy of a little more attention here.

**Understanding the Loopback Setting** In essence, the Loopback setting makes the Computer Configuration settings for a system the effective settings, no matter what other GPOs might apply to the user account at logon time. Moreover, the Loopback setting is not even configured from the Group Policy tab like the other behaviors discussed here.

It is actually a setting of the Group Policy itself. To configure the Loopback setting, you must edit the GPO that would apply to the computer and edit one of the Computer Configuration settings. The full path to the Loopback setting is Computer Configuration | Administrative Templates | System | Group Policy. The full Loopback setting policy is called User Group Policy Loopback Processing Mode.

When you double-click this setting, you have the option to enable the setting. Once in the Enabled state, the loopback behavior operates in one of two modes:

- **Replace** This replaces the GPO list obtained for the user with the GPO list obtained for the computer at startup time. It effectively overrides any user-specific settings the user might have.

- **Merge** This appends the computer GPO list with the user GPO list. Because the GPO list for the computer is applied after the user's normal GPO list received from Active Directory, any settings configured with the local GPO settings override the user's normal settings where there are conflicts. And remember, there are User Configuration settings even in the local GPO.

An example where you might use the Loopback setting is in a reception area. Let's say you have a user who is a part of the graphics OU, and a large software program is distributed to all users in the Graphics department via a GPO that makes sure they will always have the application available no matter which computer they are using. That same user logs on to a computer at the reception area to quickly check messages on the way out the door. With the Loopback setting enabled for the computer, the user then would not have the application installed on the reception computer.

 **NOTE** For further information on the Loopback setting, choose the Explain function of the setting (or any setting, for that matter), which is accessible from either the Explain tab of the Loopback setting, or by using the Extended View in the details pane of the Group Policy Object Editor. (At the bottom of the details pane, you can choose from the Standard and Extended view tabs. The Extended tab gives you access to the explain contents and lets you open the Properties dialog box of the setting with a hyperlink.)

## Disabling User and Computer Configuration Settings

Not all of your settings in a particular GPO need be configured. In fact, most settings won't be configured. For example, if you've configured a GPO whose only function is to remove the Control Panel, all Computer Configuration settings will remain untouched. However, these unconfigured settings still have to be processed come logon time.

Therefore, you can improve performance by disabling the Computer Configuration settings. In fact, Microsoft recommends this practice. You don't have to apply settings that are unconfigured, and in fact, you shouldn't. Disabling part of a GPO can speed up GPO processing at startup and log on time. This can be done at either the Computer Configuration or User configuration level. You will notice the performance increase the most when several GPOs apply to your user logon.

Here's how to disable the User or Computer settings for a given GPO:

1. Open the Group Policy Object that you want to edit.

2. In the console tree, right-click the icon or name of the Group Policy Object, and then click Properties.

3. On the General tab, select the Disable User Configuration Settings check box, and then click OK.

## Slow Link Processing

If you are accessing the settings of a GPO over a slow connection to a domain controller, those settings can take a long time to be sent over the network. This problem occurs most often when a user is logging on over a remote connection with no domain controller at the local site, although if traffic is congested, slow links can also be detected when using the LAN.

The slow link settings prevent certain GPO settings from being sent, thus improving GPO processing time. By default, however, registry-based settings applied by administrative templates, and security settings will always be applied. Other settings are not applied when a slow link is detected.

By default, a link is judged fast or slow status based on a test ping to the domain controller from where the GPO must be retrieved. If it takes less than two seconds for a response from the server, the link is considered fast, and all policy settings for the GPO will be applied.

Most of the settings that apply to slow link detection are located under the Computer Configuration\Administrative Templates\System section of the Group Policy Object Editor. Of specific note here is the Group Policy Slow Link Detection setting, which is located within the Computer Configuration\Administrative Templates\System\Group Policy node. Configuring this setting specifies what is considered a slow link for this particular GPO.

---

 **TIP** If you set the Slow Link setting value to 0, all connections will be considered fast.

---

Now that you understand the rules that govern Group Policy behavior, it's time to create a Group Policy Object. A great way to get comfortable with Group Policies is to configure one that will make changes to the user environment. These changes are relatively easy to configure (as explored previously, settings that affect the user environment are usually either Enabled, Disabled, or Not Configured), and for the most part, the changes made with these settings are hard to miss.

## Planning a Strategy for Configuring the User and Computer Environment by Using Group Policy

The following are the steps necessary to create a Group Policy Object. The one demonstrated here will be linked to the domain container, but you can create the GPO in any Active Directory container where GPOs can be linked. As you learn, you should experiment with several settings, and on several containers.

## Lab Exercise 22.3: Preventing Access to the Control Panel

The idea here is to show one example of a setting that will have an immediate impact on the desktop. Other examples will follow. Here's what to do:

1. Open the Active Directory Users and Computers MMC snap-in, and choose the Domain object.

2. Right-click, and choose Properties from the context menu. In the Properties dialog box, click the Group Policy tab.

3. As seen in Figure 22-8, the Group Policy tab has several buttons that will help you manage the Group Policy Objects linked to the domain container. All objects in Active Directory that can have a GPO linked to them will have a Group Policy tab that, except for the listing of the GPOs, will look exactly the same. Several buttons are available on this tab.

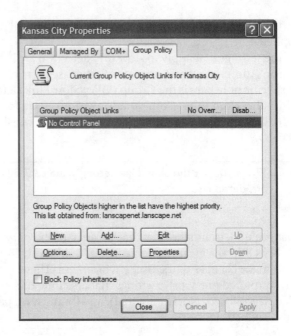

**Figure 22-8**
The Group
Policy tab

- **New** This button lets you create a new Group Policy Object from scratch. Nothing will be configured in this GPO until you edit its settings, so simply creating a GPO will have no effect on the computing environment. Further, this GPO will be linked automatically to the current Active Directory container.

- **Add** This button lets you add an existing GPO to the list of Group Policies linked to the current container. Adding a GPO places it at the bottom of the list.

- **Edit** This button opens the Group Policy Object Editor, which allows you to configure the settings of the selected Group Policy Object. After making changes to the GPO, changes are applied according to the Group Policy refresh intervals discussed in the next section.

- **Options** This button lets you configure the options of the GPO, including the option to enable or disable the GPO. It also lets you specify whether its settings may be blocked or overwritten by GPOs lower in the processing inheritance chain.

- **Delete** It seems straightforward, but there are actually a couple of facets to the delete behavior. When you have a GPO selected, clicking this button opens a dialog box that lets you either delete the link from the GPO to the container, or delete the GPO altogether. If you delete the link, the GPO is still available for processing at other containers. If you delete the GPO completely, settings that you might want applied at other levels will no longer apply.

- **Properties**  Like any other Active Directory object, the GPO has a set of properties with which you manage the object. Especially significant here is the Security tab of the GPO. This holds the access control list of the GPO. And just like the ACLs we examined earlier when looking at delegating authority over OUs, the tab specifies who can do what to the object. In the case of a GPO, you can use the ACL to control who can apply the settings of the GPO.

- **Up and Down**  These buttons become available when two or more GPOs are listed for a single Active Directory entity. These buttons let you move the GPOs up and down the list, which can significantly impact the effective settings because of the processing order. Remember that the processing occurs from bottom to top, and the last settings processed are the effective settings where conflicts are present.

Also note the Block Policy Inheritance check box at the bottom of the Group Policy tab. This option allows you to block a setting's inheritance characteristics from parent-level Group Policies, much like the blocking of NTFS permissions when configuring properties of file and folder resources. More to come about the blocking of Group Policy inheritance later in the chapter.

**NOTE**  And don't forget: when in doubt, right-click. You can right-click the GPO name in the listing on the Group Policy tab and a context menu appears, letting you configure certain aspects of behavior, such as the No Override behavior, that are also available using the buttons just described.

4. Click the New button to create a new GPO that will automatically be linked to this container. The GPO is created at the bottom of the list if an existing GPO is linked. The GPO is named New Group Policy Object. You should change this name to something that will indicate what the GPO is for. As shown previously in Figure 22-8, the new GPO is called the No Control Panel policy.

**NOTE**  Unless you're in a test environment, you shouldn't give GPOs names like My Really Neat Group Policy. No one except you would understand the significance of the GPO, and other people would have to sift through the mountain of settings available to figure it out. If, on the other hand, the policy were called Software Policy, or better yet, Service Pack Policy, other administrators would have a pretty good idea of where to start looking to make edits to the policy settings. You might even confuse yourself if, when looking at a GPO you haven't edited in a while, you stumble upon GPO names such as My Really Neat Group Policy.

5. Click the Edit button after creating a new GPO to begin modifying its settings. If you have the proper permissions, you could also edit existing GPOs you see in the list.

6. The Group Policy Object Editor (GPOE) opens, as shown in Figure 22-9. The two main nodes of the GPOE are Computer Configuration settings, and User Configuration settings. In the example here, the administrator wants to remove the Control Panel from users' desktops, so she expands the User Configuration settings, and then Administrative Templates. Then she chooses the Control Panel node.

7. To configure an Administrative Template setting, generally, you just double-click the setting, like Prohibit Access To The Control Panel, and enable the settings with a click of a check box. Sometimes, you also need to set parameters, as is the case with most of the security settings.

8. Once you've configured the settings, close the Group Policy Object Editor, and then click OK in the Active Directory object's Properties dialog box. The settings apply when the GPO is refreshed.

 **NOTE** Although you can get to the properties of almost any other file, folder, print, or Active Directory object by double-clicking, if you double-click the name of a GPO, you'll launch the Group Policy Object Editor, not the properties of the GPO.

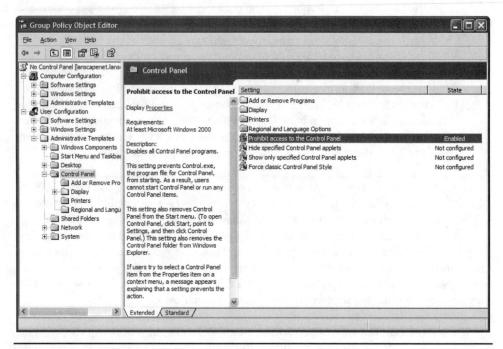

**Figure 22-9** The Group Policy Object Editor

You're done! If you've followed the preceding steps, a GPO is now linked to the domain container that will prevent all users in the domain from accessing the Control Panel. No one will be exempt from this setting until other GPOs are created for organizational units, or until exceptions are configured.

So when will the new setting take effect for clients of the domain? The next section provides the answer.

## Group Policy Refresh Interval

Active Directory domain controllers check for any changes to Group Policy Objects and refresh Group Policy application every five minutes. Member servers running Windows Server 2003 and Windows 2000 Server, or client computers running Windows 2000 Professional and XP Professional refresh their Group Policy settings every 90 minutes, with a 30-minute random offset. This prevents all client computers from refreshing their Group Policy settings from domain controllers simultaneously, thereby keeping the network free of crippling amounts of Group Policy traffic.

The refresh mechanism occurs by checking the version number of the GPO. Each time a setting is changed, the version number is incremented, and if a newer GPO is found, it is requested from the client machine. Under most circumstances, you won't have to spend any time worrying about Group Policy refreshes; they take care of themselves quite nicely. You can, however, force an immediate refresh of Group Policy settings.

## Permissions over Group Policy Objects

When you set the permissions of a Group policy object, you define two types of behaviors:

- Which users can make changes to the Group policy objects itself
- Which users will have the Group Policy apply

To understand this better, it helps to take a look at the default behaviors of a newly created GPO. When a new Group Policy is created, like in the previous example, it inherits the access control list of its parent container, if applicable. When you're working in a domain, the parent container of an organizational unit is the domain container. Organizational units, then, can be the parent containers of other OUs.

 **TIP** Just like when dealing with NTFS, printer, or share-level permissions, the Deny permission is a trump card of sorts. It is stronger than the Allow permission.

By default, the Authenticated Users group is granted the Read permission and the Apply Group Policy permission. As a result, everyone who is able to log on successfully—provided their account lives in an OU where a Group Policy has been created—will have the Group Policy processed.

This process is really not different than editing the ACL for an OU to decide who does what to the OU. The only real difference is that the Group Policy Object does not include a handy Delegation Of Control Wizard to help you through the process.

## Lab Exercise 22.4: Setting Permissions for a GPO

You use the following procedure to set permissions and/or delegate control on a Group Policy Object:

1. Open Active Directory Users and Computers and select the domain container where the Group Policy is linked for which you want to configure permissions.

2. Right-click and choose Properties, and then navigate to the Group Policy tab. Select the GPO you want to configure, and click the Properties button.

3. The GPO Properties dialog box includes the Security tab, where you set the permissions over the objects, as shown in Figure 22-10. There are several standard permissions to choose from, outlined in Table 22-1.

**Figure 22-10**
The Security
tab of the GPO
properties

| Permission | Significance |
|---|---|
| Full Control | Enables the user or group the ability to perform all administrative tasks over the GPO. This includes changing the permissions of the GPO and deleting the GPO itself. |
| Read | Allows a user or group to read the settings of the GPO. This permission is also required to apply the GPO, and it is a default permission of the Authenticated Users group. |
| Write | Lets a user or group make changes to the settings of the GPO. Note that to make changes, you also need Read permissions because to make GPO edits, you must first be able to read the GPO. |
| Create All Child Objects | Lets a user or group add objects to GPO settings. This comes into play mostly when using the Software Installation settings, as users who associate software packages with a GPO are also adding child objects. (More about the software distribution settings in Chapter 23.) |
| Delete All Child Objects | Allows removal of an object that may have been created for an OU. The inverse of the Create Child Objects permission. |
| Apply Group Policy | Applies the Group Policy settings. This permission is also granted to the Authenticated Users group by default so that users who successfully log on have the policy settings apply. |

**Table 22-1**    Standard GPO Permissions

## Delegating Control over a GPO

The bigger your Active Directory enterprise, the further you're going to be from the daily tasks of administering users. As you've seen, some of the first tasks to be delegated include adding user accounts and changing passwords. But as the organization continues to grow, this delegation ability eventually extends to your Group Policy Objects.

Fortunately, the same mechanism exists for the delegation of Group Policy control: the access control list. As you've just seen, the ACL defines who does what to the GPO. Three permissions are used to delegate control over the GPOs in your enterprise:

- Permission to create Group Policy Objects
- Permission to edit Group Policy settings
- Permission to link Group Policies

The significance of these three permissions is fairly self-explanatory by now, and the procedure for each looks almost exactly the same. In the interests of space and tree conservation, let's take a look at how to delegate the editing of any particular GPO. Here's how:

1. Open the Group Policy Object Editor.

2. In the console tree, right-click the icon or name of the Group Policy Object, and then click Properties.

3. Do any of the following:

- To add a user or group of users, click the Security tab, and then click Add. Type the name of the user or group of users, and then click OK.

- To give a user or group the ability to edit a Group Policy Object, in the Permissions For Authenticated Users section, select the appropriate check boxes for the permissions you want to give. When you are finished, click OK.

- If you do not want a policy to apply to a group or and individual user, under Permissions For Authenticated Users, clear the Allow check box for Apply Group Policy. When you are finished, click OK.

By delegating control over the settings of a GPO, a user is able to change the way a certain Active Directory container is administered without otherwise affecting the administrative structure of the Active Directory enterprise. Further, by associating many GPOs to a container, you can subdivide the settings other users can affect.

**User and Group Permission Interaction**    If you're familiar with NTFS and share-level permissions (they are briefly discussed in Chapter 4), you are aware that when access to an object is evaluated, the effective permission is the combination of the user and group permissions. That is, if a security group has the Change permission over an object, and a user has the Read permission, the effective permission for the user is Read and Change. This same behavior, by the way, also applies to Active Directory Objects like organizational units and domains: permissions are cumulative.

**NOTE**    For a detailed discussion of user and group permissions when dealing with NTFS resources, please refer to Part I of this book.

When evaluating the effective permissions to Group Policy Objects, however, we need to shift our paradigms. As you reconcile the effective Group Policy Object permissions, know that the user-level permissions take precedence over any group-level settings for which the user is a member. Again, they are not cumulative; the user permission is trump, no matter whether the permission is higher or lower than the group's setting.

For example, if a user were a part of a security group that had the Read and Create Child Objects permission, but the user account was granted only the Read permission, the effective permission for that user would be the Read permission to the GPO.

When you are creating a delegation strategy for your GPOs, also bear in mind that only members of the Domain Admins and Enterprise Admins security groups can grant the Write permission to a Group Policy Object, and thereby grant the user the ability to edit the particular GPO. Even if you have delegated a high level of administrative privileges over an OU in your enterprise, that user will still not be able to delegate the ability to change any GPOs he might create to manage that OU. That is, of course, unless his account is added to one of the aforementioned groups.

**TIP** This user-level primacy of Group Policy permissions makes the filtering of GPO scope easier to implement.

## Planning Group Policy Using the Resultant Set of Policy (RSoP)

How do you tell which Group Policy is configuring a particular setting? You don't. True, a tool in Windows 2000 lets you see which Group Policies are effective for a user, but that tool doesn't tell you anything about which settings are being configured by a particular GPO. You still have to open each of the effective GPOs to try to determine the cause of the setting you are trying to troubleshoot.

But that's no longer the case with Windows Server 2003 because of a nifty new mechanism called the Resultant Set of Policy (RSoP). This new addition to the Group Policy technology makes policy troubleshooting much easier than it was in the Windows 2000 Active Directory environment. Furthermore, you can use the RSoP engine to plan and test a set of GPOs before actual implementation.

RSoP is referred to as an engine, or a mechanism, but not a tool. That's because at its heart, the RSoP is a just reporter. You do not actually use the RSoP; rather, you use tools that are written to take advantage of the RSoP query engine. This query engine has the ability to poll both existing policies, and also any policies you plan to implement, and then reports results of those queries to the various management and reporting interfaces. In this way, it can be used to predict the effects of a new GPO before it is rolled out to the production environment. Poor anticipation of Group Policy effects can cause major problems on any network, and Group Policy settings and behavior must be carefully understood before implementation.

The RSoP engine is capable of polling policies based on site, domain, and organizational unit, as you might expect, and also the local policy effective for a domain controller.

## Using the Resultant Set of Policy (RSoP) Planning Mode

RSoP has the capability of supplying details about all policy settings configured, including Group Policy settings from Administrative Templates, Folder Redirection, Internet Explorer, Security settings, Scripts, and even Software Installation.

As you have learned, a user logging on can have multiple Group Policy Objects applied to not only his or her user account, but to the computer at startup as well. As you have also seen, these settings can sometimes conflict, and certain policies take precedence over others, depending on a variety of variables. It can be confusing to determine who got which setting from where. The RSoP helps you sort it all out.

The RSoP reporting mechanism can be used in one of two modes:

- **Planning mode** Lets you simulate what would happen if you were to apply the settings in a GPO or group of GPOs, to a computer or user.

- **Logging mode** Provides reportage about the existing policy settings, and is a wonderful troubleshooting feature for the reasons outlined previously. It lets you quickly identify the effective settings for a computer and user, and where those settings came from.

**PART IV**

It's probably easier to understand the Resultant Set of Policy feature, however, when you see it in action. The query engine relies on the use of three tools, each discussed in the following sections, to extract meaningful results about how best to configure Group Policy.

### The RSoP Snap-In
You can run an RSoP query on almost any object from within Active Directory Users and Computers using the following procedure.

## Lab Exercise 22.5: Using RSoP to Query an OU
In the example, you run a query on an OU.

1. In the console tree of Active Directory Users and Computers, right-click the organizational unit on which you want to run RSoP.

2. From the context menu, choose All Tasks, and then click Resultant Set Of Policy (Planning).

3. The Resultant Set Of Policy Wizard launches, as shown in Figure 22-11. Using the wizard, you will have the options to simulate settings for an individual user, all users in a container, an individual computer, or all computers in a container.

4. The next few screens of the wizard help you fine-tune the query, simulating changes to particular security groups.

**Figure 22-11**
Running an
RSoP query

5. When you're done, click Finish on the summary page of the wizard.

You might find the results a bit anticlimactic, however, in that there aren't any results you can view—yet. You have just created a query, but now you must use the RSoP MMC snap-in to actually view the results of your query. Fortunately, it launches after your query has finished. You can also add the Resultant Set of Policy snap-in to any custom MMC.

The Resultant Set of Policy snap-in presents you with a view similar to the Group policy Object Editor. The difference is that the query shows you only configured settings, as in Figure 22-12.

## Lab Exercise 22.6: Using RSoP in Logging Mode

You can also use the RSoP MMC snap-in in logging mode, as described earlier. Here's how:

1. With the Resultant Set of Policy snap-in loaded into an MMC, right-click the Resultant Set of Policy node, and then choose Generate RSoP Data.

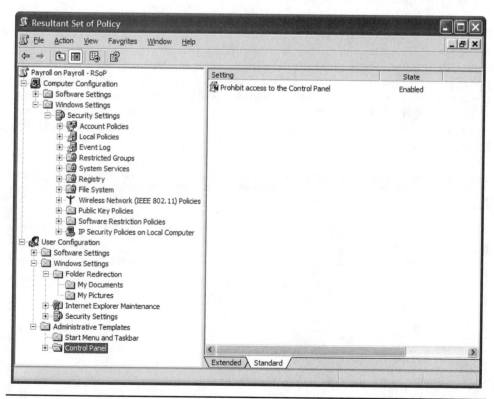

**Figure 22-12**   Results of a query in the Resultant Set of Policy snap-in

2. The Resultant Set Of Policy Wizard launches. Click Next on the welcome screen.

3. On the Mode Selection screen, choose Logging mode, and click Next. (Note that you can use this tool for planning here without using Active Directory Users and Computers.)

4. On the Computer Selection screen, specify the computer on which to run RSoP, click Next, and then do the same on the User Selection screen. Click Next.

5. The Summary Of Selections screen lets you review selections. Click Next to let RSoP finish processing the data. Then click Finish on the Completing The Resultant Set Of Policy Wizard screen.

6. In the RSoP console tree, as shown in Figure 22-13, expand the newly created RSoP query to view the data. Notice that the login data helps you identify what the effective setting is, and where that policy setting has come from.

You shouldn't be tested on the mechanics of RSoP Wizard use. Just know that the RSoP snap-in is quite a complex utility. The whys and whens to use the tool are what you need to know come test time.

## Advanced System Information – Policy

You access this tool through the Help and Support Center, but it uses the same RSoP engine to turn out meaningful information. With the Advances System Information – Policy tool, you can view a printable HTML report of Group Policy settings applied to the computer and the user currently logged on. In this way, it behaves much the same as the logging mode of the MMC snap-in, but it presents information in a more user-friendly, portable manner. There is no planning mode equivalent when using this RSoP utility.

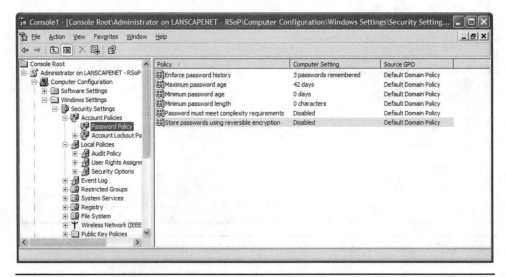

**Figure 22-13**    Viewing logging data with the RSoP snap-in

# Lab Exercise 22.7: Generating an HTML Report with RSoP

Here's the procedure to generate an HTML report using the Advanced System Information – Policy tool:

1. From the Start menu, open the Help and Support Center.

2. Click the Tools link under the Support Tasks section.

3. Under the Tools section, expand the Help and Support Center Tools, and then click Advanced System Information.

4. In the Advanced System Information details section in the right pane, choose View Group Policy settings applied.

5. After processing, a report is generated like the one shown in Figure 22-14. Scroll to locate the results you want to view.

**NOTE** At the bottom of the report is a link that lets you save the report to an .htm file.

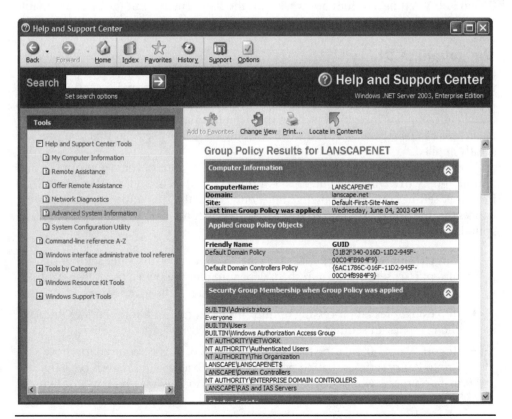

**Figure 22-14** Using Advanced System Information – Policy to view policy settings

## gpresult

The third tool that makes use of the RSoP engine is called gpresult. You can use it at the command line to produce a detailed report similar to the information generated when using the RSoP MMC utility in logging mode. One possible reason you might select gpresult over the RSoP snap-in is that it lets you export query results to a text file for use in other applications.

Here's the syntax for the gpresult utility:

```
gpresult [/s Computer [/u Domain\User /p Password]] [/user TargetUserName] [/
scope {user | computer}] [{/v | /z}]
```

You can use gpresult with the /s switch to specify the target computer on which to run the utility. The default computer on which the report will run will be the local machine. The u/ switch lets you specify a user other than the one currently logged on, and the / user switch, for example, lets you identify the name of the user whose RSoP information is to be displayed.

Because the RSoP snap-in is new to the Windows Server 2003 operating system, a familiarity with the tools that work with RSoP is highly recommended. You will likely see mention of one, if not all, utilities on the 70-294 exam.

Another command-line tool is worth knowing about that helps configure and apply Group Policy settings. It does not work with the RSoP engine, but it can be a valuable utility when you want to enforce an immediate policy refresh.

## The gpupdate Utility

Another command-line utility used to manage Group Policy Objects is the gpupdate utility. gpupdate made its debut with the Windows XP Professional operating system, and it is used most commonly to force an immediate refresh of the Group Policy at a particular computer instead of waiting the default interval for a GPO to naturally refresh. This can be especially effective when changing security settings that you want instantly applied.

Also, the command-line utility is quite flexible in its application—you can use it to refresh both Active Directory and local Group Policy Objects; and you can use it to refresh user settings only, computer settings only, or both. This utility replaces and enhances the functionality of the secedit /refreshpolicy utility used in Windows 2000. The gpupdate utility is used with the following switches:

- **/target:{computer|user}** Lets you specify that only Computer settings or current User settings get refreshed, depending on the switch used. By default, gpupdate processes both the computer settings and the user settings.

- **/force** Ignores all processing optimization settings for Group Policy Objects and reapplies all settings.

- **/logoff** Logs off after the refresh has completed. This is required for those Group Policy settings that do not process on a background refresh cycle but that do process when the user logs on. For instance, when you have configured a new Software Installation and/or Folder Redirection policy, the settings will not take effect until the user logs back on—thus, the need for the switch.

- **/boot**  Restarts the computer after the refresh has completed. This is required for Group Policy settings that do not process on a background refresh cycle but that do process when the computer starts up. A perfect use for this is when you have configured a new computer Software Installation policy.

# Configuring the User Environment by Using Group Policy

As mentioned in the beginning of the chapter, once you learn the fundamentals of Active Directory administration using Group Policy Objects, the rest of the discussion just looks at examples of what a GPO can do. Two of the uses of a Group Policy Object specifically mentioned in Microsoft exam objectives include the enrollment of a user certificate, and the redirection of special folders. Keep in mind, however, that these are just a few examples of what's possible. You might see others specified on the exam; the two discussed here are likely candidates for a question or two.

Generally, there are two ways to manipulate the end-user experience for Windows users: You can either change settings with the various applets in the Control Panel, or you can use the Administrative Templates setting when configuring Group Policies. When you edit the Control Panel, essentially, you are editing the registry of the local machine. Changes made apply either to all users of the machine, or just a single user, depending on which configuration change is made. What's more, the changes via the Control Panel can be overwritten by a user with access to the Control Panel and with knowledge of what they're doing. (Actually, knowing what to do isn't necessarily a requisite for making the changes with the Control Panel, much to the bane of many a system admin.)

The advantage of using Group Policies is that the changes you make become a permanent part of the user desktop, at least until the Group Policy is no longer effective, and these changes can be configured on multiple computers at a time. In other words, in an Active Directory environment, typically you will be managing the end-user environment using Group Policy. The following sections looks at some of the ways to effectively manage this environment.

## Automatically Enroll User Certificates by Using Group Policy

Another way a GPO can affect the end-user experience is when it is used to automatically enroll a digital certificate. These certificates can be used to positively identify users, computers, or sometimes applications in an open network. A common use of certificates is during Internet communication, when credit card or other confidential information must be passed over a public network. How do you know the computer you're sending your credit card information to is who it claims to be? Via a digital certificate.

*Certificates* present yet another way to positively identify users when accessing network resources. The end result is the same as though the user provided a user name and password, yet the process can be automated with certificates.

Before a certificate can be put to use, it must be requested and then enrolled. This enrollment process maps a digital certificate to the entity needing identification. Enrollment can be performed either manually or automatically through the settings of a Group Policy Object.

Certificates take advantage of a public/private key infrastructure. A public key value is bound to the user account, device, or application for communication with a server application service that holds the corresponding private key. The server application then uses public key technology to authenticate the (user, app, computer) using this certificate. If authenticated, the account is logged on. Once the certificate has been enrolled, all of this authentication behavior occurs transparently to the end user.

**NOTE** For more information about digital certificates, please refer to Part III of this book.

Combine this advantage with these: certificates can be widely distributed, issued by multiple parties, and furthermore, can be verified by simply examining the certificate, without having to refer to a centralized database, like the Active Directory database. For instance, think a certificate the same way you think of a driver's license: because the certificate is issued by a trusted party, you do not have to verify a person's identity against the Department of Motor Vehicles database. The certificate issued is proof enough because the certificate issuer is a trusted authority.

However, Windows Server 2003, along with other operating systems and administration tools, are built to deal only with accounts, not certificates. The workaround, then, is to create a mapping between a certificate and a user account. By doing so, administrators get the benefits of both certificates and user accounts: the operating system persists with its use of user names and passwords, while access to additional resources in nonsecure networks can be accomplished with digital certificates. Group Policy Objects can help automate this enrollment process.

When setting up a GPO to automatically enroll certificates, you'll need the following baseline information:

- The certificate type for which you want the computers to automatically enroll. Not every certificate can be enrolled automatically, because only certificate types associated with computers, not users, can be enrolled automatically. Some examples include these:
  - Computer certificates
  - IPSec certificates
  - Web Server certificates
- The identity of the certificate authority (CA) that is issuing the certificate

To aid in this setup, there is a list of predefined CAs to choose from. The CA selected must be capable of issuing a certificate of the type you have specified for automatic enrollment to occur.

Follow these steps to complete automatic certificate enrollment:

1. Open Active Directory Users and Computers, or Active Directory Sites and Services, and locate the Group Policy Object you want to edit. (Remember, you right-click the Active Directory container, choose Properties, and then select the Group Policy tab.)

2. From the GPOE, expand Computer Configuration, then Windows Settings, the Security Settings, then Public Key Policies, and select Automatic Certificate Request Settings.

3. Right-click Automatic Certificate Request Settings, and from the context menu, choose New, and then Automatic Certificate Request.

4. The Automatic Certificate Request Setup Wizard launches, as in Figure 22-15. Use the steps in the wizard to create an automatic certificate request for all computers to whom the GPO will be effective.

5. You'll get a warning right away that instructs you how to populate Active Directory with certificate templates. Complete this step opening the Run dialog box and typing **certtmpl.msc** to continue.

 **NOTE**  A certificate based on the selected template will be requested automatically after any of the following events: a user logs on, a GPO refresh occurs (including a restart), or a computer joins the domain and is subject to an existing GPO setting.

**Figure 22-15**
Automatically enrolling certificates through Group Policy

## Redirecting Folders by Using Group Policy

Windows Server 2003 makes it easier to implement folder redirection for commonly used folders like My Documents, the Start menu, and Application Data (which can include the Outlook data store, for example). With folder redirection, users store files on what they think is a local drive on their computer. Behind the scenes, however, these files are being sent to a network file server, where the files can generally be more easily secured. Whether they are copied or moved to the redirected location depends on how you configure the policy behavior.

Folder redirection is especially handy of you want to simplify a backup scheme for users' working data. What's more, it's all transparent, so redirecting folders lets you accomplish this task without educating users about where their data is stored. They can use the folders they are comfortable with—like My Documents—for their working data, instead of having to be educated about file servers, mapped network drives, and so forth.

There are many additional advantages of folder redirection, including these:

- If your network makes use of roaming profiles, only the network path to the My Documents folder is stored as part of the roaming user profile, rather than the entire contents of the My Documents folder. This is significant because the My Documents folder can become quite large. If it's the place where users store music, for example, it can quickly reach several GBs in size. Using a roaming profile, the My Documents contents are copied back and forth between the client computer and the server each time the user logs on or off, thus slowing logon times sometimes by several minutes or more. When the folder is redirected, though, just the information about the path is sent and stored, and the logon times can be dramatically improved. (This is a common cause of slow logon times, and why roaming profiles are rarely recommend, except maybe for administrators.)

- If you are not using roaming profiles and a user logs on from different computers, his or her documents in a redirected folder are always available, because while the profile does not roam, the GPOs will follow the user around.

- Data that is stored in a shared network folder can be backed up as part of routine system administration. This is safer because it requires no action on the part of the user.

- You can leverage the ability to set disk quotas on a file server (as long as the redirected location is on an NTFS drive), thus limiting the amount of space a user can commit to all those MP3s.

- You don't have to redirect to a network folder. If you redirect to a different partition than the one storing the operating system, data is safer in the event the OS needs to be reinstalled.

**NOTE** By the time you've gotten to this section, you should have seen and configured disk quotas. For instructions on disk quotas, please refer back to Part I of this book.

The Windows Server 2003 implementation is easier because you no longer have to use variables such as the *%username%* part of the redirection path. (This variable uses the user name when building the redirection path to the server.) Furthermore, an option now exists for redirecting the contents of My Documents to a user's home directory. Before Windows Server 2003, if administrators wanted to centralize backup, they would typically either redirect the My Documents folder or configure a home directory for a user, but not both. Now you can combine the two behaviors seamlessly into the end-user experience in environments where home directories are already deployed. If you have recently upgraded from a Windows NT 4.0 network, this might indeed be the case.

## Lab Exercise 22.8: Redirecting a Folder

Here is how to redirect the contents of the My Documents folder to a home directory:

1. Open Active Directory Users and Computers and select the container where you want to implement this redirection setting. This will normally apply to the domain container (to have it affect all users) or an OU (to affect a specific user), but you may have it apply to a site as well.

2. From the properties of the container, select the Group Policy tab and either edit an existing GPO or create a new one with a name like Folder Redirect, and edit its settings.

3. In the Group policy Object Editor, expand User Configuration, then Windows Settings, then Folder Redirection, and then select My Documents.

4. Right-click My Documents, and then click Properties.

5. As shown in Figure 22-16, you configure the redirection location from the Target tab. In the Setting section, click Basic - Redirect Everyone's Folder To The Same Location.

6. Under Target Folder Location, click Redirect To The User's Home Directory, and then click OK. Close the Group Policy Object Editor when you're finished.

**NOTE** You should implement redirection to a home folder location only if the network has already deployed home folders. You set the user's home directory from the Properties pages in Active Directory Users and Computers. A network share is also necessary for implementation of home folders.

PART IV

**Figure 22-16**
Redirecting folder
location for My
Documents

Redirecting My Documents to a home folder location is just one commonly used example of the control you have with Folder Redirection. Unfortunately, there is no room in this condensed format to explore all redirection settings in detail. It will be up to you to experiment with this until you get the gist of it.

You further manage the settings of Folder Redirection on the Settings tab in each folder's Properties dialog box, as shown in Figure 22-17.

Of interest here is the check box labeled Grant The User Exclusive Rights To My Documents. When you select this check box, only the user and the Local System account will have full control over the folder. All other users, administrators included, are denied access to the folder. (Administrators can still get in the folder if they want, but they have to take ownership first and edit the folder's ACL.) If you clear this check box when configuring the policy settings, no changes will be made to the permissions on the redirected folder, and any permissions currently set will remain in effect.

## Restricting Group Membership with Group Policy

You can also use Group Policies to control membership in certain Active Directory groups. One security hole that has been found in a number of audits is that the membership of some powerful groups, such as the Domain Admins or Server Operators, is not very well managed. Over time, users are added to groups like these as the people taking care of your network come and go. For example, it's not uncommon for IT consultants to add themselves to the Administrators local group, or worse, the Domain Admins group, for purposes of tweaking a network's computers.

**Figure 22-17**
Configuring
the settings of
redirected folders

Once that consultant leaves, though, it takes a vigilant administrator to remember to take those temporary accounts out of the groups they were in, and any account that's in the Domain Admins group is a potential security risk to your network.

To combat this, you can use the Restricted Groups feature. With restricted groups, group membership is defined by a Group Policy, not by the Active Directory Users and Computers MMC snap-in. You can still put members in the restricted groups you've configured using Active Directory Users and Computers, but those members will be removed anytime during a Group Policy refresh. Conversely, any members who might have been removed from the restricted groups with the Active Directory Users and Computers interface will be added.

## Lab Exercise 22.9: Using Restricted Groups

Here's how you could enforce a Restricted Groups policy:

1. Open up the GPOE on the Group Policy for which you will define a restricted group. Usually you will do this on the Default Domain policy.

2. Expand the Computer Configuration settings, then the Windows Settings, then Security settings.

3. Right-click the Restricted Groups node, and from the context menu, choose Add Group.

4. In the Add Group dialog box, type the name of the group for which you will restrict membership, or click Browse to would like restricted policy and click OK.

5. Now that you've defined the restricted group, it's time to add members to the group. To do so, perform one of the following:

- If you created a new group, click Add Members.
- If you are working with an existing group, select it in the details pane of the restricted groups Group Policy node. Right-click, choose Properties, and then click Add from the Properties dialog box.

6. To add this group as a member of any other groups, in the This Group Is A Member Of section, choose Add, and then type the name of the group, and click OK.

By configuring restricted groups for your enterprise, you can help close this significant security hold found in most networks today. In fact, when you define this policy for the Administrators group, all members not defined in the restricted groups setting will be removed from the Administrators group when the Group Policy Object is applied to the local computer.

# Chapter Review

A good 40 percent of the test will probably in some way check your understanding of Group Policy Objects, and the material in this chapter laid the groundwork for that understanding.

By the end of the review questions that follow, you should have a clear picture of what Group Policies are used for, which Active Directory objects they can be linked to, what the default processing order is for Group Policy application, and which settings take precedence when Group Policy setting conflicts are encountered during processing. You should also be aware of the inheritance behavior of Group Policy settings as they are applied through the Active Directory hierarchy. In addition, you should be aware of the many instances where exceptions to the default processing order might be made.

You should also understand how to use utilities like gpresult and gpupdate to apply Group Policy settings without waiting the default refresh interval, and how to generate reports on effective Group Policy settings using the Resultant Set of Policy tools.

Finally, you should come away with a better understanding of which kinds of settings can be managed to define the end-user experience, and how some of these settings can be configured.

## Questions

1. You are the administrator of a Windows Server 2003 domain. You configure the default domain policy GPO so that users do not have the ability to access the Shutdown command from their Start menu. However, when walking back from getting coffee later that day, you find that some users in the Accounting department still have the ability to shut down their computers from the Start

menu. Others in the organization do not have this option. What is the likely cause of the anomaly?

    A. The Accounting department users have not logged off and have not had the GPO refresh.

    B. The users are also in the Domain Admins global group, and are therefore exempt.

    C. The Accounting OU has the No Override option set for a GPO linked to it.

    D. The Accounting OU has the Allow Inheritable Permissions check box cleared on the Group Policy tab of its Properties dialog box.

2. GPO settings are stored by Active Directory domain controllers in two locations. What are they? (Choose all that apply.)

    A. SYSVOL folder

    B. Group policy template

    C. WINDOWS directory

    D. Group Policy container

3. You are the administrator of a Windows Server 2003 domain. Users in the domain do not log on and off frequently, and you want the changes to the GPO settings to refresh more quickly than the default settings. What should you configure to make these changes?

    A. Use the ntdsutil utility to change the default refresh rate from 90 minutes to 15 minutes.

    B. Change the policy refresh rate using the Group Policy Object Editor and change the system options under the User Configuration Administrative Templates.

    C. Make any GPO changes to already established GPOs; changes made to existing GPOs are refreshed immediately on client systems.

    D. Use the gpupdate utility to immediately refresh policy every time a GPO is edited.

4. You are the enterprise admin for a Windows Server 2003 network. You have set up Group Policies affecting user desktops for the OUs, Domain, and Site. One of the settings in the Group Policy controls whether users will have icons on their desktop and is named Hide And Disable All Items On The Desktop. If the same setting is enabled at site level, disabled at domain level, and not configured at OU level, will a user who is affected by all three policies have icons on her desktop?

    A. Yes.

    B. No.

**C.** The setting that is highest in the settings dialog box will win.

**D.** The setting that is lowest in the settings dialog box will win.

5. You are the enterprise admin for a Windows Server 2003 network. You have set up Group Policies affecting user desktops for the OUs, Domain, and Site. One of the settings in the Group Policy requires that a user must use a complex password. If the same setting is enabled at site level, disabled at domain level, and enabled at OU level, will a user that is affected by all three policies have to use a complex password?

**A.** Yes.

**B.** No.

**C.** The setting that is highest in the settings dialog box will win.

**D.** The setting that is lowest in the settings dialog box will win.

6. You are a domain admin for a Windows Server 2003 network. You have created a hierarchy of OUs. You wish to roll out a Group Policy that will affect one entire hierarchy of OUs, but not the entire domain. You would like to do this with the least administrative effort. How should you roll out the Group Policy?

**A.** Create the Group Policy at domain level first and then use Block Inheritance to filter out the OUs you don't want to receive the Group Policy.

**B.** Create the Group Policy at the parent OU and then link it to all of the child OUs.

**C.** Create the Group Policy unlinked to any OU and then link it to all appropriate OUs.

**D.** Create the Group Policy at the parent OU with the default inheritance setting.

7. You are an OU admin of a Windows Server 2003 domain. You have linked a Group Policy that prevents all users in your OU from accessing the Internet. Many other OU admins have used this policy with great success. Two new users, Dave and Sue, are added to your OU. You happen to be walking by Dave's desk one day and notice that he is on the Internet. Later you see that Sue is also able to access the Internet. You check to make sure the Group Policy is in force for all other users and find that it is. Why are Dave and Sue able to access the Internet?

**A.** Because their accounts were not originally created in your OU, you have no control over them.

**B.** They have been prevented from having that Group Policy applied to them by their previous OU admin.

**C.** You are not the enterprise admin.

**D.** The Group Policy should have been linked to their previous OU before the accounts were moved into your OU.

8. You are the domain admin of a Windows Server 2003 domain. You have linked three different Group Policies to the same domain and are concerned that some of the settings in the policies conflict with each other. Which are true with respect to your management of these three policies? (Choose all that apply.)

   A. The policies will all be applied to the domain.

   B. When there are settings that conflict, the last policy that is applied will be the effective setting.

   C. The policies will be applied in the order in which they are listed from top to bottom.

   D. If any user and computer settings directly conflict, the user setting will be the effective setting.

9. You are the enterprise admin for a Windows Server 2003 network. You applied a computer configuration Group Policy named Securedesk to an OU named Sales. You then created a child OU within Sales named Inside Sales. Which of the following are true? (Choose all that apply.)

   A. Securedesk will apply to all users in the Sales OU.

   B. Securedesk will apply to all computers in the Inside Sales OU.

   C. Securedesk will be listed in the Group Policy Settings dialog box for the Inside Sales OU.

   D. You can use RSoP to determine where Securedesk is applied.

10. You are the OU admin for a Windows Server 2003 network. You are currently logged on to a computer, and you would like to determine which policies are being applied against the computer. Which should you do? (Choose all that apply.)

    A. Log off and then back on. Watch closely to see the list of policies that are applied at logon.

    B. Run the Active Directory Users And Computers Wizard.

    C. Run gpresult.exe from a command prompt.

    D. Use the RSoP tool from the Web.

## Answers

1. **D.** The likely explanation here is that the option Allow Inheritable Permissions From Parent To Propagate To This Object has been cleared. Even if the users in the Accounting department were also domain admins, they would still be

subject to the settings of the GPO unless a filter had been configured, and there is no indication of that in the question. The GPO would have had the 90 minutes time to refresh, and you know this because the other computers in the building show the signs of the GPO taking effect.

2. **B** and **D.** Group Policy settings are stored in the Group Policy template, and the Group Policy container. Answer A is a bit tricky because the Group Policy template exists in subfolders of the SYSVOL directory, but the GPO are not stored directly in the SYSVOL folder.

3. **B.** Using the node mentioned in the answer, you can change the default refresh rate. The gpupdate tool will refresh the Group Policies that apply for a given user or computer, but it cannot be configured to automatically refresh when GPOs are updated. The ntdsutil utility is not used for refresh of Group Policies.

4. **A.** The processing order of Group Policies in regard to their containers is always the same with the exception of account policies. The site policies are processed first, then the domain policies, and finally, the OU policies in their hierarchical order. If multiple policies exist at any level, the policy that is highest in the order in the settings dialog box will win for that container. In this scenario, the site policy took away the icons but the domain policy gave them back. Then the OU policy did not make any other changes; therefore, the icons will be on the desktop. With account policies such as password and account lockout policies, the domain setting always overrides all others.

5. **B.** The processing order of Group Policies in regard to their containers is always the same with the exception of account policies. The site policies are processed first, then the domain policies, and finally, the OU policies in their hierarchical order. If multiple policies exist at any level, the policy that is highest in the order in the settings dialog box will win for that container. In this scenario, Password Complexity is an account policy; therefore, the domain setting will prevail.

6. **D.** Because all of the OUs are in the same hierarchy, all you need to do is create the Group Policy at the parent OU with the default inheritance setting. This will ensure that the Group Policy gets passed down to the child OUs.

7. **B.** For a Group Policy to apply to a user, that user must have Read and Apply Group Policy permissions for the policy itself. It is possible to "filter" a policy from applying to users in an OU by denying Read and/or Apply Group Policy for that individual user. If this is done and then the policy is linked to another OU, the policy is still filtered for that user. If that user is then moved into the OU where the policy is linked, then the user will still be "filtered" from having the policy applied to them.

8. **A** and **B.** All of the policies that are linked to the domain will be applied. The policies will be applied in the order on the list from the bottom up. If any user and computer settings directly conflict, the computer setting will always be the effective setting.

9. **B** and **D.** The Securedesk Group Policy is configured for computers so users will not be affected by it. Securedesk will be applied to Inside Sales because the child OU will inherit the policy by default from its parent OU. You will not see Securedesk in the Group Policy Settings dialog box for Inside Sales, but you will see it where it is linked at the parent (Sales). You can use the Resulting Set of Policies tool, which can be downloaded from the Web, to determine where Securedesk is applied.

10. **C** and **D.** You can either run gpresult.exe from a command line or download RSoP from the Microsoft site on the Web. Logging off and then back on is not necessary, and you cannot see which policies are being applied.

# CHAPTER 23

# Managing and Maintaining Group Policy

In this chapter, you will learn how to

- Configure User and Computer Security settings Group Policy
- Configure an audit policy
- Deploy software through Group Policy
- Troubleshoot issues related to Group Policy application and deployment

Once you have the basics down about Group Policy behavior, Security settings and Software settings are just two more examples of the capabilities that a Group Policy can be set to manage. If it sounds simple, stay tuned. There's still quite a bit to learn about implementing both of these technologies. Each requires specialized knowledge that you're sure to encounter on the 70-294 exam.

This chapter will help you use Group Policy Objects to configure a system's Security settings, as well as to deploy and manage software. The software managed with Group Policy can be made available to both users and computers in the Active Directory enterprise.

## Configuring User and Computer Security Settings Group Policy

In Chapter 22, we examined several ways that Group Policies could manage the computing environment. Yet another example of the settings a Group Policy can be used for include the Security settings. Several areas of the computing environment can be secured with Group Policy's many settings. You access the security areas from the Windows Settings folder in each of the User Configuration and Computer Configuration nodes, as shown in Figure 23-1.

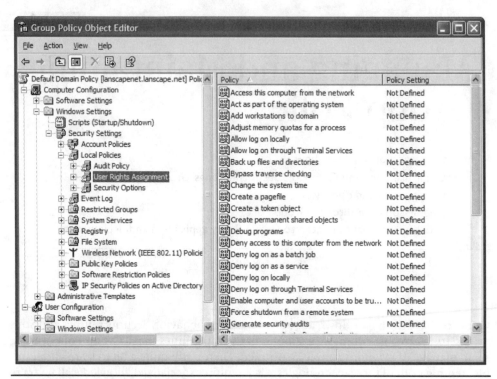

**Figure 23-1**    The multitude of security-related settings

The settings include the following:

- **Account Policies**    These settings apply to user accounts, including password, account lockout, and Kerberos-related settings.

- **Local Policies**    These settings are based on the computer you are logged on to, and they affect the abilities a user has over that system. The Local Policies settings include Audit Policies, User Rights Assignments, and Security Options.

- **Event Log**    These settings define the properties of the Application, Security, and System logs in the Event Viewer, along with access rights to each log file and retention settings.

- **Restricted Groups**    These settings are used to govern group membership. One significant security issue Microsoft found was that users, especially in larger environments, would be added to groups and then never removed. This also applied to former administrators: the person would leave the company, but the account would remain, leaving a security hazard to the domain. With Restricted Groups, you can control the membership of groups like Administrators, Power Users, Print Operators, and Domain Admins through Group Policy settings. Configuring Restricted Groups ensures the group memberships are set as specified by the editor of the Group Policy and are not subject to change.

- **System Services**  These settings are used to configure the startup behavior of services running on a computer. The configurable startup settings include Automatic, Manual, and Disabled. They also define which user accounts will have permission to read, write, delete, start, stop, or execute the service.

- **Registry**  These settings are used to configure security on specific registry keys.

- **File System**  These settings are employed to configure security on specific file paths. The Access Control List (ACL) to a file or folder is set through a Group Policy.

- **Wireless Network Policies**  These settings allow you to create and manage wireless network policies. A wizard interface will help you create each policy. They can be used to define which wireless networks a system can communicate with by using a wireless network number known as a service set identifier (SSID).

- **Public Key Policies**  These settings are used to define encrypted data recovery agents, domain roots, and trusted certificate authorities.

- **Software Restriction Policies**  These policies let you manage which software can run on a particular computer. This can be an important security level if you are worried about users downloading and running untrusted software in your network. For example, you can use these policies to block certain file type attachments from running in your e-mail program. Software Restriction Policies settings are set by first configuring a default security level of Unrestricted, which allows all programs to run within the context of the user currently logged on, or Disallowed, which does not allow programs to run. You then set up rules that provide exceptions to default security level. These rules can be based on hash algorithms or certificates, both of which are used to uniquely identify software. Other rules include path rules, which potentially let users use software if it is located in a specific directory or registry path, or Internet Zone rules, which identify software from a certain zone specified through Internet Explorer.

- **IP Security Policies**  These settings are for configuring secure IP traffic. You can use this area to set encryption rules for inbound and outbound traffic, and also specify particular networks or individual computers with which your system can communicate. Much like the Software Restriction Policies settings, IP Security Policies settings are exception-based, configured by either accepting or rejecting traffic based on a set of conditions. The different permutations of IP Security Policies are virtually infinite. There are three editable, preconfigured policies to help you on your way: Server, Client, and Secure Server.

As you can see, hundreds of settings can affect the security of a system or a network. Memorizing all of these settings is impossible and would not be helpful for purposes of the exam. However, you still need to be familiar with some of the configurable settings. Each of the Security settings could have several pages or even entire chapters of material explaining the various purposes of the settings here. Covering each of them in exhaustive detail is outside the scope of this book.

As mentioned at the beginning of Chapter 22, it would be in your best interest to experiment with some of the settings in a test environment. Of special import are the Software

Restriction Policies settings, because they are another new feature of Windows Server 2003. Microsoft doesn't want folks with a thorough knowledge of Windows 2000 to sit down and breeze through the Windows 2003 stuff.

It is important that you recognize the types of settings that help define the security environment and understand the tools used to quickly analyze and apply many of these Security settings all at once. The three tools provided to help you perform this task are the security templates, the Security Configuration and Analysis tools, which are MMC snap-ins, and the secedit command-line utility, as explained in the sections to follow.

## Security Templates

A *security template* is a single file that stores a series of security-related settings. It's a physical representation of a security configuration. By storing several security-related settings in one file, you can use this file to quickly apply tens, if not hundreds, of Security settings all at once.

The tool used to view and alter these template files is called the Security Templates MMC snap-in. With this tool, you can painlessly alter existing security templates or create new ones. You do not use the utility to create new Security settings; rather, you take existing settings and create new *configurations* of these settings. These configurations are then stored in text-based .inf files. This organization of Security settings can go a long way toward streamlining administration.

---

 **TIP** There are a couple of exceptions to what can be contained in a security template. IP Security and Public Key Policies cannot be set with a security template.

---

To use the Security Templates MMC, you must first add it to an existing MMC console or create a new one:

1. Click Start | Run, type **mmc**, and then click OK.

2. Select File | Add/Remove Snap-In.

3. In the Add/Remove Snap-In dialog box, click Add.

4. In the Available Standalone Snap-Ins window, click Security Templates, click Add, click Close, and then click OK. As shown in Figure 23-2, you will now have the ability to access the predefined template files, which are stored in the path identified in the Security Templates root node: *systemroot*\security\templates

5. Select File | Save, and name the new MMC console. It will then be added to your list of Administrative Tools.

Once you define and/or modify security templates, they can then be imported into a Group Policy Object to ease domain and organizational unit (OU) security administration. Once imported, any computer accounts or user accounts in the site, domain, and

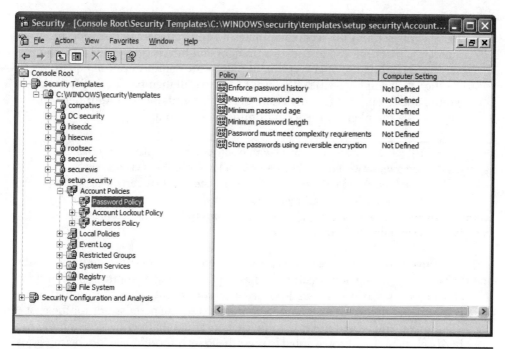

**Figure 23-2**    The predefined security templates

OU where the template has been applied will then receive the Security settings defined in the template.

Windows Server 2003 includes a collection of preconfigured security templates you can use to rapidly establish a baseline of Security settings. The predefined security templates are based on the roles computers play in a computing environment. The roles that these templates configure can be divided into three common security levels:

- **Compatible (compat.inf)**   The Compatible template is used to enable development of new applications to a standard security level in the Windows Server 2003 environment, while still allowing existing legacy applications to run under a less secure configuration. Because of the inherent security limitations that allow for maximum compatibility, you should not apply this template to domain controllers; also, you should not import it into either the default domain policy or the default domain controller policy.

- **Secure (secure*.inf)**   The Secure templates configure recommended Security settings for areas except file, folder, and registry key settings. They are commonly used to apply a range of password, audit, and account lockout policies that are much more secure than the default settings used after operating system installation.

- **Highly Secure (hisec\*.inf)** The Highly Secure templates enforce all of the Security settings the secure templates do and add even tighter security standards. They impose restrictions on data that travels between clients and servers, including use of encryption as part of the communication equation. Further, they employ restricted groups to remove all members of the Power Users group, and to ensure that only Domain Admins and the local Administrator account are members of the local Administrators group.

---

**TIP** Computers configured with highly secure templates may make communication impossible with down-level Windows clients, such as Windows 95 and 98 computers. You'll note also that certain templates, such as the Setup Security (setup security.inf) template, act as the Reset button on security for a given system, which can return the Security settings back to the way they were upon Windows installation.

---

The effective settings in the Setup Security template vary from computer to computer, and they represent the default Security settings applied during operating system installation. Other templates such as System Root Security (rootsec.inf) are used to apply security to only a very specific area of the computer—in this case, the permissions for the root of the system drive. You would use it if you were concerned that permissions on the root drive had been altered, and you wanted to press the Reset button for the root permissions.

Additionally, these predefined templates can serve as a good starting point when creating new templates. For example, you might like the Security settings of the Secure Domain Controller template (securedc.inf), with only a few modifications of the password policies. You can make the needed changes to only the password policies, and then save the changes to a new template file.

You will use the predefined security templates to complete the following security tasks based on the needs of your system:

- Reapplying default settings
- Implementing a highly secure environment
- Implementing a less secure but more compatible environment
- Securing the *systemroot* directory

---

**NOTE** For a detailed breakdown of what the predefined templates can do, open the Windows Server 2003 Help and Support Center and search for Predefined Security Templates. A somewhat lengthy overview describes the capabilities of each template. This can be important before template deployment, but it is not important for exam preparation.

---

For example, the Setup security.inf template allows you to reapply default Security settings. This template is created during setup for each computer and must be applied locally. You should not apply the predefined security templates without testing first, because some of the Security settings in the more secure templates can make a Windows Server 2003 machine incompatible with other Windows operating systems that do not support the same security features.

## Creating and Modifying Templates

You can create a new security template to best suit the needs of your organization. Or to save time and effort configuring many of the hundreds of Security settings, use one of the predefined security templates. Before making any changes to your Security settings, though, you should understand what the default settings of your system are and how they influence behavior.

## Lab Exercise 23.1: Creating a Security Template

To create your own security templates, follow these steps:

1. Open the Security Templates MMC snap-in.

2. In the console tree, right-click the default path folder (*systemroot*\security\templates), and choose New Template. Name the template and provide a description (optional), and then click OK

3. You now have an unconfigured security template you can start modifying. In the console tree of your new template, expand the template to display the security policies, and navigate to the Security setting attribute you want to modify.

4. In the details pane, right-click the security setting and choose Properties from the context menu, or simply double-click the setting.

5. From the setting's Properties dialog box, select the Define This Policy Setting In The Template check box, and make any desired changes to the setting. Figure 23-3 shows you how to make a password policy a part of the new template. Click OK when you're finished.

**Figure 23-3**
Modifying
a setting
in a template

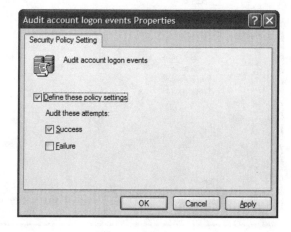

PART IV

Yet another way you can use this tool is to change existing templates. To do so, just expand one of the preconfigured templates and make changes according to the steps just outlined. When you've made the necessary tweaks, right-click the name of the policy and choose Save As from the context menu. The Save As dialog box will open to the same location where the predefined templates are stored, as shown in Figure 23-4. Name the modified template, and it should now appear in the Security Templates MMC snap-in.

## Importing a Template into a GPO

Now that you know how to create and modify security templates, it's time to put them to use. You can use these collections of Security settings by applying the template file to a Group Policy Object (GPO). This mechanism allows the templates to do their magic.

The following section details how to import a template into a Group Policy Object.

### Lab Exercise 23.2: Apply a Template to a Group Policy

This example applies a template to a domain-linked GPO, but the method is the same no matter to which GPO the template is imported:

1. Open Active Directory Users and Computers, right-click the Domain node, and select Properties. In the Properties dialog box, click the Group Policy tab, and then select the Group Policy to which you want the template applied. Click Edit.

2. Expand the Computer Configuration settings, and then select Security Settings. Right-click and choose Import Policy.

3. In the Import Policy dialog box, select the template you want to import. By default, the dialog box opens to the default template location of *systemroot\* security\templates.

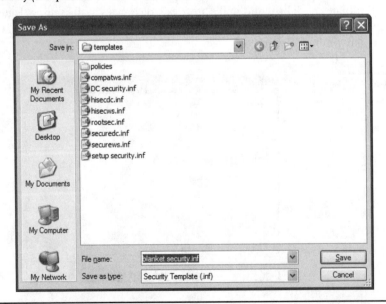

**Figure 23-4**    Saving a modified template

That's it! You can force an immediate refresh of the new Group Policy Security settings using the gpupdate utility, as seen in Chapter 22, or you can wait for the default refresh interval. A reboot will also do the trick.

Now the time spent fine-tuning the security templates has paid off. But before you leave this objective, another important tool will let you try out the security templates before putting them into play in the production environment. It's called the Security Configuration and Analysis tool.

 **CAUTION**   Exercise caution when applying templates in a production environment. When you apply a policy, it removes all existing Security settings, replacing them with the settings stored in the template file. This can cause problems in the network, because settings that are too low will put data at risk, and settings that are too high can make the network impractical for most users.

## Using the Security Configuration and Analysis Tool

This MMC utility is a powerful tool that lets you analyze Security settings, view results, resolve any discrepancies between an expected and an actual security configuration, and finally, apply those configuration changes to the local machine.

The *analysis* part of the Security Configuration and Analysis tool works by building a database of Security settings and then comparing the local Security settings of the computer against the database of settings built by the utility. The *configuration* part of Security Configuration and Analysis uses the database of Security settings to rapidly apply the settings to the system.

How are the databases of Security settings built? With the template files—both the ones already on the machine in the *systemroot*\security\templates folder, and the custom templates you configure with the Security Templates utility. Remember that the templates are merely text files full of Security settings, and just like almost any other database tool, Security Configuration and Analysis can use these kinds of files to populate the entries of a database table.

As you can see, the Security Templates and the Security Configuration and Analysis tools work hand in hand. There's even another cool way these two utilities work in harmony, as you will see later in the section. Therefore, it's common to have both MMC snap-ins loaded into the same console.

To add the Security Configuration and Analysis MMC snap-in to a console, follow the same procedure as you did when adding the Security Templates utility, only choose the Security Configuration and Analysis tool instead, of course.

## Configuring System Security

The Security Configuration and Analysis tool performs a series of complex analyses and configurations to your machine, but the tool itself is not that difficult to learn. What's more, you don't really need to, because the instructions in the details pane will help you use this tool for the first time.

Your first order of business when using this tool, however, is to set a working database of Security settings. Until this step is completed, the Security Configuration and Analysis tool really isn't capable of much.

## Lab Exercise 23.3: Using the Security Configuration and Analysis Tool

Follow these steps:

1. In the Security Configuration and Analysis snap-in, right-click Security Configuration And Analysis and choose Open Database. This will be your working database of settings that will be either analyzed or applied.

2. Name the database, and then select the security template you want to apply to the database. You can use any of the preconfigured templates or one you have created. Click Open.

3. Nothing changes except the instructions in the details pane of Security Configuration and Analysis. However, something important has occurred, at least as far as the utility is concerned. You now have a database of settings you will use for comparison or application (that is, analysis or configuration).

4. To analyze the system with the template's database of settings, right-click the Security Configuration and Analysis root node and then select Analyze Computer Now. Verify the error log location, click OK, and analysis begins, as shown in Figure 23-5.

When the processing is complete, any discrepancies between the local computer settings and the database settings will show up marked with a red *x*, while settings that match will show as a green check mark. Figure 23-6 shows you what to expect when performing the analysis. Settings that do not have either the red *x* or the green check mark are not configured in the database you just created with the template.

Once analysis has finished, you can then resolve discrepancies between the database settings and the computer settings if you want. You do this by double-clicking the settings and selecting whether to define the setting in the database, as shown in Figure 23-7, and furthermore adjusting the setting to best suit your needs.

You can also repeat the process and import multiple templates. The database will merge the many different templates to create one composite template. Any conflicts encountered will be resolved by having the last setting imported become the effective database setting.

**Figure 23-5**

The Security Configuration and Analysis tool performing its analysis

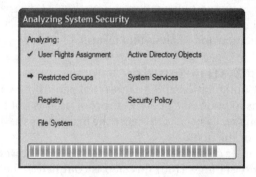

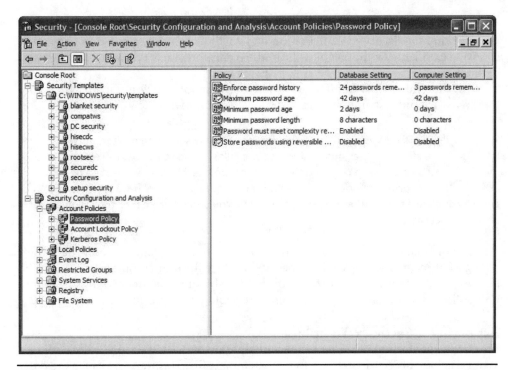

**Figure 23-6**    Results of a security analysis

**Figure 23-7**
Defining a
security setting
in the database

When you are satisfied with the settings in the database, you can apply them by right-clicking the Security Configuration and Analysis root node as before, and then choosing Configure Computer Now from the context menu. Set the error log path and click OK.

Now, with the Security Configuration and Analysis tool, you've just made potentially hundreds of Security setting changes to the local machine with a few clicks of the mouse.

**NOTE** When you apply the secure or highly secure templates, network traffic that does not conform to the rules of the template are rejected, and some of these connection and encryption technologies specified by the template are not even available on Windows 9x or NT 4.0 systems. To ensure compatibility with these operating systems, you should use either the Compatible or Setup security template.

Also note that when using the Security Configuration and Analysis tool, you are applying local Security settings. If this does not produce the results you expect, it could be because the Security settings are being overwritten by site, domain, and organizational unit policies, according to the Group Policy processing statutes outlined in Chapter 22.

### Exporting a Security Template

Another handy feature of the Security Configuration and Analysis tool is the ability to save a database of Security settings to a new template file. This way, you can take a database of carefully adjusted settings and save them for later use when configuring the Security settings of Group Policy Objects. Further, you can later redefine these settings using the Security Templates tool, using the two utilities to take Security settings back and forth as often as you please.

### Lab Exercise 23.4: Exporting a Database of Settings into a New Security Template

To export a security template, follow these steps:

1. Open the Security Configuration and Analysis console, and right-click the root Security Configuration and Analysis node.

2. If you have created a security database by importing multiple templates, you can save the database settings into a separate template file. To perform this task, choose Export Template from the context menu.

3. The Export Template To dialog box appears, set by default to the same location as the other security templates. Give the file a descriptive name and click OK.

4. Now you should see that template added to your list of manageable templates in the Security Templates console. If you don't, right-click the Templates folder and choose Refresh from the context menu.

## Using secedit

The secedit command-line utility does pretty much everything the Security Configuration and Analysis tool does, only from the command line. Its advantage is that you can use the secedit command in the syntax of a batch file or configure it as a scheduled task to automate the creation and application of security templates.

The usefulness of secedit is most evident when you have multiple computers on which security must be analyzed or configured, and these tasks must be performed without user intervention, including security analysis during off-hours.

The utility is used with the following switches:

- **/analyze**  Analyzes Security settings, working almost exactly the same as the Analyze Computer Now selection when using Security Configuration and Analysis.

- **/configure**  Configures the local computer using the settings stored in a database populated with a security template.

- **/export**  Exports the settings in the configuration database to a template file.

- **/import**  Imports a template file into a security configuration database, which can then be used to analyze or configure a local system.

- **/validate**  Validates the syntax of a template that will be imported.

- **/generaterollback**  Generates an "undo" or rollback template. The rollback template can be used to configure the system with the Security settings it had before configuration with another template. This switch is very useful.

 **NOTE**  If you are used to Windows 2000, please note that the /refreshpolicy option has been removed from secedit. The switch's functionality has been replaced by the gpupdate utility.

## Configuring an Audit Policy

By implementing auditing, you gain the ability to monitor what users are doing on the computer. *Auditing* can show you what activities are happening on a system, who is doing the activities, and what time they were doing it.

There are three main steps to implementing security-related auditing for your system.

First, you need to decide which events you wish to audit. You can audit events such as user logon and logoff, as well as access to resources on a computer. The categories of events you select will define your overall audit policy for a particular computer. When you first install Windows Server 2003, no categories are selected, and therefore no auditing occurs.

You can audit the types of events listed in Table 23-1.

After you've decided what to audit, the next step is to set the properties of the security log, including the size of the log file. These topics will be discussed in the next section.

| Event | Description |
|-------|-------------|
| account logon events | Each instance of a domain user logging on or off a domain controller. |
| account management | Events where accounts are modified. Examples include account creation, deletion, renaming, disabling, or password resetting. |
| directory service access | A user accesses an Active Directory object that has an ACL associated with it. This lets you see who has accessed objects like organizational units or Group Policy Objects. |
| logon events | Instances of a user logging on or off a particular computer. Note that this will not audit domain logon and logoff events. |
| object access | Determines whether to enable object auditing. It is then refined by defining which objects will be audited, and how they are audited. |
| policy change | Audits every incident of change to user rights policies, audit policies, or trust policies. |
| privilege use | Audits the use of user rights. |
| process tracking | Information such as program activation, process exiting, or indirect object access. Used to track the behavior of applications on a system. |
| system events | Audits events like a user shutting down a system, or any other event that would be written to the system or security log. |

**Table 23-1**    The Available Auditing Settings

Finally, depending on the audit events selected, you need to determine which objects are audited. Auditing object access, for example, can be more accurately described as the *ability* to audit object access. Once object access is enabled, you then need to select the objects for which you wan to monitor access, and set the audit settings from that object's Properties dialog box accordingly. You can furthermore set up auditing of either Success, Failure, or both when users try to access that particular file.

You configure audit policy from the Group Policy Object Editor's Audit Policy folder, which is located under the Local Policies node in the Security Settings console, as shown in Figure 23-8.

## Deciding What to Audit

When you define an audit policy, you get to choose which events to track and whether to track the success or failure of those events. Whether you should track success or failure events depends on the activities you are trying to capture. For example, do you really want to audit each and every successful logon? Probably not. Do you want to audit failed logon attempts? In a secure environment, you probably do. Keep in mind that auditing does generate overhead on the computer, so you want to audit the events that are most likely to indicate a security issue. Unnecessary auditing can negatively influence performance, so you want to focus your audits appropriately.

By default, nothing is audited, so you must configure auditing manually on a per-computer basis. It can also be a two-step process, as in the case where you would want to audit who is accessing a confidential file. You would first audit the success of object access, and you would then set the auditing on an individual resource by accessing the Properties dialog box of that resource and configuring auditing on a per-group or per-user basis through the Advanced button, as shown in Figure 23-9.

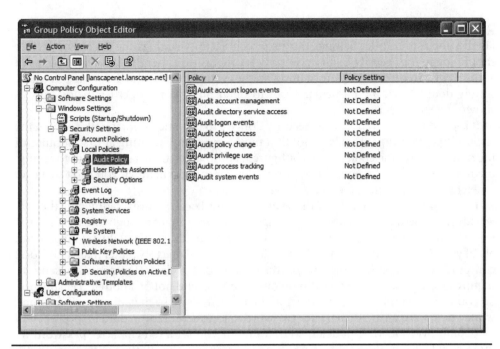

**Figure 23-8**   The audit policies

**NOTE**   Remember, you need to ensure that Simple File Sharing is turned off before you can see the Security tab on an NTFS resource. Verify that SFS is not checked by looking at the View tab in Folder Options.

**TIP**   You can audit access to resources only on NTFS partitions.

**Figure 23-9**
Auditing a
resource

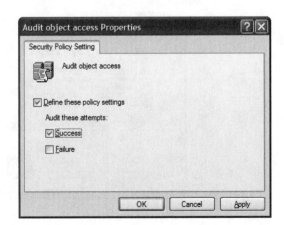

## Reviewing the Results of Your Audit Policy

Finally, the Audit Policy settings dictate which Security settings the Event Log service should log in the Security log. The Security log identifies either the failure or success of audit events. To get detailed information on the events, such as who did what and when, simply double-click the particular event to open the Event Properties dialog box, as shown in Figure 23-10.

It is good practice to use Local Security Policies to become familiar with some of the Group Policy settings. This is a tool that may seem overwhelming at first because of the number of settings that can be configured. Finding exactly what you want to configure requires patience, repeated use, and trial and error. Remember, you can't make an omelet without cracking a few eggs.

That being said, you will hardly ever configure Local Security settings in the real world. That's because most Security settings that are important enough to set at the local level should also apply to the network as a whole. So that's what you do: set most, if not all, of your Security settings at the domain level in Active Directory rather than at the local computer level. A perfect example of this is password policies. Does it make sense to require an eight-character password on one computer and not on another? Usually not. So you would set this password policy at the domain level, so that all users of your network would need an eight-character password to log on. Moreover, domain policies will by default override local policies, so that even if you set a ten-character password requirement at the local computer using the same scenario, the effective setting would still be for an eight-character password.

**Figure 23-10**
Examining
the results
of your audit

So, when might you want to change any of the local Group Policy settings? Well, your only Group Policy lever is available in a workgroup setting. In this configuration, the Local Group Policies can be quite effective on securing a machine, especially one that is shared by many people.

The greater the number of GPOs configured for a computer, and the greater the number of settings within each GPO configured, the longer it takes for a computer to start and complete the logon process. Therefore, best practice is to minimize the number of GPOs applied to a computer in a domain, and minimize the number of settings applied to a computer in a workgroup or a domain. Configure only what you need.

If you're thinking right now that this information has been covered previously, it has. Fact is, there are just some test objectives that overlap, and there are enough cross-references in this book already. To illustrate, consider these two, copied for your convenience from Microsoft's Training and Certification web site. First, this one from the 70-291 section:

> Implement security baseline settings and audit Security settings by using security templates.

Now look at this one, from the 70-294:

> Configure computer Security settings by using Group Policy.

See? An audit setting is one of the Security settings configured with a Group Policy. And Security settings in a GPO can easily be configured with Security Templates. You get the idea.

So you've read most of what's preceded. There are a few differences; a couple of details here that weren't in Chapter 10, and visa versa. They are different tests, after all. But really, there's only so many ways to define a Security Template, Audit, and so on, but you will need knowledge of these technologies going into both exams. The information is given to keep you from reading with two bookmarks at the ready, or in case you take the 70-291 exam. Each part of this book attempts to present as thorough a story of test readiness as possible.

The rest of this chapter, you can be assured, is all new information.

# Deploying Software Through Group Policy

In Chapter 22, you were introduced to Group Policy and some of the settings configurable with a Group Policy Object. If you followed along with the examples, you already have a taste of the power of a Group Policy. Distributing software just adds to the scope of that power. This chapter is dedicated to yet another configurable setting of Group Policy: a software distribution policy.

 **NOTE** Remember that a GPO can apply only to a client operating system that's compatible with Group Policy. This means you can't deploy software to Windows 9x to NT 4.0 computers. If this is your goal, you might consider implementing Microsoft's Systems Management Server (SMS), which can push software to down-level Microsoft clients. Furthermore, you can use your knowledge of SMS as an elective in your pursuit of the MCSE certification.

There are four stages of the software life cycle, each of which can be addressed through a Group Policy Object:

- **Preparation**  The preparation stage looks at issues surrounding planning for software deployment and laying groundwork for deployment. These include the creation of a Windows Installer Package (an .msi file) if one has not shipped with the software product, and configuration of a network share for storage of the .msi file and the rest of the installation files. Sometimes, applications will not ship with the newer Windows Installer package. You also check for hardware and software compatibility in the software preparation stage.

- **Deployment**  In this stage, the software is actually pushed to the target computer. The software can be configured to be installed no matter which user logs on, or to install upon the presentation of certain user credentials. Because the software is deployed using Group Policy, you have all the administrative flexibility afforded by Group Policies. All of the behaviors inherent in GPOs carry forward into the realm of software deployment. Therefore, software can be deployed to sites, entire domains, organizational units, or even individual computers at your discretion.

- **Maintenance**  Because the life cycle of a software product is ever-evolving, the GPO can be tailored to accommodate changes as the application matures. A perfect example of an evolving software product is the Windows operating system itself. Service packs are changes and updates to files that address security, stability, performance, and compatibility issues, and are released as improvements are made. Microsoft Office behaves in the same manner. As improvements are made to the code of a program, these improvements can be sent to computers via a Group Policy.

- **Removal**  The fourth stage in the software product life cycle is the removal of software. For example, if you are updating your office's installation of Microsoft Office, you will most often replace the latest and greatest (by the time you're reading this, Microsoft Office 2003) with what has preceded it (Microsoft Office XP, 2000, and so on). A user rarely needs both installations. Group Policies have the ability to both install and uninstall software. The only real caveat here is that for software to be removed through a Group Policy, it must have been installed with a Group Policy as well. And if a user does indeed need two versions of the same product, Group Policy can be configured to handle most instances of that situation, too. (Microsoft Outlook is one example of an application that won't tolerate previous installations of itself on the same computer, but most applications will.)

At the end of the day, it's all about automation. Software deployment with a Group Policy negates the need for administrators to complete the laborious, expensive, and tedious task of walking around from machine to machine, CD-ROM in hand, installing software at client computers. The automation of software deployment, repair, update, and removal that are all available through Group Policy rely on an engine called Windows Installer.

## Exploring Windows Installer Technology

At the heart of the software deployment technology used by Group Policy is the Windows Installer. This technology was first employed in large scale with the rollout of Office 2000 and has been a part of every Microsoft software application ever since. Windows Installer has two main components:

- The Windows Installer service
- The Windows Installer package

The Windows Installer *service* installs and runs on every Windows 2000, Windows XP, and Windows Server 2003 machine as a part of operating system installation. The service facilitates automated installations and also provides a mechanism to repair or change existing installations without user intervention. The service works behind the scenes to make sure applications are properly installed and remain problem-free. It's all a part of Microsoft's lower Total Cost of Ownership (TCO) initiative.

 **NOTE** As you have no doubt experienced, you don't have to use a Group Policy to take advantage of a Windows Installer package. You can also install directly from CD-ROM or any other distribution media. Some of the resiliency of the application is lost, however, when the distribution media is removed.

A Windows Installer *package* (.msi file) does not actually install the program files. Rather, it is a miniature database of all the information and settings the Windows Installer service requires to install, repair, or even remove an application. Included in the information contained in an .msi file is the location of the installation files, as well as .ini and registry setting changes that may be needed at installation time.

The .msi file is also referred to as the package file. Be aware, however, that the actual software installation package usually includes other supplementary files. When creating a software package for deployment, the Group Policy searches for .msi files. Without an .msi file, the package that a Group Policy deploys cannot be created. (There is an exception, actually, but we'll get to that later.) What's more, this .msi file can be created, even in the case when one doesn't ship with the application.

The following are some of the benefits of a Windows Installer package:

- **Resilient software** If an application's critical files are deleted or otherwise damaged, the Windows Installer service reconnects to the software distribution point and replaces the file with a working copy. (This is why the feature is less impressive when installed from a CD; you will have to search out the CD when the Windows Installer wants additional files.) This reduces the amount of time an administrator must be at deskside performing application reinstalls.

- **Clean removal** A common problem when removing software is that the deletion of one piece of software removes a file needed by another application. One of the services Windows Installer provides is tracking which files are needed by other applications. Any files critical to the operation of other applications are not removed. Files that the Windows Installer determines are no longer needed are then removed. This occurs for all applications for which the Windows Installer service has performed the installation.

- **Elevated security**   It's common for an application to require installation in the context of a user account with administrative privileges. In a properly implemented Active Directory environment, users are rarely logged on with such administrative privileges. How to proceed? With the Windows Installer service, which runs in the context of the LocalSystem account by default. Again, this prevents the administrator from visiting deskside, logging on with an administrator account, and then performing the installation (and then, often as not, forgetting to log out, opening security compromises galore).

Sometimes, though, an application does not ship with an .msi file. This is especially true if you want to deploy older applications in your network. In such a case, you can create an .msi file for the installation with a third-party tool. You can also use a .zap file in conjunction with the application's setup.exe installation program.

## Using the .zap File

There are more applications out there than there are .msi files to help them install. Prior to Microsoft Office 2000, most applications, Office included, installed by launching the setup executable, setup.exe. Microsoft was aware of this fact when they wrote the Windows Installer code, and they have accommodated the use of existing setup programs in Windows Installer deployments using a special file called a .zap file.

The .zap file gets its name from its file extension—.zap—and it is simply a text file you can create with any ASCII editor and a little know-how. Notepad, for example, will do just fine. The .zap file is really quite similar to the .msi file in that they both contain information about the program and how it is set up. For example, a typical .zap file contains the name of the setup program, the name of the application, any file extensions to be associated with the application, and other parameters used by the setup.

---

 **NOTE**   For an example of a .zap file, please see the Microsoft Windows Server 2003 Resource Kit, at www.microsoft.com/MSPress/books/5555.asp.

---

Don't get the wrong idea: package creation is preferred when possible. There are several drawbacks when comparing .zap files to their more evolved relatives, the .msi package:

- **.zap files cannot be assigned to users, only published.**   You can only publish a software package created with a .zap file, which limits several options you have when deploying the package. Specifically, it prevents you from making software installations mandatory.

- **.zap files are not self-repairing.**   They're a dream when installing software for the target user, but once the application has installed, it's on its own. You lose the benefit of a software package repairing itself when a corrupted file is detected.

- **.zap file installations usually require user intervention.** While .msi packages can sometimes install the program before the user ever sees the desktop, the same is not true of a package created with a .zap file. The .zap file's job is to summon the setup executable, and usually the user needs to provide some kind of input to complete installation. The only possible exception is if the application is configured to install in completely unattended install mode, usually with an /unattend switch following the setup executable.

- **.zap files can't install using elevated privileges.** As discussed, another significant benefit of the .msi package is the use of the LocalSystem account, which is not used by packages created with a .zap file. In other words, when using an .msi file, the Windows Installer service actually performs the install, not the user. When a .zap file is used, it calls the setup.exe file, which runs in the context of the user currently logged on. If the user does not have an account with the proper rights, the install fails, defeating the purpose of automating software deployment.

 **TIP** As always, remember that the Group Policy can be deployed only to computers that support GPOs. Clients such as Windows 98 or NT 4.0 must have software deployed through alternate means.

## Creating an .msi File

One of the options you have when an application does not ship with a Windows Installer file is to create one of your own. In most cases, this is preferable for software deployment over the use of a .zap file for the reasons just listed.

Several third-party tools and applications will help you repackage an existing application and create the necessary .msi file for software deployment through Group Policy. One of these is a utility called WinINSTALL LE, from the Veritas Corporation. The process of repackaging an application is quite involved and should be performed with two computers. Only a general overview is provided here. The purpose of this book is not to give instructions on repackaging applications, but rather, for testing purposes, to point out that it is possible and identify which tools are used.

 **NOTE** A 98-page white paper from Microsoft called "Windows Installer: Benefits and Implementation for System Administrators," outlines the many variables of the application repackaging process, among other things. One line that stands out is as follows: "The amount of time, money, and labor needed to repackage applications is often underestimated." In other words, seek out applications that already have Windows Installer files if possible.

To use WinINSTALL LE, perform the following steps:

1. Prepare a Windows 2000 Professional or Windows XP Professional computer by installing just the operating system. This machine will serve as the reference computer and should not have any other software installed.

2. Prepare a network installation folder to hold the new Windows Installer package and any supporting files. This is the location users will connect to install the application, or will be the location used by Group Policy to find the deployed application.

3. Install the WinINSTALL LE utility on a second machine. Using this second machine, take a "before" image of the reference computer's configuration.

4. Now that you have the "before" image, proceed with installing the application you want to repackage using a normal installation routine.

5. After application installation, use WinINSTALL again to take an "after" image of the reference computer. This image will scan the system for any settings changes, and will use this information to build the repackaged application to the network location, along with a new Windows Installer file.

Microsoft also recommends that when you make use of repackaged applications, you do so by running them on computers that have identical hardware and software. This can improve the reliability of repackaged software. Some common causes of failed installation or poor functionality of repackaged applications can be traced to differences in the platforms that receive them, such as these:

- Systems that are all running the same operating systems, but differ in the optional operating system components installed

- Service pack version

- Windows 2000 Professional and Windows 2000 Server

- Windows XP Professional and Windows Server 2003

- Different versions of shared components, such as Internet Explorer

- Different versions of other installed applications, such as Microsoft Office

 **NOTE** Repackaging applications into the Windows Installer format has limitations and might not be supported by every application manufacturer. You should check with each application manufacturer for additional information and recommendations.

Now that you know about a few of the files you might encounter when creating software packages, you must be familiar with a few terms that define how the packages are deployed.

## Application Advertisement

It's a term that sounds a little strange when used in the discussion of application deployment, but it's nevertheless one you must understand. When an application is advertised to a user, it is not physically installed, but a shortcut appears on the Start menu. When a user clicks the application's shortcut, the installation actually occurs.

Applications can also advertise themselves in the Add/Remove Programs section of the Control Panel. A user opening this applet sees a special section where all published applications will be listed. Any applications the user selects are automatically installed from the installation share.

This installation share is specified on every software package created. You can streamline the installation process by defining a single network location for all software packages, and then setting the default software installation location to this directory.

## Setting the Software Installation Default Location

Before we get started creating software packages, know that several default settings affect how applications are deployed, managed, and removed. Some of the choices you set with these default options will affect the dialog boxes you see as you create the software packages, so let's look at how to set these options now.

Additionally, you need to make sure the software to be deployed is available on the network. You perform this task by setting up a software distribution point, which is simply a network share that holds the packages you create (the .msi files), along with the program files and any associated files such as transform (.mst) files. This share can then be configured as the default software installation location, which streamlines the package creation process. You can even take advantage of the Distributed File System (DFS) in creating your distribution points, adding the benefits of load balancing and fault tolerance to your application management.

After you share out this folder to the network, you should verify that users who will be getting the software can read from the distribution point. They will need the Read permission to read the information in the software package, as well as the files necessary for installation.

You set the default software installation settings from the Properties dialog box of the Software Installation node in a GPO. These options affect the global properties of all new software packages created, and they can be set differently for User settings than for Computer settings.

## Lab Exercise 23.5: Configuring Default Software Installation Settings

Follow these steps to configure the default settings:

1. To access these global settings, open the Group Policy Object Editor snap-in, and under either Computer Configuration or User Configuration settings, select Software Settings.

2. Right-click the Software Installation node, and then choose Properties. You set the default software installation options from the General tab, as shown in Figure 23-11.

3. In the Default Package Location field, type or browse to the software distribution point.

PART IV

**Figure 23-11**
Configuring
default software
distribution
options

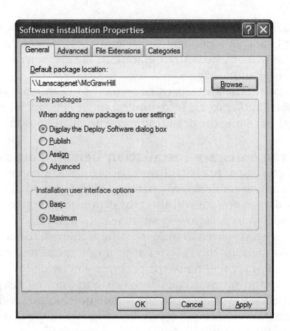

4. In the New Packages section, set the behavior for new package creation:

- **Display The Deploy Software Dialog Box**   Gives you the option of
  publishing or assigning when you create the package, and it should be
  selected for the examples to follow.

- **Publish**   Configures the default package creation option to publish the
  application. This option will be dimmed under the Computer Configuration
  section because applications can be published only to users, not computers.

- **Assign**   Assigns the package created by default with standard package
  properties. Publishing and assigning are discussed next.

5. Select from the two Installation User Interface Options section:

- **Basic**   Provides only the base display of the installation process.

- **Maximum**   Displays all installation messages and screens during the
  installation, so you can treat your users to a show if you choose Maximum.

**NOTE**   When you create a new software package, the Open dialog box
shows all .msi packages located at the software distribution point that you
specify as the default.

As you start looking at software deployment, it's important that you understand the
difference between *assigning* an application and *publishing* an application. Choosing
whether to publish or assign is a decision you must make at package creation time, and
it affects how the software is distributed.

# Publishing

When you *publish* an application, you are making it available to the users the Group Policy affects, but the application is not automatically installed. That is, no shortcuts are visible on the desktop or from the Start menu, and no changes are made to the local registry on the computer from which the user is logging on.

So how does the user even know about the application's existence in the first place? Through Active Directory. Published applications store their advertisement attributes in Active Directory. Thus, information about the application is exposed to the user account, enabling that user to install the application either through the Add/Remove Programs applet or by opening a file that is associated with the application. Both of these features are discussed in the following section.

The advantage of publishing an application is that it lets users have more control over the programs that are installed on their computers. Users install only applications they need to work with the files they are trying to open, or applications they selectively install through the Control Panel.

## Lab Exercise 23.6: Publishing an Application

To publish an application to a user, follow these steps:

1. Open Active Directory Users and Computers, navigate to the OU where you want to create the software installation Group Policy, right-click, and choose Properties.

2. From the Group Policy tab, open the Group Policy Object Editor for the Group Policy you want to configure.

3. Under the User Configuration node, expand Software Settings, and then select Software Installation.

4. Right-click the Software Installation node, and from the details pane, choose New | Package, as shown in Figure 23-12.

5. In the Open dialog box, click the Windows Installer package to be published, and then click Open.

6. In the Deploy Software dialog box, click Published.

---

 **TIP**   You do not publish applications to computers, only to users.

---

## Publishing Considerations

When publishing software to users, the application is not actually installed until the user invokes installation. There are two ways this happens:

- **File invocation**   When a user opens a file that is associated with the deployed software package, installation of the program occurs automatically. By using document invocation instead of having the application already installed on the computer's hard disk, you conserve disk space and also network bandwidth. Applications are installed on an ad hoc basis rather than having every user get every application installed all at once. For example, if a user who had the Excel spreadsheet application published to his or her account then opened a file with the .xls extension, Excel would be installed from the network software distribution location. Compare this to what might happen to network performance if all users connected to the distribution point first thing in the morning to install Excel.

- **Add/Remove Programs in the Control Panel**  If an application is published to a user account, it is listed in a special section of the Add/Remove Programs utility. This listing can sometimes be subdivided into groups of software categories, and will contain all the programs the user is able to install based on Group Policy settings. This also lets users selectively install just the applications they need to get work done, and reduces unnecessary use of disk space and network bandwidth. Once a user selects an application, Windows Installer performs the software installation on behalf of the user, so additional privileges are not needed.

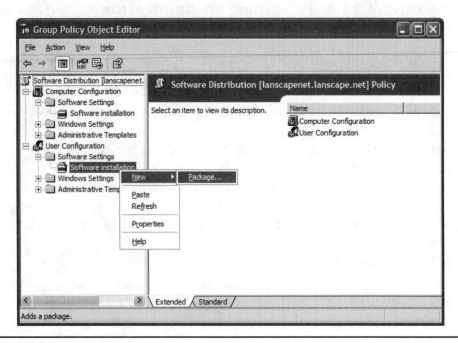

**Figure 23-12**    Creating a new software package

## Assigning

When you assign a software package with a Group Policy, you have the choice of assigning to either a computer or a user, as discussed next. The general idea behind application assignment is that it makes software installation mandatory. You can implement package assignment to make sure users always have a certain application available no matter where they go, or so that a particular computer or group of computers always has a consistent software environment. For example, you assign software when you want all systems in the office to have the same installation of—Office.

First, let's examine the significance of assigning software to a user.

## To Users

When you configure a Group Policy to assign an application to a user, the application is advertised to that user (or group of users, as will more commonly be the case) with a shortcut on the Start menu the next time the user logs on from a computer capable of processing a Group Policy Object. The application is not, however, actually installed until the user either uses the application the first time or opens a document whose file extension is associated with the application.

As previously mentioned, the real advantage of this functionality is that the application advertisement follows the user, no matter which physical computer he or she actually uses (again, as long as the system is compatible with Group Policy). For instance, suppose you want all users in your company's Sales department to have Microsoft Access installed because this database application is the front end for a database full of product and customer information. Furthermore, all users in the Sales department are kept in a single organizational unit. When you modify a Group Policy Object linked to the Sales department to assign that department the Access application, Access is advertised on the Start menu of every computer a member of the Sales OU uses.

Again, this doesn't necessarily install the application. If a user in the Sales department used a company laptop simply to check e-mail, Access would not be installed even though a shortcut would be placed on the Start menu. If the user of this same laptop were to open an .mdb file or click on the Start menu shortcut, Access would then install.

Additionally, it is possible for a user to delete an application that has been assigned to his or her account. However, the assigned application is advertised again the next time the user logs on, and, just as before, installs the next time a user selects it on the Start menu.

## Lab Exercise 23.7: Assigning an Application

To create a software package for assignment to a user, follow these steps:

1. Open Active Directory Users and Computers, navigate to the OU where you want to create the software installation Group Policy, right-click, and choose Properties.

2. From the Group Policy tab, open the Group Policy Object Editor for the Group Policy you want to configure.

3. Under the User Configuration node, expand Software Settings, and then select Software Installation.

4. Right-click and choose New | Package.

5. In the Open dialog box, navigate to the Windows Installer package for the software you want to deploy, and click Open.

6. In the Deploy Software dialog box, choose Assigned, as shown in Figure 23-13, and then click OK.

## To Computers

When you assign an application to the computer, the application is advertised on the Start menu of the computer, and the installation happens automatically when it is safe to do so. Usually, "safe to do so" means that installation occurs as the computer starts up. It takes a bit longer to be presented with the logon screen, but this ensures that no competing processes are on the computer when the application is installed.

**TIP** The preceding leads to an important point when applications are assigned to computers: they are installed when the Group Policy is applied, not just advertised, as they are to users. This distinction can be an important one to make come exam time.

The following are the steps necessary to assign an application to a computer. In this example, you create a package that applies to an organizational unit; keep in mind that you can create a software distribution policy that affects any of the Active Directory container objects where you can apply Group Policy:

1. Open Active Directory Users and Computers, navigate to the OU where you want to create the software installation Group Policy, right-click, and choose Properties.

2. From the Group Policy tab, open the Group Policy Object Editor for the Group Policy you want to configure.

**Figure 23-13**
Assigning to
a user

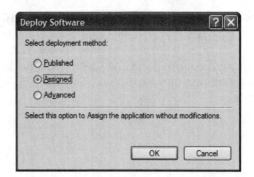

3. Under the Computer Configuration node, expand Software Settings, and then select Software Installation.

4. Right-click and choose New | Package.

5. In the Open dialog box, navigate to the Windows Installer package for the software you want to deploy, and click Open.

6. In the Deploy Software dialog box, choose Assigned, and then click OK.

---

 **NOTE** Henceforth, the directions to navigate to the Software Installation node in a Group Policy are implicit; you'll just be directed to the Software Installation node.

---

## Maintaining Installed Software by Using Group Policy

Most of the time when deploying new software, it's out with the old, in with the new. For example, when deploying Office 2003, most organizations are going to want it to replace any existing editions of Office. Group Policies can be set up to handle this task quite easily because you can also configure a software package to update any existing software applications, as you'll see in the next exercise.

## Lab Exercise 23.8: Updating an Existing Application

To configure the package to upgrade software, follow these steps:

1. Choose the appropriate Group Policy, and navigate to the Software Installation node. Create a new software installation package, choosing whether to publish or assign the application. This package will serve as the upgrade of an existing application.

2. Once the new Windows Installer package has been configured, right-click the package that will be the upgrade, choose Properties, and then choose the Upgrades tab.

3. Click Add in this dialog box to create or add to the list of packages that you want the current package to upgrade, as shown in Figure 23-14.

4. In the Add Upgrade Package dialog box, in the Choose A Package From section, you can configure one of the following:

   • Choose a current Group Policy Object (GPO).

   • Choose a specific GPO by clicking Browse, and then clicking the Group Policy Object that you want to upgrade.

5. Review the list of packages under Package To Upgrade, which lists all of the other packages that are assigned or published within the selected Group Policy Object.

**Figure 23-14**
Upgrading
an existing
application

6. Choose the existing package that you want the new package to upgrade, and then make one of these selections:

   • To replace an application with a completely different application, choose Uninstall The Existing Package, Then Install The Upgrade Package. This removes all files from an existing application, and is most commonly used to replace a product from one vendor with a product from another.

   • To install a newer version of the same product while retaining all user-specific settings the user has configured, choose Package Can Upgrade Over The Existing Package. This preserves the custom dictionary and AutoCorrect options, for example, when upgrading from Office 2000 to Office 2003.

7. Click OK to close the Add Upgrade Package dialog box. The last selection on the Upgrades tab is optional. You can make the upgrade package a mandatory upgrade by selecting the Required Upgrade For Existing Packages check box.

## Mandatory Upgrades

This last point of the preceding instructions merits a bit more discussion. You can make upgrades mandatory. This means, as the moniker implies, that the deployed application will completely replace any and all existing application files. This occurs because of an uninstall that takes place when you configure the mandatory upgrade with the Required Upgrade For Existing Packages check box described in the previous exercise.

Any time you leave this selection unchecked, the upgrade is an optional upgrade. By default, application upgrades are optional.

**TIP** if you are configuring an upgrade from the Computer Configuration settings, the Required Upgrade For Existing Packages check box is automatically selected and is also unchangeable because packages will be assigned to the computer, not published. Therefore, the upgrade will be installed on the computer automatically.

## Creating a Package Modification

You can also customize a Windows Installer application through Group Policy's support of software modification. Such software modifications, known as *transforms*, allow for the deployment of several configurations of the same piece of software. The modifications are performed with a transform file. This file has an .mst extension, and it is used in combination with an existing Windows Installer package. In other words, no .msi, no .mst.

For example, you can use a transform file to deploy Microsoft Word to make sure users in one part of the globe receive the English dictionary, and users in other parts get the Spanish dictionary. In this case, you would create an .mst file for each dictionary, and furthermore, create separate GPOs to deploy the Word software package with their separate .mst files.

These transforms allow you to transform the original package using authoring and repackaging utilities. Some applications even provide wizard-based tools that permit a user to create these transform files.

**TIP** A transform file (.mst) can be employed only *before* the application package is deployed. The transform is applied to the package at the time of assignment or publication, and the changes the file specifies are carried out at application installation. Once the software has been installed on a user's machine, it cannot be changed using an .mst file.

## Lab Exercise 23.9: Adding a Transform to a Software Package

To deploy a Microsoft transform file to modify the properties of an application deployment, follow these steps:

1. Open the Group Policy Object Editor and expand either the Computer Configuration or the User Configuration settings, and then the Software Installation node.

2. Right-click Software Installation, select New, and then click Package.

3. In the Open dialog box, choose the Windows Installer package you want to modify, and click Open.

4. In the Deploy Software dialog box, click the Advanced selection, and then click OK.

PART IV

5. In the Properties dialog box for the package, navigate to the Modifications tab, as shown in Figure 23-15. Once there, perform any of the following actions:

- To add modifications, click Add. In the Open dialog box, browse to the transform file (.mst), and then click Open.

- To remove modifications, on the Modifications tab, click the modification you want to remove, and then click Remove. Repeat this step until you have removed each modification you do not want.

6. When you are sure the modifications are configured exactly how you want them, click OK.

**NOTE** When you click OK, the package is assigned or published immediately. If the modifications are not properly configured, you will have to uninstall the package or upgrade the package with a correctly configured version.

## Distributing Updates to Software Using Group Policy

Instead of upgrading a software package, you might find it easier to merely reinstall the application on the user's machine. By redeploying the software, you cause a reinstallation. This method of upgrading software is preferable if you have changed a software package without changing the application's name, have added or removed files from the package, have included a patch or hotfix, have added shortcuts, have changed registry settings, or have changed an existing package in any other way. To make sure all users have the updated software, you will likely choose to redeploy the package.

**Figure 23-15**

Configuring
modifications
for a Windows
Installer package

Using this method, you can incorporate more comprehensive changes to the application than are typical when simply modifying or upgrading an existing package. When doing so, you should create a new Windows Installer file with a name that exactly matches the existing package, and then store the file in the same location as the original. As long as the version and the package name are identical, the application, even though it has been modified, is considered to be the same piece of software. The package can then be redeployed as needed.

## Lab Exercise 23.10: Redeploy an Application

To redeploy a software package with included changes, follow these steps:

1. Open Active Directory Users and Computers and then open the Group Policy Object Editor that contains the software deployment settings you want to change.

2. Expand either the Computer or User configuration to the Software Installation node where the original package was created.

3. Right-click the original package, and from the context menu, choose All Tasks | Redeploy Application.

4. Close the Group Policy Object Editor to save your changes to the Group Policy Object.

5. Click OK to close the container's Properties dialog box, and then close Active Directory Users and Computers.

Not only do the applications in your network need to be prepared for, deployed, and maintained, but they also need to be removed when they no longer effectively serve the needs of the computing environment.

## Software Removal

In the life cycle of a software application, installation is only part of the picture. Applications can be upgraded once installed, as you have just seen, and they can be removed. Group Policy also provides a mechanism to remove software packages once they have been deployed. As with upgrading software packages, you have two choices when removing:

- **Optional**  This allows the user to continue using the software. The application no longer appears in the list under Add/Remove Programs in the Control Panel.

- **Mandatory**  As suggested by the name, mandatory removal is forced removal, where files are deleted from the computer's hard disk. If the package was assigned to the computer, the application is removed the next time the computer restarts.

PART IV

## Lab Exercise 23.11: Application Removal

These software removal settings are configured with a dialog box that presents you with two selections as you configure the removal:

1. Open the Group Policy Object Editor, and navigate to the software package you want to remove.

2. In the details pane, right-click the application, choose All Tasks from the context menu, and then click Remove.

3. In the Remove Software dialog box, shown in Figure 23-16, choose one of the following options that will specify the removal method:

   - **Immediately Uninstall The Software From Users And Computers** The application will be removed the next time a user logs on or restarts the computer.

   - **Allow Users To Continue To Use The Software, But Prevent New Installations** Users have the option to continue using the application if they have already installed it. If users have previously removed the application, or if they've never installed it, it will not be available for installation anymore.

**NOTE** Once the decision has been made to configure an optional or mandatory removal, you cannot reverse course. The package will be removed from the Group Policy Object. If a user decides to leave an optional application on his or her system, you cannot later force the removal, because the software package will no longer exist in the GPO.

## Additional Deployment Considerations

Two other deployment considerations are worth mentioning so you're not tripped up by an exam questions that mentions them. If you right-click a software package assigned or published to users, you can access these two options from the Deployment tab, as shown in Figure 23-17. You can enable the following two check boxes independently:

- **Uninstall This Application When It Falls Out Of The Scope Of Management** This option mandates that the application will automatically be removed if and when the Group Policy Object no longer manages its deployment. For example, if there were applications assigned to a computer in one OU, and that computer then moved to another OU, the application would uninstall since the GPO that managed the software deployment no longer applied to that computer.

- **Install This Application At Logon** This option is new in Windows Server 2003, and therefore is a good candidate for subject matter on the exam. Selecting this check box will install the application using package defaults. Normally, an assigned program would just advertise itself, but the option will perform the entire install before the user gets the desktop.

**Figure 23-16**
Options for removing software with a Group Policy

When you configure the software settings of a Group Policy Object, you're dealing with only a single node in the Group Policy Object Editor. This might make it seem like something that's easy to manage, but as you have just seen, there's still quite a bit to learn about the underlying technology before you start creating and deploying software packages.

**NOTE** Remember, this presentation is condensed, optimized for purposes of providing only the information essential for your exam success. Real-world application of software distribution with a Group Policy requires more study.

Once your Group policies are configured and deployed, the next order of business is to make sure they are doing what they are supposed to do. To successfully troubleshoot Group Policy deployment, you need a thorough knowledge of the topics presented in this chapter and in Chapter 22. Troubleshooting Group Policy application will be an area that you are sure to see tested on the 70-294 exam.

**Figure 23-17**
Advanced deployment options

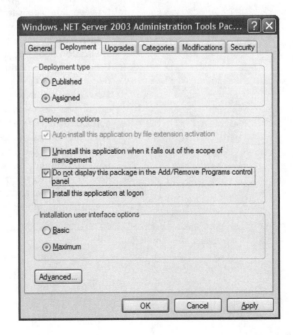

PART IV

# Troubleshooting Issues Related to Group Policy Application

Table 23-2 lists some common problems when installing software with a Group Policy Object and their possible solutions.

| Table 23-2 | Problem | Resolution |
|---|---|---|
| Common Group Policy Issues | Application cannot be installed. | Commonly, this is a problem with the permissions of the network share where the application package is stored. You should first ensure that the network location is in fact available by establishing a connection (you could use UNC syntax to do this: Start \| Run \| \\servername\sharename), and then check permissions. The permissions required for a user to install an application are the Read permission on the share, and the NTFS permission Read and Execute on the directory itself. Further, the Read and Execute permissions are required on every file that is a part of the package, not just the Windows Installer (.msi) file. |
| | Applications do not appear on the user's desktop. | You should use RSoP or the gpresult utility to check the way the application was deployed. If the application was *assigned* to the user, the shortcut for the application should appear on the user's Start menu, as assigned applications advertise themselves. If the application was published, however, the application will be installed either from the Add/Remove Programs applet in the Control Panel or via document invocation. If the application does not appear in the Add/Remove Programs applet of the Control Panel, it is possible that either the Group Policy Object has been filtered for this user (or a group the user is a part of), or was deployed to another Active Directory container than the one you expect. Yet another possibility is that the settings of a Group Policy have been blocked by a child-level organizational unit. You should check the ACL for the Group Policy Object to see if any filtering behavior has been configured, and check the properties of the organizational unit to see if inheritance has been blocked. |

| Table 23-2 Common Group Policy Issues *(continued)* | Problem | Resolution |
|---|---|---|
| | Deployed applications do not work properly after installation. | When applications are repackaged using third-party software as described in earlier in this chapter, the Windows Installer file created might not have worked properly. If, during repackaging, the application did not install certain files on the hard disk of the source system, these files will not exist in the package created. If these missing files do not exist on the target computer's hard disk, the application may not work properly after it is deployed. To correct this, you should repackage the application again, adding the necessary files to the application. |
| | Package installation removes other files. | This problem is also likely a repackaging issue. When repackaging an application, the period between the "before" snapshot and the "after" snapshot are crucial. If changes are made to the source computer prior to the "after" snapshot that includes the removal of files, this can cause the package to also include instructions to remove files as well. If the wrong files are removed, other applications may stop functioning. To fix this problem, you should repackage the application, making sure any file deletion references are not included during the creation of the Windows Installer package. |
| | Applications are not deployed at all. | This problem is mostly due to Group Policy issues, and requires a thorough knowledge of the Group Policy processing behaviors discussed in Chapter 22. Remember that when conflicts occur in Group Policy processing, the last setting processed will become the effective policy by default. Also keep in mind all of the possible exceptions to the default processing behavior. |
| | When attempting to edit a Group Policy Object, you receive the "Failed to open the Group Policy Object" error. | This is usually due to a networking problem, specifically, a problem with the Domain Name System (DNS) configuration. Because Group Policy Objects are stored in the Active Directory database, and Active Directory requires the presence of DNS to resolve domain resources, you will not be able to locate Active Directory–based GPOs without DNS. To resolve this problem, you should verify that DNS is configured and working properly. |

PART IV

| | Problem | Resolution |
|---|---|---|
| **Table 23-2** Common Group Policy Issues *(continued)* | When trying to edit a GPO, you receive a "Missing Active Directory Container" error. | This error occurs when Group Policy attempts to link a Group Policy Object to an organizational unit that it cannot find. The organizational unit might have been deleted, or it might have been created on another domain controller but not replicated to the domain controller you are using. To resolve the problem, limit the number of users who can make structural changes to Active Directory, or who can edit a Group Policy Object, at any one time. Allow changes to replicate before making changes that affect the same organizational unit or Group Policy Object. |
| | Software you have assigned to a computer has not been installed on the computer. | The client computer has not been restarted. For assigned software to be installed on the client computer, the system must first reboot. |
| | Group Policy is not taking effect on the local computer. | As discussed in Chapter 22, local Group Policies are the weakest. Any Active Directory–based policy can overwrite them. Check to see which Group Policy Objects are being applied through Active Directory and if those Group Policy Objects have settings that are in conflict with the local settings. |
| | The user opens an already installed application, and Windows Installer starts. | An application might be undergoing automatic repair, or a user-required feature is being added. There is nothing you need to do to correct and/or prevent this behavior. |
| | A user receives error messages such as "Active Directory will not allow the package to be deployed" or "Cannot prepare package for deployment." | The package might be corrupted, or there might be a networking problem. You might want to consider redeploying the package using the procedure outlined previously. You should also investigate the possibility of network problems and take appropriate action. |

# Chapter Review

The following are the word associations to keep in mind when taking the Microsoft exam:

- **.msi**  Microsoft Installer file, used for creation of software packages
- **.zap**  File used in conjunction with programs that do not have an .msi file
- **.mst**  Microsoft transform, used to modify an existing .msi deployment
- **Assign**  Automatic software installation, used for computers and users
- **Publish**  Optional software installation, used only for users, not for computers

- **Security Templates**   Tool used to make changes to security template files, which in turn can be imported into Group Policy Objects

You can also configure a wide range of Group Policy settings that affect the security behavior of the computer. These settings include Password Policies, which have been discussed previously, Audit Policies, and User Rights Assignment. And that's just the beginning.

Because the number of Security settings is so extensive, it can sometimes be difficult to remember exactly what has been set, and then take that configuration and port it to other systems on the network. You should understand how security templates are used to address this concern: how they store multiple Security settings in a single file that can be used to configure the Security settings of GPOs throughout the domain. You should also understand how to use the Security Configuration and Analysis tool to quickly analyze the potential impact of a Security Template, and how to apply the settings of that template to the local computer. You should also know how to take the settings defined with Security Configuration and Analysis and use them to populate a new Security Template file.

Finally, Microsoft will expect you to know how to troubleshoot Group Policy application when deployment doesn't go according to plan. (Of course, because computers just take instructions, it could be argued that Group Policy deployment doesn't go according to plan because of a bad plan in the first place.)

You will acquire most of these troubleshooting skills as a result of your experience with Windows Server 2003 and, more specifically, Group Policy Objects, but you will also draw heavily on how well you understand this awesome administrative technology.

This book should have helped you gain a good measure of that crucial understanding. Therefore, you should find it an essential asset on your quest toward MSCE certification.

**PART IV**

## Questions

1. You are the administrator of a Windows Server 2003 domain called bookstore.com. You have just completed a security audit of the network's resources, and you have determined that users in the Management OU need a password policy that requires more complex passwords than are currently being used. What is the most efficient way to accomplish your goal without affecting the rest of the passwords used in the network?

   A. Configure the security policy of the default Domain Controller Security Policy GPO to require password complexity.

   B. Configure the security policy of the default Domain Security Policy GPO to require password complexity.

   C. Configure the security policy of a GPO linked to the Management organizational unit to require password complexity.

   D. There is no way to accomplish your goal.

2. You are the administrator of a Windows Server 2003 domain called bookstore .com. You have created an organizational unit for all Windows 2000 client systems in the network, and you have also linked a Group Policy to that organizational unit. You want this security policy to be in effect at all times on these machines, but you are discovering that other domain admins periodically change the Security settings on the client computers when troubleshooting. You want to automate the security analysis of client computers on the network so you can track changes to the organizational unit's client machines. You want to do this without interrupting the work of the other domain admins. How should you go about the task?

A. Use the Windows Task Scheduler to schedule the secedit command to run on the client computers in the OU.

B. Remove all other user accounts from the Domain Admins global group.

C. Edit the Default Domain Security policy to configure the security policy of all client computers in the domain; changes made to this GPO will be logged in the Directory Services event log.

D. Use the Security and Configuration Analysis tool and add a Scheduled Task for all Windows 2000 clients.

3. You are the administrator of a Windows Server 2003 domain and want the passwords used in the network to be at least six characters long. To accomplish this, you edit the Default Domain Controllers Group Policy for the domain, and configure the Password options to require six character passwords. Upon inspection, however, you discover that users are still able to use passwords that do not meet this requirement. What should you do to enforce your administrative objectives?

A. Initiate replication to using the gpupdate utility to make sure the Group Policy containers and the Group Policy template (GPT) have been replicated to all replication partners.

B. Use the Security Templates tool to create a security template specifying the password requirement; then use the Security Configuration and Analysis Tool to configure each client with that template file.

C. Using the Group Policy Object Editor, edit the Default Domain Controllers Group Policy to force the passwords to meet complexity requirements.

D. Using the Group Policy Object Editor, edit the Default Domain Group Policy to require password to be at least six characters long.

4. Software applications deployed with a .zap file cannot take advantage of all features available with an .msi file, but they still offer several beneficial features. Which of the following is among these features? (Choose two.)

A. .zap files are used to deploy software applications to down-level clients like Windows 98.

    **B.** .zap packages can be used to deploy down-level software applications that ship with a setup.exe program.

    **C.** Packages built with .zap files can be used to configure registry settings and shortcuts.

    **D.** .zap packages can be used to install an application even though the user logged on may not have the rights to do so.

5. You are the administrator of a Windows Server 2003 Active Directory enterprise. All computers in the network are running Windows 2000, Windows XP, or Windows Server 2003. You have configured an audit policy for a Windows Server 2003 computer in the forest root domain that stores confidential data, and discover that it is being accessed by users outside the Active Directory forest. You are now in the process of configuring a stricter network communications security policy, and you want to require encrypted TCP/IP communication for all computers in the forest with the least amount of administrative overhead. What should you do?

    **A.** For each domain, create a domain-based GPO, and configure it to assign the Secure Server IPSec policy.

    **B.** Create a GPO for the domain, and configure it to assign the Secure Server IPSec policy and to enable Secure Channel: Require Strong Session Key.

    **C.** Implement TCP/IP packet filtering, and open only the ports required for your network services.

    **D.** Use the Security Configuration and Analysis tool to configure the local security policies on all server and client computers, and import the Highly Secure template. Then use the Configure Computer Now option to apply the template.

6. You are performing a security audit for a law firm with four offices: Salina, Fort Scott, Manhattan, and Lawrence. You are assessing the security vulnerabilities in the firm's single Windows 2003 Server Active Directory domain. The domain has been separated into four sites, one for each of the cities. There are eight domain controllers in the domain, and you adjust the Security settings on one of the domain controllers to tighten security standards for the law firm. You now want to duplicate those settings to the other domain controllers with the least amount of administrative effort. What should you do?

    **A.** Export the secured domain controllers security configuration information to a template file. Open Security Configuration and Analysis on each of the other domain controllers, and import the template file. Then select Analyze Computer Now.

    **B.** Use the Security Configuration and Analysis tool on the newly configured domain controller, and export the secured domain controller's security configuration to a template file. Copy the template file to the SYSVOL folder on each domain controller.

    C. Create a GPO for the domain. Use the Security settings of the secure domain controller to configure the domain GPO settings. Filter the GPO by assigning the Domain Users group the Deny setting for the Apply Group Policy permission.

    D. Place all the domain controllers in a single organizational unit, and create a GPO for that OU. Configure the GPO Security settings to match the settings of the secured domain controller.

7. The CFO of your company has e-mailed you, asking for a recommendation concerning upcoming software purchases. He is considering an application that ships with a setup.exe file, and another that ships with an .msi file. The application with the setup.exe file is cheaper, and the CFO is concerned primarily with keeping costs down, as both applications are comparable in terms of performance. Which deployment advantages can you recount for the CFO that might influence his decision to purchase the application with the .msi file? (Choose two.)

    A. You will be able to gather detailed information about how often the program is used.

    B. The software package created with the .msi file can be used to install using elevated privileges.

    C. You will be able to deploy the application automatically with an .msi file; there is no way to do that with the other application.

    D. The application with the .msi file can be automatically repaired should critical files become corrupted or deleted.

8. You are the domain administrator for a company whose offices are all located in a single corporate campus. There is only one Windows Server 2003 Active Directory domain, and the administration has been delegated by the creation of several organizational units, divided by job description. You instruct the administrator of the Marketing OU to forcibly remove an application that is causing system instability. The application is in use only in that single OU. The next day, however, you notice that some of the users in the OU are still using the application. On other systems, the application has been removed. What is the most likely explanation for this behavior?

    A. A group of users has been denied the ability to apply Group Policy on the Properties pages of the GPO.

    B. The users in question have been added to the local Administrators group by the Marketing OU administrator; local administrators are exempt from software removal policies.

    C. The users reinstalled the application by using the Add/Remove Programs applet in the Control Panel because the policy just removes the application advertisement.

   D. To force removal of an application, the GPO needs to be configured at the domain level, not at the OU level.

9. You are the domain administrator of a Windows Server 2003 domain, and you have decided to implement a software modification to a recently purchased accounting application. This accounting application shipped with an .msi file, and it is to be deployed with a GPO that assigns the application to all users in the domain. What should you do to deploy the change to the application with the least amount of administrative overhead?

   A. Configure the software installation package to remove the existing installation, and then recreate the package using an .mst file, which will modify the installation the next time it is redeployed.

   B. Create an .mst file and edit the default domain GPO to include the .mst file in the Software Installation settings. The .mst file will automatically change the application for which it was written throughout the domain.

   C. Create a new GPO, and in the Software Installation settings, create a new package using the .mst file. Then assign the new software package to all domain users.

   D. This cannot be done with Windows Installer technology.

10. What kind of file is used to deploy a software package using a legacy installation executable like setup.exe?

   A. .mst

   B. .zip

   C. .msi

   D. .zap

11. Which of the following are true regarding the deployment of software through Group Policy? (Choose three.)

   A. Applications can be assigned to users and computers.

   B. Applications can be published to users and computers.

   C. You can force users in the Active Directory network to upgrade an existing application.

   D. Applications deployed with an .msi file will repair themselves if a file becomes corrupted.

   E. Reporting information can be gathered about how often applications are crashing.

12. You are the administrator of a large Windows Server 2003 domain, and you need to quickly configure Security settings on all domain controllers. You would also like to have the Security settings you configure for the domain

controllers apply to the Windows Server 2003 member servers as well. Which utilities will you use to accomplish your objective? (Choose three.)

**A.** ntdsutil

**B.** Active Directory Sites and Services

**C.** Security Templates

**D.** Security Configuration and Analysis

**E.** Active Directory Users and Computers

## Answers

1. **D.** Any change to password requirements will affect all users of the domain, because users use passwords when logging on to the domain, and not to organizational units.

2. **A.** The secedit tool is the one necessary here. It can be called in a batch file, or be configured as a Scheduled Task.

3. **D.** This is what is necessary to meet your objectives here. Password policies will be configured at the domain level, and the objective can be met simply enough with an edit of the existing Domain Group Policy.

4. **B** and **C.** .zap files are used to create software installation packages when an .msi file is not available. Packages created with .zap files also have the ability to configure shortcuts and registry settings. Because they are created with a Group Policy Object, they cannot be used to deploy software to Windows 98 clients, or any other clients not Group Policy-aware.

5. **A.** The best way to do this is with a domain-wide security policy that will configure all domain computers.

6. **D.** The best way to accomplish your task here is to configure a GPO that will be effective for a single collection of Active Directory objects, in this case, all your domain controllers.

7. **B** and **D.** Using a Windows Installer file to deploy the software package, you gain several important advantages. You can assign the application to both users and computers, and the installation can occur without the user having to log on with an account with Power User or Administrative abilities. Further, files that become damaged or are missing are automatically replaced.

8. **A.** The likely reason here is that the users of these computers have been filtered from the scope of the OU with an edit of the Security tab of the GPO's Properties page. If a user or group has the Deny setting for the Apply Group Policy permission, the user won't be able to receive the settings of the GPO.

9. **C.** To deploy an application modification, all that is necessary is a change to the existing GPO that performed the deployment. Once you add the .mst file to the software package, the deployed application will be automatically modified.

10. **D and A.** .zap file can be used to deploy software through a Group Policy that does not ship with an .msi file, and where you do not choose to create one. The .zap is a text file that, among other instructions, specifies the name of the setup executable.

11. **A, C, and D.** Group Policy software deployment offers several benefits, including those mentioned in answers A, C, and D.

12. **C, D, and E.** You can use the Security Templates tool to create and modify a collection of Security settings and save them in a single file. You can then use Security Configuration and Analysis to analyze and test the collection of settings. This is also the tool for applying the template to member servers. You can use Active Directory Users and Computers to import the template file to a GPO that will be linked to the Domain Controllers OU.

# About the CD

The CD included with this book contains five practice exams—one for each of the following MCSE certification exams covered in this book:

- **Exam 70-290** Managing and Maintaining a Microsoft Windows Server 2003 Environment
- **Exam 70-291** Implementing, Managing, and Maintaining a Microsoft Windows Server 2003 Network Infrastructure
- **Exam 70-293** Planning and Maintaining a Microsoft Windows Server 2003 Network Infrastructure
- **Exam 70-294** Planning, Implementing, and Maintaining a Microsoft Windows Server 2003 Active Directory Infrastructure

Plus a bonus exam:

- **Exam 70-270** Installing, Configuring, and Administering Microsoft Windows XP Professional

The CD also includes MasterExam, an electronic version of this book, and Session #1 of LearnKey's online training. The software is easy to install on any Windows 98/NT/ 2000 computer. You must install it to access the MasterExam feature. You can, however, browse the electronic book directly from the CD without installation. To register for LearnKey's online training and a second bonus MasterExam, click the Online Training link on the Main Page and follow the directions to the free online registration.

## System Requirements

The CD software requires Windows 98 or higher, Internet Explorer 5.0 or higher, and 20MB of hard disk space for full installation. The electronic book requires Adobe Acrobat Reader. To access the online training from LearnKey, you must have RealPlayer Basic 8 or the Real1 plug-in, which is installed automatically when you launch the online training.

# LearnKey Online Training

The LearnKey Online Training link allows you to access online training from Osborne.Onlineexpert.com. The first session of this course is provided free of charge. You can purchase additional sessions for this course and other courses directly from www.LearnKey.com or by calling (800) 865-0165.

Prior to running the online training, you must add the Real plug-in and the RealCBT plug-in to your system. This is facilitated automatically when you attempt to run the training the first time. You must also register the online product. Follow the instructions for a first-time user. Please be sure to use a valid e-mail address.

# Installing and Running MasterExam

If your computer's CD-ROM drive is configured to auto-run, the CD will automatically start up when you insert it. From the opening screen, you can install MasterExam by clicking the MasterExam button. This begins the installation process and creates a program group named LearnKey. To run MasterExam, select Start | All Programs | LearnKey. If the auto-run feature does not launch your CD, browse to the CD and double-click the RunInstall icon.

## MasterExam

MasterExam simulates the actual exam. The number of questions, the type of questions, and the time allowed are intended to represent the exam environment. You have the option to take an open-book exam that includes hints, references, and answers; a closed-book exam; or the timed MasterExam simulation.

When you launch the MasterExam simulation, a digital clock appears in the top center of your screen. The clock counts down to zero unless you end the exam before the time expires.

# Electronic Book

The CD includes the entire contents of the Exam Guide in PDF. The Adobe Acrobat Reader is included on the CD to allow you to read the file.

# Help

A help file is provided and can be accessed by clicking the Help button on the main page in the lower-left corner. Individual help features are also available through MasterExam and LearnKey's online training.

# Removing Installation(s)

MasterExam is installed on your hard drive. For *best* results for removal of programs, use the Start | Programs | LearnKey | Uninstall options to remove MasterExam.

To remove RealPlayer, use the Add/Remove Programs icon in the Control Panel. You can also remove the LearnKey training program from this location.

# Technical Support

For questions regarding the technical content of the electronic book or MasterExam, please visit www.osborne.com or e-mail customer.service@mcgraw-hill.com. For customers outside the United States, please e-mail international_cs@mcgraw-hill.com.

## LearnKey Technical Support

For technical problems with the LearnKey software (installation, operation, and removing installations) and for questions regarding LearnKey online training and MasterSim content, please visit www.learnkey.com or e-mail techsupport@learnkey.com.

# INDEX

# INTERNATIONAL CONTACT INFORMATION

**AUSTRALIA**
McGraw-Hill Book Company
Australia Pty. Ltd.
TEL +61-2-9900-1800
FAX +61-2-9878-8881
http://www.mcgraw-hill.com.au
books-it_sydney@mcgraw-hill.com

**CANADA**
McGraw-Hill Ryerson Ltd.
TEL +905-430-5000
FAX +905-430-5020
http://www.mcgraw-hill.ca

**GREECE, MIDDLE EAST, & AFRICA
(Excluding South Africa)**
McGraw-Hill Hellas
TEL +30-210-6560-990
TEL +30-210-6560-993
TEL +30-210-6560-994
FAX +30-210-6545-525

**MEXICO (Also serving Latin America)**
McGraw-Hill Interamericana Editores
S.A. de C.V.
TEL +525-1500-5108
FAX +525-117-1589
http://www.mcgraw-hill.com.mx
carlos_ruiz@mcgraw-hill.com

**SINGAPORE (Serving Asia)**
McGraw-Hill Book Company
TEL +65-6863-1580
FAX +65-6862-3354
http://www.mcgraw-hill.com.sg
mghasia@mcgraw-hill.com

**SOUTH AFRICA**
McGraw-Hill South Africa
TEL +27-11-622-7512
FAX +27-11-622-9045
robyn_swanepoel@mcgraw-hill.com

**SPAIN**
McGraw-Hill/
Interamericana de España, S.A.U.
TEL +34-91-180-3000
FAX +34-91-372-8513
http://www.mcgraw-hill.es
professional@mcgraw-hill.es

**UNITED KINGDOM, NORTHERN,
EASTERN, & CENTRAL EUROPE**
McGraw-Hill Education Europe
TEL +44-1-628-502500
FAX +44-1-628-770224
http://www.mcgraw-hill.co.uk
emea_queries@mcgraw-hill.com

**ALL OTHER INQUIRIES Contact:**
McGraw-Hill/Osborne
TEL +1-510-420-7700
FAX +1-510-420-7703
http://www.osborne.com
omg_international@mcgraw-hill.com